The Sporting News
PRO FOOTBALL REGISTER
1999 EDITION

Editor/Pro Football Register
BRENDAN ROBERTS

Efrem Zimbalist III, President and Chief Executive Officer, Times Mirror Magazines; **James H. Nuckols,** President, The Sporting News; **Francis X. Farrell,** Senior Vice President, Publisher; **John D. Rawlings,** Senior Vice President, Editorial Director; **John Kastberg,** Vice President, General Manager; **Kathy Kinkeade,** Vice President, Operations; **Steve Meyerhoff,** Executive Editor; **Marilyn Kasal,** Production Director; **Bob Parajon,** Prepress Director; **Terry Shea,** Database Analyst; **Michael Behrens,** Art Director, Special Projects; **Christen Webster,** Production Artist; **Kate Bond and David Walton,** Editorial Assistants.

A Times Mirror Company

CONTENTS

Veteran players 3
This section includes all veteran NFL players who appeared in at least one NFL game during the 1998 season and many who have previous game experience in the NFL, USFL, NFL Europe or CFL and were listed on an NFL roster as of June 3, 1999.

1999 draft picks 445
This section lists college statistics for all players selected in the 1999 NFL draft.

Head coaches 495

1998 Statistical leaders 510

EXPLANATION OF ABBREVIATIONS AND TERMS

LEAGUES: AFL: American Football League. **Ar.FL., Arena Football:** Arena Football League. **CFL:** Canadian Football League. **CoFL:** Continental Football League. **NFL:** National Football League. **NFLE:** NFL Europe League. **USFL:** United States Football League. **WFL:** World Football League. **W.L.:** World League. **WLAF:** World League of American Football.

TEAMS: Birm.: Birmingham. **Jack.:** Jacksonville. **L.A. Raiders:** Los Angeles Raiders. **L.A. Rams:** Los Angeles Rams. **New Eng.:** New England. **N.Y. Giants:** New York Giants. **N.Y. Jets:** New York Jets. **N.Y./N.J.:** New York/New Jersey. **San Ant.:** San Antonio. **San Fran.:** San Francisco. **Sask.:** Saskatchewan. **StL.:** St. Louis.

STATISTICS: Att.: Attempts. **Avg.:** Average. **Blk.:** Blocked punts. **Cmp.:** Completions. **FGA:** Field goals attempted. **FGM:** Field goals made. **50+:** Field goals of 50 yards or longer. **F., Fum.:** Fumbles. **G:** Games. **In. 20:** Punts inside 20-yard line. **Int.:** Interceptions. **Lg.:** Longest made field goal. **L:** Lost. **Net avg.:** Net punting average. **No.:** Number. **Rat.:** Passer rating. **Pct.:** Percentage. **Pts.:** Points scored. **T:** Tied. **TD:** Touchdowns. **2-pt.:** Two-point conversions. **W:** Won. **XPA:** Extra points attempted. **XPM:** Extra points made. **Yds.:** Yards.

POSITIONS: C: Center. **CB:** Corner back. **DB:** Defensive back. **DE:** Defensive end. **DT:** Defensive tackle. **FB:** Full back. **G:** Guard. **K:** Kicker. **LB:** Linebacker. **OL:** Offensive lineman. **OT:** Offensive tackle. **P:** Punter. **QB:** Quarterback. **RB:** Running back. **S:** Safety. **TE:** Tight end. **WR:** Wide receiver.

SINGLE GAME HIGHS (regular season): If a player reached a single game high on numerous occasions—had one rushing touchdown in a game, for example—the most recent occurrence is listed.

EXPLANATION OF AWARDS

AWARDS: Butkus Award: Nation's top college linebacker. **Davey O'Brien Award:** Nation's top college quarterback. **Doak Walker Award:** Nation's top college junior or senior running back. **Fred Biletnikoff Award:** Nation's top college wide receiver. **Harlon Hill Trophy:** Nation's top college Division II player. **Heisman Trophy:** Nation's top college player. **Jim Thorpe Award:** Nation's top college defensive back. **Lombardi Award:** Nation's top college lineman. **Lou Groza Award:** Nation's top college kicker. **Maxwell Award:** Nation's top college player. **Outland Trophy:** Nation's top college interior lineman. **Walter Payton Award:** Nation's top college Division I-AA player.

ON THE COVER: Vikings wide receiver Randy Moss. (Cover design by Michael Behrens/THE SPORTING NEWS. Large photo by Albert Dickson/THE SPORTING NEWS, action photo by THE SPORTING NEWS.)

Copyright © 1999 by The Sporting News, a division of Times Mirror Magazines, Inc.; 10176 Corporate Square Dr., Suite 200, St. Louis, MO 63132. All rights reserved. Printed in the U.S.A.

No part of the Pro Football Register may be reproduced or transmitted in any form or by any means, electronic or mechanical, including photocopy, recording or any information storage and retrieval system now known or to be invented, without permission in writing from the publisher, except by a reviewer who wishes to quote brief passages in connection with a review written for inclusion in a magazine, newspaper or broadcast.

THE SPORTING NEWS is a registered trademark of The Sporting News, a Times Mirror Company.

ISBN: 0-89204-614-7   10 9 8 7 6 5 4 3 2 1

VETERAN PLAYERS

Please note for statistical comparisons: In 1982, only nine of 16 games were played due to the cancellation of games because of a player's strike. In 1987, only 15 of 16 games were played due to the cancellation of games in the third week because of a player's strike. Most NFL players also missed games scheduled in the fourth, fifth and sixth weeks.
Sacks became an official NFL statistic in 1982.
Two-point conversions became an official NFL statistic in 1994.

* Indicates league leader.	† Indicates tied for league lead.	... Statistics unavailable, unofficial, or mathematically
‡ Indicates NFC leader.	§ Indicates AFC leader.	impossible to calculate.
∞ Indicates tied for NFC lead.	▲ Indicates tied for AFC lead.	

ABDUL-JABBAR, KARIM — RB — DOLPHINS

PERSONAL: Born June 28, 1974, in Los Angeles. ... 5-10/205. ... Formerly known as Sharmon Shah.
HIGH SCHOOL: Dorsey (Los Angeles).
COLLEGE: UCLA.
TRANSACTIONS/CAREER NOTES: Selected after junior season by Miami Dolphins in third round (80th pick overall) of 1996 NFL draft. ... Signed by Dolphins (July 18, 1996). ... Granted free agency (February 12, 1999). ... Re-signed by Dolphins (April 13, 1999).
HONORS: Named running back on THE SPORTING NEWS college All-America second team (1995).
PRO STATISTICS: 1998—Recovered one fumble.
SINGLE GAME HIGHS (regular season): Attempts—33 (September 20, 1998, vs. Pittsburgh); yards—152 (December 22, 1996, vs. New York Jets); and rushing touchdowns—3 (November 23, 1997, vs. New England).
STATISTICAL PLATEAUS: 100-yard rushing games: 1996 (4), 1997 (2), 1998 (3). Total: 9.

			RUSHING				RECEIVING				TOTALS			
Year Team	G	GS	Att.	Yds.	Avg.	TD	No.	Yds.	Avg.	TD	TD	2pt.	Pts.	Fum.
1996—Miami NFL	16	14	307	1116	3.6	11	23	139	6.0	0	11	0	66	4
1997—Miami NFL	16	14	283	892	3.2	†15	29	261	9.0	1	*16	0	†96	3
1998—Miami NFL	15	15	270	960	3.6	6	21	102	4.9	0	6	0	36	2
Pro totals (3 years)	47	43	860	2968	3.5	32	73	502	6.9	1	33	0	198	9

ABRAHAM, DONNIE — CB — BUCCANEERS

PERSONAL: Born October 8, 1973, in Orangeburg, S.C. ... 5-10/184. ... Full name: Nathaniel Donnell Abraham.
HIGH SCHOOL: Orangeburg-Wilkinson (Orangeburg, S.C.).
COLLEGE: East Tennessee State (degree in business management, 1995).
TRANSACTIONS/CAREER NOTES: Selected by Tampa Bay Buccaneers in third round (71st pick overall) of 1996 NFL draft. ... Signed by Buccaneers (July 13, 1996).
PRO STATISTICS: 1996—Recovered two fumbles for three yards. 1997—Recovered one fumble for two yards. 1998—Recovered two fumbles.

			INTERCEPTIONS			
Year Team	G	GS	No.	Yds.	Avg.	TD
1996—Tampa Bay NFL	16	12	5	27	5.4	0
1997—Tampa Bay NFL	16	16	5	16	3.2	0
1998—Tampa Bay NFL	13	13	1	3	3.0	0
Pro totals (3 years)	45	41	11	46	4.2	0

ABRAMS, KEVIN — CB — LIONS

PERSONAL: Born February 28, 1974, in Tampa. ... 5-8/175. ... Full name: Kevin R. Abrams.
HIGH SCHOOL: Hillsborough (Tampa).
COLLEGE: Syracuse.
TRANSACTIONS/CAREER NOTES: Selected by Detroit Lions in second round (54th pick overall) of 1997 NFL draft. ... Signed by Lions (July 14, 1997).
HONORS: Named defensive back on THE SPORTING NEWS college All-America first team (1995).
PRO STATISTICS: 1998—Returned two punts for 12 yards and recovered one fumble for seven yards.

			INTERCEPTIONS				SACKS
Year Team	G	GS	No.	Yds.	Avg.	TD	No.
1997—Detroit NFL	15	4	1	29	29.0	0	2.0
1998—Detroit NFL	16	7	0	0	...	0	3.0
Pro totals (2 years)	31	11	1	29	29.0	0	5.0

ACKERMAN, TOM — C/G — SAINTS

PERSONAL: Born September 6, 1972, in Bellingham, Wash. ... 6-3/296. ... Full name: Thomas Michael Ackerman.
HIGH SCHOOL: Nooksack (Wash.) Valley.
COLLEGE: Eastern Washington.
TRANSACTIONS/CAREER NOTES: Selected by New Orleans Saints in fifth round (145th pick overall) of 1996 NFL draft. ... Signed by Saints (July 14, 1996). ... Granted free agency (February 12, 1999). ... Re-signed by Saints (April 14, 1999).
PLAYING EXPERIENCE: New Orleans NFL, 1996-1998. ... Games/Games started: 1996 (2/0), 1997 (14/0), 1998 (15/10). Total: 31/10.

ADAMS, FLOZELL — G/OT — COWBOYS

PERSONAL: Born May 10, 1975, in Chicago. ... 6-7/335. ... Full name: Flozell Jootin Adams. ... Cousin of Hersey Hawkins, guard, Seattle SuperSonics.
HIGH SCHOOL: Proviso West (Maywood, Ill.).
COLLEGE: Michigan State.
TRANSACTIONS/CAREER NOTES: Selected by Dallas Cowboys in second round (38th pick overall) of 1998 NFL draft. ... Signed by Cowboys (July 17, 1998).
PLAYING EXPERIENCE: Dallas NFL, 1998. ... Games/Games started: 16/12.
HONORS: Named offensive tackle on THE SPORTING NEWS college All-America third team (1997).
PRO STATISTICS: 1998—Recovered one fumble.

ADAMS, SAM — DT — SEAHAWKS

PERSONAL: Born June 13, 1973, in Houston. ... 6-3/300. ... Full name: Sam Aaron Adams. ... Son of Sam Adams Sr., guard with New England Patriots (1972-80) and New Orleans Saints (1981).
HIGH SCHOOL: Cypress Creek (Houston).
COLLEGE: Texas A&M.
TRANSACTIONS/CAREER NOTES: Selected after junior season by Seattle Seahawks in first round (eighth pick overall) of 1994 NFL draft. ... Signed by Seahawks (July 30, 1994).
HONORS: Named defensive lineman on THE SPORTING NEWS college All-America first team (1993).
PRO STATISTICS: 1996—Recovered one fumble for two yards. 1998—Intercepted one pass for 25 yards and a touchdown and recovered one fumble.

Year Team	G	GS	SACKS
1994—Seattle NFL	12	7	4.0
1995—Seattle NFL	16	5	3.5
1996—Seattle NFL	16	15	5.5
1997—Seattle NFL	16	16	7.0
1998—Seattle NFL	16	11	2.0
Pro totals (5 years)	76	54	22.0

ADAMS, VASHONE — S — CHIEFS

PERSONAL: Born September 12, 1973, in Aurora, Colo. ... 5-10/201. ... Full name: Vashone LaRey Adams. ... Name pronounced vash-ON.
HIGH SCHOOL: Overland (Aurora, Colo.).
JUNIOR COLLEGE: Butte College (Calif.).
COLLEGE: Fort Hays State (Kan.), then Eastern Michigan.
TRANSACTIONS/CAREER NOTES: Signed as non-drafted free agent by Cleveland Browns (May 2, 1995). ... Released by Browns (August 21, 1995). ... Re-signed by Browns to practice squad (August 30, 1995). ... Activated (November 4, 1995). ... Browns franchise moved to Baltimore and renamed Ravens for 1996 season (March 11, 1996). ... Granted unconditional free agency (February 14, 1997). ... Signed by New Orleans Saints (April 7, 1997). ... Released by Saints (September 29, 1997). ... Signed by Kansas City Chiefs (April 7, 1998). ... On injured reserve with knee injury (August 30, 1998-entire season).
PLAYING EXPERIENCE: Cleveland NFL, 1995; Baltimore NFL, 1996; New Orleans NFL, 1997. ... Games/Games started: 1995 (8/6), 1996 (16/2), 1997 (5/4). Total: 29/12.
PRO STATISTICS: 1996—Intercepted one pass for 16 yards.

AGNEW, RAY — DT — RAMS

PERSONAL: Born December 9, 1967, in Winston-Salem, N.C. ... 6-3/285. ... Full name: Raymond Mitchell Agnew.
HIGH SCHOOL: Carver (Winston-Salem, N.C.).
COLLEGE: North Carolina State.
TRANSACTIONS/CAREER NOTES: Selected by New England Patriots in first round (10th pick overall) of 1990 NFL draft. ... Signed by Patriots (July 19, 1990). ... On injured reserve with knee injury (December 29, 1990-remainder of season). ... Granted unconditional free agency (February 17, 1995). ... Signed by New York Giants (March 10, 1995). ... Released by Giants (June 4, 1997). ... Signed by Carolina Panthers (June 12, 1997). ... Released by Panthers (August 19, 1997). ... Signed by Giants (August 21, 1997). ... Granted unconditional free agency (February 13, 1998). ... Signed by St. Louis Rams (March 5, 1998).
PRO STATISTICS: 1990—Recovered one fumble. 1992—Recovered one fumble. 1995—Recovered one fumble. 1996—Intercepted one pass for 34 yards and a touchdown. 1997—Recovered one fumble. 1998—Intercepted one pass for no yards and recovered one fumble.

Year Team	G	GS	SACKS
1990—New England NFL	12	9	2.5
1991—New England NFL	13	10	2.0
1992—New England NFL	14	14	1.0
1993—New England NFL	16	1	1.5
1994—New England NFL	11	3	0.5
1995—New York Giants NFL	16	15	1.0
1996—New York Giants NFL	13	2	0.5
1997—New York Giants NFL	15	0	2.0
1998—St. Louis NFL	16	12	5.0
Pro totals (9 years)	126	66	16.0

AGUIAR, LOUIE — P — CHIEFS

PERSONAL: Born June 30, 1966, in Livermore, Calif. ... 6-2/218. ... Full name: Louis Raymond Aguiar. ... Name pronounced AG-ee-ar.
HIGH SCHOOL: Granada (Livermore, Calif.).
JUNIOR COLLEGE: Chabot Junior College (Calif.).
COLLEGE: Utah State.
TRANSACTIONS/CAREER NOTES: Signed as non-drafted free agent by Buffalo Bills (May 8, 1989). ... Released by Bills (August 14, 1989). ... Re-signed by Bills (March 27, 1990). ... Released by Bills (August 7, 1990). ... Signed by WLAF (January 8, 1991). ... Selected by Barcelona Dragons in first round (first punter) of 1991 WLAF positional draft. ... Signed by New York Jets (June 14, 1991). ... Granted free agency (February 17, 1994). ... Signed by Kansas City Chiefs (April 1994). ... Granted unconditional free agency (February 14, 1997). ... Re-signed by Chiefs (April 18, 1997).
PRO STATISTICS: NFL: 1991—Made one of two field goal attempts (23 yards), rushed once for 18 yards and recovered one fumble. 1993—Rushed three times for minus 27 yards, attempted two passes without a completion and an interception, fumbled twice and recovered one fumble for minus 10 yards. 1997— Rushed twice for 11 yards and attempted one pass with a completion for 35 yards. 1998—Recovered one fumble.

				PUNTING			
Year Team	G	No.	Yds.	Avg.	Net avg.	In. 20	Blk.
1991—Barcelona W.L.	10	49	2029	41.4	33.7	15	1
—New York Jets NFL	16	64	2521	39.4	34.6	14	0
1992—New York Jets NFL	16	73	2993	41.0	37.6	21	0
1993—New York Jets NFL	16	73	2806	38.4	34.3	21	0
1994—Kansas City NFL	16	85	3582	42.1	34.5	15	0
1995—Kansas City NFL	16	91	3990	43.8	36.5	†29	0
1996—Kansas City NFL	16	88	3667	41.7	33.7	25	0
1997—Kansas City NFL	16	82	3465	42.3	38.2	▲28	0
1998—Kansas City NFL	16	75	3226	43.0	34.4	20	1
W.L. totals (1 year)	10	49	2029	41.4	33.7	15	1
NFL totals (8 years)	128	631	26250	41.6	35.5	173	1
Pro totals (9 years)	138	680	28279	41.6	35.4	188	2

AHANOTU, CHIDI — DE — BUCCANEERS

PERSONAL: Born October 11, 1970, in Modesto, Calif. ... 6-2/285. ... Full name: Chidi Obioma Ahanotu. ... Name pronounced chee-DEE a-HA-nah-TWO.
HIGH SCHOOL: Berkeley (Calif.).
COLLEGE: California (degree in physical education).
TRANSACTIONS/CAREER NOTES: Selected by Tampa Bay Buccaneers in sixth round (145th pick overall) of 1993 NFL draft. ... Signed by Buccaneers (July 9, 1993). ... Granted free agency (February 16, 1996). ... Re-signed by Buccaneers (February 20, 1996). ... On injured reserve with shoulder injury (October 27, 1998-remainder of season). ... Designated by Buccaneers as franchise player (February 12, 1999).
PRO STATISTICS: 1996—Recovered one fumble. 1997—Recovered two fumbles.

Year Team	G	GS	SACKS
1993—Tampa Bay NFL	16	10	1.5
1994—Tampa Bay NFL	16	16	1.0
1995—Tampa Bay NFL	16	15	3.0
1996—Tampa Bay NFL	13	13	5.5
1997—Tampa Bay NFL	16	15	10.0
1998—Tampa Bay NFL	4	4	0.0
Pro totals (6 years)	81	73	21.0

AIKMAN, TROY — QB — COWBOYS

PERSONAL: Born November 21, 1966, in West Covina, Calif. ... 6-4/226. ... Full name: Troy Kenneth Aikman.
HIGH SCHOOL: Henryetta (Okla.).
COLLEGE: Oklahoma, then UCLA.
TRANSACTIONS/CAREER NOTES: Selected by Dallas Cowboys in first round (first pick overall) of 1989 NFL draft. ... Signed by Cowboys (April 20, 1989). ... On injured reserve with shoulder injury (December 28, 1990-remainder of season).
CHAMPIONSHIP GAME EXPERIENCE: Played in NFC championship game (1992-1995 seasons). ... Member of Super Bowl championship team (1992, 1993 and 1995 seasons).
HONORS: Named quarterback on THE SPORTING NEWS college All-America second team (1987). ... Davey O'Brien Award winner (1988). ... Named quarterback on THE SPORTING NEWS college All-America first team (1988). ... Played in Pro Bowl (1991, 1992 and 1994 seasons). ... Named Most Valuable Player of Super Bowl XXVII (1992 season). ... Named quarterback on THE SPORTING NEWS NFL All-Pro team (1993). ... Named to play in Pro Bowl (1993 season); replaced by Bobby Hebert due to injury. ... Named to play in Pro Bowl (1995 season); replaced by Warren Moon due to injury. ... Named to play in Pro Bowl (1996 season); replaced by Gus Frerotte due to injury.
POST SEASON RECORDS: Holds Super Bowl career record for highest percentage of passes completed (minimum 40 attempts)—70.0. ... Holds NFL postseason single-game record for longest pass completion (to Alvin Harper)—94 yards (January 8, 1995, vs. Green Bay).
PRO STATISTICS: 1989—Caught one pass for minus 13 yards, fumbled six times and recovered three fumbles. 1990—Fumbled five times and recovered one fumble. 1991—Caught one pass for minus six yards and fumbled four times. 1992—Fumbled four times and recovered one fumble. 1993—Fumbled seven times and recovered three fumbles for minus three yards. 1994—Fumbled twice and recovered two fumbles. 1995—Fumbled five times and recovered two fumbles for minus 15 yards. 1996—Fumbled six times and recovered two fumbles for minus eight yards. 1997—Fumbled six times for minus five yards. 1998—Fumbled three times for minus 20 yards.
SINGLE GAME HIGHS (regular season): Attempts—57 (November 26, 1998, vs. Minnesota); completions—34 (November 26, 1998, vs. Minnesota); yards—455 (November 26, 1998, vs. Minnesota); and touchdown passes—4 (August 31, 1997, vs. Pittsburgh).
STATISTICAL PLATEAUS: 300-yard passing games: 1989 (1), 1990 (1), 1991 (1), 1993 (1), 1994 (1), 1995 (2), 1996 (1), 1997 (2), 1998 (1). Total: 11.
MISCELLANEOUS: Regular-season record as starting NFL quarterback: 83-57 (.593). ... Postseason record as starting NFL quarterback: 11-3 (.786). ... Holds Dallas Cowboys all-time record for most yards passing (28,346).

A

Year Team	G	GS	Att.	Cmp.	Pct.	Yds.	TD	Int.	Avg.	Rat.	Att.	Yds.	Avg.	TD	TD	2pt.	Pts.
					PASSING							RUSHING				TOTALS	
1989—Dallas NFL	11	11	293	155	52.9	1749	9	18	5.97	55.7	38	302	7.9	0	0	...	0
1990—Dallas NFL	15	15	399	226	56.6	2579	11	∞18	6.46	66.6	40	172	4.3	1	1	...	6
1991—Dallas NFL	12	12	363	237	‡65.3	2754	11	10	7.59	86.7	16	5	0.3	1	1	...	6
1992—Dallas NFL	16	16	473	∞302	63.8	3445	23	14	7.28	89.5	37	105	2.8	1	1	...	6
1993—Dallas NFL	14	14	392	271	*69.1	3100	15	6	7.91	99.0	32	125	3.9	0	0	...	0
1994—Dallas NFL	14	14	361	233	64.5	2676	13	12	7.41	84.9	30	62	2.1	1	1	0	6
1995—Dallas NFL	16	16	432	280	64.8	3304	16	7	7.65	93.6	21	32	1.5	1	1	0	6
1996—Dallas NFL	15	15	465	296	63.7	3126	12	13	6.72	80.1	35	42	1.2	1	1	0	6
1997—Dallas NFL	16	16	‡518	292	56.4	3283	19	12	6.34	78.0	25	79	3.2	0	0	0	0
1998—Dallas NFL	11	11	315	187	59.4	2330	12	5	7.40	88.5	22	69	3.1	2	2	0	12
Pro totals (10 years)	140	140	4011	2479	61.8	28346	141	115	7.07	82.8	296	993	3.4	8	8	0	48

AKERS, DAVID　　　　　　　　　　K　　　　　　　　　　EAGLES

PERSONAL: Born December 9, 1974, in Lexington, Ky. ... 5-10/180. ... Full name: David Roy Akers.
HIGH SCHOOL: Tates Creek (Lexington, Ky.).
COLLEGE: Louisville.
TRANSACTIONS/CAREER NOTES: Signed as non-drafted free agent by Carolina Panthers (April 19, 1997). ... Released by Panthers (August 17, 1997). ... Signed by Atlanta Falcons for 1998 season. ... Released by Falcons (July 7, 1998). ... Re-signed by Falcons (July 21, 1998). ... Released by Falcons (August 24, 1998). ... Signed by Washington Redskins to practice squad (September 1, 1998). ... Activated (September 15, 1998). ... Released by Redskins (September 22, 1998). ... Signed by Philadelphia Eagles (January 11, 1999). ... Assigned by Eagles to Berlin Thunder in 1999 NFL Europe enhancement allocation program (February 22, 1999).

					KICKING				
Year Team	G	GS	XPM	XPA	FGM	FGA	Lg.	50+	Pts.
1998—Washington NFL	1	0	2	2	0	2	...	0-0	2

ALBRIGHT, ETHAN　　　　　　　　OL　　　　　　　　　　BILLS

PERSONAL: Born May 1, 1971, in Greensboro, N.C. ... 6-5/283. ... Full name: Lawrence Ethan Albright.
HIGH SCHOOL: Grimsley (Greensboro, N.C.).
COLLEGE: North Carolina.
TRANSACTIONS/CAREER NOTES: Signed as non-drafted free agent by Miami Dolphins (April 28, 1994). ... Released by Dolphins (August 22, 1994). ... Re-signed by Dolphins to practice squad (August 29, 1994). ... Released by Dolphins (September 14, 1994). ... Re-signed by Dolphins to practice squad (September 28, 1994). ... Released by Dolphins (November 2, 1994). ... Re-signed by Dolphins (February 16, 1995). ... On injured reserve with knee injury (November 15, 1995-remainder of season). ... Released by Dolphins (August 20, 1996). ... Signed by Buffalo Bills (August 26, 1996). ... Granted free agency (February 13, 1998). ... Re-signed by Bills (April 15, 1998). ... Granted unconditional free agency (February 12, 1999). ... Re-signed by Bills (April 1, 1999).
PLAYING EXPERIENCE: Miami NFL, 1995; Buffalo NFL, 1996-1998. ... Games/Games started: 1995 (10/0), 1996 (16/0), 1997 (16/0), 1998 (16/0). Total: 58/0.
PRO STATISTICS: 1998—Recovered one fumble.

ALDRIDGE, ALLEN　　　　　　　　LB　　　　　　　　　　LIONS

PERSONAL: Born May 30, 1972, in Houston. ... 6-1/255. ... Full name: Allen Ray Aldridge. ... Son of Allen Aldridge, defensive end with Houston Oilers (1971-72) and Cleveland Browns (1974).
HIGH SCHOOL: Willowridge (Sugar Land, Texas).
COLLEGE: Houston.
TRANSACTIONS/CAREER NOTES: Selected by Denver Broncos in second round (51st pick overall) of 1994 NFL draft. ... Signed by Broncos (July 12, 1994). ... Granted free agency (February 14, 1997). ... Re-signed by Broncos (April 15, 1997). ... Granted unconditional free agency (February 13, 1998). ... Signed by Detroit Lions (February 14, 1998).
PLAYING EXPERIENCE: Denver NFL, 1994-1997; Detroit NFL, 1998. ... Games/Games started: 1994 (16/2), 1995 (16/12), 1996 (16/16), 1997 (16/15), 1998 (16/15). Total: 80/60.
CHAMPIONSHIP GAME EXPERIENCE: Played in AFC championship game (1997 season). ... Member of Super Bowl championship team (1997 season).
PRO STATISTICS: 1995—Credited with 1 1/2 sacks and recovered one fumble. 1998—Credited with three sacks and recovered one fumble.

ALEAGA, INK　　　　　　　　　　LB　　　　　　　　　　SAINTS

PERSONAL: Born April 4, 1973, in Honolulu. ... 6-1/251.
HIGH SCHOOL: Maryknoll (Honolulu).
COLLEGE: Washington.
TRANSACTIONS/CAREER NOTES: Signed as non-drafted free agent by New Orleans Saints (April 25, 1997). ... Released by Saints (August 24, 1997). ... Re-signed by Saints to practice squad (August 25, 1997). ... Activated (October 17, 1997).
PLAYING EXPERIENCE: New Orleans NFL, 1997 and 1998. ... Games/Games started: 1997 (3/1), 1998 (15/3). Total: 18/4.
PRO STATISTICS: 1998—Credited with one sack.

ALEXANDER, BRENT　　　　　　　S　　　　　　　　　　PANTHERS

PERSONAL: Born July 10, 1971, in Gallatin, Tenn. ... 5-11/196. ... Full name: Ronald Brent Alexander.
HIGH SCHOOL: Gallatin (Tenn.).
COLLEGE: Tennessee State.

TRANSACTIONS/CAREER NOTES: Signed as non-drafted free agent by Arizona Cardinals (April 28, 1994). ... Granted unconditional free agency (February 13, 1998). ... Signed by Carolina Panthers (March 20, 1998).
PRO STATISTICS: 1995—Credited with ½ sack and recovered one fumble. 1998—Recovered one fumble for 12 yards.

				INTERCEPTIONS		
Year Team	G	GS	No.	Yds.	Avg.	TD
1994—Arizona NFL	16	7	0	0	...	0
1995—Arizona NFL	16	13	2	14	7.0	0
1996—Arizona NFL	16	15	2	3	1.5	0
1997—Arizona NFL	16	15	0	0	...	0
1998—Carolina NFL	16	16	0	0	...	0
Pro totals (5 years)	80	66	4	17	4.3	0

ALEXANDER, DERRICK — WR — CHIEFS

PERSONAL: Born November 6, 1971, in Detroit. ... 6-2/198. ... Full name: Derrick Scott Alexander.
HIGH SCHOOL: Benedictine (Detroit).
COLLEGE: Michigan (degree in sports management).
TRANSACTIONS/CAREER NOTES: Selected by Cleveland Browns in first round (29th pick overall) of 1994 NFL draft. ... Signed by Browns (August 3, 1994). ... Browns franchise moved to Baltimore and renamed Ravens for 1996 season (March 11, 1996). ... Granted unconditional free agency (February 13, 1998). ... Signed by Kansas City Chiefs (March 2, 1998).
PRO STATISTICS: 1995—Fumbled three times and recovered one fumble. 1997—Fumbled once.
SINGLE GAME HIGHS (regular season): Receptions—8 (September 7, 1997, vs. Cincinnati); yards—198 (December 1, 1996, vs. Pittsburgh); and touchdown receptions—2 (November 29, 1998, vs. Arizona).
STATISTICAL PLATEAUS: 100-yard receiving games: 1994 (3), 1996 (3), 1997 (3), 1998 (2). Total: 11.
MISCELLANEOUS: Shares Baltimore Ravens all-time records for most touchdown receptions (18) and touchdowns (18).

			RUSHING				RECEIVING				PUNT RETURNS				KICKOFF RETURNS				TOTALS		
Year Team	G	GS	Att.	Yds.	Avg.	TD	No.	Yds.	Avg.	TD	No.	Yds.	Avg.	TD	No.	Yds.	Avg.	TD	TD	2pt.	Pts.
1994—Cleveland NFL	14	12	4	38	9.5	0	48	828	17.3	2	0	0	...	0	0	0	...	0	2	1	14
1995—Cleveland NFL	14	2	1	29	29.0	0	15	216	14.4	0	9	122	13.6	†1	21	419	20.0	0	1	0	6
1996—Baltimore NFL	15	14	3	0	0.0	0	62	1099	17.7	9	1	15	15.0	0	1	13	13.0	0	9	1	56
1997—Baltimore NFL	15	13	1	0	0.0	0	65	1009	15.5	9	1	34	34.0	0	0	0	...	0	9	0	54
1998—Kansas City NFL	15	14	0	0	...	0	54	992	18.4	4	0	0	...	0	0	0	...	0	4	0	24
Pro totals (5 years)	73	55	9	67	7.4	0	244	4144	17.0	24	11	171	15.5	1	22	432	19.6	0	25	2	154

ALEXANDER, DERRICK — DE — BROWNS

PERSONAL: Born November 13, 1973, in Jacksonville. ... 6-4/286.
HIGH SCHOOL: Raines (Jacksonville).
COLLEGE: Florida State.
TRANSACTIONS/CAREER NOTES: Selected after junior season by Minnesota Vikings in first round (11th pick overall) of 1995 NFL draft. ... Signed by Vikings (August 16, 1995). ... Granted unconditional free agency (February 12, 1999). ... Signed by Cleveland Browns (April 19, 1999).
CHAMPIONSHIP GAME EXPERIENCE: Played in NFC championship game (1998 season).
HONORS: Named defensive lineman on THE SPORTING NEWS college All-America second team (1994).
PRO STATISTICS: 1995—Recovered one fumble. 1996—Recovered one fumble for three yards. 1997—Recovered one fumble.

Year Team	G	GS	SACKS
1995—Minnesota NFL	15	12	2.0
1996—Minnesota NFL	12	9	3.5
1997—Minnesota NFL	14	14	4.5
1998—Minnesota NFL	16	16	7.5
Pro totals (4 years)	57	51	17.5

ALEXANDER, ELIJAH — LB

PERSONAL: Born August 2, 1970, in Fort Worth, Texas. ... 6-2/237. ... Full name: Elijah Alfred Alexander III.
HIGH SCHOOL: Dunbar Senior (Fort Worth, Texas).
COLLEGE: Kansas State (degree in accounting).
TRANSACTIONS/CAREER NOTES: Selected by Tampa Bay Buccaneers in 10th round (254th pick overall) of 1992 NFL draft. ... Signed by Buccaneers (June 3, 1992). ... Released by Buccaneers (August 31, 1992). ... Re-signed by Buccaneers (September 1, 1992). ... Released by Buccaneers (October 16, 1992). ... Re-signed by Buccaneers to practice squad (October 22, 1992). ... Activated (November 10, 1992). ... Claimed on waivers by Denver Broncos (August 31, 1993). ... On injured reserve with shoulder injury (November 22, 1995-remainder of season). ... Granted unconditional free agency (February 16, 1996). ... Signed by Indianapolis Colts (August 6, 1996). ... Selected by Cleveland Browns from Colts in NFL expansion draft (February 9, 1999). ... Released by Browns (June 1, 1999).
PRO STATISTICS: 1994—Recovered one fumble for nine yards. 1998—Recovered two fumbles.

			INTERCEPTIONS				SACKS
Year Team	G	GS	No.	Yds.	Avg.	TD	No.
1992—Tampa Bay NFL	12	0	0	0	...	0	0.0
1993—Denver NFL	16	0	0	0	...	0	0.0
1994—Denver NFL	16	16	1	2	2.0	0	1.0
1995—Denver NFL	9	8	2	5	2.5	0	0.5
1996—Indianapolis NFL	14	3	0	0	...	0	1.0
1997—Indianapolis NFL	13	11	1	43	43.0	1	1.0
1998—Indianapolis NFL	13	9	1	12	12.0	0	0.0
Pro totals (7 years)	93	47	5	62	12.4	1	3.5

ALEXANDER, PATRISE — LB — EAGLES

PERSONAL: Born October 23, 1972, in Galveston, Texas. ... 6-1/244.
HIGH SCHOOL: Ball (Galveston, Texas).
COLLEGE: Southwestern Louisiana.
TRANSACTIONS/CAREER NOTES: Signed as non-drafted free agent by Washington Redskins (April 26, 1995). ... Released by Redskins (August 22, 1995). ... Re-signed by Redskins to practice squad (November 21, 1995). ... On physically unable to perform list with knee injury (August 25-November 6, 1998). ... Released by Redskins (November 11, 1998). ... Signed by Philadelphia Eagles (January 15, 1999).
PLAYING EXPERIENCE: Washington NFL, 1996-1998. ... Games/Games started: 1996 (16/1), 1997 (16/0), 1998 (1/0). Total: 33/1.

ALEXANDER, STEPHEN — TE — REDSKINS

PERSONAL: Born November 7, 1975, in Chickasha, Okla. ... 6-4/246.
HIGH SCHOOL: Chickasha (Okla.).
COLLEGE: Oklahoma.
TRANSACTIONS/CAREER NOTES: Selected by Washington Redskins in second round (48th pick overall) of 1998 NFL draft. ... Signed by Redskins (July 13, 1998).
SINGLE GAME HIGHS (regular season): Receptions—7 (December 13, 1998, vs. Carolina); yards—72 (November 22, 1998, vs. Arizona); and touchdown receptions—1 (December 19, 1998, vs. Tampa Bay).

				RECEIVING				TOTALS		
Year Team	G	GS	No.	Yds.	Avg.	TD	TD	2pt.	Pts.	Fum.
1998—Washington NFL	15	5	37	383	10.4	4	4	0	24	2

ALFORD, BRIAN — WR — GIANTS

PERSONAL: Born June 7, 1975, in Oak Park, Mich. ... 6-1/190. ... Full name: Brian Wayne Alford.
HIGH SCHOOL: Oak Park (Mich.).
COLLEGE: Purdue.
TRANSACTIONS/CAREER NOTES: Selected by New York Giants in third round (70th pick overall) of 1998 NFL draft. ... Signed by Giants (July 24, 1998).
PLAYING EXPERIENCE: New York Giants NFL, 1998. ... Games/Games started: 2/0.
HONORS: Named wide receiver on THE SPORTING NEWS college All-America third team (1997).
PRO STATISTICS: 1998—Caught one pass for 11 yards.
SINGLE GAME HIGHS (regular season): Receptions—1 (December 20, 1998, vs. Kansas City); yards—11 (December 20, 1998, vs. Kansas City); and touchdown receptions—0.

ALLEN, ERIC — DB — RAIDERS

PERSONAL: Born November 22, 1965, in San Diego. ... 5-10/190. ... Full name: Eric Andre Allen.
HIGH SCHOOL: Point Loma (San Diego).
COLLEGE: Arizona State (degree in broadcasting, 1988).
TRANSACTIONS/CAREER NOTES: Selected by Philadelphia Eagles in second round (30th pick overall) of 1988 NFL draft. ... Signed by Eagles (July 19, 1988). ... Granted free agency (February 1, 1992). ... Re-signed by Eagles (September 2, 1992). ... Granted roster exemption (September 2-4, 1992). ... Designated by Eagles as transition player (February 25, 1993). ... Tendered offer sheet by New Orleans Saints (March 20, 1995). ... Eagles declined to match offer (March 27, 1995). ... Traded by Saints to Oakland Raiders for fourth-round pick (DB Fred Weary) in 1998 draft (March 5, 1998). ... On injured reserve with knee injury (November 18, 1998-remainder of season).
HONORS: Played in Pro Bowl (1989 and 1991-1995 seasons).
RECORDS: Shares NFL single-season record for most touchdowns by interception—4 (1993). ... Shares NFL single-game record for most touchdowns by interception—2 (December 26, 1993, vs. New Orleans).
PRO STATISTICS: 1989—Fumbled once for seven yards. 1990—Returned one kickoff for two yards and recovered one fumble. 1991—Recovered one fumble. 1992—Recovered two fumbles. 1993—Credited with two sacks. 1994—Recovered one fumble for 30 yards.
MISCELLANEOUS: Shares Philadelphia Eagles all-time record for most interceptions (34).

				INTERCEPTIONS		
Year Team	G	GS	No.	Yds.	Avg.	TD
1988—Philadelphia NFL	16	16	5	76	15.2	0
1989—Philadelphia NFL	15	15	‡8	38	4.8	0
1990—Philadelphia NFL	16	16	3	37	12.3	1
1991—Philadelphia NFL	16	16	5	20	4.0	0
1992—Philadelphia NFL	16	16	4	49	12.3	0
1993—Philadelphia NFL	16	16	6	*201	33.5	*4
1994—Philadelphia NFL	16	16	3	61	20.3	0
1995—New Orleans NFL	16	16	2	28	14.0	0
1996—New Orleans NFL	16	16	1	33	33.0	0
1997—New Orleans NFL	16	16	2	27	13.5	0
1998—Oakland NFL	10	10	5	59	11.8	0
Pro totals (11 years)	169	168	44	629	14.3	5

ALLEN, JAMES — RB — BEARS

PERSONAL: Born March 28, 1975 ... 5-10/215.
HIGH SCHOOL: Wynnewood (Okla.).
COLLEGE: Oklahoma.
TRANSACTIONS/CAREER NOTES: Signed as non-drafted free agent by Tennessee Oilers (May 14, 1997). ... Released by Oilers (August 20, 1997). ... Signed by Philadelphia Eagles to practice squad (August 27, 1997). ... Released by Eagles (September 2, 1997). ... Re-signed by Eagles to practice squad (September 10, 1997). ... Signed by Chicago Bears off Eagles practice squad (December 9, 1997). ... Inactive for two

games (1997). ... Released by Bears (August 25, 1998). ... Re-signed by Bears to practice squad (August 31, 1998). ... Activated (October 13, 1998).
PRO STATISTICS: 1998—Recovered two fumbles.
SINGLE GAME HIGHS (regular season): Attempts—23 (December 20, 1998, vs. Baltimore); yards—163 (December 20, 1998, vs. Baltimore); and rushing touchdowns—1 (December 20, 1998, vs. Baltimore).
STATISTICAL PLATEAUS: 100-yard rushing games: 1998 (1).

				RUSHING				RECEIVING			TOTALS			
Year Team	G	GS	Att.	Yds.	Avg.	TD	No.	Yds.	Avg.	TD	TD	2pt.	Pts.	Fum.
1997—Chicago NFL							Did not play.							
1998—Chicago NFL	6	2	58	270	4.7	1	8	77	9.6	1	2	0	12	1

ALLEN, LARRY — G/OT — COWBOYS

PERSONAL: Born November 27, 1971, in Los Angeles. ... 6-3/326. ... Full name: Larry Christopher Allen.
HIGH SCHOOL: Vintage (Napa, Calif.).
JUNIOR COLLEGE: Butte College (Calif.).
COLLEGE: Sonoma State (Calif.).
TRANSACTIONS/CAREER NOTES: Selected by Dallas Cowboys in second round (46th pick overall) of 1994 NFL draft. ... Signed by Cowboys (July 16, 1994).
PLAYING EXPERIENCE: Dallas NFL, 1994-1998. ... Games/Games started: 1994 (16/10), 1995 (16/16), 1996 (16/16), 1997 (16/16), 1998 (16/16). Total: 80/74.
CHAMPIONSHIP GAME EXPERIENCE: Played in NFC championship game (1994 and 1995 seasons). ... Member of Super Bowl championship team (1995 season).
HONORS: Named guard on THE SPORTING NEWS NFL All-Pro team (1995-97). ... Played in Pro Bowl (1995-1998 seasons). ... Named offensive tackle on THE SPORTING NEWS NFL All-Pro team (1998).
PRO STATISTICS: 1995—Recovered one fumble.

ALLEN, TAJE — CB — RAMS

PERSONAL: Born November 6, 1973, in Lubbock, Texas. ... 5-10/185. ... Full name: Taje LaQuane Allen. ... Name pronounced TAH-jee.
HIGH SCHOOL: Estacado (Lubbock, Texas).
COLLEGE: Texas.
TRANSACTIONS/CAREER NOTES: Selected by St. Louis Rams in fifth round (158th pick overall) of 1997 NFL draft. ... Signed by Rams (July 3, 1997).
PLAYING EXPERIENCE: St. Louis NFL, 1997 and 1998. ... Games/Games started: 1997 (14/1), 1998 (16/0). Total: 30/1.

ALLEN, TERRY — RB

PERSONAL: Born February 21, 1968, in Commerce, Ga. ... 5-10/208. ... Full name: Terry Thomas Allen Jr.
HIGH SCHOOL: Banks County (Homer, Ga.).
COLLEGE: Clemson.
TRANSACTIONS/CAREER NOTES: Selected after junior season by Minnesota Vikings in ninth round (241st pick overall) of 1990 NFL draft. ... Signed by Vikings (July 2, 1990). ... On injured reserve with knee injury (August 28, 1990-entire season). ... On injured reserve with knee injury (August 23, 1993-entire season). ... Released by Vikings (May 8, 1995). ... Signed by Washington Redskins (June 15, 1995). ... Granted free agency (February 16, 1996). ... Re-signed by Redskins (July 17, 1996). ... Granted unconditional free agency (February 14, 1997). ... Re-signed by Redskins (February 26, 1997). ... Released by Redskins (April 19, 1999).
HONORS: Played in Pro Bowl (1996 season).
PRO STATISTICS: 1991—Returned one kickoff for 14 yards and recovered one fumble. 1992—Recovered two fumbles. 1994—Recovered two fumbles for four yards. 1995—Recovered one fumble. 1997—Recovered one fumble. 1998—Recovered one fumble.
SINGLE GAME HIGHS (regular season): Attempts—36 (September 28, 1997, vs. Jacksonville); yards—172 (December 20, 1992, vs. Pittsburgh); and rushing touchdowns—3 (December 22, 1996, vs. Dallas).
STATISTICAL PLATEAUS: 100-yard rushing games: 1991 (1), 1992 (3), 1994 (3), 1995 (4), 1996 (5), 1997 (3). Total: 19. ... 100-yard receiving games: 1992 (1).

				RUSHING				RECEIVING			TOTALS			
Year Team	G	GS	Att.	Yds.	Avg.	TD	No.	Yds.	Avg.	TD	TD	2pt.	Pts.	Fum.
1990—Minnesota NFL							Did not play.							
1991—Minnesota NFL	15	6	120	563	‡4.7	2	6	49	8.2	1	3	...	18	4
1992—Minnesota NFL	16	16	266	1201	4.5	13	49	478	9.8	2	15	...	90	9
1993—Minnesota NFL							Did not play.							
1994—Minnesota NFL	16	16	255	1031	4.0	8	17	148	8.7	0	8	1	50	3
1995—Washington NFL	16	16	338	1309	3.9	10	31	232	7.5	0	11	0	66	6
1996—Washington NFL	16	16	347	1353	3.9	*21	32	194	6.1	0	*21	0	126	4
1997—Washington NFL	10	10	210	724	3.4	4	20	172	8.6	1	5	0	30	2
1998—Washington NFL	10	10	148	700	4.7	2	17	128	7.5	0	2	0	12	4
Pro totals (7 years)	99	90	1684	6881	4.1	60	172	1401	8.1	5	65	1	392	32

ALLRED, JOHN — TE — BEARS

PERSONAL: Born September 9, 1974, in Del Mar, Calif. ... 6-4/249.
HIGH SCHOOL: Torrey Pines (Encinitas, Calif.).
COLLEGE: Southern California.
TRANSACTIONS/CAREER NOTES: Selected by Chicago Bears in second round (38th pick overall) of 1997 NFL draft. ... Signed by Bears (July 14, 1997).
PLAYING EXPERIENCE: Chicago NFL, 1997 and 1998. ... Games/Games started: 1997 (15/4), 1998 (3/0). Total: 18/4.
PRO STATISTICS: 1997—Caught eight passes for 70 yards and returned two kickoffs for 21 yards.
SINGLE GAME HIGHS (regular season): Receptions—2 (September 14, 1997, vs. Detroit); yards—26 (September 14, 1997, vs. Detroit); and touchdown receptions—0.

ALSTOTT, MIKE — FB — BUCCANEERS

PERSONAL: Born December 21, 1973, in Joliet, Ill. ... 6-1/255. ... Full name: Michael Joseph Alstott.
HIGH SCHOOL: Joliet (Ill.) Catholic.
COLLEGE: Purdue (degree in business, 1995).
TRANSACTIONS/CAREER NOTES: Selected by Tampa Bay Buccaneers in second round (35th pick overall) of 1996 NFL draft. ... Signed by Buccaneers (July 21, 1996).
HONORS: Played in Pro Bowl (1997 and 1998 seasons).
PRO STATISTICS: 1996—Returned one kickoff for 14 yards. 1997—Returned one kickoff for no yards. 1998—Attempted one pass without a completion and returned one kickoff for eight yards.
SINGLE GAME HIGHS (regular season): Attempts—24 (December 13, 1998, vs. Pittsburgh); yards—128 (November 1, 1998, vs. Minnesota); and rushing touchdowns—3 (December 27, 1998, vs. Cincinnati).
STATISTICAL PLATEAUS: 100-yard rushing games: 1998 (2).

				RUSHING				RECEIVING				TOTALS		
Year Team	G	GS	Att.	Yds.	Avg.	TD	No.	Yds.	Avg.	TD	TD	2pt.	Pts.	Fum.
1996—Tampa Bay NFL	16	16	96	377	3.9	3	65	557	8.6	3	6	0	36	4
1997—Tampa Bay NFL	15	15	176	665	3.8	7	23	178	7.7	3	10	0	60	5
1998—Tampa Bay NFL	16	16	215	846	3.9	8	22	152	6.9	1	9	0	54	5
Pro totals (3 years)	47	47	487	1888	3.9	18	110	887	8.1	7	25	0	150	14

AMBROSE, ASHLEY — CB

PERSONAL: Born September 17, 1970, in New Orleans. ... 5-10/185. ... Full name: Ashley Avery Ambrose.
HIGH SCHOOL: Fortier (New Orleans).
COLLEGE: Mississippi Valley State (degree in industrial technology).
TRANSACTIONS/CAREER NOTES: Selected by Indianapolis Colts in second round (29th pick overall) of 1992 NFL draft. ... Signed by Colts (August 11, 1992). ... On injured reserve with leg injury (September 14-October 29, 1992); on practice squad (October 21-29, 1992). ... Granted free agency (February 17, 1995). ... Re-signed by Colts (April 29, 1995). ... Granted unconditional free agency (February 16, 1996). ... Signed by Cincinnati Bengals (February 25, 1996). ... Granted unconditional free agency (February 12, 1999).
CHAMPIONSHIP GAME EXPERIENCE: Played in AFC championship game (1995 season).
HONORS: Played in Pro Bowl (1996 season).
PRO STATISTICS: 1992—Returned eight kickoffs for 126 yards. 1994—Recovered one fumble. 1997—Credited with one sack and recovered two fumbles.

			INTERCEPTIONS			
Year Team	G	GS	No.	Yds.	Avg.	TD
1992—Indianapolis NFL	10	2	0	0	...	0
1993—Indianapolis NFL	14	6	0	0	...	0
1994—Indianapolis NFL	16	4	2	50	25.0	0
1995—Indianapolis NFL	16	0	3	12	4.0	0
1996—Cincinnati NFL	16	16	8	63	7.9	1
1997—Cincinnati NFL	16	16	3	56	18.7	0
1998—Cincinnati NFL	15	15	2	0	0.0	0
Pro totals (7 years)	103	59	18	181	10.1	1

AMEY, VINCE — DE — RAIDERS

PERSONAL: Born February 9, 1975, in Hollywood, Calif. ... 6-2/289. ... Full name: Vincent Wayne Amey.
HIGH SCHOOL: James Logan (Union City, Calif.).
COLLEGE: Arizona State.
TRANSACTIONS/CAREER NOTES: Selected by Oakland Raiders in seventh round (230th pick overall) of 1998 NFL draft. ... Signed by Raiders (May 21, 1998). ... Released by Raiders (August 30, 1998). ... Re-signed by Raiders to practice squad (August 31, 1998). ... Activated (November 13, 1998). ... Assigned by Raiders to Frankfurt Galaxy in 1999 NFL Europe enhancement allocation program (February 22, 1999).
PLAYING EXPERIENCE: Oakland NFL, 1998. ... Games/Games started: 4/1.
PRO STATISTICS: 1998—Returned one kickoff for no yards.

ANDERS, KIMBLE — FB — CHIEFS

PERSONAL: Born September 10, 1966, in Galveston, Texas. ... 5-11/225. ... Full name: Kimble Lynard Anders.
HIGH SCHOOL: Ball (Galveston, Texas).
COLLEGE: Houston.
TRANSACTIONS/CAREER NOTES: Signed as non-drafted free agent by Pittsburgh Steelers (April 25, 1990). ... Released by Steelers (September 3, 1990). ... Signed by Kansas City Chiefs (March 13, 1991). ... On injured reserve with hand injury (September 15, 1991-remainder of season). ... On injured reserve with knee injury (September 12-October 17, 1992); on practice squad (October 7-17, 1992). ... Granted unconditional free agency (February 16, 1996). ... Re-signed by Chiefs (April 1, 1996).
CHAMPIONSHIP GAME EXPERIENCE: Played in AFC championship game (1993 season).
HONORS: Played in Pro Bowl (1995-1997 seasons).
PRO STATISTICS: 1994—Recovered two fumbles. 1997—Recovered one fumble. 1998—Recovered one fumble.
SINGLE GAME HIGHS (regular season): Attempts—13 (November 13, 1994, vs. San Diego); yards—75 (November 5, 1995, vs. Washington); and rushing touchdowns—1 (November 17, 1996, vs. Chicago).

			RUSHING				RECEIVING				KICKOFF RETURNS				TOTALS		
Year Team	G	GS	Att.	Yds.	Avg.	TD	No.	Yds.	Avg.	TD	No.	Yds.	Avg.	TD	TD	2pt.	Pts.	Fum.
1991—Kansas City NFL	2	0	0	0	...	0	2	30	15.0	0	0	0	...	0	0	...	0	0
1992—Kansas City NFL	11	2	1	1	1.0	0	5	65	13.0	0	1	20	20.0	0	0	...	0	1
1993—Kansas City NFL	16	13	75	291	3.9	0	40	326	8.2	1	1	47	47.0	0	1	...	6	1
1994—Kansas City NFL	16	13	62	231	3.7	2	67	525	7.8	1	2	36	18.0	0	3	0	18	1

Year Team	G	GS	Att	Rushing Yds	Avg	TD	No.	Receiving Yds	Avg	TD	No.	Kickoff Returns Yds	Avg	TD	TD	Totals 2pt	Pts	Fum
1995—Kansas City NFL	16	13	58	398	6.9	2	55	349	6.3	1	0	0	...	0	3	0	18	1
1996—Kansas City NFL	16	15	54	201	3.7	2	60	529	8.8	2	2	37	18.5	0	4	0	24	0
1997—Kansas City NFL	15	14	79	397	5.0	0	59	453	7.7	2	1	0	0.0	0	2	0	12	3
1998—Kansas City NFL	16	15	58	230	4.0	1	64	462	7.2	2	1	16	16.0	0	3	0	18	6
Pro totals (8 years)	108	85	387	1749	4.5	7	352	2739	7.8	9	8	156	19.5	0	16	0	96	13

ANDERSEN, MORTEN — K — FALCONS

PERSONAL: Born August 19, 1960, in Copenhagen, Denmark. ... 6-2/222.
HIGH SCHOOL: Ben Davis (Indianapolis).
COLLEGE: Michigan State (degrees in communications and German).
TRANSACTIONS/CAREER NOTES: Selected by New Orleans Saints in fourth round (86th pick overall) of 1982 NFL draft. ... On injured reserve with sprained ankle (September 15-November 20, 1982). ... Designated by Saints as transition player (February 25, 1993). ... Released by Saints (July 19, 1995). ... Signed by Atlanta Falcons (July 21, 1995).
CHAMPIONSHIP GAME EXPERIENCE: Played in NFC championship game (1998 season). ... Played in Super Bowl XXXIII (1998 season).
HONORS: Named kicker on THE SPORTING NEWS college All-America first team (1981). ... Named kicker on THE SPORTING NEWS NFL All-Pro team (1985-1987 and 1995). ... Played in Pro Bowl (1985-1988, 1990, 1992 and 1995 seasons).
RECORDS: Holds NFL career records for most seasons with 100 or more points—12 (1985-89, 1991-95, 1997 and 1998); for most consecutive games scoring—238 (December 11, 1983-present); and for most made field goals of 50 or more yards—35. ... Holds NFL single-season record for most made field goals of 50 or more yards—8 (1995). ... Holds NFL single-game record for most made field goals of 50 or more yards—3 (December 11, 1983, at Philadelphia).

Year Team	G	XPM	XPA	FGM	FGA	Lg.	50+	Pts.
1982—New Orleans NFL	8	6	6	2	5	45	0-1	12
1983—New Orleans NFL	16	37	38	18	24	52	3-4	91
1984—New Orleans NFL	16	34	34	20	27	53	2-3	94
1985—New Orleans NFL	16	27	29	31	35	55	3-4	120
1986—New Orleans NFL	16	30	30	26	30	53	2-5	108
1987—New Orleans NFL	12	37	37	*28	*36	52	2-6	121
1988—New Orleans NFL	16	32	33	26	36	51	1-4	110
1989—New Orleans NFL	16	44	45	20	29	49	0-4	104
1990—New Orleans NFL	16	29	29	21	27	52	3-4	92
1991—New Orleans NFL	16	38	38	25	32	60	2-4	113
1992—New Orleans NFL	16	33	34	29	34	52	3-3	∞120
1993—New Orleans NFL	16	33	33	28	35	56	1-5	117
1994—New Orleans NFL	16	32	32	28	†39	48	0-6	116
1995—Atlanta NFL	16	29	30	‡31	37	59	8-9	122
1996—Atlanta NFL	16	31	31	22	29	54	1-5	97
1997—Atlanta NFL	16	35	35	23	27	55	2-3	104
1998—Atlanta NFL	16	51	52	23	28	53	2-2	120
Pro totals (17 years)	260	558	566	401	510	60	35-72	1761

ANDERSON, ANTONIO — DT

PERSONAL: Born June 4, 1973, in Brooklyn, N.Y. ... 6-6/318. ... Full name: Antonio Kenneth Anderson. ... Cousin of Keith Jennings, tight end with Montreal Machine of World League (1991) and Chicago Bears (1991-97); cousin of Stanford Jennings, running back with Cincinnati Bengals (1984-90), New Orleans Saints (1991) and Tampa Bay Buccaneers (1992); and cousin of John Salley, forward with four NBA teams (1986-87 through 1994-95).
HIGH SCHOOL: Midwood (Brooklyn, N.Y.), then Milford (Conn.) Academy.
COLLEGE: Syracuse.
TRANSACTIONS/CAREER NOTES: Selected by Dallas Cowboys in fourth round (101st pick overall) of 1997 NFL draft. ... Signed by Cowboys (July 14, 1997). ... Selected by Cleveland Browns from Cowboys in NFL expansion draft (February 9, 1999). ... Released by Browns (April 22, 1999).
PLAYING EXPERIENCE: Dallas NFL, 1997 and 1998. ... Games/Games started: 1997 (16/5), 1998 (5/0). Total: 21/5.
PRO STATISTICS: 1997—Credited with two sacks.

ANDERSON, DARREN — CB

PERSONAL: Born January 11, 1969, in Cincinnati. ... 5-10/189. ... Full name: Darren Hunter Anderson.
HIGH SCHOOL: Walnut Hills (Cincinnati).
COLLEGE: Toledo.
TRANSACTIONS/CAREER NOTES: Selected by New England Patriots in fourth round (93rd pick overall) of 1992 NFL draft. ... Signed by Patriots (July 21, 1992). ... Released by Patriots (September 3, 1992). ... Re-signed by Patriots to practice squad (September 9, 1992). ... Activated (September 26, 1992). ... Released by Patriots (October 2, 1992). ... Re-signed by Patriots to practice squad (October 6, 1992). ... Released by Patriots (October 28, 1992). ... Signed by Tampa Bay Buccaneers to practice squad (October 31, 1992). ... Activated (December 26, 1992). ... Traded by Buccaneers to Kansas City Chiefs for seventh-round pick (DE Jeffrey Rodgers) in 1995 draft (August 23, 1994). ... Granted free agency (February 16, 1996). ... Re-signed by Chiefs (April 9, 1996). ... Released by Chiefs (April 24, 1998). ... Signed by Atlanta Falcons (September 30, 1998). ... Granted unconditional free agency (February 12, 1999).
PLAYING EXPERIENCE: New England (1)-Tampa Bay (1) NFL, 1992; Tampa Bay NFL, 1993; Kansas City NFL 1994-1997; Atlanta NFL, 1998. ... Games/Games started: 1992 (N.E.-1/0; T.B.-1/0; Total: 2/0), 1993 (14/1), 1994 (15/1), 1995 (16/0), 1996 (11/3), 1997 (11/0), 1998 (6/0). Total: 75/5.
CHAMPIONSHIP GAME EXPERIENCE: Member of Falcons for NFC championship game (1998 season); inactive. ... Member of Falcons for Super Bowl XXXIII (1998 season); inactive.
PRO STATISTICS: 1993—Intercepted one pass for six yards. 1994—Recovered one fumble. 1996—Recovered one fumble. 1997—Intercepted one pass for 55 yards and a touchdown and credited with two sacks.

ANDERSON, GARY — K — VIKINGS

PERSONAL: Born July 16, 1959, in Parys, Orange Free State, South Africa. ... 5-11/179. ... Full name: Gary Allan Anderson. ... Son of Rev. Douglas Anderson, former professional soccer player in England.
HIGH SCHOOL: Brettonwood (Durban, South Africa).
COLLEGE: Syracuse (degree in management and accounting, 1982).
TRANSACTIONS/CAREER NOTES: Selected by Buffalo Bills in seventh round (171st pick overall) of 1982 NFL draft. ... Signed by Bills for 1982 season. ... Claimed on waivers by Pittsburgh Steelers (September 7, 1982). ... Designated by Steelers as transition player (February 15, 1994). ... On reserve/did not report list (August 23-25, 1994). ... Free agency status changed by Steelers from transition to unconditional (February 17, 1995). ... Signed by Philadelphia Eagles (July 23, 1995). ... Released by Eagles (April 22, 1997). ... Signed by San Francisco 49ers (June 11, 1997). ... Granted unconditional free agency (February 13, 1998). ... Signed by Minnesota Vikings (February 20, 1998).
CHAMPIONSHIP GAME EXPERIENCE: Played in AFC championship game (1984 and 1994 seasons). ... Played in NFC championship game (1997 and 1998 seasons).
HONORS: Played in Pro Bowl (1983, 1985, 1993 and 1998 seasons). ... Named kicker on THE SPORTING NEWS NFL All-Pro team (1998).
RECORDS: Holds NFL career record for most field goals made—420; and most consecutive field goals made—40. ... Holds NFL single-season records for most PATs made without a miss—59 (1998); and most points scored without a touchdown—164 (1998). ... Shares NFL single-season record for highest field-goal percentage—100.0 (1998).
POST SEASON RECORDS: Holds NFL postseason career record for most field goals made—25. ... Holds NFL postseason record for most consecutive field goals made—16 (1989-95).
PRO STATISTICS: 1994—Rushed once for three yards.

					KICKING				
Year Team		G	XPM	XPA	FGM	FGA	Lg.	50+	Pts.
1982—Pittsburgh NFL		9	22	22	10	12	48	0-1	52
1983—Pittsburgh NFL		16	38	39	27	31	49	0-0	§119
1984—Pittsburgh NFL		16	45	45	▲24	32	55	2-3	§117
1985—Pittsburgh NFL		16	40	40	*33	*42	52	1-4	§139
1986—Pittsburgh NFL		16	32	32	21	32	45	0-3	95
1987—Pittsburgh NFL		12	21	21	22	27	52	2-2	87
1988—Pittsburgh NFL		16	34	35	28	36	52	1-2	118
1989—Pittsburgh NFL		16	28	28	21	30	49	0-0	91
1990—Pittsburgh NFL		16	32	32	20	25	48	0-2	92
1991—Pittsburgh NFL		16	31	31	23	33	54	1-6	100
1992—Pittsburgh NFL		16	29	31	28	36	49	0-2	113
1993—Pittsburgh NFL		16	32	32	28	30	46	0-0	116
1994—Pittsburgh NFL		16	32	32	24	29	50	1-2	104
1995—Philadelphia NFL		16	32	33	22	30	43	0-3	98
1996—Philadelphia NFL		16	40	40	25	29	46	0-0	115
1997—San Francisco NFL		16	38	38	29	36	51	1-3	125
1998—Minnesota NFL		16	*59	*59	‡35	∞35	53	2-2	*164
Pro totals (17 years)		261	585	590	420	525	55	11-35	1845

ANDERSON, JAMAL — RB — FALCONS

PERSONAL: Born September 30, 1972, in Woodland Hills, Calif. ... 5-11/235. ... Full name: Jamal Sharif Anderson.
HIGH SCHOOL: El Camino Real (Monterey Park, Calif.).
JUNIOR COLLEGE: Moorpark (Calif.) Junior College.
COLLEGE: Utah.
TRANSACTIONS/CAREER NOTES: Selected by Atlanta Falcons in seventh round (201st pick overall) of 1994 NFL draft. ... Signed by Falcons (June 21, 1994).
CHAMPIONSHIP GAME EXPERIENCE: Played in NFC championship game (1998 season). ... Played in Super Bowl XXXIII (1998 season).
HONORS: Named running back on THE SPORTING NEWS NFL All-Pro team (1998). ... Played in Pro Bowl (1998 season).
RECORDS: Holds NFL single-season record for most rushing attempts—410 (1998).
PRO STATISTICS: 1996—Recovered one fumble. 1997—Attempted four passes with one completion for 27 yards and a touchdown and one interception and recovered one fumble. 1998—Attempted two passes without a completion and recovered one fumble.
SINGLE GAME HIGHS (regular season): Attempts—33 (December 21, 1997, vs. Arizona); yards—188 (November 29, 1998, vs. St. Louis); and rushing touchdowns—3 (October 6, 1996, vs. Detroit).
STATISTICAL PLATEAUS: 100-yard rushing games: 1996 (3), 1997 (2), 1998 (12). Total: 17.

			RUSHING				RECEIVING				KICKOFF RETURNS				TOTALS			
Year Team	G	GS	Att.	Yds.	Avg.	TD	No.	Yds.	Avg.	TD	No.	Yds.	Avg.	TD	TD	2pt.	Pts.	Fum.
1994—Atlanta NFL	3	0	2	-1	-0.5	0	0	0	...	0	1	11	11.0	0	0	0	0	0
1995—Atlanta NFL	16	0	39	161	4.1	1	4	42	10.5	0	24	541	22.5	0	1	0	6	0
1996—Atlanta NFL	16	12	232	1055	4.5	5	49	473	9.7	1	4	80	20.0	0	6	0	36	4
1997—Atlanta NFL	16	15	290	1002	3.5	7	29	284	9.8	3	0	0	...	0	10	0	60	4
1998—Atlanta NFL	16	16	*410	‡1846	4.5	‡14	27	319	11.8	2	0	0	...	0	16	1	98	5
Pro totals (5 years)	67	43	973	4063	4.2	27	109	1118	10.3	6	29	632	21.8	0	33	1	200	13

ANDERSON, RICHIE — RB — JETS

PERSONAL: Born September 13, 1971, in Sandy Spring, Md. ... 6-2/230. ... Full name: Richard Darnoll Anderson II.
HIGH SCHOOL: Sherwood (Sandy Spring, Md.).
COLLEGE: Penn State.
TRANSACTIONS/CAREER NOTES: Selected after junior season by New York Jets in sixth round (144th pick overall) of 1993 NFL draft. ... Signed by Jets (June 10, 1993). ... On injured reserve with ankle injury (December 31, 1993-remainder of season). ... On injured reserve with ankle injury (November 30, 1995-remainder of season).
CHAMPIONSHIP GAME EXPERIENCE: Member of Jets for AFC championship game (1998 season); did not play.
PRO STATISTICS: 1993—Recovered one fumble. 1994—Recovered one fumble. 1995—Attempted one pass without a completion. 1996—Recovered one fumble. 1997—Recovered one fumble.

SINGLE GAME HIGHS (regular season): Attempts—9 (November 13, 1994, vs. Green Bay); yards—74 (November 13, 1994, vs. Green Bay); and rushing touchdowns—1 (October 27, 1996, vs. Arizona).

				RUSHING				RECEIVING				KICKOFF RETURNS				TOTALS		
Year Team	G	GS	Att.	Yds.	Avg.	TD	No.	Yds.	Avg.	TD	No.	Yds.	Avg.	TD	TD	2pt.	Pts.	Fum.
1993—New York Jets NFL	7	0	0	0	...	0	0	0	...	0	4	66	16.5	0	0	...	0	1
1994—New York Jets NFL	13	5	43	207	4.8	1	25	212	8.5	1	3	43	14.3	0	2	0	12	1
1995—New York Jets NFL	10	0	5	17	3.4	0	5	26	5.2	0	0	0	...	0	0	0	0	2
1996—New York Jets NFL	16	13	47	150	3.2	1	44	385	8.8	0	0	0	...	0	1	0	6	0
1997—New York Jets NFL	16	3	21	70	3.3	0	26	150	5.8	1	0	0	...	0	1	0	6	2
1998—New York Jets NFL	8	2	1	2	2.0	0	3	12	4.0	0	0	0	...	0	0	0	0	0
Pro totals (6 years)	70	23	117	446	3.8	2	103	785	7.6	2	7	109	15.6	0	4	0	24	6

ANDERSON, RONNIE   WR   CARDINALS

PERSONAL: Born February 27, 1974, in Cleveland. ... 6-1/189. ... Full name: Ronnie Dernell Anderson.
HIGH SCHOOL: University (Hunting Valley, Ohio).
COLLEGE: Allegheny (degrees in English and history).
TRANSACTIONS/CAREER NOTES: Signed as non-drafted free agent by Green Bay Packers (April 25, 1997). ... Released by Packers (August 18, 1997). ... Re-signed by Packers to practice squad (October 7, 1997). ... Activated (January 23, 1998). ... Claimed on waivers by Arizona Cardinals (August 31, 1998).
PLAYING EXPERIENCE: Arizona NFL, 1998. ... Games/Games started: 4/0.
CHAMPIONSHIP GAME EXPERIENCE: Member of Packers for Super Bowl XXXII (1997 season); inactive.
PRO STATISTICS: 1998—Caught one pass for eight yards and recovered one fumble.
SINGLE GAME HIGHS (regular season): Receptions—1 (November 29, 1998, vs. Kansas City); yards—8 (November 29, 1998, vs. Kansas City); and touchdown receptions—0.

ANDERSON, WILLIE   OT   BENGALS

PERSONAL: Born July 11, 1975, in Mobile, Ala. ... 6-5/340. ... Full name: Willie Aaron Anderson.
HIGH SCHOOL: Vigor (Mobile, Ala.).
COLLEGE: Auburn.
TRANSACTIONS/CAREER NOTES: Selected after junior season by Cincinnati Bengals in first round (10th pick overall) of 1996 NFL draft. ... Signed by Bengals (August 5, 1996).
PLAYING EXPERIENCE: Cincinnati NFL, 1996-1998. ... Games/Games started: 1996 (16/10), 1997 (16/16), 1998 (16/16). Total: 48/42.
PRO STATISTICS: 1998—Recovered one fumble.

ANDRUZZI, JOE   G   PACKERS

PERSONAL: Born August 23, 1975, in Brooklyn, N.Y. ... 6-3/310. ... Full name: Joseph Dominick Andruzzi.
HIGH SCHOOL: Tottenville (Staten Island, N.Y.).
COLLEGE: Southern Connecticut State.
TRANSACTIONS/CAREER NOTES: Signed as non-drafted free agent by Green Bay Packers (April 25, 1997). ... Inactive for all 16 games (1997). ... Assigned by Packers to Scottish Claymores in 1998 NFL Europe enhancement allocations program (February 18, 1998).
PLAYING EXPERIENCE: Scottish NFLE, 1998; Green Bay NFL, 1998. ... Games/Games started: NFLE 1998 (10/10), NFL 1998 (15/1). Total Pro: 25/11.
CHAMPIONSHIP GAME EXPERIENCE: Member of Packers for NFC championship game (1997 season); inactive. ... Member of Packers for Super Bowl XXXII (1997 season); inactive.
PRO STATISTICS: 1998—Recovered one fumble.

ANTHONY, REIDEL   WR   BUCCANEERS

PERSONAL: Born October 20, 1976, in South Bay, Fla. ... 5-11/178. ... Full name: Reidel Clarence Anthony. ... Name pronounced REE-dell.
HIGH SCHOOL: Glades Central (Fla.).
COLLEGE: Florida.
TRANSACTIONS/CAREER NOTES: Selected after junior season by Tampa Bay Buccaneers in first round (16th pick overall) of 1997 NFL draft. ... Signed by Buccaneers (July 20, 1997).
HONORS: Named wide receiver on THE SPORTING NEWS college All-America first team (1996).
PRO STATISTICS: 1998—Recovered one fumble.
SINGLE GAME HIGHS (regular season): Receptions—7 (November 8, 1998, vs. Tennessee); yards—126 (November 15, 1998, vs. Jacksonville); and touchdown receptions—2 (November 15, 1998, vs. Jacksonville).
STATISTICAL PLATEAUS: 100-yard receiving games: 1998 (1).

				RUSHING				RECEIVING				KICKOFF RETURNS				TOTALS		
Year Team	G	GS	Att.	Yds.	Avg.	TD	No.	Yds.	Avg.	TD	No.	Yds.	Avg.	TD	TD	2pt.	Pts.	Fum.
1997—Tampa Bay NFL	16	12	5	84	16.8	0	35	448	12.8	4	25	592	23.7	0	4	0	24	0
1998—Tampa Bay NFL	15	13	4	43	10.8	0	51	708	13.9	7	46	1118	24.3	0	7	1	44	0
Pro totals (2 years)	31	25	9	127	14.1	0	86	1156	13.4	11	71	1710	24.1	0	11	1	68	0

ARAGUZ, LEO   P   RAIDERS

PERSONAL: Born January 18, 1970, in Pharr, Texas. ... 5-11/190. ... Full name: Leobardo Jaime Araguz.
HIGH SCHOOL: Harlingen (Texas).
COLLEGE: Stephen F. Austin.

TRANSACTIONS/CAREER NOTES: Signed as non-drafted free agent by Miami Dolphins (March 28, 1994). ... Released by Dolphins prior to 1994 season. ... Signed by San Diego Chargers (1995). ... Released by Chargers prior to 1995 season. ... Signed by Rhein Fire of the World League for 1996 season. ... Signed by Oakland Raiders (December 4, 1996).
RECORDS: Holds NFL single-game record for most punts—16 (October 11, 1998, vs. San Diego).
PRO STATISTICS: 1996—Rushed once for no yards and recovered one fumble. 1997—Rushed once for no yards, fumbled once and recovered one fumble for minus 21 yards. 1998—Rushed once for minus 12 yards and attempted one pass with a completion for minus one yard.

				PUNTING			
Year Team	G	No.	Yds.	Avg.	Net avg.	In. 20	Blk.
1996—Rhein W.L.	...	41	1735	42.3	37.8	17	0
—Oakland NFL	3	13	534	41.1	34.5	4	0
1997—Oakland NFL	16	§93	§4189	45.0	*39.1	▲28	0
1998—Oakland NFL	16	§98	§4256	43.4	33.4	29	0
W.L. totals (1 year)	...	41	1735	42.3	37.8	17	0
NFL totals (3 years)	35	204	8979	44.0	36.1	61	0
Pro totals (4 years)	...	245	10714	43.7	36.4	78	0

ARCHAMBEAU, LESTER — DE — FALCONS

PERSONAL: Born June 27, 1967, in Montville, N.J. ... 6-5/275. ... Full name: Lester Milward Archambeau.
HIGH SCHOOL: Montville (N.J.).
COLLEGE: Stanford (degree in industrial engineering).
TRANSACTIONS/CAREER NOTES: Selected by Green Bay Packers in seventh round (186th pick overall) of 1990 NFL draft. ... Signed by Packers (July 22, 1990). ... On injured reserve with back injury (October 6, 1990-remainder of season). ... Granted free agency (February 1, 1992). ... Re-signed by Packers (August 12, 1992). ... Traded by Packers to Atlanta Falcons for WR James Milling (June 3, 1993). ... Granted unconditional free agency (February 17, 1994). ... Re-signed by Falcons (March 7, 1994). ... Granted unconditional free agency (February 14, 1997). ... Re-signed by Falcons (March 3, 1997).
CHAMPIONSHIP GAME EXPERIENCE: Played in NFC championship game (1998 season). ... Played in Super Bowl XXXIII (1998 season).
PRO STATISTICS: 1995—Recovered one fumble. 1997—Intercepted one pass for no yards and recovered three fumbles. 1998—Recovered two fumbles.

Year Team	G	GS	SACKS
1990—Green Bay NFL	4	0	0.0
1991—Green Bay NFL	16	0	4.5
1992—Green Bay NFL	16	0	1.0
1993—Atlanta NFL	15	11	0.0
1994—Atlanta NFL	16	12	2.0
1995—Atlanta NFL	16	7	3.0
1996—Atlanta NFL	15	15	2.0
1997—Atlanta NFL	16	16	8.5
1998—Atlanta NFL	15	15	10.0
Pro totals (9 years)	129	76	31.0

ARCHIE, MIKE — RB — TITANS

PERSONAL: Born October 14, 1972, in Sharon, Pa. ... 5-8/204. ... Full name: Michael Lamont Archie.
HIGH SCHOOL: Sharon (Pa.).
COLLEGE: Penn State.
TRANSACTIONS/CAREER NOTES: Selected by Houston Oilers in seventh round (218th pick overall) of 1996 NFL draft. ... Signed by Oilers (July 12, 1996). ... Oilers franchise moved to Tennessee for 1997 season. ... Oilers franchise renamed Tennessee Titans for 1999 season (December 26, 1998). ... Granted free agency (February 12, 1999).
PRO STATISTICS: 1997—Recovered one fumble. 1998—Attempted two passes with one completion for 18 yards and a touchdown and fumbled three times.
SINGLE GAME HIGHS (regular season): Attempts—2 (November 29, 1998, vs. Seattle); yards—20 (November 29, 1998, vs. Seattle); and rushing touchdowns—1 (November 8, 1998, vs. Tampa Bay).

			RUSHING				RECEIVING			PUNT RETURNS				KICKOFF RETURNS				TOTALS		
Year Team	G	GS	Att.	Yds.	Avg.	TD	No.	Yds.	Avg.	TD	No.	Yds.	Avg.	TD	No.	Yds.	Avg.	TD	TD	2pt.	Pts.
1996—Houston NFL	2	0	0	0	...	0	0	0	...	0	0	0	...	0	2	24	12.0	0	0	0	0
1997—Tennessee NFL	5	0	0	0	...	0	0	0	...	0	1	5	5.0	0	2	24	12.0	0	0	0	0
1998—Tennessee NFL	16	0	6	24	4.0	1	5	25	5.0	0	7	52	7.4	0	42	913	21.7	0	1	0	6
Pro totals (3 years)	23	0	6	24	4.0	1	5	25	5.0	0	8	57	7.1	0	46	961	20.9	0	1	0	6

ARMOUR, JUSTIN — WR

PERSONAL: Born January 1, 1973, in Colorado Springs, Colo. ... 6-4/209. ... Full name: Justin Hugh Armour.
HIGH SCHOOL: Manitou Springs (Colo.).
COLLEGE: Stanford.
TRANSACTIONS/CAREER NOTES: Selected by Buffalo Bills in fourth round (113th pick overall) of 1995 NFL draft. ... Signed by Bills (June 27, 1995). ... Inactive for 11 games (1996). ... On injured reserve with foot injury (November 22, 1996-remainder of season). ... Released by Bills (August 24, 1997). ... Signed by Philadelphia Eagles (September 23, 1997). ... Released by Eagles (September 27, 1997). ... Re-signed by Eagles (September 29, 1997). ... Released by Eagles (November 4, 1997). ... Signed by San Francisco 49ers (December 8, 1997). ... Released by 49ers after 1997 season. ... Signed by Denver Broncos (February 24, 1998). ... Selected by Cleveland Browns from Broncos in NFL expansion draft (February 9, 1999). ... Released by Browns (May 24, 1999).
PLAYING EXPERIENCE: Buffalo NFL, 1995; Philadelphia NFL, 1997; Denver NFL, 1998. ... Games/Games started: 1995 (15/9), 1997 (1/0), 1998 (7/0). Total: 23/9.
CHAMPIONSHIP GAME EXPERIENCE: Member of 49ers for NFC championship game (1997 season); inactive. ... Member of Broncos for AFC championship game (1998 season); inactive. ... Member of Super Bowl championship team (1998 season); inactive.

PRO STATISTICS: 1995—Rushed four times for minus five yards, caught 26 passes for 300 yards and three touchdowns, attempted one pass without a completion, fumbled once and recovered two fumbles. 1998—Caught one pass for 23 yards.
SINGLE GAME HIGHS (regular season): Receptions—6 (November 26, 1995, vs. New England); yards—66 (November 26, 1995, vs. New England); and touchdown receptions—1 (December 24, 1995, vs. Houston).

ARMSTEAD, JESSIE   LB   GIANTS

PERSONAL: Born October 26, 1970, in Dallas. ... 6-1/240. ... Full name: Jessie W. Armstead.
HIGH SCHOOL: David W. Carter (Dallas).
COLLEGE: Miami, Fla. (degree in criminal justice, 1992).
TRANSACTIONS/CAREER NOTES: Selected by New York Giants in eighth round (207th pick overall) of 1993 NFL draft. ... Signed by Giants (July 19, 1993).
HONORS: Named outside linebacker on THE SPORTING NEWS NFL All-Pro team (1997). ... Played in Pro Bowl (1997 and 1998 seasons).
PRO STATISTICS: 1995—Recovered one fumble. 1996—Fumbled once and recovered two fumbles. 1997—Recovered one fumble.

			INTERCEPTIONS				SACKS
Year Team	G	GS	No.	Yds.	Avg.	TD	No.
1993—New York Giants NFL	16	0	1	0	0.0	0	0.0
1994—New York Giants NFL	16	0	1	0	0.0	0	3.0
1995—New York Giants NFL	16	2	1	58	58.0	1	0.5
1996—New York Giants NFL	16	16	2	23	11.5	0	3.0
1997—New York Giants NFL	16	16	2	57	28.5	1	3.5
1998—New York Giants NFL	16	16	2	4	2.0	0	5.0
Pro totals (6 years)	96	50	9	142	15.8	2	15.0

ARMSTRONG, BRUCE   OT   PATRIOTS

PERSONAL: Born September 7, 1965, in Miami. ... 6-4/295. ... Full name: Bruce Charles Armstrong.
HIGH SCHOOL: Central (Miami).
COLLEGE: Louisville.
TRANSACTIONS/CAREER NOTES: Selected by New England Patriots in first round (23rd pick overall) of 1987 NFL draft. ... Signed by Patriots (July 23, 1987). ... On injured reserve with knee injury (November 2, 1992-remainder of season). ... On physically unable to perform list with knee injury (July 16-27, 1993). ... Granted unconditional free agency (February 13, 1998). ... Re-signed by Patriots (February 13, 1998).
PLAYING EXPERIENCE: New England NFL, 1987-1998. ... Games: 1987 (12/12), 1988 (16/16), 1989 (16/16), 1990 (16/16), 1991 (16/16), 1992 (8/8), 1993 (16/16), 1994 (16/16), 1995 (16/16), 1996 (16/16), 1997 (16/16), 1998 (16/16). Total: 180/180.
CHAMPIONSHIP GAME EXPERIENCE: Played in AFC championship game (1996 season). ... Played in Super Bowl XXXI (1996 season).
HONORS: Named offensive tackle on THE SPORTING NEWS NFL All-Pro team (1988). ... Played in Pro Bowl (1990, 1991 and 1994-1997 seasons).
PRO STATISTICS: 1990—Recovered two fumbles for four yards. 1992—Recovered one fumble. 1993—Recovered one fumble for one yard. 1995—Recovered one fumble. 1998—Recovered three fumbles.

ARMSTRONG, TRACE   DE   DOLPHINS

PERSONAL: Born October 5, 1965, in Bethesda, Md. ... 6-4/270. ... Full name: Raymond Lester Armstrong.
HIGH SCHOOL: John Carroll (Birmingham, Ala.).
COLLEGE: Arizona State, then Florida (degree in psychology, 1989).
TRANSACTIONS/CAREER NOTES: Selected by Chicago Bears in first round (12th pick overall) of 1989 NFL draft. ... Signed by Bears (August 18, 1989). ... On injured reserve with knee injury (September 24-November 3, 1991). ... Granted free agency (March 1, 1993). ... Re-signed by Bears (March 14, 1993). ... Traded by Bears to Miami Dolphins for second- (P Todd Sauerbrun) and third-round (G Evan Pilgrim) picks in 1995 draft (April 4, 1995).
HONORS: Named defensive lineman on THE SPORTING NEWS college All-America first team (1988).
PRO STATISTICS: 1989—Recovered one fumble. 1990—Recovered two fumbles. 1992—Recovered one fumble. 1993—Recovered three fumbles for three yards. 1995—Recovered one fumble. 1996—Recovered two fumbles. 1997—Recovered three fumbles. 1998—Recovered one fumble for two yards.

Year Team	G	GS	SACKS
1989—Chicago NFL	15	14	5.0
1990—Chicago NFL	16	16	10.0
1991—Chicago NFL	12	12	1.5
1992—Chicago NFL	14	14	6.5
1993—Chicago NFL	16	16	11.5
1994—Chicago NFL	15	15	7.5
1995—Miami NFL	15	0	4.5
1996—Miami NFL	16	9	12.0
1997—Miami NFL	16	16	5.5
1998—Miami NFL	16	0	10.5
Pro totals (10 years)	151	112	74.5

ARMSTRONG, TYJI   TE

PERSONAL: Born October 3, 1970, in Inkster, Mich. ... 6-4/250. ... Full name: Tyji Donrapheal Armstrong. ... Name pronounced TY-JAY.
HIGH SCHOOL: Robichaud (Dearborn, Mich.).
JUNIOR COLLEGE: Iowa Central Community College.
COLLEGE: Mississippi.
TRANSACTIONS/CAREER NOTES: Selected by Tampa Bay Buccaneers in third round (79th pick overall) of 1992 NFL draft. ... Signed by Buccaneers (July 27, 1992). ... Granted free agency (February 17, 1995). ... Re-signed by Buccaneers (May 19, 1995). ... Released by

Buccaneers (August 25, 1996). ... Signed by Dallas Cowboys (August 27, 1996). ... Granted unconditional free agency (February 14, 1997). ... Signed by St. Louis Rams (January 21, 1998). ... Assigned by Rams to Amsterdam Admirals in 1998 NFL Europe enhancement allocation program (February 18, 1998). ... Granted unconditional free agency (February 12, 1999).
PRO STATISTICS: 1993—Rushed twice for five yards. 1994—Rushed once for minus one yard, returned one kickoff for six yards and recovered one fumble. 1995—Returned one kickoff for six yards and recovered one fumble.
SINGLE GAME HIGHS (regular season): Receptions—4 (December 24, 1994, vs. Green Bay); yards—81 (December 6, 1992, vs. Los Angeles Rams); and touchdown receptions—1 (December 24, 1994, vs. Green Bay).

			RECEIVING				TOTALS			
Year Team	G	GS	No.	Yds.	Avg.	TD	TD	2pt.	Pts.	Fum.
1992—Tampa Bay NFL	15	7	7	138	19.7	1	1	...	6	0
1993—Tampa Bay NFL	12	7	9	86	9.6	1	1	...	6	0
1994—Tampa Bay NFL	16	9	22	265	12.0	1	1	0	6	2
1995—Tampa Bay NFL	16	3	7	68	9.7	0	0	0	0	1
1996—Dallas NFL	16	7	2	10	5.0	0	0	0	0	0
1997—					Did not play.					
1998—St. Louis NFL	12	0	6	54	9.0	0	0	0	0	0
Pro totals (6 years)	87	33	53	621	11.7	3	3	0	18	3

ARNOLD, JAHINE　　　　　WR　　　　　　　　　PACKERS

PERSONAL: Born June 19, 1973, in Cupertino, Calif. ... 6-0/180. ... Full name: Jahine Amid Arnold. ... Name pronounced JAH-heen.
HIGH SCHOOL: Homestead (Cupertino, Calif.).
JUNIOR COLLEGE: De Anza College (Calif.).
COLLEGE: Fresno State.
TRANSACTIONS/CAREER NOTES: Selected by Pittsburgh Steelers in fourth round (132nd pick overall) of 1996 NFL draft. ... Signed by Steelers (July 16, 1996). ... On injured reserve with knee injury (August 19, 1997-entire season). ... On injured reserve with finger injury (November 20, 1998-remainder of season). ... Granted free agency (February 12, 1999). ... Re-signed by Steelers (April 6, 1999). ... Traded by Steelers to Green Bay Packers for past considerations (April 6, 1999).
PRO STATISTICS: 1996—Rushed once for minus three yards and returned two punts for six yards. 1998—Returned four punts for 19 yards.
SINGLE GAME HIGHS (regular season): Receptions—2 (December 22, 1996, vs. Carolina); yards—26 (October 7, 1996, vs. Kansas City); and touchdown receptions—0.

			RECEIVING				KICKOFF RETURNS				TOTALS			
Year Team	G	GS	No.	Yds.	Avg.	TD	No.	Yds.	Avg.	TD	TD	2pt.	Pts.	Fum.
1996—Pittsburgh NFL	9	0	6	76	12.7	0	19	425	22.4	0	0	0	0	1
1997—Pittsburgh NFL							Did not play.							
1998—Pittsburgh NFL	2	0	0	0	...	0	3	78	26.0	0	0	0	0	0
Pro totals (2 years)	11	0	6	76	12.7	0	22	503	22.9	0	0	0	0	1

ASHER, JAMIE　　　　　TE　　　　　　　　　EAGLES

PERSONAL: Born October 31, 1972, in Indianapolis. ... 6-3/245.
HIGH SCHOOL: Warren Central (Indianapolis), then Clay County (Clay, Ky.).
COLLEGE: Louisville.
TRANSACTIONS/CAREER NOTES: Selected by Washington Redskins in fifth round (137th pick overall) of 1995 NFL draft. ... Signed by Redskins (June 1, 1995). ... Granted free agency (February 13, 1998). ... Re-signed by Redskins (April 24, 1998). ... On injured reserve with knee injury (November 13, 1998-remainder of season). ... Granted unconditional free agency (February 12, 1999). ... Signed by Philadelphia Eagles (April 14, 1999).
PRO STATISTICS: 1995—Returned one kickoff for 13 yards. 1996—Returned one kickoff for 13 yards and recovered two fumbles. 1997—Returned one kickoff for 17 yards and recovered two fumbles. 1998—Returned one kickoff for eight yards and recovered one fumble.
SINGLE GAME HIGHS (regular season): Receptions—6 (September 7, 1997, vs. Pittsburgh); yards—74 (September 20, 1998, vs. Seattle); and touchdown receptions—2 (November 17, 1996, vs. Philadelphia).

			RECEIVING				TOTALS			
Year Team	G	GS	No.	Yds.	Avg.	TD	TD	2pt.	Pts.	Fum.
1995—Washington NFL	7	1	14	172	12.3	0	0	0	0	0
1996—Washington NFL	16	12	42	481	11.5	4	4	0	24	0
1997—Washington NFL	16	13	49	474	9.7	1	1	0	6	0
1998—Washington NFL	9	7	28	294	10.5	0	0	0	0	0
Pro totals (4 years)	48	33	133	1421	10.7	5	5	0	30	0

ASHMORE, DARRYL　　　　OT　　　　　　　　RAIDERS

PERSONAL: Born November 1, 1969, in Peoria, Ill. ... 6-7/310. ... Full name: Darryl Allan Ashmore.
HIGH SCHOOL: Peoria (Ill.) Central.
COLLEGE: Northwestern (degree in business).
TRANSACTIONS/CAREER NOTES: Selected by Los Angeles Rams in seventh round (171st pick overall) of 1992 NFL draft. ... Signed by Rams (July 13, 1992). ... On injured reserve with knee injury (September 3-October 7, 1992). ... On practice squad (October 7, 1992-remainder of season). ... Granted free agency (February 17, 1995). ... Rams franchise moved to St. Louis (April 12, 1995). ... Re-signed by Rams (July 20, 1995). ... Released by Rams (October 14, 1996). ... Signed by Washington Redskins (October 26, 1996). ... Granted unconditional free agency (February 14, 1997). ... Re-signed by Redskins (May 9, 1997). ... Granted unconditional free agency (February 13, 1998). ... Signed by Oakland Raiders (April 25, 1998).
PLAYING EXPERIENCE: Los Angeles Rams NFL, 1993 and 1994; St. Louis NFL, 1995; St. Louis (6)-Washington (5) NFL, 1996; Washington NFL, 1997; Oakland NFL, 1998. ... Games/Games started: 1993 (9/7), 1994 (11/3), 1995 (16/15), 1996 (St.L-6/0; Wash.-5/0; Total: 11/0), 1997 (11/2), 1998 (15/4). Total: 73/31.
PRO STATISTICS: 1998—Recovered one fumble for one yard and a touchdown.

ATKINS, JAMES — OL — RAVENS

PERSONAL: Born January 28, 1970, in Amite, La. ... 6-6/306.
HIGH SCHOOL: Woodland (Amite, La.).
COLLEGE: Southwestern Louisiana.
TRANSACTIONS/CAREER NOTES: Signed as non-drafted free agent by Houston Oilers (May 26, 1993). ... Released by Oilers (August 31, 1993). ... Signed by Seattle Seahawks to practice squad (October 11, 1993). ... Released by Seahawks (February 27, 1998). ... Signed by Baltimore Ravens (March 25, 1998).
PLAYING EXPERIENCE: Seattle NFL, 1994-1997; Baltimore NFL, 1998. ... Games/Games started: 1994 (4/2), 1995 (16/16), 1996 (16/16), 1997 (13/3), 1998 (9/6). Total: 58/43.
PRO STATISTICS: 1995—Recovered one fumble. 1996—Recovered two fumbles. 1997—Recovered one fumble. 1998—Caught one pass for no yards.

ATWATER, STEVE — S — JETS

PERSONAL: Born October 28, 1966, in Chicago. ... 6-3/217. ... Full name: Stephen Dennis Atwater. ... Cousin of Mark Ingram, wide receiver with four NFL teams (1987-96).
HIGH SCHOOL: Lutheran North (St. Louis).
COLLEGE: Arkansas (degree in business administration, 1989).
TRANSACTIONS/CAREER NOTES: Selected by Denver Broncos in first round (20th pick overall) of 1989 NFL draft. ... Signed by Broncos (August 1, 1989). ... Designated by Broncos as transition player (February 25, 1993). ... Designated by Broncos as franchise player (February 15, 1995). ... Released by Broncos (February 17, 1999). ... Signed by New York Jets (March 2, 1999).
CHAMPIONSHIP GAME EXPERIENCE: Played in AFC championship game (1989, 1991, 1997 and 1998 seasons). ... Played in Super Bowl XXIV (1989 season). ... Member of Super Bowl championship team (1997 and 1998 seasons).
HONORS: Named defensive back on THE SPORTING NEWS college All-America second team (1988). ... Played in Pro Bowl (1990-1995 and 1998 seasons). ... Named free safety on THE SPORTING NEWS NFL All-Pro team (1992). ... Named to play in Pro Bowl (1996 season); replaced by Eric Turner due to injury.
PRO STATISTICS: 1989—Recovered one fumble for 29 yards. 1990—Returned one kickoff for no yards. 1991—Recovered one fumble. 1992—Recovered two fumbles for one yard. 1994—Recovered two fumbles for 17 yards. 1996—Fumbled once. 1997—Recovered two fumbles.

				INTERCEPTIONS			SACKS
Year Team	G	GS	No.	Yds.	Avg.	TD	No.
1989—Denver NFL	16	16	3	34	11.3	0	0.0
1990—Denver NFL	15	15	2	32	16.0	0	1.0
1991—Denver NFL	16	16	5	104	20.8	0	1.0
1992—Denver NFL	15	15	2	22	11.0	0	1.0
1993—Denver NFL	16	16	2	81	40.5	0	1.0
1994—Denver NFL	14	14	1	24	24.0	0	0.0
1995—Denver NFL	16	16	3	54	18.0	0	0.0
1996—Denver NFL	16	16	3	11	3.7	0	0.0
1997—Denver NFL	15	15	2	42	21.0	1	1.0
1998—Denver NFL	16	16	1	4	4.0	0	0.0
Pro totals (10 years)	155	155	24	408	17.0	1	5.0

AUSTIN, BILLY — DB — COLTS

PERSONAL: Born March 8, 1975, in Washington, D.C. ... 5-10/195.
HIGH SCHOOL: Kempner (Sugar Land, Texas).
COLLEGE: New Mexico.
TRANSACTIONS/CAREER NOTES: Signed as non-drafted free agent by St. Louis Rams (April 20, 1998). ... Released by Rams (July 8, 1998). ... Re-signed by Rams (July 21, 1998). ... Released by Rams (August 24, 1998). ... Signed by Indianapolis Colts to practice squad (September 9, 1998). ... Activated (December 16, 1998).
PLAYING EXPERIENCE: Indianapolis NFL, 1998. ... Games/Games started: 1/0.

AUSTIN, RAY — S — BEARS

PERSONAL: Born December 21, 1974, in Greensboro, N.C. ... 5-11/198. ... Full name: Raymond Demont Austin.
HIGH SCHOOL: Leilehua (Hawaii), then Eisenhower (Lawton, Okla.).
COLLEGE: Tennessee.
TRANSACTIONS/CAREER NOTES: Selected by New York Jets in fifth round (145th pick overall) of 1997 NFL draft. ... Signed by Jets (June 15, 1997). ... Claimed on waivers by Chicago Bears (August 31, 1998).
PLAYING EXPERIENCE: New York Jets NFL, 1997; Chicago NFL, 1998. ... Games/Games started: 1997 (16/0), 1998 (12/0). Total: 28/0.

AVERY, JOHN — RB — DOLPHINS

PERSONAL: Born January 11, 1976, in Richmond, Va. ... 5-9/190. ... Full name: John Edward Avery III.
HIGH SCHOOL: Asheville (N.C.).
JUNIOR COLLEGE: Northwest Mississippi Community College.
COLLEGE: Mississippi.
TRANSACTIONS/CAREER NOTES: Selected by Miami Dolphins in first round (29th pick overall) of 1998 NFL draft. ... Signed by Dolphins (July 17, 1998).
PRO STATISTICS: 1998—Recovered two fumbles.
SINGLE GAME HIGHS (regular season): Attempts—21 (November 8, 1998, vs. Indianapolis); yards—99 (November 8, 1998, vs. Indianapolis); and rushing touchdowns (November 8, 1998, vs. Indianapolis).

			RUSHING				RECEIVING				KICKOFF RETURNS				TOTALS		
Year Team	G	GS	Att.	Yds.	Avg.	TD	No.	Yds.	Avg.	TD	No.	Yds.	Avg.	TD	TD	2pt.	Pts.	Fum.
1998—Miami NFL	16	0	143	503	3.5	2	10	67	6.7	1	43	1085	25.2	0	3	0	18	5

AYANBADEJO, OBAFEMI   FB   VIKINGS

PERSONAL: Born March 5, 1975, in Chicago. ... 6-2/235. ... Name pronounced oh-bah-FEH-mee eye-yon-bah-DAY-zho.
HIGH SCHOOL: Santa Cruz (Calif.).
JUNIOR COLLEGE: Cabrillo Junior College (Calif.).
COLLEGE: San Diego State.
TRANSACTIONS/CAREER NOTES: Signed as non-drafted free agent by Minnesota Vikings (April 25, 1997). ... Released by Vikings (August 18, 1997). ... Re-signed by Vikings (February 6, 1998). ... Assigned by Vikings to England Monarchs in 1998 NFL Europe enhancement allocation program (February 17, 1998). ... Released by Vikings (August 24, 1998). ... Re-signed by Vikings to practice squad (August 31, 1998). ... Activated (December 1, 1998). ... Released by Vikings (December 23, 1998). ... Re-signed by Vikings to practice squad (December 24, 1998).
PLAYING EXPERIENCE: England Monarchs NFLE, 1998; Minnesota NFL, 1998. ... Games/Games started: NFLE 1998 (games played unavailable), NFL 1998 (1/0).
PRO STATISTICS: NFLE: 1998—Caught two passes for 28 yards.

BADGER, BRAD   G   REDSKINS

PERSONAL: Born January 11, 1975, in Corvallis, Ore. ... 6-4/298.
HIGH SCHOOL: Corvallis (Ore.).
COLLEGE: Stanford.
TRANSACTIONS/CAREER NOTES: Selected by Washington Redskins in fifth round (162nd pick overall) of 1997 NFL draft. ... Signed by Redskins (May 5, 1997).
PLAYING EXPERIENCE: Washington NFL, 1997 and 1998. ... Games/Games started: 1997 (12/2), 1998 (16/16). Total: 28/18.

BAILEY, AARON   WR/KR

PERSONAL: Born October 24, 1971, in Ann Arbor, Mich. ... 5-10/185. ... Full name: Aaron Duane Bailey.
HIGH SCHOOL: Pioneer (Ann Arbor, Mich.).
COLLEGE: College of DuPage (Ill.), then Louisville.
TRANSACTIONS/CAREER NOTES: Signed as non-drafted free agent by Indianapolis Colts (May 5, 1994). ... Released by Colts (April 12, 1999).
CHAMPIONSHIP GAME EXPERIENCE: Played in AFC championship game (1995 season).
PRO STATISTICS: 1995—Rushed once for 34 yards and recovered one fumble. 1996—Recovered one fumble. 1997—Rushed three times for 20 yards and recovered one fumble. 1998—Recovered one fumble.
SINGLE GAME HIGHS (regular season): Receptions—7 (September 21, 1997, vs. Buffalo); yards—96 (September 21, 1997, vs. Buffalo); and touchdown receptions—1 (November 30, 1997, vs. New England).

				RECEIVING				PUNT RETURNS				KICKOFF RETURNS			TOTALS			
Year Team	G	GS	No.	Yds.	Avg.	TD	No.	Yds.	Avg.	TD	No.	Yds.	Avg.	TD	TD	2pt.	Pts.	Fum.
1994—Indianapolis NFL	13	0	2	30	15.0	0	...	...	...	...	0	0	...	0	0	0	0	0
1995—Indianapolis NFL	15	3	21	379	18.0	3	...	...	...	...	21	495	23.6	1	4	0	24	0
1996—Indianapolis NFL	14	2	18	302	16.8	0	...	...	...	...	43	1041	24.2	▲1	1	0	6	3
1997—Indianapolis NFL	13	4	26	329	12.7	3	1	19	19.0	0	55	1206	21.9	0	3	0	18	2
1998—Indianapolis NFL	9	0	0	0	...	0	19	176	9.3	0	34	759	22.3	0	0	0	0	2
Pro totals (5 years)	64	9	67	1040	15.5	6	20	195	9.8	0	153	3501	22.9	2	8	0	48	7

BAILEY, ROBERT   CB   LIONS

PERSONAL: Born September 3, 1968, in Barbados. ... 5-9/174. ... Full name: Robert Martin Luther Bailey.
HIGH SCHOOL: Miami Southridge Senior.
COLLEGE: Miami, Fla. (degree in science).
TRANSACTIONS/CAREER NOTES: Selected by Los Angeles Rams in fourth round (107th pick overall) of 1991 NFL draft. ... Signed by Rams (July 17, 1991). ... On injured reserve with broken hand (August 27-October 11, 1991). ... On injured reserve with finger injury (November 19, 1991-remainder of season). ... On injured reserve with knee injury (December 11, 1993-remainder of season). ... Granted free agency (February 17, 1994). ... Re-signed by Rams (June 10, 1994). ... Released by Rams (August 22, 1995). ... Signed by Washington Redskins (September 11, 1995). ... Released by Redskins (October 17, 1995). ... Signed by Dallas Cowboys (October 19, 1995). ... Granted unconditional free agency (February 16, 1996). ... Signed by Miami Dolphins (March 7, 1996). ... Released by Dolphins (March 20, 1997). ... Signed by Detroit Lions (April 24, 1997). ... Released by Lions (June 20, 1997). ... Re-signed by Lions (July 22, 1997). ... Granted unconditional free agency (February 13, 1998). ... Re-signed by Lions (March 6, 1998).
CHAMPIONSHIP GAME EXPERIENCE: Played in NFC championship game (1995 season). ... Member of Super Bowl championship team (1995 season).
RECORDS: Holds NFL record for longest punt return—103 yards, touchdown (October 23, 1994, at New Orleans).
PRO STATISTICS: 1994—Returned one punt for 103 yards and a touchdown and recovered one fumble. 1996—Credited with one sack. 1997—Credited with two sacks.

			INTERCEPTIONS			
Year Team	G	GS	No.	Yds.	Avg.	TD
1991—Los Angeles Rams NFL	6	0	0	0	...	0
1992—Los Angeles Rams NFL	16	6	3	61	20.3	1
1993—Los Angeles Rams NFL	9	3	2	41	20.5	0
1994—Los Angeles Rams NFL	16	2	0	0	...	0
1995—Washington NFL	4	0	0	0	...	0
—Dallas NFL	9	0	0	0	...	0
1996—Miami NFL	14	0	0	0	...	0
1997—Detroit NFL	15	0	1	0	0.0	0
1998—Detroit NFL	16	0	0	0	...	0
Pro totals (8 years)	105	11	6	102	17.0	1

BALL, JERRY — DT — BROWNS

PERSONAL: Born December 15, 1964, in Beaumont, Texas. ... 6-1/320. ... Full name: Jerry Lee Ball. ... Nephew of Mel Farr Sr., running back with Detroit Lions (1967-1973); cousin of Mel Farr Jr., running back with Los Angeles Rams (1989) and Sacramento Surge of World League (1991); and cousin of Mike Farr, wide receiver with Detroit Lions (1990-1992).
HIGH SCHOOL: Westbrook (Texas).
COLLEGE: Southern Methodist.
TRANSACTIONS/CAREER NOTES: Selected by Detroit Lions in third round (63rd pick overall) of 1987 NFL draft. ... Signed by Lions (July 6, 1987). ... On injured reserve with knee injury (December 12, 1991-remainder of season). ... On injured reserve with ankle injury (December 13, 1992-remainder of season). ... Traded by Lions to Cleveland Browns for third-round pick (LB Antonio London) in 1993 draft (April 23, 1993). ... Granted unconditional free agency (February 17, 1994). ... Signed by Los Angeles Raiders (June 21, 1994). ... Raiders franchise moved to Oakland (July 21, 1995). ... Released by Raiders (February 14, 1997). ... Signed by Minnesota Vikings (September 24, 1997). ... Granted unconditional free agency (February 12, 1999). ... Signed by Browns (April 28, 1999).
CHAMPIONSHIP GAME EXPERIENCE: Played in NFC championship game (1998 season).
HONORS: Played in Pro Bowl (1989 and 1990 seasons). ... Named to play in Pro Bowl (1991 season); replaced by Henry Thomas due to injury.
PRO STATISTICS: 1987—Returned two kickoffs for 23 yards. 1989—Recovered three fumbles. 1991—Credited with a safety. 1992—Recovered three fumbles for 21 yards and a touchdown. 1994—Recovered one fumble. 1995—Recovered one fumble. 1996—Intercepted one pass for 66 yards and a touchdown and recovered one fumble. 1997—Recovered two fumbles. 1998—Recovered one fumble.

Year Team	G	GS	SACKS
1987—Detroit NFL	12	12	1.0
1988—Detroit NFL	16	16	2.0
1989—Detroit NFL	16	16	9.0
1990—Detroit NFL	15	16	2.0
1991—Detroit NFL	13	13	2.0
1992—Detroit NFL	12	12	2.5
1993—Cleveland NFL	16	7	3.0
1994—Los Angeles Raiders NFL	16	14	3.0
1995—Oakland NFL	15	15	3.0
1996—Oakland NFL	16	0	3.0
1997—Minnesota NFL	12	6	0.0
1998—Minnesota NFL	16	16	0.0
Pro totals (12 years)	175	143	30.5

BALLARD, HOWARD — OT — SEAHAWKS

PERSONAL: Born November 3, 1963, in Ashland, Ala. ... 6-6/325. ... Full name: Howard Louis Ballard. ... Nickname: The House.
HIGH SCHOOL: Clay County (Ashland, Ala.).
COLLEGE: Alabama A&M.
TRANSACTIONS/CAREER NOTES: Selected by Buffalo Bills in 11th round (283rd pick overall) of 1987 NFL draft (elected to return to college for final year of eligibility). ... Signed by Bills (March 30, 1988). ... Granted unconditional free agency (February 17, 1994). ... Signed by Seattle Seahawks (February 28, 1994).
PLAYING EXPERIENCE: Buffalo NFL, 1988-1993; Seattle NFL, 1994-1998. ... Games: 1988 (16/0), 1989 (16/16), 1990 (16/16), 1991 (16/16), 1992 (16/16), 1993 (16/16), 1994 (16/16), 1995 (16/16), 1996 (16/16), 1997 (10/10), 1998 (16/16). Total: 170/154.
CHAMPIONSHIP GAME EXPERIENCE: Played in AFC championship game (1988 and 1990-1993 seasons). ... Played in Super Bowl XXV (1990 season), Super Bowl XXVI (1991 season), Super Bowl XXVII (1992 season) and Super Bowl XXVIII (1993 season).
HONORS: Played in Pro Bowl (1992 and 1993 seasons).
PRO STATISTICS: 1996—Recovered one fumble. 1998—Recovered two fumbles.

BANKS, ANTONIO — CB — VIKINGS

PERSONAL: Born March 12, 1973, in Ivor, Va. ... 5-10/195. ... Full name: Antonio Dontral Banks.
HIGH SCHOOL: Warwick (Newport News, Va.).
COLLEGE: Virginia Tech.
TRANSACTIONS/CAREER NOTES: Selected by Minnesota Vikings in fourth round (113th pick overall) of 1997 NFL draft. ... Signed by Vikings (June 9, 1997). ... On injured reserve with foot injury (August 18, 1997-entire season). ... Assigned by Vikings to Amsterdam Admirals in 1998 NFL Europe enhancement allocation program (February 18, 1998). ... Released by Vikings (August 30, 1998). ... Re-signed by Vikings to practice squad (November 10, 1998). ... Activated (December 3, 1998).
PLAYING EXPERIENCE: Amsterdam Admirals NFLE, 1998; Minnesota NFL, 1998. ... Games/Games started: NFLE 1998 (games played unavailable), NFL 1998 (4/0).
CHAMPIONSHIP GAME EXPERIENCE: Played in NFC championship game (1998 season).
PRO STATISTICS: NFLE: 1998—Credited with three sacks.

BANKS, CHRIS — G — BRONCOS

PERSONAL: Born April 4, 1973, in Lexington, Mo. ... 6-1/300. ... Full name: Warren Christopher Banks.
HIGH SCHOOL: Lexington (Mo.).
COLLEGE: Kansas.
TRANSACTIONS/CAREER NOTES: Selected by Denver Broncos in seventh round (226th pick overall) of 1996 NFL draft. ... Signed by Broncos (July 16, 1996). ... On injured reserve with knee injury (August 25-September 6, 1996). ... Released by Broncos (September 6, 1996). ... Re-signed by Broncos (January 29, 1997). ... Assigned by Broncos to Barcelona Dragons in 1997 World League enhancement allocation program (February 19, 1997). ... Released by Broncos (August 24, 1997). ... Re-signed by Broncos to practice squad (August 25, 1997). ... Released by Broncos (January 26, 1998). ... Re-signed by Broncos to practice squad (January 30, 1998).
PLAYING EXPERIENCE: Barcelona W.L., 1997; Denver NFL, 1998. ... Games/Games started: W.L. 1997 (games played unavailable), 1998 (4/0).
CHAMPIONSHIP GAME EXPERIENCE: Member of Broncos for AFC championship game (1998 season); inactive. ... Member of Super Bowl championship team (1998 season); inactive.

BANKS, TAVIAN — RB — JAGUARS

PERSONAL: Born February 17, 1974, in Davenport, Iowa. ... 5-10/194. ... Full name: Tavian Remond Banks.
HIGH SCHOOL: Bettendorf (Iowa).
COLLEGE: Iowa (degree in sports management, 1997).
TRANSACTIONS/CAREER NOTES: Selected by Jacksonville Jaguars in fourth round (101st pick overall) of 1998 NFL draft. ... Signed by Jaguars (May 26, 1998).
PRO STATISTICS: 1998—Recovered one fumble.
SINGLE GAME HIGHS (regular season): Attempts—9 (October 12, 1998, vs. Miami); yards—75 (October 12, 1998, vs. Miami); and rushing touchdowns—1 (October 18, 1998, vs. Buffalo).

				RUSHING				RECEIVING				KICKOFF RETURNS				TOTALS		
Year Team	G	GS	Att.	Yds.	Avg.	TD	No.	Yds.	Avg.	TD	No.	Yds.	Avg.	TD	TD	2pt.	Pts.	Fum.
1998—Jacksonville NFL	6	1	26	140	5.4	1	4	20	5.0	0	5	133	26.6	0	1	0	6	2

BANKS, TONY — QB — RAVENS

PERSONAL: Born April 5, 1973, in San Diego. ... 6-4/215. ... Full name: Anthony Lamar Banks. ... Cousin of Chip Banks, linebacker with Cleveland Browns (1982-86), San Diego Chargers (1987) and Indianapolis Colts (1989-92).
HIGH SCHOOL: Hoover (San Diego).
JUNIOR COLLEGE: San Diego Mesa College.
COLLEGE: Michigan State.
TRANSACTIONS/CAREER NOTES: Selected by St. Louis Rams in second round (42nd pick overall) of 1996 NFL draft. ... Signed by Rams (July 15, 1996). ... On injured reserve with knee injury (December 14, 1998-remainder of season). ... Granted free agency (February 12, 1999). ... Re-signed by Rams (April 17, 1999). ... Traded by Rams to Baltimore Ravens for fifth-round pick (G Cameron Spikes) in 1999 draft and seventh-round pick in 2000 draft (April 17, 1999).
RECORDS: Holds NFL single-season record for most fumbles—21 (1996).
PRO STATISTICS: 1996—Led league with 21 fumbles and recovered four fumbles for minus 17 yards. 1997—Tied for NFC lead with 15 fumbles and recovered three fumbles for minus 27 yards. 1998—Fumbled 10 times and recovered eight fumbles for minus 23 yards.
SINGLE GAME HIGHS (regular season): Attempts—49 (September 28, 1997, vs. Oakland); completions—29 (September 6, 1998, vs. New Orleans); yards—401 (November 2, 1997, vs. Atlanta); and touchdown passes—3 (December 7, 1997, vs. New Orleans).
STATISTICAL PLATEAUS: 300-yard passing games: 1996 (2), 1997 (1). Total: 3.
MISCELLANEOUS: Regular-season record as starting NFL quarterback: 14-29 (.326).

					PASSING						RUSHING				TOTALS		
Year Team	G	GS	Att.	Cmp.	Pct.	Yds.	TD	Int.	Avg.	Rat.	Att.	Yds.	Avg.	TD	TD	2pt.	Pts.
1996—St. Louis NFL	14	13	368	192	52.2	2544	15	15	6.91	71.0	61	212	3.5	0	0	1	2
1997—St. Louis NFL	16	16	487	252	51.7	3254	14	13	6.68	71.5	47	186	4.0	0	1	0	6
1998—St. Louis NFL	14	14	408	241	59.1	2535	7	14	6.21	68.6	40	156	3.9	3	3	1	20
Pro totals (3 years)	44	43	1263	685	54.2	8333	36	42	6.60	70.4	148	554	3.7	4	4	2	28

RECORD AS BASEBALL PLAYER

TRANSACTIONS/CAREER NOTES: Threw right, batted right. ... Selected by Minnesota Twins organization in 10th round of free-agent draft (June 3, 1991).

						BATTING							FIELDING		
Year Team (League)	Pos.	G	AB	R	H	2B	3B	HR	RBI	Avg.	BB	SO	SB	PO	A	E	Avg.
1991—GC Twins (GCL)	DH	17	57	7	13	3	0	0	1	.228	4	16	2	...	...	...	...

BANKSTON, MICHAEL — DE — BENGALS

PERSONAL: Born March 12, 1970, in East Bernard, Texas. ... 6-5/285.
HIGH SCHOOL: East Bernard (Texas).
COLLEGE: Sam Houston State.
TRANSACTIONS/CAREER NOTES: Selected by Phoenix Cardinals in fourth round (100th pick overall) of 1992 NFL draft. ... Signed by Cardinals (July 20, 1992). ... Cardinals franchise renamed Arizona Cardinals for 1994 season. ... Granted unconditional free agency (February 14, 1997). ... Re-signed by Cardinals (April 2, 1997). ... Granted unconditional free agency (February 13, 1998). ... Tendered offer sheet by Cincinnati Bengals (February 13, 1998). ... Cardinals declined to match offer (February 14, 1998).
PRO STATISTICS: 1993—Recovered five fumbles for 16 yards. 1994—Recovered one fumble for two yards. 1995—Intercepted one pass for 28 yards and fumbled once. 1996—Recovered one fumble. 1998—Recovered one fumble for five yards.

Year Team	G	GS	SACKS
1992—Phoenix NFL	16	6	2.0
1993—Phoenix NFL	16	12	3.0
1994—Arizona NFL	16	16	7.0
1995—Arizona NFL	16	16	2.0
1996—Arizona NFL	16	16	0.5
1997—Arizona NFL	16	16	2.0
1998—Cincinnati NFL	16	16	4.5
Pro totals (7 years)	112	98	21.0

BANTA, BRAD — TE — COLTS

PERSONAL: Born December 14, 1970, in Baton Rouge, La. ... 6-6/260. ... Full name: Dennis Bradford Banta.
HIGH SCHOOL: University (Baton Rouge, La.).
COLLEGE: Southern California.
TRANSACTIONS/CAREER NOTES: Selected by Indianapolis Colts in fourth round (106th pick overall) of 1994 NFL draft. ... Signed by Colts (July 22, 1994). ... Granted free agency (February 14, 1997). ... Re-signed by Colts (May 14, 1997).

PLAYING EXPERIENCE: Indianapolis NFL, 1994-1998. ... Games/Games started: 1994 (16/0), 1995 (16/2), 1996 (13/0), 1997 (15/0), 1998 (16/0). Total: 76/2.
CHAMPIONSHIP GAME EXPERIENCE: Played in AFC championship game (1995 season).
PRO STATISTICS: 1995—Caught one pass for six yards. 1998—Caught one pass for seven yards and recovered one fumble.
SINGLE GAME HIGHS (regular season): Receptions—1 (November 1, 1998, vs. New England); yards—7 (November 1, 1998, vs. New England); and touchdown receptions—0.

BARBER, MICHAEL   LB   COLTS

PERSONAL: Born November 9, 1971, in Edgemore, S.C. ... 6-0/246.
HIGH SCHOOL: Lewisville (Edgemore, S.C.).
COLLEGE: Clemson.
TRANSACTIONS/CAREER NOTES: Signed as non-drafted free agent by Seattle Seahawks (April 26, 1995). ... Granted free agency (February 13, 1998). ... Re-signed by Seahawks (May 13, 1998). ... Claimed on waivers by Indianapolis Colts (August 31, 1998).
PLAYING EXPERIENCE: Seattle NFL, 1995-1997; Indianapolis NFL, 1998. ... Games/Games started: 1995 (2/0), 1996 (13/7), 1997 (8/2), 1998 (12/6). Total: 35/15.
PRO STATISTICS: 1996—Returned one kickoff for 12 yards and recovered one fumble. 1997—Recovered one fumble. 1998—Intercepted one pass for no yards and credited with two sacks.

BARBER, RONDE   CB   BUCCANEERS

PERSONAL: Born April 7, 1975, in Montgomery County, Va. ... 5-10/180. ... Full name: Jamael Oronde Barber. ... Twin brother of Tiki Barber, running back, New York Giants. ... Name pronounced RON-day.
HIGH SCHOOL: Cave Spring (Roanoke, Va.).
COLLEGE: Virginia (degree in commerce, 1996).
TRANSACTIONS/CAREER NOTES: Selected after junior season by Tampa Bay Buccaneers in third round (66th pick overall) of 1997 NFL draft. ... Signed by Buccaneers (July 18, 1997).
PRO STATISTICS: 1998—Returned one punt for 23 yards and a touchdown.

				INTERCEPTIONS			SACKS
Year Team	G	GS	No.	Yds.	Avg.	TD	No.
1997—Tampa Bay NFL	1	0	0	0	...	0	0.0
1998—Tampa Bay NFL	16	9	2	67	33.5	0	3.0
Pro totals (2 years)	17	9	2	67	33.5	0	3.0

BARBER, SHAWN   LB   REDSKINS

PERSONAL: Born January 14, 1975, in Richmond, Va. ... 6-2/224.
HIGH SCHOOL: Hermitage (Richmond, Va.).
COLLEGE: Richmond.
TRANSACTIONS/CAREER NOTES: Selected by Washington Redskins in fourth round (113th pick overall) of 1998 NFL draft. ... Signed by Redskins (May 13, 1998).
PLAYING EXPERIENCE: Washington NFL, 1998. ... Games/Games started: 16/1.
PRO STATISTICS: 1998—Intercepted one pass for no yards.

BARBER, TIKI   RB   GIANTS

PERSONAL: Born April 7, 1975, in Roanoke, Va. ... 5-10/205. ... Full name: Atiim Kiambu Barber. ... Twin Brother of Ronde Barber, cornerback, Tampa Bay Buccaneers. ... Name pronounced TEE-kee.
HIGH SCHOOL: Cave Spring (Roanake, Va.).
COLLEGE: Virginia.
TRANSACTIONS/CAREER NOTES: Selected by New York Giants in second round (36th pick overall) of 1997 NFL draft. ... Signed by Giants for 1997 season.
SINGLE GAME HIGHS (regular season): Attempts—21 (December 7, 1997, vs. Philadelphia); yards—114 (December 7, 1997, vs. Philadelphia); and rushing touchdowns—1 (September 14, 1997, vs. Baltimore).
STATISTICAL PLATEAUS: 100-yard rushing games: 1997 (1).

			RUSHING				RECEIVING				KICKOFF RETURNS				TOTALS		
Year Team	G	GS	Att.	Yds.	Avg.	TD	No.	Yds.	Avg.	TD	No.	Yds.	Avg.	TD	TD 2pt.	Pts.	Fum.
1997—New York Giants NFL	12	6	136	511	3.8	3	34	299	8.8	1	0	0	...	0	4 1	26	3
1998—New York Giants NFL	16	4	52	166	3.2	0	42	348	8.3	3	14	250	17.9	0	3 0	18	1
Pro totals (2 years)	28	10	188	677	3.6	3	76	647	8.5	4	14	250	17.9	0	7 1	44	4

BARKER, BRYAN   P   JAGUARS

PERSONAL: Born June 28, 1964, in Jacksonville Beach, Fla. ... 6-2/201. ... Full name: Bryan Christopher Barker.
HIGH SCHOOL: Miramonte (Orinda, Calif.).
COLLEGE: Santa Clara (degree in economics).
TRANSACTIONS/CAREER NOTES: Signed as non-drafted free agent by Denver Broncos (May 1988). ... Released by Broncos (July 19, 1988). ... Signed by Seattle Seahawks (1989). ... Released by Seahawks (August 30, 1989). ... Signed by Kansas City Chiefs (May 1, 1990). ... Released by Chiefs (August 28, 1990). ... Re-signed by Chiefs (September 26, 1990). ... Granted unconditional free agency (February 1-April 1, 1991). ... Re-signed by Chiefs for 1991 season. ... Granted unconditional free agency (February 1-April 1, 1992). ... Re-signed by Chiefs for 1992 season. ... Released by Chiefs (1994). ... Signed by Minnesota Vikings (May 18, 1994). ... Released by Vikings (August 30, 1994). ...

Signed by Philadelphia Eagles (October 11, 1994). ... Granted unconditional free agency (February 17, 1995). ... Signed by Jacksonville Jaguars (March 7, 1995).
CHAMPIONSHIP GAME EXPERIENCE: Played in AFC championship game (1993 and 1996 seasons).
HONORS: Played in Pro Bowl (1997 season).
PRO STATISTICS: 1997—Rushed once for no yards, attempted one pass with a completion for 22 yards and fumbled once for minus 19 yards.

				PUNTING			
Year Team	G	No.	Yds.	Avg.	Net avg.	In. 20	Blk.
1990—Kansas City NFL	13	64	2479	38.7	33.3	16	0
1991—Kansas City NFL	16	57	2303	40.4	35.0	14	0
1992—Kansas City NFL	15	75	3245	43.3	35.2	16	1
1993—Kansas City NFL	16	76	3240	42.6	35.3	19	1
1994—Philadelphia NFL	11	66	2696	40.8	‡36.2	20	0
1995—Jacksonville NFL	16	82	3591	43.8	*38.6	19	0
1996—Jacksonville NFL	16	69	3016	43.7	35.6	16	0
1997—Jacksonville NFL	16	66	2964	44.9	38.8	27	0
1998—Jacksonville NFL	16	85	3824	45.0	38.5	28	0
Pro totals (9 years)	135	640	27358	42.7	36.4	175	2

BARKER, ROY — DE — BROWNS

PERSONAL: Born February 24, 1969, in New York. ... 6-5/290.
HIGH SCHOOL: Central Islip (N.Y.).
COLLEGE: North Carolina (degree in speech communications, 1991).
TRANSACTIONS/CAREER NOTES: Selected by Minnesota Vikings in fourth round (98th pick overall) of 1992 NFL draft. ... Signed by Vikings (July 16, 1992). ... On injured reserve with knee injury (September 1-30, 1992). ... Granted unconditional free agency (February 16, 1996). ... Signed by San Francisco 49ers (February 28, 1996). ... Traded by 49ers with TE Irv Smith to Cleveland Browns for past considerations (February 12, 1999).
CHAMPIONSHIP GAME EXPERIENCE: Played in NFC championship game (1997 season).
PRO STATISTICS: 1993—Recovered one fumble. 1994—Recovered one fumble. 1995—Intercepted one pass for minus two yards. 1998—Intercepted one pass for minus four yards.

Year Team	G	GS	SACKS
1992—Minnesota NFL	8	0	0.0
1993—Minnesota NFL	16	16	6.0
1994—Minnesota NFL	16	15	3.5
1995—Minnesota NFL	16	16	3.0
1996—San Francisco NFL	16	16	12.5
1997—San Francisco NFL	13	12	5.5
1998—San Francisco NFL	16	16	12.0
Pro totals (7 years)	101	91	42.5

BARLOW, REGGIE — WR/PR/KR — JAGUARS

PERSONAL: Born January 22, 1973, in Montgomery, Ala. ... 6-0/191. ... Full name: Reggie Devon Barlow.
HIGH SCHOOL: Lanier (Montgomery, Ala.).
COLLEGE: Alabama State.
TRANSACTIONS/CAREER NOTES: Selected by Jacksonville Jaguars in fourth round (110th pick overall) of 1996 NFL draft. ... Signed by Jaguars (May 28, 1996). ... Granted free agency (February 12, 1999). ... Re-signed by Jaguars (March 23, 1999).
CHAMPIONSHIP GAME EXPERIENCE: Played in AFC championship game (1996 season).
PRO STATISTICS: 1997—Recovered one fumble. 1998—Recovered one fumble.
SINGLE GAME HIGHS (regular season): Receptions—4 (October 12, 1998, vs. Miami); yards—50 (October 12, 1998, vs. Miami); and touchdown receptions—0.

			RECEIVING				PUNT RETURNS				KICKOFF RETURNS				TOTALS			
Year Team	G	GS	No.	Yds.	Avg.	TD	No.	Yds.	Avg.	TD	No.	Yds.	Avg.	TD	TD	2pt.	Pts.	Fum.
1996—Jacksonville NFL	7	0	0	0	...	0	0	0	...	0	0	0	...	0	0	0	0	0
1997—Jacksonville NFL	16	0	5	74	14.8	0	36	412	11.4	0	10	267	26.7 ▲1		2	0	12	2
1998—Jacksonville NFL	16	2	11	168	15.3	0	43	*555	§12.9	1	30	747	24.9	0	1	0	6	1
Pro totals (3 years)	39	2	16	242	15.1	0	79	967	12.2	1	40	1014	25.4	1	3	0	18	3

BARNDT, TOM — DT — CHIEFS

PERSONAL: Born March 14, 1972, in Mentor, Ohio. ... 6-3/301. ... Full name: Thomas Allen Barndt.
HIGH SCHOOL: Mentor (Ohio).
COLLEGE: Pittsburgh.
TRANSACTIONS/CAREER NOTES: Selected by Kansas City Chiefs in sixth round (207th pick overall) of 1995 NFL draft. ... Signed by Chiefs for the 1995 season. ... Released by Chiefs (August 27, 1995). ... Re-signed by Chiefs to practice squad (August 29, 1995). ... Assigned by Chiefs to Scottish Claymores in 1996 World League enhancement allocation program (February 19, 1996). ... Granted free agency (February 12, 1999). ... Re-signed by Chiefs (May 4, 1999).
PRO STATISTICS: 1998—Recovered two fumbles.

Year Team	G	GS	SACKS
1995—Kansas City NFL	Did not play.		
1996—Kansas City NFL	13	0	0.0
1997—Kansas City NFL	16	1	2.0
1998—Kansas City NFL	16	16	3.5
Pro totals (3 years)	45	17	5.5

BARNHARDT, TOMMY   P

PERSONAL: Born June 11, 1963, in China Grove, N.C. ... 6-2/228. ... Full name: Tommy Ray Barnhardt.
HIGH SCHOOL: South Rowan (China Grove, N.C.).
COLLEGE: East Carolina, then North Carolina (degree in industrial relations, 1986).
TRANSACTIONS/CAREER NOTES: Selected by Baltimore Stars in 1986 USFL territorial draft. ... Selected by Tampa Bay Buccaneers in ninth round (223rd pick overall) of 1986 NFL draft. ... Signed by Buccaneers (July 16, 1986). ... Released by Buccaneers (August 25, 1986). ... Re-signed by Buccaneers (February 6, 1987). ... Released by Buccaneers (August 5, 1987). ... Signed as replacement player by New Orleans Saints (September 23, 1987). ... Released by Saints (November 3, 1987). ... Signed by Chicago Bears (December 16, 1987). ... Released by Bears (August 24, 1988). ... Signed by Washington Redskins (September 9, 1988). ... On injured reserve with pulled quadricep (October 11, 1988-remainder of season). ... Granted unconditional free agency (February 1-April 1, 1989). ... Re-signed by Redskins (May 11, 1989). ... Released by Redskins (June 27, 1989). ... Signed by Detroit Lions (July 20, 1989). ... Released by Lions (August 30, 1989). ... Signed by Saints (October 11, 1989). ... Granted unconditional free agency (February 1-April 1, 1992). ... Re-signed by Saints for 1992 season. ... Granted unconditional free agency (March 1, 1993). ... Re-signed by Saints (July 15, 1993). ... Granted unconditional free agency (February 17, 1995). ... Signed by Carolina Panthers (March 2, 1995). ... Released by Panthers (May 7, 1996). ... Signed by Buccaneers (May 13, 1996). ... On injured reserve with broken collarbone (October 9, 1997-remainder of season). ... Granted unconditional free agency (February 12, 1999).
PRO STATISTICS: 1987—Rushed once for minus 13 yards. 1991—Rushed once for no yards. 1992—Rushed four times for minus two yards and fumbled twice for minus 16 yards. 1993—Rushed once for 18 yards and attempted one pass with a completion for seven yards. 1994—Rushed once for 21 yards and attempted one pass without a completion. 1996—Rushed twice for 27 yards. 1997—Attempted one pass with a completion for 25 yards.

		PUNTING				
Year Team	G	No.	Yds.	Avg.	Net avg.	In. 20	Blk.
1987—New Orleans NFL	3	11	483	43.9	...	4	0
—Chicago NFL	2	6	236	39.3	35.2	2	0
1988—Washington NFL	4	15	628	41.9	34.2	1	0
1989—New Orleans NFL	11	55	2179	39.6	35.0	17	0
1990—New Orleans NFL	16	70	2990	42.7	36.2	20	1
1991—New Orleans NFL	16	86	*3743	43.5	35.2	20	1
1992—New Orleans NFL	16	67	2947	44.0	37.7	19	0
1993—New Orleans NFL	16	77	3356	43.6	37.5	26	0
1994—New Orleans NFL	16	67	2920	43.6	33.5	14	0
1995—Carolina NFL	16	‡95	‡3906	41.1	35.2	27	0
1996—Tampa Bay NFL	16	70	3015	43.1	37.7	24	1
1997—Tampa Bay NFL	6	29	1304	45.0	39.1	12	0
1998—Tampa Bay NFL	16	81	3340	41.2	35.3	19	0
Pro totals (12 years)	154	729	31047	42.6	35.5	205	3

BARROW, MICHEAL   LB   PANTHERS

PERSONAL: Born April 19, 1970, in Homestead, Fla. ... 6-2/236. ... Full name: Micheal Colvin Barrow.
HIGH SCHOOL: Homestead (Fla.) Senior.
COLLEGE: Miami, Fla. (degree in accounting, 1992).
TRANSACTIONS/CAREER NOTES: Selected by Houston Oilers in second round (47th pick overall) of 1993 NFL draft. ... Signed by Oilers (July 30, 1993). ... Granted free agency (February 16, 1996). ... Re-signed by Oilers (August 9, 1996). ... Granted unconditional free agency (February 14, 1997). ... Signed by Carolina Panthers (February 20, 1997).
HONORS: Named linebacker on THE SPORTING NEWS college All-America first team (1992).
PRO STATISTICS: 1995—Recovered one fumble. 1996—Recovered one fumble. 1997—Recovered two fumbles. 1998—Intercepted one pass for 10 yards and recovered two fumbles.

Year Team	G	GS	SACKS
1993—Houston NFL	16	0	1.0
1994—Houston NFL	16	16	2.5
1995—Houston NFL	13	12	3.0
1996—Houston NFL	16	16	6.0
1997—Carolina NFL	16	16	8.5
1998—Carolina NFL	16	16	4.0
Pro totals (6 years)	93	76	25.0

BARTON, HARRIS   OT   49ERS

PERSONAL: Born April 19, 1964, in Atlanta. ... 6-4/292. ... Full name: Harris Scott Barton.
HIGH SCHOOL: Dunwoody (Ga.).
COLLEGE: North Carolina (bachelor of science degree, 1987).
TRANSACTIONS/CAREER NOTES: Selected by San Francisco 49ers in first round (22nd pick overall) of 1987 NFL draft. ... Signed by 49ers (July 22, 1987). ... Granted free agency (February 1, 1990). ... Re-signed by 49ers (July 30, 1990). ... Inactive for eight games (1997). ... On injured reserve with knee injury (October 31, 1997-remainder of season). ... On injured reserve with leg injury (August 30, 1998-entire season).
PLAYING EXPERIENCE: San Francisco NFL, 1987-1996. ... Games/Games started: 1987 (12/9), 1988 (16/15), 1989 (16/16), 1990 (16/16), 1991 (16/16), 1992 (13/13), 1993 (15/15), 1994 (9/9), 1995 (12/12), 1996 (13/13). Total: 138/134.
CHAMPIONSHIP GAME EXPERIENCE: Played in NFC championship game (1988-1990 and 1992-1994 seasons). ... Member of Super Bowl championship team (1988, 1989 and 1994 seasons). ... Member of 49ers for NFC championship game (1997 season); inactive.
HONORS: Named offensive tackle on THE SPORTING NEWS college All-America second team (1986). ... Named offensive tackle on THE SPORTING NEWS NFL All-Pro team (1993). ... Played in Pro Bowl (1993 season).
PRO STATISTICS: 1987—Recovered one fumble. 1991—Recovered one fumble.

BARTRUM, MIKE — TE — PATRIOTS

PERSONAL: Born June 23, 1970, in Galliapolis, Ohio. ... 6-5/245. ... Full name: Michael Weldon Bartrum.
HIGH SCHOOL: Meigs (Pomeroy, Ohio).
COLLEGE: Marshall (degree in education).
TRANSACTIONS/CAREER NOTES: Signed as non-drafted free agent by Kansas City Chiefs (May 5, 1993). ... Released by Chiefs (August 30, 1993). ... Re-signed by Chiefs to practice squad (August 31, 1993). ... Activated (October 27, 1993). ... Released by Chiefs (August 23, 1994). ... Signed by Green Bay Packers (January 20, 1995). ... On injured reserve with broken arm (October 11, 1995-remainder of season). ... Traded by Packers with DE Walter Scott to New England Patriots for past considerations (August 25, 1996). ... On injured reserve with forearm injury (November 12, 1997-remainder of season). ... Granted unconditional free agency (February 13, 1998). ... Re-signed by Patriots (April 7, 1998).
PLAYING EXPERIENCE: Kansas City NFL, 1993; Green Bay NFL, 1995; New England NFL, 1996-1998. ... Games/Games started: 1993 (3/0), 1995 (4/0), 1996 (16/0), 1997 (9/0), 1998 (16/0). Total: 48/0.
CHAMPIONSHIP GAME EXPERIENCE: Member of Chiefs for AFC championship game (1993 season); inactive. ... Played in AFC championship game (1996 season). ... Played in Super Bowl XXXI (1996 season).
PRO STATISTICS: 1996—Caught one pass for one yard and a touchdown.
SINGLE GAME HIGHS (regular season): Receptions—1 (October 6, 1996, vs. Baltimore); yards—1 (October 6, 1996, vs. Baltimore); and touchdown receptions—1 (October 6, 1996, vs. Baltimore).

BASS, ANTHONY — DB — VIKINGS

PERSONAL: Born March 26, 1975, in St. Alban, W.Va. ... 6-1/203.
HIGH SCHOOL: South Charleston (W.Va.).
COLLEGE: Bethune-Cookman.
TRANSACTIONS/CAREER NOTES: Signed as non-drafted free agent by Minnesota Vikings (April 23, 1998). ... Released by Vikings (August 24, 1998). ... Signed by Green Bay Packers to practice squad (September 9, 1998). ... Released by Packers (September 12, 1998). ... Signed by Vikings to practice squad (September 17, 1998). ... Activated (November 10, 1998).
PLAYING EXPERIENCE: Minnesota NFL, 1998. ... Games/Games started: 3/0.
CHAMPIONSHIP GAME EXPERIENCE: Played in NFC championship game (1998 season).

BATCH, CHARLIE — QB — LIONS

PERSONAL: Born December 5, 1974, in Homestead, Pa. ... 6-2/216. ... Full name: Charles D'Donte Batch.
HIGH SCHOOL: Steel Valley (Homestead, Pa.).
COLLEGE: Eastern Michigan (degree in business, 1997).
TRANSACTIONS/CAREER NOTES: Selected by Detroit Lions in second round (60th pick overall) of 1998 NFL draft. ... Signed by Lions (July 19, 1998). ... On injured reserve with back injury (December 24, 1998-remainder of season).
RECORDS: Holds NFL rookie-season record for lowest interception percentage—1.98.
PRO STATISTICS: 1998—Fumbled twice.
SINGLE GAME HIGHS (regular season): Attempts—40 (September 20, 1998, vs. Minnesota); completions—20 (October 25, 1998, vs. Minnesota); yards—268 (October 4, 1998, vs. Chicago) and touchdown passes—2 (December 6, 1998, vs. Jacksonville).
MISCELLANEOUS: Regular-season record as starting NFL quarterback: 5-7 (.417).

				PASSING						RUSHING				TOTALS	
Year Team	G	GS	Att.	Cmp.	Pct.	Yds.	TD	Int.	Avg.	Rat.	Att.	Yds.	Avg.	TD	TD 2pt. Pts.
1998—Detroit NFL	12	12	303	173	57.1	2178	11	6	7.19	83.5	41	229	5.6	1	1 0 6

BATES, MARIO — RB — CARDINALS

PERSONAL: Born January 16, 1973, in Tucson, Ariz. ... 6-1/217. ... Full name: Mario Doniel Bates. ... Brother of Michael Bates, kick returner, Carolina Panthers.
HIGH SCHOOL: Amphitheater (Tucson, Ariz.).
COLLEGE: Arizona State.
TRANSACTIONS/CAREER NOTES: Selected after junior season by New Orleans Saints in second round (44th pick overall) of 1994 NFL draft. ... Signed by Saints (July 6, 1994). ... Granted free agency (February 14, 1997). ... Re-signed by Saints (June 12, 1997). ... Granted unconditional free agency (February 13, 1998). ... Signed by Arizona Cardinals (March 6, 1998).
PRO STATISTICS: 1994—Returned one kickoff for 20 yards and recovered one fumble. 1995—Recovered one fumble. 1997—Attempted one pass with a completion for 21 yards and a touchdown.
SINGLE GAME HIGHS (regular season): Attempts—32 (December 15, 1996, vs. New York Giants); yards—162 (September 21, 1997, vs. Detroit); and rushing touchdowns—3 (December 4, 1994, vs. Los Angeles Rams).
STATISTICAL PLATEAUS: 100-yard rushing games: 1994 (1), 1995 (3), 1996 (1), 1997 (1). Total: 6.

			RUSHING				RECEIVING				TOTALS			
Year Team	G	GS	Att.	Yds.	Avg.	TD	No.	Yds.	Avg.	TD	TD	2pt.	Pts.	Fum.
1994—New Orleans NFL	11	7	151	579	3.8	6	8	62	7.8	0	6	0	36	3
1995—New Orleans NFL	16	16	244	951	3.9	7	18	114	6.3	0	7	0	42	2
1996—New Orleans NFL	14	10	164	584	3.6	4	13	44	3.4	0	4	0	24	4
1997—New Orleans NFL	12	7	119	440	3.7	4	5	42	8.4	0	4	0	24	2
1998—Arizona NFL	16	1	60	165	2.8	6	1	14	14.0	0	6	0	36	0
Pro totals (5 years)	69	41	738	2719	3.7	27	45	276	6.1	0	27	0	162	11

BATES, MICHAEL — KR — PANTHERS

PERSONAL: Born December 19, 1969, in Tucson, Ariz. ... 5-10/189. ... Full name: Michael Dion Bates. ... Brother of Mario Bates, running back, Arizona Cardinals.
HIGH SCHOOL: Amphitheater (Tucson, Ariz.).
COLLEGE: Arizona.

TRANSACTIONS/CAREER NOTES: Selected after sophomore season by Seattle Seahawks in sixth round (151st pick overall) of 1992 NFL draft. ... Missed 1992 season due to contract dispute. ... Signed by Seahawks (March 7, 1993). ... Claimed on waivers by Carolina Panthers (August 28, 1995). ... Traded by Panthers to Cleveland Browns for LB Travis Hill (August 29, 1995). ... Granted unconditional free agency (February 16, 1996). ... Signed by Panthers (March 12, 1996). ... Granted unconditional free agency (February 13, 1998). ... Re-signed by Panthers (March 4, 1998).
CHAMPIONSHIP GAME EXPERIENCE: Played in NFC championship game (1996 season).
HONORS: Named kick returner on THE SPORTING NEWS NFL All-Pro team (1996 and 1997). ... Played in Pro Bowl (1996-1998 seasons).
PRO STATISTICS: 1993—Rushed twice for 12 yards and recovered two fumbles for three yards. 1994—Rushed twice for minus four yards. 1997—Returned one punt for eight yards and recovered two fumbles.
SINGLE GAME HIGHS (regular season): Receptions—1 (December 24, 1994, vs. Cleveland); yards—40 (September 11, 1994, vs. Los Angeles Raiders); and touchdown receptions—1 (September 11, 1994, vs. Los Angeles Raiders).
MISCELLANEOUS: Won bronze medal in 200-meter dash in 1992 Summer Olympics.

				RECEIVING				KICKOFF RETURNS				TOTALS		
Year Team	G	GS	No.	Yds.	Avg.	TD	No.	Yds.	Avg.	TD	TD	2pt.	Pts.	Fum.
1992—Seattle NFL								Did not play.						
1993—Seattle NFL	16	1	1	6	6.0	0	30	603	20.1	0	0	...	0	1
1994—Seattle NFL	15	0	5	112	22.4	1	26	508	19.5	0	1	0	6	3
1995—Cleveland NFL	13	0	0	0	...	0	9	176	19.6	0	0	0	0	0
1996—Carolina NFL	14	0	0	0	...	0	33	998	*30.2	1	1	0	6	2
1997—Carolina NFL	16	0	0	0	...	0	47	1281	*27.3	0	0	0	0	4
1998—Carolina NFL	14	0	0	0	...	0	59	1480	25.1	1	1	0	6	1
Pro totals (6 years)	88	1	6	118	19.7	1	204	5046	24.7	2	3	0	18	11

BATISTE, MICHAEL   G

PERSONAL: Born December 24, 1970, in Beaumont, Texas. ... 6-3/325.
HIGH SCHOOL: Westbrook (Texas).
COLLEGE: Tulane.
TRANSACTIONS/CAREER NOTES: Signed as non-drafted free agent by Dallas Cowboys (April 28, 1994). ... Released by Cowboys (August 23, 1994). ... Re-signed by Cowboys (April 10, 1995). ... Released by Cowboys (August 25, 1996). ... Signed by Washington Redskins (February 27, 1997). ... Released by Redskins (August 24, 1997). ... Re-signed by Redskins (February 11, 1998). ... Released by Redskins (October 20, 1998). ... Selected by Barcelona Dragons in 1999 NFL Europe draft (February 23, 1999).
PLAYING EXPERIENCE: Dallas NFL, 1995; Washington NFL, 1998. ... Games/Games started: 1995 (2/0), 1998 (6/0). Total: 8/0.
CHAMPIONSHIP GAME EXPERIENCE: Member of Cowboys for NFC championship game (1995 season); inactive.

BATTAGLIA, MARCO   TE   BENGALS

PERSONAL: Born January 25, 1973, in Howard Beach, N.Y. ... 6-3/252.
HIGH SCHOOL: St. Francis (Queens, N.Y.).
COLLEGE: Rutgers.
TRANSACTIONS/CAREER NOTES: Selected by Cincinnati Bengals in second round (39th pick overall) of 1996 NFL draft. ... Signed by Bengals (July 15, 1996). ... Granted free agency (February 12, 1999). ... Re-signed by Bengals (May 25, 1999).
HONORS: Named tight end on THE SPORTING NEWS college All-America first team (1995).
PRO STATISTICS: 1996—Returned one kickoff for eight yards and recovered one fumble. 1997—Recovered two fumbles. 1998—Returned one kickoff for five yards and recovered three fumbles.
SINGLE GAME HIGHS (regular season): Receptions—3 (November 9, 1997, vs. Indianapolis); yards—42 (December 21, 1997, vs. Baltimore); and touchdown receptions—1 (November 1, 1998, vs. Denver).

				RECEIVING				TOTALS		
Year Team	G	GS	No.	Yds.	Avg.	TD	TD	2pt.	Pts.	Fum.
1996—Cincinnati NFL	16	0	8	79	9.9	0	0	0	0	0
1997—Cincinnati NFL	16	0	12	149	12.4	1	1	0	6	2
1998—Cincinnati NFL	16	0	10	47	4.7	1	1	0	6	1
Pro totals (3 years)	48	0	30	275	9.2	2	2	0	12	3

BAXTER, FRED   TE   JETS

PERSONAL: Born June 14, 1971, in Brundidge, Ala. ... 6-3/265. ... Full name: Frederick Denard Baxter.
HIGH SCHOOL: Pike County (Brundidge, Ala.).
COLLEGE: Auburn.
TRANSACTIONS/CAREER NOTES: Selected by New York Jets in fifth round (115th pick overall) of 1993 NFL draft. ... Signed by Jets (July 13, 1993).
CHAMPIONSHIP GAME EXPERIENCE: Played in AFC championship game (1998 season).
PRO STATISTICS: 1994—Returned one kickoff for 20 yards and recovered one fumble. 1995—Returned six kickoffs for 36 yards and recovered two fumbles for eight yards. 1997—Returned one kickoff for no yards. 1998—Returned one kickoff for eight yards and recovered one fumble.
SINGLE GAME HIGHS (regular season): Receptions—6 (September 17, 1995, vs. Jacksonville); yards—99 (September 17, 1995, vs. Jacksonville); and touchdown receptions—1 (November 23, 1997, vs. Minnesota).

				RECEIVING				TOTALS		
Year Team	G	GS	No.	Yds.	Avg.	TD	TD	2pt.	Pts.	Fum.
1993—New York Jets NFL	7	0	3	48	16.0	1	1	...	6	0
1994—New York Jets NFL	11	1	3	11	3.7	1	1	0	6	0
1995—New York Jets NFL	15	3	18	222	12.3	1	1	0	6	1
1996—New York Jets NFL	16	4	7	114	16.3	0	0	0	0	1
1997—New York Jets NFL	16	9	27	276	10.2	3	3	0	18	1
1998—New York Jets NFL	14	1	3	50	16.7	0	0	0	0	0
Pro totals (6 years)	79	18	61	721	11.8	6	6	0	36	3

BAYNE, CHRIS — S — FALCONS

PERSONAL: Born March 22, 1975, in Riverside, Calif. ... 6-1/215. ... Full name: Christopher Oliver Bayne.
HIGH SCHOOL: North (Riverside, Calif.).
JUNIOR COLLEGE: San Bernardino (Calif.) Valley.
COLLEGE: Fresno State.
TRANSACTIONS/CAREER NOTES: Selected by Atlanta Falcons in seventh round (222nd pick overall) of 1997 NFL draft. ... Signed by Falcons (June 11, 1997).
PLAYING EXPERIENCE: Atlanta NFL, 1997 and 1998. ... Games/Games started: 1997 (13/0), 1998 (10/0). Total: 23/0.
CHAMPIONSHIP GAME EXPERIENCE: Played in NFC championship game (1998 season). ... Member of Falcons for Super Bowl XXXIII (1998 season); inactive.

B BEASLEY, AARON — CB — JAGUARS

PERSONAL: Born July 7, 1973, in Pottstown, Pa. ... 6-0/202. ... Full name: Aaron Bruce Beasley.
HIGH SCHOOL: Pottstown (Pa.), then Valley Forge Military Academy (Wayne, Pa.).
COLLEGE: West Virginia.
TRANSACTIONS/CAREER NOTES: Selected by Jacksonville Jaguars in third round (63rd pick overall) of 1996 NFL draft. ... Signed by Jaguars (May 24, 1996). ... Granted free agency (February 12, 1999). ... Re-signed by Jaguars (March 3, 1999).
CHAMPIONSHIP GAME EXPERIENCE: Played in AFC championship game (1996 season).
PRO STATISTICS: 1998—Recovered one fumble for 90 yards and a touchdown and ran 30 yards on a lateral from punt return.

			INTERCEPTIONS				SACKS
Year Team	G	GS	No.	Yds.	Avg.	TD	No.
1996—Jacksonville NFL	9	7	1	0	0.0	0	1.0
1997—Jacksonville NFL	9	7	1	5	5.0	0	0.0
1998—Jacksonville NFL	16	15	3	35	11.7	0	0.0
Pro totals (3 years)	34	29	5	40	8.0	0	1.0

BEASLEY, FRED — RB — 49ERS

PERSONAL: Born September 18, 1974, in Montgomery, Ala. ... 6-0/220. ... Full name: Frederick Jerome Beasley.
HIGH SCHOOL: Robert E. Lee (Montgomery, Ala.).
COLLEGE: Auburn.
TRANSACTIONS/CAREER NOTES: Selected by San Francisco 49ers in sixth round (180th pick overall) of 1998 NFL draft. ... Signed by 49ers (July 18, 1998).
PLAYING EXPERIENCE: San Francisco NFL, 1998. ... Games/Games started: 16/0.
PRO STATISTICS: 1998—Caught one pass for 11 yards.

BECH, BRETT — WR — SAINTS

PERSONAL: Born August 20, 1971, in Slidell, La. ... 6-1/201. ... Full name: Brett Lamar Bech.
HIGH SCHOOL: Slidell (La.).
COLLEGE: Louisiana State.
TRANSACTIONS/CAREER NOTES: Signed as non-drafted free agent by Jacksonville Jaguars (April 24, 1995). ... Released by Jaguars (June 7, 1995). ... Signed by San Antonio Texans of CFL (July 1995). ... Signed by New Orleans Saints to practice squad (November 13, 1996). ... Activated (December 19, 1996); did not play. ... Released by Saints (August 24, 1997). ... Re-signed by Saints to practice squad (August 25, 1997). ... Activated (September 27, 1997). ... On injured reserve with hand and shoulder injuries (December 12, 1997-remainder of season).
PRO STATISTICS: 1997—Recovered one fumble.
SINGLE GAME HIGHS (regular season): Receptions—4 (December 27, 1998, vs. Buffalo); yards—113 (December 27, 1998, vs. Buffalo); and touchdown receptions—2 (December 27, 1998, vs. Buffalo).
STATISTICAL PLATEAUS: 100-yard receiving games: 1998 (1).

			RECEIVING				KICKOFF RETURNS				TOTALS			
Year Team	G	GS	No.	Yds.	Avg.	TD	No.	Yds.	Avg.	TD	TD	2pt.	Pts.	Fum.
1995—San Antonio CFL	5	...	0	0	...	0	0	0	...	0	0	...	0	0
1996—New Orleans NFL							Did not play.							
1997—New Orleans NFL	10	0	3	50	16.7	0	3	47	15.7	0	0	0	0	0
1998—New Orleans NFL	16	0	14	264	18.9	3	1	20	20.0	0	3	0	18	0
CFL totals (1 year)	5	...	0	0	...	0	0	0	...	0	0	...	0	0
NFL totals (2 years)	26	0	17	314	18.5	3	4	67	16.8	0	3	0	18	0
Pro totals (3 years)	31	...	17	314	18.5	3	4	67	16.8	0	3	0	18	0

BECKLES, IAN — G

PERSONAL: Born July 20, 1967, in Montreal. ... 6-1/304. ... Full name: Ian Harold Beckles.
HIGH SCHOOL: Lindsay Place (Montreal).
JUNIOR COLLEGE: Waldorf Junior College (Iowa).
COLLEGE: Indiana (degree in general studies).
TRANSACTIONS/CAREER NOTES: Selected by Tampa Bay Buccaneers in fifth round (114th pick overall) of 1990 NFL draft. ... Signed by Buccaneers (July 19, 1990). ... Granted free agency (February 1, 1992). ... Re-signed by Buccaneers (July 17, 1992). ... On injured reserve with knee injury (September 1-October 16, 1992). ... On injured reserve with knee injury (December 22, 1993-remainder of season). ... Granted unconditional free agency (February 17, 1994). ... Re-signed by Buccaneers (March 29, 1994). ... Granted unconditional free agency (February 14, 1997). ... Signed by Philadelphia Eagles (June 4, 1997). ... Granted unconditional free agency (February 12, 1999).
PLAYING EXPERIENCE: Tampa Bay NFL, 1990-1997; Philadelphia NFL, 1998. ... Games/Games started: 1990 (16/16), 1991 (16/16), 1992 (11/7), 1993 (14/14), 1994 (16/16), 1995 (15/15), 1996 (13/13), 1997 (9/8), 1998 (16/16). Total: 126/121.
PRO STATISTICS: 1993—Recovered one fumble. 1994—Recovered two fumbles. 1995—Recovered two fumbles. 1997—Recovered two fumbles. 1998—Recovered two fumbles.

– 26 –

BEEDE, FRANK — G — SEAHAWKS

PERSONAL: Born May 1, 1973, in Antioch, Calif. ... 6-4/296.
HIGH SCHOOL: Antioch (Calif.).
COLLEGE: Panhandle State (Okla.).
TRANSACTIONS/CAREER NOTES: Signed as non-drafted free agent by Seattle Seahawks (April 22, 1996). ... On injured reserve with knee injury (August 25, 1998-entire season). ... Granted free agency (February 12, 1999). ... Re-signed by Seahawks (April 7, 1999).
PLAYING EXPERIENCE: Seattle NFL, 1996 and 1997. ... Games/Games started: 1996 (14/2), 1997 (16/6). Total: 30/8.
PRO STATISTICS: 1997—Returned one kick for no yards and fumbled once.

BELL, MYRON — S — BENGALS

PERSONAL: Born September 15, 1971, in Toledo, Ohio. ... 5-11/203. ... Full name: Myron Corey Bell.
HIGH SCHOOL: Macomber-Whitney (Toledo, Ohio).
COLLEGE: Michigan State.
TRANSACTIONS/CAREER NOTES: Selected by Pittsburgh Steelers in fifth round (140th pick overall) of 1994 NFL draft. ... Signed by Steelers (July 18, 1994). ... Granted free agency (February 14, 1997). ... Re-signed by Steelers (April 15, 1997). ... Granted unconditional free agency (February 13, 1998). ... Signed by Cincinnati Bengals (June 26, 1998).
CHAMPIONSHIP GAME EXPERIENCE: Played in AFC championship game (1994, 1995 and 1997 seasons). ... Played in Super Bowl XXX (1995 season).
PRO STATISTICS: 1995—Recovered one fumble. 1996—Credited with two sacks and recovered two fumbles. 1997—Credited with 1 1/2 sacks and recovered one fumble. 1998—Credited with one sack.

				INTERCEPTIONS		
Year Team	G	GS	No.	Yds.	Avg.	TD
1994—Pittsburgh NFL	15	0	0	0	...	0
1995—Pittsburgh NFL	16	9	2	4	2.0	0
1996—Pittsburgh NFL	16	4	0	0	...	0
1997—Pittsburgh NFL	16	8	1	10	10.0	0
1998—Cincinnati NFL	16	2	0	0	...	0
Pro totals (5 years)	79	23	3	14	4.7	0

BELL, RICKY — CB — BEARS

PERSONAL: Born October 2, 1974, in Columbia, S.C. ... 5-10/194.
HIGH SCHOOL: Eau Claire (Columbia, S.C.).
COLLEGE: North Carolina State.
TRANSACTIONS/CAREER NOTES: Signed as non-drafted free agent by Pittsburgh Steelers (April 29, 1996). ... Released by Steelers (August 24, 1996). ... Re-signed by Steelers to practice squad (August 27, 1996). ... Activated (September 10, 1996); did not play. ... Claimed on waivers by Jacksonville Jaguars (September 25, 1996). ... Released by Jaguars (August 19, 1997). ... Signed by Chicago Bears (September 9, 1997). ... On non-football injury list for personal reasons (October 25, 1997-remainder of season). ... Assigned by Bears to Barcelona Dragons in 1999 NFL Europe enhancement allocation program (February 22, 1999).
PLAYING EXPERIENCE: Jacksonville NFL, 1996; Chicago NFL, 1997 and 1998. ... Games/Games started: 1996 (12/0), 1997 (5/0), 1998 (14/0). Total: 31/0.
CHAMPIONSHIP GAME EXPERIENCE: Played in AFC championship game (1996 season).
PRO STATISTICS: 1996—Returned six kickoffs for 119 yards and fumbled once. 1998—Recovered one fumble.

BELLAMY, JAY — S — SEAHAWKS

PERSONAL: Born July 8, 1972, in Perth Amboy, N.J. ... 5-11/199. ... Full name: John Lee Bellamy.
HIGH SCHOOL: Matawan (N.J.).
COLLEGE: Rutgers.
TRANSACTIONS/CAREER NOTES: Signed as non-drafted free agent by Seattle Seahawks (April 27, 1994). ... On injured reserve with shoulder injury (November 11, 1994-remainder of season).
PRO STATISTICS: 1997—Credited with two sacks. 1998—Credited with one sack and recovered two fumbles.

				INTERCEPTIONS		
Year Team	G	GS	No.	Yds.	Avg.	TD
1994—Seattle NFL	3	0	0	0	...	0
1995—Seattle NFL	14	0	0	0	...	0
1996—Seattle NFL	16	0	3	18	6.0	0
1997—Seattle NFL	16	7	1	13	13.0	0
1998—Seattle NFL	16	16	3	40	13.3	0
Pro totals (5 years)	65	23	7	71	10.1	0

BELLISARI, GREG — LB — RAIDERS

PERSONAL: Born June 21, 1975, in Boynton Beach, Fla. ... 6-0/236. ... Full name: Greg Ernest Bellisari.
HIGH SCHOOL: Community (Boca Raton, Fla.).
COLLEGE: Ohio State.
TRANSACTIONS/CAREER NOTES: Signed as non-drafted free agent by Tampa Bay Buccaneers (April 21, 1997). ... Released by Buccaneers (September 17, 1998). ... Signed by Oakland Raiders (March 10, 1999).
PLAYING EXPERIENCE: Tampa Bay NFL, 1997 and 1998. ... Games/Games started: 1997 (14/0), 1998 (2/0). Total: 16/0.
PRO STATISTICS: 1998—Recovered one fumble.

BELSER, JASON — DB — COLTS

PERSONAL: Born May 28, 1970, in Kansas City, Mo. ... 5-9/196. ... Full name: Jason Daks Belser. ... Son of Caeser Belser, defensive back with Kansas City Chiefs (1968-71) and linebacker with San Francisco 49ers (1974).
HIGH SCHOOL: Raytown (Mo.) South.
COLLEGE: Oklahoma.
TRANSACTIONS/CAREER NOTES: Selected by Indianapolis Colts in eighth round (197th pick overall) of 1992 NFL draft. ... Signed by Colts (July 22, 1992). ... Granted free agency (February 17, 1995). ... Tendered offer sheet by Carolina Panthers (April 17, 1995). ... Offer matched by Colts (April 19, 1995).
CHAMPIONSHIP GAME EXPERIENCE: Played in AFC championship game (1995 season).
PRO STATISTICS: 1992—Fumbled once and recovered two fumbles. 1993—Recovered three fumbles. 1995—Returned one kickoff for 15 yards and recovered two fumbles. 1996—Credited with one sack and recovered one fumble. 1997—Credited with one sack. 1998—Returned one punt for 53 yards, credited with one sack and recovered one fumble.

			INTERCEPTIONS			
Year Team	G	GS	No.	Yds.	Avg.	TD
1992—Indianapolis NFL	16	2	3	27	9.0	0
1993—Indianapolis NFL	16	16	1	14	14.0	0
1994—Indianapolis NFL	13	12	1	31	31.0	0
1995—Indianapolis NFL	16	16	1	0	0.0	0
1996—Indianapolis NFL	16	16	4	81	20.3	†2
1997—Indianapolis NFL	16	16	2	121	60.5	1
1998—Indianapolis NFL	16	16	1	19	19.0	0
Pro totals (7 years)	109	94	13	293	22.5	3

BENNETT, BRANDON — RB

PERSONAL: Born February 3, 1973, in Taylors, S.C. ... 5-11/220.
HIGH SCHOOL: Riverside (Taylors, S.C.).
COLLEGE: South Carolina.
TRANSACTIONS/CAREER NOTES: Signed as non-drafted free agent by Cleveland Browns (July 25, 1995). ... Released by Browns (August 18, 1995). ... Signed by Chicago Bears to practice squad (December 6, 1995). ... Released by Bears (August 19, 1996). ... Re-signed by Bears to practice squad (September 24, 1996). ... Released by Bears (November 1, 1996). ... Signed by Miami Dolphins to practice squad (November 5, 1996). ... Activated (December 17, 1996); did not play. ... Released by Dolphins (August 12, 1997). ... Signed by Cincinnati Bengals (April 20, 1998). ... Released by Bengals (August 30, 1998). ... Re-signed by Bengals (September 7, 1998). ... Released by Bengals (June 3, 1999).
PRO STATISTICS: 1998—Recovered one fumble.
SINGLE GAME HIGHS (regular season): Attempts—25 (December 20, 1998, vs. Pittsburgh); yards—87 (December 13, 1998, vs. Indianapolis); and rushing touchdowns—1 (December 13, 1998, vs. Indianapolis).
STATISTICAL PLATEAUS: 100-yard receiving games: 1998 (1).

			RUSHING				RECEIVING				KICKOFF RETURNS				TOTALS			
Year Team	G	GS	Att.	Yds.	Avg.	TD	No.	Yds.	Avg.	TD	No.	Yds.	Avg.	TD	TD	2pt.	Pts.	Fum.
1995—Chicago NFL								Did not play.										
1996—Miami NFL								Did not play.										
1997—								Did not play.										
1998—Cincinnati NFL	14	1	77	243	3.2	2	8	153	19.1	0	3	61	20.3	0	2	0	12	1

BENNETT, CORNELIUS — LB — COLTS

PERSONAL: Born August 25, 1965, in Birmingham, Ala. ... 6-2/240. ... Full name: Cornelius O'landa Bennett.
HIGH SCHOOL: Ensley (Birmingham, Ala.).
COLLEGE: Alabama.
TRANSACTIONS/CAREER NOTES: Selected by Indianapolis Colts in first round (second pick overall) of 1987 NFL draft. ... Placed on reserve/unsigned list (August 31-October 30, 1987). ... Rights traded by Colts to Buffalo Bills in exchange for Bills trading first-round pick (RB Gaston Green) in 1988 draft, first-(RB Cleveland Gary) and second-round (CB Darryl Henley) picks in 1989 draft and RB Greg Bell to Los Angeles Rams (October 31, 1987); Rams also traded RB Eric Dickerson to Colts for first-(WR Aaron Cox) and second-round (LB Fred Strickland) picks in 1988 draft, second-round pick (LB Frank Stams) in 1989 draft and RB Owen Gill. ... Signed by Bills (October 31, 1987). ... Granted roster exemption (October 31-November 7, 1987). ... Granted free agency (February 1, 1992). ... Re-signed by Bills (August 31, 1992). ... Designated by Bills as franchise player (February 15, 1995). ... Granted unconditional free agency (February 16, 1996). ... Signed by Atlanta Falcons (March 1, 1996). ... Released by Falcons (February 17, 1999). ... Signed by Indianapolis Colts (March 1, 1999).
CHAMPIONSHIP GAME EXPERIENCE: Played in AFC championship game (1988 and 1990-1993 seasons). ... Played in Super Bowl XXV (1990 season), Super Bowl XXVI (1991 season), Super Bowl XXVII (1992 season), Super Bowl XXVIII (1993 season) and Super Bowl XXXIII (1998 season). ... Played in NFC championship game (1998 season).
HONORS: Named linebacker on THE SPORTING NEWS college All-America first team (1984-1986). ... Lombardi Award winner (1986). ... Named outside linebacker on THE SPORTING NEWS NFL All-Pro team (1988). ... Played in Pro Bowl (1988 and 1990-1993 seasons).
PRO STATISTICS: 1988—Recovered three fumbles. 1989—Recovered two fumbles for five yards. 1990—Returned blocked field-goal attempt 80 yards for a touchdown and recovered two fumbles. 1991—Recovered two fumbles for nine yards and a touchdown. 1992—Recovered three fumbles. 1993—Recovered two fumbles for 40 yards and fumbled once. 1994—Recovered three fumbles for 14 yards. 1995—Recovered two fumbles. 1996—Recovered two fumbles. 1997—Recovered one fumble. 1998—Recovered two fumbles for 10 yards.

			INTERCEPTIONS				SACKS
Year Team	G	GS	No.	Yds.	Avg.	TD	No.
1987—Buffalo NFL	8	7	0	0	...	0	8.5
1988—Buffalo NFL	16	16	2	30	15.0	0	9.5
1989—Buffalo NFL	12	12	2	5	2.5	0	5.5
1990—Buffalo NFL	16	16	0	0	...	0	4.0
1991—Buffalo NFL	16	16	0	0	...	0	9.0
1992—Buffalo NFL	15	15	0	0	...	0	4.0
1993—Buffalo NFL	16	16	1	5	5.0	0	5.0
1994—Buffalo NFL	16	16	0	0	...	0	5.0

Year Team	G	GS	INTERCEPTIONS No.	Yds.	Avg.	TD	SACKS No.
1995—Buffalo NFL	14	14	1	69	69.0	▲1	2.0
1996—Atlanta NFL	13	13	1	3	3.0	0	3.0
1997—Atlanta NFL	16	16	0	0	...	0	7.0
1998—Atlanta NFL	16	16	0	0	...	0	1.0
Pro totals (12 years)	174	173	7	112	16.0	1	63.5

BENNETT, DARREN P CHARGERS

PERSONAL: Born January 9, 1965, in Sydney, Australia. ... 6-5/235. ... Full name: Darren Leslie Bennett.
HIGH SCHOOL: Applecross (Perth, Western Australia).
COLLEGE: None.
TRANSACTIONS/CAREER NOTES: Played Australian Rules Football (1987-1993). ... Signed as non-drafted free agent by San Diego Chargers (April 14, 1994). ... Released by Chargers (August 28, 1994). ... Re-signed by Chargers to practice squad (August 29, 1994). ... Assigned by Chargers to Amsterdam Admirals in 1995 World League enhancement allocation program (February 20, 1995).
HONORS: Named punter on THE SPORTING NEWS NFL All-Pro team (1995). ... Played in Pro Bowl (1995 season).
PRO STATISTICS: 1998—Fumbled once and recovered one fumble.

Year Team	G	No.	PUNTING Yds.	Avg.	Net avg.	In. 20	Blk.
1995—Amsterdam W.L.	10	60	2296	38.3	35.1	24	1
—San Diego NFL	16	72	3221	44.7	36.6	28	0
1996—San Diego NFL	16	87	3967	45.6	37.2	23	0
1997—San Diego NFL	16	89	3972	44.6	37.7	26	1
1998—San Diego NFL	16	95	4174	43.9	36.8	27	0
W.L. totals (1 year)	10	60	2296	38.3	35.1	24	1
NFL totals (4 years)	64	343	15334	44.7	37.1	104	1
Pro totals (5 years)	74	403	17630	43.7	36.8	128	2

BENNETT, DONNELL RB CHIEFS

PERSONAL: Born September 14, 1972, in Fort Lauderdale, Fla. ... 6-0/235.
HIGH SCHOOL: Cardinal Gibbons (Fort Lauderdale, Fla.).
COLLEGE: Miami (Fla.).
TRANSACTIONS/CAREER NOTES: Selected after junior season by Kansas City Chiefs in second round (58th pick overall) of 1994 NFL draft. ... Signed by Chiefs (May 6, 1994). ... On injured reserve with knee injury (December 20, 1994-remainder of season). ... On physically unable to perform list with knee injury (August 22-October 31, 1995). ... Granted free agency (February 14, 1997). ... Re-signed by Chiefs (April 22, 1997).
PRO STATISTICS: 1994—Returned one kickoff for 12 yards and recovered one fumble.
SINGLE GAME HIGHS (regular season): Attempts—30 (September 20, 1998, vs. San Deigo); yards—115 (September 6, 1998, vs. Oakland); and rushing touchdowns—3 (September 27, 1998, vs. Philadelphia).
STATISTICAL PLATEAUS: 100-yard rushing games: 1998 (1).

Year Team	G	GS	RUSHING Att.	Yds.	Avg.	TD	RECEIVING No.	Yds.	Avg.	TD	TOTALS TD	2pt.	Pts.	Fum.
1994—Kansas City NFL	15	0	46	178	3.9	2	7	53	7.6	0	2	0	12	2
1995—Kansas City NFL	3	1	7	11	1.6	0	1	12	12.0	0	0	0	0	0
1996—Kansas City NFL	16	0	36	166	4.6	0	8	21	2.6	0	0	0	0	0
1997—Kansas City NFL	14	1	94	369	3.9	1	7	5	0.7	0	1	0	6	0
1998—Kansas City NFL	16	10	148	527	3.6	5	16	91	5.7	1	6	0	36	4
Pro totals (5 years)	64	12	331	1251	3.8	8	39	182	4.7	1	9	0	54	6

BENNETT, EDGAR RB BEARS

PERSONAL: Born February 15, 1969, in Jacksonville. ... 6-0/218. ... Full name: Edgar Bennett III.
HIGH SCHOOL: Robert E. Lee Senior (Jacksonville).
COLLEGE: Florida State.
TRANSACTIONS/CAREER NOTES: Selected by Green Bay Packers in fourth round (103rd pick overall) of 1992 NFL draft. ... Signed by Packers (July 22, 1992). ... Granted free agency (February 17, 1995). ... Re-signed by Packers (May 5, 1995). ... On injured reserve with knee injury (August 18, 1997-entire season). ... Granted unconditional free agency (February 13, 1998). ... Signed by Chicago Bears (February 20, 1998).
CHAMPIONSHIP GAME EXPERIENCE: Played in NFC championship game (1995 and 1996 seasons). ... Member of Super Bowl championship team (1996 season).
PRO STATISTICS: 1992—Returned five kickoffs for 104 yards. 1993—Recovered one fumble. 1994—Recovered one fumble. 1995—Recovered one fumble. 1996—Recovered one fumble. 1998—Attempted two passes with one completion for 18 yards and a touchdown and recovered one fumble.
SINGLE GAME HIGHS (regular season): Attempts—30 (September 11, 1995, vs. Chicago); yards—121 (October 29, 1995, vs. Detroit); and rushing touchdowns—2 (October 31, 1994, vs. Chicago).
STATISTICAL PLATEAUS: 100-yard rushing games: 1992 (1), 1994 (3), 1995 (1), 1996 (1). Total: 6. ... 100-yard receiving games: 1994 (1).

Year Team	G	GS	RUSHING Att.	Yds.	Avg.	TD	RECEIVING No.	Yds.	Avg.	TD	TOTALS TD	2pt.	Pts.	Fum.
1992—Green Bay NFL	16	2	61	214	3.5	0	13	93	7.2	0	0	...	0	2
1993—Green Bay NFL	16	14	159	550	3.5	9	59	457	7.7	1	10	0	60	0
1994—Green Bay NFL	16	15	178	623	3.5	5	78	546	7.0	4	9	0	54	1
1995—Green Bay NFL	16	16	316	1067	3.4	3	61	648	10.6	4	7	0	42	2
1996—Green Bay NFL	16	15	222	899	4.0	2	31	176	5.7	1	3	‡2	22	2
1997—Green Bay NFL								Did not play.						
1998—Chicago NFL	16	13	173	611	3.5	2	28	209	7.5	0	2	0	12	2
Pro totals (6 years)	96	75	1109	3964	3.6	21	270	2129	7.9	10	31	2	190	9

– 29 –

BENNETT, TOMMY — S — CARDINALS

PERSONAL: Born February 19, 1973, in Las Vegas, Nev. ... 6-2/219.
HIGH SCHOOL: Morse (San Diego).
COLLEGE: UCLA.
TRANSACTIONS/CAREER NOTES: Signed as a non-drafted free agent by Arizona Cardinals (April 23, 1996). ... Granted free agency (February 12, 1999).
PRO STATISTICS: 1997—Recovered blocked punt in end zone for a touchdown.

			INTERCEPTIONS				TOTALS		
Year Team	G	GS	No.	Yds.	Avg.	TD	TD	2pt.	Pts.	Fum.
1996—Arizona NFL	16	1	0	0	...	0	0	0	0	0
1997—Arizona NFL	13	7	1	0	0.0	0	1	0	6	0
1998—Arizona NFL	16	16	2	100	50.0	1	1	0	6	0
Pro totals (3 years)	45	24	3	100	33.3	1	2	0	12	0

BERCICH, PETE — LB — VIKINGS

PERSONAL: Born December 23, 1971, in Joliet, Ill. ... 6-1/239. ... Full name: Peter James Bercich. ... Son of Bob Bercich, safety with Dallas Cowboys (1960 and 1961). ... Name pronounced BURR-sitch.
HIGH SCHOOL: Providence Catholic (New Lenox, Ill.).
COLLEGE: Notre Dame (degree in finance, 1993).
TRANSACTIONS/CAREER NOTES: Selected by Minnesota Vikings in seventh round (211th pick overall) of 1994 NFL draft. ... Signed by Vikings (July 11, 1994). ... Released by Vikings (August 28, 1994). ... Re-signed by Vikings to practice squad (August 29, 1994). ... Granted free agency (February 13, 1998). ... Re-signed by Vikings (April 27, 1998). ... Granted unconditional free agency (February 12, 1999). ... Re-signed by Vikings (April 16, 1999).
PLAYING EXPERIENCE: Minnesota NFL, 1995-1998. ... Games/Games started: 1995 (9/0), 1996 (15/1), 1997 (16/0), 1998 (15/1). Total: 55/2.
CHAMPIONSHIP GAME EXPERIENCE: Played in NFC championship game (1998 season).
PRO STATISTICS: 1996—Recovered one fumble.

BERGER, MITCH — P — VIKINGS

PERSONAL: Born June 24, 1972, in Kamloops, B.C. ... 6-2/217.
HIGH SCHOOL: North Delta (Vancouver).
JUNIOR COLLEGE: Tyler (Texas) Junior College.
COLLEGE: Colorado.
TRANSACTIONS/CAREER NOTES: Selected by Philadelphia Eagles in sixth round (193rd pick overall) of 1994 NFL draft. ... Signed by Eagles (July 11, 1994). ... Released by Eagles (October 10, 1994). ... Signed by Cincinnati Bengals to practice squad (October 13, 1994). ... Released by Bengals (November 30, 1994). ... Signed by Chicago Bears (March 7, 1995). ... Released by Bears (May 4, 1995). ... Signed by Indianapolis Colts (May 16, 1995). ... Claimed on waivers by Green Bay Packers (August 24, 1995). ... Released by Packers (August 27, 1995). ... Signed by Bears (November 7, 1995). ... Released by Bears (November 13, 1995). ... Signed by Minnesota Vikings (April 19, 1996).
CHAMPIONSHIP GAME EXPERIENCE: Played in NFC championship game (1998 season).
PRO STATISTICS: 1997—Rushed once for no yards and fumbled once for minus nine yards.

		PUNTING					
Year Team	G	No.	Yds.	Avg.	Net avg.	In. 20	Blk.
1994—Philadelphia NFL	5	25	951	38.0	31.3	8	0
1995—				Did not play.			
1996—Minnesota NFL	16	88	3616	41.1	32.3	26	2
1997—Minnesota NFL	14	73	3133	42.9	34.1	22	0
1998—Minnesota NFL	16	55	2458	44.7	37.0	17	0
Pro totals (4 years)	51	241	10158	42.1	33.8	73	2

BERRY, BERT — LB — COLTS

PERSONAL: Born August 15, 1975, in Houston. ... 6-2/248. ... Full name: Bertrand Demond Berry.
HIGH SCHOOL: Humble (Texas).
COLLEGE: Notre Dame.
TRANSACTIONS/CAREER NOTES: Selected by Indianapolis Colts in third round (86th pick overall) of 1997 NFL draft. ... Signed by Colts (July 9, 1997).

Year Team	G	GS	SACKS
1997—Indianapolis NFL	10	1	0.0
1998—Indianapolis NFL	16	12	4.0
Pro totals (2 years)	26	13	4.0

BERTI, TONY — OT — BRONCOS

PERSONAL: Born June 21, 1972, in Rock Springs, Wyo. ... 6-6/300. ... Full name: Charles Anton Berti Jr.
HIGH SCHOOL: Skyview (Thornton, Colo.).
COLLEGE: Colorado.
TRANSACTIONS/CAREER NOTES: Selected by San Diego Chargers in sixth round (200th pick overall) of 1995 NFL draft. ... Signed by Chargers (July 12, 1995). ... On injured reserve with shoulder injury (August 25-November 25, 1998). ... Released by Chargers (November 25, 1998). ... Signed by Seattle Seahawks (November 25, 1998). ... Inactive for five games (1998). ... Granted unconditional free agency (February 12, 1999). ... Signed by Denver Broncos (February 17, 1999).
PLAYING EXPERIENCE: San Diego NFL, 1995-1997. ... Games/Games started: 1995 (1/0), 1996 (16/14), 1997 (16/16). Total: 33/30.
PRO STATISTICS: 1997—Recovered one fumble.

BETTIS, JEROME — RB — STEELERS

PERSONAL: Born February 16, 1972, in Detroit. ... 5-11/250. ... Full name: Jerome Abram Bettis. ... Nickname: The Bus.
HIGH SCHOOL: Mackenzie (Detroit).
COLLEGE: Notre Dame.
TRANSACTIONS/CAREER NOTES: Selected after junior season by Los Angeles Rams in first round (10th pick overall) of 1993 NFL draft. ... Signed by Rams (July 22, 1993). ... Rams franchise moved to St. Louis (April 12, 1995). ... Traded by Rams with third-round pick (LB Steven Conley) in 1996 draft to Pittsburgh Steelers for second-round pick (TE Ernie Conwell) in 1996 draft and fourth-round pick (traded to Miami) in 1997 draft (April 20, 1996). ... Granted unconditional free agency (February 14, 1997). ... Re-signed by Steelers (February 17, 1997).
CHAMPIONSHIP GAME EXPERIENCE: Played in AFC championship game (1997 season).
HONORS: Named NFL Rookie of the Year by THE SPORTING NEWS (1993). ... Played in Pro Bowl (1993, 1994, 1996 and 1997 seasons).
PRO STATISTICS: 1994—Recovered three fumbles. 1995—Recovered two fumbles. 1996—Recovered two fumbles. 1997—Recovered one fumble.
SINGLE GAME HIGHS (regular season): Attempts—39 (January 2, 1994, vs. Chicago); yards—212 (December 12, 1993, vs. New Orleans); and rushing touchdowns—3 (November 30, 1997, vs. Arizona).
STATISTICAL PLATEAUS: 100-yard rushing games: 1993 (7), 1994 (4), 1996 (10), 1997 (10), 1998 (6). Total: 37.

				RUSHING				RECEIVING				TOTALS			
Year Team	G	GS	Att.	Yds.	Avg.	TD	No.	Yds.	Avg.	TD	TD	2pt.	Pts.	Fum.
1993—Los Angeles Rams NFL	16	12	‡294	1429	4.9	7	26	244	9.4	0	7	...	42	4
1994—Los Angeles Rams NFL	16	16	319	1025	3.2	3	31	293	9.5	1	4	∞2	28	5
1995—St. Louis NFL	15	13	183	637	3.5	3	18	106	5.9	0	3	0	18	4
1996—Pittsburgh NFL	16	12	320	1431	4.5	11	22	122	5.5	0	11	0	66	7
1997—Pittsburgh NFL	15	15	*375	1665	4.4	7	15	110	7.3	2	9	0	54	6
1998—Pittsburgh NFL	15	15	316	1185	3.8	3	16	90	5.6	0	3	0	18	2
Pro totals (6 years)	93	83	1807	7372	4.1	34	128	965	7.5	3	37	2	226	28

BEUERLEIN, STEVE — QB — PANTHERS

PERSONAL: Born March 7, 1965, in Hollywood, Calif. ... 6-3/220. ... Full name: Stephen Taylor Beuerlein. ... Name pronounced BURR-line.
HIGH SCHOOL: Servite (Anaheim, Calif.).
COLLEGE: Notre Dame (degree in American studies, 1987).
TRANSACTIONS/CAREER NOTES: Selected by Los Angeles Raiders in fourth round (110th pick overall) of 1987 NFL draft. ... Signed by Raiders (July 24, 1987). ... On injured reserve with elbow and shoulder injuries (September 7, 1987-entire season). ... Granted free agency (February 1, 1990). ... Re-signed by Raiders (September 3, 1990). ... Granted roster exemption (September 3-16, 1990). ... Inactive for all 16 games (1990). ... Granted free agency (February 1, 1991). ... Re-signed by Raiders (July 8, 1991). ... Traded by Raiders to Dallas Cowboys for fourth-round pick (traded to Indianapolis) in 1992 draft (August 25, 1991). ... Granted unconditional free agency (March 1, 1993). ... Signed by Phoenix Cardinals (April 21, 1993). ... Cardinals franchise renamed Arizona Cardinals for 1994 season. ... Selected by Jacksonville Jaguars from Cardinals in NFL expansion draft (February 15, 1995). ... Granted free agency (February 16, 1996). ... Signed by Carolina Panthers (April 10, 1996).
CHAMPIONSHIP GAME EXPERIENCE: Member of Raiders for AFC championship game (1990 season); inactive. ... Played in NFC championship game (1992 season). ... Member of Super Bowl championship team (1992 season). ... Member of Panthers for NFC championship game (1996 season); did not play.
PRO STATISTICS: 1988—Caught one pass for 21 yards, fumbled six times and recovered two fumbles for minus one yard. 1989—Fumbled six times and recovered three fumbles for minus eight yards. 1993—Fumbled eight times and recovered two fumbles. 1994—Fumbled eight times and recovered three fumbles for minus 13 yards. 1995—Fumbled three times. 1996—Fumbled nine times and recovered two fumbles for minus seven yards. 1997—Fumbled once. 1998—Fumbled 13 times and recovered five fumbles for minus 19 yards.
SINGLE GAME HIGHS (regular season): Attempts—53 (December 19, 1993, vs. Seattle); completions—34 (December 19, 1993, vs. Seattle); yards—431 (December 19, 1993, vs. Seattle); and touchdown passes—3 (December 6, 1998, vs. San Francisco).
STATISTICAL PLATEAUS: 300-yard passing games: 1988 (1), 1993 (2). Total: 3.
MISCELLANEOUS: Regular-season record as starting NFL quarterback: 30-35 (.462). ... Postseason record as starting NFL quarterback: 1-1 (.500).

					PASSING					RUSHING				TOTALS		
Year Team	G	GS	Att.	Cmp.	Pct.	Yds.	TD	Int.	Avg.	Rat.	Att.	Yds.	Avg.	TD	TD	2pt.	Pts.
1987—L.A. Raiders NFL						Did not play.											
1988—L.A. Raiders NFL	10	8	238	105	44.1	1643	8	7	6.90	66.6	30	35	1.2	0	0	...	0
1989—L.A. Raiders NFL	10	7	217	108	49.8	1677	13	9	7.73	78.4	16	39	2.4	0	0	...	0
1990—L.A. Raiders NFL						Did not play.											
1991—Dallas NFL	8	4	137	68	49.6	909	5	2	6.64	77.2	7	-14	-2.0	0	0	...	0
1992—Dallas NFL	16	0	18	12	66.7	152	0	1	8.44	69.7	4	-7	-1.8	0	0	...	0
1993—Phoenix NFL	16	14	418	258	61.7	3164	18	17	7.57	82.5	22	45	2.0	0	0	...	0
1994—Arizona NFL	9	7	255	130	51.0	1545	5	9	6.06	61.6	22	39	1.8	1	1	0	6
1995—Jacksonville NFL	7	6	142	71	50.0	952	4	7	6.70	60.5	5	32	6.4	0	0	0	0
1996—Carolina NFL	8	4	123	69	56.1	879	8	2	7.15	93.5	12	17	1.4	0	0	0	0
1997—Carolina NFL	7	3	153	89	58.2	1032	6	3	6.75	83.6	4	32	8.0	0	0	0	0
1998—Carolina NFL	12	12	343	216	63.0	2613	17	12	7.62	88.2	22	26	1.2	0	0	0	0
Pro totals (10 years)	103	65	2044	1126	55.1	14566	84	69	7.13	77.3	144	244	1.7	1	1	0	6

BEVERLY, ERIC — C — LIONS

PERSONAL: Born March 28, 1974, in Cleveland. ... 6-3/279. ... Full name: Eric Raymonde Beverly.
HIGH SCHOOL: Bedford Heights (Ohio).
COLLEGE: Miami (Ohio).
TRANSACTIONS/CAREER NOTES: Signed as non-drafted free agent by Detroit Lions (April 24, 1997). ... Released by Lions (August 24, 1997). ... Re-signed by Lions to practice squad (August 26, 1997). ... Activated (December 20, 1997). ... Active for one game (1997); did not play.
PLAYING EXPERIENCE: Detroit NFL, 1998. ... Games/Games started: 16/0.

BIAKABUTUKA, TSHIMANGA — RB — PANTHERS

PERSONAL: Born January 24, 1974, in Kinsasha, Zaire. ... 6-0/215. ... Name pronounced Tee-MONG-uh Bee-ock-uh-bah-TWO-kah. ... Nickname: Tim.
HIGH SCHOOL: John Jacques Rosseau (Longueuil, Que.), then Vanier College (Montreal).
COLLEGE: Michigan.
TRANSACTIONS/CAREER NOTES: Selected after junior season by Carolina Panthers in first round (eighth pick overall) of 1996 NFL draft. ... Signed by Panthers (August 16, 1996). ... On injured reserve with knee injury (October 1, 1996-remainder of season).
SINGLE GAME HIGHS (regular season): Attempts—26 (September 1, 1996, vs. Atlanta); yards—109 (December 27, 1998, vs. Indianapolis); and rushing touchdowns—2 (October 26, 1997, vs. Atlanta).
STATISTICAL PLATEAUS: 100-yard rushing games: 1997 (1), 1998 (2). Total: 3.

			RUSHING				RECEIVING				TOTALS		
Year Team	G	GS	Att.	Yds.	Avg.	TD	No.	Yds.	Avg.	TD	TD	2pt.	Pts.	Fum.
1996—Carolina NFL	4	4	71	229	3.2	0	0	0	...	0	0	0	0	0
1997—Carolina NFL	8	2	75	299	4.0	2	0	0	...	0	2	0	12	1
1998—Carolina NFL	11	3	101	427	4.2	3	8	138	17.3	1	4	0	24	1
Pro totals (3 years)	23	9	247	955	3.9	5	8	138	17.3	1	6	0	36	2

BIEKERT, GREG — LB — RAIDERS

PERSONAL: Born March 14, 1969, in Iowa City, Iowa. ... 6-2/245. ... Name pronounced BEEK-ert.
HIGH SCHOOL: Longmont (Colo.).
COLLEGE: Colorado (degree in marketing, 1992).
TRANSACTIONS/CAREER NOTES: Selected by Los Angeles Raiders in seventh round (181st pick overall) of 1993 NFL draft. ... Signed by Raiders (July 13, 1993). ... Raiders franchise moved to Oakland (July 21, 1995).
PRO STATISTICS: 1994—Intercepted one pass for 11 yards. 1996—Recovered one fumble. 1997—Returned one kickoff for 16 yards. 1998—Recovered one fumble.

Year Team	G	GS	SACKS
1993—Los Angeles Raiders NFL	16	0	0.0
1994—Los Angeles Raiders NFL	16	14	1.5
1995—Oakland NFL	16	14	1.0
1996—Oakland NFL	16	15	0.0
1997—Oakland NFL	16	16	2.5
1998—Oakland NFL	16	16	3.0
Pro totals (6 years)	96	75	8.0

BIENIEMY, ERIC — RB — EAGLES

PERSONAL: Born August 15, 1969, in New Orleans. ... 5-9/205. ... Full name: Eric Bieniemy Jr.
HIGH SCHOOL: Bishop Amat (La Puente, Calif.).
COLLEGE: Colorado.
TRANSACTIONS/CAREER NOTES: Selected by San Diego Chargers in second round (39th pick overall) of 1991 NFL draft. ... Signed by Chargers (July 19, 1991). ... Granted free agency (February 17, 1994). ... Re-signed by Chargers (June 6, 1994). ... Granted unconditional free agency (February 17, 1995). ... Signed by Cincinnati Bengals (March 27, 1995). ... Granted unconditional free agency (February 12, 1999). ... Signed by Philadelphia Eagles (May 7, 1999).
CHAMPIONSHIP GAME EXPERIENCE: Played in AFC championship game (1994 season). ... Played in Super Bowl XXIX (1994 season).
HONORS: Named running back on THE SPORTING NEWS college All-America first team (1990).
PRO STATISTICS: 1992—Fumbled four times and recovered one fumble. 1993—Fumbled once. 1994—Fumbled once and recovered one fumble. 1995—Attempted two passes without a completion, fumbled once and recovered one fumble. 1996—Fumbled once. 1997—Fumbled twice. 1998—Fumbled once.
SINGLE GAME HIGHS (regular season): Attempts—19 (November 12, 1995, vs. Houston); yards—65 (September 10, 1995, vs. Jacksonville); and rushing touchdowns—1 (December 14, 1997, vs. Dallas).

			RUSHING				RECEIVING				PUNT RETURNS				KICKOFF RETURNS				TOTALS		
Year Team	G	GS	Att.	Yds.	Avg.	TD	No.	Yds.	Avg.	TD	No.	Yds.	Avg.	TD	No.	Yds.	Avg.	TD	TD	2pt.	Pts.
1991—San Diego NFL	15	0	3	17	5.7	0	0	0	...	0	0	0	...	0	0	0	...	0	0	...	0
1992—San Diego NFL	15	0	74	264	3.6	3	5	49	9.8	0	30	229	7.6	0	15	257	17.1	0	3	...	18
1993—San Diego NFL	16	0	33	135	4.1	1	1	0	0.0	0	0	0	...	0	7	110	15.7	0	1	...	6
1994—San Diego NFL	16	0	73	295	4.0	0	5	48	9.6	0	0	0	...	0	0	0	...	0	0	0	0
1995—Cincinnati NFL	16	1	98	381	3.9	3	43	424	9.9	0	7	47	6.7	0	8	168	21.0	0	3	0	18
1996—Cincinnati NFL	16	0	56	269	4.8	2	32	272	8.5	0	0	0	...	0	0	0	...	0	2	0	12
1997—Cincinnati NFL	16	0	21	97	4.6	1	31	249	8.0	0	0	0	...	0	34	789	23.2 ▲1	2	0	12
1998—Cincinnati NFL	16	0	17	56	3.3	0	27	153	5.7	0	0	0	...	0	5	87	17.4	0	0	0	0
Pro totals (8 years)	126	1	375	1514	4.0	10	144	1195	8.3	0	37	276	7.5	0	69	1411	20.4	1	11	0	66

BILLUPS, TERRY — CB — COWBOYS

PERSONAL: Born February 9, 1975, in Weisboden, Germany ... 5-9/179. ... Full name: Terry Michael Billups.
HIGH SCHOOL: Oak Ridge (Orlando).
COLLEGE: North Carolina.
TRANSACTIONS/CAREER NOTES: Signed as non-drafted free agent by New England Patriots (April 19, 1998). ... Released by Patriots (August 25, 1998). ... Re-signed by Patriots to practice squad (August 31, 1998). ... Released by Patriots (September 10, 1998). ... Signed by Miami Dolphins to practice squad (September 15, 1998). ... Released by Dolphins (September 30, 1998). ... Signed by Dallas Cowboys to practice squad (October 5, 1998). ... Activated (November 24, 1998). ... Released by Cowboys (December 7, 1998). ... Re-signed by Cowboys to practice squad (December 9, 1998). ... Assigned by Cowboys to Scottish Claymores in 1999 NFL Europe enhancement allocation program (February 22, 1999).
PLAYING EXPERIENCE: Dallas NFL, 1998. ... Games/Games started: 1/0.

BINN, DAVID   C   CHARGERS

PERSONAL: Born February 6, 1972, in San Mateo, Calif. ... 6-3/245. ... Full name: David Aaron Binn.
HIGH SCHOOL: San Mateo (Calif.).
COLLEGE: California (degree in ecology and the social system, 1993).
TRANSACTIONS/CAREER NOTES: Signed as non-drafted free agent by San Diego Chargers (April 28, 1994). ... Granted unconditional free agency (February 13, 1998). ... Re-signed by Chargers (February 25, 1998).
PLAYING EXPERIENCE: San Diego NFL, 1994-1998. ... Games/Games started: 1994 (16/0), 1995 (16/0), 1996 (16/0), 1997 (16/0), 1998 (15/0). Total: 79/0.
CHAMPIONSHIP GAME EXPERIENCE: Played in AFC championship game (1994 season). ... Played in Super Bowl XXIX (1994 season).

BIRK, MATT   OT   VIKINGS

PERSONAL: Born July 23, 1976, in St. Paul, Minn. ... 6-4/310. ... Full name: Matthew Robert Birk.
HIGH SCHOOL: Cretin-Derham Hall (St. Paul, Minn.).
COLLEGE: Harvard (degree in economics, 1998).
TRANSACTIONS/CAREER NOTES: Selected by Minnesota Vikings in sixth round (173rd pick overall) of 1998 NFL draft. ... Signed by Vikings (June 24, 1998).
PLAYING EXPERIENCE: Minnesota NFL, 1998. ... Games/Games started: 7/0.
CHAMPIONSHIP GAME EXPERIENCE: Member of Vikings for NFC championship game (1998 season); did not play.

BISHOP, BLAINE   S   TITANS

PERSONAL: Born July 24, 1970, in Indianapolis. ... 5-9/203. ... Full name: Blaine Elwood Bishop.
HIGH SCHOOL: Cathedral (Indianapolis).
COLLEGE: Saint Joseph's College (Ind.), then Ball State (degree in insurance, 1993).
TRANSACTIONS/CAREER NOTES: Selected by Houston Oilers in eighth round (214th pick overall) of 1993 NFL draft. ... Signed by Oilers (July 16, 1993). ... Granted free agency (February 16, 1996). ... Re-signed by Oilers (June 17, 1996). ... Designated by Oilers as franchise player (February 14, 1997). ... Oilers franchise moved to Tennessee for 1997 season. ... Re-signed by Oilers (August 27, 1997). ... Oilers franchise renamed Tennessee Titans for 1999 season (December 26, 1998).
HONORS: Played in Pro Bowl (1995 and 1997 seasons). ... Named to play in Pro Bowl (1996 season); replaced by Tyrone Braxton due to injury.
PRO STATISTICS: 1993—Fumbled once and recovered one fumble. 1994—Returned two kickoffs for 18 yards and recovered one fumble. 1995—Recovered four fumbles for six yards. 1997—Recovered two fumbles. 1998—Recovered one fumble.

			INTERCEPTIONS				SACKS
Year Team	G	GS	No.	Yds.	Avg.	TD	No.
1993—Houston NFL	16	2	1	1	1.0	0	1.0
1994—Houston NFL	16	13	1	21	21.0	0	1.5
1995—Houston NFL	16	16	1	62	62.0	▲1	1.5
1996—Houston NFL	15	15	1	6	6.0	0	0.0
1997—Tennessee NFL	14	14	0	0	...	0	1.5
1998—Tennessee NFL	13	13	1	13	13.0	0	3.0
Pro totals (6 years)	90	73	5	103	20.6	1	8.5

BISHOP, GREG   G   FALCONS

PERSONAL: Born May 2, 1971, in Stockton, Calif. ... 6-5/315. ... Full name: Gregory Lawrence Bishop.
HIGH SCHOOL: Lodi (Calif.).
COLLEGE: Pacific.
TRANSACTIONS/CAREER NOTES: Selected by New York Giants in fourth round (93rd pick overall) of 1993 NFL draft. ... Signed by Giants (July 19, 1993). ... Granted unconditional free agency (February 12, 1999). ... Signed by Atlanta Falcons (March 29, 1999).
PLAYING EXPERIENCE: New York Giants NFL, 1993-1998. ... Games/Games started: 1993 (8/0), 1994 (16/1), 1995 (16/16), 1996 (16/16), 1997 (16/16), 1998 (16/16). Total: 88/65.
PRO STATISTICS: 1994—Recovered two fumbles. 1995—Recovered one fumble. 1996—Recovered one fumble. 1997—Recovered one fumble.

BISHOP, HAROLD   TE   STEELERS

PERSONAL: Born April 8, 1970, in Boonville, Miss. ... 6-5/250. ... Full name: Harold Lucius Bishop Jr.
HIGH SCHOOL: Central East (Tuscaloosa, Ala.).
COLLEGE: Louisiana State.
TRANSACTIONS/CAREER NOTES: Selected by Tampa Bay Buccaneers in third round (69th pick overall) of 1994 NFL draft. ... Signed by Buccaneers (July 19, 1994). ... Traded by Buccaneers to Cleveland Browns for second-round pick (FB Mike Alstott) in 1996 draft (May 19, 1995). ... Browns franchise moved to Baltimore and renamed Ravens for 1996 season (March 11, 1996). ... Released by Ravens (October 29, 1996). ... Signed by Washington Redskins (December 18, 1996). ... Released by Redskins (April 30, 1997). ... Selected by Rhein Fire in 1998 NFL Europe draft (February 18, 1998). ... Signed by Pittsburgh Steelers (June 23, 1998).
SINGLE GAME HIGHS (regular season): Receptions—4 (October 29, 1995, vs. Cincinnati); yards—28 (October 22, 1995, vs. Jacksonville); and touchdown receptions—0.

			RECEIVING			
Year Team	G	GS	No.	Yds.	Avg.	TD
1994—Tampa Bay NFL	6	0	0	0	...	0
1995—Cleveland NFL	13	3	16	135	8.4	0
1996—Baltimore NFL	8	2	2	22	11.0	0
1997—			Did not play.			
1998—Rhein NFLE	...	...	19	239	12.6	2
—Pittsburgh NFL	6	1	1	4	4.0	0
NFL Europe totals (1 year)	...	...	19	239	12.6	2
NFL totals (4 years)	33	6	19	161	8.5	0
Pro totals (5 years)	...	...	38	400	10.5	2

BJORNSON, ERIC — TE — COWBOYS

PERSONAL: Born December 15, 1971, in San Francisco. ... 6-4/236. ... Name pronounced buh-YORN-sun.
HIGH SCHOOL: Bishop O'Dowd (Oakland).
COLLEGE: Washington.
TRANSACTIONS/CAREER NOTES: Selected by Dallas Cowboys in fourth round (110th pick overall) of 1995 NFL draft. ... Signed by Cowboys (July 18, 1995). ... Granted free agency (February 13, 1998). ... Re-signed by Cowboys (July 13, 1998).
CHAMPIONSHIP GAME EXPERIENCE: Played in NFC championship game (1995 season). ... Member of Super Bowl championship team (1995 season).
PRO STATISTICS: 1998—Rushed once for seven yards and a touchdown.
SINGLE GAME HIGHS (regular season): Receptions—8 (November 10, 1996, vs. San Francisco); yards—71 (October 5, 1997, vs. New York Giants); and touchdown receptions—1 (November 8, 1998, vs. New York Giants).

			RECEIVING					TOTALS		
Year Team	G	GS	No.	Yds.	Avg.	TD	TD	2pt.	Pts.	Fum.
1995—Dallas NFL	14	1	7	53	7.6	0	0	0	0	0
1996—Dallas NFL	14	10	48	388	8.1	3	3	1	20	1
1997—Dallas NFL	14	14	47	442	9.4	0	0	1	2	2
1998—Dallas NFL	16	4	15	218	14.5	1	2	0	12	0
Pro totals (4 years)	58	29	117	1101	9.4	4	5	2	34	3

BLACKMAN, KEN — G — BENGALS

PERSONAL: Born November 8, 1972, in Abilene, Texas. ... 6-6/320.
HIGH SCHOOL: Wylie (Abilene, Texas).
COLLEGE: Illinois.
TRANSACTIONS/CAREER NOTES: Selected by Cincinnati Bengals in third round (69th pick overall) of 1996 NFL draft. ... Signed by Bengals (July 16, 1996). ... On non-football injury list with back injury (July 20-August 3, 1998). ... On injured reserve with knee injury (November 3, 1998-remainder of season). ... Granted free agency (February 12, 1999). ... Re-signed by Bengals (May 4, 1999).
PLAYING EXPERIENCE: Cincinnati NFL, 1996-1998. ... Games/Games started: 1996 (14/10), 1997 (13/13), 1998 (8/8). Total: 35/31.

BLACKMON, ROBERT — S

PERSONAL: Born May 12, 1967, in Bay City, Texas. ... 6-0/208. ... Full name: Robert James Blackmon.
HIGH SCHOOL: Van Vleck (Texas).
COLLEGE: Baylor.
TRANSACTIONS/CAREER NOTES: Selected by Seattle Seahawks in second round (34th pick overall) of 1990 NFL draft. ... Signed by Seahawks (July 29, 1990). ... Granted free agency (March 1, 1993). ... Tendered offer sheet by Philadelphia Eagles (April 21, 1993). ... Offer matched by Seahawks (April 23, 1993). ... Designated by Seahawks as franchise player (February 16, 1996). ... Granted unconditional free agency (February 14, 1997). ... Signed by Indianapolis Colts (June 3, 1997). ... Released by Colts (April 28, 1999).
PRO STATISTICS: 1990—Recovered one fumble. 1991—Recovered one fumble. 1992—Recovered one fumble for nine yards. 1993—Recovered one fumble for five yards and a touchdown. 1993—Recovered one fumble for five yards. 1994—Recovered three fumbles for 18 yards. 1996—Returned blocked field-goal attempt 61 yards for a touchdown and recovered one fumble for five yards. 1997—Recovered one fumble for 18 yards and a touchdown.

			INTERCEPTIONS				SACKS
Year Team	G	GS	No.	Yds.	Avg.	TD	No.
1990—Seattle NFL	15	5	0	0	...	0	0.0
1991—Seattle NFL	16	16	3	59	19.7	0	1.0
1992—Seattle NFL	15	15	1	69	69.0	0	3.5
1993—Seattle NFL	16	16	2	0	0.0	0	0.0
1994—Seattle NFL	15	15	1	24	24.0	0	0.0
1995—Seattle NFL	13	13	5	46	9.2	0	1.0
1996—Seattle NFL	16	16	3	48	16.0	0	1.0
1997—Indianapolis NFL	14	14	1	2	2.0	0	3.0
1998—Indianapolis NFL	15	9	1	14	14.0	0	1.0
Pro totals (9 years)	135	119	17	262	15.4	0	10.5

BLACKMON, ROOSEVELT — CB — BENGALS

PERSONAL: Born September 10, 1974, in Pahokee, Fla. ... 6-1/185. ... Full name: Roosevelt Blackmon III.
HIGH SCHOOL: Belle Glade (Fla.).
COLLEGE: Morris Brown (Ga.).
TRANSACTIONS/CAREER NOTES: Selected by Green Bay Packers in fourth round (121st pick overall) of 1998 NFL draft. ... Signed by Packers (July 17, 1998). ... Claimed on waivers by Cincinnati Bengals (October 1, 1998).
PLAYING EXPERIENCE: Green Bay (3)-Cincinnati (12) NFL, 1998. ... Games/Games started: 1998 (G.B.-3/0; Cin.-12/0; Total: 14/0).

BLACKSHEAR, JEFF — G — RAVENS

PERSONAL: Born March 29, 1969, in Fort Pierce, Fla. ... 6-6/323. ... Full name: Jeffrey Leon Blackshear.
HIGH SCHOOL: Westwood (Fort Pierce, Fla.).
JUNIOR COLLEGE: Northwest Mississippi Junior College.
COLLEGE: Northeast Louisiana.
TRANSACTIONS/CAREER NOTES: Selected by Seattle Seahawks in eighth round (197th pick overall) of 1993 NFL draft. ... Signed by Seahawks (July 15, 1993). ... Traded by Seahawks to Cleveland Browns for fourth-round pick (traded to Atlanta) in 1997 draft (March 12, 1996). ...

Browns franchise moved to Baltimore and renamed Ravens for 1996 season (March 11, 1996). ... Granted unconditional free agency (February 14, 1997). ... Re-signed by Ravens (March 13, 1997).
PLAYING EXPERIENCE: Seattle NFL, 1993 and 1994; Cleveland NFL, 1995; Baltimore NFL, 1996-1998. ... Games/Games started: 1993 (15/2), 1994 (16/16), 1995 (16/3), 1996 (16/12), 1997 (16/16), 1998 (16/16). Total: 95/65.

BLACKWELL, KORY   DB   BROWNS

PERSONAL: Born August 3, 1972, in New York. ... 5-11/185.
HIGH SCHOOL: Stevenson (Queens, N.Y.).
COLLEGE: Massachusetts.
TRANSACTIONS/CAREER NOTES: Signed as non-drafted free agent by New York Giants (April 28, 1997). ... Released by Giants (August 19, 1997). ... Re-signed by Giants to practice squad (August 27, 1997). ... Activated (December 23, 1997); did not play. ... Assigned by Giants to Scottish Claymores in 1998 NFL Europe enhancement allocation program (February 18, 1998). ... Selected by Cleveland Browns from Giants in NFL expansion draft (February 9, 1999).
PLAYING EXPERIENCE: Scottish Claymores NFLE, 1998; New York Giants NFL, 1998. ... Games/Games started: NFLE 1998 (games played unavailable); NFL 1998 (5/0).
PRO STATISTICS: NFLE: 1998—Intercepted three passes for 65 yards and one touchdown and returned one kickoff for 21 yards.

BLACKWELL, WILL   WR   STEELERS

PERSONAL: Born July 6, 1975, in Texarkana, Texas. ... 6-0/190. ... Full name: William Herman Blackwell Jr.
HIGH SCHOOL: Skyline (Oakland).
COLLEGE: San Diego State.
TRANSACTIONS/CAREER NOTES: Selected after junior season by Pittsburgh Steelers in second round (53rd pick overall) of 1997 NFL draft. ... Signed by Steelers (July 15, 1997).
CHAMPIONSHIP GAME EXPERIENCE: Played in AFC championship game (1997 season).
PRO STATISTICS: 1997—Recovered two fumbles.
SINGLE GAME HIGHS (regular season): Receptions—4 (November 23, 1997, vs. Philadelphia); yards—68 (September 28, 1997, vs. Tennessee); and touchdown receptions—1 (November 26, 1998, vs. Detroit).

			RECEIVING				PUNT RETURNS				KICKOFF RETURNS				TOTALS		
Year Team	G	GS	No.	Yds.	Avg.	TD	No.	Yds.	Avg.	TD	No.	Yds.	Avg.	TD	TD	2pt.	Pts.	Fum.
1997—Pittsburgh NFL	14	0	12	168	14.0	1	23	149	6.5	0	32	791	24.7 ▲1	2	0	12	3
1998—Pittsburgh NFL	16	2	32	297	9.3	1	4	22	5.5	0	20	382	19.1	0	1	1	8	1
Pro totals (2 years)	30	2	44	465	10.6	2	27	171	6.3	0	52	1173	22.6	1	3	1	20	4

BLADES, BRIAN   WR

PERSONAL: Born July 24, 1965, in Fort Lauderdale, Fla. ... 5-11/190. ... Full name: Brian Keith Blades. ... Brother of Bennie Blades, safety with Detroit Lions (1988-96) and Seattle Seahawks (1997); and cousin of Daryl Porter, cornerback, Buffalo Bills.
HIGH SCHOOL: Piper (Sunrise, Fla.).
COLLEGE: Miami (Fla.).
TRANSACTIONS/CAREER NOTES: Selected by Seattle Seahawks in second round (49th pick overall) of 1988 NFL draft. ... Signed by Seahawks (May 19, 1988). ... Granted free agency (February 1, 1992). ... Re-signed by Seahawks (September 2, 1992). ... Granted roster exemption (September 2-5, 1992). ... On injured reserve with broken collarbone (September 8-November 25, 1992); on practice squad (November 18-25, 1992). ... Designated by Seahawks as transition player (February 25, 1993). ... Free agency status changed from transitional to unconditional (February 17, 1994). ... Re-signed by Seahawks (May 17, 1994). ... Granted unconditional free agency (February 16, 1996). ... Re-signed by Seahawks (April 10, 1996). ... On injured reserve with hand injury (November 19, 1997-remainder of season). ... Granted unconditional free agency (February 12, 1999). ... Re-signed by Seahawks (March 29, 1999). ... Released by Seahawks (June 4, 1999).
HONORS: Played in Pro Bowl (1989 season).
PRO STATISTICS: 1988—Recovered one fumble. 1989—Recovered one fumble. 1994—Recovered two fumbles.
SINGLE GAME HIGHS (regular season): Receptions—12 (September 1, 1991, vs. New Orleans); yards—160 (September 1, 1991 vs. New Orleans); and touchdown receptions—2 (November 5, 1995, vs. New York Giants).
STATISTICAL PLATEAUS: 100-yard receiving games: 1988 (2), 1989 (5), 1991 (3), 1992 (1), 1993 (2), 1994 (1), 1995 (3). Total: 17.

			RUSHING				RECEIVING				TOTALS			
Year Team	G	GS	Att.	Yds.	Avg.	TD	No.	Yds.	Avg.	TD	TD	2pt.	Pts.	Fum.
1988—Seattle NFL	16	7	5	24	4.8	0	40	682	17.1	8	8	...	48	1
1989—Seattle NFL	16	14	1	3	3.0	0	77	1063	13.8	5	5	...	30	3
1990—Seattle NFL	16	16	3	19	6.3	0	49	525	10.7	3	3	...	18	0
1991—Seattle NFL	16	16	2	17	8.5	0	70	1003	14.3	2	2	...	12	1
1992—Seattle NFL	6	5	1	5	5.0	0	19	256	13.5	1	1	...	6	1
1993—Seattle NFL	16	14	5	52	10.4	0	80	945	11.8	3	3	...	18	1
1994—Seattle NFL	16	16	2	32	16.0	0	81	1086	13.4	4	4	1	26	1
1995—Seattle NFL	16	16	2	4	2.0	0	77	1001	13.0	4	4	0	24	0
1996—Seattle NFL	11	9	0	0	...	0	43	556	12.9	2	2	0	12	1
1997—Seattle NFL	11	3	0	0	...	0	30	319	10.6	2	2	0	12	1
1998—Seattle NFL	16	6	0	0	...	0	15	184	12.3	0	0	0	0	1
Pro totals (11 years)	156	122	21	156	7.4	0	581	7620	13.1	34	34	1	206	11

BLAIR, MICHAEL   RB   BROWNS

PERSONAL: Born November 26, 1974, in Chicago. ... 5-11/245. ... Full name: Michaelangelo Christopher Blair.
HIGH SCHOOL: Thornwood (South Holland, Ill.).
COLLEGE: Ball State.

TRANSACTIONS/CAREER NOTES: Signed as non-drafted free agent by Kansas City Chiefs (April 28, 1997). ... Released by Chiefs (August 15, 1997). ... Selected by Frankfurt Galaxy in 1998 NFL Europe draft (February 18, 1998). ... Signed by Green Bay Packers (April 22, 1998). ... Released by Packers (August 25, 1998). ... Re-signed by Packers to practice squad (September 1, 1998). ... Activated (September 5, 1998). ... Claimed on waivers by Cincinnati Bengals (September 30, 1998). ... Claimed on waivers by Packers (November 11, 1998). ... Selected by Cleveland Browns from Packers in NFL expansion draft (February 9, 1999).
PRO STATISTICS: 1998—Recovered one fumble.
SINGLE GAME HIGHS (regular season): Attempts—2 (September 13, 1998, vs. Tampa Bay); yards—4 (November 8, 1998, vs. Jacksonville); and rushing touchdowns—0.

				RUSHING				RECEIVING			TOTALS		
Year Team	G	GS	Att.	Yds.	Avg.	TD	No.	Yds.	Avg.	TD	TD	2pt.	Pts.	Fum.
1998—Green Bay NFL	11	0	2	3	1.5	0	2	13	6.5	0	0	0	0	0
—Cincinnati NFL	2	0	1	4	4.0	0	1	7	7.0	0	0	0	0	1
Pro totals (1 years)	13	0	3	7	2.3	0	3	20	6.7	0	0	0	0	1

BLAKE, JEFF   QB   BENGALS

PERSONAL: Born December 4, 1970, in Daytona Beach, Fla. ... 6-0/210. ... Son of Emory Blake, running back with Toronto Argonauts of CFL (1974).
HIGH SCHOOL: Seminole (Sanford, Fla.).
COLLEGE: East Carolina.
TRANSACTIONS/CAREER NOTES: Selected by New York Jets in sixth round (166th pick overall) of 1992 NFL draft. ... Signed by Jets (July 14, 1992). ... Inactive for all 16 games (1993). ... Claimed on waivers by Cincinnati Bengals (August 29, 1994). ... Granted free agency (February 17, 1995). ... Re-signed by Bengals (May 8, 1995). ... On injured reserve with wrist injury (December 24, 1998-remainder of season).
HONORS: Played in Pro Bowl (1995 season).
PRO STATISTICS: 1992—Fumbled once. 1994—Fumbled six times. 1995—Fumbled 10 times for minus seven yards. 1996—Fumbled seven times and recovered one fumble for minus five yards. 1997—Fumbled seven times. 1998—Fumbled once.
SINGLE GAME HIGHS (regular season): Attempts—46 (December 17, 1995, vs. Cleveland); completions—31 (November 6, 1994, vs. Seattle); yards—387 (November 6, 1994, vs. Seattle); and touchdown passes—4 (November 24, 1996, vs. Atlanta).
STATISTICAL PLATEAUS: 300-yard passing games: 1994 (2), 1995 (1), 1996 (2), 1997 (1), 1998 (1). Total: 7.
MISCELLANEOUS: Regular-season record as starting NFL quarterback: 22-32 (.407).

			PASSING							RUSHING				TOTALS		
Year Team	G	GS	Att.	Cmp.	Pct.	Yds.	TD	Int.	Avg.	Rat.	Att.	Yds.	Avg.	TD	TD	2pt.	Pts.
1992—New York Jets NFL	3	0	9	4	44.4	40	0	1	4.44	18.1	2	-2	-1.0	0	0	...	0
1993—New York Jets NFL						Did not play.											
1994—Cincinnati NFL	10	9	306	156	51.0	2154	14	9	7.04	76.9	37	204	5.5	1	1	1	8
1995—Cincinnati NFL	16	16	567	§326	57.5	3822	§28	17	6.74	82.1	53	309	5.8	2	2	1	14
1996—Cincinnati NFL	16	16	549	308	56.1	3624	24	14	6.60	80.3	72	317	4.4	2	2	0	12
1997—Cincinnati NFL	11	11	317	184	58.0	2125	8	7	6.70	77.6	45	234	5.2	3	3	0	18
1998—Cincinnati NFL	9	2	93	51	54.8	739	3	3	7.95	78.2	15	103	6.9	0	0	0	0
Pro totals (6 years)	65	54	1841	1029	55.9	12504	77	51	6.79	79.4	224	1165	5.2	8	8	2	52

BLANCHARD, CARY   K   REDSKINS

PERSONAL: Born November 5, 1968, in Fort Worth, Texas. ... 6-1/232. ... Full name: Robert Cary Blanchard.
HIGH SCHOOL: L.D. Bell (Hurst, Texas).
COLLEGE: Oklahoma State.
TRANSACTIONS/CAREER NOTES: Signed as non-drafted free agent by Dallas Cowboys (April 25, 1991). ... Released by Cowboys (August 4, 1991). ... Signed by Sacramento Surge of World League (1992). ... Signed by New Orleans Saints (July 7, 1992). ... Released by Saints (August 31, 1992). ... Re-signed by Saints to practice squad (September 7, 1992). ... Activated (September 14, 1992). ... Active for one game with Saints (1992); did not play. ... Claimed on waivers by New York Jets (September 29, 1992). ... Released by Jets (June 24, 1994). ... Signed by Minnesota Vikings (July 12, 1994). ... Released by Vikings (August 28, 1994). ... Signed by New Orleans Saints (April 18, 1995). ... Released by Saints (August 27, 1995). ... Signed by Indianapolis Colts (October 3, 1995). ... Released by Colts (August 30, 1998). ... Signed by Washington Redskins (September 22, 1998). ... Granted unconditional free agency (February 12, 1999). ... Re-signed by Redskins (April 20, 1999).
CHAMPIONSHIP GAME EXPERIENCE: Played in AFC championship game (1995 season).
HONORS: Named kicker on THE SPORTING NEWS NFL All-Pro team (1996). ... Played in Pro Bowl (1996 season).
PRO STATISTICS: 1998—Punted three times for 113 yards.

				KICKING				
Year Team	G	XPM	XPA	FGM	FGA	Lg.	50+	Pts.
1992—Sacramento W.L.	4	17	17	5	8	42	0-0	32
—New York Jets NFL	11	17	17	16	22	47	0-1	65
1993—New York Jets NFL	16	31	31	17	26	45	0-2	82
1994—				Did not play.				
1995—Indianapolis NFL	12	25	25	19	24	50	1-1	82
1996—Indianapolis NFL	16	27	27	§36	§40	52	5-5	§135
1997—Indianapolis NFL	16	21	21	§32	†41	50	1-3	117
1998—Washington NFL	13	30	31	11	17	54	1-2	63
W.L. totals (1 year)	4	17	17	5	8	42	0-0	32
NFL totals (5 years)	84	151	152	131	170	54	8-14	544
Pro totals (6 years)	88	168	169	136	178	54	8-0	576

BLAND, TONY   WR   VIKINGS

PERSONAL: Born December 12, 1972, in St. Petersburg, Fla. ... 6-3/213.
HIGH SCHOOL: Pinellas Park (St. Petersburg, Fla.).
COLLEGE: Florida A&M.

TRANSACTIONS/CAREER NOTES: Signed as non-drafted free agent by Minnesota Vikings (April 26, 1996). ... Released by Vikings (August 20, 1996). ... Re-signed by Vikings to practice squad (August 26, 1996). ... Activated (December 20, 1996); did not play. ... Released by Vikings (August 24, 1997). ... Re-signed by Vikings to practice squad (August 25, 1997). ... Activated (November 29, 1997). ... Released by Vikings (August 30, 1998). ... Re-signed by Vikings (December 23, 1998). ... Released by Vikings (February 12, 1999). ... Signed by Tampa Bay Buccaneers (March 9, 1999); later voided because he failed physical. ... Signed by Vikings (April 15, 1999).
PLAYING EXPERIENCE: Minnesota NFL, 1997 and 1998. ... Games/Games started: 1997 (2/0), 1998 (1/0). Total: 3/0.
CHAMPIONSHIP GAME EXPERIENCE: Member of Vikings for NFC championship game (1998 season); inactive.

BLANTON, SCOTT   K

PERSONAL: Born July 1, 1973, in Norman, Okla. ... 6-2/221.
HIGH SCHOOL: Norman (Okla.).
COLLEGE: Oklahoma.
TRANSACTIONS/CAREER NOTES: Signed as non-drafted free agent by Washington Redskins (April 26, 1995). ... On injured reserve with groin injury (August 27, 1995-entire season). ... Granted free agency (February 13, 1998). ... Re-signed by Redskins (May 7, 1998). ... Released by Redskins (September 15, 1998).
PRO STATISTICS: 1997—Recovered one fumble.

				KICKING				
Year Team	G	XPM	XPA	FGM	FGA	Lg.	50+	Pts.
1995—Washington NFL				Did not play.				
1996—Washington NFL	16	40	40	26	32	53	2-3	118
1997—Washington NFL	15	34	34	16	24	50	1-4	82
1998—Washington NFL	2	4	4	2	4	46	0-0	10
Pro totals (3 years)	33	78	78	44	60	53	3-7	210

BLEDSOE, DREW   QB   PATRIOTS

PERSONAL: Born February 14, 1972, in Ellensburg, Wash. ... 6-5/233.
HIGH SCHOOL: Walla Walla (Wash.).
COLLEGE: Washington State.
TRANSACTIONS/CAREER NOTES: Selected after junior season by New England Patriots in first round (first pick overall) of 1993 NFL draft. ... Signed by Patriots (July 6, 1993).
CHAMPIONSHIP GAME EXPERIENCE: Played in AFC championship game (1996 season). ... Played in Super Bowl XXXI (1996 season).
HONORS: Played in Pro Bowl (1994, 1996 and 1997 seasons).
RECORDS: Holds NFL single-season record for most passes attempted—691 (1994). ... Holds NFL single-game records for most passes completed—45; most passes attempted—70; and most passes attempted without an interception—70 (November 13, 1994, vs. Minnesota).
POST SEASON RECORDS: Shares Super Bowl single-game record for most passes intercepted—4 (January 26, 1997, vs. New England).
PRO STATISTICS: 1993—Fumbled eight times and recovered five fumbles for minus 23 yards. 1994—Fumbled nine times and recovered three fumbles for minus five yards. 1995—Caught one pass for minus nine yards, fumbled 11 times and recovered one fumble for minus eight yards. 1996—Fumbled nine times and recovered one fumble for minus two yards. 1997—Fumbled four times and recovered three fumbles for minus four yards. 1998—Fumbled nine times and recovered four fumbles for minus 10 yards.
SINGLE GAME HIGHS (regular season): Attempts—70 (November 13, 1994, vs. Minnesota); completions—45 (November 13, 1994, vs. Minnesota); yards—426 (November 13, 1994, vs. Minnesota); and touchdown passes—4 (September 7, 1997, vs. Indianapolis).
STATISTICAL PLATEAUS: 300-yard passing games: 1993 (1), 1994 (6), 1995 (2), 1996 (4), 1997 (3), 1998 (4). Total: 20.
MISCELLANEOUS: Regular-season record as starting NFL quarterback: 50-39 (.562). ... Postseason record as starting NFL quarterback: 3-3 (.500).

				PASSING						RUSHING				TOTALS		
Year Team	G	GS	Att.	Cmp.	Pct.	Yds.	TD	Int.	Avg.	Rat.	Att.	Yds.	Avg.	TD	TD	2pt.	Pts.
1993—New England NFL	13	12	429	214	49.9	2494	15	15	5.81	65.0	32	82	2.6	0	0	...	0
1994—New England NFL	16	16	*691	*400	57.9	*4555	25	*27	6.59	73.6	44	40	0.9	0	0	0	0
1995—New England NFL	15	15	*636	323	50.8	3507	13	16	5.51	63.7	20	28	1.4	0	0	0	0
1996—New England NFL	16	16	*623	*373	59.9	4086	27	15	6.56	83.7	24	27	1.1	0	0	0	0
1997—New England NFL	16	16	522	314	60.2	3706	28	15	7.10	87.7	28	55	2.0	0	0	0	0
1998—New England NFL	14	14	481	263	54.7	3633	20	14	7.55	80.9	28	44	1.6	0	0	0	0
Pro totals (6 years)	90	89	3382	1887	55.8	21981	128	102	6.50	75.7	176	276	1.6	0	0	0	0

BLEVINS, TONY   DB   COLTS

PERSONAL: Born January 29, 1975, in Rockford, Ill. ... 6-0/165.
HIGH SCHOOL: Rockhurst (Kansas City, Mo.).
COLLEGE: Kansas.
TRANSACTIONS/CAREER NOTES: Signed as non-drafted free agent by San Francisco 49ers (April 24, 1998). ... Released by 49ers (August 25, 1998). ... Re-signed by 49ers to practice squad (September 1, 1998). ... Activated (September 26, 1998). ... Released by 49ers (September 29, 1998). ... Re-signed by 49ers to practice squad (October 1, 1998). ... Activated (October 7, 1998). ... Claimed on waivers by Indianapolis Colts (October 30, 1998).
PLAYING EXPERIENCE: San Francisco (2)-Indianapolis (3) NFL, 1998. ... Games/Games started: 1998 (S.F.-2/0; Ind.-3/0; Total: 5/0).

BOBO, ORLANDO   G   BROWNS

PERSONAL: Born February 9, 1974, in Westpoint, Miss. ... 6-3/299.
HIGH SCHOOL: Westpoint (Miss.).
JUNIOR COLLEGE: East Mississippi Community College.
COLLEGE: Northeast Louisiana.

– 37 –

TRANSACTIONS/CAREER NOTES: Signed as non-drafted free agent by Minnesota Vikings (April 26, 1996). ... Released by Vikings (August 20, 1996). ... Re-signed by Vikings to practice squad (August 26, 1996). ... Released by Vikings (August 27, 1997). ... Re-signed by Vikings to practice squad (August 29, 1997). ... Activated (September 12, 1997). ... On injured reserve with leg injury (October 27, 1998-remainder of season). ... Selected by Cleveland Browns from Vikings in NFL expansion draft (February 9, 1999).
PLAYING EXPERIENCE: Minnesota NFL, 1997 and 1998. ... Games/Games started: 1997 (5/0), 1998 (4/0). Total: 9/0.

BOCK, JOHN G DOLPHINS

PERSONAL: Born February 11, 1971, in Chicago. ... 6-3/298. ... Full name: John Matthew Bock. ... Nephew of Wayne Bock, offensive tackle with Chicago Cardinals (1957).
HIGH SCHOOL: Crystal Lake (Ill.).
COLLEGE: Louisville, then Indiana State (degree in sociology).
TRANSACTIONS/CAREER NOTES: Signed as non-drafted free agent by Buffalo Bills (May 7, 1994). ... Released by Bills (August 22, 1994). ... Selected by Amsterdam Admirals in 1995 World League draft. ... Signed by New York Jets (June 22, 1995). ... Released by Jets (August 29, 1996). ... Signed by Miami Dolphins (October 16, 1996). ... Granted unconditional free agency (February 12, 1999). ... Re-signed by Dolphins (March 23, 1999).
PLAYING EXPERIENCE: Amsterdam W.L., 1995; New York Jets NFL, 1995; Miami NFL, 1996-1998. ... Games/Games started: W.L. 1995 (10/10), NFL 1995 (10/7), 1996 (2/0), 1997 (14/3), 1998 (16/6). Total W.L.: 10/10. Total NFL: 42/16. Total Pro: 52/26.
PRO STATISTICS: 1995—Fumbled once for minus one yard.

BOHLINGER, ROB OL PANTHERS

PERSONAL: Born June 14, 1975, in Minneapolis. ... 6-9/310. ... Full name: Robert Paul Bohlinger.
HIGH SCHOOL: Totino Grace (Maple Grove, Minn.).
COLLEGE: Wyoming.
TRANSACTIONS/CAREER NOTES: Signed as non-drafted free agent by Carolina Panthers (April 18, 1998).
PLAYING EXPERIENCE: Carolina NFL, 1998. ... Games/Games started: 13/1.
PRO STATISTICS: 1998—Recovered one fumble.

BOLDEN, JURAN CB CHIEFS

PERSONAL: Born June 27, 1974, in Tampa. ... 6-2/201.
HIGH SCHOOL: Hillsborough (Tampa).
JUNIOR COLLEGE: Mississippi Delta Community College.
COLLEGE: None.
TRANSACTIONS/CAREER NOTES: Played for Winnipeg Blue Bombers in CFL (1995). ... Selected by Atlanta Falcons in fourth round (127th pick overall) of 1996 NFL draft. ... Signed by Falcons (July 20, 1996). ... On injured reserve with knee injury (December 9, 1996-remainder of season). ... Claimed on waivers by Green Bay Packers (September 30, 1998). ... Claimed on waivers by Carolina Panthers (October 27, 1998). ... Released by Panthers (February 12, 1999). ... Signed by Kansas City Chiefs (April 20, 1999).
PLAYING EXPERIENCE: Winnipeg CFL, 1995; Atlanta NFL, 1996 and 1997; Atlanta (3)-Green Bay (3)-Carolina (6) NFL, 1998. ... Games/Games started: 1995 (9/9), 1996 (9/0), 1997 (14/1), 1998 (Atl.-3/0; G.B.-3/0; Car.-6/0; Total: 12/0). Total CFL: 9/9. Total NFL: 35/1. Total Pro: 44/10.
PRO STATISTICS: CFL: 1995—Intercepted six passes for 28 yards and returned one kickoff for two yards. NFL: 1997—Returned five kickoffs for 106 yards. 1998—Recovered one fumble.

BONHAM, SHANE DT 49ERS

PERSONAL: Born October 18, 1970, in Fairbanks, Alaska. ... 6-2/286. ... Full name: Steven Shane Bonham. ... Name pronounced BON-um.
HIGH SCHOOL: Lathrop (Fairbanks, Alaska).
COLLEGE: Air Force, then Tennessee.
TRANSACTIONS/CAREER NOTES: Selected by Detroit Lions in third round (93rd pick overall) of 1994 NFL draft. ... Signed by Lions (July 21, 1994). ... Granted free agency (February 14, 1997). ... Re-signed by Lions (May 22, 1997). ... Granted unconditional free agency (February 13, 1998). ... Signed by San Francisco 49ers (April 21, 1998).

Year Team	G	GS	SACKS
1994—Detroit NFL	15	1	0.0
1995—Detroit NFL	15	0	1.0
1996—Detroit NFL	15	2	2.0
1997—Detroit NFL	16	0	1.0
1998—San Francisco NFL	8	0	0.0
Pro totals (5 years)	69	3	4.0

BONIOL, CHRIS K EAGLES

PERSONAL: Born December 9, 1971, in Alexandria, La. ... 5-11/167. ... Name pronounced BONE-yol.
HIGH SCHOOL: Alexandria (La.).
COLLEGE: Louisiana Tech.
TRANSACTIONS/CAREER NOTES: Signed as non-drafted free agent by Dallas Cowboys (April 28, 1994). ... Granted free agency (February 14, 1997). ... Tendered offer sheet by Philadelphia Eagles (March 7, 1997). ... Cowboys declined to match offer (March 14, 1997).
CHAMPIONSHIP GAME EXPERIENCE: Played in NFC championship game (1994 and 1995 season). ... Member of Super Bowl championship team (1995 season).
RECORDS: Shares NFL single-game record for most field goals—7 (November 18, 1996, vs. Green Bay).
PRO STATISTICS: 1995—Punted twice for 77 yards.

				KICKING					
Year	Team	G	XPM	XPA	FGM	FGA	Lg.	50+	Pts.
1994	—Dallas NFL	16	48	48	22	29	47	0-1	114
1995	—Dallas NFL	16	46	†48	27	28	45	0-0	127
1996	—Dallas NFL	16	24	25	32	36	52	1-2	120
1997	—Philadelphia NFL	16	33	33	22	31	49	0-1	99
1998	—Philadelphia NFL	16	15	17	14	21	50	1-1	57
Pro totals (5 years)		80	166	171	117	145	52	2-5	517

BONO, STEVE   QB   PANTHERS

PERSONAL: Born May 11, 1962, in Norristown, Pa. ... 6-4/212. ... Full name: Steven Christopher Bono.
HIGH SCHOOL: Norristown (Pa.).
COLLEGE: UCLA.
TRANSACTIONS/CAREER NOTES: Selected by Memphis Showboats in 1985 USFL territorial draft. ... Selected by Minnesota Vikings in sixth round (142nd pick overall) of 1985 NFL draft. ... Signed by Vikings (July 10, 1985). ... Released by Vikings (October 4, 1986). ... Re-signed by Vikings (November 19, 1986). ... Released by Vikings (December 9, 1986). ... Signed by Pittsburgh Steelers (March 25, 1987). ... Released by Steelers (September 7, 1987). ... Re-signed as replacement player by Steelers (September 24, 1987). ... Released by Steelers (April 13, 1989). ... Signed by San Francisco 49ers (June 13, 1989). ... Active for seven games (1990); did not play. ... Granted free agency (February 1, 1991). ... Re-signed by 49ers (1991). ... Granted unconditional free agency (March 1, 1993). ... Re-signed by 49ers (April 7, 1993). ... Released by 49ers (April 29, 1994). ... Re-signed by 49ers (May 2, 1994). ... Traded by 49ers to Kansas City Chiefs for fourth-round pick (traded to Cleveland) in 1995 draft (May 2, 1994). ... Released by Chiefs (June 12, 1997). ... Signed by Green Bay Packers (June 20, 1997). ... Traded by Packers to St. Louis Rams for future considerations (April 6, 1998). ... Granted unconditional free agency (February 12, 1999). ... Signed by Carolina Panthers (March 19, 1999).
CHAMPIONSHIP GAME EXPERIENCE: Member of 49ers for NFC championship game (1989 and 1990 seasons); inactive. ... Member of Super Bowl championship team (1989 season). ... Played in NFC championship game (1992 and 1993 seasons). ... Member of Packers for NFC championship game (1997 season); did not play. ... Member of Packers for Super Bowl XXXII (1997 season); did not play.
HONORS: Played in Pro Bowl (1995 season).
PRO STATISTICS: 1987—Caught one pass for two yards, fumbled five times and recovered three fumbles. 1991—Fumbled seven times for minus eight yards. 1992—Fumbled twice and recovered one fumble for minus three yards. 1995—Fumbled 10 times and recovered one fumble for minus five yards. 1996—Fumbled five times. 1997—Fumbled once. 1998—Fumbled four times for minus 11 yards.
SINGLE GAME HIGHS (regular season): Attempts—55 (December 12, 1994, vs. Miami); completions—33 (December 12, 1994, vs. Miami); yards—347 (December 1, 1991, vs. New Orleans); and touchdown passes—3 (December 27, 1998, vs. San Francisco).
STATISTICAL PLATEAUS: 300-yard passing games: 1991 (2), 1994 (2). Total: 4.
MISCELLANEOUS: Regular-season record as starting NFL quarterback: 28-14 (.667). ... Postseason record as starting NFL quarterback: 0-1.

				PASSING							RUSHING				TOTALS		
Year Team	G	GS	Att.	Cmp.	Pct.	Yds.	TD	Int.	Avg.	Rat.	Att.	Yds.	Avg.	TD	TD	2pt.	Pts.
1985—Minnesota NFL	1	0	10	1	10.0	5	0	0	0.50	39.6	0	0	...	0	0	...	0
1986—Minnesota NFL	1	0	1	1	100.0	3	0	0	3.00	79.2	0	0	...	0	0	...	0
1987—Pittsburgh NFL	3	3	74	34	45.9	438	5	2	5.92	76.3	8	27	3.4	1	1	...	6
1988—Pittsburgh NFL	2	0	35	10	28.6	110	1	2	3.14	25.9	0	0	...	0	0	...	0
1989—San Francisco NFL	1	0	5	4	80.0	62	1	0	12.40	157.9	0	0	...	0	0	...	0
1990—San Francisco NFL							Did not play.										
1991—San Francisco NFL	9	6	237	141	59.5	1617	11	4	6.82	88.5	17	46	2.7	0	0	...	0
1992—San Francisco NFL	16	0	56	36	64.3	463	2	1	8.27	87.1	15	23	1.5	0	0	...	0
1993—San Francisco NFL	8	0	61	39	63.9	416	0	1	6.82	76.9	12	14	1.2	1	1	...	6
1994—Kansas City NFL	7	2	117	66	56.4	796	4	4	6.80	74.6	4	-1	-0.3	0	0	0	0
1995—Kansas City NFL	16	16	520	293	56.3	3121	21	10	6.00	79.5	28	113	4.0	5	5	0	30
1996—Kansas City NFL	13	13	438	235	53.7	2572	12	13	5.87	68.0	26	27	1.0	0	0	0	0
1997—Green Bay NFL	2	0	10	5	50.0	29	0	0	2.90	56.3	3	-3	-1.0	0	0	0	0
1998—St. Louis NFL	6	2	136	69	50.7	807	5	4	5.93	69.1	10	13	1.3	0	0	1	2
Pro totals (13 years)	85	42	1700	934	54.9	10439	62	42	6.14	75.3	123	259	2.1	7	7	1	44

BOOKER, MICHAEL   CB   FALCONS

PERSONAL: Born April 27, 1975, in Oceanside, Calif. ... 6-2/200. ... Full name: Michael Allen Booker.
HIGH SCHOOL: El Camino (Calif.).
COLLEGE: Nebraska.
TRANSACTIONS/CAREER NOTES: Selected by Atlanta Falcons in first round (11th pick overall) of 1997 NFL draft. ... Signed by Falcons (July 16, 1997).
CHAMPIONSHIP GAME EXPERIENCE: Played in NFC championship game (1998 season). ... Played in Super Bowl XXXIII (1998 season).
PRO STATISTICS: 1998—Fumbled once and recovered one fumble for five yards.

			INTERCEPTIONS			
Year Team	G	GS	No.	Yds.	Avg.	TD
1997—Atlanta NFL	15	2	3	16	5.3	0
1998—Atlanta NFL	14	6	1	27	27.0	0
Pro totals (2 years)	29	8	4	43	10.8	0

BOOKER, VAUGHN   DE   PACKERS

PERSONAL: Born February 24, 1968, in Cincinnati. ... 6-5/300. ... Full name: Vaughn Jamel Booker.
HIGH SCHOOL: Taft (Cincinnati).
COLLEGE: Cincinnati.
TRANSACTIONS/CAREER NOTES: Signed by Winnipeg Blue Bombers of CFL (June 1992). ... Granted free agency after 1993 season. ... Signed as non-drafted free agent by Kansas City Chiefs (May 2, 1994). ... Traded by Chiefs to Green Bay Packers for DT Darius Holland (May 13, 1998).

PRO STATISTICS: CFL: 1992—Recovered four fumbles and returned one kickoff for three yards. NFL: 1994—Recovered two fumbles for six yards and returned two kickoffs for 10 yards. 1995—Recovered one fumble for 14 yards and a touchdown. 1996—Recovered one fumble. 1997—Recovered one fumble.
MISCELLANEOUS: Served in U.S. Army (1988-90).

Year Team	G	GS	SACKS
1992—Winnipeg CFL	15	...	2.0
1993—Winnipeg CFL	9	...	4.0
1994—Kansas City NFL	13	0	0.0
1995—Kansas City NFL	16	10	1.5
1996—Kansas City NFL	14	12	1.0
1997—Kansas City NFL	13	13	4.0
1998—Green Bay NFL	16	4	3.0
CFL totals (2 years)	24	...	6.0
NFL totals (5 years)	72	39	9.5
Pro totals (7 years)	96	...	15.5

BOOSE, DORIAN DE JETS

PERSONAL: Born January 29, 1974, in Frankfurt, West Germany. ... 6-5/292. ... Full name: Dorian Alexander Boose.
HIGH SCHOOL: Foss (Tacoma, Wash.).
JUNIOR COLLEGE: Walla Walla (Wash.) Community College.
COLLEGE: Washington State.
TRANSACTIONS/CAREER NOTES: Selected by New York Jets in second round (56th pick overall) of 1998 NFL draft. ... Signed by Jets (July 8, 1998).
PLAYING EXPERIENCE: New York Jets NFL, 1998. ... Games/Games started: 12/0.
CHAMPIONSHIP GAME EXPERIENCE: Member of Jets for AFC championship game (1998 season); inactive.

BORDANO, CHRIS LB SAINTS

PERSONAL: Born December 30, 1974, in San Antonio. ... 6-1/248.
HIGH SCHOOL: Southwest (San Antonio).
COLLEGE: Southern Methodist.
TRANSACTIONS/CAREER NOTES: Selected by New Orleans Saints in sixth round (161st pick overall) of 1998 NFL draft. ... Signed by Saints (June 11, 1998).
PLAYING EXPERIENCE: New Orleans NFL, 1998. ... Games/Games started: 16/6.
PRO STATISTICS: 1998—Credited with one sack.

BOSELLI, TONY OT JAGUARS

PERSONAL: Born April 17, 1972, in Boulder, Colo. ... 6-7/324. ... Full name: Don Anthony Boselli Jr.
HIGH SCHOOL: Fairview (Boulder, Colo.).
COLLEGE: Southern California (degree in business administration, 1995).
TRANSACTIONS/CAREER NOTES: Selected by Jacksonville Jaguars in first round (second pick overall) of 1995 NFL draft. ... Signed by Jaguars (June 1, 1995).
PLAYING EXPERIENCE: Jacksonville NFL, 1995-1998. ... Games/Games started: 1995 (13/12), 1996 (16/16), 1997 (12/12), 1998 (15/15). Total: 56/55.
CHAMPIONSHIP GAME EXPERIENCE: Played in AFC championship game (1996 season).
HONORS: Named offensive lineman on THE SPORTING NEWS college All-America first team (1994). ... Played in Pro Bowl (1996-1998 seasons). ... Named offensive tackle on THE SPORTING NEWS NFL All-Pro team (1997 and 1998).
PRO STATISTICS: 1996—Recovered one fumble. 1998—Recovered one fumble for two yards.

BOSTIC, JAMES RB EAGLES

PERSONAL: Born March 13, 1972, in Fort Lauderdale, Fla. ... 5-11/225. ... Full name: James Edward Bostic.
HIGH SCHOOL: Dillard (Fort Lauderdale, Fla.).
COLLEGE: Auburn.
TRANSACTIONS/CAREER NOTES: Selected after junior season by Los Angeles Rams in third round (83rd pick overall) of 1994 NFL draft. ... Signed by Rams (July 6, 1994). ... Active for 10 games (1994); did not play. ... On injured reserve with wrist injury (November 16, 1994-remainder of season). ... Rams franchise moved to St. Louis (April 12, 1995). ... Released by Rams (August 27, 1995). ... Signed by Green Bay Packers (January 10, 1996). ... On injured reserve with knee injury (August 20, 1996-entire season). ... Released by Packers (June 24, 1997). ... Signed by Kansas City Chiefs (April 7, 1998). ... Released by Chiefs (August 30, 1998). ... Signed by Miami Dolphins to practice squad (September 9, 1998). ... Released by Dolphins (September 30, 1998). ... Signed by Philadelphia Eagles to practice squad (October 7, 1998). ... Activated (November 27, 1998).
PLAYING EXPERIENCE: Philadelphia NFL, 1998. ... Games/Games started: 2/0.

BOUIE, TONY S

PERSONAL: Born August 7, 1972, in New Orleans. ... 5-10/193. ... Full name: Tony Vanderson Bouie.
HIGH SCHOOL: Holy Cross (New Orleans).
COLLEGE: Arizona (degree in media arts, 1994).
TRANSACTIONS/CAREER NOTES: Signed as non-drafted free agent by Tampa Bay Buccaneers (April 26, 1995). ... Released by Buccaneers (August 21, 1995). ... Re-signed by Buccaneers to practice squad (October 4, 1995). ... Activated (October 17, 1995). ... Granted free agency (February 13, 1998). ... Re-signed by Buccaneers (June 15, 1998). ... Granted unconditional free agency (February 12, 1999).

PLAYING EXPERIENCE: Tampa Bay NFL, 1995-1998. ... Games/Games started: 1995 (9/3), 1996 (16/0), 1997 (16/1), 1998 (16/0). Total: 57/4.
HONORS: Named defensive back on THE SPORTING NEWS college All-America second team (1994).
PRO STATISTICS: 1995—Intercepted one pass for 19 yards. 1997—Caught one pass for 25 yards and recovered one fumble. 1998—Recovered one fumble.

BOULWARE, PETER   LB   RAVENS

PERSONAL: Born December 18, 1974, in Columbia, S.C. ... 6-4/255. ... Full name: Peter Nicholas Boulware. ... Name pronounced BOWL-ware.
HIGH SCHOOL: Spring Valley (Columbia, S.C.).
COLLEGE: Florida State (degree in management information systems, 1997).
TRANSACTIONS/CAREER NOTES: Selected after junior season by Baltimore Ravens in first round (fourth pick overall) of 1997 NFL draft. ... Signed by Ravens (August 16, 1997).
HONORS: Named defensive end on THE SPORTING NEWS college All-America first team (1996). ... Played in Pro Bowl (1998 season).
PRO STATISTICS: 1998—Recovered one fumble.

Year Team	G	GS	SACKS
1997—Baltimore NFL	16	16	11.5
1998—Baltimore NFL	16	16	8.5
Pro totals (2 years)	32	32	20.0

BOUTTE, MARC   DT   REDSKINS

PERSONAL: Born July 26, 1969, in Lake Charles, La. ... 6-4/307. ... Full name: Marc Anthony Boutte. ... Name pronounced BOO-TAY.
HIGH SCHOOL: William Oscar Boston (Lake Charles, La.).
COLLEGE: Louisiana State.
TRANSACTIONS/CAREER NOTES: Selected by Los Angeles Rams in third round (57th pick overall) of 1992 NFL draft. ... Signed by Rams (July 13, 1992). ... Claimed on waivers by Washington Redskins (August 29, 1994). ... Granted free agency (February 17, 1995). ... Re-signed by Redskins (April 21, 1995). ... Granted unconditional free agency (February 16, 1996). ... Re-signed by Redskins (February 17, 1996). ... On injured reserve with knee injury (October 13, 1996-remainder of season).
PRO STATISTICS: 1993—Recovered one fumble. 1995—Recovered one fumble. 1996—Intercepted one pass for no yards. 1997—Intercepted one pass for 10 yards. 1998—Credited with a safety.

Year Team	G	GS	SACKS
1992—Los Angeles Rams NFL	16	15	1.0
1993—Los Angeles Rams NFL	16	16	1.0
1994—Washington NFL	9	3	0.0
1995—Washington NFL	16	16	2.0
1996—Washington NFL	10	10	0.0
1997—Washington NFL	16	13	2.0
1998—Washington NFL	13	1	2.0
Pro totals (7 years)	96	74	8.0

BOWDEN, JOE   LB   TITANS

PERSONAL: Born February 25, 1970, in Dallas. ... 5-11/235. ... Full name: Joseph Tarrod Bowden. ... Name pronounced BOW-din.
HIGH SCHOOL: North Mesquite (Mesquite, Texas).
COLLEGE: Oklahoma.
TRANSACTIONS/CAREER NOTES: Selected by Houston Oilers in fifth round (133rd pick overall) of 1992 NFL draft. ... Signed by Oilers (July 16, 1992). ... Granted free agency (February 17, 1995). ... Re-signed by Oilers (June 6, 1995). ... Granted unconditional free agency (February 16, 1996). ... Re-signed by Oilers (March 4, 1996). ... Oilers franchise moved to Tennessee for 1997 season. ... Oilers franchise renamed Tennessee Titans for 1999 season (December 26, 1998).
PRO STATISTICS: 1993—Recovered one fumble. 1995—Returned one kickoff for six yards and recovered one fumble. 1997—Recovered one fumble. 1998—Intercepted one pass for one yard and a touchdown and recovered two fumbles for 17 yards and one touchdown.

Year Team	G	GS	SACKS
1992—Houston NFL	14	0	0.0
1993—Houston NFL	16	6	1.0
1994—Houston NFL	14	1	0.0
1995—Houston NFL	16	14	1.0
1996—Houston NFL	16	16	3.0
1997—Tennessee NFL	16	16	2.5
1998—Tennessee NFL	16	16	1.5
Pro totals (7 years)	108	69	9.0

BOWENS, TIM   DT   DOLPHINS

PERSONAL: Born February 7, 1973, in Okolona, Miss. ... 6-4/315. ... Full name: Timothy L. Bowens.
HIGH SCHOOL: Okolona (Miss.).
JUNIOR COLLEGE: Itawamba Junior College (Miss.).
COLLEGE: Mississippi.
TRANSACTIONS/CAREER NOTES: Selected after junior season by Miami Dolphins in first round (20th pick overall) of 1994 NFL draft. ... Signed by Dolphins (June 2, 1994). ... Designated by Dolphins as franchise player (February 13, 1998). ... Re-signed by Dolphins (August 21, 1998). ... On injured reserve with torn biceps muscle (January 3, 1999-remainder of playoffs).
HONORS: Named to play in Pro Bowl (1998 season); replaced by Cortez Kennedy due to injury.
PRO STATISTICS: 1994—Recovered one fumble. 1995—Recovered two fumbles. 1996—Recovered one fumble. 1997—Recovered one fumble in end zone for a touchdown.

Year Team	G	GS	SACKS
1994—Miami NFL	16	15	3.0
1995—Miami NFL	16	16	2.0
1996—Miami NFL	16	16	3.0
1997—Miami NFL	16	16	5.0
1998—Miami NFL	16	16	0.0
Pro totals (5 years)	80	79	13.0

BOWIE, LARRY — FB — REDSKINS

PERSONAL: Born March 21, 1973, in Anniston, Ala. ... 6-0/249.
HIGH SCHOOL: Anniston (Ala.).
COLLEGE: Northeast Oklahoma A&M, then Georgia.
TRANSACTIONS/CAREER NOTES: Signed as non-drafted free agent by Washington Redskins (May 1, 1996). ... On injured reserve with leg injury (October 6, 1998-remainder of season).
PRO STATISTICS: 1997—Returned one kickoff for 15 yards and recovered one fumble.
SINGLE GAME HIGHS (regular season): Attempts—6 (December 7, 1997, vs. Arizona); yards—23 (December 21, 1997, vs. Philadelphia); and rushing touchdowns—1 (December 21, 1997, vs. Philadelphia).

			RUSHING				RECEIVING				TOTALS			
Year Team	G	GS	Att.	Yds.	Avg.	TD	No.	Yds.	Avg.	TD	TD	2pt.	Pts.	Fum.
1996—Washington NFL	3	0	0	0	...	0	3	17	5.7	0	0	0	0	0
1997—Washington NFL	15	13	28	100	3.6	2	34	388	11.4	2	4	0	24	2
1998—Washington NFL	5	4	4	8	2.0	0	7	53	7.6	1	1	0	6	0
Pro totals (3 years)	23	17	32	108	3.4	2	44	458	10.4	3	5	0	30	2

BOWNES, FABIEN — WR — BEARS

PERSONAL: Born February 29, 1972, in Aurora, Ill. ... 5-11/190. ... Name pronounced BOW-ens.
HIGH SCHOOL: Waubonsie Valley (Aurora, Ill.).
COLLEGE: Western Illinois.
TRANSACTIONS/CAREER NOTES: Signed as non-drafted free agent by Chicago Bears (April 27, 1995). ... Released by Bears (August 27, 1995). ... Re-signed by Bears to practice squad (August 29, 1995). ... Activated (December 14, 1995). ... Released by Bears (August 19, 1996). ... Re-signed by Bears to practice squad (October 15, 1996).
PRO STATISTICS: 1997—Recovered one fumble.
SINGLE GAME HIGHS (regular season): Receptions—4 (November 2, 1997, vs. Washington); yards—56 (September 27, 1998, vs. Minnesota); and touchdown receptions—1 (October 4, 1998, vs. Detroit).

			RECEIVING				KICKOFF RETURNS				TOTALS			
Year Team	G	GS	No.	Yds.	Avg.	TD	No.	Yds.	Avg.	TD	TD	2pt.	Pts.	Fum.
1995—Chicago NFL	1	0	0	0	...	0	0	0	...	0	0	0	0	0
1996—Chicago NFL							Did not play.							
1997—Chicago NFL	16	0	12	146	12.2	0	19	396	20.8	0	0	0	0	0
1998—Chicago NFL	16	0	5	69	13.8	1	1	19	19.0	0	1	0	6	0
Pro totals (3 years)	33	0	17	215	12.6	1	20	415	20.8	0	1	0	6	0

BOYD, STEPHEN — LB — LIONS

PERSONAL: Born August 22, 1972, in Valley Stream, N.Y. ... 6-0/247. ... Full name: Stephen Gerard Boyd.
HIGH SCHOOL: Valley Stream (N.Y.).
COLLEGE: Boston College (degree in human development).
TRANSACTIONS/CAREER NOTES: Selected by Detroit Lions in fifth round (141st pick overall) of 1995 NFL draft. ... Signed by Lions (July 19, 1995). ... Granted free agency (February 13, 1998). ... Re-signed by Lions (April 17, 1998). ... On injured reserve with shoulder injury (December 23, 1998-remainder of season). ... Granted unconditional free agency (February 12, 1999). ... Re-signed by Lions (February 23, 1999).
PLAYING EXPERIENCE: Detroit NFL, 1995-1998. ... Games/Games started: 1995 (16/0), 1996 (8/5), 1997 (16/16), 1998 (13/13). Total: 53/34.
HONORS: Named linebacker on THE SPORTING NEWS college All-America first team (1994).
RECORDS: Shares NFL single-game record for most opponents' fumbles recovered—3 (October 4, 1998, vs. Chicago).
PRO STATISTICS: 1997—Intercepted one pass for four yards and recovered one fumble for 42 yards and a touchdown. 1998—Credited with four sacks and recovered four fumbles for one yard.

BOYD, TOMMIE — WR — BENGALS

PERSONAL: Born December 21, 1971 ... 6-0/195.
HIGH SCHOOL: Lansing (Mich.) Eastern.
COLLEGE: Toledo (degree in communications).
TRANSACTIONS/CAREER NOTES: Signed as non-drafted free agent by Detroit Lions (April 24, 1995). ... Released by Lions (August 18, 1995). ... Re-signed by Lions (January 22, 1996). ... Played with Rhein Fire of World League (1996). ... Released by Lions (August 21, 1996). ... Re-signed by Lions (February 19, 1997). ... Released by Lions (March 31, 1999). ... Signed by Cincinnati Bengals (April 7, 1999).
SINGLE GAME HIGHS (regular season): Receptions—3 (December 21, 1997, vs. New York Jets); yards—37 (December 20, 1998, vs. Atlanta); and touchdown receptions—1 (December 20, 1998, vs. Atlanta).

			RECEIVING				PUNT RETURNS				KICKOFF RETURNS				TOTALS			
Year Team	G	GS	No.	Yds.	Avg.	TD	No.	Yds.	Avg.	TD	No.	Yds.	Avg.	TD	TD	2pt.	Pts.	Fum.
1996—Rhein W.L.	...	...	22	204	9.3	1	17	164	9.6	0	0	0	...	0	1	0	6	0
1997—Detroit NFL	16	1	10	142	14.2	0	0.	0	...	0	0	0	...	0	0	0	0	0
1998—Detroit NFL	9	0	4	52	13.0	1	4	11	2.8	0	8	163	20.4	0	1	0	6	0
W.L. totals (1 year)	...	...	22	204	9.3	1	17	164	9.6	0	0	0	...	0	1	0	6	0
NFL totals (2 years)	25	1	14	194	13.9	1	4	11	2.8	0	8	163	20.4	0	1	0	6	0
Pro totals (3 years)	...	...	36	398	11.1	2	21	175	8.3	0	8	163	20.4	0	2	0	12	0

BOYER, BRANT — LB — JAGUARS

PERSONAL: Born June 27, 1971, in Ogden, Utah. ... 6-1/232. ... Full name: Brant T. Boyer.
HIGH SCHOOL: North Summit (Coalville, Utah).
JUNIOR COLLEGE: Snow College (Utah).
COLLEGE: Arizona.
TRANSACTIONS/CAREER NOTES: Selected by Miami Dolphins in sixth round (177th pick overall) of 1994 NFL draft. ... Signed by Dolphins (July 11, 1994). ... Released by Dolphins (September 21, 1994). ... Re-signed by Dolphins to practice squad (September 22, 1994). ... Activated (October 5, 1994). ... Selected by Jacksonville Jaguars from Dolphins in NFL expansion draft (February 15, 1995). ... Released by Jaguars (August 27, 1995). ... Re-signed by Jaguars (December 13, 1995). ... Released by Jaguars (August 25, 1996). ... Re-signed by Jaguars (September 24, 1996). ... Released by Jaguars (September 25, 1996). ... Re-signed by Jaguars (September 27, 1996). ... Granted free agency (February 13, 1998). ... Re-signed by Jaguars (March 18, 1998). ... On injured reserve with neck injury (December 2, 1998-remainder of season). ... Granted unconditional free agency (February 12, 1999). ... Re-signed by Jaguars (March 12, 1999).
PLAYING EXPERIENCE: Miami NFL, 1994; Jacksonville NFL, 1995-1998. ... Games/Games started: 1994 (14/0), 1995 (2/0), 1996 (12/0), 1997 (16/2), 1998 (11/0). Total: 55/2.
CHAMPIONSHIP GAME EXPERIENCE: Played in AFC championship game (1996 season).
PRO STATISTICS: 1997—Credited with 1½ sacks. 1998—Credited with one sack.

BRACKENS, TONY — DE — JAGUARS

PERSONAL: Born December 26, 1974, in Fairfield, Texas. ... 6-4/260. ... Full name: Tony Lynn Brackens Jr.
HIGH SCHOOL: Fairfield (Texas).
COLLEGE: Texas.
TRANSACTIONS/CAREER NOTES: Selected after junior season by Jacksonville Jaguars in second round (33rd pick overall) of 1996 NFL draft. ... Signed by Jaguars (May 28, 1996).
CHAMPIONSHIP GAME EXPERIENCE: Played in AFC championship game (1996 season).
HONORS: Named defensive lineman on THE SPORTING NEWS college All-America first team (1995).
PRO STATISTICS: 1996—Intercepted one pass for 27 yards and recovered three fumbles. 1997—Recovered one fumble. 1998—Recovered three fumbles for eight yards.

Year Team	G	GS	SACKS
1996—Jacksonville NFL	16	1	7.0
1997—Jacksonville NFL	15	3	7.0
1998—Jacksonville NFL	12	8	3.5
Pro totals (3 years)	43	12	17.5

BRADFORD, COREY — WR — PACKERS

PERSONAL: Born December 8, 1975, in Baton Rouge, La. ... 6-1/197. ... Full name: Corey Lamon Bradford.
HIGH SCHOOL: Clinton (La.).
JUNIOR COLLEGE: Hinds Community College (Miss.).
COLLEGE: Jackson State.
TRANSACTIONS/CAREER NOTES: Selected by Green Bay Packers in fifth round (150th pick overall) of 1998 NFL draft. ... Signed by Packers (July 17, 1998).
SINGLE GAME HIGHS (regular season): Receptions—1 (December 7, 1998, vs. Tampa Bay); yards—18 (November 15, 1998, vs. New York Giants); and touchdown receptions—0.

			RECEIVING				KICKOFF RETURNS			TOTALS			
Year Team	G	GS	No.	Yds.	Avg.	TD	No.	Yds.	Avg.	TD	TD	2pt.	Pts.	Fum.
1998—Green Bay NFL	8	0	3	27	9.0	0	2	33	16.5	0	0	0	0	1

BRADFORD, RONNIE — CB — FALCONS

PERSONAL: Born October 1, 1970, in Minot, N.D. ... 5-10/195. ... Full name: Ronald L. Bradford.
HIGH SCHOOL: Adams City (Commerce City, Colo.).
COLLEGE: Colorado.
TRANSACTIONS/CAREER NOTES: Selected by Miami Dolphins in fourth round (105th pick overall) of 1993 NFL draft. ... Signed by Dolphins (July 14, 1993). ... Released by Dolphins (August 24, 1993). ... Signed by Denver Broncos to practice squad (September 1, 1993). ... Activated (October 12, 1993). ... On injured reserve with knee injury (September 28, 1995-remainder of season). ... Released by Broncos (August 25, 1996). ... Signed by Arizona Cardinals (August 27, 1996). ... Granted unconditional free agency (February 14, 1997). ... Signed by Atlanta Falcons (April 11, 1997). ... Granted unconditional free agency (February 12, 1999). ... Re-signed by Falcons (March 8, 1999).
CHAMPIONSHIP GAME EXPERIENCE: Played in NFC championship game (1998 season). ... Played in Super Bowl XXXIII (1998 season).
PRO STATISTICS: 1993—Returned one punt for no yards and fumbled once. 1994—Credited with one sack and recovered two fumbles. 1996—Recovered one fumble. 1998—Credited with a safety and recovered one fumble.

			INTERCEPTIONS				TOTALS			
Year Team	G	GS	No.	Yds.	Avg.	TD	TD	2pt.	Pts.	Fum.
1993—Denver NFL	10	3	1	0	0.0	0	0	0	0	1
1994—Denver NFL	12	0	0	0	...	0	0	0	0	0
1995—Denver NFL	4	0	0	0	...	0	0	0	0	0
1996—Arizona NFL	15	11	1	0	0.0	0	0	0	0	0
1997—Atlanta NFL	16	15	4	9	2.3	0	0	0	0	0
1998—Atlanta NFL	14	10	3	11	3.7	1	1	0	8	0
Pro totals (6 years)	71	39	9	20	2.2	1	1	0	8	1

BRADY, DONNY — DB

PERSONAL: Born November 24, 1973, in North Bellmore, N.Y. ... 6-2/195. ... Full name: Donald Maynard Brady.
HIGH SCHOOL: Mepham (Bellmore, N.Y.).
JUNIOR COLLEGE: Nassau Community College (N.Y.).
COLLEGE: Wisconsin.
TRANSACTIONS/CAREER NOTES: Signed as non-drafted free agent by Cleveland Browns (May 2, 1995). ... Released by Browns (August 21, 1995). ... Re-signed by Browns to practice squad (December 13, 1995). ... Activated (December 16, 1995). ... Browns franchise moved to Baltimore and renamed Ravens for 1996 season (March 11, 1996). ... Granted free agency (February 12, 1999).
PLAYING EXPERIENCE: Cleveland NFL, 1995; Baltimore NFL, 1996-1998. ... Games/Games started: 1995 (2/0), 1996 (16/13), 1997 (16/5), 1998 (13/0). Total: 47/18.
PRO STATISTICS: 1996—Recovered one fumble. 1997—Recovered one fumble. 1998—Credited with one sack.

BRADY, JEFF — LB

PERSONAL: Born November 9, 1968, in Cincinnati. ... 6-1/243. ... Full name: Jeffrey Thomas Brady.
HIGH SCHOOL: Newport (Ky.) Central Catholic.
COLLEGE: Kentucky (degree in telecommunications, 1990).
TRANSACTIONS/CAREER NOTES: Selected by Pittsburgh Steelers in 12th round (323rd pick overall) of 1991 NFL draft. ... Signed by Steelers (July 10, 1991). ... Granted unconditional free agency (February 1, 1992). ... Signed by Green Bay Packers (March 30, 1992). ... On injured reserve with knee injury (September 26-November 21, 1992). ... Claimed on waivers by Los Angeles Rams (August 31, 1993). ... Released by Rams (October 20, 1993). ... Signed by San Diego Chargers (October 25, 1993). ... Granted free agency (February 17, 1994). ... Signed by Tampa Bay Buccaneers (May 4, 1994). ... Granted unconditional free agency (February 17, 1995). ... Signed by Minnesota Vikings (April 13, 1995). ... Granted unconditional free agency (February 16, 1996). ... Re-signed by Vikings (February 28, 1996). ... Granted unconditional free agency (February 14, 1997). ... Re-signed by Vikings (March 1, 1997). ... On injured reserve with hamstring injury (December 30, 1997-remainder of playoffs). ... Released by Vikings (February 13, 1998). ... Signed by Carolina Panthers (March 31, 1998). ... Granted unconditional free agency (February 12, 1999).
PRO STATISTICS: 1993—Recovered one fumble. 1995—Recovered two fumbles. 1996—Recovered three fumbles. 1997—Recovered three fumbles for 30 yards and one touchdown. 1998—Returned one kickoff for eight yards, fumbled once and recovered one fumble.

				INTERCEPTIONS				SACKS
Year Team	G	GS	No.	Yds.	Avg.	TD	No.
1991—Pittsburgh NFL	16	0	0	0	...	0	0.0
1992—Green Bay NFL	8	0	0	0	...	0	0.0
1993—Los Angeles Rams NFL	6	0	0	0	...	0	0.0
—San Diego NFL	3	0	0	0	...	0	0.0
1994—Tampa Bay NFL	16	0	0	0	...	0	0.0
1995—Minnesota NFL	16	7	2	7	3.5	0	3.0
1996—Minnesota NFL	16	16	3	20	6.7	0	1.5
1997—Minnesota NFL	15	14	0	0	...	0	0.0
1998—Carolina NFL	16	16	4	85	21.3	0	4.0
Pro totals (8 years)	112	53	9	112	12.4	0	8.5

BRADY, KYLE — TE — JAGUARS

PERSONAL: Born January 14, 1972, in New Cumberland, Pa. ... 6-6/268. ... Full name: Kyle James Brady.
HIGH SCHOOL: Cedar Cliff (Camp Hill, Pa.).
COLLEGE: Penn State.
TRANSACTIONS/CAREER NOTES: Selected by New York Jets in first round (ninth pick overall) of 1995 NFL draft. ... Signed by Jets (July 17, 1995). ... Designated by Jets as transition player (February 12, 1999). ... Tendered offer sheet by Jacksonville Jaguars (February 16, 1999). ... Jets declined to match offer (February 18, 1999).
CHAMPIONSHIP GAME EXPERIENCE: Played in AFC championship game (1998 season).
HONORS: Named tight end on THE SPORTING NEWS college All-America second team (1994).
PRO STATISTICS: 1995—Returned two kickoffs for 25 yards. 1996—Returned two kickoffs for 26 yards. 1998—Returned one kickoff for 20 yards.
SINGLE GAME HIGHS (regular season): Receptions—5 (October 19, 1998, vs. New England); yards—48 (November 1, 1998, vs. Kansas City); and touchdown receptions—2 (October 19, 1998, vs. New England).

			RECEIVING				TOTALS			
Year Team	G	GS	No.	Yds.	Avg.	TD	TD	2pt.	Pts.	Fum.
1995—New York Jets NFL	15	11	26	252	9.7	2	2	0	12	0
1996—New York Jets NFL	16	16	15	144	9.6	1	1	1	8	1
1997—New York Jets NFL	16	14	22	238	10.8	2	2	0	12	1
1998—New York Jets NFL	16	16	30	315	10.5	5	5	0	30	1
Pro totals (4 years)	63	57	93	949	10.2	10	10	1	62	3

BRAHAM, RICH — G — BENGALS

PERSONAL: Born November 6, 1970, in Morgantown, W.Va. ... 6-4/305. ... Name pronounced bray-HAM.
HIGH SCHOOL: University (Morgantown, W.Va.).
COLLEGE: West Virginia (degree in finance).
TRANSACTIONS/CAREER NOTES: Selected by Arizona Cardinals in third round (76th pick overall) of 1994 NFL draft. ... Signed by Cardinals (July 30, 1994). ... Claimed on waivers by Cincinnati Bengals (November 18, 1994). ... On injured reserve with ankle injury (August 29, 1995-entire season). ... Granted free agency (February 14, 1997). ... Tendered offer sheet by New England Patriots (April 8, 1997). ... Offer matched by Bengals (April 15, 1997). ... On injured reserve with knee injury (December 3, 1998-remainder of season).
PLAYING EXPERIENCE: Cincinnati NFL, 1994 and 1996-98. ... Games/Games started: 1994 (3/0), 1996 (16/16), 1997 (16/16), 1998 (12/12). Total: 47/44.
HONORS: Named offensive lineman on THE SPORTING NEWS college All-America second team (1993).

BRANCH, CALVIN — RB — RAIDERS

PERSONAL: Born May 8, 1974, in Lexington, Ky. ... 5-11/195. ... Full name: Calvin Stanley Branch.
HIGH SCHOOL: Klein (Spring, Texas).
COLLEGE: Iowa State, then Colorado State.
TRANSACTIONS/CAREER NOTES: Selected by Oakland Raiders in sixth round (172nd pick overall) of 1997 NFL draft. ... Signed by Raiders (July 21, 1997). ... Assigned by Raiders to Barcelona Dragons in 1999 NFL Europe enhancement allocation program (February 22, 1999).
PLAYING EXPERIENCE: Oakland NFL, 1997 and 1998. ... Games/Games started: 1997 (6/0), 1998 (16/0). Total: 22/0.
PRO STATISTICS: 1998—Returned five kickoffs for 70 yards, fumbled once and recovered one fumble.

BRANDENBURG, DAN — LB — BILLS

PERSONAL: Born February 16, 1973, in Rensselaer, Ind. ... 6-2/255. ... Full name: Daniel James Brandenburg.
HIGH SCHOOL: Rensselaer (Ind.) Central.
COLLEGE: Indiana State.
TRANSACTIONS/CAREER NOTES: Selected by Buffalo Bills in seventh round (237th pick overall) of 1996 NFL draft. ... Signed by Bills (July 9, 1996). ... Released by Bills (August 20, 1996). ... Re-signed by Bills to practice squad (August 26, 1996). ... Activated (November 22, 1996). ... Inactive for five games (1996).
PLAYING EXPERIENCE: Buffalo NFL, 1997 and 1998. ... Games/Games started: 1997 (12/0), 1998 (16/1). Total: 28/1.
PRO STATISTICS: 1997—Recovered one fumble.

BRATZKE, CHAD — DE — COLTS

PERSONAL: Born September 15, 1971, in Brandon, Fla. ... 6-4/275. ... Full name: Chad Allen Bratzke.
HIGH SCHOOL: Bloomingdale (Valrco, Fla.).
COLLEGE: Eastern Kentucky.
TRANSACTIONS/CAREER NOTES: Selected by New York Giants in fifth round (155th pick overall) of 1994 NFL draft. ... Signed by Giants (July 17, 1994). ... On injured reserve with knee injury (November 12, 1997-remainder of season). ... Granted unconditional free agency (February 12, 1999). ... Signed by Indianapolis Colts (March 1, 1999).
PRO STATISTICS: 1996—Recovered two fumbles. 1997—Recovered two fumbles. 1998—Recovered one fumble.

Year Team	G	GS	SACKS
1994—New York Giants NFL	2	0	0.0
1995—New York Giants NFL	6	0	0.0
1996—New York Giants NFL	16	16	5.0
1997—New York Giants NFL	10	10	3.5
1998—New York Giants NFL	16	16	11.0
Pro totals (5 years)	**50**	**42**	**19.5**

BRAXTON, TYRONE — S — BRONCOS

PERSONAL: Born December 17, 1964, in Madison, Wis. ... 5-11/190. ... Full name: Tyrone Scott Braxton. ... Related to Jim Braxton, fullback with Buffalo Bills (1971-78) and Miami Dolphins (1978).
HIGH SCHOOL: James Madison Memorial (Madison, Wis.).
COLLEGE: North Dakota State.
TRANSACTIONS/CAREER NOTES: Selected by Denver Broncos in 12th round (334th pick overall) of 1987 NFL draft. ... Signed by Broncos (July 18, 1987). ... On injured reserve with shoulder injury (September 1-December 18, 1987). ... On injured reserve with knee injury (September 25, 1990-remainder of season). ... Granted unconditional free agency (February 17, 1994). ... Signed by Miami Dolphins (May 13, 1994). ... Released by Dolphins (April 20, 1995). ... Signed by Broncos (May 5, 1995). ... Granted unconditional free agency (February 16, 1996). ... Re-signed by Broncos (March 1, 1996).
CHAMPIONSHIP GAME EXPERIENCE: Played in AFC championship game (1987, 1989, 1991, 1997 and 1998 seasons). ... Played in Super Bowl XXII (1987 season) and Super Bowl XXIV (1989 season). ... Member of Super Bowl championship team (1997 and 1998 seasons).
HONORS: Played in Pro Bowl (1996 season).
PRO STATISTICS: 1988—Recovered one fumble. 1989—Recovered two fumbles for 35 yards. 1991—Fumbled once and recovered one fumble. 1993—Recovered two fumbles for six yards. 1994—Returned one kickoff for 34 yards. 1996—Recovered one fumble for 20 yards. 1997—Recovered three fumbles for 45 yards.

Year Team	G	GS	INTERCEPTIONS No.	Yds.	Avg.	TD	SACKS No.
1987—Denver NFL	2	0	0	0	...	0	0.0
1988—Denver NFL	16	0	2	6	3.0	0	1.0
1989—Denver NFL	16	16	6	103	17.2	1	0.0
1990—Denver NFL	3	2	1	10	10.0	0	0.0
1991—Denver NFL	16	15	4	55	13.8	1	1.0
1992—Denver NFL	16	14	2	54	27.0	0	0.0
1993—Denver NFL	16	16	3	37	12.3	0	0.0
1994—Miami NFL	16	0	2	3	1.5	0	0.0
1995—Denver NFL	16	16	2	36	18.0	0	0.0
1996—Denver NFL	16	16	†9	128	14.2	1	0.0
1997—Denver NFL	16	16	4	113	28.3	1	0.5
1998—Denver NFL	16	6	1	72	72.0	0	0.0
Pro totals (12 years)	**165**	**117**	**36**	**617**	**17.1**	**4**	**2.5**

BRIEN, DOUG — K — SAINTS

PERSONAL: Born November 24, 1970, in Bloomfield, N.J. ... 6-0/180. ... Full name: Douglas Robert Zachariah Brien.
HIGH SCHOOL: De La Salle Catholic (Concord, Calif.).
COLLEGE: California (degree in political economies).
TRANSACTIONS/CAREER NOTES: Selected by San Francisco 49ers in third round (85th pick overall) of 1994 NFL draft. ... Signed by 49ers (July 27, 1994). ... Released by 49ers (October 16, 1995). ... Signed by New Orleans Saints (October 31, 1995). ... Granted free agency (February 14, 1997). ... Re-signed by Saints (July 17, 1997).
CHAMPIONSHIP GAME EXPERIENCE: Played in NFC championship game (1994 season). ... Member of Super Bowl championship team (1994 season).
POST SEASON RECORDS: Shares Super Bowl single-game record for most extra points—7 (January 29, 1995, vs. San Diego).
PRO STATISTICS: 1998—Punted twice for 72 yards.

				KICKING				
Year Team	G	XPM	XPA	FGM	FGA	Lg.	50+	Pts.
1994—San Francisco NFL	16	*60	*62	15	20	48	0-1	105
1995—San Francisco NFL	6	19	19	7	12	51	1-1	40
—New Orleans NFL	8	16	16	12	17	47	0-1	52
1996—New Orleans NFL	16	18	18	21	25	54	3-4	81
1997—New Orleans NFL	16	22	22	23	27	53	4-5	91
1998—New Orleans NFL	16	31	31	20	22	56	4-6	91
Pro totals (5 years)	78	166	168	98	123	56	12-18	460

BRIGANCE, O.J. — LB — DOLPHINS

PERSONAL: Born September 29, 1969, in Houston. ... 6-0/236. ... Full name: Orenthial James Brigance.
HIGH SCHOOL: Willowridge (Sugar Land, Texas).
COLLEGE: Rice (degree in managerial studies).
TRANSACTIONS/CAREER NOTES: Signed by B.C. Lions of CFL (May 1991). ... Granted free agency (February 1994). ... Signed by Baltimore Stallions of CFL (April 1994). ... Granted free agency (February 16, 1996). ... Signed as non-drafted free agent by Miami Dolphins (May 17, 1996). ... Granted free agency (February 12, 1999). ... Re-signed by Dolphins (May 20, 1999).
PRO STATISTICS: CFL: 1991—Intercepted one pass for seven yards. 1992—Returned five kickoffs for 40 yards and recovered three fumbles. 1993—Recovered one fumble for 27 yards. 1994—Recovered two fumbles. 1995—Intercepted one pass for 13 yards and recovered three fumbles for 10 yards. NFL: 1997—Recovered one fumble.

Year Team	G	GS	SACKS
1991—British Columbia CFL	18	...	2.0
1992—British Columbia CFL	18	...	0.0
1993—British Columbia CFL	18	...	20.0
1994—Baltimore CFL	18	...	6.0
1995—Baltimore CFL	18	...	7.0
1996—Miami NFL	12	0	0.0
1997—Miami NFL	16	0	0.0
1998—Miami NFL	16	0	0.0
CFL totals (5 years)	90	...	35.0
NFL totals (3 years)	44	0	0.0
Pro totals (8 years)	134	...	35.0

BRIGHAM, JEREMY — TE — RAIDERS

PERSONAL: Born March 22, 1975, in Boston. ... 6-6/255.
HIGH SCHOOL: Saguara (Scottsdale, Ariz.).
COLLEGE: Washington.
TRANSACTIONS/CAREER NOTES: Selected by Oakland Raiders in fifth round (127th pick overall) of 1998 NFL draft. ... Signed by Raiders (July 18, 1998).
PLAYING EXPERIENCE: Oakland NFL, 1998. ... Games/Games started: 2/0.

BRILZ, DARRICK — C

PERSONAL: Born February 14, 1964, in Richmond, Calif. ... 6-3/295. ... Full name: Darrick Joseph Brilz.
HIGH SCHOOL: Pinole (Calif.) Valley.
COLLEGE: Oregon State (degree in industrial engineering).
TRANSACTIONS/CAREER NOTES: Signed as non-drafted free agent by Washington Redskins (May 1, 1987). ... Released by Redskins (August 31, 1987). ... Re-signed as replacement player by Redskins (September 23, 1987). ... On injured reserve with pinched nerve in neck (December 12, 1987-remainder of season). ... Claimed on waivers by San Diego Chargers (August 30, 1988). ... Released by Chargers (August 1, 1989). ... Signed by Seattle Seahawks (August 16, 1989). ... Released by Seahawks (September 5, 1989). ... Re-signed by Seahawks (September 21, 1989). ... Granted unconditional free agency (February 17, 1994). ... Signed by Cincinnati Bengals (March 28, 1994). ... Granted unconditional free agency (February 12, 1997).
PLAYING EXPERIENCE: Washington NFL, 1987; San Diego NFL, 1988; Seattle NFL, 1989-1993; Cincinnati NFL, 1994-1998. ... Games/Games started 1987 (7/4), 1988 (14/0), 1989 (14/0), 1990 (16/5), 1991 (16/7), 1992 (16/16), 1993 (16/16), 1994 (15/15), 1995 (16/16), 1996 (13/13), 1997 (16/16), 1998 (16/16). Total: 175/124.
PRO STATISTICS: 1991—Recovered one fumble. 1994—Recovered one fumble. 1997—Recovered one fumble.

BRISBY, VINCENT — WR — PATRIOTS

PERSONAL: Born January 25, 1971, in Houston. ... 6-3/193. ... Full name: Vincent Cole Brisby.
HIGH SCHOOL: Washington-Marion Magnet (Lake Charles, La.).
COLLEGE: Northeast Louisiana (degree in business administration, 1993).

TRANSACTIONS/CAREER NOTES: Selected by New England Patriots in second round (56th pick overall) of 1993 NFL draft. ... Signed by Patriots (July 30, 1993). ... Granted free agency (February 16, 1996). ... Re-signed by Patriots (May 31, 1996). ... On injured reserve with broken finger and hamstring injury (November 21, 1998-remainder of season).
CHAMPIONSHIP GAME EXPERIENCE: Played in AFC championship game (1996 season). ... Played in Super Bowl XXXI (1996 season).
PRO STATISTICS: 1993—Recovered one fumble.
SINGLE GAME HIGHS (regular season): Receptions—9 (October 1, 1995, vs. Atlanta); yards—161 (October 1, 1995, vs. Atlanta); and touchdown receptions—2 (December 18, 1994, vs. Buffalo).
STATISTICAL PLATEAUS: 100-yard receiving games: 1994 (2), 1995 (3). Total: 5.

				RECEIVING				TOTALS			
Year Team	G	GS	No.	Yds.	Avg.	TD	TD	2pt.	Pts.	Fum.
1993—New England NFL	16	12	45	626	13.9	2	2	...	12	1
1994—New England NFL	14	11	58	904	15.6	5	5	0	30	1
1995—New England NFL	16	16	66	974	14.8	3	3	0	18	0
1996—New England NFL	3	0	0	0	...	0	0	0	0	0
1997—New England NFL	16	4	23	276	12.0	2	2	0	12	0
1998—New England NFL	6	1	7	96	13.7	2	2	0	12	0
Pro totals (6 years)	71	44	199	2876	14.5	14	14	0	84	2

BRISTER, BUBBY   QB   BRONCOS

PERSONAL: Born August 15, 1962, in Alexandria, La. ... 6-3/205. ... Full name: Walter Andrew Brister III.
HIGH SCHOOL: Neville (Monroe, La.).
COLLEGE: Tulane, then Northeast Louisiana.
TRANSACTIONS/CAREER NOTES: Selected by Pittsburgh Steelers in third round (67th pick overall) of 1986 NFL draft. ... Selected by New Jersey Generals in 11th round (80th pick overall) of 1986 USFL draft; did not sign. ... Signed by Steelers (July 25, 1986). ... Granted free agency (February 1, 1992). ... Re-signed by Steelers (June 16, 1992). ... Released by Steelers (June 4, 1993). ... Signed by Philadelphia Eagles (July 19, 1993). ... Granted unconditional free agency (February 17, 1994). ... Re-signed by Eagles (April 6, 1994). ... Granted unconditional free agency (February 17, 1995). ... Signed by New York Jets (March 17, 1995). ... Released by Jets (February 29, 1996). ... Signed by Denver Broncos (April 7, 1997).
CHAMPIONSHIP GAME EXPERIENCE: Member of Broncos for AFC championship game (1997 season); did not play. ... Member of Super Bowl championship team (1997 season); did not play. ... Member of Broncos for AFC championship game (1998 season); did not play. ... Member of Super Bowl championship team (1998 season).
PRO STATISTICS: 1986—Fumbled once. 1988—Recovered two fumbles. 1989—Caught one pass for minus 10 yards, fumbled eight times and recovered one fumble. 1990—Fumbled nine times. 1991—Fumbled four times and recovered two fumbles. 1992—Fumbled twice and recovered two fumbles for minus two yards. 1993—Fumbled three times. 1995—Caught one pass for two yards, fumbled four times and recovered three fumbles for minus nine yards. 1998—Fumbled twice and recovered one fumble for minus one yard.
SINGLE GAME HIGHS (regular season): Attempts—48 (December 12, 1993, vs. Buffalo); completions—28 (December 12, 1993, vs. Buffalo); yards—353 (October 14, 1990, vs. Denver); and touchdown passes—4 (October 4, 1998, vs. Philadelphia).
STATISTICAL PLATEAUS: 300-yard passing games: 1988 (2), 1993 (1), 1994 (1). Total: 4.
MISCELLANEOUS: Regular-season record as starting NFL quarterback: 37-38 (.493). ... Postseason record as starting NFL quarterback: 1-1 (.500).

			PASSING							RUSHING				TOTALS		
Year Team	G	GS	Att.	Cmp.	Pct.	Yds.	TD	Int.	Avg.	Rat.	Att.	Yds.	Avg.	TD	TD	2pt.	Pts.
1986—Pittsburgh NFL	2	2	60	21	35.0	291	0	2	4.85	37.6	6	10	1.7	1	1	...	6
1987—Pittsburgh NFL	2	0	12	4	33.3	20	0	3	1.67	2.8	0	0	...	0	0	...	0
1988—Pittsburgh NFL	13	13	370	175	47.3	2634	11	14	7.12	65.3	45	209	4.6	6	6	...	36
1989—Pittsburgh NFL	14	14	342	187	54.7	2365	9	10	6.92	73.1	27	25	0.9	0	0	...	0
1990—Pittsburgh NFL	16	16	387	223	57.6	2725	20	14	7.04	81.6	25	64	2.6	0	0	...	0
1991—Pittsburgh NFL	8	8	190	103	54.2	1350	9	9	7.11	72.9	11	17	1.5	0	0	...	0
1992—Pittsburgh NFL	6	4	116	63	54.3	719	2	5	6.20	61.0	10	16	1.6	0	0	...	0
1993—Philadelphia NFL	10	8	309	181	58.6	1905	14	5	6.17	84.9	20	39	2.0	0	0	...	0
1994—Philadelphia NFL	7	2	76	51	67.1	507	2	1	6.67	89.1	1	7	7.0	0	0	0	0
1995—New York Jets NFL	9	4	170	93	54.7	726	4	8	4.27	53.7	16	18	1.1	0	0	0	0
1997—Denver NFL	1	0	9	6	66.7	48	0	0	5.33	79.9	4	2	0.5	0	0	0	0
1998—Denver NFL	7	4	131	78	59.5	986	10	3	7.53	99.0	19	102	5.4	1	1	0	6
Pro totals (12 years)	95	75	2172	1185	54.6	14276	81	74	6.57	73.2	184	509	2.8	8	8	0	48

RECORD AS BASEBALL PLAYER

TRANSACTIONS/CAREER NOTES: Threw right, batted right. ... Selected by Detroit Tigers organization in fourth round of free-agent draft (June 8, 1981). ... On suspended list (June 22, 1982-entire season). ... Placed on restricted list (October 7, 1982).

				BATTING									FIELDING			
Year Team (League)	Pos.	G	AB	R	H	2B	3B	HR	RBI	Avg.	BB	SO	SB	PO	A	E	Avg.
1981—Bristol (Appal.)	OF-SS	39	111	12	20	7	0	0	10	.180	16	27	5	46	11	9	.864
1982—						Did not play.											

BROCK, FRED   WR   GIANTS

PERSONAL: Born November 15, 1974, in Montgomery, Ala. ... 5-11/181.
HIGH SCHOOL: Jefferson Davis (Montgomery, Ala.).
COLLEGE: Southern Mississippi.
TRANSACTIONS/CAREER NOTES: Signed as non-drafted free agent by Arizona Cardinals (April 23, 1996). ... Released by Cardinals (August 20, 1996). ... Re-signed by Cardinals to practice squad (August 27, 1996). ... Selected by Cleveland Browns from Cardinals in NFL expansion draft (February 9, 1999). ... Released by Browns (April 29, 1999). ... Signed by New York Giants (May 20, 1999).
PRO STATISTICS: 1998—Recovered one fumble for 19 yards.
SINGLE GAME HIGHS (regular season): Receptions—1 (November 8, 1998, vs. Washington); yards—29 (November 9, 1997, vs. Dallas); and touchdown receptions—0.

			RECEIVING				TOTALS			
Year Team	G	GS	No.	Yds.	Avg.	TD	TD	2pt.	Pts.	Fum.
1996—Arizona NFL					Did not play.					
1997—Arizona NFL	2	0	1	29	29.0	0	0	0	0	0
1998—Arizona NFL	12	0	2	12	6.0	0	0	0	0	0
Pro totals (2 years)	14	0	3	41	13.7	0	0	0	0	0

BROCKERMEYER, BLAKE — OT — BEARS

PERSONAL: Born April 11, 1973, in Fort Worth, Texas. ... 6-4/305. ... Full name: Blake Weeks Brockermeyer.
HIGH SCHOOL: Arlington Heights (Texas).
COLLEGE: Texas.
TRANSACTIONS/CAREER NOTES: Selected after junior season by Carolina Panthers in first round (29th pick overall) of 1995 NFL draft. ... Signed by Panthers (July 14, 1995). ... Granted unconditional free agency (February 12, 1999). ... Signed by Chicago Bears (March 8, 1999).
PLAYING EXPERIENCE: Carolina NFL, 1995-1998. ... Games/Games started: 1995 (16/16), 1996 (12/12), 1997 (16/13), 1998 (14/14). Total: 58/55.
CHAMPIONSHIP GAME EXPERIENCE: Played in NFC championship game (1996 season).
HONORS: Named offensive lineman on THE SPORTING NEWS college All-America first team (1994).
PRO STATISTICS: 1998—Recovered two fumbles.

BROMELL, LORENZO — DE — DOLPHINS

PERSONAL: Born September 23, 1975, in Georgetown, S.C. ... 6-6/266. ... Full name: Lorenzo Alexis Bromell.
HIGH SCHOOL: Choppee (Georgetown, S.C.).
JUNIOR COLLEGE: Georgia Military College.
COLLEGE: Clemson.
TRANSACTIONS/CAREER NOTES: Selected by Miami Dolphins in fourth round (102nd pick overall) of 1998 draft. ... Signed by Dolphins (July 10, 1998).
PRO STATISTICS: 1998—Recovered one fumble.

Year Team	G	GS	SACKS
1998—Miami NFL	14	0	8.0

BRONSON, ZACK — S — 49ERS

PERSONAL: Born January 28, 1974, in Jasper, Texas. ... 6-1/191. ... Full name: Robert Bronson.
HIGH SCHOOL: Jasper (Texas).
COLLEGE: McNeese State.
TRANSACTIONS/CAREER NOTES: Signed as non-drafted free agent by San Francisco 49ers (May 2, 1997).
CHAMPIONSHIP GAME EXPERIENCE: Played in NFC championship game (1997 season).
PRO STATISTICS: 1997—Recovered one fumble for three yards.

			INTERCEPTIONS			
Year Team	G	GS	No.	Yds.	Avg.	TD
1997—San Francisco NFL	16	0	1	22	22.0	0
1998—San Francisco NFL	11	0	4	34	8.5	0
Pro totals (2 years)	27	0	5	56	11.2	0

BROOKING, KEITH — LB — FALCONS

PERSONAL: Born October 30, 1975, in Senoia, Ga. ... 6-2/242. ... Full name: Keith Howard Brooking.
HIGH SCHOOL: East Coweta (Ga.).
COLLEGE: Georgia Tech.
TRANSACTIONS/CAREER NOTES: Selected by Atlanta Falcons in first round (12th pick overall) of 1998 NFL draft. ... Signed by Falcons (June 29, 1998).
PLAYING EXPERIENCE: Atlanta NFL, 1998. ... Games/Games started: 15/0.
CHAMPIONSHIP GAME EXPERIENCE: Played in NFC championship game (1998 season). ... Played in Super Bowl XXXIII (1998 season).
PRO STATISTICS: 1998—Intercepted one pass for 12 yards.

BROOKS, BARRETT — OT — LIONS

PERSONAL: Born May 5, 1972, in St. Louis. ... 6-4/320.
HIGH SCHOOL: McCluer North (Florissant, Mo.).
COLLEGE: Kansas State.
TRANSACTIONS/CAREER NOTES: Selected by Philadelphia Eagles in second round (58th pick overall) of 1995 NFL draft. ... Signed by Eagles (July 19, 1995). ... Granted free agency (February 13, 1998). ... Re-signed by Eagles (April 21, 1998). ... Granted unconditional free agency (February 12, 1999). ... Signed by Detroit Lions (April 12, 1999).
PLAYING EXPERIENCE: Philadelphia NFL, 1995-1998. ... Games/Games started: 1995 (16/16), 1996 (16/15), 1997 (16/14), 1998 (16/1). Total: 64/46.
PRO STATISTICS: 1996—Returned one kickoff for no yards and recovered one fumble. 1997—Recovered two fumbles. 1998—Returned one kickoff for seven yards.

BROOKS, BUCKY — DB — RAIDERS

PERSONAL: Born January 22, 1971, in Raleigh, N.C. ... 6-0/192. ... Full name: William Eldridge Brooks Jr.
HIGH SCHOOL: Millbrook (Raleigh, N.C.).
COLLEGE: North Carolina (degree in speech communications).
TRANSACTIONS/CAREER NOTES: Selected by Buffalo Bills in second round (48th pick overall) of 1994 NFL draft. ... Signed by Bills (July 15, 1994). ... On injured reserve with knee injury (November 17, 1994-remainder of season). ... Released by Bills (August 22, 1995). ... Signed by Green Bay Packers (December 12, 1995). ... Inactive for two games (1995). ... Claimed on waivers by Jacksonville Jaguars (October 29, 1996). ... Claimed on waivers by Packers (September 24, 1997). ... Released by Packers (November 25, 1997). ... Signed by Kansas City Chiefs (December 3, 1997). ... Released by Chiefs (November 3, 1998). ... Signed by Oakland Raiders (November 18, 1998).
CHAMPIONSHIP GAME EXPERIENCE: Member of Packers for NFC championship game (1995 season); inactive. ... Played in AFC championship game (1996 season).
PRO STATISTICS: 1994—Recovered one fumble. 1998—Returned one punt for no yards.

			KICKOFF RETURNS				TOTALS			
Year Team	G	GS	No.	Yds.	Avg.	TD	TD	2pt.	Pts.	Fum.
1994—Buffalo NFL	3	0	9	162	18.0	0	0	0	0	1
1995—Green Bay NFL						Did not play.				
1996—Green Bay NFL	2	0	0	0	...	0	0	0	0	0
—Jacksonville NFL	6	1	17	412	24.2	0	0	0	0	0
1997—Jacksonville NFL	3	0	0	0	...	0	0	0	0	0
—Green Bay NFL	3	0	0	0	...	0	0	0	0	0
—Kansas City NFL	3	0	0	0	...	0	0	0	0	0
1998—Kansas City NFL	6	0	0	0	...	0	0	0	0	0
—Oakland NFL	6	0	0	0	...	0	0	0	0	1
Pro totals (4 years)	32	1	26	574	22.1	0	0	0	0	2

BROOKS, DERRICK — LB — BUCCANEERS

PERSONAL: Born April 18, 1973, in Pensacola, Fla. ... 6-0/229. ... Full name: Derrick Dewan Brooks.
HIGH SCHOOL: Booker T. Washington (Pensacola, Fla.).
COLLEGE: Florida State (degree in communications, 1994).
TRANSACTIONS/CAREER NOTES: Selected by Tampa Bay Buccaneers in first round (28th pick overall) of 1995 NFL draft. ... Signed by Buccaneers (May 3, 1995).
HONORS: Named linebacker on THE SPORTING NEWS college All-America first team (1993 and 1994). ... Played in Pro Bowl (1997 and 1998 seasons).
PRO STATISTICS: 1997—Fumbled once and recovered one fumble.

			INTERCEPTIONS				SACKS
Year Team	G	GS	No.	Yds.	Avg.	TD	No.
1995—Tampa Bay NFL	16	13	0	0	...	0	1.0
1996—Tampa Bay NFL	16	16	1	6	6.0	0	0.0
1997—Tampa Bay NFL	16	16	2	13	6.5	0	1.5
1998—Tampa Bay NFL	16	16	1	25	25.0	0	0.0
Pro totals (4 years)	64	61	4	44	11.0	0	2.5

BROOKS, ETHAN — OT — RAMS

PERSONAL: Born April 27, 1972, in Hartford, Conn. ... 6-6/300.
HIGH SCHOOL: Westminster (Simsbury, Conn.).
COLLEGE: Williams, Conn. (degree in psychology, 1995).
TRANSACTIONS/CAREER NOTES: Selected by Atlanta Falcons in seventh round (229th pick overall) of 1996 NFL draft. ... Signed by Falcons (June 7, 1996). ... Assigned by Falcons to Frankfurt Galaxy in 1997 World League enhancement allocation program (February 19, 1997). ... Released by Falcons (August 27, 1997). ... Signed by St. Louis Rams (November 20, 1997). ... Inactive for five games (1997).
PLAYING EXPERIENCE: Atlanta NFL, 1996; Frankfurt W.L., 1997; St. Louis NFL, 1998. ... Games/Games started: 1996 (2/0), 1997 (games played unavailable), 1998 (15/0). Total NFL: 17/0.

BROOKS, ROBERT — WR — PACKERS

PERSONAL: Born June 23, 1970, in Greenwood, S.C. ... 6-0/180. ... Full name: Robert Darren Brooks.
HIGH SCHOOL: Greenwood (S.C.).
COLLEGE: South Carolina (bachelor of science degree in retailing).
TRANSACTIONS/CAREER NOTES: Selected by Green Bay Packers in third round (62nd pick overall) of 1992 NFL draft. ... Signed by Packers (July 22, 1992). ... Granted free agency (February 17, 1995). ... Re-signed by Packers (June 1, 1995). ... On injured reserve with knee injury (October 26, 1996-remainder of season). ... Granted unconditional free agency (February 13, 1998). ... Re-signed by Packers (February 13, 1998).
CHAMPIONSHIP GAME EXPERIENCE: Played in NFC championship game (1995 and 1997 seasons). ... Member of Super Bowl championship team (1996 season); inactive. ... Played in Super Bowl XXXII (1997 season).
RECORDS: Shares NFL record for longest pass reception (from Brett Favre)—99 yards, touchdown (September 11, 1995, at Chicago).
POST SEASON RECORDS: Holds NFL postseason career record for highest average punt return (minimum 10 returns)—15.3.
PRO STATISTICS: 1993—Fumbled once and recovered one fumble. 1994—Fumbled four times and recovered one fumble.
SINGLE GAME HIGHS (regular season): Receptions—11 (December 24, 1995, vs. Pittsburgh); yards—164 (September 28, 1997, vs. Detroit); and touchdown receptions—2 (September 9, 1996, vs. Philadelphia).
STATISTICAL PLATEAUS: 100-yard receiving games: 1994 (1), 1995 (9), 1996 (2), 1997 (1). Total: 13.

Year Team	G	GS	RUSHING Att.	Yds.	Avg.	TD	RECEIVING No.	Yds.	Avg.	TD	PUNT RETURNS No.	Yds.	Avg.	TD	KICKOFF RETURNS No.	Yds.	Avg.	TD	TOTALS TD	2pt.	Pts.
1992—Green Bay NFL	16	1	2	14	7.0	0	12	126	10.5	1	11	102	9.3	0	18	338	18.8	0	1	...	6
1993—Green Bay NFL	14	0	3	17	5.7	0	20	180	9.0	0	16	135	8.4	0	23	611	*26.6	†1	1	...	6
1994—Green Bay NFL	16	16	1	0	0.0	0	58	648	11.2	4	40	352	8.8	1	9	260	28.9	1	6	0	36
1995—Green Bay NFL	16	15	4	21	5.3	0	102	1497	14.7	13	0	0	...	0	1	28	28.0	0	13	0	78
1996—Green Bay NFL	7	7	4	2	0.5	0	23	344	15.0	4	0	0	...	0	0	0	...	0	4	0	24
1997—Green Bay NFL	15	15	2	19	9.5	0	60	1010	‡16.8	7	0	0	...	0	0	0	...	0	7	0	42
1998—Green Bay NFL	12	12	1	2	2.0	0	31	420	13.5	3	0	0	...	0	0	0	...	0	3	0	18
Pro totals (7 years)	96	66	17	75	4.4	0	306	4225	13.8	32	67	589	8.8	1	51	1237	24.3	2	35	0	210

BROUGHTON, LUTHER TE PANTHERS

PERSONAL: Born November 30, 1974, in Charleston, S.C. ... 6-2/248. ... Full name: Luther Rashard Broughton Jr.
HIGH SCHOOL: Cainhoy (Huger, S.C.).
COLLEGE: Furman.
TRANSACTIONS/CAREER NOTES: Selected by Philadelphia Eagles in fifth round (155th pick overall) of 1997 NFL draft. ... Signed by Eagles (July 15, 1997). ... Active for one game with Eagles (1997); did not play. ... Released by Eagles (November 5, 1997). ... Re-signed by Eagles to practice squad (November 5, 1997). ... Signed by Carolina Panthers from Eagles practice squad (December 15, 1997). ... Inactive for one game with Panthers (1997).
PRO STATISTICS: 1998—Recovered one fumble.
SINGLE GAME HIGHS (regular season): Receptions—2 (December 20, 1998, vs. St. Louis); yards—78 (December 20, 1998, vs. St. Louis); and touchdown receptions—1 (December 20, 1998, vs. St. Louis).

Year Team	G	GS	RECEIVING No.	Yds.	Avg.	TD	TOTALS TD	2pt.	Pts.	Fum.
1997—Philadelphia NFL							Did not play.			
1998—Carolina NFL	16	4	6	142	23.7	1	1	0	6	1

BROUSSARD, STEVE RB RAVENS

PERSONAL: Born February 22, 1967, in Los Angeles. ... 5-7/201. ... Full name: Steve N. Broussard. ... Name pronounced BREW-sard.
HIGH SCHOOL: Manual Arts (Los Angeles).
COLLEGE: Washington State.
TRANSACTIONS/CAREER NOTES: Selected by Atlanta Falcons in first round (20th pick overall) of 1990 NFL draft. ... Signed by Falcons (July 12, 1990). ... Released by Falcons (February 17, 1994). ... Signed by Cincinnati Bengals (April 8, 1994). ... On injured reserve with concussion (December 21, 1994-remainder of season). ... Released by Bengals (May 3, 1995). ... Signed by Seattle Seahawks (June 13, 1995). ... Granted unconditional free agency (February 13, 1998). ... Re-signed by Seahawks (March 2, 1998). ... Released by Seahawks (February 10, 1999). ... Signed by Baltimore Ravens (April 21, 1999).
HONORS: Named running back on THE SPORTING NEWS college All-America second team (1988).
PRO STATISTICS: 1992—Recovered one fumble for minus two yards. 1994—Attempted one pass without a completion and recovered one fumble. 1995—Recovered one fumble. 1998—Recovered one fumble.
SINGLE GAME HIGHS (regular season): Attempts—26 (December 19, 1993, vs. Washington); yards—162 (December 19, 1993, vs. Washington); and rushing touchdowns—2 (October 5, 1997, vs. Tennessee).
STATISTICAL PLATEAUS: 100-yard rushing games: 1991 (2), 1993 (1), 1997 (1). Total: 4.

Year Team	G	GS	RUSHING Att.	Yds.	Avg.	TD	RECEIVING No.	Yds.	Avg.	TD	KICKOFF RETURNS No.	Yds.	Avg.	TD	TOTALS TD	2pt.	Pts.	Fum.
1990—Atlanta NFL	13	10	126	454	3.6	4	24	160	6.7	0	3	45	15.0	0	4	...	24	6
1991—Atlanta NFL	14	5	99	449	4.5	4	12	120	10.0	1	0	0	...	0	5	...	30	1
1992—Atlanta NFL	15	1	84	363	4.3	1	11	96	8.7	1	0	0	...	0	2	...	12	3
1993—Atlanta NFL	8	0	39	206	5.3	1	1	4	4.0	0	0	0	...	0	1	...	6	0
1994—Cincinnati NFL	13	3	94	403	4.3	2	34	218	6.4	0	0	0	...	0	2	1	14	5
1995—Seattle NFL	15	1	46	222	4.8	1	10	94	9.4	0	7	115	16.4	0	1	0	6	4
1996—Seattle NFL	12	0	15	106	7.1	1	6	26	4.3	0	43	1064	24.7	0	1	0	6	2
1997—Seattle NFL	16	1	70	418	6.0	5	24	143	6.0	1	43	979	22.8	0	6	0	36	0
1998—Seattle NFL	15	0	5	4	0.8	0	4	21	5.3	0	50	1076	21.5	0	0	0	0	0
											29	781	26.9	▲1				
Pro totals (9 years)	121	21	578	2625	4.5	19	126	882	7.0	3	175	4060	23.2	1	23	1	140	22

BROWN, ANTHONY OT/G STEELERS

PERSONAL: Born November 6, 1972, in Okinawa, Japan. ... 6-5/315.
HIGH SCHOOL: American (Wurzburg, West Germany).
COLLEGE: Utah.
TRANSACTIONS/CAREER NOTES: Signed as non-drafted free agent by Cincinnati Bengals (April 26, 1995). ... Granted free agency (February 13, 1998). ... Re-signed by Bengals (April 13, 1998). ... Granted unconditional free agency (February 12, 1999). ... Signed by Pittsburgh Steelers (April 23, 1999).
PLAYING EXPERIENCE: Cincinnati NFL, 1995-1998. ... Games/Games started: 1995 (7/1), 1996 (7/0), 1997 (6/0), 1998 (16/5). Total: 36/6.

BROWN, CHAD LB SEAHAWKS

PERSONAL: Born July 12, 1970, in Altadena, Calif. ... 6-2/240. ... Full name: Chadwick Everett Brown.
HIGH SCHOOL: John Muir (Pasadena, Calif.).
COLLEGE: Colorado (degree in marketing, 1992).
TRANSACTIONS/CAREER NOTES: Selected by Pittsburgh Steelers in second round (44th pick overall) of 1993 NFL draft. ... Signed by Steelers (July 26, 1993). ... Granted unconditional free agency (February 14, 1997). ... Signed by Seattle Seahawks (February 15, 1997).
CHAMPIONSHIP GAME EXPERIENCE: Played in AFC championship game (1994 and 1995 seasons). ... Played in Super Bowl XXX (1995 season).

HONORS: Named linebacker on THE SPORTING NEWS NFL All-Pro team (1996 and 1998). ... Played in Pro Bowl (1996 and 1998 seasons).
PRO STATISTICS: 1996—Fumbled once and recovered two fumbles. 1997—Recovered four fumbles for 68 yards and two touchdowns. 1998—Recovered one fumble.

				INTERCEPTIONS			SACKS
Year Team	G	GS	No.	Yds.	Avg.	TD	No.
1993—Pittsburgh NFL	16	9	0	0	...	0	3.0
1994—Pittsburgh NFL	16	16	1	9	9.0	0	8.5
1995—Pittsburgh NFL	10	10	0	0	...	0	5.5
1996—Pittsburgh NFL	14	14	2	20	10.0	0	13.0
1997—Seattle NFL	15	15	0	0	...	0	6.5
1998—Seattle NFL	16	16	1	11	11.0	0	7.5
Pro totals (6 years)	87	80	4	40	10.0	0	44.0

BROWN, CORNELL   LB   RAVENS   B

PERSONAL: Born March 15, 1975, in Englewood, N.J. ... 6-0/240. ... Full name: Cornell Desmond Brown. ... Brother of Ruben Brown, guard, Buffalo Bills.
HIGH SCHOOL: E.C. Glass (Lynchburg, Va.).
COLLEGE: Virginia Tech.
TRANSACTIONS/CAREER NOTES: Selected by Baltimore Ravens in sixth round (194th pick overall) of 1997 NFL draft. ... Signed by Ravens (July 10, 1997).
PLAYING EXPERIENCE: Baltimore NFL, 1997 and 1998. ... Games/Games started: 1997 (16/1), 1998 (16/1). Total: 32/2.
HONORS: Named defensive lineman on THE SPORTING NEWS college All-America first team (1995).
PRO STATISTICS: 1997—Intercepted one pass for 21 yards and credited with $1/2$ sack.

BROWN, CORWIN   S   JETS

PERSONAL: Born April 25, 1970, in Chicago. ... 6-1/205. ... Full name: Corwin Alan Brown.
HIGH SCHOOL: Percy L. Julian (Chicago).
COLLEGE: Michigan (degree in English).
TRANSACTIONS/CAREER NOTES: Selected by New England Patriots in fourth round (110th pick overall) of 1993 NFL draft. ... Signed by Patriots (July 16, 1993). ... Granted free agency (February 16, 1996). ... Re-signed by Patriots (February 27, 1996). ... Released by Patriots (August 24, 1997). ... Signed by New York Jets (August 25, 1997).
PLAYING EXPERIENCE: New England NFL, 1993-1996; New York Jets NFL, 1997 and 1998. ... Games/Games started: 1993 (15/12), 1994 (16/0), 1995 (16/2), 1996 (14/0), 1997 (16/0), 1998 (16/1). Total: 93/15.
CHAMPIONSHIP GAME EXPERIENCE: Played in AFC championship game (1996 and 1998 seasons). ... Played in Super Bowl XXXI (1996 season).
PRO STATISTICS: 1993—Recovered one fumble. 1995—Recovered one fumble. 1996—Recovered one fumble for 42 yards and a touchdown. 1997—Caught one pass for 26 yards. 1998—Intercepted one pass for no yards and recovered one fumble for 16 yards.

BROWN, CYRON   DE   BRONCOS

PERSONAL: Born June 28, 1975, in Chicago. ... 6-5/265. ... Full name: Cyron DeAndre Brown.
HIGH SCHOOL: Lane Tech (Chicago).
COLLEGE: Illinois, then Western Illinois.
TRANSACTIONS/CAREER NOTES: Signed as non-drafted free agent by Denver Broncos (May 1, 1998).
PLAYING EXPERIENCE: Denver NFL, 1998. ... Games/Games started: 4/0.
CHAMPIONSHIP GAME EXPERIENCE: Member of Broncos for AFC championship game (1998 season); inactive. ... Member of Super Bowl championship team (1998 season); inactive.

BROWN, DAVE   QB   CARDINALS

PERSONAL: Born February 25, 1970, in Summit, N.J. ... 6-5/230. ... Full name: David Michael Brown.
HIGH SCHOOL: Westfield (N.J.).
COLLEGE: Duke (degrees in history and political science, 1992).
TRANSACTIONS/CAREER NOTES: Selected by New York Giants in first round of 1992 NFL supplemental draft. ... Signed by Giants (August 12, 1992). ... On injured reserve with thumb injury (December 18, 1992-remainder of season). ... Granted unconditional free agency (February 16, 1996). ... Re-signed by Giants (May 3, 1996). ... Released by Giants (February 20, 1998). ... Signed by Arizona Cardinals (April 29, 1998).
PRO STATISTICS: 1994—Punted twice for 57 yards, fumbled 11 times and recovered four fumbles for minus 15 yards. 1995—Punted once for 15 yards, fumbled 10 times and recovered two fumbles for minus eight yards. 1996—Fumbled nine times and recovered one fumble for minus three yards. 1997—Fumbled once.
SINGLE GAME HIGHS (regular season): Attempts—50 (September 17, 1995, vs. Green Bay); completions—28 (September 14, 1997, vs. Baltimore); yards—299 (November 5, 1995, vs. Seattle); and touchdown passes—2 (September 28, 1997, vs. New Orleans).
MISCELLANEOUS: Regular-season record as starting NFL quarterback: 23-30 (.434).

			PASSING							RUSHING				TOTALS		
Year Team	G	GS	Att.	Cmp.	Pct.	Yds.	TD	Int.	Avg.	Rat.	Att.	Yds.	Avg.	TD	TD	2pt.	Pts.
1992—N.Y. Giants NFL	2	0	7	4	57.1	21	0	0	3.00	62.2	2	-1	-0.5	0	0	...	0
1993—N.Y. Giants NFL	1	0	0	0	...	0	0	0	...	...	3	-4	-1.3	0	0	...	0
1994—N.Y. Giants NFL	15	15	350	201	57.4	2536	12	16	7.25	72.5	60	196	3.3	2	2	0	12
1995—N.Y. Giants NFL	16	16	456	254	55.7	2814	11	10	6.17	73.1	45	228	5.1	4	4	0	24
1996—N.Y. Giants NFL	16	16	398	214	53.8	2412	12	20	6.06	61.3	50	170	3.4	0	0	0	0
1997—N.Y. Giants NFL	8	6	180	93	51.7	1023	5	3	5.68	71.1	17	29	1.7	1	1	0	6
1998—Arizona NFL	1	0	5	2	40.0	31	0	0	6.20	61.3	1	2	2.0	0	0	0	0
Pro totals (7 years)	59	53	1396	768	55.0	8837	40	49	6.33	69.2	178	620	3.5	7	7	0	42

BROWN, DEREK   TE

PERSONAL: Born March 31, 1970, in Fairfax, Va. ... 6-6/264. ... Full name: Derek Vernon Brown.
HIGH SCHOOL: Merritt Island (Fla.).
COLLEGE: Notre Dame.
TRANSACTIONS/CAREER NOTES: Selected by New York Giants in first round (14th pick overall) of 1992 NFL draft. ... Signed by Giants (July 29, 1992). ... Selected by Jacksonville Jaguars from Giants in NFL expansion draft (February 15, 1995). ... Inactive for six games (1995). ... On injured reserve with rib injury (October 10, 1995-remainder of season). ... Granted unconditional free agency (February 14, 1997). ... Re-signed by Jaguars (February 26, 1997). ... Granted unconditional free agency (February 13, 1998). ... Signed by Oakland Raiders (May 13, 1998). ... Granted unconditional free agency (February 12, 1999).
CHAMPIONSHIP GAME EXPERIENCE: Played in AFC championship game (1996 season).
PRO STATISTICS: 1994—Returned one kickoff for one yard and recovered one fumble. 1998—Recovered one fumble.
SINGLE GAME HIGHS (regular season): Receptions—3 (November 22, 1998, vs. Denver); yards—38 (November 22, 1998, vs. Denver); and touchdown receptions—1 (October 19, 1997, vs. Dallas).

			RECEIVING				TOTALS			
Year Team	G	GS	No.	Yds.	Avg.	TD	TD	2pt.	Pts.	Fum.
1992—New York Giants NFL	16	7	4	31	7.8	0	0	...	0	0
1993—New York Giants NFL	16	0	7	56	8.0	0	0	...	0	0
1994—New York Giants NFL	13	0	0	0	...	0	0	0	0	0
1995—Jacksonville NFL						Did not play.				
1996—Jacksonville NFL	16	14	17	141	8.3	0	0	0	0	0
1997—Jacksonville NFL	13	7	8	84	10.5	1	1	0	6	0
1998—Oakland NFL	16	4	7	89	12.7	0	0	0	0	0
Pro totals (6 years)	90	32	43	401	9.3	1	1	0	6	0

BROWN, DOUG   DT   REDSKINS

PERSONAL: Born September 29, 1974, in New Westminster, B.C. ... 6-7/290.
HIGH SCHOOL: Port Moody (B.C.) Senior Secondary.
COLLEGE: Simon Fraser (B.C.).
TRANSACTIONS/CAREER NOTES: Signed as non-drafted free agent by Buffalo Bills (May 20, 1997). ... Released by Bills (August 24, 1997). ... Re-signed by Bills to practice squad (August 26, 1997). ... Granted free agency after 1997 season. ... Signed by Washington Redskins (February 17, 1998).
PLAYING EXPERIENCE: Washington NFL, 1998. ... Games/Games started: 10/8.

BROWN, ERIC   S   BRONCOS

PERSONAL: Born March 20, 1975, in San Antonio. ... 6-0/210. ... Full name: Eric Jon Brown.
HIGH SCHOOL: Converse-Judson (San Antonio).
JUNIOR COLLEGE: Blinn College (Texas).
COLLEGE: Mississippi State.
TRANSACTIONS/CAREER NOTES: Selected by Denver Broncos in second round (61st pick overall) of 1998 NFL draft. ... Signed by Broncos (July 16, 1998).
PLAYING EXPERIENCE: Denver NFL, 1998. ... Games/Games started: 11/10.
CHAMPIONSHIP GAME EXPERIENCE: Member of Broncos for AFC championship game (1998 season); inactive. ... Member of Super Bowl championship team (1998 season); inactive.
PRO STATISTICS: 1998—Recovered one fumble.

BROWN, GARY   RB   GIANTS

PERSONAL: Born July 1, 1969, in Williamsport, Pa. ... 5-11/230. ... Full name: Gary Leroy Brown.
HIGH SCHOOL: Williamsport (Pa.) Area.
COLLEGE: Penn State.
TRANSACTIONS/CAREER NOTES: Selected by Houston Oilers in eighth round (214th pick overall) of 1991 NFL draft. ... Signed by Oilers (July 15, 1991). ... Granted free agency (February 17, 1994). ... Re-signed by Oilers (July 15, 1994). ... Released by Oilers (April 19, 1996). ... Signed by San Diego Chargers (February 24, 1997). ... Granted unconditional free agency (February 13, 1998). ... Signed by New York Giants (April 21, 1998).
PRO STATISTICS: 1992—Recovered one fumble. 1993—Recovered two fumbles for four yards. 1995—Recovered one fumble. 1998—Recovered one fumble.
SINGLE GAME HIGHS (regular season): Attempts—36 (October 5, 1997, vs. Oakland); yards—194 (November 21, 1993, vs. Cleveland); and rushing touchdowns—2 (September 11, 1994, vs. Dallas).
STATISTICAL PLATEAUS: 100-yard rushing games: 1993 (5), 1995 (1), 1997 (2), 1998 (6). Total: 14.

			RUSHING				RECEIVING				KICKOFF RETURNS				TOTALS		
Year Team	G	GS	Att.	Yds.	Avg.	TD	No.	Yds.	Avg.	TD	No.	Yds.	Avg.	TD	TD	2pt.	Pts. Fum.
1991—Houston NFL	11	0	8	85	10.6	1	2	1	0.5	0	3	30	10.0	0	1	...	6 0
1992—Houston NFL	16	0	19	87	4.6	1	1	5	5.0	0	1	15	15.0	0	1	...	6 0
1993—Houston NFL	16	8	195	1002	§5.1	6	21	240	11.4	2	2	29	14.5	0	8	...	48 4
1994—Houston NFL	12	8	169	648	3.8	4	18	194	10.8	1	0	0	...	0	5	0	30 6
1995—Houston NFL	9	4	86	293	3.4	0	6	16	2.7	0	0	0	...	0	0	0	0 2
1996—									Did not play.								
1997—San Diego NFL	15	14	253	945	3.7	4	21	137	6.5	0	0	0	...	0	4	0	24 0
1998—New York Giants NFL	16	11	247	1063	4.3	5	13	36	2.8	0	0	0	...	0	5	0	30 1
Pro totals (7 years)	95	45	977	4123	4.2	21	82	629	7.7	3	6	74	12.3	0	24	0	144 15

BROWN, GILBERT — DT — PACKERS

PERSONAL: Born February 22, 1971, in Detroit. ... 6-2/350. ... Full name: Gilbert Jesse Brown.
HIGH SCHOOL: Mackenzie (Detroit).
COLLEGE: Kansas.
TRANSACTIONS/CAREER NOTES: Selected by Minnesota Vikings in third round (79th pick overall) of 1993 NFL draft. ... Signed by Vikings (July 16, 1993). ... Claimed on waivers by Green Bay Packers (August 31, 1993). ... On injured reserve with knee injury (December 6, 1994-remainder of season). ... Granted unconditional free agency (February 14, 1997). ... Re-signed by Packers (February 18, 1997).
CHAMPIONSHIP GAME EXPERIENCE: Played in NFC championship game (1995-97 seasons). ... Member of Super Bowl championship team (1996 season). ... Played in Super Bowl XXXII (1997 season).

Year Team	G	GS	SACKS
1993—Green Bay NFL	2	0	0.0
1994—Green Bay NFL	13	1	3.0
1995—Green Bay NFL	13	7	0.0
1996—Green Bay NFL	16	16	1.0
1997—Green Bay NFL	12	12	3.0
1998—Green Bay NFL	16	16	0.0
Pro totals (6 years)	72	52	7.0

BROWN, J.B. — CB

PERSONAL: Born January 5, 1967, in Washington, D.C. ... 6-0/191. ... Full name: James Harold Brown.
HIGH SCHOOL: DeMatha Catholic (Hyattsville, Md.).
COLLEGE: Maryland.
TRANSACTIONS/CAREER NOTES: Selected by Miami Dolphins in 12th round (315th pick overall) of 1989 NFL draft. ... Signed by Dolphins (July 16, 1989). ... Granted free agency (February 1, 1991). ... Re-signed by Dolphins to practice squad (August 29, 1991). ... Activated (September 7, 1991). ... Granted free agency (March 1, 1993). ... Re-signed by Dolphins (July 21, 1993). ... Released by Dolphins (February 3, 1997). ... Signed by Pittsburgh Steelers (February 7, 1997). ... Traded by Steelers to Arizona Cardinals for seventh-round pick (K Kris Brown) in 1999 draft (August 25, 1998). ... Released by Cardinals after 1998 season.
CHAMPIONSHIP GAME EXPERIENCE: Played in AFC championship game (1992 and 1997 seasons).
PRO STATISTICS: 1990—Credited with one sack. 1992—Recovered one fumble. 1993—Fumbled once. 1995—Fumbled once and recovered two fumbles. 1998—Recovered one fumble.

			INTERCEPTIONS			
Year Team	G	GS	No.	Yds.	Avg.	TD
1989—Miami NFL	16	0	0	0	...	0
1990—Miami NFL	16	16	0	0	...	0
1991—Miami NFL	15	11	1	0	0.0	0
1992—Miami NFL	16	16	4	119	29.8	1
1993—Miami NFL	16	16	5	43	8.6	0
1994—Miami NFL	16	16	3	82	27.3	0
1995—Miami NFL	13	12	2	20	10.0	0
1996—Miami NFL	14	1	1	29	29.0	0
1997—Pittsburgh NFL	13	0	0	0	...	0
1998—Arizona NFL	15	6	0	0	...	0
Pro totals (10 years)	150	94	16	293	18.3	1

BROWN, JAMES — OT — DOLPHINS

PERSONAL: Born November 30, 1970, in Philadelphia. ... 6-6/330. ... Full name: James Lamont Brown.
HIGH SCHOOL: Mastbaum Area Vo-Tech (Philadelphia).
COLLEGE: Virginia State.
TRANSACTIONS/CAREER NOTES: Selected by Dallas Cowboys in third round (82nd pick overall) of 1992 NFL draft. ... Signed by Cowboys (July 15, 1992). ... Released by Cowboys (August 17, 1992). ... Signed by Indianapolis Colts (August 19, 1992). ... Released by Colts (August 31, 1992). ... Signed by New York Jets to practice squad (September 2, 1992). ... Traded by Jets to Miami Dolphins for fifth-round pick (DB Raymond Austin) in 1997 draft (March 4, 1996). ... Granted unconditional free agency (February 13, 1998). ... Re-signed by Dolphins (March 3, 1998).
PLAYING EXPERIENCE: New York Jets NFL, 1993-1995; Miami NFL, 1996-1998. ... Games/Games started: 1993 (14/1), 1994 (16/6), 1995 (14/12), 1996 (16/16), 1997 (16/16), 1998 (16/16). Total: 92/67.
PRO STATISTICS: 1994—Recovered one fumble.

BROWN, JAMIE — OT — REDSKINS

PERSONAL: Born April 24, 1972, in Miami. ... 6-8/318. ... Full name: Jamie Shepard Brown. ... Brother-in-law of Michael Irvin, wide receiver, Dallas Cowboys.
HIGH SCHOOL: Miami Killian.
COLLEGE: Florida A&M.
TRANSACTIONS/CAREER NOTES: Selected by Denver Broncos in fourth round (121st pick overall) of 1995 NFL draft. ... Signed by Broncos (May 25, 1995). ... On injured reserve with foot injury (November 29, 1995-remainder of season). ... Granted free agency (February 13, 1998). ... Re-signed by Broncos (April 15, 1998). ... Traded by Broncos to San Francisco 49ers for second-round pick (DE Montae Reagor) in 1999 draft (April 15, 1998). ... On reserve/suspended list (August 25-September 15, 1998). ... Released by 49ers (February 9, 1999). ... Signed by Washington Redskins (March 18, 1999).
PLAYING EXPERIENCE: Denver NFL, 1995-1997; San Francisco NFL, 1998. ... Games/Games started: 1995 (6/0), 1996 (12/2), 1997 (11/2), 1998 (8/5). Total: 37/9.
CHAMPIONSHIP GAME EXPERIENCE: Member of Broncos for AFC championship game (1997 season); inactive. ... Member of Super Bowl championship team (1997 season); inactive.

BROWN, JONATHON — DE — PACKERS

PERSONAL: Born November 28, 1975, in Chickasha, Okla. ... 6-4/265. ... Full name: Jonathon Bernard Brown.
HIGH SCHOOL: Booker T. Washington (Tulsa, Okla.).
COLLEGE: Tennessee.
TRANSACTIONS/CAREER NOTES: Selected by Green Bay Packers in third round (90th pick overall) of 1998 NFL draft. ... Signed by Packers (June 12, 1998).
PLAYING EXPERIENCE: Green Bay NFL, 1998. ... Games/Games started: 4/0.

BROWN, LANCE — DB — STEELERS

PERSONAL: Born February 2, 1972, in Jacksonville. ... 6-2/203.
HIGH SCHOOL: Terry Parker (Jacksonville).
COLLEGE: Indiana.
TRANSACTIONS/CAREER NOTES: Selected by Pittsburgh Steelers in fifth round (161st pick overall) of 1995 NFL draft. ... Signed by Steelers (July 18, 1995). ... Claimed on waivers by Arizona Cardinals (September 25, 1995). ... Released by Cardinals (September 10, 1996). ... Signed by New York Jets to practice squad (November 19, 1996). ... Released by Jets (August 7, 1997). ... Signed by Steelers (February 13, 1998).
PLAYING EXPERIENCE: Arizona NFL, 1995 and 1996; Pittsburgh NFL, 1998. ... Games/Games started: 1995 (11/5), 1996 (1/0), 1998 (16/0). Total: 28/5.
PRO STATISTICS: 1995—Recovered one fumble. 1998—Recovered two fumbles for one yard.

BROWN, LARRY — CB

PERSONAL: Born November 30, 1969, in Miami. ... 5-11/186. ... Full name: Larry Brown Jr.
HIGH SCHOOL: Los Angeles.
JUNIOR COLLEGE: Southwestern College (Calif.).
COLLEGE: Texas Christian (degree in criminal justice).
TRANSACTIONS/CAREER NOTES: Selected by Dallas Cowboys in 12th round (320th pick overall) of 1991 NFL draft. ... Granted unconditional free agency (February 16, 1996). ... Signed by Oakland Raiders (February 20, 1996). ... Released by Raiders (June 2, 1998). ... Signed by Minnesota Vikings (June 16, 1998). ... Released by Vikings (August 30, 1998). ... Signed by Cowboys (December 2, 1998). ... Granted unconditional free agency (February 12, 1999).
CHAMPIONSHIP GAME EXPERIENCE: Played in NFC championship game (1992-1995 seasons). ... Member of Super Bowl championship team (1992, 1993 and 1995 seasons).
HONORS: Named Most Valuable Player of Super Bowl XXX (1995 season).
POST SEASON RECORDS: Shares Super Bowl career record for most interceptions—3.
PRO STATISTICS: 1991—Recovered one fumble. 1992—Recovered one fumble.

				INTERCEPTIONS		
Year Team	G	GS	No.	Yds.	Avg.	TD
1991—Dallas NFL	16	13	2	31	15.5	0
1992—Dallas NFL	16	15	1	30	30.0	0
1993—Dallas NFL	16	16	0	0	...	0
1994—Dallas NFL	15	15	4	21	5.3	0
1995—Dallas NFL	16	15	6	124	20.7	†2
1996—Oakland NFL	8	1	1	4	4.0	0
1997—Oakland NFL	4	0	0	0	...	0
1998—Dallas NFL	4	0	0	0	...	0
Pro totals (8 years)	95	75	14	210	15.0	2

BROWN, LOMAS — OT — BROWNS

PERSONAL: Born March 30, 1963, in Miami. ... 6-4/290. ... Full name: Lomas Brown Jr. ... Cousin of Joe Taylor, defensive back with Chicago Bears (1967-74); cousin of Guy McIntyre, guard with San Francisco 49ers (1984-93), Green Bay Packers (1994) and Philadelphia Eagles (1995 and 1996); and cousin of Eric Curry, defensive end, Jacksonville Jaguars.
HIGH SCHOOL: Miami Springs Senior.
COLLEGE: Florida (degree in public recreation, 1996).
TRANSACTIONS/CAREER NOTES: Selected by Orlando Renegades in second round (18th pick overall) of 1985 USFL draft. ... Selected by Detroit Lions in first round (sixth pick overall) of 1985 NFL draft. ... Signed by Lions (August 9, 1985). ... Designated by Lions as franchise player (February 25, 1993). ... Granted roster exemption (September 1-3, 1993). ... Designated by Lions as franchise player (February 15, 1995). ... Re-signed by Lions (September 7, 1995). ... Granted unconditional free agency (February 16, 1996). ... Signed by Arizona Cardinals (February 28, 1996). ... Granted unconditional free agency (February 12, 1999). ... Signed by Cleveland Browns (March 9, 1999).
PLAYING EXPERIENCE: Detroit NFL, 1985-1995; Arizona NFL, 1996-1998. ... Games/Games started: 1985 (16/16), 1986 (16/16), 1987 (11/11), 1988 (16/16), 1989 (16/16), 1990 (16/16), 1991 (15/15), 1992 (16/16), 1993 (11/11), 1994 (16/16), 1995 (15/14), 1996 (16/16), 1997 (14/14), 1998 (16/16). Total: 210/209.
CHAMPIONSHIP GAME EXPERIENCE: Played in NFC championship game (1991 season).
HONORS: Named tackle on THE SPORTING NEWS college All-America first team (1984). ... Played in Pro Bowl (1990-1996 seasons). ... Named offensive tackle on THE SPORTING NEWS NFL All-Pro team (1992).
PRO STATISTICS: 1989—Rushed once for three yards and recovered one fumble. 1991—Recovered one fumble.

BROWN, OMAR — S — FALCONS

PERSONAL: Born March 28, 1975, in York, Pa. ... 5-10/200. ... Full name: Omar L. Brown.
HIGH SCHOOL: William Penn (York, Pa.).
COLLEGE: North Carolina.

TRANSACTIONS/CAREER NOTES: Selected by Atlanta Falcons in fourth round (103rd pick overall) of 1998 NFL draft. ... Signed by Falcons (July 2, 1998).
PLAYING EXPERIENCE: Atlanta NFL, 1998. ... Games/Games started: 2/0.
CHAMPIONSHIP GAME EXPERIENCE: Member of Falcons for NFC championship game (1998 season); inactive. ... Member of Falcons for Super Bowl XXXIII (1998 season); inactive.

BROWN, ORLANDO   OT   BROWNS

PERSONAL: Born December 20, 1970, in Washington, D.C. ... 6-7/350. ... Full name: Orlando Claude Brown.
HIGH SCHOOL: Howard D. Woodson (Washington, D.C.).
COLLEGE: Central State (Ohio), then South Carolina State.
TRANSACTIONS/CAREER NOTES: Signed as non-drafted free agent by Cleveland Browns (May 13, 1993). ... On injured reserve with shoulder injury (August 30, 1993-entire season). ... Browns franchise moved to Baltimore and renamed Ravens for 1996 season (March 11, 1996). ... Granted unconditional free agency (February 12, 1999). ... Signed by Browns (February 17, 1999).
PLAYING EXPERIENCE: Cleveland NFL, 1994 and 1995; Baltimore NFL, 1996-1998. ... Games/Games started: 1994 (14/8), 1995 (16/16), 1996 (16/16), 1997 (16/16), 1998 (13/13). Total: 75/69.
PRO STATISTICS: 1995—Recovered one fumble.

BROWN, RAY   G   49ERS

PERSONAL: Born December 12, 1962, in Marion, Ark. ... 6-5/318. ... Full name: Leonard Ray Brown Jr.
HIGH SCHOOL: Marion (Ark.).
COLLEGE: Memphis State, then Arizona State, then Arkansas State.
TRANSACTIONS/CAREER NOTES: Selected by St. Louis Cardinals in eighth round (201st pick overall) of 1986 NFL draft. ... Signed by Cardinals (July 14, 1986). ... On injured reserve with knee injury (October 17-November 21, 1986). ... Released by Cardinals (September 7, 1987). ... Re-signed by Cardinals as replacement player (September 25, 1987). ... On injured reserve with finger injury (November 12-December 12, 1987). ... Cardinals franchise moved to Phoenix (March 15, 1988). ... Granted unconditional free agency (February 1, 1989). ... Signed by Washington Redskins (March 10, 1989). ... On injured reserve with knee injury (September 5-November 4, 1989). ... On injured reserve with knee injury (September 4, 1990-January 4, 1991). ... Granted unconditional free agency (February 1-April 1, 1991). ... Re-signed by Redskins for 1991 season. ... On injured reserve with elbow injury (August 27, 1991-entire season). ... Granted unconditional free agency (February 16, 1996). ... Signed by San Francisco 49ers (March 1, 1996).
PLAYING EXPERIENCE: St. Louis NFL, 1986 and 1987; Phoenix NFL, 1988; Washington NFL, 1989, 1992-1995; San Francisco NFL, 1996-1998. ... Games/Games started: 1986 (11/4), 1987 (7/3), 1988 (15/1), 1989 (7/0), 1992 (16/8), 1993 (16/14), 1994 (16/16), 1995 (16/16), 1996 (16/16), 1997 (15/15), 1998 (16/16). Total: 151/109.
CHAMPIONSHIP GAME EXPERIENCE: Played in NFC championship game (1997 season).

BROWN, REGGIE   FB   SEAHAWKS

PERSONAL: Born June 26, 1973, in Highland Park, Mich. ... 6-0/244. ... Full name: Regilyn Brown.
HIGH SCHOOL: Henry Ford (Detroit).
JUNIOR COLLEGE: College of the Desert (Calif.).
COLLEGE: Fresno State.
TRANSACTIONS/CAREER NOTES: Selected by Seattle Seahawks in third round (91st pick overall) of 1996 NFL draft. ... Signed by Seahawks (July 17, 1996). ... On injured reserve with knee injury (October 23, 1996-remainder of season). ... On injured reserve with knee injury (December 17, 1997-remainder of season). ... Granted free agency (February 12, 1999). ... Re-signed by Seahawks April 14, 1999).
PRO STATISTICS: 1998—Rushed once for two yards.
SINGLE GAME HIGHS (regular season): Attempts—1 (September 6, 1998, vs. Philadelphia); yards—2 (September 6, 1998, vs. Philadelphia); and rushing touchdowns—0.

			KICKOFF RETURNS				TOTALS			
Year Team	G	GS	No.	Yds.	Avg.	TD	TD	2pt.	Pts.	Fum.
1996—Seattle NFL	7	0	4	51	12.8	0	0	0	0	0
1997—Seattle NFL	11	0	1	16	16.0	0	0	0	0	0
1998—Seattle NFL	15	1	4	44	11.0	0	0	0	0	0
Pro totals (3 years)	33	1	9	111	12.3	0	0	0	0	0

BROWN, RUBEN   G   BILLS

PERSONAL: Born February 13, 1972, in Englewood, N.J. ... 6-3/304. ... Full name: Ruben Pernell Brown. ... Brother of Cornell Brown, linebacker, Baltimore Ravens.
HIGH SCHOOL: E.C. Glass (Lynchburg, Va.).
COLLEGE: Pittsburgh.
TRANSACTIONS/CAREER NOTES: Selected by Buffalo Bills in first round (14th pick overall) of 1995 NFL draft. ... Signed by Bills (June 20, 1995).
PLAYING EXPERIENCE: Buffalo NFL, 1995-1998. ... Games/Games started: 1995 (16/16), 1996 (14/14), 1997 (16/16), 1998 (13/13). Total: 59/59.
HONORS: Named offensive lineman on THE SPORTING NEWS college All-America second team (1994). ... Played in Pro Bowl (1996-1998 seasons).
PRO STATISTICS: 1997—Recovered one fumble.

BROWN, TIM   WR   RAIDERS

PERSONAL: Born July 22, 1966, in Dallas. ... 6-0/195. ... Full name: Timothy Donell Brown.
HIGH SCHOOL: Woodrow Wilson (Dallas).
COLLEGE: Notre Dame (degree in sociology).

TRANSACTIONS/CAREER NOTES: Selected by Los Angeles Raiders in first round (sixth pick overall) of 1988 NFL draft. ... Signed by Raiders (July 14, 1988). ... On injured reserve with knee injury (September 12, 1989-remainder of season). ... Granted free agency (February 1, 1992). ... Re-signed by Raiders (August 13, 1992). ... Designated by Raiders as transition player (February 25, 1993). ... Tendered offer sheet by Denver Broncos (March 11, 1994). ... Offer matched by Raiders (March 16, 1994). ... Raiders franchise moved to Oakland (July 21, 1995).
CHAMPIONSHIP GAME EXPERIENCE: Played in AFC championship game (1990 season).
HONORS: Named wide receiver on THE SPORTING NEWS college All-America first team (1986 and 1987). ... Heisman Trophy winner (1987). ... Named College Football Player of the Year by THE SPORTING NEWS (1987). ... Named kick returner on THE SPORTING NEWS NFL All-Pro team (1988). ... Played in Pro Bowl (1988, 1991 and 1993-1997 seasons). ... Named wide receiver on THE SPORTING NEWS NFL All-Pro team (1997).
RECORDS: Holds NFL rookie-season record for most combined yards gained—2,317 (1988).
PRO STATISTICS: 1988—Fumbled five times and recovered one fumble for seven yards. 1989—Fumbled once. 1990—Fumbled three times. 1991—Fumbled once. 1992—Fumbled six times and recovered one fumble. 1993—Fumbled once. 1994—Fumbled three times. 1995—Recovered one fumble for three yards. 1996—Fumbled three times and recovered one fumble. 1997—Fumbled once. 1998—Fumbled three times and recovered two fumbles.
SINGLE GAME HIGHS (regular season): Receptions—14 (December 21, 1997, vs. Jacksonville); yards—183 (December 5, 1993, vs. Buffalo); and touchdown receptions—3 (August 31, 1997, vs. Tennessee).
STATISTICAL PLATEAUS: 100-yard receiving games: 1988 (1), 1991 (1), 1992 (1), 1993 (4), 1994 (4), 1995 (6), 1996 (2), 1997 (7), 1998 (3). Total: 29.
MISCELLANEOUS: Holds Raiders franchise all-time record for most receptions (680) and most yards receiving (9,600).

				RUSHING				RECEIVING				PUNT RETURNS				KICKOFF RETURNS				TOTALS		
Year Team	G	GS	Att.	Yds.	Avg.	TD	No.	Yds.	Avg.	TD	No.	Yds.	Avg.	TD	No.	Yds.	Avg.	TD	TD	2pt.	Pts.
1988—L.A. Raiders NFL	16	9	14	50	3.6	1	43	725	16.9	5	§49	§444	9.1	0	†41	*1098	*26.8	†1	7	...	42
1989—L.A. Raiders NFL	1	1	0	0	...	0	1	8	8.0	0	4	43	10.8	0	3	63	21.0	0	0	...	0
1990—L.A. Raiders NFL	16	0	0	0	...	0	18	265	14.7	3	34	295	8.7	0	0	0	...	0	3	...	18
1991—L.A. Raiders NFL	16	1	5	16	3.2	0	36	554	15.4	5	29	§330	11.4	▲1	1	29	29.0	0	6	...	36
1992—L.A. Raiders NFL	15	12	3	-4	-1.3	0	49	693	14.1	7	37	383	10.4	0	2	14	7.0	0	7	...	42
1993—L.A. Raiders NFL	16	16	2	7	3.5	0	80	§1180	14.8	7	40	§465	11.6	1	0	0	...	0	8	...	48
1994—L.A. Raiders NFL	16	16	0	0	...	0	89	§1309	14.7	9	40	*487	12.2	0	0	0	...	0	9	0	54
1995—Oakland NFL	16	16	0	0	...	0	89	§1342	15.1	10	36	364	10.1	0	0	0	...	0	10	0	60
1996—Oakland NFL	16	16	6	35	5.8	0	90	1104	12.3	9	32	272	8.5	0	1	24	24.0	0	9	0	54
1997—Oakland NFL	16	16	5	19	3.8	0	†104	§1408	13.5	5	0	0	...	0	1	7	7.0	0	5	1	32
1998—Oakland NFL	16	16	1	-7	-7.0	0	81	1012	12.5	9	3	23	7.7	0	0	0	...	0	9	0	54
Pro totals (11 years)	160	119	36	116	3.2	1	680	9600	14.1	69	304	3106	10.2	2	49	1235	25.2	1	73	1	440

BROWN, TROY — WR — PATRIOTS

PERSONAL: Born July 2, 1971, in Barnwell, S.C. ... 5-10/190. ... Full name: Troy Fitzgerald Brown.
HIGH SCHOOL: Blackville (S.C.)-Hilda.
JUNIOR COLLEGE: Lees-McRae College (N.C.).
COLLEGE: Marshall.
TRANSACTIONS/CAREER NOTES: Selected by New England Patriots in eighth round (198th pick overall) of 1993 NFL draft. ... Signed by Patriots (July 16, 1993). ... On injured reserve with quadriceps injury (December 31, 1993-remainder of season). ... Released by Patriots (August 28, 1994). ... Re-signed by Patriots (October 19, 1994). ... Granted unconditional free agency (February 14, 1997). ... Re-signed by Patriots (March 10, 1997).
CHAMPIONSHIP GAME EXPERIENCE: Played in AFC championship game (1996 season). ... Member of Patriots for Super Bowl XXXI (1996 season); inactive.
PRO STATISTICS: 1993—Recovered one fumble. 1994—Recovered two fumbles. 1995—Recovered one fumble for 75 yards and a touchdown. 1997—Rushed once for minus 18 yards.
SINGLE GAME HIGHS (regular season): Receptions—7 (December 21, 1996, vs. New York Giants); yards—125 (October 19, 1997, vs. New York Jets); and touchdown receptions—1 (September 7, 1998, vs. Denver).
STATISTICAL PLATEAUS: 100-yard receiving games: 1997 (2).

			RECEIVING				PUNT RETURNS				KICKOFF RETURNS				TOTALS			
Year Team	G	GS	No.	Yds.	Avg.	TD	No.	Yds.	Avg.	TD	No.	Yds.	Avg.	TD	TD	2pt.	Pts.	Fum.
1993—New England NFL	12	0	2	22	11.0	0	25	224	9.0	0	15	243	16.2	0	0	...	0	2
1994—New England NFL	9	0	0	0	...	0	24	202	8.4	0	1	14	14.0	0	0	0	0	2
1995—New England NFL	16	0	14	159	11.4	0	0	0	...	0	31	672	21.7	0	1	0	6	1
1996—New England NFL	16	0	21	222	10.6	0	0	0	...	0	29	634	21.9	0	0	0	0	0
1997—New England NFL	16	6	41	607	14.8	6	0	0	...	0	0	0	...	0	6	0	36	0
1998—New England NFL	10	0	23	346	15.0	1	17	225	13.2	0	0	0	...	0	1	0	6	0
Pro totals (6 years)	79	6	101	1356	13.4	7	66	651	9.9	0	76	1563	20.6	0	8	0	48	5

BROWNING, JOHN — DE — CHIEFS

PERSONAL: Born September 30, 1973, in Miami. ... 6-4/295.
HIGH SCHOOL: North Miami (Fla.).
COLLEGE: West Virginia.
TRANSACTIONS/CAREER NOTES: Selected by Kansas City Chiefs in third round (68th pick overall) of 1996 NFL draft. ... Signed by Chiefs (July 24, 1996).
PRO STATISTICS: 1997—Recovered one fumble.

Year Team	G	GS	SACKS
1996—Kansas City NFL	13	2	2.0
1997—Kansas City NFL	14	13	4.0
1998—Kansas City NFL	8	8	0.0
Pro totals (3 years)	35	23	6.0

BRUCE, AUNDRAY — DE

PERSONAL: Born April 30, 1966, in Montgomery, Ala. ... 6-5/265. ... Uncle of Ricky Shaw, linebacker with New York Giants (1988 and 1989) and Philadelphia Eagles (1989 and 1990).
HIGH SCHOOL: George Washington Carver (Montgomery, Ala.).
COLLEGE: Auburn.
TRANSACTIONS/CAREER NOTES: Signed by Atlanta Falcons (April 6, 1988). ... Selected officially by Falcons in first round (first pick overall) of 1988 NFL draft. ... Granted unconditional free agency (February 1, 1992). ... Signed by Los Angeles Raiders (February 14, 1992). ... Granted unconditional free agency (February 17, 1995). ... Re-signed by Oakland Raiders (September 6, 1995). ... Raiders franchise moved to Oakland (July 21, 1995). ... Released by Raiders (August 24, 1997). ... Re-signed by Raiders (October 1, 1997). ... Released by Raiders (February 12, 1998). ... Re-signed by Raiders (April 25, 1998). ... Released by Raiders (February 11, 1999).
HONORS: Named linebacker on THE SPORTING NEWS college All-America first team (1987).
PRO STATISTICS: 1989—Returned one kickoff for 15 yards. 1991—Caught one pass for 11 yards. 1993—Recovered one fumble. 1996—Recovered one fumble for three yards.

			INTERCEPTIONS				SACKS
Year Team	G	GS	No.	Yds.	Avg.	TD	No.
1988—Atlanta NFL	16	16	2	10	5.0	0	6.0
1989—Atlanta NFL	16	13	1	0	0.0	0	6.0
1990—Atlanta NFL	16	3	0	0	...	0	4.0
1991—Atlanta NFL	14	2	0	0	...	0	0.0
1992—Los Angeles Raiders NFL	16	4	0	0	...	0	3.5
1993—Los Angeles Raiders NFL	16	0	0	0	...	0	2.0
1994—Los Angeles Raiders NFL	16	0	0	0	...	0	0.0
1995—Oakland NFL	14	0	1	1	1.0	▲1	5.5
1996—Oakland NFL	16	0	0	0	...	0	4.0
1997—Oakland NFL	10	3	0	0	...	0	1.0
1998—Oakland NFL	1	0	0	0	...	0	0.0
Pro totals (11 years)	151	41	4	11	2.8	1	32.0

BRUCE, ISAAC — WR — RAMS

PERSONAL: Born November 10, 1972, in Fort Lauderdale, Fla. ... 6-0/188. ... Full name: Isaac Isidore Bruce. ... Cousin of Derrick Moore, running back with Detroit Lions (1993 and 1994) and Carolina Panthers (1995).
HIGH SCHOOL: Dillard (Fort Lauderdale, Fla.).
JUNIOR COLLEGE: West Los Angeles Junior College, then Santa Monica (Calif.) Junior College.
COLLEGE: Memphis State.
TRANSACTIONS/CAREER NOTES: Selected by Los Angeles Rams in second round (33rd pick overall) of 1994 NFL draft. ... Signed by Rams (July 13, 1994). ... On injured reserve with sprained right knee (December 9, 1994-remainder of season). ... Rams franchise moved to St. Louis (April 12, 1995). ... On injured reserve with hamstring injury (December 9, 1998-remainder of season).
HONORS: Played in Pro Bowl (1996 season).
PRO STATISTICS: 1995—Ran 52 yards with lateral from punt return and recovered one fumble. 1996—Attempted two passes with one completion for 15 yards and one interception.
SINGLE GAME HIGHS (regular season): Receptions—15 (December 24, 1995, vs. Miami); yards—233 (November 2, 1997, vs. Atlanta); and touchdown receptions—2 (December 7, 1997, vs. New Orleans).
STATISTICAL PLATEAUS: 100-yard receiving games: 1995 (9), 1996 (4), 1997 (2), 1998 (2). Total: 17.

			RUSHING				RECEIVING				TOTALS			
Year Team	G	GS	Att.	Yds.	Avg.	TD	No.	Yds.	Avg.	TD	TD	2pt.	Pts.	Fum.
1994—Los Angeles Rams NFL	12	0	1	2	2.0	0	21	272	13.0	3	3	0	18	0
1995—St. Louis NFL	16	16	3	17	5.7	0	119	1781	15.0	13	13	1	80	2
1996—St. Louis NFL	16	16	1	4	4.0	0	84	*1338	15.9	7	7	0	42	1
1997—St. Louis NFL	12	12	0	0	...	0	56	815	14.6	5	5	0	30	1
1998—St. Louis NFL	5	5	1	30	30.0	0	32	457	14.3	1	1	0	6	0
Pro totals (5 years)	61	49	6	53	8.8	0	312	4663	14.9	29	29	1	176	4

BRUENER, MARK — TE — STEELERS

PERSONAL: Born September 16, 1972, in Olympia, Wash. ... 6-4/261. ... Full name: Mark Frederick Bruener. ... Name pronounced BREW-ner.
HIGH SCHOOL: Aberdeen (Wash.).
COLLEGE: Washington (degree in economics).
TRANSACTIONS/CAREER NOTES: Selected by Pittsburgh Steelers in first round (27th pick overall) of 1995 NFL draft. ... Signed by Steelers (July 25, 1995). ... On injured reserve with knee injury (November 29, 1996-remainder of season).
CHAMPIONSHIP GAME EXPERIENCE: Played in AFC championship game (1995 and 1997 seasons). ... Played in Super Bowl XXX (1995 season).
PRO STATISTICS: 1995—Returned two kickoffs for 19 yards. 1998—Lost seven yards with lateral from kickoff return.
SINGLE GAME HIGHS (regular season): Receptions—5 (December 13, 1997, vs. New England); yards—43 (December 13, 1997, vs. New England); and touchdown receptions—1 (November 22, 1998, vs. Jacksonville).

			RECEIVING				TOTALS			
Year Team	G	GS	No.	Yds.	Avg.	TD	TD	2pt.	Pts.	Fum.
1995—Pittsburgh NFL	16	13	26	238	9.2	3	3	0	18	0
1996—Pittsburgh NFL	12	12	12	141	11.8	0	0	1	2	0
1997—Pittsburgh NFL	16	16	18	117	6.5	6	6	0	36	1
1998—Pittsburgh NFL	16	16	19	157	8.3	2	2	0	12	0
Pro totals (4 years)	60	57	75	653	8.7	11	11	1	68	1

BRUNELL, MARK — QB — JAGUARS

PERSONAL: Born September 17, 1970, in Los Angeles. ... 6-1/211. ... Full name: Mark Allen Brunell.
HIGH SCHOOL: St. Joseph (Santa Maria, Calif.).
COLLEGE: Washington (degree in history).
TRANSACTIONS/CAREER NOTES: Selected by Green Bay Packers in fifth round (118th pick overall) of 1993 NFL draft. ... Signed by Packers (July 1, 1993). ... Traded by Packers to Jacksonville Jaguars for third- (FB William Henderson) and fifth-round (RB Travis Jervey) picks in 1995 draft (April 21, 1995).
CHAMPIONSHIP GAME EXPERIENCE: Played in AFC championship game (1996 season).
HONORS: Played in Pro Bowl (1996 and 1997 seasons). ... Named Outstanding Player of Pro Bowl (1996 season).
PRO STATISTICS: 1994—Fumbled once. 1995—Fumbled five times and recovered three fumbles. 1996—Led AFC with 14 fumbles and recovered five fumbles for minus 14 yards. 1997—Fumbled four times for minus five yards. 1998—Fumbled three times and recovered two fumbles for minus one yard.
SINGLE GAME HIGHS (regular season): Attempts—52 (October 20, 1996, vs. St. Louis); completions—37 (October 20, 1996, vs. St. Louis); yards—432 (September 22, 1996, vs. New England); and touchdown passes—4 (November 29, 1998, vs. Cincinnati).
STATISTICAL PLATEAUS: 300-yard passing games: 1995 (2), 1996 (6), 1997 (3), 1998 (2). Total: 13.
MISCELLANEOUS: Regular-season record as starting NFL quarterback: 31-22 (.525). ... Postseason record as starting NFL quarterback: 3-3 (.500). ... Holds Jacksonville Jaguars all-time record for most yards passing (12,417) and most touchdown passes (72).

					PASSING						RUSHING				TOTALS	
Year Team	G	GS	Att.	Cmp.	Pct.	Yds.	TD	Int.	Avg.	Rat.	Att.	Yds.	Avg.	TD	TD	2pt.	Pts.
1993—Green Bay NFL						Did not play.											
1994—Green Bay NFL	2	0	27	12	44.4	95	0	0	3.52	53.8	6	7	1.2	1	1	0	6
1995—Jacksonville NFL	13	10	346	201	58.1	2168	15	7	6.27	82.6	67	480	7.2	4	4	0	24
1996—Jacksonville NFL	16	16	557	353	§63.4	*4367	19	§20	*7.84	84.0	80	396	5.0	3	3	2	22
1997—Jacksonville NFL	14	14	435	264	60.7	3281	18	7	§7.54	§91.2	48	257	5.4	2	2	0	12
1998—Jacksonville NFL	13	13	354	208	58.8	2601	20	9	7.35	89.9	49	192	3.9	0	0	0	0
Pro totals (5 years)	58	53	1719	1038	60.4	12512	72	43	7.28	86.3	250	1332	5.3	10	10	2	64

BRUSCHI, TEDY — LB — PATRIOTS

PERSONAL: Born June 9, 1973, in San Francisco. ... 6-1/245. ... Full name: Tedy Lacap Bruschi. ... Stepson of Ronald Sandys, former professional tennis player. ... Name pronounced BREW-ski.
HIGH SCHOOL: Roseville (Calif.).
COLLEGE: Arizona (degree in communications).
TRANSACTIONS/CAREER NOTES: Selected by New England Patriots in third round (86th pick overall) of 1996 NFL draft. ... Signed by Patriots (July 17, 1996). ... Granted free agency (February 12, 1999).
CHAMPIONSHIP GAME EXPERIENCE: Played in AFC championship game (1996 season). ... Played in Super Bowl XXXI (1996 season).
HONORS: Named defensive lineman on THE SPORTING NEWS college All-America first team (1994 and 1995).
PRO STATISTICS: 1996—Returned blocked punt four yards for a touchdown. 1997—Recovered two fumbles. 1998—Returned one kickoff for four yards.

Year Team	G	GS	SACKS
1996—New England NFL	16	0	4.0
1997—New England NFL	16	1	4.0
1998—New England NFL	16	7	2.0
Pro totals (3 years)	48	8	10.0

BRYANT, JUNIOR — DT — 49ERS

PERSONAL: Born January 16, 1971, in Omaha, Neb. ... 6-4/278. ... Full name: Edward E. Bryant.
HIGH SCHOOL: Creighton Prep (Omaha, Neb.).
COLLEGE: Notre Dame.
TRANSACTIONS/CAREER NOTES: Signed as non-drafted free agent by San Francisco 49ers (May 3, 1993). ... Released by 49ers (August 30, 1993). ... Re-signed by 49ers to practice squad (August 31, 1993). ... Released by 49ers (August 27, 1994). ... Re-signed by 49ers to practice squad (August 31, 1994).
CHAMPIONSHIP GAME EXPERIENCE: Played in NFC championship game (1997 season).
PRO STATISTICS: 1996—Recovered one fumble.

Year Team	G	GS	SACKS
1993—San Francisco NFL		Did not play.	
1994—San Francisco NFL		Did not play.	
1995—San Francisco NFL	16	4	1.0
1996—San Francisco NFL	16	1	0.5
1997—San Francisco NFL	16	3	2.5
1998—San Francisco NFL	16	16	5.0
Pro totals (4 years)	64	24	9.0

BUCHANAN, RAY — CB — FALCONS

PERSONAL: Born September 29, 1971, in Chicago. ... 5-9/185. ... Full name: Raymond Louis Buchanan.
HIGH SCHOOL: Proviso East (Chicago).
COLLEGE: Louisville.
TRANSACTIONS/CAREER NOTES: Selected by Indianapolis Colts in third round (65th pick overall) of 1993 NFL draft. ... Signed by Colts (July 26, 1993). ... Designated by Colts as transition player (February 13, 1997). ... Tendered offer sheet by Atlanta Falcons (February 25, 1997). ... Colts declined to match offer (March 3, 1997).
CHAMPIONSHIP GAME EXPERIENCE: Played in AFC championship game (1995 season). ... Played in NFC championship game (1998 season). ... Played in Super Bowl XXXIII (1998 season).
HONORS: Played in Pro Bowl (1998 season).

PRO STATISTICS: 1994—Credited with one sack and recovered one fumble. 1995—Returned one kickoff for 22 yards, credited with one sack and recovered two fumbles. 1996—Returned one kickoff for 20 yards. 1997—Ran 37 yards with lateral from punt return.

				INTERCEPTIONS				PUNT RETURNS				TOTALS		
Year Team	G	GS	No.	Yds.	Avg.	TD	No.	Yds.	Avg.	TD	TD	2pt.	Pts.	Fum.
1993—Indianapolis NFL	16	5	4	45	11.3	0	0	0	...	0	0	...	0	0
1994—Indianapolis NFL	16	16	8	221	27.6	†3	0	0	...	0	3	0	18	0
1995—Indianapolis NFL	16	16	2	60	30.0	0	16	113	7.1	0	0	0	0	1
1996—Indianapolis NFL	13	13	2	32	16.0	0	12	201	16.8	0	0	0	0	0
1997—Atlanta NFL	16	16	5	49	9.8	0	0	37	...	0	0	0	0	0
1998—Atlanta NFL	16	16	7	102	14.6	0	1	4	4.0	0	0	0	0	0
Pro totals (6 years)	93	82	28	509	18.2	3	29	355	12.2	0	3	0	18	1

BUCKEY, JEFF   OT   BROWNS

PERSONAL: Born August 7, 1974, in Bakersfield, Calif. ... 6-5/305. ... Full name: Jeffery Michael Buckey.
HIGH SCHOOL: Bakersfield (Calif.).
COLLEGE: Stanford (degree in economics).
TRANSACTIONS/CAREER NOTES: Selected by Miami Dolphins in seventh round (230th pick overall) of 1996 NFL draft. ... Signed by Dolphins for 1996 season. ... On injured reserve with back injury (November 11, 1998-remainder of season). ... Selected by Cleveland Browns from Dolphins in NFL expansion draft (February 9, 1999). ... Granted free agency (February 12, 1999).
PLAYING EXPERIENCE: Miami NFL, 1996-1998. ... Games/Games started: 1996 (15/1), 1997 (16/12), 1998 (7/0). Totals: 38/13.

BUCKLEY, CURTIS   S   GIANTS

PERSONAL: Born September 25, 1970, in Oakdale, Calif. ... 6-0/182. ... Full name: Curtis LaDonn Buckley.
HIGH SCHOOL: Silsbee (Texas).
JUNIOR COLLEGE: Kilgore (Texas) College.
COLLEGE: East Texas State.
TRANSACTIONS/CAREER NOTES: Signed as non-drafted free agent by Tampa Bay Buccaneers (May 3, 1993). ... Released by Buccaneers (August 30, 1993). ... Re-signed by Buccaneers (August 31, 1993). ... Released by Buccaneers (September 7, 1993). ... Re-signed by Buccaneers to practice squad (September 9, 1993). ... Activated (November 5, 1993). ... Released by Buccaneers (August 30, 1994). ... Re-signed by Buccaneers (September 7, 1994). ... Released by Buccaneers (September 17, 1994). ... Re-signed by Buccaneers (September 30, 1994). ... Granted free agency (February 16, 1996). ... Tendered offer sheet by San Francisco 49ers (February 21, 1996). ... Buccaneers declined to match offer (February 28, 1996). ... Claimed on waivers by New York Giants (November 13, 1998).
CHAMPIONSHIP GAME EXPERIENCE: Played in NFC championship game (1997 season).
PRO STATISTICS: 1994—Recovered two fumbles. 1996—Recovered two fumbles. 1997—Recovered one fumble.

			KICKOFF RETURNS				TOTALS			
Year Team	G	GS	No.	Yds.	Avg.	TD	TD	2pt.	Pts.	Fum.
1993—Tampa Bay NFL	10	2	0	0	...	0	0	...	0	0
1994—Tampa Bay NFL	13	0	8	177	22.1	0	0	0	0	1
1995—Tampa Bay NFL	15	0	2	29	14.5	0	0	0	0	0
1996—San Francisco NFL	15	0	0	0	...	0	0	0	0	0
1997—San Francisco NFL	15	0	0	0	...	0	0	0	0	0
1998—San Francisco NFL	8	0	0	0	...	0	0	0	0	0
—New York Giants NFL	6	0	0	0	...	0	0	0	0	0
Pro totals (6 years)	82	2	10	206	20.6	0	0	0	0	1

BUCKLEY, MARCUS   LB   GIANTS

PERSONAL: Born February 3, 1971, in Fort Worth, Texas. ... 6-3/240. ... Full name: Marcus Wayne Buckley.
HIGH SCHOOL: Eastern Hills (Fort Worth, Texas).
COLLEGE: Texas A&M.
TRANSACTIONS/CAREER NOTES: Selected by New York Giants in third round (66th pick overall) of 1993 NFL draft. ... Signed by Giants (July 23, 1993). ... Granted free agency (February 16, 1996). ... Re-signed by Giants (April 15, 1996). ... Granted unconditional free agency (February 13, 1998). ... Re-signed by Giants (February 19, 1998).
PLAYING EXPERIENCE: New York Giants NFL, 1993-1998. ... Games/Games started: 1993 (16/2), 1994 (16/1), 1995 (16/5), 1996 (15/2), 1997 (12/3), 1998 (14/12). Total: 89/25.
HONORS: Named linebacker on THE SPORTING NEWS college All-America first team (1992).
PRO STATISTICS: 1993—Recovered one fumble. 1995—Recovered one fumble. 1997—Recovered one fumble. 1998—Intercepted one pass for no yards, credited with 1 1/2 sacks and recovered one fumble.

BUCKLEY, TERRELL   CB   DOLPHINS

PERSONAL: Born June 7, 1971, in Pascagoula, Miss. ... 5-10/180. ... Full name: Douglas Terrell Buckley.
HIGH SCHOOL: Pascagoula (Miss.).
COLLEGE: Florida State.
TRANSACTIONS/CAREER NOTES: Selected after junior season by Green Bay Packers in first round (fifth pick overall) of 1992 NFL draft. ... Signed by Packers (September 11, 1992). ... Granted roster exemption for one game (September 1992). ... Traded by Packers to Miami Dolphins for past considerations (April 3, 1995).
HONORS: Named defensive back on THE SPORTING NEWS college All-America second team (1990). ... Jim Thorpe Award winner (1991). ... Named defensive back on THE SPORTING NEWS college All-America first team (1991).
PRO STATISTICS: 1992—Recovered four fumbles. 1994—Recovered one fumble. 1995—Returned one kickoff for 16 yards. 1996—Returned one kickoff for 48 yards and recovered two fumbles. 1997—Recovered two fumbles for 23 yards and one touchdown. 1998—Recovered two fumbles.

Year Team	G	GS	INTERCEPTIONS No.	Yds.	Avg.	TD	PUNT RETURNS No.	Yds.	Avg.	TD	TOTALS TD	2pt.	Pts.	Fum.
1992—Green Bay NFL	14	12	3	33	11.0	1	21	211	10.0	1	2	...	12	7
1993—Green Bay NFL	16	16	2	31	15.5	0	11	76	6.9	0	0	...	0	1
1994—Green Bay NFL	16	16	5	38	7.6	0	0	0	...	0	0	0	0	0
1995—Miami NFL	16	4	1	0	0.0	0	0	0	...	0	0	0	0	0
1996—Miami NFL	16	16	6	*164	27.3	1	3	24	8.0	0	1	0	6	1
1997—Miami NFL	16	16	4	26	6.5	0	4	58	14.5	0	1	0	6	0
1998—Miami NFL	16	16	8	157	19.6	1	29	354	12.2	0	1	0	6	1
Pro totals (7 years)	110	96	29	449	15.5	3	68	723	10.6	1	5	0	30	10

BUCKNER, BRENTSON   DE   49ERS

PERSONAL: Born September 30, 1971, in Columbus, Ga. ... 6-2/305. ... Full name: Brentson Andre Buckner. ... Name pronounced BRENT-son.
HIGH SCHOOL: Carver (Columbus, Ga.).
COLLEGE: Clemson (degree in English, 1993).
TRANSACTIONS/CAREER NOTES: Selected by Pittsburgh Steelers in second round (50th pick overall) of 1994 NFL draft. ... Signed by Steelers (July 23, 1994). ... Traded by Steelers to Kansas City Chiefs for seventh-round pick (traded to San Diego) in 1997 draft (April 4, 1997). ... Claimed on waivers by Cincinnati Bengals (August 25, 1997). ... Granted unconditional free agency (February 13, 1998). ... Signed by San Francisco 49ers (May 26, 1998). ... On physically unable to perform list with pulled quadricep muscle (July 17-August 15, 1998). ... Granted unconditional free agency (February 12, 1999). ... Re-signed by 49ers (April 7, 1999).
CHAMPIONSHIP GAME EXPERIENCE: Played in AFC championship game (1994 and 1995 seasons). ... Played in Super Bowl XXX (1995 season).
PRO STATISTICS: 1994—Recovered one fumble. 1995—Recovered one fumble for 46 yards and a touchdown. 1996—Fumbled once and recovered one fumble for 13 yards. 1998—Recovered one fumble.

Year Team	G	GS	SACKS
1994—Pittsburgh NFL	13	5	2.0
1995—Pittsburgh NFL	16	16	3.0
1996—Pittsburgh NFL	15	14	3.0
1997—Cincinnati NFL	14	5	0.0
1998—San Francisco NFL	13	0	0.5
Pro totals (5 years)	71	40	8.5

BURGER, TODD   G

PERSONAL: Born March 20, 1970, in Clark, N.J. ... 6-3/303. ... Full name: Todd R. Burger.
HIGH SCHOOL: A.L. Johnson Regional (Clark, N.J.).
COLLEGE: Penn State.
TRANSACTIONS/CAREER NOTES: Signed as non-drafted free agent by Chicago Bears (April 29, 1993). ... Released by Bears (August 30, 1993). ... Re-signed by Bears to practice squad (August 31, 1993). ... Activated (December 12, 1993); did not play. ... Granted free agency (February 14, 1997). ... Re-signed by Bears (March 7, 1997). ... Granted unconditional free agency (February 13, 1998). ... Signed by New York Jets (February 25, 1998). ... Released by Jets (March 29, 1999).
PLAYING EXPERIENCE: Chicago NFL, 1994-1997; New York Jets NFL, 1998. ... Games/Games started: 1994 (4/0); 1995 (16/1); 1996 (11/8); 1997 (15/15), 1998 (16/16). Total: 62/40.
CHAMPIONSHIP GAME EXPERIENCE: Played in AFC championship game (1998 season).
PRO STATISTICS: 1996—Recovered one fumble. 1997—Recovered one fumble. 1998—Recovered two fumbles.

BURGESS, JAMES   LB

PERSONAL: Born March 31, 1974, in Miami. ... 5-11/230. ... Full name: James Paul Burgess. ... Half-brother of Fernanza Burgess, wide receiver with New York Jets (1984) and Miami Dolphins (1984).
HIGH SCHOOL: Homestead (Fla.).
COLLEGE: Miami (Fla.).
TRANSACTIONS/CAREER NOTES: Signed as non-drafted free agent by Kansas City Chiefs (April 25, 1997). ... Released by Chiefs (August 19, 1997). ... Signed by Dallas Cowboys to practice squad (August 28, 1997). ... Signed by San Diego Chargers off Cowboys practice squad (September 2, 1997). ... Released by Chargers (February 12, 1999).
PLAYING EXPERIENCE: San Diego NFL, 1997 and 1998. ... Games/Games started: 1997 (15/4), 1998 (16/0). Total: 31/4.

BURKE, JOHN   TE   CHARGERS

PERSONAL: Born September 7, 1971, in Elizabeth, N.J. ... 6-3/248. ... Full name: John Richard Burke.
HIGH SCHOOL: Holmdel (N.J.).
COLLEGE: Virginia Tech.
TRANSACTIONS/CAREER NOTES: Selected by New England Patriots in fourth round (121st pick overall) of 1994 NFL draft. ... Signed by Patriots (May 25, 1994). ... Granted free agency (February 14, 1997). ... Re-signed by Patriots (June 20, 1997). ... Claimed on waivers by New York Jets (August 25, 1997). ... Granted unconditional free agency (February 13, 1998). ... Signed by San Diego Chargers (April 13, 1998).
CHAMPIONSHIP GAME EXPERIENCE: Played in AFC championship game (1996 season). ... Played in Super Bowl XXXI (1996 season).
PRO STATISTICS: 1995—Recovered one fumble.
SINGLE GAME HIGHS (regular season): Receptions—4 (October 8, 1995, vs. Denver); yards—41 (December 18, 1994, vs. Buffalo); and touchdown receptions—0.

Year Team	G	GS	RECEIVING No.	Yds.	Avg.	TD	KICKOFF RETURNS No.	Yds.	Avg.	TD	TOTALS TD	2pt.	Pts.	Fum.
1994—New England NFL	16	6	9	86	9.6	0	3	11	3.7	0	0	0	0	0
1995—New England NFL	16	4	15	136	9.1	0	1	7	7.0	0	0	0	0	0
1996—New England NFL	11	2	1	19	19.0	0	0	0	...	0	0	0	0	0
1997—New York Jets NFL	7	1	0	0	...	0	0	0	...	0	0	0	0	0
1998—San Diego NFL	10	6	3	32	10.7	0	1	5	5.0	0	0	0	0	0
Pro totals (5 years)	60	19	28	273	9.8	0	5	23	4.6	0	0	0	0	0

BURNETT, CHESTER   LB   REDSKINS

PERSONAL: Born April 15, 1975, in Denver. ... 5-10/238. ... Full name: Chester Dean Burnett.
HIGH SCHOOL: Mullen (Denver).
COLLEGE: Arizona.
TRANSACTIONS/CAREER NOTES: Selected by Minnesota Vikings in seventh round (208th pick overall) of 1998 NFL draft. ... Signed by Vikings (July 14, 1998). ... On physically unable to perform list with knee injury (July 27-August 3, 1998). ... Released by Vikings (August 30, 1998). ... Signed by Washington Redskins to practice squad (October 7, 1998). ... Activated (November 27, 1998).
PLAYING EXPERIENCE: Washington NFL, 1998. ... Games/Games started: 5/0.
PRO STATISTICS: 1998—Returned one kickoff for five yards.

BURNETT, ROB   DE   RAVENS

PERSONAL: Born August 27, 1967, in Livingston, N.J. ... 6-4/280. ... Full name: Robert Barry Burnett.
HIGH SCHOOL: Newfield (Selden, N.Y.).
COLLEGE: Syracuse (degree in economics).
TRANSACTIONS/CAREER NOTES: Selected by Cleveland Browns in fifth round (129th pick overall) of 1990 NFL draft. ... Signed by Browns (July 22, 1990). ... Granted free agency (March 1, 1993). ... Re-signed by Browns (June 11, 1993). ... Browns franchise moved to Baltimore and renamed Ravens for 1996 season (March 11, 1996).
HONORS: Played in Pro Bowl (1994 season).
PRO STATISTICS: 1991—Recovered one fumble for nine yards. 1992—Recovered two fumbles. 1993—Recovered two fumbles. 1994—Recovered one fumble. 1995—Recovered one fumble. 1997—Recovered one fumble. 1998—Credited with a safety and recovered one fumble.

Year—Team	G	GS	SACKS
1990—Cleveland NFL	16	6	2.0
1991—Cleveland NFL	13	8	3.0
1992—Cleveland NFL	16	16	9.0
1993—Cleveland NFL	16	16	9.0
1994—Cleveland NFL	16	16	10.0
1995—Cleveland NFL	16	16	7.5
1996—Baltimore NFL	6	6	3.0
1997—Baltimore NFL	15	15	4.0
1998—Baltimore NFL	16	16	2.5
Pro totals (9 years)	130	115	50.0

BURNS, KEITH   LB   BEARS

PERSONAL: Born May 16, 1972, in Greelyville, S.C. ... 6-2/245. ... Full name: Keith Bernard Burns.
HIGH SCHOOL: T. C. Williams (Alexandria, Va.).
JUNIOR COLLEGE: Navarro College (Texas).
COLLEGE: Oklahoma State.
TRANSACTIONS/CAREER NOTES: Selected by Denver Broncos in seventh round (210th pick overall) of 1994 NFL draft. ... Signed by Broncos (July 12, 1994). ... Granted free agency (February 14, 1997). ... Re-signed by Broncos (June 30, 1997). ... Granted unconditional free agency (February 12, 1999). ... Signed by Chicago Bears (April 6, 1999).
PLAYING EXPERIENCE: Denver NFL, 1994-1998. ... Games/Games started: 1994 (11/1), 1995 (16/0), 1996 (16/0), 1997 (16/0), 1998 (16/0). Total: 75/1.
CHAMPIONSHIP GAME EXPERIENCE: Played in AFC championship game (1997 and 1998 seasons). ... Member of Super Bowl championship team (1997 and 1998 seasons).
PRO STATISTICS: 1995—Credited with 1 1/2 sacks, returned one kickoff for five yards and recovered two fumbles. 1997—Returned four kickoffs for 45 yards. 1998—Returned two kickoffs for 17 yards, fumbled once and recovered one fumble.

BURRIS, JEFF   DB   COLTS

PERSONAL: Born June 7, 1972, in Rock Hill, S.C. ... 6-0/190. ... Full name: Jeffrey Lamar Burris.
HIGH SCHOOL: Northwestern (Rock Hill, S.C.).
COLLEGE: Notre Dame.
TRANSACTIONS/CAREER NOTES: Selected by Buffalo Bills in first round (27th pick overall) of 1994 NFL draft. ... Signed by Bills (July 18, 1994). ... On injured reserve with knee injury (November 20, 1995-remainder of season). ... Granted unconditional free agency (February 13, 1998). ... Signed by Indianapolis Colts (February 18, 1998).
HONORS: Named defensive back on THE SPORTING NEWS college All-America second team (1993).
PRO STATISTICS: 1994—Recovered one fumble. 1996—Recovered one fumble. 1997—Returned one kickoff for 10 yards and recovered one fumble.

			INTERCEPTIONS				PUNT RETURNS				TOTALS			
Year—Team	G	GS	No.	Yds.	Avg.	TD	No.	Yds.	Avg.	TD	TD	2pt.	Pts.	Fum.
1994—Buffalo NFL	16	0	2	24	12.0	0	32	332	10.4	0	0	0	0	2
1995—Buffalo NFL	9	9	1	19	19.0	0	20	229	11.5	0	0	0	0	0
1996—Buffalo NFL	15	15	1	28	28.0	0	27	286	10.6	0	0	0	0	1
1997—Buffalo NFL	14	14	2	19	9.5	0	21	198	9.4	0	0	0	0	3
1998—Indianapolis NFL	14	14	1	0	0.0	0	0	0	...	0	0	0	0	0
Pro totals (5 years)	68	52	7	90	12.9	0	100	1045	10.5	0	0	0	0	6

BURROUGH, JOHN DE VIKINGS

PERSONAL: Born May 17, 1972, in Laramie, Wyo. ... 6-5/275.
HIGH SCHOOL: Pinedale (Wyo.).
COLLEGE: Wyoming.
TRANSACTIONS/CAREER NOTES: Selected by Atlanta Falcons in seventh round (245th pick overall) of 1995 NFL draft. ... Signed by Falcons (June 30, 1995). ... Granted free agency (February 13, 1998). ... Re-signed by Falcons (April 1, 1998). ... Granted unconditional free agency (February 12, 1999). ... Signed by Minnesota Vikings (February 18, 1999).
PLAYING EXPERIENCE: Atlanta NFL, 1995-1998. ... Games/Games started: 1995 (16/0), 1996 (16/1), 1997 (16/1), 1998 (16/3). Total: 64/5.
CHAMPIONSHIP GAME EXPERIENCE: Played in NFC championship game (1998 season). ... Played in Super Bowl XXXIII (1998 season).
PRO STATISTICS: 1997—Returned one kickoff for six yards and credited with one sack. 1998—Credited with $1/2$ sack and recovered one fumble.

BURTON, SHANE DT DOLPHINS

PERSONAL: Born January 18, 1974, in Logan, W.Va. ... 6-6/305. ... Full name: Franklin Shane Burton.
HIGH SCHOOL: Bandys (Catawba, N.C.).
COLLEGE: Tennessee.
TRANSACTIONS/CAREER NOTES: Selected by Miami Dolphins in fifth round (150th pick overall) of 1996 NFL draft. ... Signed by Dolphins (June 18, 1996). ... Granted free agency (February 12, 1999). ... Re-signed by Dolphins (April 13, 1999).
PRO STATISTICS: 1996—Recovered one fumble. 1997—Recovered one fumble. 1998—Recovered one fumble.

Year Team	G	GS	SACKS
1996—Miami NFL	16	8	3.0
1997—Miami NFL	16	4	4.0
1998—Miami NFL	15	0	2.0
Pro totals (3 years)	47	12	9.0

BUSH, DEVIN S RAMS

PERSONAL: Born July 3, 1973, in Miami. ... 5-11/210.
HIGH SCHOOL: Hialeah (Fla.) Miami Lakes.
COLLEGE: Florida State.
TRANSACTIONS/CAREER NOTES: Selected after junior season by Atlanta Falcons in first round (26th pick overall) of 1995 NFL draft. ... Signed by Falcons (August 8, 1995). ... Granted unconditional free agency (February 12, 1999). ... Signed by St. Louis Rams (February 19, 1999).
CHAMPIONSHIP GAME EXPERIENCE: Member of Falcons for NFC championship game (1998 season); inactive. ... Played in Super Bowl XXXIII (1998 season).
PRO STATISTICS: 1995—Recovered one fumble. 1996—Recovered one fumble. 1997—Recovered one fumble.

			INTERCEPTIONS			
Year Team	G	GS	No.	Yds.	Avg.	TD
1995—Atlanta NFL	11	5	1	0	0.0	0
1996—Atlanta NFL	16	15	1	2	2.0	0
1997—Atlanta NFL	16	16	1	4	4.0	0
1998—Atlanta NFL	13	0	0	0	...	0
Pro totals (4 years)	56	36	3	6	2.0	0

BUSH, LEW LB CHARGERS

PERSONAL: Born December 2, 1969, in Atlanta. ... 6-2/245. ... Full name: Lewis Fitzgerald Bush.
HIGH SCHOOL: Washington (Tacoma, Wash.).
COLLEGE: Washington State.
TRANSACTIONS/CAREER NOTES: Selected by San Diego Chargers in fourth round (99th pick overall) of 1993 NFL draft. ... Signed by Chargers (July 9, 1993). ... Granted free agency (February 16, 1996). ... Re-signed by Chargers (June 14, 1996). ... Granted unconditional free agency (February 14, 1997). ... Re-signed by Chargers (May 13, 1997). ... On injured reserve with knee injury (December 26, 1998-remainder of season).
PLAYING EXPERIENCE: San Diego NFL, 1993-1998. ... Games/Games started: 1993 (16/0), 1994 (16/0), 1995 (16/15), 1996 (16/16), 1997 (14/13), 1998 (10/10). Total: 88/54.
CHAMPIONSHIP GAME EXPERIENCE: Played in AFC championship game (1994 season). ... Played in Super Bowl XXIX (1994 season).
PRO STATISTICS: 1994—Recovered one fumble. 1995—Intercepted one pass and recovered two fumbles. 1996—Credited with one sack and recovered two fumbles. 1998—Credited with one sack.

BUSH, STEVE TE/FB BENGALS

PERSONAL: Born July 4, 1974, in Phoenix. ... 6-3/258. ... Full name: Steven Jack Bush.
HIGH SCHOOL: Paradise Valley (Phoenix).
COLLEGE: Arizona State.
TRANSACTIONS/CAREER NOTES: Signed as non-drafted free agent by Cincinnati Bengals (April 25, 1997).
SINGLE GAME HIGHS (regular season): Receptions—1 (November 29, 1998, vs. Jacksonville); yards—18 (November 22, 1998, vs. Baltimore); and touchdown receptions—0.

			RECEIVING				TOTALS			
Year Team	G	GS	No.	Yds.	Avg.	TD	TD	2pt.	Pts.	Fum.
1997—Cincinnati NFL	16	0	0	0	...	0	0	0	0	0
1998—Cincinnati NFL	12	2	4	39	9.8	0	0	0	0	0
Pro totals (2 years)	28	2	4	39	9.8	0	0	0	0	0

BUTLER, DUANE — DB — BROWNS

PERSONAL: Born November 29, 1973, in Trotwood, Ohio. ... 6-1/203.
HIGH SCHOOL: Madison (Trotwood, Ohio).
COLLEGE: Eastern Michigan, then Illinois State.
TRANSACTIONS/CAREER NOTES: Signed as a non-drafted free agent by New York Jets (April 25, 1997). ... Released by Jets (August 10, 1997). ... Signed by Minnesota Vikings (August 13, 1997). ... Released by Vikings (August 18, 1997). ... Re-signed by Vikings to practice squad (August 25, 1997). ... Activated (October 8, 1997). ... Released by Vikings (November 13, 1997). ... Re-signed by Vikings to practice squad (November 14, 1997). ... Activated (November 26, 1997). ... Assigned by Vikings to England Monarchs in 1998 NFL Europe enhancement allocation program (February 18, 1998). ... Selected by Cleveland Browns from Vikings in NFL expansion draft (February 9, 1999).
PLAYING EXPERIENCE: Minnesota NFL, 1997 and 1998; England Monarchs NFLE, 1998. ... Games/Games started: 1997 (3/0), NFLE 1998 (games played unavailable), NFL 1998 (14/0). Total NFL: 17/0.
CHAMPIONSHIP GAME EXPERIENCE: Played in NFC championship game (1998 season).

BUTLER, HILLARY — LB — SEAHAWKS

PERSONAL: Born January 5, 1971, in San Francisco ... 6-2/244.
HIGH SCHOOL: Lakes (Tacoma, Wash.).
COLLEGE: Washington (degree in public relations).
TRANSACTIONS/CAREER NOTES: Signed as non-drafted free agent by Seattle Seahawks (April 26, 1994). ... Released by Seahawks (August 23, 1994). ... Signed by Jacksonville Jaguars (December 15, 1994); did not play. ... Released by Jaguars (August 20, 1995). ... Played for Frankfurt Galaxy of World League (1996-1997). ... Signed by San Francisco 49ers (July 11, 1997). ... Released by 49ers (August 20, 1997). ... Signed by Denver Broncos to practice squad (September 24, 1997). ... Released by Broncos (August 30, 1998). ... Re-signed by Broncos to practice squad (August 31, 1998). ... Released by Broncos (September 8, 1998). ... Re-signed by Broncos to practice squad (September 23, 1998). ... Released by Broncos (October 30, 1998). ... Signed by Seattle Seahawks to practice squad (November 4, 1998). ... Activated (November 6, 1998).
PLAYING EXPERIENCE: Frankfurt Galaxy W.L., 1996 and 1997; Frankfurt NFLE, 1998; Seattle NFL, 1998. ... Games/Games started: 1996 (games played unavailable), 1997 (-), NFLE 1998 (-), NFL 1998 (7/0).
PRO STATISTICS: NFLE: 1998—Credited with one sack.

BUTLER, LeROY — S — PACKERS

PERSONAL: Born July 19, 1968, in Jacksonville. ... 6-0/198. ... Full name: LeRoy Butler III.
HIGH SCHOOL: Robert E. Lee Senior (Jacksonville).
COLLEGE: Florida State.
TRANSACTIONS/CAREER NOTES: Selected by Green Bay Packers in second round (48th pick overall) of 1990 NFL draft. ... Signed by Packers (July 25, 1990). ... On suspended list (December 9, 1992). ... Designated by Packers as transition player (February 15, 1994).
CHAMPIONSHIP GAME EXPERIENCE: Played in NFC championship game (1995-97 seasons). ... Member of Super Bowl championship team (1996 season). ... Played in Super Bowl XXXII (1997 season).
HONORS: Named strong safety on THE SPORTING NEWS NFL All-Pro team (1993 and 1996-1998). ... Played in Pro Bowl (1993 and 1996-1998 seasons).
PRO STATISTICS: 1991—Recovered one fumble. 1992—Recovered one fumble for 17 yards. 1993—Ran 25 yards with lateral from fumble recovery for a touchdown. 1996—Recovered two fumbles for two yards. 1997—Recovered one fumble. 1998—Recovered two fumbles for 32 yards and one touchdown.

				INTERCEPTIONS				SACKS
Year Team		G	GS	No.	Yds.	Avg.	TD	No.
1990—Green Bay NFL		16	0	3	42	14.0	0	0.0
1991—Green Bay NFL		16	16	3	6	2.0	0	0.0
1992—Green Bay NFL		15	15	1	0	0.0	0	0.0
1993—Green Bay NFL		16	16	6	131	21.8	0	1.0
1994—Green Bay NFL		13	13	3	68	22.7	0	1.0
1995—Green Bay NFL		16	16	5	105	21.0	0	1.0
1996—Green Bay NFL		16	16	5	149	29.8	1	6.5
1997—Green Bay NFL		16	16	5	4	0.8	0	3.0
1998—Green Bay NFL		16	16	3	3	1.0	0	4.0
Pro totals (9 years)		140	124	34	508	14.9	1	16.5

BYARS, KEITH — FB

PERSONAL: Born October 14, 1963, in Dayton, Ohio. ... 6-1/255. ... Full name: Keith Alan Byars.
HIGH SCHOOL: Nettie Lee Roth (Dayton, Ohio).
COLLEGE: Ohio State.
TRANSACTIONS/CAREER NOTES: Selected by New Jersey Generals in 1986 USFL territorial draft. ... Selected by Philadelphia Eagles in first round (10th pick overall) of 1986 NFL draft. ... Signed by Eagles (July 25, 1986). ... Granted free agency (February 1, 1990). ... Re-signed by Eagles (August 10, 1990). ... Granted unconditional free agency (March 1, 1993). ... Signed by Miami Dolphins (July 15, 1993). ... On injured reserve with knee injury (November 9, 1994-remainder of season). ... Released by Dolphins (February 15, 1996). ... Re-signed by Dolphins (March 21, 1996). ... Released by Dolphins (October 1, 1996). ... Signed by New England Patriots (October 15, 1996). ... Granted unconditional free agency (February 13, 1998). ... Signed by New York Jets (February 25, 1998). ... Granted unconditional free agency (February 12, 1999).
CHAMPIONSHIP GAME EXPERIENCE: Played in AFC championship game (1996 and 1998 seasons). ... Played in Super Bowl XXXI (1996 season).
HONORS: Named running back on THE SPORTING NEWS college All-America first team (1984). ... Played in Pro Bowl (1993 season).
PRO STATISTICS: 1986—Attempted two passes with one completion for 55 yards and a touchdown, returned two kickoffs for 47 yards and recovered two fumbles. 1987—Recovered two fumbles. 1988—Attempted two passes without a completion, returned two kickoffs for 20 yards and recovered two fumbles for 14 yards. 1989—Recovered four fumbles for six yards and returned one kickoff for 27 yards. 1990—Attempted four passes with four completions for 53 yards and four touchdowns and recovered one fumble. 1991—Attempted two passes without a completion and with one interception. 1992—Attempted one pass without a completion and recovered one fumble. 1993—Attempted two passes with one completion for 11 yards and a touchdown.

SINGLE GAME HIGHS (regular season): Attempts—24 (December 7, 1986, vs. St. Louis); yards—127 (December 7, 1986, vs. St. Louis); and rushing touchdowns—2 (October 29, 1989, vs. Denver).
STATISTICAL PLATEAUS: 100-yard rushing games: 1986 (1), 1987 (1). Total: 2. ... 100-yard receiving games: 1989 (2), 1990 (2), 1991 (1). Total: 5.

				RUSHING				RECEIVING				TOTALS			
Year Team	G	GS	Att.	Yds.	Avg.	TD	No.	Yds.	Avg.	TD	TD	2pt.	Pts.	Fum.
1986—Philadelphia NFL	16	8	177	577	3.3	1	11	44	4.0	0	1	...	6	3
1987—Philadelphia NFL	10	8	116	426	3.7	3	21	177	8.4	1	4	...	24	3
1988—Philadelphia NFL	16	16	152	517	3.4	6	72	705	9.8	4	10	...	60	5
1989—Philadelphia NFL	16	15	133	452	3.4	5	68	721	10.6	0	5	...	30	4
1990—Philadelphia NFL	16	15	37	141	3.8	0	81	819	10.1	3	3	...	18	4
1991—Philadelphia NFL	16	16	94	383	4.1	1	62	564	9.1	3	4	...	24	5
1992—Philadelphia NFL	15	15	41	176	4.3	1	56	502	9.0	2	3	...	18	1
1993—Miami NFL	16	16	64	269	4.2	3	61	613	10.0	3	6	...	36	3
1994—Miami NFL	9	9	19	64	3.4	2	49	418	8.5	5	7	0	42	0
1995—Miami NFL	16	16	15	44	2.9	1	51	362	7.1	2	3	0	18	0
1996—Miami NFL	4	4	0	0	...	0	5	40	8.0	0	0	0	0	0
—New England NFL	10	6	2	2	1.0	0	27	249	9.2	2	2	1	14	0
1997—New England NFL	16	8	11	24	2.2	0	20	189	9.5	3	0	0	18	1
1998—New York Jets NFL	13	9	4	34	8.5	0	26	258	9.9	3	3	0	18	0
Pro totals (13 years)	189	161	865	3109	3.6	23	610	5661	9.3	31	54	1	326	29

BYNUM, KENNY — RB — CHARGERS

PERSONAL: Born May 29, 1974, in Gainesville, Fla. ... 5-11/191. ... Full name: Kenneth Bernard Bynum.
HIGH SCHOOL: Gainesville (Fla.).
COLLEGE: South Carolina State.
TRANSACTIONS/CAREER NOTES: Selected by San Diego Chargers in fifth round (138th pick overall) of 1997 NFL draft. ... Signed by Chargers (June 16, 1997). ... Assigned by Chargers to Rhein Fire in 1999 NFL Europe enhancement allocation program (February 22, 1999).
PRO STATISTICS: 1998—Recovered two fumbles.
SINGLE GAME HIGHS (regular season): Attempts—11 (November 23, 1997, vs. San Francisco); yards—64 (November 23, 1997, vs. San Francisco); and rushing touchdowns—0.

			RUSHING				RECEIVING				KICKOFF RETURNS				TOTALS			
Year Team	G	GS	Att.	Yds.	Avg.	TD	No.	Yds.	Avg.	TD	No.	Yds.	Avg.	TD	TD	2pt.	Pts.	Fum.
1997—San Diego NFL	13	0	30	97	3.2	0	2	4	2.0	0	38	814	21.4	0	0	0	0	0
1998—San Diego NFL	10	0	11	23	2.1	0	4	27	6.8	0	19	345	18.2	0	0	0	0	3
Pro totals (2 years)	23	0	41	120	2.9	0	6	31	5.2	0	57	1159	20.3	0	0	0	0	3

BYRD, ISAAC — WR — TITANS

PERSONAL: Born November 16, 1974, in St. Louis. ... 6-1/188. ... Full name: Isaac Byrd III. ... Brother of Israel Byrd, cornerback, Tennessee Titans.
HIGH SCHOOL: Parkway Central (Chesterfield, Mo.).
COLLEGE: Kansas.
TRANSACTIONS/CAREER NOTES: Selected by Kansas City Chiefs in sixth round (195th pick overall) of 1997 NFL draft. ... Signed by Chiefs (May 6, 1997). ... Released by Chiefs (August 23, 1997). ... Re-signed by Chiefs to practice squad (August 25, 1997). ... Signed by Tennessee Oilers off Chiefs practice squad (November 7, 1997). ... Oilers franchise renamed Tennessee Titans for 1999 season (December 26, 1998).
PRO STATISTICS: 1998—Recovered one fumble.
SINGLE GAME HIGHS (regular season): Receptions—5 (October 18, 1998, vs. Cincinnati); yards—53 (October 18, 1998, vs. Cincinnati); and touchdown receptions—0.
MISCELLANEOUS: Selected by San Diego Padres organization in 24th round of free-agent draft (June 3, 1993).

			RECEIVING				TOTALS			
Year Team	G	GS	No.	Yds.	Avg.	TD	TD	2pt.	Pts.	Fum.
1997—Tennessee NFL	2	0	0	0	...	0	0	0	0	0
1998—Tennessee NFL	4	3	6	71	11.8	0	0	0	0	0
Pro totals (2 years)	6	3	6	71	11.8	0	0	0	0	0

RECORD AS BASEBALL PLAYER

TRANSACTIONS/CAREER NOTES: Batted right, threw right. ... Selected by San Diego Padres organization in 24th round of free-agent draft (June 3, 1993); did not sign. ... Selected by St. Louis Cardinals organization in 11th round of free agent draft (June 2, 1996).

					BATTING								FIELDING		
Year Team (League)	Pos.	G	AB	R	H	2B	3B	HR	RBI	Avg.	BB	SO	SB	PO	A	E	Avg.
1996—Johnson City (Appal.)	OF	24	94	16	26	6	1	2	15	.277	8	19	5	37	1	1	.974

CADREZ, GLENN — LB — BRONCOS

PERSONAL: Born January 2, 1970, in El Centro, Calif. ... 6-3/240. ... Full name: Glenn E. Cadrez. ... Name pronounced kuh-DREZ.
HIGH SCHOOL: Central Union (El Centro, Calif.).
JUNIOR COLLEGE: Chaffey College (Calif.).
COLLEGE: Houston.
TRANSACTIONS/CAREER NOTES: Selected by New York Jets in sixth round (154th pick overall) of 1992 NFL draft. ... Signed by Jets (July 13, 1992). ... Released by Jets (September 19, 1995). ... Signed by Denver Broncos (September 27, 1995).
PLAYING EXPERIENCE: New York Jets NFL, 1992-1994; New York Jets (1)-Denver (10) NFL, 1995; Denver NFL, 1996-1998. ... Games/Games started: 1992 (16/0), 1993 (16/0), 1994 (16/0), 1995 (NYJ: 1/0; Den.:10/7; Total: 11/7), 1996 (16/0), 1997 (16/0), 1998 (16/15). Total: 107/22.
CHAMPIONSHIP GAME EXPERIENCE: Played in AFC championship game (1997 and 1998 seasons). ... Member of Super Bowl championship team (1997 and 1998 seasons).
PRO STATISTICS: 1992—Recovered one fumble. 1994—Returned one kickoff for 10 yards and recovered one fumble. 1995—Credited with two sacks and recovered one fumble. 1996—Recovered one fumble. 1998—Intercepted two passes for 11 yards and credited with four sacks.

CALDWELL, MIKE — LB — EAGLES

PERSONAL: Born August 31, 1971, in Oak Ridge, Tenn. ... 6-2/237. ... Full name: Mike Isiah Caldwell. ... Nickname: Zeke.
HIGH SCHOOL: Oak Ridge (Tenn.).
COLLEGE: Middle Tennessee State (degree in business administration, 1996).
TRANSACTIONS/CAREER NOTES: Selected by Cleveland Browns in third round (83rd pick overall) of 1993 NFL draft. ... Signed by Browns (July 14, 1993). ... Granted free agency (February 16, 1996). ... Browns franchise moved to Baltimore and renamed Ravens for 1996 season (March 11, 1996). ... Re-signed by Ravens for 1996 season. ... Granted unconditional free agency (February 17, 1997). ... Signed by Arizona Cardinals (July 16, 1997). ... Granted unconditional free agency (February 13, 1998). ... Signed by Philadelphia Eagles (April 9, 1998).
PRO STATISTICS: 1993—Recovered one fumble. 1994—Returned one punt for two yards.

			INTERCEPTIONS				SACKS
Year Team	G	GS	No.	Yds.	Avg.	TD	No.
1993—Cleveland NFL	15	1	0	0	...	0	0.0
1994—Cleveland NFL	16	1	1	0	0.0	0	0.0
1995—Cleveland NFL	16	6	2	24	12.0	▲1	0.0
1996—Baltimore NFL	9	9	1	45	45.0	0	4.5
1997—Arizona NFL	16	0	1	5	5.0	0	2.0
1998—Philadelphia NFL	16	8	1	33	33.0	0	1.0
Pro totals (6 years)	88	25	6	107	17.8	2	7.5

CALLOWAY, CHRIS — WR — FALCONS

PERSONAL: Born March 29, 1968, in Chicago. ... 5-10/188. ... Full name: Christopher Fitzpatrick Calloway.
HIGH SCHOOL: Mount Carmel (Chicago).
COLLEGE: Michigan (degree in communications and film, 1990).
TRANSACTIONS/CAREER NOTES: Selected by Pittsburgh Steelers in fourth round (97th pick overall) of 1990 NFL draft. ... Signed by Steelers (July 18, 1990). ... On injured reserve with knee injury (November 25, 1991-remainder of season). ... Granted unconditional free agency (February 1, 1992). ... Signed by New York Giants (April 1, 1992). ... Granted unconditional free agency (February 17, 1994). ... Re-signed by Giants (July 18, 1994). ... Granted unconditional free agency (February 16, 1996). ... Re-signed by Giants (April 2, 1996). ... Released by Giants (February 17, 1999). ... Signed by Atlanta Falcons (February 26, 1999).
PRO STATISTICS: 1991—Recovered one fumble. 1992—Returned two kickoffs for 29 yards. 1993—Returned six kickoffs for 89 yards and recovered one fumble. 1996—Recovered one fumble for seven yards.
SINGLE GAME HIGHS (regular season): Receptions—9 (October 20, 1996, vs. Washington); yards—145 (October 19, 1997, vs. Detroit); and touchdown receptions—2 (December 27, 1998, vs. Philadelphia).
STATISTICAL PLATEAUS: 100-yard receiving games: 1995 (1), 1996 (1), 1997 (1). Total: 3.

			RUSHING				RECEIVING				TOTALS			
Year Team	G	GS	Att.	Yds.	Avg.	TD	No.	Yds.	Avg.	TD	TD	2pt.	Pts.	Fum.
1990—Pittsburgh NFL	16	2	0	0	...	0	10	124	12.4	1	1	...	6	0
1991—Pittsburgh NFL	12	0	0	0	...	0	15	254	16.9	1	1	...	6	0
1992—New York Giants NFL	16	1	0	0	...	0	27	335	12.4	1	1	...	6	0
1993—New York Giants NFL	16	9	0	0	...	0	35	513	14.7	3	3	...	18	0
1994—New York Giants NFL	16	14	8	77	9.6	0	43	666	15.5	2	2	0	12	1
1995—New York Giants NFL	16	15	2	-9	-4.5	0	56	796	14.2	3	3	0	18	0
1996—New York Giants NFL	16	15	1	2	2.0	0	53	739	13.9	4	4	0	24	1
1997—New York Giants NFL	16	16	1	-1	-1.0	0	58	849	14.6	8	8	0	48	0
1998—New York Giants NFL	16	16	0	0	...	0	62	812	13.1	6	6	0	36	1
Pro totals (9 years)	140	88	12	69	5.8	0	359	5088	14.2	29	29	0	174	3

CAMPBELL, JESSE — S

PERSONAL: Born April 11, 1969, in Washington, N.C. ... 6-1/211.
HIGH SCHOOL: West Craven (Vanceboro, N.C.).
COLLEGE: North Carolina State.
TRANSACTIONS/CAREER NOTES: Selected after junior season by Philadelphia Eagles in second round (48th pick overall) of 1991 NFL draft. ... Signed by Eagles (July 17, 1991). ... On injured reserve with knee injury (August 27-October 23, 1991). ... On practice squad (October 23, 1991-remainder of season). ... Released by Eagles (September 4, 1992). ... Signed by New York Giants (September 7, 1992). ... Released by Giants (September 21, 1992). ... Signed by Giants to practice squad (September 23, 1992). ... Activated (October 21, 1992). ... Granted free agency (February 17, 1994). ... Re-signed by Giants (July 17, 1994). ... Granted unconditional free agency (February 17, 1995). ... Re-signed by Giants (June 24, 1995). ... Released by Giants (February 14, 1997). ... Signed by Washington Redskins (April 5, 1997). ... On injured reserve with knee injury (November 27, 1998-remainder of season). ... Released by Redskins (February 16, 1999).
HONORS: Named defensive back on THE SPORTING NEWS college All-America first team (1990).
PRO STATISTICS: 1992—Recovered one fumble. 1994—Recovered two fumbles for three yards. 1996—Recovered one fumble. 1997—Recovered two fumbles for minus one yard. 1998—Fumbled once.

			INTERCEPTIONS			
Year Team	G	GS	No.	Yds.	Avg.	TD
1991—Philadelphia NFL			Did not play.			
1992—New York Giants NFL	11	0	0	0	...	0
1993—New York Giants NFL	16	0	1	0	0.0	0
1994—New York Giants NFL	14	10	2	3	1.5	0
1995—New York Giants NFL	16	16	0	0	...	0
1996—New York Giants NFL	16	16	2	14	7.0	0
1997—Washington NFL	16	16	1	7	7.0	0
1998—Washington NFL	3	3	1	4	4.0	0
Pro totals (7 years)	92	61	7	28	4.0	0

CAMPBELL, LAMAR   CB   LIONS

PERSONAL: Born August 29, 1976, in Chester, Pa. ... 5-11/182.
HIGH SCHOOL: Strath Haven (Wallingford, Pa.).
COLLEGE: Wisconsin.
TRANSACTIONS/CAREER NOTES: Signed as non-drafted free agent by Detroit Lions (April 24, 1998).
PLAYING EXPERIENCE: Detroit NFL, 1998. ... Games/Games started: 12/0.

CAMPBELL, MATT   G   PANTHERS

PERSONAL: Born July 14, 1972, in North Augusta, S.C. ... 6-4/300. ... Full name: Mathew Thomas Campbell.
HIGH SCHOOL: North Augusta (S.C.).
COLLEGE: South Carolina.
TRANSACTIONS/CAREER NOTES: Signed as non-drafted free agent by New Orleans Saints (April 28, 1994). ... Released by Saints (August 23, 1994). ... Re-signed by Saints to practice squad (August 30, 1994). ... Released by Saints (September 20, 1994). ... Signed by Carolina Panthers (December 15, 1994). ... Granted free agency (February 13, 1998). ... Tendered offer sheet by Miami Dolphins (February 20, 1998). ... Offer matched by Panthers (February 27, 1998).
PLAYING EXPERIENCE: Carolina NFL, 1995-1998. ... Games/Games started: 1995 (10/1), 1996 (9/8), 1997 (16/14), 1998 (10/10). Total: 45/33.
CHAMPIONSHIP GAME EXPERIENCE: Played in NFC championship game (1996 season).
PRO STATISTICS: 1995—Caught three passes for 32 yards and fumbled once.
MISCELLANEOUS: Played tight end during 1995 season.

CANNIDA, JAMES   DT   BUCCANEERS

PERSONAL: Born January 3, 1975, in Savannah, Ga. ... 6-2/285. ... Full name: James Thomas Cannida II.
HIGH SCHOOL: American (Fremont, Calif.).
COLLEGE: Nevada-Reno.
TRANSACTIONS/CAREER NOTES: Selected by Tampa Bay Buccaneers in sixth round (175th pick overall) of 1998 NFL draft. ... Signed by Buccaneers (June 4, 1998).
PLAYING EXPERIENCE: Tampa Bay NFL, 1998. ... Games/Games started: 10/0.

CANTY, CHRIS   CB

PERSONAL: Born March 30, 1976, in Long Beach, Calif. ... 5-9/185. ... Full name: Christopher Shawn Patrick Canty.
HIGH SCHOOL: Eastern (Voorhees, N.J.).
COLLEGE: Kansas State.
TRANSACTIONS/CAREER NOTES: Selected after junior season by New England Patriots in first round (29th pick overall) of 1997 NFL draft. ... Signed by Patriots (July 17, 1997). ... Released by Patriots (June 8, 1999).
HONORS: Named defensive back on THE SPORTING NEWS college All-America first team (1995). ... Named cornerback on THE SPORTING NEWS college All-America first team (1996).
PRO STATISTICS: 1997—Recovered two fumbles for nine yards.

			INTERCEPTIONS			SACKS	PUNT RETURNS				KICKOFF RETURNS				TOTALS			
Year Team	G	GS	No.	Yds.	Avg.	TD	No.	No.	Yds.	Avg.	TD	No.	Yds.	Avg.	TD	TD	2pt.	Pts.	Fum.
1997—New England NFL......	16	1	0	0	...	0	2.0	0	0	...	0	4	115	28.8	0	0	0	0	0
1998—New England NFL......	16	9	1	12	12.0	0	1.0	16	170	10.6	0	11	198	18.0	0	0	0	0	2
Pro totals (2 years)	32	10	1	12	12.0	0	3.0	16	170	10.6	0	15	313	20.9	0	0	0	0	2

CARNEY, JOHN   K   CHARGERS

PERSONAL: Born April 20, 1964, in Hartford, Conn. ... 5-11/170. ... Full name: John Michael Carney.
HIGH SCHOOL: Cardinal Newman (West Palm Beach, Fla.).
COLLEGE: Notre Dame (degree in marketing, 1987).
TRANSACTIONS/CAREER NOTES: Signed as non-drafted free agent by Cincinnati Bengals (May 1, 1987). ... Released by Bengals (August 10, 1987). ... Signed as replacement player by Tampa Bay Buccaneers (September 24, 1987). ... Released by Buccaneers (October 14, 1987). ... Re-signed by Buccaneers (April 5, 1988). ... Released by Buccaneers (August 23, 1988). ... Re-signed by Buccaneers (November 22, 1988). ... Granted unconditional free agency (February 1-April 1, 1989). ... Re-signed by Buccaneers (April 13, 1989). ... Released by Buccaneers (September 5, 1989). ... Re-signed by Buccaneers (December 13, 1989). ... Granted unconditional free agency (February 1, 1990). ... Signed by San Diego Chargers (April 1, 1990). ... Released by Chargers (August 28, 1990). ... Signed by Los Angeles Rams (September 21, 1990). ... Released by Rams (September 26, 1990). ... Signed by Chargers (October 3, 1990). ... Granted free agency (February 1, 1992). ... Re-signed by Chargers (July 27, 1992). ... Granted free agency (March 1, 1993). ... Re-signed by Chargers (June 9, 1993). ... Granted unconditional free agency (February 17, 1994). ... Re-signed by Chargers (April 6, 1994). ... On injured reserve with knee injury (November 15, 1997-remainder of season).
CHAMPIONSHIP GAME EXPERIENCE: Played in AFC championship game (1994 season). ... Played in Super Bowl XXIX (1994 season).
HONORS: Named kicker on THE SPORTING NEWS NFL All-Pro team (1994). ... Played in Pro Bowl (1994 season).
RECORDS: Holds NFL career record for highest field-goal percentage—81.06.
PRO STATISTICS: 1993—Punted four times for 155 yards (38.8-yard average).

			KICKING						
Year Team	G	XPM	XPA	FGM	FGA	Lg.	50+	Pts.
1988—Tampa Bay NFL	4	6	6	2	5	29	0-0	12
1989—Tampa Bay NFL	1	0	0	0	0	...	0-0	0
1990—Los Angeles Rams NFL	1	0	0	0	0	...	0-0	0
—San Diego NFL	12	27	28	19	21	43	0-1	84
1991—San Diego NFL	16	31	31	19	29	54	2-4	88
1992—San Diego NFL	16	35	35	26	32	50	1-3	113
1993—San Diego NFL	16	31	33	31	40	51	2-3	124
1994—San Diego NFL	16	33	33	†34	§38	50	2-2	*135
1995—San Diego NFL	16	32	33	21	26	45	0-2	95
1996—San Diego NFL	16	31	31	29	36	53	3-3	118
1997—San Diego NFL	4	5	5	7	7	41	0-0	26
1998—San Diego NFL	16	19	19	26	30	54	2-3	97
Pro totals (11 years)	134	250	254	214	264	54	12-21	892

CARPENTER, RON   S   RAMS

PERSONAL: Born January 20, 1970, in Cincinnati. ... 6-1/188.
HIGH SCHOOL: Princeton (Cincinnati).
COLLEGE: Miami (Ohio).
TRANSACTIONS/CAREER NOTES: Signed as non-drafted free agent by Minnesota Vikings (May 1, 1993). ... Claimed on waivers by Cincinnati Bengals (November 3, 1993). ... Released by Bengals (July 29, 1994). ... Signed by Minnesota Vikings (August 2, 1994). ... Released by Vikings (August 22, 1994). ... Selected by Amsterdam Admirals in fifth round (27th pick overall) of 1995 World League draft. ... Signed by New York Jets (June 28, 1995). ... Released by Jets (September 18, 1996). ... Signed by St. Louis Rams (July 16, 1997). ... Released by Rams (August 24, 1997). ... Played for New York Cityhawks of Arena Football League (1998). ... Signed by Rams (November 17, 1998).

			INTERCEPTIONS				KICKOFF RETURNS				TOTALS		
Year Team	G	GS	No.	Yds.	Avg.	TD	No.	Yds.	Avg.	TD	TD	2pt.	Pts.	Fum.
1993—Minnesota NFL	7	0	0	0	...	0	0	0	...	0	0	...	0	0
—Cincinnati NFL	6	0	0	0	...	0	0	0	...	0	0	...	0	0
1994—								Did not play.						
1995—Amsterdam W.L.	...	...	7	93	13.3	1	7	219	31.3	0	1	0	6	...
—New York Jets NFL	13	4	0	0	...	0	20	553	*27.7	0	0	0	0	2
1996—New York Jets NFL	2	0	0	0	...	0	6	107	17.8	0	0	0	0	0
1997—Amsterdam W.L.	...	...	2	45	22.5	0	23	580	25.2	0	0	0	0	...
1998—St. Louis NFL	6	0	0	0	...	0	0	0	...	0	0	0	0	0
W.L. totals (2 years)	...	...	9	138	15.3	1	30	799	26.6	0	1	0	6	0
NFL totals (4 years)	34	4	0	0	...	0	26	660	25.4	0	0	0	0	2
Pro totals (6 years)	...	...	9	138	15.3	1	56	1459	26.1	0	1	0	6	2

CARRIER, MARK   WR

PERSONAL: Born October 28, 1965, in Lafayette, La. ... 6-0/185. ... Full name: John Mark Carrier. ... Related to Mark Carrier, safety, Detroit Lions.
HIGH SCHOOL: Church Point (La.).
COLLEGE: Nicholls State (La.).
TRANSACTIONS/CAREER NOTES: Selected by Tampa Bay Buccaneers in third round (57th pick overall) of 1987 NFL draft. ... Signed by Buccaneers (July 18, 1987). ... Granted free agency (February 1, 1990). ... Re-signed by Buccaneers (August 13, 1990). ... Granted unconditional free agency (March 1, 1993). ... Signed by Cleveland Browns (April 7, 1993). ... Selected by Carolina Panthers from Browns in NFL expansion draft (February 15, 1995). ... Granted unconditional free agency (February 16, 1996). ... Re-signed by Panthers (April 2, 1996). ... Granted unconditional free agency (February 14, 1997). ... Re-signed by Panthers (September 17, 1997). ... On injured reserve with hand injury (December 5, 1997-remainder of season). ... Granted unconditional free agency (February 13, 1998). ... Re-signed by Panthers (February 26, 1998). ... Released by Panthers (April 1, 1999).
CHAMPIONSHIP GAME EXPERIENCE: Played in NFC championship game (1996 season).
HONORS: Played in Pro Bowl (1989 season).
PRO STATISTICS: 1987—Returned one kickoff for no yards. 1991—Recovered one fumble. 1993—Rushed four times for 26 yards and one touchdown. 1994—Rushed once for 14 yards and a touchdown and recovered one fumble. 1995—Rushed three times for minus four yards and recovered one fumble.
SINGLE GAME HIGHS (regular season): Receptions—10 (December 10, 1989, vs. Houston); yards—212 (December 6, 1987, vs. New Orleans); and touchdown receptions—2 (September 29, 1996, vs. Jacksonville).
STATISTICAL PLATEAUS: 100-yard receiving games: 1987 (1), 1988 (1), 1989 (8), 1990 (1), 1991 (1), 1992 (1), 1993 (2), 1995 (3), 1996 (1), 1998 (1). Total: 20.
MISCELLANEOUS: Holds Carolina Panthers all-time records for most receptions (176) and most yards receiving (2,547).

			RECEIVING				PUNT RETURNS				TOTALS		
Year Team	G	GS	No.	Yds.	Avg.	TD	No.	Yds.	Avg.	TD	TD	2pt.	Pts.	Fum.
1987—Tampa Bay NFL	10	5	26	423	16.3	3	0	0	...	0	3	...	18	0
1988—Tampa Bay NFL	16	16	57	970	17.0	5	0	0	...	0	5	...	30	2
1989—Tampa Bay NFL	16	15	86	1422	16.5	9	0	0	...	0	9	...	54	1
1990—Tampa Bay NFL	16	16	49	813	16.6	4	0	0	...	0	4	...	24	0
1991—Tampa Bay NFL	16	16	47	698	14.9	2	0	0	...	0	2	...	12	2
1992—Tampa Bay NFL	14	12	56	692	12.4	4	0	0	...	0	4	...	24	1
1993—Cleveland NFL	16	16	43	746	17.3	3	6	92	15.3	1	5	...	30	0
1994—Cleveland NFL	16	6	29	452	15.6	6	9	112	12.4	0	6	0	36	1
1995—Carolina NFL	16	15	66	1002	15.2	3	6	25	4.2	0	3	0	18	0
1996—Carolina NFL	16	15	58	808	13.9	6	0	0	...	0	6	0	36	0
1997—Carolina NFL	9	6	33	436	13.2	2	0	0	...	0	2	0	12	1
1998—Carolina NFL	16	1	19	301	15.8	2	0	0	...	0	2	0	12	0
Pro totals (12 years)	177	139	569	8763	15.4	48	21	229	10.9	1	51	0	306	8

– 67 –

CARRIER, MARK   S   LIONS

PERSONAL: Born April 28, 1968, in Lake Charles, La. ... 6-1/192. ... Full name: Mark Anthony Carrier III. ... Related to Mark Carrier, wide receiver with Tampa Bay Buccaneers (1987-92), Cleveland Browns (1993 and 1994) and Carolina Panthers (1995-98).
HIGH SCHOOL: Polytechnic (Long Beach, Calif.).
COLLEGE: Southern California (degree in communications).
TRANSACTIONS/CAREER NOTES: Selected after junior season by Chicago Bears in first round (sixth pick overall) of 1990 NFL draft. ... Signed by Bears (April 22, 1990). ... Designated by Bears as transition player (February 25, 1993). ... Released by Bears (June 1, 1997). ... Signed by Detroit Lions (June 20, 1997).
HONORS: Named defensive back on THE SPORTING NEWS college All-America second team (1988). ... Jim Thorpe Award winner (1989). ... Named defensive back on THE SPORTING NEWS college All-America first team (1989). ... Played in Pro Bowl (1990, 1991 and 1993 seasons). ... Named free safety on THE SPORTING NEWS NFL All-Pro team (1991).
PRO STATISTICS: 1990—Recovered two fumbles for 16 yards. 1991—Recovered one fumble for two yards. 1992—Recovered two fumbles. 1995—Recovered one fumble. 1996—Recovered one fumble. 1997—Returned one punt for no yards and fumbled once. 1998—Fumbled once.

			INTERCEPTIONS			
Year Team	G	GS	No.	Yds.	Avg.	TD
1990—Chicago NFL	16	16	*10	39	3.9	0
1991—Chicago NFL	16	16	2	54	27.0	0
1992—Chicago NFL	16	14	0	0	...	0
1993—Chicago NFL	16	16	4	94	23.5	1
1994—Chicago NFL	16	15	2	10	5.0	0
1995—Chicago NFL	16	15	0	0	...	0
1996—Chicago NFL	13	13	2	0	0.0	0
1997—Detroit NFL	16	16	5	94	18.8	0
1998—Detroit NFL	13	13	3	33	11.0	0
Pro totals (9 years)	138	134	28	324	11.6	1

CARRUTH, RAE   WR   PANTHERS

PERSONAL: Born January 20, 1974, in Sacramento. ... 5-11/195. ... Full name: Rae Lamar Carruth.
HIGH SCHOOL: Valley (Sacramento).
COLLEGE: Colorado.
TRANSACTIONS/CAREER NOTES: Selected by Carolina Panthers in first round (27th pick overall) of 1997 NFL draft. ... Signed by Panthers (July 18, 1997). ... On injured reserve with foot injury (November 28, 1998-remainder of season).
HONORS: Named wide receiver on THE SPORTING NEWS college All-America first team (1996).
SINGLE GAME HIGHS (regular season): Receptions—8 (September 21, 1997, vs. Kansas City); yards—110 (September 21, 1997, vs. Kansas City); and touchdown receptions—1 (December 20, 1997, vs. St. Louis).
STATISTICAL PLATEAUS: 100-yard receiving games: 1997 (2).

			RUSHING				RECEIVING				TOTALS			
Year Team	G	GS	Att.	Yds.	Avg.	TD	No.	Yds.	Avg.	TD	TD	2pt.	Pts.	Fum.
1997—Carolina NFL	15	14	6	23	3.8	0	44	545	12.4	4	4	0	24	2
1998—Carolina NFL	2	1	0	0	...	0	4	59	14.8	0	0	0	0	0
Pro totals (2 years)	17	15	6	23	3.8	0	48	604	12.6	4	4	0	24	2

CARSWELL, DWAYNE   TE   BRONCOS

PERSONAL: Born January 18, 1972, in Jacksonville. ... 6-3/260.
HIGH SCHOOL: University Christian (Jacksonville).
COLLEGE: Liberty (Va.).
TRANSACTIONS/CAREER NOTES: Signed as non-drafted free agent by Denver Broncos (May 2, 1994). ... Released by Broncos (August 26, 1994). ... Re-signed by Broncos to practice squad (August 30, 1994). ... Activated (November 25, 1994).
CHAMPIONSHIP GAME EXPERIENCE: Played in AFC championship game (1997 and 1998 seasons). ... Member of Super Bowl championship team (1997 and 1998 seasons).
PRO STATISTICS: 1994—Returned one kickoff for no yards and recovered one fumble. 1997—Recovered one fumble.
SINGLE GAME HIGHS (regular season): Receptions—4 (September 14, 1997, vs. St. Louis); yards—47 (September 14, 1997, vs. St. Louis); and touchdown receptions—1 (September 14, 1997, vs. St. Louis).

			RECEIVING				TOTALS		
Year Team	G	GS	No.	Yds.	Avg.	TD	TD	2pt.	Pts.	Fum.
1994—Denver NFL	4	0	0	0	...	0	0	0	0	0
1995—Denver NFL	9	2	3	37	12.3	0	0	0	0	0
1996—Denver NFL	16	2	15	85	5.7	0	0	0	0	0
1997—Denver NFL	16	3	12	96	8.0	1	1	0	6	0
1998—Denver NFL	16	1	4	51	12.8	0	0	0	0	0
Pro totals (5 years)	61	8	34	269	7.9	1	1	0	6	0

CARTER, CHRIS   S   PATRIOTS

PERSONAL: Born September 27, 1974, in Tyler, Texas. ... 6-1/201. ... Full name: Christopher Cary Carter. ... Cousin of Joe Carter, first baseman/outfielder with five major league baseball teams (1984-98).
HIGH SCHOOL: John Tyler (Tyler, Texas).
COLLEGE: Texas.
TRANSACTIONS/CAREER NOTES: Selected by New England Patriots in third round (89th pick overall) of 1997 NFL draft. ... Signed by Patriots (July 15, 1997).
PLAYING EXPERIENCE: New England NFL, 1997 and 1998. ... Games/Games started: 1997 (16/0), 1998 (16/0). Total: 32/0.
PRO STATISTICS: 1998—Credited with one sack.

CARTER, CRIS — WR — VIKINGS

PERSONAL: Born November 25, 1965, in Troy, Ohio. ... 6-3/214. ... Full name: Christopher D. Carter. ... Brother of Butch Carter, head coach, Toronto Raptors.
HIGH SCHOOL: Middletown (Ohio).
COLLEGE: Ohio State.
TRANSACTIONS/CAREER NOTES: Selected by Philadelphia Eagles in fourth round of 1987 NFL supplemental draft (September 4, 1987). ... Signed by Eagles (September 17, 1987). ... Granted roster exemption (September 17-October 26, 1987). ... Claimed on waivers by Minnesota Vikings (September 4, 1990). ... Granted free agency (February 1, 1991). ... Re-signed by Vikings (July 9, 1991). ... Granted free agency (February 1, 1992). ... Re-signed by Vikings (July 26, 1992). ... On injured reserve with broken collarbone (December 4-30, 1992).
CHAMPIONSHIP GAME EXPERIENCE: Played in NFC championship game (1998 season).
HONORS: Played in Pro Bowl (1993-1998 seasons). ... Named wide receiver on THE SPORTING NEWS NFL All-Pro team (1994).
PRO STATISTICS: 1987—Attempted one pass without a completion and returned 12 kickoffs for 241 yards. 1988—Recovered one fumble in end zone for a touchdown. 1989—Recovered one fumble. 1993—Recovered one fumble. 1996—Returned one kickoff for three yards and recovered one fumble.
SINGLE GAME HIGHS (regular season): Receptions—14 (October 2, 1994, vs. Arizona); yards—167 (October 2, 1994, vs. Arizona); and touchdown receptions—3 (December 21, 1997, vs. Indianapolis).
STATISTICAL PLATEAUS: 100-yard receiving games: 1988 (1), 1989 (1), 1990 (2), 1991 (4), 1992 (1), 1993 (3), 1994 (5), 1995 (5), 1996 (1), 1997 (4), 1998 (3). Total: 30.
MISCELLANEOUS: Holds Minnesota Vikings all-time records for most receptions (745), most yards receiving (8,997), most touchdowns (82) and most touchdown receptions (82).

				RUSHING				RECEIVING				TOTALS		
Year Team	G	GS	Att.	Yds.	Avg.	TD	No.	Yds.	Avg.	TD	TD	2pt.	Pts.	Fum.
1987—Philadelphia NFL	9	0	0	0	...	0	5	84	16.8	2	2	...	12	0
1988—Philadelphia NFL	16	16	1	1	1.0	0	39	761	19.5	6	7	...	42	0
1989—Philadelphia NFL	16	15	2	16	8.0	0	45	605	13.4	11	11	...	66	1
1990—Minnesota NFL	16	5	2	6	3.0	0	27	413	15.3	3	3	...	18	0
1991—Minnesota NFL	16	16	0	0	...	0	72	962	13.4	5	5	...	30	1
1992—Minnesota NFL	12	12	5	15	3.0	0	53	681	12.8	6	6	...	36	1
1993—Minnesota NFL	16	16	0	0	...	0	86	1071	12.5	9	9	...	54	0
1994—Minnesota NFL	16	16	0	0	...	0	*122	1256	10.3	7	7	2	46	4
1995—Minnesota NFL	16	16	1	0	0.0	0	122	1371	11.2	†17	17	0	102	0
1996—Minnesota NFL	16	16	0	0	...	0	96	1163	12.1	10	10	0	60	1
1997—Minnesota NFL	16	16	0	0	...	0	89	1069	12.0	*13	13	3	84	3
1998—Minnesota NFL	16	16	1	-1	-1.0	0	78	1011	13.0	12	12	0	72	0
Pro totals (12 years)	181	160	12	37	3.1	0	834	10447	12.5	101	102	5	622	11

CARTER, DALE — CB — BRONCOS

PERSONAL: Born November 28, 1969, in Covington, Ga. ... 6-1/188. ... Full name: Dale Lavelle Carter. ... Brother of Jake Reed, wide receiver, Minnesota Vikings.
HIGH SCHOOL: Newton County (Covington, Ga.).
JUNIOR COLLEGE: Ellsworth (Iowa) Community College.
COLLEGE: Tennessee.
TRANSACTIONS/CAREER NOTES: Selected by Kansas City Chiefs in first round (20th pick overall) of 1992 NFL draft. ... Signed by Chiefs (June 2, 1992). ... Designated by Chiefs as transition player (February 25, 1993). ... On injured reserve with broken arm (January 7, 1994-remainder of 1993 playoffs). ... Tendered offer sheet by Minnesota Vikings (July 12, 1996). ... Offer matched by Chiefs (July 19, 1996). ... Granted unconditional free agency (February 12, 1999). ... Signed by Denver Broncos (February 19, 1999).
HONORS: Named kick returner on THE SPORTING NEWS college All-America first team (1990). ... Named defensive back on THE SPORTING NEWS college All-America first team (1991). ... Played in Pro Bowl (1994, 1995 and 1997 seasons). ... Named cornerback on THE SPORTING NEWS NFL All-Pro team (1996). ... Named to play in Pro Bowl (1996 season); replaced by Terry McDaniel due to injury.
PRO STATISTICS: 1992—Recovered two fumbles. 1993—Rushed once for two yards and recovered two fumbles. 1994—Recovered one fumble. 1995—Recovered two fumbles. 1996—Rushed once for three yards, caught six passes for 89 yards and a touchdown, and recovered two fumbles for seven yards.

			INTERCEPTIONS				PUNT RETURNS				KICKOFF RETURNS				TOTALS		
Year Team	G	GS	No.	Yds.	Avg.	TD	No.	Yds.	Avg.	TD	No.	Yds.	Avg.	TD	TD	2pt.	Pts.	Fum.
1992—Kansas City NFL	16	9	7	65	9.3	1	38	398	10.5	†2	11	190	17.3	0	3	...	18	7
1993—Kansas City NFL	15	11	1	0	0.0	0	27	247	9.1	0	0	0	...	0	0	...	0	4
1994—Kansas City NFL	16	16	2	24	12.0	0	16	124	7.8	0	0	0	...	0	0	0	0	1
1995—Kansas City NFL	16	14	4	45	11.3	0	0	0	...	0	0	0	...	0	0	0	0	0
1996—Kansas City NFL	14	14	3	17	5.7	0	2	18	9.0	0	0	0	...	0	1	0	6	1
1997—Kansas City NFL	16	15	2	9	4.5	0	0	0	...	0	0	0	...	0	0	0	0	0
1998—Kansas City NFL	11	9	2	23	11.5	0	0	0	...	0	0	0	...	0	0	0	0	0
Pro totals (7 years)	104	88	21	183	8.7	1	83	787	9.5	2	11	190	17.3	0	4	0	24	13

CARTER, KEVIN — DE — RAMS

PERSONAL: Born September 21, 1973, in Miami. ... 6-5/280. ... Full name: Kevin Louis Carter. ... Brother of Bernard Carter, linebacker with Jacksonville Jaguars (1995).
HIGH SCHOOL: Lincoln (Tallahassee, Fla.).
COLLEGE: Florida.
TRANSACTIONS/CAREER NOTES: Selected by St. Louis Rams in first round (sixth pick overall) of 1995 NFL draft. ... Signed by Rams (July 17, 1995).
HONORS: Named defensive lineman on THE SPORTING NEWS college All-America first team (1994).
PRO STATISTICS: 1995—Recovered one fumble. 1996—Recovered two fumbles. 1997—Recovered two fumbles for five yards.

Year Team	G	GS	SACKS
1995—St. Louis NFL	16	16	6.0
1996—St. Louis NFL	16	16	9.5
1997—St. Louis NFL	16	16	7.5
1998—St. Louis NFL	16	16	12.0
Pro totals (4 years)	64	64	35.0

CARTER, KI-JANA — RB — BENGALS

PERSONAL: Born September 12, 1973, in Westerville, Ohio. ... 5-10/222. ... Full name: Kenneth Leonard Carter. ... Name pronounced ki-JOHN-ah.
HIGH SCHOOL: Westerville (Ohio) South.
COLLEGE: Penn State.
TRANSACTIONS/CAREER NOTES: Selected after junior season by Cincinnati Bengals in first round (first pick overall) of 1995 NFL draft. ... Signed by Bengals (July 19, 1995). ... On injured reserve with knee injury (August 22, 1995-entire season). ... On injured reserve with wrist injury (September 7, 1998-remainder of season).
HONORS: Named running back on THE SPORTING NEWS college All-America first team (1994).
PRO STATISTICS: 1996—Recovered two fumbles for minus eight yards. 1997—Attempted one pass without a completion, returned one kickoff for nine yards and recovered two fumbles.
SINGLE GAME HIGHS (regular season): Attempts—19 (August 31, 1997, vs. Arizona); yards—104 (September 21, 1997, vs. Denver); and rushing touchdowns—2 (August 31, 1997, vs. Arizona).
STATISTICAL PLATEAUS: 100-yard rushing games: 1997 (1).

			RUSHING				RECEIVING				TOTALS			
Year Team	G	GS	Att.	Yds.	Avg.	TD	No.	Yds.	Avg.	TD	TD	2pt.	Pts.	Fum.
1995—Cincinnati NFL							Did not play.							
1996—Cincinnati NFL	16	4	91	264	2.9	8	22	169	7.7	1	9	0	54	2
1997—Cincinnati NFL	15	10	128	464	3.6	7	21	157	7.5	0	7	0	42	3
1998—Cincinnati NFL	1	0	2	4	2.0	0	6	25	4.2	0	0	0	0	0
Pro totals (3 years)	32	14	221	732	3.3	15	49	351	7.2	1	16	0	96	5

CARTER, MARTY — S — FALCONS

PERSONAL: Born December 17, 1969, in LaGrange, Ga. ... 6-1/210. ... Full name: Marty LaVincent Carter.
HIGH SCHOOL: LaGrange (Ga.).
COLLEGE: Middle Tennessee State.
TRANSACTIONS/CAREER NOTES: Selected by Tampa Bay Buccaneers in eighth round (207th pick overall) of 1991 NFL draft. ... Signed by Buccaneers (July 19, 1991). ... Granted unconditional free agency (February 17, 1995). ... Signed by Chicago Bears (March 3, 1995). ... Granted unconditional free agency (February 12, 1999). ... Signed by Atlanta Falcons (March 12, 1999).
PRO STATISTICS: 1993—Recovered two fumbles. 1994—Caught one pass for 21 yards and returned one kickoff for no yards. 1995—Recovered one fumble. 1998—Recovered two fumbles.

			INTERCEPTIONS				SACKS
Year Team	G	GS	No.	Yds.	Avg.	TD	No.
1991—Tampa Bay NFL	14	11	1	5	5.0	0	0.0
1992—Tampa Bay NFL	16	16	3	1	0.3	0	2.0
1993—Tampa Bay NFL	16	14	1	0	0.0	0	0.0
1994—Tampa Bay NFL	16	14	0	0	...	0	1.0
1995—Chicago NFL	16	16	2	20	10.0	0	0.0
1996—Chicago NFL	16	16	3	34	11.3	0	0.0
1997—Chicago NFL	15	15	1	14	14.0	0	1.0
1998—Chicago NFL	16	16	0	0	...	0	0.0
Pro totals (8 years)	125	118	11	74	6.7	0	4.0

CARTER, PERRY — DB — RAIDERS

PERSONAL: Born August 5, 1971, in McComb, Miss. ... 6-0/185. ... Full name: Perry Lynn Carter.
HIGH SCHOOL: South Pike (Magnolia, Miss.).
COLLEGE: Southern Mississippi.
TRANSACTIONS/CAREER NOTES: Selected by Arizona Cardinals in fourth round (107th pick overall) of 1994 NFL draft. ... Signed by Cardinals for 1994 season. ... Released by Cardinals (August 27, 1994). ... Re-signed by Cardinals to practice squad (August 30, 1994). ... Released by Cardinals (September 5, 1994). ... Signed by Washington Redskins to practice squad (September 13, 1994). ... Released by Redskins (September 20, 1994). ... Signed by Kansas City Chiefs to practice squad (December 15, 1994). ... Released by Chiefs (August 22, 1995). ... Re-signed by Chiefs to practice squad (August 29, 1995). ... Activated (December 10, 1995). ... Released by Chiefs (August 25, 1996). ... Signed by Oakland Raiders (November 20, 1996).
PLAYING EXPERIENCE: Kansas City NFL, 1995; Oakland NFL, 1996-1998. ... Games/Games started: 1995 (2/0), 1996 (4/0), 1997 (16/7), 1998 (6/0). Total: 28/7.

CARTER, TOM — CB — BEARS

PERSONAL: Born September 5, 1972, in St. Petersburg, Fla. ... 6-0/189. ... Full name: Thomas Carter III.
HIGH SCHOOL: Lakeland (St. Petersburg, Fla.).
COLLEGE: Notre Dame (degree in finance, 1996).
TRANSACTIONS/CAREER NOTES: Selected after junior season by Washington Redskins in first round (17th pick overall) of 1993 NFL draft. ... Signed by Redskins for 1993 season. ... Designated by Redskins as transition player (February 15, 1994). ... Designated by Redskins as transition player (February 12, 1997). ... Tendered offer sheet by Chicago Bears (March 31, 1997). ... Redskins declined to match offer (April 7, 1997). ... On injured reserve with broken collarbone (September 30, 1998-remainder of season).

Year	Team	G	GS	INTERCEPTIONS No.	Yds.	Avg.	TD
1993	Washington NFL	14	11	6	54	9.0	0
1994	Washington NFL	16	16	3	58	19.3	0
1995	Washington NFL	16	16	4	116	29.0	1
1996	Washington NFL	16	16	5	24	4.8	0
1997	Chicago NFL	16	16	3	12	4.0	0
1998	Chicago NFL	4	4	2	20	10.0	0
Pro totals (6 years)		82	79	23	284	12.3	1

CARTER, TONY — FB — PATRIOTS

PERSONAL: Born August 23, 1972, in Columbus, Ohio. ... 6-0/230. ... Full name: Antonio Marcus Carter.
HIGH SCHOOL: South (Columbus, Ohio).
COLLEGE: Minnesota.
TRANSACTIONS/CAREER NOTES: Signed as non-drafted free agent by Chicago Bears (April 28, 1994). ... Granted unconditional free agency (February 13, 1998). ... Signed by New England Patriots (February 25, 1998).
PRO STATISTICS: 1996—Recovered one fumble. 1997—Recovered one fumble.
SINGLE GAME HIGHS (regular season): Attempts—6 (October 13, 1996, vs. New Orleans); yards—37 (October 13, 1996, vs. New Orleans); and rushing touchdowns—0.

				RUSHING				RECEIVING				KICKOFF RETURNS				TOTALS			
Year	Team	G	GS	Att.	Yds.	Avg.	TD	No.	Yds.	Avg.	TD	No.	Yds.	Avg.	TD	TD	2pt.	Pts.	Fum.
1994—Chicago NFL		14	0	0	0	...	0	1	24	24.0	0	6	99	16.5	0	0	0	0	0
1995—Chicago NFL		16	11	10	34	3.4	0	40	329	8.2	1	3	24	8.0	0	1	0	6	1
1996—Chicago NFL		16	11	11	43	3.9	0	41	233	5.7	0	0	0	...	0	0	0	0	1
1997—Chicago NFL		16	10	9	56	6.2	0	24	152	6.3	0	2	34	17.0	0	0	0	0	0
1998—New England NFL		11	7	2	3	1.5	0	18	166	9.2	0	0	0	...	0	0	0	0	0
Pro totals (5 years)		73	39	32	136	4.3	0	124	904	7.3	1	11	157	14.3	0	1	0	6	2

CASCADDEN, CHAD — LB — JETS

PERSONAL: Born May 14, 1972, in Two Rivers, Wis. ... 6-1/240.
HIGH SCHOOL: Chippewa Falls (Wis.).
COLLEGE: Wisconsin (degree in kinesiology).
TRANSACTIONS/CAREER NOTES: Signed as non-drafted free agent by New York Jets (April 28, 1995). ... Released by Jets (August 27, 1995). ... Re-signed by Jets to practice squad (August 29, 1995). ... Activated (September 19, 1995). ... Granted free agency (February 13, 1998). ... Tendered offer sheet by St. Louis Rams (April 6, 1998). ... Offer matched by Jets (April 13, 1998).
CHAMPIONSHIP GAME EXPERIENCE: Played in AFC championship game (1998 season).
PRO STATISTICS: 1996—Recovered one fumble. 1997—Recovered one fumble. 1998—Recovered two fumbles for 23 yards and one touchdown.

Year	Team	G	GS	SACKS
1995—New York Jets NFL		12	0	0.0
1996—New York Jets NFL		16	8	3.0
1997—New York Jets NFL		15	0	0.0
1998—New York Jets NFL		13	4	5.0
Pro totals (4 years)		56	12	8.0

CASE, STONEY — QB — COLTS

PERSONAL: Born July 7, 1972, in Odessa, Texas. ... 6-3/201. ... Full name: Stoney Jarrod Case.
HIGH SCHOOL: Permian (Odessa, Texas).
COLLEGE: New Mexico (degree in biology, 1995).
TRANSACTIONS/CAREER NOTES: Selected by Arizona Cardinals in third round (80th pick overall) of 1995 NFL draft. ... Signed by Cardinals for 1995 season. ... Inactive for 16 games (1996). ... Assigned by Cardinals to Barcelona Dragons in 1997 World League enhancement allocation program (February 19, 1997). ... Granted free agency (February 13, 1998). ... Re-signed by Cardinals (April 28, 1998). ... Granted unconditional free agency (February 12, 1999). ... Signed by Indianapolis Colts (March 8, 1999).
PRO STATISTICS: 1997—Fumbled three times.
SINGLE GAME HIGHS (regular season): Attempts—33 (October 12, 1997, vs. New York Giants); completions—18 (October 12, 1997, vs. New York Giants); yards—222 (October 12, 1997, vs. New York Giants); and touchdown passes—0.
MISCELLANEOUS: Regular-season record as starting NFL quarterback: 0-1.

				PASSING							RUSHING				TOTALS		
Year	Team	G	GS	Att.	Cmp.	Pct.	Yds.	TD	Int.	Avg.	Rat.	Att.	Yds.	Avg.	TD	TD	2pt.	Pts.
1995—Arizona NFL		2	0	2	1	50.0	19	0	1	9.50	43.8	1	4	4.0	0	0	0	0
1996—Arizona NFL									Did not play.									
1997—Arizona NFL		3	1	55	29	52.7	316	0	2	5.75	54.8	7	8	1.1	1	1	0	6
1998—Arizona NFL		1	0	0	0	...	0	0	0	...	...	0	0	...	0	0	0	0
Pro totals (3 years)		6	1	57	30	52.6	335	0	3	5.88	48.5	8	12	1.5	1	1	0	6

CAVIL, BEN — G — BROWNS

PERSONAL: Born January 31, 1972, in Galveston, Texas ... 6-2/310. ... Full name: Ben Anthony Cavil. ... Name pronounced Gavel. ... Nickname: Big Ben.
HIGH SCHOOL: LaMarque (Texas).
COLLEGE: Oklahoma.

TRANSACTIONS/CAREER NOTES: Signed as non-drafted free agent by San Diego Chargers (April 27, 1995). ... Released by Chargers (September 4, 1995). ... Re-signed by Chargers (March 11, 1996). ... Claimed on waivers by Philadelphia Eagles (August 20, 1996). ... Released by Eagles (August 30, 1996). ... Re-signed by Eagles to practice squad (September 2, 1996). ... Traded by Eagles to Baltimore Ravens for future considerations (August 24, 1997); Eagles acquired CB Willie Clark to complete deal (August 27, 1997). ... Selected by Cleveland Browns from Ravens in NFL expansion draft (February 9, 1999).
PLAYING EXPERIENCE: Baltimore NFL, 1997 and 1998. ... Games/Games started: 1997 (15/8); 1998 (16/6). Total: 31/14.

CENTERS, LARRY — FB — CARDINALS

PERSONAL: Born June 1, 1968, in Tatum, Texas. ... 6-0/225. ... Full name: Larry E. Centers.
HIGH SCHOOL: Tatum (Texas).
COLLEGE: Stephen F. Austin State.
TRANSACTIONS/CAREER NOTES: Selected by Phoenix Cardinals in fifth round (115th pick overall) of 1990 NFL draft. ... Signed by Cardinals (July 23, 1990). ... On injured reserve with broken foot (September 11-October 30, 1991). ... Granted free agency (February 1, 1992). ... Re-signed by Cardinals (July 23, 1992). ... Granted unconditional free agency (February 17, 1994). ... Re-signed by Cardinals (March 15, 1994). ... Cardinals franchise renamed Arizona Cardinals for 1994 season. ... Granted unconditional free agency (February 14, 1997). ... Re-signed by Cardinals (March 14, 1997).
HONORS: Played in Pro Bowl (1995 and 1996 seasons).
PRO STATISTICS: 1991—Returned five punts for 30 yards and recovered two fumbles. 1993—Recovered two fumbles. 1994—Recovered two fumbles for 27 yards. 1995—Had only pass attempt intercepted and recovered one fumble. 1996—Recovered one fumble.
SINGLE GAME HIGHS (regular season): Attempts—15 (September 4, 1994, vs. Los Angeles Rams); yards—62 (November 26, 1995, vs. Atlanta); and rushing touchdowns—2 (December 4, 1994, vs. Houston).
STATISTICAL PLATEAUS: 100-yard receiving games: 1995 (2), 1996 (1). Total: 3.
MISCELLANEOUS: Holds Cardinals franchise all-time record for most receptions (535).

			RUSHING				RECEIVING				KICKOFF RETURNS				TOTALS			
Year Team	G	GS	Att.	Yds.	Avg.	TD	No.	Yds.	Avg.	TD	No.	Yds.	Avg.	TD	TD	2pt.	Pts.	Fum.
1990—Phoenix NFL	6	0	0	0	...	0	0	0	...	0	16	272	17.0	0	0	...	0	1
1991—Phoenix NFL	9	2	14	44	3.1	0	19	176	9.3	0	16	330	20.6	0	0	...	0	4
1992—Phoenix NFL	16	1	37	139	3.8	0	50	417	8.3	2	0	0	...	0	2	...	12	1
1993—Phoenix NFL	16	9	25	152	6.1	0	66	603	9.1	3	0	0	...	0	3	...	18	1
1994—Arizona NFL	16	5	115	336	2.9	5	77	647	8.4	2	0	0	...	0	7	0	42	2
1995—Arizona NFL	16	10	78	254	3.3	2	101	962	9.5	2	1	15	15.0	0	4	0	24	2
1996—Arizona NFL	16	14	116	425	3.7	2	99	766	7.7	7	0	0	...	0	9	0	54	1
1997—Arizona NFL	15	14	101	276	2.7	1	54	409	7.6	1	0	0	...	0	2	0	12	1
1998—Arizona NFL	16	12	31	110	3.5	0	69	559	8.1	2	0	0	...	0	2	0	12	1
Pro totals (9 years)	126	67	517	1736	3.4	10	535	4539	8.5	19	33	617	18.7	0	29	0	174	14

CHALENSKI, MIKE — DE

PERSONAL: Born January 28, 1970, in Elizabeth, N.J. ... 6-5/280.
HIGH SCHOOL: David Brearley Regional (Kenilworth, N.J.).
COLLEGE: Pittsburgh, then UCLA.
TRANSACTIONS/CAREER NOTES: Signed as non-drafted free agent by Philadelphia Eagles (April 30, 1993). ... On injured reserve with knee injury (August 23, 1994-entire season). ... Granted unconditional free agency (February 16, 1996). ... Signed by New York Jets (April 25, 1996). ... Granted unconditional free agency (February 14, 1997). ... Signed by Minnesota Vikings (June 9, 1997). ... Released by Vikings (August 24, 1997). ... Signed by Miami Dolphins (October 21, 1997). ... Granted unconditional free agency (February 13, 1998). ... Re-signed by Dolphins (March 23, 1998). ... Released by Dolphins (August 17, 1998). ... Signed by Detroit Lions (August 25, 1998). ... Granted unconditional free agency (February 12, 1999).
PLAYING EXPERIENCE: Philadelphia NFL, 1993 and 1995; New York Jets NFL, 1996; Miami NFL, 1997; Detroit NFL, 1998. ... Games/Games started: 1993 (15/0), 1995 (9/0), 1996 (15/7), 1997 (8/0), 1998 (8/0). Total: 55/7.
PRO STATISTICS: 1996—Recovered one fumble.

CHAMBERLAIN, BYRON — TE — BRONCOS

PERSONAL: Born October 17, 1971, in Honolulu. ... 6-1/242.
HIGH SCHOOL: Eastern Hills (Fort Worth, Texas).
COLLEGE: Missouri, then Wayne State (Neb.).
TRANSACTIONS/CAREER NOTES: Selected by Denver Broncos in seventh round (222nd pick overall) of 1995 NFL draft. ... Signed by Broncos (August 27, 1995). ... Released by Broncos (August 27, 1995). ... Re-signed by Broncos to practice squad (August 28, 1995). ... Activated (November 24, 1995). ... Assigned by Broncos to Rhein Fire in 1996 World League enhancement allocation program (February 19, 1996).
CHAMPIONSHIP GAME EXPERIENCE: Played in AFC championship game (1997 and 1998 seasons). ... Member of Super Bowl championship team (1997 season); did not play. ... Member of Super Bowl championship team (1998 season).
PRO STATISTICS: W.L.: 1996—Rushed once for four yards and returned one kickoff for eight yards. NFL: 1996—Returned three kickoffs for 49 yards. 1997—Returned one kickoff for 13 yards.
SINGLE GAME HIGHS (regular season): Receptions—5 (December 15, 1996, vs. Oakland); yards—61 (December 15, 1996, vs. Oakland); and touchdown receptions—0.

			RECEIVING				TOTALS			
Year Team	G	GS	No.	Yds.	Avg.	TD	TD	2pt.	Pts.	Fum.
1995—Denver NFL	5	0	1	11	11.0	0	0	0	0	0
1996—Rhein W.L.	10	10	58	685	11.8	8	8	0	48	...
—Denver NFL	11	0	12	129	10.8	0	0	0	0	1
1997—Denver NFL	10	0	2	18	9.0	0	0	0	0	1
1998—Denver NFL	16	0	3	35	11.7	0	0	0	0	0
W.L. totals (1 year)	10	10	58	685	11.8	8	8	0	48	0
NFL totals (4 years)	42	0	18	193	10.7	0	0	0	0	2
Pro totals (5 years)	52	10	76	878	11.6	8	8	0	48	2

CHANCEY, ROBERT — FB — BEARS

PERSONAL: Born September 7, 1972, in Macon, Ala. ... 6-0/250. ... Full name: Robert Dewayne Chancey.
HIGH SCHOOL: Stanhope Elmore (Millbrook, Ala.).
COLLEGE: None.
TRANSACTIONS/CAREER NOTES: Signed as non-drafted free agent by San Diego Chargers (April 7, 1997). ... Released by Chargers (August 24, 1997). ... Re-signed by Chargers to practice squad (August 25, 1997). ... Activated (November 4, 1997). ... Released by Chargers (July 23, 1998). ... Signed by Chicago Bears (July 26, 1998).
PRO STATISTICS: 1998—Returned two kickoffs for 18 yards.
SINGLE GAME HIGHS (regular season): Attempts—6 (December 20, 1998, vs. Baltimore); yards—19 (December 27, 1998, vs. Green Bay) and rushing touchdowns—1 (December 20, 1998, vs. Baltimore).

				RUSHING				RECEIVING			TOTALS		
Year Team	G	GS	Att.	Yds.	Avg.	TD	No.	Yds.	Avg.	TD	TD	2pt.	Pts.	Fum.
1997—San Diego NFL	6	0	0	0	...	0	0	0	...	0	0	0	0	0
1998—Chicago NFL	16	1	29	122	4.2	2	11	102	9.3	0	2	0	12	2
Pro totals (2 years)	22	1	29	122	4.2	2	11	102	9.3	0	2	0	12	2

RECORD AS BASEBALL PLAYER

TRANSACTIONS/CAREER NOTES: Selected by Baltimore Orioles organization in sixth round of free-agent draft (June 1, 1992). ... Released by Gulf Coast Orioles, Orioles organization (September 30, 1993). ... Signed by Pittsfield, New York Mets organization (April 15, 1996). ... On Pittsfield temporarily inactive list (May 10-June 10, 1996). ... Released by Kingsport, Mets organization (July 1, 1996).
STATISTICAL NOTES: Led Gulf Coast League outfielders with seven errors (1992).

						BATTING							FIELDING		
Year Team (League)	Pos.	G	AB	R	H	2B	3B	HR	RBI	Avg.	BB	SO	SB	PO	A	E	Avg.
1992—GC Orioles (GCL)	OF	43	141	22	41	3	3	1	23	.291	7	50	13	70	5	7	.915
1993—GC Orioles (GCL)	OF	29	84	7	12	3	0	0	3	.143	4	39	3	31	3	6	.850
1996—Kingsport (Appal.)	OF	6	19	4	5	0	0	1	3	.263	2	5	1	7	0	1	.875

CHANDLER, CHRIS — QB — FALCONS

PERSONAL: Born October 12, 1965, in Everett, Wash. ... 6-4/225. ... Full name: Christopher Mark Chandler. ... Brother of Greg Chandler, catcher with San Francisco Giants organization (1978); and son-in-law of John Brodie, quarterback with San Francisco 49ers (1957-73).
HIGH SCHOOL: Everett (Wash.).
COLLEGE: Washington (degree in economics, 1988).
TRANSACTIONS/CAREER NOTES: Selected by Indianapolis Colts in third round (76th pick overall) of 1988 NFL draft. ... Signed by Colts (July 23, 1988). ... On injured reserve with knee injury (October 3, 1989-remainder of season). ... Traded by Colts to Tampa Bay Buccaneers for first round pick (DL Steve Emtman) in 1992 draft (August 7, 1990). ... Claimed on waivers by Phoenix Cardinals (November 6, 1991). ... Granted unconditional free agency (February 17, 1994). ... Signed by Los Angeles Rams (May 6, 1994). ... Granted unconditional free agency (February 17, 1995). ... Signed by Houston Oilers (March 10, 1995). ... Traded by Oilers to Atlanta Falcons for fourth- (WR Derrick Mason) and sixth-round (traded to New Orleans) picks in 1997 draft (February 24, 1997).
CHAMPIONSHIP GAME EXPERIENCE: Played in NFC championship game (1998 season). ... Played in Super Bowl XXXIII (1998 season).
HONORS: Played in Pro Bowl (1997 and 1998 seasons).
PRO STATISTICS: 1988—Fumbled eight times and recovered five fumbles for minus six yards. 1990—Fumbled five times and recovered one fumble for minus two yards. 1991—Fumbled six times and recovered two fumbles for minus seven yards. 1992—Fumbled nine times and recovered two fumbles for minus 11 yards. 1993—Fumbled twice. 1994—Fumbled three times. 1995—Tied for AFC lead with 12 fumbles and recovered five fumbles for minus nine yards. 1996—Fumbled eight times and recovered three fumbles for minus four yards. 1997—Fumbled nine times and recovered three fumbles for minus 18 yards. 1998—Caught one pass for 22 yards, fumbled six times and recovered one fumble for minus four yards.
SINGLE GAME HIGHS (regular season): Attempts—47 (October 1, 1995, vs. Jacksonville); completions—28 (September 20, 1992, vs. Dallas); yards—383 (September 20, 1992, vs. Dallas); and touchdown passes—4 (September 24, 1995, vs. Cincinnati).
STATISTICAL PLATEAUS: 300-yard passing games: 1992 (1), 1995 (1), 1998 (1). Total: 3.
MISCELLANEOUS: Regular-season record as starting NFL quarterback: 48-50 (.490). ... Postseason record as starting NFL quarterback: 2-1 (.667).

					PASSING						RUSHING			TOTALS		
Year Team	G	GS	Att.	Cmp.	Pct.	Yds.	TD	Int.	Avg.	Rat.	Att.	Yds.	Avg.	TD	TD	2pt.	Pts.
1988—Indianapolis NFL	15	13	233	129	55.4	1619	8	12	6.95	67.2	46	139	3.0	3	3	...	18
1989—Indianapolis NFL	3	3	80	39	48.8	537	2	3	6.71	63.4	7	57	8.1	1	1	...	6
1990—Tampa Bay NFL	7	3	83	42	50.6	464	1	6	5.59	41.4	13	71	5.5	1	1	...	6
1991—Tampa Bay NFL	6	3	104	53	51.0	557	4	8	5.36	47.6	18	79	4.4	0	0	...	0
—Phoenix NFL	3	2	50	25	50.0	289	1	2	5.78	57.8	8	32	4.0	0	0	...	0
1992—Phoenix NFL	15	13	413	245	59.3	2832	15	15	6.86	77.1	36	149	4.1	1	1	...	6
1993—Phoenix NFL	4	2	103	52	50.5	471	3	2	4.57	64.8	3	2	0.7	0	0	...	0
1994—L.A. Rams NFL	12	6	176	108	61.4	1352	7	2	7.68	93.8	18	61	3.4	1	1	0	6
1995—Houston NFL	13	13	356	225	63.2	2460	17	10	6.91	87.8	28	58	2.1	2	2	1	14
1996—Houston NFL	12	12	320	184	57.5	2099	16	11	6.56	79.7	28	113	4.0	0	0	0	0
1997—Atlanta NFL	14	14	342	202	59.1	2692	20	7	7.87	95.1	43	158	3.7	0	0	0	0
1998—Atlanta NFL	14	14	327	190	58.1	3154	25	12	*9.65	100.9	36	121	3.4	2	2	0	12
Pro totals (11 years)	118	98	2587	1494	57.8	18526	119	90	7.16	80.9	284	1040	3.7	11	11	1	68

CHAVOUS, COREY — S — CARDINALS

PERSONAL: Born January 15, 1976, in Aiken, S.C. ... 6-0/204. ... Cousin of Fred Vinson, cornerback, Green Bay Packers.
HIGH SCHOOL: Silver Bluff (Aiken, S.C.).
COLLEGE: Vanderbilt.
TRANSACTIONS/CAREER NOTES: Selected by Arizona Cardinals in second round (33rd pick overall) of 1998 NFL draft. ... Signed by Cardinals (July 23, 1998).
PRO STATISTICS: 1998—Recovered one fumble.

			INTERCEPTIONS			
Year Team	G	GS	No.	Yds.	Avg.	TD
1998—Arizona NFL	16	5	2	0	0.0	0

CHERRY, JE'ROD DB SAINTS

PERSONAL: Born May 30, 1973, in Charlotte. ... 6-1/208. ... Full name: Je'Rod L. Cherry. ... Name pronounced juh-ROD.
HIGH SCHOOL: Berkeley (Calif.).
COLLEGE: California (degree in political science, 1995).
TRANSACTIONS/CAREER NOTES: Selected by New Orleans Saints in second round (40th pick overall) of 1996 NFL draft. ... Signed by Saints (July 3, 1996). ... Granted free agency (February 12, 1999).
PLAYING EXPERIENCE: New Orleans NFL, 1996-1998. ... Games/Games started: 1996 (13/0), 1997 (16/0), 1998 (14/0). Total: 43/0.
PRO STATISTICS: 1996—Recovered one fumble. 1998—Credited with two sacks.

CHERRY, MIKE QB GIANTS

PERSONAL: Born December 15, 1973, in Texarkana, Ark. ... 6-3/225. ... Full name: Michael Cherry.
HIGH SCHOOL: Arkansas (Texarkana, Ark.).
COLLEGE: Murray State.
TRANSACTIONS/CAREER NOTES: Selected by New York Giants in sixth round (171st pick overall) of 1997 NFL draft. ... Signed by Giants for 1997 season. ... Assigned by Giants to Rhein Fire in 1999 NFL Europe enhancement allocation program (February 22, 1999).
PLAYING EXPERIENCE: New York Giants NFL, 1997 and 1998. ... Games/Games started: 1997 (1/0), 1998 (1/0). Total: 2/0.
PRO STATISTICS: 1997—Rushed once for minus two yards. 1998—Rushed three times for minus three yards and attempted one pass without a completion.
SINGLE GAME HIGHS (regular season): Attempts—1 (December 20, 1998, vs. Kansas City); completions—0; yards—0; and touchdown passes—0.

CHESTER, LARRY DT COLTS

PERSONAL: Born October 17, 1975, in Hammond, La. ... 6-2/305.
HIGH SCHOOL: Hammond (La.).
JUNIOR COLLEGE: Southeast Mississippi Junior College.
COLLEGE: Temple.
TRANSACTIONS/CAREER NOTES: Signed as non-drafted free agent by Indianapolis Colts (April 24, 1998). ... Released by Colts (August 31, 1998). ... Re-signed by Colts to practice squad (September 2, 1998). ... Activated (September 11, 1998).

Year Team	G	GS	SACKS
1998—Indianapolis NFL	14	2	3.0

CHMURA, MARK TE PACKERS

PERSONAL: Born February 22, 1969, in Deerfield, Mass. ... 6-5/255. ... Full name: Mark William Chmura. ... Name pronounced cha-MER-ah.
HIGH SCHOOL: Frontier Regional (South Deerfield, Mass.).
COLLEGE: Boston College.
TRANSACTIONS/CAREER NOTES: Selected by Green Bay Packers in sixth round (157th pick overall) of 1992 NFL draft. ... Signed by Packers (July 2, 1992). ... On injured reserve with back injury (August 24, 1992-entire season).
CHAMPIONSHIP GAME EXPERIENCE: Played in NFC championship game (1995-97 seasons). ... Member of Super Bowl championship team (1996 season). ... Played in Super Bowl XXXII (1997 season).
HONORS: Named tight end on THE SPORTING NEWS college All-America second team (1991). ... Played in Pro Bowl (1995, 1997 and 1998 seasons).
POST SEASON RECORDS: Shares Super Bowl and NFL postseason career and single-game records for most two-point conversions—1 (January 26, 1997, vs. New England).
PRO STATISTICS: 1993—Returned one kickoff for no yards and recovered one fumble.
SINGLE GAME HIGHS (regular season): Receptions—7 (December 3, 1995, vs. Cincinnati); yards—109 (December 3, 1995, vs. Cincinnati); and touchdown receptions—2 (December 7, 1998, vs. Tampa Bay).
STATISTICAL PLATEAUS: 100-yard receiving games: 1995 (2).

			RECEIVING				TOTALS			
Year Team	G	GS	No.	Yds.	Avg.	TD	TD	2pt.	Pts.	Fum.
1992—Green Bay NFL					Did not play.					
1993—Green Bay NFL	14	0	2	13	6.5	0	0	...	0	1
1994—Green Bay NFL	14	4	14	165	11.8	0	0	0	0	0
1995—Green Bay NFL	16	15	54	679	12.6	7	7	1	44	0
1996—Green Bay NFL	13	13	28	370	13.2	0	0	0	0	0
1997—Green Bay NFL	15	14	38	417	11.0	6	6	0	36	1
1998—Green Bay NFL	15	14	47	554	11.8	4	4	0	24	1
Pro totals (6 years)	87	60	183	2198	12.0	17	17	1	104	3

CHORAK, JASON LB COLTS

PERSONAL: Born September 23, 1974, in Vashon, Wash. ... 6-4/253.
HIGH SCHOOL: Vashon (Wash.).
COLLEGE: Washington.
TRANSACTIONS/CAREER NOTES: Selected by St. Louis Rams in seventh round (236th pick overall) of 1998 NFL draft. ... Signed by Rams (July 8, 1998). ... Released by Rams (August 30, 1998). ... Re-signed by Rams to practice squad (September 1, 1998). ... Signed by Indianapolis Colts off Rams practice squad (October 21, 1998).
HONORS: Named outside linebacker on THE SPORTING NEWS college All-America first team (1996).

Year Team	G	GS	SACKS
1998—Indianapolis NFL	8	0	1.0

CHREBET, WAYNE   WR   JETS

PERSONAL: Born August 14, 1973, in Garfield, N.J. ... 5-10/185. ... Name pronounced kra-BET.
HIGH SCHOOL: Garfield (N.J.).
COLLEGE: Hofstra.
TRANSACTIONS/CAREER NOTES: Signed as non-drafted free agent by New York Jets (April 25, 1995).
CHAMPIONSHIP GAME EXPERIENCE: Played in AFC championship game (1998 season).
PRO STATISTICS: 1995—Rushed once for one yard. 1996—Recovered two fumbles. 1997—Returned one kickoff for five yards.
SINGLE GAME HIGHS (regular season): Receptions—12 (October 13, 1996, vs. Jacksonville); yards—162 (October 13, 1996, vs. Jacksonville); and touchdown receptions—2 (November 29, 1998, vs. Carolina).
STATISTICAL PLATEAUS: 100-yard receiving games: 1996 (1), 1997 (1), 1998 (5). Total: 7.

				RECEIVING			PUNT RETURNS			TOTALS			
Year Team	G	GS	No.	Yds.	Avg.	TD	No.	Yds.	Avg.	TD	TD	2pt.	Pts.	Fum.
1995—New York Jets NFL	16	16	66	726	11.0	4	0	0	...	0	4	0	24	1
1996—New York Jets NFL	16	9	84	909	10.8	3	28	139	5.0	0	3	0	18	5
1997—New York Jets NFL	16	1	58	799	13.8	3	0	0	...	0	3	0	18	0
1998—New York Jets NFL	16	15	75	1083	14.4	8	0	0	...	0	8	0	48	0
Pro totals (4 years)	64	41	283	3517	12.4	18	28	139	5.0	0	18	0	108	6

CHRISTIAN, BOB   FB   FALCONS

PERSONAL: Born November 14, 1968, in St. Louis. ... 5-11/232. ... Full name: Robert Douglas Christian.
HIGH SCHOOL: McCluer North (Florissant, Mo.).
COLLEGE: Northwestern.
TRANSACTIONS/CAREER NOTES: Selected by Atlanta Falcons in 12th round (310th pick overall) of 1991 NFL draft. ... Signed by Falcons (July 18, 1991). ... Released by Falcons (August 20, 1991). ... Selected by London Monarchs in 16th round (175th pick overall) of 1992 World League draft. ... Signed by San Diego Chargers (July 10, 1992). ... Released by Chargers (August 25, 1992). ... Signed by Chicago Bears to practice squad (September 8, 1992). ... Activated (December 18, 1992). ... On injured reserve with knee injury (December 2, 1994-remainder of season). ... Selected by Carolina Panthers from Bears in NFL expansion draft (February 15, 1995). ... Granted free agency (February 16, 1996). ... Re-signed by Panthers (July 19, 1996). ... On injured reserve with shoulder injury (August 25, 1996-entire season). ... Granted unconditional free agency (February 14, 1997). ... Signed by Falcons (March 6, 1997). ... On injured reserve with knee injury (December 15, 1998-remainder of season).
PRO STATISTICS: 1995—Recovered one fumble. 1997—Recovered one fumble. 1998—Recovered two fumbles.
SINGLE GAME HIGHS (regular season): Attempts—6 (December 3, 1995, vs. Indianapolis); yards—39 (November 26, 1995, vs. New Orleans); and rushing touchdowns—0.

			RUSHING				RECEIVING				TOTALS			
Year Team	G	GS	Att.	Yds.	Avg.	TD	No.	Yds.	Avg.	TD	TD	2pt.	Pts.	Fum.
1992—Chicago NFL	2	0	0	0	...	0	0	0	...	0	0	...	0	0
1993—Chicago NFL	14	1	8	19	2.4	0	16	160	10.0	0	0	...	0	0
1994—Chicago NFL	12	0	7	29	4.1	0	2	30	15.0	0	0	0	0	0
1995—Carolina NFL	14	12	41	158	3.9	0	29	255	8.8	1	1	1	8	1
1996—Carolina NFL								Did not play.						
1997—Atlanta NFL	16	12	7	8	1.1	0	22	154	7.0	1	1	0	6	3
1998—Atlanta NFL	14	11	8	21	2.6	2	19	214	11.3	1	3	0	18	1
Pro totals (6 years)	72	36	71	235	3.3	2	88	813	9.2	3	5	1	32	5

CHRISTIE, STEVE   K   BILLS

PERSONAL: Born November 13, 1967, in Oakville, Ont. ... 6-0/185. ... Full name: Geoffrey Stephen Christie.
HIGH SCHOOL: Trafalgar (Oakville, Ont.).
COLLEGE: William & Mary.
TRANSACTIONS/CAREER NOTES: Signed as non-drafted free agent by Tampa Bay Buccaneers (May 8, 1990). ... Granted unconditional free agency (February 1, 1992). ... Signed by Buffalo Bills (February 5, 1992).
CHAMPIONSHIP GAME EXPERIENCE: Played in AFC championship game (1992 and 1993 seasons). ... Played in Super Bowl XXVII (1992 season) and Super Bowl XXVIII (1993 season).
POST SEASON RECORDS: Holds Super Bowl single-game record for longest field goal—54 yards (January 30, 1994, vs. Dallas). ... Shares NFL postseason single-game record for most field goals—5; and most field goals attempted—6 (January 17, 1993, at Miami).
PRO STATISTICS: 1994—Recovered one fumble.

		KICKING						
Year Team	G	XPM	XPA	FGM	FGA	Lg.	50+	Pts.
1990—Tampa Bay NFL	16	27	27	23	27	54	2-2	96
1991—Tampa Bay NFL	16	22	22	15	20	49	0-0	67
1992—Buffalo NFL	16	§43	§44	24	30	†54	3-5	115
1993—Buffalo NFL	16	36	37	23	32	*59	1-6	105
1994—Buffalo NFL	16	§38	§38	24	28	52	2-2	110
1995—Buffalo NFL	16	33	35	31	40	51	2-5	126
1996—Buffalo NFL	16	33	33	24	29	48	0-1	105
1997—Buffalo NFL	16	21	21	24	30	†55	1-2	93
1998—Buffalo NFL	16	41	41	33	*41	52	1-3	§140
Pro totals (9 years)	144	294	298	221	277	59	12-26	957

CHRISTY, JEFF   C   VIKINGS

PERSONAL: Born February 3, 1969, in Natrona Heights, Pa. ... 6-3/285. ... Full name: Jeffrey Allen Christy. ... Brother of Greg Christy, offensive tackle with Buffalo Bills (1985).
HIGH SCHOOL: Freeport (Pa.) Area.
COLLEGE: Pittsburgh.

TRANSACTIONS/CAREER NOTES: Selected by Phoenix Cardinals in fourth round (91st pick overall) of 1992 NFL draft. ... Signed by Cardinals (July 21, 1992). ... Released by Cardinals (August 31, 1992). ... Signed by Minnesota Vikings (March 16, 1993). ... On injured reserve with ankle injury (November 26, 1997-remainder of season).
PLAYING EXPERIENCE: Minnesota NFL, 1993-1998. ... Games/Games started: 1993 (9/0), 1994 (16/16), 1995 (16/16), 1996 (16/16), 1997 (12/12), 1998 (16/16). Total: 85/76.
CHAMPIONSHIP GAME EXPERIENCE: Played in NFC championship game (1998 season).
HONORS: Played in Pro Bowl (1998 season).

CHRYPLEWICZ, PETE — TE — LIONS

PERSONAL: Born April 27, 1974, in Detroit. ... 6-5/253. ... Full name: Peter Gerald Chryplewicz.
HIGH SCHOOL: Stevenson (Sterling Heights, Mich.).
COLLEGE: Notre Dame (degree in business administration, 1996).
TRANSACTIONS/CAREER NOTES: Selected by Detroit Lions in fifth round (135th pick overall) of 1997 NFL draft. ... Signed by Lions (July 10, 1997).
SINGLE GAME HIGHS (regular season): Receptions—2 (October 15, 1998, vs. Green Bay); yards—23 (September 21, 1997, vs. New Orleans); and touchdown receptions—1 (October 15, 1998, vs. Green Bay).

			RECEIVING				TOTALS			
Year Team	G	GS	No.	Yds.	Avg.	TD	TD	2pt.	Pts.	Fum.
1997—Detroit NFL	10	0	3	27	9.0	1	1	0	6	0
1998—Detroit NFL	16	2	4	20	5.0	2	2	0	12	1
Pro totals (2 years)	26	2	7	47	6.7	3	3	0	18	1

CLARK, GREG — TE — 49ERS

PERSONAL: Born April 7, 1972, in Centerville, Utah. ... 6-4/251. ... Full name: Gregory Jay Clark.
HIGH SCHOOL: Viewmont (Bountiful, Utah).
JUNIOR COLLEGE: Ricks College (Idaho).
COLLEGE: Stanford (degree in psychology, 1996).
TRANSACTIONS/CAREER NOTES: Selected by San Francisco 49ers in third round (77th pick overall) of 1997 NFL draft. ... Signed by 49ers (July 17, 1997).
CHAMPIONSHIP GAME EXPERIENCE: Played in NFC championship game (1997 season).
POST SEASON RECORDS: Shares NFL postseason career record for most two-point conversions—1.
SINGLE GAME HIGHS (regular season): Receptions—3 (December 27, 1998, vs. St. Louis); yards—46 (December 27, 1998, vs. St. Louis); and touchdown receptions—1 (October 11, 1998, vs. New Orleans).

			RECEIVING				TOTALS			
Year Team	G	GS	No.	Yds.	Avg.	TD	TD	2pt.	Pts.	Fum.
1997—San Francisco NFL	15	4	8	96	12.0	1	1	0	6	0
1998—San Francisco NFL	13	8	12	124	10.3	1	1	1	8	0
Pro totals (2 years)	28	12	20	220	11.0	2	2	1	14	0

CLARK, JON — OT — CARDINALS

PERSONAL: Born April 11, 1973, in Philadelphia. ... 6-6/345.
HIGH SCHOOL: John Bartram (Philadelphia).
COLLEGE: Temple.
TRANSACTIONS/CAREER NOTES: Selected by Chicago Bears in sixth round (187th pick overall) of 1996 NFL draft. ... Signed by Bears (July 11, 1996). ... Released by Bears (October 7, 1997). ... Signed by New York Jets (December 8, 1997). ... Released by Jets (December 12, 1997). ... Signed by Arizona Cardinals (February 18, 1998). ... Released by Cardinals (September 12, 1998). ... Re-signed by Cardinals to practice squad (September 16, 1998). ... Activated (November 19, 1998).
PLAYING EXPERIENCE: Chicago NFL, 1996 and 1997; Arizona NFL, 1998. ... Games/Games started: 1996 (1/0), 1997 (1/0), 1998 (6/0). Total: 8/0.

CLARK, RICO — DB — COLTS

PERSONAL: Born June 6, 1974, in Atlanta. ... 5-10/181. ... Full name: Rico Cornell Clark.
HIGH SCHOOL: Lakeside (Atlanta).
COLLEGE: Louisville.
TRANSACTIONS/CAREER NOTES: Signed as non-drafted free agent by Indianapolis Colts (April 27, 1997). ... Released by Colts (August 18, 1997). ... Re-signed by Colts to practice squad (August 25, 1997). ... Released by Colts (October 8, 1997). ... Re-signed by Colts to practice squad (November 4, 1997). ... Activated (November 25, 1997).
PRO STATISTICS: 1998—Returned three kickoffs for 38 yards.

			INTERCEPTIONS			
Year Team	G	GS	No.	Yds.	Avg.	TD
1997—Indianapolis NFL	4	2	1	14	14.0	0
1998—Indianapolis NFL	16	0	1	30	30.0	0
Pro totals (2 years)	20	2	2	44	22.0	0

CLARK, WILLIE — CB

PERSONAL: Born January 6, 1972, in New Haven, Conn. ... 5-10/186. ... Full name: Willie Calvin Clark Jr.
HIGH SCHOOL: Wheatland (Calif.).
COLLEGE: Notre Dame.
TRANSACTIONS/CAREER NOTES: Selected by San Diego Chargers in third round (82nd pick overall) of 1994 NFL draft. ... Signed by Chargers (July 12, 1994). ... Granted free agency (February 14, 1997). ... Re-signed by Chargers (April 18, 1997). ... Claimed on waivers by Baltimore

Ravens (August 24, 1997). ... Traded by Ravens to Philadelphia Eagles (August 27, 1997); completing deal in which Eagles traded G Ben Cavil to Ravens for future considerations (August 24, 1997). ... Granted unconditional free agency (February 13, 1998). ... Signed by St. Louis Rams (May 6, 1998). ... Released by Rams (August 24, 1998). ... Re-signed by Rams (August 27, 1998). ... Released by Rams (September 2, 1998). ... Signed by San Diego Chargers (November 25, 1998). ... Granted unconditional free agency (February 12, 1999).
CHAMPIONSHIP GAME EXPERIENCE: Played in AFC championship game (1994 season). ... Played in Super Bowl XXIX (1994 season).
PRO STATISTICS: 1995—Recovered one fumble. 1996—Recovered one fumble for nine yards. 1997—Returned one kickoff for 39 yards and a touchdown.

				INTERCEPTIONS		
Year Team	G	GS	No.	Yds.	Avg.	TD
1994—San Diego NFL	6	0	0	0	...	0
1995—San Diego NFL	16	2	2	14	7.0	0
1996—San Diego NFL	16	4	2	83	41.5	1
1997—Philadelphia NFL	16	2	0	0	...	0
1998—San Diego NFL	5	0	0	0	...	0
Pro totals (5 years)	59	8	4	97	24.3	1

CLAY, HAYWARD TE COWBOYS

PERSONAL: Born July 5, 1973, in Snyder, Texas. ... 6-3/260. ... Full name: Hayward John Clay.
HIGH SCHOOL: Snyder (Texas).
COLLEGE: Texas.
TRANSACTIONS/CAREER NOTES: Selected by St. Louis Rams in sixth round (201st pick overall) of 1996 NFL draft. ... Signed by Rams (July 10, 1996). ... Released by Rams (August 17, 1997). ... Selected by Barcelona Dragons in 1998 NFL Europe draft (February 18, 1998). ... Signed by Chicago Bears (June 23, 1998). ... Claimed on waivers by Dallas Cowboys (August 31, 1998).
PRO STATISTICS: 1996—Recovered one fumble.
SINGLE GAME HIGHS (regular season): Receptions—2 (October 27, 1996, vs. Baltimore); yards—34 (December 1, 1996, vs. New Orleans); and touchdown receptions—0.

C

				RECEIVING		
Year Team	G	GS	No.	Yds.	Avg.	TD
1996—St. Louis NFL	11	4	4	51	12.8	0
1997—				Did not play.		
1998—Rhein NFLE	...	...	6	112	18.7	0
—Dallas NFL	3	2	1	27	27.0	0
NFL Europe totals (1 year)	...	...	6	112	18.7	0
NFL totals (2 years)	14	6	5	78	15.6	0
Pro totals (3 years)	...	...	11	190	17.3	0

CLAY, WILLIE S PATRIOTS

PERSONAL: Born September 5, 1970, in Pittsburgh. ... 5-10/200. ... Full name: Willie James Clay.
HIGH SCHOOL: Linsly (Wheeling, W.Va.).
COLLEGE: Georgia Tech.
TRANSACTIONS/CAREER NOTES: Selected by Detroit Lions in eighth round (221st pick overall) of 1992 NFL draft. ... Signed by Lions (July 25, 1992). ... Released by Lions (September 4, 1992). ... Re-signed by Lions to practice squad (September 8, 1992). ... Activated (November 20, 1992). ... Granted free agency (February 17, 1995). ... Re-signed by Lions (May 16, 1995). ... Granted unconditional free agency (February 16, 1996). ... Signed by New England Patriots (March 14, 1996).
CHAMPIONSHIP GAME EXPERIENCE: Played in AFC championship game (1996 season). ... Played in Super Bowl XXXI (1996 season).
HONORS: Named defensive back on THE SPORTING NEWS college All-America second team (1991).
PRO STATISTICS: 1993—Credited with one sack, returned two kickoffs for 34 yards and recovered two fumbles for 54 yards and two touchdowns. 1996—Recovered one fumble for 17 yards. 1997—Recovered two fumbles. 1998—Recovered one fumble for three yards.

				INTERCEPTIONS		
Year Team	G	GS	No.	Yds.	Avg.	TD
1992—Detroit NFL	6	0	0	0	...	0
1993—Detroit NFL	16	1	0	0	...	0
1994—Detroit NFL	16	16	3	54	18.0	1
1995—Detroit NFL	16	16	8	*173	21.6	0
1996—New England NFL	16	16	4	50	12.5	0
1997—New England NFL	16	16	6	109	18.2	1
1998—New England NFL	16	16	3	19	6.3	0
Pro totals (7 years)	102	81	24	405	16.9	2

CLEELAND, CAM TE SAINTS

PERSONAL: Born April 15, 1975, in Sedro Woolley, Wash. ... 6-4/272. ... Full name: Cameron Cleeland. ... Nephew of Phil Misley, pitcher in Milwaukee Braves organization (1956-58).
HIGH SCHOOL: Sedro Woolley (Wash.).
COLLEGE: Washington.
TRANSACTIONS/CAREER NOTES: Selected by New Orleans Saints in second round (40th pick overall) of 1998 NFL draft. ... Signed by Saints (June 9, 1998).
PRO STATISTICS: 1998—Recovered two fumbles for seven yards.
SINGLE GAME HIGHS (regular season): Receptions—10 (December 27, 1998, vs. Buffalo); yards—112 (December 27, 1998, vs. Buffalo); and touchdown receptions—1 (December 27, 1998, vs. Buffalo).
STATISTICAL PLATEAUS: 100-yard receiving games: 1998 (1).

			RECEIVING				TOTALS			
Year Team	G	GS	No.	Yds.	Avg.	TD	TD	2pt.	Pts.	Fum.
1998—New Orleans NFL	16	16	54	684	12.7	6	6	0	36	1

– 77 –

CLEMENT, ANTHONY — OT — CARDINALS

PERSONAL: Born April 10, 1976, in Lafayette, La. ... 6-7/355.
HIGH SCHOOL: Cecilia (Breaux Bridge, La.).
COLLEGE: Southwestern Louisiana.
TRANSACTIONS/CAREER NOTES: Selected by Arizona Cardinals in second round (36th pick overall) of 1998 NFL draft. ... Signed by Cardinals (June 16, 1998). ... On injured reserve with back injury (November 17, 1998-remainder of season).
PLAYING EXPERIENCE: Arizona NFL, 1998. ... Games/Games started: 1/0.

CLEMONS, CHARLIE — LB — RAMS

PERSONAL: Born July 4, 1972, in Griffin, Ga. ... 6-2/255. ... Full name: Charlie Fitzgerald Clemons.
HIGH SCHOOL: Griffin (Ga.).
JUNIOR COLLEGE: Northeast Oklahoma.
COLLEGE: Georgia (degree in recreation and leisure studies, 1993).
TRANSACTIONS/CAREER NOTES: Signed by Winnipeg Blue Bombers of CFL (May 1994). ... Transferred to Ottawa Rough Riders of CFL (August 1995). ... Transferred back to Blue Bombers (January 1996). ... Signed as non-drafted free agent by St. Louis Rams (February 19, 1997). ... On injured reserve with hamstring injury (November 24, 1997-remainder of season).
PRO STATISTICS: CFL: 1994—Recovered one fumble. 1995—Returned one kickoff for 10 yards. NFL: 1998—Returned one kickoff for no yards.

Year Team	G	GS	SACKS
1994—Winnipeg CFL	7	...	0.0
1995—Winnipeg CFL	6	...	3.0
—Ottawa CFL	7	...	3.0
1996—Ottawa CFL	14	...	6.0
1997—St. Louis NFL	5	0	0.0
1998—St. Louis NFL	16	0	2.0
CFL totals (3 years)	34	...	12.0
NFL totals (2 years)	21	0	2.0
Pro totals (5 years)	55	...	14.0

CLEMONS, DUANE — DE — VIKINGS

PERSONAL: Born May 23, 1974, in Riverside, Calif. ... 6-5/272.
HIGH SCHOOL: John W. North (Riverside, Calif.).
COLLEGE: California (degree in ethnic studies, 1993).
TRANSACTIONS/CAREER NOTES: Selected after junior season by Minnesota Vikings in first round (16th pick overall) of 1996 NFL draft. ... Signed by Vikings (July 25, 1996).
CHAMPIONSHIP GAME EXPERIENCE: Played in NFC championship game (1998 season).
PRO STATISTICS: 1996—Recovered one fumble for eight yards. 1997—Recovered one fumble.

Year Team	G	GS	SACKS
1996—Minnesota NFL	13	0	0.0
1997—Minnesota NFL	13	3	7.0
1998—Minnesota NFL	16	4	2.5
Pro totals (3 years)	42	7	9.5

COAKLEY, DEXTER — LB — COWBOYS

PERSONAL: Born October 20, 1972, in Charleston, S.C. ... 5-10/228. ... Full name: William Dexter Coakley.
HIGH SCHOOL: Wando (Mt. Pleasant, S.C.), then Fork Union (Va.) Military Academy.
COLLEGE: Appalachian State.
TRANSACTIONS/CAREER NOTES: Selected by Dallas Cowboys in third round (65th pick overall) of 1997 NFL draft. ... Signed by Cowboys (July 14, 1997).
PRO STATISTICS: 1997—Recovered one fumble for 16 yards and a touchdown. 1998—Recovered one fumble.

			INTERCEPTIONS				SACKS
Year Team	G	GS	No.	Yds.	Avg.	TD	No.
1997—Dallas NFL	16	16	1	6	6.0	0	2.5
1998—Dallas NFL	16	16	1	18	18.0	0	2.0
Pro totals (2 years)	32	32	2	24	12.0	0	4.5

COATES, BEN — TE — PATRIOTS

PERSONAL: Born August 16, 1969, in Greenwood, S.C. ... 6-5/245. ... Full name: Ben Terrence Coates.
HIGH SCHOOL: Greenwood (S.C.).
COLLEGE: Livingstone College, N.C. (degree in sports management).
TRANSACTIONS/CAREER NOTES: Selected after junior season by New England Patriots in fifth round (124th pick overall) of 1991 NFL draft. ... Signed by Patriots (April 25, 1991). ... Granted free agency (February 17, 1994). ... Re-signed by Patriots (April 2, 1994).
CHAMPIONSHIP GAME EXPERIENCE: Played in AFC championship game (1996 season). ... Played in Super Bowl XXXI (1996 season).
HONORS: Named tight end on THE SPORTING NEWS NFL All-Pro team (1994 and 1995). ... Played in Pro Bowl (1994-1998 seasons).
RECORDS: Holds NFL single-season record for most receptions by tight end—96 (1994).
PRO STATISTICS: 1991—Rushed once for minus six yards and returned one kickoff for six yards. 1992—Rushed once for two yards. 1994—Rushed once for no yards and recovered two fumbles. 1997—Returned one kickoff for 20 yards.
SINGLE GAME HIGHS (regular season): Receptions—12 (November 27, 1994, vs. Indianapolis); yards—161 (September 4, 1994, vs. Miami); and touchdown receptions—3 (November 26, 1995, vs. Buffalo).
STATISTICAL PLATEAUS: 100-yard receiving games: 1993 (1), 1994 (5), 1995 (1), 1996 (1), 1998 (1). Total: 9.

Year Team	G	GS	RECEIVING No.	Yds.	Avg.	TD	TOTALS TD	2pt.	Pts.	Fum.
1991—New England NFL	16	2	10	95	9.5	1	1	...	6	0
1992—New England NFL	16	2	20	171	8.6	3	3	...	18	1
1993—New England NFL	16	10	53	659	12.4	8	8	...	48	0
1994—New England NFL	16	16	§96	1174	12.2	7	7	0	42	2
1995—New England NFL	16	15	84	915	10.9	6	6	0	36	4
1996—New England NFL	16	15	62	682	11.0	9	9	1	56	1
1997—New England NFL	16	16	66	737	11.2	8	8	0	48	0
1998—New England NFL	14	14	67	668	10.0	6	6	0	36	0
Pro totals (8 years)	126	90	458	5101	11.1	48	48	1	290	8

COGHILL, GEORGE   S   BRONCOS

PERSONAL: Born March 30, 1970, in Fredericksburg. Va. ... 6-0/210.
HIGH SCHOOL: James Madison (Fredericksburg, Va.).
COLLEGE: Wake Forest.
TRANSACTIONS/CAREER NOTES: Signed as non-drafted free agent by New Orleans Saints (April 27, 1993). ... On injured reserve with knee injury (August 12, 1993-entire season). ... Released by Saints (August 22, 1994). ... Played for Scottish Claymores of World League (1995-1997). ... Signed by Denver Broncos (July 16, 1997). ... Released by Broncos (August 24, 1997). ... Re-signed by Broncos to practice squad (August 25, 1997). ... Released by Broncos (January 26, 1998). ... Re-signed by Broncos (January 28, 1998).
PLAYING EXPERIENCE: Scottish Claymores W.L., 1995-1997; Denver NFL, 1998. ... Games/Games started: 1995 (games played unavailable), 1996 (-), 1997 (-), 1998 (9/0).
CHAMPIONSHIP GAME EXPERIENCE: Played in AFC championship game (1998 season). ... Member of Super Bowl championship team (1998 season).
PRO STATISTICS: 1998—Intercepted one pass for 20 yards and returned three punts for 20 yards.

COLEMAN, ANDRE   WR/KR

PERSONAL: Born September 19, 1972, in Charlotte, N.C. ... 5-9/165. ... Full name: Andre Clintonian Coleman.
HIGH SCHOOL: Hickory (Hermitage, Pa.).
COLLEGE: Kansas State.
TRANSACTIONS/CAREER NOTES: Selected by San Diego Chargers in third round (70th pick overall) of 1994 NFL draft. ... Signed by Chargers (July 12, 1994). ... Granted free agency (February 14, 1997). ... Re-signed by Chargers (June 2, 1997). ... Released by Chargers (August 19, 1997). ... Signed by Seattle Seahawks (August 26, 1997). ... Released by Seahawks (October 1, 1997). ... Signed by Pittsburgh Steelers (October 14, 1997). ... Released by Steelers (October 13, 1998).
CHAMPIONSHIP GAME EXPERIENCE: Played in AFC championship game (1994 and 1997 seasons). ... Played in Super Bowl XXIX (1994 season).
POST SEASON RECORDS: Shares Super Bowl and NFL postseason career and single-game records for most touchdowns by kickoff return—1. ... Holds Super Bowl and NFL postseason single-game records for most kickoff returns—8; and most yards by kickoff returns—244 (January 29, 1995, vs. San Francisco). ... Shares Super Bowl and NFL postseason single-game records for most yards by combined kick returns—244 (January 29, 1995, vs. San Francisco).
PRO STATISTICS: 1994—Recovered one fumble. 1995—Recovered three fumbles. 1996—Recovered three fumbles.
SINGLE GAME HIGHS (regular season): Receptions—5 (September 15, 1996, vs. Green Bay); yards—70 (September 8, 1996, vs. Cincinnati); and touchdown receptions—1 (September 13, 1998, vs. Chicago).

Year Team	G	GS	RECEIVING No.	Yds.	Avg.	TD	PUNT RETURNS No.	Yds.	Avg.	TD	KICKOFF RETURNS No.	Yds.	Avg.	TD	TOTALS TD	2pt.	Pts.	Fum.
1994—San Diego NFL	13	0	0	0	...	0	0	0	...	0	§49	§1293	26.4	▲2	2	0	12	3
1995—San Diego NFL	15	0	4	78	19.5	0	28	326	§11.6	†1	§62	§1411	22.8	†2	3	0	18	10
1996—San Diego NFL	16	10	36	486	13.5	2	0	0	...	0	§55	1210	22.0	0	2	0	12	4
1997—Seattle NFL	2	0	0	0	...	0	0	0	...	0	3	65	21.7	0	0	0	0	1
—Pittsburgh NFL	8	0	0	0	...	0	5	5	1.0	0	24	487	20.3	0	0	0	0	1
1998—Pittsburgh NFL	4	0	4	49	12.3	1	10	53	5.3	0	0	0	...	0	1	0	6	1
Pro totals (5 years)	58	10	44	613	13.9	3	43	384	8.9	1	193	4466	23.1	4	8	0	48	20

COLEMAN, BEN   G/OT   JAGUARS

PERSONAL: Born May 18, 1971, in South Hill, Va. ... 6-5/327. ... Full name: Benjamin Leon Coleman.
HIGH SCHOOL: Park View Senior (South Hill, Va.).
COLLEGE: Wake Forest.
TRANSACTIONS/CAREER NOTES: Selected by Phoenix Cardinals in second round (32nd pick overall) of 1993 NFL draft. ... Signed by Cardinals (July 6, 1993). ... Cardinals franchise renamed Arizona Cardinals for 1994 season. ... Claimed on waivers by Jacksonville Jaguars (September 27, 1995). ... Granted free agency (February 16, 1996). ... Re-signed by Jaguars (June 6, 1996). ... Granted unconditional free agency (February 14, 1997). ... Re-signed by Jaguars (March 3, 1997).
PLAYING EXPERIENCE: Phoenix NFL, 1993; Arizona NFL, 1994; Arizona (3)-Jacksonville (10) NFL, 1995; Jacksonville NFL, 1996-1998. ... Games/Games started: 1993 (12/0), 1994 (15/13), 1995 (Ariz.-3/0; Jack.-10/5; Total: 13/5), 1996 (16/16), 1997 (16/16), 1998 (16/16). Total: 88/66.
CHAMPIONSHIP GAME EXPERIENCE: Played in AFC championship game (1996 season).
PRO STATISTICS: 1995—Recovered one fumble.

COLEMAN, MARCO   DE   REDSKINS

PERSONAL: Born December 18, 1969, in Dayton, Ohio. ... 6-3/267. ... Full name: Marco Darnell Coleman.
HIGH SCHOOL: Patterson Co-op (Dayton, Ohio).
COLLEGE: Georgia Tech.

TRANSACTIONS/CAREER NOTES: Selected after junior season by Miami Dolphins in first round (12th pick overall) of 1992 NFL draft. ... Signed by Dolphins (August 1, 1992). ... Designated by Dolphins as transition player (February 25, 1993). ... Tendered offer sheet by San Diego Chargers (February 28, 1996). ... Dolphins declined to match offer (March 7, 1996). ... Granted unconditional free agency (February 12, 1999). ... Signed by Washington Redskins (June 3, 1999).
CHAMPIONSHIP GAME EXPERIENCE: Played in AFC championship game (1992 season).
HONORS: Named linebacker on The Sporting News college All-America second team (1991).
PRO STATISTICS: 1997—Intercepted one pass for two yards. 1998—Recovered two fumbles.

Year Team	G	GS	SACKS
1992—Miami NFL	16	15	6.0
1993—Miami NFL	15	15	5.5
1994—Miami NFL	16	16	6.0
1995—Miami NFL	16	16	6.5
1996—San Diego NFL	16	15	4.0
1997—San Diego NFL	16	16	2.0
1998—San Diego NFL	16	16	3.5
Pro totals (7 years)	111	109	33.5

COLEMAN, MARCUS — DB — JETS

PERSONAL: Born May 24, 1974, in Dallas. ... 6-2/210.
HIGH SCHOOL: Lake Highlands (Dallas).
COLLEGE: Texas Tech.
TRANSACTIONS/CAREER NOTES: Selected by New York Jets in fifth round (133rd pick overall) of 1996 NFL draft. ... Signed by Jets (July 11, 1996).
CHAMPIONSHIP GAME EXPERIENCE: Played in AFC championship game (1998 season).
PRO STATISTICS: 1997—Recovered one fumble.

			INTERCEPTIONS			
Year Team	G	GS	No.	Yds.	Avg.	TD
1996—New York Jets NFL	13	4	1	23	23.0	0
1997—New York Jets NFL	16	2	1	24	24.0	0
1998—New York Jets NFL	14	0	0	0	...	0
Pro totals (3 years)	43	6	2	47	23.5	0

COLINET, STALIN — DE — VIKINGS

PERSONAL: Born July 19, 1974, in Bronx, N.Y. ... 6-6/284. ... Name pronounced KAWL-i-nay.
HIGH SCHOOL: Cardinal Hayes (Bronx, N.Y.).
COLLEGE: Boston College (degree in sociology, 1996).
TRANSACTIONS/CAREER NOTES: Selected by Minnesota Vikings in third round (78th pick overall) of 1997 NFL draft. ... Signed by Vikings (June 30, 1997).
PLAYING EXPERIENCE: Minnesota NFL, 1997 and 1998. ... Games/games started: 1997 (10/2), 1998 (11/3). Total: 21/5.
CHAMPIONSHIP GAME EXPERIENCE: Played in NFC championship game (1998 season).
PRO STATISTICS: 1998—Credited with one sack.

Year Team	G	GS	SACKS
1997—Minnesota NFL	10	2	0.0
1998—Minnesota NFL	11	3	1.0
Pro totals (2 years)	21	5	1.0

COLLINS, ANDRE — LB — BEARS

PERSONAL: Born May 4, 1968, in Riverside, N.J. ... 6-1/240. ... Full name: Andre Pierre Collins.
HIGH SCHOOL: Cinnaminson (N.J.).
COLLEGE: Penn State (degree in health planning and administration, 1991).
TRANSACTIONS/CAREER NOTES: Selected by Washington Redskins in second round (46th pick overall) of 1990 NFL draft. ... Signed by Redskins (July 22, 1990). ... Granted free agency (March 1, 1993). ... Re-signed by Redskins for 1993 season. ... Released by Redskins (April 11, 1995). ... Signed by Cincinnati Bengals (May 7, 1995). ... Granted free agency (February 16, 1996). ... Re-signed by Bengals (August 22, 1996). ... Granted free agency (February 14, 1997). ... Re-signed by Bengals (July 2, 1997). ... Granted unconditional free agency (February 13, 1998). ... Signed by Chicago Bears (May 27, 1998).
CHAMPIONSHIP GAME EXPERIENCE: Played in NFC championship game (1991 season). ... Member of Super Bowl championship team (1991 season).
HONORS: Named inside linebacker on The Sporting News college All-America second team (1989).
PRO STATISTICS: 1991—Fumbled once. 1992—Recovered one fumble for 40 yards. 1994—Returned one kickoff for no yards and recovered one fumble for 16 yards. 1995—Returned one kickoff for minus three yards. 1997—Recovered one fumble.

			INTERCEPTIONS				SACKS
Year Team	G	GS	No.	Yds.	Avg.	TD	No.
1990—Washington NFL	16	16	0	0	...	0	6.0
1991—Washington NFL	16	16	2	33	16.5	∞1	3.0
1992—Washington NFL	14	14	1	59	59.0	0	2.0
1993—Washington NFL	13	13	1	5	5.0	0	6.0
1994—Washington NFL	16	16	4	150	37.5	2	1.5
1995—Cincinnati NFL	16	6	2	3	1.5	0	4.0
1996—Cincinnati NFL	14	0	0	0	...	0	0.0
1997—Cincinnati NFL	16	0	0	0	...	0	3.0
1998—Chicago NFL	16	2	3	29	9.7	0	0.0
Pro totals (9 years)	137	83	13	279	21.5	3	25.5

COLLINS, CALVIN — C/G — FALCONS

PERSONAL: Born January 5, 1974, in Beaumont, Texas. ... 6-2/305. ... Full name: Calvin Lewis Collins.
HIGH SCHOOL: West Brook (Beaumont, Texas).
COLLEGE: Texas A&M.
TRANSACTIONS/CAREER NOTES: Selected by Atlanta Falcons in sixth round (180th pick overall) of 1997 NFL draft. ... Signed by Falcons (June 22, 1997).
PLAYING EXPERIENCE: Atlanta NFL, 1997 and 1998. ... Games/Games started: 1997 (15/13), 1998 (16/16). Total: 31/29.
CHAMPIONSHIP GAME EXPERIENCE: Played in NFC championship game (1998 season). ... Played in Super Bowl XXXIII (1998 season).
PRO STATISTICS: 1998—Recovered one fumble.

COLLINS, KERRY — QB — GIANTS

PERSONAL: Born December 30, 1972, in Lebanon, Pa. ... 6-5/240. ... Full name: Kerry Michael Collins.
HIGH SCHOOL: Wilson (West Lawn, Pa.).
COLLEGE: Penn State.
TRANSACTIONS/CAREER NOTES: Selected by Carolina Panthers in first round (fifth pick overall) of 1995 NFL draft. ... Signed by Panthers (July 17, 1995). ... Granted free agency (February 13, 1998). ... Re-signed by Panthers (July 24, 1998). ... Claimed on waivers by New Orleans Saints (October 14, 1998). ... Granted unconditional free agency (February 12, 1999). ... Signed by New York Giants (February 22, 1999).
CHAMPIONSHIP GAME EXPERIENCE: Played in NFC championship game (1996 season).
HONORS: Maxwell Award winner (1994). ... Davey O'Brien Award winner (1994). ... Named quarterback on The Sporting News college All-America first team (1994). ... Played in Pro Bowl (1996 season).
PRO STATISTICS: 1995—Fumbled 13 times and recovered four fumbles for minus 15 yards. 1996—Fumbled six times and recovered one fumble. 1997—Fumbled eight times and recovered two fumbles for minus 14 yards. 1998—Caught one pass for minus 11 yards, fumbled 13 times and recovered two fumbles for minus nine yards.
SINGLE GAME HIGHS (regular season): Attempts—53 (September 27, 1998, vs. Green Bay); completions—26 (December 15, 1996, vs. Baltimore); yards—335 (November 26, 1995, vs. New Orleans); and touchdown passes—3 (October 4, 1998, vs. Atlanta).
STATISTICAL PLATEAUS: 300-yard passing games: 1995 (2), 1996 (1), 1997 (1), 1998 (2). Total: 6.
MISCELLANEOUS: Selected by Detroit Tigers organization in 26th round of free-agent draft (June 4, 1990); did not sign. ... Selected by Toronto Blue Jays organization in 58th round of free-agent draft (June 4, 1994); did not sign. ... Regular-season record as starting NFL quarterback: 24-25 (.490). ... Postseason record as starting NFL quarterback: 1-1 (.500). ... Holds Carolina Panthers all-time records for most yards passing (8,306) and most touchdown passes (47).

				PASSING						RUSHING				TOTALS	
Year Team	G	GS	Att.	Cmp.	Pct.	Yds.	TD	Int.	Avg.	Rat.	Att.	Yds.	Avg.	TD	TD	2pt.	Pts.
1995—Carolina NFL	15	13	433	214	49.4	2717	14	19	6.27	61.9	42	74	1.8	3	3	0	18
1996—Carolina NFL	13	12	364	204	56.0	2454	14	9	6.74	79.4	32	38	1.2	0	0	1	2
1997—Carolina NFL	13	13	381	200	52.5	2124	11	*21	5.57	55.7	26	65	2.5	1	1	0	6
1998—Carolina NFL	4	4	162	76	46.9	1011	8	5	6.24	70.8	7	40	5.7	0	0	1	2
—New Orleans NFL	7	7	191	94	49.2	1202	4	10	6.29	54.5	23	113	4.9	1	1	0	6
Pro totals (4 years)	52	49	1531	788	51.5	9508	51	64	6.21	64.5	130	330	2.5	5	5	2	34

COLLINS, MARK — S — SEAHAWKS

PERSONAL: Born January 16, 1964, in St. Louis. ... 5-10/196. ... Full name: Mark Anthony Collins.
HIGH SCHOOL: Pacific (San Bernardino, Calif.).
COLLEGE: Cal State Fullerton.
TRANSACTIONS/CAREER NOTES: Selected by New York Giants in second round (44th pick overall) of 1986 NFL draft. ... Signed by Giants (July 30, 1986). ... On injured reserve with back injury (December 23, 1987-remainder of season). ... On injured reserve with pulled groin (December 3, 1988-remainder of season). ... On injured reserve with sprained ankle (September 19-October 19, 1990). ... Granted free agency (February 1, 1992). ... Re-signed by Giants (August 7, 1992). ... On injured reserve with rib injury (December 24, 1992-remainder of season). ... Granted unconditional free agency (February 17, 1994). ... Signed by Kansas City Chiefs (April 26, 1994). ... Released by Chiefs (May 9, 1997). ... Signed by Green Bay Packers (November 27, 1997). ... Granted unconditional free agency (February 13, 1998). ... Signed by Seattle Seahawks (April 21, 1998).
CHAMPIONSHIP GAME EXPERIENCE: Played in NFC championship game (1986 and 1990 seasons). ... Member of Super Bowl championship team (1986 and 1990 seasons). ... Member of Packers for NFC championship game (1997 season); inactive. ... Played in Super Bowl XXXII (1997 season).
HONORS: Named defensive back on The Sporting News college All-America first team (1985).
PRO STATISTICS: 1986—Returned three punts for 11 yards and recovered three fumbles for five yards. 1988—Credited with one safety. 1989—Recovered two fumbles for eight yards. 1991—Recovered two fumbles. 1994—Recovered two fumbles. 1995—Recovered one fumble for 34 yards and a touchdown. 1996—Recovered one fumble.

			INTERCEPTIONS				SACKS	KICKOFF RETURNS				TOTALS		
Year Team	G	GS	No.	Yds.	Avg.	TD	No.	No.	Yds.	Avg.	TD	TD	2pt.	Pts.	Fum.
1986—New York Giants NFL	15	9	1	0	0.0	0	0.0	11	204	18.5	0	0	...	0	2
1987—New York Giants NFL	11	11	2	28	14.0	0	1.5	0	0	...	0	0	...	0	0
1988—New York Giants NFL	11	11	1	13	13.0	0	0.0	4	67	16.8	0	0	...	2	0
1989—New York Giants NFL	16	16	2	12	6.0	0	1.0	1	0	0.0	0	0	...	0	0
1990—New York Giants NFL	13	12	2	0	0.0	0	0.0	0	0	...	0	0	...	0	0
1991—New York Giants NFL	16	15	4	77	19.3	0	0.0	0	0	...	0	0	...	0	0
1992—New York Giants NFL	14	14	1	0	0.0	0	0.0	0	0	...	0	0	...	0	0
1993—New York Giants NFL	16	16	4	77	19.3	1	1.0	0	0	...	0	1	...	6	0
1994—Kansas City NFL	14	13	2	83	41.5	1	2.0	0	0	...	0	1	0	6	0
1995—Kansas City NFL	16	15	1	8	8.0	0	0.0	0	0	...	0	1	0	6	1
1996—Kansas City NFL	16	15	6	45	7.5	0	1.0	0	0	...	0	0	0	0	0
1997—Green Bay NFL	1	0	0	0	...	0	0.0	0	0	...	0	0	0	0	0
1998—Seattle NFL	9	0	1	0	0.0	0	1.5	0	0	...	0	0	0	0	0
Pro totals (13 years)	168	147	27	343	12.7	2	8.0	16	271	16.9	0	3	0	20	3

COLLINS, MO   OT   RAIDERS

PERSONAL: Born September 22, 1976, in Charlotte, N.C. ... 6-4/325. ... Full name: Damon Jamal Collins.
HIGH SCHOOL: West Charlotte (N.C.).
COLLEGE: Florida.
TRANSACTIONS/CAREER NOTES: Selected after junior season by Oakland Raiders in first round (23rd pick overall) of 1998 NFL draft. ... Signed by Raiders (July 15, 1998).
PLAYING EXPERIENCE: Oakland NFL, 1998. ... Games/Games started: 16/11.

COLLINS, TODD   LB   RAMS

PERSONAL: Born May 27, 1970, in New Market, Tenn. ... 6-2/248. ... Full name: Todd Franklin Collins.
HIGH SCHOOL: Jefferson County (Dandridge, Tenn.).
COLLEGE: Georgia (did not play football), then Tennessee (did not play football), then Carson-Newman (Tenn.).
TRANSACTIONS/CAREER NOTES: Selected after junior season by New England Patriots in third round (64th pick overall) of 1992 NFL draft. ... Signed by Patriots (July 23, 1992). ... On injured reserve with neck injury (October 16-November 13, 1992); on practice squad (November 11-13, 1992). ... On injured reserve with knee injury (November 15, 1994-remainder of season). ... Granted free agency (February 17, 1995). ... Re-signed by Patriots (April 20, 1995). ... On reserved/retired list (July 21, 1995-April 16, 1996). ... Granted unconditional free agency (February 14, 1997). ... Re-signed by Patriots (April 4, 1997). ... Granted unconditional free agency (February 12, 1999). ... Signed by St. Louis Rams (March 12, 1999).
PLAYING EXPERIENCE: New England NFL, 1992-1994 and 1996-1998. ... Games/Games started: 1992 (10/0), 1993 (16/12), 1994 (7/7), 1996 (16/9), 1997 (15/15), 1998 (12/10). Total: 76/53.
CHAMPIONSHIP GAME EXPERIENCE: Played in AFC championship game (1996 season). ... Played in Super Bowl XXXI (1996 season).
PRO STATISTICS: 1992—Recovered two fumbles. 1993—Credited with one sack, intercepted one pass for eight yards and recovered one fumble for two yards. 1996—Intercepted one pass for seven yards. 1997—Credited with 1$\frac{1}{2}$ sacks.

COLLONS, FERRIC   DE

PERSONAL: Born December 4, 1969, in Scott Air Force Base (Belleville, Ill.). ... 6-6/285. ... Full name: Ferric Jason Collons.
HIGH SCHOOL: Jesuit (Carmichael, Calif.).
COLLEGE: California.
TRANSACTIONS/CAREER NOTES: Signed as non-drafted free agent by Los Angeles Raiders (April 1992). ... Released by Raiders (August 31, 1992). ... Re-signed by Raiders to practice squad (September 2, 1992). ... Inactive for all 16 games (1993). ... Released by Raiders (August 23, 1994). ... Signed by Jacksonville Jaguars (December 15, 1994). ... Inactive for two games (1994). ... Released by Jaguars (May 1, 1995). ... Signed by Green Bay Packers (May 22, 1995). ... Traded by Packers to New England Patriots for past considerations (August 27, 1995). ... Granted free agency (February 14, 1997). ... Tendered offer sheet by Philadelphia Eagles (April 14, 1997). ... Offer matched by Patriots (April 18, 1997). ... On injured reserve with shoulder injury (October 30, 1997-remainder of season). ... Released by Patriots (February 11, 1999).
CHAMPIONSHIP GAME EXPERIENCE: Played in AFC championship game (1996 season). ... Played in Super Bowl XXXI (1996 season).
PRO STATISTICS: 1997—Recovered one fumble for five yards.

Year Team	G	GS	SACKS
1992—Los Angeles Raiders NFL	Did not play.		
1993—Los Angeles Raiders NFL	Did not play.		
1994—Jacksonville NFL	Did not play.		
1995—New England NFL	16	4	4.0
1996—New England NFL	15	5	0.5
1997—New England NFL	6	5	1.0
1998—New England NFL	14	13	0.0
Pro totals (4 years)	**51**	**27**	**5.5**

COLMAN, DOUG   LB   GIANTS

PERSONAL: Born June 4, 1973, in Somers Point, N.J. ... 6-2/250.
HIGH SCHOOL: Ocean City (N.J.).
COLLEGE: Nebraska.
TRANSACTIONS/CAREER NOTES: Selected by New York Giants in sixth round (171st pick overall) of 1996 NFL draft. ... Signed by Giants (June 18, 1996). ... Granted free agency (February 12, 1999).
PLAYING EXPERIENCE: New York Giants NFL, 1996-1998. ... Games/Games started: 1996 (13/0), 1997 (14/0), 1998 (16/0). Total: 43/0.

COMELLA, GREG   FB   GIANTS

PERSONAL: Born July 29, 1975, in Wellesley, Mass. ... 6-1/240.
HIGH SCHOOL: Xaverian Brothers (Wellesley, Mass.).
COLLEGE: Stanford.
TRANSACTIONS/CAREER NOTES: Signed as non-drafted free agent by New York Giants (April 24, 1998).
PLAYING EXPERIENCE: New York Giants NFL, 1998. ... Games/Games started: 16/0.
PRO STATISTICS: 1998—Rushed once for six yards, caught one pass for three yards, returned one kickoff for 12 yards and recovered one fumble.
SINGLE GAME HIGHS (regular season): Attempts—1 (September 21, 1998, vs. Dallas); yards—6 (September 21, 1998, vs. Dallas); and rushing touchdowns—0.

COMPTON, MIKE   G   LIONS

PERSONAL: Born September 18, 1970, in Richlands, Va. ... 6-6/297. ... Full name: Michael Eugene Compton.
HIGH SCHOOL: Richlands (Va.).
COLLEGE: West Virginia.
TRANSACTIONS/CAREER NOTES: Selected by Detroit Lions in third round (68th pick overall) of 1993 NFL draft. ... Signed by Lions (June 4, 1993).
PLAYING EXPERIENCE: Detroit NFL, 1993-1998. ... Games/Games started: 1993 (8/0), 1994 (2/0), 1995 (16/8), 1996 (15/15), 1997 (16/16), 1998 (16/16). Total: 73/55.
HONORS: Named center on THE SPORTING NEWS college All-America first team (1992).
PRO STATISTICS: 1996—Fumbled once.

CONATY, BILLY   OL   BILLS

PERSONAL: Born March 8, 1973, in Baltimore. ... 6-2/306. ... Full name: William B. Conaty. ... Name pronounced con-ah-TEE.
HIGH SCHOOL: Milford (Conn.) Academy, then Camden (N.J.) Catholic.
COLLEGE: Virginia Tech.
TRANSACTIONS/CAREER NOTES: Signed as non-drafted free agent by Buffalo Bills (April 25, 1997). ... Released by Bills (August 24, 1997). ... Re-signed by Bills to practice squad (August 26, 1997). ... Activated (September 6, 1997). ... Released by Bills (September 22, 1997). ... Re-signed by Bills to practice squad (September 24, 1997).
PLAYING EXPERIENCE: Buffalo NFL, 1997 and 1998. ... Games/Games started: 1997 (1/0), 1998 (15/1). Totals: 16/1.
HONORS: Named center on THE SPORTING NEWS college All-America first team (1996).

CONLEY, STEVEN   LB   PANTHERS

PERSONAL: Born January 18, 1972, in Chicago. ... 6-5/240. ... Full name: Donald Steven Conley.
HIGH SCHOOL: Luther South (Chicago).
COLLEGE: Arkansas.
TRANSACTIONS/CAREER NOTES: Selected by Pittsburgh Steelers in third round (72nd pick overall) of 1996 NFL draft. ... Signed by Steelers (July 12, 1996). ... Traded by Steelers to Indianapolis Colts for fifth-round pick (TE Jerame Tuman) in 1999 draft (August 30, 1998). ... Released by Colts (September 16, 1998). ... Signed by Steelers (October 28, 1998). ... Released by Steelers (November 13, 1998). ... Re-signed by Steelers (November 17, 1998). ... Released by Steelers (November 25, 1998). ... Signed by Carolina Panthers (February 10, 1999).
PLAYING EXPERIENCE: Pittsburgh NFL, 1996 and 1997; Indianapolis (1)-Pittsburgh (2) NFL, 1998. ... Games/Games started: 1996 (2/0), 1997 (16/0), 1998 (Ind.-1/0; Pit.-2/1; Total: 3/1). Total: 21/1.
CHAMPIONSHIP GAME EXPERIENCE: Played in AFC championship game (1997 season).
PRO STATISTICS: 1997—Intercepted one pass for minus three yards and credited with four sacks.

CONNELL, ALBERT   WR   REDSKINS

PERSONAL: Born May 13, 1974, in Fort Lauderdale, Fla. ... 6-0/179. ... Full name: Albert Gene Anthony Connell.
HIGH SCHOOL: Piper (Fort Lauderdale, Fla.).
JUNIOR COLLEGE: Trinity Valley Community College (Texas).
COLLEGE: Texas A&M.
TRANSACTIONS/CAREER NOTES: Selected by Washington Redskins in fourth round (115th pick overall) of 1997 NFL draft. ... Signed by Redskins (May 28, 1997).
PRO STATISTICS: 1997—Rushed once for three yards.
SINGLE GAME HIGHS (regular season): Receptions—8 (December 13, 1998, vs. Carolina); yards—116 (December 13, 1998, vs. Carolina); and touchdown receptions—1 (December 13, 1998, vs. Carolina).
STATISTICAL PLATEAUS: 100-yard receiving games: 1998 (1).

			RECEIVING				TOTALS		
Year Team	G	GS	No.	Yds.	Avg.	TD	TD	2pt.	Pts.	Fum.
1997—Washington NFL	5	1	9	138	15.3	2	2	0	12	0
1998—Washington NFL	14	5	28	451	16.1	2	2	0	12	0
Pro totals (2 years)	19	6	37	589	15.9	4	4	0	24	0

CONRAD, CHRIS   OT   STEELERS

PERSONAL: Born May 27, 1975, in Fullerton, Calif. ... 6-6/310. ... Full name: Christopher Lee Conrad.
HIGH SCHOOL: Olinda (Brea, Calif.).
COLLEGE: Fresno State.
TRANSACTIONS/CAREER NOTES: Selected by Pittsburgh Steelers in third round (66th pick overall) of 1998 NFL draft. ... Signed by Steelers (July 9, 1998).
PLAYING EXPERIENCE: Pittsburgh NFL, 1998. ... Games/Games started: 6/1.

CONWAY, BRETT   K   REDSKINS

PERSONAL: Born March 8, 1975, in Atlanta. ... 6-2/192. ... Full name: Brett Alan Conway.
HIGH SCHOOL: Parkview (Lilburn, Ga.).
COLLEGE: Penn State.
TRANSACTIONS/CAREER NOTES: Selected by Green Bay Packers in third round (90th pick overall) of 1997 NFL draft. ... Signed by Packers (July 8, 1997). ... On injured reserve with thigh injury (September 3, 1997-entire season). ... Traded by Packers to New York Jets for an undisclosed draft pick (August 21, 1998). ... Released by Jets (August 30, 1998). ... Re-signed by Jets to practice squad (September 1, 1998). ... Released by Jets (September 23, 1998). ... Signed by Washington Redskins (November 12, 1998).
PLAYING EXPERIENCE: Washington NFL, 1998. ... Games/Games started: 6/0.

CONWAY, CURTIS — WR — BEARS

PERSONAL: Born March 13, 1971, in Los Angeles. ... 6-0/194. ... Full name: Curtis LaMont Conway.
HIGH SCHOOL: Hawthorne (Calif.).
JUNIOR COLLEGE: El Camino College (Calif.).
COLLEGE: Southern California.
TRANSACTIONS/CAREER NOTES: Selected after junior season by Chicago Bears in first round (seventh pick overall) of 1993 NFL draft. ... Signed by Bears (May 24, 1993). ... Granted free agency (February 16, 1996). ... Re-signed by Bears (March 4, 1996).
HONORS: Named kick returner on THE SPORTING NEWS college All-America second team (1992).
PRO STATISTICS: 1993—Fumbled once. 1994—Attempted one pass with a completion for 23 yards and a touchdown, fumbled twice and recovered one fumble. 1994—Returned eight punts for 63 yards. 1995—Attempted one pass without a completion. 1996—Attempted one pass with a completion for 33 yards and a touchdown. 1997—Attempted one pass without a completion. 1998—Attempted one pass without a completion and recovered one fumble.
SINGLE GAME HIGHS (regular season): Receptions—9 (December 22, 1996, vs. Tampa Bay); yards—148 (September 12, 1994, vs. Philadelphia); and touchdown receptions—3 (October 15, 1995, vs. Jacksonville).
STATISTICAL PLATEAUS: 100-yard receiving games: 1994 (1), 1995 (3), 1996 (4), 1997 (3). Total: 11.

			RUSHING			RECEIVING				KICKOFF RETURNS				TOTALS			
Year Team	G	GS	Att.	Yds.	Avg.	TD	No.	Yds.	Avg.	TD	No.	Yds.	Avg.	TD	TD	2pt.	Pts.	Fum.
1993—Chicago NFL	16	7	5	44	8.8	0	19	231	12.2	2	21	450	21.4	0	2	...	12	1
1994—Chicago NFL	13	12	6	31	5.2	0	39	546	14.0	2	10	228	22.8	0	2	1	14	2
1995—Chicago NFL	16	16	5	77	15.4	0	62	1037	16.7	12	0	0	...	0	12	0	72	0
1996—Chicago NFL	16	16	8	50	6.3	0	81	1049	13.0	7	0	0	...	0	7	0	42	1
1997—Chicago NFL	7	7	3	17	5.7	0	30	476	15.9	1	0	0	...	0	1	0	6	0
1998—Chicago NFL	15	15	5	48	9.6	0	54	733	13.6	3	0	0	...	0	3	0	18	1
Pro totals (6 years)	83	73	32	267	8.3	0	285	4072	14.3	27	31	678	21.9	0	27	1	164	5

CONWELL, ERNIE — TE — RAMS

PERSONAL: Born August 17, 1972, in Renton, Wash. ... 6-1/265. ... Full name: Ernest Harold Conwell.
HIGH SCHOOL: Kentwood (Kent, Wash.).
COLLEGE: Washington (degree in sociology, 1995).
TRANSACTIONS/CAREER NOTES: Selected by St. Louis Rams in second round (59th pick overall) of 1996 NFL draft. ... Signed by Rams (June 25, 1996). ... On injured reserve with knee injury (October 28, 1998-remainder of season).
PRO STATISTICS: 1996—Recovered one fumble. 1997—Recovered one fumble.
SINGLE GAME HIGHS (regular season): Receptions—5 (September 13, 1998, vs. Minnesota); yards—75 (November 23, 1997, vs. Carolina); and touchdown receptions—1 (December 20, 1997, vs. Carolina).

			RECEIVING				TOTALS			
Year Team	G	GS	No.	Yds.	Avg.	TD	TD	2pt.	Pts.	Fum.
1996—St. Louis NFL	10	8	15	164	10.9	0	0	0	0	0
1997—St. Louis NFL	16	16	38	404	10.6	4	4	0	24	0
1998—St. Louis NFL	7	7	15	105	7.0	0	0	0	0	0
Pro totals (3 years)	33	31	68	673	9.9	4	4	0	24	0

COOK, ANTHONY — DE — REDSKINS

PERSONAL: Born May 30, 1972, in Bennettsville, S.C. ... 6-3/295. ... Full name: Anthony Andrew Cook.
HIGH SCHOOL: Marlboro County (Bennettsville, S.C.).
COLLEGE: South Carolina State.
TRANSACTIONS/CAREER NOTES: Selected by Houston Oilers in second round (35th pick overall) of 1995 NFL draft. ... Signed by Oilers (July 20, 1995). ... Oilers franchise moved to Tennessee for 1997 season. ... On injured reserve with chest injury (December 12, 1998-remainder of season). ... Granted unconditional free agency (February 12, 1999). ... Signed by Washington Redskins (April 7, 1999).
PRO STATISTICS: 1997—Recovered two fumbles.

Year Team	G	GS	SACKS
1995—Houston NFL	11	5	4.5
1996—Houston NFL	12	11	7.5
1997—Tennessee NFL	16	16	0.0
1998—Tennessee NFL	13	3	2.0
Pro totals (4 years)	52	35	14.0

COOKS, KERRY — S — PACKERS

PERSONAL: Born March 28, 1974, in Irving, Texas. ... 5-11/202.
HIGH SCHOOL: Nimitz (Irving, Texas).
COLLEGE: Iowa.
TRANSACTIONS/CAREER NOTES: Selected by Minnesota Vikings in fifth round (144th pick overall) of 1998 NFL draft. ... Signed by Vikings (July 20, 1998). ... Claimed on waivers by Green Bay Packers (September 17, 1998).
PLAYING EXPERIENCE: Green Bay NFL, 1998. ... Games/Games started: 9/0.
PRO STATISTICS: 1998—Recovered one fumble.

COOPER, RICHARD — OT

PERSONAL: Born November 1, 1964, in Memphis, Tenn. ... 6-5/290. ... Full name: Richard Warren Cooper.
HIGH SCHOOL: Melrose (Memphis, Tenn.).
COLLEGE: Tennessee.
TRANSACTIONS/CAREER NOTES: Signed as non-drafted free agent by Seattle Seahawks (May 1988). ... Released by Seahawks (August 1, 1988). ... Signed by New Orleans Saints (February 2, 1989). ... Released by Saints (September 5, 1989). ... Re-signed by Saints to develop-

mental squad (September 6, 1989). ... Released by Saints (December 29, 1989). ... Re-signed by Saints (February 2, 1990). ... Granted free agency (March 1, 1993). ... Re-signed by Saints (April 19, 1993). ... On injured reserve with elbow injury (December 22, 1994-remainder of season). ... Granted unconditional free agency (February 16, 1996). ... Signed by Philadelphia Eagles (February 29, 1996). ... On injured reserve with arm injury (August 19, 1997-entire season). ... Released by Eagles (April 21, 1999).
PLAYING EXPERIENCE: New Orleans NFL, 1990-1995; Philadelphia NFL, 1996 and 1998. ... Games: 1990 (2/1), 1991 (15/11), 1992 (16/16), 1993 (16/16), 1994 (14/14), 1995 (14/14), 1996 (16/16), 1998 (15/15). Total: 108/103.
PRO STATISTICS: 1991—Recovered one fumble. 1992—Recovered one fumble. 1993—Recovered one fumble. 1995—Recovered one fumble.

COPELAND, HORACE   WR

PERSONAL: Born January 2, 1971, in Orlando. ... 6-3/208. ... Full name: Horace Cornellious Copeland.
HIGH SCHOOL: Maynard Evans (Orlando).
COLLEGE: Miami, Fla. (degree in criminal justice, 1992).
TRANSACTIONS/CAREER NOTES: Selected by Tampa Bay Buccaneers in fourth round (104th pick overall) of 1993 NFL draft. ... Signed by Buccaneers (June 22, 1993). ... On injured reserve with knee injury (August 18, 1996-entire season). ... Released by Buccaneers (August 30, 1998). ... Signed by Miami Dolphins (October 1, 1998). ... Released by Dolphins (November 4, 1998). ... Signed by Buccaneers (December 22, 1998). ... Inactive for one game with Buccaneers (1998). ... Granted unconditional free agency (February 12, 1999).
PRO STATISTICS: 1993—Rushed three times for 34 yards.
SINGLE GAME HIGHS (regular season): Receptions—8 (December 10, 1995, vs. Green Bay); yards—155 (September 3, 1995, vs. Philadelphia); and touchdown receptions—2 (October 31, 1993, vs. Atlanta).
STATISTICAL PLATEAUS: 100-yard receiving games: 1993 (2), 1995 (2), 1997 (1). Total: 5.

			RECEIVING				TOTALS			
Year Team	G	GS	No.	Yds.	Avg.	TD	TD	2pt.	Pts.	Fum.
1993—Tampa Bay NFL	14	8	30	633	21.1	4	4	...	24	0
1994—Tampa Bay NFL	16	2	17	308	18.1	0	0	1	2	0
1995—Tampa Bay NFL	15	7	35	605	17.3	2	2	0	12	0
1996—Tampa Bay NFL					Did not play.					
1997—Tampa Bay NFL	13	11	33	431	13.1	1	1	0	6	3
1998—Miami NFL	2	0	0	0	...	0	0	0	0	0
Pro totals (5 years)	60	28	115	1977	17.2	7	7	1	44	3

COPELAND, JOHN   DE   BENGALS

PERSONAL: Born September 20, 1970, in Lanett, Ala. ... 6-3/280.
HIGH SCHOOL: Valley (Ala.).
JUNIOR COLLEGE: Hinds Community College (Miss.).
COLLEGE: Alabama.
TRANSACTIONS/CAREER NOTES: Selected by Cincinnati Bengals in first round (fifth pick overall) of 1993 NFL draft. ... Signed by Bengals (August 13, 1993). ... Granted unconditional free agency (February 13, 1998). ... Re-signed by Bengals (February 20, 1998). ... On physically unable to perform list with heel injury (August 25-November 17, 1998).
HONORS: Named defensive lineman on THE SPORTING NEWS college All-America first team (1992).
PRO STATISTICS: 1997—Recovered two fumbles for 25 yards and one touchdown. 1998—Intercepted one pass for three yards.

Year Team	G	GS	SACKS
1993—Cincinnati NFL	14	14	3.0
1994—Cincinnati NFL	12	12	1.0
1995—Cincinnati NFL	16	16	9.0
1996—Cincinnati NFL	13	13	3.0
1997—Cincinnati NFL	15	15	3.0
1998—Cincinnati NFL	5	0	0.0
Pro totals (6 years)	75	70	19.0

COPELAND, RUSSELL   WR

PERSONAL: Born November 4, 1971, in Tupelo, Miss. ... 6-0/200. ... Full name: Russell S. Copeland.
HIGH SCHOOL: Tupelo (Miss.).
COLLEGE: Memphis State.
TRANSACTIONS/CAREER NOTES: Selected after junior season by Buffalo Bills in fourth round (111th pick overall) of 1993 NFL draft. ... Signed by Bills (July 12, 1993). ... Granted free agency (February 16, 1996). ... Re-signed by Bills (June 5, 1996). ... Granted unconditional free agency (February 14, 1997). ... Signed by Philadelphia Eagles (June 2, 1997). ... Released by Eagles (August 24, 1997). ... Re-signed by Eagles (November 4, 1997). ... Active for one game (1997); did not play. ... Released by Eagles (December 4, 1998). ... Signed by Green Bay Packers (December 9, 1998). ... Granted unconditional free agency (February 12, 1999).
CHAMPIONSHIP GAME EXPERIENCE: Played in AFC championship game (1993 season). ... Played in Super Bowl XXVIII (1993 season).
PRO STATISTICS: 1994—Rushed once for minus seven yards. 1995—Rushed once for minus one yard and recovered one fumble. 1996—Recovered one fumble.
SINGLE GAME HIGHS (regular season): Receptions—6 (October 18, 1998, vs. San Diego); yards—112 (September 10, 1995, vs. Carolina); and touchdown receptions—1 (September 10, 1995, vs. Carolina).
STATISTICAL PLATEAUS: 100-yard receiving games: 1995 (1).

			RECEIVING				PUNT RETURNS				KICKOFF RETURNS				TOTALS			
Year Team	G	GS	No.	Yds.	Avg.	TD	No.	Yds.	Avg.	TD	No.	Yds.	Avg.	TD	TD	2pt.	Pts.	Fum.
1993—Buffalo NFL	16	2	13	242	18.6	0	31	274	8.8	1	24	436	18.2	0	1	...	6	1
1994—Buffalo NFL	15	4	21	255	12.1	1	1	11	11.0	0	12	232	19.3	0	1	0	6	0
1995—Buffalo NFL	16	15	42	646	15.4	1	2	8	4.0	0	0	0	...	0	1	0	6	1
1996—Buffalo NFL	11	0	7	85	12.1	0	14	119	8.5	0	6	136	22.7	0	0	0	0	2
1997—Philadelphia NFL								Did not play.										
1998—Philadelphia NFL	11	0	18	221	12.3	0	0	0	...	0	3	52	17.3	0	0	0	0	1
—Green Bay NFL	3	1	2	11	5.5	0	0	0	...	0	0	0	...	0	0	0	0	0
Pro totals (5 years)	72	22	103	1460	14.2	2	48	412	8.6	1	45	856	19.0	0	3	0	18	5

– 85 –

COSTELLO, BRAD   P   BENGALS

PERSONAL: Born December 12, 1974, in Burlington, N.J. ... 6-1/230. ... Full name: Bradford L. Costello.
HIGH SCHOOL: Fairfield (Conn.) Prep, then Holy Cross (Delran, N.J.).
COLLEGE: Boston University (school of hospitality administration, 1998).
TRANSACTIONS/CAREER NOTES: Signed as non-drafted free agent by Cincinnati Bengals (April 23, 1998). ... Released by Bengals (August 25, 1998). ... Re-signed by Bengals to practice squad (November 11, 1998). ... Activated (December 7, 1998).
PRO STATISTICS: 1998—Rushed once for no yards.

		PUNTING					
Year Team	G	No.	Yds.	Avg.	Net avg.	In. 20	Blk.
1998—Cincinnati NFL	3	10	495	49.5	32.7	0	1

COTA, CHAD   DB   COLTS

PERSONAL: Born August 8, 1971, in Ashland, Ore. ... 6-1/198. ... Full name: Chad Garrett Cota.
HIGH SCHOOL: Ashland (Ore.).
COLLEGE: Oregon (degree in sociology).
TRANSACTIONS/CAREER NOTES: Selected by Carolina Panthers in seventh round (209th pick overall) of 1995 NFL draft. ... Signed by Panthers (July 14, 1995). ... Granted free agency (February 13, 1998). ... Tendered offer sheet by New Orleans Saints (March 11, 1998). ... Panthers declined to match offer (March 19, 1998). ... Granted unconditional free agency (February 12, 1999). ... Signed by Indianapolis Colts (February 23, 1999).
CHAMPIONSHIP GAME EXPERIENCE: Played in NFC championship game (1996 season).
PRO STATISTICS: 1995—Recovered one fumble. 1996—Credited with one sack, fumbled once and recovered one fumble. 1997—Credited with one sack and recovered one fumble. 1998—Credited with two sacks and recovered one fumble.

			INTERCEPTIONS			
Year Team	G	GS	No.	Yds.	Avg.	TD
1995—Carolina NFL	16	0	0	0	...	0
1996—Carolina NFL	16	2	5	63	12.6	0
1997—Carolina NFL	16	16	2	28	14.0	0
1998—New Orleans NFL	16	16	4	16	4.0	0
Pro totals (4 years)	64	34	11	107	9.7	0

COTTON, KENYON   FB   RAVENS

PERSONAL: Born February 23, 1974, in Bossier City, La. ... 6-0/255. ... Full name: Timothy Kenyon Cotton.
HIGH SCHOOL: Minden (La.).
COLLEGE: Southwestern Louisiana.
TRANSACTIONS/CAREER NOTES: Signed as non-drafted free agent by Baltimore Ravens (April 25, 1997).
SINGLE GAME HIGHS (regular season): Attempts—1 (November 1, 1998, vs. Jacksonville); yards—7 (November 1, 1998, vs. Jacksonville); and rushing touchdowns—1 (November 30, 1997, vs. Jacksonville).

			RUSHING				KICKOFF RETURNS				TOTALS		
Year Team	G	GS	Att.	Yds.	Avg.	TD	No.	Yds.	Avg.	TD	TD	2pt.	Pts.	Fum.
1997—Baltimore NFL	16	0	2	2	1.0	1	0	0	...	0	1	0	6	0
1998—Baltimore NFL	12	0	2	8	4.0	0	2	33	16.5	0	0	0	0	0
Pro totals (2 years)	28	0	4	10	2.5	1	2	33	16.5	0	1	0	6	0

COTTRELL, DANA   LB   PATRIOTS

PERSONAL: Born January 11, 1974, in Boston. ... 6-3/244. ... Full name: Dana Robert Cottrell.
HIGH SCHOOL: Billerica (Mass.) Memorial.
COLLEGE: Syracuse.
TRANSACTIONS/CAREER NOTES: Signed as non-drafted free agent by New England Patriots (April 20, 1997). ... Released by Patriots (August 24, 1997). ... Re-signed by Patriots to practice squad (August 26, 1997). ... Assigned by Patriots to England Monarchs in 1998 NFL Europe enhancement allocation program (February 18, 1998). ... Released by Patriots (August 25, 1998). ... Re-signed by Patriots to practice squad (December 9, 1998). ... Activated (December 18, 1998).
PLAYING EXPERIENCE: England Monarchs NFLE, 1998; New England NFL, 1998. ... Games/Games started: NFLE 1998 (games played unavailable), NFL 1998 (2/0).
PRO STATISTICS: NFLE: 1998—Credited with one sack.

COUSIN, TERRY   CB   BEARS

PERSONAL: Born April 11, 1975 ... 5-9/182.
HIGH SCHOOL: Miami Beach (Fla.) Senior.
COLLEGE: South Carolina.
TRANSACTIONS/CAREER NOTES: Signed as non-drafted free agent by Chicago Bears (April 25, 1997). ... Released by Bears (August 24, 1997). ... Re-signed by Bears to practice squad (August 26, 1997). ... Activated (October 25, 1997). ... Released by Bears (October 28, 1997). ... Re-signed by Bears to practice squad (October 30, 1997). ... Activated (November 15, 1997).
PLAYING EXPERIENCE: Chicago NFL, 1997 and 1998. ... Games/Games started: 1997 (6/0), 1998 (16/12). Total: 22/12.
PRO STATISTICS: 1998—Intercepted one pass for no yards and recovered two fumbles.

COWART, SAM — LB — BILLS

PERSONAL: Born February 26, 1975, in Jacksonville. ... 6-2/239.
HIGH SCHOOL: Mandarin (Jacksonville).
COLLEGE: Florida State.
TRANSACTIONS/CAREER NOTES: Selected by Buffalo Bills in second round (39th pick overall) of 1998 NFL draft. ... Signed by Bills (July 20, 1998).
HONORS: Named outside linebacker on THE SPORTING NEWS college All-America first team (1997).
PLAYING EXPERIENCE: Buffalo NFL, 1998. ... Games/Games started: 16/11.
PRO STATISTICS: 1998—Intercepted two passes for 23 yards.

COX, BRYAN — LB — JETS

PERSONAL: Born February 17, 1968, in St. Louis. ... 6-4/250. ... Full name: Bryan Keith Cox.
HIGH SCHOOL: East St. Louis (Ill.) Senior.
COLLEGE: Western Illinois (bachelor of science degree in mass communications).
TRANSACTIONS/CAREER NOTES: Selected by Miami Dolphins in fifth round (113th pick overall) of 1991 NFL draft. ... Signed by Dolphins (July 11, 1991). ... On injured reserve with sprained ankle (October 5-November 2, 1991). ... Granted unconditional free agency (February 16, 1996). ... Signed by Chicago Bears (February 20, 1996). ... On injured reserve with thumb injury (November 5, 1996-remainder of season). ... Released by Bears (June 2, 1998). ... Signed by New York Jets (August 1, 1998).
CHAMPIONSHIP GAME EXPERIENCE: Played in AFC championship game (1992 and 1998 seasons).
HONORS: Played in Pro Bowl (1992, 1994 and 1995 seasons).
PRO STATISTICS: 1992—Recovered one fumble. 1993—Recovered four fumbles for one yard. 1995—Recovered one fumble. 1996—Recovered three fumbles, including one in end zone for a touchdown. 1997—Recovered one fumble. 1998—Credited with a safety.

				INTERCEPTIONS				SACKS
Year Team	G	GS	No.	Yds.	Avg.	TD		No.
1991—Miami NFL	13	13	0	0	...	0		2.0
1992—Miami NFL	16	16	1	0	0.0	0		14.0
1993—Miami NFL	16	16	1	26	26.0	0		5.0
1994—Miami NFL	16	16	0	0	...	0		3.0
1995—Miami NFL	16	16	1	12	12.0	0		7.5
1996—Chicago NFL	9	9	0	0	...	0		3.0
1997—Chicago NFL	16	15	0	0	...	0		5.0
1998—New York Jets NFL	16	10	0	0	...	0		6.0
Pro totals (8 years)	118	111	3	38	12.7	0		45.5

CRAFTS, JERRY — OT/G — EAGLES

PERSONAL: Born January 6, 1968, in Tulsa, Okla. ... 6-5/334. ... Full name: Jerry Wayne Crafts.
HIGH SCHOOL: Metro Christian Academy (Tulsa, Okla.).
COLLEGE: Oklahoma, then Louisville.
TRANSACTIONS/CAREER NOTES: Selected by Indianapolis Colts in 11th round (293rd pick overall) of 1991 NFL draft. ... Signed by Colts (July 13, 1991). ... Released by Colts (August 16, 1991). ... Selected by Orlando Thunder in 16th round (170th pick overall) of 1992 World League draft. ... Signed by Buffalo Bills (July 7, 1992). ... On injured reserve with knee injury (October 26, 1992-remainder of season). ... Granted unconditional free agency (February 17, 1995). ... Signed by Green Bay Packers (March 17, 1995). ... Released by Packers (August 21, 1995). ... Selected by Amsterdam Admirals in 1996 World League draft (February 22, 1996). ... Signed by Philadelphia Eagles (July 8, 1997). ... Granted unconditional free agency (February 13, 1998). ... Re-signed by Eagles (February 19, 1998).
PLAYING EXPERIENCE: Orlando W.L., 1992; Buffalo NFL, 1992-1994; Amsterdam W.L., 1996; Philadelphia NFL, 1997 and 1998. ... Games/Games started: W.L. 1992 (9/9); NFL 1992 (6/0), 1993 (16/0), 1994 (16/7), 1996 (games played unavailable), 1997 (15/6), 1998 (1/0). Total NFL: 39/13. Total Pro: 63/22.
CHAMPIONSHIP GAME EXPERIENCE: Played in AFC championship game (1993 season). ... Played in Super Bowl XXVIII (1993 season).
PRO STATISTICS: 1994—Recovered two fumbles. W.L. 1996—Returned one punt for five yards.

CRAVER, AARON — FB — SAINTS

PERSONAL: Born December 18, 1968, in Los Angeles. ... 6-0/232. ... Full name: Aaron LeRenze Craver.
HIGH SCHOOL: Compton (Calif.).
JUNIOR COLLEGE: El Camino College (Calif.).
COLLEGE: Fresno State.
TRANSACTIONS/CAREER NOTES: Selected by Miami Dolphins in third round (60th pick overall) of 1991 NFL draft. ... Signed by Dolphins (July 23, 1991). ... On injured reserve with pulled hamstring (October 21-December 12, 1992). ... On practice squad (December 12-January 9, 1993). ... On injured reserve with knee injury (August 23, 1993-entire season). ... Granted free agency (February 17, 1994). ... Re-signed by Dolphins (May 31, 1994). ... Released by Dolphins (August 28, 1994). ... Re-signed by Dolphins (September 26, 1994). ... Released by Dolphins (October 4, 1994). ... Re-signed by Dolphins (November 9, 1994). ... Granted unconditional free agency (February 17, 1995). ... Signed by Denver Broncos (March 9, 1995). ... Granted unconditional free agency (February 14, 1997). ... Signed by San Diego Chargers (April 24, 1997). ... Granted unconditional free agency (February 13, 1998). ... Signed by New Orleans Saints (April 16, 1998). ... Granted unconditional free agency (February 12, 1999). ... Re-signed by Saints (February 23, 1999).
CHAMPIONSHIP GAME EXPERIENCE: Played in AFC championship game (1992 season).
PRO STATISTICS: 1991—Recovered two fumbles. 1994—Recovered one fumble. 1995—Recovered one fumble. 1996—Attempted one pass without a completion. 1997—Recovered one fumble. 1998—Attempted one pass without a completion and recovered one fumble.
SINGLE GAME HIGHS (regular season): Attempts—20 (December 24, 1995, vs. Oakland); yards—108 (December 24, 1995, vs. Oakland); and rushing touchdowns—1 (December 27, 1998, vs. Buffalo).
STATISTICAL PLATEAUS: 100-yard rushing games: 1995 (1).

Year Team	G	GS	RUSHING Att.	Yds.	Avg.	TD	RECEIVING No.	Yds.	Avg.	TD	KICKOFF RETURNS No.	Yds.	Avg.	TD	TOTALS TD	2pt.	Pts.	Fum.
1991—Miami NFL	14	0	20	58	2.9	1	8	67	8.4	0	32	615	19.2	0	1	...	6	2
1992—Miami NFL	6	0	3	9	3.0	0	0	0	...	0	8	174	21.8	0	0	...	0	0
1993—Miami NFL									Did not play.									
1994—Miami NFL	8	0	6	43	7.2	0	24	237	9.9	0	0	0	...	0	0	1	2	1
1995—Denver NFL	16	10	73	333	4.6	5	43	369	8.6	1	7	50	7.1	0	6	0	36	1
1996—Denver NFL	15	15	59	232	3.9	2	39	297	7.6	1	0	0	...	0	3	0	18	1
1997—San Diego NFL	15	5	20	71	3.6	0	4	26	6.5	0	3	68	22.7	0	0	0	0	0
1998—New Orleans NFL	16	10	45	180	4.0	2	33	214	6.5	2	7	212	30.3	1	5	0	30	2
Pro totals (7 years)	90	40	226	926	4.1	10	151	1210	8.0	4	57	1119	19.6	1	15	1	92	7

CRAWFORD, KEITH　　　WR　　　CHIEFS

PERSONAL: Born November 21, 1970, in Palestine, Texas. ... 6-2/195. ... Full name: Keith L. Crawford.
HIGH SCHOOL: Westwood (Palestine, Texas).
COLLEGE: Howard Payne University (Texas).
TRANSACTIONS/CAREER NOTES: Signed as non-drafted free agent by New York Giants (May 1, 1993). ... Released by Giants (October 7, 1993). ... Re-signed by Giants to practice squad (October 8, 1993). ... Activated (October 20, 1993). ... Released by Giants (August 22, 1994). ... Signed by Green Bay Packers (October 28, 1994). ... Inactive for four games (1994). ... Released by Packers (November 22, 1994). ... Re-signed by Packers (December 27, 1994). ... Claimed on waivers by St. Louis Rams (August 26, 1996). ... Granted free agency (February 14, 1997). ... Re-signed by Rams (May 20, 1997). ... Granted unconditional free agency (February 13, 1998). ... Signed by Atlanta Falcons (March 16, 1998). ... Released by Falcons (August 29, 1998). ... Signed by Kansas City Chiefs (November 3, 1998).
PLAYING EXPERIENCE: New York Giants NFL, 1993; Green Bay NFL, 1995; St. Louis NFL, 1996 and 1997; Kansas City NFL, 1998. ... Games/Games started: 1993 (7/0), 1995 (13/0), 1996 (16/0), 1997 (15/2), 1998 (8/0). Total: 59/2.
CHAMPIONSHIP GAME EXPERIENCE: Played in NFC championship game (1995 season).
PRO STATISTICS: 1993—Caught one pass for six yards. 1996—Returned four kickoffs for 47 yards. 1997—Rushed twice for 32 yards, caught 11 passes for 232 yards and recovered one fumble.
SINGLE GAME HIGHS (regular season): Receptions—4 (October 26, 1997, vs. Kansas City); yards—86 (October 12, 1997, vs. San Francisco); and touchdown receptions—0.

CRAWFORD, VERNON　　　LB　　　PATRIOTS

PERSONAL: Born June 25, 1974, in Texas City, Texas ... 6-4/245. ... Full name: Vernon Dean Crawford Jr.
HIGH SCHOOL: Texas City (Texas).
JUNIOR COLLEGE: San Francisco City College.
COLLEGE: Florida State.
TRANSACTIONS/CAREER NOTES: Selected by New England Patriots in fifth round (159th pick overall) of 1997 NFL draft. ... Signed by Patriots (June 19, 1997).
PLAYING EXPERIENCE: New England NFL, 1997 and 1998. ... Games/games started: 1997 (16/0), 1998 (16/1). Total: 32/1.
PRO STATISTICS: 1997—Recovered one fumble.

CRISWELL, JEFF　　　OT　　　CHIEFS

PERSONAL: Born March 7, 1964, in Grinnell, Iowa. ... 6-7/294. ... Full name: Jeffrey L. Criswell.
HIGH SCHOOL: Lynnville-Sully (Sully, Iowa).
COLLEGE: Graceland College, Iowa (degree in physical education, health and secondary education).
TRANSACTIONS/CAREER NOTES: Signed as free-agent replacement player by Indianapolis Colts (September 26, 1987). ... Released by Colts (October 19, 1987). ... Signed by New York Jets (May 3, 1988). ... On injured reserve with foot injury (December 24, 1992-remainder of season). ... Granted unconditional free agency (February 17, 1995). ... Signed by Kansas City Chiefs (March 9, 1995).
PLAYING EXPERIENCE: Indianapolis NFL, 1987; New York Jets NFL, 1988-1994; Kansas City NFL, 1995-1998. ... Games/Games started: 1987 (3/3), 1988 (15/12), 1989 (16/16), 1990 (16/16), 1991 (16/16), 1992 (14/13), 1993 (16/16), 1994 (15/15), 1995 (15/4), 1996 (15/5), 1997 (16/16), 1998 (14/14). Total: 171/146.
PRO STATISTICS: 1989—Recovered one fumble. 1990—Recovered one fumble. 1994—Recovered one fumble.

CROCKETT, HENRI　　　LB　　　FALCONS

PERSONAL: Born October 28, 1974, in Pompano Beach, Fla. ... 6-2/238. ... Full name: Henri W. Crockett. ... Brother of Zack Crockett, fullback, Oakland Raiders.
HIGH SCHOOL: Ely (Pompano Beach, Fla.).
COLLEGE: Florida State (degree in criminology, 1996).
TRANSACTIONS/CAREER NOTES: Selected by Atlanta Falcons in fourth round (100th pick overall) of 1997 NFL draft. ... Signed by Falcons (July 14, 1997).
CHAMPIONSHIP GAME EXPERIENCE: Played in NFC championship game (1998 season). ... Played in Super Bowl XXXIII (1998 season).
PRO STATISTICS: 1997—Recovered one fumble.

Year Team	G	GS	SACKS
1997—Atlanta NFL	16	10	2.0
1998—Atlanta NFL	10	10	1.0
Pro totals (2 years)	26	20	3.0

CROCKETT, RAY — CB — BRONCOS

PERSONAL: Born January 5, 1967, in Dallas. ... 5-10/184. ... Full name: Donald Ray Crockett.
HIGH SCHOOL: Duncanville (Texas).
COLLEGE: Baylor.
TRANSACTIONS/CAREER NOTES: Selected by Detroit Lions in fourth round (86th pick overall) of 1989 NFL draft. ... Signed by Lions (July 18, 1989). ... Granted unconditional free agency (February 17, 1994). ... Signed by Denver Broncos (March 9, 1994).
CHAMPIONSHIP GAME EXPERIENCE: Played in NFC championship game (1991 season). ... Played in AFC championship game (1997 and 1998 seasons). ... Member of Super Bowl championship team (1997 and 1998 seasons).
PRO STATISTICS: 1989—Returned one kickoff for eight yards and recovered one fumble. 1990—Recovered two fumbles for 22 yards and a touchdown. 1992—Recovered one fumble for 15 yards. 1993—Recovered one fumble. 1994—Recovered two fumbles for 43 yards. 1995—Ran four yards with lateral from punt return and recovered one fumble for 50 yards and a touchdown.

Year—Team	G	GS	INTERCEPTIONS No.	Yds.	Avg.	TD	SACKS No.
1989—Detroit NFL	16	0	1	5	5.0	0	0.0
1990—Detroit NFL	16	6	3	17	5.7	0	1.0
1991—Detroit NFL	16	16	∞6	141	23.5	∞1	1.0
1992—Detroit NFL	15	15	4	50	12.5	0	1.0
1993—Detroit NFL	16	16	2	31	15.5	0	1.0
1994—Denver NFL	14	14	2	6	3.0	0	0.0
1995—Denver NFL	16	16	0	0	...	0	3.0
1996—Denver NFL	15	15	2	34	17.0	0	4.0
1997—Denver NFL	16	16	4	18	4.5	0	0.0
1998—Denver NFL	16	16	3	105	35.0	1	0.5
Pro totals (10 years)	156	130	27	407	15.1	2	11.5

CROCKETT, ZACK — RB — RAIDERS

PERSONAL: Born December 2, 1972, in Pompano Beach, Fla. ... 6-2/246. ... Brother of Henri Crockett, linebacker, Atlanta Falcons.
HIGH SCHOOL: Ely (Pompano Beach, Fla.).
JUNIOR COLLEGE: Hinds Community College (Miss.).
COLLEGE: Florida State.
TRANSACTIONS/CAREER NOTES: Selected by Indianapolis Colts in third round (79th pick overall) of 1995 NFL draft. ... Signed by Colts (July 21, 1995). ... On injured reserve with knee injury (October 22, 1996-remainder of season). ... Granted free agency (February 13, 1998). ... Re-signed by Colts (July 23, 1998). ... Claimed on waivers by Jacksonville Jaguars (October 21, 1998). ... Granted unconditional free agency (February 12, 1999). ... Signed by Oakland Raiders (March 16, 1999).
CHAMPIONSHIP GAME EXPERIENCE: Played in AFC championship game (1995 season).
SINGLE GAME HIGHS (regular season): Attempts—15 (December 7, 1997, vs. New York Jets); yards—81 (November 2, 1997, vs. Tampa Bay); and rushing touchdowns—1 (December 7, 1997, vs. New York Jets).

Year—Team	G	GS	RUSHING Att.	Yds.	Avg.	TD	RECEIVING No.	Yds.	Avg.	TD	TOTALS TD	2pt.	Pts.	Fum.
1995—Indianapolis NFL	16	0	1	0	0.0	0	2	35	17.5	0	0	0	0	0
1996—Indianapolis NFL	5	5	31	164	5.3	0	11	96	8.7	1	1	0	6	2
1997—Indianapolis NFL	16	12	95	300	3.2	1	15	112	7.5	0	1	0	6	3
1998—Indianapolis NFL	2	1	2	5	2.5	0	1	1	1.0	0	0	0	0	1
—Jacksonville NFL	10	1	0	0	...	0	1	4	4.0	0	0	0	0	0
Pro totals (4 years)	49	19	129	469	3.6	1	30	248	8.3	1	2	0	12	6

CROEL, MIKE — LB

PERSONAL: Born June 6, 1969, in Detroit. ... 6-3/235. ... Name pronounced KROLL.
HIGH SCHOOL: Lincoln-Sudbury (Mass.) Regional.
COLLEGE: Nebraska.
TRANSACTIONS/CAREER NOTES: Selected by Denver Broncos in first round (fourth pick overall) of 1991 NFL draft. ... Signed by Broncos (August 9, 1991). ... Released by Broncos (March 7, 1995). ... Signed by New York Giants (April 5, 1995). ... Granted unconditional free agency (February 16, 1996). ... Signed by Baltimore Ravens (July 16, 1996). ... Granted unconditional free agency (February 14, 1997). ... Signed by Atlanta Falcons (May 22, 1997). ... Released by Falcons (August 4, 1997). ... Signed by Rhein Fire of NFL Europe League (February 1998). ... Signed by Seattle Seahawks (July 15, 1998). ... Granted unconditional free agency (February 12, 1999).
CHAMPIONSHIP GAME EXPERIENCE: Played in AFC championship game (1991 season).
HONORS: Named linebacker on The Sporting News college All-America second team (1990). ... Named NFL Rookie of the Year by The Sporting News (1991).
PRO STATISTICS: 1992—Recovered one fumble. 1993—Intercepted one pass for 22 yards and a touchdown and recovered two fumbles. 1996—Intercepted one pass for 16 yards.

Year—Team	G	GS	SACKS
1991—Denver NFL	13	10	10.0
1992—Denver NFL	16	16	5.0
1993—Denver NFL	16	16	5.0
1994—Denver NFL	13	12	0.0
1995—New York Giants NFL	16	14	1.0
1996—Baltimore NFL	16	16	3.0
1997—	Did not play.		
1998—Rhein NFLE	...	...	6.0
—Seattle NFL	11	0	0.0
NFL Europe totals (1 year)	...	...	6.0
NFL totals (7 years)	101	84	24.0
Pro totals (8 years)	...	...	30.0

CROSS, HOWARD — TE — GIANTS

PERSONAL: Born August 8, 1967, in Huntsville, Ala. ... 6-5/275. ... Full name: Howard E. Cross.
HIGH SCHOOL: New Hope (Ala.).
COLLEGE: Alabama.
TRANSACTIONS/CAREER NOTES: Selected by New York Giants in sixth round (158th pick overall) of 1989 NFL draft. ... Signed by Giants (July 24, 1989). ... Granted free agency (February 1, 1991). ... Re-signed by Giants (July 24, 1991). ... Granted free agency (March 1, 1993). ... Re-signed by Giants (July 16, 1993). ... Designated by Giants as transition player (February 15, 1994).
CHAMPIONSHIP GAME EXPERIENCE: Played in NFC championship game (1990 season). ... Member of Super Bowl championship team (1990 season).
PRO STATISTICS: 1992—Recovered one fumble. 1993—Recovered one fumble. 1994—Recovered one fumble. 1997—Recovered one fumble.
SINGLE GAME HIGHS (regular season): Receptions—6 (September 13, 1992, vs. Dallas); yards—77 (September 13, 1992, vs. Dallas); and touchdown receptions—2 (September 11, 1994, vs. Arizona).

				RECEIVING			KICKOFF RETURNS			TOTALS			
Year Team	G	GS	No.	Yds.	Avg.	TD	No.	Yds.	Avg.	TD	TD	2pt.	Pts.	Fum.
1989—New York Giants NFL	16	4	6	107	17.8	1	0	0	...	0	1	...	6	1
1990—New York Giants NFL	16	8	8	106	13.3	0	1	10	10.0	0	0	...	0	0
1991—New York Giants NFL	16	16	20	283	14.2	2	1	11	11.0	0	2	...	12	1
1992—New York Giants NFL	16	16	27	357	13.2	2	0	0	...	0	2	...	12	2
1993—New York Giants NFL	16	16	21	272	13.0	5	2	15	7.5	0	5	0	30	0
1994—New York Giants NFL	16	16	31	364	11.7	4	0	0	...	0	4	0	24	0
1995—New York Giants NFL	15	15	18	197	10.9	0	0	0	...	0	0	0	0	0
1996—New York Giants NFL	16	16	22	178	8.1	1	0	0	...	0	1	0	6	1
1997—New York Giants NFL	16	16	21	150	7.1	2	0	0	...	0	2	0	12	1
1998—New York Giants NFL	16	16	13	90	6.9	0	0	0	...	0	0	0	0	2
Pro totals (10 years)	159	139	187	2104	11.3	17	4	36	9.0	0	17	0	102	8

CROWELL, GERMANE — WR — LIONS

PERSONAL: Born September 13, 1976, in Winston-Salem, N.C. ... 6-3/213. ... Full name: Germane L. Crowell. ... Name pronounced jur-MANE KROLL.
HIGH SCHOOL: North Forsyth (Winston-Salem, N.C.).
COLLEGE: Virginia.
TRANSACTIONS/CAREER NOTES: Selected by Detroit Lions in second round (50th pick overall) of 1998 NFL draft. ... Signed by Lions (July 20, 1998).
SINGLE GAME HIGHS (regular season): Receptions—5 (December 14, 1998, vs. San Francisco); yards—83 (December 14, 1998, vs. San Francisco); and touchdown receptions—1 (December 6, 1998, vs. Jacksonville).

			RUSHING				RECEIVING				TOTALS		
Year Team	G	GS	Att.	Yds.	Avg.	TD	No.	Yds.	Avg.	TD	TD	2pt.	Pts.	Fum.
1998—Detroit NFL	14	2	1	35	35.0	0	25	464	18.6	3	3	0	18	1

CRUMPLER, CARLESTER — TE — VIKINGS

PERSONAL: Born September 5, 1971, in Greenville, N.C. ... 6-6/260. ... Full name: Carlester Crumpler Jr.
HIGH SCHOOL: J.H. Rose (Greenville, N.C.).
COLLEGE: East Carolina (degree in finance, 1995).
TRANSACTIONS/CAREER NOTES: Selected by Seattle Seahawks in seventh round (202nd pick overall) of 1994 NFL draft. ... Signed by Seahawks (July 6, 1994). ... Granted unconditional free agency (February 13, 1998). ... Re-signed by Seahawks (April 21, 1998). ... Granted unconditional free agency (February 12, 1999). ... Signed by Minnesota Vikings (April 13, 1999).
HONORS: Named tight end on THE SPORTING NEWS college All-America second team (1993).
SINGLE GAME HIGHS (regular season): Receptions—6 (December 15, 1996, vs. Jacksonville); yards—59 (October 29, 1995, vs. Arizona); and touchdown receptions—1 (November 1, 1998, vs. Oakland).

			RECEIVING				TOTALS			
Year Team	G	GS	No.	Yds.	Avg.	TD	TD	2pt.	Pts.	Fum.
1994—Seattle NFL	9	4	2	19	9.5	0	0	0	0	0
1995—Seattle NFL	16	7	23	254	11.0	1	1	0	6	1
1996—Seattle NFL	16	7	26	258	9.9	0	0	0	0	1
1997—Seattle NFL	15	12	31	361	11.6	1	1	0	6	0
1998—Seattle NFL	11	1	6	52	8.7	1	1	0	6	0
Pro totals (5 years)	67	31	88	944	10.7	3	3	0	18	2

CRUTCHFIELD, BUDDY — CB — REDSKINS

PERSONAL: Born March 7, 1976, in Raleigh, N.C. ... 6-0/196.
HIGH SCHOOL: Athens (Raleigh, N.C.).
COLLEGE: North Carolina Central.
TRANSACTIONS/CAREER NOTES: Signed as non-drafted free agent by Washington Redskins (April 24, 1998).
PLAYING EXPERIENCE: Washington NFL, 1998. ... Games/Games started: 2/0.

CULLORS, DERRICK — RB/KR — PATRIOTS

PERSONAL: Born December 26, 1972, in Dallas. ... 6-0/195. ... Full name: Derrick Shane Cullors.
HIGH SCHOOL: Sunset (Dallas), then Lake Highlands (Texas).

COLLEGE: Texas Christian, then Murray State.
TRANSACTIONS/CAREER NOTES: Signed as non-drafted free agent by Baltimore Ravens (April 26, 1996). ... Released by Ravens (August 25, 1996). ... Signed by New England Patriots to practice squad (September 18, 1996).
SINGLE GAME HIGHS (regular season): Attempts—10 (December 22, 1997, vs. Miami); yards—41 (November 16, 1997, vs. Tampa Bay); and rushing touchdowns—0.

				RUSHING				RECEIVING				KICKOFF RETURNS				TOTALS		
Year Team	G	GS	Att.	Yds.	Avg.	TD	No.	Yds.	Avg.	TD	No.	Yds.	Avg.	TD	TD	2pt.	Pts.	Fum.
1997—New England NFL	15	1	22	101	4.6	0	2	8	4.0	0	15	386	25.7	▲1	1	0	6	3
1998—New England NFL	16	0	18	48	2.7	0	14	146	10.4	1	45	1085	24.1	0	1	0	6	1
Pro totals (2 years)	31	1	40	149	3.7	0	16	154	9.6	1	60	1471	24.5	1	2	0	12	4

CULPEPPER, BRAD   DT   BUCCANEERS

PERSONAL: Born May 8, 1969, in Tallahassee, Fla. ... 6-1/270. ... Full name: John Broward Culpepper.
HIGH SCHOOL: Leon (Tallahassee, Fla.).
COLLEGE: Florida (degree in history, 1991).
TRANSACTIONS/CAREER NOTES: Selected by Minnesota Vikings in 10th round (264th pick overall) of 1992 NFL draft. ... Signed by Vikings (July 20, 1992). ... On injured reserve with toe injury (November 23, 1992-remainder of season). ... Claimed on waivers by Tampa Bay Buccaneers (August 30, 1994).
HONORS: Named defensive lineman on THE SPORTING NEWS college All-America first team (1991).
PRO STATISTICS: 1994—Returned two kickoffs for 30 yards and recovered one fumble. 1995—Recovered one fumble for 12 yards. 1998—Recovered one fumble.

Year Team	G	GS	SACKS
1992—Minnesota NFL	11	2	0.0
1993—Minnesota NFL	15	0	0.0
1994—Tampa Bay NFL	16	15	4.0
1995—Tampa Bay NFL	16	4	4.0
1996—Tampa Bay NFL	13	13	1.5
1997—Tampa Bay NFL	16	16	8.5
1998—Tampa Bay NFL	16	16	9.0
Pro totals (7 years)	103	66	27.0

CUMMINGS, JOE   LB   BILLS

PERSONAL: Born June 8, 1974, in Missoula, Mont. ... 6-2/242. ... Full name: Joe Edward Cummings. ... Son of Ed Cummings, linebacker with New York Jets (1964) and Denver Broncos (1965).
HIGH SCHOOL: Stevensville (Mont.).
COLLEGE: Wyoming.
TRANSACTIONS/CAREER NOTES: Signed as non-drafted free agent by Philadelphia Eagles (April 26, 1996). ... Released by Eagles (August 20, 1996). ... Signed by San Diego Chargers (October 5, 1996). ... Released by Chargers (October 9, 1996). ... Re-signed by Chargers to practice squad (October 11, 1996). ... Activated (October 25, 1996). ... Released by Chargers (November 12, 1996). ... Re-signed by Chargers to practice squad (November 20, 1996). ... Activated (November 20, 1996). ... Released by Chargers (June 2, 1997). ... Signed by Green Bay Packers (June 3, 1997). ... Released by Packers (August 24, 1997). ... Signed by Buffalo Bills (February 2, 1998). ... Assigned to Bills to Barcelona Dragons in 1998 NFL Europe enhancement allocation program (February 18, 1998). ... Released by Bills (August 30, 1998). ... Re-signed by Bills to practice squad (August 31, 1998). ... Activated (Sepember 30, 1998).
PLAYING EXPERIENCE: San Diego NFL, 1996; Barcelona Dragons NFLE, 1998; Buffalo NFL, 1998. ... Games/Games started: 1996 (3/0), NFLE 1998 (games played unavailable), NFL 1998 (9/2). Total NFL: 12/2.
PRO STATISTICS: 1998—Returned one kickoff for 21 yards.

CUNNINGHAM, RANDALL   QB   VIKINGS

PERSONAL: Born March 27, 1963, in Santa Barbara, Calif. ... 6-4/215. ... Son of Sam Cunningham, running back with New England Patriots (1973-79 and 1981).
HIGH SCHOOL: Santa Barbara (Calif.).
COLLEGE: UNLV.
TRANSACTIONS/CAREER NOTES: Selected by Arizona Outlaws in 1985 USFL territorial draft. ... Selected by Philadelphia Eagles in second round (37th pick overall) of 1985 NFL draft. ... Signed by Eagles (July 22, 1985). ... On injured reserve with knee injury (September 3, 1991-remainder of season). ... Granted unconditional free agency (February 16, 1996). ... On retired list (August 30, 1996-April 15, 1997). ... Signed by Minnesota Vikings (April 15, 1997). ... Granted unconditional free agency (February 13, 1998). ... Re-signed by Vikings (March 24, 1998).
CHAMPIONSHIP GAME EXPERIENCE: Played in NFC championship game (1998 season).
HONORS: Named punter on THE SPORTING NEWS college All-America first team (1984). ... Played in Pro Bowl (1988-1990 and 1998 seasons). ... Named Outstanding Player of Pro Bowl (1988 season).
RECORDS: Holds NFL single-season record for most times sacked—72 (1986). ... Shares NFL single-game records for most own fumbles recovered—4 (November 30, 1986, OT, at Los Angeles Raiders); and most own and opponents' fumbles recovered—4 (November 30, 1986, OT, at Los Angeles Raiders).
PRO STATISTICS: 1985—Fumbled three times. 1986—Punted twice for 54 yards, fumbled seven times and recovered four fumbles. 1987—Caught one pass for minus three yards, led league with 12 fumbles and recovered six fumbles for minus seven yards. 1988—Punted three times for 167 yards, led league with 12 fumbles and recovered six fumbles. 1989—Punted six times for 319 yards, led the NFC with 17 fumbles and recovered four fumbles for minus six yards. 1990—Fumbled nine times and recovered three fumbles for minus four yards. 1992—Led league with 13 fumbles and recovered three fumbles. 1993—Fumbled three times. 1994—Punted once for 80 yards, fumbled 10 times and recovered two fumbles for minus 15 yards. 1995—Fumbled three times and recovered one fumble for minus five yards. 1997—Fumbled four times and recovered two fumbles. 1998—Caught one pass for minus three yards and fumbled twice.
SINGLE GAME HIGHS (regular season): Attempts—62 (October 2, 1989, vs. Chicago); completions—34 (September 17, 1989, vs. Washington); yards—447 (September 17, 1989, vs. Washington); and touchdown passes—5 (September 17, 1989, vs. Washington).
STATISTICAL PLATEAUS: 300-yard passing games: 1987 (1), 1988 (1), 1989 (3), 1992 (1), 1993 (1), 1994 (4), 1998 (4). Total: 16. ... 100-yard rushing games: 1986 (1), 1990 (1), 1992 (1). Total: 3.
MISCELLANEOUS: Regular-season record as starting NFL quarterback: 77-46-1 (.625). ... Postseason record as starting NFL quarterback: 3-6 (.333).

Year	Team	G	GS	Att.	Cmp.	Pct.	Yds.	TD	Int.	Avg.	Rat.	Att.	Yds.	Avg.	TD	TD	2pt.	Pts.
						PASSING							RUSHING				TOTALS	
1985—Philadelphia NFL		6	4	81	34	42.0	548	1	8	6.77	29.8	29	205	7.1	0	0	...	0
1986—Philadelphia NFL		15	5	209	111	53.1	1391	8	7	6.66	72.9	66	540	8.2	5	5	...	30
1987—Philadelphia NFL		12	12	406	223	54.9	2786	23	12	6.86	83.0	76	505	6.6	3	3	...	18
1988—Philadelphia NFL		16	16	‡560	301	53.8	3808	24	16	6.80	77.6	93	624	6.7	6	6	...	36
1989—Philadelphia NFL		16	16	532	290	54.5	3400	21	15	6.39	75.5	104	621	*6.0	4	4	...	24
1990—Philadelphia NFL		16	16	465	271	58.3	3466	‡30	13	7.45	91.6	118	942	*8.0	5	5	...	30
1991—Philadelphia NFL		1	1	4	1	25.0	19	0	0	4.75	46.9	0	0	...	0	0	...	0
1992—Philadelphia NFL		15	15	384	233	60.7	2775	19	11	7.23	87.3	87	549	6.3	5	5	...	30
1993—Philadelphia NFL		4	4	110	76	69.1	850	5	5	7.73	88.1	18	110	6.1	1	1	...	6
1994—Philadelphia NFL		14	14	490	265	54.1	3229	16	13	6.59	74.4	65	288	4.4	3	3	0	18
1995—Philadelphia NFL		7	4	121	69	57.0	605	3	5	5.00	61.5	21	98	4.7	0	0	0	0
1996—								Did not play.										
1997—Minnesota NFL		6	3	88	44	50.0	501	6	4	5.69	71.3	19	127	6.7	0	0	0	0
1998—Minnesota NFL		15	14	425	259	60.9	3704	34	10	8.72	*106.0	32	132	4.1	1	1	1	8
Pro totals (13 years)		143	124	3875	2177	56.2	27082	190	119	6.99	81.6	728	4741	6.5	33	33	1	200

CUNNINGHAM, RICHIE   K   COWBOYS

PERSONAL: Born August 18, 1970, in Terrebonne, La. ... 5-10/167. ... Full name: Richard Anthony Cunningham.
HIGH SCHOOL: Terrebonne (La.).
COLLEGE: Southwestern Louisiana (degree in marketing).
TRANSACTIONS/CAREER NOTES: Signed as non-drafted free agent by Dallas Cowboys (May 2, 1994). ... Released by Cowboys (August 17, 1994). ... Signed by Green Bay Packers (April 22, 1996). ... Released by Packers (August 19, 1996). ... Signed by Cowboys (April 15, 1997).
HONORS: Named kicker on THE SPORTING NEWS NFL All-Pro team (1997).

					KICKING				
Year Team	G	XPM	XPA	FGM	FGA	Lg.	50+	Pts.
1997—Dallas NFL	16	24	24	*34	∞37	53	1-1	‡126
1998—Dallas NFL	16	40	40	29	35	54	1-3	127
Pro totals (2 years)	32	64	64	63	72	54	2-4	253

CUNNINGHAM, RICK   OT   RAIDERS

PERSONAL: Born January 4, 1967, in Los Angeles. ... 6-7/305. ... Full name: Patrick Dante Ross Cunningham.
HIGH SCHOOL: Beverly Hills (Calif.).
JUNIOR COLLEGE: Sacramento Community College.
COLLEGE: Oregon State, then Texas A&M.
TRANSACTIONS/CAREER NOTES: Selected by Indianapolis Colts in fourth round (106th pick overall) of 1990 NFL draft. ... Signed by Colts (July 17, 1990). ... Released by Colts (August 26, 1991). ... Selected by Orlando Thunder in third round (28th pick overall) of 1992 World League draft. ... Signed by Phoenix Cardinals (June 16, 1992). ... On injured reserve with forearm injury (December 4, 1992-remainder of season). ... Cardinals franchise renamed Arizona Cardinals for 1994 season. ... Granted unconditional free agency (February 17, 1995). ... Signed by Minnesota Vikings (April 3, 1995). ... Granted unconditional free agency (February 16, 1996). ... Signed by Oakland Raiders (July 24, 1996).
PLAYING EXPERIENCE: Indianapolis NFL, 1990; Orlando W.L., 1992; Phoenix NFL, 1992 and 1993; Arizona NFL, 1994; Minnesota NFL, 1995; Oakland NFL, 1996-1998. ... Games/Games started: 1990 (2/0), W.L. 1992 (10/10), NFL 1992 (8/6), 1993 (16/16), 1994 (11/10), 1995 (11/1), 1996 (13/0), 1997 (7/0), 1998 (12/0). Total W.L.: 10/10. Total NFL: 80/33. Total Pro: 90/43.
HONORS: Named offensive tackle on All-World League team (1992).
PRO STATISTICS: W.L.: 1992—Recovered one fumble. NFL: 1993—Recovered one fumble. 1995—Recovered one fumble. 1996—Caught one pass for three yards and a touchdown.

CURRY, ERIC   DE   JAGUARS

PERSONAL: Born February 3, 1970, in Thomasville, Ga. ... 6-6/269. ... Full name: Eric Felece Curry. ... Cousin of William Andrews, running back with Atlanta Falcons (1979-83 and 1986); cousin of Lomas Brown, offensive tackle, Cleveland Browns; and cousin of Guy McIntyre, guard with San Francisco 49ers (1984-93), Green Bay Packers (1994) and Philadelphia Eagles (1995 and 1996).
HIGH SCHOOL: Thomasville (Ga.).
COLLEGE: Alabama (degree in criminal justice, 1992).
TRANSACTIONS/CAREER NOTES: Selected by Tampa Bay Buccaneers in first round (sixth pick overall) of 1993 NFL draft. ... Signed by Buccaneers (August 16, 1993). ... Designated by Buccaneers as transition player (February 15, 1994). ... Released by Buccaneers (August 23, 1997). ... Re-signed by Buccaneers (August 25, 1997). ... Granted unconditional free agency (February 13, 1998). ... Signed by Green Bay Packers (April 2, 1998). ... Released by Packers (August 30, 1998). ... Signed by Jacksonville Jaguars (September 9, 1998). ... Granted unconditional free agency (February 12, 1999). ... Re-signed by Jaguars (April 8, 1999).
HONORS: Named defensive lineman on THE SPORTING NEWS college All-America first team (1992).
PRO STATISTICS: Recovered one fumble. 1995—Recovered one fumble.

Year Team	G	GS	SACKS
1993—Tampa Bay NFL	10	10	5.0
1994—Tampa Bay NFL	15	14	3.0
1995—Tampa Bay NFL	16	16	2.0
1996—Tampa Bay NFL	12	3	2.0
1997—Tampa Bay NFL	6	1	0.0
1998—Jacksonville NFL	11	0	0.0
Pro totals (6 years)	70	44	12.0

CURTIS, CANUTE — LB — BENGALS

PERSONAL: Born August 4, 1974, in Amityville, N.Y. ... 6-2/256. ... Name pronounced kuh-NOOT.
HIGH SCHOOL: Farmingdale (N.Y.).
COLLEGE: West Virginia.
TRANSACTIONS/CAREER NOTES: Selected by Cincinnati Bengals in sixth round (176th pick overall) of 1997 NFL draft. ... Signed by Bengals (July 11, 1997). ... Released by Bengals (August 24, 1997). ... Re-signed by Bengals to practice squad (August 26, 1997). ... Activated (October 21, 1997). ... Released by Bengals (August 30, 1998). ... Re-signed by Bengals to practice squad (August 31, 1998). ... Activated (November 10, 1998).
PLAYING EXPERIENCE: Cincinnati NFL, 1997 and 1998. ... Games/games started: 1997 (3/0), 1998 (5/0). Total: 8/0.
HONORS: Named outside linebacker on THE SPORTING NEWS college All-America first team (1996).

DALMAN, CHRIS — C — 49ERS

PERSONAL: Born March 15, 1970, in Salinas, Calif. ... 6-3/297. ... Full name: Christopher William Dalman.
HIGH SCHOOL: Palma (Salinas, Calif.).
COLLEGE: Stanford (degree in political science, 1992).
TRANSACTIONS/CAREER NOTES: Selected by San Francisco 49ers in sixth round (166th pick overall) of 1993 NFL draft. ... Signed by 49ers (June 24, 1993). ... Granted unconditional free agency (February 14, 1997). ... Re-signed by 49ers (April 25, 1997).
PLAYING EXPERIENCE: San Francisco NFL, 1993-1998. ... Games/Games started: 1993 (15/0), 1994 (16/4), 1995 (15/1), 1996 (16/16), 1997 (13/13), 1998 (15/15). Total: 90/49.
CHAMPIONSHIP GAME EXPERIENCE: Played in NFC championship game (1993, 1994 and 1997 seasons). ... Member of Super Bowl championship team (1994 season).
PRO STATISTICS: 1993—Recovered one fumble. 1994—Fumbled once. 1995—Caught one pass for minus one yard, returned three kickoffs for 29 yards and recovered one fumble. 1997—Recovered one fumble.

DALTON, LIONAL — DT — RAVENS

PERSONAL: Born February 21, 1975, in Detroit. ... 6-1/320.
HIGH SCHOOL: Cooley (Detroit).
COLLEGE: Eastern Michigan.
TRANSACTIONS/CAREER NOTES: Signed as non-drafted free agent by Baltimore Ravens (April 23, 1998).
PLAYING EXPERIENCE: Baltimore NFL, 1998. ... Games/Games started: 2/1.

DALUISO, BRAD — K — GIANTS

PERSONAL: Born December 31, 1967, in San Diego. ... 6-2/215. ... Full name: Bradley William Daluiso. ... Name pronounced DOLL-uh-WEE-so.
HIGH SCHOOL: Valhalla (El Cajon, Calif.).
JUNIOR COLLEGE: Grossmont College (Calif.).
COLLEGE: San Diego State, then UCLA.
TRANSACTIONS/CAREER NOTES: Signed as non-drafted free agent by Green Bay Packers (May 2, 1991). ... Traded by Packers to Atlanta Falcons for an undisclosed pick in 1992 draft (August 26, 1991). ... Claimed on waivers by Buffalo Bills (September 10, 1991). ... Granted unconditional free agency (February 1, 1992). ... Signed by Dallas Cowboys (February 18, 1992). ... Claimed on waivers by Denver Broncos (September 1, 1992). ... Released by Broncos (August 23, 1993). ... Signed by New York Giants (September 1, 1993). ... Granted free agency (February 17, 1994). ... Re-signed by Giants (June 21, 1994). ... Granted unconditional free agency (February 17, 1995). ... Re-signed by Giants (February 22, 1995). ... Granted unconditional free agency (February 13, 1998). ... Re-signed by Giants (February 13, 1998).
CHAMPIONSHIP GAME EXPERIENCE: Played in AFC championship game (1991 season). ... Played in Super Bowl XXVI (1991 season).
PRO STATISTICS: 1992—Punted 10 times for 467 yards.

		KICKING						
Year Team	G	XPM	XPA	FGM	FGA	Lg.	50+	Pts.
1991—Atlanta NFL	2	2	2	2	3	23	0-0	8
—Buffalo NFL	14	0	0	0	0	...	0-0	0
1992—Denver NFL	16	0	0	0	1	0	0-1	0
1993—New York Giants NFL	15	0	0	1	3	54	1-3	3
1994—New York Giants NFL	16	5	5	11	11	52	1-1	38
1995—New York Giants NFL	16	28	28	20	28	51	2-2	88
1996—New York Giants NFL	16	22	22	24	27	46	0-0	94
1997—New York Giants NFL	16	27	29	22	32	52	1-4	93
1998—New York Giants NFL	16	32	32	21	27	51	1-1	95
Pro totals (8 years)	127	116	118	101	132	54	6-12	419

DANIELS, JEROME — OL — CARDINALS

PERSONAL: Born September 13, 1974, in Hartford, Conn. ... 6-5/350. ... Full name: Jerome Alvonne Daniels.
HIGH SCHOOL: Bloomfield (Conn.).
COLLEGE: Northeastern (degree in English, 1997).
TRANSACTIONS/CAREER NOTES: Selected by Miami Dolphins in fourth round (121st pick overall) of 1997 NFL draft. ... Signed by Dolphins (June 10, 1997). ... Claimed on waivers by Baltimore Ravens (August 19, 1997). ... Released by Ravens (August 24, 1997). ... Re-signed by Ravens to practice squad (August 26, 1997). ... Signed by Arizona Cardinals off Ravens practice squad (November 27, 1997). ... Inactive for four games (1997).
PLAYING EXPERIENCE: Arizona NFL, 1998. ... Games/Games started: 8/5.

DANIELS, PHILLIP — DE — SEAHAWKS

PERSONAL: Born March 4, 1973, in Donalsonville, Ga. ... 6-5/263. ... Full name: Phillip Bernard Daniels.
HIGH SCHOOL: Seminole County (Ga.).
COLLEGE: Georgia.
TRANSACTIONS/CAREER NOTES: Selected by Seattle Seahawks in fourth round (99th pick overall) of 1996 NFL draft. ... Signed by Seahawks (July 17, 1996). ... Granted free agency (February 12, 1999). ... Re-signed by Seahawks (April 6, 1999).
PRO STATISTICS: 1996—Recovered one fumble. 1997—Returned one kickoff for minus two yards and fumbled once. 1998—Recovered two fumbles.

Year Team	G	GS	SACKS
1996—Seattle NFL	15	0	2.0
1997—Seattle NFL	13	10	4.0
1998—Seattle NFL	16	15	6.5
Pro totals (3 years)	44	25	12.5

DAR DAR, KIRBY — WR — CHIEFS

PERSONAL: Born March 27, 1972, in Morgan City, La. ... 5-9/192. ... Full name: Kirby David Dar Dar.
HIGH SCHOOL: Thomas Jefferson (Tampa).
COLLEGE: Syracuse.
TRANSACTIONS/CAREER NOTES: Signed as non-drafted free agent by Miami Dolphins (April 27, 1995). ... Released by Dolphins (August 22, 1995). ... Re-signed by Dolphins to practice squad (August 30, 1995). ... Activated (December 23, 1995). ... Released by Dolphins (August 20, 1996). ... Re-signed by Dolphins (August 24, 1996). ... On injured reserve with knee injury (August 18, 1997-entire season). ... Released by Dolphins (October 1, 1998). ... Signed by Kansas City Chiefs (March 4, 1999).
PLAYING EXPERIENCE: Miami NFL, 1995, 1996 and 1998. ... Games/Games started: 1995 (1/0), 1996 (11/0), 1998 (2/0). Total: 14/0.
PRO STATISTICS: 1995—Returned one kickoff for 22 yards. 1996—Returned seven kickoffs for 132 yards.

DARIUS, DONOVIN — S — JAGUARS

PERSONAL: Born August 12, 1975, in Camden, N.J. ... 6-1/213. ... Full name: Donovin Lee Darius.
HIGH SCHOOL: Woodrow Wilson (Camden, N.J.).
COLLEGE: Syracuse (degree in exercise science, 1997).
TRANSACTIONS/CAREER NOTES: Selected by Jacksonville Jaguars in first round (25th pick overall) of 1998 NFL draft. ... Signed by Jaguars (July 23, 1998).
PLAYING EXPERIENCE: Jacksonville NFL, 1998. ... Games/Games started: 14/14.
HONORS: Named free safety on THE SPORTING NEWS college All-America first team (1997).
PRO STATISTICS: 1998—Recovered one fumble for 83 yards and a touchdown.

DARLING, JAMES — LB — EAGLES

PERSONAL: Born December 29, 1974, in Denver. ... 6-0/250. ... Full name: James Jackson Darling.
HIGH SCHOOL: Kettle Falls (Wash.).
COLLEGE: Washington State.
TRANSACTIONS/CAREER NOTES: Selected by Philadelphia Eagles in second round (57th pick overall) of 1997 NFL draft. ... Signed by Eagles (July 16, 1997).
PLAYING EXPERIENCE: Philadelphia NFL, 1997 and 1998. ... Games/Games started: 1997 (16/6), 1998 (12/8). Total: 28/14.
HONORS: Named inside linebacker on THE SPORTING NEWS college All-America second team (1996).
PRO STATISTICS: 1998—Credited with two sacks.

DAVIDDS-GARRIDO, NORBERTO — OT — PANTHERS

PERSONAL: Born October 4, 1972, in La Puenta, Calif. ... 6-5/315. ... Full name: Norberto Davidds-Garrido Jr. ... Formerly known as Norberto Garrido. ... Name pronounced No-BURR-toe DAY-vids Gah-REE-do.
HIGH SCHOOL: Workman (La Puenta, Calif.).
JUNIOR COLLEGE: Mt. San Antonio College (Walnut, Calif.).
COLLEGE: Southern California.
TRANSACTIONS/CAREER NOTES: Selected by Carolina Panthers in fourth round (106th pick overall) of 1996 NFL draft. ... Signed by Panthers (June 17, 1996). ... On injured reserve with ankle injury (December 15, 1997-remainder of season). ... Granted free agency (February 12, 1999).
PLAYING EXPERIENCE: Carolina NFL, 1996-1998. ... Games/Games started: 1996 (12/8), 1997 (15/15), 1998 (16/16). Total: 43/39.
CHAMPIONSHIP GAME EXPERIENCE: Played in NFC championship game (1996 season).
PRO STATISTICS: 1998—Recovered one fumble.

DAVIS, ANTHONY — LB

PERSONAL: Born March 7, 1969, in Kennewick, Wash. ... 6-0/235. ... Full name: Anthony D. Davis.
HIGH SCHOOL: Pasco (Wash.).
JUNIOR COLLEGE: Spokane Falls Community College (Wash.).
COLLEGE: Utah.
TRANSACTIONS/CAREER NOTES: Selected by Houston Oilers in 11th round (301st pick overall) of 1992 NFL draft. ... Signed by Oilers prior to 1992 season. ... Released by Oilers (August 24, 1992). ... Re-signed by Oilers to practice squad (September 2, 1992). ... Released by Oilers (October 6, 1992). ... Signed by Seattle Seahawks to practice squad (December 9, 1992). ... Released by Seahawks (August 30, 1993). ... Re-

signed by Seahawks to practice squad (September 1, 1993). ... Activated (October 11, 1993). ... Released by Seahawks (August 22, 1994). ... Signed by Kansas City Chiefs (November 24, 1994). ... Granted unconditional free agency (February 12, 1999).
PRO STATISTICS: 1997—Recovered one fumble for two yards.

				INTERCEPTIONS				SACKS
Year Team	G	GS	No.	Yds.	Avg.	TD		No.
1993—Seattle NFL	10	0	0	0	...	0		0.0
1994—Kansas City NFL	5	0	0	0	...	0		0.0
1995—Kansas City NFL	16	2	1	11	11.0	0		2.0
1996—Kansas City NFL	16	15	2	37	18.5	0		2.5
1997—Kansas City NFL	15	15	0	0	...	0		3.5
1998—Kansas City NFL	16	16	2	27	13.5	0		4.5
Pro totals (6 years)	78	48	5	75	15.0	0		12.5

DAVIS, BILLY　　　　　WR

PERSONAL: Born July 6, 1972, in El Paso, Texas. ... 6-1/205. ... Full name: William Augusta Davis III.
HIGH SCHOOL: Irvin (El Paso, Texas).
COLLEGE: Pittsburgh.
TRANSACTIONS/CAREER NOTES: Signed as non-drafted free agent by Dallas Cowboys (April 27, 1995). ... Granted free agency (February 13, 1998). ... Re-signed by Cowboys (February 27, 1998). ... Released by Cowboys (June 1, 1999).
CHAMPIONSHIP GAME EXPERIENCE: Played in NFC championship game (1995 season). ... Member of Super Bowl championship team (1995 season).
PRO STATISTICS: 1998—Returned one kickoff for 10 yards and recovered one fumble.
SINGLE GAME HIGHS (regular season): Receptions—4 (December 27, 1998, vs. Washington); yards—87 (September 27, 1998, vs. Oakland); and touchdown receptions—1 (November 22, 1998, vs. Seattle).

			RUSHING				RECEIVING				TOTALS			
Year Team	G	GS	Att.	Yds.	Avg.	TD	No.	Yds.	Avg.	TD	TD	2pt.	Pts.	Fum.
1995—Dallas NFL	16	0	0	0	...	0	0	0	...	0	0	0	0	0
1996—Dallas NFL	13	0	0	0	...	0	0	0	...	0	0	0	0	0
1997—Dallas NFL	16	0	0	0	...	0	3	33	11.0	0	0	0	0	0
1998—Dallas NFL	16	11	4	15	3.8	0	39	691	17.7	3	3	0	18	1
Pro totals (4 years)	61	11	4	15	3.8	0	42	724	17.2	3	3	0	18	1

DAVIS, DON　　　　　LB　　　　　BUCCANEERS

PERSONAL: Born December 17, 1972, in Olathe, Kan. ... 6-1/240.
HIGH SCHOOL: South (Olathe, Kan.).
COLLEGE: Kansas.
TRANSACTIONS/CAREER NOTES: Signed as non-drafted free agent by New York Jets (April 28, 1995). ... Released by Jets (August 27, 1995). ... Signed by Kansas City Chiefs (January 9, 1996). ... Released by Chiefs (August 20, 1996). ... Signed by New Orleans Saints to practice squad (August 27, 1996). ... Activated (October 4, 1996). ... On injured reserve with wrist injury (November 19, 1997-remainder of season). ... Claimed on waivers by Tampa Bay Buccaneers (November 25, 1998). ... Granted free agency (February 12, 1999). ... Re-signed by Buccaneers (May 21, 1999).
PLAYING EXPERIENCE: New Orleans NFL, 1996 and 1997; New Orleans (4)-Tampa Bay (5) NFL, 1998. ... Games/Games started: 1996 (11/0), 1997 (11/0), 1998 (N.O.-4/0; T.B.-5/0; Total: 9/0). Total: 31/0.
PRO STATISTICS: 1996—Recovered one fumble.

DAVIS, ERIC　　　　　CB　　　　　PANTHERS

PERSONAL: Born January 26, 1968, in Anniston, Ala. ... 5-11/185. ... Full name: Eric Wayne Davis.
HIGH SCHOOL: Anniston (Ala.).
COLLEGE: Jacksonville (Ala.) State.
TRANSACTIONS/CAREER NOTES: Selected by San Francisco 49ers in second round (53rd pick overall) of 1990 NFL draft. ... Signed by 49ers (July 28, 1990). ... On injured reserve with shoulder injury (September 11, 1991-remainder of season). ... Granted free agency (March 1, 1993). ... Re-signed by 49ers (July 20, 1993). ... Granted unconditional free agency (February 16, 1996). ... Signed by Carolina Panthers (February 21, 1996).
CHAMPIONSHIP GAME EXPERIENCE: Played in NFC championship game (1990, 1992-1994 and 1996 seasons). ... Member of Super Bowl championship team (1994 season).
HONORS: Played in Pro Bowl (1995 and 1996 seasons).
POST SEASON RECORDS: Shares NFL postseason career record for most consecutive games with one or more interception—3.
PRO STATISTICS: 1990—Returned five punts for 38 yards and recovered one fumble for 34 yards. 1992—Recovered two fumbles. 1993—Recovered one fumble for 47 yards and a touchdown. 1994—Recovered two fumbles. 1995—Credited with one sack. 1997—Recovered one fumble for two yards. 1998—Credited with one sack and recovered one fumble.
MISCELLANEOUS: Holds Carolina Panthers all-time record for most interceptions (15).

			INTERCEPTIONS			
Year Team	G	GS	No.	Yds.	Avg.	TD
1990—San Francisco NFL	16	0	1	13	13.0	0
1991—San Francisco NFL	2	2	0	0	...	0
1992—San Francisco NFL	16	16	3	52	17.3	0
1993—San Francisco NFL	16	16	4	45	11.3	1
1994—San Francisco NFL	16	16	1	8	8.0	0
1995—San Francisco NFL	15	15	3	84	28.0	1
1996—Carolina NFL	16	16	5	57	11.4	0
1997—Carolina NFL	14	14	5	25	5.0	0
1998—Carolina NFL	16	16	5	81	16.2	2
Pro totals (9 years)	127	111	27	365	13.5	4

DAVIS, GREG   K

PERSONAL: Born October 29, 1965, in Rome, Ga. ... 6-0/205. ... Full name: Gregory Brian Davis.
HIGH SCHOOL: Lakeside (Atlanta).
COLLEGE: The Citadel (degree in physical education, 1987).
TRANSACTIONS/CAREER NOTES: Selected by Tampa Bay Buccaneers in ninth round (246th pick overall) of 1987 NFL draft. ... Signed by Buccaneers (July 18, 1987). ... Released by Buccaneers (September 7, 1987). ... Signed as replacement player by Atlanta Falcons (September 24, 1987). ... Claimed on waivers by Buccaneers (October 20, 1987). ... Released by Buccaneers (November 2, 1987). ... Signed by Falcons (December 24, 1987). ... Granted unconditional free agency (February 1, 1989). ... Signed by New England Patriots (March 9, 1989). ... Released by Patriots (November 8, 1989). ... Signed by Falcons (November 15, 1989). ... Granted unconditional free agency (February 1, 1991). ... Signed by Phoenix Cardinals (February 21, 1991). ... Granted unconditional free agency (March 1, 1993). ... Re-signed by Cardinals (July 15, 1993). ... Cardinals franchise renamed Arizona Cardinals for 1994 season. ... Released by Cardinals (November 5, 1996). ... Signed by Minnesota Vikings (April 11, 1997). ... Released by Vikings (September 24, 1997). ... Signed by San Diego Chargers (September 24, 1997). ... Granted unconditional free agency (February 13, 1998). ... Signed by Oakland Raiders (June 16, 1998). ... Granted unconditional free agency (February 12, 1999).

			KICKING						
Year Team	G	XPM	XPA	FGM	FGA	Lg.	50+	Pts.
1987—Atlanta NFL	3	6	6	3	4	42	0-0	15
1988—Atlanta NFL	16	25	27	19	30	52	1-4	82
1989—New England NFL	9	13	16	16	23	52	2-2	61
—Atlanta NFL	6	12	12	7	11	47	0-0	33
1990—Atlanta NFL	16	40	40	22	33	53	2-5	106
1991—Phoenix NFL	16	19	19	21	30	52	3-7	82
1992—Phoenix NFL	16	28	28	13	26	49	0-3	67
1993—Phoenix NFL	16	37	37	21	28	55	4-5	100
1994—Arizona NFL	14	17	17	20	26	51	1-4	77
1995—Arizona NFL	16	19	19	30	‡39	55	1-6	109
1996—Arizona NFL	9	12	12	9	14	49	0-0	39
1997—Minnesota NFL	4	10	10	7	10	43	0-0	31
—San Diego NFL	12	21	22	19	24	45	0-0	78
1998—Oakland NFL	16	31	31	17	27	51	1-2	82
Pro totals (12 years)	**169**	**290**	**296**	**224**	**325**	**55**	**15-38**	**962**

DAVIS, JOHN   TE   BUCCANEERS

PERSONAL: Born May 14, 1973, in Jasper, Texas. ... 6-4/262.
HIGH SCHOOL: Jasper (Texas).
JUNIOR COLLEGE: Cisco (Texas) Junior College.
COLLEGE: Emporia (Kan.) State.
TRANSACTIONS/CAREER NOTES: Selected by Dallas Cowboys in fifth round of 1994 supplemental draft. ... Signed by Cowboys for 1994 season. ... Released by Cowboys (August 28, 1994). ... Re-signed by Cowboys to practice squad (August 30, 1994). ... On injured reserve with ankle injury (prior to 1995 season-October 1995). ... Released by Cowboys (October 1995). ... Signed by New Orleans Saints (June 3, 1996). ... Released by Saints (August 12, 1996). ... Signed by Tampa Bay Buccaneers (January 20, 1997). ... Granted free agency (February 12, 1999). ... Re-signed by Buccaneers (April 23, 1999).
SINGLE GAME HIGHS (regular season): Receptions—1 (November 15, 1998, vs. Jacksonville); yards—16 (December 21, 1997, vs. Chicago); and touchdown receptions—1 (November 15, 1998, vs. Jacksonville).

			RECEIVING				TOTALS		
Year Team	G	GS	No.	Yds.	Avg.	TD	TD	2pt.	Pts.	Fum.
1997—Tampa Bay NFL	8	2	3	35	11.7	0	0	0	0	0
1998—Tampa Bay NFL	16	0	2	12	6.0	1	1	0	6	0
Pro totals (2 years)	**24**	**2**	**5**	**47**	**9.4**	**1**	**1**	**0**	**6**	**0**

DAVIS, ROB   C   PACKERS

PERSONAL: Born December 10, 1968, in Washington, D.C. ... 6-3/290. ... Full name: Robert Emmett Davis.
HIGH SCHOOL: Eleanor Roosevelt (Greenbelt, Md.).
COLLEGE: Shippensburg, Pa. (degree in criminal justice/law enforcement).
TRANSACTIONS/CAREER NOTES: Signed as non-drafted free agent by New York Jets (April 27, 1993). ... Released by Jets (August 24, 1993). ... Re-signed by Jets (April 29, 1994). ... Released by Jets (August 22, 1994). ... Signed by Baltimore Stallions of CFL (April 1995). ... Signed by Kansas City Chiefs (April 22, 1996). ... Released by Chiefs (August 20, 1996). ... Signed by Chicago Bears (August 28, 1996). ... Released by Bears (August 27, 1997). ... Signed by Green Bay Packers (November 4, 1997). ... On physically unable to perform list with back injury (July 18-August 10, 1998).
PLAYING EXPERIENCE: Baltimore CFL, 1995; Chicago NFL, 1996; Green Bay NFL, 1997 and 1998. ... Games/Games started: 1995 (18/0), 1996 (16/0), 1997 (7/0), 1998 (16/0). Total CFL: 18/0. Total NFL: 39/0. Total Pro: 57/0.
CHAMPIONSHIP GAME EXPERIENCE: Played in NFC championship game (1997 season). ... Played in Super Bowl XXXII (1997 season).

DAVIS, STEPHEN   RB   REDSKINS

PERSONAL: Born March 1, 1974, in Spartanburg, S.C. ... 6-0/234.
HIGH SCHOOL: Spartanburg (S.C.).
COLLEGE: Auburn (degree in vocational education, 1995).
TRANSACTIONS/CAREER NOTES: Selected by Washington Redskins in fourth round (102nd pick overall) of 1996 NFL draft. ... Signed by Redskins (July 16, 1996). ... Granted free agency (February 12, 1999). ... Re-signed by Redskins (May 12, 1999).
PRO STATISTICS: 1997—Returned three kickoffs for 62 yards and recovered one fumble.

SINGLE GAME HIGHS (regular season): Attempts—22 (October 13, 1997, vs. Dallas); yards—94 (October 13, 1997, vs. Dallas); and rushing touchdowns—2 (October 13, 1997, vs. Dallas).
STATISTICAL PLATEAUS: 100-yard receiving games: 1998 (1).

				RUSHING				RECEIVING				TOTALS		
Year Team	G	GS	Att.	Yds.	Avg.	TD	No.	Yds.	Avg.	TD	TD	2pt.	Pts.	Fum.
1996—Washington NFL	12	0	23	139	6.0	2	0	0	...	0	2	0	12	0
1997—Washington NFL	14	6	141	567	4.0	3	18	134	7.4	0	3	0	18	1
1998—Washington NFL	16	12	34	109	3.2	0	21	263	12.5	2	2	0	12	0
Pro totals (3 years)	42	18	198	815	4.1	5	39	397	10.2	2	7	0	42	1

DAVIS, TERRELL — RB — BRONCOS

PERSONAL: Born October 28, 1972, in San Diego. ... 5-11/210.
HIGH SCHOOL: Abraham Lincoln Prep (San Diego).
COLLEGE: Long Beach State, then Georgia.
TRANSACTIONS/CAREER NOTES: Selected by Denver Broncos in sixth round (196th pick overall) of 1995 NFL draft. ... Signed by Broncos (June 30, 1995).
CHAMPIONSHIP GAME EXPERIENCE: Played in AFC championship game (1997 and 1998 seasons). ... Member of Super Bowl championship team (1997 and 1998 seasons).
HONORS: Named running back on THE SPORTING NEWS NFL All-Pro team (1996-1998). ... Played in Pro Bowl (1996 and 1997 seasons). ... Named Most Valuable Player of Super Bowl XXXII (1997 season). ... Named to play in Pro Bowl (1998 season); replaced by Curtis Martin due to injury. ... Named NFL Player of the Year by THE SPORTING NEWS (1998).
POST SEASON RECORDS: Holds Super Bowl single-game record for most rushing touchdowns—3 (January 25, 1998, vs. Green Bay). ... Shares Super Bowl single-game records for most points—18; and most touchdowns—3 (January 25, 1998, vs. Green Bay). ... Holds NFL postseason career record for highest average gain—5.41. ... Holds NFL postseason record for most consecutive games with 100 or more yards rushing—7 (1997-present). ... Shares NFL postseason career record for most games with 100 or more yards rushing—7.
PRO STATISTICS: 1995—Recovered one fumble. 1996—Recovered two fumbles. 1997—Recovered two fumbles for minus seven yards. 1998—Recovered one fumble.
SINGLE GAME HIGHS (regular season): Attempts—42 (October 26, 1997, vs. Buffalo); yards—215 (September 21, 1997, vs. Cincinnati); and rushing touchdowns—3 (December 6, 1998, vs. Kansas City).
STATISTICAL PLATEAUS: 100-yard rushing games: 1995 (3), 1996 (6), 1997 (10), 1998 (11). Total: 30.
MISCELLANEOUS: Holds Denver Broncos all-time records for most yards rushing (6,413), most touchdowns (61) and most rushing touchdowns (56).

				RUSHING				RECEIVING				TOTALS		
Year Team	G	GS	Att.	Yds.	Avg.	TD	No.	Yds.	Avg.	TD	TD	2pt.	Pts.	Fum.
1995—Denver NFL	14	14	237	1117	§4.7	7	49	367	7.5	1	8	0	48	5
1996—Denver NFL	16	16	§345	§1538	4.5	13	36	310	8.6	2	15	0	90	5
1997—Denver NFL	15	15	369	§1750	4.7	†15	42	287	6.8	0	15	3	†96	4
1998—Denver NFL	16	16	§392	*2008	*5.1	*21	25	217	8.7	2	*23	0	138	2
Pro totals (4 years)	61	61	1343	6413	4.8	56	152	1181	7.8	5	61	3	372	16

DAVIS, TRAVIS — S — STEELERS

PERSONAL: Born January 10, 1973, in Harbor City, Calif. ... 6-0/209. ... Full name: Travis Horace Davis.
HIGH SCHOOL: Banning (Wilmington, Calif.).
COLLEGE: Notre Dame (degree in psychology, 1997).
TRANSACTIONS/CAREER NOTES: Selected by New Orleans Saints in seventh round (242nd pick overall) of 1995 NFL draft. ... Signed by Saints (July 14, 1995). ... Released by Saints (September 5, 1995). ... Re-signed by Saints to practice squad (September 6, 1995). ... Signed by Jacksonville Jaguars off Saints practice squad (October 17, 1995). ... Granted free agency (February 13, 1998). ... Re-signed by Jaguars (June 12, 1998). ... Granted unconditional free agency (February 12, 1999). ... Signed by Pittsburgh Steelers (April 19, 1999).
CHAMPIONSHIP GAME EXPERIENCE: Played in AFC championship game (1996 season).
PRO STATISTICS: 1995—Recovered one fumble. 1996—Recovered two fumbles. 1997—Credited with two sacks, returned one kickoff for nine yards and recovered three fumbles for 10 yards. 1998—Credited with 1/2 sack and recovered one fumble.

			INTERCEPTIONS			
Year Team	G	GS	No.	Yds.	Avg.	TD
1995—Jacksonville NFL	9	5	0	0	...	0
1996—Jacksonville NFL	16	7	2	0	0.0	0
1997—Jacksonville NFL	16	16	1	23	23.0	0
1998—Jacksonville NFL	16	5	2	34	17.0	0
Pro totals (4 years)	57	33	5	57	11.4	0

DAVIS, TROY — RB — SAINTS

PERSONAL: Born September 14, 1975, in Miami. ... 5-7/191.
HIGH SCHOOL: Southridge (Miami).
COLLEGE: Iowa State.
TRANSACTIONS/CAREER NOTES: Selected after junior season by New Orleans Saints in third round (62nd pick overall) of 1997 NFL draft. ... Signed by Saints (June 13, 1997).
HONORS: Named running back on THE SPORTING NEWS college All-America first team (1995 and 1996).
SINGLE GAME HIGHS (regular season): Attempts—18 (October 25, 1998, vs. Tampa Bay); yards—48 (October 25, 1998, vs. Tampa Bay); and rushing touchdowns—1 (December 27, 1998, vs. Buffalo).

				RUSHING				RECEIVING				KICKOFF RETURNS			TOTALS		
Year Team	G	GS	Att.	Yds.	Avg.	TD	No.	Yds.	Avg.	TD	No.	Yds.	Avg.	TD	TD	2pt.	Pts.	Fum.
1997—New Orleans NFL	16	7	75	271	3.6	0	13	85	6.5	0	9	173	19.2	0	0	0	0	3
1998—New Orleans NFL	14	2	55	143	2.6	1	16	99	6.2	0	2	21	10.5	0	1	0	6	1
Pro totals (2 years)	30	9	130	414	3.2	1	29	184	6.3	0	11	194	17.6	0	1	0	6	4

DAVIS, TYRONE — TE — PACKERS

PERSONAL: Born June 30, 1972, in Halifax, Va. ... 6-4/252.
HIGH SCHOOL: Halifax (Va.), then Fork Union (Va.) Military Academy.
COLLEGE: Virginia.
TRANSACTIONS/CAREER NOTES: Selected by New York Jets in fourth round (107th pick overall) of 1995 NFL draft. ... Signed by Jets (June 14, 1995). ... Released by Jets (September 13, 1995). ... Re-signed by Jets to practice squad (September 15, 1995). ... Activated (December 11, 1995). ... Granted free agency (February 14, 1997). ... Re-signed by Jets for 1997 season. ... Traded by Jets to Green Bay Packers for past considerations (August 25, 1997). ... Released by Packers (September 24, 1997). ... Re-signed by Packers (September 29, 1997).
CHAMPIONSHIP GAME EXPERIENCE: Played in NFC championship game (1997 season). ... Played in Super Bowl XXXII (1997 season).
PRO STATISTICS: 1997—Recovered one fumble in end zone for touchdown.
SINGLE GAME HIGHS (regular season): Receptions—3 (November 22, 1998, vs. Minnesota); yards—83 (November 15, 1998, vs. New York Giants); and touchdown receptions—2 (November 22, 1998, vs. Minnesota).

				RECEIVING			TOTALS			
Year Team	G	GS	No.	Yds.	Avg.	TD	TD	2pt.	Pts.	Fum.
1995—New York Jets NFL	4	0	1	9	9.0	0	0	0	0	0
1996—New York Jets NFL	2	0	1	6	6.0	0	0	0	0	0
1997—Green Bay NFL	13	0	2	28	14.0	1	2	0	12	0
1998—Green Bay NFL	13	1	18	250	13.9	7	7	0	42	1
Pro totals (4 years)	32	1	22	293	13.3	8	9	0	54	1

DAVIS, WENDELL — TE — CHARGERS

PERSONAL: Born October 24, 1975, in Escatawapa, Miss. ... 6-2/246.
HIGH SCHOOL: Moss Point (Miss.).
JUNIOR COLLEGE: Mississippi Gulf Coast Junior College.
COLLEGE: Temple.
TRANSACTIONS/CAREER NOTES: Signed as non-drafted free agent by San Diego Chargers (April 20, 1998). ... Released by Chargers (August 30, 1998). ... Re-signed by Chargers to practice squad (September 2, 1998). ... Activated (September 29, 1998).
PLAYING EXPERIENCE: San Diego NFL, 1998. ... Games/Games started: 11/7.
PRO STATISTICS: 1998—Caught four passes for 23 yards and recovered one fumble.

DAVIS, WILLIE — WR

PERSONAL: Born October 10, 1967, in Little Rock, Ark. ... 6-0/182. ... Full name: Willie Clark Davis. ... Brother of Tyree Davis, wide receiver with Tampa Bay Buccaneers (1993-95), Cincinnati Bengals (1996) and Seattle Seahawks (1997).
HIGH SCHOOL: Altheimer (Ark.).
COLLEGE: Central Arkansas.
TRANSACTIONS/CAREER NOTES: Signed as non-drafted free agent by Kansas City Chiefs (May 2, 1990). ... Released by Chiefs (September 3, 1990). ... Re-signed by Chiefs to practice squad (September 5, 1990). ... Released by Chiefs (August 26, 1991). ... Re-signed by Chiefs to practice squad (August 28, 1991). ... Activated (November 23, 1991). ... Moved to practice squad (November 26, 1991). ... Assigned by Chiefs to Orlando Thunder in 1992 World League enhancement allocation program (February 20, 1992). ... Granted unconditional free agency (February 16, 1996). ... Signed by Houston Oilers (March 26, 1996). ... Oilers franchise moved to Tennessee for 1997 season. ... Released by Oilers (February 12, 1999).
CHAMPIONSHIP GAME EXPERIENCE: Played in AFC championship game (1993 season).
PRO STATISTICS: W.L.: 1992—Recovered one fumble and rushed once for 12 yards. NFL: 1992—Rushed once for minus 11 yards. 1996—Rushed once for 15 yards. 1997—Attempted one pass with a completion for 22 yards and a touchdown.
SINGLE GAME HIGHS (regular season): Receptions—7 (October 17, 1994, vs. Denver); yards—167 (October 11, 1992, vs. Philadelphia); and touchdown receptions—2 (October 12, 1997, vs. Cincinnati).
STATISTICAL PLATEAUS: 100-yard receiving games: 1992 (3), 1993 (2), 1994 (2), 1995 (1). Total: 8.

				RECEIVING			TOTALS			
Year Team	G	GS	No.	Yds.	Avg.	TD	TD	2pt.	Pts.	Fum.
1990—Kansas City NFL					Did not play.					
1991—Kansas City NFL	1	0	0	0	...	0	0	...	0	0
1992—Orlando W.L.	6	3	20	242	12.1	1	1	...	6	0
—Kansas City NFL	16	14	36	756	*21.0	3	3	...	18	0
1993—Kansas City NFL	16	15	52	909	17.5	7	7	...	42	0
1994—Kansas City NFL	14	13	51	822	16.1	5	5	1	32	0
1995—Kansas City NFL	16	16	33	527	16.0	5	5	0	30	0
1996—Houston NFL	16	14	39	464	11.9	6	6	0	36	1
1997—Tennessee NFL	16	15	43	564	13.1	4	4	0	24	0
1998—Tennessee NFL	13	10	32	461	14.4	3	3	0	18	0
W.L. totals (1 year)	6	3	20	242	12.1	1	1	0	6	0
NFL totals (8 years)	108	97	286	4503	15.7	33	33	1	200	2
Pro totals (9 years)	114	100	306	4745	15.5	34	34	1	206	2

DAWKINS, BRIAN — S — EAGLES

PERSONAL: Born October 13, 1973, in Jacksonville. ... 5-11/200.
HIGH SCHOOL: Raines (Jacksonville).
COLLEGE: Clemson (degree in education, 1995).
TRANSACTIONS/CAREER NOTES: Selected by Philadelphia Eagles in second round (61st pick overall) of 1996 NFL draft. ... Signed by Eagles (July 17, 1996).
HONORS: Named defensive back on THE SPORTING NEWS college All-America second team (1995).
PRO STATISTICS: 1996—Recovered two fumbles for 23 yards. 1998—Recovered one fumble.

			INTERCEPTIONS				SACKS
Year Team	G	GS	No.	Yds.	Avg.	TD	No.
1996—Philadelphia NFL	14	13	3	41	13.7	0	1.0
1997—Philadelphia NFL	15	15	3	76	25.3	1	0.0
1998—Philadelphia NFL	14	14	2	39	19.5	0	1.0
Pro totals (3 years)	43	42	8	156	19.5	1	2.0

DAWKINS, SEAN   WR   SEAHAWKS

PERSONAL: Born February 3, 1971, in Red Bank, N.J. ... 6-4/218. ... Full name: Sean Russell Dawkins.
HIGH SCHOOL: Homestead (Cupertino, Calif.).
COLLEGE: California.
TRANSACTIONS/CAREER NOTES: Selected after junior season by Indianapolis Colts in first round (16th pick overall) of 1993 NFL draft. ... Signed by Colts (August 4, 1993). ... Granted unconditional free agency (February 13, 1998). ... Signed by New Orleans Saints (May 1, 1998). ... Granted unconditional free agency (February 12, 1999). ... Signed by Seattle Seahawks (April 15, 1999).
CHAMPIONSHIP GAME EXPERIENCE: Played in AFC championship game (1995 season).
HONORS: Named wide receiver on THE SPORTING NEWS college All-America first team (1992).
SINGLE GAME HIGHS (regular season): Receptions—8 (November 22, 1998, vs. San Francisco); yards—148 (November 22, 1998, vs. San Francisco); and touchdown receptions—1 (September 13, 1998, vs. Carolina).
STATISTICAL PLATEAUS: 100-yard receiving games: 1993 (1), 1994 (1), 1995 (2), 1997 (1), 1998 (3). Total: 8.

			RECEIVING				TOTALS			
Year Team	G	GS	No.	Yds.	Avg.	TD	TD	2pt.	Pts.	Fum.
1993—Indianapolis NFL	16	7	26	430	16.5	1	1	...	6	0
1994—Indianapolis NFL	16	16	51	742	14.5	5	5	0	30	1
1995—Indianapolis NFL	16	13	52	784	15.1	3	3	0	18	1
1996—Indianapolis NFL	15	14	54	751	13.9	1	1	0	6	1
1997—Indianapolis NFL	14	12	68	804	11.8	2	2	0	12	0
1998—New Orleans NFL	15	15	53	823	15.5	1	1	0	6	2
Pro totals (6 years)	92	77	304	4334	14.3	13	13	0	78	5

DAWSON, DERMONTTI   C   STEELERS

PERSONAL: Born June 17, 1965, in Lexington, Ky. ... 6-2/292. ... Full name: Dermontti Farra Dawson. ... Cousin of Marc Logan, running back with four NFL teams (1987-97); and cousin of George Adams, running back with New York Giants (1985-89) and New England Patriots (1990-91).
HIGH SCHOOL: Bryan Station (Lexington, Ky.).
COLLEGE: Kentucky (degree in kinesiology and health promotions, 1988).
TRANSACTIONS/CAREER NOTES: Selected by Pittsburgh Steelers in second round (44th pick overall) of 1988 NFL draft. ... Signed by Steelers (August 1, 1988). ... On injured reserve with knee injury (September 26-November 26, 1988). ... Designated by Steelers as transition player (February 25, 1993).
PLAYING EXPERIENCE: Pittsburgh NFL, 1988-1998. ... Games: 1988 (8/5), 1989 (16/16), 1990 (16/16), 1991 (16/16), 1992 (16/16), 1993 (16/16), 1994 (16/16), 1995 (16/16), 1996 (16/16), 1997 (16/16), 1998 (16/16). Total: 168/165.
CHAMPIONSHIP GAME EXPERIENCE: Played in AFC championship game (1994, 1995 and 1997 seasons). ... Played in Super Bowl XXX (1995 season).
HONORS: Played in Pro Bowl (1992-1998 seasons). ... Named center on THE SPORTING NEWS NFL All-Pro team (1994-1998).
PRO STATISTICS: 1991—Fumbled twice and recovered one fumble for two yards. 1993—Fumbled once. 1998—Fumbled once for minus 25 yards.

DAWSON, PHIL   K   BROWNS

PERSONAL: Born January 23, 1975, in West Palm Beach, Fla. ... 5-11/190.
HIGH SCHOOL: Lake Highlands (Dallas).
COLLEGE: Texas.
TRANSACTIONS/CAREER NOTES: Signed as non-drafted free agent by Oakland Raiders (April 1998). ... Claimed on waivers by New England Patriots (August 21, 1998). ... Released by Patriots (August 30, 1998). ... Re-signed by Patriots to practice squad (August 31, 1998). ... Granted free agency after 1998 season. ... Signed by Cleveland Browns (March 26, 1999).

DeBERG, STEVE   QB

PERSONAL: Born January 19, 1954, in Oakland. ... 6-3/220. ... Full name: Steven L. DeBerg.
HIGH SCHOOL: Savanna (Anaheim, Calif.).
JUNIOR COLLEGE: Fullerton (Calif.) College.
COLLEGE: San Jose State (degree in human performance, 1980).
TRANSACTIONS/CAREER NOTES: Selected by Dallas Cowboys in 10th round (275th pick overall) of 1977 NFL draft. ... Signed by Cowboys for 1977 season. ... Claimed on waivers by San Francisco 49ers (September 12, 1977). ... Active for five games (1977); did not play. ... Traded by 49ers to Denver Broncos for fourth-round pick (traded to Los Angeles Rams) in 1983 draft (August 31, 1981). ... USFL rights traded by Oakland Invaders to Denver Gold for rights to TE John Thompson and OT Randy Van Divier (October 7, 1983). ... On injured reserve with separated shoulder (November 16-December 22, 1983). ... Granted free agency (February 1, 1984). ... Re-signed by Broncos and traded to Tampa Bay Buccaneers for fourth-round pick (DB Randy Robbins) in 1984 draft and second-round pick (WR Vance Johnson) in 1985 draft (April 24, 1984). ... Granted free agency (February 1, 1988). ... Re-signed by Buccaneers and traded to Kansas City Chiefs for S Mark Robinson and fourth- (G John Bruhin) and eighth-round (RB Anthony Simpson) picks in 1988 draft (March 31, 1988). ... Granted free agency (February 1, 1991). ... Re-signed by Chiefs (August 6, 1991). ... Granted unconditional free agency (February 1, 1992). ... Signed by Buccaneers (March 31, 1992). ... Released by Buccaneers (November 2, 1993). ... Signed by Miami Dolphins (November 10, 1993). ... Granted unconditional free agency (February 17, 1994). ... Served as New York Giants quarterbacks coach (1994 and 1995 seasons). ... Out of pro football (1996 and 1997 seasons). ... Signed by Atlanta Falcons (July 6, 1998). ... Granted unconditional free agency (February 12, 1999).

CHAMPIONSHIP GAME EXPERIENCE: Member of Falcons for NFC championship game (1998 season); did not play.
RECORDS: Holds NFL record for being the oldest quarterback to start a game—44 (October 25, 1998).
PRO STATISTICS: 1978—Recovered two fumbles for minus five yards. 1979—Recovered two fumbles for minus 17 yards. 1984— Recovered two fumbles for minus eight yards. 1986— Recovered one fumble for minus five yards. 1987— Recovered two fumbles for minus two yards. 1989—Recovered three fumbles for minus 26 yards. 1990—Recovered three fumbles for minus 31 yards. 1991—Recovered four fumbles for minus 19 yards. 1998—Fumbled twice and recovered one fumble.
SINGLE GAME HIGHS (regular season): Attempts—54 (October 28, 1984, vs. Kansas City); completions—32 (September 28, 1980); yards—395 (September 17, 1990, vs. Denver); and touchdown passes—5 (September 13, 1987, vs. Atlanta).
STATISTICAL PLATEAUS: 300-yard passing games: 1983 (1), 1984 (2), 1985 (2), 1987 (2), 1988 (1), 1989 (1), 1990 (2), 1991 (1). Total: 12.

				PASSING							RUSHING				TOTALS		
Year Team	G	GS	Att.	Cmp.	Pct.	Yds.	TD	Int.	Avg.	Rat.	Att.	Yds.	Avg.	TD	TD	2pt.	Pts.
1977—San Francisco NFL									Did not play.								
1978—San Francisco NFL	12	...	302	137	45.4	1570	8	22	5.20	40.0	15	20	1.3	1	1	...	6
1979—San Francisco NFL	16	...	*578	*347	60.0	3652	17	21	6.32	73.1	17	10	0.6	0	0	...	0
1980—San Francisco NFL	11	...	321	186	57.9	1998	12	17	6.22	66.7	6	4	0.7	0	0	...	0
1981—Denver NFL	14	...	108	64	59.3	797	6	6	7.38	77.6	9	40	4.4	0	0	...	0
1982—Denver NFL	9	...	223	131	58.7	1405	7	11	6.30	67.2	8	27	3.4	1	1	...	6
1983—Denver NFL	10	...	215	119	55.3	1617	9	7	7.52	79.9	13	28	2.2	1	1	...	6
1984—Tampa Bay NFL	16	...	509	308	60.5	3554	19	18	6.98	79.3	28	59	2.1	2	2	...	12
1985—Tampa Bay NFL	11	...	370	197	53.2	2488	19	18	6.72	71.3	9	28	3.1	0	0	...	0
1986—Tampa Bay NFL	16	...	96	50	52.1	610	5	12	6.35	49.7	2	1	0.5	1	1	...	6
1987—Tampa Bay NFL	12	...	275	159	57.8	1891	14	7	6.88	85.3	8	-8	-1.0	0	0	...	0
1988—Kansas City NFL	13	...	414	224	54.1	2935	16	16	7.09	73.5	18	30	1.7	1	1	...	6
1989—Kansas City NFL	12	...	324	196	§60.5	2529	11	16	7.81	75.8	14	-8	-0.6	0	0	...	0
1990—Kansas City NFL	16	...	444	258	58.1	3444	23	4	7.76	96.3	21	-5	-0.2	0	0	...	0
1991—Kansas City NFL	16	...	434	256	59.0	2965	17	14	6.83	79.3	21	-15	-0.7	0	0	...	0
1992—Tampa Bay NFL	6	2	125	76	60.8	710	3	4	5.68	71.1	3	3	1.0	0	0	...	0
1993—Tampa Bay NFL	3	1	39	23	59.0	186	1	3	4.77	47.6	0	0	...	0	0	...	0
—Miami NFL	5	4	188	113	60.1	1521	6	7	8.09	81.0	4	-4	-1.0	0	0	...	0
1994—									Did not play.								
1995—									Did not play.								
1996—									Did not play.								
1997—									Did not play.								
1998—Atlanta NFL	8	1	59	30	50.8	369	3	1	6.25	80.4	8	-10	-1.3	0	0	0	0
Pro totals (17 years)	206	...	5024	2874	57.2	34241	196	204	6.82	74.2	204	200	1.0	7	7	0	42

DEESE, DERRICK   OT   49ERS

PERSONAL: Born May 17, 1970, in Culver City, Calif. ... 6-3/289.
HIGH SCHOOL: Culver City (Calif.).
JUNIOR COLLEGE: El Camino Junior College (Calif.).
COLLEGE: Southern California.
TRANSACTIONS/CAREER NOTES: Signed as non-drafted free agent by San Francisco 49ers (May 8, 1992). ... On injured reserve with elbow injury (August 4, 1992-entire season). ... Inactive for six games (1993). ... On injured reserve with broken wrist (October 23, 1993-remainder of season). ... Granted free agency (February 17, 1995). ... Tendered offer sheet by St. Louis Rams (April 20, 1995). ... Offer matched by 49ers (April 21, 1995). ... Granted unconditional free agency (February 16, 1996). ... Re-signed by 49ers (June 4, 1996). ... Granted unconditional free agency (February 14, 1997). ... Re-signed by 49ers (April 22, 1997).
PLAYING EXPERIENCE: San Francisco NFL, 1994-1998. ... Games/Games started: 1994 (16/15), 1995 (2/2), 1996 (16/0), 1997 (16/13), 1998 (16/16). Total: 66/46.
CHAMPIONSHIP GAME EXPERIENCE: Played in NFC championship game (1994 and 1997 seasons). ... Member of Super Bowl championship team (1994 season).
PRO STATISTICS: 1996—Returned two kickoffs for 20 yards. 1997—Recovered one fumble. 1998—Recovered one fumble.

DeGRAFFENREID, ALLEN   OL   CARDINALS

PERSONAL: Born June 3, 1974, in Kansas City, Mo. ... 6-4/293.
HIGH SCHOOL: Dunwoody (Ga.).
COLLEGE: Vanderbilt (degree in human and organizational development, 1997).
TRANSACTIONS/CAREER NOTES: Signed as non-drafted free agent by Arizona Cardinals (April 21, 1997). ... Released by Cardinals (August 19, 1997). ... Re-signed by Cardinals to practice squad (August 26, 1997).
PLAYING EXPERIENCE: Arizona NFL, 1998. ... Games/Games started: 5/0.

DEL GRECO, AL   K   TITANS

PERSONAL: Born March 2, 1962, in Providence, R.I. ... 5-10/202. ... Full name: Albert Louis Del Greco Jr.
HIGH SCHOOL: Coral Gables (Fla.).
COLLEGE: Auburn (degree in business transportation).
TRANSACTIONS/CAREER NOTES: Signed as non-drafted free agent by Miami Dolphins (May 17, 1984). ... Released by Dolphins (August 27, 1984). ... Signed by Green Bay Packers (October 17, 1984). ... Released by Packers (November 25, 1987). ... Signed by St. Louis Cardinals (December 8, 1987). ... Cardinals franchise moved to Phoenix (March 15, 1988). ... Granted unconditional free agency (February 1-April 1, 1991). ... Re-signed by Cardinals (July 1, 1991). ... Released by Cardinals (August 19, 1991). ... Signed by Houston Oilers (November 5, 1991). ... Granted unconditional free agency (February 1-April 1, 1992). ... Re-signed by Oilers for 1992 season. ... Granted unconditional free agency (February 1, 1995). ... Re-signed by Oilers (June 2, 1995). ... Oilers franchise moved to Tennessee for 1997 season. ... Oilers franchise renamed Tennessee Titans for 1999 season (December 26, 1998).
PRO STATISTICS: 1988—Rushed once for eight yards. 1990—Recovered one fumble. 1995—Punted once for 15 yards. 1997—Punted once for 32 yards.

			KICKING						
Year Team	G	XPM	XPA	FGM	FGA	Lg.	50+	Pts.
1984—Green Bay NFL	9	34	34	9	12	45	0-1	61
1985—Green Bay NFL	16	38	40	19	26	46	0-1	95
1986—Green Bay NFL	16	29	29	17	27	50	2-4	80
1987—Green Bay NFL	5	11	11	5	10	47	0-0	26
—St. Louis NFL	3	8	9	4	5	37	0-0	20
1988—Phoenix NFL	16	42	44	12	21	51	1-2	78
1989—Phoenix NFL	16	28	29	18	26	50	1-2	82
1990—Phoenix NFL	16	31	31	17	27	50	2-6	82
1991—Houston NFL	7	16	16	10	13	52	1-1	46
1992—Houston NFL	16	41	41	21	27	54	1-1	104
1993—Houston NFL	16	39	40	29	34	52	4-7	126
1994—Houston NFL	16	18	18	16	20	50	1-3	66
1995—Houston NFL	16	33	33	27	31	53	3-5	114
1996—Houston NFL	16	35	35	32	38	56	1-3	131
1997—Tennessee NFL	16	32	32	27	35	52	2-2	113
1998—Tennessee NFL	16	28	28	*36	39	48	0-0	136
Pro totals (15 years)	216	463	470	299	391	56	19-38	1360

DELLENBACH, JEFF   C/G

PERSONAL: Born February 14, 1963, in Wausau, Wis. ... 6-6/300. ... Full name: Jeffrey Alan Dellenbach. ... Name pronounced del-en-BOK.
HIGH SCHOOL: East (Wausau, Wis.).
COLLEGE: Wisconsin.
TRANSACTIONS/CAREER NOTES: Selected by Jacksonville Bulls in 1985 USFL territorial draft. ... Selected by Miami Dolphins in fourth round (111th pick overall) of 1985 NFL draft. ... Signed by Dolphins (July 15, 1985). ... Granted free agency (February 1, 1990). ... Re-signed by Dolphins (August 30, 1990). ... Granted roster exemption (August 30-September 8, 1990). ... Granted free agency (February 1, 1992). ... Re-signed by Dolphins (May 4, 1992). ... Granted unconditional free agency (February 17, 1995). ... Signed by New England Patriots (March 6, 1995). ... Released by Patriots (September 10, 1996). ... Signed by Green Bay Packers (December 3, 1996). ... Granted unconditional free agency (February 14, 1997). ... Re-signed by Packers (July 25, 1997). ... Granted unconditional free agency (February 13, 1998). ... Re-signed by Packers (July 18, 1998). ... Granted unconditional free agency (February 12, 1999).
PLAYING EXPERIENCE: Miami NFL, 1985-1994; New England NFL, 1995; New England (2)-Green Bay (3) NFL, 1996; Green Bay NFL, 1997 and 1998. ... Games/Games started: 1985 (11/1), 1986 (13/6), 1987 (11/6), 1988 (16/16), 1989 (16/16), 1990 (15/0), 1991 (15/2), 1992 (16/8), 1993 (16/16), 1994 (16/16), 1995 (15/5), 1996 (N.E.-2/0; G.B.-3/0; Total: 5/0), 1997 (13/5), 1998 (16/3). Total: 194/100.
CHAMPIONSHIP GAME EXPERIENCE: Played in AFC championship game (1985 and 1992 seasons). ... Played in NFC championship game (1996 season). ... Member of Super Bowl championship team (1996 season). ... Member of Packers for NFC championship game (1997 season); did not play. ... Member of Packers for Super Bowl XXXII (1997 season); did not play.
PRO STATISTICS: 1987—Fumbled once for minus 13 yards. 1988—Fumbled once for minus nine yards. 1991—Returned one kickoff for no yards. 1992—Recovered one fumble. 1993—Fumbled once and recovered one fumble for minus six yards. 1994—Fumbled once. 1998—Recovered two fumbles.

DeLONG, GREG   TE   RAVENS

PERSONAL: Born April 3, 1973, in Orefield, Pa. ... 6-4/250. ... Full name: Gregory A. DeLong.
HIGH SCHOOL: Parkland Senior (Orefield, Pa.).
COLLEGE: North Carolina.
TRANSACTIONS/CAREER NOTES: Signed as non-drafted free agent by Cleveland Browns (May 2, 1995). ... Released by Browns (August 21, 1995). ... Signed by Minnesota Vikings to practice squad (August 28, 1995). ... Activated (November 15, 1995). ... Granted free agency (February 13, 1998). ... Re-signed by Vikings (April 23, 1998). ... Granted unconditional free agency (February 12, 1999). ... Signed by Baltimore Ravens (February 26, 1999).
CHAMPIONSHIP GAME EXPERIENCE: Played in NFC championship game (1998 season).
PRO STATISTICS: 1996—Returned one kickoff for three yards and recovered one fumble.
SINGLE GAME HIGHS (regular season): Receptions—4 (December 18, 1995, vs. San Francisco); yards—28 (September 20, 1998, vs. Detroit); and touchdown receptions—0.

			RECEIVING				TOTALS		
Year Team	G	GS	No.	Yds.	Avg.	TD	TD	2pt.	Pts.	Fum.
1995—Minnesota NFL	2	2	6	38	6.3	0	0	0	0	0
1996—Minnesota NFL	16	8	8	34	4.3	0	0	0	0	1
1997—Minnesota NFL	16	3	8	75	9.4	0	0	0	0	0
1998—Minnesota NFL	15	5	8	58	7.3	0	0	0	0	0
Pro totals (4 years)	49	18	30	205	6.8	0	0	0	0	1

DeMARCO, BRIAN   G   BENGALS

PERSONAL: Born April 9, 1972, in Berea, Ohio. ... 6-7/323. ... Full name: Brian Thomas DeMarco.
HIGH SCHOOL: Admiral King (Lorain, Ohio).
COLLEGE: Michigan State.
TRANSACTIONS/CAREER NOTES: Selected by Jacksonville Jaguars in second round (40th pick overall) of 1995 NFL draft. ... Signed by Jaguars (June 1, 1995). ... Granted unconditional free agency (February 12, 1999). ... Signed by Cincinnati Bengals (April 2, 1999).
PLAYING EXPERIENCE: Jacksonville NFL, 1995-1998. ... Games/Games started: 1995 (16/16), 1996 (10/9), 1997 (14/5), 1998 (16/9). Total: 56/39.
CHAMPIONSHIP GAME EXPERIENCE: Played in AFC championship game (1996 season).

DENSON, DAMON — G — PATRIOTS

PERSONAL: Born February 8, 1975, in Pittsburgh. ... 6-4/305. ... Full name: Damon Michael Denson.
HIGH SCHOOL: Baldwin (Pittsburgh).
COLLEGE: Michigan.
TRANSACTIONS/CAREER NOTES: Selected by New England Patriots in fourth round (97th pick overall) of 1997 NFL draft. ... Signed by Patriots (July 16, 1997).
PLAYING EXPERIENCE: New England NFL, 1997 and 1998. ... Games/Games started: 1997 (2/0), 1998 (11/4). Total: 13/4.

DENTON, TIM — DB — REDSKINS

PERSONAL: Born February 2, 1973, in Galveston, Texas ... 5-11/182.
HIGH SCHOOL: Ball (Galveston, Texas).
JUNIOR COLLEGE: Blinn College (Texas).
COLLEGE: Oklahoma, then Sam Houston State.
TRANSACTIONS/CAREER NOTES: Signed as non-drafted free agent by Atlanta Falcons (April 22, 1996). ... Released by Falcons (August 31, 1996). ... Re-signed by Falcons (February 10, 1997). ... Released by Falcons (August 18, 1997). ... Re-signed by Falcons to practice squad (August 26, 1997). ... Granted free agency after 1997 season. ... Signed by Washington Redskins (July 15, 1998). ... Assigned by Redskins to Rhein Fire in 1998 NFL Europe enhancement allocation program (February 18, 1998).
PLAYING EXPERIENCE: Rhein Fire NFLE, 1998; Washington NFL, 1998. ... Games/Games started: NFLE 1998 (games played unavailable), NFL 1998 (16/0).
PRO STATISTICS: NFLE: 1998—Intercepted two passes for no yards.

DETMER, KOY — QB — EAGLES

PERSONAL: Born July 5, 1973, in San Antonio. ... 6-1/195. ... Brother of Ty Detmer, quarterback, Cleveland Browns.
HIGH SCHOOL: Mission (Texas).
COLLEGE: Colorado (degree in communications, 1996).
TRANSACTIONS/CAREER NOTES: Selected by Philadelphia Eagles in seventh round (207th pick overall) of 1997 NFL draft. ... Signed by Eagles (June 4, 1997). ... On injured reserve with knee injury (August 22, 1997-entire season).
PRO STATISTICS: 1998—Fumbled once.
SINGLE GAME HIGHS (regular season): Attempts—43 (December 20, 1998, vs. Dallas); completions—24 (December 20, 1998, vs. Dallas); yards—231 (December 20, 1998, vs. Dallas); and touchdown passes—2 (December 3, 1998, vs. St. Louis).
MISCELLANEOUS: Regular-season record as starting NFL quarterback: 1-4 (.200).

				PASSING							RUSHING				TOTALS	
Year Team	G	GS	Att.	Cmp.	Pct.	Yds.	TD	Int.	Avg.	Rat.	Att.	Yds.	Avg.	TD	TD	2pt.	Pts.
1997—Philadelphia NFL								Did not play.									
1998—Philadelphia NFL	8	5	181	97	53.6	1011	5	5	5.59	67.7	7	20	2.9	0	0	0	0

DETMER, TY — QB — BROWNS

PERSONAL: Born October 30, 1967, in San Marcos, Texas. ... 6-0/194. ... Full name: Ty Hubert Detmer. ... Brother of Koy Detmer, quarterback, Philadelphia Eagles.
HIGH SCHOOL: Southwest (San Antonio).
COLLEGE: Brigham Young (degree in recreation administration, 1991).
TRANSACTIONS/CAREER NOTES: Selected by Green Bay Packers in ninth round (230th pick overall) of 1992 NFL draft. ... Signed by Packers (July 22, 1992). ... Active for two games (1992); did not play. ... Active for five games (1994); did not play. ... On injured reserve with thumb injury (November 8, 1995-remainder of season). ... Granted unconditional free agency (February 16, 1996). ... Signed by Philadelphia Eagles (March 1, 1996). ... Granted unconditional free agency (February 13, 1998). ... Signed by San Francisco 49ers (March 12, 1998). ... Traded by 49ers with fourth-round pick (LB Wali Rainer) in 1999 draft to Cleveland Browns for fourth- (traded to Indianapolis) and fifth-round (traded to Miami) picks in 1999 draft (February 23, 1999).
HONORS: Heisman Trophy winner (1990). ... Maxwell Award winner (1990). ... Davey O'Brien Award winner (1990 and 1991). ... Named quarterback on THE SPORTING NEWS college All-America first team (1990 and 1991).
PRO STATISTICS: 1995—Fumbled once and recovered one fumble. 1996—Fumbled seven times and recovered one fumble. 1997—Fumbled six times and recovered one fumble for minus two yards. 1998—Fumbled once.
SINGLE GAME HIGHS (regular season): Attempts—45 (September 28, 1997, vs. Minnesota); completions—28 (September 28, 1997, vs. Minnesota); yards—342 (October 27, 1996, vs. Carolina); and touchdown passes—4 (October 20, 1996, vs. Miami).
STATISTICAL PLATEAUS: 300-yard passing games: 1996 (3).
MISCELLANEOUS: Regular-season record as starting NFL quarterback: 10-9 (.526). ... Postseason record as starting NFL quarterback: 0-1.

				PASSING							RUSHING				TOTALS		
Year Team	G	GS	Att.	Cmp.	Pct.	Yds.	TD	Int.	Avg.	Rat.	Att.	Yds.	Avg.	TD	TD	2pt.	Pts.
1992—Green Bay NFL								Did not play.									
1993—Green Bay NFL	3	0	5	3	60.0	26	0	0	5.20	73.8	1	-2	-2.0	0	0	...	0
1994—Green Bay NFL								Did not play.									
1995—Green Bay NFL	4	0	16	8	50.0	81	1	1	5.06	59.6	3	3	1.0	0	0	0	0
1996—Philadelphia NFL	13	11	401	238	59.4	2911	15	13	7.26	80.8	31	59	1.9	0	1	0	6
1997—Philadelphia NFL	8	7	244	134	54.9	1567	7	6	6.42	73.9	14	46	3.3	1	1	0	6
1998—San Francisco NFL	16	1	38	24	63.2	312	4	3	8.21	91.1	8	7	0.9	0	0	0	0
Pro totals (5 years)	44	19	704	407	57.8	4897	27	23	6.96	78.4	57	113	2.0	2	2	0	12

DEVINE, KEVIN — DB — BROWNS

PERSONAL: Born December 11, 1974, in Jackson, Miss. ... 5-9/179. ... Full name: Kevin L. Devine.
HIGH SCHOOL: West Nogales (West Covina, Calif.).
COLLEGE: California.

TRANSACTIONS/CAREER NOTES: Signed as non-drafted free agent by Jacksonville Jaguars (April 21, 1997). ... Assigned by Jaguars to Amsterdam Admirals in 1998 NFL Europe enhancement allocation program (February 18, 1998). ... Selected by Cleveland Browns from Jaguars in NFL expansion draft (February 9, 1999).
PLAYING EXPERIENCE: Jacksonville NFL, 1997 and 1998. ... Games/Games started: 1997 (12/0), 1998 (5/0). Total: 17/0.
PRO STATISTICS: 1998—Intercepted one pass for no yards.

DEVLIN, MIKE   C   CARDINALS

PERSONAL: Born November 16, 1969, in Blacksburg, Va. ... 6-2/318. ... Full name: Michael R. Devlin. ... Cousin of Joe Devlin, offensive tackle/guard with Buffalo Bills (1976-82 and 1984-89).
HIGH SCHOOL: Cherokee (Marlton, N.J.).
COLLEGE: Iowa.
TRANSACTIONS/CAREER NOTES: Selected by Buffalo Bills in fifth round (136th pick overall) of 1993 NFL draft. ... Signed by Bills (July 12, 1993). ... Granted unconditional free agency (February 16, 1996). ... Signed by Arizona Cardinals (March 8, 1996). ... Granted unconditional free agency (February 14, 1997). ... Re-signed by Cardinals (February 25, 1997). ... Granted unconditional free agency (February 12, 1999). ... Re-signed by Cardinals (April 12, 1999).
PLAYING EXPERIENCE: Buffalo NFL, 1993-1995; Arizona NFL, 1996-1998. ... Games/Games started: 1993 (12/0), 1994 (16/0), 1995 (16/0), 1996 (11/11), 1997 (15/13), 1998 (15/3). Total: 85/27.
CHAMPIONSHIP GAME EXPERIENCE: Played in AFC championship game (1993 season). ... Played in Super Bowl XXVIII (1993 season).
PRO STATISTICS: 1997—Recovered one fumble. 1998—Recovered one fumble.

DEXTER, JAMES   OT   CARDINALS

PERSONAL: Born March 3, 1973, in Fort Ord, Calif. ... 6-7/319.
HIGH SCHOOL: West Springfield (Va.).
COLLEGE: South Carolina (degree in criminal justice, 1996).
TRANSACTIONS/CAREER NOTES: Selected by Arizona Cardinals in fifth round (137th pick overall) of 1996 NFL draft. ... Signed by Cardinals (July 21, 1996). ... Granted free agency (February 12, 1999). ... Re-signed by Cardinals (May 21, 1999).
PLAYING EXPERIENCE: Arizona NFL, 1996-1998. ... Games/Games started: 1996 (6/1), 1997 (10/9), 1998 (16/16). Total: 32/26.
PRO STATISTICS: 1998—Recovered two fumbles.

DIAZ, JORGE   G   BUCCANEERS

PERSONAL: Born November 15, 1973, in New York. ... 6-4/315. ... Full name: Jorge Armando Diaz.
HIGH SCHOOL: Katy (Texas).
JUNIOR COLLEGE: Kilgore (Texas) College.
COLLEGE: Texas A&M-Kingsville.
TRANSACTIONS/CAREER NOTES: Signed as a non-drafted free agent by Tampa Bay Buccaneers (April 23, 1996).
PLAYING EXPERIENCE: Tampa Bay NFL, 1996-1998. ... Games/Games started: 1996 (11/6), 1997 (16/16), 1998 (12/12). Total: 39/34.
PRO STATISTICS: 1997—Recovered one fumble.

DIAZ-INFANTE, DAVID   G   BRONCOS

PERSONAL: Born March 31, 1964, in San Jose, Calif. ... 6-3/296. ... Full name: Gustavo David Mienez Diaz-Infante.
HIGH SCHOOL: Bellarmine Prep (San Jose, Calif.).
COLLEGE: San Jose State.
TRANSACTIONS/CAREER NOTES: Signed as non-drafted free agent by San Diego Chargers prior to 1987 season. ... Released by Chargers prior to 1987 season. ... Re-signed by Chargers as replacement player for 1987 season. ... Released by Chargers (October 1987). ... Signed by Los Angeles Rams for 1988 season. ... Released by Rams prior to 1988 season. ... Re-signed by Rams for 1989 season. ... Released by Rams prior to 1989 season. ... Selected by Franfurt Galaxy in third round (fourth offensive lineman) of 1991 WLAF positional draft. ... Signed by Galaxy (January 11, 1991). ... Signed by San Francisco 49ers (May 25, 1993). ... Released by 49ers (August 22, 1993). ... Signed by Sacramento Gold Miners of CFL (September 1993). ... Signed by Denver Broncos (March 30, 1995). ... Released by Broncos (August 27, 1995). ... Re-signed by Broncos to practice squad (August 28, 1995).
PLAYING EXPERIENCE: San Diego NFL, 1987; Frankfurt WL, 1991 and 1992; Sacramento CFL, 1993 and 1994; Denver NFL, 1996-1998. ... Games/Games started: 1987 (3/0; replacement games), 1991, 1992 and 1994 games played unavailable, 1993 (8/-), 1996 (9/2), 1997 (16/7), 1998 (10/0). Total NFL: 38/9; including 3/0 as replacement player.
CHAMPIONSHIP GAME EXPERIENCE: Played in AFC championship game (1997 and 1998 seasons). ... Member of Super Bowl championship team (1997 and 1998 seasons).

DILFER, TRENT   QB   BUCCANEERS

PERSONAL: Born March 13, 1972, in Santa Cruz, Calif. ... 6-4/237. ... Full name: Trent Farris Dilfer.
HIGH SCHOOL: Aptos (Calif.).
COLLEGE: Fresno State.
TRANSACTIONS/CAREER NOTES: Selected after junior season by Tampa Bay Buccaneers in first round (sixth pick overall) of 1994 NFL draft. ... Signed by Buccaneers (August 3, 1994).
HONORS: Played in Pro Bowl (1997 season).
PRO STATISTICS: 1994—Fumbled twice. 1995—Fumbled 13 times and recovered one fumble for minus nine yards. 1996—Fumbled 10 times and recovered four fumbles for minus four yards. 1997—Fumbled nine times and recovered three fumbles for minus 22 yards. 1998—Fumbled nine times and recovered two fumbles for minus five yards.
SINGLE GAME HIGHS (regular season): Attempts—48 (November 26, 1995, vs. Green Bay); completions—30 (November 17, 1996, vs. San Diego); yards—327 (November 17, 1996, vs. San Diego); and touchdown passes—4 (September 21, 1997, vs. Miami).
STATISTICAL PLATEAUS: 300-yard passing games: 1995 (1), 1996 (1). Total: 2.
MISCELLANEOUS: Regular-season record as starting NFL quarterback: 31-35 (.470). ... Postseason record as starting NFL quarterback: 1-1 (.500).

Year	Team	G	GS	Att.	Cmp.	Pct.	Yds.	TD	Int.	Avg.	Rat.	Att.	Yds.	Avg.	TD	TD	2pt.	Pts.
						PASSING							RUSHING				TOTALS	
1994—Tampa Bay NFL		5	2	82	38	46.3	433	1	6	5.28	36.3	2	27	13.5	0	0	0	0
1995—Tampa Bay NFL		16	16	415	224	54.0	2774	4	18	6.68	60.1	23	115	5.0	2	2	0	12
1996—Tampa Bay NFL		16	16	482	267	55.4	2859	12	19	5.93	64.8	32	124	3.9	0	0	0	0
1997—Tampa Bay NFL		16	16	386	217	56.2	2555	21	11	6.62	82.8	33	99	3.0	1	1	0	6
1998—Tampa Bay NFL		16	16	429	225	52.4	2729	21	15	6.36	74.0	40	141	3.5	2	2	0	12
Pro totals (5 years)		69	66	1794	971	54.1	11350	59	69	6.33	68.5	130	506	3.9	5	5	0	30

DILGER, KEN — TE — COLTS

PERSONAL: Born February 2, 1971, in Mariah Hill, Ind. ... 6-5/259. ... Full name: Kenneth Ray Dilger.
HIGH SCHOOL: Heritage Hills (Lincoln City, Ind.).
COLLEGE: Illinois (degree in marketing).
TRANSACTIONS/CAREER NOTES: Selected by Indianapolis Colts in second round (48th pick overall) of 1995 NFL draft. ... Signed by Colts (July 15, 1995).
CHAMPIONSHIP GAME EXPERIENCE: Played in AFC championship game (1995 season).
PRO STATISTICS: 1998—Returned one kickoff for 14 yards.
SINGLE GAME HIGHS (regular season): Receptions—7 (September 8, 1996, vs. New York Jets); yards—156 (September 8, 1996, vs. New York Jets); and touchdown receptions—3 (December 14, 1997, vs. Miami).
STATISTICAL PLATEAUS: 100-yard receiving games: 1995 (1), 1996 (1), 1997 (1). Total: 3.

Year	Team	G	GS	No.	Yds.	Avg.	TD	TD	2pt.	Pts.	Fum.
				RECEIVING				TOTALS			
1995—Indianapolis NFL		16	13	42	635	15.1	4	4	0	24	0
1996—Indianapolis NFL		16	16	42	503	12.0	4	4	0	24	1
1997—Indianapolis NFL		14	14	27	380	14.1	3	3	0	18	0
1998—Indianapolis NFL		16	16	31	303	9.8	1	1	1	8	0
Pro totals (4 years)		62	59	142	1821	12.8	12	12	1	74	1

DILLON, COREY — RB — BENGALS

PERSONAL: Born October 24, 1975, in Seattle. ... 6-1/225.
HIGH SCHOOL: Franklin (Seattle).
JUNIOR COLLEGE: Garden City (Kan.) Community College, then Dixie College (Utah).
COLLEGE: Washington.
TRANSACTIONS/CAREER NOTES: Selected after junior season by Cincinnati Bengals in second round (43rd pick overall) of 1997 NFL draft. ... Signed by Bengals (July 21, 1997).
HONORS: Named running back on THE SPORTING NEWS college All-America second team (1996).
PRO STATISTICS: 1997—Recovered one fumble for four yards.
SINGLE GAME HIGHS (regular season): Attempts—39 (December 4, 1997, vs. Tennessee); yards—246 (December 4, 1997, vs. Tennessee); and rushing touchdowns—4 (December 4, 1997, vs. Tennessee).
STATISTICAL PLATEAUS: 100-yard rushing games: 1997 (4), 1998 (4). Total: 8.
MISCELLANEOUS: Selected by San Diego Padres organization in 34th round of free agent draft (June 3, 1993); did not sign.

Year	Team	G	GS	Att.	Yds.	Avg.	TD	No.	Yds.	Avg.	TD	No.	Yds.	Avg.	TD	TD	2pt.	Pts.	Fum.
				RUSHING				RECEIVING				KICKOFF RETURNS				TOTALS			
1997—Cincinnati NFL		16	6	233	1129	4.8	10	27	259	9.6	0	6	182	30.3	0	10	0	60	1
1998—Cincinnati NFL		15	15	262	1130	4.3	4	28	178	6.4	1	0	0	...	0	5	0	30	2
Pro totals (2 years)		31	21	495	2259	4.6	14	55	437	7.9	1	6	182	30.3	0	15	0	90	3

DIMRY, CHARLES — CB — CHARGERS

PERSONAL: Born January 31, 1966, in San Diego. ... 6-0/176. ... Full name: Charles Louis Dimry III.
HIGH SCHOOL: Oceanside (Calif.).
COLLEGE: UNLV.
TRANSACTIONS/CAREER NOTES: Selected by Atlanta Falcons in fifth round (110th pick overall) of 1988 NFL draft. ... Signed by Falcons (July 16, 1988). ... Granted unconditional free agency (February 1, 1991). ... Signed by Denver Broncos (March 28, 1991). ... Granted unconditional free agency (February 17, 1994). ... Signed by Tampa Bay Buccaneers (May 23, 1994). ... Released by Buccaneers (July 20, 1997). ... Signed by Philadelphia Eagles (July 29, 1997). ... Granted unconditional free agency (February 13, 1998). ... Signed by San Diego Chargers (June 10, 1998).
CHAMPIONSHIP GAME EXPERIENCE: Played in AFC championship game (1991 season).
PRO STATISTICS: 1989—Credited with one sack. 1991—Recovered one fumble. 1992—Returned one punt for four yards. 1994—Recovered one fumble. 1995—Recovered two fumbles. 1996—Recovered one fumble. 1997—Fumbled once and recovered two fumbles for 34 yards.

Year	Team	G	GS	No.	Yds.	Avg.	TD
				INTERCEPTIONS			
1988—Atlanta NFL		16	1	0	0	...	0
1989—Atlanta NFL		16	4	2	72	36.0	0
1990—Atlanta NFL		16	12	3	16	5.3	0
1991—Denver NFL		16	1	3	35	11.7	1
1992—Denver NFL		16	6	1	2	2.0	0
1993—Denver NFL		12	11	1	0	0.0	0
1994—Tampa Bay NFL		16	16	1	0	0.0	0
1995—Tampa Bay NFL		16	16	1	0	0.0	0
1996—Tampa Bay NFL		16	7	2	1	0.5	0
1997—Philadelphia NFL		15	9	2	25	12.5	0
1998—San Diego NFL		16	15	3	38	12.7	0
Pro totals (11 years)		171	98	19	189	9.9	1

DISHMAN, CHRIS — G — CARDINALS

PERSONAL: Born February 27, 1974, in Cozad, Neb. ... 6-3/320.
HIGH SCHOOL: Cozad (Neb.).
COLLEGE: Nebraska.
TRANSACTIONS/CAREER NOTES: Selected by Arizona Cardinals in fourth round (106th pick overall) of 1997 NFL draft. ... Signed by Cardinals (July 9, 1997).
PLAYING EXPERIENCE: Arizona NFL, 1997 and 1998. ... Games/Games started: 1997 (8/0), 1998 (12/11). Total: 20/11.
PRO STATISTICS: 1998—Recovered one fumble.

DISHMAN, CRIS — CB — CHIEFS

PERSONAL: Born August 13, 1965, in Louisville, Ky. ... 6-0/195. ... Full name: Cris Edward Dishman.
HIGH SCHOOL: DeSales (Louisville, Ky.).
COLLEGE: Purdue.
TRANSACTIONS/CAREER NOTES: Selected by Houston Oilers in fifth round (125th pick overall) of 1988 NFL draft. ... Signed by Oilers (July 15, 1988). ... Granted free agency (February 1, 1991). ... Re-signed by Oilers (August 18, 1991). ... Granted free agency (February 1, 1992). ... Re-signed by Oilers (September 10, 1992). ... Designated by Oilers as transition player (February 15, 1994). ... Free agency status changed by Oilers from transitional to franchise player (February 15, 1996). ... Granted unconditional free agency (February 14, 1997). ... Signed by Washington Redskins (April 5, 1997). ... Released by Redskins (April 19, 1999). ... Signed by Kansas City Chiefs (May 13, 1999).
HONORS: Played in Pro Bowl (1991 and 1997 seasons).
PRO STATISTICS: 1988—Returned blocked punt 10 yards for a touchdown and recovered one fumble. 1989—Returned blocked punt seven yards for a touchdown and recovered one fumble. 1991—Recovered three fumbles for 19 yards and one touchdown. 1993—Recovered two fumbles for 69 yards and one touchdown. 1994—Returned one punt for no yards and recovered one fumble for 29 yards. 1995—Recovered two fumbles for 15 yards. 1996—Recovered two fumbles. 1997—Credited with 1$^1/_2$ sacks and recovered one fumble.

			INTERCEPTIONS			
Year Team	G	GS	No.	Yds.	Avg.	TD
1988—Houston NFL	15	2	0	0	...	0
1989—Houston NFL	16	0	4	31	7.8	0
1990—Houston NFL	16	14	4	50	12.5	0
1991—Houston NFL	15	15	6	61	10.2	0
1992—Houston NFL	15	15	3	34	11.3	0
1993—Houston NFL	16	16	6	74	12.3	0
1994—Houston NFL	16	16	4	74	18.5	1
1995—Houston NFL	15	15	3	17	5.7	0
1996—Houston NFL	16	16	1	7	7.0	0
1997—Washington NFL	16	15	4	47	11.8	1
1998—Washington NFL	16	16	2	60	30.0	0
Pro totals (11 years)	172	140	37	455	12.3	2

DIXON, DAVID — G — VIKINGS

PERSONAL: Born January 5, 1969, in Papakura, New Zealand. ... 6-5/352. ... Full name: David Tukatahi Dixon.
HIGH SCHOOL: Pukekohe (New Zealand).
JUNIOR COLLEGE: Ricks College (Idaho).
COLLEGE: Arizona State.
TRANSACTIONS/CAREER NOTES: Selected by New England Patriots in ninth round (232nd pick overall) of 1992 NFL draft. ... Signed by Patriots for 1992 season. ... Released by Patriots (August 1992). ... Signed by Minnesota Vikings to practice squad (October 20, 1992). ... Released by Vikings (August 23, 1993). ... Signed by Dallas Cowboys to practice squad (September 8, 1993). ... Granted free agency after 1993 season. ... Signed by Vikings (July 12, 1994). ... Granted free agency (February 14, 1997). ... Re-signed by Vikings (May 1, 1997). ... Granted unconditional free agency (February 13, 1998). ... Re-signed by Vikings (February 17, 1998).
PLAYING EXPERIENCE: Minnesota NFL, 1994-1998. ... Games/Games started: 1994 (1/0), 1995 (15/6), 1996 (13/6), 1997 (13/13), 1998 (16/16). Total: 58/41.
CHAMPIONSHIP GAME EXPERIENCE: Played in NFC championship game (1998 season).
PRO STATISTICS: 1998—Recovered one fumble.

DIXON, ERNEST — LB — CHIEFS

PERSONAL: Born October 17, 1971, in Fort Mill, S.C. ... 6-1/240. ... Full name: Ernest James Dixon.
HIGH SCHOOL: Fort Mill (S.C.).
COLLEGE: South Carolina (degree in psychology).
TRANSACTIONS/CAREER NOTES: Signed as non-drafted free agent by New Orleans Saints (April 28, 1994). ... Granted unconditional free agency (February 14, 1997). ... Re-signed by Saints (June 2, 1997). ... Granted unconditional free agency (February 13, 1998). ... Signed by Carolina Panthers (February 19, 1998). ... Released by Panthers (August 30, 1998). ... Signed by Oakland Raiders (October 19, 1998). ... Released by Raiders (November 13, 1998). ... Signed by Kansas City Chiefs (November 18, 1998).
PLAYING EXPERIENCE: New Orleans NFL, 1994-1997; Oakland (2)-Kansas City (1) NFL, 1998. ... Games/Games started: 1994 (15/1), 1995 (16/5), 1996 (16/0), 1997 (15/0), 1998 (Oak.-3/0; K.C.-1/0; Total: 4/0). Total: 66/6.
PRO STATISTICS: 1995—Intercepted two passes for 17 yards, credited with four sacks and fumbled once. 1996—Recovered one fumble for 22 yards. 1997—Credited with $^1/_2$ sack.

DIXON, GERALD — LB — CHARGERS

PERSONAL: Born June 20, 1969, in Charlotte. ... 6-3/250. ... Full name: Gerald Scott Dixon.
HIGH SCHOOL: Rock Hill (S.C.).
JUNIOR COLLEGE: Garden City (Kan.) Community College.
COLLEGE: South Carolina.

TRANSACTIONS/CAREER NOTES: Selected by Cleveland Browns in third round (78th pick overall) of 1992 NFL draft. ... Signed by Browns (July 15, 1992). ... On injured reserve with ankle injury (September 2, 1992-entire season). ... Granted free agency (February 17, 1995). ... Re-signed by Browns for 1995 season. ... Granted unconditional free agency (February 16, 1996). ... Signed by Cincinnati Bengals (March 14, 1996). ... Granted unconditional free agency (February 13, 1998). ... Signed by San Diego Chargers (March 24, 1998).
PRO STATISTICS: 1995—Intercepted two passes for 48 yards and one touchdown, returned one kickoff for 10 yards and recovered one fumble.

Year Team	G	GS	SACKS
1992—Cleveland NFL	Did not play.		
1993—Cleveland NFL	11	0	0.0
1994—Cleveland NFL	16	0	1.0
1995—Cleveland NFL	16	9	0.0
1996—Cincinnati NFL	16	1	0.0
1997—Cincinnati NFL	15	12	8.5
1998—San Diego NFL	16	6	2.5
Pro totals (6 years)	90	28	12.0

DIXON, MARK   G   DOLPHINS

PERSONAL: Born November 6, 1970, in Charlottesville, N.C. ... 6-4/300. ... Full name: Mark Keller Dixon.
HIGH SCHOOL: Ragsdale (Jamestown, N.C.).
COLLEGE: Virginia.
TRANSACTIONS/CAREER NOTES: Signed as non-drafted free agent by Philadelphia Eagles (April 1994). ... Released by Eagles (August 1994). ... Signed by Atlanta Falcons (July 18, 1995). ... Released by Falcons (August 21, 1995). ... Played with Frankfurt Galaxy of World League (1995). ... Signed by Baltimore Stallions of CFL (August 30, 1995). ... Signed by Miami Dolphins (January 22, 1998). ... On injured reserve with neck injury (November 24, 1998-remainder of season).
PLAYING EXPERIENCE: Frankfurt Galaxy W.L., 1995; Baltimore Stallions CFL, 1995, Montreal Alouettes CFL, 1996 and 1997. Miami NFL, 1998. ... Games/Games started: W.L. 1995 (games played unavailable), CFL 1995 (8/5), 1996 (18/18), 1997 (7/7). 1998 (11/10). Total CFL: 33/30. Total NFL: 11/10. Total Pro: 44/40.
CHAMPIONSHIP GAME EXPERIENCE: Member of CFL championship team (1995).
PRO STATISTICS: 1998—Recovered two fumbles.

DIXON, RONNIE   DT   CHIEFS

PERSONAL: Born May 10, 1971, in Clinton, N.C. ... 6-3/310. ... Full name: Ronnie Christopher Dixon.
HIGH SCHOOL: Clinton (N.C.).
COLLEGE: Cincinnati.
TRANSACTIONS/CAREER NOTES: Selected by New Orleans Saints in sixth round (165th pick overall) of 1993 NFL draft. ... Signed by Saints (July 2, 1993). ... Released by Saints (August 30, 1993). ... Re-signed by Saints (August 31, 1993). ... Released by Saints (August 22, 1994). ... Selected by Frankfurt Galaxy in 17th round (98th pick overall) of 1995 World League Draft. ... Signed by Cleveland Browns for 1995 season. ... Traded by Browns to Philadelphia Eagles for seventh-round pick (QB Jon Stark) in 1996 draft (August 21, 1995). ... Released by Eagles to New York Jets for seventh-round pick (QB Koy Detmer) in 1997 draft (April 18, 1997). ... Released by Jets (October 24, 1997). ... Re-signed by Jets (October 29, 1997). ... Released by Jets (November 22, 1997). ... Re-signed by Jets (November 27, 1997). ... Released by Jets (December 8, 1997). ... Re-signed by Jets (December 15, 1997). ... Released by Jets (August 25, 1998). ... Signed by Kansas City Chiefs (October 19, 1998).
PLAYING EXPERIENCE: New Orleans NFL, 1993; Philadelphia NFL, 1995 and 1996; New York Jets NFL, 1997; Kansas City NFL, 1998. ... Games/Games started: 1993 (2/0), 1995 (16/10), 1996 (16/4), 1997 (6/3), 1998 (4/0). Total: 44/17.

DODGE, DEDRICK   S

PERSONAL: Born June 14, 1967, in Neptune, N.J. ... 6-2/187. ... Full name: Dedrick Allen Dodge. ... Name pronounced DEAD-rik.
HIGH SCHOOL: East Brunswick (N.J.) and Mulberry (Fla.).
COLLEGE: Florida State (degree in criminology).
TRANSACTIONS/CAREER NOTES: Signed as non-drafted free agent by Seattle Seahawks (May 1, 1990). ... Released by Seahawks (August 29, 1990). ... Signed by WLAF (January 31, 1991). ... Selected by London Monarchs in fourth round (40th defensive back) of 1991 WLAF positional draft. ... Signed by Seahawks (August 13, 1991). ... Released by Seahawks (August 26, 1991). ... Re-signed by Seahawks to practice squad (August 28, 1991). ... Activated (October 5, 1991). ... Assigned by Seahawks to Monarchs in 1992 World League enhancement allocation program (February 20, 1992). ... On injured reserve with knee injury (December 19, 1992-remainder of season). ... Granted free agency (March 1, 1993). ... Re-signed by Seahawks (July 2, 1993). ... Released by Seahawks (August 30, 1993). ... Signed by San Francisco 49ers (June 1, 1994). ... Granted unconditional free agency (February 17, 1995). ... Re-signed by 49ers (April 13, 1995). ... Released by 49ers (February 3, 1997). ... Signed by Denver Broncos (February 25, 1997). ... Released by Broncos (June 15, 1998). ... Signed by Carolina Panthers (July 27, 1998). ... Released by Panthers (August 30, 1998). ... Signed by San Diego Chargers (November 2, 1998). ... Granted unconditional free agency (February 12, 1999).
CHAMPIONSHIP GAME EXPERIENCE: Played in NFC championship game (1994 season). ... Member of Super Bowl championship team (1994 and 1997 seasons). ... Played in AFC championship game (1997 season).
HONORS: Named strong safety on All-World League team (1992).
PRO STATISTICS: W.L.: 1991—Recovered one fumble. NFL: 1992—Credited with a sack. 1997—Recovered one fumble.

				INTERCEPTIONS		
Year Team	G	GS	No.	Yds.	Avg.	TD
1991—London W.L.	10	...	6	202	33.7	*2
—Seattle NFL	11	0	0	0	...	0
1992—London W.L.	10	10	3	35	11.7	0
—Seattle NFL	14	0	1	13	13.0	0
1993—				Did not play.		
1994—San Francisco NFL	15	0	0	0	...	0
1995—San Francisco NFL	16	0	1	13	13.0	0
1996—San Francisco NFL	16	3	3	27	9.0	0
1997—Denver NFL	16	1	0	0	...	0
1998—San Diego NFL	8	0	0	0	...	0
W.L. totals (2 years)	20	...	9	237	26.3	2
NFL totals (7 years)	96	4	5	53	10.6	0
Pro totals (9 years)	116	...	14	290	20.7	2

DOGINS, KEVIN — C/G — BUCCANEERS

PERSONAL: Born December 7, 1972, in Eagle Lake, Texas. ... 6-1/298. ... Full name: Kevin Ray Dogins.
HIGH SCHOOL: Rice (Eagle Lake, Texas).
COLLEGE: Texas A&M-Kingsville.
TRANSACTIONS/CAREER NOTES: Signed as non-drafted free agent by Dallas Cowboys (April 25, 1996). ... Released by Cowboys (August 19, 1996). ... Signed by Tampa Bay Buccaneers to practice squad (August 27, 1996). ... Activated (December 17, 1996). ... Inactive for all 16 games (1997).
PLAYING EXPERIENCE: Tampa Bay NFL, 1996 and 1998. ... Games/Games started: 1996 (1/0), 1998 (6/4). Total: 7/4.

DOLEMAN, CHRIS — DE

PERSONAL: Born October 16, 1961, in Indianapolis. ... 6-5/289. ... Full name: Christopher John Doleman.
HIGH SCHOOL: William Penn (York, Pa.).
COLLEGE: Pittsburgh.
TRANSACTIONS/CAREER NOTES: Selected by Baltimore Stars in 1985 USFL territorial draft. ... Selected by Minnesota Vikings in first round (fourth pick overall) of 1985 NFL draft. ... Signed by Vikings (August 8, 1985). ... Granted free agency (February 1, 1991). ... Re-signed by Vikings (July 25, 1991). ... Traded by Vikings with second-round pick (WR Bert Emanuel) in 1994 draft to Atlanta Falcons for second-round pick (RB/WR/KR David Palmer) in 1994 draft and first-round pick (DE Derrick Alexander) in 1995 draft (April 24, 1994). ... Granted unconditional free agency (February 16, 1996). ... Signed by San Francisco 49ers (March 14, 1996). ... Announced retirement (January 9, 1999).
CHAMPIONSHIP GAME EXPERIENCE: Played in NFC championship game (1987 and 1997 seasons).
HONORS: Played in Pro Bowl (1987-1990, 1992, 1993, 1995 and 1997 seasons). ... Named defensive end on THE SPORTING NEWS NFL All-Pro team (1989 and 1992).
PRO STATISTICS: 1985—Recovered three fumbles. 1989—Recovered five fumbles for seven yards. 1990—Credited with one safety. 1991—Recovered two fumbles for seven yards. 1992—Credited with one safety and recovered three fumbles. 1993—Recovered one fumble. 1995—Recovered two fumbles. 1996—Recovered three fumbles for 13 yards and one touchdown. 1997—Recovered one fumble. 1998—Recovered two fumbles.

			INTERCEPTIONS				SACKS
Year Team	G	GS	No.	Yds.	Avg.	TD	No.
1985—Minnesota NFL	16	13	1	5	5.0	0	0.5
1986—Minnesota NFL	16	9	1	59	59.0	1	3.0
1987—Minnesota NFL	12	12	0	0	...	0	11.0
1988—Minnesota NFL	16	16	0	0	...	0	8.0
1989—Minnesota NFL	16	16	0	0	...	0	*21.0
1990—Minnesota NFL	16	16	1	30	30.0	0	11.0
1991—Minnesota NFL	16	16	0	0	...	0	7.0
1992—Minnesota NFL	16	16	1	27	27.0	1	14.5
1993—Minnesota NFL	16	16	1	-3	-3.0	0	12.5
1994—Atlanta NFL	14	7	1	2	2.0	0	7.0
1995—Atlanta NFL	16	16	0	0	...	0	9.0
1996—San Francisco NFL	16	16	2	1	0.5	0	11.0
1997—San Francisco NFL	16	16	0	0	...	0	12.0
1998—San Francisco NFL	16	16	0	0	...	0	15.0
Pro totals (14 years)	218	201	8	121	15.1	2	142.5

DONNALLEY, KEVIN — G — DOLPHINS

PERSONAL: Born June 10, 1968, in St. Louis. ... 6-5/305. ... Full name: Kevin Thomas Donnalley. ... Brother of Rick Donnalley, center with Pittsburgh Steelers (1982 and 1983), Washington Redskins (1984 and 1985) and Kansas City Chiefs (1986 and 1987).
HIGH SCHOOL: Athens Drive Senior (Raleigh, N.C.).
COLLEGE: Davidson, then North Carolina (degree in economics).
TRANSACTIONS/CAREER NOTES: Selected by Houston Oilers in third round (79th pick overall) of 1991 NFL draft. ... Signed by Oilers (July 10, 1991). ... Granted free agency (February 17, 1994). ... Tendered offer sheet by Los Angeles Rams (March 17, 1994). ... Offer matched by Oilers (March 23, 1994). ... Oilers franchise moved to Tennessee for 1997 season. ... Granted unconditional free agency (February 13, 1998). ... Signed by Miami Dolphins (February 17, 1998).
PLAYING EXPERIENCE: Houston NFL, 1991-1996; Tennessee NFL, 1997; Miami NFL, 1998. ... Games/Games started: 1991 (16/0), 1992 (16/2), 1993 (16/6), 1994 (13/11), 1995 (16/16), 1996 (16/16), 1997 (16/16), 1998 (14/14). Total: 123/81.
PRO STATISTICS: 1995—Recovered one fumble. 1998—Recovered one fumble.

DORSETT, ANTHONY — CB — TITANS

PERSONAL: Born September 14, 1973, in Aliquippa, Pa. ... 5-11/200. ... Full name: Anthony Drew Dorsett Jr. ... Son of Tony Dorsett, Hall of Fame running back with Dallas Cowboys (1977-87) and Denver Broncos (1988).
HIGH SCHOOL: Richland (Dallas), then J.J. Pearce (Dallas).
COLLEGE: Pittsburgh.
TRANSACTIONS/CAREER NOTES: Selected by Houston Oilers in sixth round (177th pick overall) of 1996 NFL draft. ... Signed by Oilers (June 21, 1996). ... Assigned by Oilers to Barcelona Dragons in 1997 World League enhancement allocation program (February 19, 1997). ... Oilers franchise moved to Tennessee for 1997 season. ... Oilers franchise renamed Tennessee Titans for 1999 season (December 26, 1998). ... Granted free agency (February 12, 1999).
PLAYING EXPERIENCE: Houston NFL, 1996; Tennessee NFL, 1997 and 1998. ... Games/Games started: 1996 (8/0), 1997 (16/0), 1998 (16/0). Total: 40/0.

DOTSON, EARL — OT — PACKERS

PERSONAL: Born December 17, 1970, in Beaumont, Texas. ... 6-4/315. ... Full name: Earl Christopher Dotson.
HIGH SCHOOL: Westbrook (Beaumont, Texas).
JUNIOR COLLEGE: Tyler (Texas) Junior College.
COLLEGE: Texas A&I.
TRANSACTIONS/CAREER NOTES: Selected by Green Bay Packers in third round (81st pick overall) of 1993 NFL draft. ... Signed by Packers (June 14, 1993).
PLAYING EXPERIENCE: Green Bay NFL, 1993-1998. ... Games/Games started: 1993 (13/0), 1994 (4/0), 1995 (16/16), 1996 (15/15), 1997 (13/13), 1998 (16/16). Total: 77/60.
CHAMPIONSHIP GAME EXPERIENCE: Played in NFC championship game (1995-97 seasons). ... Member of Super Bowl championship team (1996 season). ... Played in Super Bowl XXXII (1997 season).
PRO STATISTICS: 1996—Recovered one fumble. 1997—Recovered one fumble.

DOTSON, SANTANA — DT — PACKERS

PERSONAL: Born December 19, 1969, in New Orleans. ... 6-5/286. ... Full name: Santana N. Dotson. ... Son of Alphonse Dotson, defensive tackle with Kansas City Chiefs (1965), Miami Dolphins (1966) and Oakland Raiders (1968-70).
HIGH SCHOOL: Jack Yates (Houston).
COLLEGE: Baylor.
TRANSACTIONS/CAREER NOTES: Selected by Tampa Bay Buccaneers in fifth round (132nd pick overall) of 1992 NFL draft. ... Signed by Buccaneers (July 7, 1992). ... Granted free agency (February 17, 1995). ... Re-signed by Buccaneers (June 14, 1995). ... Granted unconditional free agency (February 16, 1996). ... Signed by Green Bay Packers (March 7, 1996). ... Granted unconditional free agency (February 12, 1999). ... Re-signed by Packers (February 19, 1999).
CHAMPIONSHIP GAME EXPERIENCE: Played in NFC championship game (1996 and 1997 seasons). ... Member of Super Bowl championship team (1996 season). ... Played in Super Bowl XXXII (1997 season).
HONORS: Named defensive lineman on THE SPORTING NEWS college All-America first team (1991). ... Named NFL Rookie of the Year by THE SPORTING NEWS (1992).
PRO STATISTICS: 1992—Recovered two fumbles for 42 yards and one touchdown. 1995—Recovered two fumbles. 1996—Recovered one fumble for eight yards. 1998—Recovered one fumble.

Year Team	G	GS	SACKS
1992—Tampa Bay NFL	16	16	10.0
1993—Tampa Bay NFL	16	13	5.0
1994—Tampa Bay NFL	16	9	3.0
1995—Tampa Bay NFL	16	8	5.0
1996—Green Bay NFL	16	15	5.5
1997—Green Bay NFL	16	16	5.5
1998—Green Bay NFL	16	16	3.0
Pro totals (7 years)	112	93	37.0

DOUGLAS, HUGH — LB/DE — EAGLES

PERSONAL: Born August 23, 1971, in Mansfield, Ohio. ... 6-2/280.
HIGH SCHOOL: Mansfield (Ohio).
COLLEGE: Central State (Ohio).
TRANSACTIONS/CAREER NOTES: Selected after junior season by New York Jets in first round (16th pick overall) of 1995 NFL draft. ... Signed by Jets (June 8, 1995). ... Traded by Jets to Philadelphia Eagles for second- (traded to Pittsburgh) and fifth-round (LB Casey Dailey) picks in 1998 draft (March 13, 1998).
PRO STATISTICS: 1995—Recovered two fumbles. 1996—Recovered three fumbles for 64 yards and a touchdown.

Year Team	G	GS	SACKS
1995—New York Jets NFL	15	3	10.0
1996—New York Jets NFL	10	10	8.0
1997—New York Jets NFL	15	15	4.0
1998—Philadelphia NFL	15	13	12.5
Pro totals (4 years)	55	41	34.5

DOWNS, GARY — RB — FALCONS

PERSONAL: Born June 6, 1972, in Columbus, Ga. ... 6-1/218. ... Full name: Gary McLinton Downs.
HIGH SCHOOL: William H. Spencer (Columbus, Ga.).
COLLEGE: North Carolina State.
TRANSACTIONS/CAREER NOTES: Selected by New York Giants in third round (95th pick overall) of 1994 NFL draft. ... Signed by Giants (July 19, 1994). ... Released by Giants (August 27, 1995). ... Signed by Denver Broncos (August 28, 1995). ... Released by Broncos (August 28, 1996). ... Signed by Giants (October 31, 1996). ... Signed by Atlanta Falcons (February 14, 1997). ... Signed by Atlanta Falcons (March 17, 1997). ... Granted unconditional free agency (February 13, 1998). ... Re-signed by Falcons (March 13, 1998).
CHAMPIONSHIP GAME EXPERIENCE: Played in NFC championship game (1998 season). ... Played in Super Bowl XXXIII (1998 season).
PRO STATISTICS: 1996—Recovered one fumble.
SINGLE GAME HIGHS (regular season): Attempts—22 (December 21, 1996, vs. New England); yards—52 (December 21, 1996, vs. New England); and rushing touchdowns—0.

			RUSHING				RECEIVING			TOTALS			
Year Team	G	GS	Att.	Yds.	Avg.	TD	No.	Yds.	Avg.	TD	TD	2pt.	Pts.	Fum.
1994—New York Giants NFL	14	0	15	51	3.4	0	2	15	7.5	0	0	0	0	1
1995—Denver NFL	1	0	0	0	...	0	0	0	...	0	0	0	0	0
1996—New York Giants NFL	6	1	29	94	3.2	0	3	20	6.7	0	0	0	0	1
1997—Atlanta NFL	16	0	0	0	...	0	0	0	...	0	0	0	0	0
1998—Atlanta NFL	16	1	1	4	4.0	0	4	31	7.8	0	0	0	0	0
Pro totals (5 years)	53	2	45	149	3.3	0	9	66	7.3	0	0	0	0	2

DOXZON, TODD — WR — DOLPHINS

PERSONAL: Born March 28, 1975, in Sioux City, Iowa. ... 6-0/186.
HIGH SCHOOL: Millard Smith (Omaha, Neb.).
COLLEGE: Iowa State.
TRANSACTIONS/CAREER NOTES: Signed as non-drafted free agent by New York Jets (April 25, 1997). ... Released by Jets (August 18, 1997). ... Played with Amsterdam Admirals of NFL Europe (1997). ... Signed by New England Patriots (February 13, 1998). ... Assigned by Patriots to Amsterdam Admirals in 1998 NFL Europe enhancement allocation program (February 18, 1998). ... Released by Patriots (August 19, 1998). ... Signed by Miami Dolphins to practice squad (October 7, 1998). ... Activated (October 14, 1998). ... Assigned by Dolphins to Amsterdam Admirals in 1999 NFL Europe enhancement allocation program (February 22, 1999).
PLAYING EXPERIENCE: Amsterdam Admirals W.L., 1997; Amsterdam Admirals NFLE, 1998; Miami NFL, 1998. ... Games/Games started: W.L. 1997 (games played unavailable), NFLE 1998 (games played unavailable), NFL 1998 (9/0).
PRO STATISTICS: NFLE: 1998—Caught eight passes for 135 yards and two touchdowns. NFL: 1998—Rushed twice for six yards.

DRAFT, CHRIS — LB — BEARS

PERSONAL: Born February 26, 1976, in Anaheim. ... 5-11/222.
HIGH SCHOOL: Valencia (Calif.).
COLLEGE: Stanford.
TRANSACTIONS/CAREER NOTES: Selected by Chicago Bears in sixth round (157th pick overall) of 1998 NFL draft. ... Signed by Bears (June 16, 1998). ... Released by Bears (August 30, 1998). ... Re-signed by Bears to practice squad (August 31, 1998). ... Activated (December 2, 1998).
PLAYING EXPERIENCE: Chicago NFL, 1998. ... Games/Games started: 1/0.

DRAKE, JERRY — DE — CARDINALS

PERSONAL: Born July 9, 1969, in Kingston, N.Y. ... 6-5/310.
HIGH SCHOOL: Kingston (N.Y.).
JUNIOR COLLEGE: Ulster Community College (N.Y.).
COLLEGE: Hastings (Neb.) College.
TRANSACTIONS/CAREER NOTES: Signed as non-drafted free agent by Arizona Cardinals (May 2, 1995). ... Released by Cardinals (August 21, 1995). ... Re-signed by Cardinals to practice squad (August 30, 1995). ... Activated (November 24, 1995). ... Assigned by Cardinals to London Monarchs in 1996 World League enhancement allocation program (February 19, 1996). ... On injured reserve with neck injury (August 19, 1997-entire season). ... On injured reserve with back injury (October 2, 1998-remainder of season).
PLAYING EXPERIENCE: Arizona NFL, 1995, 1996 and 1998.; London W.L., 1996. ... Games/Games started: 1995 (2/0), W.L. 1996 (10/10), NFL 1996 (11/0), 1998 (1/1). Total: W.L.: 10/10. Total NFL: 14/1. Total Pro: 24/11.
PRO STATISTICS: W.L.: 1996—Credited with eight sacks.

DRAKE, TROY — OT

PERSONAL: Born May 15, 1972, in Rockford, Ill. ... 6-6/305.
HIGH SCHOOL: Byron (Ill.).
COLLEGE: Indiana (degree in business marketing).
TRANSACTIONS/CAREER NOTES: Signed as non-drafted free agent by Philadelphia Eagles (April 26, 1995). ... Released by Eagles (October 23, 1995). ... Re-signed by Eagles to practice squad (October 25, 1995). ... Activated (November 12, 1995). ... Released by Eagles (November 14, 1995). ... Re-signed by Eagles to practice squad (November 15, 1995). ... Granted free agency (February 13, 1998). ... Signed by Washington Redskins (April 6, 1998). ... On injured reserve with knee injury (November 24, 1998-remainder of season). ... Granted unconditional free agency (February 12, 1999).
PLAYING EXPERIENCE: Philadelphia NFL, 1995-1997; Washington NFL, 1998. ... Games/Games started: 1995 (1/0), 1996 (11/0), 1997 (9/2), 1998 (11/2). Total: 32/4.

DRAKEFORD, TYRONNE — CB — SAINTS

PERSONAL: Born June 21, 1971, in Camden, S.C. ... 5-11/185. ... Full name: Tyronne James Drakeford.
HIGH SCHOOL: North Central (Camden, S.C.).
COLLEGE: Virginia Tech (degree in finance).
TRANSACTIONS/CAREER NOTES: Selected by San Francisco 49ers in second round (62nd pick overall) of 1994 NFL draft. ... Signed by 49ers (July 20, 1994). ... Granted free agency (February 14, 1997). ... Re-signed by 49ers (April 8, 1997). ... Granted unconditional free agency (February 13, 1998). ... Signed by New Orleans Saints (February 19, 1998).
CHAMPIONSHIP GAME EXPERIENCE: Played in NFC championship game (1994 and 1997 seasons). ... Member of Super Bowl championship team (1994 season).
PRO STATISTICS: 1995—Fumbled once and recovered one fumble for 12 yards. 1996—Recovered one fumble for eight yards. 1997—Returned one kickoff for 24 yards.

			INTERCEPTIONS				SACKS
Year Team	G	GS	No.	Yds.	Avg.	TD	No.
1994—San Francisco NFL	13	0	1	6	6.0	0	0.0
1995—San Francisco NFL	16	2	5	54	10.8	0	1.0
1996—San Francisco NFL	16	16	1	11	11.0	0	2.0
1997—San Francisco NFL	16	2	5	15	3.0	0	0.0
1998—New Orleans NFL	16	15	4	76	19.0	1	0.0
Pro totals (5 years)	77	35	16	162	10.1	1	3.0

DRAYTON, TROY — TE — DOLPHINS

PERSONAL: Born June 29, 1970, in Harrisburg, Pa. ... 6-3/270. ... Full name: Troy Anthony Drayton. ... Cousin of Kevin Mitchell, linebacker, New Orleans Saints.
HIGH SCHOOL: Highspire (Steelton, Pa.).
COLLEGE: Penn State.
TRANSACTIONS/CAREER NOTES: Selected by Los Angeles Rams in second round (39th pick overall) of 1993 NFL draft. ... Signed by Rams (July 20, 1993). ... Rams franchise moved to St. Louis (April 12, 1995). ... Granted free agency (February 16, 1996). ... Re-signed by Rams (April 17, 1996). ... Traded by Rams to Miami Dolphins for OT Bill Milner (October 1, 1996).
PRO STATISTICS: 1993—Rushed once for seven yards and returned one kickoff for minus 15 yards. 1994—Rushed once for four yards. 1996—Recovered one fumble.
SINGLE GAME HIGHS (regular season): Receptions—8 (November 19, 1995, vs. Atlanta); yards—106 (September 24, 1995, vs. Chicago); and touchdown receptions—2 (October 12, 1998, vs. Jacksonville).
STATISTICAL PLATEAUS: 100-yard receiving games: 1995 (1).

			RECEIVING					TOTALS		
Year Team	G	GS	No.	Yds.	Avg.	TD	TD	2pt.	Pts.	Fum.
1993—Los Angeles Rams NFL	16	2	27	319	11.8	4	4	...	24	1
1994—Los Angeles Rams NFL	16	16	32	276	8.6	6	6	0	36	0
1995—St. Louis NFL	16	16	47	458	9.7	4	4	0	24	2
1996—St. Louis NFL	3	3	2	11	5.5	0	0	0	0	0
—Miami NFL	10	10	26	320	12.3	0	0	1	2	0
1997—Miami NFL	16	15	39	558	14.3	4	4	0	24	0
1998—Miami NFL	15	15	30	334	11.1	3	3	0	18	0
Pro totals (6 years)	92	77	203	2276	11.2	21	21	1	128	3

DRONETT, SHANE — DE — FALCONS

PERSONAL: Born January 12, 1971, in Orange, Texas. ... 6-6/298.
HIGH SCHOOL: Bridge City (Texas).
COLLEGE: Texas.
TRANSACTIONS/CAREER NOTES: Selected after junior season by Denver Broncos in second round (54th pick overall) of 1992 NFL draft. ... Signed by Broncos (July 15, 1992). ... Granted free agency (February 17, 1995). ... Re-signed by Broncos (May 12, 1995). ... Granted unconditional free agency (February 16, 1996). ... Signed by Atlanta Falcons (April 9, 1996). ... Released by Falcons (October 7, 1996). ... Signed by Detroit Lions (October 9, 1996). ... Granted unconditional free agency (February 14, 1997). ... Re-signed by Lions for 1997 season. ... Released by Lions (August 24, 1997). ... Signed by Falcons (August 27, 1997). ... Granted unconditional free agency (February 13, 1998). ... Re-signed by Falcons (February 20, 1998).
CHAMPIONSHIP GAME EXPERIENCE: Played in NFC championship game (1998 season). ... Played in Super Bowl XXXIII (1998 season).
PRO STATISTICS: 1992—Recovered two fumbles for minus five yards. 1993—Intercepted two passes for 13 yards. 1998—Recovered one fumble.

Year Team	G	GS	SACKS
1992—Denver NFL	16	2	6.5
1993—Denver NFL	16	16	7.0
1994—Denver NFL	16	15	6.0
1995—Denver NFL	13	2	2.0
1996—Atlanta NFL	5	0	0.0
—Detroit NFL	7	0	0.0
1997—Atlanta NFL	16	1	3.0
1998—Atlanta NFL	16	16	6.5
Pro totals (7 years)	105	52	31.0

DRUCKENMILLER, JIM — QB — 49ERS

PERSONAL: Born September 19, 1972, in Northhampton, Pa. ... 6-4/241. ... Full name: James David Druckenmiller Jr. ... Name pronounced DRUCK-en-miller.
HIGH SCHOOL: Northhampton (Pa.), then Fork Union (Va.) Military Academy.
COLLEGE: Virginia Tech.
TRANSACTIONS/CAREER NOTES: Selected by San Francisco 49ers in first round (26th pick overall) of 1997 NFL draft. ... Signed by 49ers (July 31, 1997).
CHAMPIONSHIP GAME EXPERIENCE: Member of 49ers for NFC championship game (1997 season); inactive.
SINGLE GAME HIGHS (regular season): Attempts—28 (September 7, 1997, vs. St. Louis); completions—10 (September 7, 1997, vs. St. Louis); yards—102 (September 7, 1997, vs. St. Louis); and touchdown passes—1 (September 7, 1997, vs. St. Louis).
MISCELLANEOUS: Regular-season record as starting NFL quarterback: 1-0.

			PASSING						RUSHING				TOTALS		
Year Team	G	GS	Att.	Cmp.	Pct.	Yds.	TD	Int.	Avg.	Rat.	Att.	Yds.	Avg.	TD	TD	2pt.	Pts.
1997—San Francisco NFL	4	1	52	21	40.4	239	1	4	4.60	29.2	10	-6	-0.6	0	0	0	0
1998—San Francisco NFL	2	0	0	0	...	0	0	0	...	...	3	-4	-1.3	0	0	0	0
Pro totals (2 years)	6	1	52	21	40.4	239	1	4	4.60	29.2	13	-10	-0.8	0	0	0	0

DUDLEY, RICKEY — TE — RAIDERS

PERSONAL: Born July 15, 1972, in Henderson, Texas. ... 6-6/250.
HIGH SCHOOL: Henderson (Texas).
COLLEGE: Ohio State.
TRANSACTIONS/CAREER NOTES: Selected by Oakland Raiders in first round (ninth pick overall) of 1996 NFL draft. ... Signed by Raiders (July 12, 1996).

– 110 –

PRO STATISTICS: 1998—Rushed once for minus two yards.
SINGLE GAME HIGHS (regular season): Receptions—6 (November 8, 1998, vs. Baltimore); yards—116 (November 9, 1997, vs. New Orleans); and touchdown receptions—2 (September 28, 1997, vs. St. Louis).
STATISTICAL PLATEAUS: 100-yard receiving games: 1997 (2), 1998 (1). Total: 3.
MISCELLANEOUS: Member of Ohio State basketball team (1991-92 through 1993-94).

				RECEIVING				TOTALS		
Year Team	G	GS	No.	Yds.	Avg.	TD	TD	2pt.	Pts.	Fum.
1996—Oakland NFL	16	15	34	386	11.4	4	4	0	24	1
1997—Oakland NFL	16	16	48	787	16.4	7	7	0	42	0
1998—Oakland NFL	16	15	36	549	15.3	5	5	1	32	1
Pro totals (3 years)	48	46	118	1722	14.6	16	16	1	98	2

DUFF, JAMAL   DE   BEARS

PERSONAL: Born March 11, 1972, in Columbus, Ohio. ... 6-7/285. ... Full name: Jamal Edwin Duff. ... Brother of John Duff, tight end with Los Angeles Raiders (1993-94) and Philadelphia Eagles (1997).
HIGH SCHOOL: Foothill (Tustin, Calif.).
COLLEGE: San Diego State.
TRANSACTIONS/CAREER NOTES: Selected by New York Giants in sixth round (204th pick overall) of 1995 NFL draft. ... Signed by Giants (July 23, 1995). ... On injured reserve with foot injury (August 26, 1996-entire season). ... On physically unable to perform list with ankle injury (July 19-21, 1997). ... Claimed on waivers by Washington Redskins (August 20, 1997). ... Granted free agency (February 13, 1998). ... Re-signed by Redskins (May 7, 1998). ... Granted unconditional free agency (February 12, 1999). ... Signed by Chicago Bears (March 24, 1999).

Year Team	G	GS	SACKS
1995—New York Giants NFL	15	2	4.0
1996—New York Giants NFL	Did not play.		
1997—Washington NFL	13	5	2.0
1998—Washington NFL	13	3	3.0
Pro totals (3 years)	41	10	9.0

DUFFY, ROGER   G/C   STEELERS

PERSONAL: Born July 16, 1967, in Pittsburgh. ... 6-3/299. ... Full name: Roger Thomas Duffy.
HIGH SCHOOL: Canton (Ohio) Central Catholic.
COLLEGE: Penn State (degree in communications, 1990).
TRANSACTIONS/CAREER NOTES: Selected by New York Jets in eighth round (196th pick overall) of 1990 NFL draft. ... Signed by Jets (July 18, 1990). ... Granted free agency (February 1, 1992). ... Re-signed by Jets (May 15, 1992). ... Granted unconditional free agency (February 17, 1994). ... Re-signed by Jets (March 2, 1994). ... Granted unconditional free agency (February 16, 1996). ... Re-signed by Jets (April 1, 1996). ... Granted unconditional free agency (February 13, 1998). ... Signed by Pittsburgh Steelers (March 13, 1998).
PLAYING EXPERIENCE: New York Jets NFL, 1990-1997; Pittsburgh NFL, 1998. ... Games/Games started: 1990 (16/2), 1991 (12/0), 1992 (16/6), 1993 (16/1), 1994 (16/14), 1995 (16/16), 1996 (16/16), 1997 (15/15), 1998 (15/4). Total: 138/74.
PRO STATISTICS: 1991—Returned one kickoff for eight yards. 1992—Returned one kickoff for seven yards and recovered one fumble. 1993—Recovered one fumble. 1995—Recovered two fumbles. 1996—Recovered one fumble. 1997—Fumbled twice and recovered one fumble for minus 22 yards.

DULANEY, MIKE   FB

PERSONAL: Born September 9, 1970, in Kingsport, Tenn. ... 6-0/245. ... Full name: Michael Faulkerson Dulaney. ... Formerly known as Mike Faulkerson.
HIGH SCHOOL: Dobyns-Bennett (Kingsport, Tenn.).
COLLEGE: North Carolina.
TRANSACTIONS/CAREER NOTES: Played in Arena Football League with Albany Firebirds (1995). ... Signed as non-drafted free agent by Chicago Bears (July 17, 1995). ... Released by Bears (August 27, 1995). ... Re-signed by Bears to practice squad (August 29, 1995). ... Activated (September 22, 1995). ... Released by Bears (September 25, 1995). ... Re-signed by Bears to practice squad (September 27, 1995). ... Activated (November 29, 1995). ... Released by Bears (August 24, 1997). ... Re-signed by Bears (October 28, 1997). ... Released by Bears following 1997 season. ... Signed by Carolina Panthers (March 24, 1998). ... Granted free agency (February 12, 1999).
PLAYING EXPERIENCE: Chicago NFL, 1995-1997; Carolina NFL, 1998. ... Games/Games started: 1995 (5/1), 1996 (16/0), 1997 (7/0), 1998 (8/0). Total: 36/1.
PRO STATISTICS: 1995—Caught two passes for 22 yards. 1996—Caught one pass for one yard and a touchdown and returned four kickoffs for 63 yards. 1997—Returned one punt for no yards and fumbled once.

DUMAS, MIKE   S   CHARGERS

PERSONAL: Born March 18, 1969, in Grand Rapids, Mich. ... 6-0/202. ... Full name: Michael Dion Dumas.
HIGH SCHOOL: Lowell (Mich.).
COLLEGE: Indiana.
TRANSACTIONS/CAREER NOTES: Selected by Houston Oilers in second round (28th pick overall) of 1991 NFL draft. ... Signed by Oilers (August 12, 1991). ... On injured reserve with Achilles' tendon injury (August 23, 1993-entire season). ... Granted free agency (February 17, 1994). ... Re-signed by Oilers (June 1994). ... Released by Oilers (July 14, 1994). ... Signed by Buffalo Bills (July 25, 1994). ... Granted unconditional free agency (February 17, 1995). ... Signed by Jacksonville Jaguars (April 24, 1995). ... Released by Jaguars (April 24, 1996). ... Signed by San Diego Chargers (March 4, 1997). ... Granted unconditional free agency (February 13, 1998). ... Re-signed by Chargers (February 20, 1998). ... On injured reserve with knee injury (September 26, 1998-remainder of season).
HONORS: Named defensive back on THE SPORTING NEWS college All-America second team (1990).
PRO STATISTICS: 1991—Recovered three fumbles for 19 yards and one touchdown. 1992—Recovered one fumble. 1994—Recovered two fumbles for 40 yards. 1995—Recovered two fumbles. 1997—Credited with one sack and recovered one fumble. 1998—Credited with one sack.

Year Team	G	GS	INTERCEPTIONS No.	Yds.	Avg.	TD
1991—Houston NFL	13	0	1	19	19.0	0
1992—Houston NFL	16	1	1	0	0.0	0
1993—Houston NFL			Did not play.			
1994—Buffalo NFL	14	0	0	...	...	0
1995—Jacksonville NFL	14	8	1	0	0.0	0
1996—			Did not play.			
1997—San Diego NFL	16	15	1	0	0.0	0
1998—San Diego NFL	3	3	0	0	...	0
Pro totals (6 years)	76	27	4	19	4.8	0

DUNCAN, JAMIE   LB   BUCCANEERS

PERSONAL: Born July 20, 1975, in Wilmington, Del. ... 6-0/220.
HIGH SCHOOL: Christiana (Wilmington, Del.).
COLLEGE: Vanderbilt (degree in human and organizational development, 1998).
TRANSACTIONS/CAREER NOTES: Selected by Tampa Bay Buccaneers in third round (84th pick overall) of 1998 NFL draft. ... Signed by Buccaneers (July 10, 1998).
PLAYING EXPERIENCE: Tampa Bay NFL, 1998. ... Games/Games started: 14/6.
HONORS: Named inside linebacker on THE SPORTING NEWS college All-America second team (1997).

DUNN, DAVID   WR   STEELERS

PERSONAL: Born June 10, 1972, in San Diego. ... 6-2/220.
HIGH SCHOOL: Samuel F.B. Morse (San Diego).
JUNIOR COLLEGE: Bakersfield (Calif.) College.
COLLEGE: Fresno State.
TRANSACTIONS/CAREER NOTES: Selected by Cincinnati Bengals in fifth round (139th pick overall) of 1995 NFL draft. ... Signed by Bengals (July 31, 1995). ... Granted free agency (February 13, 1998). ... Re-signed by Bengals (April 23, 1998). ... Released by Bengals (September 9, 1998). ... Signed by Pittsburgh Steelers (October 14, 1998).
HONORS: Named kick returner on THE SPORTING NEWS college All-America second team (1994).
PRO STATISTICS: 1995—Rushed once for minus 13 yards. 1996—Returned seven punts for 54 yards. 1997—Recovered one fumble.
SINGLE GAME HIGHS (regular season): Receptions—7 (December 15, 1996, vs. Houston); yards—95 (December 15, 1996, vs. Houston); and touchdown receptions—1 (December 14, 1997, vs. Dallas).

			RECEIVING				KICKOFF RETURNS				TOTALS			
Year Team	G	GS	No.	Yds.	Avg.	TD	No.	Yds.	Avg.	TD	TD	2pt.	Pts.	Fum.
1995—Cincinnati NFL	16	0	17	209	12.3	1	50	1092	21.8	0	1	0	6	2
1996—Cincinnati NFL	16	0	32	509	15.9	1	35	782	22.3	▲1	3	0	18	1
1997—Cincinnati NFL	14	5	27	414	15.3	2	19	487	25.6	0	2	0	12	1
1998—Cincinnati NFL	1	0	0	0	...	0	0	0	...	0	0	0	0	0
—Pittsburgh NFL	10	0	9	87	9.7	0	21	525	25.0	0	0	0	0	1
Pro totals (4 years)	57	5	85	1219	14.3	4	125	2886	23.1	1	6	0	36	5

DUNN, JASON   TE   EAGLES

PERSONAL: Born November 15, 1973, in Harrodsburg, Ky. ... 6-4/257. ... Full name: Jason Adam Dunn.
HIGH SCHOOL: Harrodsburg (Ky.).
COLLEGE: Eastern Kentucky.
TRANSACTIONS/CAREER NOTES: Selected by Philadelphia Eagles in second round (54th pick overall) of 1996 NFL draft. ... Signed by Eagles (July 17, 1996). ... On injured reserve with knee injury (December 1, 1998-remainder of season). ... Granted free agency (February 12, 1999).
PRO STATISTICS: 1996—Recovered one fumble. 1997—Returned two kickoffs for 32 yards. 1998—Rushed once for minus five yards and recovered one fumble.
SINGLE GAME HIGHS (regular season): Receptions—4 (November 15, 1998, vs. Washington); yards—58 (September 22, 1996, vs. Atlanta); and touchdown receptions—1 (December 21, 1997, vs. Washington).

			RECEIVING				TOTALS			
Year Team	G	GS	No.	Yds.	Avg.	TD	TD	2pt.	Pts.	Fum.
1996—Philadelphia NFL	16	12	15	332	22.1	2	2	0	12	0
1997—Philadelphia NFL	15	4	7	93	13.3	2	2	0	12	0
1998—Philadelphia NFL	10	10	18	132	7.3	0	0	0	0	1
Pro totals (3 years)	41	26	40	557	13.9	4	4	0	24	1

DUNN, WARRICK   RB   BUCCANEERS

PERSONAL: Born January 5, 1975, in Baton Rouge, La. ... 5-8/176. ... Full name: Warrick De'Mon Dunn.
HIGH SCHOOL: Catholic (Baton Rouge, La.).
COLLEGE: Florida State (degree in information studies, 1997).
TRANSACTIONS/CAREER NOTES: Selected by Tampa Bay Buccaneers in first round (12th pick overall) of 1997 NFL draft. ... Signed by Buccaneers (July 24, 1997).
HONORS: Named NFL Rookie of the Year by THE SPORTING NEWS (1997). ... Played in Pro Bowl (1997 season).
PRO STATISTICS: 1997—Returned five punts for 48 yards and recovered four fumbles. 1998—Recovered one fumble.
SINGLE GAME HIGHS (regular season): Attempts—24 (November 30, 1997, vs. New York Giants); yards—130 (September 7, 1997, vs. Detroit); and rushing touchdowns—1 (November 1, 1998, vs. Minnesota).
STATISTICAL PLATEAUS: 100-yard rushing games: 1997 (5), 1998 (2). Total: 7. ... 100-yard receiving games: 1997 (1).

				RUSHING				RECEIVING				KICKOFF RETURNS				TOTALS		
Year	Team	G	GS	Att.	Yds.	Avg.	TD	No.	Yds.	Avg.	TD	No.	Yds.	Avg.	TD	TD	2pt.	Pts.	Fum.
1997—Tampa Bay NFL		16	10	224	978	4.4	4	39	462	11.8	3	6	129	21.5	0	7	0	42	4
1998—Tampa Bay NFL		16	14	245	1026	4.2	2	44	344	7.8	0	1	25	25.0	0	2	0	12	1
Pro totals (2 years)		32	24	469	2004	4.3	6	83	806	9.7	3	7	154	22.0	0	9	0	54	5

DWIGHT, TIM — WR/KR — FALCONS

PERSONAL: Born July 13, 1975, in Iowa City, Iowa. ... 5-8/180.
HIGH SCHOOL: Iowa City (Iowa) High.
COLLEGE: Iowa.
TRANSACTIONS/CAREER NOTES: Selected by Atlanta Falcons in fourth round (114th pick overall) of 1998 NFL draft. ... Signed by Falcons (June 25, 1998).
CHAMPIONSHIP GAME EXPERIENCE: Played in NFC championship game (1998 season). ... Played in Super Bowl XXXIII (1998 season).
HONORS: Named kick returner on THE SPORTING NEWS college All-America second team (1996). ... Named kick returner on THE SPORTING NEWS college All-America first team (1997).
POST SEASON RECORDS: Holds Super Bowl career record for highest kickoff return average (minimum four returns)—42.0. ... Shares Super Bowl single-game record for most touchdowns by kickoff return—1 (January 31, 1999, vs. Denver).
PRO STATISTICS: 1998—Attempted two passes with one completion for 22 yards and fumbled three times.
SINGLE GAME HIGHS (regular season): Receptions—1 (November 29, 1998, vs. St. Louis); yards—44 (September 6, 1998, vs. Carolina); and touchdown receptions—1 (September 6, 1998, vs. Carolina).

				RUSHING				RECEIVING				PUNT RETURNS				KICKOFF RETURNS				TOTALS		
Year	Team	G	GS	Att.	Yds.	Avg.	TD	No.	Yds.	Avg.	TD	No.	Yds.	Avg.	TD	No.	Yds.	Avg.	TD	TD	2pt.	Pts.
1998—Atlanta NFL		12	0	8	19	2.4	0	4	94	23.5	1	31	263	8.5	0	36	973	27.0	1	2	0	12

DYSON, KEVIN — WR — TITANS

PERSONAL: Born June 23, 1975, in Logan, Utah ... 6-1/201.
HIGH SCHOOL: Clearfield (Utah).
COLLEGE: Utah.
TRANSACTIONS/CAREER NOTES: Selected by Tennessee Oilers in first round (16th pick overall) of 1998 NFL draft. ... Signed by Oilers (July 24, 1998). ... Oilers franchise renamed Tennessee Titans for 1999 season (December 26, 1998).
PRO STATISTICS: 1998—Rushed once for four yards.
SINGLE GAME HIGHS (regular season): Receptions—4 (November 15, 1998, vs. Pittsburgh); yards—82 (October 18, 1998, vs. Cincinnati); and touchdown receptions—1 (November 1, 1998, vs. Pittsburgh).

				RECEIVING				TOTALS			
Year	Team	G	GS	No.	Yds.	Avg.	TD	TD	2pt.	Pts.	Fum.
1998—Tennessee NFL		13	9	21	263	12.5	2	2	0	12	0

EARLY, QUINN — WR

PERSONAL: Born April 13, 1965, in West Hempstead, N.Y. ... 6-0/190. ... Full name: Quinn Remar Early.
HIGH SCHOOL: Great Neck (N.Y.).
COLLEGE: Iowa (degree in art, 1988).
TRANSACTIONS/CAREER NOTES: Selected by San Diego Chargers in third round (60th pick overall) of 1988 NFL draft. ... Signed by Chargers (July 11, 1988). ... On injured reserve with knee injury (October 21-December 13, 1989). ... On developmental squad (December 14-15, 1989). ... Activated (December 16, 1989). ... Granted unconditional free agency (February 1, 1991). ... Signed by New Orleans Saints (April 1, 1991). ... Granted unconditional free agency (February 16, 1996). ... Signed by Buffalo Bills (March 8, 1996). ... Released by Bills (February 10, 1999).
PRO STATISTICS: 1991—Returned nine kickoffs for 168 yards.
SINGLE GAME HIGHS (regular season): Receptions—9 (November 19, 1995, vs. Minnesota); yards—150 (November 19, 1995, vs. Minnesota); and touchdown receptions—2 (November 23, 1997, vs. Tennessee).
STATISTICAL PLATEAUS: 100-yard receiving games: 1991 (1), 1994 (1), 1995 (2), 1996 (2), 1997 (2). Total: 8.

				RUSHING				RECEIVING				TOTALS			
Year	Team	G	GS	Att.	Yds.	Avg.	TD	No.	Yds.	Avg.	TD	TD	2pt.	Pts.	Fum.
1988—San Diego NFL		16	10	7	63	9.0	0	29	375	12.9	4	4	...	24	1
1989—San Diego NFL		6	3	1	19	19.0	0	11	126	11.5	0	0	...	0	0
1990—San Diego NFL		14	4	0	0	...	0	15	238	15.9	1	1	...	6	0
1991—New Orleans NFL		15	12	3	13	4.3	0	32	541	16.9	2	2	...	12	2
1992—New Orleans NFL		16	16	3	-1	-0.3	0	30	566	18.9	5	5	...	30	0
1993—New Orleans NFL		16	15	2	32	16.0	0	45	670	14.9	6	6	...	36	1
1994—New Orleans NFL		16	13	2	10	5.0	0	82	894	10.9	4	4	...	24	0
1995—New Orleans NFL		16	15	2	-3	-1.5	0	81	1087	13.4	8	8	...	48	1
1996—Buffalo NFL		16	13	3	39	13.0	0	50	798	16.0	4	4	1	26	0
1997—Buffalo NFL		16	16	0	0	...	0	60	853	14.2	5	5	0	30	0
1998—Buffalo NFL		16	2	0	0	...	0	19	217	11.4	1	1	0	6	0
Pro totals (11 years)		163	119	23	172	7.5	0	454	6365	14.0	40	40	1	242	5

EATON, CHAD — DT — PATRIOTS

PERSONAL: Born April 6, 1972, in Exeter, N.H. ... 6-5/300. ... Full name: Chad Everett Eaton.
HIGH SCHOOL: Rogers (Puyallup, Wash.).
COLLEGE: Washington State.

TRANSACTIONS/CAREER NOTES: Selected by Arizona Cardinals in seventh round (241st pick overall) of 1995 NFL draft. ... Signed by Cardinals (July 24, 1995). ... Released by Cardinals (August 14, 1995). ... Signed by New York Jets (August 15, 1995). ... Released by Jets (August 27, 1995). ... Signed by Cleveland Browns to practice squad (September 28, 1995). ... Activated (December 15, 1995); did not play. ... Browns franchise moved to Baltimore and renamed Ravens for 1996 season (March 11, 1996). ... Released by Ravens (August 19, 1996). ... Signed by New England Patriots to practice squad (August 27, 1996). ... Activated (November 28, 1996).
CHAMPIONSHIP GAME EXPERIENCE: Played in AFC championship game (1996 season). ... Played in Super Bowl XXXI (1996 season).
HONORS: Named defensive lineman on THE SPORTING NEWS college All-America second team (1994).
PRO STATISTICS: 1998—Returned one kickoff for 13 yards and recovered one fumble for two yards.

Year Team	G	GS	SACKS
1995—Cleveland NFL	Did not play.		
1996—New England NFL	4	0	1.0
1997—New England NFL	16	1	1.0
1998—New England NFL	15	14	6.0
Pro totals (3 years)	35	15	8.0

EDWARDS, ANTONIO — DE — PANTHERS

PERSONAL: Born March 10, 1970, in Moultrie, Ga. ... 6-3/271.
HIGH SCHOOL: Colquitt County (Moultrie, Ga.).
COLLEGE: Valdosta (Ga.) State.
TRANSACTIONS/CAREER NOTES: Selected by Seattle Seahawks in eighth round (204th pick overall) of 1993 NFL draft. ... Signed by Seahawks (July 14, 1993). ... Released by Seahawks (August 5, 1997). ... Re-signed by Seahawks (September 23, 1997). ... Released by Seahawks (October 20, 1997). ... Signed by New York Giants (December 2, 1997). ... Granted unconditional free agency (February 13, 1998). ... Signed by Atlanta Falcons (June 19, 1998). ... Granted unconditional free agency (February 12, 1999). ... Signed by Carolina Panthers (March 3, 1999).
CHAMPIONSHIP GAME EXPERIENCE: Played in NFC championship game (1998 season). ... Played in Super Bowl XXXIII (1998 season).
PRO STATISTICS: 1993—Credited with a safety. 1995—Recovered one fumble for 83 yards and a touchdown. 1998—Recovered one fumble for two yards and a touchdown.

Year Team	G	GS	SACKS
1993—Seattle NFL	9	0	3.0
1994—Seattle NFL	15	14	2.5
1995—Seattle NFL	13	8	5.5
1996—Seattle NFL	12	3	2.0
1997—Seattle NFL	1	0	0.0
—New York Giants NFL	3	0	0.0
1998—Atlanta NFL	15	0	1.0
Pro totals (6 years)	68	25	14.0

EDWARDS, DIXON — LB

PERSONAL: Born March 25, 1968, in Cincinnati. ... 6-1/233. ... Full name: Dixon Voldean Edwards III.
HIGH SCHOOL: Aiken (Cincinnati).
COLLEGE: Michigan State.
TRANSACTIONS/CAREER NOTES: Selected by Dallas Cowboys in second round (37th pick overall) of 1991 NFL draft. ... Signed by Cowboys (April 22, 1991). ... On injured reserve with hamstring injury (August 27-September 25, 1991). ... Granted unconditional free agency (February 16, 1996). ... Signed by Minnesota Vikings (February 26, 1996). ... Released by Vikings (June 2, 1999).
CHAMPIONSHIP GAME EXPERIENCE: Played in NFC championship game (1992-1995 and 1998 seasons). ... Member of Super Bowl championship team (1992, 1993 and 1995 seasons).
PRO STATISTICS: 1991—Intercepted one pass for 36 yards and a touchdown. 1992—Returned one kickoff for no yards. 1993—Recovered one fumble. 1994—Recovered one fumble for 21 yards. 1996—Intercepted one pass for 18 yards. 1997—Recovered one fumble. 1998—Recovered one fumble.

Year Team	G	GS	SACKS
1991—Dallas NFL	11	1	0.0
1992—Dallas NFL	16	1	0.0
1993—Dallas NFL	16	15	1.5
1994—Dallas NFL	16	15	1.0
1995—Dallas NFL	15	15	0.0
1996—Minnesota NFL	14	13	3.5
1997—Minnesota NFL	16	16	1.5
1998—Minnesota NFL	15	14	0.0
Pro totals (8 years)	119	90	7.5

EDWARDS, DONNIE — LB — CHIEFS

PERSONAL: Born April 6, 1973, in San Diego ... 6-2/236. ... Full name: Donnie Lewis Edwards Jr.
HIGH SCHOOL: Chula Vista (San Diego).
COLLEGE: UCLA (degree in political science).
TRANSACTIONS/CAREER NOTES: Selected by Kansas City Chiefs in fourth round (98th pick overall) of 1996 NFL draft. ... Signed by Chiefs (July 24, 1996).
PRO STATISTICS: 1997—Recovered one fumble. 1998—Recovered one fumble.

Year Team	G	GS	INTERCEPTIONS No.	Yds.	Avg.	TD	SACKS No.
1996—Kansas City NFL	15	1	1	22	22.0	0	0.0
1997—Kansas City NFL	16	16	2	15	7.5	0	2.5
1998—Kansas City NFL	15	15	0	0	...	0	6.0
Pro totals (3 years)	46	32	3	37	12.3	0	8.5

EDWARDS, MARC — FB — BROWNS

PERSONAL: Born November 17, 1974, in Cincinnati. ... 6-0/229. ... Full name: Marc Alexander Edwards.
HIGH SCHOOL: Norwood (Ohio).
COLLEGE: Notre Dame (degree in business management, 1996).
TRANSACTIONS/CAREER NOTES: Selected by San Francisco 49ers in second round (55th pick overall) of 1997 NFL draft. ... Signed by 49ers (July 23, 1997). ... On physically unable to perform list with back injury (July 17-August 10, 1998). ... Traded by 49ers to Cleveland Browns for fourth-round pick (DB Pierson Prioleau) in 1999 draft (April 17, 1999).
CHAMPIONSHIP GAME EXPERIENCE: Played in NFC championship game (1997 season).
PRO STATISTICS: 1997—Returned one kickoff for 30 yards.
SINGLE GAME HIGHS (regular season): Attempts—3 (December 27, 1998, vs. St. Louis); yards—41 (September 27, 1998, vs. Atlanta); and rushing touchdowns—1 (September 27, 1998, vs. Atlanta).

			RUSHING				RECEIVING				TOTALS			
Year Team	G	GS	Att.	Yds.	Avg.	TD	No.	Yds.	Avg.	TD	TD	2pt.	Pts.	Fum.
1997—San Francisco NFL	15	1	5	17	3.4	0	6	48	8.0	0	0	0	0	0
1998—San Francisco NFL	16	11	22	94	4.3	1	22	218	9.9	2	3	0	18	0
Pro totals (2 years)	31	12	27	111	4.1	1	28	266	9.5	2	3	0	18	0

EDWARDS, ROBERT — RB — PATRIOTS

PERSONAL: Born October 2, 1974, in Tennille, Ga. ... 5-11/218. ... Full name: Robert Lee Edwards III.
HIGH SCHOOL: Washington County (Tennille, Ga.).
COLLEGE: Georgia.
TRANSACTIONS/CAREER NOTES: Selected by New England Patriots in first round (18th pick overall) of 1998 NFL draft. ... Signed by Patriots (July 17, 1998).
PRO STATISTICS: 1998—Recovered two fumbles.
SINGLE GAME HIGHS (regular season): Attempts—28 (December 6, 1998, vs. Pittsburgh); yards—196 (December 13, 1998, vs. St. Louis); and rushing touchdowns—1 (December 20, 1998, vs. San Francisco).
STATISTICAL PLATEAUS: 100-yard rushing games: 1998 (4).

			RUSHING				RECEIVING				TOTALS			
Year Team	G	GS	Att.	Yds.	Avg.	TD	No.	Yds.	Avg.	TD	TD	2pt.	Pts.	Fum.
1998—New England NFL	16	15	291	1115	3.8	9	35	331	9.5	3	12	0	72	5

ELAM, JASON — K — BRONCOS

PERSONAL: Born March 8, 1970, in Fort Walton Beach, Fla. ... 5-11/200.
HIGH SCHOOL: Brookwood (Snellville, Ga.).
COLLEGE: Hawaii.
TRANSACTIONS/CAREER NOTES: Selected by Denver Broncos in third round (70th pick overall) of 1993 NFL draft. ... Signed by Broncos (July 12, 1993).
CHAMPIONSHIP GAME EXPERIENCE: Played in AFC championship game (1997 and 1998 seasons). ... Member of Super Bowl championship team (1997 and 1998 seasons).
HONORS: Named kicker on THE SPORTING NEWS college All-America second team (1989 and 1991). ... Played in Pro Bowl (1995 and 1998 seasons).
RECORDS: Holds NFL career record for highest PAT percentage—99.62. ... Shares NFL career record for longest field goal—63 (October 25, 1998, vs. Jacksonville).
PRO STATISTICS: 1995—Punted once for 17 yards.

				KICKING				
Year Team	G	XPM	XPA	FGM	FGA	Lg.	50+	Pts.
1993—Denver NFL	16	§41	§42	26	35	54	4-6	119
1994—Denver NFL	16	29	29	30	37	†54	1-3	119
1995—Denver NFL	16	39	39	31	38	§56	5-7	132
1996—Denver NFL	16	§46	§46	21	28	51	1-3	109
1997—Denver NFL	15	§46	§46	26	36	53	3-5	124
1998—Denver NFL	16	§58	§58	23	27	*63	3-4	§127
Pro totals (6 years)	95	259	260	157	201	63	17-28	730

ELIAS, KEITH — RB — COLTS

PERSONAL: Born February 3, 1972, in Lacey Township, N.J. ... 5-9/203.
HIGH SCHOOL: Lacey Township (N.J.).
COLLEGE: Princeton.
TRANSACTIONS/CAREER NOTES: Signed as non-drafted free agent by New York Giants (April 29, 1994). ... On injured reserve with knee injury (December 19, 1996-remainder of season). ... Granted unconditional free agency (February 14, 1997). ... Signed by Indianapolis Colts (January 12, 1998).
SINGLE GAME HIGHS (regular season): Attempts—3 (September 20, 1998, vs. New York Jets); yards—11 (November 26, 1995, vs. Chicago); and rushing touchdowns—0.

			RUSHING				RECEIVING				KICKOFF RETURNS				TOTALS			
Year Team	G	GS	Att.	Yds.	Avg.	TD	No.	Yds.	Avg.	TD	No.	Yds.	Avg.	TD	TD	2pt.	Pts.	Fum.
1994—New York Giants NFL	2	0	2	4	2.0	0	0	0	...	0	0	0	...	0	0	0	0	0
1995—New York Giants NFL	15	0	10	44	4.4	0	9	69	7.7	0	0	0	...	0	0	0	0	0
1996—New York Giants NFL	9	0	9	24	2.7	0	8	51	6.4	0	0	0	...	0	0	0	0	0
1997—									Did not play.									
1998—Indianapolis NFL	13	0	8	24	3.0	0	1	11	11.0	0	14	317	22.6	0	0	0	0	0
Pro totals (4 years)	39	0	29	96	3.3	0	18	131	7.3	0	14	317	22.6	0	0	0	0	0

ELLARD, HENRY — WR

PERSONAL: Born July 21, 1961, in Fresno, Calif. ... 5-11/188. ... Full name: Henry Austin Ellard. ... Name pronounced EL-lard.
HIGH SCHOOL: Hoover (Fresno, Calif.).
COLLEGE: Fresno State.
TRANSACTIONS/CAREER NOTES: Selected by Oakland Invaders in 1983 USFL territorial draft. ... Selected by Los Angeles Rams in second round (32nd pick overall) of 1983 NFL draft. ... Signed by Rams (July 22, 1983). ... Granted free agency (February 1, 1986). ... Re-signed by Rams (October 22, 1986). ... Granted roster exemption (October 22-25, 1986). ... Granted unconditional free agency (February 17, 1994). ... Signed by Washington Redskins (April 13, 1994). ... Granted unconditional free agency (February 16, 1996). ... Re-signed by Redskins (February 17, 1996). ... Granted unconditional free agency (February 13, 1998). ... Signed by New England Patriots (October 28, 1998). ... Released by Patriots (December 1, 1998). ... Signed by Redskins (December 8, 1998). ... Granted unconditional free agency (February 12, 1999).
CHAMPIONSHIP GAME EXPERIENCE: Played in NFC championship game (1985 and 1989 seasons).
HONORS: Named punt returner on THE SPORTING NEWS NFL All-Pro team (1984 and 1985). ... Played in Pro Bowl (1984, 1988 and 1989 seasons). ... Named wide receiver on THE SPORTING NEWS NFL All-Pro team (1988).
PRO STATISTICS: 1983—Fumbled twice and recovered two fumbles. 1984—Fumbled four times and recovered two fumbles. 1985—Fumbled three times and recovered five fumbles. 1986—Fumbled three times and recovered one fumble. 1987—Fumbled three times and recovered one fumble. 1988—Fumbled three times. 1990—Fumbled four times. 1991—Fumbled once and recovered one fumble. 1994—Fumbled once. 1995—Fumbled once.
SINGLE GAME HIGHS (regular season): Receptions—12 (September 17, 1989, vs. Indianapolis); yards—230 (September 17, 1989, vs. Indianapolis); and touchdown receptions—3 (September 17, 1989, vs. Indianapolis).
STATISTICAL PLATEAUS: 100-yard receiving games: 1985 (2), 1986 (2), 1987 (1), 1988 (5), 1989 (5), 1990 (6), 1991 (1), 1993 (3), 1994 (5), 1995 (3), 1996 (3). Total: 36.
MISCELLANEOUS: Holds Rams franchise all-time records for most receptions (593) and most yards receiving (9,761).

				RUSHING			RECEIVING				PUNT RETURNS				KICKOFF RETURNS				TOTALS		
Year Team	G	GS	Att.	Yds.	Avg.	TD	No.	Yds.	Avg.	TD	No.	Yds.	Avg.	TD	No.	Yds.	Avg.	TD	TD	2pt.	Pts.
1983—L.A. Rams NFL....	12	0	3	7	2.3	0	16	268	16.8	0	16	217*13.6		†1	15	314	20.9	0	1	...	6
1984—L.A. Rams NFL....	16	16	3	-5	-1.7	0	34	622	18.3	6	30	403‡13.4		*2	2	24	12.0	0	8	...	48
1985—L.A. Rams NFL....	16	16	3	8	2.7	0	54	811	15.0	5	37	‡501‡13.5		∞1	0	0	...	0	6	...	36
1986—L.A. Rams NFL....	9	8	1	-15	-15.0	0	34	447	13.1	4	14	127	9.1	0	1	18	18.0	0	4	...	24
1987—L.A. Rams NFL....	12	12	1	4	4.0	0	51	799	15.7	3	15	107	7.1	0	1	8	8.0	0	3	...	18
1988—L.A. Rams NFL....	16	16	1	7	7.0	0	‡86	*1414	16.4	10	17	119	7.0	0	0	0	...	0	10	...	60
1989—L.A. Rams NFL....	14	12	2	10	5.0	0	70	1382	19.7	8	2	20	10.0	0	0	0	...	0	8	...	48
1990—L.A. Rams NFL....	15	15	2	21	10.5	0	76	1294	17.0	4	2	15	7.5	0	0	0	...	0	4	...	24
1991—L.A. Rams NFL....	16	16	0	0	...	0	64	1052	16.4	3	0	0	...	0	0	0	...	0	3	...	18
1992—L.A. Rams NFL....	16	15	0	0	...	0	47	727	15.5	3	0	0	...	0	0	0	...	0	3	...	18
1993—L.A. Rams NFL....	16	16	2	18	9.0	0	61	945	15.5	2	2	18	9.0	0	0	0	...	0	2	...	12
1994—Washington NFL.	16	16	1	-5	-5.0	0	74	1397	18.9	6	0	0	...	0	0	0	...	0	6	0	36
1995—Washington NFL.	15	15	0	0	...	0	56	1005	17.9	5	0	0	...	0	0	0	...	0	5	0	30
1996—Washington NFL.	16	16	0	0	...	0	52	1014	*19.5	2	0	0	...	0	0	0	...	0	2	0	12
1997—Washington NFL.	16	11	0	0	...	0	32	485	15.2	4	0	0	...	0	0	0	...	0	4	0	24
1998—New England NFL	5	0	0	0	...	0	5	86	17.2	0	0	0	...	0	0	0	...	0	0	0	0
—Washington NFL .	2	0	0	0	...	0	2	29	14.5	0	0	0	...	0	0	0	...	0	0	0	0
Pro totals (16 years)......	228	200	19	50	2.6	0	814	13777	16.9	65	135	1527	11.3	4	19	364	19.2	0	69	0	414

ELLIOTT, JUMBO — OT — JETS

PERSONAL: Born April 1, 1965, in Lake Ronkonkoma, N.Y. ... 6-7/308. ... Full name: John Elliott.
HIGH SCHOOL: Sachem (Lake Ronkonkoma, N.Y.).
COLLEGE: Michigan.
TRANSACTIONS/CAREER NOTES: Selected by New York Giants in second round (36th pick overall) of 1988 NFL draft. ... Signed by Giants (July 18, 1988). ... Granted free agency (February 1, 1991). ... Re-signed by Giants (August 22, 1991). ... Designated by Giants as franchise player (February 25, 1993). ... On injured reserve with back injury (January 7, 1994-remainder of 1993 playoffs). ... Granted unconditional free agency (February 16, 1996). ... Signed by New York Jets (February 24, 1996). ... On injured reserve with ankle injury (December 1, 1997-remainder of season).
PLAYING EXPERIENCE: New York Giants NFL, 1988-1995; New York Jets NFL, 1996-1998. ... Games/Games started: 1988 (16/5), 1989 (13/11), 1990 (8/8), 1991 (16/16), 1992 (16/16), 1993 (11/11), 1994 (15/15), 1995 (16/16), 1996 (14/14), 1997 (13/13), 1998 (16/16). Total: 155/141.
CHAMPIONSHIP GAME EXPERIENCE: Played in NFC championship game (1990 season). ... Member of Super Bowl championship team (1990 season). ... Played in AFC championship game (1998 season).
HONORS: Played in Pro Bowl (1993 season).
PRO STATISTICS: 1988—Recovered one fumble.

ELLIS, ED — OT — PATRIOTS

PERSONAL: Born October 13, 1975, in Hamden, Conn. ... 6-7/340. ... Full name: Edward Key Ellis.
HIGH SCHOOL: Hamden (Conn.).
COLLEGE: Buffalo.
TRANSACTIONS/CAREER NOTES: Selected by New England Patriots in fourth round (125th pick overall) of 1997 NFL draft. ... Signed by Patriots (June 19, 1997).
PLAYING EXPERIENCE: New England NFL, 1997 and 1998. ... Games/Games started: 1997 (1/0), 1998 (7/0). Total: 8/0.

ELLIS, GREG — DE — COWBOYS

PERSONAL: Born August 14, 1975, in Wendell. N.C. ... 6-6/286. ... Full name: Gregory Lemont Ellis.
HIGH SCHOOL: East Wake (Wendell, N.C.).

COLLEGE: North Carolina.
TRANSACTIONS/CAREER NOTES: Selected by Dallas Cowboys in first round (eighth pick overall) of 1998 NFL draft. ... Signed by Cowboys (July 13, 1998).
HONORS: Named defensive end on THE SPORTING NEWS college All-America second team (1996 and 1997).
PRO STATISTICS: 1998—Recovered one fumble for two yards.

Year Team	G	GS	SACKS
1998—Dallas NFL	16	16	3.0

ELLISON, JERRY   RB

PERSONAL: Born December 20, 1971, in Augusta, Ga. ... 5-10/204. ... Full name: Jerry Ernest Ellison.
HIGH SCHOOL: Glenn Hills (Augusta, Ga.).
COLLEGE: Tennessee-Chattanooga.
TRANSACTIONS/CAREER NOTES: Signed as non-drafted free agent by Tampa Bay Buccaneers (May 5, 1994). ... Released by Buccaneers (August 23, 1994). ... Re-signed by Buccaneers to practice squad (September 7, 1994). ... Released by Buccaneers (September 12, 1994). ... Re-signed by Buccaneers to practice squad (September 27, 1994). ... Granted free agency (February 13, 1998). ... Re-signed by Buccaneers (June 11, 1998). ... Granted unconditional free agency (February 12, 1999).
PRO STATISTICS: 1995—Recovered one fumble. 1996—Recovered one fumble. 1997—Recovered one fumble. 1998—Recovered two fumbles.
SINGLE GAME HIGHS (regular season): Attempts—8 (September 8, 1996, vs. Detroit); yards—91 (December 23, 1995, vs. Detroit); and rushing touchdowns—2 (November 12, 1995, vs. Detroit).

			RUSHING				RECEIVING				KICKOFF RETURNS				TOTALS		
Year Team	G	GS	Att.	Yds.	Avg.	TD	No.	Yds.	Avg.	TD	No.	Yds.	Avg.	TD	TD	2pt.	Pts.	Fum.
1994—Tampa Bay NFL									Did not play.									
1995—Tampa Bay NFL	16	3	26	218	8.4	5	7	44	6.3	0	15	261	17.4	0	5	0	30	0
1996—Tampa Bay NFL	16	2	35	106	3.0	0	18	208	11.6	0	0	0	...	0	0	0	0	2
1997—Tampa Bay NFL	16	0	2	10	5.0	0	1	8	8.0	0	2	61	30.5	0	0	0	0	0
1998—Tampa Bay NFL	16	0	9	24	2.7	0	0	0	...	0	1	19	19.0	0	0	0	0	0
Pro totals (4 years)	64	5	72	358	5.0	5	26	260	10.0	0	18	341	18.9	0	5	0	30	2

ELLISS, LUTHER   DT   LIONS

PERSONAL: Born March 22, 1973, in Mancos, Colo. ... 6-5/315.
HIGH SCHOOL: Mancos (Colo.).
COLLEGE: Utah.
TRANSACTIONS/CAREER NOTES: Selected by Detroit Lions in first round (20th pick overall) of 1995 NFL draft. ... Signed by Lions (July 19, 1995).
HONORS: Named defensive lineman on THE SPORTING NEWS college All-America first team (1994).
PRO STATISTICS: 1997—Recovered two fumbles. 1998—Recovered one fumble.

Year Team	G	GS	SACKS
1995—Detroit NFL	16	16	0.0
1996—Detroit NFL	14	14	6.5
1997—Detroit NFL	16	16	8.5
1998—Detroit NFL	16	16	3.0
Pro totals (4 years)	62	62	18.0

ELLSWORTH, PERCY   S   GIANTS

PERSONAL: Born October 19, 1974, in Drewryville, Va. ... 6-2/225.
HIGH SCHOOL: Southhampton (Drewryville, Va.).
COLLEGE: Virginia.
TRANSACTIONS/CAREER NOTES: Signed as non-drafted free agent by New York Giants (April 27, 1996). ... Granted free agency (February 12, 1999).
PRO STATISTICS: 1996—Recovered one fumble. 1997—Recovered two fumbles for 24 yards.

			INTERCEPTIONS			
Year Team	G	GS	No.	Yds.	Avg.	TD
1996—New York Giants NFL	14	4	3	62	20.7	0
1997—New York Giants NFL	16	1	4	40	10.0	0
1998—New York Giants NFL	16	9	5	92	18.4	2
Pro totals (3 years)	46	14	12	194	16.2	2

ELOMS, JOEY   CB   SEAHAWKS

PERSONAL: Born April 4, 1976, in Fort Wayne, Ind. ... 5-10/183.
HIGH SCHOOL: Concordia (Ind.).
COLLEGE: Indiana.
TRANSACTIONS/CAREER NOTES: Signed as non-drafted free agent by Seattle Seahawks (April 28, 1998). ... Released by Seahawks (August 30, 1998). ... Re-signed by Seahawks to practice squad (August 31, 1998). ... Released by Seahawks (September 9, 1998). ... Re-signed by Seahawks to practice squad (September 22, 1998). ... Activated (November 28, 1998). ... Assigned by Seahawks to Scottish Claymores in 1999 NFL Europe enhancement allocation program (February 22, 1999).
PLAYING EXPERIENCE: Seattle NFL, 1998. ... Games/Games started: 1/0.

ELWAY, JOHN — QB

PERSONAL: Born June 28, 1960, in Port Angeles, Wash. ... 6-3/215. ... Full name: John Albert Elway Jr. ... Son of Jack Elway, director of pro scouting, Denver Broncos.
HIGH SCHOOL: Granada Hills (Calif.).
COLLEGE: Stanford (degree in economics, 1983).
TRANSACTIONS/CAREER NOTES: Selected by Oakland Invaders in 1983 USFL territorial draft. ... Selected by Baltimore Colts in first round (first pick overall) of 1983 NFL draft. ... Rights traded by Colts to Denver Broncos for QB Mark Herrmann, rights to OL Chris Hinton and first-round pick (G Ron Solt) in 1984 draft (May 2, 1983). ... Signed by Broncos (May 2, 1983). ... Announced retirement (May 2, 1999).
CHAMPIONSHIP GAME EXPERIENCE: Played in AFC championship game (1986, 1987, 1989, 1991, 1997 and 1998 seasons). ... Played in Super Bowl XXI (1986 season), Super Bowl XXII (1987 season) and Super Bowl XXIV (1989 season). ... Member of Super Bowl championship team (1997 and 1998 seasons).
HONORS: Named quarterback on The Sporting News college All-America first team (1980 and 1982). ... Played in Pro Bowl (1986, 1987, 1993, 1994 and 1998 seasons). ... Named quarterback on The Sporting News NFL All-Pro team (1987). ... Named to play in Pro Bowl (1989 season); replaced by Dave Krieg due to injury. ... Named to play in Pro Bowl as replacement for Dan Marino (1991); replaced by Ken O'Brien due to injury. ... Named to play in Pro Bowl (1996 season); replaced by Mark Brunell due to injury. ... Named to play in Pro Bowl (1997 season); replaced by Warren Moon due to injury. ... Named Most Valuable Player of Super Bowl XXXIII (1998 season).
RECORDS: Holds NFL career records for most regular-season wins as a starting NFL quarterback—148; and most times sacked—516.
POST SEASON RECORDS: Holds Super Bowl career records for most passes attempted—152; and most passes intercepted—8. ... Holds Super Bowl record for oldest player to score a touchdown—37 (January 25, 1998, vs. Green Bay). ... Shares Super Bowl career record for most fumbles recovered—2.
PRO STATISTICS: 1983—Fumbled six times and recovered three fumbles. 1984—Fumbled 14 times and recovered five fumbles for minus 10 yards. 1985—Fumbled seven times and recovered two fumbles for minus 35 yards. 1986—Caught one pass for 23 yards and a touchdown, fumbled eight times and recovered one fumble for minus 13 yards. 1987—Punted once for 31 yards and fumbled twice. 1988—Punted three times for 117 yards, fumbled seven times and recovered five fumbles for minus nine yards. 1989—Punted once for 34 yards, fumbled nine times and recovered two fumbles for minus four yards. 1990—Punted once for 37 yards, fumbled eight times and recovered one fumble for minus three yards. 1991—Caught one pass for 24 yards, punted once for 34 yards, led league with 12 fumbles and recovered two fumbles. 1992—Tied for the lead with 12 fumbles and recovered one fumble. 1993—Fumbled eight times and recovered five fumbles for minus five yards. 1994—Tied for AFC lead with 11 fumbles and recovered two fumbles for minus five yards. 1995—Fumbled nine times and recovered one fumble for minus seven yards. 1996—Fumbled six times and recovered two fumbles for minus four yards. 1997—Fumbled 11 times and recovered one fumble for minus 21 yards. 1998—Caught one pass for 14 yards, fumbled seven times and recovered two fumbles for minus 18 yards.
SINGLE GAME HIGHS (regular season): Attempts—59 (October 10, 1993, vs. Green Bay); completions—36 (September 4, 1994, vs. San Diego); yards—432 (December 20, 1985, vs. Seattle); and touchdown passes—5 (November 18, 1984, vs. Minnesota).
STATISTICAL PLATEAUS: 300-yard passing games: 1983 (1), 1984 (1), 1985 (3), 1986 (2), 1987 (4), 1988 (1), 1989 (1), 1990 (2), 1991 (1), 1992 (1), 1993 (3), 1994 (4), 1995 (5), 1996 (4), 1997 (1), 1998 (2). Total: 36.
MISCELLANEOUS: Regular-season record as starting NFL quarterback: 148-82-1 (.643). ... Postseason record as starting NFL quarterback: 14-7 (.667). ... Holds Denver Broncos all-time records for most yards passing (51,475) and most touchdown passes (300).

					PASSING						RUSHING				TOTALS	
Year Team	G	GS	Att.	Cmp.	Pct.	Yds.	TD	Int.	Avg.	Rat.	Att.	Yds.	Avg.	TD	TD	2pt.	Pts.
1983—Denver NFL	11	10	259	123	47.5	1663	7	14	6.42	54.9	28	146	5.2	1	1	...	6
1984—Denver NFL	15	14	380	214	56.3	2598	18	15	6.84	76.8	56	237	4.2	1	1	...	6
1985—Denver NFL	16	16	*605	327	54.0	3891	22	§23	6.43	70.2	51	253	5.0	0	0	...	0
1986—Denver NFL	16	16	504	280	55.6	3485	19	13	6.91	79.0	52	257	4.9	1	2	...	12
1987—Denver NFL	12	12	410	224	54.6	3198	19	12	§7.80	83.4	66	304	4.6	4	4	...	24
1988—Denver NFL	15	15	496	274	55.2	3309	17	19	6.67	71.4	54	234	4.3	1	1	...	6
1989—Denver NFL	15	15	416	223	53.6	3051	18	18	7.33	73.7	48	244	5.1	3	3	...	18
1990—Denver NFL	16	16	502	294	58.6	3526	15	14	7.02	78.5	50	258	5.2	3	3	...	18
1991—Denver NFL	16	16	451	242	53.7	3253	13	12	7.21	75.4	55	255	4.6	6	6	...	36
1992—Denver NFL	12	12	316	174	55.1	2242	10	17	7.09	65.7	34	94	2.8	2	2	...	12
1993—Denver NFL	16	16	*551	*348	§63.2	*4030	§25	10	7.31	§92.8	44	153	3.5	0	0	...	0
1994—Denver NFL	14	14	494	307	62.1	3490	16	10	7.06	85.7	58	235	4.1	4	4	0	24
1995—Denver NFL	16	16	542	316	58.3	§3970	26	14	7.32	86.4	41	176	4.3	1	1	1	8
1996—Denver NFL	15	15	466	287	61.6	3328	26	14	7.14	§89.2	50	249	5.0	4	4	0	24
1997—Denver NFL	16	16	502	280	55.8	3635	27	11	7.24	87.5	50	218	4.4	1	1	0	6
1998—Denver NFL	13	12	356	210	59.0	2806	22	10	§7.88	93.0	37	94	2.5	1	1	0	6
Pro totals (16 years)	234	231	7250	4123	56.9	51475	300	226	7.10	79.9	774	3407	4.4	33	34	1	206

RECORD AS BASEBALL PLAYER

TRANSACTIONS//CAREER NOTES: Threw right, batted left. ... Selected by Kansas City Royals organization in 18th round of free-agent draft (June 5, 1979); did not sign. ... Selected by New York Yankees organization in second round of free-agent draft (June 8, 1981). ... On temporary inactive list (August 2-September 13, 1982). ... On suspended list (April 8-18, 1983). ... Placed on restricted list (April 18, 1983).

						BATTING							FIELDING		
Year Team (League)	Pos.	G	AB	R	H	2B	3B	HR	RBI	Avg.	BB	SO	SB	PO	A	E	Avg.
1982—Oneonta (NYP)	OF	42	151	26	48	6	2	4	25	.318	28	25	13	69	8	0	1.000

EMANUEL, BERT — WR — BUCCANEERS

PERSONAL: Born October 28, 1970, in Kansas City, Mo. ... 5-10/175. ... Full name: Bert Tyrone Emanuel.
HIGH SCHOOL: Langham Creek (Houston).
COLLEGE: UCLA, then Rice (degree in business, 1993).
TRANSACTIONS/CAREER NOTES: Selected by Atlanta Falcons in second round (45th pick overall) of 1994 NFL draft. ... Signed by Falcons (July 11, 1994). ... Granted free agency (February 14, 1997). ... Re-signed by Falcons (July 16, 1997). ... Designated by Falcons as transition player (February 13, 1998). ... Tendered offer sheet by Tampa Bay Buccaneers (April 10, 1998). ... Falcons declined to match offer (April 14, 1998).
PRO STATISTICS: 1994—Rushed twice for four yards and had only pass attempt intercepted. 1995—Rushed once for no yards. 1997—Recovered two fumbles. 1998—Rushed once for 11 yards.
SINGLE GAME HIGHS (regular season): Receptions—9 (December 15, 1996, vs. St. Louis); yards—173 (December 15, 1996, vs. St. Louis); and touchdown receptions—2 (November 2, 1997, vs. St. Louis).

STATISTICAL PLATEAUS: 100-yard receiving games: 1994 (1), 1995 (4), 1996 (3), 1997 (1), 1998 (1). Total: 10.
MISCELLANEOUS: Selected by Toronto Blue Jays organization in 75th round of free-agent baseball draft (June 5, 1989); did not sign. ... Selected by Pittsburgh Pirates organization in 49th round of free-agent baseball draft (June 1, 1992); did not sign.

				RECEIVING				TOTALS		
Year Team	G	GS	No.	Yds.	Avg.	TD	TD	2pt.	Pts.	Fum.
1994—Atlanta NFL	16	16	46	649	14.1	4	4	0	24	0
1995—Atlanta NFL	16	16	74	1039	14.0	5	5	0	30	2
1996—Atlanta NFL	14	13	75	921	12.3	6	6	0	36	0
1997—Atlanta NFL	16	16	65	991	15.2	9	9	0	54	2
1998—Tampa Bay NFL	11	11	41	636	15.5	2	2	0	12	0
Pro totals (5 years)	73	72	301	4236	14.1	26	26	0	156	4

EMMONS, CARLOS   LB   STEELERS

PERSONAL: Born September 3, 1973, in Greenwood, Miss. ... 6-5/250. ... Name pronounced EM-mins.
HIGH SCHOOL: Greenwood (Miss.).
COLLEGE: Arkansas State (degree in business management, 1995).
TRANSACTIONS/CAREER NOTES: Selected by Pittsburgh Steelers in seventh round (242nd pick overall) of 1996 NFL draft. ... Signed by Steelers (July 16, 1996). ... Granted free agency (February 12, 1999). ... Re-signed by Steelers (April 26, 1999).
CHAMPIONSHIP GAME EXPERIENCE: Played in AFC championship game (1997 season).
PRO STATISTICS: 1996—Recovered one fumble. 1998—Intercepted one pass for two yards and recovered one fumble.

Year Team	G	GS	SACKS
1996—Pittsburgh NFL	15	0	2.5
1997—Pittsburgh NFL	5	0	0.0
1998—Pittsburgh NFL	15	13	3.5
Pro totals (3 years)	35	13	6.0

ENGLER, DEREK   C   GIANTS

PERSONAL: Born July 11, 1974, in St. Paul, Minn. ... 6-5/300.
HIGH SCHOOL: Cretin-Derham Hall (St. Paul, Minn.).
COLLEGE: Wisconsin.
TRANSACTIONS/CAREER NOTES: Signed as non-drafted free agent by New York Giants (April 28, 1997).
PLAYING EXPERIENCE: New York Giants NFL, 1997 and 1998. ... Games/Games started: 1997 (5/5), 1998 (11/0). Total: 16/5.
PRO STATISTICS: 1997—Fumbled once for minus two yards.

ENGRAM, BOBBY   WR   BEARS

PERSONAL: Born January 7, 1973, in Camden, S.C. ... 5-10/192. ... Full name: Simon Engram III.
HIGH SCHOOL: Camden (S.C.).
COLLEGE: Penn State.
TRANSACTIONS/CAREER NOTES: Selected by Chicago Bears in second round (52nd pick overall) of 1996 NFL draft. ... Signed by Bears (July 17, 1996). ... Granted free agency (February 12, 1999). ... Re-signed by Bears (April 16, 1999).
HONORS: Named wide receiver on THE SPORTING NEWS college All-America second team (1994 and 1995).
PRO STATISTICS: 1997—Recovered one fumble. 1998—Rushed once for three yards.
SINGLE GAME HIGHS (regular season): Receptions—9 (December 6, 1998, vs. Minnesota); yards—142 (October 11, 1998, vs. Arizona); and touchdown receptions—2 (September 27, 1998, vs. Minnesota).
STATISTICAL PLATEAUS: 100-yard receiving games: 1998 (3).

			RECEIVING				PUNT RETURNS				KICKOFF RETURNS			TOTALS			
Year Team	G	GS	No.	Yds.	Avg.	TD	No.	Yds.	Avg.	TD	No.	Yds.	Avg.	TD	TD	2pt.	Pts.	Fum.
1996—Chicago NFL	16	2	33	389	11.8	6	31	282	9.1	0	25	580	23.2	0	6	0	36	2
1997—Chicago NFL	11	11	45	399	8.9	2	1	4	4.0	0	2	27	13.5	0	2	1	14	1
1998—Chicago NFL	16	16	64	987	15.4	5	0	0	...	0	0	0	...	0	5	0	30	1
Pro totals (3 years)	43	29	142	1775	12.5	13	32	286	8.9	0	27	607	22.5	0	13	1	80	4

ENIS, CURTIS   RB   BEARS

PERSONAL: Born June 15, 1976, in Union City, Ohio. ... 6-0/242. ... Full name: Curtis D. Enis.
HIGH SCHOOL: Mississinawa Valley (Union City, Ohio), then Kiski Prep (Saltsburg, Pa.).
COLLEGE: Penn State.
TRANSACTIONS/CAREER NOTES: Selected after junior season by Chicago Bears in first round (fifth pick overall) of 1998 NFL draft. ... Signed by Bears (August 18, 1998). ... On injured reserve with knee injury (November 11, 1998-remainder of season).
HONORS: Named running back on THE SPORTING NEWS college All-America second team (1997).
SINGLE GAME HIGHS (regular season): Attempts—22 (September 13, 1998, vs. Pittsburgh); yards—94 (September 13, 1998, vs. Pittsburgh); and rushing touchdowns—0.

			RUSHING				RECEIVING				TOTALS			
Year Team	G	GS	Att.	Yds.	Avg.	TD	No.	Yds.	Avg.	TD	TD	2pt.	Pts.	Fum.
1998—Chicago NFL	9	1	133	497	3.7	0	6	20	3.3	0	0	0	0	1

ERICKSON, CRAIG   QB   DOLPHINS

PERSONAL: Born May 17, 1969, in Boynton Beach, Fla. ... 6-2/215. ... Full name: Craig Neil Erickson.
HIGH SCHOOL: Cardinal Newman (West Palm Beach, Fla.).

COLLEGE: Miami, Fla. (degree in business).
TRANSACTIONS/CAREER NOTES: Selected by Philadelphia Eagles in fifth round (131st pick overall) of 1991 NFL draft; did not sign. ... Selected by Tampa Bay Buccaneers in fourth round (86th pick overall) of 1992 NFL draft. ... Signed by Buccaneers (July 10, 1992). ... Granted free agency (February 17, 1995). ... Re-signed by Buccaneers (April 26, 1995). ... Traded by Buccaneers to Indianapolis Colts for first-round (DT Marcus Jones) in 1996 draft (April 26, 1995). ... Released by Colts (August 25, 1996). ... Signed by Miami Dolphins (September 2, 1996). ... Granted unconditional free agency (February 13, 1998). ... Re-signed by Dolphins (March 5, 1998). ... Active for seven games (1998); did not play. ... On injured reserve with elbow injury (October 28, 1998-remainder of season).
CHAMPIONSHIP GAME EXPERIENCE: Member of Colts for AFC championship game (1995 season); did not play.
PRO STATISTICS: 1993—Fumbled nine times and recovered six fumbles for minus two yards. 1994—Fumbled six times and recovered one fumble for minus one yard. 1995—Fumbled twice for minus four yards. 1996—Fumbled four times and recovered three fumbles for minus three yards. 1997—Fumbled twice and recovered two fumbles for minus 13 yards.
SINGLE GAME HIGHS (regular season): Attempts—41 (January 2, 1994, vs. San Diego); completions—22 (November 20, 1994, vs. Seattle); yards—318 (October 31, 1993, vs. Atlanta); and touchdown passes—4 (October 31, 1993, vs. Atlanta).
STATISTICAL PLATEAUS: 300-yard passing games: 1993 (1), 1994 (1). Total: 2.
MISCELLANEOUS: Graduate assistant football coach, University of Georgia (1991). ... Started one game at wide receiver (1994). ... Regular-season record as starting NFL quarterback: 14-21 (.400).

					PASSING						RUSHING				TOTALS	
Year Team	G	GS	Att.	Cmp.	Pct.	Yds.	TD	Int.	Avg.	Rat.	Att.	Yds.	Avg.	TD	TD	2pt.	Pts.
1992—Tampa Bay NFL	6	0	26	15	57.7	121	0	0	4.65	69.6	1	-1	-1.0	0	0	...	0
1993—Tampa Bay NFL	16	15	457	233	51.0	3054	18	21	6.68	66.4	26	96	3.7	0	0	...	0
1994—Tampa Bay NFL	15	15	399	225	56.4	2919	16	10	7.32	82.5	26	68	2.6	1	1	0	6
1995—Indianapolis NFL	6	3	83	50	60.2	586	3	4	7.06	73.7	9	14	1.6	0	0	0	0
1996—Miami NFL	7	3	99	55	55.6	780	4	2	7.88	86.3	11	16	1.5	0	0	0	0
1997—Miami NFL	2	0	28	13	46.4	165	0	1	5.89	50.4	4	8	2.0	0	0	0	0
1998—Miami NFL						Did not play.											
Pro totals (6 years)	52	36	1092	591	54.1	7625	41	38	6.98	74.3	77	201	2.6	1	1	0	6

EVANS, CHUCK — FB — RAVENS

PERSONAL: Born April 16, 1967, in Augusta, Ga. ... 6-1/245. ... Full name: Charles Evans Jr.
HIGH SCHOOL: Glenn Hills (Augusta, Ga.).
COLLEGE: Clark Atlanta University.
TRANSACTIONS/CAREER NOTES: Selected by Minnesota Vikings in 11th round (295th pick overall) of 1992 NFL draft. ... Signed by Vikings (June 10, 1992). ... Released by Vikings (August 31, 1992). ... Re-signed by Vikings (February 10, 1993). ... On injured reserve with wrist injury (October 11, 1993-remainder of season). ... Granted free agency (February 16, 1996). ... Re-signed by Vikings (May 9, 1996). ... Granted unconditional free agency (February 14, 1997). ... Re-signed by Vikings (April 11, 1997). ... Granted unconditional free agency (February 12, 1999). ... Signed by Baltimore Ravens (February 17, 1999).
CHAMPIONSHIP GAME EXPERIENCE: Played in NFC championship game (1998 season).
PRO STATISTICS: 1993—Returned one kickoff for 11 yards. 1994—Returned one kickoff for four yards. 1997—Recovered one fumble.
SINGLE GAME HIGHS (regular season): Attempts—10 (December 9, 1995, vs. Cleveland); yards—50 (November 9, 1997, vs. Chicago); and rushing touchdowns—1 (November 9, 1997, vs. Chicago).

			RUSHING				RECEIVING				TOTALS		
Year Team	G	GS	Att.	Yds.	Avg.	TD	No.	Yds.	Avg.	TD	TD	2pt.	Pts.	Fum.
1993—Minnesota NFL	3	0	14	32	2.3	0	4	39	9.8	0	0	...	0	0
1994—Minnesota NFL	14	0	6	20	3.3	0	1	2	2.0	0	0	0	0	0
1995—Minnesota NFL	16	7	19	59	3.1	1	18	119	6.6	1	2	0	12	0
1996—Minnesota NFL	16	6	13	29	2.2	0	22	135	6.1	0	0	0	0	0
1997—Minnesota NFL	16	13	43	157	3.7	2	21	152	7.2	0	2	1	14	0
1998—Minnesota NFL	16	8	23	67	2.9	1	12	84	7.0	0	1	0	6	0
Pro totals (6 years)	81	34	118	364	3.1	4	78	531	6.8	1	5	1	32	0

EVANS, DOUG — CB — PANTHERS

PERSONAL: Born May 13, 1970, in Shreveport, La. ... 6-1/190. ... Full name: Douglas Edwards Evans. ... Brother of Bobby Evans, safety with Winnipeg Blue Bombers of the CFL (1990-94).
HIGH SCHOOL: Haynesville (La.).
COLLEGE: Louisiana Tech (degree in finance).
TRANSACTIONS/CAREER NOTES: Selected by Green Bay Packers in sixth round (141st pick overall) of 1993 NFL draft. ... Signed by Packers (July 9, 1993). ... Granted unconditional free agency (February 13, 1998). ... Signed by Carolina Panthers (February 18, 1998). ... On injured reserve with broken collarbone (November 10, 1998-remainder of season).
CHAMPIONSHIP GAME EXPERIENCE: Played in NFC championship game (1995-97 seasons). ... Member of Super Bowl championship team (1996 season). ... Played in Super Bowl XXXII (1997 season).
PRO STATISTICS: 1993—Recovered two fumbles. 1994—Recovered one fumble for three yards. 1995—Returned one punt for no yards and fumbled once. 1996—Fumbled once and recovered one fumble for two yards.

			INTERCEPTIONS				SACKS
Year Team	G	GS	No.	Yds.	Avg.	TD	No.
1993—Green Bay NFL	16	0	1	0	0.0	0	0.0
1994—Green Bay NFL	16	15	1	0	0.0	0	1.0
1995—Green Bay NFL	16	16	2	24	12.0	0	1.0
1996—Green Bay NFL	16	16	5	102	20.4	1	3.0
1997—Green Bay NFL	15	15	3	33	11.0	0	1.0
1998—Carolina NFL	9	7	2	18	9.0	0	0.0
Pro totals (6 years)	88	69	14	177	12.6	1	6.0

EVANS, GREG — S — REDSKINS

PERSONAL: Born June 28, 1971, in Daingerfield, Texas. ... 6-1/208. ... Full name: Gregory Evans.
HIGH SCHOOL: Daingerfield (Texas).
COLLEGE: Texas Christian (degree in criminal justice).
TRANSACTIONS/CAREER NOTES: Signed as non-drafted free agent by Buffalo Bills (May 19, 1994). ... Released by Bills (August 22, 1994). ... Re-signed by Bills to practice squad (August 29, 1994). ... Activated (December 24, 1994); did not play. ... Released by Bills (August 19, 1996). ... Signed by Washington Redskins (February 19, 1997). ... Assigned by Redskins to Frankfurt Galaxy in 1997 World League enhancement allocation program (February 19, 1997). ... Released by Redskins (August 21, 1997). ... Re-signed by Redskins (August 20, 1998). ... Released by Redskins (August 25, 1998). ... Re-signed by Redskins (September 23, 1998). ... Released by Redskins (October 29, 1998). ... Re-signed by Redskins (October 30, 1998).
PRO STATISTICS: 1995—Recovered one fumble for three yards. 1997—Credited with one sack. 1998—NFL: Recovered one fumble.

				INTERCEPTIONS		
Year Team	G	GS	No.	Yds.	Avg.	TD
1994—Buffalo NFL				Did not play.		
1995—Buffalo NFL	16	4	1	18	18.0	0
1996—				Did not play.		
1997—Frankfurt W.L.	...	...	4	45	11.3	0
1998—Frankfurt NFLE	...	...	3	52	17.3	0
—Washington NFL	13	0	0	0	...	0
NFL Europe totals (1 year)	...	...	3	52	17.3	0
W.L. totals (1 year)	...	...	4	45	11.3	0
NFL totals (2 years)	29	4	1	18	18.0	0
Pro totals (4 years)	...	...	8	115	14.4	0

EVANS, JOSH — DT/DE — TITANS

PERSONAL: Born September 6, 1972, in Langdale, Ala. ... 6-2/288. ... Full name: Mijoshki Antwon Evans.
HIGH SCHOOL: Lanett (Ala.).
COLLEGE: Alabama-Birmingham.
TRANSACTIONS/CAREER NOTES: Signed as non-drafted free agent by Dallas Cowboys (April 27, 1995). ... Released by Cowboys (August 22, 1995). ... Signed by Houston Oilers to practice squad (September 1, 1995). ... Activated (November 10, 1995). ... On injured reserve with knee injury (November 29, 1996-remainder of season). ... Oilers franchise moved to Tennessee for 1997 season. ... Granted free agency (February 13, 1998). ... Re-signed by Oilers (July 25, 1998). ... Oilers franchise renamed Tennessee Titans for 1999 season (December 26, 1998).
PLAYING EXPERIENCE: Houston NFL, 1995 and 1996; Tennessee NFL, 1997 and 1998. ... Games/Games started: 1995 (7/0), 1996 (8/0), 1997 (15/0), 1998 (14/11). Total: 44/11.
PRO STATISTICS: 1997—Credited with two sacks and recovered one fumble. 1998—Credited with $3^1/_2$ sacks.

EVANS, LEOMONT — S — REDSKINS

PERSONAL: Born July 12, 1974, in Abbeville, S.C. ... 6-1/202.
HIGH SCHOOL: Abbeville (S.C.).
COLLEGE: Clemson.
TRANSACTIONS/CAREER NOTES: Selected by Washington Redskins in fifth round (138th pick overall) of 1996 NFL draft. ... Signed by Redskins (June 4, 1996). ... Granted free agency (February 12, 1999). ... Re-signed by Redskins (March 2, 1999).
PLAYING EXPERIENCE: Washington NFL, 1996-1998. ... Games/Games started: 1996 (12/0), 1997 (16/0), 1998 (16/13). Total: 44/13.
PRO STATISTICS: 1997—Recovered one fumble. 1998—Intercepted three passes for 77 yards and credited with one sack.

EVERITT, STEVE — C — EAGLES

PERSONAL: Born August 21, 1970, in Miami. ... 6-5/310. ... Full name: Steven Michael Everitt.
HIGH SCHOOL: Southridge (Miami).
COLLEGE: Michigan (degree in fine arts, 1993).
TRANSACTIONS/CAREER NOTES: Selected by Cleveland Browns in first round (14th pick overall) of 1993 NFL draft. ... Signed by Browns (July 15, 1993). ... Designated by Browns as transition player (February 15, 1994). ... Browns franchise moved to Baltimore and renamed Ravens for 1996 season (March 11, 1996). ... Free agency status changed by Ravens from transitional to unconditional (February 14, 1997). ... Signed by Philadelphia Eagles (March 6, 1997).
PLAYING EXPERIENCE: Cleveland NFL, 1993-1995; Baltimore NFL, 1996; Philadelphia NFL, 1997 and 1998. ... Games/Games started: 1993 (16/16), 1994 (15/15), 1995 (15/14), 1996 (8/7), 1997 (16/16), 1998 (13/13). Total: 83/81.
HONORS: Named center on The Sporting News college All-America second team (1992).
PRO STATISTICS: 1993—Recovered two fumbles. 1995—Recovered one fumble. 1997—Recovered one fumble.

FABINI, JASON — OT — JETS

PERSONAL: Born August 25, 1974, in Fort Wayne, Ind. ... 6-7/312.
HIGH SCHOOL: Bishop Dwenger (Fort Wayne, Ind.).
COLLEGE: Cincinnati.
TRANSACTIONS/CAREER NOTES: Selected by New York Jets in fourth round (111th pick overall) of 1998 NFL draft. ... Signed by Jets (July 13, 1998).
PLAYING EXPERIENCE: New York Jets NFL, 1998. ... Games/Games started: 16/16.
CHAMPIONSHIP GAME EXPERIENCE: Played in AFC championship game (1998 season).

FAIR, TERRY   CB   LIONS

PERSONAL: Born July 20, 1976, in Phoenix. ... 5-9/185. ... Full name: Terrance Delon Fair.
HIGH SCHOOL: South Mountain (Phoenix).
COLLEGE: Tennessee.
TRANSACTIONS/CAREER NOTES: Selected by Detroit Lions in first round (20th pick overall) of 1998 NFL draft. ... Signed by Lions (July 20, 1998).
HONORS: Named kick returner on THE SPORTING NEWS NFL All-Pro team (1998).
PRO STATISTICS: 1998—Credited with one sack and recovered one fumble.

				PUNT RETURNS			KICKOFF RETURNS			TOTALS			
Year Team	G	GS	No.	Yds.	Avg.	TD	No.	Yds.	Avg.	TD	TD	2pt.	Pts.	Fum.
1998—Detroit NFL	14	10	30	189	6.3	0	51	1428	*28.0	†2	2	0	12	5

FANECA, ALAN   G   STEELERS

PERSONAL: Born December 7, 1976, in New Orleans. ... 6-4/315. ... Full name: Alan Joseph Faneca Jr. ... Name pronounced FAN-ee-ka.
HIGH SCHOOL: John Curtis (New Orleans), then Lamar (Houston).
COLLEGE: Louisiana State.
TRANSACTIONS/CAREER NOTES: Selected after junior season by Pittsburgh Steelers in first round (26th pick overall) of 1998 NFL draft. ... Signed by Steelers (July 29, 1998).
PLAYING EXPERIENCE: Pittsburgh NFL, 1998. ... Games/Games started: 16/12.
HONORS: Named guard on THE SPORTING NEWS college All-America first team (1997).

FANN, CHAD   TE   49ERS

PERSONAL: Born June 7, 1970, in Jacksonville. ... 6-3/256. ... Full name: Chad Fitzgerald Fann.
HIGH SCHOOL: Jean Ribault (Jacksonville).
COLLEGE: Mississippi, then Florida A&M.
TRANSACTIONS/CAREER NOTES: Signed as non-drafted free agent by Phoenix Cardinals (April 28, 1993). ... Released by Cardinals (August 23, 1993). ... Re-signed by Cardinals to practice squad (October 24, 1993). ... Activated (November 4, 1993). ... Cardinals franchise renamed Arizona Cardinals for 1994 season. ... Granted free agency (February 16, 1996). ... Signed by San Francisco 49ers (June 11, 1996). ... Released by 49ers (August 21, 1996). ... Re-signed by 49ers (January 29, 1997). ... Granted unconditional free agency (February 13, 1998). ... Re-signed by 49ers (June 1, 1998). ... Granted unconditional free agency (February 12, 1999). ... Re-signed by 49ers (March 2, 1999).
CHAMPIONSHIP GAME EXPERIENCE: Played in NFC championship game (1997 season).
PRO STATISTICS: 1997—Returned one kickoff for no yards.
SINGLE GAME HIGHS (regular season): Receptions—6 (November 27, 1994, vs. Chicago); yards—50 (December 21, 1997, vs. Seattle); and touchdown receptions—0.

			RECEIVING				TOTALS			
Year Team	G	GS	No.	Yds.	Avg.	TD	TD	2pt.	Pts.	Fum.
1993—Phoenix NFL	1	0	0	0	...	0	0	...	0	0
1994—Arizona NFL	16	9	12	96	8.0	0	0	0	0	1
1995—Arizona NFL	16	3	5	41	8.2	0	0	0	0	1
1996—						Did not play.				
1997—San Francisco NFL	11	0	5	78	15.6	0	0	0	0	0
1998—San Francisco NFL	12	0	0	0	...	0	0	0	0	0
Pro totals (5 years)	56	12	22	215	9.8	0	0	0	0	2

FARMER, RAY   LB

PERSONAL: Born July 1, 1974, in White Plains, N.Y. ... 6-3/225.
HIGH SCHOOL: Glenn (Kernersville, N.C.).
COLLEGE: Duke (degree in sociology, 1995).
TRANSACTIONS/CAREER NOTES: Selected by Philadelphia Eagles in fourth round (121st pick overall) of 1996 NFL draft. ... Signed by Eagles (June 20, 1996). ... Released by Eagles (September 17, 1998). ... Signed by Carolina Panthers (February 16, 1999). ... Released by Panthers (April 1, 1999).
PLAYING EXPERIENCE: Philadelphia NFL, 1996-1998. ... Games/Games started: 1996 (16/11), 1997 (14/5), 1998 (2/0). Total: 32/16.
PRO STATISTICS: 1996—Intercepted one pass for no yards, credited with one sack, fumbled once and recovered three fumbles for 10 yards. 1997—Credited with one sack and recovered one fumble.
MISCELLANEOUS: Selected by Seattle Mariners in 26th round of free-agent draft (June 1, 1992); did not sign. ...

FARQUHAR, JOHN   TE   SAINTS

PERSONAL: Born March 22, 1972, in Menlo, Calif. ... 6-6/278. ... Full name: John Christian Mowat Farquhar. ... Name pronounced far-QUAR.
HIGH SCHOOL: Menlo (Calif.).
COLLEGE: Duke.
TRANSACTIONS/CAREER NOTES: Signed as non-drafted free agent by Denver Broncos (April 28, 1995). ... Released by Broncos (May 25, 1995). ... Signed by Pittsburgh Steelers (February 29, 1996). ... Released by Steelers (August 24, 1996). ... Re-signed by Steelers to practice squad (August 27, 1996). ... Released by Steelers (October 23, 1996). ... Signed by Tampa Bay Buccaneers (October 23, 1996). ... Released by Buccaneers (November 12, 1996). ... Signed by Steelers to practice squad (November 18, 1996). ... Activated (November 29, 1996). ... Released by Steelers (August 23, 1997). ... Signed by New Orleans Saints (September 8, 1997). ... On physically unable to perform list with ankle injury (August 30-November 4, 1998). ... Granted free agency (February 12, 1999).
SINGLE GAME HIGHS (regular season): Receptions—4 (October 12, 1997, vs. Atlanta); yards—82 (September 28, 1997, vs. New York Giants); and touchdown receptions—1 (December 14, 1997, vs. Arizona).

Year Team	G	GS	RECEIVING No.	Yds.	Avg.	TD	TOTALS TD	2pt.	Pts.	Fum.
1996—Tampa Bay NFL	1	0	0	0	...	0	0	0	0	0
—Pittsburgh NFL	4	0	0	0	...	0	0	0	0	0
1997—New Orleans NFL	12	8	17	253	14.9	1	1	0	6	0
1998—New Orleans NFL	5	0	1	13	13.0	0	0	0	0	0
Pro totals (3 years)	22	8	18	266	14.8	1	1	0	6	0

FARR, D'MARCO   DT   RAMS

PERSONAL: Born June 9, 1971, in San Pablo, Calif. ... 6-1/280. ... Full name: D'Marco Marcellus Farr.
HIGH SCHOOL: John F. Kennedy (Richmond, Calif.).
COLLEGE: Washington (degree in society and justice, 1993).
TRANSACTIONS/CAREER NOTES: Signed as non-drafted free agent by Los Angeles Rams (May 4, 1994). ... On injured reserve with dislocated left elbow (December 7, 1994-remainder of season). ... Rams franchise moved to St. Louis (April 12, 1995).
PRO STATISTICS: 1994—Returned one kickoff for 16 yards. 1995—Intercepted one pass for five yards. 1996—Intercepted one pass for five yards. 1997—Intercepted one pass for 22 yards and recovered two fumbles. 1998—Recovered one fumble for 18 yards.

Year Team	G	GS	SACKS
1994—Los Angeles Rams NFL	10	3	1.0
1995—St. Louis NFL	16	16	11.5
1996—St. Louis NFL	16	16	4.5
1997—St. Louis NFL	16	16	3.0
1998—St. Louis NFL	16	16	7.0
Pro totals (5 years)	74	67	27.0

FARRIOR, JAMES   LB   JETS

PERSONAL: Born January 6, 1975, in Ettrick, Va. ... 6-2/242. ... Full name: James Alfred Farrior.
HIGH SCHOOL: Matoaca (Ettrick, Va.).
COLLEGE: Virginia.
TRANSACTIONS/CAREER NOTES: Selected by New York Jets in first round (eighth pick overall) of 1997 NFL draft. ... Signed by Jets (July 20, 1997).
CHAMPIONSHIP GAME EXPERIENCE: Played in AFC championship game (1998 season).
PRO STATISTICS: 1998—Recovered one fumble.

Year Team	G	GS	SACKS
1997—New York Jets NFL	16	15	1.5
1998—New York Jets NFL	12	2	0.0
Pro totals (2 years)	28	17	1.5

FAULK, MARSHALL   RB   RAMS

PERSONAL: Born February 26, 1973, in New Orleans. ... 5-10/211. ... Full name: Marshall William Faulk.
HIGH SCHOOL: George Washington Carver (New Orleans).
COLLEGE: San Diego State.
TRANSACTIONS/CAREER NOTES: Selected after junior season by Indianapolis Colts in first round (second pick overall) of 1994 NFL draft. ... Signed by Colts (July 24, 1994). ... Traded by Colts to St. Louis Rams for second- (LB Mike Peterson) and fifth-round (DE Brad Scioli) picks in 1999 draft (April 15, 1999).
CHAMPIONSHIP GAME EXPERIENCE: Member of Colts for AFC championship game (1995 season); inactive due to injury.
HONORS: Named running back on THE SPORTING NEWS college All-America first team (1991-1993). ... Named NFL Rookie of the Year by THE SPORTING NEWS (1994). ... Played in Pro Bowl (1994, 1995 and 1998 seasons). ... Named Outstanding Player of Pro Bowl (1994 season).
PRO STATISTICS: 1994—Recovered one fumble. 1995—Recovered one fumble. 1997—Recovered one fumble. 1998—Recovered two fumbles for 13 yards.
SINGLE GAME HIGHS (regular season): Attempts—29 (September 13, 1998, vs. New England); yards—192 (November 29, 1998, vs. Baltimore); and rushing touchdowns—3 (October 1, 1995, vs. St. Louis).
STATISTICAL PLATEAUS: 100-yard rushing games: 1994 (4), 1995 (1), 1996 (1), 1997 (3), 1998 (4). Total: 14. ... 100-yard receiving games: 1994 (1), 1998 (3). Total: 4.

Year Team	G	GS	RUSHING Att.	Yds.	Avg.	TD	RECEIVING No.	Yds.	Avg.	TD	TOTALS TD	2pt.	Pts.	Fum.
1994—Indianapolis NFL	16	16	314	1282	4.1	11	52	522	10.0	1	▲12	0	72	5
1995—Indianapolis NFL	16	16	289	1078	3.7	11	56	475	8.5	3	14	0	84	8
1996—Indianapolis NFL	13	13	198	587	3.0	7	56	428	7.6	0	7	0	42	2
1997—Indianapolis NFL	16	16	264	1054	4.0	7	47	471	10.0	1	8	0	48	5
1998—Indianapolis NFL	16	15	324	1319	4.1	6	86	908	10.6	4	10	0	60	3
Pro totals (5 years)	77	76	1389	5320	3.8	42	297	2804	9.4	9	51	0	306	23

FAURIA, CHRISTIAN   TE   SEAHAWKS

PERSONAL: Born September 22, 1971, in Harbor City, Calif. ... 6-4/245. ... Name pronounced FOUR-ee-a.
HIGH SCHOOL: Crespi Carmelite (Encino, Calif.).
COLLEGE: Colorado (degree in communications, 1995).
TRANSACTIONS/CAREER NOTES: Selected by Seattle Seahawks in second round (39th pick overall) of 1995 NFL draft. ... Signed by Seahawks (July 17, 1995). ... Granted free agency (February 13, 1998). ... Re-signed by Seahawks (April 20, 1998). ... Granted unconditional free agency (February 12, 1999). ... Re-signed by Seahawks (March 5, 1999).
PRO STATISTICS: 1996—Returned one kickoff for eight yards. 1998—Returned one kickoff for no yards and recovered one fumble.
SINGLE GAME HIGHS (regular season): Receptions—5 (December 27, 1998, vs. Denver); yards—67 (December 27, 1998, vs. Denver); and touchdown receptions—1 (November 15, 1998, vs. Oakland).

Year Team	G	GS	RECEIVING No.	Yds.	Avg.	TD	TOTALS TD	2pt.	Pts.	Fum.
1995—Seattle NFL	14	9	17	181	10.6	1	1	0	6	0
1996—Seattle NFL	10	9	18	214	11.9	1	1	0	6	0
1997—Seattle NFL	16	3	10	110	11.0	0	0	0	0	0
1998—Seattle NFL	16	15	37	377	10.2	2	2	0	12	1
Pro totals (4 years)	56	36	82	882	10.8	4	4	0	24	1

FAVORS, GREGORY — LB — CHIEFS

PERSONAL: Born September 30, 1974, in Atlanta. ... 6-1/236. ... Full name: Gregory Bernard Favors.
HIGH SCHOOL: Southside (Atlanta).
COLLEGE: Mississippi State (degree in correction, 1997).
TRANSACTIONS/CAREER NOTES: Selected by Kansas City Chiefs in fourth round (120th pick overall) of 1998 NFL draft. ... Signed by Chiefs (July 17, 1998).
PRO STATISTICS: 1998—Recovered one fumble for 41 yards.

Year Team	G	GS	SACKS
1998—Kansas City NFL	16	4	2.0

FAVRE, BRETT — QB — PACKERS

PERSONAL: Born October 10, 1969, in Gulfport, Miss. ... 6-2/230. ... Full name: Brett Lorenzo Favre. ... Name pronounced FAHRV.
HIGH SCHOOL: Hancock North Central (Kiln, Miss.).
COLLEGE: Southern Mississippi.
TRANSACTIONS/CAREER NOTES: Selected by Atlanta Falcons in second round (33rd pick overall) of 1991 NFL draft. ... Signed by Falcons (July 18, 1991). ... Traded by Falcons to Green Bay Packers for first-round pick (OT Bob Whitfield) in 1992 draft (February 11, 1992). ... Granted free agency (February 17, 1994). ... Re-signed by Packers (July 14, 1994).
CHAMPIONSHIP GAME EXPERIENCE: Played in NFC championship game (1995-97 seasons). ... Member of Super Bowl championship team (1996 season). ... Played in Super Bowl XXXII (1997 season).
HONORS: Played in Pro Bowl (1992, 1993, 1995 and 1996 seasons). ... Named NFL Player of the Year by THE SPORTING NEWS (1995 and 1996). ... Named quarterback on THE SPORTING NEWS NFL All-Pro team (1995-97). ... Named to play in Pro Bowl (1997 season); replaced by Chris Chandler due to injury.
RECORDS: Shares NFL record for longest pass completion (to Robert Brooks)—99 yards, touchdown (September 11, 1995, at Chicago).
POST SEASON RECORDS: Holds Super Bowl record for longest pass completion (to Antonio Freeman)—81 yards (January 26, 1997, vs. New England).
PRO STATISTICS: 1992—Caught one pass for minus seven yards, fumbled 12 times and recovered three fumbles for minus 12 yards. 1993—Fumbled 12 times and recovered two fumbles for minus one yard. 1994—Fumbled seven times and recovered one fumble for minus two yards. 1995—Fumbled eight times. 1996—Fumbled 11 times and recovered five fumbles for minus 10 yards. 1997—Fumbled seven times and recovered one fumble for minus 10 yards. 1998—Fumbled eight times and recovered three fumbles for minus one yard.
SINGLE GAME HIGHS (regular season): Attempts—61 (October 14, 1996, vs. San Francisco); completions—36 (December 5, 1993, vs. Chicago); yards—402 (December 5, 1993, vs. Chicago); and touchdown passes—5 (September 27, 1998, vs. Carolina).
STATISTICAL PLATEAUS: 300-yard passing games: 1993 (1), 1994 (4), 1995 (7), 1996 (2), 1997 (2), 1998 (4). Total: 20.
MISCELLANEOUS: Regular-season record as starting NFL quarterback: 74-35 (.679). ... Postseason record as starting NFL quarterback: 9-5 (.643). ... Holds Green Bay Packers all-time records for most yards passing (26,803) and most touchdown passes (213).

Year Team	G	GS	PASSING Att.	Cmp.	Pct.	Yds.	TD	Int.	Avg.	Rat.	RUSHING Att.	Yds.	Avg.	TD	TOTALS TD	2pt.	Pts.
1991—Atlanta NFL	2	0	5	0	0.0	0	0	2	...	0.0	0	0	...	0	0	...	0
1992—Green Bay NFL	15	13	471	∞302	64.1	3227	18	13	6.85	85.3	47	198	4.2	1	1	...	6
1993—Green Bay NFL	16	16	‡522	‡318	60.9	3303	19	*24	6.33	72.2	58	216	3.7	1	1	...	6
1994—Green Bay NFL	16	16	582	363	62.4	3882	33	14	6.67	90.7	42	202	4.8	2	2	0	12
1995—Green Bay NFL	16	16	570	359	63.0	*4413	*38	13	‡7.74	‡99.5	39	181	4.6	3	3	0	18
1996—Green Bay NFL	16	16	‡543	‡325	59.9	‡3899	*39	13	7.18	95.8	49	136	2.8	2	2	0	12
1997—Green Bay NFL	16	16	513	‡304	59.3	‡3867	*35	16	7.54	92.6	58	187	3.2	1	1	0	6
1998—Green Bay NFL	16	16	‡551	*347	*63.0	*4212	31	‡23	7.64	87.8	40	133	3.3	1	1	0	6
Pro totals (8 years)	113	109	3757	2318	61.7	26803	213	118	7.13	89.0	333	1253	3.8	11	11	0	66

FEAGLES, JEFF — P — SEAHAWKS

PERSONAL: Born August 7, 1966, in Anaheim. ... 6-1/207. ... Full name: Jeffrey Allan Feagles.
HIGH SCHOOL: Gerard Catholic (Phoenix).
JUNIOR COLLEGE: Scottsdale (Ariz.) Community College.
COLLEGE: Miami, Fla. (degree in business administration, 1988).
TRANSACTIONS/CAREER NOTES: Signed as non-drafted free agent by New England Patriots (May 1, 1988). ... Claimed on waivers by Philadelphia Eagles (June 5, 1990). ... Granted unconditional free agency (February 1-April 1, 1992). ... Re-signed by Eagles for 1992 season. ... Granted unconditional free agency (February 17, 1994). ... Signed by Phoenix Cardinals (March 2, 1994). ... Cardinals franchise renamed Arizona Cardinals for 1994 season. ... Granted unconditional free agency (February 13, 1998). ... Signed by Seattle Seahawks (March 4, 1998).
HONORS: Played in Pro Bowl (1995 season).
PRO STATISTICS: 1988—Rushed once for no yards and recovered one fumble. 1989—Attempted two passes without a completion, fumbled once and recovered one fumble. 1990—Rushed twice for three yards and attempted one pass without a completion. 1991—Rushed three times for minus one yard, fumbled once and recovered one fumble. 1993—Rushed twice for six yards and recovered one fumble. 1994—Rushed twice for eight yards. 1995—Rushed twice for four yards and fumbled once for minus 22 yards. 1996—Rushed once for no yards and fumbled once for minus seven yards. 1997—Fumbled once and recovered one fumble.

					PUNTING			
Year Team	G	No.	Yds.	Avg.	Net avg.	In. 20	Blk.	
1988—New England NFL	16	▲91	3482	38.3	34.1	24	0	
1989—New England NFL	16	63	2392	38.0	31.3	13	1	
1990—Philadelphia NFL	16	72	3026	42.0	35.5	20	2	
1991—Philadelphia NFL	16	*87	3640	41.8	34.0	*29	1	
1992—Philadelphia NFL	16	‡82	‡3459	42.2	36.8	‡26	0	
1993—Philadelphia NFL	16	83	3323	40.0	35.2	*31	0	
1994—Arizona NFL	16	*98	‡3997	40.8	36.0	‡33	0	
1995—Arizona NFL	16	72	3150	43.8	‡38.2	20	0	
1996—Arizona NFL	16	76	3328	43.8	36.3	23	1	
1997—Arizona NFL	16	91	4028	44.3	36.8	24	1	
1998—Seattle NFL	16	81	3568	44.0	36.5	27	0	
Pro totals (11 years)	176	896	37393	41.7	35.6	270	6	

FERGUSON, JASON — DT — JETS

PERSONAL: Born November 28, 1974, in Nettleton, Miss. ... 6-3/305. ... Full name: Jason O. Ferguson. ... Cousin of Terance Mathis, wide receiver, Atlanta Falcons.
HIGH SCHOOL: Nettleton (Miss.).
JUNIOR COLLEGE: Itawamba Junior College (Miss.).
COLLEGE: Georgia.
TRANSACTIONS/CAREER NOTES: Selected by New York Jets in seventh round (229th pick overall) of 1997 NFL draft. ... Signed by Jets (April 30, 1997).
CHAMPIONSHIP GAME EXPERIENCE: Played in AFC championship game (1998 season).
PRO STATISTICS: 1997—Returned one kickoff for one yard.

Year Team	G	GS	SACKS
1997—New York Jets NFL	13	1	3.5
1998—New York Jets NFL	16	16	4.0
Pro totals (2 years)	29	17	7.5

FIALA, JOHN — LB — STEELERS

PERSONAL: Born November 25, 1973, in Fullerton, Calif. ... 6-2/235. ... Full name: John Charles Fiala. ... Name pronounced FEE-ah-lah.
HIGH SCHOOL: Lake Washington (Bellevue, Wash.).
COLLEGE: Washington.
TRANSACTIONS/CAREER NOTES: Selected by Miami Dolphins in sixth round (166th pick overall) of 1997 NFL draft. ... Signed by Dolphins (June 17, 1997). ... Released by Dolphins (July 31, 1997). ... Signed by Pittsburgh Steelers to practice squad (August 26, 1997).
PLAYING EXPERIENCE: Pittsburgh NFL, 1998. ... Games/Games started: 16/0.

FIEDLER, JAY — QB — JAGUARS

PERSONAL: Born December 29, 1971, in Oceanside, N.Y. ... 6-2/224.
HIGH SCHOOL: Oceanside (N.Y.).
COLLEGE: Dartmouth.
TRANSACTIONS/CAREER NOTES: Signed as non-drafted free agent by Philadelphia Eagles (April, 1994). ... Inactive for 16 games (1994). ... Claimed on waivers by Cincinnati Bengals (July 31, 1996). ... Released by Bengals (August 25, 1996). ... Played for Amsterdam Admirals of World League (1997). ... Signed by Minnesota Vikings (April 3, 1998). ... Released by Vikings (August 30, 1998). ... Re-signed by Vikings (September 15, 1998). ... Granted free agency (February 12, 1999). ... Signed by Jacksonville Jaguars (April 16, 1999).
CHAMPIONSHIP GAME EXPERIENCE: Member of Vikings for NFC championship game (1998 season); inactive.
SINGLE GAME HIGHS (regular season): Attempts—4 (October 18, 1998, vs. Washington); completions—2 (October 18, 1998, vs. Washington); yards—29 (October 18, 1998, vs. Washington); and touchdown passes—0.

			PASSING							RUSHING				TOTALS		
Year Team	G	GS	Att.	Cmp.	Pct.	Yds.	TD	Int.	Avg.	Rat.	Att.	Yds.	Avg.	TD	TD	2pt.	Pts.
1994—Philadelphia NFL							Did not play.										
1995—Philadelphia NFL	1	0	0	0	...	0	0	0	...	...	0	0	...	0	0	0	0
1996—							Did not play.										
1997—Amsterdam W.L.			109	46	42.2	678	2	8	6.22	38.7	16	93	5.8	0	0	...	0
1998—Minnesota NFL	5	0	7	3	42.9	41	0	1	5.86	22.6	4	-6	-1.5	0	0	0	0
W.L. totals (1 year)	...	...	109	46	42.2	678	2	8	6.22	38.7	16	93	5.8	0	0	...	0
NFL totals (2 years)	6	0	7	3	42.9	41	0	1	5.86	22.6	4	-6	-1.5	0	0	0	0
Pro totals (3 years)	...	...	116	49	42.2	719	2	9	6.20	36.5	20	87	4.4	0	0	0	0

FIELDS, MARK — LB — SAINTS

PERSONAL: Born November 9, 1972, in Los Angeles. ... 6-2/244. ... Full name: Mark Lee Fields.
HIGH SCHOOL: Washington (Cerritos, Calif.).
JUNIOR COLLEGE: Los Angeles Southwest Community College.
COLLEGE: Washington State.
TRANSACTIONS/CAREER NOTES: Selected by New Orleans Saints in first round (13th pick overall) of 1995 NFL draft. ... Signed by Saints (July 20, 1995).
PRO STATISTICS: 1996—Recovered one fumble for 20 yards. 1997—Recovered two fumbles for 28 yards and one touchdown. 1998—Recovered one fumble for 36 yards and a touchdown.

Year Team	G	GS	SACKS
1995—New Orleans NFL	16	3	1.0
1996—New Orleans NFL	16	15	2.0
1997—New Orleans NFL	16	15	8.0
1998—New Orleans NFL	15	15	6.0
Pro totals (4 years)	63	48	17.0

FIGURES, DEON — CB — JAGUARS

PERSONAL: Born January 20, 1970, in Bellflower, Calif. ... 6-0/192. ... Full name: Deon Juniel Figures.
HIGH SCHOOL: Skyline (Oakland).
COLLEGE: Colorado (degree in sociology and criminology, 1993).
TRANSACTIONS/CAREER NOTES: Selected by Pittsburgh Steelers in first round (23rd pick overall) of 1993 NFL draft. ... Signed by Steelers (July 21, 1993). ... Granted unconditional free agency (February 14, 1997). ... Signed by Jacksonville Jaguars (March 5, 1997).
CHAMPIONSHIP GAME EXPERIENCE: Played in AFC championship game (1994 and 1995 seasons). ... Played in Super Bowl XXX (1995 season).
HONORS: Jim Thorpe Award winner (1992). ... Named defensive back on THE SPORTING NEWS college All-America first team (1992).
PRO STATISTICS: 1993—Returned five punts for 15 yards and recovered two fumbles for six yards. 1994—Credited with one sack and recovered one fumble. 1996—Recovered one fumble.

			INTERCEPTIONS			
Year Team	G	GS	No.	Yds.	Avg.	TD
1993—Pittsburgh NFL	15	4	1	78	78.0	0
1994—Pittsburgh NFL	16	15	0	0	...	0
1995—Pittsburgh NFL	14	1	0	0	...	0
1996—Pittsburgh NFL	16	3	2	13	6.5	0
1997—Jacksonville NFL	16	12	5	48	9.6	0
1998—Jacksonville NFL	16	4	1	0	0.0	0
Pro totals (6 years)	93	39	9	139	15.4	0

FINA, JOHN — OT — BILLS

PERSONAL: Born March 11, 1969, in Rochester, Minn. ... 6-4/285. ... Full name: John Joseph Fina. ... Name pronounced FEE-nuh.
HIGH SCHOOL: Salpointe Catholic (Tucson, Ariz.).
COLLEGE: Arizona.
TRANSACTIONS/CAREER NOTES: Selected by Buffalo Bills in first round (27th pick overall) of 1992 NFL draft. ... Signed by Bills (July 21, 1992). ... Designated by Bills as franchise player (February 16, 1996).
PLAYING EXPERIENCE: Buffalo NFL, 1992-1998. ... Games/Games started: 1992 (16/0), 1993 (16/16), 1994 (12/12), 1995 (16/16), 1996 (15/15), 1997 (16/16), 1998 (14/14). Total: 105/89.
CHAMPIONSHIP GAME EXPERIENCE: Played in AFC championship game (1992 and 1993 seasons). ... Played in Super Bowl XXVII (1992 season) and Super Bowl XXVIII (1993 season).
PRO STATISTICS: 1992—Caught one pass for one yard and a touchdown. 1993—Rushed once for minus two yards. 1996—Recovered two fumbles for minus one yard. 1997—Recovered one fumble.

FIORE, DAVE — OT — 49ERS

PERSONAL: Born August 10, 1974, in Hackensack, N.J. ... 6-4/288. ... Full name: David Fiore.
HIGH SCHOOL: Waldwick (N.J.).
COLLEGE: Hofstra.
TRANSACTIONS/CAREER NOTES: Signed as non-drafted free agent by San Francisco 49ers (April 23, 1996). ... Claimed on waivers by New York Jets (October 14, 1996). ... Active for nine games (1996); did not play. ... Released by Jets (July 31, 1997). ... Signed by 49ers (August 1, 1997). ... On injured reserve with knee injury (August 19, 1997-entire season).
PLAYING EXPERIENCE: San Francisco NFL, 1998. ... Games/Games started: 9/3.

FISCHER, MARK — C — REDSKINS

PERSONAL: Born July 29, 1974, in Cincinnati. ... 6-3/293. ... Full name: Mark Raymond Fischer.
HIGH SCHOOL: LaSalle (Cincinnati).
COLLEGE: Purdue.
TRANSACTIONS/CAREER NOTES: Selected by Washington Redskins in fifth round (140th pick overall) of 1998 NFL draft. ... Signed by Redskins (May 26, 1998).
PLAYING EXPERIENCE: Washington NFL, 1998. ... Games/Games started: 6/0.

FISK, JASON — DT — TITANS

PERSONAL: Born September 4, 1972, in Davis, Calif. ... 6-3/295.
HIGH SCHOOL: Davis (Calif.).
COLLEGE: Stanford.
TRANSACTIONS/CAREER NOTES: Selected by Minnesota Vikings in seventh round (243rd pick overall) of 1995 NFL draft. ... Signed by Vikings (July 24, 1995). ... Granted unconditional free agency (February 12, 1999). ... Signed by Tennessee Titans (March 15, 1999).
CHAMPIONSHIP GAME EXPERIENCE: Played in NFC championship game (1998 season).
PRO STATISTICS: 1996—Intercepted one pass for no yards and recovered one fumble. 1997—Intercepted one pass for one yard and recovered one fumble. 1998—Recovered one fumble.

Year Team	G	GS	SACKS
1995—Minnesota NFL	8	0	...
1996—Minnesota NFL	16	6	1.0
1997—Minnesota NFL	16	10	3.0
1998—Minnesota NFL	16	0	1.5
Pro totals (4 years)	56	16	5.5

FLANAGAN, MIKE   C   PACKERS

PERSONAL: Born November 10, 1973, in Washington, D.C. ... 6-5/290. ... Full name: Michael Christopher Flanagan.
HIGH SCHOOL: Rio Americano (Sacramento).
COLLEGE: UCLA.
TRANSACTIONS/CAREER NOTES: Selected by Green Bay Packers in third round (90th pick overall) of 1996 NFL draft. ... Signed by Packers (July 17, 1996). ... On injured reserve with leg injury (August 19, 1996-entire season). ... On physically unable to perform list with ankle injury (August 19, 1997-entire season). ... Traded by Packers to Carolina Panthers for an undisclosed draft pick (August 31, 1998); trade later voided because Flanagan failed physical (September 1, 1998). ... Granted free agency (February 12, 1999). ... Re-signed by Packers (March 25, 1999).
PLAYING EXPERIENCE: Green Bay NFL, 1998. ... Games/Games started: 2/0.

FLANIGAN, JIM   DT   BEARS

PERSONAL: Born August 27, 1971, in Green Bay. ... 6-2/288. ... Full name: James Michael Flanigan. ... Son of Jim Flanigan, linebacker with Green Bay Packers (1967-70) and New Orleans Saints (1971).
HIGH SCHOOL: Southern Door (Brussels, Wis.).
COLLEGE: Notre Dame.
TRANSACTIONS/CAREER NOTES: Selected by Chicago Bears in third round (74th pick overall) of 1994 NFL draft. ... Signed by Bears (July 14, 1994). ... Granted free agency (February 14, 1997). ... Re-signed by Bears (June 1, 1997). ... Granted unconditional free agency (February 13, 1998). ... Re-signed by Bears (February 13, 1998).
PRO STATISTICS: 1994—Returned two kickoffs for 26 yards. 1995—Rushed once for no yards, caught two passes for six yards and two touchdowns and recovered one fumble. 1996—Caught one pass for one yard and a touchdown. 1997—Recovered three fumbles for three yards and credited with one two-point conversion. 1998—Recovered one fumble.

Year Team	G	GS	SACKS
1994—Chicago NFL	14	0	0.0
1995—Chicago NFL	16	12	11.0
1996—Chicago NFL	14	14	5.0
1997—Chicago NFL	16	16	6.0
1998—Chicago NFL	16	16	8.5
Pro totals (5 years)	76	58	30.5

FLANNERY, JOHN   C   RAMS

PERSONAL: Born January 13, 1969, in Pottsville, Pa. ... 6-4/295. ... Full name: John Joseph Flannery.
HIGH SCHOOL: Pottsville (Pa.) Area.
COLLEGE: Syracuse (degree in political science, 1991).
TRANSACTIONS/CAREER NOTES: Selected by Houston Oilers in second round (44th pick overall) of 1991 NFL draft. ... Signed by Oilers (July 21, 1991). ... On injured reserve with knee injury (August 23, 1993-entire season). ... Released by Oilers (August 8, 1995). ... Signed by Dallas Cowboys (October 3, 1996). ... Granted unconditional free agency (February 13, 1998). ... Signed by St. Louis Rams (April 2, 1998).
PLAYING EXPERIENCE: Houston NFL, 1991, 1992 and 1994; Dallas NFL, 1996 and 1997; St. Louis NFL, 1998. ... Games/Games started: 1991 (16/9), 1992 (15/2), 1994 (16/16), 1996 (1/0), 1997 (16/4), 1998 (16/15). Total: 80/46.
HONORS: Named center on THE SPORTING NEWS college All-America first team (1990).
PRO STATISTICS: 1991—Returned one kickoff for no yards and recovered one fumble. 1992—Returned one kickoff for 12 yards and recovered two fumbles. 1994—Recovered two fumbles. 1998—Caught one pass for two yards and fumbled twice for minus five yards.

FLETCHER, LONDON   LB   RAMS

PERSONAL: Born May 19, 1975, in Cleveland. ... 6-0/241. ... Full name: London Levi Fletcher.
HIGH SCHOOL: Villa Angela-St. Joseph (Cleveland).
COLLEGE: John Carroll (degree in sociology).
TRANSACTIONS/CAREER NOTES: Signed as non-drafted free agent by St. Louis Rams (April 28, 1998).
PLAYING EXPERIENCE: St. Louis NFL, 1998. ... Games/Games started: 16/1.
PRO STATISTICS: 1998—Returned five kickoffs for 72 yards and fumbled once.

FLETCHER, TERRELL   RB   CHARGERS

PERSONAL: Born September 14, 1973, in St. Louis. ... 5-8/196. ... Full name: Terrell Antoine Fletcher.
HIGH SCHOOL: Hazelwood East (St. Louis).
COLLEGE: Wisconsin (degree in English, 1994).
TRANSACTIONS/CAREER NOTES: Selected by San Diego Chargers in second round (51st pick overall) of 1995 NFL draft. ... Signed by Chargers (July 12, 1995). ... On injured reserve with knee injury (December 17, 1997-remainder of season). ... Granted free agency (February 13, 1998). ... Re-signed by Chargers (June 1998).
PRO STATISTICS: 1995—Fumbled twice and recovered two fumbles. 1996—Fumbled once and recovered one fumble. 1997—Fumbled four times. 1998—Attempted one pass with a completion for 23 yards and a touchdown, fumbled once and recovered two fumbles for 21 yards.

SINGLE GAME HIGHS (regular season): Attempts—34 (December 6, 1998, vs. Washington); yards—127 (December 27, 1998, vs. Arizona); and rushing touchdowns—2 (November 22, 1998, vs. Kansas City).
STATISTICAL PLATEAUS: 100-yard rushing games: 1998 (2).

			RUSHING				RECEIVING				PUNT RETURNS				KICKOFF RETURNS				TOTALS		
Year Team	G	GS	Att.	Yds.	Avg.	TD	No.	Yds.	Avg.	TD	No.	Yds.	Avg.	TD	No.	Yds.	Avg.	TD	TD	2pt.	Pts.
1995—San Diego NFL	16	0	26	140	5.4	1	3	26	8.7	0	3	12	4.0	0	4	65	16.3	0	1	0	6
1996—San Diego NFL	16	0	77	282	3.7	0	61	476	7.8	2	0	0	...	0	0	0	...	0	2	0	12
1997—San Diego NFL	13	1	51	161	3.2	0	39	292	7.5	0	0	0	...	0	0	0	...	0	0	0	0
1998—San Diego NFL	12	5	153	543	3.5	5	30	188	6.3	0	0	0	...	0	3	71	23.7	0	5	0	30
Pro totals (4 years)	57	6	307	1126	3.7	6	133	982	7.4	2	3	12	4.0	0	7	136	19.4	0	8	0	48

FLOWERS, LEE S STEELERS

PERSONAL: Born January 14, 1973, in Columbia, S.C. ... 6-0/211. ... Full name: Lethon Flowers III. ... Name pronounced LEE-thon.
HIGH SCHOOL: Spring Valley (Columbia, S.C.).
COLLEGE: Georgia Tech.
TRANSACTIONS/CAREER NOTES: Selected by Pittsburgh Steelers in fifth round (151st pick overall) of 1995 NFL draft. ... Signed by Steelers (July 18, 1995). ... Granted free agency (February 13, 1998). ... Re-signed by Steelers (June 9, 1998). ... Granted unconditional free agency (February 12, 1999). ... Re-signed by Steelers (February 16, 1999).
PLAYING EXPERIENCE: Pittsburgh NFL, 1995-1998. ... Games/Games started: 1995 (10/0), 1996 (16/0), 1997 (10/0), 1998 (16/16). Total: 52/16.
CHAMPIONSHIP GAME EXPERIENCE: Played in AFC championship game (1995 and 1997 seasons). ... Played in Super Bowl XXX (1995 season).
PRO STATISTICS: 1997—Recovered one fumble. 1998—Intercepted one pass for two yards, credited with one sack and recovered two fumbles.

FLOYD, CHRIS FB PATRIOTS

PERSONAL: Born June 23, 1975, in Detroit. ... 6-0/231. ... Full name: Christopher Michael Floyd.
HIGH SCHOOL: Cooley (Detroit).
COLLEGE: Michigan (degree in sports management and communications).
TRANSACTIONS/CAREER NOTES: Selected by New England Patriots in third round (81st pick overall) of 1998 NFL draft. ... Signed by Patriots (July 15, 1998).
SINGLE GAME HIGHS (regular season): Attempts—3 (October 11, 1998, vs. Kansas City); yards—14 (December 20, 1998, vs. San Francisco); and rushing touchdowns—0.

			RUSHING				RECEIVING				TOTALS			
Year Team	G	GS	Att.	Yds.	Avg.	TD	No.	Yds.	Avg.	TD	TD	2pt.	Pts.	Fum.
1998—New England NFL	16	2	6	22	3.7	0	1	6	6.0	0	0	0	0	0

FLOYD, WILLIAM FB PANTHERS

PERSONAL: Born February 17, 1972, in St. Petersburg, Fla. ... 6-1/242. ... Full name: William Ali Floyd.
HIGH SCHOOL: Lakewood Senior (St. Petersburg, Fla.).
COLLEGE: Florida State.
TRANSACTIONS/CAREER NOTES: Selected after junior season by San Francisco 49ers in first round (28th pick overall) of 1994 NFL draft. ... Signed by 49ers (July 28, 1994). ... On injured reserve with knee injury (October 31, 1995-remainder of season). ... On physically unable to perform list with knee injury (August 20-October 12, 1996). ... Granted unconditional free agency (February 13, 1998). ... Signed by Carolina Panthers (March 6, 1998).
CHAMPIONSHIP GAME EXPERIENCE: Played in NFC championship game (1994 and 1997 seasons). ... Member of Super Bowl championship team (1994 season).
POST SEASON RECORDS: Holds postseason single-game record for most touchdowns by rookie—3 (January 7, 1995, vs Chicago).
PRO STATISTICS: 1996—Recovered one fumble. 1998—Had only pass attempt intercepted, returned one kickoff for 22 yards and recovered one fumble.
SINGLE GAME HIGHS (regular season): Attempts—12 (October 1, 1995, vs. New York Giants); yards—61 (December 4, 1994, vs. Atlanta); and rushing touchdowns—2 (December 17, 1994, vs. Denver).

			RUSHING				RECEIVING				TOTALS			
Year Team	G	GS	Att.	Yds.	Avg.	TD	No.	Yds.	Avg.	TD	TD	2pt.	Pts.	Fum.
1994—San Francisco NFL	16	11	87	305	3.5	6	19	145	7.6	0	6	0	36	0
1995—San Francisco NFL	8	8	64	237	3.7	2	47	348	7.4	1	3	0	18	1
1996—San Francisco NFL	9	8	47	186	4.0	2	26	197	7.6	1	3	0	18	4
1997—San Francisco NFL	15	15	78	231	3.0	3	37	321	8.7	1	4	0	24	2
1998—Carolina NFL	16	13	28	71	2.5	3	24	123	5.1	1	4	0	24	1
Pro totals (5 years)	64	55	304	1030	3.4	16	153	1134	7.4	4	20	0	120	8

FLUTIE, DOUG QB BILLS

PERSONAL: Born October 23, 1962, in Manchester, Md. ... 5-10/175. ... Full name: Douglas Richard Flutie. ... Brother of Darren Flutie, wide receiver with San Diego Chargers (1988), B.C. Lions of CFL (1991-95) and Edmonton Eskimos of CFL (1996-98).
HIGH SCHOOL: Natick (Mass.).
COLLEGE: Boston College (degrees in computer science and speech communications, 1984).
TRANSACTIONS/CAREER NOTES: Selected by New Jersey Generals in 1985 USFL territorial draft. ... Signed by Generals (February 4, 1985). ... Granted roster exemption (February 4-14, 1985). ... Activated (February 15, 1985). ... On developmental squad for three games with Generals (1985). ... Selected by Los Angeles Rams in 11th round (285th pick overall) of 1985 NFL draft. ... On developmental squad (June 10, 1995-remainder of season). ... Rights traded by Rams with fourth-round pick in 1987 draft to Chicago Bears for third- and sixth-round picks in 1987 draft (October 14, 1986). ... Signed by Bears (October 21, 1986). ... Granted roster exemption (October 21-November 3, 1986). ... Activated (November 4, 1986). ... Crossed picket line during players strike (October 13, 1987). ... Traded by Bears to New England Patriots

for eighth-round pick in 1988 draft (October 13, 1987). ... Released by Patriots after 1989 season. ... Signed by B.C. Lions of CFL (June 1990). ... Granted free agency (February 1992). ... Signed by Calgary Stampeders of CFL (March 1992). ... Rights assigned to Toronto Argonauts of CFL (March 15, 1996). ... Signed by Buffalo Bills (January 16, 1998).
CHAMPIONSHIP GAME EXPERIENCE: Member of CFL championship team (1992 and 1996). ... Named Most Valuable Player of Grey Cup, CFL championship game (1992 and 1996). ... Played in Grey Cup (1993).
HONORS: Heisman Trophy winner (1984). ... Named College Football Player of the Year by THE SPORTING NEWS (1984). ... Named quarterback on THE SPORTING NEWS college All-America first team (1984). ... Most Outstanding Player of CFL (1991-1994 seasons). ... Played in Pro Bowl (1998 season).
PRO STATISTICS: USFL: 1985—Recovered two fumbles. NFL: 1986—Recovered two fumbles and fumbled three times for minus four yards. 1987—Recovered one fumble. 1988—Fumbled three times. 1989—Fumbled once. CFL: 1990—Fumbled six times. 1991—Fumbled seven times. 1992—Fumbled five times. 1993—Caught one pass for 11 yards and fumbled five times. 1994—Fumbled eight times. 1995—Fumbled twice. 1996—Fumbled once. 1997—Fumbled three times. NFL: 1998—Fumbled three times and recovered four fumbles for minus 13 yards.
SINGLE GAME HIGHS (regular season): Attempts—41 (October 1, 1989, vs. Buffalo); completions—23 (October 11, 1998, vs. Indianapolis); yards—339 (November 29, 1998, vs. New England); and touchdown passes—4 (October 30, 1988, vs. Chicago).
STATISTICAL PLATEAUS: 300-yard passing games: 1998 (2).
MISCELLANEOUS: Regular-season record as starting NFL quarterback: 16-8 (.667). ... Postseason record as starting NFL quarterback: 0-2.

				PASSING							RUSHING				TOTALS		
Year Team	G	GS	Att.	Cmp.	Pct.	Yds.	TD	Int.	Avg.	Rat.	Att.	Yds.	Avg.	TD	TD	2pt.	Pts.
1985—New Jersey USFL........	15	...	281	134	47.7	2109	13	14	7.51	67.8	65	465	7.2	6	6	0	36
1986—Chicago NFL................	4	1	46	23	50.0	361	3	2	7.85	80.1	9	36	4.0	1	1	...	6
1987—Chicago NFL................						Did not play.											
—New England NFL........	1	1	25	15	60.0	199	1	0	7.96	98.6	6	43	7.2	0	0	...	0
1988—New England NFL........	11	9	179	92	51.4	1150	8	10	6.42	63.3	38	179	4.7	1	1	...	6
1989—New England NFL........	5	3	91	36	39.6	493	2	5	5.42	46.6	16	87	5.4	0	0	...	0
1990—British Columbia CFL ..	16	...	392	207	52.8	2960	16	19	7.55	71.0	79	662	8.4	3	3	0	18
1991—British Columbia CFL ..	18	...	730	466	63.8	6619	38	24	9.07	96.7	120	610	5.1	14	14	1	86
1992—Calgary CFL.................	18	...	688	396	57.6	5945	32	30	8.64	83.4	96	669	7.0	11	11	0	66
1993—Calgary CFL.................	18	...	703	416	59.2	6092	44	17	8.67	98.3	74	373	5.0	11	11	0	66
1994—Calgary CFL.................	18	...	659	403	61.2	5726	48	19	8.69	101.5	96	760	7.9	8	8	0	48
1995—Calgary CFL.................	12	...	332	223	67.2	2788	16	5	8.40	102.8	46	288	6.3	5	5	0	30
1996—Toronto CFL.................	18	...	677	434	64.1	5720	29	17	8.45	94.5	101	756	7.5	9	9	0	54
1997—Toronto CFL.................	18	18	673	430	63.9	5505	47	24	8.18	97.8	92	542	5.9	9	9	0	54
1998—Buffalo NFL..................	13	10	354	202	57.1	2711	20	11	7.66	87.4	48	248	5.2	1	1	0	6
USFL totals (1 year)...............	15	...	281	134	47.7	2109	13	14	7.51	67.8	65	465	7.2	6	6	...	36
CFL totals (8 years)..............	136	...	4854	2975	61.3	41355	270	155	8.52	93.9	704	4660	6.6	70	70	1	422
NFL totals (5 years)..............	34	24	695	368	52.9	4914	34	27	7.07	75.8	117	593	5.1	3	3	0	18
Pro totals (14 years).............	185	...	5830	3477	59.6	48378	317	196	8.30	90.5	886	5718	6.5	79	79	...	476

FLYNN, MIKE   OL   RAVENS

PERSONAL: Born June 15, 1974, in Doylestown, Pa. ... 6-3/295. ... Full name: Michael Patrick Flynn.
HIGH SCHOOL: Cathedral (Springfield, Mass.).
COLLEGE: Maine.
TRANSACTIONS/CAREER NOTES: Signed as non-drafted free agent by Baltimore Ravens (April 25, 1997). ... Released by Ravens (August 24, 1997). ... Signed by Tampa Bay Buccaneers to practice squad (August 27, 1997). ... Released by Buccaneers (September 2, 1997). ... Signed by Jacksonville Jaguars to practice squad (November 4, 1997). ... Signed by Ravens off Jaguars practice squad (December 3, 1997). ... Inactive for three games (1997).
PLAYING EXPERIENCE: Baltimore NFL, 1998. ... Games/Games started: 2/0.

FOLAU, SPENCER   OT   RAVENS

PERSONAL: Born April 5, 1973, in Nuk 'Alofa, Tonga, Samoan Islands. ... 6-5/300. ... Full name: Spencer Sione Folau. ... Name pronounced fah-LOWE.
HIGH SCHOOL: Sequoia (Redwood City, Calif.).
COLLEGE: Idaho.
TRANSACTIONS/CAREER NOTES: Signed as non-drafted free agent by Baltimore Ravens (April 26, 1996). ... Released by Ravens (August 25, 1996). ... Re-signed by Ravens to practice squad (October 29, 1996). ... Assigned by Ravens to Rhein Fire in 1997 World League enhancement allocation program (February 1997). ... Released by Ravens (October 28, 1998). ... Re-signed by Ravens (November 3, 1998).
PLAYING EXPERIENCE: Rhein Fire W.L., 1997; Baltimore NFL, 1997 and 1998. ... Games/Games started: W.L.: 1997 (games played unavailable), NFL 1997 (10/0), 1998 (3/3). Total NFL: 13/3.

FOLEY, GLENN   QB   SEAHAWKS

PERSONAL: Born October 10, 1970, in Cherry Hill, N.J. ... 6-2/220. ... Full name: Glenn Edward Foley.
HIGH SCHOOL: Cherry Hill (N.J.) East.
COLLEGE: Boston College (degree in sociology).
TRANSACTIONS/CAREER NOTES: Selected by New York Jets in seventh round (208th pick overall) of 1994 NFL draft. ... Signed by Jets (June 21, 1994). ... On injured reserve with shoulder injury (November 8, 1995-remainder of season). ... On physically unable to perform list with knee injury (July 18-21, 1997). ... Traded by Jets to Seattle Seahawks for seventh-round pick (OT Ryan Young) in 1999 draft (March 19, 1999).
CHAMPIONSHIP GAME EXPERIENCE: Member of Jets for AFC championship game (1998 season); inactive.
PRO STATISTICS: 1995—Caught one pass for minus nine yards. 1996—Fumbled once for minus four yards. 1997—Fumbled once. 1998—Fumbled once.
SINGLE GAME HIGHS (regular season): Attempts—58 (September 6, 1998, vs. San Francisco); completions—30 (September 6, 1998, vs. San Francisco); yards—415 (September 6, 1998, vs. San Francisco); and touchdown passes—3 (September 6, 1998, vs. San Francisco).
STATISTICAL PLATEAUS: 300-yard passing games: 1997 (1), 1998 (1). Total: 2.
MISCELLANEOUS: Regular-season record as starting NFL quarterback: 1-7 (.125).

				PASSING						RUSHING				TOTALS	
Year Team	G	GS	Att.	Cmp.	Pct.	Yds.	TD	Int.	Avg.	Rat.	Att.	Yds.	Avg.	TD	TD	2pt.	Pts.
1994—New York Jets NFL	1	0	8	5	62.5	45	0	1	5.63	38.0	0	0	...	0	0	0	0
1995—New York Jets NFL	1	0	29	16	55.2	128	0	1	4.41	52.1	1	9	9.0	0	0	0	0
1996—New York Jets NFL	5	3	110	54	49.1	559	3	7	5.08	46.7	7	40	5.7	0	0	0	0
1997—New York Jets NFL	6	2	97	56	57.7	705	3	1	7.27	86.5	3	-5	-1.7	0	0	0	0
1998—New York Jets NFL	5	3	108	58	53.7	749	4	6	6.94	64.9	5	-11	-2.2	0	0	0	0
Pro totals (5 years)	18	8	352	189	53.7	2186	10	16	6.21	63.2	16	33	2.1	0	0	0	0

FOLEY, STEVE — LB — BENGALS

PERSONAL: Born September 9, 1975, in Little Rock, Ark. ... 6-3/260.
HIGH SCHOOL: Hall (Little Rock, Ark.).
COLLEGE: Northeast Louisiana.
TRANSACTIONS/CAREER NOTES: Selected by Cincinnati Bengals in third round (75th pick overall) of 1998 NFL draft. ... Signed by Bengals (July 19, 1998).

Year Team	G	GS	SACKS
1998—Cincinnati NFL	10	1	2.0

FOLSTON, JAMES — LB — RAIDERS

PERSONAL: Born August 14, 1971, in Cocoa, Fla. ... 6-3/240. ... Full name: James Edward Folston.
HIGH SCHOOL: Cocoa (Fla.).
COLLEGE: Northeast Louisiana.
TRANSACTIONS/CAREER NOTES: Selected by Los Angeles Raiders in second round (52nd pick overall) of 1994 NFL draft. ... Signed by Raiders (July 13, 1994). ... Raiders franchise moved to Oakland (July 21, 1995). ... Granted free agency (February 14, 1997). ... Re-signed by Raiders for 1997 season.
PLAYING EXPERIENCE: Los Angeles Raiders NFL, 1994; Oakland NFL, 1995-1998. ... Games/Games started: 1994 (7/0), 1995 (15/0), 1996 (12/0), 1997 (16/7), 1998 (16/5). Total: 66/12.
PRO STATISTICS: 1997—Recovered one fumble. 1998—Caught one pass for minus one yard and credited with one sack.

FONTENOT, AL — DE — CHARGERS

PERSONAL: Born September 17, 1970, in Houston. ... 6-4/287. ... Full name: Albert Paul Fontenot. ... Name pronounced FAHN-tuh-no.
HIGH SCHOOL: Jack Yates (Houston).
JUNIOR COLLEGE: Navarro College (Texas).
COLLEGE: Baylor (degree in communications).
TRANSACTIONS/CAREER NOTES: Selected by Chicago Bears in fourth round (112th pick overall) of 1993 NFL draft. ... Signed by Bears (July 16, 1993). ... Granted free agency (February 16, 1996). ... Re-signed by Bears (April 18, 1996). ... Granted unconditional free agency (February 14, 1997). ... Signed by Indianapolis Colts (April 3, 1997). ... On injured reserve with calf injury (November 25, 1998-remainder of season). ... Released by Colts (April 28, 1999). ... Signed by San Diego Chargers (May 12, 1999).
PRO STATISTICS: 1993—Returned one kickoff for eight yards. 1995—Credited with one safety and recovered one fumble. 1997—Recovered three fumbles for 35 yards and one touchdown. 1998—Recovered one fumble.

Year Team	G	GS	SACKS
1993—Chicago NFL	16	0	1.0
1994—Chicago NFL	16	8	4.0
1995—Chicago NFL	13	5	2.5
1996—Chicago NFL	16	15	4.5
1997—Indianapolis NFL	16	16	4.5
1998—Indianapolis NFL	7	5	1.0
Pro totals (6 years)	84	49	17.5

FONTENOT, CHRIS — TE — EAGLES

PERSONAL: Born July 11, 1974, in Lafayette, La. ... 6-3/250. ... Full name: Christopher Dwight Fontenot.
HIGH SCHOOL: Iota (La.).
COLLEGE: McNeese State.
TRANSACTIONS/CAREER NOTES: Signed as non-drafted free agent by Miami Dolphins (April 23, 1998). ... Released by Dolphins (August 30, 1998). ... Signed by Kansas City Chiefs to practice squad (September 1, 1998). ... Signed by Philadelphia Eagles off Chiefs practice squad (October 29, 1998).
SINGLE GAME HIGHS (regular season): Receptions—4 (December 13, 1998, vs. Arizona); yards—47 (December 13, 1998, vs. Arizona); and touchdown receptions—0.

			RECEIVING				TOTALS		
Year Team	G	GS	No.	Yds.	Avg.	TD	TD	2pt.	Pts.	Fum.
1998—Philadelphia NFL	5	3	8	90	11.3	0	0	0	0	0

FONTENOT, JERRY — C — SAINTS

PERSONAL: Born November 21, 1966, in Lafayette, La. ... 6-3/300. ... Full name: Jerry Paul Fontenot. ... Name pronounced FAHN-tuh-no.
HIGH SCHOOL: Lafayette (La.).
COLLEGE: Texas A&M.
TRANSACTIONS/CAREER NOTES: Selected by Chicago Bears in third round (65th pick overall) of 1989 NFL draft. ... Signed by Bears (July 27, 1989). ... Granted free agency (March 1, 1993). ... Re-signed by Bears (June 16, 1993). ... Granted free agency (February 16, 1996). ...

Re-signed by Bears (July 10, 1996). ... Granted unconditional free agency (February 14, 1997). ... Signed by New Orleans Saints (May 28, 1997). ... On injured reserve with knee injury (October 14, 1998-remainder of season). ... Granted unconditional free agency (February 12, 1999). ... Re-signed by Saints (February 23, 1999).
PLAYING EXPERIENCE: Chicago NFL, 1989-1996; New Orleans NFL, 1997 and 1998. ... Games/Games started: 1989 (16/0), 1990 (16/2), 1991 (16/7), 1992 (16/16), 1993 (16/16), 1994 (16/16), 1995 (16/16), 1996 (16/16), 1997 (16/16), 1998 (4/4). Total: 148/109.
PRO STATISTICS: 1989—Recovered one fumble. 1990—Fumbled once. 1992—Fumbled once for minus two yards. 1993—Recovered one fumble. 1997—Fumbled three times.

FOOTMAN, DAN — DE

PERSONAL: Born January 13, 1969, in Tampa. ... 6-5/290. ... Full name: Dan Ellis Footman Jr.
HIGH SCHOOL: Hillsborough (Tampa).
COLLEGE: Florida State.
TRANSACTIONS/CAREER NOTES: Selected by Cleveland Browns in second round (42nd pick overall) of 1993 NFL draft. ... Signed by Browns (July 15, 1993). ... Granted free agency (February 16, 1996). ... Browns franchise moved to Baltimore and renamed Ravens for 1996 season (March 11, 1996). ... Signed by Ravens (April 3, 1996). ... Released by Ravens (June 2, 1997). ... Signed by Indianapolis Colts (June 20, 1997). ... On injured reserve with knee injury (October 6, 1998-remainder of season). ... Granted unconditional free agency (February 12, 1999).
PRO STATISTICS: 1995—Recovered one fumble. 1997—Recovered two fumbles for 14 yards.

Year Team	G	GS	SACKS
1993—Cleveland NFL	8	0	1.0
1994—Cleveland NFL	16	2	2.5
1995—Cleveland NFL	16	16	5.0
1996—Baltimore NFL	10	8	0.5
1997—Indianapolis NFL	16	10	10.5
1998—Indianapolis NFL	3	3	0.0
Pro totals (6 years)	69	39	19.5

FORBES, MARLON — DB — BROWNS

PERSONAL: Born December 25, 1971, in Long Island, N.Y. ... 6-1/215.
HIGH SCHOOL: Central Islip (N.Y.).
COLLEGE: Penn State.
TRANSACTIONS/CAREER NOTES: Signed as non-drafted free agent by Chicago Bears (April 1995). ... Released by Bears (August 27, 1995). ... Re-signed by Bears to practice squad (December 1, 1995). ... Released by Bears (August 27, 1996). ... Re-signed by Bears to practice squad (September 4, 1996). ... Activated (September 9, 1996). ... Selected by Cleveland Browns from Bears in NFL expansion draft (February 9, 1999). ... Granted free agency (February 12, 1999).
PLAYING EXPERIENCE: Chicago NFL, 1996-1998. ... Games/Games started: 1996 (15/0), 1997 (16/1), 1998 (16/2). Total: 47/3.
PRO STATISTICS: 1996—Recovered one fumble.

FORD, COLE — K

PERSONAL: Born December 31, 1972, in Tucson, Ariz. ... 6-2/210.
HIGH SCHOOL: Sabino (Tucson, Ariz.).
COLLEGE: Southern California.
TRANSACTIONS/CAREER NOTES: Selected by Pittsburgh Steelers in seventh round (247th pick overall) of 1995 NFL draft. ... Signed by Steelers (July 17, 1995). ... Released by Steelers (August 15, 1995). ... Signed by Oakland Raiders to practice squad (August 31, 1995). ... Activated (September 2, 1995). ... Released by Raiders (September 5, 1995). ... Re-signed by Raiders to practice squad (September 6, 1995). ... Activated (September 9, 1995). ... Granted free agency (February 13, 1998). ... Re-signed by Raiders (April 28, 1998). ... Claimed on waivers by Buffalo Bills (August 26, 1998). ... Released by Bills (September 29, 1998).

				KICKING				
Year Team	G	XPM	XPA	FGM	FGA	Lg.	50+	Pts.
1995—Oakland NFL	5	17	18	8	9	46	0-1	41
1996—Oakland NFL	16	36	36	24	31	47	0-1	108
1997—Oakland NFL	16	33	35	13	22	53	1-1	72
1998—Buffalo NFL	1	0	0	0	0	0	0-0	0
Pro totals (4 years)	38	86	89	45	62	53	1-3	221

FORD, HENRY — DT — TITANS

PERSONAL: Born October 30, 1971, in Fort Worth, Texas. ... 6-3/295.
HIGH SCHOOL: Trimble Technical (Fort Worth, Texas).
COLLEGE: Arkansas.
TRANSACTIONS/CAREER NOTES: Selected by Houston Oilers in first round (26th pick overall) of 1994 NFL draft. ... Signed by Oilers (June 16, 1994). ... Oilers franchise moved to Tennessee for 1997 season. ... Granted unconditional free agency (February 13, 1998). ... Re-signed by Oilers (March 2, 1998). ... Oilers franchise renamed Tennessee Titans for 1999 season (December 26, 1998).
PRO STATISTICS: 1997—Recovered two fumbles for 13 yards. 1998—Recovered one fumble.

Year Team	G	GS	SACKS
1994—Houston NFL	11	0	0.0
1995—Houston NFL	16	16	4.5
1996—Houston NFL	15	14	1.0
1997—Tennessee NFL	16	16	5.0
1998—Tennessee NFL	13	5	1.5
Pro totals (5 years)	71	51	12.0

FORDHAM, TODD — G/OT — JAGUARS

PERSONAL: Born October 9, 1973, in Atlanta. ... 6-5/308. ... Full name: Lindsey Todd Fordham.
HIGH SCHOOL: Tift County (Tifton, Ga.).
COLLEGE: Florida State (degree in business, 1996).
TRANSACTIONS/CAREER NOTES: Signed as non-drafted free agent by Jacksonville Jaguars (April 21, 1997). ... Released by Jaguars (August 24, 1997). ... Re-signed by Jaguars to practice squad (August 25, 1997). ... Activated (September 23, 1997).
PLAYING EXPERIENCE: Jacksonville NFL, 1997 and 1998. ... Games/Games started: 1997 (1/0), 1998 (11/1). Total: 12/1.
PRO STATISTICS: 1998—Returned one kickoff for no yards and recovered one fumble.

FORTIN, ROMAN — C/G — CHARGERS

PERSONAL: Born February 26, 1967, in Columbus, Ohio. ... 6-5/297. ... Full name: Roman Brian Fortin.
HIGH SCHOOL: Ventura (Calif.).
COLLEGE: Oregon, then San Diego State.
TRANSACTIONS/CAREER NOTES: Selected by Detroit Lions in eighth round (203rd pick overall) of 1990 NFL draft. ... On injured reserve (September 5, 1990-entire season). ... Granted unconditional free agency (February 1, 1992). ... Signed by Atlanta Falcons (March 31, 1992). ... Granted unconditional free agency (February 17, 1994). ... Re-signed by Falcons (February 24, 1994). ... Granted unconditional free agency (February 16, 1996). ... Re-signed by Falcons (February 20, 1996). ... Released by Falcons (February 11, 1998). ... Signed by San Diego Chargers (March 17, 1998).
PLAYING EXPERIENCE: Detroit NFL, 1991; Atlanta NFL, 1992-1997; San Diego NFL, 1998. ... Games/Games started: 1991 (16/2), 1992 (16/1), 1993 (16/1), 1994 (16/16), 1995 (16/16), 1996 (16/16), 1997 (3/3), 1998 (16/16). Total: 115/71.
CHAMPIONSHIP GAME EXPERIENCE: Played in NFC championship game (1991 season).
PRO STATISTICS: 1991—Caught one pass for four yards. 1992—Returned one kickoff for five yards and recovered one fumble. 1995—Fumbled twice for minus six yards. 1996—Recovered two fumbles.

FOX, MIKE — DE

PERSONAL: Born August 5, 1967, in Akron, Ohio. ... 6-8/295. ... Full name: Michael James Fox.
HIGH SCHOOL: Akron (Ohio) North.
COLLEGE: West Virginia.
TRANSACTIONS/CAREER NOTES: Selected by New York Giants in second round (51st pick overall) of 1990 NFL draft. ... Signed by Giants (July 31, 1990). ... Granted free agency (March 1, 1993). ... Re-signed by Giants (August 13, 1993). ... Granted unconditional free agency (February 17, 1995). ... Signed by Carolina Panthers (February 20, 1995). ... Released by Panthers (February 10, 1999).
CHAMPIONSHIP GAME EXPERIENCE: Played in NFC championship game (1990 and 1996 seasons). ... Member of Super Bowl championship team (1990 season).
PRO STATISTICS: 1993—Recovered one fumble for two yards.

Year Team	G	GS	SACKS
1990—New York Giants NFL	16	0	1.5
1991—New York Giants NFL	15	5	0.0
1992—New York Giants NFL	16	4	2.5
1993—New York Giants NFL	16	16	4.5
1994—New York Giants NFL	16	16	1.0
1995—Carolina NFL	16	16	4.5
1996—Carolina NFL	11	11	2.0
1997—Carolina NFL	11	9	0.0
1998—Carolina NFL	16	7	1.0
Pro totals (9 years)	**133**	**84**	**17.0**

FRANCIS, JAMES — LB — BENGALS

PERSONAL: Born August 4, 1968, in Houston. ... 6-5/257. ... Brother of Ron Francis, cornerback with Dallas Cowboys (1987-90).
HIGH SCHOOL: La Marque (Texas).
COLLEGE: Baylor.
TRANSACTIONS/CAREER NOTES: Selected by Cincinnati Bengals in first round (12th pick overall) of 1990 NFL draft. ... Signed by Bengals (July 19, 1990). ... On injured reserve with knee injury (December 26, 1992-remainder of season). ... Designated by Bengals as transition player (February 25, 1993). ... On injured reserve with broken leg (November 22, 1995-remainder of season).
HONORS: Named special-teams player on THE SPORTING NEWS college All-America first team (1989).
PRO STATISTICS: 1990—Credited with one safety. 1991—Recovered one fumble. 1992—Recovered two fumbles for three yards. 1993—Recovered one fumble. 1996—Recovered three fumbles. 1997—Recovered one fumble.

			INTERCEPTIONS				SACKS
Year Team	G	GS	No.	Yds.	Avg.	TD	No.
1990—Cincinnati NFL	16	16	1	17	17.0	▲1	8.0
1991—Cincinnati NFL	16	16	1	0	0.0	0	3.0
1992—Cincinnati NFL	14	13	3	108	36.0	1	6.0
1993—Cincinnati NFL	14	12	2	12	6.0	0	2.0
1994—Cincinnati NFL	16	16	0	0	...	0	4.5
1995—Cincinnati NFL	11	11	0	0	...	0	3.0
1996—Cincinnati NFL	16	15	3	61	20.3	1	3.0
1997—Cincinnati NFL	16	16	1	7	7.0	0	3.5
1998—Cincinnati NFL	14	14	0	0	...	0	0.0
Pro totals (9 years)	**133**	**129**	**11**	**205**	**18.6**	**3**	**33.0**

FRASE, PAUL — DE/DT

PERSONAL: Born May 5, 1965, in Elmira, N.Y. ... 6-5/267. ... Full name: Paul Miles Frase. ... Name pronounced FRAZE.
HIGH SCHOOL: Spaulding (Rochester, N.H.).
COLLEGE: Syracuse (degree in psychology).
TRANSACTIONS/CAREER NOTES: Selected by New York Jets in sixth round (146th pick overall) of 1988 NFL draft. ... Signed by Jets (June 21, 1988). ... On reserve/non-football illness list with hyperthyroidism (August 27, 1990-entire season). ... Granted unconditional free agency (February 1-April 1, 1991). ... Re-signed by Jets for 1991 season. ... Granted free agency (February 1, 1992). ... Re-signed by Jets (July 13, 1992). ... Granted free agency (March 1, 1993). ... Re-signed by Jets (April 12, 1993). ... Granted unconditional free agency (February 17, 1994). ... Re-signed by Jets (April 6, 1994). ... Selected by Jacksonville Jaguars from Jets in NFL expansion draft (February 15, 1995). ... Granted unconditional free agency (February 14, 1997). ... Re-signed by Jaguars (April 28, 1997). ... Traded by Jaguars to Green Bay Packers for sixth-round pick (RB Kevin McLeod) in 1998 draft (August 24, 1997). ... Granted unconditional free agency (February 13, 1998). ... Re-signed by Packers (April 24, 1998). ... Released by Packers (August 25, 1998). ... Signed by Baltimore Ravens (October 14, 1998). ... Granted unconditional free agency (February 12, 1999).
CHAMPIONSHIP GAME EXPERIENCE: Played in AFC championship game (1996 season). ... Played in NFC championship game (1997 season). ... Member of Packers for Super Bowl XXXII (1997 season); inactive.
PRO STATISTICS: 1991—Fumbled once. 1993—Recovered two fumbles. 1994—Recovered one fumble.

Year — Team	G	GS	SACKS
1988—New York Jets NFL	16	7	1.0
1989—New York Jets NFL	16	14	2.0
1990—New York Jets NFL	Did not play.		
1991—New York Jets NFL	16	2	0.0
1992—New York Jets NFL	16	12	5.0
1993—New York Jets NFL	16	4	1.0
1994—New York Jets NFL	16	5	1.0
1995—Jacksonville NFL	9	5	1.0
1996—Jacksonville NFL	14	0	0.0
1997—Green Bay NFL	9	0	0.0
1998—Baltimore NFL	11	0	0.0
Pro totals (10 years)	139	49	11.0

FREDERICK, MIKE — DE — JETS

PERSONAL: Born August 6, 1972, in Abington, Pa. ... 6-5/280. ... Full name: Thomas Michael Frederick.
HIGH SCHOOL: Neshaminy (Langhorne, Pa.).
COLLEGE: Virginia (degree in management).
TRANSACTIONS/CAREER NOTES: Selected by Cleveland Browns in third round (94th pick overall) of 1995 NFL draft. ... Signed by Browns (July 14, 1995). ... Browns franchise moved to Baltimore and renamed Ravens for 1996 season (March 11, 1996). ... Granted free agency (February 13, 1998). ... Re-signed by Ravens (June 10, 1998). ... Granted unconditional free agency (February 12, 1999). ... Signed by New York Jets (February 17, 1999).
PLAYING EXPERIENCE: Cleveland NFL, 1995; Baltimore NFL, 1996-1998. ... Games/Games started: 1995 (16/0), 1996 (16/11), 1997 (16/1), 1998 (10/0). Total: 58/12.
PRO STATISTICS: 1995—Credited with one sack and returned two kickoffs for 16 yards. 1996—Lost one yard with lateral from kickoff return. 1997—Recovered one fumble.

FREDRICKSON, ROB — LB — CARDINALS

PERSONAL: Born May 13, 1971, in Saint Joseph, Mich. ... 6-4/240. ... Full name: Robert J. Fredrickson.
HIGH SCHOOL: Saint Joseph (Mich.) Senior.
COLLEGE: Michigan State.
TRANSACTIONS/CAREER NOTES: Selected by Los Angeles Raiders in first round (22nd pick overall) of 1994 NFL draft. ... Signed by Raiders (July 19, 1994). ... Raiders franchise moved to Oakland (July 21, 1995). ... On injured reserve with shoulder injury (November 20, 1996-remainder of season). ... Traded by Raiders to Detroit Lions for fourth-round pick (traded to Washington) in 1998 draft (March 25, 1998). ... Granted unconditional free agency (February 12, 1999). ... Signed by Arizona Cardinals (March 29, 1999).
PRO STATISTICS: 1995—Intercepted one pass for 14 yards and recovered four fumbles for 35 yards and one touchdown. 1998—Intercepted one pass for no yards.

Year — Team	G	GS	SACKS
1994—Los Angeles Raiders NFL	16	12	3.0
1995—Oakland NFL	16	15	0.0
1996—Oakland NFL	10	10	0.0
1997—Oakland NFL	16	13	2.0
1998—Detroit NFL	16	16	2.5
Pro totals (5 years)	74	66	7.5

FREEMAN, ANTONIO — WR — PACKERS

PERSONAL: Born May 27, 1972, in Baltimore. ... 6-1/198. ... Full name: Antonio Michael Freeman.
HIGH SCHOOL: Polytechnic (Baltimore).
COLLEGE: Virginia Tech.
TRANSACTIONS/CAREER NOTES: Selected by Green Bay Packers in third round (90th pick overall) of 1995 NFL draft. ... Signed by Packers (June 22, 1995). ... Granted free agency (February 13, 1998). ... Re-signed by Packers (June 16, 1998). ... Designated by Packers as franchise player (February 12, 1999).
CHAMPIONSHIP GAME EXPERIENCE: Played in NFC championship game (1995-97 seasons). ... Member of Super Bowl championship team (1996 season). ... Played in Super Bowl XXXII (1997 season).
HONORS: Named wide receiver on THE SPORTING NEWS NFL All-Pro team (1998). ... Played in Pro Bowl (1998 season).
POST SEASON RECORDS: Holds Super Bowl record for longest pass reception (from Brett Favre)—81 yards (January 26, 1997, vs. New England). ... Shares NFL postseason record for most touchdowns by punt return—1 (December 31, 1995, vs. Atlanta).

PRO STATISTICS: 1995—Recovered four fumbles. 1996—Recovered one fumble for 14 yards. 1997—Rushed once for 14 yards. 1998—Rushed three times for five yards.
SINGLE GAME HIGHS (regular season): Receptions—10 (December 14, 1997, vs. Carolina); yards—193 (November 1, 1998, vs. San Francisco); and touchdown receptions—3 (December 20, 1998, vs. Tennessee).
STATISTICAL PLATEAUS: 100-yard receiving games: 1996 (4), 1997 (3), 1998 (6). Total: 13.

				RECEIVING				PUNT RETURNS				KICKOFF RETURNS				TOTALS		
Year Team	G	GS	No.	Yds.	Avg.	TD	No.	Yds.	Avg.	TD	No.	Yds.	Avg.	TD	TD	2pt.	Pts.	Fum.
1995—Green Bay NFL	11	0	8	106	13.3	1	37	292	7.9	0	24	556	23.2	0	1	0	6	7
1996—Green Bay NFL	12	12	56	933	16.7	9	0	0	...	0	1	16	16.0	0	9	0	54	3
1997—Green Bay NFL	16	16	81	1243	15.3	12	0	0	...	0	0	0	...	0	12	0	72	1
1998—Green Bay NFL	15	15	84	*1424	17.0	14	0	0	...	0	0	0	...	0	14	1	86	0
Pro totals (4 years)	54	43	229	3706	16.2	36	37	292	7.9	0	25	572	22.9	0	36	1	218	11

FREROTTE, GUS   QB   LIONS

PERSONAL: Born August 3, 1971, in Kittanning, Pa. ... 6-3/240. ... Full name: Gustave Joseph Frerotte. ... Brother of Mitch Frerotte, guard with Buffalo Bills (1987 and 1990-92).
HIGH SCHOOL: Ford City (Pa.) Junior-Senior.
COLLEGE: Tulsa.
TRANSACTIONS/CAREER NOTES: Selected by Washington Redskins in seventh round (197th pick overall) of 1994 NFL draft. ... Signed by Redskins (July 19, 1994). ... Granted free agency (February 14, 1997). ... Re-signed by Redskins (July 18, 1997). ... On injured reserve with hip injury (December 2, 1997-remainder of season). ... Released by Redskins (February 11, 1999). ... Signed by Detroit Lions (March 3, 1999).
HONORS: Played in Pro Bowl (1996 season).
PRO STATISTICS: 1994—Fumbled four times and recovered two fumbles for minus four yards. 1995—Fumbled seven times and recovered four fumbles for minus 16 yards. 1996—Fumbled 12 times and recovered one fumble for minus 12 yards. 1997—Fumbled eight times and recovered two fumbles for minus 16 yards.
SINGLE GAME HIGHS (regular season): Attempts—45 (November 30, 1997, vs. St. Louis); completions—22 (December 22, 1996, vs. Dallas); yards—346 (December 22, 1996, vs. Dallas); and touchdown passes—3 (September 28, 1997, vs. Jacksonville).
STATISTICAL PLATEAUS: 300-yard passing games: 1995 (1), 1996 (1). Total: 2.
MISCELLANEOUS: Regular-season record as starting NFL quarterback: 19-26-1 (.413).

				PASSING							RUSHING				TOTALS		
Year Team	G	GS	Att.	Cmp.	Pct.	Yds.	TD	Int.	Avg.	Rat.	Att.	Yds.	Avg.	TD	TD	2pt.	Pts.
1994—Washington NFL	4	4	100	46	46.0	600	5	5	6.00	61.3	4	1	0.3	0	0	0	0
1995—Washington NFL	16	11	396	199	50.3	2751	13	13	6.95	70.2	22	16	0.7	1	1	0	6
1996—Washington NFL	16	16	470	270	57.4	3453	12	11	7.35	79.3	28	16	0.6	0	0	0	0
1997—Washington NFL	13	13	402	204	50.7	2682	17	12	6.67	73.8	24	65	2.7	2	2	0	12
1998—Washington NFL	3	2	54	25	46.3	283	1	3	5.24	45.5	3	20	6.7	0	0	0	0
Pro totals (5 years)	52	46	1422	744	52.3	9769	48	44	6.87	72.7	81	118	1.5	3	3	0	18

FRIESZ, JOHN   QB   PATRIOTS

PERSONAL: Born May 19, 1967, in Missoula, Mont. ... 6-4/223. ... Full name: John Melvin Friesz. ... Name pronounced FREEZE.
HIGH SCHOOL: Coeur D'Alene (Idaho).
COLLEGE: Idaho.
TRANSACTIONS/CAREER NOTES: Selected by San Diego Chargers in sixth round (138th pick overall) of 1990 NFL draft. ... Signed by Chargers (July 20, 1990). ... On injured reserve with elbow injury (September 4-October 3, 1990). ... On practice squad (October 3-December 28, 1990). ... Granted free agency (February 1, 1992). ... Re-signed by Chargers (July 27, 1992). ... On injured reserve with knee injury (August 25, 1992-entire season). ... Granted unconditional free agency (February 17, 1994). ... Signed by Washington Redskins (April 18, 1994). ... Granted unconditional free agency (February 17, 1995). ... Signed by Seattle Seahawks (March 17, 1995). ... Released by Seahawks (February 10, 1999). ... Signed by New England Patriots (April 22, 1999).
HONORS: Walter Payton Award winner (1989).
PRO STATISTICS: 1991—Fumbled 10 times and recovered two fumbles for minus 21 yards. 1993—Fumbled twice and recovered one fumble for minus three yards. 1994—Fumbled twice and recovered one fumble. 1995—Fumbled twice and recovered one fumble for minus three yards. 1996—Fumbled seven times and recovered two fumbles for minus six yards. 1997—Fumbled once and recovered one fumble for minus two yards.
SINGLE GAME HIGHS (regular season): Attempts—54 (October 20, 1991, vs. Cleveland); completions—33 (October 20, 1991, vs. Cleveland); yards—381 (September 18, 1994, vs. New York Giants); and touchdown passes—4 (September 11, 1994, vs. New Orleans).
STATISTICAL PLATEAUS: 300-yard passing games: 1991 (2), 1994 (1), 1996 (1). Total: 4.
MISCELLANEOUS: Regular-season record as starting NFL quarterback: 13-25 (.342).

				PASSING							RUSHING				TOTALS		
Year Team	G	GS	Att.	Cmp.	Pct.	Yds.	TD	Int.	Avg.	Rat.	Att.	Yds.	Avg.	TD	TD	2pt.	Pts.
1990—San Diego NFL	1	1	22	11	50.0	98	1	1	4.45	58.5	1	3	3.0	0	0	...	0
1991—San Diego NFL	16	16	487	262	53.8	2896	12	15	5.95	67.1	10	18	1.8	0	0	...	0
1992—San Diego NFL							Did not play.										
1993—San Diego NFL	12	6	238	128	53.8	1402	6	4	5.89	72.8	10	3	0.3	0	0	0	0
1994—Washington NFL	16	4	180	105	58.3	1266	10	9	7.03	77.7	1	1	1.0	0	0	0	0
1995—Seattle NFL	6	3	120	64	53.3	795	6	3	6.63	80.4	11	0	0.0	0	0	0	0
1996—Seattle NFL	8	6	211	120	56.9	1629	8	4	7.72	86.4	12	1	0.1	0	0	0	0
1997—Seattle NFL	2	1	36	15	41.7	138	0	3	3.83	18.1	1	0	0.0	0	0	0	0
1998—Seattle NFL	6	1	49	29	59.2	409	2	2	8.35	82.8	5	5	1.0	0	0	0	0
Pro totals (8 years)	67	38	1343	734	54.7	8633	45	41	6.43	72.9	51	31	0.6	0	0	0	0

FROST, SCOTT   S   JETS

PERSONAL: Born January 4, 1975, in Wood River, Neb. ... 6-3/219.
HIGH SCHOOL: Wood River (Neb.).

COLLEGE: Stanford, then Nebraska (degree in finance, 1997).
TRANSACTIONS/CAREER NOTES: Selected by New York Jets in third round (67th pick overall) of 1998 NFL draft. ... Signed by Jets (July 21, 1998).
PLAYING EXPERIENCE: New York Jets NFL, 1998. ... Games/Games started: 13/0.
CHAMPIONSHIP GAME EXPERIENCE: Played in AFC championship game (1998 season).
PRO STATISTICS: 1998—Returned one punt for no yards and fumbled once.

FRYAR, IRVING WR

PERSONAL: Born September 28, 1962, in Mount Holly, N.J. ... 6-0/200. ... Full name: Irving Dale Fryar.
HIGH SCHOOL: Rancocas Valley (Mount Holly, N.J.).
COLLEGE: Nebraska (degree in bible study).
TRANSACTIONS/CAREER NOTES: Selected by Chicago Blitz in first round (third pick overall) of 1984 USFL draft. ... Signed by New England Patriots (April 11, 1984). ... Selected officially by Patriots in first round (first pick overall) of 1984 NFL draft. ... Traded by Patriots to Miami Dolphins for second-round pick (OL Todd Rucci) in 1993 draft and third-round pick (C Joe Burch) in 1994 draft (April 1, 1993). ... Granted unconditional free agency (February 16, 1996). ... Signed by Philadelphia Eagles (March 19, 1996). ... Announced retirement (December 23, 1998).
CHAMPIONSHIP GAME EXPERIENCE: Played in Super Bowl XX (1985 season).
HONORS: Named wide receiver on THE SPORTING NEWS college All-America first team (1983). ... Played in Pro Bowl (1985, 1993, 1994, 1996 and 1997 seasons).
PRO STATISTICS: 1984—Fumbled four times and recovered one fumble. 1985—Fumbled four times. 1986—Fumbled four times and recovered one fumble. 1987—Fumbled twice. 1988—Fumbled twice. 1989—Fumbled twice. 1990—Fumbled once and recovered one fumble. 1991—Attempted one pass without a completion and fumbled twice. 1994—Ran two yards with lateral from reception for a touchdown and recovered one fumble for seven yards. 1997—Fumbled once.
SINGLE GAME HIGHS (regular season): Receptions—10 (October 12, 1997, vs. Jacksonville); yards—211 (September 4, 1994, vs. New England); and touchdown receptions—4 (October 20, 1996, vs. Miami).
STATISTICAL PLATEAUS: 100-yard receiving games: 1985 (1), 1986 (2), 1987 (1), 1988 (1), 1989 (1), 1990 (1), 1991 (3), 1992 (2), 1993 (2), 1994 (6), 1995 (2), 1996 (4), 1997 (6). Total: 32.

				RUSHING				RECEIVING				PUNT RETURNS				KICKOFF RETURNS			TOTALS		
Year Team	G	GS	Att.	Yds.	Avg.	TD	No.	Yds.	Avg.	TD	No.	Yds.	Avg.	TD	No.	Yds.	Avg.	TD	TD	2pt.	Pts.
1984—New England NFL	14	2	2	-11	-5.5	0	11	164	14.9	1	36	347	9.6	0	5	95	19.0	0	1	...	6
1985—New England NFL	16	14	7	27	3.9	1	39	670	17.2	7	37	520*14.1		†2	3	39	13.0	0	10	...	60
1986—New England NFL	14	13	4	80	20.0	0	43	737	17.1	6	35	366	10.5	▲1	10	192	19.2	0	7	...	42
1987—New England NFL	12	12	9	52	5.8	0	31	467	15.1	5	18	174	9.7	0	6	119	19.8	0	5	...	30
1988—New England NFL	15	14	6	12	2.0	0	33	490	14.8	5	38	398	10.5	0	1	3	3.0	0	5	...	30
1989—New England NFL	11	5	2	15	7.5	0	29	537	18.5	3	12	107	8.9	0	1	47	47.0	0	3	...	18
1990—New England NFL	16	15	0	0	...	0	54	856	15.9	4	28	133	4.8	0	0	0	...	0	4	...	24
1991—New England NFL	16	15	2	11	5.5	0	68	1014	14.9	3	2	10	5.0	0	0	0	...	0	3	...	18
1992—New England NFL	15	14	1	6	6.0	0	55	791	14.4	4	0	0	...	0	0	0	...	0	4	...	24
1993—Miami NFL	16	16	3	-4	-1.3	0	64	1010	15.8	5	0	0	...	0	1	10	10.0	0	5	...	30
1994—Miami NFL	16	16	0	0	...	0	73	1270	17.4	7	0	0	...	0	0	0	...	0	7	2	46
1995—Miami NFL	16	16	0	0	...	0	62	910	14.7	8	0	0	...	0	0	0	...	0	8	0	48
1996—Philadelphia NFL	16	16	1	-4	-4.0	0	88	1195	13.6	11	0	0	...	0	0	0	...	0	11	0	66
1997—Philadelphia NFL	16	16	0	0	...	0	86	1316	15.3	6	0	0	...	0	0	0	...	0	6	0	36
1998—Philadelphia NFL	16	16	3	46	15.3	0	48	556	11.6	2	0	0	...	0	0	0	...	0	2	0	12
Pro totals (15 years)	225	200	40	230	5.8	1	784	11983	15.3	77	206	2055	10.0	3	27	505	18.7	0	81	2	490

FUAMATU-MA'AFALA, CHRIS RB STEELERS

PERSONAL: Born March 4, 1977, in Honolulu. ... 5-11/252. ... Name pronounced fu-ah-MAH-tu my-ah-FAH-la.
HIGH SCHOOL: St. Louis (Honolulu).
COLLEGE: Utah.
TRANSACTIONS/CAREER NOTES: Selected after junior season by Pittsburgh Steelers in sixth round (178th pick overall) of 1998 NFL draft. ... Signed by Steelers (July 10, 1998).
SINGLE GAME HIGHS (regular season): Attempts—2 (October 18, 1998, vs. Baltimore); yards—10 (September 27, 1998, vs. Seattle); and rushing touchdowns—1 (November 9, 1998, vs. Green Bay).

			RUSHING				RECEIVING				TOTALS			
Year Team	G	GS	Att.	Yds.	Avg.	TD	No.	Yds.	Avg.	TD	2pt.	Pts.	Fum.
1998—Pittsburgh NFL	12	0	7	30	4.3	2	9	84	9.3	1	3	0	18	0

FULLER, COREY DB BROWNS

PERSONAL: Born May 1, 1971, in Tallahassee, Fla. ... 5-10/217.
HIGH SCHOOL: James S. Rickards (Tallahassee, Fla.).
COLLEGE: Florida State (degree in criminology and child development, 1994).
TRANSACTIONS/CAREER NOTES: Selected by Minnesota Vikings in second round (55th pick overall) of 1995 NFL draft. ... Signed by Vikings (July 24, 1995). ... Granted unconditional free agency (February 12, 1999). ... Signed by Cleveland Browns (February 18, 1999).
CHAMPIONSHIP GAME EXPERIENCE: Played in NFC championship game (1998 season).
PRO STATISTICS: 1995—Credited with 1/2 sack and recovered one fumble for 12 yards and a touchdown. 1998—Credited with one sack.

			INTERCEPTIONS			
Year Team	G	GS	No.	Yds.	Avg.	TD
1995—Minnesota NFL	16	11	1	0	0.0	0
1996—Minnesota NFL	16	14	3	3	1.0	0
1997—Minnesota NFL	16	16	2	24	12.0	0
1998—Minnesota NFL	16	16	4	36	9.0	0
Pro totals (4 years)	64	57	10	63	6.3	0

FULLER, RANDY — CB — FALCONS

PERSONAL: Born June 2, 1970, in Griffin, Ga. ... 5-10/184. ... Full name: Randy Lamar Fuller.
HIGH SCHOOL: William H. Spencer (Columbus, Ga.).
COLLEGE: Tennessee State.
TRANSACTIONS/CAREER NOTES: Selected by Denver Broncos in fourth round (123rd pick overall) of 1994 NFL draft. ... Signed by Broncos (July 22, 1994). ... Released by Broncos (August 22, 1995). ... Signed by Pittsburgh Steelers (September 12, 1995). ... Granted free agency (February 14, 1997). ... Re-signed by Steelers for 1997 season. ... Granted unconditional free agency (February 13, 1998). ... Signed by Atlanta Falcons (March 19, 1998).
PLAYING EXPERIENCE: Denver NFL, 1994; Pittsburgh NFL, 1995-1997; Atlanta NFL, 1998. ... Games/Games started: 1994 (10/1), 1995 (13/0), 1996 (14/1), 1997 (12/3), 1998 (13/0). Total: 62/5.
CHAMPIONSHIP GAME EXPERIENCE: Played in AFC championship game (1995 and 1997 seasons). ... Played in Super Bowl XXX (1995 season) and Super Bowl XXXIII (1998 season). ... Played in NFC championship game (1998 season).
PRO STATISTICS: 1996—Intercepted one pass for no yards. 1997—Credited with one sack. 1998—Credited with two sacks and recovered two fumbles.

FULLER, WILLIAM — DE

PERSONAL: Born March 8, 1962, in Norfolk, Va. ... 6-3/280. ... Full name: William Henry Fuller Jr.
HIGH SCHOOL: Indian River (Chesapeake, Va.).
COLLEGE: North Carolina (degree in psychology, 1983).
TRANSACTIONS/CAREER NOTES: Selected by Philadelphia Stars in 1984 USFL territorial draft. ... Signed by Stars (February 6, 1984). ... On injured reserve with fractured ankle (May 18-June 23, 1984). ... Selected by Los Angeles Rams in first round (21st pick overall) of 1984 NFL supplemental draft. ... Stars franchise moved to Baltimore (November 1, 1984). ... Granted free agency when USFL suspended operations (August 7, 1986). ... Signed by Rams (September 10, 1986). ... Traded by Rams with G Kent Hill, first- (WR Haywood Jeffires) and fifth-round (RB Spencer Tillman) picks in 1987 draft and first-round pick (traded to Los Angeles Raiders) in 1988 draft to Houston Oilers for rights to QB Jim Everett (September 18, 1986). ... Granted roster exemption (September 18-22, 1986). ... Granted free agency (February 1, 1992). ... Re-signed by Oilers (September 11, 1992). ... Granted unconditional free agency (February 17, 1994). ... Signed by Philadelphia Eagles (March 31, 1994). ... Granted unconditional free agency (February 14, 1997). ... Signed by San Diego Chargers (April 14, 1997). ... Granted unconditional free agency (February 12, 1999).
CHAMPIONSHIP GAME EXPERIENCE: Played in USFL championship game (1984 and 1985 seasons).
HONORS: Named defensive tackle on THE SPORTING NEWS college All-America first team (1983). ... Named defensive end on THE SPORTING NEWS USFL All-Star team (1985). ... Played in Pro Bowl (1991 and 1994-1996 seasons).
PRO STATISTICS: USFL: 1984—Recovered one fumble. 1985—Intercepted one pass for 35 yards and recovered four fumbles for 17 yards. NFL: 1987—Returned one kickoff for no yards and recovered one fumble. 1988—Intercepted one pass for nine yards. 1990—Recovered one fumble. 1991—Recovered two fumbles for three yards. 1992—Recovered one fumble for 10 yards and a touchdown. 1994—Credited with one safety and recovered one fumble. 1995—Recovered one fumble. 1996—Recovered one fumble. 1997—Intercepted one pass for no yards.

Year Team	G	GS	SACKS
1984—Philadelphia USFL	13	12	2.0
1985—Baltimore USFL	18	...	8.5
1986—Houston NFL	13	0	1.0
1987—Houston NFL	12	1	2.0
1988—Houston NFL	16	15	8.5
1989—Houston NFL	15	8	6.5
1990—Houston NFL	16	16	8.0
1991—Houston NFL	16	16	§15.0
1992—Houston NFL	15	14	8.0
1993—Houston NFL	16	16	10.0
1994—Philadelphia NFL	16	16	9.5
1995—Philadelphia NFL	14	13	∞13.0
1996—Philadelphia NFL	16	16	13.0
1997—San Diego NFL	16	16	3.0
1998—San Diego NFL	13	13	3.0
USFL totals (2 years)	31	...	10.5
NFL totals (13 years)	194	160	100.5
Pro totals (15 years)	225	...	111.0

GADSDEN, ORONDE — WR — DOLPHINS

PERSONAL: Born August 20, 1971, in Charleston, S.C. ... 6-2/218. ... Full name: Oronde Benjamin Gadsden.
HIGH SCHOOL: Burke (Charleston, S.C.).
COLLEGE: Winston-Salem (degree in marketing).
TRANSACTIONS/CAREER NOTES: Signed as non-drafted free agent by Dallas Cowboys (April 24, 1995). ... Released by Cowboys (August 22, 1995). ... Re-signed by Cowboys to practice squad (August 30, 1995). ... Activated by Cowboys (January 8, 1996). ... On injured reserve with left ankle sprain (January 11, 1996-remainder of season). ... Released by Cowboys (August 27, 1996). ... Signed by Pittsburgh Steelers (August 5, 1997). ... Released by Steelers (August 19, 1997). ... Signed by Cowboys (August 21, 1997). ... Released by Cowboys (August 24, 1997). ... Played with Portland Forest Dragons of Arena League (1998). ... Signed by Miami Dolphins (August 3, 1998).
SINGLE GAME HIGHS (regular season): Receptions—9 (December 27, 1998, vs. Atlanta); yards—153 (December 27, 1998, vs. Atlanta); and touchdown receptions—2 (November 23, 1998, vs. New England).
STATISTICAL PLATEAUS: 100-yard receiving games: 1998 (1).

			RECEIVING				TOTALS		
Year Team	G	GS	No.	Yds.	Avg.	TD	TD	2pt.	Pts.	Fum.
1995—Dallas NFL						Did not play.				
1996—						Did not play.				
1997—						Did not play.				
1998—Miami NFL	16	12	48	713	14.9	7	7	0	42	2

GAITER, TONY — PR/KR — CHARGERS

PERSONAL: Born July 15, 1974, in Miami. ... 5-8/170. ... Full name: Tony Bernard Gaiter.
HIGH SCHOOL: Killian (Miami).
JUNIOR COLLEGE: San Bernardino (Calif.) Valley.
COLLEGE: Miami (Fla.).
TRANSACTIONS/CAREER NOTES: Selected by New England Patriots in sixth round (192nd pick overall) of 1997 NFL draft. ... Signed by Patriots (July 16, 1997). ... Released by Patriots (August 24, 1997). ... Re-signed by Patriots to practice squad (August 26, 1997). ... Activated (November 28, 1997). ... Released by Patriots (August 25, 1998). ... Re-signed by Patriots (October 22, 1998). ... Active for one game with Patriots (1998); did not play. ... Released by Patriots (October 28, 1998). ... Signed by San Diego Chargers (November 24, 1998).

				PUNT RETURNS				KICKOFF RETURNS				TOTALS		
Year Team	G	GS	No.	Yds.	Avg.	TD	No.	Yds.	Avg.	TD	TD	2pt.	Pts.	Fum.
1997—New England NFL	1	0	0	0	...	0	0	0	...	0	0	0	0	0
1998—San Diego NFL	5	0	13	155	11.9	0	16	295	18.4	0	0	0	0	1
Pro totals (2 years)	6	0	13	155	11.9	0	16	295	18.4	0	0	0	0	1

GALBRAITH, SCOTT — TE

PERSONAL: Born January 7, 1967, in Sacramento. ... 6-2/254. ... Full name: Alan Scott Galbraith. ... Name pronounced GAL-breath.
HIGH SCHOOL: Highlands (North Highlands, Calif.).
COLLEGE: Southern California.
TRANSACTIONS/CAREER NOTES: Selected by Cleveland Browns in seventh round (178th pick overall) of 1990 NFL draft. ... Signed by Browns (July 17, 1990). ... Granted free agency (February 1, 1992). ... Re-signed by Browns (August 30, 1992). ... Activated (September 15, 1992). ... Granted free agency (March 1, 1993). ... Released by Browns (July 24, 1993). ... Signed by Browns (August 30, 1993). ... Signed by Dallas Cowboys (November 11, 1993). ... Granted unconditional free agency (February 17, 1995). ... Signed by Washington Redskins (May 16, 1995). ... Granted unconditional free agency (February 16, 1996). ... Re-signed by Redskins (April 17, 1996). ... Released by Redskins (June 4, 1997). ... Signed by Cowboys (July 16, 1997). ... Granted unconditional free agency (February 13, 1998). ... Signed by Green Bay Packers (December 23, 1998). ... Released by Packers (December 29, 1998).
CHAMPIONSHIP GAME EXPERIENCE: Played in NFC championship game (1993 and 1994 seasons). ... Member of Super Bowl championship team (1993 season).
PRO STATISTICS: 1990—Returned three kickoffs for 16 yards and recovered one fumble. 1991—Returned two kickoffs for 13 yards and recovered one fumble. 1997—Returned two kickoffs for 24 yards.
SINGLE GAME HIGHS (regular season): Receptions—4 (December 15, 1991, vs. Houston); yards—60 (December 9, 1990, vs. Houston); and touchdown receptions—1 (September 22, 1996, vs. St. Louis).

			RECEIVING				TOTALS			
Year Team	G	GS	No.	Yds.	Avg.	TD	TD	2pt.	Pts.	Fum.
1990—Cleveland NFL	16	1	4	62	15.5	0	0	...	0	0
1991—Cleveland NFL	16	13	27	328	12.1	0	0	...	0	0
1992—Cleveland NFL	14	2	4	63	15.8	1	1	...	6	0
1993—Dallas NFL	7	0	1	1	1.0	1	1	...	6	0
1994—Dallas NFL	16	2	4	31	7.8	0	0	0	0	0
1995—Washington NFL	16	16	10	80	8.0	2	2	0	12	0
1996—Washington NFL	16	6	8	89	11.1	2	2	0	12	0
1997—Dallas NFL	16	0	2	16	8.0	0	0	0	0	0
1998—Green Bay NFL	1	0	0	0	...	0	0	0	0	0
Pro totals (9 years)	118	40	60	670	11.2	6	6	0	36	0

GALLERY, NICK — P — DOLPHINS

PERSONAL: Born February 15, 1975, in Manchester, Iowa. ... 6-4/245. ... Full name: Nick Patrick Gallery.
HIGH SCHOOL: East Buchanan (Winthrop, Iowa).
COLLEGE: Iowa.
TRANSACTIONS/CAREER NOTES: Signed as a non-drafted free agent by Kansas City Chiefs (April 26, 1997). ... Released by Chiefs (August 12, 1997). ... Signed by New York Jets to practice squad (October 20, 1997). ... Released by Jets (September 13, 1998). ... Signed by Philadelphia Eagles to practice squad (December 14, 1998). ... Granted free agency after 1998 season. ... Signed by Miami Dolphins (February 3, 1999).

			PUNTING				
Year Team	G	No.	Yds.	Avg.	Net avg.	In. 20	Blk.
1997—New York Jets NFL			Did not play.				
1998—New York Jets NFL	1	6	238	39.7	33.3	2	0

GALLOWAY, JOEY — WR — SEAHAWKS

PERSONAL: Born November 20, 1971, in Bellaire, Ohio. ... 5-11/188.
HIGH SCHOOL: Bellaire (Ohio).
COLLEGE: Ohio State (degree in business/marketing, 1994).
TRANSACTIONS/CAREER NOTES: Selected by Seattle Seahawks in first round (eighth pick overall) of 1995 NFL draft. ... Signed by Seahawks (July 20, 1995).
PRO STATISTICS: 1995—Fumbled once. 1996—Fumbled twice. 1997—Fumbled once and recovered one fumble. 1998—Fumbled once.
SINGLE GAME HIGHS (regular season): Receptions—8 (November 2, 1997, vs. Denver); yards—142 (September 6, 1998, vs. Philadelphia); and touchdown receptions—3 (October 26, 1997, vs. Oakland).
STATISTICAL PLATEAUS: 100-yard receiving games: 1995 (3), 1996 (2), 1997 (3), 1998 (4). Total: 12.

			RUSHING				RECEIVING				PUNT RETURNS				KICKOFF RETURNS				TOTALS		
Year Team	G	GS	Att.	Yds.	Avg.	TD	No.	Yds.	Avg.	TD	No.	Yds.	Avg.	TD	No.	Yds.	Avg.	TD	TD	2pt.	Pts.
1995—Seattle NFL	16	16	11	154	14.0	1	67	1039	15.5	7	36	360	10.0	†1	2	30	15.0	0	9	0	54
1996—Seattle NFL	16	16	15	127	8.5	0	57	987	17.3	7	15	158	10.5	▲1	0	0	...	0	8	0	48
1997—Seattle NFL	15	15	9	72	8.0	0	72	1049	14.6▲12	0	0	...	0	0	0	...	0	12	0	72
1998—Seattle NFL	16	16	9	26	2.9	0	65	1047	16.1	10	25	251	10.0	†2	0	0	...	0	12	0	72
Pro totals (4 years)	63	63	44	379	8.6	1	261	4122	15.8	36	76	769	10.1	4	2	30	15.0	0	41	0	246

GALYON, SCOTT — LB — GIANTS

PERSONAL: Born March 23, 1974, in Seymour, Tenn. ... 6-2/245.
HIGH SCHOOL: Seymour (Tenn.).
COLLEGE: Tennessee.
TRANSACTIONS/CAREER NOTES: Selected by New York Giants in sixth round (182nd pick overall) of 1996 NFL draft. ... Signed by Giants (July 17, 1996). ... On injured reserve with knee injury (December 8, 1998-remainder of season). ... Granted free agency (February 12, 1999). ... Re-signed by Giants (May 3, 1999).
PLAYING EXPERIENCE: New York Giants NFL, 1996-1998. ... Games/Games started: 1996 (16/0), 1997 (16/0), 1998 (10/1). Total: 42/1.
PRO STATISTICS: 1997—Credited with three sacks. 1998—Credited with one sack and recovered one fumble.

GAMMON, KENDALL — C — SAINTS

PERSONAL: Born October 23, 1968, in Wichita, Kan. ... 6-4/265. ... Full name: Kendall Robert Gammon.
HIGH SCHOOL: Rose Hill (Kan.).
COLLEGE: Pittsburg (Kan.) State (degree in physical education).
TRANSACTIONS/CAREER NOTES: Selected by Pittsburgh Steelers in 11th round (291st pick overall) of 1992 NFL draft. ... Signed by Steelers (July 14, 1992). ... Released by Steelers (August 30, 1993). ... Re-signed by Steelers (August 31, 1993). ... Granted unconditional free agency (February 17, 1995). ... Re-signed by Steelers (May 8, 1995). ... Released by Steelers (August 26, 1996). ... Signed by New Orleans Saints (August 28, 1996).
PLAYING EXPERIENCE: Pittsburgh NFL, 1992-1995; New Orleans NFL, 1996-1998. ... Games/Games started: 1992 (16/0), 1993 (16/0), 1994 (16/0), 1995 (16/0), 1996 (16/0), 1997 (16/0), 1998 (16/0). Total: 112/0.
CHAMPIONSHIP GAME EXPERIENCE: Played in AFC championship game (1994 and 1995 seasons). ... Played in Super Bowl XXX (1995 season).

GANDY, WAYNE — OT — STEELERS

PERSONAL: Born February 10, 1971, in Haines City, Fla. ... 6-5/310. ... Full name: Wayne Lamar Gandy.
HIGH SCHOOL: Haines City (Fla.).
COLLEGE: Auburn.
TRANSACTIONS/CAREER NOTES: Selected by Los Angeles Rams in first round (15th pick overall) of 1994 NFL draft. ... Signed by Rams (July 23, 1994). ... Rams franchise moved to St. Louis (April 12, 1995). ... Granted unconditional free agency (February 12, 1999). ... Signed by Pittsburgh Steelers (April 6, 1999).
PLAYING EXPERIENCE: Los Angeles Rams NFL, 1994; St. Louis NFL, 1995-1998. ... Games/Games started: 1994 (16/9), 1995 (16/16), 1996 (16/16), 1997 (16/16), 1998 (16/16). Total: 80/73.
HONORS: Named offensive lineman on THE SPORTING NEWS college All-America first team (1993).

GANNON, RICH — QB — RAIDERS

PERSONAL: Born December 20, 1965, in Philadelphia. ... 6-3/210. ... Full name: Richard Joseph Gannon.
HIGH SCHOOL: St. Joseph's Prep (Philadelphia).
COLLEGE: Delaware (degree in criminal justice, 1987).
TRANSACTIONS/CAREER NOTES: Selected by New England Patriots in fourth round (98th pick overall) of 1987 NFL draft. ... Rights traded by Patriots to Minnesota Vikings for fourth- (WR Sammy Martin) and 11th-round (traded) picks in 1988 draft (May 6, 1987). ... Signed by Vikings (July 30, 1987). ... Active for 13 games (1989); did not play. ... Granted free agency (February 1, 1990). ... Re-signed by Vikings (July 30, 1990). ... Granted free agency (February 1, 1991). ... Re-signed by Vikings (July 25, 1991). ... Granted free agency (February 1, 1992). ... Re-signed by Vikings (August 8, 1992). ... Traded by Vikings to Washington Redskins for conditional draft pick (August 20, 1993). ... Granted unconditional free agency (February 1, 1994). ... Signed by Kansas City Chiefs (March 29, 1995). ... Released by Chiefs (February 15, 1996). ... Re-signed by Chiefs (April 3, 1996). ... Granted unconditional free agency (February 12, 1999). ... Signed by Oakland Raiders (February 16, 1999).
CHAMPIONSHIP GAME EXPERIENCE: Member of Vikings for NFC championship game (1987 season); did not play.
PRO STATISTICS: 1990—Recovered six fumbles for minus three yards. 1991—Caught one pass for no yards. 1993—Recovered one fumble. 1996—Fumbled once. 1997—Fumbled five times. 1998—Fumbled nine times and recovered four fumbles for minus 15 yards.
SINGLE GAME HIGHS (regular season): Attempts—63 (October 20, 1991, vs. New England); completions—35 (October 20, 1991, vs. New England); yards—318 (September 27, 1992, vs. Cincinnati); and touchdown passes—4 (September 27, 1992, vs. Cincinnati).
STATISTICAL PLATEAUS: 300-yard passing games: 1991 (1), 1992 (1), 1997 (1), 1998 (1). Total: 4.
MISCELLANEOUS: Regular-season record as starting NFL quarterback: 31-27 (.534).

				PASSING							RUSHING				TOTALS		
Year Team	G	GS	Att.	Cmp.	Pct.	Yds.	TD	Int.	Avg.	Rat.	Att.	Yds.	Avg.	TD	TD	2pt.	Pts.
1987—Minnesota NFL	4	0	6	2	33.3	18	0	1	3.00	2.8	0	0	...	0	0	...	0
1988—Minnesota NFL	3	0	15	7	46.7	90	0	0	6.00	66.0	4	29	7.3	0	0	...	0
1989—Minnesota NFL						Did not play.											
1990—Minnesota NFL	14	12	349	182	52.1	2278	16	16	6.53	68.9	52	268	5.2	1	1	...	6
1991—Minnesota NFL	15	11	354	211	59.6	2166	12	6	6.12	81.5	43	236	5.5	2	2	...	12
1992—Minnesota NFL	12	12	279	159	57.0	1905	12	13	6.83	72.9	45	187	4.2	0	0	...	0
1993—Washington NFL	8	4	125	74	59.2	704	3	7	5.63	59.6	21	88	4.2	1	1	...	6
1994—						Did not play.											
1995—Kansas City NFL	2	0	11	7	63.6	57	0	0	5.18	76.7	8	25	3.1	0	0	0	0
1996—Kansas City NFL	4	3	90	54	60.0	491	6	1	5.46	92.4	12	81	6.8	0	0	0	0
1997—Kansas City NFL	9	6	175	98	56.0	1144	7	4	6.54	79.8	33	109	3.3	2	2	0	12
1998—Kansas City NFL	12	10	354	206	58.2	2305	10	6	6.51	80.1	44	168	3.8	3	3	0	18
Pro totals (10 years)	83	58	1758	1000	56.9	11158	66	54	6.35	75.6	262	1191	4.5	10	9	0	54

GARCIA, FRANK — C — PANTHERS

PERSONAL: Born January 28, 1972, in Phoenix. ... 6-2/302. ... Full name: Frank Christopher Garcia.
HIGH SCHOOL: Maryvale (Phoenix).
COLLEGE: Washington.
TRANSACTIONS/CAREER NOTES: Selected by Carolina Panthers in fourth round (132nd pick overall) of 1995 NFL draft. ... Signed by Panthers (July 14, 1995). ... Granted free agency (February 13, 1998). ... Re-signed by Panthers (March 16, 1998).
PLAYING EXPERIENCE: Carolina NFL, 1995-1998. ... Games/Games started: 1995 (15/14), 1996 (14/8), 1997 (16/16), 1998 (14/14). Total: 59/52.
CHAMPIONSHIP GAME EXPERIENCE: Played in NFC championship game (1996 season).
PRO STATISTICS: 1995—Fumbled once and recovered one fumble for 10 yards. 1996—Recovered two fumbles. 1997—Returned one kick-off for 11 yards. 1998—Recovered two fumbles for two yards.

GARCIA, JEFF — QB — 49ERS

PERSONAL: Born February 24, 1970, in Gilroy, Calif. ... 6-1/195.
HIGH SCHOOL: Gilroy (Calif.).
JUNIOR COLLEGE: Gavilan College (Calif.).
COLLEGE: San Jose State.
TRANSACTIONS/CAREER NOTES: Signed by Calgary Stampeders of CFL (1994). ... Granted free agency (February 16, 1997). ... Re-signed by Stampeders (April 30, 1997). ... Signed as non-drafted free agent by San Francisco 49ers (February 16, 1999).
CHAMPIONSHIP GAME EXPERIENCE: Played in Grey Cup (1995 and 1998). ... Member of CFL championship team (1998). ... Named Most Valuable Player of Grey Cup, CFL championship game (1998).

				PASSING							RUSHING				TOTALS	
Year Team	G	GS	Att.	Cmp.	Pct.	Yds.	TD	Int.	Avg.	Rat.	Att.	Yds.	Avg.	TD	TD	2pt.	Pts.
1994—Calgary CFL	7	...	3	2	66.7	10	0	0	3.33	71.5	2	3	1.5	0	0	...	0
1995—Calgary CFL	18	...	364	230	63.2	3358	25	7	9.23	108.1	61	396	6.5	5	5	...	30
1996—Calgary CFL	18	...	537	315	58.7	4225	25	16	7.87	86.9	92	657	7.1	6	6	...	36
1997—Calgary CFL	17	...	566	354	62.5	4573	33	14	8.08	97.0	135	727	5.4	7	7	...	42
1998—Calgary CFL		...	554	348	62.8	4276	28	15	7.72	92.3	94	575	6.1	6	6	...	36
Pro totals (5 years)		...	2024	1249	61.7	16442	111	52	8.12	94.9	384	2358	6.1	24	24	...	144

GARDENER, DARYL — DT — DOLPHINS

PERSONAL: Born February 25, 1973, in Baltimore. ... 6-6/315. ... Full name: Daryl Ronald Gardener.
HIGH SCHOOL: Lawton (Okla.).
COLLEGE: Baylor.
TRANSACTIONS/CAREER NOTES: Selected by Miami Dolphins in first round (20th pick overall) of 1996 NFL draft. ... Signed by Dolphins (June 6, 1996).
PRO STATISTICS: 1996—Recovered one fumble. 1997—Recovered one fumble. 1998—Intercepted one pass for minus one yard.

Year Team	G	GS	SACKS
1996—Miami NFL	16	12	1.0
1997—Miami NFL	16	16	1.5
1998—Miami NFL	16	16	1.0
Pro totals (3 years)	48	44	3.5

GARDOCKI, CHRIS — P — BROWNS

PERSONAL: Born February 7, 1970, in Stone Mountain, Ga. ... 6-1/200. ... Full name: Christopher Allen Gardocki.
HIGH SCHOOL: Redan (Stone Mountain, Ga.).
COLLEGE: Clemson.
TRANSACTIONS/CAREER NOTES: Selected after junior season by Chicago Bears in third round (78th pick overall) of 1991 NFL draft. ... Signed by Bears (June 24, 1991). ... On injured reserve with groin injury (August 27-November 27, 1991). ... Granted unconditional free agency (February 17, 1995). ... Signed by Indianapolis Colts (February 24, 1995). ... Granted unconditional free agency (February 12, 1999). ... Signed by Cleveland Browns (February 16, 1999).
CHAMPIONSHIP GAME EXPERIENCE: Played in AFC championship game (1995 season).
HONORS: Named kicker on THE SPORTING NEWS college All-America second team (1990). ... Named punter on THE SPORTING NEWS NFL All-Pro team (1996). ... Played in Pro Bowl (1996 season).
PRO STATISTICS: 1992—Attempted three passes with one completion for 43 yards and recovered one fumble. 1993—Attempted two passes without a completion, fumbled once and recovered one fumble. 1995—Attempted one pass without a completion.

			PUNTING			
Year Team	G	No.	Yds.	Avg.	Net avg.	In. 20	Blk.
1991—Chicago NFL	4	0	0	...	...	0	0
1992—Chicago NFL	16	79	3393	42.9	36.2	19	0
1993—Chicago NFL	16	80	3080	38.5	36.6	28	0
1994—Chicago NFL	16	76	2871	37.8	32.3	23	0
1995—Indianapolis NFL	16	63	2681	42.6	33.3	16	0
1996—Indianapolis NFL	16	68	3105	45.7	§39.0	23	0
1997—Indianapolis NFL	16	67	3034	45.3	36.2	18	0
1998—Indianapolis NFL	16	79	3583	45.4	37.1	23	0
Pro totals (8 years)	116	512	21747	42.5	35.8	150	0

GARNER, CHARLIE — RB

PERSONAL: Born February 13, 1972, in Falls Church, Va. ... 5-9/187.
HIGH SCHOOL: Jeb Stuart (Falls Church, Va.).
JUNIOR COLLEGE: Scottsdale (Ariz.) Community College.
COLLEGE: Tennessee.
TRANSACTIONS/CAREER NOTES: Selected by Philadelphia Eagles in second round (42nd pick overall) of 1994 NFL draft. ... Signed by Eagles (July 18, 1994). ... Granted free agency (February 14, 1997). ... Re-signed by Eagles (June 16, 1997). ... Granted unconditional free agency (February 13, 1998). ... Re-signed by Eagles (February 23, 1998). ... On injured reserve with rib injury (December 10, 1998-remainder of season). ... Released by Eagles (April 20, 1999).
SINGLE GAME HIGHS (regular season): Attempts—28 (October 9, 1994, vs. Washington); yards—129 (November 8, 1998, vs. Detroit); and rushing touchdowns—3 (October 8, 1995, vs. Washington).
STATISTICAL PLATEAUS: 100-yard rushing games: 1994 (2), 1995 (1), 1997 (1), 1998 (1). Total: 5.

			RUSHING				RECEIVING				KICKOFF RETURNS				TOTALS			
Year Team	G	GS	Att.	Yds.	Avg.	TD	No.	Yds.	Avg.	TD	No.	Yds.	Avg.	TD	TD	2pt.	Pts.	Fum.
1994—Philadelphia NFL	10	8	109	399	3.7	3	8	74	9.3	0	0	0	...	0	3	0	18	3
1995—Philadelphia NFL	15	2	108	588	*5.4	6	10	61	6.1	0	29	590	20.3	0	6	0	36	2
1996—Philadelphia NFL	15	1	66	346	5.2	1	14	92	6.6	0	6	117	19.5	0	1	0	6	1
1997—Philadelphia NFL	16	2	116	547	4.7	3	24	225	9.4	0	0	0	...	0	3	0	18	1
1998—Philadelphia NFL	10	3	96	381	4.0	4	19	110	5.8	0	0	0	...	0	4	0	24	1
Pro totals (5 years)	66	16	495	2261	4.6	17	75	562	7.5	0	35	707	20.2	0	17	0	102	8

GARNES, SAM — S — GIANTS

PERSONAL: Born July 12, 1974, in Bronx, N.Y. ... 6-3/225. ... Full name: Sam Aaron Garnes.
HIGH SCHOOL: DeWitt Clinton (Bronx, N.Y.).
COLLEGE: Cincinnati.
TRANSACTIONS/CAREER NOTES: Selected by New York Giants in fifth round (136th pick overall) of 1997 NFL draft. ... Signed by Giants for 1997 season.

			INTERCEPTIONS			
Year Team	G	GS	No.	Yds.	Avg.	TD
1997—New York Giants NFL	16	15	1	95	95.0	1
1998—New York Giants NFL	11	11	1	13	13.0	0
Pro totals (2 years)	27	26	2	108	54.0	1

GARRETT, JASON — QB — COWBOYS

PERSONAL: Born March 28, 1966, in Abington, Pa. ... 6-2/195. ... Full name: Jason Calvin Garrett. ... Son of Jim Garrett, scout, Dallas Cowboys; brother of John Garrett, wide receiver with Cincinnati Bengals (1989) and San Antonio Riders of World League (1991); and brother of Judd Garrett, running back with London of World League (1991-92).
HIGH SCHOOL: University (Chargin Falls, Ohio).
COLLEGE: Princeton (degree in history).
TRANSACTIONS/CAREER NOTES: Signed as non-drafted free agent by New Orleans Saints (1989). ... Released by Saints (August 30, 1989). ... Re-signed by Saints to developmental squad (September 6, 1989). ... Released by Saints (December 29, 1989). ... Re-signed by Saints for 1990 season. ... Released by Saints (September 3, 1990). ... Signed by WLAF (January 3, 1991). ... Selected by San Antonio Riders in first round (seventh quarterback) of 1991 WLAF positional draft. ... Signed by Ottawa Rough Riders of CFL (1991). ... Released by San Antonio Riders (March 3, 1992). ... Signed by Dallas Cowboys (March 23, 1992). ... Released by Cowboys (August 31, 1992). ... Re-signed by Cowboys to practice squad (September 1, 1992). ... Granted unconditional free agency (February 16, 1996). ... Re-signed by Cowboys (April 3, 1996). ... Granted unconditional free agency (February 14, 1997). ... Re-signed by Cowboys (April 8, 1997).
CHAMPIONSHIP GAME EXPERIENCE: Member of Cowboys for NFC championship game (1993-1995 seasons); inactive. ... Member of Super Bowl championship game (1993 and 1995 seasons).
PRO STATISTICS: W.L.: 1991—Fumbled twice. CFL: 1991—Fumbled once. NFL: 1993—Fumbled once. 1994—Recovered one fumble. 1998—Fumbled four times for minus 17 yards.
SINGLE GAME HIGHS (regular season): Attempts—33 (September 27, 1998, vs. Oakland); completions—18 (September 27, 1998, vs. Oakland); yards—311 (November 24, 1994, vs. Green Bay); and touchdown passes—2 (October 11, 1998, vs. Carolina).
STATISTICAL PLATEAUS: 300-yard passing games: 1994 (1).
MISCELLANEOUS: Regular-season record as starting NFL quarterback: 5-2 (.714).

			PASSING								RUSHING				TOTALS		
Year Team	G	GS	Att.	Cmp.	Pct.	Yds.	TD	Int.	Avg.	Rat.	Att.	Yds.	Avg.	TD	TD	2pt.	Pts.
1991—San Antonio W.L.	5	3	113	66	58.4	609	3	3	5.39	71.0	7	7	1.0	0	0	...	0
—Ottawa CFL	13	0	3	2	66.7	28	0	0	9.33	96.5	0	0	...	0	0	...	0
1992—Dallas NFL						Did not play.											
1993—Dallas NFL	5	1	19	9	47.4	61	0	0	3.21	54.9	8	-8	-1.0	0	0	...	0
1994—Dallas NFL	2	1	31	16	51.6	315	2	1	10.16	95.5	3	-2	-0.7	0	0	...	0
1995—Dallas NFL	1	0	5	4	80.0	46	1	0	9.20	144.6	1	-1	-1.0	0	0	0	0
1996—Dallas NFL	1	0	3	3	100.0	44	0	0	14.67	118.8	0	0	...	0	0	0	0
1997—Dallas NFL	1	0	14	10	71.4	56	0	0	4.00	78.3	0	0	...	0	0	0	0
1998—Dallas NFL	8	5	158	91	57.6	1206	5	3	7.63	84.5	11	14	1.3	0	0	0	0
W.L. totals (1 year)	5	3	113	66	58.4	609	3	3	5.39	71.0	7	7	1.0	0	0	0	0
CFL totals (1 year)	13	0	3	2	66.7	28	0	0	9.33	96.5	0	0	...	0	0	0	0
NFL totals (6 years)	18	7	230	133	57.8	1728	8	4	7.51	85.9	23	3	0.1	0	0	0	0
Pro totals (8 years)	36	10	346	201	58.1	2365	11	7	6.84	81.1	30	10	0.3	0	0	0	0

GASH, SAM — FB — BILLS

PERSONAL: Born March 7, 1969, in Hendersonville, N.C. ... 6-0/235. ... Full name: Samuel Lee Gash Jr. ... Cousin of Thane Gash, safety with Cleveland Browns (1988-90) and San Francisco 49ers (1992).
HIGH SCHOOL: Hendersonville (N.C.).
COLLEGE: Penn State (degree in liberal arts).
TRANSACTIONS/CAREER NOTES: Selected by New England Patriots in eighth round (205th pick overall) of 1992 NFL draft. ... Signed by Patriots (June 10, 1992). ... Granted free agency (February 17, 1995). ... Re-signed by Patriots (May 5, 1995). ... On injured reserve with knee injury (December 10, 1996-remainder of season). ... Granted unconditional free agency (February 13, 1998). ... Signed by Buffalo Bills (March 5, 1998).
HONORS: Played in Pro Bowl (1998 season).
PRO STATISTICS: 1992—Recovered two fumbles. 1994—Returned one kickoff for nine yards and recovered one fumble. 1998—Returned three kickoffs for 41 yards.
SINGLE GAME HIGHS (regular season): Attempts—15 (December 18, 1994, vs. Buffalo); yards—56 (December 18, 1994, vs. Buffalo); and rushing touchdowns—1 (September 19, 1993, vs. Seattle).

			RUSHING				RECEIVING				TOTALS			
Year Team	G	GS	Att.	Yds.	Avg.	TD	No.	Yds.	Avg.	TD	TD	2pt.	Pts.	Fum.
1992—New England NFL	15	0	5	7	1.4	1	0	0	...	0	1	...	6	1
1993—New England NFL	15	4	48	149	3.1	1	14	93	6.6	0	1	...	6	1
1994—New England NFL	13	6	30	86	2.9	0	9	61	6.8	0	0	0	0	1
1995—New England NFL	15	12	8	24	3.0	0	26	242	9.3	1	1	0	6	0
1996—New England NFL	14	9	8	15	1.9	0	33	276	8.4	2	2	1	14	0
1997—New England NFL	16	5	6	10	1.7	0	22	154	7.0	3	3	0	18	0
1998—Buffalo NFL	16	13	11	32	2.9	0	19	165	8.7	3	3	0	18	0
Pro totals (7 years)	104	49	116	323	2.8	2	123	991	8.1	9	11	1	68	3

GEDNEY, CHRIS — TE — CARDINALS

PERSONAL: Born August 9, 1970, in Liverpool, N.Y. ... 6-5/250. ... Full name: Christopher Joseph Gedney.
HIGH SCHOOL: Liverpool (N.Y.).
COLLEGE: Syracuse (degree in speech communications, 1993).
TRANSACTIONS/CAREER NOTES: Selected by Chicago Bears in third round (61st pick overall) of 1993 NFL draft. ... Signed by Bears (June 16, 1994). ... On injured reserve with broken fibula (October 24, 1994-remainder of season). ... Granted free agency (February 16, 1996). ... Re-signed by Bears (March 29, 1996). ... On injured reserve with ankle injury (September 20, 1996-entire season). ... Granted unconditional free agency (February 14, 1997). ... Signed by Arizona Cardinals (February 28, 1997). ... Granted unconditional free agency (February 13, 1998). ... Re-signed by Cardinals (February 24, 1998).
HONORS: Named tight end on THE SPORTING NEWS college All-America first team (1992).
PRO STATISTICS: 1997—Rushed once for 15 yards and returned two kickoffs for 26 yards. 1998—Returned two kickoffs for 12 yards.
SINGLE GAME HIGHS (regular season): Receptions—6 (October 25, 1993, vs. Minnesota); yards—69 (October 25, 1993, vs. Minnesota); and touchdown receptions—2 (September 4, 1994, vs. Tampa Bay).

			RECEIVING				TOTALS			
Year Team	G	GS	No.	Yds.	Avg.	TD	TD	2pt.	Pts.	Fum.
1993—Chicago NFL	7	4	10	98	9.8	0	0	...	0	1
1994—Chicago NFL	7	7	13	157	12.1	3	3	0	18	1
1995—Chicago NFL	14	1	5	52	10.4	0	0	0	0	0
1996—Chicago NFL					Did not play.					
1997—Arizona NFL	16	3	23	261	11.3	4	4	0	24	1
1998—Arizona NFL	16	3	22	271	12.3	1	1	0	6	1
Pro totals (6 years)	60	18	73	839	11.5	8	8	0	48	4

GEORGE, EDDIE — RB — TITANS

PERSONAL: Born September 24, 1973, in Philadelphia. ... 6-3/240. ... Full name: Edward Nathan George.
HIGH SCHOOL: Abington (Philadelphia), then Fork Union (Va.) Military Academy.
COLLEGE: Ohio State.
TRANSACTIONS/CAREER NOTES: Selected by Houston Oilers in first round (14th pick overall) of 1996 NFL draft. ... Signed by Oilers (July 20, 1996). ... Oilers franchise moved to Tennessee for 1997 season. ... Oilers franchise renamed Tennessee Titans for 1999 season (December 26, 1998).
HONORS: Heisman Trophy winner (1995). ... Maxwell Award winner (1995). ... Doak Walker Award winner (1995). ... Named running back on THE SPORTING NEWS college All-America first team (1995). ... Named NFL Rookie of the Year by THE SPORTING NEWS (1996). ... Played in Pro Bowl (1997 and 1998 seasons).
PRO STATISTICS: 1996—Recovered one fumble. 1998—Recovered five fumbles.
SINGLE GAME HIGHS (regular season): Attempts—35 (August 31, 1997, vs. Oakland); yards—216 (August 31, 1997, vs. Oakland); and rushing touchdowns—2 (October 19, 1997, vs. Washington).
STATISTICAL PLATEAUS: 100-yard rushing games: 1996 (4), 1997 (8), 1998 (6). Total: 18.

			RUSHING				RECEIVING				TOTALS			
Year Team	G	GS	Att.	Yds.	Avg.	TD	No.	Yds.	Avg.	TD	TD	2pt.	Pts.	Fum.
1996—Houston NFL	16	16	335	1368	4.1	8	23	182	7.9	0	8	0	48	3
1997—Tennessee NFL	16	16	357	1399	3.9	6	7	44	6.3	1	7	1	44	4
1998—Tennessee NFL	16	16	348	1294	3.7	5	37	310	8.4	1	6	1	38	7
Pro totals (3 years)	48	48	1040	4061	3.9	19	67	536	8.0	2	21	2	130	14

GEORGE, JEFF — QB — VIKINGS

PERSONAL: Born December 8, 1967, in Indianapolis. ... 6-4/215. ... Full name: Jeffrey Scott George.
HIGH SCHOOL: Warren Central (Indianapolis).
COLLEGE: Purdue, then Illinois (degree in speech communications, 1991).
TRANSACTIONS/CAREER NOTES: Signed after junior season by Indianapolis Colts (April 20, 1990). ... Selected officially by Colts in first round (first pick overall) of 1990 NFL draft. ... On reserve/did not report list (July 23-August 20, 1993). ... Traded by Colts to Atlanta Falcons for first- (LB Trev Alberts) and third-round (OT Jason Mathews) picks in 1994 draft and a first-round pick (WR Marvin Harrison) in 1996 draft (March 24, 1994). ... Designated by Falcons as transition player (February 16, 1996). ... Released by Falcons (October 22, 1996). ... Signed by Oakland Raiders (February 15, 1997). ... Granted unconditional free agency (February 12, 1999). ... Signed by Minnesota Vikings (April 6, 1999).
PRO STATISTICS: 1990—Fumbled four times and recovered two fumbles. 1991—Fumbled eight times and recovered two fumbles for minus four yards. 1992—Fumbled six times and recovered one fumble for minus 10 yards. 1993—Fumbled four times. 1994—Led league with 12 fumbles and recovered six fumbles for minus 12 yards. 1995—Fumbled six times and recovered two fumbles for minus 15 yards. 1996—Fumbled three times and recovered two fumbles for minus 24 yards. 1997—Fumbled seven times and recovered three fumbles for minus 14 yards. 1998—Fumbled seven times and recovered one fumble for minus six yards.
SINGLE GAME HIGHS (regular season): Attempts—59 (November 7, 1993, vs. Washington); completions—37 (November 7, 1993, vs. Washington); yards—386 (September 17, 1995, vs. New Orleans); and touchdown passes—4 (September 28, 1997, vs. St. Louis).
STATISTICAL PLATEAUS: 300-yard passing games: 1991 (2), 1992 (3), 1993 (2), 1994 (2), 1995 (3), 1997 (2), 1998 (1). Total: 15.
MISCELLANEOUS: Regular-season record as starting NFL quarterback: 37-70 (.346). ... Postseason record as starting NFL quarterback: 0-1.

				PASSING						RUSHING				TOTALS		
Year Team	G	GS	Att.	Cmp.	Pct.	Yds.	TD	Int.	Avg.	Rat.	Att.	Yds.	Avg.	TD	TD	2pt.	Pts.
1990—Indianapolis NFL	13	12	334	181	54.2	2152	16	13	6.44	73.8	11	2	0.2	1	1	...	6
1991—Indianapolis NFL	16	16	485	292	60.2	2910	10	12	6.00	73.8	16	36	2.3	0	0	...	0
1992—Indianapolis NFL	10	10	306	167	54.6	1963	7	15	6.42	61.5	14	26	1.9	1	1	...	6
1993—Indianapolis NFL	13	11	407	234	57.5	2526	8	6	6.21	76.3	13	39	3.0	0	0	...	0
1994—Atlanta NFL	16	16	524	322	61.5	3734	23	18	7.13	83.3	30	66	2.2	0	0	0	0
1995—Atlanta NFL	16	16	557	336	60.3	4143	24	11	7.44	89.5	27	17	0.6	0	0	0	0
1996—Atlanta NFL	3	3	99	56	56.6	698	3	3	7.05	76.1	5	10	2.0	0	0	0	0
1997—Oakland NFL	16	16	521	290	55.7	*3917	§29	9	7.52	91.2	17	44	2.6	0	0	0	0
1998—Oakland NFL	8	7	169	93	55.0	1186	4	5	7.02	72.7	8	2	0.3	0	0	0	0
Pro totals (9 years)	111	107	3402	1971	57.9	23229	124	92	6.83	79.7	141	242	1.7	2	2	0	12

GEORGE, MATT — K

PERSONAL: Born January 13, 1975, in Santa Clarita, Calif. ... 5-11/190. ... Full name: Matthew Michael George.
HIGH SCHOOL: Canyon (Anaheim).
COLLEGE: Chapman University (Calif.).
TRANSACTIONS/CAREER NOTES: Signed as non-drafted free agent by Pittsbrugh Steelers (April 24, 1998). ... Released by Steelers (August 24, 1998). ... Re-signed by Steelers (November 13, 1998). ... Released by Steelers (November 16, 1998). ... Signed by Tampa Bay Buccaneers (January 15, 1999). ... Assigned by Buccaneers to Amsterdam Admirals in 1999 NFL Europe enhancement allocation program (February 22, 1999). ... Released by Buccaneers (April 7, 1999).

			KICKING					
Year Team	G	XPM	XPA	FGM	FGA	Lg.	50+	Pts.
1998—Pittsburgh NFL	1	2	2	0	1	0	0-0	2

GEORGE, RON — LB — CHIEFS

PERSONAL: Born March 20, 1970, in Heidelberg, West Germany. ... 6-2/241. ... Full name: Ronald L. George.
HIGH SCHOOL: Heidelberg (West Germany) American.
COLLEGE: Air Force, then Stanford (degree in economics, 1992).
TRANSACTIONS/CAREER NOTES: Selected by Atlanta Falcons in fifth round (121st pick overall) of 1993 NFL draft. ... Signed by Falcons (June 4, 1993). ... Granted free agency (February 16, 1996). ... Re-signed by Falcons (June 12, 1996). ... Granted unconditional free agency (February 14, 1997). ... Signed by Minnesota Vikings (June 9, 1997). ... Released by Vikings (February 11, 1998). ... Signed by Kansas City Chiefs (April 6, 1998).
PLAYING EXPERIENCE: Atlanta NFL, 1993-1996; Minnesota NFL, 1997; Kansas City NFL, 1998. ... Games/Games started: 1993 (12/4), 1994 (16/9), 1995 (16/0), 1996 (16/15), 1997 (16/0), 1998 (16/0). Total: 92/28.
HONORS: Named linebacker on THE SPORTING NEWS college All-America second team (1992).
PRO STATISTICS: 1993—Credited with one sack. 1994—Recovered one fumble. 1995—Returned three kickoffs for 45 yards. 1996—Credited with two sacks and recovered three fumbles for 14 yards. 1997—Returned one kickoff for 10 yards. 1998—Recovered one fumble.

GEORGE, SPENCER — RB — TITANS

PERSONAL: Born October 28, 1973, in Beaumont, Texas. ... 5-9/200. ... Full name: Spencer James George.
HIGH SCHOOL: Hamshire-Fannett (Hamshire, Texas).
COLLEGE: Rice (degree in managerial studies/economics).
TRANSACTIONS/CAREER NOTES: Signed as non-drafted free agent by Tennessee Oilers (May 5, 1997). ... Released by Oilers (August 25, 1997). ... Re-signed by Oilers to practice squad (August 26, 1997). ... Activated (November 18, 1997). ... Released by Oilers (August 30, 1998). ... Re-signed by Oilers to practice squad (September 29, 1998). ... Activated (November 4, 1998). ... Transferred by Oilers to practice squad (December 16, 1998).
PLAYING EXPERIENCE: Tennessee NFL, 1997 and 1998. ... Games/Games started: 1997 (5/0), 1998 (5/0). Total: 10/0.

GERMAN, JAMMI — WR — FALCONS

PERSONAL: Born July 4, 1974, in Fort Myers, Fla. ... 6-1/192. ... Full name: Jammi Darnell German. ... Name pronounced JAY-me.
HIGH SCHOOL: Fort Myers (Fla.).
COLLEGE: Miami (Fla.).
TRANSACTIONS/CAREER NOTES: Selected by Atlanta Falcons in third round (74th pick overall) of 1998 NFL draft. ... Signed by Falcons (July 8, 1998). ... On injured reserve with knee injury (November 10, 1998-remainder of season).
PLAYING EXPERIENCE: Atlanta NFL, 1998. ... Games/Games started: 6/0.

GIBSON, DAMON — WR — BROWNS

PERSONAL: Born February 25, 1975, in Houston. ... 5-9/184.
HIGH SCHOOL: Forest Brook (Houston).
COLLEGE: Iowa.
TRANSACTIONS/CAREER NOTES: Signed as non-drafted free agent by Cincinnati Bengals (April 20, 1998). ... Selected by Cleveland Browns from Bengals in NFL expansion draft (February 9, 1999).
PRO STATISTICS: 1998—Rushed once for nine yards and recovered one fumble.
SINGLE GAME HIGHS (regular season): Receptions—3 (November 1, 1998, vs. Denver); yards—76 (October 18, 1998, vs. Tennessee); and touchdown receptions—1 (November 8, 1998, vs. Jacksonville).

			RECEIVING			PUNT RETURNS			KICKOFF RETURNS			TOTALS			
Year Team	G	GS	No.	Yds.	Avg.	TD	No.	Yds.	Avg.	TD	No.	Yds.	Avg.	TD	TD 2pt. Pts. Fum.
1998—Cincinnati NFL	16	0	19	258	13.6	3	27	218	8.1	1	17	372	21.9	0	4 0 24 3

GIBSON, OLIVER — DT — BENGALS

PERSONAL: Born March 15, 1972, in Chicago. ... 6-2/290. ... Full name: Oliver Donnovan Gibson. ... Cousin of Godfrey Myles, linebacker with Dallas Cowboys (1991-96).
HIGH SCHOOL: Romeoville (Ill.).
COLLEGE: Notre Dame (degree in economics, 1994).
TRANSACTIONS/CAREER NOTES: Selected by Pittsburgh Steelers in fourth round (120th pick overall) of 1995 NFL draft. ... Signed by Steelers (July 18, 1995). ... Granted free agency (February 13, 1998). ... Re-signed by Steelers (June 9, 1998). ... Granted unconditional free agency (February 12, 1999). ... Signed by Cincinnati Bengals (March 9, 1999).
CHAMPIONSHIP GAME EXPERIENCE: Member of Steelers for AFC championship game (1995 season); inactive. ... Played in AFC championship game (1997 season).
HONORS: Earned first-team All-Independent honors from THE SPORTING NEWS (1994).
PRO STATISTICS: 1995—Returned one kickoff for 10 yards. 1997—Recovered one fumble. 1998—Returned one kickoff for nine yards.

Year Team	G	GS	SACKS
1995—Pittsburgh NFL	12	0	0.0
1996—Pittsburgh NFL	16	0	2.5
1997—Pittsburgh NFL	16	0	1.0
1998—Pittsburgh NFL	16	0	2.0
Pro totals (4 years)	60	0	5.5

GILBERT, SEAN — DE — PANTHERS

PERSONAL: Born April 10, 1970, in Aliquippa, Pa. ... 6-5/318.
HIGH SCHOOL: Aliquippa (Pa.).
COLLEGE: Pittsburgh.
TRANSACTIONS/CAREER NOTES: Selected after junior season by Los Angeles Rams in first round (third pick overall) of 1992 NFL draft. ... Signed by Rams (July 28, 1992). ... Designated by Rams as transition player (February 25, 1993). ... Rams franchise moved to St. Louis (April 12, 1995). ... Traded by Rams to Washington Redskins for first-round pick (RB Lawrence Phillips) in 1996 draft (April 8, 1996). ... Designated by Redskins as franchise player (February 12, 1997). ... Sat out 1997 season due to contract dispute. ... Designated by Redskins as franchise player (February 11, 1998). ... Tendered offer sheet by Carolina Panthers (March 24, 1998). ... Redskins declined to match offer (April 21, 1998).
HONORS: Played in Pro Bowl (1993 season).
PRO STATISTICS: 1992—Recovered one fumble. 1994—Credited with one safety. 1995—Recovered one fumble.

Year Team	G	GS	SACKS
1992—Los Angeles Rams NFL	16	16	5.0
1993—Los Angeles Rams NFL	16	16	10.5
1994—Los Angeles Rams NFL	14	14	3.0
1995—St. Louis NFL	14	14	5.5
1996—Washington NFL	16	16	3.0
1997—Washington NFL		Did not play.	
1998—Carolina NFL	16	16	6.0
Pro totals (6 years)	92	92	33.0

GILDON, JASON — LB — STEELERS

PERSONAL: Born July 31, 1972, in Altus, Okla. ... 6-3/255. ... Full name: Jason Larue Gildon. ... Related to Wendall Gaines, guard, Philadelphia Eagles.
HIGH SCHOOL: Altus (Okla.).
COLLEGE: Oklahoma State.

TRANSACTIONS/CAREER NOTES: Selected by Pittsburgh Steelers in third round (88th pick overall) of 1994 NFL draft. ... Signed by Steelers (July 15, 1994). ... Granted free agency (February 14, 1997). ... Re-signed by Steelers (July 21, 1997). ... Granted unconditional free agency (February 13, 1998). ... Re-signed by Steelers (April 7, 1998).
CHAMPIONSHIP GAME EXPERIENCE: Played in AFC championship game (1994, 1995 and 1997 seasons). ... Played in Super Bowl XXX (1995 season).
PRO STATISTICS: 1995—Recovered one fumble. 1997—Recovered two fumbles for 32 yards and one touchdown. 1998—Recovered one fumble.

Year Team	G	GS	SACKS
1994—Pittsburgh NFL	16	1	2.0
1995—Pittsburgh NFL	16	0	3.0
1996—Pittsburgh NFL	14	13	7.0
1997—Pittsburgh NFL	16	16	5.0
1998—Pittsburgh NFL	16	16	11.0
Pro totals (5 years)	78	46	28.0

GISLER, MIKE   C/G   JETS

PERSONAL: Born August 26, 1969, in Runge, Texas. ... 6-4/295. ... Full name: Michael Gisler.
HIGH SCHOOL: Runge (Texas).
COLLEGE: Houston.
TRANSACTIONS/CAREER NOTES: Selected by New Orleans Saints in 11th round (303rd pick overall) of 1992 NFL draft. ... Signed by Saints (July 15, 1992). ... Released by Saints (August 31, 1992). ... Re-signed by Saints to practice squad (September 2, 1992). ... Released by Saints (September 7, 1992). ... Signed by Houston Oilers to practice squad (September 9, 1992). ... Granted free agency after 1992 season. ... Signed by New England Patriots (March 3, 1993). ... Granted free agency (February 16, 1996). ... Re-signed by Patriots (May 20, 1996). ... Released by Patriots (August 25, 1996). ... Re-signed by Patriots (September 10, 1996). ... Granted unconditional free agency (February 14, 1997). ... Re-signed by Patriots (April 22, 1997). ... Granted unconditional free agency (February 13, 1998). ... Signed by New York Jets (February 18, 1998).
PLAYING EXPERIENCE: New England NFL, 1993-1997; New York Jets NFL, 1998. ... Games/Games started: 1993 (12/0), 1994 (15/5), 1995 (16/0), 1996 (14/0), 1997 (16/2), 1998 (16/0). Total: 89/7.
CHAMPIONSHIP GAME EXPERIENCE: Played in AFC championship game (1996 and 1998 seasons). ... Played in Super Bowl XXXI (1996 season).
PRO STATISTICS: 1995—Returned two kickoffs for 19 yards and fumbled once. 1996—Returned one kickoff for nine yards.

GIVENS, REGGIE   LB   49ERS

PERSONAL: Born October 3, 1971, in Emporia, Va. ... 6-0/234. ... Full name: Reginald Alonzo Givens.
HIGH SCHOOL: Sussex (Va.) Central.
COLLEGE: Penn State.
TRANSACTIONS/CAREER NOTES: Selected by Dallas Cowboys in eighth round (213rd pick overall) of 1993 NFL draft. ... Signed by Cowboys (July 15, 1993). ... Released by Cowboys (August 30, 1993). ... Signed by Chicago Bears (April 20, 1994). ... Released by Bears (August 18, 1994). ... Signed by Winnipeg Blue Bombers of CFL (October 1994). ... Released by Blue Bombers (July 11, 1995). ... Signed by Baltimore Stallions of CFL (August 9, 1995). ... Transferred to Saskatchewan Roughriders of CFL (May 16, 1996). ... Released by Roughriders (June 3, 1996). ... Signed by Toronto Argonauts of CFL (June 6, 1996). ... Granted free agency (February 16, 1998). ... Signed by San Francisco 49ers (March 12, 1998).
PLAYING EXPERIENCE: Winnipeg CFL, 1994; Winnipeg (1)-Baltimore (4) CFL, 1995; Toronto CFL, 1996 and 1997; San Francisco NFL, 1998. ... Games/Games started: 1994 (4/games started unavailable), 1995 (Win.-1/-/ Bal.-4/-/ Total: 5/-), 1996 (18/-), 1997 (18/-), 1998 (16/0). Total CFL: 45/-. Total NFL: 16/0. Total Pro: 61/-.
PRO STATISTICS: CFL: 1994—Intercepted one pass for no yards and credited with two sacks. 1996—Rushed once for one yard, intercepted one pass for no yards, credited with eight sacks, fumbled once and recovered four fumbles. 1997—Intercepted one pass for six yards, credited with six sacks and recovered two fumbles for 182 yards and two touchdowns.

GLENN, AARON   CB/KR   JETS

PERSONAL: Born July 16, 1972, in Humble, Texas. ... 5-9/185. ... Full name: Aaron DeVon Glenn.
HIGH SCHOOL: Nimitz (Irving, Texas).
JUNIOR COLLEGE: Navarro College (Texas).
COLLEGE: Texas A&M.
TRANSACTIONS/CAREER NOTES: Selected by New York Jets in first round (12th pick overall) of 1994 NFL draft. ... Signed by Jets (July 21, 1994).
CHAMPIONSHIP GAME EXPERIENCE: Played in AFC championship game (1998 season).
HONORS: Named defensive back on The Sporting News college All-America first team (1993). ... Played in Pro Bowl (1997 season). ... Named to play in Pro Bowl (1998 season); replaced by Charles Woodson due to injury.
PRO STATISTICS: 1994—Recovered one fumble. 1995—Recovered one fumble. 1998—Recovered one fumble and returned a missed field goal attempt 104 yards for a touchdown.

			INTERCEPTIONS			KICKOFF RETURNS			TOTALS			
Year Team	G	GS	No.	Yds.	Avg.	TD	No.	Yds.	Avg.	TD	TD	2pt.	Pts.	Fum.
1994—New York Jets NFL	15	15	0	0	...	0	27	582	21.6	0	0	0	0	2
1995—New York Jets NFL	16	16	1	17	17.0	0	1	12	12.0	0	0	0	0	0
1996—New York Jets NFL	16	16	4	113	28.3	†2	1	6	6.0	0	2	0	12	0
1997—New York Jets NFL	16	16	1	5	5.0	0	28	741	§26.5	▲1	1	0	6	1
1998—New York Jets NFL	13	13	6	23	3.8	0	24	585	24.4	0	1	0	6	1
Pro totals (5 years)	76	76	12	158	13.2	2	81	1926	23.8	1	4	0	24	4

GLENN, TARIK   OT   COLTS

PERSONAL: Born May 25, 1976, in Cleveland. ... 6-5/335.
HIGH SCHOOL: Bishop O'Dowd (Oakland).

COLLEGE: California.
TRANSACTIONS/CAREER NOTES: Selected by Indianapolis Colts in first round (19th pick overall) of 1997 NFL draft. ... Signed by Colts (August 11, 1997).
PLAYING EXPERIENCE: Indianapolis NFL, 1997 and 1998. ... Games/Games started: 1997 (16/16), 1998 (16/16). Total: 32/32.
HONORS: Named offensive tackle on THE SPORTING NEWS college All-America second team (1996).
PRO STATISTICS: 1997—Caught one pass for three yards and recovered one fumble.

GLENN, TERRY WR PATRIOTS

PERSONAL: Born July 23, 1974, in Columbus, Ohio. ... 5-11/185.
HIGH SCHOOL: Brookhaven (Columbus, Ohio).
COLLEGE: Ohio State.
TRANSACTIONS/CAREER NOTES: Selected after junior season by New England Patriots in first round (seventh pick overall) of 1996 NFL draft. ... Signed by Patriots (July 12, 1996). ... On injured reserve with fractured ankle (December 18, 1998-remainder of season).
CHAMPIONSHIP GAME EXPERIENCE: Played in AFC championship game (1996 season). ... Played in Super Bowl XXXI (1996 season).
HONORS: Fred Biletnikoff Award winner (1995). ... Named wide receiver on THE SPORTING NEWS college All-America first team (1995).
RECORDS: Holds NFL single-season record for most receptions by a rookie—90 (1996).
SINGLE GAME HIGHS (regular season): Receptions—10 (November 3, 1996, vs. Miami); yards—193 (December 6, 1998, vs. Pittsburgh); and touchdown receptions—1 (December 6, 1998, vs. Pittsburgh).
STATISTICAL PLATEAUS: 100-yard receiving games: 1996 (2), 1997 (1), 1998 (4). Total: 7.

			RUSHING				RECEIVING				TOTALS			
Year Team	G	GS	Att.	Yds.	Avg.	TD	No.	Yds.	Avg.	TD	TD	2pt.	Pts.	Fum.
1996—New England NFL	15	15	5	42	8.4	0	90	1132	12.6	6	6	0	36	1
1997—New England NFL	9	9	0	0	...	0	27	431	16.0	2	2	0	12	1
1998—New England NFL	10	9	2	-1	-0.5	0	50	792	15.8	3	3	0	18	0
Pro totals (3 years)	34	33	7	41	5.9	0	167	2355	14.1	11	11	0	66	2

GLOVER, ANDREW TE VIKINGS

PERSONAL: Born August 12, 1967, in New Orleans. ... 6-6/252. ... Full name: Andrew Lee Glover.
HIGH SCHOOL: East Ascension (Gonzales, La.).
COLLEGE: Grambling State (degree in criminal justice, 1990).
TRANSACTIONS/CAREER NOTES: Selected by Los Angeles Raiders in 10th round (274th pick overall) of 1991 NFL draft. ... Signed by Raiders (1991). ... On injured reserve with knee injury (December 27, 1993-remainder of season). ... Raiders franchise moved to Oakland (July 21, 1995). ... Granted unconditional free agency (February 16, 1996). ... Re-signed by Raiders (May 24, 1996). ... Granted unconditional free agency (February 14, 1997). ... Signed by Minnesota Vikings (July 28, 1997). ... Granted unconditional free agency (February 13, 1998). ... Re-signed by Vikings (February 18, 1998).
CHAMPIONSHIP GAME EXPERIENCE: Played in NFC championship game (1998 season).
PRO STATISTICS: 1992—Recovered one fumble.
SINGLE GAME HIGHS (regular season): Receptions—9 (November 8, 1998, vs. New Orleans); yards—93 (November 8, 1998, vs. New Orleans); and touchdown receptions—2 (December 20, 1998, vs. Jacksonville).

			RECEIVING				TOTALS			
Year Team	G	GS	No.	Yds.	Avg.	TD	TD	2pt.	Pts.	Fum.
1991—Los Angeles Raiders NFL	16	1	5	45	9.0	3	3	...	18	0
1992—Los Angeles Raiders NFL	16	2	15	178	11.9	1	1	...	6	1
1993—Los Angeles Raiders NFL	15	0	4	55	13.8	1	1	0	6	0
1994—Los Angeles Raiders NFL	16	16	33	371	11.2	2	2	0	12	0
1995—Oakland NFL	16	7	26	220	8.5	3	3	0	18	0
1996—Oakland NFL	14	4	9	101	11.2	1	1	0	6	0
1997—Minnesota NFL	13	11	32	378	11.8	3	3	0	18	0
1998—Minnesota NFL	16	12	35	522	14.9	5	5	0	30	0
Pro totals (8 years)	122	53	159	1870	11.8	19	19	0	114	1

GLOVER, KEVIN C SEAHAWKS

PERSONAL: Born June 17, 1963, in Washington, D.C. ... 6-2/282. ... Full name: Kevin Bernard Glover.
HIGH SCHOOL: Largo (Md.).
COLLEGE: Maryland.
TRANSACTIONS/CAREER NOTES: Selected by Tampa Bay Bandits in 1985 USFL territorial draft. ... Selected by Detroit Lions in second round (34th pick overall) of 1985 NFL draft. ... Signed by Lions (July 23, 1985). ... On injured reserve with knee injury (December 7, 1985-remainder of season). ... On injured reserve with knee injury (September 29-December 20, 1986). ... Granted free agency (February 1, 1992). ... Re-signed by Lions (August 25, 1992). ... On injured reserve with ankle injury (October 27, 1992-remainder of season). ... Designated by Lions as franchise player (February 16, 1996). ... Granted unconditional free agency (February 13, 1998). ... Signed by Seattle Seahawks (February 21, 1998). ... On injured reserve with back injury (November 29, 1998-remainder of season).
PLAYING EXPERIENCE: Detroit NFL, 1985-1997; Seattle NFL, 1998. ... Games/Games started: 1985 (10/0), 1986 (4/1), 1987 (12/9), 1988 (16/16), 1989 (16/16), 1990 (16/16), 1991 (16/16), 1992 (7/7), 1993 (16/16), 1994 (16/16), 1995 (16/16), 1996 (16/16), 1997 (16/16), 1998 (8/8). Total: 185/169.
CHAMPIONSHIP GAME EXPERIENCE: Played in NFC championship game (1991 season).
HONORS: Named center on THE SPORTING NEWS college All-America first team (1984). ... Played in Pro Bowl (1995-1997 seasons).
PRO STATISTICS: 1987—Returned one kickoff for 19 yards. 1988—Recovered two fumbles. 1990—Recovered one fumble. 1992—Recovered one fumble. 1995—Fumbled twice and recovered one fumble for minus 14 yards. 1996—Recovered two fumbles. 1997—Recovered one fumble.

GLOVER, LA'ROI   DT   SAINTS

PERSONAL: Born July 4, 1974, in San Diego. ... 6-2/285. ... Full name: La'Roi Damon Glover. ... Name pronounced luh-ROY.
HIGH SCHOOL: Point Loma (San Diego).
COLLEGE: San Diego State.
TRANSACTIONS/CAREER NOTES: Selected by Oakland Raiders in fifth round (166th pick overall) of 1996 NFL draft. ... Signed by Raiders (July 12, 1996). ... Assigned by Raiders to Barcelona Dragons in 1997 World League enhancement allocation program (February 19, 1997). ... Claimed on waivers by New Orleans Saints (August 25, 1997).
PRO STATISTICS: 1997—Recovered one fumble. 1998—Intercepted one pass for no yards.

Year Team	G	GS	SACKS
1996—Oakland NFL	2	0	0.0
1997—Barcelona W.L.	10	10	6.5
—New Orleans NFL	15	2	6.5
1998—New Orleans NFL	16	15	10.0
W.L. totals (1 year)	10	10	6.5
NFL totals (3 years)	33	17	16.5
Pro totals (4 years)	43	27	23.0

GODFREY, RANDALL   LB   COWBOYS

PERSONAL: Born April 6, 1973, in Valdosta, Ga. ... 6-2/245. ... Full name: Randall Euralentris Godfrey.
HIGH SCHOOL: Lowndes County (Valdosta, Ga.).
COLLEGE: Georgia.
TRANSACTIONS/CAREER NOTES: Selected by Dallas Cowboys in second round (49th pick overall) of 1996 NFL draft. ... Signed by Cowboys (July 17, 1996). ... Granted free agency (February 12, 1999).
PLAYING EXPERIENCE: Dallas NFL, 1996-1998. ... Games/Games started: 1996 (16/6), 1997 (16/16), 1998 (16/16). Total: 48/38.
PRO STATISTICS: 1997—Credited with one sack and recovered one fumble. 1998—Intercepted one pass for no yards, credited with three sacks and recovered one fumble.

GOFF, MIKE   G   BENGALS

PERSONAL: Born January 6, 1976, in Spring Valley, Ill. ... 6-5/316. ... Full name: Michael J. Goff.
HIGH SCHOOL: Lasalle-Peru (Peru, Ill.).
COLLEGE: Iowa.
TRANSACTIONS/CAREER NOTES: Selected by Cincinnati Bengals in third round (78th pick overall) of 1998 NFL draft. ... Signed by Bengals (July 20, 1998).
PLAYING EXPERIENCE: Cincinnati NFL, 1998. ... Games/Games started: 10/5.

GOGAN, KEVIN   G   DOLPHINS

PERSONAL: Born November 2, 1964, in Pacifica, Calif. ... 6-7/330. ... Full name: Kevin Patrick Gogan.
HIGH SCHOOL: Sacred Heart (San Francisco).
COLLEGE: Washington (degree in sociology, 1987).
TRANSACTIONS/CAREER NOTES: Selected by Dallas Cowboys in eighth round (206th pick overall) of 1987 NFL draft. ... Signed by Cowboys (July 18, 1987). ... On non-football injury list with substance abuse problem (August 5-31, 1988). ... Granted roster exemption (August 31-September 5, 1988). ... Granted unconditional free agency (February 17, 1994). ... Signed by Los Angeles Raiders (April 18, 1994). ... Raiders franchise moved to Oakland (July 21, 1995). ... Granted unconditional free agency (February 14, 1997). ... Signed by San Francisco 49ers (February 25, 1997). ... On physically unable to perform list with hamstring injury (July 21-28, 1998). ... Traded by 49ers to Miami Dolphins for fifth-round pick (RB Terry Jackson) in 1999 draft (March 1, 1999).
PLAYING EXPERIENCE: Dallas NFL, 1987-1993; Los Angeles Raiders NFL, 1994; Oakland NFL, 1995 and 1996; San Francisco NFL, 1997 and 1998. ... Games/Games started: 1987 (11/10), 1988 (15/15), 1989 (13/13), 1990 (16/4), 1991 (16/16), 1992 (16/1), 1993 (16/16), 1994 (16/16), 1995 (16/16), 1996 (16/16), 1997 (16/16), 1998 (16/16). Total: 183/155.
CHAMPIONSHIP GAME EXPERIENCE: Played in NFC championship game (1992, 1993 and 1997 seasons). ... Member of Super Bowl championship team (1992 and 1993 seasons).
HONORS: Played in Pro Bowl (1994, 1997 and 1998 seasons).
PRO STATISTICS: 1987—Recovered one fumble. 1990—Recovered one fumble. 1996—Recovered one fumble.

GONZALEZ, TONY   TE   CHIEFS

PERSONAL: Born February 27, 1976, in Torrance, Calif. ... 6-4/250. ... Full name: Anthony Gonzalez.
HIGH SCHOOL: Huntington Beach (Calif.).
COLLEGE: California.
TRANSACTIONS/CAREER NOTES: Selected by Kansas City Chiefs in first round (13th pick overall) of 1997 NFL draft. ... Signed by Chiefs (July 29, 1997).
HONORS: Named tight end on THE SPORTING NEWS college All-America first team (1996).
SINGLE GAME HIGHS (regular season): Receptions—7 (September 13, 1998, vs. Jacksonville); yards—76 (December 26, 1998, vs. Oakland); and touchdown receptions—1 (December 26, 1998, vs. Oakland).

			RECEIVING				TOTALS		
Year Team	G	GS	No.	Yds.	Avg.	TD	TD	2pt.	Pts.	Fum.
1997—Kansas City NFL	16	0	33	368	11.2	2	2	1	14	0
1998—Kansas City NFL	16	16	59	621	10.5	2	2	0	12	3
Pro totals (2 years)	32	16	92	989	10.8	4	4	1	26	3

GOOCH, JEFF — LB — BUCCANEERS

PERSONAL: Born October 31, 1974, in Nashville. ... 5-11/219. ... Full name: Jeffery Lance Gooch.
HIGH SCHOOL: Overton (Nashville).
COLLEGE: Austin Peay State.
TRANSACTIONS/CAREER NOTES: Signed as non-drafted free agent by Tampa Bay Buccaneers (April 23, 1996). ... On injured reserve with knee injury (December 17, 1996-remainder of season). ... Granted free agency (February 12, 1999). ... Re-signed by Buccaneers (April 13, 1999).
PLAYING EXPERIENCE: Tampa Bay NFL, 1996-1998. ... Games/Games started: 1996 (15/0), 1997 (14/5), 1998 (16/16). Total: 45/21.
PRO STATISTICS: 1996—Recovered one fumble. 1998—Credited with one sack and recovered one fumble.

GOODWIN, HUNTER — TE — DOLPHINS

PERSONAL: Born October 10, 1972, in Bellville, Texas. ... 6-5/275. ... Full name: Robert Hunter Goodwin.
HIGH SCHOOL: Bellville (Texas).
COLLEGE: Texas A&M-Kingsville, then Texas A&M.
TRANSACTIONS/CAREER NOTES: Selected by Minnesota Vikings in fourth round (97th pick overall) of 1996 NFL draft. ... Signed by Vikings (July 20, 1996). ... Granted free agency (February 12, 1999). ... Tendered offer sheet by Miami Dolphins (April 8, 1999). ... Vikings declined to match offer (April 9, 1999).
CHAMPIONSHIP GAME EXPERIENCE: Played in NFC championship game (1998 season).
PRO STATISTICS: 1998—Recovered one fumble.
SINGLE GAME HIGHS (regular season): Receptions—2 (September 7, 1997, vs. Chicago); yards—24 (December 1, 1996, vs. Arizona); and touchdown receptions—0.

			RECEIVING				TOTALS		
Year Team	G	GS	No.	Yds.	Avg.	TD	TD	2pt.	Pts.	Fum.
1996—Minnesota NFL	9	6	1	24	24.0	0	0	0	0	0
1997—Minnesota NFL	16	5	7	61	8.7	0	0	0	0	0
1998—Minnesota NFL	15	0	3	16	5.3	0	0	0	0	0
Pro totals (3 years)	40	11	11	101	9.2	0	0	0	0	0

GORDON, DARRIEN — CB — RAIDERS

PERSONAL: Born November 14, 1970, in Shawnee, Okla. ... 5-11/178. ... Full name: Darrien X. Jamal Gordon.
HIGH SCHOOL: Shawnee (Okla.).
COLLEGE: Stanford.
TRANSACTIONS/CAREER NOTES: Selected by San Diego Chargers in first round (22nd pick overall) of 1993 NFL draft. ... Signed by Chargers (July 16, 1993). ... Inactive for all 16 games due to shoulder injury (1995 season). ... Granted unconditional free agency (February 14, 1997). ... Signed by Denver Broncos (April 30, 1997). ... Granted unconditional free agency (February 12, 1999). ... Signed by Oakland Raiders (June 9, 1999).
CHAMPIONSHIP GAME EXPERIENCE: Played in AFC championship game (1994, 1997 and 1998 seasons). ... Played in Super Bowl XXIX (1994 season). ... Member of Super Bowl championship team (1997 and 1998 seasons).
HONORS: Named punt returner on THE SPORTING NEWS NFL All-Pro team (1997).
RECORDS: Shares NFL single-game records for most touchdowns by punt return—2; and most touchdowns by combined kick return—2 (November 9, 1997, vs. Carolina).
POST SEASON RECORDS: Holds Super Bowl career and single-game records for most interception return yards—108 (January 31, 1999, vs. Atlanta).
PRO STATISTICS: 1993—Recovered two fumbles for minus two yards. 1994—Recovered three fumbles for 15 yards. 1996—Credited with two sacks. 1997—Credited with two sacks and recovered four fumbles. 1998—Recovered one fumble.

			INTERCEPTIONS				PUNT RETURNS				TOTALS			
Year Team	G	GS	No.	Yds.	Avg.	TD	No.	Yds.	Avg.	TD	TD	2pt.	Pts.	Fum.
1993—San Diego NFL	16	7	1	3	3.0	0	31	395	12.7	0	0	...	0	4
1994—San Diego NFL	16	16	4	32	8.0	0	36	475	§13.2	†2	2	0	12	2
1995—San Diego NFL							Did not play.							
1996—San Diego NFL	16	6	2	55	27.5	0	36	537	§14.9	▲1	1	0	6	3
1997—Denver NFL	16	16	4	64	16.0	1	40	543	13.6	†3	4	0	24	3
1998—Denver NFL	16	16	4	125	31.3	1	34	379	11.1	0	1	0	6	1
Pro totals (5 years)	80	61	15	279	18.6	2	177	2329	13.2	6	8	0	48	13

GORDON, DWAYNE — LB — JETS

PERSONAL: Born November 2, 1969, in White Plains, N.Y. ... 6-1/240. ... Full name: Dwayne K. Gordon.
HIGH SCHOOL: Arlington North (LaGrangeville, N.Y.).
COLLEGE: New Hampshire.
TRANSACTIONS/CAREER NOTES: Selected by Miami Dolphins in eighth round (218th pick overall) of 1993 NFL draft. ... Released by Dolphins (July 12, 1993). ... Signed by Atlanta Falcons (July 19, 1993). ... Released by Falcons (August 27, 1995). ... Signed by San Diego Chargers (August 28, 1995). ... Granted free agency (February 16, 1996). ... Re-signed by Chargers (June 14, 1996). ... Granted unconditional free agency (February 17, 1997). ... Signed by New York Jets (June 4, 1997). ... Granted unconditional free agency (February 12, 1999). ... Re-signed by Jets (March 10, 1999).
PLAYING EXPERIENCE: Atlanta NFL, 1993 and 1994; San Diego NFL, 1995 and 1996; New York Jets NFL, 1997 and 1998. ... Games/Games started: 1993 (5/0), 1994 (16/0), 1995 (16/3), 1996 (13/0), 1997 (16/8), 1998 (16/4). Total: 82/15.
CHAMPIONSHIP GAME EXPERIENCE: Played in AFC championship game (1998 season).
PRO STATISTICS: 1993—Fumbled once. 1995—Credited with one sack and recovered one fumble. 1997—Credited with one sack. 1998—Intercepted one pass for 31 yards and a touchdown.

GORDON, STEVE — C — BROWNS

PERSONAL: Born April 15, 1969, in Fort Ord, Calif. ... 6-3/288. ... Full name: Steve Duane Gordon.
HIGH SCHOOL: Nevada Union (Grass Valley, Calif.).
COLLEGE: California (degree in political science).
TRANSACTIONS/CAREER NOTES: Selected by New England Patriots in 10th round (277th pick overall) of 1992 NFL draft. ... Signed by Patriots (July 24, 1992). ... Released by Patriots (August 31, 1992). ... Re-signed by Patriots to practice squad (September 2, 1992). ... Activated (December 9, 1992). ... Active for two games (1992); did not play. ... Released by Patriots (September 8, 1993). ... Re-signed by Patriots to practice squad (September 9, 1993). ... Released by Patriots (October 27, 1993). ... Signed by New Orleans Saints to practice squad (November 17, 1993). ... Granted free agency after 1993 season. ... Signed by Seattle Seahawks (April 15, 1994). ... Released by Seahawks (August 28, 1994). ... Signed by San Francisco 49ers (February 15, 1995). ... Released by 49ers (August 19, 1995). ... Re-signed by 49ers (January 9, 1996). ... Released by 49ers (August 27, 1996). ... Re-signed by 49ers (January 23, 1997). ... Released by 49ers (September 4, 1997). ... Signed by Denver Broncos (August 12, 1998). ... Traded by Broncos with DT David Richie to 49ers for past considerations (August 25, 1998). ... Selected by Cleveland Browns from 49ers in NFL expansion draft (February 9, 1999).
PLAYING EXPERIENCE: San Francisco NFL, 1998. ... Games/Games started: 13/1.

GOUVEIA, KURT — LB

PERSONAL: Born September 14, 1964, in Honolulu. ... 6-1/240. ... Full name: Kurt Keola Gouveia. ... Name pronounced goo-VAY-uh.
HIGH SCHOOL: Waianae (Hawaii).
COLLEGE: Brigham Young.
TRANSACTIONS/CAREER NOTES: Selected by Washington Redskins in eighth round (213th pick overall) of 1986 NFL draft. ... Signed by Redskins (July 18, 1986). ... On injured reserve with knee injury (August 25, 1986-entire season). ... Granted unconditional free agency (March 1, 1992). ... Re-signed by Redskins for 1993 season. ... Granted unconditional free agency (February 17, 1995). ... Signed by Philadelphia Eagles (April 23, 1995). ... Granted unconditional free agency (February 16, 1996). ... Signed by San Diego Chargers (February 27, 1996). ... On injured reserve with neck injury (October 22, 1997-remainder of season). ... Granted unconditional free agency (February 12, 1999).
CHAMPIONSHIP GAME EXPERIENCE: Played in NFC championship game (1987 and 1991 seasons). ... Member of Super Bowl championship team (1987 and 1991 seasons).
POST SEASON RECORDS: Shares NFL postseason career record for most consecutive games with one or more interception—3.
PRO STATISTICS: 1990—Recovered one fumble for 39 yards and a touchdown. 1995—Recovered one fumble.

			INTERCEPTIONS			SACKS	KICKOFF RETURNS				TOTALS		
Year Team	G	GS	No.	Yds.	Avg.	TD	No.	No.	Yds.	Avg.	TD	TD 2pt.	Pts. Fum.
1986—Washington NFL								Did not play.					
1987—Washington NFL	11	1	0	0	...	0	0.0	0	0	...	0	0 ...	0 0
1988—Washington NFL	16	0	0	0	...	0	0.0	0	0	...	0	0 ...	0 0
1989—Washington NFL	15	1	1	1	1.0	0	0.0	1	0	0.0	0	0 ...	0 0
1990—Washington NFL	16	7	0	0	...	0	1.0	2	23	11.5	0	1 ...	6 0
1991—Washington NFL	14	1	1	22	22.0	0	0.0	3	12	4.0	0	0 ...	0 0
1992—Washington NFL	16	14	3	43	14.3	0	1.0	1	7	7.0	0	0 ...	0 0
1993—Washington NFL	16	16	1	59	59.0	1	1.5	0	0	...	0	1 ...	6 0
1994—Washington NFL	14	1	1	7	7.0	0	0.0	0	0	...	0	0 0	0 0
1995—Philadelphia NFL	16	16	1	20	20.0	0	0.0	0	0	...	0	0 ...	0 0
1996—San Diego NFL	16	16	3	41	13.7	0	1.0	0	0	...	0	0 ...	0 0
1997—San Diego NFL	7	6	1	0	0.0	0	0.0	0	0	...	0	0 ...	0 0
1998—San Diego NFL	15	12	0	0	...	0	0.5	0	0	...	0	0 ...	0 0
Pro totals (12 years)	172	91	12	193	16.1	1	5.0	7	42	6.0	0	2 0	12 0

GOWIN, TOBY — P — COWBOYS

PERSONAL: Born March 30, 1975, in Jacksonville, Texas ... 5-10/167.
HIGH SCHOOL: Jacksonville (Texas).
COLLEGE: North Texas (degree in kinesiology).
TRANSACTIONS/CAREER NOTES: Signed as non-drafted free agent by Dallas Cowboys (April 24, 1997).

		PUNTING						KICKING					
Year Team	G	No.	Yds.	Avg.	Net avg.	In. 20	Blk.	XPM	XPA	FGM	FGA	Lg.	50+	Pts.
1997—Dallas NFL	16	86	3592	41.8	35.4	26	0	0	0	0	1	0	0-1	0
1998—Dallas NFL	16	77	3342	43.4	36.6	31	∞1	0	0	0	0	...	0-0	0
Pro totals (2 years)	32	163	6934	42.5	36.0	57	1	0	0	0	1	...	0-1	0

GRAGG, SCOTT — OT — GIANTS

PERSONAL: Born February 28, 1972, in Silverton, Ore. ... 6-8/325.
HIGH SCHOOL: Silverton (Ore.) Union.
COLLEGE: Montana.
TRANSACTIONS/CAREER NOTES: Selected by New York Giants in second round (54th pick overall) of 1995 NFL draft. ... Signed by Giants (July 23, 1995). ... Granted free agency (February 13, 1998). ... Re-signed by Giants (September 4, 1998).
PLAYING EXPERIENCE: New York Giants NFL, 1995-1998. ... Games/Games started: 1995 (13/0), 1996 (16/16), 1997 (16/16), 1998 (16/16). Total: 61/48.
PRO STATISTICS: 1997—Recovered one fumble. 1998—Recovered one fumble.

GRAHAM, AARON — C — CARDINALS

PERSONAL: Born May 22, 1973, in Las Vegas, N.M. ... 6-4/293.
HIGH SCHOOL: Denton (Texas).

COLLEGE: Nebraska.
TRANSACTIONS/CAREER NOTES: Selected by Arizona Cardinals in fourth round (112th pick overall) of 1996 NFL draft. ... Signed by Cardinals for 1996 season. ... Granted free agency (February 12, 1999). ... Re-signed by Cardinals (May 21, 1999).
PLAYING EXPERIENCE: Arizona NFL, 1996-1998. ... Games/Games started: 1996 (16/7), 1997 (16/4), 1998 (14/13). Total: 46/24.
PRO STATISTICS: 1997—Recovered one fumble.

GRAHAM, DERRICK — G

PERSONAL: Born March 18, 1967, in Groveland, Fla. ... 6-4/315. ... Full name: Deltrice Andrew Graham.
HIGH SCHOOL: Groveland (Fla.).
COLLEGE: Appalachian State (degree in criminal justice).
TRANSACTIONS/CAREER NOTES: Selected by Kansas City Chiefs in fifth round (124th pick overall) of 1990 NFL draft. ... Signed by Chiefs (July 28, 1990). ... On injured reserve with ankle injury (November 3, 1990-remainder of season). ... On injured reserve with knee injury (September 16, 1992-remainder of season). ... Granted unconditional free agency (February 17, 1995). ... Signed by Carolina Panthers (February 21, 1995). ... Released by Panthers (February 14, 1996). ... Signed by Seattle Seahawks (February 29, 1996). ... Granted unconditional free agency (February 13, 1998). ... Signed by Oakland Raiders (June 13, 1998). ... Granted unconditional free agency (February 12, 1999).
PLAYING EXPERIENCE: Kansas City NFL, 1990-1994; Carolina NFL, 1995; Seattle NFL, 1996 and 1997; Oakland NFL, 1998. ... Games/Games started: 1990 (6/0), 1991 (16/1), 1992 (2/2), 1993 (11/2), 1994 (16/11), 1995 (11/7), 1996 (16/16), 1997 (9/9), 1998 (12/12). Total: 99/60.
CHAMPIONSHIP GAME EXPERIENCE: Played in AFC championship game (1993 season).

GRAHAM, JAY — RB — RAVENS

PERSONAL: Born July 14, 1975, in Concord, N.C. ... 5-11/220. ... Full name: Herman Jason Graham.
HIGH SCHOOL: Concord (N.C.).
COLLEGE: Tennessee.
TRANSACTIONS/CAREER NOTES: Selected by Baltimore Ravens in third round (64th pick overall) of 1997 NFL draft. ... Signed by Ravens (June 19, 1997). ... On injured reserve with knee injury (December 10, 1998-remainder of season).
PRO STATISTICS: 1997—Returned six kickoffs for 115 yards and recovered one fumble. 1998—Returned three kickoffs for 52 yards.
SINGLE GAME HIGHS (regular season): Attempts—35 (November 16, 1997, vs. Philadelphia); yards—154 (November 16, 1997, vs. Philadelphia); and rushing touchdowns—1 (September 14, 1997, vs. New York Giants).
STATISTICAL PLATEAUS: 100-yard rushing games: 1997 (1).

			RUSHING				RECEIVING			TOTALS		
Year Team	G	GS	Att.	Yds.	Avg.	TD	No.	Yds.	Avg.	TD	TD	2pt.	Pts.	Fum.
1997—Baltimore NFL	13	3	81	299	3.7	2	12	51	4.3	0	2	0	12	2
1998—Baltimore NFL	5	2	35	109	3.1	0	5	41	8.2	0	0	0	0	0
Pro totals (2 years)	18	5	116	408	3.5	2	17	92	5.4	0	2	0	12	2

GRAHAM, JEFF — WR — CHARGERS

PERSONAL: Born February 14, 1969, in Dayton, Ohio. ... 6-2/206. ... Full name: Jeff Todd Graham.
HIGH SCHOOL: Archbishop Alter (Kettering, Ohio).
COLLEGE: Ohio State.
TRANSACTIONS/CAREER NOTES: Selected by Pittsburgh Steelers in second round (46th pick overall) of 1991 NFL draft. ... Signed by Steelers (August 3, 1991). ... Traded by Steelers to Chicago Bears for fifth-round pick (DB Lethon Flowers) in 1995 draft (April 29, 1994). ... Granted unconditional free agency (February 16, 1996). ... Signed by New York Jets (March 14, 1996). ... Traded by Jets to Philadelphia Eagles for sixth-round pick (DE Eric Ogbogu) in 1998 draft (April 19, 1998). ... Released by Eagles (February 13, 1999). ... Signed by San Diego Chargers (March 19, 1999).
PRO STATISTICS: 1991—Returned three kickoffs for 48 yards. 1994—Recovered one fumble. 1995—Returned one kickoff for 12 yards. 1997—Recovered one fumble.
SINGLE GAME HIGHS (regular season): Receptions—9 (November 17, 1996, vs. Indianapolis); yards—192 (December 19, 1993, vs. Houston); and touchdown receptions—3 (November 17, 1996, vs. Indianapolis).
STATISTICAL PLATEAUS: 100-yard receiving games: 1992 (2), 1993 (2), 1994 (2), 1995 (7), 1996 (3), 1997 (1). Total: 17.

			RECEIVING				PUNT RETURNS			TOTALS		
Year Team	G	GS	No.	Yds.	Avg.	TD	No.	Yds.	Avg.	TD	TD	2pt.	Pts.	Fum.
1991—Pittsburgh NFL	13	1	2	21	10.5	0	8	46	5.8	0	0	...	0	0
1992—Pittsburgh NFL	14	10	49	711	14.5	1	0	0	...	0	1	...	6	0
1993—Pittsburgh NFL	15	12	38	579	15.2	0	0	0	...	0	0	...	0	0
1994—Chicago NFL	16	15	68	944	13.9	4	15	140	9.3	1	5	1	32	1
1995—Chicago NFL	16	16	82	1301	15.9	4	23	183	8.0	0	4	0	24	3
1996—New York Jets NFL	11	9	50	788	15.8	6	0	0	...	0	6	0	36	0
1997—New York Jets NFL	16	16	42	542	12.9	2	0	0	...	0	2	0	12	0
1998—Philadelphia NFL	15	15	47	600	12.8	2	0	0	...	0	2	0	12	0
Pro totals (8 years)	116	94	378	5486	14.5	19	46	369	8.0	1	20	1	122	4

GRAHAM, KENT — QB — GIANTS

PERSONAL: Born November 1, 1968, in Wheaton, Ill. ... 6-5/240. ... Full name: Kent Douglas Graham.
HIGH SCHOOL: Wheaton (Ill.) North.
COLLEGE: Notre Dame, then Ohio State.
TRANSACTIONS/CAREER NOTES: Selected by New York Giants in eighth round (211th pick overall) of 1992 NFL draft. ... Signed by Giants (July 21, 1992). ... On injured reserve with elbow injury (September 18-October 14, 1992). ... Granted free agency (February 17, 1995). ... Re-signed by Giants (July 1995). ... Released by Giants (August 30, 1995). ... Signed by Detroit Lions (September 5, 1995). ... Granted unconditional free agency (February 16, 1996). ... Signed by Arizona Cardinals (March 7, 1996). ... Granted unconditional free agency (February 13, 1998). ... Signed by New York Giants (February 17, 1998).

PRO STATISTICS: 1992—Fumbled once and recovered one fumble. 1994—Fumbled twice and recovered one fumble. 1996—Fumbled five times. 1997—Fumbled five times. 1998—Caught one pass for 16 yards and fumbled twice for minus three yards.
SINGLE GAME HIGHS (regular season): Attempts—58 (September 29, 1996, vs. St. Louis); completions—37 (September 29, 1996, vs. St. Louis); yards—366 (September 29, 1996, vs. St. Louis); and touchdown passes—4 (September 29, 1996, vs. St. Louis).
STATISTICAL PLATEAUS: 300-yard passing games: 1996 (1), 1997 (1). Total: 2.
MISCELLANEOUS: Regular-season record as starting NFL quarterback: 10-14 (.417).

				PASSING							RUSHING				TOTALS		
Year Team	G	GS	Att.	Cmp.	Pct.	Yds.	TD	Int.	Avg.	Rat.	Att.	Yds.	Avg.	TD	TD	2pt.	Pts.
1992—N.Y. Giants NFL	6	3	97	42	43.3	470	1	4	4.85	44.6	6	36	6.0	0	0	...	0
1993—N.Y. Giants NFL	9	0	22	8	36.4	79	0	0	3.59	47.3	2	-3	-1.5	0	0	...	0
1994—N.Y. Giants NFL	13	1	53	24	45.3	295	3	2	5.57	66.2	2	11	5.5	0	0	0	0
1995—Detroit NFL	2	0	0	0	...	0	0	0	...	...	0	0	...	0	0	0	0
1996—Arizona NFL	10	8	274	146	53.3	1624	12	7	5.93	75.1	21	87	4.1	0	0	0	0
1997—Arizona NFL	8	6	250	130	52.0	1408	4	5	5.63	65.9	13	23	1.8	2	2	0	12
1998—N.Y. Giants NFL	11	6	205	105	51.2	1219	7	5	5.95	70.8	27	138	5.1	2	2	0	12
Pro totals (7 years)	59	24	901	455	50.5	5095	27	23	5.65	67.1	71	292	4.1	4	4	0	24

GRANVILLE, BILLY — LB — BENGALS

PERSONAL: Born March 11, 1974, in Lawrenceville, N.J. ... 6-3/252.
HIGH SCHOOL: Lawrenceville (N.J.).
COLLEGE: Duke (degree in sociology, 1997).
TRANSACTIONS/CAREER NOTES: Signed as non-drafted free agent by Cincinnati Bengals (April 25, 1997).
PLAYING EXPERIENCE: Cincinnati NFL, 1997 and 1998. ... Games/Games started: 1997 (12/4), 1998 (16/0). Total: 28/4.
PRO STATISTICS: 1998—Recovered one fumble.

GRASMANIS, PAUL — DT — BEARS

PERSONAL: Born August 2, 1974, in Grand Rapids, Mich. ... 6-2/298. ... Full name: Paul Ryan Grasmanis.
HIGH SCHOOL: Jenison (Mich.).
COLLEGE: Notre Dame.
TRANSACTIONS/CAREER NOTES: Selected by Chicago Bears in fourth round (116th pick overall) of 1996 NFL draft. ... Signed by Bears (June 13, 1996). ... Granted free agency (February 12, 1999). ... Re-signed by Bears (April 14, 1999).
PLAYING EXPERIENCE: Chicago NFL, 1996-1998. ... Games/Games started: 1996 (14/3), 1997 (16/0), 1998 (15/0). Total: 45/3.
PRO STATISTICS: 1997—Credited with 1/2 sack and recovered one fumble. 1998—Credited with one sack.

GRAY, CARLTON — CB — CHIEFS

PERSONAL: Born June 26, 1971, in Cincinnati. ... 6-0/200. ... Full name: Carlton Patrick Gray.
HIGH SCHOOL: Forest Park (Cincinnati).
COLLEGE: UCLA.
TRANSACTIONS/CAREER NOTES: Selected by Seattle Seahawks in second round (30th pick overall) of 1993 NFL draft. ... Signed by Seahawks (July 22, 1993). ... On injured reserve with forearm injury (November 23, 1994-remainder of season). ... Granted free agency (February 16, 1996). ... Re-signed by Seahawks (February 16, 1996). ... Granted unconditional free agency (February 14, 1997). ... Signed by Indianapolis Colts (March 3, 1997). ... Released by Colts (September 3, 1998). ... Signed by New York Giants (September 9, 1998). ... Released by Giants (February 11, 1999). ... Signed by Kansas City Chiefs (February 18, 1999).
HONORS: Named defensive back on THE SPORTING NEWS college All-America first team (1992).
PRO STATISTICS: 1993—Credited with one sack. 1995—Fumbled once. 1996—Ran three yards with lateral from interception return and recovered one fumble for 62 yards. 1998—Credited with one sack.

			INTERCEPTIONS			
Year Team	G	GS	No.	Yds.	Avg.	TD
1993—Seattle NFL	10	2	3	33	11.0	0
1994—Seattle NFL	11	11	2	0	0.0	0
1995—Seattle NFL	16	16	4	45	11.3	0
1996—Seattle NFL	16	16	0	3	...	0
1997—Indianapolis NFL	15	13	2	0	0.0	0
1998—New York Giants NFL	14	3	1	36	36.0	0
Pro totals (6 years)	82	61	12	117	9.8	0

GRAY, CHRIS — G — SEAHAWKS

PERSONAL: Born June 19, 1970, in Birmingham, Ala. ... 6-4/305. ... Full name: Christopher William Gray.
HIGH SCHOOL: Homewood (Ala.).
COLLEGE: Auburn (degree in marketing, 1992).
TRANSACTIONS/CAREER NOTES: Selected by Miami Dolphins in fifth round (132nd pick overall) of 1993 NFL draft. ... Signed by Dolphins (July 12, 1993). ... On injured reserve with ankle injury (November 15, 1995-remainder of season). ... On injured reserve with broken leg (November 19, 1996-remainder of season). ... Released by Dolphins (August 12, 1997). ... Signed by Chicago Bears (September 9, 1997). ... Granted unconditional free agency (February 13, 1998). ... Signed by Seattle Seahawks (February 20, 1998).
PLAYING EXPERIENCE: Miami NFL, 1993-1996; Chicago NFL, 1997; Seattle NFL, 1998. ... Games/Games started: 1993 (5/0), 1994 (16/2), 1995 (10/10), 1996 (11/11), 1997 (8/2), 1998 (15/8). Total: 65/33.
PRO STATISTICS: 1994—Recovered one fumble.

GRAY, DERWIN — DB

PERSONAL: Born April 9, 1971, in San Antonio. ... 5-11/210. ... Full name: Derwin Lamont Gray.
HIGH SCHOOL: Judson-Converse (San Antonio).
COLLEGE: Brigham Young (degree in sports business management, 1992).
TRANSACTIONS/CAREER NOTES: Selected by Indianapolis Colts in fourth round (92nd pick overall) of 1993 NFL draft. ... Signed by Colts (July 20, 1993). ... Granted free agency (February 16, 1996). ... Re-signed by Colts (July 16, 1996). ... Granted unconditional free agency (February 13, 1998). ... Signed by Carolina Panthers (April 15, 1998). ... Released by Panthers (August 24, 1998). ... Re-signed by Panthers (September 21, 1998). ... On injured reserve with knee injury (October 13, 1998-remainder of season). ... Granted unconditional free agency (February 12, 1999).
PLAYING EXPERIENCE: Indianapolis NFL, 1993-1997; Carolina NFL, 1998. ... Games/Games started: 1993 (11/0), 1994 (16/2), 1995 (16/0), 1996 (10/1), 1997 (11/0), 1998 (3/0). Total: 67/3.
CHAMPIONSHIP GAME EXPERIENCE: Played in AFC championship game (1995 season).
PRO STATISTICS: 1993—Recovered one fumble. 1994—Ran four yards with lateral from kickoff return. 1995—Intercepted one pass for 10 yards and recovered one fumble.

GRAY, TORRIAN — S — VIKINGS

PERSONAL: Born March 18, 1974, in Bartow, Fla. ... 6-0/200. ... Full name: Torrian Deshon Gray.
HIGH SCHOOL: Kathleen (Lakeland, Fla.).
COLLEGE: Virginia Tech.
TRANSACTIONS/CAREER NOTES: Selected by Minnesota Vikings in second round (49th pick overall) of 1997 NFL draft. ... Signed by Vikings (June 5, 1997). ... On injured reserve with knee injury (November 10, 1998-remainder of season).
PLAYING EXPERIENCE: Minnesota NFL, 1997 and 1998. ... Games/Games started: 1997 (16/3), 1998 (9/1). Total: 25/4.
PRO STATISTICS: 1998—Intercepted one pass for 11 yards, credited with one sack and recovered one fumble for 14 yards.

GRAZIANI, TONY — QB — FALCONS

PERSONAL: Born December 23, 1973, in Las Vegas, Nev. ... 6-2/215. ... Full name: Anthony Robert Graziani.
HIGH SCHOOL: Downey (Modesto, Calif.).
COLLEGE: Oregon.
TRANSACTIONS/CAREER NOTES: Selected by Atlanta Falcons in seventh round (204th pick overall) of 1997 NFL draft. ... Signed by Falcons for 1997 season.
CHAMPIONSHIP GAME EXPERIENCE: Member of Falcons for NFC championship game (1998 season); inactive. ... Member of Falcons for Super Bowl XXXIII (1998 season); inactive.
SINGLE GAME HIGHS (regular season): Attempts—18 (November 29, 1998, vs. St. Louis); completions—8 (November 29, 1998, vs. St. Louis); yards—102 (November 29, 1998, vs. St. Louis); and touchdown passes—0.
MISCELLANEOUS: Regular-season record as starting NFL quarterback: 1-1 (.500).

				PASSING							RUSHING				TOTALS	
Year Team	G	GS	Att.	Cmp.	Pct.	Yds.	TD	Int.	Avg.	Rat.	Att.	Yds.	Avg.	TD	TD	2pt.	Pts.
1997—Atlanta NFL	3	1	23	7	30.4	41	0	2	1.78	3.7	3	19	6.3	0	0	0	0
1998—Atlanta NFL	4	1	33	16	48.5	199	0	2	6.03	42.4	4	21	5.3	0	0	0	0
Pro totals (2 years)	7	2	56	23	41.1	240	0	4	4.29	24.4	7	40	5.7	0	0	0	0

GRBAC, ELVIS — QB — CHIEFS

PERSONAL: Born August 13, 1970, in Cleveland. ... 6-5/232.
HIGH SCHOOL: St. Joseph (Cleveland).
COLLEGE: Michigan (degree in graphic design, 1993).
TRANSACTIONS/CAREER NOTES: Selected by San Francisco 49ers in eighth round (219th pick overall) of 1993 NFL draft. ... Signed by 49ers (July 13, 1993). ... Inactive for all 16 games (1993). ... Granted unconditional free agency (February 14, 1997). ... Signed by Kansas City Chiefs (March 17, 1997).
CHAMPIONSHIP GAME EXPERIENCE: Member of 49ers for NFC championship game (1993 season); inactive. ... Member of 49ers for NFC championship game (1994 season); did not play. ... Member of Super Bowl championship team (1994 season).
PRO STATISTICS: 1994—Fumbled five times. 1995—Fumbled twice and recovered two fumbles for minus one yard. 1997—Fumbled once. 1998—Fumbled once and recovered one fumble.
SINGLE GAME HIGHS (regular season): Attempts—42 (October 29, 1995, vs. New Orleans); completions—31 (November 20, 1995, vs. Miami); yards—382 (November 20, 1995, vs. Miami); and touchdown passes—4 (November 20, 1995, vs. Miami).
STATISTICAL PLATEAUS: 300-yard passing games: 1995 (3), 1997 (1). Total: 4.
MISCELLANEOUS: Regular-season record as starting NFL quarterback: 16-9 (.640). ... Postseason record as starting NFL quarterback: 0-1.

				PASSING							RUSHING				TOTALS	
Year Team	G	GS	Att.	Cmp.	Pct.	Yds.	TD	Int.	Avg.	Rat.	Att.	Yds.	Avg.	TD	TD	2pt.	Pts.
1993—San Francisco NFL							Did not play.										
1994—San Francisco NFL	11	0	50	35	70.0	393	2	1	7.86	98.2	13	1	0.1	0	0	0	0
1995—San Francisco NFL	16	5	183	127	69.4	1469	8	5	8.03	96.6	20	33	1.7	2	2	0	12
1996—San Francisco NFL	15	4	197	122	61.9	1236	8	10	6.27	72.2	23	21	0.9	2	2	0	12
1997—Kansas City NFL	10	10	314	179	57.0	1943	11	6	6.19	79.1	30	168	5.6	1	1	0	6
1998—Kansas City NFL	8	6	188	98	52.1	1142	5	12	6.07	53.1	7	27	3.9	0	0	0	0
Pro totals (5 years)	60	25	932	561	60.2	6183	34	34	6.63	76.8	93	250	2.7	5	5	0	30

GREEN, AHMAN — RB — SEAHAWKS

PERSONAL: Born February 16, 1977, in Omaha, Neb. ... 6-0/213.
HIGH SCHOOL: North (Omaha, Neb.), then Central Christian (Omaha, Neb.).
COLLEGE: Nebraska.
TRANSACTIONS/CAREER NOTES: Selected after junior season by Seattle Seahawks in third round (76th pick overall) of 1998 NFL draft. ... Signed by Seahawks (July 18, 1998).
HONORS: Named running back on THE SPORTING NEWS college All-America second team (1997).
PRO STATISTICS: 1998—Recovered one fumble.
SINGLE GAME HIGHS (regular season): Attempts—7 (September 13, 1998, vs. Arizona); yards—100 (September 6, 1998, vs. Philadelphia); and rushing touchdowns—1 (September 6, 1998, vs. Philadelphia).
STATISTICAL PLATEAUS: 100-yard rushing games: 1998 (1).

			RUSHING				RECEIVING				KICKOFF RETURNS				TOTALS			
Year Team	G	GS	Att.	Yds.	Avg.	TD	No.	Yds.	Avg.	TD	No.	Yds.	Avg.	TD	TD	2pt.	Pts.	Fum.
1998—Seattle NFL	16	0	35	209	6.0	1	3	2	0.7	0	27	620	23.0	0	1	0	6	1

GREEN, DARRELL — CB — REDSKINS

PERSONAL: Born February 15, 1960, in Houston. ... 5-8/184.
HIGH SCHOOL: Jesse H. Jones Senior (Houston).
COLLEGE: Texas A&I.
TRANSACTIONS/CAREER NOTES: Selected by Denver Gold in 10th round (112th pick overall) of 1983 USFL draft. ... Selected by Washington Redskins in first round (28th pick overall) of 1983 NFL draft. ... Signed by Redskins (June 10, 1983). ... On injured reserve with broken hand (December 13, 1988-remainder of season). ... On injured reserve with broken bone in wrist (October 24, 1989-remainder of season). ... Granted free agency (February 1, 1992). ... Re-signed by Redskins (August 25, 1992). ... On injured reserve with broken forearm (September 16-November 23, 1992). ... Granted unconditional free agency (February 17, 1995). ... Re-signed by Redskins (March 10, 1995). ... Granted unconditional free agency (February 14, 1997). ... Re-signed by Redskins (April 25, 1997).
CHAMPIONSHIP GAME EXPERIENCE: Played in NFC championship game (1983, 1986, 1987 and 1991 seasons). ... Played in Super Bowl XVIII (1983 season). ... Member of Super Bowl championship team (1987 and 1991 seasons).
HONORS: Played in Pro Bowl (1984, 1986, 1987, 1990, 1991, 1996 and 1997 seasons). ... Named cornerback on THE SPORTING NEWS NFL All-Pro team (1991).
POST SEASON RECORDS: Shares NFL postseason career record for most touchdowns by punt return—1 (January 10, 1988, at Chicago).
PRO STATISTICS: 1983—Recovered one fumble. 1985—Rushed once for six yards and recovered one fumble. 1986—Recovered one fumble. 1987—Recovered one fumble for 26 yards and a touchdown. 1988—Credited with one sack and recovered one fumble. 1989—Recovered one fumble. 1993—Recovered one fumble for 78 yards and a touchdown. 1996—Recovered one fumble for 15 yards. 1997—Returned one kickoff for nine yards.
MISCELLANEOUS: Holds Washington Redskins all-time record for most interceptions (47).

			INTERCEPTIONS				PUNT RETURNS				TOTALS			
Year Team	G	GS	No.	Yds.	Avg.	TD	No.	Yds.	Avg.	TD	TD	2pt.	Pts.	Fum.
1983—Washington NFL	16	16	2	7	3.5	0	4	29	7.3	0	0	...	0	1
1984—Washington NFL	16	16	5	91	18.2	1	2	13	6.5	0	1	...	6	0
1985—Washington NFL	16	16	2	0	0.0	0	16	214	13.4	0	0	...	0	2
1986—Washington NFL	16	15	5	9	1.8	0	12	120	10.0	0	0	...	0	1
1987—Washington NFL	12	12	3	65	21.7	0	5	53	10.6	0	1	...	6	0
1988—Washington NFL	15	15	1	12	12.0	0	9	103	11.4	0	0	...	0	1
1989—Washington NFL	7	7	2	0	0.0	0	1	11	11.0	0	0	...	0	0
1990—Washington NFL	16	16	4	20	5.0	1	1	6	6.0	0	1	...	6	0
1991—Washington NFL	16	16	5	47	9.4	0	0	0	...	0	0	...	0	0
1992—Washington NFL	8	7	1	15	15.0	0	0	0	...	0	0	...	0	0
1993—Washington NFL	16	16	4	10	2.5	0	1	27	27.0	0	1	...	6	0
1994—Washington NFL	16	16	3	32	10.7	1	0	0	...	0	1	0	6	0
1995—Washington NFL	16	16	3	42	14.0	1	0	0	...	0	1	0	6	0
1996—Washington NFL	16	16	3	84	28.0	1	0	0	...	0	1	0	6	0
1997—Washington NFL	16	16	1	83	83.0	1	0	0	...	0	1	0	6	0
1998—Washington NFL	16	16	3	36	12.0	0	0	0	...	0	0	0	0	0
Pro totals (16 years)	234	232	47	553	11.8	6	51	576	11.3	0	8	0	48	6

GREEN, E.G. — WR — COLTS

PERSONAL: Born June 28, 1975, in Fort Walton Beach, Fla. ... 5-11/187. ... Full name: Ernie G. Green.
HIGH SCHOOL: Fort Walton Beach (Fla.).
COLLEGE: Florida State.
TRANSACTIONS/CAREER NOTES: Selected by Indianapolis Colts in third round (71st pick overall) of 1998 NFL draft. ... Signed by Colts (July 21, 1998).
SINGLE GAME HIGHS (regular season): Receptions—4 (December 13, 1998, vs. Cincinnati); yards—52 (December 20, 1998, vs. Seattle); and touchdown receptions—1 (December 13, 1998, vs. Cincinnati).

			RECEIVING				TOTALS			
Year Team	G	GS	No.	Yds.	Avg.	TD	TD	2pt.	Pts.	Fum.
1998—Indianapolis NFL	12	0	15	177	11.8	1	1	0	6	0

GREEN, ERIC — TE — JETS

PERSONAL: Born June 22, 1967, in Savannah, Ga. ... 6-5/285. ... Full name: Bernard Eric Green.
HIGH SCHOOL: A.E. Beach (Savannah, Ga.).
COLLEGE: Liberty University, Va. (degree in finance, 1991).

TRANSACTIONS/CAREER NOTES: Selected by Pittsburgh Steelers in first round (21st pick overall) of 1990 NFL draft. ... Signed by Steelers (September 10, 1990). ... Granted roster exemption (September 10-24, 1990). ... On injured reserve with ankle injury (November 23, 1991-remainder of season). ... On injured reserve with shoulder injury (September 9-October 5, 1992). ... On practice squad (October 5-10, 1992). ... On reserve/suspended list for substance abuse (November 9-December 21, 1992). ... Granted roster exemption (December 21-27, 1992). ... Designated by Steelers as franchise player (February 15, 1994). ... Free agency status changed by Steelers from franchise to unconditional (February 15, 1995). ... Signed by Miami Dolphins (March 10, 1995). ... Released by Dolphins (July 9, 1996). ... Signed by Baltimore Ravens (September 24, 1996). ... Granted unconditional free agency (February 14, 1997). ... Re-signed by Ravens (July 18, 1997). ... Granted unconditional free agency (February 13, 1998). ... Re-signed by Ravens (February 18, 1998). ... Granted unconditional free agency (February 12, 1999). ... Signed by New York Jets (February 17, 1999).
CHAMPIONSHIP GAME EXPERIENCE: Played in AFC championship game (1994 season).
HONORS: Played in Pro Bowl (1993 and 1994 seasons).
PRO STATISTICS: 1990—Returned one kickoff for 16 yards and recovered one fumble.
SINGLE GAME HIGHS (regular season): Receptions—9 (November 2, 1997, vs. New York Jets); yards—158 (September 22, 1991, vs. Philadelphia); and touchdown receptions—3 (October 14, 1990, vs. Denver).
STATISTICAL PLATEAUS: 100-yard receiving games: 1990 (1), 1991 (1), 1993 (2). Total: 4.

				RECEIVING				TOTALS			
Year Team	G	GS	No.	Yds.	Avg.	TD	TD	2pt.	Pts.	Fum.
1990—Pittsburgh NFL	13	7	34	387	11.4	7	7	...	42	1
1991—Pittsburgh NFL	11	11	41	582	14.2	6	6	...	36	2
1992—Pittsburgh NFL	7	5	14	152	10.9	2	2	...	12	0
1993—Pittsburgh NFL	16	16	63	942	15.0	5	5	...	30	3
1994—Pittsburgh NFL	15	14	46	618	13.4	4	4	0	24	2
1995—Miami NFL	14	14	43	499	11.6	3	3	1	20	0
1996—Baltimore NFL	6	3	15	150	10.0	1	1	0	6	0
1997—Baltimore NFL	16	15	65	601	9.2	5	5	0	30	1
1998—Baltimore NFL	12	12	34	422	12.4	1	1	0	6	4
Pro totals (9 years)	110	97	355	4353	12.3	34	34	1	206	13

GREEN, HAROLD RB

PERSONAL: Born January 29, 1968, in Sacramento. ... 6-2/222. ... Full name: Harold Green Jr.
HIGH SCHOOL: Stratford (Goose Creek, S.C.).
COLLEGE: South Carolina.
TRANSACTIONS/CAREER NOTES: Selected by Cincinnati Bengals in second round (38th pick overall) of 1990 NFL draft. ... Signed by Bengals (August 1, 1990). ... Designated by Bengals as transition player (February 25, 1993). ... Free agency status changed by Bengals from transitional to unconditional (February 16, 1996). ... Signed by St. Louis Rams (July 10, 1996). ... Granted unconditional free agency (February 14, 1997). ... Signed by Atlanta Falcons (June 16, 1997). ... Granted unconditional free agency (February 13, 1998). ... Re-signed by Falcons (February 28, 1998). ... Released by Falcons (February 12, 1999).
CHAMPIONSHIP GAME EXPERIENCE: Played in NFC championship game (1998 season). ... Played in Super Bowl XXXIII (1998 season).
HONORS: Played in Pro Bowl (1992 season).
PRO STATISTICS: 1990—Recovered two fumbles. 1991—Returned four kickoffs for 66 yards. 1992—Recovered one fumble. 1994—Returned five kickoffs for 113 yards and recovered one fumble. 1995—Recovered one fumble. 1996—Recovered one fumble. 1997—Returned one kickoff for 23 yards and recovered one fumble. 1998—Returned one kickoff for 24 yards.
SINGLE GAME HIGHS (regular season): Attempts—31 (December 20, 1992, vs. New England); yards—190 (December 20, 1992, vs. New England); and rushing touchdowns—2 (November 10, 1996, vs. Atlanta).
STATISTICAL PLATEAUS: 100-yard rushing games: 1991 (3), 1992 (5), 1996 (1). Total: 9.

			RUSHING				RECEIVING				TOTALS			
Year Team	G	GS	Att.	Yds.	Avg.	TD	No.	Yds.	Avg.	TD	TD	2pt.	Pts.	Fum.
1990—Cincinnati NFL	12	9	83	353	4.3	1	12	90	7.5	1	2	...	12	2
1991—Cincinnati NFL	14	10	158	731	4.6	2	16	136	8.5	0	2	...	12	2
1992—Cincinnati NFL	16	15	265	1170	4.4	2	41	214	5.2	0	2	...	12	1
1993—Cincinnati NFL	15	15	215	589	2.7	0	22	115	5.2	0	0	...	0	3
1994—Cincinnati NFL	14	11	76	223	2.9	1	27	267	9.9	1	2	0	12	1
1995—Cincinnati NFL	15	15	171	661	3.9	2	27	182	6.7	1	3	0	18	2
1996—St. Louis NFL	16	5	127	523	4.1	4	37	246	6.6	1	5	1	32	2
1997—Atlanta NFL	16	1	36	78	2.2	1	29	360	12.4	0	1	0	6	0
1998—Atlanta NFL	6	0	20	37	1.9	0	2	34	17.0	0	0	0	0	1
Pro totals (9 years)	124	81	1151	4365	3.8	13	213	1644	7.7	4	17	1	104	14

GREEN, JACQUEZ WR BUCCANEERS

PERSONAL: Born January 15, 1976, in Fort Valley, Ga. ... 5-9/172. ... Full name: D'Tanyian Jacquez Green.
HIGH SCHOOL: Peach County (Fort Valley, Ga.).
COLLEGE: Florida.
TRANSACTIONS/CAREER NOTES: Selected after junior season by Tampa Bay Buccaneers in second round (34th pick overall) of 1998 NFL draft. ... Signed by Buccaneers (July 19, 1998).
HONORS: Named wide receiver on The Sporting News college All-America second team (1997).
PRO STATISTICS: 1998—Fumbled five times and recovered two fumbles.
SINGLE GAME HIGHS (regular season): Receptions—3 (December 27, 1998, vs. Cincinnati); yards—98 (November 22, 1998, vs. Detroit); and touchdown receptions—1 (December 7, 1998, vs. Green Bay).

			RUSHING				RECEIVING				PUNT RETURNS				KICKOFF RETURNS				TOTALS		
Year Team	G	GS	Att.	Yds.	Avg.	TD	No.	Yds.	Avg.	TD	No.	Yds.	Avg.	TD	No.	Yds.	Avg.	TD	TD	2pt.	Pts.
1998—Tampa Bay NFL	12	1	3	12	4.0	0	14	251	17.9	2	30	453	15.1	1	10	229	22.9	0	3	0	18

GREEN, TRENT — QB — RAMS

PERSONAL: Born July 9, 1970, in Cedar Rapids, Iowa. ... 6-3/215. ... Full name: Trent Jason Green.
HIGH SCHOOL: Vianney (St. Louis).
COLLEGE: Indiana.
TRANSACTIONS/CAREER NOTES: Selected by San Diego Chargers in eighth round (222nd pick overall) of 1993 NFL draft. ... Signed by Chargers (July 15, 1993). ... Inactive for all 16 games (1993). ... Released by Chargers (August 22, 1994). ... Signed by Washington Redskins (April 5, 1995). ... Inactive for all 16 games (1995). ... Inactive for all 16 games (1996). ... Granted free agency (February 14, 1997). ... Re-signed by Redskins (June 6, 1997). ... Granted unconditional free agency (February 12, 1999). ... Signed by St. Louis Rams (February 17, 1999).
PRO STATISTICS: 1998—Caught two passes for minus eight yards, led NFL with 14 fumbles and recovered four fumbles.
SINGLE GAME HIGHS (regular season): Attempts—54 (September 20, 1998, vs. Seattle); completions—30 (November 22, 1998, vs. Arizona); yards—383 (September 20, 1998, vs. Seattle); and touchdown passes—4 (November 22, 1998, vs. Arizona).
STATISTICAL PLATEAUS: 300-yard passing games: 1998 (2).
MISCELLANEOUS: Regular-season record as starting NFL quarterback: 6-8 (.429).

				PASSING						RUSHING			TOTALS		
Year Team	G	GS	Att.	Cmp.	Pct.	Yds.	TD	Int.	Avg.	Rat.	Att.	Yds.	Avg.	TD	TD	2pt.	Pts.
1993—San Diego NFL						Did not play.										
1994—						Did not play.										
1995—Washington NFL						Did not play.										
1996—Washington NFL						Did not play.										
1997—Washington NFL	1	0	1	0	0.0	0	0	0	...	39.6	0	0	...	0	0	0	0
1998—Washington NFL	15	14	509	278	54.6	3441	23	11	6.76	81.8	42	117	2.8	2	2	0	12
Pro totals (2 years)	16	14	510	278	54.5	3441	23	11	6.75	81.7	42	117	2.8	2	2	0	12

GREEN, VICTOR — S — JETS

PERSONAL: Born December 8, 1969, in Americus, Ga. ... 5-11/205. ... Full name: Victor Bernard Green. ... Cousin of Tommy Sims, defensive back with Indianapolis Colts (1986).
HIGH SCHOOL: Americus (Ga.).
JUNIOR COLLEGE: Copiah-Lincoln Junior College (Miss.).
COLLEGE: Akron (degree in criminal justice, 1993).
TRANSACTIONS/CAREER NOTES: Signed as non-drafted free agent by New York Jets (April 29, 1993). ... Released by Jets (August 30, 1993). ... Re-signed by Jets to practice squad (September 1, 1993). ... Activated (September 28, 1993).
CHAMPIONSHIP GAME EXPERIENCE: Played in AFC championship game (1998 season).
PRO STATISTICS: 1994—Recovered one fumble. 1995—Recovered one fumble. 1996—Recovered three fumbles. 1998—Recovered one fumble.

			INTERCEPTIONS				SACKS
Year Team	G	GS	No.	Yds.	Avg.	TD	No.
1993—New York Jets NFL	11	0	0	0	...	0	0.0
1994—New York Jets NFL	16	0	0	0	...	0	1.0
1995—New York Jets NFL	16	12	1	2	2.0	0	2.0
1996—New York Jets NFL	16	16	2	27	13.5	0	2.0
1997—New York Jets NFL	16	16	3	89	29.7	0	1.0
1998—New York Jets NFL	16	16	4	99	24.8	0	1.0
Pro totals (6 years)	91	60	10	217	21.7	0	7.0

GREEN, WILLIE — WR — DOLPHINS

PERSONAL: Born April 2, 1966, in Athens, Ga. ... 6-4/191. ... Full name: Willie Aaron Green.
HIGH SCHOOL: Clarke Central (Athens, Ga.), then Tennessee Military Academy.
COLLEGE: Mississippi.
TRANSACTIONS/CAREER NOTES: Selected by Detroit Lions in eighth round (194th pick overall) of 1990 NFL draft. ... Signed by Lions for 1990 season. ... On injured reserve with shoulder injury (September 5, 1990-entire season). ... Granted free agency (February 1, 1992). ... Re-signed by Lions (August 11, 1992). ... On suspended list (December 7-14, 1992). ... Released by Lions (June 9, 1994). ... Signed by Tampa Bay Buccaneers (July 5, 1994). ... Released by Buccaneers (October 11, 1994). ... Signed by Carolina Panthers (December 15, 1994). ... Granted unconditional free agency (February 14, 1997). ... Signed by Denver Broncos (March 21, 1997). ... Released by Broncos (February 11, 1999). ... Signed by Miami Dolphins (February 26, 1999).
CHAMPIONSHIP GAME EXPERIENCE: Played in NFC championship game (1991 and 1996 seasons). ... Played in AFC championship game (1997 and 1998 seasons). ... Member of Super Bowl championship team (1997 and 1998 seasons).
PRO STATISTICS: 1996—Rushed once for one yard.
SINGLE GAME HIGHS (regular season): Receptions—9 (November 3, 1996, vs. Atlanta); yards—157 (December 8, 1996, vs. San Francisco); and touchdown receptions—2 (November 24, 1996, vs. Houston).
STATISTICAL PLATEAUS: 100-yard receiving games: 1992 (2), 1993 (1), 1995 (4), 1996 (1). Total: 8.

			RECEIVING				TOTALS			
Year Team	G	GS	No.	Yds.	Avg.	TD	TD	2pt.	Pts.	Fum.
1990—Detroit NFL						Did not play.				
1991—Detroit NFL	16	15	39	592	15.2	7	7	...	42	0
1992—Detroit NFL	15	13	33	586	17.8	5	5	...	30	1
1993—Detroit NFL	16	6	28	462	16.5	2	2	...	12	0
1994—Tampa Bay NFL	5	0	9	150	16.7	0	0	0	0	0
1995—Carolina NFL	16	7	47	882	‡18.8	6	6	0	36	1
1996—Carolina NFL	15	10	46	614	13.3	3	3	0	18	0
1997—Denver NFL	16	1	19	240	12.6	2	2	0	12	0
1998—Denver NFL	15	1	16	194	12.1	1	1	0	6	0
Pro totals (8 years)	114	53	237	3720	15.7	26	26	0	156	2

GREENE, ANDREW — G

PERSONAL: Born September 24, 1969, in Kingston, Jamaica. ... 6-3/304.
HIGH SCHOOL: Pickering (Ajax, Ont.).
COLLEGE: Indiana.
TRANSACTIONS/CAREER NOTES: Selected by Miami Dolphins in second round (53rd pick overall) of 1995 NFL draft. ... Signed by Dolphins (June 30, 1995). ... Released by Dolphins (August 25, 1996). ... Signed by Seattle Seahawks (January 30, 1997). ... Released by Seahawks (August 24, 1997). ... Re-signed by Seahawks (February 14, 1998). ... Released by Seahawks (November 6, 1998). ... Re-signed by Seahawks (November 11, 1998). ... Released by Seahawks (November 25, 1998). ... Signed by Jacksonville Jaguars to practice squad (December 16, 1998). ... Released by Jaguars (April 18, 1999).
PLAYING EXPERIENCE: Miami NFL, 1995; Seattle NFL, 1998. ... Games/Games started: 1995 (6/1), 1998 (4/0). Total: 10/1.

GREENE, KEVIN — LB — PANTHERS

PERSONAL: Born July 31, 1962, in New York. ... 6-3/247. ... Full name: Kevin Darwin Greene.
HIGH SCHOOL: South (Granite City, Ill.).
COLLEGE: Auburn.
TRANSACTIONS/CAREER NOTES: Selected by Birmingham Stallions in 1985 USFL territorial draft. ... Selected by Los Angeles Rams in fifth round (113th pick overall) of 1985 NFL draft. ... Signed by Rams (July 12, 1985). ... Crossed picket line during players strike (October 14, 1987). ... Granted free agency (February 1, 1990). ... Re-signed by Rams (September 1, 1990). ... Granted roster exemption (September 1-7, 1990). ... Granted unconditional free agency (March 1, 1993). ... Signed by Pittsburgh Steelers (April 3, 1993). ... Granted unconditional free agency (February 16, 1996). ... Signed by Carolina Panthers (May 3, 1996). ... On reserve/did not report list (July 21-August 25, 1997). ... Released by Panthers (August 25, 1997). ... Signed by San Francisco 49ers (August 28, 1997). ... Released by 49ers (February 9, 1998). ... Signed by Panthers (March 16, 1998).
CHAMPIONSHIP GAME EXPERIENCE: Played in NFC championship game (1985, 1989, 1996 and 1997 seasons). ... Played in AFC championship game (1994 and 1995 seasons). ... Played in Super Bowl XXX (1995 season).
HONORS: Named outside linebacker on THE SPORTING NEWS NFL All-Pro team (1989 and 1994). ... Played in Pro Bowl (1989, 1994-1996 and 1998 seasons).
PRO STATISTICS: 1986—Recovered one fumble for 13 yards. 1987—Intercepted one pass for 25 yards. 1988—Credited with a safety and intercepted one pass for 10 yards. 1989—Recovered two fumbles. 1990—Recovered four fumbles. 1991—Credited with one safety. 1992—Credited with one safety and recovered four fumbles for two yards. 1993—Recovered three fumbles for five yards. 1994—Recovered three fumbles. 1995—Intercepted one pass for no yards. 1996—Recovered three fumbles for 66 yards and a touchdown. 1997—Recovered two fumbles for 40 yards and one touchdown. 1998—Intercepted two passes for 18 yards and recovered one fumble for two yards.
MISCELLANEOUS: Holds Carolina Panthers all-time record for most sacks (29.5).

Year Team	G	GS	SACKS
1985—Los Angeles Rams NFL	15	0	0.0
1986—Los Angeles Rams NFL	16	0	7.0
1987—Los Angeles Rams NFL	9	0	6.5
1988—Los Angeles Rams NFL	16	14	16.5
1989—Los Angeles Rams NFL	16	16	16.5
1990—Los Angeles Rams NFL	15	15	13.0
1991—Los Angeles Rams NFL	16	16	3.0
1992—Los Angeles Rams NFL	16	16	10.0
1993—Pittsburgh NFL	16	16	12.5
1994—Pittsburgh NFL	16	16	*14.0
1995—Pittsburgh NFL	16	16	9.0
1996—Carolina NFL	16	16	*14.5
1997—San Francisco NFL	14	4	10.5
1998—Carolina NFL	15	15	15.0
Pro totals (14 years)	**212**	**160**	**148.0**

GREENE, SCOTT — RB — COLTS

PERSONAL: Born June 1, 1972, in Honeoye, N.Y. ... 5-11/230. ... Full name: Scott Clayton Greene.
HIGH SCHOOL: Canandaigua (N.Y.) Academy.
COLLEGE: Michigan State.
TRANSACTIONS/CAREER NOTES: Selected by Carolina Panthers in sixth round (193rd pick overall) of 1996 NFL draft. ... Signed by Panthers (July 17, 1996). ... Released by Panthers (August 21, 1996). ... Re-signed by Panthers to practice squad (August 27, 1996). ... Activated (October 29, 1996). ... Released by Panthers (August 26, 1998). ... Signed by Indianapolis Colts (October 20, 1998). ... Granted free agency (February 12, 1999).
CHAMPIONSHIP GAME EXPERIENCE: Played in NFC championship game (1996 season).
PRO STATISTICS: 1996—Returned two kickoffs for 10 yards. 1997—Returned three kickoffs for 18 yards.
SINGLE GAME HIGHS (regular season): Attempts—7 (November 30, 1997, vs. New Orleans); yards—30 (November 30, 1997, vs. New Orleans); and rushing touchdowns—1 (November 2, 1997, vs. Oakland).

			RUSHING				RECEIVING			TOTALS			
Year Team	G	GS	Att.	Yds.	Avg.	TD	No.	Yds.	Avg.	TD	TD	2pt.	Pts.	Fum.
1996—Carolina NFL	8	0	0	0	...	0	2	7	3.5	1	1	0	6	0
1997—Carolina NFL	16	14	45	157	3.5	1	40	277	6.9	1	2	0	12	1
1998—Indianapolis NFL	5	0	0	0	...	0	1	2	2.0	0	0	0	0	0
Pro totals (3 years)	**29**	**14**	**45**	**157**	**3.5**	**1**	**43**	**286**	**6.7**	**2**	**3**	**0**	**18**	**1**

GREER, DONOVAN — DB — BILLS

PERSONAL: Born September 11, 1974, in Houston. ... 5-9/178.
HIGH SCHOOL: Elsik (Alief, Texas).
COLLEGE: Texas A&M.

TRANSACTIONS/CAREER NOTES: Signed as non-drafted free agent by New Orleans Saints (April 25, 1997). ... Released by Saints (August 24, 1997). ... Signed by Atlanta Falcons (August 26, 1997). ... Released by Falcons (September 3, 1997). ... Signed by Saints to practice squad (September 4, 1997). ... Activated (November 15, 1997). ... Released by Saints (August 24, 1998). ... Signed by Buffalo Bills to practice squad (September 9, 1998). ... Activated (September 30, 1998).
PLAYING EXPERIENCE: Atlanta (1)-New Orleans (6) NFL, 1997; Buffalo NFL, 1998. ... Games/Games started: 1997 (Atl.-1/0; N.O.-6/1; Total: 7/1), 1998 (11/2). Total: 18/3.
PRO STATISTICS: 1998—Recovered one fumble for 18 yards.

GRIESE, BRIAN — QB — BRONCOS

PERSONAL: Born March 18, 1975, in Miami. ... 6-3/215. ... Full name: Brian David Griese. ... Son of Bob Griese, Hall of Fame quarterback with Miami Dolphins (1967-80).
HIGH SCHOOL: Columbus (Miami).
COLLEGE: Michigan.
TRANSACTIONS/CAREER NOTES: Selected by Denver Broncos in third round (91st pick overall) of 1998 NFL draft. ... Signed by Broncos (July 22, 1998).
CHAMPIONSHIP GAME EXPERIENCE: Member of Broncos for AFC championship game (1998 season); inactive. ... Member of Super Bowl championship team (1998 season); inactive.
PRO STATISTICS: 1998—Fumbled once for minus one yard.
SINGLE GAME HIGHS (regular season): Attempts—3 (October 4, 1998, vs. Philadelphia); completions—1 (October 4, 1998, vs. Phildelphia); yards—2 (October 4, 1998, vs. Philadelphia); and touchdown passes—0.

			PASSING						RUSHING				TOTALS		
Year Team	G	GS	Att.	Cmp.	Pct.	Yds.	TD	Int.	Avg.	Rat.	Att.	Yds.	Avg.	TD	TD	2pt.	Pts.
1998—Denver NFL	1	0	3	1	33.3	2	0	1	0.67	2.8	4	-4	-1.0	0	...	0	...

GRIFFITH, HOWARD — FB — BRONCOS

PERSONAL: Born November 17, 1967, in Chicago. ... 6-0/230. ... Full name: Howard Thomas Griffith.
HIGH SCHOOL: Percy L. Julian (Chicago).
COLLEGE: Illinois.
TRANSACTIONS/CAREER NOTES: Selected by Indianapolis Colts in ninth round (237th pick overall) of 1991 NFL draft. ... Signed by Colts (July 12, 1991). ... Released by Colts (August 26, 1991). ... Signed by Buffalo Bills to practice squad (September 4, 1991). ... Released by Bills (August 31, 1992). ... Re-signed by Bills to practice squad (September 2, 1992). ... Released by Bills (October 21, 1992). ... Signed by San Diego Chargers to practice squad (October 23, 1992). ... Released by Chargers (October 28, 1992). ... Re-signed by Chargers to practice squad (October 30, 1992). ... Released by Chargers (December 9, 1992). ... Re-signed by Chargers to practice squad (December 14, 1992). ... Released by Chargers (August 30, 1993). ... Signed by Los Angeles Rams (September 2, 1993). ... Selected by Carolina Panthers from Rams in NFL expansion draft (February 15, 1995). ... Granted free agency (February 16, 1996). ... Re-signed by Panthers (July 20, 1996). ... Granted unconditional free agency (February 14, 1997). ... Signed by Denver Broncos (February 18, 1997).
CHAMPIONSHIP GAME EXPERIENCE: Played in NFC championship game (1996 season). ... Played in AFC championship game (1997 and 1998 seasons). ... Member of Super Bowl championship team (1997 and 1998 seasons).
PRO STATISTICS: 1995—Recovered one fumble. 1996—Recovered one fumble. 1997—Recovered one fumble.
SINGLE GAME HIGHS (regular season): Attempts—25 (November 19, 1995, vs. Arizona); yards—88 (November 19, 1995, vs. Arizona); and rushing touchdowns—1 (December 1, 1996, vs. Tampa Bay).

			RUSHING				RECEIVING				KICKOFF RETURNS				TOTALS			
Year Team	G	GS	Att.	Yds.	Avg.	TD	No.	Yds.	Avg.	TD	No.	Yds.	Avg.	TD	TD	2pt.	Pts.	Fum.
1991—Buffalo NFL								Did not play.										
1992—San Diego NFL								Did not play.										
1993—L.A. Rams NFL	15	0	0	0	...	0	0	0	...	0	8	169	21.1	0	0	...	0	0
1994—L.A. Rams NFL	16	10	9	30	3.3	0	16	113	7.1	1	2	35	17.5	0	1	0	6	0
1995—Carolina NFL	15	7	65	197	3.0	1	11	63	5.7	0	0	0	...	0	2	0	12	1
1996—Carolina NFL	16	14	12	7	0.6	1	27	223	8.3	1	0	0	...	0	2	0	12	1
1997—Denver NFL	15	13	9	34	3.8	0	11	55	5.0	0	0	0	...	0	0	0	0	0
1998—Denver NFL	14	13	4	13	3.3	0	15	97	6.5	3	0	0	...	0	3	0	18	0
Pro totals (6 years)	91	57	99	281	2.8	2	80	551	6.9	6	10	204	20.4	0	8	0	48	2

GRIFFITH, RICH — TE — JAGUARS

PERSONAL: Born July 31, 1969, in Tucson, Ariz. ... 6-5/261. ... Full name: Richard Pope Griffith.
HIGH SCHOOL: Catalina (Tucson, Ariz.).
COLLEGE: Arizona (degree in communications, 1993).
TRANSACTIONS/CAREER NOTES: Selected by New England Patriots in fifth round (138th pick overall) of 1993 NFL draft. ... Signed by Patriots (July 16, 1993). ... Released by Patriots (August 20, 1994). ... Signed by Jacksonville Jaguars (January 6, 1995). ... Granted free agency (February 14, 1997). ... Re-signed by Jaguars (April 15, 1997). ... Granted unconditional free agency (February 13, 1998). ... Re-signed by Jaguars (February 15, 1998). ... On injured reserve with knee injury (October 28, 1998-remainder of season).
PLAYING EXPERIENCE: New England NFL, 1993; Jacksonville NFL, 1995-1998. ... Games/Games started: 1993 (3/0), 1995 (16/15), 1996 (16/2), 1997 (16/1), 1998 (7/0). Total: 58/18.
CHAMPIONSHIP GAME EXPERIENCE: Played in AFC championship game (1996 season).
PRO STATISTICS: 1995—Caught 16 passes for 243 yards and returned one kickoff for nine yards. 1996—Caught five passes for 53 yards, returned two kickoffs for 24 yards and recovered one fumble.
SINGLE GAME HIGHS (regular season): Receptions—4 (December 10, 1995, vs. Indianapolis); yards—54 (December 10, 1995, vs. Indianapolis); and touchdown receptions—0.

GRIFFITH, ROBERT — S — VIKINGS

PERSONAL: Born November 30, 1970, in Landham, Md. ... 5-11/195. ... Full name: Robert Otis Griffith.
HIGH SCHOOL: Mount Miguel (Spring Valley, Calif.).
COLLEGE: San Diego State.
TRANSACTIONS/CAREER NOTES: Signed by Sacramento Gold Miners of CFL to practice squad (August 8, 1993). ... Granted free agency after 1993 season. ... Signed as non-drafted free agent by Minnesota Vikings (April 21, 1994). ... Granted free agency (February 14, 1997). ... Re-signed by Vikings (May 7, 1997).
CHAMPIONSHIP GAME EXPERIENCE: Played in NFC championship game (1998 season).
HONORS: Named safety on THE SPORTING NEWS NFL All-Pro team (1998).
PRO STATISTICS: 1996—Fumbled once.

			INTERCEPTIONS				SACKS
Year Team	G	GS	No.	Yds.	Avg.	TD	No.
1994—Minnesota NFL	15	0	0	0	...	0	0.0
1995—Minnesota NFL	16	0	0	0	...	0	0.5
1996—Minnesota NFL	14	14	4	67	16.8	0	2.0
1997—Minnesota NFL	16	16	2	26	13.0	0	0.0
1998—Minnesota NFL	16	16	5	25	5.0	0	0.0
Pro totals (5 years)	77	46	11	118	10.7	0	2.5

GRUBER, PAUL — OT — BUCCANEERS

PERSONAL: Born February 24, 1965, in Madison, Wis. ... 6-5/292. ... Full name: Paul Blake Gruber.
HIGH SCHOOL: Sauk Prairie (Prairie du Sac, Wis.).
COLLEGE: Wisconsin (degree in communication arts, 1988).
TRANSACTIONS/CAREER NOTES: Selected by Tampa Bay Buccaneers in first round (fourth pick overall) of 1988 NFL draft. ... Signed by Buccaneers (August 7, 1988). ... Designated by Buccaneers as franchise player (February 25, 1993). ... Re-signed by Buccaneers (October 20, 1993). ... Granted roster exemption (October 20-23, 1993).
PLAYING EXPERIENCE: Tampa Bay NFL, 1988-1998. ... Games/Games started: 1988 (16/16), 1989 (16/16), 1990 (16/16), 1991 (16/16), 1992 (16/16), 1993 (10/10), 1994 (16/16), 1995 (16/16), 1996 (13/13), 1997 (16/16), 1998 (16/16). Total: 167/167.
HONORS: Named offensive tackle on THE SPORTING NEWS college All-America first team (1987).
PRO STATISTICS: 1988—Recovered two fumbles. 1990—Recovered one fumble. 1991—Recovered one fumble. 1992—Recovered one fumble. 1994—Recovered one fumble. 1995—Recovered two fumbles. 1997—Recovered one fumble.

GRUNHARD, TIM — C — CHIEFS

PERSONAL: Born May 17, 1968, in Chicago. ... 6-2/307. ... Full name: Timothy Gerard Grunhard.
HIGH SCHOOL: St. Laurence (Burbank, Ill.).
COLLEGE: Notre Dame (degree in political science).
TRANSACTIONS/CAREER NOTES: Selected by Kansas City Chiefs in second round (40th pick overall) of 1990 NFL draft. ... Signed by Chiefs (July 22, 1990).
PLAYING EXPERIENCE: Kansas City NFL, 1990-1998. ... Games/Games started: 1990 (14/9), 1991 (16/16), 1992 (12/12), 1993 (16/16), 1994 (16/16), 1995 (16/16), 1996 (16/16), 1997 (16/16), 1998 (16/16). Total: 138/133.
CHAMPIONSHIP GAME EXPERIENCE: Played in AFC championship game (1993 season).
PRO STATISTICS: 1991—Recovered one fumble. 1992—Recovered two fumbles. 1993—Fumbled once. 1995—Recovered one fumble. 1996—Recovered one fumble. 1997—Recovered one fumble.

GRUTTADAURIA, MIKE — C — RAMS

PERSONAL: Born December 6, 1972, in Fort Lauderdale, Fla. ... 6-3/297. ... Full name: Michael Jason Gruttadauria.
HIGH SCHOOL: Tarpon Springs (Fla.).
COLLEGE: Central Florida.
TRANSACTIONS/CAREER NOTES: Signed as non-drafted free agent by Dallas Cowboys (April 26, 1995). ... Released by Cowboys (August 22, 1995). ... Signed by St. Louis Rams (February 9, 1996). ... Granted free agency (February 12, 1999).
PLAYING EXPERIENCE: St. Louis NFL, 1996-1998. ... Games/Games started: 1996 (9/3), 1997 (14/14), 1998 (12/3). Total: 35/20.
PRO STATISTICS: 1997—Caught one pass for no yards.

GULIFORD, ERIC — WR

PERSONAL: Born October 25, 1969, in Peoria, Ariz. ... 5-8/165. ... Full name: Eric Andre Guliford.
HIGH SCHOOL: Peoria (Ariz.).
COLLEGE: Arizona State.
TRANSACTIONS/CAREER NOTES: Signed as non-drafted free agent by Minnesota Vikings (May 3, 1993). ... Selected by Carolina Panthers from Vikings in NFL expansion draft (February 15, 1995). ... On injured reserve with hamstring injury (December 13, 1995-remainder of season). ... Granted unconditional free agency (February 16, 1996). ... Signed by Winnipeg Blue Bombers of CFL (May 26, 1996). ... Released by Blue Bombers (November 23, 1996). ... Signed by New Orleans Saints (May 19, 1997). ... On non-football injury list with Achilles' tendon injury (August 25-November 24, 1998). ... Released by Saints (March 2, 1999).
PRO STATISTICS: 1995—Attempted two passes with one completion for 46 yards and an interception, rushed twice for two yards and recovered one fumble. 1997—Rushed once for minus two yards and recovered one fumble. 1998—Recovered one fumble.
SINGLE GAME HIGHS (regular season): Receptions—7 (October 29, 1995, vs. New England); yards— 94 (October 29, 1995, vs. New England); and touchdown receptions—1 (December 14, 1997, vs. Arizona).

Year Team	G	GS	RECEIVING No. Yds. Avg. TD	PUNT RETURNS No. Yds. Avg. TD	KICKOFF RETURNS No. Yds. Avg. TD	TOTALS TD 2pt. Pts. Fum.
1993—Minnesota NFL	10	0	1 45 45.0 0	29 212 7.3 0	5 101 20.2 0	0 0 0 1
1994—Minnesota NFL	7	1	0 0 ... 0	5 14 2.8 0	0 0 ... 0	0 0 0 1
1995—Carolina NFL	14	9	29 444 15.3 1	43 ‡475 11.0 †1	0 0 ... 0	2 0 12 1
1996—Winnipeg CFL	11	...	47 758 16.1 3	44 546 12.4 0	31 634 20.5 0	3 0 18 0
1997—New Orleans NFL	16	2	27 362 13.4 1	47 498 10.6 0	43 1128 26.2 1	2 0 12 2
1998—New Orleans NFL	5	1	10 124 12.4 0	10 101 10.1 0	18 431 23.9 0	0 0 0 1
CFL totals (1 year)	11	...	47 758 16.1 3	44 546 12.4 0	31 634 20.5 0	3 0 18 0
NFL totals (5 years)	52	13	67 975 14.6 2	134 1300 9.7 1	66 1660 25.2 1	4 0 24 6
Pro totals (6 years)	63	...	114 1733 15.2 5	178 1846 10.4 1	97 2294 23.6 1	7 0 42 6

GUTIERREZ, BROCK G/C BENGALS

PERSONAL: Born September 25, 1973 in Charlotte, Mich. ... 6-3/304. ... Name pronounced goo-TARE-ez.
HIGH SCHOOL: Charlotte (Mich.).
COLLEGE: Central Michigan.
TRANSACTIONS/CAREER NOTES: Signed as non-drafted free agent by Cincinnati Bengals (April 23, 1996). ... Active for two games (1996). ... Released by Bengals (August 30, 1998). ... Re-signed by Bengals (November 4, 1998). ... Released by Bengals (November 17, 1998). ... Signed by Jacksonville Jaguars to practice squad (November 30, 1998). ... Signed by Bengals off Jaguars practice squad (December 15, 1998).
PLAYING EXPERIENCE: Cincinnati NFL, 1997 and 1998. ... Games/Games started: 1997 (5/0), 1998 (1/0). Total: 6/0.

HAASE, ANDY TE GIANTS

PERSONAL: Born July 10, 1974, in Odessa, Wash. ... 6-4/260.
HIGH SCHOOL: Rampart (Colorado Springs, Colo.).
COLLEGE: Northern Colorado.
TRANSACTIONS/CAREER NOTES: Signed as non-drafted free agent by New York Giants (April 24, 1998). ... Released by Giants (September 9, 1998). ... Re-signed by Giants to practice squad (September 10, 1998). ... Activated (November 17, 1998). ... Assigned by Giants to Rhein Fire in 1999 NFL Europe enhancement allocation program (February 22, 1999).
PLAYING EXPERIENCE: New York Giants NFL, 1998. ... Games/Games started: 7/1.
PRO STATISTICS: 1998—Caught two passes for 33 yards.
SINGLE GAME HIGHS (regular season): Receptions—1 (December 6, 1998, vs. Arizona); yards—27 (November 30, 1998, vs. San Francisco); and touchdown receptions—0.

HABIB, BRIAN G SEAHAWKS

PERSONAL: Born December 2, 1964, in Ellensburg, Wash. ... 6-7/299. ... Full name: Brian Richard Habib.
HIGH SCHOOL: Ellensburg (Wash.).
COLLEGE: Washington.
TRANSACTIONS/CAREER NOTES: Selected by Minnesota Vikings in 10th round (264th pick overall) of 1988 NFL draft. ... Signed by Vikings (July 19, 1988). ... On injured reserve with shoulder injury (September 3-December 24, 1988). ... Granted free agency (February 1, 1991). ... Re-signed by Vikings (July 18, 1991). ... Granted free agency (February 1, 1992). ... Re-signed by Vikings (July 24, 1992). ... Granted unconditional free agency (March 1, 1993). ... Signed by Denver Broncos (March 8, 1993). ... Granted unconditional free agency (February 13, 1998). ... Signed by Seattle Seahawks (March 6, 1998).
PLAYING EXPERIENCE: Minnesota NFL, 1989-1992; Denver NFL, 1993-1997; Seattle NFL, 1998. ... Games/Games started: 1989 (16/0), 1990 (16/0), 1991 (16/8), 1992 (16/15), 1993 (16/16), 1994 (16/16), 1995 (16/16), 1996 (16/16), 1997 (14/14), 1998 (16/16). Total: 158/117.
CHAMPIONSHIP GAME EXPERIENCE: Played in AFC championship game (1997 season). ... Member of Super Bowl championship team (1997 season).
PRO STATISTICS: 1994—Recovered one fumble. 1998—Recovered two fumbles.

HAKIM, AZ-ZAHIR WR RAMS

PERSONAL: Born June 3, 1977, in Los Angeles. ... 5-10/178. ... Full name: Az-zahir Ali Hakim. ... Name pronounced oz-aa-HERE ha-KEEM.
HIGH SCHOOL: Fairfax (Los Angeles).
COLLEGE: San Diego State.
TRANSACTIONS/CAREER NOTES: Selected by St. Louis Rams in fourth round (96th pick overall) of 1998 NFL draft. ... Signed by Rams (July 13, 1998).
SINGLE GAME HIGHS (regular season): Receptions—4 (December 20, 1998, vs. Carolina); yards—50 (December 13, 1998, vs. New England); and touchdown receptions—1 (December 13, 1998, vs. New England).

Year Team	G	GS	RUSHING Att. Yds. Avg. TD	RECEIVING No. Yds. Avg. TD	KICKOFF RETURNS No. Yds. Avg. TD	TOTALS TD 2pt. Pts. Fum.
1998—St. Louis NFL	9	4	2 30 15.0 1	20 247 12.4 1	0 0 ... 0	2 0 12 1

HALL, JOHN K JETS

PERSONAL: Born March 17, 1974, in Port Charlotte, Fla. ... 6-3/223.
HIGH SCHOOL: Port Charlotte (Fla.).
COLLEGE: Wisconsin.
TRANSACTIONS/CAREER NOTES: Signed as non-drafted free agent by New York Jets (April 25, 1997).
CHAMPIONSHIP GAME EXPERIENCE: Played in AFC championship game (1998 season).
PRO STATISTICS: 1997—Punted three times for 144 yards.

Year Team	G	XPM	XPA	FGM	FGA	Lg.	50+	Pts.
				KICKING				
1997—New York Jets NFL	16	36	36	28	†41	55	4-6	120
1998—New York Jets NFL	16	45	46	25	35	54	1-3	120
Pro totals (2 years)	32	81	82	53	76	55	5-9	240

HALL, LEMANSKI — LB — BEARS

PERSONAL: Born November 24, 1970, in Valley, Ala. ... 6-0/235. ... Full name: Lemanski S. Hall. ... Name pronounced LA-man-ski.
HIGH SCHOOL: Valley (Ala.).
COLLEGE: Alabama.
TRANSACTIONS/CAREER NOTES: Selected by Houston Oilers in seventh round (220th pick overall) of 1994 NFL draft. ... Signed by Oilers (June 20, 1994). ... Released by Oilers (August 28, 1994). ... Re-signed by Oilers to practice squad (August 30, 1994). ... Activated (December 23, 1994); did not play. ... Assigned by Oilers to Frankfurt Galaxy in 1995 World League enhancement allocation program (February 20, 1995). ... Assigned by Oilers to Amsterdam Admirals in 1996 World League enhancement allocation program (February 19, 1996). ... Oilers franchise moved to Tennessee for 1997 season. ... Granted free agency (February 13, 1998). ... Re-signed by Oilers (May 28, 1998). ... Traded by Oilers to Chicago Bears for seventh-round pick in 2000 draft (September 1, 1998).
PLAYING EXPERIENCE: Frankfurt W.L., 1995; Houston NFL, 1995 and 1996; Amsterdam W.L. 1996; Tennessee NFL, 1997; Chicago NFL, 1998. ... Games/Games started: W.L. 1995 (games played unavailable), NFL 1995 (12.0), W.L. 1996 (-), NFL 1996 (3/0), 1997 (16/2), 1998 (15/0). Total NFL: 46/2.
PRO STATISTICS: 1997—Credited with two sacks. 1998—Recovered one fumble for five yards.

HALL, RHETT — DT

PERSONAL: Born December 5, 1968, in San Jose, Calif. ... 6-2/276. ... Full name: Rhett Floyd Hall.
HIGH SCHOOL: Live Oak (Morgan Hill, Calif.).
JUNIOR COLLEGE: Gavilan College (Calif.).
COLLEGE: California.
TRANSACTIONS/CAREER NOTES: Selected by Tampa Bay Buccaneers in sixth round (147th pick overall) of 1991 NFL draft. ... Signed by Buccaneers (July 18, 1991). ... Released by Buccaneers (August 31, 1992). ... Re-signed by Buccaneers (September 1, 1992). ... Released by Buccaneers (September 2, 1992). ... Re-signed by Buccaneers (September 4, 1992). ... Released by Buccaneers (September 23, 1992). ... Re-signed by Buccaneers (December 9, 1992). ... Released by Buccaneers (August 30, 1993). ... Re-signed by Buccaneers (August 31, 1993). ... Released by Buccaneers (September 11, 1993). ... Re-signed by Buccaneers (November 23, 1993). ... Granted free agency (February 17, 1994). ... Signed by San Francisco 49ers (June 1, 1994). ... Released by 49ers (September 7, 1994). ... Re-signed by 49ers (September 14, 1994). ... Granted unconditional free agency (February 17, 1995). ... Signed by Philadelphia Eagles (March 9, 1995). ... Designated by Eagles as transition player (February 12, 1998). ... Re-signed by Eagles (June 8, 1998). ... On injured reserve with knee injury (September 25, 1998-remainder of season). ... Granted unconditional free agency (February 12, 1999).
CHAMPIONSHIP GAME EXPERIENCE: Played in NFC championship game (1994 season). ... Member of Super Bowl championship team (1994 season).
PRO STATISTICS: 1994—Recovered one fumble. 1996—Recovered two fumbles for 32 yards and a touchdown. 1997—Intercepted one pass for 39 yards.

Year Team	G	GS	SACKS
1991—Tampa Bay NFL	16	0	1.0
1992—Tampa Bay NFL	4	0	0.0
1993—Tampa Bay NFL	1	0	0.0
1994—San Francisco NFL	12	2	4.0
1995—Philadelphia NFL	3	1	1.0
1996—Philadelphia NFL	16	16	4.5
1997—Philadelphia NFL	15	15	8.0
1998—Philadelphia NFL	2	0	0.0
Pro totals (8 years)	69	34	18.5

HALL, TRAVIS — DT — FALCONS

PERSONAL: Born August 3, 1972, in Kenai, Alaska. ... 6-5/298.
HIGH SCHOOL: West Jordan (Utah).
COLLEGE: Brigham Young.
TRANSACTIONS/CAREER NOTES: Selected by Atlanta Falcons in sixth round (181st pick overall) of 1995 NFL draft. ... Signed by Falcons (June 30, 1995).
CHAMPIONSHIP GAME EXPERIENCE: Played in NFC championship game (1998 season). ... Played in Super Bowl XXXIII (1998 season).
PRO STATISTICS: 1996—Recovered one fumble. 1997—Recovered one fumble. 1998—Recovered four fumbles.

Year Team	G	GS	SACKS
1995—Atlanta NFL	1	0	0.0
1996—Atlanta NFL	14	13	6.0
1997—Atlanta NFL	16	16	10.5
1998—Atlanta NFL	14	13	4.5
Pro totals (4 years)	45	42	21.0

HALLEN, BOB — C/G — FALCONS

PERSONAL: Born March 9, 1975, in Mentor, Ohio. ... 6-4/292. ... Full name: Robert Joseph Hallen.
HIGH SCHOOL: Mentor (Ohio).
COLLEGE: Kent.
TRANSACTIONS/CAREER NOTES: Selected by Atlanta Falcons in second round (53rd pick overall) of 1998 NFL draft. ... Signed by Falcons (June 3, 1998).
PLAYING EXPERIENCE: Atlanta NFL, 1998. ... Games/Games started: 12/0.
CHAMPIONSHIP GAME EXPERIENCE: Played in NFC championship game (1998 season). ... Played in Super Bowl XXXIII (1998 season).

HALLOCK, TY — FB — BEARS

PERSONAL: Born April 30, 1971, in Grand Rapids, Mich. ... 6-2/256. ... Full name: Ty Edward Hallock.
HIGH SCHOOL: Greenville (Mich.).
COLLEGE: Michigan State (degree in employee relations, 1997).
TRANSACTIONS/CAREER NOTES: Selected by Detroit Lions in seventh round (174th pick overall) of 1993 NFL draft. ... Signed by Lions (July 15, 1993). ... Released by Lions (August 30, 1993). ... Re-signed by Lions to practice squad (August 31, 1993). ... Activated (September 3, 1993). ... Traded by Lions to Jacksonville Jaguars for CB Corey Raymond (May 30, 1995). ... On reserve/retired list (July 10, 1995-February 12, 1996). ... Granted free agency (February 14, 1997). ... Re-signed by Jaguars (June 9, 1997). ... Granted unconditional free agency (February 13, 1998). ... Signed by Chicago Bears (February 16, 1998).
CHAMPIONSHIP GAME EXPERIENCE: Played in AFC championship game (1996 season).
PRO STATISTICS: 1993—Returned one kickoff for 11 yards. 1997—Returned one kickoff for six yards. 1998—Recovered one fumble.
SINGLE GAME HIGHS (regular season): Attempts—3 (December 6, 1998, vs. Minnesota); yards—17 (December 6, 1998, vs. Minnesota); and rushing touchdowns—1 (October 25, 1998, vs. Tennessee).

				RUSHING				RECEIVING				TOTALS		
Year Team	G	GS	Att.	Yds.	Avg.	TD	No.	Yds.	Avg.	TD	TD	2pt.	Pts.	Fum.
1993—Detroit NFL	16	4	0	0	...	0	8	88	11.0	2	2	...	12	0
1994—Detroit NFL	15	10	0	0	...	0	7	75	10.7	0	0	0	0	0
1995—Jacksonville NFL							Did not play.							
1996—Jacksonville NFL	7	0	0	0	...	0	1	5	5.0	0	0	0	0	0
1997—Jacksonville NFL	15	8	4	21	5.3	0	18	131	7.3	1	1	0	6	0
1998—Chicago NFL	16	12	13	41	3.2	1	25	166	6.6	0	1	0	6	3
Pro totals (5 years)	69	34	17	62	3.6	1	59	465	7.9	3	4	0	24	3

HAMBRICK, DARREN — LB — COWBOYS

PERSONAL: Born August 30, 1975, in Lacoochee, Fla. ... 6-2/227. ... Nephew of Mudcat Grant, pitcher for seven major league teams (1958-71).
HIGH SCHOOL: Pasco (Dade City, Fla.).
COLLEGE: Florida, then South Carolina.
TRANSACTIONS/CAREER NOTES: Selected by Dallas Cowboys in fifth round (130th pick overall) of 1998 NFL draft. ... Signed by Cowboys (July 14, 1998).
PLAYING EXPERIENCE: Dallas NFL, 1998. ... Games/Games started: 14/0.

HAMILTON, BOBBY — DE/DT — JETS

PERSONAL: Born January 7, 1971, in Denver. ... 6-5/280.
HIGH SCHOOL: East Marion (Columbia, Miss.).
COLLEGE: Southern Mississippi.
TRANSACTIONS/CAREER NOTES: Signed as non-drafted free agent by Seattle Seahawks (April 19, 1994). ... On injured reserve with knee injury (August 17, 1994-entire season). ... Assigned by Seahawks to Amsterdam Admirals in 1995 World League enhancement allocation draft. ... Released by Seahawks (August 15, 1996). ... Signed by New York Jets (September 2, 1996). ... Released by Jets (August 24, 1996). ... Re-signed by Jets to practice squad (August 26, 1996). ... Activated (September 4, 1996).
CHAMPIONSHIP GAME EXPERIENCE: Played in AFC championship game (1998 season).
PRO STATISTICS: 1996—Recovered one fumble for seven yards. 1997—Returned one kickoff for no yards.

Year Team	G	GS	SACKS
1994—Seattle NFL	Did not play.		
1995—Amsterdam W.L.	10	9	5.0
1996—Amsterdam W.L.	11	9	5.0
—New York Jets NFL	15	11	4.5
1997—New York Jets NFL	16	0	1.0
1998—New York Jets NFL	16	1	0.0
W.L. totals (2 years)	21	18	10.0
NFL totals (3 years)	47	12	5.5
Pro totals (5 years)	68	30	15.5

HAMILTON, CONRAD — CB — GIANTS

PERSONAL: Born November 5, 1974, in Alamogordo, N.M. ... 5-10/195.
HIGH SCHOOL: Alamogordo (N.M.).
JUNIOR COLLEGE: New Mexico Military Institute.
COLLEGE: Eastern New Mexico.
TRANSACTIONS/CAREER NOTES: Selected by New York Giants in seventh round (214th pick overall) of 1996 NFL draft. ... Signed by Giants (July 18, 1996). ... Granted free agency (February 12, 1999). ... Re-signed by Giants (May 13, 1999).
PRO STATISTICS: 1998—Credited with one sack and recovered one fumble.

			INTERCEPTIONS				KICKOFF RETURNS				TOTALS		
Year Team	G	GS	No.	Yds.	Avg.	TD	No.	Yds.	Avg.	TD	TD	2pt.	Pts.	Fum.
1996—New York Giants NFL	15	1	1	29	29.0	0	19	382	20.1	0	0	0	0	0
1997—New York Giants NFL	14	0	1	18	18.0	0	0	0	...	0	0	0	0	0
1998—New York Giants NFL	16	15	1	17	17.0	0	0	0	...	0	0	0	0	0
Pro totals (3 years)	45	16	3	64	21.3	0	19	382	20.1	0	0	0	0	0

HAMILTON, JAMES — LB — JAGUARS

PERSONAL: Born April 17, 1974, in Hartford, Conn. ... 6-5/245. ... Full name: James Samuel Hamilton.
HIGH SCHOOL: Richmond County (Hamlet, N.C.).
COLLEGE: North Carolina (degree in sociology, 1997).
TRANSACTIONS/CAREER NOTES: Selected by Jacksonville Jaguars in third round (79th pick overall) of 1997 NFL draft. ... Signed by Jaguars (May 23, 1997). ... On injured reserve with knee injury (November 24, 1998-remainder of season).
PLAYING EXPERIENCE: Jacksonville NFL, 1997 and 1998. ... Games/Games started: 1997 (9/0), 1998 (7/0). Total: 16/0.

HAMILTON, KEITH — DT — GIANTS

PERSONAL: Born May 25, 1971, in Paterson, N.J. ... 6-6/300. ... Full name: Keith Lamarr Hamilton.
HIGH SCHOOL: Heritage (Lynchburg, Va.).
COLLEGE: Pittsburgh.
TRANSACTIONS/CAREER NOTES: Selected after junior season by New York Giants in fourth round (99th pick overall) of 1992 NFL draft. ... Signed by Giants (July 21, 1992).
PRO STATISTICS: 1992—Recovered one fumble for four yards. 1993—Credited with a safety and recovered one fumble for 10 yards. 1994—Recovered three fumbles. 1995—Fumbled once and recovered three fumbles for 87 yards. 1997—Recovered three fumbles. 1998—Recovered one fumble.

Year Team	G	GS	SACKS
1992—New York Giants NFL	16	0	3.5
1993—New York Giants NFL	16	16	11.5
1994—New York Giants NFL	15	15	6.5
1995—New York Giants NFL	14	14	2.0
1996—New York Giants NFL	14	14	3.0
1997—New York Giants NFL	16	16	8.0
1998—New York Giants NFL	16	16	7.0
Pro totals (7 years)	**107**	**91**	**41.5**

HAMILTON, MALCOLM — LB — REDSKINS

PERSONAL: Born December 31, 1972, in Dallas. ... 6-1/235.
HIGH SCHOOL: Permian (Odessa, Texas).
COLLEGE: Baylor.
TRANSACTIONS/CAREER NOTES: Signed as non-drafted free agent by Washington Redskins (April 28, 1997). ... Released by Redskins (August 19, 1997). ... Re-signed by Redskins to practice squad (September 2, 1997). ... Released by Redskins (August 29, 1998). ... Signed by Atlanta Falcons to practice squad (September 23, 1998). ... Released by Falcons (November 25, 1998). ... Signed by Redskins (November 25, 1998). ... On injured reserve with shoulder injury (December 15, 1998-remainder of season).
PLAYING EXPERIENCE: Washington NFL, 1998. ... Games/Games started: 2/0.

HAMILTON, MICHAEL — LB — CHARGERS

PERSONAL: Born December 3, 1973, in Greenville, S.C. ... 6-2/245. ... Full name: Michael Antonio Hamilton.
HIGH SCHOOL: Southside (Greenville, S.C.).
COLLEGE: North Carolina A&T.
TRANSACTIONS/CAREER NOTES: Selected by San Diego Chargers in third round (74th pick overall) of 1997 NFL draft. ... Signed by Chargers (June 11, 1997). ... Released by Chargers (September 2, 1997). ... Re-signed by Chargers to practice squad (September 3, 1997). ... Activated (November 4, 1997).
PLAYING EXPERIENCE: San Diego NFL, 1997 and 1998. ... Games/Games started: 1997 (6/0), 1998 (13/0). Total: 19/0.
PRO STATISTICS: 1998—Recovered one fumble.

HAMILTON, RUFFIN — LB — FALCONS

PERSONAL: Born March 2, 1971, in Detroit. ... 6-1/235. ... Full name: Ruffin Hamilton III.
HIGH SCHOOL: Northeast (Zachary, La.).
COLLEGE: Tulane.
TRANSACTIONS/CAREER NOTES: Selected by Green Bay Packers in sixth round (175th pick overall) of 1994 NFL draft. ... Signed by Packers (July 19, 1994). ... Released by Packers (October 6, 1994). ... Re-signed by Packers to practice squad (October 7, 1994). ... Activated (December 6, 1994). ... Released by Packers (August 27, 1995). ... Signed by Atlanta Falcons (January 30, 1996). ... Released by Falcons (August 25, 1996). ... Re-signed by Falcons (February 13, 1997).
PLAYING EXPERIENCE: Green Bay NFL, 1994; Atlanta NFL, 1997 and 1998. ... Games/Games started: 1994 (5/0), 1997 (13/0), 1998 (16/0). Total: 34/0.
CHAMPIONSHIP GAME EXPERIENCE: Played in NFC championship game (1998 season). ... Played in Super Bowl XXXIII (1998 season).

HAND, NORMAN — DT — CHARGERS

PERSONAL: Born September 4, 1972, in Queens, N.Y. ... 6-3/313. ... Full name: Norman L. Hand.
HIGH SCHOOL: Walterboro (S.C.).
JUNIOR COLLEGE: Itawamba Community College (Miss.).
COLLEGE: Mississippi.
TRANSACTIONS/CAREER NOTES: Selected by Miami Dolphins in fifth round (158th pick overall) of 1995 NFL draft. ... Signed by Dolphins (May 17, 1995). ... Inactive for all 16 games (1995). ... Claimed on waivers by San Diego Chargers (August 25, 1997). ... Granted free agency (February 13, 1998). ... Re-signed by Chargers (July 14, 1998).
PRO STATISTICS: 1998—Intercepted two passes for 47 yards.

Year Team	G	GS	SACKS
1995—Miami NFL	Did not play.		
1996—Miami NFL	9	0	0.5
1997—San Diego NFL	15	1	1.0
1998—San Diego NFL	16	16	6.0
Pro totals (3 years)	**40**	**17**	**7.5**

HANKS, MERTON — S — 49ERS

PERSONAL: Born March 12, 1968, in Dallas. ... 6-2/181. ... Full name: Merton Edward Hanks.
HIGH SCHOOL: Lake Highlands (Dallas).
COLLEGE: Iowa (degree in liberal arts, 1990).
TRANSACTIONS/CAREER NOTES: Selected by San Francisco 49ers in fifth round (122nd pick overall) of 1991 NFL draft. ... Signed by 49ers (July 10, 1991).
CHAMPIONSHIP GAME EXPERIENCE: Played in NFC championship game (1992-1994 and 1997 seasons). ... Member of Super Bowl championship team (1994 season).
HONORS: Named free safety on THE SPORTING NEWS NFL All-Pro team (1994 and 1995). ... Played in Pro Bowl (1994, 1995 and 1997 seasons).
PRO STATISTICS: 1991—Recovered two fumbles. 1992—Returned one punt for 48 yards. 1993—Recovered one fumble. 1994—Credited with $1/2$ sack, fumbled once and recovered two fumbles. 1995—Returned one punt for no yards and recovered two fumbles for 69 yards and one touchdown. 1997—Recovered two fumbles for 38 yards and one touchdown. 1998—Credited with $1/2$ sack and recovered one fumble.

			INTERCEPTIONS			
Year Team	G	GS	No.	Yds.	Avg.	TD
1991—San Francisco NFL	13	8	0	0	...	0
1992—San Francisco NFL	16	5	2	5	2.5	0
1993—San Francisco NFL	16	14	3	104	34.7	1
1994—San Francisco NFL	16	16	7	93	13.3	0
1995—San Francisco NFL	16	16	5	31	6.2	0
1996—San Francisco NFL	16	16	4	7	1.8	0
1997—San Francisco NFL	16	16	6	103	17.2	1
1998—San Francisco NFL	16	16	4	37	9.3	0
Pro totals (8 years)	125	107	31	380	12.3	2

HANKTON, KARL — WR — EAGLES

PERSONAL: Born July 24, 1970, in New Orleans. ... 6-2/202.
HIGH SCHOOL: De La Salle (New Orleans).
JUNIOR COLLEGE: Valley Forge Military Academy (Pa.).
COLLEGE: Louisiana State, then Trinity (Ill.).
TRANSACTIONS/CAREER NOTES: Signed as non-drafted free agent by Washington Redskins (April 1, 1997). ... Released by Redskins (March 2, 1998). ... Signed by Philadelphia Eagles (April 9, 1998). ... Released by Eagles (August 31, 1998). ... Re-signed by Eagles to practice squad (September 2, 1998). ... Released by Eagles (August 31, 1998). ... Re-signed by Eagles to practice squad (September 25, 1998). ... Activated (September 25, 1998).
PLAYING EXPERIENCE: Philadelphia NFL, 1998. ... Games/Games started: 10/0.
PRO STATISTICS: 1998—Rushed once for minus four yards and returned one kickoff for 18 yards.

HANSEN, BRIAN — P

PERSONAL: Born October 26, 1960, in Hawarden, Iowa. ... 6-4/215. ... Full name: Brian Dean Hansen.
HIGH SCHOOL: West Sioux Community (Hawarden, Iowa).
COLLEGE: Sioux Falls (S.D.) College.
TRANSACTIONS/CAREER NOTES: Selected by New Orleans Saints in ninth round (237th pick overall) of 1984 NFL draft. ... Signed by Saints for 1984 season. ... Released by Saints (September 5, 1989). ... Signed by New England Patriots (May 3, 1990). ... Granted unconditional free agency (February 1, 1991). ... Signed by Cleveland Browns (April 1, 1991). ... Granted unconditional free agency (February 1-April 1, 1992). ... Re-signed by Browns for 1992 season. ... Granted unconditional free agency (February 17, 1994). ... Signed by New York Jets (April 19, 1994). ... Released by Jets (August 25, 1997). ... Re-signed by Jets (August 27, 1997). ... Traded by Jets to Green Bay Packers for undisclosed terms (August 17, 1998). ... Released by Packers (August 21, 1998). ... Signed by Jets (September 13, 1998). ... Released by Jets (November 3, 1998).
HONORS: Played in Pro Bowl (1984 season).
PRO STATISTICS: 1984—Rushed twice for minus 27 yards. 1985—Attempted one pass with a completion for eight yards. 1986—Rushed once for no yards, fumbled once and recovered one fumble. 1987—Rushed twice for minus six yards. 1988—Rushed once for 10 yards. 1990—Rushed once for no yards, fumbled once and recovered two fumbles for minus 18 yards. 1991—Attempted one pass with a completion for 11 yards and a touchdown, rushed twice for minus three yards and recovered one fumble. 1992—Fumbled once and recovered a fumble. 1996—Rushed once for one yard. 1997—Attempted one pass with a completion for 26 yards.

				PUNTING			
Year Team	G	No.	Yds.	Avg.	Net avg.	In. 20	Blk.
1984—New Orleans NFL	16	69	3020	43.8	33.2	9	1
1985—New Orleans NFL	16	89	3763	42.3	36.5	14	0
1986—New Orleans NFL	16	81	3456	42.7	36.6	17	1
1987—New Orleans NFL	12	52	2104	40.5	35.6	19	0
1988—New Orleans NFL	16	72	2913	40.5	34.2	19	1
1989—				Did not play.			
1990—New England NFL	16	*90	*3752	41.7	33.6	18	2
1991—Cleveland NFL	16	80	3397	42.5	36.1	20	0
1992—Cleveland NFL	16	74	3083	41.7	36.1	28	1
1993—Cleveland NFL	16	82	3632	44.3	35.6	15	2
1994—New York Jets NFL	16	84	3534	42.1	36.1	25	0
1995—New York Jets NFL	16	*99	*4090	41.3	31.8	23	1
1996—New York Jets NFL	16	74	3293	44.5	36.5	13	0
1997—New York Jets NFL	15	71	3068	43.2	35.3	20	1
1998—New York Jets NFL	7	31	1233	39.8	32.7	6	0
Pro totals (14 years)	210	1048	44338	42.3	35.0	246	10

HANSEN, CARL — DT — JETS

PERSONAL: Born January 25, 1976, in Houston. ... 6-5/280.
HIGH SCHOOL: Stratford (Houston).
COLLEGE: Stanford.
TRANSACTIONS/CAREER NOTES: Selected by Seattle Seahawks in sixth round (162nd pick overall) of 1998 NFL draft. ... Signed by Seahawks (June 5, 1998). ... Released by Seahawks (August 30, 1998). ... Re-signed by Seahawks to practice squad (August 31, 1998). ... Signed by New York Jets off Seahawks practice squad (October 7, 1998).
PLAYING EXPERIENCE: New York Jets NFL, 1998. ... Games/Games started: 5/0.
CHAMPIONSHIP GAME EXPERIENCE: Member of Jets for AFC championship game (1998 season); inactive.

HANSEN, PHIL — DE — BILLS

PERSONAL: Born May 20, 1968, in Ellendale, N.D. ... 6-5/278. ... Full name: Phillip Allen Hansen.
HIGH SCHOOL: Oakes (N.D.).
COLLEGE: North Dakota State (degree in agricultural economics).
TRANSACTIONS/CAREER NOTES: Selected by Buffalo Bills in second round (54th pick overall) of 1991 NFL draft. ... Signed by Bills (July 10, 1991). ... Granted free agency (February 17, 1994). ... Re-signed by Bills (April 29, 1994).
CHAMPIONSHIP GAME EXPERIENCE: Played in AFC championship game (1991-1993 seasons). ... Played in Super Bowl XXVI (1991 season), Super Bowl XXVII (1992 season) and Super Bowl XXVIII (1993 season).
PRO STATISTICS: 1991—Recovered one fumble. 1995—Recovered one fumble. 1996—Recovered two fumbles. 1997—Credited with a safety. 1998—Recovered three fumbles for 13 yards and one touchdown.

Year Team	G	GS	SACKS
1991—Buffalo NFL	14	10	2.0
1992—Buffalo NFL	16	16	8.0
1993—Buffalo NFL	11	9	3.5
1994—Buffalo NFL	16	16	5.5
1995—Buffalo NFL	16	16	10.0
1996—Buffalo NFL	16	16	8.0
1997—Buffalo NFL	16	16	6.0
1998—Buffalo NFL	15	15	7.5
Pro totals (8 years)	120	114	50.5

HANSHAW, TIM — G

PERSONAL: Born April 27, 1970, in Spokane, Wash. ... 6-5/302. ... Full name: Timothy Eugene Hanshaw.
HIGH SCHOOL: West Valley (Spokane, Wash.).
COLLEGE: Brigham Young (degree in history, 1994).
TRANSACTIONS/CAREER NOTES: Selected by San Francisco 49ers in fourth round (127th pick overall) of 1995 NFL draft. ... Signed by 49ers (July 17, 1995). ... Inactive for all 16 games (1995). ... Released by 49ers (October 22, 1996). ... Re-signed by 49ers (October 30, 1996). ... Released by 49ers (November 15, 1996). ... Re-signed by 49ers (November 25, 1996). ... Active for one game (1996); did not play. ... Granted free agency (February 13, 1998). ... Re-signed by 49ers (April 24, 1998). ... Granted unconditional free agency (February 12, 1999).
PLAYING EXPERIENCE: San Francisco NFL, 1997 and 1998. ... Games/Games started: 1997 (13/3), 1998 (16/0). Total: 29/3.
CHAMPIONSHIP GAME EXPERIENCE: Played in NFC championship game (1997 season).

HANSON, JASON — K — LIONS

PERSONAL: Born June 17, 1970, in Spokane, Wash. ... 5-11/183. ... Full name: Jason Douglas Hanson.
HIGH SCHOOL: Mead (Spokane, Wash.).
COLLEGE: Washington State (degree in pre-med).
TRANSACTIONS/CAREER NOTES: Selected by Detroit Lions in second round (56th pick overall) of 1992 NFL draft. ... Signed by Lions (July 23, 1992). ... Designated by Lions as transition player (February 15, 1994).
HONORS: Named kicker on THE SPORTING NEWS college All-America first team (1989). ... Named kicker on THE SPORTING NEWS NFL All-Pro team (1993). ... Played in Pro Bowl (1997 season).
PRO STATISTICS: 1995—Punted once for 34 yards. 1996—Punted once for 24 yards. 1998—Punted three times for 94 yards.

Year Team	G	XPM	XPA	FGM	FGA	Lg.	50+	Pts.
1992—Detroit NFL	16	30	30	21	26	52	2-5	93
1993—Detroit NFL	16	28	28	‡34	‡43	53	3-7	‡130
1994—Detroit NFL	16	39	40	18	27	49	0-5	93
1995—Detroit NFL	16	*48	†48	28	34	56	1-1	132
1996—Detroit NFL	16	36	36	12	17	51	1-3	72
1997—Detroit NFL	16	39	40	26	29	†55	3-5	117
1998—Detroit NFL	16	27	29	29	33	51	1-3	114
Pro totals (7 years)	112	247	251	168	209	56	11-29	751

(KICKING)

HANSPARD, BYRON — RB — FALCONS

PERSONAL: Born January 23, 1976, in Dallas. ... 5-10/200. ... Cousin of Essex Johnson, running back with Cincinnati Bengals (1968-75).
HIGH SCHOOL: DeSoto (Texas).
COLLEGE: Texas Tech.
TRANSACTIONS/CAREER NOTES: Selected by Atlanta Falcons in second round (41st pick overall) of 1997 NFL draft. ... Signed by Falcons (July 14, 1997). ... On injured reserve with knee injury (August 30, 1998-entire season).

HONORS: Doak Walker Award winner (1996). ... Named running back on THE SPORTING NEWS college All-America first team (1996).
PRO STATISTICS: 1997—Recovered two fumbles.
SINGLE GAME HIGHS (regular season): Attempts—8 (September 28, 1997, vs. Denver); yards—84 (September 14, 1997, vs. Oakland); and rushing touchdowns—0.

				RUSHING				RECEIVING			KICKOFF RETURNS				TOTALS		
Year	Team	G	GS	Att.	Yds.	Avg.	TD	No.	Yds.	Avg.	TD	No.	Yds.	Avg.	TD	TD	2pt.	Pts.	Fum.
1997—Atlanta NFL		16	0	53	335	6.3	0	6	53	8.8	1	40	987	24.7	*2	3	0	18	3
1998—Atlanta NFL											Did not play.								

HAPE, PATRICK   TE   BUCCANEERS

PERSONAL: Born June 6, 1974, in Killen, Ala. ... 6-4/247. ... Full name: Patrick Stephen Hape.
HIGH SCHOOL: Brooks (Killen, Ala.).
COLLEGE: Alabama.
TRANSACTIONS/CAREER NOTES: Selected by Tampa Bay Buccaneers in fifth round (137th pick overall) of 1997 NFL draft. ... Signed by Buccaneers (July 20, 1997).
PRO STATISTICS: 1997—Rushed once for one yard.
SINGLE GAME HIGHS (regular season): Receptions—2 (September 6, 1998, vs. Minnesota); yards—13 (October 5, 1997, vs. Green Bay); and touchdown receptions—1 (September 7, 1997, vs. Detroit).

				RECEIVING				TOTALS			
Year Team	G	GS	No.	Yds.	Avg.	TD	TD	2pt.	Pts.	Fum.
1997—Tampa Bay NFL	14	3	4	22	5.5	1	1	0	6	1
1998—Tampa Bay NFL	16	2	4	27	6.8	0	0	1	2	1
Pro totals (2 years)	30	5	8	49	6.1	1	1	1	8	2

HARBAUGH, JIM   QB   CHARGERS

PERSONAL: Born December 23, 1963, in Toledo, Ohio. ... 6-3/215. ... Full name: James Joseph Harbaugh. ... Son of Jack Harbaugh, head coach, Western Kentucky University; and cousin of Mike Gottfried, ESPN college football analyst; and former head coach, Murray State University, University of Cincinnati, University of Kansas and University of Pittsburgh.
HIGH SCHOOL: Pioneer (Ann Arbor, Mich.), then Palo Alto (Calif.).
COLLEGE: Michigan (degree in communications, 1987).
TRANSACTIONS/CAREER NOTES: Selected by Chicago Bears in first round (26th pick overall) of 1987 NFL draft. ... Signed by Bears (August 3, 1987). ... On injured reserve with separated shoulder (December 19, 1990-remainder of season). ... Granted free agency (February 1, 1991). ... Re-signed by Bears (July 22, 1991). ... Granted unconditional free agency (March 1, 1993). ... Re-signed by Bears (March 19, 1993). ... Released by Bears (March 16, 1994). ... Signed by Indianapolis Colts (April 7, 1994). ... Designated by Colts as franchise player (February 16, 1996). ... Traded by Colts with fourth-round pick (traded to Tampa Bay) in 1998 draft to Baltimore Ravens for third- (WR E.G. Green) and fourth-round (traded back to Baltimore) picks in 1998 draft (February 14, 1998). ... Traded by Ravens to San Diego Chargers for conditional fourth- or fifth-round pick in 2000 draft (March 22, 1999).
CHAMPIONSHIP GAME EXPERIENCE: Member of Bears for NFC championship game (1988 season); did not play. ... Played in AFC championship game (1995 season).
HONORS: Played in Pro Bowl (1995 season).
PRO STATISTICS: 1988—Fumbled once. 1989—Fumbled twice. 1990—Fumbled eight times and recovered three fumbles for minus four yards. 1991—Fumbled six times. 1992—Fumbled six times and recovered three fumbles. 1993—Caught one pass for one yard, led league with 15 fumbles and recovered four fumbles for minus one yard. 1994—Fumbled once. 1995—Caught one pass for minus nine yards, fumbled four times and recovered one fumble for minus 20 yards. 1996—Fumbled eight times and recovered four fumbles for minus three yards. 1997—Fumbled four times and recovered one fumble. 1998—Fumbled seven times and recovered three fumbles for minus seven yards.
SINGLE GAME HIGHS (regular season): Attempts—47 (November 28, 1991, vs. Detroit); completions—30 (September 7, 1997, vs. New England); yards—319 (October 8, 1995, vs. Miami); and touchdown passes—4 (December 14, 1997, vs. Miami).
STATISTICAL PLATEAUS: 300-yard passing games: 1991 (1), 1992 (1), 1995 (1), 1997 (1). Total: 4.
MISCELLANEOUS: Regular-season record as starting NFL quarterback: 60-63 (.488). ... Postseason record as starting NFL quarterback: 2-3 (.400).

				PASSING						RUSHING				TOTALS		
Year Team	G	GS	Att.	Cmp.	Pct.	Yds.	TD	Int.	Avg.	Rat.	Att.	Yds.	Avg.	TD	TD	2pt.	Pts.
1987—Chicago NFL	6	0	11	8	72.7	62	0	0	5.64	86.2	4	15	3.8	0	0	...	0
1988—Chicago NFL	10	2	97	47	48.5	514	0	2	5.30	55.9	19	110	5.8	1	1	...	6
1989—Chicago NFL	12	5	178	111	62.4	1204	5	9	6.76	70.5	45	276	6.1	3	3	...	18
1990—Chicago NFL	14	14	312	180	57.7	2178	10	6	6.98	81.9	51	321	6.3	4	4	...	24
1991—Chicago NFL	16	16	478	275	57.5	3121	15	16	6.53	73.7	70	338	4.8	2	2	...	12
1992—Chicago NFL	16	13	358	202	56.4	2486	13	12	6.94	76.2	47	272	5.8	1	1	...	6
1993—Chicago NFL	15	15	325	200	61.5	2002	7	11	6.16	72.1	60	277	4.6	4	4	...	24
1994—Indianapolis NFL	12	9	202	125	61.9	1440	9	6	7.13	85.8	39	223	5.7	0	0	...	0
1995—Indianapolis NFL	15	12	314	200	63.7	2575	17	5	*8.20	*100.7	52	235	4.5	2	2	...	12
1996—Indianapolis NFL	14	14	405	232	57.3	2630	13	11	6.49	76.3	48	192	4.0	1	1	0	6
1997—Indianapolis NFL	12	11	309	189	§61.2	2060	10	4	6.67	86.2	36	206	5.7	0	0	0	0
1998—Baltimore NFL	14	12	293	164	56.0	1839	12	11	6.28	72.9	40	172	4.3	0	0	0	0
Pro totals (12 years)	156	123	3282	1933	58.9	22111	111	93	6.74	78.7	511	2637	5.2	18	18	0	108

HARDY, KEVIN   LB   JAGUARS

PERSONAL: Born July 24, 1973, in Evansville, Ind. ... 6-4/250. ... Full name: Kevin Lamont Hardy.
HIGH SCHOOL: Harrison (Evansville, Ind.).
COLLEGE: Illinois (degree in marketing, 1995).
TRANSACTIONS/CAREER NOTES: Selected by Jacksonville Jaguars in first round (second pick overall) of 1996 NFL draft. ... Signed by Jaguars (July 17, 1996).

– 164 –

CHAMPIONSHIP GAME EXPERIENCE: Played in AFC championship game (1996 season).
HONORS: Butkus Award winner (1995). ... Named linebacker on THE SPORTING NEWS college All-America first team (1995).
PRO STATISTICS: 1996—Recovered one fumble for 13 yards. 1998—Recovered one fumble.

				INTERCEPTIONS			SACKS
Year Team	G	GS	No.	Yds.	Avg.	TD	No.
1996—Jacksonville NFL	16	15	2	19	9.5	0	5.5
1997—Jacksonville NFL	13	11	0	0	...	0	2.5
1998—Jacksonville NFL	16	16	2	40	20.0	0	1.5
Pro totals (3 years)	45	42	4	59	14.8	0	9.5

HARDY, TERRY   TE   CARDINALS

PERSONAL: Born May 31, 1976, in Montgomery, Ala. ... 6-4/266.
HIGH SCHOOL: Carver (Montgomery, Ala.).
COLLEGE: Southern Mississippi (degree in coaching and sports information, 1997).
TRANSACTIONS/CAREER NOTES: Selected by Arizona Cardinals in fifth round (125th pick overall) of 1998 NFL draft. ... Signed by Cardinals (June 15, 1998).
PLAYING EXPERIENCE: Arizona NFL, 1998. ... Games/Games started: 9/0.

HARLOW, PAT   OT   RAIDERS

PERSONAL: Born March 16, 1969, in Norco, Calif. ... 6-6/295. ... Full name: Patrick Christopher Harlow.
HIGH SCHOOL: Norco (Calif.).
COLLEGE: Southern California (degree in public administration).
TRANSACTIONS/CAREER NOTES: Selected by New England Patriots in first round (11th pick overall) of 1991 NFL draft. ... Signed by Patriots (July 15, 1991). ... Granted free agency (February 17, 1994). ... Re-signed by Patriots (April 2, 1994). ... Traded by Patriots to Oakland Raiders for second-round pick (traded to Oakland) in 1996 NFL draft (April 17, 1996). ... On injured reserve with back injury (October 24, 1998-remainder of season).
PLAYING EXPERIENCE: New England NFL, 1991-1995; Oakland NFL, 1996-1998. ... Games/Games started: 1991 (16/16), 1992 (16/16), 1993 (16/16), 1994 (16/16), 1995 (10/0), 1996 (10/9), 1997 (16/16), 1998 (5/5). Total: 105/94.
PRO STATISTICS: 1998—Recovered two fumbles.

HARPER, DWAYNE   CB   CHARGERS

PERSONAL: Born March 29, 1966, in Orangeburg, S.C. ... 5-11/175. ... Full name: Dwayne Anthony Harper.
HIGH SCHOOL: Orangeburg-Wilkinson (Orangeburg, S.C.).
COLLEGE: South Carolina State (degree in marketing, 1987).
TRANSACTIONS/CAREER NOTES: Selected by Seattle Seahawks in 11th round (299th pick overall) of 1988 NFL draft. ... Signed by Seahawks (July 16, 1988). ... Granted free agency (February 1, 1992). ... Re-signed by Seahawks (August 10, 1992). ... Granted unconditional free agency (February 17, 1994). ... Signed by San Diego Chargers (March 3, 1994). ... Granted unconditional free agency (February 14, 1997). ... Re-signed by Chargers (February 16, 1997). ... On injured reserve with hamstring injury (December 17, 1997-remainder of season). ... On injured reserve with neck injury (October 21, 1998-remainder of season).
CHAMPIONSHIP GAME EXPERIENCE: Played in AFC championship game (1994 season). ... Played in Super Bowl XXIX (1994 season).
PRO STATISTICS: 1988—Credited with a sack and recovered one fumble. 1989—Recovered one fumble. 1991—Returned one punt for five yards. 1992—Fumbled once and recovered two fumbles for 52 yards and a touchdown. 1993—Recovered one fumble. 1995—Recovered one fumble for one yard. 1997—Recovered one fumble.

			INTERCEPTIONS			
Year Team	G	GS	No.	Yds.	Avg.	TD
1988—Seattle NFL	16	1	0	0	...	0
1989—Seattle NFL	16	13	2	15	7.5	0
1990—Seattle NFL	16	16	3	69	23.0	0
1991—Seattle NFL	16	16	4	84	21.0	0
1992—Seattle NFL	16	16	3	74	24.7	0
1993—Seattle NFL	14	14	1	0	0.0	0
1994—San Diego NFL	16	16	3	28	9.3	0
1995—San Diego NFL	16	16	4	12	3.0	0
1996—San Diego NFL	6	6	1	0	0.0	0
1997—San Diego NFL	12	12	2	43	21.5	0
1998—San Diego NFL	1	1	1	12	12.0	0
Pro totals (11 years)	145	127	24	337	14.0	0

HARRIS, AL   CB   EAGLES

PERSONAL: Born December 7, 1974, in Pompano Beach, Fla. ... 6-0/185. ... Full name: Alshinard Harris.
HIGH SCHOOL: Ely (Pompano Beach, Fla.).
JUNIOR COLLEGE: Trinity Valley Community College (Texas).
COLLEGE: Texas A&M-Kingsville.
TRANSACTIONS/CAREER NOTES: Selected by Tampa Bay Buccaneers in sixth round (169th pick overall) of 1997 NFL draft. ... Signed by Buccaneers (July 1, 1997). ... Released by Buccaneers (August 24, 1997). ... Re-signed by Buccaneers to practice squad (August 26, 1997). ... Claimed on waivers by Philadelphia Eagles (August 31, 1998).
PLAYING EXPERIENCE: Philadelphia NFL, 1998. ... Games/Games started: 16/7.
PRO STATISTICS: 1998—Returned one punt for minus two yards and fumbled once.

HARRIS, ANTHONY — LB — DOLPHINS

PERSONAL: Born January 25, 1973, in Fort Pierce, Fla. ... 6-1/240. ... Full name: Anthony Jerrod Harris.
HIGH SCHOOL: Westwood (Fort Pierce, Fla.).
COLLEGE: Auburn.
TRANSACTIONS/CAREER NOTES: Signed as non-drafted free agent by Miami Dolphins (April 21, 1996). ... Granted free agency (February 12, 1999). ... Re-signed by Dolphins (April 8, 1999).
PLAYING EXPERIENCE: Miami NFL, 1996-1998. ... Games/Games started: 1996 (7/3), 1997 (16/16), 1998 (5/0). Total: 28/19.
PRO STATISTICS: 1996—Recovered one fumble. 1997—Returned one kickoff for no yards and credited with one sack.

HARRIS, BERNARDO — LB — PACKERS

PERSONAL: Born October 15, 1971, in Chapel Hill, N.C. ... 6-2/248. ... Full name: Bernardo Jamaine Harris.
HIGH SCHOOL: Chapel Hill (N.C.).
COLLEGE: North Carolina.
TRANSACTIONS/CAREER NOTES: Signed as non-drafted free agent by Kansas City Chiefs (June 2, 1994). ... Released by Chiefs (August 2, 1994). ... Signed by Green Bay Packers (January 20, 1995).
PLAYING EXPERIENCE: Green Bay NFL, 1995-1998. ... Games/Games started: 1995 (11/0), 1996 (16/0), 1997 (16/16), 1998 (16/16). Total: 59/32.
CHAMPIONSHIP GAME EXPERIENCE: Played in NFC championship game (1995-97 seasons). ... Member of Super Bowl championship team (1996 season). ... Played in Super Bowl XXXII (1997 season).
PRO STATISTICS: 1997—Intercepted one pass for no yards and credited with one sack. 1998—Credited with two sacks.

HARRIS, COREY — CB — RAVENS

PERSONAL: Born October 25, 1969, in Indianapolis. ... 5-11/205. ... Full name: Corey Lamont Harris.
HIGH SCHOOL: Ben Davis (Indianapolis).
COLLEGE: Vanderbilt (degree in human resources).
TRANSACTIONS/CAREER NOTES: Selected by Houston Oilers in third round (77th pick overall) of 1992 NFL draft. ... Signed by Oilers (August 5, 1992). ... Claimed on waivers by Green Bay Packers (October 14, 1992). ... Granted free agency (February 17, 1995). ... Tendered offer sheet by Seattle Seahawks (March 3, 1995). ... Packers declined to match offer (March 10, 1995). ... Granted unconditional free agency (February 14, 1997). ... Signed by Miami Dolphins (March 17, 1997). ... Released by Dolphins (August 3, 1998). ... Signed by Baltimore Ravens (August 17, 1998). ... Granted unconditional free agency (February 12, 1999). ... Re-signed by Ravens (May 17, 1999).
PRO STATISTICS: 1992—Rushed twice for 10 yards and returned six punts for 17 yards. 1993—Caught two passes for 11 yards. 1994—Recovered one fumble. 1995—Recovered one fumble for 57 yards and a touchdown. 1996—Credited with one sack and recovered three fumbles for 28 yards. 1998—Credited with one sack and recovered one fumble.
MISCELLANEOUS: Played wide receiver (1992 and 1993).

				INTERCEPTIONS				KICKOFF RETURNS				TOTALS		
Year Team	G	GS	No.	Yds.	Avg.	TD	No.	Yds.	Avg.	TD	TD	2pt.	Pts.	Fum.
1992—Houston NFL	5	0	0	0	...	0	0	0	...	0	0	...	0	0
—Green Bay NFL	10	0	0	0	...	0	33	691	20.9	0	0	...	0	0
1993—Green Bay NFL	11	0	0	0	...	0	16	482	30.1	0	0	...	0	0
1994—Green Bay NFL	16	2	0	0	...	0	29	618	21.3	0	0	0	0	1
1995—Seattle NFL	16	16	3	-5	-1.7	0	19	397	20.9	0	1	0	6	0
1996—Seattle NFL	16	16	1	25	25.0	0	7	166	23.7	0	0	0	0	0
1997—Miami NFL	16	7	0	0	...	0	11	224	20.4	0	0	0	0	0
1998—Baltimore NFL	16	6	0	0	...	0	35	965	§27.6	▲1	1	0	6	2
Pro totals (7 years)	106	47	4	20	5.0	0	150	3543	23.6	1	2	0	12	3

HARRIS, DERRICK — RB — RAMS

PERSONAL: Born September 18, 1972, in Angleton, Texas. ... 6-0/252. ... Full name: Sidney Derrick Harris.
HIGH SCHOOL: Angleton (Texas), then Willowridge (Texas).
COLLEGE: Miami, Fla. (degree in business management, 1995).
TRANSACTIONS/CAREER NOTES: Selected by St. Louis Rams in sixth round (175th pick overall) of 1996 NFL draft. ... Signed by Rams (July 9, 1996). ... Active for one game (1997); did not play. ... Granted free agency (February 12, 1999).
PRO STATISTICS: 1996—Recovered one fumble. 1998—Recovered two fumbles.
SINGLE GAME HIGHS (regular season): Attempts—5 (October 11, 1998, vs. New York Jets); yards—15 (September 20, 1998, vs. Buffalo); and rushing touchdowns—0.

			RUSHING				RECEIVING				TOTALS		
Year Team	G	GS	Att.	Yds.	Avg.	TD	No.	Yds.	Avg.	TD	2pt.	Pts.	Fum.
1996—St. Louis NFL	11	6	3	5	1.7	0	4	17	4.3	0	0	0	0
1997—St. Louis NFL							Did not play.						
1998—St. Louis NFL	16	14	14	38	2.7	0	12	57	4.8	2	2	0	12	1
Pro totals (2 years)	27	20	17	43	2.5	0	16	74	4.6	2	2	0	12	1

HARRIS, JACKIE — TE — TITANS

PERSONAL: Born January 4, 1968, in Pine Bluff, Ark. ... 6-4/250. ... Full name: Jackie Bernard Harris.
HIGH SCHOOL: Dollarway (Ark.).
COLLEGE: Northeast Louisiana.
TRANSACTIONS/CAREER NOTES: Selected by Green Bay Packers in fourth round (102nd pick overall) of 1990 NFL draft. ... Signed by Packers (July 22, 1990). ... Granted free agency (February 1, 1992). ... Re-signed by Packers (August 14, 1992). ... Designated by Packers as transi-

tion player (February 25, 1993). ... Tendered offer sheet by Tampa Bay Buccaneers (June 15, 1994). ... Packers declined to match offer (June 22, 1994). ... On injured reserve with shoulder injury (November 22, 1994-remainder of season). ... On injured reserve with hernia (January 2, 1998-remainder of 1997 playoffs). ... Granted unconditional free agency (February 13, 1998). ... Signed by Tennessee Oilers (March 11, 1998). ... Oilers franchise renamed Tennessee Titans for 1999 season (December 26, 1998).
PRO STATISTICS: 1991—Rushed once for one yard and recovered one fumble. 1998—Returned one kickoff for three yards.
SINGLE GAME HIGHS (regular season): Receptions—10 (November 26, 1995, vs. Green Bay); yards—128 (October 10, 1993, vs. Denver); and touchdown receptions—1 (December 13, 1998, vs. Minnesota).
STATISTICAL PLATEAUS: 100-yard receiving games: 1993 (1), 1995 (2). Total: 3.

				RECEIVING				TOTALS		
Year Team	G	GS	No.	Yds.	Avg.	TD	TD	2pt.	Pts.	Fum.
1990—Green Bay NFL	16	3	12	157	13.1	0	0	...	0	0
1991—Green Bay NFL	16	6	24	264	11.0	3	3	...	18	1
1992—Green Bay NFL	16	11	55	595	10.8	2	2	...	12	1
1993—Green Bay NFL	12	12	42	604	14.4	4	4	...	24	0
1994—Tampa Bay NFL	9	9	26	337	13.0	3	3	1	20	0
1995—Tampa Bay NFL	16	16	62	751	12.1	1	1	0	6	2
1996—Tampa Bay NFL	13	12	30	349	11.6	1	1	1	8	1
1997—Tampa Bay NFL	12	11	19	197	10.4	1	1	0	6	0
1998—Tennessee NFL	16	16	43	412	9.6	2	2	0	12	0
Pro totals (9 years)	126	96	313	3666	11.7	17	17	2	106	5

HARRIS, JAMES　　　DE　　　RAIDERS

PERSONAL: Born May 13, 1968, in East St. Louis, Ill. ... 6-6/280. ... Full name: James Edward Harris.
HIGH SCHOOL: East St. Louis (Ill.) Senior, then East St. Louis (Ill.) Lincoln.
COLLEGE: Temple.
TRANSACTIONS/CAREER NOTES: Signed as non-drafted free agent by Seattle Seahawks (April 30, 1992). ... Released by Seahawks (August 24, 1992). ... Signed by Minnesota Vikings to practice squad (September 8, 1992). ... On injured reserve with ankle injury (October 29, 1992-remainder of season). ... On physically unable to perform list with foot injury (July 24-September 10, 1995). ... Granted unconditional free agency (February 16, 1996). ... Signed by St. Louis Rams (April 23, 1996). ... Granted unconditional free agency (February 14, 1997). ... Re-signed by Rams (Febraury 24, 1997). ... Released by Rams (August 17, 1997). ... Signed by Oakland Raiders (March 11, 1998).
PRO STATISTICS: 1994—Intercepted one pass for 21 yards, fumbled twice and recovered three fumbles for 18 yards and one touchdown, . 1995—Recovered one fumble. 1996—Recovered one fumble for 22 yards. 1998—Recovered one fumble for one yard.

Year Team	G	GS	SACKS
1993—Minnesota NFL	6	0	0.0
1994—Minnesota NFL	16	16	3.0
1995—Minnesota NFL	12	3	1.0
1996—St. Louis NFL	16	0	2.0
1998—Oakland NFL	16	16	1.0
Pro totals (5 years)	66	35	7.0

HARRIS, JON　　　DE　　　EAGLES

PERSONAL: Born June 9, 1974, in Inwood, N.Y. ... 6-7/300. ... Full name: Jonathon Cecil Harris.
HIGH SCHOOL: Kellenberg (Inwood, N.Y.).
COLLEGE: Virginia (degree in psychology, 1996).
TRANSACTIONS/CAREER NOTES: Selected by Philadelphia Eagles in first round (25th pick overall) of 1997 NFL draft. ... Signed by Eagles (June 10, 1997).
PRO STATISTICS: 1998—Recovered one fumble.

Year Team	G	GS	SACKS
1997—Philadelphia NFL	8	4	1.0
1998—Philadelphia NFL	16	4	1.0
Pro totals (2 years)	24	8	2.0

HARRIS, MARK　　　WR　　　49ERS

PERSONAL: Born April 28, 1970, in Clovis, N.M ... 6-4/201. ... Full name: Mark Edward Harris.
HIGH SCHOOL: Box Elder (Brigham City, Utah).
JUNIOR COLLEGE: Ricks College (Idaho).
COLLEGE: Southern Utah, then Stanford (degree in psychology, 1995).
TRANSACTIONS/CAREER NOTES: Signed as non-drafted free agent by Dallas Cowboys (April, 25, 1996). ... Released by Cowboys (July 30, 1996). ... Signed by San Francisco 49ers (August 8, 1996). ... Released by 49ers (August 21, 1996). ... Re-signed by 49ers to practice squad (August 26, 1996). ... Activated (October 21, 1996). ... Released by 49ers (October 21, 1996). ... Re-signed by 49ers to practice squad (October 23, 1996).
CHAMPIONSHIP GAME EXPERIENCE: Member of 49ers for NFC championship game (1997 season); inactive.
SINGLE GAME HIGHS (regular season): Receptions—2 (October 12, 1997, vs. St. Louis); yards—42 (November 15, 1998, vs. Atlanta); and touchdown receptions—0.

				RECEIVING				TOTALS		
Year Team	G	GS	No.	Yds.	Avg.	TD	TD	2pt.	Pts.	Fum.
1996—San Francisco NFL	1	0	0	0	0	0	0	0	0	0
1997—San Francisco NFL	10	0	5	53	10.6	0	0	0	0	0
1998—San Francisco NFL	10	0	2	67	33.5	0	0	0	0	0
Pro totals (3 years)	21	0	7	120	17.1	0	0	0	0	0

HARRIS, RAYMONT — RB

PERSONAL: Born December 23, 1970, in Lorain, Ohio. ... 6-0/225. ... Full name: Raymont LeShawn Harris.
HIGH SCHOOL: Admiral King (Lorain, Ohio).
COLLEGE: Ohio State.
TRANSACTIONS/CAREER NOTES: Selected by Chicago Bears in fourth round (114th pick overall) of 1994 NFL draft. ... Signed by Bears (June 21, 1994). ... On injured reserve with broken collarbone (November 29, 1995-remainder of season). ... Granted free agency (February 14, 1997). ... On injured reserve with ankle injury (December 9, 1997-remainder of season). ... Designated by Bears as transition player (February 12, 1998). ... Free agency status changed from transitional to unconditional (April 20, 1998). ... Signed by Green Bay Packers (July 20, 1998). ... Released by Packers (December 8, 1998).
PRO STATISTICS: 1994—Returned one kickoff for 18 yards and recovered three fumbles.
SINGLE GAME HIGHS (regular season): Attempts—33 (November 23, 1997, vs. Tampa Bay); yards—122 (September 1, 1997, vs. Green Bay); and rushing touchdowns—2 (September 1, 1997, vs. Green Bay).
STATISTICAL PLATEAUS: 100-yard rushing games: 1996 (3), 1997 (5). Total: 8. ... 100-yard receiving games: 1996 (1).

				RUSHING				RECEIVING				TOTALS		
Year Team	G	GS	Att.	Yds.	Avg.	TD	No.	Yds.	Avg.	TD	TD	2pt.	Pts.	Fum.
1994—Chicago NFL	16	11	123	464	3.8	1	39	236	6.1	0	1	0	6	1
1995—Chicago NFL	2	1	0	0	...	0	1	4	4.0	0	0	0	0	0
1996—Chicago NFL	12	10	194	748	3.9	4	32	296	9.3	1	5	0	30	3
1997—Chicago NFL	13	13	275	1033	3.8	10	28	115	4.1	0	10	0	60	1
1998—Green Bay NFL	8	3	79	228	2.9	1	10	68	6.8	0	1	0	6	3
Pro totals (5 years)	51	38	671	2473	3.7	16	110	719	6.5	1	17	0	102	8

HARRIS, ROBERT — DT — GIANTS

PERSONAL: Born June 13, 1969, in Riviera Beach, Fla. ... 6-4/300. ... Full name: Robert Lee Harris.
HIGH SCHOOL: Sun Coast (Riviera Beach, Fla.).
COLLEGE: Southern.
TRANSACTIONS/CAREER NOTES: Selected by Minnesota Vikings in second round (39th pick overall) of 1992 NFL draft. ... Signed by Vikings (July 20, 1992). ... On injured reserve with knee injury (September 30-November 12, 1992). ... Granted free agency (February 17, 1995). ... Tendered offer sheet by New York Giants (March 13, 1995). ... Vikings declined to match offer (March 20, 1995).
PRO STATISTICS: 1995—Recovered two fumbles for five yards. 1997—Recovered two fumbles.

Year Team	G	GS	SACKS
1992—Minnesota NFL	7	0	0.0
1993—Minnesota NFL	16	0	1.0
1994—Minnesota NFL	11	1	2.0
1995—New York Giants NFL	15	15	5.0
1996—New York Giants NFL	16	16	4.5
1997—New York Giants NFL	16	16	10.0
1998—New York Giants NFL	10	10	3.5
Pro totals (7 years)	91	58	26.0

HARRIS, RONNIE — WR — FALCONS

PERSONAL: Born June 4, 1970, in Granada Hills, Calif. ... 5-11/185. ... Full name: Ronnie James Harris.
HIGH SCHOOL: Valley Christian (San Jose, Calif.).
COLLEGE: Oregon (degree in business and management, 1992).
TRANSACTIONS/CAREER NOTES: Signed as non-drafted free agent by New England Patriots (April 30, 1993). ... Released by Patriots (August 23, 1993). ... Re-signed by Patriots to practice squad (August 31, 1993). ... Activated (December 3, 1993). ... Released by Patriots (August 20, 1994). ... Re-signed by Patriots to practice squad (August 30, 1994). ... Activated (October 15, 1994). ... Released by Patriots (October 19, 1994). ... Re-signed by Patriots to practice squad (October 19, 1994). ... Released by Patriots (November 23, 1994). ... Signed by Seattle Seahawks to practice squad (November 29, 1994). ... Activated (December 11, 1994). ... Granted free agency (February 13, 1998). ... Re-signed by Seahawks (February 27, 1998). ... Released by Seahawks (November 2, 1998). ... Signed by Atlanta Falcons (November 11, 1998). ... Granted unconditional free agency (February 12, 1999). ... Re-signed by Falcons (March 8, 1999).
CHAMPIONSHIP GAME EXPERIENCE: Played in NFC championship game (1998 season). ... Played in Super Bowl XXXIII (1998 season).
RECORDS: Shares NFL single-game record for most combined kick returns—13 (December 5, 1993, at Pittsburgh).
PRO STATISTICS: 1993—Recovered one fumble. 1997—Recovered two fumbles. 1998—Recovered one fumble.
SINGLE GAME HIGHS (regular season): Receptions—2 (September 14, 1997, vs. Indianapolis); yards—38 (September 14, 1997, vs. Indianapolis); and touchdown receptions—0.

			RECEIVING				PUNT RETURNS				KICKOFF RETURNS				TOTALS		
Year Team	G	GS	No.	Yds.	Avg.	TD	No.	Yds.	Avg.	TD	No.	Yds.	Avg.	TD	TD	2pt.	Pts.	Fum.
1993—New England NFL	5	0	0	0	...	0	23	201	8.7	0	6	90	15.0	0	0	...	0	2
1994—New England NFL	1	0	1	11	11.0	0	3	26	8.7	0	0	0	...	0	0	0	0	1
—Seattle NFL	1	0	0	0	...	0	0	0	...	0	0	0	...	0	0	0	0	0
1995—Seattle NFL	13	0	0	0	...	0	3	23	7.7	0	1	29	29.0	0	0	0	0	0
1996—Seattle NFL	15	0	2	26	13.0	0	19	194	10.2	0	12	240	20.0	0	0	0	0	0
1997—Seattle NFL	13	0	4	81	20.3	0	21	144	6.9	0	14	318	22.7	0	0	0	0	4
1998—Seattle NFL	2	0	0	0	...	0	1	-5	-5.0	0	0	0	...	0	0	0	0	1
—Atlanta NFL	6	0	1	14	14.0	0	1	-1	-1.0	0	1	16	16.0	0	0	0	0	1
Pro totals (6 years)	56	0	8	132	16.5	0	71	582	8.2	0	34	693	20.4	0	0	0	0	9

HARRIS, SEAN — LB — BEARS

PERSONAL: Born February 25, 1972, in Tucson, Ariz. ... 6-3/248. ... Full name: Sean Eugene Harris.
HIGH SCHOOL: Tucson (Ariz.) High Magnet School.
COLLEGE: Arizona.

TRANSACTIONS/CAREER NOTES: Selected by Chicago Bears in third round (83rd pick overall) of 1995 NFL draft. ... Signed by Bears (July 18, 1995). ... Granted free agency (February 13, 1998). ... Re-signed by Bears (May 12, 1998). ... Granted unconditional free agency (February 12, 1999). ... Re-signed by Bears (March 26, 1999).
PLAYING EXPERIENCE: Chicago NFL, 1995-1998. ... Games/Games started: 1995 (11/0), 1996 (15/0), 1997 (11/1), 1998 (16/14). Total: 53/15.
PRO STATISTICS: 1998—Intercepted one pass for no yards and credited with one sack.

HARRIS, WALT   CB   BEARS

PERSONAL: Born August 10, 1974, in LaGrange, Ga. ... 5-11/195. ... Full name: Walter Lee Harris.
HIGH SCHOOL: LaGrange (Ga.).
COLLEGE: Mississippi State.
TRANSACTIONS/CAREER NOTES: Selected by Chicago Bears in first round (13th pick overall) of 1996 NFL draft. ... Signed by Bears (July 11, 1996). ... On injured reserve with knee injury (December 22, 1998-remainder of season).
PRO STATISTICS: 1996—Recovered two fumbles for eight yards. 1997—Fumbled once and recovered one fumble. 1998—Recovered one fumble.

				INTERCEPTIONS		
Year Team	G	GS	No.	Yds.	Avg.	TD
1996—Chicago NFL	15	13	2	0	0.0	0
1997—Chicago NFL	16	16	5	30	6.0	0
1998—Chicago NFL	14	14	4	41	10.3	1
Pro totals (3 years)	**45**	**43**	**11**	**71**	**6.5**	**1**

HARRISON, MARVIN   WR   COLTS

PERSONAL: Born August 25, 1972, in Philadelphia. ... 6-0/181. ... Full name: Marvin Daniel Harrison.
HIGH SCHOOL: Roman Catholic (Philadelphia).
COLLEGE: Syracuse.
TRANSACTIONS/CAREER NOTES: Selected by Indianapolis Colts in first round (19th pick overall) of 1996 NFL draft. ... Signed by Colts (July 8, 1996). ... On injured reserve with shoulder injury (December 2, 1998-remainder of season).
HONORS: Named kick returner on THE SPORTING NEWS All-America first team (1995).
PRO STATISTICS: 1996—Rushed three times for 15 yards. 1997—Recovered one fumble for five yards.
SINGLE GAME HIGHS (regular season): Receptions—9 (November 15, 1998, vs. New York Jets); yards—128 (November 15, 1998, vs. New York Jets); and touchdown receptions—3 (October 18, 1998, vs. San Francisco).
STATISTICAL PLATEAUS: 100-yard receiving games: 1996 (2), 1998 (2). Total: 4.

			RECEIVING				PUNT RETURNS			TOTALS			
Year Team	G	GS	No.	Yds.	Avg.	TD	No.	Yds.	Avg.	TD	TD	2pt.	Pts.	Fum.
1996—Indianapolis NFL	16	15	64	836	13.1	8	18	177	9.8	0	8	0	48	1
1997—Indianapolis NFL	16	15	73	866	11.9	6	0	0	...	0	6	2	40	2
1998—Indianapolis NFL	12	12	59	776	13.2	7	0	0	...	0	7	1	44	0
Pro totals (3 years)	**44**	**42**	**196**	**2478**	**12.6**	**21**	**18**	**177**	**9.8**	**0**	**21**	**3**	**132**	**3**

HARRISON, NOLAN   DE   STEELERS

PERSONAL: Born January 25, 1969, in Chicago. ... 6-5/291. ... Full name: Nolan Harrison III.
HIGH SCHOOL: Homewood-Flossmoor (Flossmoor, Ill.).
COLLEGE: Indiana (degree in criminal justice, 1991).
TRANSACTIONS/CAREER NOTES: Selected by Los Angeles Raiders in sixth round (146th pick overall) of 1991 NFL draft. ... Signed by Raiders (1991). ... Raiders franchise moved to Oakland (July 21, 1995). ... Granted unconditional free agency (February 16, 1996). ... Signed by Pittsburgh Steelers (May 20, 1997).
CHAMPIONSHIP GAME EXPERIENCE: Played in AFC championship game (1997 season).
PRO STATISTICS: 1992—Credited with a safety. 1993—Recovered one fumble for five yards. 1994—Recovered two fumbles.

Year Team	G	GS	SACKS
1991—Los Angeles Raiders NFL	14	3	1.0
1992—Los Angeles Raiders NFL	14	14	2.5
1993—Los Angeles Raiders NFL	16	14	3.0
1994—Los Angeles Raiders NFL	16	16	5.0
1995—Oakland NFL	7	6	0.0
1996—Oakland NFL	15	2	2.0
1997—Pittsburgh NFL	16	16	4.0
1998—Pittsburgh NFL	9	7	3.5
Pro totals (8 years)	**107**	**78**	**21.0**

HARRISON, RODNEY   S   CHARGERS

PERSONAL: Born December 15, 1972, in Markham, Ill. ... 6-1/207. ... Full name: Rodney Scott Harrison.
HIGH SCHOOL: Marian Catholic (Chicago Heights, Ill.).
COLLEGE: Western Illinois.
TRANSACTIONS/CAREER NOTES: Selected after junior season by San Diego Chargers in fifth round (145th pick overall) of 1994 NFL draft. ... Signed by Chargers (June 29, 1994).
CHAMPIONSHIP GAME EXPERIENCE: Played in AFC championship game (1994 season). ... Played in Super Bowl XXIX (1994 season).
HONORS: Named safety on THE SPORTING NEWS NFL All-Pro team (1998). ... Played in Pro Bowl (1998 season).
PRO STATISTICS: 1994—Recovered one fumble. 1996—Returned one kickoff for 10 yards, fumbled once and recovered two fumbles for four yards. 1997—Returned one punt for no yards, returned one kickoff for 40 yards and a touchdown and recovered three fumbles, including one in end zone for a touchdown.

Year Team	G	GS	No.	Yds.	Avg.	TD	Sacks No.
1994—San Diego NFL	15	0	0	0	...	0	0.0
1995—San Diego NFL	11	0	5	22	4.4	0	0.0
1996—San Diego NFL	16	16	5	56	11.2	0	1.0
1997—San Diego NFL	16	16	2	75	37.5	1	4.0
1998—San Diego NFL	16	16	3	42	14.0	0	4.0
Pro totals (5 years)	74	48	15	195	13.0	1	9.0

HARTINGS, JEFF — G — LIONS

PERSONAL: Born September 7, 1972, in Henry, Ohio. ... 6-3/283. ... Full name: Jeffrey Allen Hartings.
HIGH SCHOOL: St. Henry (Ohio).
COLLEGE: Penn State.
TRANSACTIONS/CAREER NOTES: Selected by Detroit Lions in first round (23rd pick overall) of 1996 NFL draft. ... Signed by Lions (September 27, 1996).
PLAYING EXPERIENCE: Detroit NFL, 1996-1998. ... Games/Games started: 1996 (11/10), 1997 (16/16), 1998 (13/13). Total: 40/39.
HONORS: Named offensive lineman on THE SPORTING NEWS college All-America second team (1994). ... Named offensive lineman on THE SPORTING NEWS college All-America first team (1995).
PRO STATISTICS: 1996—Recovered one fumble.

HARTLEY, FRANK — TE

PERSONAL: Born December 15, 1967, in Chicago. ... 6-2/268.
HIGH SCHOOL: Bogan (Chicago).
COLLEGE: Illinois (degree in political science).
TRANSACTIONS/CAREER NOTES: Signed as non-drafted free agent by Los Angeles Rams to practice squad (December 4, 1991). ... Released by Rams (August 31, 1992). ... Signed by San Francisco 49ers to practice squad (September 23, 1992). ... Released by 49ers (October 5, 1992). ... Signed by Atlanta Falcons (May 26, 1993). ... Released by Falcons (August 30, 1993). ... Signed by Cleveland Browns (February 21, 1994). ... Released by Browns (August 23, 1994). ... Re-signed by Browns (October 10, 1994). ... Browns franchise moved to Baltimore and renamed Ravens for 1996 season (March 11, 1996). ... Granted unconditional free agency (February 14, 1997). ... Signed by San Diego Chargers (June 3, 1997). ... Granted unconditional free agency (February 13, 1998). ... Re-signed by Chargers (March 9, 1998). ... Released by Chargers (February 11, 1999).
PRO STATISTICS: 1995—Recovered one fumble. 1998—Returned one kickoff for 11 yards.
SINGLE GAME HIGHS (regular season): Receptions—4 (December 14, 1997, vs. Kansas City); yards—54 (December 14, 1997, vs. Kansas City); and touchdown receptions—1 (October 26, 1997, vs. Indianapolis).

			RECEIVING				TOTALS			
Year Team	G	GS	No.	Yds.	Avg.	TD	TD	2pt.	Pts.	Fum.
1992—San Francisco NFL					Did not play.					
1993—					Did not play.					
1994—Cleveland NFL	10	5	3	13	4.3	1	1	0	6	0
1995—Cleveland NFL	15	13	11	137	12.5	1	1	0	6	1
1996—Baltimore NFL	8	0	0	0	...	0	0	0	0	0
1997—San Diego NFL	16	16	19	246	12.9	1	1	0	6	0
1998—San Diego NFL	16	3	2	28	14.0	0	0	0	0	0
Pro totals (5 years)	65	37	35	424	12.1	3	3	0	18	1

HARVEY, KEN — LB — REDSKINS

PERSONAL: Born May 6, 1965, in Austin, Texas. ... 6-2/237. ... Full name: Kenneth Ray Harvey.
HIGH SCHOOL: Lanier (Austin, Texas).
JUNIOR COLLEGE: Laney College (Calif.).
COLLEGE: California.
TRANSACTIONS/CAREER NOTES: Selected by Phoenix Cardinals in first round (12th pick overall) of 1988 NFL draft. ... Signed by Cardinals (June 17, 1988). ... Granted free agency (February 1, 1992). ... Re-signed by Cardinals (July 28, 1992). ... On injured reserve with knee injury (November 18, 1992-remainder of season). ... Designated by Cardinals as transition player (February 25, 1993). ... Free agency status changed by Cardinals from transitional to unconditional (February 17, 1994). ... Signed by Washington Redskins (March 5, 1994). ... Granted unconditional free agency (February 13, 1998). ... Re-signed by Redskins (February 13, 1998). ... On injured reserve with knee injury (December 1, 1998-remainder of season).
HONORS: Played in Pro Bowl (1994-1996 seasons). ... Named to play in Pro Bowl (1997 season); replaced by Lee Woodall due to injury.
PRO STATISTICS: 1988—Credited with one safety. 1990—Recovered one fumble. 1991—Recovered two fumbles. 1992—Recovered two fumbles. 1994—Recovered one fumble. 1995—Recovered two fumbles. 1996—Intercepted one pass for two yards, fumbled once and recovered two fumbles. 1998—Recovered one fumble.

Year Team	G	GS	SACKS
1988—Phoenix NFL	16	0	6.0
1989—Phoenix NFL	16	16	7.0
1990—Phoenix NFL	16	16	10.0
1991—Phoenix NFL	16	16	9.0
1992—Phoenix NFL	10	10	6.0
1993—Phoenix NFL	16	6	9.5
1994—Washington NFL	16	16	∞13.5
1995—Washington NFL	16	16	7.5
1996—Washington NFL	16	16	9.0
1997—Washington NFL	15	14	9.5
1998—Washington NFL	11	9	2.0
Pro totals (11 years)	164	135	89.0

HARVEY, RICHARD — LB — RAIDERS

PERSONAL: Born September 11, 1966, in Pascagoula, Miss. ... 6-1/235. ... Full name: Richard Clemont Harvey. ... Son of Richard Harvey Sr., defensive back with Philadelphia Eagles (1970) and New Orleans Saints (1971).
HIGH SCHOOL: Pascagoula (Miss.).
COLLEGE: Tulane.
TRANSACTIONS/CAREER NOTES: Selected by Buffalo Bills in 11th round (305th pick overall) of 1989 NFL draft. ... Signed by Bills for 1989 season. ... On injured reserve with shoulder injury (September 4, 1989-entire season). ... Granted unconditional free agency (February 1, 1990). ... Signed by New England Patriots (March 23, 1990). ... Released by Patriots (September 2, 1991). ... Signed by Bills (February 3, 1992). ... Selected by Ohio Glory in first round of 1992 World League supplemental draft. ... Granted unconditional free agency (February 17, 1994). ... Signed by Denver Broncos (May 9, 1994). ... Granted unconditional free agency (February 14, 1995). ... Signed by New Orleans Saints (April 3, 1995). ... Granted unconditional free agency (February 14, 1997). ... Re-signed by Saints (May 1, 1997). ... On injured reserve with foot injury (December 20, 1997-remainder of season). ... Granted unconditional free agency (February 13, 1998). ... Re-signed by Saints (March 2, 1998). ... Released by Saints (August 24, 1998). ... Signed by Oakland Raiders (August 26, 1998).
CHAMPIONSHIP GAME EXPERIENCE: Member of Bills for AFC championship game (1992 season); inactive. ... Member of Bills for Super Bowl XXVII (1992 season); inactive. ... Played in AFC championship game (1993 season). ... Played in Super Bowl XXVIII (1993 season).
PRO STATISTICS: 1992—Recovered one fumble. 1994—Recovered one fumble. 1997—Intercepted one pass for seven yards and recovered one fumble. 1998—Intercepted one pass for two yards.

Year Team	G	GS	SACKS
1989—Buffalo NFL	Did not play.		
1990—New England NFL	16	9	0.0
1991—New England NFL	1	0	0.0
1992—Buffalo NFL	12	0	0.0
1993—Buffalo NFL	15	0	0.0
1994—Denver NFL	16	1	0.0
1995—New Orleans NFL	16	14	2.0
1996—New Orleans NFL	14	7	2.0
1997—New Orleans NFL	14	13	3.0
1998—Oakland NFL	16	16	4.0
Pro totals (9 years)	**120**	**60**	**11.0**

HASKINS, JON — LB — CHARGERS

PERSONAL: Born October 6, 1975, in Des Moines, Iowa ... 6-2/245. ... Full name: Jon Radcliffe Haskins.
HIGH SCHOOL: Riverview (Sarasota, Fla.).
COLLEGE: Stanford.
TRANSACTIONS/CAREER NOTES: Selected by San Diego Chargers in seventh round (194th pick overall) of 1998 NFL draft. ... Signed by Chargers (July 10, 1998). ... Released by Chargers (August 30, 1998). ... Re-signed by Chargers to practice squad (August 31, 1998). ... Activated (November 21, 1998). ... Claimed on waivers by Philadelphia Eagles (December 4, 1998). ... Inactive for three games with Eagles (1998). ... Released by Eagles after 1998 season. ... Signed by Chargers (May 12, 1999).
PLAYING EXPERIENCE: San Diego NFL, 1998. ... Games/Games started: 2/0.

HASSELBACH, HARALD — DE — BRONCOS

PERSONAL: Born September 22, 1967, in Amsterdam, Holland. ... 6-6/285.
HIGH SCHOOL: South Delta (Delta, B.C.).
COLLEGE: Washington.
TRANSACTIONS/CAREER NOTES: Selected by Calgary Stampeders in fifth round (34th pick overall) of 1989 CFL draft. ... Granted free agency after 1993 season. ... Signed as non-drafted free agent by Denver Broncos (April 11, 1994).
CHAMPIONSHIP GAME EXPERIENCE: Played in Grey Cup (1992). ... Played in AFC championship game (1997 and 1998 seasons). ... Member of Super Bowl championship team (1997 and 1998 seasons).
PRO STATISTICS: CFL: 1992—Recovered two fumbles. 1993—Recovered four fumbles for 16 yards, intercepted one pass for no yards and fumbled once. NFL: 1995—Recovered four fumbles.

Year Team	G	GS	SACKS
1990—Calgary CFL	3	...	0.0
1991—Calgary CFL	11	...	3.0
1992—Calgary CFL	18	...	4.0
1993—Calgary CFL	18	...	7.0
1994—Denver NFL	16	9	2.0
1995—Denver NFL	16	10	4.0
1996—Denver NFL	16	1	2.0
1997—Denver NFL	16	3	1.5
1998—Denver NFL	16	3	3.0
CFL totals (4 years)	**50**	**...**	**14.0**
NFL totals (5 years)	**80**	**26**	**12.5**
Pro totals (9 years)	**130**	**...**	**26.5**

HASTINGS, ANDRE — WR — SAINTS

PERSONAL: Born November 7, 1970, in Atlanta. ... 6-1/190. ... Full name: Andre Orlando Hastings.
HIGH SCHOOL: Morrow (Ga.).
COLLEGE: Georgia.
TRANSACTIONS/CAREER NOTES: Selected after junior season by Pittsburgh Steelers in third round (76th pick overall) of 1993 NFL draft. ... Signed by Steelers (July 18, 1993). ... Granted free agency (February 16, 1996). ... Re-signed by Steelers (August 9, 1996). ... Granted unconditional free agency (February 14, 1997). ... Signed by New Orleans Saints (May 28, 1997). ... Released by Saints (February 10, 1998). ... Re-signed by Saints (March 6, 1998).

CHAMPIONSHIP GAME EXPERIENCE: Played in AFC championship game (1994 and 1995 seasons). ... Played in Super Bowl XXX (1995 season).
PRO STATISTICS: 1996—Recovered one fumble. 1998—Recovered one fumble.
SINGLE GAME HIGHS (regular season): Receptions—10 (September 18, 1995, vs. Miami); yards—122 (December 6, 1998, vs. Dallas); and touchdown receptions—2 (December 1, 1996, vs. Baltimore).
STATISTICAL PLATEAUS: 100-yard receiving games: 1997 (1), 1998 (1). Total: 2.

				RUSHING				RECEIVING				PUNT RETURNS				KICKOFF RETURNS				TOTALS		
Year Team	G	GS	Att.	Yds.	Avg.	TD	No.	Yds.	Avg.	TD	No.	Yds.	Avg.	TD	No.	Yds.	Avg.	TD	TD	2pt.	Pts.
1993—Pittsburgh NFL....	6	0	0	0	...	0	3	44	14.7	0	0	0	...	0	12	177	14.8	0	0	...	0
1994—Pittsburgh NFL....	16	8	0	0	...	0	20	281	14.1	2	2	15	7.5	0	0	0	...	0	2	0	12
1995—Pittsburgh NFL....	16	0	1	14	14.0	0	48	502	10.5	1	48	474	9.9	†1	0	0	...	0	2	0	12
1996—Pittsburgh NFL....	16	10	4	71	17.8	0	72	739	10.3	6	37	242	6.5	0	1	42	42.0	0	6	0	36
1997—New Orleans NFL	16	16	4	35	8.8	0	48	722	15.0	5	1	-2	-2.0	0	0	0	...	0	5	1	32
1998—New Orleans NFL	16	12	3	32	10.7	0	35	455	13.0	3	22	307	14.0	0	1	16	16.0	0	3	0	18
Pro totals (6 years)	86	46	12	152	12.7	0	226	2743	12.1	17	110	1036	9.4	1	14	235	16.8	0	18	1	110

HASTY, JAMES CB CHIEFS

PERSONAL: Born May 23, 1965, in Seattle. ... 6-0/208. ... Full name: James Edward Hasty.
HIGH SCHOOL: Franklin (Seattle).
COLLEGE: Central Washington, then Washington State (degree in communications, 1988).
TRANSACTIONS/CAREER NOTES: Selected by New York Jets in third round (74th pick overall) of 1988 NFL draft. ... Signed by Jets (July 12, 1988). ... Designated by Jets as transition player (February 25, 1993). ... Tendered offer sheet by Cincinnati Bengals (April 29, 1993). ... Offer matched by Jets (May 4, 1993). ... Granted unconditional free agency (February 17, 1995). ... Signed by Kansas City Chiefs (March 29, 1995). ... On reserve/did not report list (July 20-August 3, 1997). ... Granted unconditional free agency (February 13, 1998). ... Re-signed by Chiefs (February 17, 1998).
HONORS: Played in Pro Bowl (1997 season).
PRO STATISTICS: 1988—Recovered three fumbles for 35 yards. 1989—Fumbled once and recovered two fumbles for two yards. 1990—Returned one punt for no yards, fumbled once and recovered three fumbles. 1991—Recovered four fumbles for seven yards. 1992—Recovered two fumbles. 1993—Recovered two fumbles for 28 yards. 1994—Recovered two fumbles. 1995—Recovered one fumble for 20 yards. 1996—Recovered one fumble for 80 yards and a touchdown. 1997—Recovered one fumble. 1998—Recovered one fumble.

			INTERCEPTIONS				SACKS
Year Team	G	GS	No.	Yds.	Avg.	TD	No.
1988—New York Jets NFL	15	15	5	20	4.0	0	1.0
1989—New York Jets NFL	16	16	5	62	12.4	1	0.0
1990—New York Jets NFL	16	16	2	0	0.0	0	0.0
1991—New York Jets NFL	16	16	3	39	13.0	0	0.0
1992—New York Jets NFL	16	16	2	18	9.0	0	0.0
1993—New York Jets NFL	16	16	2	22	11.0	0	0.0
1994—New York Jets NFL	16	16	5	90	18.0	0	3.0
1995—Kansas City NFL	16	16	3	89	29.7	▲1	0.0
1996—Kansas City NFL	15	14	0	0	...	0	1.0
1997—Kansas City NFL	16	15	3	22	7.3	0	2.0
1998—Kansas City NFL	16	14	4	42	10.5	0	1.0
Pro totals (11 years)	174	170	34	404	11.9	2	8.0

HATCHETTE, MATTHEW WR VIKINGS

PERSONAL: Born May 1, 1974, in Cleveland. ... 6-2/198. ... Full name: Matthew Isaac Hatchette.
HIGH SCHOOL: Jefferson (Cleveland).
COLLEGE: Mercyhurst College (Pa.), then Langston University (Okla.).
TRANSACTIONS/CAREER NOTES: Selected by Minnesota Vikings in seventh round (235th pick overall) of 1997 NFL draft. ... Signed by Vikings (June 20, 1997).
CHAMPIONSHIP GAME EXPERIENCE: Played in NFC championship game (1998 season).
SINGLE GAME HIGHS (regular season): Receptions—6 (December 13, 1998, vs. Baltimore); yards—95 (December 13, 1998, vs. Baltimore); and touchdown receptions—0.

			RECEIVING				TOTALS			
Year Team	G	GS	No.	Yds.	Avg.	TD	TD	2pt.	Pts.	Fum.
1997—Minnesota NFL	16	0	3	54	18.0	0	0	0	0	0
1998—Minnesota NFL	5	0	15	216	14.4	0	0	0	0	0
Pro totals (2 years)	21	0	18	270	15.0	0	0	0	0	0

HAUCK, TIM S EAGLES

PERSONAL: Born December 20, 1966, in Butte, Mont. ... 5-10/187. ... Full name: Timothy Christian Hauck. ... Name pronounced HOWK.
HIGH SCHOOL: Sweet Grass County (Big Timber, Mont.).
COLLEGE: Pacific (Ore.), then Montana.
TRANSACTIONS/CAREER NOTES: Signed as non-drafted free agent by New England Patriots (May 1, 1990). ... Released by Patriots (August 26, 1990). ... Re-signed by Patriots to practice squad (October 1, 1990). ... Activated (October 27, 1990). ... Granted unconditional free agency (February 1, 1991). ... Signed by Green Bay Packers (April 1, 1991). ... Granted unconditional free agency (February 1-April 1, 1992). ... Re-signed by Packers for 1992 season. ... Granted free agency (March 1, 1993). ... Re-signed by Packers (July 13, 1993). ... Granted unconditional free agency (February 17, 1994). ... Re-signed by Packers (July 20, 1994). ... Granted unconditional free agency (February 17, 1995). ... Signed by Denver Broncos (March 6, 1995). ... Granted unconditional free agency (February 14, 1997). ... Signed by Seattle Seahawks (June 2, 1997). ... Granted unconditional free agency (February 13, 1998). ... Signed by Indianapolis Colts (July 26, 1998). ... Granted unconditional free agency (February 12, 1999). ... Signed by Philadelphia Eagles (April 20, 1999).

PLAYING EXPERIENCE: New England NFL, 1990; Green Bay NFL, 1991-1994; Denver NFL, 1995 and 1996; Seattle NFL, 1997; Indianapolis NFL, 1998. ... Games/Games started: 1990 (10/0), 1991 (16/0), 1992 (16/0), 1993 (13/0), 1994 (13/3), 1995 (16/0), 1996 (16/0), 1997 (16/0), 1998 (16/7). Total: 132/10.
PRO STATISTICS: 1991—Recovered one fumble. 1992—Returned one punt for two yards. 1993—Recovered one fumble. 1997—Recovered one fumble for eight yards.

HAWKINS, ARTRELL   CB   BENGALS

PERSONAL: Born November 24, 1975, in Johnstown, Pa. ... 5-10/190. ... Cousin of Carlton Haselrig, offensive guard with Pittsburgh Steelers (1990-93) and New York Jets (1995).
HIGH SCHOOL: Bishop McCort (Johnstown, Pa.).
COLLEGE: Cincinnati.
TRANSACTIONS/CAREER NOTES: Selected by Cincinnati Bengals in second round (43rd pick overall) of 1998 NFL draft. ... Signed by Bengals (May 14, 1998).
PRO STATISTICS: 1998—Recovered one fumble for 25 yards.

				INTERCEPTIONS			SACKS
Year Team	G	GS	No.	Yds.	Avg.	TD	No.
1998—Cincinnati NFL	16	16	3	21	7.0	0	1.0

HAWKINS, COURTNEY   WR   STEELERS

PERSONAL: Born December 12, 1969, in Flint, Mich. ... 5-9/190. ... Full name: Courtney Tyrone Hawkins Jr. ... Cousin of Roy Marble, guard/forward with Atlanta Hawks and Denver Nuggets of NBA (1990-91 and 1993-94).
HIGH SCHOOL: Beecher (Flint, Mich.).
COLLEGE: Michigan State.
TRANSACTIONS/CAREER NOTES: Selected by Tampa Bay Buccaneers in second round (44th pick overall) of 1992 NFL draft. ... Signed by Buccaneers (July 16, 1992). ... On injured reserve with knee injury (December 16, 1994-remainder of season). ... Granted free agency (February 17, 1995). ... Re-signed by Buccaneers (July 21, 1995). ... Granted unconditional free agency (February 16, 1996). ... Re-signed by Buccaneers (April 27, 1996). ... Granted free agency (February 14, 1997). ... Signed by Pittsburgh Steelers (June 2, 1997).
CHAMPIONSHIP GAME EXPERIENCE: Played in AFC championship game (1997 season).
PRO STATISTICS: 1992—Returned nine kickoffs for 118 yards and recovered one fumble. 1995—Rushed four times for five yards. 1996—Rushed once for minus 10 yards. 1998—Rushed 10 times for 41 yards and recovered one fumble.
SINGLE GAME HIGHS (regular season): Receptions—14 (November 1, 1998, vs. Tennessee); yards—147 (November 1, 1998, vs. Tennessee); and touchdown receptions—2 (November 20, 1994, vs. Seattle).
STATISTICAL PLATEAUS: 100-yard receiving games: 1992 (1), 1993 (2), 1996 (1), 1998 (1). Total: 5.

			RECEIVING				PUNT RETURNS				TOTALS		
Year Team	G	GS	No.	Yds.	Avg.	TD	No.	Yds.	Avg.	TD	TD	2pt.	Pts.	Fum.
1992—Tampa Bay NFL	16	5	20	336	16.8	2	13	53	4.1	0	2	...	12	2
1993—Tampa Bay NFL	16	12	62	933	15.0	5	15	166	11.1	0	5	...	30	2
1994—Tampa Bay NFL	13	12	37	438	11.8	5	5	28	5.6	0	5	0	30	0
1995—Tampa Bay NFL	16	3	41	493	12.0	0	0	0	...	0	0	0	0	1
1996—Tampa Bay NFL	16	16	46	544	11.8	1	1	-1	-1.0	0	1	0	6	1
1997—Pittsburgh NFL	15	3	45	555	12.3	3	4	68	17.0	0	3	0	18	1
1998—Pittsburgh NFL	15	14	66	751	11.4	1	15	175	11.7	0	1	0	6	1
Pro totals (7 years)	107	65	317	4050	12.8	17	53	489	9.2	0	17	0	102	8

HAYDEN, AARON   RB   EAGLES

PERSONAL: Born April 13, 1973, in Detroit. ... 6-0/216. ... Full name: Aaron Chautezz Hayden. ... Name pronounced HEY-den.
HIGH SCHOOL: Mumford (Detroit).
COLLEGE: Tennessee.
TRANSACTIONS/CAREER NOTES: Selected by San Diego Chargers in fourth round (104th pick overall) of 1995 NFL draft. ... Signed by Chargers (July 17, 1995). ... On physically unable to perform list with leg injury (August 22-November 10, 1995). ... Claimed on waivers by Green Bay Packers (July 10, 1997). ... Granted free agency (February 13, 1998). ... Re-signed by Packers for 1998 season. ... Claimed on waivers by Philadelphia Eagles (July 22, 1998). ... On injured reserve with shoulder injury (September 9, 1998-remainder of season). ... Granted unconditional free agency (February 12, 1999). ... Re-signed by Eagles (March 30, 1999).
CHAMPIONSHIP GAME EXPERIENCE: Played in NFC championship game (1997 season). ... Played in Super Bowl XXXII (1997 season).
PRO STATISTICS: 1996—Recovered one fumble. 1997—Returned six kickoffs for 141 yards. 1998—Returned one kickoff for 22 yards.
SINGLE GAME HIGHS (regular season): Attempts—32 (December 3, 1995, vs. Cleveland); yards—127 (December 3, 1995, vs. Cleveland); and rushing touchdowns—2 (December 3, 1995, vs. Cleveland).
STATISTICAL PLATEAUS: 100-yard rushing games: 1995 (1).

			RUSHING				RECEIVING				TOTALS		
Year Team	G	GS	Att.	Yds.	Avg.	TD	No.	Yds.	Avg.	TD	TD	2pt.	Pts.	Fum.
1995—San Diego NFL	7	4	128	470	3.7	3	5	53	10.6	0	3	0	18	0
1996—San Diego NFL	11	0	55	166	3.0	0	1	10	10.0	0	0	0	0	1
1997—Green Bay NFL	14	0	32	148	4.6	1	2	11	5.5	0	1	0	6	0
1998—Philadelphia NFL	1	0	0	0	...	0	0	0	...	0	0	0	0	0
Pro totals (4 years)	33	4	215	784	3.6	4	8	74	9.3	0	4	0	24	1

HAYES, CHRIS   S   JETS

PERSONAL: Born May 7, 1972, in San Bernardino, Calif. ... 6-0/206.
HIGH SCHOOL: San Gorgonio (San Bernardino, Calif.).
COLLEGE: Washington State.

TRANSACTIONS/CAREER NOTES: Selected by New York Jets in seventh round (210th pick overall) of 1996 NFL draft. ... Signed by Jets (June 26, 1996). ... Released by Jets (August 19, 1996). ... Signed by Washington Redskins to practice squad (September 11, 1996). ... Released by Redskins (October 2, 1996). ... Signed by Green Bay Packers to practice squad (October 4, 1996). ... Activated (December 9, 1996). ... Traded by Packers to Jets for CB Carl Greenwood (June 5, 1997).
PLAYING EXPERIENCE: Green Bay NFL, 1996; New York Jets NFL, 1997 and 1998. ... Games/Games started: 1996 (2/0), 1997 (16/0), 1998 (15/0). Total: 33/0.
CHAMPIONSHIP GAME EXPERIENCE: Played in NFC championship game (1996 season). ... Member of Super Bowl championship team (1996 season). ... Played in AFC championship game (1998 season).

HAYES, DONALD — WR — PANTHERS

PERSONAL: Born July 13, 1975, in Madison, Wis. ... 6-4/208. ... Full name: Donald Ross Hayes Jr.
HIGH SCHOOL: East (Madison, Wis.).
COLLEGE: Wisconsin.
TRANSACTIONS/CAREER NOTES: Selected by Carolina Panthers in fourth round (106th pick overall) of 1998 NFL draft. ... Signed by Panthers (July 8, 1998).
SINGLE GAME HIGHS (regular season): Receptions—1 (December 27, 1998, vs. Indianapolis); yards—35 (November 22, 1998, vs. St. Louis); and touchdown receptions—0.

				RECEIVING		
Year Team	G	GS	No.	Yds.	Avg.	TD
1998—Carolina NFL	8	0	3	62	20.7	0

HAYES, JARIUS — FB/TE — CARDINALS

PERSONAL: Born March 27, 1973, in Sheffield, Ala. ... 6-3/266.
HIGH SCHOOL: Muscle Shoals (Ala.).
COLLEGE: North Alabama.
TRANSACTIONS/CAREER NOTES: Selected by Arizona Cardinals in seventh round (212th pick overall) of 1996 NFL draft. ... Signed by Cardinals (July 21, 1996). ... Assigned by Cardinals to Barcelona Dragons in 1997 World League enhancement allocation program (February 19, 1997). ... Released by Cardinals (August 24, 1997). ... Selected by Amsterdam Admirals in 1998 NFL Europe draft (February 18, 1998). ... Re-signed by Cardinals (June 15, 1998).
PLAYING EXPERIENCE: Arizona NFL, 1996 and 1998; Amsterdam Admirals NFLE, 1998. ... Games/Games started: 1996 (4/0), NFLE 1998 (games played unavailable), NFL 1998 (16/0). Total NFL: 20/0.
PRO STATISTICS: NFLE: 1998—Caught five passes for 49 yards.

HEARST, GARRISON — RB — 49ERS

PERSONAL: Born January 4, 1971, in Lincolnton, Ga. ... 5-11/219. ... Full name: Gerald Garrison Hearst.
HIGH SCHOOL: Lincoln County (Lincolnton, Ga.).
COLLEGE: Georgia.
TRANSACTIONS/CAREER NOTES: Selected after junior season by Phoenix Cardinals in first round (third pick overall) of 1993 NFL draft. ... Signed by Cardinals (August 28, 1993). ... On injured reserve with knee injury (November 4, 1993-remainder of season). ... Cardinals franchise renamed Arizona Cardinals for 1994 season. ... On physically unable to perform list with knee injury (August 23-October 13, 1994). ... Granted free agency (February 16, 1996). ... Re-signed by Cardinals (May 23, 1996). ... Claimed on waivers by Cincinnati Bengals (August 21, 1996). ... Granted unconditional free agency (February 14, 1997). ... Signed by San Francisco 49ers (March 7, 1997).
CHAMPIONSHIP GAME EXPERIENCE: Played in NFC championship game (1997 season).
HONORS: Doak Walker Award winner (1992). ... Named running back on THE SPORTING NEWS college All-America first team (1992). ... Named to play in Pro Bowl (1998 season); replaced by Emmitt Smith due to injury.
PRO STATISTICS: 1993—Had only pass attempt intercepted. 1994—Attempted one pass with one completion for 10 yards and a touchdown. 1995—Attempted two passes with one completion for 16 yards and recovered two fumbles. 1996—Recovered one fumble. 1997—Recovered two fumbles. 1998—Recovered one fumble.
SINGLE GAME HIGHS (regular season): Attempts—28 (September 29, 1997, vs. Carolina); yards—198 (December 14, 1998, vs. Detroit); and rushing touchdowns—2 (September 6, 1998, vs. New York Jets).
STATISTICAL PLATEAUS: 100-yard rushing games: 1995 (3), 1997 (3), 1998 (6). Total: 12. ... 100-yard receiving games: 1998 (2).

			RUSHING				RECEIVING				TOTALS			
Year Team	G	GS	Att.	Yds.	Avg.	TD	No.	Yds.	Avg.	TD	TD	2pt.	Pts.	Fum.
1993—Phoenix NFL	6	5	76	264	3.5	1	6	18	3.0	0	1	...	6	2
1994—Arizona NFL	8	0	37	169	4.6	1	6	49	8.2	0	1	0	6	0
1995—Arizona NFL	16	15	284	1070	3.8	1	29	243	8.4	1	2	0	12	12
1996—Cincinnati NFL	16	12	225	847	3.8	0	12	131	10.9	1	1	1	8	1
1997—San Francisco NFL	13	13	234	1019	4.4	4	21	194	9.2	2	6	0	36	2
1998—San Francisco NFL	16	16	310	1570	‡5.1	7	39	535	13.7	2	9	1	56	4
Pro totals (6 years)	75	61	1166	4939	4.2	14	113	1170	10.4	6	20	2	124	21

HEBRON, VAUGHN — RB

PERSONAL: Born October 7, 1970, in Baltimore. ... 5-8/198. ... Full name: Vaughn Harlen Hebron.
HIGH SCHOOL: Cardinal Gibbons (Baltimore).
COLLEGE: Virginia Tech.
TRANSACTIONS/CAREER NOTES: Signed as non-drafted free agent by Philadelphia Eagles (April 29, 1993). ... On injured reserve with knee injury (August 22, 1995-entire season). ... Granted unconditional free agency (February 16, 1996). ... Re-signed by Eagles (April 18, 1996). ... Released by Eagles (August 22, 1996). ... Signed by Denver Broncos (August 28, 1996). ... Granted unconditional free agency (February 12, 1999).
CHAMPIONSHIP GAME EXPERIENCE: Played in AFC championship game (1997 and 1998 seasons). ... Member of Super Bowl championship team (1997 and 1998 seasons).

PRO STATISTICS: 1993—Recovered one fumble. 1996—Recovered one fumble. 1997—Recovered one fumble. 1998—Recovered one fumble.
SINGLE GAME HIGHS (regular season): Attempts—16 (December 24, 1994, vs. Cincinnati); yards—73 (October 27, 1996, vs. Kansas City); and rushing touchdowns—1 (November 22, 1998, vs. Oakland).

				RUSHING				RECEIVING				KICKOFF RETURNS				TOTALS		
Year	Team	G	GS	Att.	Yds.	Avg.	TD	No.	Yds.	Avg.	TD	No.	Yds.	Avg.	TD	TD	2pt.	Pts.	Fum.
1993—Philadelphia NFL		16	4	84	297	3.5	3	11	82	7.5	0	3	35	11.7	0	3	...	18	5
1994—Philadelphia NFL		16	2	82	325	4.0	2	18	137	7.6	0	21	443	21.1	0	2	0	12	0
1995—Philadelphia NFL									Did not play.										
1996—Denver NFL		16	0	49	262	5.3	0	7	43	6.1	0	45	1099	24.4	0	0	0	0	3
1997—Denver NFL		16	1	49	222	4.5	1	3	36	12.0	0	43	1009	23.5	0	1	0	6	1
1998—Denver NFL		15	0	9	31	3.4	1	2	5	2.5	0	46§1216		26.4	▲1	2	0	12	0
Pro totals (5 years)		79	7	273	1137	4.2	7	41	303	7.4	0	158	3802	24.1	1	8	0	48	9

HECK, ANDY — OT

PERSONAL: Born January 1, 1967, in Fargo, N.D. ... 6-6/298. ... Full name: Andrew Robert Heck.
HIGH SCHOOL: W.T. Woodson (Fairfax, Va.).
COLLEGE: Notre Dame (degree in American studies, 1989).
TRANSACTIONS/CAREER NOTES: Selected by Seattle Seahawks in first round (15th pick overall) of 1989 NFL draft. ... Signed by Seahawks (July 31, 1989). ... On injured reserve with ankle injury (October 21-November 20, 1992); on practice squad (November 18-20, 1992). ... Designated by Seahawks as transition player (February 25, 1993). ... Tendered offer sheet by Chicago Bears (February 21, 1994). ... Seahawks declined to match offer (March 1, 1994). ... Released by Bears (June 2, 1999).
PLAYING EXPERIENCE: Seattle NFL, 1989-1993; Chicago NFL, 1994-1998. ... Games/Games started: 1989 (16/9), 1990 (16/16), 1991 (16/16), 1992 (13/13), 1993 (16/16), 1994 (14/14), 1995 (16/16), 1996 (16/16), 1997 (16/16), 1998 (14/14). Total: 153/146.
HONORS: Named offensive tackle on THE SPORTING NEWS college All-America first team (1988).
PRO STATISTICS: 1989—Recovered one fumble. 1990—Recovered one fumble. 1993—Recovered two fumbles.

HEGAMIN, GEORGE — OT/G — EAGLES

PERSONAL: Born February 14, 1973, in Camden, N.J. ... 6-7/331. ... Full name: George Russell Hegamin. ... Name pronounced HEG-a-min.
HIGH SCHOOL: Camden (N.J.).
COLLEGE: North Carolina State.
TRANSACTIONS/CAREER NOTES: Selected after junior season by Dallas Cowboys in third round (102nd pick overall) of 1994 NFL draft. ... Signed by Cowboys (July 15, 1994). ... Active for four games (1995); did not play. ... Assigned by Cowboys to Frankfurt Galaxy in 1996 World League enhancement allocation program (February 19, 1996). ... Granted unconditional free agency (February 13, 1998). ... Signed by Philadelphia Eagles (February 19, 1998).
PLAYING EXPERIENCE: Dallas NFL, 1994, 1996 and 1997; Frankfurt W.L., 1996; Philadelphia NFL, 1998. ... Games/Games started: 1994 (2/0), W.L. 1996 (games played unavailable), NFL 1996 (16/1), 1997 (13/9), 1998 (16/6). Total: 47/16.
CHAMPIONSHIP GAME EXPERIENCE: Member of Cowboys for NFC championship game (1994 season); inactive. ... Member of Cowboys for NFC championship game (1995 season); did not play. ... Member of Super Bowl championship team (1995 season).
PRO STATISTICS: 1997—Recovered one fumble.

HELLESTRAE, DALE — G/C

PERSONAL: Born July 11, 1962, in Phoenix. ... 6-5/291. ... Full name: Dale Robert Hellestrae. ... Name pronounced hell-us-TRAY.
HIGH SCHOOL: Saguaro (Scottsdale, Ariz.).
COLLEGE: Southern Methodist (degree in business administration).
TRANSACTIONS/CAREER NOTES: Selected by Houston Gamblers in 1985 USFL territorial draft. ... Selected by Buffalo Bills in fourth round (112th pick overall) of 1985 NFL draft. ... Signed by Bills (July 19, 1985). ... On injured reserve with broken thumb (October 4, 1985-remainder of season). ... On injured reserve with broken wrist (September 17-November 15, 1986). ... On injured reserve with hip injury (September 1, 1987-entire season). ... Granted unconditional free agency (February 1, 1989). ... Signed by Los Angeles Raiders (February 24, 1989). ... On injured reserve with broken leg (August 29, 1989-entire season). ... Traded by Raiders to Dallas Cowboys for seventh-round pick (traded to Chicago) in 1991 draft (August 20, 1990). ... Granted unconditional free agency (February 1-April 1, 1991). ... Re-signed by Cowboys for 1991 season. ... Granted unconditional free agency (February 1-April 1, 1992). ... Re-signed by Cowboys for 1992 season. ... Released by Cowboys (August 31, 1992). ... Re-signed by Cowboys (September 2, 1992). ... Granted unconditional free agency (March 1, 1993). ... Re-signed by Cowboys (June 2, 1993). ... Released by Cowboys (August 30, 1993). ... Re-signed by Cowboys (August 31, 1993). ... Granted unconditional free agency (February 17, 1994). ... Re-signed by Cowboys (July 14, 1994). ... Granted unconditional free agency (February 16, 1996). ... Re-signed by Cowboys (April 9, 1996). ... Granted unconditional free agency (February 13, 1998). ... Re-signed by Cowboys (April 7, 1998). ... Granted unconditional free agency (February 12, 1999).
PLAYING EXPERIENCE: Buffalo NFL, 1985, 1986 and 1988; Dallas NFL, 1990-1998. ... Games/Games started: 1985 (4/0), 1986 (8/0), 1988 (16/2), 1990 (16/0), 1991 (16/0), 1992 (16/0), 1993 (16/0), 1994 (16/0), 1995 (16/0), 1996 (16/0), 1997 (16/0), 1998 (16/0). Total: 172/2.
CHAMPIONSHIP GAME EXPERIENCE: Played in AFC championship game (1988 season). ... Played in NFC championship game (1992-1995 seasons). ... Member of Super Bowl championship team (1992, 1993 and 1995 seasons).
PRO STATISTICS: 1986—Fumbled once for minus 14 yards.

HEMSLEY, NATE — LB — COWBOYS

PERSONAL: Born May 15, 1974, in Willingboro, N.J. ... 6-0/228. ... Full name: Nathaniel Richard Hemsley.
HIGH SCHOOL: Delran (N.J.).
COLLEGE: Syracuse.
TRANSACTIONS/CAREER NOTES: Signed as non-drafted free agent by Tennessee Oilers (April 23, 1997). ... Released by Oilers (August 13, 1997). ... Signed by Dallas Cowboys to practice squad (September 3, 1997). ... Activated (December 10, 1997). ... On injured reserve with ankle injury (October 5, 1998-remainder of season).
PLAYING EXPERIENCE: Dallas NFL, 1997 and 1998. ... Games/Games started: 1997 (2/0), 1998 (3/0). Total: 5/0.

HENDERSON, JEROME — CB

PERSONAL: Born August 8, 1969, in Portsmouth, Va. ... 5-10/200. ... Full name: Jerome Virgil Henderson.
HIGH SCHOOL: West Iredel (Statesville, N.C.).
COLLEGE: Clemson.
TRANSACTIONS/CAREER NOTES: Selected by New England Patriots in second round (41st pick overall) of 1991 NFL draft. ... Signed by Patriots (July 15, 1991). ... Released by Patriots (October 11, 1993). ... Signed by Buffalo Bills (October 15, 1993). ... Granted free agency (February 17, 1994). ... Re-signed by Bills (May 27, 1994). ... Granted unconditional free agency (February 17, 1995). ... Signed by Philadelphia Eagles (March 22, 1995). ... Released by Eagles (August 20, 1996). ... Signed by Patriots (November 5, 1996). ... Granted unconditional free agency (February 14, 1997). ... Signed by New York Jets (March 17, 1997). ... Released by Jets (March 2, 1999).
CHAMPIONSHIP GAME EXPERIENCE: Member of Bills for AFC championship game (1993 season); inactive. ... Played in Super Bowl XXVIII (1993 season) and Super Bowl XXXI (1996 season). ... Played in AFC championship game (1996 season). ... Member of Jets for AFC championship game (1998 season); inactive.
PRO STATISTICS: 1991—Recovered one fumble. 1995—Recovered one fumble in end zone for touchdown. 1998—Credited with one sack and recovered one fumble for 53 yards and a touchdown.

				INTERCEPTIONS				PUNT RETURNS				TOTALS		
Year Team	G	GS	No.	Yds.	Avg.	TD	No.	Yds.	Avg.	TD	TD	2pt.	Pts.	Fum.
1991—New England NFL	16	1	2	2	1.0	0	27	201	7.4	0	0	...	0	2
1992—New England NFL	16	9	3	43	14.3	0	0	0	...	0	0	...	0	0
1993—New England NFL	1	0	0	0	...	0	0	0	...	0	0	...	0	0
—Buffalo NFL	2	0	0	0	...	0	0	0	...	0	0	...	0	0
1994—Buffalo NFL	12	0	0	0	...	0	0	0	...	0	0	0	0	0
1995—Philadelphia NFL	15	0	0	0	...	0	0	0	...	0	1	0	6	0
1996—New England NFL	7	0	2	7	3.5	0	0	0	...	0	0	0	0	0
1997—New York Jets NFL	16	14	1	45	45.0	0	0	0	...	0	0	0	0	0
1998—New York Jets NFL	13	9	1	21	21.0	0	0	0	...	0	1	0	6	1
Pro totals (8 years)	98	33	9	118	13.1	0	27	201	7.4	0	2	0	12	3

HENDERSON, WILLIAM — FB — PACKERS

PERSONAL: Born February 19, 1971, in Richmond, Va. ... 6-1/245. ... Full name: William Terrelle Henderson.
HIGH SCHOOL: Thomas Dale (Chester, Va.).
COLLEGE: North Carolina.
TRANSACTIONS/CAREER NOTES: Selected by Green Bay Packers in third round (66th pick overall) of 1995 NFL draft. ... Signed by Packers (July 17, 1995). ... Granted free agency (February 13, 1998). ... Re-signed by Packers (June 15, 1998). ... Granted unconditional free agency (February 12, 1999). ... Re-signed by Packers (April 6, 1999).
CHAMPIONSHIP GAME EXPERIENCE: Played in NFC championship game (1995-97 seasons). ... Member of Super Bowl championship team (1996 season). ... Played in Super Bowl XXXII (1997 season).
PRO STATISTICS: 1996—Returned two kickoffs for 38 yards. 1997—Recovered two fumbles.
SINGLE GAME HIGHS (regular season): Attempts—6 (September 29, 1997, vs. Philadelphia); yards—40 (September 9, 1996, vs. Philadelphia); and rushing touchdowns—1 (November 29, 1998, vs. Philadelphia).

			RUSHING				RECEIVING				TOTALS			
Year Team	G	GS	Att.	Yds.	Avg.	TD	No.	Yds.	Avg.	TD	TD	2pt.	Pts.	Fum.
1995—Green Bay NFL	15	2	7	35	5.0	0	3	21	7.0	0	0	0	0	0
1996—Green Bay NFL	16	11	39	130	3.3	0	27	203	7.5	1	1	0	6	1
1997—Green Bay NFL	16	14	31	113	3.6	0	41	367	9.0	1	1	0	6	1
1998—Green Bay NFL	16	10	23	70	3.0	2	37	241	6.5	1	3	0	18	1
Pro totals (4 years)	63	37	100	348	3.5	2	108	832	7.7	3	5	0	30	3

HENLEY, JUNE — RB — RAMS

PERSONAL: Born September 4, 1975, in Columbus, Ohio. ... 5-10/226. ... Full name: Charles Lee Henley Jr.
HIGH SCHOOL: Brookhaven (Columbus, Ohio).
COLLEGE: Kansas.
TRANSACTIONS/CAREER NOTES: Selected by Kansas City Chiefs in fifth round (163rd pick overall) of 1997 NFL draft. ... Signed by Chiefs (May 5, 1997). ... Released by Chiefs (August 24, 1997). ... Signed by St. Louis Rams to practice squad (August 25, 1997).
PRO STATISTICS: 1998—Returned one kickoff for 13 yards and recovered one fumble.
SINGLE GAME HIGHS (regular season): Attempts—24 (December 13, 1998, vs. New England); yards—86 (December 13, 1998, vs. New England); and rushing touchdowns—2 (December 13, 1998, vs. New England).

			RUSHING				RECEIVING				TOTALS			
Year Team	G	GS	Att.	Yds.	Avg.	TD	No.	Yds.	Avg.	TD	TD	2pt.	Pts.	Fum.
1997—St. Louis NFL							Did not play.							
1998—St. Louis NFL	11	3	88	313	3.6	3	35	252	7.2	0	3	0	18	1
Pro totals (1 years)	11	3	88	313	3.6	3	35	252	7.2	0	3	0	18	1

HENNINGS, CHAD — DT — COWBOYS

PERSONAL: Born October 20, 1965, in Elberton, Iowa. ... 6-6/291. ... Full name: Chad William Hennings.
HIGH SCHOOL: Benton Community (Van Horne, Iowa).
COLLEGE: Air Force (degree in management).
TRANSACTIONS/CAREER NOTES: Selected by Dallas Cowboys in 11th round (290th pick overall) of 1988 NFL draft. ... Signed by Cowboys (November 22, 1988). ... Served in military (1988-1992). ... Granted unconditional free agency (February 17, 1994). ... Re-signed by Cowboys for 1994 season.
CHAMPIONSHIP GAME EXPERIENCE: Played in NFC championship game (1992, 1994 and 1995 seasons). ... Member of Cowboys for NFC championship game (1993 season); inactive. ... Member of Super Bowl championship team (1992, 1993 and 1995 seasons).
HONORS: Outland Trophy winner (1987). ... Named defensive lineman on THE SPORTING NEWS college All-America first team (1987).
PRO STATISTICS: 1993—Returned one kickoff for seven yards. 1994—Recovered one fumble. 1995—Recovered one fumble. 1996—Recovered one fumble. 1997—Recovered one fumble for four yards and a touchdown. 1998—Recovered one fumble.

Year Team	G	GS	SACKS
1992—Dallas NFL	8	0	0.0
1993—Dallas NFL	13	0	0.0
1994—Dallas NFL	16	0	7.0
1995—Dallas NFL	16	7	5.5
1996—Dallas NFL	15	15	4.5
1997—Dallas NFL	11	10	4.5
1998—Dallas NFL	16	16	1.0
Pro totals (7 years)	95	48	22.5

HENRY, KEVIN — DE — STEELERS

PERSONAL: Born October 23, 1968, in Mound Bayou, Miss. ... 6-4/285. ... Full name: Kevin Lerell Henry. ... Name pronounced KEE-vin.
HIGH SCHOOL: John F. Kennedy (Mound Bayou, Miss.).
COLLEGE: Mississippi State.
TRANSACTIONS/CAREER NOTES: Selected by Pittsburgh Steelers in fourth round (108th pick overall) of 1993 NFL draft. ... Signed by Steelers (July 9, 1993). ... Granted free agency (February 16, 1996). ... Re-signed by Steelers (August 2, 1996). ... Granted unconditional free agency (February 14, 1997). ... Re-signed by Steelers (April 3, 1997).
CHAMPIONSHIP GAME EXPERIENCE: Played in AFC championship game (1994, 1995 and 1997 seasons). ... Played in Super Bowl XXX (1995 season).
PRO STATISTICS: 1993—Intercepted one pass for 10 yards. 1994—Recovered one fumble. 1996—Recovered one fumble for four yards. 1997—Intercepted one pass for 36 yards and recovered two fumbles.

Year Team	G	GS	SACKS
1993—Pittsburgh NFL	12	1	1.0
1994—Pittsburgh NFL	16	5	0.0
1995—Pittsburgh NFL	13	5	2.0
1996—Pittsburgh NFL	12	10	1.5
1997—Pittsburgh NFL	16	16	4.5
1998—Pittsburgh NFL	16	16	4.0
Pro totals (6 years)	85	53	13.0

HENTRICH, CRAIG — P — TITANS

PERSONAL: Born May 18, 1971, in Alton, Ill. ... 6-3/205. ... Full name: Craig Anthony Hentrich. ... Name pronounced HEN-trick.
HIGH SCHOOL: Marquette (Alton, Ill.).
COLLEGE: Notre Dame.
TRANSACTIONS/CAREER NOTES: Selected by New York Jets in eighth round (200th pick overall) of 1993 NFL draft. ... Signed by Jets (July 14, 1993). ... Released by Jets (August 24, 1993). ... Signed by Green Bay Packers to practice squad (September 7, 1993). ... Activated (January 14, 1994); did not play. ... Granted unconditional free agency (February 13, 1998). ... Signed by Tennessee Oilers (February 19, 1998). ... Oilers franchise renamed Tennessee Titans for 1999 season (December 26, 1998).
CHAMPIONSHIP GAME EXPERIENCE: Played in NFC championship game (1995-97 seasons). ... Member of Super Bowl championship team (1996 season). ... Played in Super Bowl XXXII (1997 season).
HONORS: Named punter on THE SPORTING NEWS NFL All-Pro team (1998). ... Played in Pro Bowl (1998 season).
PRO STATISTICS: 1996—Attempted one pass without a completion and recovered one fumble. 1998—Rushed once for minus one yard and attempted one pass with a completion for 13 yards.

			PUNTING						KICKING				
Year Team	G	No.	Yds.	Avg.	Net avg.	In. 20	Blk.	XPM	XPA	FGM	FGA	Lg.	50+	Pts.
1993—Green Bay NFL								Did not play.						
1994—Green Bay NFL	16	81	3351	41.4	35.5	24	0	0	0	0	0	...	0-0	0
1995—Green Bay NFL	16	65	2740	42.2	34.6	26	2	5	5	3	5	49	0-0	14
1996—Green Bay NFL	16	68	2886	42.4	36.2	28	0	0	0	0	0	...	0-0	0
1997—Green Bay NFL	16	75	3378	45.0	36.0	26	0	0	0	0	0	...	0-0	0
1998—Tennessee NFL	16	69	3258	47.2	39.2	18	0	0	0	0	1	0	0-0	0
Pro totals (5 years)	80	358	15613	43.6	36.3	122	2	5	5	3	6	49	0-0	14

HERNDON, JIMMY — OT — BEARS

PERSONAL: Born August 30, 1973, in Baytown, Texas. ... 6-8/318.
HIGH SCHOOL: Lee (Baytown, Texas).
COLLEGE: Houston (degree in sociology, 1996).
TRANSACTIONS/CAREER NOTES: Selected by Jacksonville Jaguars in fifth round (146th pick overall) of 1996 NFL draft. ... Signed by Jaguars (May 24, 1996). ... Active for eight games (1996); did not play. ... Traded by Jaguars to Chicago Bears for seventh-round pick (WR Alvis Whitted) in 1998 draft (August 24, 1997).
PLAYING EXPERIENCE: Chicago NFL, 1997 and 1998. ... Games/Games started: 1997 (7/0), 1998 (9/2). Total: 16/2.
CHAMPIONSHIP GAME EXPERIENCE: Member of Jaguars for AFC championship game (1996 season); inactive.

HERRING, KIM — S — RAVENS

PERSONAL: Born September 10, 1975, in Cleveland. ... 5-11/210. ... Full name: Kimani Masai Herring.
HIGH SCHOOL: Solon (Ohio).
COLLEGE: Penn State.
TRANSACTIONS/CAREER NOTES: Selected by Baltimore Ravens in second round (58th pick overall) of 1997 NFL draft. ... Signed by Ravens (July 18, 1997). ... On injured reserve with shoulder injury (December 2, 1998-remainder of season).
PLAYING EXPERIENCE: Baltimore NFL, 1997 and 1998. ... Games/Games started: 1997 (15/4), 1998 (7/7). Total: 22/11.
HONORS: Named free safety on THE SPORTING NEWS college All-America first team (1996).
PRO STATISTICS: 1997—Credited with one sack and recovered one fumble.

HERROD, JEFF — LB

PERSONAL: Born September 29, 1966, in Birmingham, Ala. ... 6-0/249. ... Full name: Jeff Sylvester Herrod.
HIGH SCHOOL: Banks (Birmingham, Ala.).
COLLEGE: Mississippi.
TRANSACTIONS/CAREER NOTES: Selected by Indianapolis Colts in ninth round (243rd pick overall) of 1988 NFL draft. ... Signed by Colts (July 13, 1988). ... Granted free agency (February 1, 1990). ... Re-signed by Colts (September 12, 1990). ... Released by Colts (July 19, 1995). ... Re-signed by Colts (July 20, 1995). ... Released by Colts (June 18, 1997). ... Signed by Philadelphia Eagles (September 2, 1997). ... Granted unconditional free agency (February 13, 1998). ... Signed by Indianapolis Colts (February 23, 1998). ... Granted unconditional free agency (February 12, 1999).
CHAMPIONSHIP GAME EXPERIENCE: Played in AFC championship game (1995 season).
HONORS: Named linebacker on THE SPORTING NEWS college All-America second team (1986).
PRO STATISTICS: 1991—Recovered three fumbles. 1993—Recovered one fumble in end zone for a touchdown.

			INTERCEPTIONS				SACKS
Year Team	G	GS	No.	Yds.	Avg.	TD	No.
1988—Indianapolis NFL	16	0	0	0	...	0	1.0
1989—Indianapolis NFL	15	14	0	0	...	0	2.0
1990—Indianapolis NFL	13	13	1	12	12.0	0	4.0
1991—Indianapolis NFL	14	14	1	25	25.0	0	2.5
1992—Indianapolis NFL	16	16	1	4	4.0	0	2.0
1993—Indianapolis NFL	14	14	1	29	29.0	0	2.0
1994—Indianapolis NFL	15	15	0	0	...	0	1.0
1995—Indianapolis NFL	16	16	0	0	...	0	0.0
1996—Indianapolis NFL	14	14	1	68	68.0	1	0.0
1997—Philadelphia NFL	10	2	0	0	...	0	0.0
1998—Indianapolis NFL	10	7	0	0	...	0	0.0
Pro totals (11 years)	153	125	5	138	27.6	1	14.5

HESSE, JON — LB — RAMS

PERSONAL: Born June 6, 1973, in Lincoln, Neb. ... 6-3/247. ... Full name: Jon Andrew Hesse.
HIGH SCHOOL: Southeast (Lincoln, Neb.).
COLLEGE: Nebraska.
TRANSACTIONS/CAREER NOTES: Selected by Jacksonville Jaguars in seventh round (221st pick overall) of 1997 NFL draft. ... Signed by Jaguars (May 23, 1997). ... Released by Jaguars (August 19, 1997). ... Signed by Green Bay Packers to practice squad (August 26, 1997). ... Signed by Denver Broncos off Packers practice squad (December 19, 1997). ... Inactive for one game (1997). ... Released by Broncos (August 25, 1998). ... Signed by Oakland Raiders to practice squad (October 7, 1998). ... Released by Raiders (October 19, 1998). ... Signed by St. Louis Rams to practice squad (October 21, 1998). ... Activated (November 6, 1998). ... Assigned by Rams to Scottish Claymores in 1999 NFL Europe enhancement allocation program (February 22, 1999).
PLAYING EXPERIENCE: St. Louis NFL, 1998. ... Games/Games started: 5/0.
CHAMPIONSHIP GAME EXPERIENCE: Member of Broncos for AFC championship game (1997 season); inactive. ... Member of Super Bowl championship team (1997 season); inactive.

HETHERINGTON, CHRIS — FB — PANTHERS

PERSONAL: Born November 27, 1972, in North Branford, Conn. ... 6-3/249. ... Full name: Christopher Raymond Hetherington.
HIGH SCHOOL: Avon (Conn.) Old Farms.
COLLEGE: Yale (degree in psychology).
TRANSACTIONS/CAREER NOTES: Signed as non-drafted free agent by Cincinnati Bengals (April 23, 1996). ... Released by Bengals (August 21, 1996). ... Re-signed by Bengals to practice squad (August 26, 1996). ... Signed by Indianapolis Colts off Bengals practice squad (October 22, 1996). ... Released by Colts (August 24, 1998). ... Re-signed by Colts (August 31, 1998). ... Released by Colts (February 12, 1999). ... Signed by Carolina Panthers (March 8, 1999).

			KICKOFF RETURNS				TOTALS			
Year Team	G	GS	No.	Yds.	Avg.	TD	TD	2pt.	Pts.	Fum.
1996—Indianapolis NFL	6	0	1	16	16.0	0	0	0	0	0
1997—Indianapolis NFL	16	0	2	23	11.5	0	0	0	0	0
1998—Indianapolis NFL	14	1	5	71	14.2	0	0	0	0	1
Pro totals (3 years)	36	1	8	110	13.8	0	0	0	0	1

HEWITT, CHRIS — S — SAINTS

PERSONAL: Born July 22, 1974, in Kingston, Jamaica. ... 6-0/210. ... Full name: Christopher Horace Hewitt.
HIGH SCHOOL: Dwight Morrow (Englewood, N.J.).
COLLEGE: Cincinnati.
TRANSACTIONS/CAREER NOTES: Signed as non-drafted free agent by New Orleans Saints (April 25, 1997). ... Released by Saints (August 18, 1997). ... Re-signed by Saints to practice squad (August 25, 1997). ... Activated (October 1, 1997).
PLAYING EXPERIENCE: New Orleans NFL, 1997 and 1998. ... Games/Games started: 1997 (11/2), 1998 (16/2). Total: 27/4.
PRO STATISTICS: 1997—Recovered one fumble. 1998—Credited with two sacks.

HEYWARD, CRAIG — FB

PERSONAL: Born September 26, 1966, in Passaic, N.J. ... 5-11/265. ... Full name: Craig William Heyward. ... Nickname: Ironhead.
HIGH SCHOOL: Passaic (N.J.).
COLLEGE: Pittsburgh.

TRANSACTIONS/CAREER NOTES: Selected by New Orleans Saints in first round (24th pick overall) of 1988 NFL draft. ... Signed by Saints (July 8, 1988). ... Granted free agency (February 1, 1991). ... Re-signed by Saints (July 12, 1991). ... On injured reserve with foot injury (November 6-December 11, 1991). ... On suspended list (December 11, 1991-remainder of season). ... Granted unconditional free agency (March 1, 1993). ... Signed by Chicago Bears (April 11, 1993). ... Released by Bears (April 26, 1994). ... Signed by Atlanta Falcons (June 21, 1994). ... Granted unconditional free agency (February 14, 1997). ... Signed by St. Louis Rams (March 6, 1997). ... On reserve/did not report list (July 24-September 2, 1998). ... Released by Rams (September 2, 1998). ... Signed by Indianapolis Colts (September 30, 1998). ... On non-football injury list with head injury (November 9, 1998-remainder of season). ... Granted unconditional free agency (February 12, 1999).
HONORS: Named running back on THE SPORTING NEWS college All-America first team (1987).
PRO STATISTICS: 1988—Recovered one fumble. 1989—Recovered one fumble. 1990—Attempted one pass without a completion. 1991—Attempted one pass with a completion for 44 yards. 1992—Returned one kickoff for 14 yards and recovered one fumble. 1993—Returned one kickoff for 12 yards. 1994—Returned one kickoff for seven yards and recovered two fumbles. 1995—Recovered three fumbles. 1996—Returned one punt for no yards and returned one kickoff for 18 yards.
SINGLE GAME HIGHS (regular season): Attempts—25 (September 17, 1995, vs. New Orleans); yards—155 (November 11, 1990, vs. Tampa Bay); and rushing touchdowns—2 (November 12, 1995, vs. Buffalo).
STATISTICAL PLATEAUS: 100-yard rushing games: 1988 (1), 1990 (2), 1995 (3). Total: 6.

				RUSHING				RECEIVING				TOTALS		
Year Team	G	GS	Att.	Yds.	Avg.	TD	No.	Yds.	Avg.	TD	TD	2pt.	Pts.	Fum.
1988—New Orleans NFL	11	8	74	355	4.8	1	13	105	8.1	0	1	...	6	0
1989—New Orleans NFL	16	6	49	183	3.7	1	13	69	5.3	0	1	...	6	2
1990—New Orleans NFL	16	15	129	599	4.6	4	18	121	6.7	0	4	...	24	3
1991—New Orleans NFL	7	4	76	260	3.4	4	4	34	8.5	1	5	...	30	0
1992—New Orleans NFL	16	13	104	416	4.0	3	19	159	8.4	0	3	...	18	1
1993—Chicago NFL	16	14	68	206	3.0	0	16	132	8.3	0	0	...	0	1
1994—Atlanta NFL	16	11	183	779	4.3	7	32	335	10.5	1	8	0	48	5
1995—Atlanta NFL	16	16	236	1083	4.6	6	37	350	9.5	2	8	0	48	3
1996—Atlanta NFL	15	5	72	321	4.5	3	16	168	10.5	0	3	0	18	0
1997—St. Louis NFL	16	12	34	84	2.5	1	8	77	9.6	0	1	0	6	1
1998—Indianapolis NFL	4	3	6	15	2.5	0	1	9	9.0	0	0	0	0	0
Pro totals (11 years)	149	107	1031	4301	4.2	30	177	1559	8.8	4	34	0	204	16

HICKMAN, KEVIN — TE

PERSONAL: Born August 20, 1971, in Cherry Hill, N.J. ... 6-4/258. ... Full name: Kevin J. Hickman.
HIGH SCHOOL: Holy Cross (Delran, N.J.), then Marine Military Academy (Harlingen, Texas).
COLLEGE: Navy.
TRANSACTIONS/CAREER NOTES: Selected by Detroit Lions in sixth round (186th pick overall) of 1995 NFL draft. ... Signed by Lions (July 19, 1995). ... On injured reserve with knee injury (December 21, 1995-remainder of season). ... On injured reserve with knee injury (August 20, 1996-entire season). ... Released by Lions (August 19, 1997). ... Re-signed by Lions (September 19, 1997). ... Released by Lions (October 30, 1997). ... Signed by Philadelphia Eagles (April 29, 1998). ... Released by Eagles (August 17, 1998). ... Signed by Lions (August 31, 1998). ... Released by Lions (October 27, 1998).
PLAYING EXPERIENCE: Detroit NFL, 1995, 1997 and 1998. ... Games/Games started: 1995 (7/0), 1997 (4/0), 1998 (3/0). Total: 14/0.

HICKS, ERIC — DE — CHIEFS

PERSONAL: Born June 17, 1976, in Erie, Pa. ... 6-6/261. ... Full name: Eric David Hicks.
HIGH SCHOOL: Mercyhurst (Erie, Pa.).
COLLEGE: Maryland.
TRANSACTIONS/CAREER NOTES: Signed as non-drafted free agent by Kansas City Chiefs (April 25, 1998).
PLAYING EXPERIENCE: Kansas City NFL, 1998. ... Games/Games started: 3/0.
PRO STATISTICS: 1998—Recovered one fumble.

HICKS, ROBERT — OT — BILLS

PERSONAL: Born November 17, 1974, in Atlanta ... 6-7/338. ... Full name: Robert Otis Hicks Jr.
HIGH SCHOOL: Douglass (Atlanta).
COLLEGE: Mississippi State.
TRANSACTIONS/CAREER NOTES: Selected by Buffalo Bills in third round (68th pick overall) of 1998 NFL draft. ... Signed by Bills (July 20, 1998).
PLAYING EXPERIENCE: Buffalo NFL, 1998. ... Games/Games started: 9/2.

HICKS, SKIP — RB — REDSKINS

PERSONAL: Born October 13, 1974, in Corsicana, Texas. ... 6-0/230. ... Full name: Brian LaVell Hicks.
HIGH SCHOOL: Burkburnett (Texas).
COLLEGE: UCLA.
TRANSACTIONS/CAREER NOTES: Selected by Washington Redskins in third round (69th pick overall) of 1998 NFL draft. ... Signed by Redskins (July 7, 1998).
HONORS: Named running back on THE SPORTING NEWS college All-America first team (1997).
SINGLE GAME HIGHS (regular season): Attempts—26 (November 15, 1998, vs. Philadelphia); yards—94 (November 15, 1998, vs. Philadelphia); and rushing touchdowns—3 (November 15, 1998, vs. Philadelphia).

				RUSHING				RECEIVING				TOTALS		
Year Team	G	GS	Att.	Yds.	Avg.	TD	No.	Yds.	Avg.	TD	TD	2pt.	Pts.	Fum.
1998—Washington NFL	9	5	122	433	3.5	8	4	23	5.8	0	8	0	48	0

HILL, ERIC — LB — CHARGERS

PERSONAL: Born November 14, 1966, in Galveston, Texas. ... 6-2/265.
HIGH SCHOOL: Ball (Galveston, Texas).
COLLEGE: Louisiana State.
TRANSACTIONS/CAREER NOTES: Selected by Phoenix Cardinals in first round (10th pick overall) of 1989 NFL draft. ... Signed by Cardinals (August 18, 1989). ... Granted free agency (March 1, 1993). ... Re-signed by Cardinals (September 4, 1993). ... Activated (September 26, 1993). ... Designated by Cardinals as transition player (February 15, 1994). ... Cardinals franchise renamed Arizona Cardinals for 1994 season. ... Granted unconditional free agency (February 13, 1998). ... Signed by St. Louis Rams (February 26, 1998). ... Released by Rams (March 11, 1999). ... Signed by San Diego Chargers (March 26, 1999).
PRO STATISTICS: 1989—Recovered one fumble. 1991—Recovered one fumble for 85 yards and a touchdown. 1992—Fumbled once and recovered one fumble for minus two yards. 1993—Recovered one fumble. 1998—Intercepted one pass for no yards.

Year Team	G	GS	SACKS
1989—Phoenix NFL	15	14	1.0
1990—Phoenix NFL	16	16	1.5
1991—Phoenix NFL	16	15	1.0
1992—Phoenix NFL	16	16	0.0
1993—Phoenix NFL	13	12	1.0
1994—Arizona NFL	16	15	1.5
1995—Arizona NFL	14	14	2.0
1996—Arizona NFL	16	16	0.0
1997—Arizona NFL	11	10	0.0
1998—St. Louis NFL	15	13	1.0
Pro totals (10 years)	148	141	9.0

HILL, GREG — RB — RAMS

PERSONAL: Born February 23, 1972, in Dallas. ... 5-11/212. ... Full name: Gregory Lamonte' Hill.
HIGH SCHOOL: David W. Carter (Dallas).
COLLEGE: Texas A&M.
TRANSACTIONS/CAREER NOTES: Selected after junior season by Kansas City Chiefs in first round (25th pick overall) of 1994 NFL draft. ... Signed by Chiefs (August 2, 1994). ... Granted unconditional free agency (February 13, 1998). ... Signed by St. Louis Rams (August 4, 1998). ... On injured reserve with broken leg (September 29, 1998-remainder of season).
HONORS: Named running back on THE SPORTING NEWS college All-America second team (1992).
SINGLE GAME HIGHS (regular season): Attempts—21 (September 13, 1998, vs. Minnesota); yards—158 (September 20, 1998, vs. Buffalo); and rushing touchdowns—2 (September 20, 1998, vs. Buffalo).
STATISTICAL PLATEAUS: 100-yard rushing games: 1995 (2), 1996 (2), 1998 (1). Total: 5.

			RUSHING				RECEIVING				TOTALS		
Year Team	G	GS	Att.	Yds.	Avg.	TD	No.	Yds.	Avg.	TD	TD	2pt.	Pts.	Fum.
1994—Kansas City NFL	16	1	141	574	4.1	1	16	92	5.8	0	1	0	6	1
1995—Kansas City NFL	16	1	155	667	4.3	1	7	45	6.4	0	1	0	6	2
1996—Kansas City NFL	15	1	135	645	4.8	4	3	60	20.0	1	5	0	30	1
1997—Kansas City NFL	16	16	157	550	3.5	0	12	126	10.5	0	0	0	0	1
1998—St. Louis NFL	2	2	40	240	6.0	4	1	6	6.0	0	4	0	24	0
Pro totals (5 years)	65	21	628	2676	4.3	10	39	329	8.4	1	11	0	66	5

HILL, RAY — CB — DOLPHINS

PERSONAL: Born August 7, 1975, in Detroit. ... 6-0/182. ... Full name: Raymond Millous Hill.
HIGH SCHOOL: Chadsey (Detroit).
COLLEGE: Michigan State.
TRANSACTIONS/CAREER NOTES: Signed as non-drafted free agent by Buffalo Bills (April 23, 1998). ... Released by Bills (August 30, 1998). ... Re-signed by Bills to practice squad (August 31, 1998). ... Activated (September 9, 1998). ... Claimed on waivers by Miami Dolphins (November 19, 1998).
PLAYING EXPERIENCE: Buffalo (4)-Miami (2) NFL, 1998. ... Games/Games started: 1998 (Buf.-4/0; Mia.-2/0; Total: 6/0).

HILLIARD, IKE — WR — GIANTS

PERSONAL: Born April 5, 1976, in Patterson, La. ... 5-11/195. ... Full name: Isaac Jason Hilliard. ... Nephew of Dalton Hilliard, running back with New Orleans Saints (1986-93).
HIGH SCHOOL: Patterson (La.).
COLLEGE: Florida.
TRANSACTIONS/CAREER NOTES: Selected by New York Giants in first round (seventh pick overall) of 1997 NFL draft. ... Signed by Giants (July 19, 1997). ... On injured reserve with neck injury (September 30, 1997-remainder of season).
PRO STATISTICS: 1998—Rushed once for four yards.
SINGLE GAME HIGHS (regular season): Receptions—8 (September 13, 1998, vs. Oakland); yards—141 (November 30, 1998, vs. San Francisco); and touchdown receptions—1 (November 1, 1998, vs. Washington).
STATISTICAL PLATEAUS: 100-yard receiving games: 1998 (1).

			RECEIVING				TOTALS			
Year Team	G	GS	No.	Yds.	Avg.	TD	TD	2pt.	Pts.	Fum.
1997—New York Giants NFL	2	2	2	42	21.0	0	0	0	0	0
1998—New York Giants NFL	16	16	51	715	14.0	2	2	0	12	2
Pro totals (2 years)	18	18	53	757	14.3	2	2	0	12	2

HILLIARD, RANDY — CB

PERSONAL: Born February 6, 1967, in New Orleans. ... 5-11/168.
HIGH SCHOOL: East Jefferson (Metairie, La.).
COLLEGE: Northwestern (La.) State.
TRANSACTIONS/CAREER NOTES: Selected by Cleveland Browns in sixth round (157th pick overall) of 1990 NFL draft. ... Signed by Browns (July 22, 1990). ... Granted free agency (February 1, 1992). ... Re-signed by Browns (July 28, 1992). ... Granted free agency (March 1, 1993). ... Re-signed by Browns (July 19, 1993). ... Granted unconditional free agency (February 17, 1994). ... Signed by Denver Broncos (May 16, 1994). ... Granted unconditional free agency (February 16, 1996). ... Re-signed by Broncos (February 26, 1996). ... Released by Broncos (February 11, 1998). ... Re-signed by Broncos (April 29, 1998). ... Released by Broncos (August 30, 1998). ... Signed by Chicago Bears (September 30, 1998). ... Granted unconditional free agency (February 12, 1999).
CHAMPIONSHIP GAME EXPERIENCE: Played in AFC championship game (1997 season). ... Member of Super Bowl championship team (1997 season).
PRO STATISTICS: 1991—Recovered one fumble. 1992—Recovered one fumble. 1996—Recovered one fumble.

Year — Team	G	GS	INTERCEPTIONS No.	Yds.	Avg.	TD	SACKS No.
1990—Cleveland NFL	15	0	0	0	...	0	0.0
1991—Cleveland NFL	14	10	1	19	19.0	0	2.0
1992—Cleveland NFL	16	4	0	0	...	0	1.0
1993—Cleveland NFL	12	5	1	54	54.0	0	0.0
1994—Denver NFL	15	6	2	8	4.0	0	0.0
1995—Denver NFL	12	0	0	0	...	0	0.0
1996—Denver NFL	13	3	1	27	27.0	0	0.0
1997—Denver NFL	14	0	0	0	...	0	0.0
1998—Chicago NFL	9	2	0	0	...	0	0.0
Pro totals (9 years)	120	30	5	108	21.6	0	3.0

HILLS, KENO — G/OT — SAINTS

PERSONAL: Born June 13, 1973, in Tampa. ... 6-6/305. ... Full name: Keno J. Hills. ... Name pronounced KEY-no.
HIGH SCHOOL: Tampa Tech.
COLLEGE: Kent, then Southwestern Louisiana.
TRANSACTIONS/CAREER NOTES: Selected by New Orleans Saints in sixth round (179th pick overall) of 1996 NFL draft. ... Signed by Saints (July 13, 1996). ... On physically unable to perform list with hamstring injury (July 18-October 16, 1997). ... Granted free agency (February 12, 1999). ... Re-signed by Saints (April 15, 1999).
PLAYING EXPERIENCE: New Orleans NFL, 1996-1998. ... Games/Games started: 1996 (1/0), 1997 (9/6), 1998 (12/1). Total: 22/7.

HITCHCOCK, JIMMY — CB — VIKINGS

PERSONAL: Born November 9, 1971, in Concord, N.C. ... 5-10/187. ... Full name: Jimmy Davis Hitchcock Jr.
HIGH SCHOOL: Concord (N.C.).
COLLEGE: North Carolina.
TRANSACTIONS/CAREER NOTES: Selected by New England Patriots in third round (88th pick overall) of 1995 NFL draft. ... Signed by Patriots (July 19, 1995). ... Granted free agency (February 13, 1998). ... Re-signed by Patriots (April 18, 1998). ... Traded by Patriots to Minnesota Vikings for third-round pick (S Tony George) in 1999 draft (April 18, 1998).
CHAMPIONSHIP GAME EXPERIENCE: Member of Patriots for AFC championship game (1996 season); inactive. ... Member of Patriots for Super Bowl XXXI (1996 season); inactive. ... Played in NFC championship game (1998 season).
PRO STATISTICS: 1998—Recovered one fumble for one yard.

Year — Team	G	GS	INTERCEPTIONS No.	Yds.	Avg.	TD
1995—New England NFL	8	0	0	0	...	0
1996—New England NFL	13	5	2	14	7.0	0
1997—New England NFL	15	15	2	104	52.0	1
1998—Minnesota NFL	16	16	7	*242	‡34.6	*3
Pro totals (4 years)	52	36	11	360	32.7	4

HOARD, LEROY — RB — VIKINGS

PERSONAL: Born May 15, 1968, in New Orleans. ... 5-11/224.
HIGH SCHOOL: St. Augustine (New Orleans).
COLLEGE: Michigan.
TRANSACTIONS/CAREER NOTES: Selected after junior season by Cleveland Browns in second round (45th pick overall) of 1990 NFL draft. ... Signed by Browns (July 29, 1990). ... Granted free agency (March 1, 1993). ... Re-signed by Browns for 1993 season. ... On physically unable to perform list with rib injury (July 22-24, 1995). ... On injured reserve with rib injury (December 16, 1995-remainder of season). ... Browns franchise moved to Baltimore and renamed Ravens for 1996 season (March 11, 1996). ... Released by Ravens (September 24, 1996). ... Signed by Carolina Panthers (October 1, 1996). ... Released by Panthers (October 22, 1996). ... Signed by Minnesota Vikings (November 5, 1996). ... Granted unconditional free agency (February 14, 1997). ... Re-signed by Vikings (April 3, 1997).
CHAMPIONSHIP GAME EXPERIENCE: Played in NFC championship game (1998 season).
HONORS: Played in Pro Bowl (1994 season).
PRO STATISTICS: 1991—Recovered one fumble for four yards. 1992—Recovered one fumble. 1993—Attempted one pass without a completion. 1998—Recovered one fumble.
SINGLE GAME HIGHS (regular season): Attempts—26 (December 13, 1998, vs. Baltimore); yards—123 (November 6, 1994, vs. New England); and rushing touchdowns—2 (November 26, 1998, vs. Dallas).
STATISTICAL PLATEAUS: 100-yard rushing games: 1994 (2), 1996 (2). Total: 4. ... 100-yard receiving games: 1991 (1).

Year	Team	G	GS	RUSHING Att.	Yds.	Avg.	TD	RECEIVING No.	Yds.	Avg.	TD	KICKOFF RETURNS No.	Yds.	Avg.	TD	TOTALS TD	2pt.	Pts.	Fum.
1990	Cleveland NFL	14	5	58	149	2.6	3	10	73	7.3	0	2	18	9.0	0	3	...	18	6
1991	Cleveland NFL	16	9	37	154	4.2	2	48	567	11.8	9	0	0	...	0	11	...	66	1
1992	Cleveland NFL	16	9	54	236	4.4	0	26	310	11.9	1	2	34	17.0	0	1	...	6	3
1993	Cleveland NFL	16	7	56	227	4.1	0	35	351	10.0	0	13	286	22.0	0	0	...	0	4
1994	Cleveland NFL	16	12	209	890	4.3	5	45	445	9.9	4	2	30	15.0	0	9	0	54	8
1995	Cleveland NFL	12	12	136	547	4.0	0	13	103	7.9	0	1	13	13.0	0	0	0	0	5
1996	Baltimore NFL	2	1	15	61	4.1	0	1	4	4.0	0	0	0	...	0	0	0	0	0
—	Carolina NFL	3	0	5	11	2.2	0	0	0	...	0	1	19	19.0	0	0	0	0	0
—	Minnesota NFL	6	6	105	420	4.0	3	10	129	12.9	0	0	0	...	0	3	0	18	3
1997	Minnesota NFL	12	1	80	235	2.9	0	11	84	7.6	0	0	0	...	0	4	0	24	0
1998	Minnesota NFL	16	1	115	479	4.2	9	22	198	9.0	1	0	0	...	0	10	0	60	1
Pro totals (9 years)		129	63	870	3409	3.9	26	221	2264	10.2	15	21	400	19.0	0	41	0	246	31

HOBERT, BILLY JOE QB SAINTS

PERSONAL: Born January 8, 1971, in Puyallup, Wash. ... 6-3/230.
HIGH SCHOOL: Puyallup (Wash.).
COLLEGE: Washington.
TRANSACTIONS/CAREER NOTES: Selected after junior season by Los Angeles Raiders in third round (58th pick overall) of 1993 NFL draft. ... Raiders franchise moved to Oakland (July 21, 1995). ... Traded by Raiders to Buffalo Bills for undisclosed draft pick (February 17, 1997). ... Released by Bills (October 15, 1997). ... Signed by New Orleans Saints (November 19, 1997). ... On injured reserve with Achilles' tendon injury (September 9, 1998-remainder of season).
PRO STATISTICS: 1996—Punted nine times for 371 yards (41.2 avg./35.1 net avg.) and fumbled six times. 1997—Fumbled three times and recovered one fumble for minus five yards.
SINGLE GAME HIGHS (regular season): Attempts—42 (December 7, 1997, vs. St. Louis); completions—20 (December 10, 1995, vs. Pittsburgh); yards—259 (December 7, 1997, vs. St. Louis); and touchdown passes—3 (December 14, 1997, vs. Arizona).
MISCELLANEOUS: Regular-season record as starting quarterback: 3-7 (.300).

Year	Team	G	GS	PASSING Att.	Cmp.	Pct.	Yds.	TD	Int.	Avg.	Rat.	RUSHING Att.	Yds.	Avg.	TD	TOTALS TD	2pt.	Pts.
1995	Oakland NFL	4	2	80	44	55.0	540	6	4	6.75	80.2	3	5	1.7	0	0	0	0
1996	Oakland NFL	8	3	104	57	54.8	667	4	5	6.41	67.3	2	13	6.5	0	0	0	0
1997	Buffalo NFL	2	0	30	17	56.7	133	0	2	4.43	40.0	2	7	3.5	0	0	0	0
—	New Orleans NFL	5	4	131	61	46.6	891	6	8	6.80	59.0	12	36	3.0	0	0	0	0
1998	New Orleans NFL	1	1	23	11	47.8	170	1	0	7.39	87.2	2	13	6.5	0	0	0	0
Pro totals (4 years)		20	10	368	190	51.6	2401	17	19	6.52	66.2	21	74	3.5	0	0	0	0

RECORD AS BASEBALL PLAYER

TRANSACTIONS/CAREER NOTES: Threw right, batted left. ... Selected by Chicago White Sox organization in 16th round of free-agent baseball draft (June 3, 1993).

Year	Team (League)	Pos.	G	AB	R	H	BATTING 2B	3B	HR	RBI	Avg.	BB	SO	SB	FIELDING PO	A	E	Avg.
1988	GC White Sox (GCL)	OF	15	39	3	10	2	0	0	4	.256	6	5	1	13	1	0	1.000

HOELSCHER, DAVID DT REDSKINS

PERSONAL: Born November 27, 1975, in Coldwater, Ohio ... 6-5/285. ... Full name: David Henry Hoelscher.
HIGH SCHOOL: Versailles (Ohio).
COLLEGE: Eastern Kentucky.
TRANSACTIONS/CAREER NOTES: Signed as non-drafted by Green Bay Packers (April 24, 1998). ... Released by Packers (August 25, 1998). ... Signed by Washington Redskins to practice squad (November 3, 1998). ... Activated (November 11, 1998). ... Assigned by Redskins to Frankfurt Galaxy in 1999 NFL Europe enhancement allocation program (February 22, 1999).
PLAYING EXPERIENCE: Washington NFL, 1998. ... Games/Games started: 1/0.

HOLCOMB, KELLY QB COLTS

PERSONAL: Born July 9, 1973, in Fayetteville, Tenn. ... 6-2/212. ... Full name: Bryan Kelly Holcomb.
HIGH SCHOOL: Lincoln County (Fayetteville, Tenn.).
COLLEGE: Middle Tennessee State.
TRANSACTIONS/CAREER NOTES: Signed as non-drafted free agent by Tampa Bay Buccaneers (May 1, 1995). ... Released by Buccaneers (August 22, 1995). ... Re-signed by Buccaneers to practice squad (August 29, 1995). ... Released by Buccaneers (September 19, 1995). ... Re-signed by Buccaneers to practice squad (October 4, 1995). ... Released by Buccaneers (October 17, 1995). ... Re-signed by Buccaneers to practice squad (December 19, 1995). ... Played for Barcelona Dragons of World League (1996). ... Released by Buccaneers (August 19, 1996). ... Signed by Indianapolis Colts to practice squad (November 27, 1996). ... Activated (December 12, 1996). ... Active for all 16 games (1998); did not play.
PRO STATISTICS: W.L.: 1995—Caught one pass for minus eight yards. 1997—Fumbled four times and recovered one fumble for minus eight yards.
SINGLE GAME HIGHS (regular season): Attempts—32 (November 9, 1997, vs. Cincinnati); completions—19 (November 9, 1997, vs. Cincinnati); yards—236 (November 9, 1997, vs. Cincinnati); touchdown passes—1 (November 9, 1997, vs. Cincinnati).
MISCELLANEOUS: Regular-season record as starting NFL quarterback: 0-1.

Year	Team	G	GS	PASSING Att.	Cmp.	Pct.	Yds.	TD	Int.	Avg.	Rat.	RUSHING Att.	Yds.	Avg.	TD	TOTALS TD	2pt.	Pts.
1995	Tampa Bay NFL							Did not play.										
1996	Barcelona W.L.	10	10	319	191	59.9	2382	14	16	7.47	76.8	38	111	2.9	2	2	0	12
—	Indianapolis NFL							Did not play.										
1997	Indianapolis NFL	5	1	73	45	61.6	454	1	8	6.22	44.3	5	5	1.0	0	0	0	0
1998	Indianapolis NFL							Did not play.										
W.L. totals (1 year)		10	10	319	191	59.9	2382	14	16	7.47	76.8	38	111	2.9	2	2	0	12
NFL totals (2 years)		5	1	73	45	61.6	454	1	8	6.22	44.3	5	5	1.0	0	0	0	0
Pro totals (3 years)		15	11	392	236	60.2	2836	15	24	7.23	69.6	43	116	2.7	2	2	0	12

HOLCOMBE, ROBERT — RB — RAMS

PERSONAL: Born December 11, 1975, in Houston. ... 5-11/220. ... Full name: Robert Wayne Holcombe.
HIGH SCHOOL: Jeff Davis Senior (Houston), then Mesa (Ariz.).
COLLEGE: Illinois.
TRANSACTIONS/CAREER NOTES: Selected by St. Louis Rams in second round (37th pick overall) of 1998 NFL draft. ... Signed by Rams (July 2, 1998).
SINGLE GAME HIGHS (regular season): Attempts—21 (September 27, 1998, vs. Arizona); yards—84 (September 27, 1998, vs. Arizona); and rushing touchdowns—2 (September 27, 1998, vs. Arizona).

				RUSHING				RECEIVING				TOTALS		
Year Team	G	GS	Att.	Yds.	Avg.	TD	No.	Yds.	Avg.	TD	TD	2pt.	Pts.	Fum.
1998—St. Louis NFL	13	7	98	230	2.3	2	6	34	5.7	0	2	0	12	0

HOLECEK, JOHN — LB — BILLS

PERSONAL: Born May 7, 1972, in Steger, Ill. ... 6-2/242. ... Full name: John Francis Holecek. ... Name pronounced hol-e-SECK.
HIGH SCHOOL: Marian Catholic (Chicago Heights, Ill.).
COLLEGE: Illinois.
TRANSACTIONS/CAREER NOTES: Selected by Buffalo Bills in fifth round (144th pick overall) of 1995 NFL draft. ... Signed by Bills (June 12, 1995). ... On physically unable to perform list with hamstring injury (August 22-November 21, 1995). ... On injured reserve with knee injury (August 16, 1996-entire season). ... Granted free agency (February 13, 1998). ... Re-signed by Bills (April 27, 1998).
PLAYING EXPERIENCE: Buffalo NFL, 1995, 1997 and 1998. ... Games: 1995 (1/0), 1997 (14/8), 1998 (13/13). Total: 28/21.
PRO STATISTICS: 1997—Credited with 1$^{1}/_{2}$ sacks.

HOLLAND, DARIUS — DT — BROWNS

PERSONAL: Born November 10, 1973, in Petersburg, Va. ... 6-5/320. ... Full name: Darius Jerome Holland.
HIGH SCHOOL: Mayfield (Las Cruces, N.M.).
COLLEGE: Colorado.
TRANSACTIONS/CAREER NOTES: Selected by Green Bay Packers in third round (65th pick overall) of 1995 NFL draft. ... Signed by Packers (July 18, 1995). ... Granted free agency (February 13, 1998). ... Re-signed by Packers (April 10, 1998). ... Traded by Packers to Kansas City Chiefs for DE Vaughn Booker (May 13, 1998). ... Released by Chiefs (October 13, 1998). ... Signed by Detroit Lions (October 19, 1998). ... Granted unconditional free agency (February 12, 1999). ... Signed by Cleveland Browns (April 23, 1999).
PLAYING EXPERIENCE: Green Bay NFL, 1995-1997; Kansas City (6)-Detroit (10) NFL, 1998. ... Games/Games started: 1995 (14/4), 1996 (16/0), 1997 (12/1), 1998 (K.C.-6/0; Det.-10/4; Total: 16/4). Total: 58/9.
CHAMPIONSHIP GAME EXPERIENCE: Played in NFC championship game (1995-97 seasons). ... Member of Super Bowl championship team (1996 season). ... Played in Super Bowl XXXII (1997 season).
PRO STATISTICS: 1995—Credited with 1$^{1}/_{2}$ sacks.

HOLLAS, DONALD — QB

PERSONAL: Born November 22, 1967, in Kingsville, Texas. ... 6-3/215. ... Full name: Donald Wayne Hollas.
HIGH SCHOOL: Lamar (Rosenberg, Texas).
COLLEGE: Rice (degree in political science and managerial studies).
TRANSACTIONS/CAREER NOTES: Selected by Cincinnati Bengals in fourth round (99th pick overall) of 1991 NFL draft. ... Signed by Bengals (July 15, 1991). ... On physically unable to perform list with knee injury (November 23, 1993-remainder of season). ... On injured reserve with separated left shoulder (November 7, 1994-remainder of season). ... Granted unconditional free agency (February 17, 1995). ... Signed by Detroit Lions (April 18, 1995). ... Released by Lions (August 28, 1995). ... Signed by Houston Oilers (May 31, 1996). ... Released by Oilers (August 25, 1996). ... Signed by Washington Redskins (February 21, 1997). ... Released by Redskins (May 6, 1997). ... Signed by Oakland Raiders (May 15, 1997). ... Inactive for all 16 games (1997). ... Granted unconditional free agency (February 12, 1998).
PRO STATISTICS: 1991—Fumbled three times. 1992—Fumbled six times and recovered five fumbles for minus five yards. 1998—Led AFC with 10 fumbles and recovered four fumbles.
SINGLE GAME HIGHS (regular season): Attempts—35 (November 22, 1998, vs. Denver); completions—20 (November 22, 1998, vs. Denver); yards—270 (November 22, 1998, vs. Denver); and touchdown passes—2 (November 29, 1998, vs. Washington).
MISCELLANEOUS: Regular-season record as starting NFL quarterback: 4-4 (.500).

					PASSING						RUSHING			TOTALS		
Year Team	G	GS	Att.	Cmp.	Pct.	Yds.	TD	Int.	Avg.	Rat.	Att.	Yds.	Avg.	TD	TD	2pt.	Pts.
1991—Cincinnati NFL	8	1	55	32	58.2	310	1	4	5.64	49.7	12	66	5.5	0	0	...	0
1992—Cincinnati NFL	10	1	58	35	60.3	335	2	0	5.78	87.9	20	109	5.5	0	0	...	0
1993—Cincinnati NFL									Did not play.								
1994—Cincinnati NFL	2	0	2	0	0.0	0	0	1	...	0.0	0	0	...	0	0	0	0
1995—									Did not play.								
1996—									Did not play.								
1997—Oakland NFL									Did not play.								
1998—Oakland NFL	12	6	260	135	51.9	1754	10	16	6.75	60.6	29	120	4.1	1	1	0	6
Pro totals (4 years)	32	8	375	202	53.9	2399	13	21	6.40	61.9	61	295	4.8	1	1	0	6

HOLLIDAY, VONNIE — DE — PACKERS

PERSONAL: Born December 11, 1975, in Camden, S.C. ... 6-5/296. ... Full name: Dimetry Giovonni Holliday. ... Cousin of Corey Holliday, wide receiver with Pittsburgh Steelers (1995-97).
HIGH SCHOOL: Camden (S.C.).
COLLEGE: North Carolina.
TRANSACTIONS/CAREER NOTES: Selected by Green Bay Packers in first round (19th pick overall) of 1998 NFL draft. ... Signed by Packers (June 15, 1998).
PRO STATISTICS: 1998—Recovered two fumbles.

Year Team	G	GS	SACKS
1998—Green Bay NFL	12	12	8.0

HOLLIER, DWIGHT   LB   DOLPHINS

PERSONAL: Born April 21, 1969, in Hampton, Va. ... 6-2/242. ... Full name: Dwight Leon Hollier Jr.
HIGH SCHOOL: Kecoughtan (Hampton, Va.).
COLLEGE: North Carolina (degree in speech communications and psychology).
TRANSACTIONS/CAREER NOTES: Selected by Miami Dolphins in fourth round (97th pick overall) of 1992 NFL draft. ... Signed by Dolphins (July 10, 1992). ... Granted free agency (February 17, 1995). ... Re-signed by Dolphins (May 9, 1995). ... Granted unconditional free agency (February 14, 1997). ... Re-signed by Dolphins (April 17, 1997).
PLAYING EXPERIENCE: Miami NFL, 1992-1998. ... Games/Games started: 1992 (16/5), 1993 (16/10), 1994 (11/7), 1995 (16/14), 1996 (16/15), 1997 (16/3), 1998 (16/0). Total: 107/54.
CHAMPIONSHIP GAME EXPERIENCE: Played in AFC championship game (1992 season).
PRO STATISTICS: 1992—Credited with one sack and recovered three fumbles. 1993—Recovered one fumble. 1994—Intercepted one pass for 36 yards. 1995—Recovered one fumble. 1996—Intercepted one pass for 11 yards and credited with one sack. 1997—Returned one kickoff for no yards. 1998—Recovered one fumble.

HOLLINQUEST, LAMONT   LB   CHIEFS

PERSONAL: Born October 24, 1970, in Los Angeles. ... 6-3/250. ... Full name: Lamont Bertrell Hollinquest. ... Cousin of Charlie Smith, wide receiver with Philadelphia Eagles (1974-81) and Boston/New Orleans Breakers of USFL (1983-84).
HIGH SCHOOL: Pius X (Downey, Calif.).
COLLEGE: Southern California.
TRANSACTIONS/CAREER NOTES: Selected by Washington Redskins in eighth round (212th pick overall) of 1993 NFL draft. ... Signed by Redskins (July 15, 1993). ... Claimed on waivers by Cincinnati Bengals (December 21, 1994). ... Released by Bengals (August 21, 1995). ... Signed by Green Bay Packers (January 18, 1996). ... Granted free agency (February 14, 1997). ... Re-signed by Packers (June 12, 1997). ... Granted unconditional free agency (February 12, 1999). ... Signed by Kansas City Chiefs (March 5, 1999).
PLAYING EXPERIENCE: Washington NFL, 1993 and 1994; Green Bay NFL, 1996-1998. ... Games/Games started: 1993 (16/0), 1994 (14/0), 1996 (16/0), 1997 (16/0), 1998 (14/2). Total: 76/2.
CHAMPIONSHIP GAME EXPERIENCE: Played in NFC championship game (1996 and 1997 seasons). ... Member of Super Bowl championship team (1996 season). ... Played in Super Bowl XXXII (1997 season).
PRO STATISTICS: 1994—Intercepted one pass for 39 yards, credited with $1/2$ sack and recovered one fumble. 1996—Intercepted one pass for two yards.

HOLLIS, MIKE   K   JAGUARS

PERSONAL: Born May 22, 1972, in Kellogg, Idaho. ... 5-7/175. ... Full name: Michael Shane Hollis.
HIGH SCHOOL: Central Valley (Veradale, Wash.).
COLLEGE: Idaho (degree in sports science, 1996).
TRANSACTIONS/CAREER NOTES: Signed as non-drafted free agent by San Diego Chargers (May 6, 1994). ... Released by Chargers (August 22, 1994). ... Signed by Jacksonville Jaguars (June 5, 1995).
CHAMPIONSHIP GAME EXPERIENCE: Played in AFC championship game (1996 season).
HONORS: Played in Pro Bowl (1997 season).

				KICKING				
Year Team	G	XPM	XPA	FGM	FGA	Lg.	50+	Pts.
1995—Jacksonville NFL	16	27	28	20	27	53	2-3	87
1996—Jacksonville NFL	16	27	27	30	36	53	2-3	117
1997—Jacksonville NFL	16	41	41	31	36	52	2-2	*134
1998—Jacksonville NFL	16	45	45	21	26	47	0-1	108
Pro totals (4 years)	64	140	141	102	125	53	6-9	446

HOLMBERG, ROB   LB   JETS

PERSONAL: Born May 6, 1971, in McKeesport, Pa. ... 6-3/230. ... Full name: Robert Anthony Holmberg.
HIGH SCHOOL: Mt. Pleasant (Pa.).
COLLEGE: Navy, then Penn State.
TRANSACTIONS/CAREER NOTES: Selected by Los Angeles Raiders in seventh round (217th pick overall) of 1994 NFL draft. ... Signed by Raiders for 1994 season. ... Raiders franchise moved to Oakland (July 21, 1995). ... Released by Raiders (August 30, 1998). ... Signed by Indianapolis Colts (September 9, 1998). ... Released by Colts (September 29, 1998). ... Signed by New York Jets (October 27, 1998).
PLAYING EXPERIENCE: Los Angeles Raiders NFL, 1994; Oakland NFL, 1995-1997; Indianapolis (3)-New York Jets (9) NFL, 1998. ... Games/Games started: 1994 (16/0), 1995 (16/0), 1996 (13/1), 1997 (16/0), 1998 (Ind.-3/0; NYJ-9/0; Total: 12/0). Total: 73/1.
CHAMPIONSHIP GAME EXPERIENCE: Played in AFC championship game (1998 season).
PRO STATISTICS: 1995—Credited with one sack and recovered one fumble. 1996—Credited with one sack. 1997—Returned one kickoff for 15 yards and recovered one fumble.

HOLMES, DARICK   RB   COLTS

PERSONAL: Born July 1, 1971, in Pasadena, Calif. ... 6-0/226.
HIGH SCHOOL: John Muir (Pasadena, Calif.).
JUNIOR COLLEGE: Sacramento City College.
COLLEGE: Portland State.
TRANSACTIONS/CAREER NOTES: Selected by Buffalo Bills in seventh round (244th pick overall) of 1995 NFL draft. ... Signed by Bills (June 19, 1995). ... Granted free agency (February 13, 1998). ... Re-signed by Bills (April 24, 1998). ... Traded by Bills to Green Bay Packers for fourth-round pick (TE Bobby Collins) in 1999 draft (September 29, 1998). ... Granted unconditional free agency (February 12, 1999). ... Signed by Indianapolis Colts (April 12, 1999).

PRO STATISTICS: 1995—Recovered two fumbles. 1996—Recovered one fumble. 1997—Recovered one fumble. 1998—Recovered one fumble.
SINGLE GAME HIGHS (regular season): Attempts—30 (December 1, 1996 vs. Indianapolis); yards—163 (November 29, 1998, vs. Philadelphia); and rushing touchdowns—3 (November 3, 1996, vs. Washington).
STATISTICAL PLATEAUS: 100-yard rushing games: 1996 (1), 1998 (2). Total: 3.

				RUSHING				RECEIVING				KICKOFF RETURNS				TOTALS		
Year Team	G	GS	Att.	Yds.	Avg.	TD	No.	Yds.	Avg.	TD	No.	Yds.	Avg.	TD	TD	2pt.	Pts.	Fum.
1995—Buffalo NFL	16	2	172	698	4.1	4	24	214	8.9	0	39	799	20.5	0	4	0	24	4
1996—Buffalo NFL	16	1	189	571	3.0	4	16	102	6.4	0	0	0	...	0	5	1	32	2
1997—Buffalo NFL	13	0	22	106	4.8	2	13	106	8.2	0	23	430	18.7	0	2	0	12	1
1998—Buffalo NFL	3	0	2	8	4.0	0	1	9	9.0	0	1	20	20.0	0	0	0	0	0
—Green Bay NFL	11	4	93	386	4.2	1	19	179	9.4	0	0	0	...	0	1	0	6	1
Pro totals (4 years)	59	7	478	1769	3.7	11	73	610	8.4	1	63	1249	19.8	0	12	1	74	8

HOLMES, EARL — LB — STEELERS

PERSONAL: Born April 28, 1973, in Tallahassee, Fla. ... 6-2/250. ... Full name: Earl L. Holmes.
HIGH SCHOOL: Florida A&M University (Tallahassee, Fla.).
COLLEGE: Florida A&M.
TRANSACTIONS/CAREER NOTES: Selected by Pittsburgh Steelers in fourth round (126th pick overall) of 1996 NFL draft. ... Signed by Steelers (July 16, 1996).
CHAMPIONSHIP GAME EXPERIENCE: Played in AFC championship game (1997 season).
PRO STATISTICS: 1997—Recovered one fumble. 1998—Intercepted one pass for 36 yards.

Year Team	G	GS	SACKS
1996—Pittsburgh NFL	3	1	1.0
1997—Pittsburgh NFL	16	16	4.0
1998—Pittsburgh NFL	14	14	1.5
Pro totals (3 years)	33	31	6.5

HOLMES, KENNY — DE — TITANS

PERSONAL: Born October 24, 1973, in Vero Beach, Fla. ... 6-4/270. ... Full name: Kenneth Holmes.
HIGH SCHOOL: Vero Beach (Fla.).
COLLEGE: Miami, Fla. (degree in criminal justice).
TRANSACTIONS/CAREER NOTES: Selected by Houston Oilers in first round (18th pick overall) of 1997 NFL draft. ... Oilers franchise moved to Tennessee for 1997 season. ... Signed by Oilers (July 18, 1997). ... Oilers franchise renamed Tennessee Titans for 1999 season (December 26, 1998).
PRO STATISTICS: 1997—Recovered one fumble.

Year Team	G	GS	SACKS
1997—Tennessee NFL	16	5	7.0
1998—Tennessee NFL	14	11	2.5
Pro totals (2 years)	30	16	9.5

HOLMES, LESTER — G — CARDINALS

PERSONAL: Born September 27, 1969, in Tylertown, Miss. ... 6-4/315.
HIGH SCHOOL: Tylertown (Miss.).
COLLEGE: Jackson State.
TRANSACTIONS/CAREER NOTES: Selected by Philadelphia Eagles in first round (19th pick overall) of 1993 NFL draft. ... Signed by Eagles (August 2, 1993). ... On injured reserve with knee injury (November 28, 1995-remainder of season). ... Granted free agency (February 16, 1996). ... Re-signed by Eagles (July 17, 1996). ... Granted unconditional free agency (February 14, 1997). ... Signed by Oakland Raiders (May 17, 1997). ... Released by Raiders (February 12, 1998). ... Signed by Arizona Cardinals (February 26, 1998).
PLAYING EXPERIENCE: Philadelphia NFL, 1993-1996; Oakland NFL, 1997; Arizona NFL, 1998. ... Games/Games started: 1993 (12/6), 1994 (16/16), 1995 (2/2), 1996 (14/14), 1997 (15/15), 1998 (16/16). Total: 77/69.
PRO STATISTICS: 1993—Recovered one fumble. 1994—Recovered three fumbles.

HOLMES, PRIEST — RB — RAVENS

PERSONAL: Born October 7, 1973, in Fort Smith, Ark. ... 5-9/205. ... Full name: Priest Anthony Holmes.
HIGH SCHOOL: Marshall (San Antonio).
COLLEGE: Texas.
TRANSACTIONS/CAREER NOTES: Signed as non-drafted free agent by Baltimore Ravens (April 25, 1997).
PRO STATISTICS: 1997—Returned one kickoff for 14 yards. 1998—Attempted one pass with an interception, returned two kickoffs for 30 yards and recovered one fumble for one yard.
SINGLE GAME HIGHS (regular season): Attempts—36 (November 22, 1998, vs. Cincinnati); yards—227 (November 22, 1998, vs. Cincinnati); and rushing touchdowns—2 (November 29, 1998, vs. Indianapolis).
STATISTICAL PLATEAUS: 100-yard rushing games: 1998 (4).

			RUSHING				RECEIVING				TOTALS			
Year Team	G	GS	Att.	Yds.	Avg.	TD	No.	Yds.	Avg.	TD	TD	2pt.	Pts.	Fum.
1997—Baltimore NFL	7	0	0	0	...	0	0	0	...	0	0	0	0	0
1998—Baltimore NFL	16	13	233	1008	4.3	7	43	260	6.0	0	7	0	42	3
Pro totals (2 years)	23	13	233	1008	4.3	7	43	260	6.0	0	7	0	42	3

HOLSEY, BERNARD — DE — GIANTS

PERSONAL: Born December 10, 1973, in Cave Spring, Ga. ... 6-2/295.
HIGH SCHOOL: Coosa (Cave Spring, Ga.).
COLLEGE: Duke.
TRANSACTIONS/CAREER NOTES: Signed as non-drafted free agent by New York Giants (April 26, 1996). ... Granted free agency (February 12, 1999).
PLAYING EXPERIENCE: New York Giants NFL, 1996-1998. ... Games/Games started: 1996 (16/0), 1997 (16/4), 1998 (16/0). Total: 48/4.
PRO STATISTICS: 1997—Credited with 3 $1/2$ sacks.

HOPKINS, BRAD — OT — TITANS

PERSONAL: Born September 5, 1970, in Columbia, S.C. ... 6-3/305. ... Full name: Bradley D. Hopkins.
HIGH SCHOOL: Moline (Ill.).
COLLEGE: Illinois (degree in speech communications, 1993).
TRANSACTIONS/CAREER NOTES: Selected by Houston Oilers in first round (13th pick overall) of 1993 NFL draft. ... Signed by Oilers (August 10, 1993). ... Granted unconditional free agency (February 14, 1997). ... Re-signed by Oilers (March 10, 1997). ... Oilers franchise moved to Tennessee for 1997 season. ... Oilers franchise renamed Tennessee Titans for 1999 season (December 26, 1998).
PLAYING EXPERIENCE: Houston NFL, 1993-1996; Tennessee NFL, 1997 and 1998. ... Games/Games started: 1993 (16/11), 1994 (16/15), 1995 (16/16), 1996 (16/16), 1997 (16/16), 1998 (13/13). Total: 93/87.
PRO STATISTICS: 1994—Recovered one fumble. 1995—Recovered three fumbles. 1996—Recovered one fumble. 1997—Recovered one fumble.

HORAN, MIKE — P

PERSONAL: Born February 1, 1959, in Orange, Calif. ... 5-11/192. ... Full name: Michael William Horan. ... Name pronounced hor-RAN.
HIGH SCHOOL: Sunny Hills (Fullerton, Calif.).
JUNIOR COLLEGE: Fullerton (Calif.) College.
COLLEGE: Long Beach State (degree in mechanical engineering).
TRANSACTIONS/CAREER NOTES: Selected by Atlanta Falcons in ninth round (235th pick overall) of 1982 NFL draft. ... Signed by Falcons for 1982 season. ... Released by Falcons (September 4, 1982). ... Signed by Green Bay Packers (March 15, 1983). ... Released by Packers after failing physical (May 6, 1983). ... Signed by Buffalo Bills (May 25, 1983). ... Released by Bills (August 22, 1983). ... Signed by Philadelphia Eagles (May 7, 1984). ... Released by Eagles (August 28, 1986). ... Signed by Minnesota Vikings (October 31, 1986). ... Active for one game with Vikings (1986); did not play. ... Released by Vikings (November 3, 1986). ... Signed by Denver Broncos (November 25, 1986). ... Granted unconditional free agency (February 1-April 1, 1991). ... Re-signed by Broncos for 1991 season. ... On injured reserve with knee injury (October 22, 1992-remainder of season). ... Released by Broncos (August 30, 1993). ... Signed by New York Giants (November 9, 1993). ... Granted unconditional free agency (February 16, 1996). ... Re-signed by Giants (May 6, 1996). ... Released by Giants (February 14, 1997). ... Signed by St. Louis Rams (October 12, 1997). ... Granted unconditional free agency (February 13, 1998). ... Signed by Chicago Bears (September 23, 1998). ... Granted unconditional free agency (February 12, 1999).
CHAMPIONSHIP GAME EXPERIENCE: Played in AFC championship game (1986, 1987, 1989 and 1991 seasons). ... Played in Super Bowl XXI (1986 season), Super Bowl XXII (1987 season) and Super Bowl XXIV (1989 season).
HONORS: Named punter on THE SPORTING NEWS NFL All-Pro team (1988). ... Played in Pro Bowl (1988 season).
POST SEASON RECORDS: Shares NFL postseason career record for longest punt—76 yards (January 12, 1991, at Buffalo).
PRO STATISTICS: 1985—Rushed once for 12 yards. 1986—Rushed once for no yards, fumbled once and recovered one fumble for minus 12 yards. 1991—Rushed twice for nine yards and recovered one fumble. 1995—Rushed once for no yards, fumbled once and recovered one fumble for minus 18 yards. 1997—Rushed once for minus three yards. 1998—Attempted two passes with one completion for 18 yards and a touchdown.

			PUNTING			
Year Team	G	No.	Yds.	Avg.	Net avg.	In. 20	Blk.
1984—Philadelphia NFL	16	‡92	‡3880	42.2	35.6	21	0
1985—Philadelphia NFL	16	‡91	‡3777	41.5	34.2	20	0
1986—Denver NFL	4	13	571	43.9	34.5	8	0
1987—Denver NFL	12	44	1807	41.1	33.1	11	*2
1988—Denver NFL	16	65	2861	44.0	*37.8	19	0
1989—Denver NFL	16	77	3111	40.4	34.2	24	0
1990—Denver NFL	15	58	2575	*44.4	*38.9	14	1
1991—Denver NFL	16	72	3012	41.8	36.7	24	1
1992—Denver NFL	7	37	1681	45.4	40.2	7	1
1993—New York Giants NFL	8	44	1882	42.8	*39.9	13	0
1994—New York Giants NFL	16	85	3521	41.4	35.2	25	*2
1995—New York Giants NFL	16	72	3063	42.5	36.2	15	0
1996—New York Giants NFL	16	*102	*4289	42.0	35.8	*32	0
1997—St. Louis NFL	10	53	2272	42.9	36.3	10	0
1998—Chicago NFL	13	64	2643	41.3	35.4	12	0
Pro totals (15 years)	197	969	40545	42.3	36.1	255	7

HORN, JOE — WR — CHIEFS

PERSONAL: Born January 16, 1972, in New Haven, Conn. ... 6-1/199. ... Full name: Joseph Horn.
HIGH SCHOOL: Douglas Bird (Fayetteville, N.C.).
JUNIOR COLLEGE: Itawamba Junior College (Miss.).
COLLEGE: None.

TRANSACTIONS/CAREER NOTES: Signed by Memphis Mad Dogs of CFL (March 25, 1995). ... Selected by Kansas City Chiefs in fifth round (135th pick overall) of 1996 NFL draft. ... Signed by Chiefs (June 25, 1996). ... Granted free agency (February 12, 1999). ... Re-signed by Chiefs (April 21, 1999).
PRO STATISTICS: 1996—Rushed once for eight yards. 1998—Rushed once for no yards, returned one punt for six yards and recovered three fumbles for minus eight yards.
SINGLE GAME HIGHS (regular season): Receptions—2 (December 6, 1998, vs. Denver); yards—68 (September 27, 1998, vs. Philadelphia); and touchdown receptions—1 (December 6, 1998, vs. Denver).

				RECEIVING				KICKOFF RETURNS				TOTALS			
Year Team	G	GS	No.	Yds.	Avg.	TD	No.	Yds.	Avg.	TD	TD	2pt.	Pts.	Fum.
1995—Memphis CFL	17	17	71	1415	19.9	5	2	17	8.5	0	5	0	30	0
1996—Kansas City NFL	9	0	2	30	15.0	0	0	0	...	0	0	0	0	0
1997—Kansas City NFL	8	0	2	65	32.5	0	0	0	...	0	0	0	0	0
1998—Kansas City NFL	16	1	14	198	14.1	1	11	233	21.2	0	1	0	6	2
CFL totals (1 year)	17	17	71	1415	19.9	5	2	17	8.5	0	5	0	30	0
NFL totals (3 years)	33	1	18	293	16.3	1	11	233	21.2	0	1	0	6	2
Pro totals (4 years)	50	18	89	1708	19.2	6	13	250	19.2	0	6	0	36	2

HORNE, TONY   WR   RAMS

PERSONAL: Born March 21, 1976, in Montgomery County, N.C. ... 5-9/173. ... Full name: Tony Tremaine Horne.
HIGH SCHOOL: Richmond City (Rockingham, N.C.).
COLLEGE: Clemson.
TRANSACTIONS/CAREER NOTES: Signed as non-drafted free agent by St. Louis Rams (April 20, 1998).
RECORDS: Holds NFL rookie-season record for most kickoff returns—56 (1998).
PRO STATISTICS: 1998—Returned one punt for no yards.

			KICKOFF RETURNS				TOTALS			
Year Team	G	GS	No.	Yds.	Avg.	TD	TD	2pt.	Pts.	Fum.
1998—St. Louis NFL	16	0	56	1306	23.3	1	1	0	6	1

HOUSTON, BOBBY   LB

PERSONAL: Born October 26, 1967, in Washington, D.C. ... 6-2/245.
HIGH SCHOOL: DeMatha Catholic (Hyattsville, Md.).
COLLEGE: North Carolina State (degree in accounting, 1989).
TRANSACTIONS/CAREER NOTES: Selected by Green Bay Packers in third round (75th pick overall) of 1990 NFL draft. ... Signed by Packers (July 23, 1990). ... On reserve/non-football injury list with pneumonia (September 22-December 19, 1990). ... Claimed on waivers by Atlanta Falcons (December 21, 1990). ... On inactive list for two games with Falcons (1990). ... Granted unconditional free agency (February 1, 1991). ... Signed by New York Jets (March 27, 1991). ... Granted unconditional free agency (February 17, 1995). ... Re-signed by Jets (February 17, 1995). ... Released by Jets (July 21, 1997). ... Signed by Kansas City Chiefs (August 4, 1997). ... Released by Chiefs (October 9, 1997). ... Signed by San Diego Chargers (October 22, 1997). ... On injured reserve with leg injury (November 4, 1997-remainder of season). ... Granted unconditional free agency (February 13, 1998). ... Signed by Minnesota Vikings (March 24, 1998). ... Granted unconditional free agency (February 12, 1999).
CHAMPIONSHIP GAME EXPERIENCE: Played in NFC championship game (1998 season).
PRO STATISTICS: 1991—Recovered one fumble. 1993—Recovered one fumble. 1994—Recovered one fumble. 1995—Recovered three fumbles. 1996—Recovered one fumble. 1998—Recovered one fumble for 14 yards.

			INTERCEPTIONS				SACKS
Year Team	G	GS	No.	Yds.	Avg.	TD	No.
1990—Green Bay NFL	1	0	0	0	...	0	0.0
1991—New York Jets NFL	15	0	0	0	...	0	1.0
1992—New York Jets NFL	16	15	1	20	20.0	1	4.0
1993—New York Jets NFL	16	14	1	0	0.0	0	3.0
1994—New York Jets NFL	16	16	0	0	...	0	3.5
1995—New York Jets NFL	16	15	0	0	...	0	3.0
1996—New York Jets NFL	15	15	2	3	1.5	0	0.0
1997—Kansas City NFL	5	0	0	0	...	0	0.0
—San Diego NFL	2	0	0	0	...	0	0.0
1998—Minnesota NFL	8	1	0	0	...	0	0.0
Pro totals (9 years)	110	76	4	23	5.8	1	14.5

HOWARD, CHRIS   RB   JAGUARS

PERSONAL: Born May 5, 1975, in River Ridge, La. ... 5-10/223.
HIGH SCHOOL: John Curtis (River Ridge, La.).
COLLEGE: Michigan.
TRANSACTIONS/CAREER NOTES: Selected by Denver Broncos in fifth round (153rd pick overall) of 1998 NFL draft. ... Signed by Broncos (July 22, 1998). ... Released by Broncos (August 30, 1998). ... Re-signed by Broncos to practice squad (September 8, 1998). ... Released by Broncos (September 22, 1998). ... Signed by Jacksonville Jaguars (September 22, 1998).
SINGLE GAME HIGHS (regular season): Attempts—7 (October 18, 1998, vs. Buffalo); yards—16 (October 18, 1998, vs. Buffalo); and rushing touchdowns—0.

			RUSHING				RECEIVING				TOTALS			
Year Team	G	GS	Att.	Yds.	Avg.	TD	No.	Yds.	Avg.	TD	TD	2pt.	Pts.	Fum.
1998—Jacksonville NFL	8	0	7	16	2.3	0	1	3	3.0	0	0	0	0	0

HOWARD, DESMOND — WR

PERSONAL: Born May 15, 1970, in Cleveland. ... 5-10/185. ... Full name: Desmond Kevin Howard.
HIGH SCHOOL: St. Joseph (Cleveland).
COLLEGE: Michigan (degree in communication studies).
TRANSACTIONS/CAREER NOTES: Selected by Washington Redskins in first round (fourth pick overall) of 1992 NFL draft. ... Signed by Redskins (August 25, 1992). ... On injured reserve with separated shoulder (December 29, 1992-remainder of 1992 season playoffs). ... Selected by Jacksonville Jaguars from Redskins in NFL expansion draft (February 15, 1995). ... Granted unconditional free agency (February 16, 1996). ... Signed by Green Bay Packers (July 11, 1996). ... Granted unconditional free agency (February 14, 1997). ... Signed by Oakland Raiders (March 4, 1997). ... Released by Raiders (June 9, 1999).
CHAMPIONSHIP GAME EXPERIENCE: Played in NFC championship game (1996 season). ... Member of Super Bowl championship team (1996 season).
HONORS: Heisman Trophy winner (1991). ... Named College Football Player of the Year by THE SPORTING NEWS (1991). ... Maxwell Award winner (1991). ... Named wide receiver on THE SPORTING NEWS college All-America first team (1991). ... Named punt returner on THE SPORTING NEWS NFL All-Pro team (1996). ... Named Most Valuable Player of Super Bowl XXXI (1996 season).
RECORDS: Holds NFL single-season record for most yards by punt return—875 (1996).
POST SEASON RECORDS: Holds Super Bowl and NFL postseason record for longest kickoff return—99 yards (January 26, 1997, vs. New England). ... Holds Super Bowl single-game record for most yards by punt return—90 (January 26, 1997, vs. New England). ... Shares Super Bowl career and single-game records for most punt returns—6. ... Shares Super Bowl single-game records for most combined yards—244; most combined yards by kick returns—244; most touchdowns by kickoff return—1 (January 26, 1997, vs. New England). ... Shares NFL postseason single-game record for most combined yards —244; most combined kick return yards—244; and most touchdowns by kickoff return—1 (January 26, 1997, vs. New England).
PRO STATISTICS: 1992—Fumbled once. 1996—Fumbled twice and recovered one fumble. 1997—Fumbled twice and recovered two fumbles. 1998—Fumbled four times.
SINGLE GAME HIGHS (regular season): Receptions—7 (November 20, 1994, vs. Dallas); yards—130 (December 4, 1994, vs. Tampa Bay); and touchdown receptions—1 (October 1, 1995, vs. Houston).
STATISTICAL PLATEAUS: 100-yard receiving games: 1994 (2).

				RUSHING				RECEIVING				PUNT RETURNS				KICKOFF RETURNS				TOTALS		
Year Team	G	GS	Att.	Yds.	Avg.	TD	No.	Yds.	Avg.	TD	No.	Yds.	Avg.	TD	No.	Yds.	Avg.	TD	TD	2pt.	Pts.
1992—Washington NFL	16	1	3	14	4.7	0	3	20	6.7	0	6	84	14.0	1	22	462	21.0	0	1	...	6
1993—Washington NFL	16	5	2	17	8.5	0	23	286	12.4	0	4	25	6.3	0	21	405	19.3	0	0	...	0
1994—Washington NFL	16	15	1	4	4.0	0	40	727	18.2	5	0	0	...	0	0	0	...	0	5	1	32
1995—Jacksonville NFL	13	7	1	8	8.0	0	26	276	10.6	1	24	246	10.3	0	10	178	17.8	0	1	0	6
1996—Green Bay NFL	16	0	0	0	...	0	13	95	7.3	0	*58	*875	*15.1	*3	22	460	20.9	0	3	0	18
1997—Oakland NFL	15	0	0	0	...	0	4	30	7.5	0	27	210	7.8	0	*61	§1318	21.6	0	0	0	0
1998—Oakland NFL	15	1	0	0	...	0	2	16	8.0	0	§45	541	12.0	†2	§49	1040	21.2	0	2	0	12
Pro totals (7 years)	107	29	7	43	6.1	0	111	1450	13.1	6	164	1981	12.1	6	185	3863	20.9	0	12	1	74

HOWARD, EDDIE — P — BUCCANEERS

PERSONAL: Born October 6, 1972, in West Covina, Calif. ... 6-1/203.
HIGH SCHOOL: Covina (Calif.).
COLLEGE: Idaho.
TRANSACTIONS/CAREER NOTES: Signed as non-drafted free agent by Green Bay Packers (July 26, 1995). ... Released by Packers (August 17, 1995). ... Signed by Detroit Lions (April 26, 1996). ... Released by Lions (June 25, 1996). ... Signed by Chicago Bears (June 17, 1997). ... Relesed by Bears (August 5, 1997). ... Signed by Washington Redskins (April 23, 1998). ... Released by Redskins (August 29, 1998). ... Signed by San Francisco 49ers (September 2, 1998). ... Released by 49ers (September 15, 1998). ... Signed by Tampa Bay Buccaneers (February 24, 1999).

				PUNTING			
Year Team	G	No.	Yds.	Avg.	Net avg.	In. 20	Blk.
1998—San Francisco NFL	2	9	324	36.0	32.8	2	0

HOWARD, TY — CB — CARDINALS

PERSONAL: Born November 30, 1973, in Columbus, Ohio. ... 5-9/185.
HIGH SCHOOL: Briggs (Columbus, Ohio).
COLLEGE: Ohio State.
TRANSACTIONS/CAREER NOTES: Selected by Arizona Cardinals in third round (84th pick overall) of 1997 NFL draft. ... Signed by Cardinals (June 10, 1997).
PLAYING EXPERIENCE: Arizona NFL, 1997 and 1998. ... Games/Games started: 1997 (15/2), 1998 (9/0). Total: 24/2.
PRO STATISTICS: 1997—Credited with one sack.

HOYING, BOBBY — QB — EAGLES

PERSONAL: Born September 20, 1972, in St. Henry, Ohio. ... 6-3/221. ... Full name: Robert Carl Hoying.
HIGH SCHOOL: St. Henry (Ohio).
COLLEGE: Ohio State (degree in production and operations management).
TRANSACTIONS/CAREER NOTES: Selected by Philadelphia Eagles in third round (85th pick overall) of 1996 NFL draft. ... Signed by Eagles (July 15, 1996). ... Granted free agency (February 12, 1999). ... Re-signed by Eagles (April 15, 1999).
PRO STATISTICS: 1997—Fumbled seven times and recovered one fumble. 1998—Fumbled six times and recovered two fumbles for minus two yards.
SINGLE GAME HIGHS (regular season): Attempts—42 (November 30, 1997, vs. Cincinnati); completions—26 (November 30, 1997, vs. Cincinnati); yards—313 (November 30, 1997, vs. Cincinnati); and touchdown passes—4 (November 30, 1997, vs. Cincinnati).
STATISTICAL PLATEAUS: 300-yard passing games: 1997 (1).
MISCELLANEOUS: Regular-season record as starting NFL quarterback: 3-9-1 (.269).

					PASSING					RUSHING				TOTALS	
Year Team	G	GS	Att.	Cmp.	Pct.	Yds.	TD	Int.	Avg.	Rat.	Att.	Yds.	Avg.	TD	TD	2pt.	Pts.
1996—Philadelphia NFL	1	0	0	0	...	0	0	0	...	...	0	0	...	0	0	0	0
1997—Philadelphia NFL	7	6	225	128	56.9	1573	11	6	6.99	83.7	16	78	4.9	0	0	0	0
1998—Philadelphia NFL	8	7	224	114	50.9	961	0	9	4.29	45.6	22	84	3.8	0	0	0	0
Pro totals (3 years)	16	13	449	242	53.9	2534	11	15	5.64	64.8	38	162	4.3	0	0	0	0

HUARD, DAMON — QB — DOLPHINS

PERSONAL: Born July 9, 1973, in Yakima, Wash. ... 6-3/215.
HIGH SCHOOL: Puyallup (Wash.).
COLLEGE: Washington.
TRANSACTIONS/CAREER NOTES: Signed as non-drafted free agent by Cincinnati Bengals (April 23, 1996). ... Released by Bengals (August 19, 1996). ... Signed by Miami Dolphins (April 24, 1997). ... Released by Dolphins (August 24, 1997). ... Re-signed by Dolphins to practice squad (August 26, 1997). ... Activated (September 6, 1997); did not play. ... Played with Frankfurt Galaxy of NFL Europe League (February 1998).
SINGLE GAME HIGHS (regular season): Attempts—6 (December 27, 1998, vs. Atlanta); completions—4 (December 27, 1998, vs. Atlanta); yards—64 (December 27, 1998, vs. Atlanta); and touchdown passes—0.

					PASSING					RUSHING				TOTALS	
Year Team	G	GS	Att.	Cmp.	Pct.	Yds.	TD	Int.	Avg.	Rat.	Att.	Yds.	Avg.	TD	TD	2pt.	Pts.
1997—Miami NFL						Did not play.											
1998—Frankfurt NFLE	10	10	290	159	54.8	1857	12	7	6.40	78.2	28	65	2.3	1	1	...	6
—Miami NFL	2	0	9	6	66.7	85	0	1	9.44	57.4	0	0	...	0	0	0	0
NFL Europe totals (1 year)	10	10	290	159	54.8	1857	12	7	6.40	78.2	28	65	2.3	1	1	0	6
NFL totals (1 year)	2	0	9	6	66.7	85	0	1	9.44	57.4	0	0	...	0	0	0	0
Pro totals (2 years)	12	10	299	165	55.2	1942	12	8	6.49	77.4	28	65	2.3	1	1	0	6

HUDSON, CHRIS — S — BEARS

PERSONAL: Born October 6, 1971, in Houston. ... 5-10/199. ... Full name: Christopher Reshard Hudson.
HIGH SCHOOL: E.E. Worthing (Houston).
COLLEGE: Colorado (degree in business, 1995).
TRANSACTIONS/CAREER NOTES: Selected by Jacksonville Jaguars in third round (71st pick overall) of 1995 NFL draft. ... Signed by Jaguars (June 1, 1995). ... On injured reserve with groin injury (September 28, 1995-remainder of season). ... Granted free agency (February 13, 1998). ... Re-signed by Jaguars (June 10, 1998). ... Granted unconditional free agency (February 12, 1999). ... Signed by Chicago Bears (April 22, 1999).
CHAMPIONSHIP GAME EXPERIENCE: Played in AFC championship game (1996 season).
HONORS: Jim Thorpe Award winner (1994).
PRO STATISTICS: 1996—Recovered two fumbles. 1997—Returned blocked field goal attempt 58 yards for a touchdown and recovered two fumbles for 32 yards and one touchdown. 1998—Recovered one fumble.
MISCELLANEOUS: Holds Jacksonville Jaguars all-time record for most interceptions (8).

			INTERCEPTIONS				PUNT RETURNS				TOTALS		
Year Team	G	GS	No.	Yds.	Avg.	TD	No.	Yds.	Avg.	TD	TD	2pt.	Pts.	Fum.
1995—Jacksonville NFL	1	0	0	0	...	0	0	0	...	0	0	0	0	0
1996—Jacksonville NFL	16	16	2	25	12.5	0	32	348	10.9	0	0	0	0	3
1997—Jacksonville NFL	16	16	3	26	8.7	0	0	0	...	0	2	0	12	1
1998—Jacksonville NFL	13	13	3	10	3.3	0	0	0	...	0	0	0	0	0
Pro totals (4 years)	46	45	8	61	7.6	0	32	348	10.9	0	2	0	12	4

HUDSON, JOHN — C/G — JETS

PERSONAL: Born January 29, 1968, in Memphis, Tenn. ... 6-2/270. ... Full name: John Lewis Hudson.
HIGH SCHOOL: Henry County (Paris, Tenn.).
COLLEGE: Auburn.
TRANSACTIONS/CAREER NOTES: Selected by Philadelphia Eagles in 11th round (294th pick overall) of 1990 NFL draft. ... Signed by Eagles (July 31, 1990). ... On physically unable to perform list with knee laceration (August 2, 1990-entire season). ... Granted unconditional free agency (February 1-April 1, 1992). ... Re-signed by Eagles (July 23, 1992). ... On injured reserve with broken hand (September 28, 1992-remainder of season). ... Granted free agency (March 1, 1993). ... Re-signed by Eagles (May 12, 1993). ... Granted unconditional free agency (February 17, 1994). ... Re-signed by Eagles (April 7, 1994). ... Granted unconditional free agency (February 16, 1996). ... Signed by New York Jets (February 26, 1996).
PLAYING EXPERIENCE: Philadelphia NFL, 1991-1995; New York Jets NFL, 1996-1998. ... Games/Games started: 1991 (16/0), 1992 (3/0), 1993 (16/0), 1994 (16/0), 1995 (16/0), 1996 (16/0), 1997 (16/0), 1998 (16/0). Total: 115/0.
CHAMPIONSHIP GAME EXPERIENCE: Played in AFC championship game (1998 season).
PRO STATISTICS: 1991—Fumbled once. 1993—Fumbled once.

HUGHES, DANAN — WR — SAINTS

PERSONAL: Born December 11, 1970, in Bayonne, N.J. ... 6-2/211. ... Full name: Robert Danan Hughes. ... Name pronounced DAY-nin.
HIGH SCHOOL: Bayonne (N.J.).
COLLEGE: Iowa (degree in communications).
TRANSACTIONS/CAREER NOTES: Selected by Kansas City Chiefs in seventh round (186th pick overall) of 1993 NFL draft. ... Signed by Chiefs (May 27, 1993). ... Released by Chiefs (September 6, 1993). ... Re-signed by Chiefs to practice squad (September 8, 1993). ... Activated (November 17, 1993). ... Granted free agency (February 16, 1996). ... Re-signed by Chiefs (May 6, 1996). ... Granted unconditional free agency (February 13, 1998). ... Re-signed by Chiefs (April 24, 1998). ... Released by Chiefs (February 26, 1999). ... Signed by New Orleans Saints (April 23, 1999).

CHAMPIONSHIP GAME EXPERIENCE: Played in AFC championship game (1993 season).
PRO STATISTICS: 1995—Rushed once for five yards. 1996—Attempted one pass with a completion for 30 yards. 1997—Recovered two fumbles for seven yards and one touchdown. 1998—Attempted one pass with a completion for 25 yards and recovered two fumbles.
SINGLE GAME HIGHS (regular season): Receptions—5 (September 15, 1996, vs. Seattle); yards—53 (November 13, 1994, vs. San Diego); and touchdown receptions—1 (November 16, 1997, vs. Denver).

				RECEIVING				PUNT RETURNS				KICKOFF RETURNS				TOTALS		
Year Team	G	GS	No.	Yds.	Avg.	TD	No.	Yds.	Avg.	TD	No.	Yds.	Avg.	TD	TD	2pt.	Pts.	Fum.
1993—Kansas City NFL	6	0	0	0	...	0	3	49	16.3	0	14	266	19.0	0	0	...	0	0
1994—Kansas City NFL	16	0	7	80	11.4	0	27	192	7.1	0	9	190	21.1	0	0	0	0	0
1995—Kansas City NFL	16	0	14	103	7.4	1	3	9	3.0	0	1	18	18.0	0	1	0	6	0
1996—Kansas City NFL	15	2	17	167	9.8	1	0	0	...	0	2	42	21.0	0	1	0	6	0
1997—Kansas City NFL	16	1	7	65	9.3	2	0	0	...	0	1	21	21.0	0	3	0	18	0
1998—Kansas City NFL	16	0	1	10	10.0	0	2	10	5.0	0	0	0	...	0	0	0	0	0
Pro totals (6 years)	85	3	46	425	9.2	4	35	260	7.4	0	27	537	19.9	0	5	0	30	0

HUGHES, TYRONE — CB/KR

PERSONAL: Born January 14, 1970, in New Orleans. ... 5-9/175. ... Full name: Tyrone Christopher Hughes.
HIGH SCHOOL: St. Augustine (New Orleans).
COLLEGE: Nebraska.
TRANSACTIONS/CAREER NOTES: Selected by New Orleans Saints in fifth round (137th pick overall) of 1993 NFL draft. ... Signed by Saints (July 16, 1993). ... Granted unconditional free agency (February 14, 1997). ... Signed by Chicago Bears (April 11, 1997). ... Released by Bears (April 24, 1998). ... Signed by Baltimore Ravens (July 30, 1998). ... Released by Ravens (August 25, 1998). ... Signed by Dallas Cowboys (December 3, 1998). ... Granted unconditional free agency (February 12, 1999).
HONORS: Played in Pro Bowl (1993 season).
RECORDS: Holds NFL single-season records for most kickoff returns—70 (1996); and yards by kickoff return—1,791 (1996). ... Holds NFL single-game records for most kickoff returns—304; and most yards by combined kick return—347 (October 23, 1994, vs. Los Angeles Rams). ... Shares NFL single-season record for most touchdowns by fumble recovery—2 (1994); and most touchdowns by recovery of opponents' fumbles—2 (1994). ... Shares NFL single-game records for most touchdowns by kickoff return—2; and most touchdowns by combined kick return—2 (October 23, 1994, vs. Los Angeles Rams).
PRO STATISTICS: 1994—Rushed twice for six yards and recovered three fumbles for 128 yards and two touchdowns. 1997—Rushed once for three yards, caught eight passes for 68 yards and recovered two fumbles.

			INTERCEPTIONS				PUNT RETURNS				KICKOFF RETURNS				TOTALS			
Year Team	G	GS	No.	Yds.	Avg.	TD	No.	Yds.	Avg.	TD	No.	Yds.	Avg.	TD	TD	2pt.	Pts.	Fum.
1993—New Orleans NFL	16	0	0	0	...	0	‡37	*503	*13.6	†2	30	753	25.1	†1	3	...	18	0
1994—New Orleans NFL	15	5	2	31	15.5	0	21	143	6.8	0	*63	*1556	24.7	2	4	0	24	7
1995—New Orleans NFL	16	2	2	19	9.5	0	28	262	9.4	0	*66	*1617	24.5	0	0	0	0	2
1996—New Orleans NFL	16	1	0	0	...	0	30	152	5.1	0	*70	*1791	25.6	0	0	0	0	2
1997—Chicago NFL	14	0	0	0	...	0	36	258	7.2	0	43	1008	23.4	0	0	0	0	2
1998—Dallas NFL	4	0	0	0	...	0	10	93	9.3	0	11	274	24.9	0	0	0	0	1
Pro totals (6 years)	81	8	4	50	12.5	0	162	1411	8.7	2	283	6999	24.7	3	7	0	42	14

HUNDON, JAMES — WR — BENGALS

PERSONAL: Born April 9, 1971, in Daly City, Calif. ... 6-1/173.
HIGH SCHOOL: Jefferson (Daly City, Calif.).
JUNIOR COLLEGE: San Francisco Community College.
COLLEGE: Portland State.
TRANSACTIONS/CAREER NOTES: Signed as non-drafted free agent by Cincinnati Bengals (April 23, 1996). ... Released by Bengals (August 27, 1996). ... Re-signed by Bengals to practice squad (November 19, 1996). ... Activated (November 22, 1996).
PRO STATISTICS: 1996—Returned one punt for minus seven yards.
SINGLE GAME HIGHS (regular season): Receptions—5 (November 30, 1997, vs. Philadelphia); yards—118 (November 30, 1997, vs. Philadelphia); and touchdown receptions—2 (November 30, 1997, vs. Philadelphia).
STATISTICAL PLATEAUS: 100-yard receiving games: 1997 (1).

			RECEIVING				KICKOFF RETURNS				TOTALS			
Year Team	G	GS	No.	Yds.	Avg.	TD	No.	Yds.	Avg.	TD	TD	2pt.	Pts.	Fum.
1996—Cincinnati NFL	5	0	1	14	14.0	1	10	237	23.7	0	1	0	6	1
1997—Cincinnati NFL	16	0	16	285	17.8	2	10	169	16.9	0	2	0	12	1
1998—Cincinnati NFL	9	3	10	112	11.2	1	0	0	...	0	1	0	6	0
Pro totals (3 years)	30	3	27	411	15.2	4	20	406	20.3	0	4	0	24	2

HUNTER, BRICE — WR — BUCCANEERS

PERSONAL: Born April 21, 1974, in Valdosta, Ga. ... 6-2/209. ... Full name: Brice H. Hunter.
HIGH SCHOOL: Valdosta (Ga.).
COLLEGE: Georgia.
TRANSACTIONS/CAREER NOTES: Selected by Miami Dolphins in seventh round (251st pick overall) of 1996 NFL draft. ... Signed by Dolphins for 1996 season. ... Released by Dolphins (August 24, 1996). ... Signed by San Francisco 49ers to practice squad (September 16, 1996). ... Released by 49ers (September 26, 1996). ... Signed by Tampa Bay Buccaneers to practice squad (October 16, 1996). ... Released by Buccaneers (August 24, 1997). ... Re-signed by Buccaneers to practice squad (August 26, 1997). ... Activated (August 30, 1997). ... Released by Buccaneers (September 16, 1997). ... Re-signed by Buccaneers to practice squad (September 18, 1997). ... Activated (November 28, 1997). ... Released by Buccaneers (December 8, 1997). ... Re-signed by Buccaneers to practice squad (December 9, 1997). ... On injured reserve with knee injury (December 22, 1998-remainder of season).
SINGLE GAME HIGHS (regular season): Receptions—1 (December 13, 1998, vs. Pittsburgh); yards—45 (November 29, 1998, vs. Chicago); and touchdown receptions—1 (November 29, 1998, vs. Chicago).

				RECEIVING			TOTALS			
Year Team	G	GS	No.	Yds.	Avg.	TD	TD	2pt.	Pts.	Fum.
1996—Tampa Bay NFL						Did not play.				
1997—Tampa Bay NFL	3	0	0	0	...	0	0	0	0	0
1998—Tampa Bay NFL	10	0	4	73	18.3	1	1	1	8	0
Pro totals (2 years)	13	0	4	73	18.3	1	1	1	8	0

HUNTINGTON, GREG G BEARS

PERSONAL: Born September 22, 1970, in Mountain Brook, Ala. ... 6-3/308. ... Full name: Gregory Gerard Huntington.
HIGH SCHOOL: Moeller (Cincinnati).
COLLEGE: Penn State (degree in economics).
TRANSACTIONS/CAREER NOTES: Selected by Washington Redskins in fifth round (128th pick overall) of 1993 NFL draft. ... Signed by Redskins for 1993 season. ... Released by Redskins (August 28, 1994). ... Signed by Jacksonville Jaguars (December 15, 1994). ... Released by Jaguars (November 21, 1995). ... Re-signed by Jaguars (December 26, 1995). ... Released by Jaguars (August 25, 1996). ... Re-signed by Jaguars (October 1, 1996). ... Released by Jaguars (October 15, 1996). ... Re-signed by Jaguars (November 19, 1996). ... Granted free agency (February 14, 1997). ... Re-signed by Jaguars (May 9, 1997). ... Released by Jaguars (August 24, 1997). ... Signed by Chicago Bears (October 28, 1997).
PLAYING EXPERIENCE: Washington NFL, 1993; Jacksonville NFL, 1995 and 1996; Chicago NFL, 1997 and 1998. ... Games/Games started: 1993 (9/0), 1995 (4/0), 1996 (2/0), 1997 (1/0), 1998 (3/0). Total: 19/0.
CHAMPIONSHIP GAME EXPERIENCE: Member of Jaguars for AFC championship game (1996 season); inactive.

HUNTLEY, RICHARD RB STEELERS

PERSONAL: Born September 18, 1972, in Monroe, N.C. ... 5-11/225. ... Full name: Richard Earl Huntley.
HIGH SCHOOL: Monroe (N.C.).
COLLEGE: Winston-Salem (N.C.) State.
TRANSACTIONS/CAREER NOTES: Selected by Atlanta Falcons in fourth round (117th pick overall) of 1996 NFL draft. ... Signed by Falcons for 1996 season. ... Released by Falcons (August 18, 1997). ... Signed by Pittsburgh Steelers (February 13, 1998).
SINGLE GAME HIGHS (regular season): Attempts—21 (October 18, 1998, vs. Baltimore); yards—85 (October 11, 1998, vs. Cincinnati); and rushing touchdowns—1 (October 11, 1998, vs. Cincinnati).

			RUSHING				RECEIVING				KICKOFF RETURNS				TOTALS			
Year Team	G	GS	Att.	Yds.	Avg.	TD	No.	Yds.	Avg.	TD	No.	Yds.	Avg.	TD	TD	2pt.	Pts.	Fum.
1996—Atlanta NFL	1	0	2	8	4.0	0	1	14	14.0	0	0	0	...	0	0	0	0	0
1997—									Did not play.									
1998—Pittsburgh NFL	16	1	55	242	4.4	1	3	18	6.0	0	6	119	19.8	0	1	0	6	5
Pro totals (2 years)	17	1	57	250	4.4	1	4	32	8.0	0	6	119	19.8	0	1	0	6	5

HUSTED, MICHAEL K RAIDERS

PERSONAL: Born June 16, 1970, in El Paso, Texas. ... 6-0/190. ... Full name: Michael James Husted.
HIGH SCHOOL: Hampton (Va.).
COLLEGE: Virginia (degree in sociology, 1992).
TRANSACTIONS/CAREER NOTES: Signed as non-drafted free agent by Tampa Bay Buccaneers (May 3, 1993). ... Granted free agency (February 16, 1996). ... Tendered offer sheet by San Francisco 49ers (February 21, 1996). ... Offer matched by Buccaneers (February 28, 1996). ... Released by Buccaneers (February 11, 1999). ... Signed by Oakland Raiders (February 24, 1999).
PRO STATISTICS: 1994—Punted twice for 53 yards. 1998—Rushed once for 20 yards.

				KICKING				
Year Team	G	XPM	XPA	FGM	FGA	Lg.	50+	Pts.
1993—Tampa Bay NFL	16	27	27	16	22	57	3-5	75
1994—Tampa Bay NFL	16	20	20	23	35	53	1-5	89
1995—Tampa Bay NFL	16	25	25	19	26	53	3-3	82
1996—Tampa Bay NFL	16	18	19	25	32	50	1-3	93
1997—Tampa Bay NFL	16	32	35	13	17	54	1-3	71
1998—Tampa Bay NFL	16	29	30	21	28	52	1-1	92
Pro totals (6 years)	96	151	156	117	160	57	10-20	502

HUTSON, TONY G/OT COWBOYS

PERSONAL: Born March 13, 1974, in Houston ... 6-3/306.
HIGH SCHOOL: MacArthur (Houston).
JUNIOR COLLEGE: Kilgore (Texas) College.
COLLEGE: Northeastern Oklahoma State.
TRANSACTIONS/CAREER NOTES: Signed as non-drafted free agent by Dallas Cowboys (April 23, 1996). ... Released by Cowboys (August 25, 1996). ... Re-signed by Cowboys to practice squad (August 27, 1996). ... Activated (January 5, 1997). ... Released by Cowboys (August 24, 1997). ... Re-signed by Cowboys to practice squad (August 26, 1997). ... Activated (November 4, 1997).
PLAYING EXPERIENCE: Dallas NFL, 1997 and 1998. ... Games/Games started: 1997 (5/1), 1998 (9/1). Total: 14/2.

HUTTON, TOM P

PERSONAL: Born July 8, 1972, in Memphis. ... 6-1/193. ... Full name: William Thomas Hutton.
HIGH SCHOOL: Memphis University High.
COLLEGE: Tennessee (degree in public relations, 1994).

TRANSACTIONS/CAREER NOTES: Signed as non-drafted free agent by Philadelphia Eagles (April 26, 1995). ... Granted unconditional free agency (February 12, 1999).
PRO STATISTICS: 1995—Fumbled once for minus 19 yards. 1996—Recovered one fumble. 1997—Rushed once for no yards, fumbled once and recovered one fumble for minus one yard.

				PUNTING			
Year Team	G	No.	Yds.	Avg.	Net avg.	In. 20	Blk.
1995—Philadelphia NFL	16	85	3682	43.3	3.3	20	1
1996—Philadelphia NFL	16	73	3107	42.6	35.1	17	1
1997—Philadelphia NFL	16	87	3660	42.1	34.6	19	1
1998—Philadelphia NFL	16	*104	4339	41.7	34.9	21	0
Pro totals (4 years)	64	349	14788	42.4	27.2	77	3

IRVIN, KEN   CB   BILLS

PERSONAL: Born July 11, 1972, in Rome, Ga. ... 5-10/186. ... Full name: Kenneth Irvin.
HIGH SCHOOL: Pepperell (Lindale, Ga.).
COLLEGE: Memphis (degree in criminal justice, 1998).
TRANSACTIONS/CAREER NOTES: Selected by Buffalo Bills in fourth round (109th pick overall) of 1995 NFL draft. ... Signed by Bills (July 10, 1995). ... Granted free agency (February 13, 1998). ... Re-signed by Bills (April 17, 1998). ... Granted unconditional free agency (February 12, 1999). ... Re-signed by Bills (March 17, 1999).
PLAYING EXPERIENCE: Buffalo NFL, 1995-1998. ... Games/Games started: 1995 (16/3), 1996 (16/1), 1997 (16/0), 1998 (16/16). Total: 64/20.
PRO STATISTICS: 1995—Returned one kickoff for 12 yards. 1996—Credited with two sacks and recovered one fumble. 1997—Intercepted two passes for 28 yards. 1998—Intercepted one pass for 43 yards.

IRVIN, MICHAEL   WR   COWBOYS

PERSONAL: Born March 5, 1966, in Fort Lauderdale, Fla. ... 6-2/207. ... Full name: Michael Jerome Irvin. ... Cousin of Sedrick Irvin, running back, Detroit Lions.
HIGH SCHOOL: St. Thomas Aquinas (Fort Lauderdale, Fla.).
COLLEGE: Miami, Fla. (degree in business management, 1988).
TRANSACTIONS/CAREER NOTES: Selected by Dallas Cowboys in first round (11th pick overall) of 1988 NFL draft. ... Signed by Cowboys (July 9, 1988). ... On injured reserve with knee injury (October 17, 1989-remainder of season). ... On injured reserve with knee injury (September 4-October 7, 1990). ... Granted free agency (February 1, 1992). ... Re-signed by Cowboys (September 3, 1992). ... Designated by Cowboys as transition player (February 25, 1993). ... On suspended list for violating league substance abuse policy (August 26-October 1, 1996).
CHAMPIONSHIP GAME EXPERIENCE: Played in NFC championship game (1992-1995 seasons). ... Member of Super Bowl championship team (1992, 1993 and 1995 seasons).
HONORS: Named wide receiver on THE SPORTING NEWS college All-America second team (1986). ... Named wide receiver on THE SPORTING NEWS NFL All-Pro team (1991). ... Played in Pro Bowl (1991-1995 seasons). ... Named Outstanding Player of Pro Bowl (1991 season).
RECORDS: Holds NFL single-season record for most games with 100 or more yards receiving—11 (1995). ... Shares NFL record for most consecutive games with 100 or more yards receiving—7 (1995).
PRO STATISTICS: 1988—Rushed once for two yards. 1989—Rushed once for six yards and recovered one fumble. 1991—Recovered one fumble. 1992—Rushed once for minus nine yards and recovered one fumble. 1993—Rushed twice for six yards. 1998—Rushed once for one yard.
SINGLE GAME HIGHS (regular season): Receptions—12 (October 27, 1996, vs. Miami); yards—210 (September 20, 1992, vs. Arizona); and touchdown receptions—3 (September 20, 1992, vs. Arizona).
STATISTICAL PLATEAUS: 100-yard receiving games: 1988 (1), 1989 (1), 1991 (7), 1992 (6), 1993 (5), 1994 (5), 1995 (11), 1996 (3), 1997 (4), 1998 (3). Total: 46.
MISCELLANEOUS: Holds Dallas Cowboys all-time records for most receptions (740) and most yards receiving (11,737).

			RECEIVING				TOTALS			
Year Team	G	GS	No.	Yds.	Avg.	TD	TD	2pt.	Pts.	Fum.
1988—Dallas NFL	14	10	32	654	‡20.4	5	5	...	30	0
1989—Dallas NFL	6	6	26	378	14.5	2	2	...	12	0
1990—Dallas NFL	12	7	20	413	20.7	5	5	...	30	0
1991—Dallas NFL	16	16	‡93	*1523	16.4	8	8	...	48	3
1992—Dallas NFL	16	14	78	1396	17.9	7	7	...	42	1
1993—Dallas NFL	16	16	88	1330	15.1	7	7	...	42	0
1994—Dallas NFL	16	16	79	1241	15.7	6	6	0	36	0
1995—Dallas NFL	16	16	111	1603	14.4	10	10	0	60	1
1996—Dallas NFL	11	11	64	962	15.0	2	2	1	14	1
1997—Dallas NFL	16	16	75	1180	15.7	9	9	0	54	0
1998—Dallas NFL	16	15	74	1057	14.3	1	1	0	6	1
Pro totals (11 years)	155	143	740	11737	15.9	62	62	1	374	7

IRVING, TERRY   LB   CARDINALS

PERSONAL: Born July 3, 1971, in Galveston, Texas. ... 6-2/236. ... Full name: Terry Duane Irving.
HIGH SCHOOL: Ball (Galveston, Texas).
COLLEGE: McNeese State (degree in electrical engineering, 1994).
TRANSACTIONS/CAREER NOTES: Selected by Arizona Cardinals in fourth round (115th pick overall) of 1994 NFL draft. ... Signed by Cardinals (July 15, 1994). ... Granted unconditional free agency (February 13, 1998). ... Re-signed by Cardinals (February 25, 1998).
PLAYING EXPERIENCE: Arizona NFL, 1994-1998. ... Games/Games started: 1994 (16/0), 1995 (16/8), 1996 (16/0), 1997 (16/6), 1998 (6/1). Total: 70/15.
PRO STATISTICS: 1994—Recovered one fumble. 1995—Recovered three fumbles for minus two yards. 1996—Recovered one fumble for five yards. 1997—Recovered one fumble.

IRWIN, HEATH   G   PATRIOTS

PERSONAL: Born June 27, 1973, in Boulder, Colo. ... 6-4/300. ... Nephew of Hale Irwin, professional golfer.
HIGH SCHOOL: Boulder (Colo.).
COLLEGE: Colorado.
TRANSACTIONS/CAREER NOTES: Selected by New England Patriots in fourth round (101st pick overall) of 1996 NFL draft. ... Signed by Patriots (July 17, 1996). ... Inactive for all 16 games (1996). ... Granted free agency (February 12, 1999).
PLAYING EXPERIENCE: New England NFL, 1997 and 1998. ... Games/Games started: 1997 (15/1), 1998 (13/3). Total: 28/4.
CHAMPIONSHIP GAME EXPERIENCE: Member of Patriots for AFC championship game (1996 season); inactive. ... Member of Patriots for Super Bowl XXXI (1996 season); inactive.

ISMAIL, QADRY   WR/KR   RAVENS

PERSONAL: Born November 8, 1970, in Newark, N.J. ... 6-0/195. ... Full name: Qadry Rahmadan Ismail. ... Brother of Rocket Ismail, wide receiver, Dallas Cowboys. ... Name pronounced KAH-dree ISS-mile.
HIGH SCHOOL: Elmer L. Meyers (Wilkes-Barre, Pa.).
COLLEGE: Syracuse (degree in communications).
TRANSACTIONS/CAREER NOTES: Selected by Minnesota Vikings in second round (52nd pick overall) of 1993 NFL draft. ... Signed by Vikings (July 20, 1993). ... Granted unconditional free agency (February 14, 1997). ... Signed by Green Bay Packers (June 2, 1997). ... Traded by Packers to Miami Dolphins for first-round pick (DT Vonnie Holliday) in 1998 draft (August 24, 1997). ... Granted unconditional free agency (February 13, 1998). ... Signed by New Orleans Saints (February 27, 1998). ... Released by Saints (February 10, 1999). ... Signed by Baltimore Ravens (April 27, 1999).
HONORS: Named kick returner on THE SPORTING NEWS college All-America second team (1991).
PRO STATISTICS: 1993—Rushed three times for 14 yards. 1994—Recovered one fumble. 1995—Rushed once for seven yards. 1996—Recovered one fumble.
SINGLE GAME HIGHS (regular season): Receptions—7 (October 30, 1995, vs. Chicago); yards—142 (November 19, 1995, vs. New Orleans); an dtouchdown receptions—1 (December 1, 1996, vs. Arizona).
STATISTICAL PLATEAUS: 100-yard receiving games: 1994 (2), 1995 (1). Total: 3.

			RECEIVING				KICKOFF RETURNS				TOTALS		
Year Team	G	GS	No.	Yds.	Avg.	TD	No.	Yds.	Avg.	TD	TD	2pt.	Pts.	Fum.
1993—Minnesota NFL	15	3	19	212	11.2	1	‡42	902	21.5	0	1	...	6	1
1994—Minnesota NFL	16	3	45	696	15.5	5	35	807	23.1	0	5	0	30	2
1995—Minnesota NFL	16	2	32	597	18.7	3	42	1037	24.7	0	3	0	18	3
1996—Minnesota NFL	16	2	22	351	16.0	3	28	527	18.8	0	3	0	18	2
1997—Miami NFL	3	0	0	0	...	0	8	166	20.8	0	0	0	0	0
1998—New Orleans NFL	10	1	0	0	...	0	28	590	21.1	0	0	0	0	2
Pro totals (6 years)	76	11	118	1856	15.7	12	183	4029	22.0	0	12	0	72	10

ISMAIL, ROCKET   WR/KR   COWBOYS

PERSONAL: Born November 18, 1969, in Elizabeth, N.J. ... 5-11/176. ... Full name: Raghib Ramadian Ismail. ... Brother of Qadry Ismail, wide receiver/kick returner, Baltimore Ravens. ... Name pronounced rahg-HEEB ISS-mile.
HIGH SCHOOL: Elmer L. Meyers (Wilkes-Barre, Pa.).
COLLEGE: Notre Dame (degree in sociology, 1994).
TRANSACTIONS/CAREER NOTES: Signed after junior season by Toronto Argonauts of CFL (April 21, 1991). ... Selected by Los Angeles Raiders in fourth round (100th pick overall) of 1991 NFL draft. ... Granted free agency from Argonauts (February 15, 1993). ... Signed by Raiders (August 30, 1993). ... Raiders franchise moved to Oakland (July 21, 1995). ... Granted free agency (February 16, 1996). ... Traded by Raiders to Carolina Panthers for fifth-round pick (traded to Miami) in 1997 draft (August 25, 1996). ... Granted unconditional free agency (February 14, 1997). ... Re-signed by Panthers (February 26, 1997). ... Granted unconditional free agency (February 13, 1998). ... Re-signed by Panthers (June 2, 1998). ... Granted unconditional free agency (February 12, 1999). ... Signed by Dallas Cowboys (April 16, 1999).
CHAMPIONSHIP GAME EXPERIENCE: Played in Grey Cup, CFL championship game (1991). ... Played in NFC championship game (1996 season).
HONORS: Named kick returner on THE SPORTING NEWS college All-America first team (1989). ... Named College Football Player of the Year by THE SPORTING NEWS (1990). ... Named wide receiver on THE SPORTING NEWS college All-America first team (1990).
PRO STATISTICS: CFL: 1991—Returned two unsuccessful field-goals for 90 yards, attempted one pass without a completion, fumbled eight times and recovered two fumbles. 1992—Fumbled seven times and recovered two fumbles. NFL: 1993—Recovered one fumble. 1995—Fumbled four times and recovered one fumble. 1998—Fumbled twice and recovered one fumble.
SINGLE GAME HIGHS (regular season): Receptions—7 (December 27, 1998, vs. Indianapolis); yards—125 (October 22, 1995, vs. Indianapolis); and touchdown receptions—2 (October 11, 1998, vs. Dallas).
STATISTICAL PLATEAUS: 100-yard receiving games: 1995 (1), 1996 (1), 1997 (1), 1998 (3). Total: 6.

			RUSHING				RECEIVING				PUNT RETURNS				KICKOFF RETURNS				TOTALS		
Year Team	G	GS	Att.	Yds.	Avg.	TD	No.	Yds.	Avg.	TD	No.	Yds.	Avg.	TD	No.	Yds.	Avg.	TD	TD	2pt.	Pts.
1991—Toronto CFL	17	17	36	271	7.5	3	64	1300	20.3	9	48	602	12.5	1	31	786	25.4	0	13	1	80
1992—Toronto CFL	16	16	34	154	4.5	3	36	651	18.1	4	59	614	10.4	1	43	*1139	26.5	0	8	...	48
1993—L.A. Raiders NFL	13	0	4	-5	-1.3	0	26	353	13.6	1	0	0	...	0	25	605	§24.2	0	1	...	6
1994—L.A. Raiders NFL	16	0	4	31	7.8	0	34	513	15.1	5	0	0	...	0	43	923	21.5	0	5	0	30
1995—Oakland NFL	16	16	6	29	4.8	0	28	491	17.5	3	0	0	...	0	36	706	19.6	0	3	0	18
1996—Carolina NFL	13	5	8	80	10.0	1	12	214	17.8	0	0	0	...	0	5	100	20.0	0	1	0	6
1997—Carolina NFL	13	2	4	32	8.0	0	36	419	11.6	2	0	0	...	0	0	0	...	0	2	0	12
1998—Carolina NFL	16	15	3	42	14.0	0	69	1024	14.8	8	0	0	...	0	0	0	...	0	8	0	48
CFL totals (2 years)	33	33	70	425	6.1	6	100	1951	19.5	13	107	1216	11.4	2	74	1925	26.0	0	21	1	128
NFL totals (6 years)	87	38	29	209	7.2	1	205	3014	14.7	19	0	0	...	0	109	2334	21.4	0	20	0	120
Pro totals (8 years)	120	71	99	634	6.4	7	305	4965	16.3	32	107	1216	11.4	2	183	4259	23.3	0	41	1	248

ISRAEL, STEVE — CB — PATRIOTS

PERSONAL: Born March 16, 1969, in Lawnside, N.J. ... 5-11/194. ... Full name: Steven Douglas Israel.
HIGH SCHOOL: Haddon Heights (N.J.).
COLLEGE: Pittsburgh (degree in economics).
TRANSACTIONS/CAREER NOTES: Selected by Los Angeles Rams in second round (30th pick overall) of 1992 NFL draft. ... Signed by Rams (August 23, 1992). ... Granted roster exemption (August 25-September 4, 1992). ... Claimed on waivers by Green Bay Packers (August 7, 1995). ... Released by Packers (August 25, 1995). ... Signed by San Francisco 49ers (October 3, 1995). ... Granted unconditional free agency (February 16, 1996). ... Re-signed by 49ers (March 1, 1996). ... Granted unconditional free agency (February 14, 1997). ... Signed by New England Patriots (March 24, 1997).
PLAYING EXPERIENCE: Los Angeles Rams NFL, 1992-1994; San Francisco, NFL, 1995 and 1996; New England NFL, 1997 and 1998. ... Games/Games started: 1992 (16/1), 1993 (16/12), 1994 (10/2), 1995 (8/0), 1996 (14/2), 1997 (5/0), 1998 (11/7). Total: 80/24.
PRO STATISTICS: 1992—Returned one kickoff for minus three yards and recovered one fumble. 1993—Returned five kickoffs for 92 yards. 1996—Intercepted one pass for three yards and recovered one fumble. 1997—Credited with one sack. 1998—Intercepted three passes for 13 yards and credited with two sacks.

IZZO, LARRY — LB — DOLPHINS

PERSONAL: Born September 26, 1974, in Fort Belvoir, Va. ... 5-10/228. ... Full name: Lawrence Alexander Izzo.
HIGH SCHOOL: McCullough (Houston).
COLLEGE: Rice.
TRANSACTIONS/CAREER NOTES: Signed as non-drafted free agent by Miami Dolphins (April 25, 1996). ... On injured reserve with foot injury (August 18, 1997-entire season). ... Granted free agency (February 12, 1999). ... Re-signed by Dolphins (March 31, 1999).
PLAYING EXPERIENCE: Miami NFL, 1996 and 1998. ... Games/Games started: 1996 (16/0), 1998 (13/0). Total: 29/0.
PRO STATISTICS: 1996—Rushed once for 26 yards.

JACKE, CHRIS — K — CARDINALS

PERSONAL: Born March 12, 1966, in Richmond, Va. ... 6-0/205. ... Full name: Christopher Lee Jacke. ... Name pronounced JACK-ee.
HIGH SCHOOL: J.J. Pearce (Richardson, Texas).
COLLEGE: Texas-El Paso (degree in business, 1989).
TRANSACTIONS/CAREER NOTES: Selected by Green Bay Packers in sixth round (142nd pick overall) of 1989 NFL draft. ... Signed by Packers (July 28, 1989). ... Granted free agency (February 1, 1991). ... Re-signed by Packers (August 26, 1991). ... Granted unconditional free agency (February 14, 1997). ... Signed by Pittsburgh Steelers (July 9, 1997). ... Released by Steelers (October 14, 1997). ... Signed by Washington Redskins (December 16, 1997). ... Released by Redskins (February 3, 1998). ... Signed by Arizona Cardinals (December 1, 1998). ... Granted unconditional free agency (February 12, 1999). ... Re-signed by Cardinals (April 14, 1999).
CHAMPIONSHIP GAME EXPERIENCE: Played in NFC championship game (1995 of 1996 seasons). ... Member of Super Bowl championship team (1996 season).

		KICKING						
Year Team	G	XPM	XPA	FGM	FGA	Lg.	50+	Pts.
1989—Green Bay NFL	16	42	42	22	28	52	1-3	108
1990—Green Bay NFL	16	28	29	23	30	53	2-4	97
1991—Green Bay NFL	16	31	31	18	24	53	1-1	85
1992—Green Bay NFL	16	30	30	22	29	53	2-3	96
1993—Green Bay NFL	16	35	35	31	37	54	6-7	128
1994—Green Bay NFL	16	41	43	19	26	50	1-3	98
1995—Green Bay NFL	14	43	43	17	23	51	3-4	94
1996—Green Bay NFL	16	*51	*53	21	27	53	1-1	114
1997—Washington NFL	1	5	5	0	0	0	0-0	5
1998—Arizona NFL	4	6	6	10	14	52	1-2	36
Pro totals (10 years)	131	312	317	183	238	54	18-28	861

JACKSON, CALVIN — S — DOLPHINS

PERSONAL: Born October 28, 1972, in Miami. ... 5-9/195. ... Full name: Calvin Bernard Jackson.
HIGH SCHOOL: Dillard (Fort Lauderdale, Fla.).
COLLEGE: Auburn.
TRANSACTIONS/CAREER NOTES: Signed as non-drafted free agent by Miami Dolphins (July 21, 1994). ... Released by Dolphins (August 22, 1994). ... Re-signed by Dolphins to practice squad (August 29, 1994). ... Activated (September 17, 1994). ... Released by Dolphins (October 26, 1994). ... Re-signed by Dolphins to practice squad (October 27, 1994). ... On practice squad injured reserve with knee injury (December 24, 1994-remainder of season). ... Released by Dolphins (August 27, 1995). ... Re-signed by Dolphins to practice squad (August 30, 1995). ... Activated (September 9, 1995).
PRO STATISTICS: 1996—Credited with one sack and fumbled once. 1997—Credited with 1/2 sack and recovered one fumble. 1998—Credited with one sack.

			INTERCEPTIONS			
Year Team	G	GS	No.	Yds.	Avg.	TD
1994—Miami NFL	2	0	0	0	...	0
1995—Miami NFL	9	1	1	23	23.0	0
1996—Miami NFL	16	15	3	82	27.3	1
1997—Miami NFL	16	16	0	0	...	0
1998—Miami NFL	16	15	0	0	...	0
Pro totals (5 years)	59	47	4	105	26.3	1

JACKSON, GRADY — DE — RAIDERS

PERSONAL: Born January 21, 1973, in Greensboro, Ala. ... 6-2/320.
HIGH SCHOOL: Greensboro (Ala.) East.
JUNIOR COLLEGE: Hinds Community College (Miss.).
COLLEGE: Knoxville (Tenn.) College.
TRANSACTIONS/CAREER NOTES: Selected by Oakland Raiders in sixth round (193rd pick overall) of 1997 NFL draft. ... Signed by Raiders for 1997 season.
PLAYING EXPERIENCE: Oakland NFL, 1997 and 1998. ... Games/Games started: 1997 (5/0), 1998 (15/1). Total: 20/1.
PRO STATISTICS: 1998—Credited with three sacks and recovered one fumble for two yards.

JACKSON, GREG — S

PERSONAL: Born August 20, 1966, in Hialeah, Fla. ... 6-1/217. ... Full name: Greg Allen Jackson.
HIGH SCHOOL: American (Miami).
COLLEGE: Louisiana State.
TRANSACTIONS/CAREER NOTES: Selected by New York Giants in third round (78th pick overall) of 1989 NFL draft. ... Signed by Giants (July 24, 1989). ... Granted free agency (February 1, 1992). ... Re-signed by Giants (August 3, 1992). ... Granted unconditional free agency (February 17, 1994). ... Signed by Philadelphia Eagles (June 30, 1994). ... Granted unconditional free agency (February 16, 1996). ... Signed by New Orleans Saints (June 18, 1996). ... Granted unconditional free agency (February 14, 1997). ... Signed by San Diego Chargers (June 13, 1997). ... On injured reserve with leg injury (December 1, 1997-remainder of season). ... Re-signed by Chargers (May 4, 1998). ... Released by Chargers (August 26, 1998). ... Re-signed by Chargers (August 30, 1998). ... Granted unconditional free agency (February 12, 1999).
CHAMPIONSHIP GAME EXPERIENCE: Played in NFC championship game (1990 season). ... Member of Super Bowl championship team (1990 season).
PRO STATISTICS: 1989—Recovered one fumble. 1990—Credited with four sacks. 1991—Fumbled once. 1992—Recovered one fumble. 1993—Recovered three fumbles for three yards. 1995—Recovered three fumbles for 45 yards and one touchdown. 1996—Fumbled once. 1997—Returned one punt for no yards and recovered one fumble for 41 yards and a touchdown. 1998—Recovered one fumble.

				INTERCEPTIONS		
Year Team	G	GS	No.	Yds.	Avg.	TD
1989—New York Giants NFL	16	1	0	0	...	0
1990—New York Giants NFL	14	14	5	8	1.6	0
1991—New York Giants NFL	13	12	1	3	3.0	0
1992—New York Giants NFL	16	16	4	71	17.8	0
1993—New York Giants NFL	16	16	4	32	8.0	0
1994—Philadelphia NFL	16	16	6	86	14.3	1
1995—Philadelphia NFL	16	16	1	18	18.0	0
1996—New Orleans NFL	16	15	3	24	8.0	0
1997—San Diego NFL	13	0	2	37	18.5	1
1998—San Diego NFL	16	13	6	50	8.3	0
Pro totals (10 years)	152	119	32	329	10.3	2

JACKSON, JOHN — OT — CHARGERS

PERSONAL: Born January 4, 1965, in Camp Kwe, Okinawa, Japan. ... 6-6/297.
HIGH SCHOOL: Woodward (Cincinnati).
COLLEGE: Eastern Kentucky (degree in police administration, 1991).
TRANSACTIONS/CAREER NOTES: Selected by Pittsburgh Steelers in 10th round (252nd pick overall) of 1988 NFL draft. ... Signed by Steelers (May 17, 1988). ... Granted unconditional free agency (February 13, 1998). ... Signed by San Diego Chargers (February 18, 1998).
PLAYING EXPERIENCE: Pittsburgh NFL, 1988-1997; San Diego NFL, 1998. ... Games/Games started: 1988 (16/0), 1989 (14/12), 1990 (16/16), 1991 (16/16), 1992 (16/13), 1993 (16/16), 1994 (16/16), 1995 (11/9), 1996 (16/16), 1997 (16/16), 1998 (16/16). Total: 169/146.
CHAMPIONSHIP GAME EXPERIENCE: Played in AFC championship game (1994, 1995 and 1997 seasons). ... Played in Super Bowl XXX (1995 season).
PRO STATISTICS: 1988—Returned one kickoff for 10 yards. 1991—Recovered one fumble. 1993—Recovered one fumble. 1994—Recovered two fumbles. 1996—Recovered one fumble.

JACKSON, MICHAEL — WR

PERSONAL: Born April 12, 1969, in Tangipahoa, La. ... 6-4/195. ... Full name: Michael Dwayne Jackson. ... Formerly known as Michael Dyson.
HIGH SCHOOL: Kentwood (La.).
COLLEGE: Southern Mississippi.
TRANSACTIONS/CAREER NOTES: Selected by Cleveland Browns in sixth round (141st pick overall) of 1991 NFL draft. ... Granted free agency (February 17, 1994). ... Re-signed by Browns for 1994 season. ... Browns franchise moved to Baltimore and renamed Ravens for 1996 season (March 11, 1996). ... Granted unconditional free agency (February 14, 1997). ... Re-signed by Ravens (February 28, 1997). ... Granted unconditional free agency (February 12, 1999).
PRO STATISTICS: 1992—Rushed once for 21 yards. 1993—Attempted one pass with a completion for 25 yards, rushed once for one yard and recovered one fumble. 1994—Attempted two passes without a completion. 1995—Had only pass intercepted and recovered one fumble. 1996—Recovered one fumble.
SINGLE GAME HIGHS (regular season): Receptions—9 (November 24, 1996, vs. Jacksonville); yards—157 (September 3, 1995, vs. New England); and touchdown receptions—3 (December 22, 1996, vs. Houston).
STATISTICAL PLATEAUS: 100-yard receiving games: 1993 (2), 1995 (2), 1996 (4), 1997 (1). Total: 9.
MISCELLANEOUS: Holds Baltimore Ravens all-time records for most yards receiving (2,596) and most receptions (183). ... Shares Baltimore Ravens all-time records for most touchdown receptions (18) and touchdowns (18).

Year Team	G	GS	RECEIVING No.	Yds.	Avg.	TD	TOTALS TD	2pt.	Pts.	Fum.
1991—Cleveland NFL	16	7	17	268	15.8	2	2	...	12	0
1992—Cleveland NFL	16	14	47	755	16.1	7	7	...	42	0
1993—Cleveland NFL	15	11	41	756	18.4	8	8	...	48	1
1994—Cleveland NFL	9	7	21	304	14.5	2	2	0	12	0
1995—Cleveland NFL	13	10	44	714	16.2	9	9	0	54	1
1996—Baltimore NFL	16	16	76	1201	15.8	†14	14	2	88	0
1997—Baltimore NFL	16	15	69	918	13.3	4	4	1	26	2
1998—Baltimore NFL	13	12	38	477	12.6	0	0	0	0	1
Pro totals (8 years)	114	92	353	5393	15.3	46	46	3	282	5

JACKSON, RAYMOND   DB   BROWNS

PERSONAL: Born February 17, 1973, in East Chicago, Ind. ... 5-10/189. ... Full name: Raymond DeWayne Jackson.
HIGH SCHOOL: Montbello (Denver).
COLLEGE: Colorado State.
TRANSACTIONS/CAREER NOTES: Selected by Buffalo Bills in fifth round (156th pick overall) of 1996 NFL draft. ... Signed by Bills (June 25, 1996). ... Selected by Cleveland Browns from Bills in NFL expansion draft (February 9, 1999). ... Granted free agency (February 12, 1999). ... Re-signed by Browns (April 14, 1999).
PRO STATISTICS: 1997—Returned one punt for no yards and fumbled once.

Year Team	G	GS	INTERCEPTIONS No.	Yds.	Avg.	TD
1996—Buffalo NFL	12	0	1	0	0.0	0
1997—Buffalo NFL	9	0	0	0	...	0
1998—Buffalo NFL	14	0	2	27	13.5	0
Pro totals (3 years)	35	0	3	27	9.0	0

JACKSON, STEVE   CB   TITANS

PERSONAL: Born April 8, 1969, in Houston. ... 5-8/188. ... Full name: Steven Wayne Jackson.
HIGH SCHOOL: Klein Forest (Houston).
COLLEGE: Purdue.
TRANSACTIONS/CAREER NOTES: Selected by Houston Oilers in third round (71st pick overall) of 1991 NFL draft. ... Signed by Oilers (July 11, 1991). ... Granted free agency (February 17, 1994). ... Re-signed by Oilers (June 10, 1994). ... Granted unconditional free agency (February 14, 1997). ... Re-signed by Oilers (March 26, 1997). ... Oilers franchise moved to Tennessee for 1997 season. ... Oilers franchise renamed Tennessee Titans for 1999 season (December 26, 1998).
PRO STATISTICS: 1991—Returned one punt for no yards and recovered two fumbles. 1994—Returned 14 kickoffs for 285 yards. 1996—Credited with a safety and recovered one fumble.

Year Team	G	GS	INTERCEPTIONS No.	Yds.	Avg.	TD	SACKS No.
1991—Houston NFL	15	2	0	0	...	0	1.0
1992—Houston NFL	16	1	3	18	6.0	0	1.0
1993—Houston NFL	16	12	5	54	10.8	▲1	0.0
1994—Houston NFL	11	0	1	0	0.0	0	1.0
1995—Houston NFL	10	1	2	0	0.0	0	1.0
1996—Houston NFL	16	1	0	0	...	0	2.0
1997—Tennessee NFL	12	6	0	0	...	0	1.0
1998—Tennessee NFL	14	4	1	0	0.0	0	1.5
Pro totals (8 years)	110	27	12	72	6.0	1	8.5

JACKSON, TYOKA   DE/DT   BUCCANEERS

PERSONAL: Born November 22, 1971, in Washington, D.C. ... 6-2/274.
HIGH SCHOOL: Bishop McNamara (Forestville, Md.).
COLLEGE: Penn State.
TRANSACTIONS/CAREER NOTES: Signed as non-drafted free agent by Atlanta Falcons (May 2, 1994). ... Released by Falcons (August 29, 1994). ... Re-signed by Falcons to practice squad (August 30, 1994). ... Signed by Miami Dolphins off Falcons practice squad (November 16, 1994). ... Released by Dolphins (August 27, 1995). ... Signed by Tampa Bay Buccaneers (December 27, 1995). ... Granted free agency (February 13, 1998). ... Re-signed by Buccaneers (June 22, 1998).
PLAYING EXPERIENCE: Miami NFL, 1994; Tampa Bay NFL, 1996-1998. ... Games/Games started: 1994 (1/0), 1996 (13/2), 1997 (12/0), 1998 (16/12). Total: 42/14.
PRO STATISTICS: 1994—Recovered one fumble. 1997—Credited with 2½ sacks. 1998—Credited with three sacks.

JACKSON, WAVERLY   OT   COLTS

PERSONAL: Born December 19, 1972, in South Hill, Va. ... 6-2/310.
HIGH SCHOOL: Park View (Va.).
COLLEGE: Virginia Tech.
TRANSACTIONS/CAREER NOTES: Signed as non-drafted free agent by Carolina Panthers (April 19, 1997). ... Released by Panthers (August 25, 1997). ... Re-signed by Panthers to practice squad (August 26, 1997). ... Granted free agency after 1997 season. ... Signed by Indianapolis Colts (January 12, 1998).
PLAYING EXPERIENCE: Indianapolis NFL, 1998. ... Games/Games started: 7/2.

JACKSON, WILLIE — WR — BENGALS

PERSONAL: Born August 16, 1971, in Gainesville, Fla. ... 6-1/212. ... Full name: Willie Bernard Jackson Jr.
HIGH SCHOOL: P.K. Yonge (Gainesville, Fla.).
COLLEGE: Florida (degree in telecommunications, 1993).
TRANSACTIONS/CAREER NOTES: Selected by Dallas Cowboys in fourth round (109th pick overall) of 1994 NFL draft. ... Signed by Cowboys (July 16, 1994). ... Inactive for 16 games (1994). ... Selected by Jacksonville Jaguars from Cowboys in NFL expansion draft (February 15, 1995). ... Granted free agency (February 14, 1997). ... Re-signed by Jaguars (March 26, 1997). ... Released by Jaguars (August 30, 1998). ... Signed by Cincinnati Bengals (September 10, 1998).
CHAMPIONSHIP GAME EXPERIENCE: Member of Cowboys for NFC championship game (1994 season); inactive. ... Played in AFC championship game (1996 season).
PRO STATISTICS: 1995—Returned one punt for minus two yards and recovered one fumble. 1996—Rushed once for two yards. 1997—Rushed three times for 14 yards.
SINGLE GAME HIGHS (regular season): Receptions—8 (November 17, 1996, vs. Pittsburgh); yards—113 (December 10, 1995, vs. Indianapolis); and touchdown receptions—2 (December 10, 1995, vs. Indianapolis).
STATISTICAL PLATEAUS: 100-yard receiving games: 1995 (1), 1996 (1). Total: 2.

				RECEIVING				KICKOFF RETURNS				TOTALS			
Year Team	G	GS	No.	Yds.	Avg.	TD	No.	Yds.	Avg.	TD	TD	2pt.	Pts.	Fum.	
1994—Dallas NFL								Did not play.							
1995—Jacksonville NFL	14	10	53	589	11.1	5	19	404	21.3	0	5	1	32	2	
1996—Jacksonville NFL	16	2	33	486	14.7	3	7	149	21.3	0	3	1	20	0	
1997—Jacksonville NFL	16	1	17	206	12.1	2	32	653	20.4	0	2	1	14	1	
1998—Cincinnati NFL	8	0	7	165	23.6	0	0	0	...	0	0	0	0	0	
Pro totals (4 years)	54	13	110	1446	13.1	10	58	1206	20.8	0	10	3	66	3	

JACOBY, MITCH — TE — RAMS

PERSONAL: Born December 8, 1973, in Port Washington, Wis. ... 6-4/260. ... Full name: Mitchel Ray Jacoby.
HIGH SCHOOL: Fredonia (Wis.).
COLLEGE: Northern Illinois.
TRANSACTIONS/CAREER NOTES: Signed as non-drafted free agent by St. Louis Rams (April 29, 1997). ... Released by Rams (August 30, 1998). ... Re-signed by Rams (November 17, 1998).
PLAYING EXPERIENCE: St. Louis NFL, 1997 and 1998. ... Games/Games started: 1997 (14/2), 1998 (5/0). Total: 19/2.
PRO STATISTICS: 1997—Caught two passes for 10 yards.
SINGLE GAME HIGHS (regular season): Receptions—1 (November 23, 1997, vs. Carolina); yards—10 (September 28, 1997, vs. Oakland); and touchdown receptions—0.

JACOX, KENDYL — C — CHARGERS

PERSONAL: Born June 10, 1975, in Dallas. ... 6-2/330. ... Full name: Kendyl LaMarc Jacox.
HIGH SCHOOL: Carter (Texas).
COLLEGE: Kansas State.
TRANSACTIONS/CAREER NOTES: Signed as non-drafted free agent by San Diego Chargers (April 20, 1998).
PLAYING EXPERIENCE: San Diego NFL, 1998. ... Games/Games started: 16/6.
PRO STATISTICS: 1998—Returned one kickoff for no yards.

JACQUET, NATE — WR — DOLPHINS

PERSONAL: Born September 2, 1975, in Duarte, Calif. ... 6-0/173. ... Full name: Nathaniel Martin Jacquet.
HIGH SCHOOL: Duarte (Calif.).
JUNIOR COLLEGE: Mt. San Antonio College (Calif.).
COLLEGE: San Diego State.
TRANSACTIONS/CAREER NOTES: Selected by Indianapolis Colts in fifth round (150th pick overall) of 1997 NFL draft. ... Signed by Colts (June 26, 1997). ... Released by Colts (August 24, 1997). ... Re-signed by Colts to practice squad (August 25, 1997). ... Activated (November 4, 1997). ... Released by Colts (August 25, 1998). ... Claimed on waivers by Miami Dolphins (August 26, 1998). ... Released by Dolphins (August 30, 1998). ... Re-signed by Dolphins to practice squad (August 31, 1998). ... Activated (September 9, 1998).
PRO STATISTICS: 1997—Recovered one fumble.
SINGLE GAME HIGHS (regular season): Receptions—5 (December 13, 1998, vs. New York Jets); yards—68 (December 13, 1998, vs. New York Jets); and touchdown receptions—0.

			RECEIVING				PUNT RETURNS				KICKOFF RETURNS				TOTALS			
Year Team	G	GS	No.	Yds.	Avg.	TD	No.	Yds.	Avg.	TD	No.	Yds.	Avg.	TD	TD	2pt.	Pts.	Fum.
1997—Indianapolis NFL	5	0	0	0	...	0	13	96	7.4	0	8	156	19.5	0	0	0	0	1
1998—Miami NFL	15	0	8	122	15.3	0	0	0	...	0	4	103	25.8	0	0	0	0	0
Pro totals (2 years)	20	0	8	122	15.3	0	13	96	7.4	0	12	259	21.6	0	0	0	0	1

JAEGER, JEFF — K — BEARS

PERSONAL: Born November 26, 1964, in Tacoma, Wash. ... 5-11/190. ... Full name: Jeff Todd Jaeger. ... Name pronounced JAY-ger.
HIGH SCHOOL: Meridian (Kent, Wash.).
COLLEGE: Washington.
TRANSACTIONS/CAREER NOTES: Selected by Cleveland Browns in third round (82nd pick overall) of 1987 NFL draft. ... Signed by Browns (July 26, 1987). ... Crossed picket line during players strike (October 14, 1987). ... On injured reserve with foot injury (August 26, 1988-entire season). ... Granted unconditional free agency (February 1, 1989). ... Signed by Los Angeles Raiders (March 20, 1989). ... Granted free agency

(February 1, 1991). ... Re-signed by Raiders (July 13, 1991). ... Released by Raiders (August 30, 1993). ... Re-signed by Raiders (August 31, 1993). ... Raiders franchise moved to Oakland (July 21, 1995). ... Released by Raiders (August 25, 1996). ... Signed by Chicago Bears (September 17, 1996).
CHAMPIONSHIP GAME EXPERIENCE: Played in AFC championship game (1990 season).
HONORS: Played in Pro Bowl (1991 season).
PRO STATISTICS: 1987—Attempted one pass without a completion and recovered one fumble. 1997—Punted once for 18 yards. 1998—Punted once for 27 yards.

					KICKING				
Year Team	G	XPM	XPA	FGM	FGA	Lg.	50+	Pts.
1987—Cleveland NFL	10	33	33	14	22	48	0-1	75
1988—Cleveland NFL				Did not play.				
1989—Los Angeles Raiders NFL	16	34	34	23	34	50	1-2	103
1990—Los Angeles Raiders NFL	16	40	42	15	20	50	1-2	85
1991—Los Angeles Raiders NFL	16	29	30	29	34	53	2-4	116
1992—Los Angeles Raiders NFL	16	28	28	15	26	54	3-6	73
1993—Los Angeles Raiders NFL	16	27	29	*35	*44	53	4-7	*132
1994—Los Angeles Raiders NFL	16	31	31	22	28	51	2-2	97
1995—Oakland NFL	11	22	22	13	18	46	0-1	61
1996—Chicago NFL	13	23	23	19	23	49	0-0	80
1997—Chicago NFL	16	20	20	21	26	52	1-1	83
1998—Chicago NFL	16	27	28	21	26	52	1-1	90
Pro totals (11 years)	162	314	320	227	301	54	15-27	995

JAMES, TORY CB BRONCOS

PERSONAL: Born May 18, 1973, in New Orleans. ... 6-1/195. ... Full name: Tory Steven James.
HIGH SCHOOL: Archbishop Shaw (Marrero, La.).
COLLEGE: Louisiana State.
TRANSACTIONS/CAREER NOTES: Selected by Denver Broncos in second round (44th pick overall) of 1996 NFL draft. ... Signed by Broncos (July 22, 1996). ... On injured reserve with knee injury (August 18, 1997-entire season).
PLAYING EXPERIENCE: Denver NFL, 1996 and 1998. ... Games/Games started: 1996 (16/2), 1998 (16/0). Total: 32/2.
CHAMPIONSHIP GAME EXPERIENCE: Played in AFC championship game (1998 season). ... Member of Super Bowl championship team (1998 season).
PRO STATISTICS: 1996—Intercepted two passes for 15 yards and recovered one fumble for 15 yards. 1998—Recovered one fumble.

JAMISON, GEORGE LB

PERSONAL: Born September 30, 1962, in Bridgeton, N.J. ... 6-1/235. ... Full name: George R. Jamison Jr. ... Cousin of Anthony (Bubba) Green, defensive tackle with Baltimore Colts (1981); and cousin of Larry Milbourne, infielder with six major league teams (1975-84).
HIGH SCHOOL: Bridgeton (N.J.).
COLLEGE: Cincinnati (degree in human resource development).
TRANSACTIONS/CAREER NOTES: Selected by Philadelphia Stars in second round (34th pick overall) of 1984 USFL draft. ... Signed by Stars (January 17, 1984). ... On developmental squad for two games (February 24-March 2 and June 21, 1984-remainder of season). ... Selected by Detroit Lions in second round (47th pick overall) of 1984 NFL supplemental draft. ... Stars franchise moved to Baltimore (November 1, 1984). ... On developmental squad for one game (May 3-10, 1985). ... Granted free agency when USFL suspended operations (August 7, 1986). ... Signed by Lions (August 17, 1986). ... On injured reserve with Achilles' tendon injury (August 30, 1986-entire season). ... On injured reserve with knee injury (December 21, 1989-remainder of season). ... Granted free agency (February 1, 1992). ... Re-signed by Lions (July 23, 1992). ... Granted unconditional free agency (February 17, 1994). ... Signed by Kansas City Chiefs (July 15, 1994). ... On reserve/non-football injury list with foot injury (August 20-November 16, 1996). ... Signed by Lions (March 5, 1997). ... Granted unconditional free agency (February 13, 1998). ... Re-signed by Lions (July 23, 1998). ... Granted unconditional free agency (February 12, 1999).
CHAMPIONSHIP GAME EXPERIENCE: Played in USFL championship game (1984 and 1985 seasons). ... Played in NFC championship game (1991 season).
PRO STATISTICS: 1987—Credited with one safety. 1988—Recovered three fumbles for four yards and one touchdown. 1990—Recovered one fumble. 1991—Fumbled once and recovered one fumble. 1992—Recovered one fumble. 1993—Returned one kickoff. 1994—Recovered three fumbles for 22 yards. 1995—Recovered two fumbles. 1997—Recovered one fumble.

			INTERCEPTIONS				SACKS
Year Team	G	GS	No.	Yds.	Avg.	TD	No.
1984—Philadelphia USFL	15	...	0	0	...	0	4.0
1985—Baltimore USFL	17	...	1	16	16.0	0	5.0
1986—Detroit NFL			Did not play.				
1987—Detroit NFL	12	0	0	0	...	0	1.0
1988—Detroit NFL	16	11	3	56	18.7	1	5.5
1989—Detroit NFL	10	6	0	0	...	0	2.0
1990—Detroit NFL	14	7	0	0	...	0	2.0
1991—Detroit NFL	16	16	3	52	17.3	0	4.0
1992—Detroit NFL	16	16	0	0	...	0	2.0
1993—Detroit NFL	16	16	2	48	24.0	1	2.0
1994—Kansas City NFL	13	12	0	0	...	0	1.0
1995—Kansas City NFL	14	14	0	0	...	0	0.0
1996—Kansas City NFL	5	0	0	0	...	0	0.0
1997—Detroit NFL	16	10	0	0	...	0	1.0
1998—Detroit NFL	14	0	1	21	21.0	0	0.0
USFL totals (2 years)	32	...	1	16	16.0	0	9.0
NFL totals (12 years)	162	108	9	177	19.7	2	20.5
Pro totals (14 years)	194	...	10	193	19.3	2	29.5

JANUS, PAUL   OL   PANTHERS

PERSONAL: Born March 17, 1975, in Edgerton, Wis. ... 6-4/294. ... Full name: Paul Scott Janus.
HIGH SCHOOL: Edgerton (Wis.).
COLLEGE: Northwestern.
TRANSACTIONS/CAREER NOTES: Signed as non-drafted free agent by Carolina Panthers (April 18, 1998). ... Released by Panthers (October 13, 1998). ... Re-signed by Panthers to practice squad (October 15, 1998).
PLAYING EXPERIENCE: Carolina NFL, 1998. ... Games/Games started: 5/1.

JASPER, ED   DT   FALCONS

PERSONAL: Born January 18, 1973, in Tyler, Texas. ... 6-2/305. ... Full name: Edward Vidal Jasper.
HIGH SCHOOL: Troup (Texas).
COLLEGE: Texas A&M.
TRANSACTIONS/CAREER NOTES: Selected by Philadelphia Eagles in sixth round (198th pick overall) of 1997 NFL draft. ... Signed by Eagles (July 16, 1997). ... Released by Eagles (August 30, 1998). ... Re-signed by Eagles (September 17, 1998). ... Released by Eagles (October 23, 1998). ... Re-signed by Eagles (December 9, 1998). ... Released by Eagles (February 12, 1999). ... Signed by Atlanta Falcons (March 5, 1999).
PLAYING EXPERIENCE: Philadelphia NFL, 1997 and 1998. ... Games/Games started: 1997 (9/1), 1998 (7/0). Total: 16/1.

JEFFERS, PATRICK   WR   PANTHERS

PERSONAL: Born February 2, 1973, in Fort Campbell, Ky. ... 6-3/218. ... Full name: Patrick Christopher Jeffers.
HIGH SCHOOL: Fort Worth (Texas) Country Day.
COLLEGE: Virginia.
TRANSACTIONS/CAREER NOTES: Selected by Denver Broncos in fifth round (159th pick overall) of 1996 NFL draft. ... Signed by Broncos (July 17, 1996). ... Traded by Broncos to Dallas Cowboys for past considerations (August 30, 1998). ... Granted free agency (February 12, 1999). ... Tendered offer sheet by Carolina Panthers (April 12, 1999). ... Cowboys declined to match offer (April 15, 1999).
CHAMPIONSHIP GAME EXPERIENCE: Played in AFC championship game (1997 season). ... Member of Super Bowl championship team (1997 season).
PRO STATISTICS: 1996—Returned one kickoff for 18 yards.
SINGLE GAME HIGHS (regular season): Receptions—5 (December 13, 1998, vs. Kansas City); yards—92 (November 26, 1998, vs. MInnesota); and touchdown receptions—1 (December 13, 1998, vs. Kansas City).

			RECEIVING					TOTALS		
Year Team	G	GS	No.	Yds.	Avg.	TD	TD	2pt.	Pts.	Fum.
1996—Denver NFL	4	0	0	0	...	0	0	0	0	0
1997—Denver NFL	10	0	3	24	8.0	0	0	0	0	0
1998—Dallas NFL	8	1	18	330	18.3	2	2	0	12	0
Pro totals (3 years)	22	1	21	354	16.9	2	2	0	12	0

JEFFERSON, GREG   DE   EAGLES

PERSONAL: Born August 31, 1971, in Orlando. ... 6-3/280. ... Full name: Greg Benton Jefferson.
HIGH SCHOOL: Bartow (Fla.).
COLLEGE: Central Florida.
TRANSACTIONS/CAREER NOTES: Selected by Philadelphia Eagles in third round (72nd pick overall) of 1995 NFL draft. ... Signed by Eagles (June 29, 1995). ... On injured reserve with knee injury (September 21, 1995-remainder of season). ... Granted free agency (February 13, 1998). ... Re-signed by Eagles (June 3, 1998).
PRO STATISTICS: 1997—Recovered one fumble.

Year Team	G	GS	SACKS
1995—Philadelphia NFL	3	0	0.0
1996—Philadelphia NFL	11	0	2.5
1997—Philadelphia NFL	12	11	3.0
1998—Philadelphia NFL	15	14	4.0
Pro totals (4 years)	41	25	9.5

JEFFERSON, SHAWN   WR   PATRIOTS

PERSONAL: Born February 22, 1969, in Jacksonville. ... 5-11/180. ... Full name: Vanchi LaShawn Jefferson.
HIGH SCHOOL: Raines (Jacksonville).
COLLEGE: Central Florida.
TRANSACTIONS/CAREER NOTES: Selected by Houston Oilers in ninth round (240th pick overall) of 1991 NFL draft. ... Signed by Oilers (July 15, 1991). ... Traded by Oilers with first-round pick (DE Chris Mims) in 1992 draft to San Diego Chargers for DL Lee Williams (August 22, 1991). ... Granted free agency (March 1, 1993). ... Re-signed by Chargers (July 15, 1993). ... Granted free agency (February 17, 1994). ... Re-signed by Chargers (May 2, 1994). ... Released by Chargers (February 29, 1996). ... Signed by New England Patriots (March 14, 1996).
CHAMPIONSHIP GAME EXPERIENCE: Played in AFC championship game (1994 and 1996 seasons). ... Played in Super Bowl XXIX (1994 season) and Super Bowl XXXI (1996 season).
PRO STATISTICS: 1998—Recovered one fumble.
SINGLE GAME HIGHS (regular season): Receptions—7 (December 22, 1997, vs. Miami); yards—131 (November 23, 1998, vs. Miami); and touchdown receptions—2 (October 6, 1996, vs. Baltimore).
STATISTICAL PLATEAUS: 100-yard receiving games: 1995 (1), 1997 (1), 1998 (2). Total: 4.

Year Team	G	GS	RUSHING Att.	Yds.	Avg.	TD	RECEIVING No.	Yds.	Avg.	TD	TOTALS TD	2pt.	Pts.	Fum.
1991—San Diego NFL	16	3	1	27	27.0	0	12	125	10.4	1	1	...	6	0
1992—San Diego NFL	16	1	0	0	...	0	29	377	13.0	2	2	...	12	0
1993—San Diego NFL	16	4	5	53	10.6	0	30	391	13.0	2	2	...	12	0
1994—San Diego NFL	16	16	3	40	13.3	0	43	627	14.6	3	3	0	18	0
1995—San Diego NFL	16	15	2	1	0.5	0	48	621	12.9	2	2	0	12	0
1996—New England NFL	15	15	1	6	6.0	0	50	771	15.4	4	4	0	24	2
1997—New England NFL	16	14	0	0	...	0	54	841	15.6	2	2	0	12	2
1998—New England NFL	16	16	1	15	15.0	0	34	771	*22.7	2	2	0	12	0
Pro totals (8 years)	127	84	13	142	10.9	0	300	4524	15.1	18	18	0	108	4

JEFFRIES, GREG   CB   DOLPHINS

PERSONAL: Born October 16, 1971, in High Point, N.C. ... 5-9/185. ... Full name: Greg Lemont Jeffries.
HIGH SCHOOL: T.W. Andrews (High Point, N.C.).
COLLEGE: Virginia.
TRANSACTIONS/CAREER NOTES: Selected by Detroit Lions in sixth round (147th pick overall) of 1993 NFL draft. ... Signed by Lions (July 17, 1993). ... Granted unconditional free agency (February 14, 1997). ... Re-signed by Lions (February 19, 1997). ... Granted unconditional free agency (February 12, 1999). ... Signed by Miami Dolphins (February 19, 1999).
PLAYING EXPERIENCE: Detroit NFL, 1993-1998. ... Games/Games started: 1993 (7/0), 1994 (16/1), 1995 (14/0), 1996 (16/4), 1997 (15/2), 1998 (15/3). Total: 83/10.
PRO STATISTICS: 1993—Recovered one fumble. 1995—Credited with 1/2 sack. 1996—Intercepted one pass for no yards. 1997—Intercepted one pass for no yards and credited with one sack. 1998—Recovered one fumble.

JELLS, DIETRICH   WR   EAGLES

PERSONAL: Born April 11, 1972, in Brooklyn, N.Y. ... 5-10/185. ... Name pronounced DEE-trick.
HIGH SCHOOL: Tech Memorial (Erie, Pa.).
COLLEGE: Pittsburgh (degree in business).
TRANSACTIONS/CAREER NOTES: Selected by Kansas City Chiefs in sixth round (176th pick overall) of 1996 NFL draft. ... Signed by Chiefs (July 26, 1996). ... Claimed on waivers by New England Patriots (August 21, 1996). ... Traded by Patriots to Philadelphia Eagles for conditional draft pick (August 30, 1998). ... Granted free agency (February 12, 1999). ... Re-signed by Eagles (March 29, 1999).
CHAMPIONSHIP GAME EXPERIENCE: Member of Patriots for AFC championship game (1996 season); inactive. ... Member of Patriots for Super Bowl XXXI (1996 season); inactive.
PRO STATISTICS: 1998—Rushed twice for nine yards.
SINGLE GAME HIGHS (regular season): Receptions—1 (December 27, 1998, vs. New York Giants); yards—37 (December 27, 1998, vs. New York Giants); and touchdown receptions—0.

Year Team	G	GS	RECEIVING No.	Yds.	Avg.	TD	TOTALS TD	2pt.	Pts.	Fum.
1996—New England NFL	7	1	1	5	5.0	0	0	0	0	0
1997—New England NFL	11	0	1	9	9.0	0	0	0	0	0
1998—Philadelphia NFL	9	0	2	53	26.5	0	0	0	0	0
Pro totals (3 years)	27	1	4	67	16.8	0	0	0	0	0

JENKINS, BILLY   S   RAMS

PERSONAL: Born July 8, 1974, in Albuquerque, N.M. ... 5-10/205.
HIGH SCHOOL: Albuquerque (N.M.).
COLLEGE: Howard.
TRANSACTIONS/CAREER NOTES: Signed as non-drafted free agent by St. Louis Rams (April 29, 1997).
PLAYING EXPERIENCE: St. Louis NFL, 1997 and 1998. ... Games/Games started: 1997 (16/2), 1998 (16/13). Total: 32/15.
PRO STATISTICS: 1998—Intercepted two passes for 31 yards and credited with three sacks.

JENKINS, DeRON   CB   RAVENS

PERSONAL: Born November 14, 1973, in St. Louis. ... 5-11/190. ... Full name: DeRon Charles Jenkins.
HIGH SCHOOL: Ritenour (St. Louis).
COLLEGE: Tennessee.
TRANSACTIONS/CAREER NOTES: Selected by Baltimore Ravens in second round (55th pick overall) of 1996 NFL draft. ... Signed by Ravens (July 19, 1996). ... Granted free agency (February 12, 1999).
PLAYING EXPERIENCE: Baltimore NFL, 1996-1998. ... Games/Games started: 1996 (15/2), 1997 (16/6), 1998 (16/7). Total: 47/15.
PRO STATISTICS: 1996—Recovered one fumble. 1997—Intercepted one pass for 15 yards and recovered one fumble. 1998—Intercepted one pass for no yards and recovered one fumble.

JENKINS, JAMES   TE   REDSKINS

PERSONAL: Born August 17, 1967, in Staten Island, N.Y. ... 6-2/249.
HIGH SCHOOL: Curtis (Staten Island, N.Y.).
COLLEGE: Rutgers.
TRANSACTIONS/CAREER NOTES: Signed as non-drafted free agent by Washington Redskins (April 25, 1991). ... Released by Redskins (August 26, 1991). ... Re-signed by Redskins to practice squad (August 27, 1991). ... Activated (November 30, 1991). ... Released by Redskins (August 31, 1992). ... Re-signed by Redskins (September 1, 1992). ... On injured reserve with back injury (September-November 28, 1992).

... On injured reserve with shoulder injury (December 28, 1993-remainder of season). ... Granted free agency (February 17, 1995). ... Re-signed by Redskins (July 19, 1995). ... Granted unconditional free agency (February 14, 1997). ... Re-signed by Redskins (July 16, 1997). ... Granted unconditional free agency (February 12, 1999). ... Re-signed by Redskins (May 12, 1999).
CHAMPIONSHIP GAME EXPERIENCE: Played in NFC championship game (1991 season). ... Member of Super Bowl championship team (1991 season).
PRO STATISTICS: 1994—Returned one kickoff for four yards. 1995—Returned one kickoff for 12 yards and recovered one fumble. 1996—Recovered one fumble. 1998—Returned one kickoff for no yards and recovered one fumble.
SINGLE GAME HIGHS (regular season): Receptions—2 (October 23, 1994, vs. Indianapolis); yards—20 (November 23, 1997, vs. New York Giants); and touchdown receptions—2 (October 23, 1994, vs. Indianapolis).

				RECEIVING			TOTALS			
Year Team	G	GS	No.	Yds.	Avg.	TD	TD	2pt.	Pts.	Fum.
1991—Washington NFL	4	0	0	0	...	0	0	...	0	0
1992—Washington NFL	5	1	0	0	...	0	0	...	0	0
1993—Washington NFL	15	5	0	0	...	0	0	...	0	0
1994—Washington NFL	16	3	8	32	4.0	4	4	0	24	0
1995—Washington NFL	16	5	1	2	2.0	0	0	...	0	0
1996—Washington NFL	16	5	1	7	7.0	0	0	...	0	0
1997—Washington NFL	16	4	4	43	10.8	3	3	0	18	0
1998—Washington NFL	16	4	0	0	...	0	0	...	0	0
Pro totals (8 years)	104	27	14	84	6.0	7	7	0	42	0

JENKINS, JOHN DB

PERSONAL: Born May 11, 1975, in East McKeesport, Pa. ... 6-0/188. ... Full name: John Eric Jenkins.
HIGH SCHOOL: East Allegheny (North Versailles, Pa.).
COLLEGE: Pittsburgh.
TRANSACTIONS/CAREER NOTES: Signed as non-drafted free agent by Pittsburgh Steelers (April 24, 1998). ... Released by Steelers (August 24, 1998). ... Re-signed by Steelers to practice squad (September 22, 1998). ... Activated (September 26, 1998). ... Released by Steelers (September 28, 1998). ... Re-signed by Steelers to practice squad (September 30, 1998). ... Released by Steelers (October 6, 1998).
PLAYING EXPERIENCE: Pittsburgh NFL, 1998. ... Games/Games started: 1/0.

JENKINS, KERRY OT/G JETS

PERSONAL: Born September 6, 1973, in Tuscaloosa, Ala. ... 6-5/310.
HIGH SCHOOL: Holt (Tuscaloosa, Ala.).
COLLEGE: Louisiana State, then Troy (Ala.) State.
TRANSACTIONS/CAREER NOTES: Signed as non-drafted free agent by Chicago Bears (April 25, 1997). ... Released by Bears (August 24, 1997). ... Re-signed by Bears to practice squad (August 27, 1997). ... Signed by New York Jets off Bears practice squad (December 3, 1997).
PLAYING EXPERIENCE: New York Jets NFL, 1997 and 1998. ... Games/Games started: 1997 (2/2), 1998 (16/0). Total: 18/2.
CHAMPIONSHIP GAME EXPERIENCE: Played in AFC championship game (1998 season).

JENSEN, JERRY LB PANTHERS

PERSONAL: Born February 26, 1975, in Downey, Calif. ... 6-0/235. ... Full name: Jerry Joe Jensen.
HIGH SCHOOL: Cascade (Everett, Wash.).
COLLEGE: Washington.
TRANSACTIONS/CAREER NOTES: Selected by Carolina Panthers in fifth round (136th pick overall) of 1998 NFL draft. ... Signed by Panthers (July 24, 1998).
PLAYING EXPERIENCE: Carolina NFL, 1998. ... Games/Games started: 10/0.
PRO STATISTICS: 1998—Returned one kickoff for nine yards and fumbled once for minus 20 yards.

JERVEY, TRAVIS RB 49ERS

PERSONAL: Born May 5, 1972, in Columbia, S.C. ... 6-0/222. ... Full name: Travis Richard Jervey.
HIGH SCHOOL: Wando (Mount Pleasant, S.C.).
COLLEGE: The Citadel.
TRANSACTIONS/CAREER NOTES: Selected by Green Bay Packers in fifth round (170th pick overall) of 1995 NFL draft. ... Signed by Packers (May 23, 1995). ... Granted free agency (February 13, 1998). ... Re-signed by Packers (June 16, 1998). ... On injured reserve with knee and ankle injuries (November 11, 1998-remainder of season). ... Granted unconditional free agency (February 12, 1999). ... Signed by San Francisco 49ers (March 22, 1999).
CHAMPIONSHIP GAME EXPERIENCE: Played in NFC championship game (1995-97 seasons). ... Member of Super Bowl championship team (1996 season). ... Played in Super Bowl XXXII (1997 season).
HONORS: Played in Pro Bowl (1997 season).
PRO STATISTICS: 1995—Recovered one fumble. 1996—Recovered one fumble.
SINGLE GAME HIGHS (regular season): Attempts—29 (October 25, 1998, vs. Baltimore); yards—95 (November 1, 1998, vs. San Francisco); and rushing touchdowns—1 (November 1, 1998, vs. San Francisco).

			RUSHING				RECEIVING				KICKOFF RETURNS				TOTALS		
Year Team	G	GS	Att.	Yds.	Avg.	TD	No.	Yds.	Avg.	TD	No.	Yds.	Avg.	TD	TD	2pt.	Pts.	Fum.
1995—Green Bay NFL	16	0	0	0	...	0	0	0	...	0	8	165	20.6	0	0	0	0	0
1996—Green Bay NFL	16	0	26	106	4.1	0	0	0	...	0	1	17	17.0	0	0	0	0	4
1997—Green Bay NFL	16	0	0	0	...	0	0	0	...	0	0	0	...	0	0	0	0	0
1998—Green Bay NFL	8	5	83	325	3.9	1	9	33	3.7	0	0	0	...	0	1	0	6	0
Pro totals (4 years)	56	5	109	431	4.0	1	9	33	3.7	0	9	182	20.2	0	1	0	6	4

JETT, JAMES — WR — RAIDERS

PERSONAL: Born December 28, 1970, in Charles Town, W.Va. ... 5-10/165.
HIGH SCHOOL: Jefferson (Shenandoah Junction, W.Va.).
COLLEGE: West Virginia.
TRANSACTIONS/CAREER NOTES: Signed as non-drafted free agent by Los Angeles Raiders (May 1993). ... Raiders franchise moved to Oakland (July 21, 1995).
PRO STATISTICS: 1993—Rushed once for no yards. 1994—Recovered two fumbles for 15 yards. 1997—Recovered one fumble. 1998—Rushed once for three yards and recovered one fumble for four yards.
SINGLE GAME HIGHS (regular season): Receptions—7 (October 13, 1996, vs. Detroit); yards—148 (September 21, 1997, vs. New York Jets); and touchdown receptions—2 (October 26, 1997, vs. Seattle).
STATISTICAL PLATEAUS: 100-yard receiving games: 1993 (2), 1996 (1), 1997 (1), 1998 (2). Total: 6.

			RECEIVING					TOTALS		
Year Team	G	GS	No.	Yds.	Avg.	TD	TD	2pt.	Pts.	Fum.
1993—Los Angeles Raiders NFL	16	1	33	771	*23.4	3	3	...	18	1
1994—Los Angeles Raiders NFL	16	1	15	253	16.9	0	0	0	0	0
1995—Oakland NFL	16	0	13	179	13.8	1	1	0	6	1
1996—Oakland NFL	16	16	43	601	14.0	4	4	0	24	0
1997—Oakland NFL	16	16	46	804	17.5	▲12	12	0	72	2
1998—Oakland NFL	16	16	45	882	19.6	6	6	0	36	0
Pro totals (6 years)	96	50	195	3490	17.9	26	26	0	156	4

JETT, JOHN — P — LIONS

PERSONAL: Born November 11, 1968, in Richmond, Va. ... 6-0/199.
HIGH SCHOOL: Northumberland (Heathsville, Va.).
COLLEGE: East Carolina.
TRANSACTIONS/CAREER NOTES: Signed as non-drafted free agent by Minnesota Vikings (June 22, 1992). ... Released by Vikings (August 25, 1992). ... Signed by Dallas Cowboys (March 10, 1993). ... Granted unconditional free agency (February 16, 1996). ... Re-signed by Cowboys (April 15, 1996). ... Granted unconditional free agency (February 14, 1997). ... Signed by Detroit Lions (March 7, 1997).
CHAMPIONSHIP GAME EXPERIENCE: Played in NFC championship game (1993-1995 seasons). ... Member of Super Bowl championship team (1993 and 1995 seasons).
PRO STATISTICS: 1996—Rushed once for minus 23 yards. 1998—Attempted one pass without a completion.

				PUNTING			
Year Team	G	No.	Yds.	Avg.	Net avg.	In. 20	Blk.
1993—Dallas NFL	16	56	2342	41.8	37.7	22	0
1994—Dallas NFL	16	70	2935	41.9	35.3	26	0
1995—Dallas NFL	16	53	2166	40.9	34.5	17	0
1996—Dallas NFL	16	74	3150	42.6	36.7	22	0
1997—Detroit NFL	16	84	3576	42.6	35.6	24	†2
1998—Detroit NFL	14	66	2892	43.8	36.0	17	0
Pro totals (6 years)	94	403	17061	42.3	36.0	128	2

JOHNSON, ALONZO — WR — SAINTS

PERSONAL: Born April 18, 1973, in Tuscaloosa, Ala. ... 5-11/186.
HIGH SCHOOL: Bount (Tuscaloosa, Ala.).
COLLEGE: Central State (Ohio).
TRANSACTIONS/CAREER NOTES: Signed as non-drafted free agent by New York Jets (April 25, 1997). ... Released by Jets (August 23, 1997). ... Re-signed by Jets to practice squad (August 26, 1997). ... Claimed on waivers by New Orleans Saints (August 25, 1998). ... Released by Saints (August 30, 1998). ... Re-signed by Saints to practice squad (September 1, 1998). ... Activated (December 19, 1998). ... Assigned by Saints to Barcelona Dragons in 1999 NFL Europe enhancement allocation program (February 22, 1999).
PLAYING EXPERIENCE: New Orleans NFL, 1998. ... Games/Games started: 1/0.

JOHNSON, ANDRE — OT — LIONS

PERSONAL: Born August 25, 1973, in Southampton, N.Y. ... 6-5/314. ... Full name: Andre T. Johnson.
HIGH SCHOOL: Southhampton (N.Y.).
COLLEGE: Penn State.
TRANSACTIONS/CAREER NOTES: Selected by Washington Redskins in first round (30th pick overall) of 1996 NFL draft. ... Signed by Redskins (July 17, 1996). ... Inactive for all 16 games (1996). ... Claimed on waivers by Miami Dolphins (August 26, 1997). ... Inactive for four games with Dolphins (1997). ... Released by Dolphins (September 29, 1997). ... Signed by Detroit Lions (October 7, 1997). ... Inactive for 10 games with Lions (1997). ... Granted free agency (February 12, 1999). ... Re-signed by Lions (April 12, 1999).
PLAYING EXPERIENCE: Detroit NFL, 1998. ... Games/Games started: 3/0.

JOHNSON, ANTHONY — RB — PANTHERS

PERSONAL: Born October 25, 1967, in Indianapolis. ... 6-0/225. ... Full name: Anthony Scott Johnson.
HIGH SCHOOL: John Adams (South Bend, Ind.).
COLLEGE: Notre Dame.
TRANSACTIONS/CAREER NOTES: Selected by Indianapolis Colts in second round (36th pick overall) of 1990 NFL draft. ... Signed by Colts (July 27, 1990). ... On injured reserve with eye injury (November 5, 1991-remainder of season). ... Granted unconditional free agency (February 17, 1994). ... Signed by New York Jets (June 21, 1994). ... Granted unconditional free agency (February 17, 1995). ... Signed by

Chicago Bears (March 21, 1995). ... Claimed on waivers by Carolina Panthers (November 7, 1995). ... Granted unconditional free agency (February 14, 1997). ... Re-signed by Panthers (February 24, 1997).
CHAMPIONSHIP GAME EXPERIENCE: Played in NFC championship game (1996 season).
PRO STATISTICS: 1992—Attempted one pass without a completion and recovered four fumbles. 1993—Had only pass attempt intercepted and recovered two fumbles. 1994—Returned one punt for three yards. 1997—Recovered two fumbles. 1998—Returned two kickoffs for 12 yards and recovered one fumble.
SINGLE GAME HIGHS (regular season): Attempts—29 (October 20, 1996, vs. New Orleans); yards—134 (August 31, 1997, vs. Seattle); and rushing touchdowns—1 (December 15, 1996, vs. Baltimore).
STATISTICAL PLATEAUS: 100-yard rushing games: 1996 (5), 1997 (1). Total: 6. ... 100-yard receiving games: 1991 (1), 1992 (1). Total: 2.
MISCELLANEOUS: Holds Carolina Panthers all-time record for most yards rushing (1,723).

				RUSHING				RECEIVING				TOTALS		
Year Team	G	GS	Att.	Yds.	Avg.	TD	No.	Yds.	Avg.	TD	TD	2pt.	Pts.	Fum.
1990—Indianapolis NFL	16	0	0	0	...	0	5	32	6.4	2	2	...	12	0
1991—Indianapolis NFL	9	6	22	94	4.3	0	42	344	8.2	0	0	...	0	2
1992—Indianapolis NFL	15	13	178	592	3.3	0	49	517	10.6	3	3	...	18	6
1993—Indianapolis NFL	13	8	95	331	3.5	1	55	443	8.1	0	1	...	6	5
1994—New York Jets NFL	15	0	5	12	2.4	0	5	31	6.2	0	0	0	0	0
1995—Chicago NFL	8	0	6	30	5.0	0	13	86	6.6	0	0	0	0	2
—Carolina NFL	7	0	24	110	4.6	1	16	121	7.6	0	1	0	6	0
1996—Carolina NFL	16	11	300	1120	3.7	6	26	192	7.4	0	6	0	36	2
1997—Carolina NFL	16	7	97	358	3.7	0	21	158	7.5	1	1	1	8	2
1998—Carolina NFL	16	2	36	135	3.8	0	27	242	9.0	1	1	0	6	3
Pro totals (9 years)	131	47	763	2782	3.6	8	259	2166	8.4	7	15	1	92	22

JOHNSON, BILL   DT   EAGLES

PERSONAL: Born December 9, 1968, in Chicago. ... 6-4/305. ... Full name: William Edward Johnson.
HIGH SCHOOL: Neal F. Simeon (Chicago).
COLLEGE: Michigan State.
TRANSACTIONS/CAREER NOTES: Selected by Cleveland Browns in third round (65th pick overall) of 1992 NFL draft. ... Signed by Browns (July 19, 1992). ... Granted free agency (February 17, 1995). ... Re-signed by Browns (April 13, 1995). ... Claimed on waivers by Cincinnati Bengals (August 1, 1995); released after failing physical. ... Signed by Pittsburgh Steelers (October 25, 1995). ... Granted unconditional free agency (February 14, 1997). ... Signed by St. Louis Rams (June 10, 1997). ... Granted unconditional free agency (February 13, 1998). ... Signed by Philadelphia Eagles (February 21, 1998). ... On injured reserve with knee injury (December 4, 1998-remainder of season).
CHAMPIONSHIP GAME EXPERIENCE: Played in AFC championship game (1995 season). ... Played in Super Bowl XXX (1995 season).
PRO STATISTICS: 1994—Recovered one fumble. 1995—Recovered one fumble. 1996—Recovered one fumble. 1997—Recovered one fumble.

Year Team	G	GS	SACKS
1992—Cleveland NFL	16	2	2.0
1993—Cleveland NFL	10	0	1.0
1994—Cleveland NFL	14	13	1.0
1995—Pittsburgh NFL	9	0	0.0
1996—Pittsburgh NFL	15	8	1.0
1997—St. Louis NFL	16	16	4.0
1998—Philadelphia NFL	13	13	2.5
Pro totals (7 years)	93	52	11.5

JOHNSON, BRAD   QB   REDSKINS

PERSONAL: Born September 13, 1968, in Marietta, Ga. ... 6-5/224. ... Full name: James Bradley Johnson.
HIGH SCHOOL: Charles D. Owen (Swannanoa, N.C.).
COLLEGE: Florida State (degree in physical education, 1991).
TRANSACTIONS/CAREER NOTES: Selected by Minnesota Vikings in ninth round (227th pick overall) of 1992 NFL draft. ... Signed by Vikings (July 17, 1992). ... Active for one game (1992); did not play. ... Inactive for all 16 games (1993). ... Granted free agency (February 17, 1995). ... Assigned by Vikings to London Monarchs in 1995 World League enhancement allocation program (February 20, 1995). ... Re-signed by Vikings (March 27, 1995). ... On injured reserve with neck injury (December 5, 1997-remainder of season). ... Traded by Vikings to Washington Redskins for first- (QB Daunte Culpepper) and third-round (traded to Pittsburgh) picks in 1999 draft and second-round pick in 2000 draft (February 15, 1999).
CHAMPIONSHIP GAME EXPERIENCE: Member of Vikings for NFC championship game (1998 season); did not play.
PRO STATISTICS: 1995—Fumbled twice. 1996—Fumbled five times and recovered three fumbles for minus eight yards. 1997—Caught one pass for three yards and a touchdown, fumbled four times and recovered three fumbles. 1998—Fumbled once.
SINGLE GAME HIGHS (regular season): Attempts—44 (September 14, 1997, vs. Tampa Bay); completions—33 (September 7, 1997, vs. Chicago); yards—334 (September 14, 1997, vs. Tampa Bay); and touchdown passes—4 (September 6, 1998, vs. Tampa Bay).
STATISTICAL PLATEAUS: 300-yard passing games: 1997 (2), 1998 (1). Total: 3.
MISCELLANEOUS: Regular-season record as starting NFL quarterback: 15-8 (.652). ... Postseason record as starting NFL quarterback: 0-1.

			PASSING							RUSHING			TOTALS		
Year Team	G	GS	Att.	Cmp.	Pct.	Yds.	TD	Int.	Avg.	Rat.	Att.	Yds.	Avg.	TD	TD	2pt.	Pts.
1992—Minnesota NFL						Did not play.										
1993—Minnesota NFL						Did not play.										
1994—Minnesota NFL	4	0	37	22	59.5	150	0	0	4.05	68.5	2	-2	-1.0	0	0	0	0
1995—London W.L.	...	...	328	194	59.1	2227	13	14	6.79	75.1	24	99	4.1	1	1	1	8
—Minnesota NFL	5	0	36	25	69.4	272	0	2	7.56	68.3	9	-9	-1.0	0	0	0	0
1996—Minnesota NFL	12	8	311	195	62.7	2258	17	10	7.26	89.4	34	90	2.6	1	1	0	6
1997—Minnesota NFL	13	13	452	275	60.8	3036	20	12	6.72	84.5	35	139	4.0	0	1	2	10
1998—Minnesota NFL	4	2	101	65	64.4	747	7	5	7.40	89.0	12	15	1.3	0	0	0	0
W.L. totals (1 year)	...	...	328	194	59.1	2227	13	14	6.79	75.1	24	99	4.1	1	1	1	8
NFL totals (5 years)	38	23	937	582	62.1	6463	44	29	6.90	85.3	92	233	2.5	1	2	2	16
Pro totals (6 years)	...	...	1265	776	61.3	8690	57	43	6.87	82.7	116	332	2.9	2	3	3	24

JOHNSON, CHARLES — WR — EAGLES

PERSONAL: Born January 3, 1972, in San Bernardino, Calif. ... 6-0/200. ... Full name: Charles Everett Johnson.
HIGH SCHOOL: Cajon (San Bernardino, Calif.).
COLLEGE: Colorado (degree in marketing, 1993).
TRANSACTIONS/CAREER NOTES: Selected by Pittsburgh Steelers in first round (17th pick overall) of 1994 NFL draft. ... Signed by Steelers (July 21, 1994). ... On injured reserve with knee injury (December 23, 1995-remainder of season). ... Granted unconditional free agency (February 12, 1999). ... Signed by Philadelphia Eagles (February 16, 1999).
CHAMPIONSHIP GAME EXPERIENCE: Played in AFC championship game (1994 and 1997 seasons).
HONORS: Named wide receiver on THE SPORTING NEWS college All-America second team (1993).
RECORDS: Shares NFL single-game record for most two-point converstions—2 (November 1, 1998).
PRO STATISTICS: 1994—Fumbled twice. 1995—Recovered one fumble. 1996—Fumbled once.
SINGLE GAME HIGHS (regular season): Receptions—9 (November 1, 1998, vs. Tennessee); yards—165 (December 24, 1994, vs. San Diego); and touchdown receptions—3 (November 1, 1998, vs. Tennessee).
STATISTICAL PLATEAUS: 100-yard receiving games: 1994 (1), 1996 (4), 1997 (1), 1998 (1). Total: 7.

			RUSHING				RECEIVING				PUNT RETURNS				KICKOFF RETURNS				TOTALS		
Year Team	G	GS	Att.	Yds.	Avg.	TD	No.	Yds.	Avg.	TD	No.	Yds.	Avg.	TD	No.	Yds.	Avg.	TD	TD	2pt.	Pts.
1994—Pittsburgh NFL	16	9	4	-1	-0.3	0	38	577	15.2	3	15	90	6.0	0	16	345	21.6	0	3	0	18
1995—Pittsburgh NFL	14	12	1	-10	-10.0	0	38	432	11.4	0	0	0	...	0	2	47	23.5	0	0	0	0
1996—Pittsburgh NFL	16	12	0	0	...	0	60	1008	16.8	3	0	0	...	0	6	111	18.5	0	3	1	20
1997—Pittsburgh NFL	13	11	0	0	...	0	46	568	12.3	2	0	0	...	0	0	0	...	0	2	0	12
1998—Pittsburgh NFL	16	16	1	4	4.0	0	65	815	12.5	7	0	0	...	0	0	0	...	0	7	†2	46
Pro totals (5 years)	75	60	6	-7	-1.2	0	247	3400	13.8	15	15	90	6.0	0	24	503	21.0	0	15	3	96

JOHNSON, DARRIUS — CB — BRONCOS

PERSONAL: Born September 17, 1972, in Terrell, Texas. ... 5-9/185.
HIGH SCHOOL: Terrell (Texas).
COLLEGE: Oklahoma.
TRANSACTIONS/CAREER NOTES: Selected by Denver Broncos in fourth round (122nd pick overall) of 1996 NFL draft. ... Signed by Broncos (July 17, 1996).
PLAYING EXPERIENCE: Denver NFL, 1996-1998. ... Games/Games started: 1996 (13/0), 1997 (16/0), 1998 (16/2). Total: 45/2.
CHAMPIONSHIP GAME EXPERIENCE: Played in AFC championship game (1997 and 1998 seasons). ... Member of Super Bowl championship team (1997 and 1998 seasons).
PRO STATISTICS: 1997—Recovered one fumble for six yards and a touchdown. 1998—Intercepted two passes for 79 yards and credited with one sack.

JOHNSON, ELLIS — DT — COLTS

PERSONAL: Born October 30, 1973, in Wildwood, Fla. ... 6-2/292. ... Full name: Ellis Bernard Johnson.
HIGH SCHOOL: Wildwood (Fla.).
COLLEGE: Florida.
TRANSACTIONS/CAREER NOTES: Selected by Indianapolis Colts in first round (15th pick overall) of 1995 NFL draft. ... Signed by Colts (June 7, 1995).
CHAMPIONSHIP GAME EXPERIENCE: Played in AFC championship game (1995 season).
PRO STATISTICS: 1997—Intercepted one pass for 18 yards and recovered two fumbles.

Year Team	G	GS	SACKS
1995—Indianapolis NFL	16	2	4.5
1996—Indianapolis NFL	12	6	0.0
1997—Indianapolis NFL	15	15	4.5
1998—Indianapolis NFL	16	16	8.0
Pro totals (4 years)	59	39	17.0

JOHNSON, JASON — C — COLTS

PERSONAL: Born February 6, 1974, in Kansas City, Mo. ... 6-3/290. ... Full name: Jason Joseph Johnson.
HIGH SCHOOL: Oak Park (Mo.).
COLLEGE: Kansas State.
TRANSACTIONS/CAREER NOTES: Signed as non-drafted free agent by Indianapolis Colts (April 25, 1997). ... Released by Colts (September 13, 1997). ... Re-signed by Colts to practice squad (September 15, 1997).
PLAYING EXPERIENCE: Indianapolis NFL, 1998. ... Games/Games started: 14/0.

JOHNSON, JIMMIE — TE

PERSONAL: Born October 6, 1966, in Augusta, Ga. ... 6-2/257. ... Full name: Jimmie O. Johnson Jr.
HIGH SCHOOL: T.W. Josey (Augusta, Ga.).
COLLEGE: Howard (degree in consumer studies, 1989).
TRANSACTIONS/CAREER NOTES: Selected by Washington Redskins in 12th round (316th pick overall) of 1989 NFL draft. ... Signed by Redskins (July 23, 1989). ... On injured reserve with pinched nerve in neck (October 12, 1991-remainder of season). ... Granted unconditional free agency (February 1, 1992). ... Signed by Detroit Lions (April 1, 1992). ... On active/non-football injury list (July 16-August 23, 1993). ... On reserve/non-football injury list (August 23-October 15, 1993). ... Released by Lions (November 29, 1993). ... Signed by Kansas City Chiefs (1994). ... Released by Chiefs (August 29, 1994). ... Re-signed by Chiefs (October 12, 1994). ... Released by Chiefs (March 30, 1995). ... Signed by Philadelphia Eagles (August 2, 1995). ... Granted unconditional free agency (February 16, 1996). ... Re-signed by Eagles (April 18, 1996). ... Granted unconditional free agency (February 14, 1997). ... Re-signed by Eagles (June 2, 1997). ... Released by Eagles (October 29, 1998).

PRO STATISTICS: 1992—Returned one kickoff for no yards. 1997—Returned three kickoffs for 22 yards.
SINGLE GAME HIGHS (regular season): Receptions—4 (November 23, 1997, vs. Pittsburgh); yards—55 (November 18, 1990, vs. New Orleans); and touchdown receptions—1 (November 30, 1997, vs. Cincinnati).

				RECEIVING			TOTALS			
Year Team	G	GS	No.	Yds.	Avg.	TD	TD	2pt.	Pts.	Fum.
1989—Washington NFL	16	0	4	84	21.0	0	0	...	0	0
1990—Washington NFL	16	5	15	218	14.5	2	2	...	12	1
1991—Washington NFL	6	0	3	7	2.3	2	2	...	12	0
1992—Detroit NFL	16	5	6	34	5.7	0	0	...	0	0
1993—Detroit NFL	6	4	2	18	9.0	0	0	...	0	0
1994—Kansas City NFL	7	1	2	7	3.5	0	0	0	0	0
1995—Philadelphia NFL	16	1	6	37	6.2	0	0	0	0	0
1996—Philadelphia NFL	16	3	7	127	18.1	0	0	0	0	0
1997—Philadelphia NFL	16	11	14	177	12.6	1	1	0	6	1
1998—Philadelphia NFL	3	3	2	14	7.0	0	0	0	0	0
Pro totals (10 years)	118	33	61	723	11.9	5	5	0	30	2

JOHNSON, JOE — DE — SAINTS

PERSONAL: Born July 11, 1972, in St. Louis. ... 6-4/270. ... Full name: Joe T. Johnson.
HIGH SCHOOL: Jennings (Mo.).
COLLEGE: Louisville.
TRANSACTIONS/CAREER NOTES: Selected after junior season by New Orleans Saints in first round (13th pick overall) of 1994 NFL draft. ... Signed by Saints (June 7, 1994). ... Designated by Saints as franchise player (February 13, 1998). ... Re-signed by Saints (September 2, 1998).
HONORS: Played in Pro Bowl (1998 season).
PRO STATISTICS: 1994—Recovered one fumble. 1997—Recovered one fumble. 1998—Recovered one fumble for five yards and a touchdown.

Year Team	G	GS	SACKS
1994—New Orleans NFL	15	14	1.0
1995—New Orleans NFL	14	14	5.5
1996—New Orleans NFL	13	13	7.5
1997—New Orleans NFL	16	16	8.5
1998—New Orleans NFL	16	16	7.0
Pro totals (5 years)	74	73	29.5

JOHNSON, KEYSHAWN — WR — JETS

PERSONAL: Born July 22, 1972, in Los Angeles. ... 6-3/212. ... Cousin of Chris Miller, wide receiver with Green Bay Packers (1997), Detroit Lions (1997) and Chicago Bears (1998).
HIGH SCHOOL: Dorsey (Los Angeles).
JUNIOR COLLEGE: West Los Angeles College.
COLLEGE: Southern California (degree in history).
TRANSACTIONS/CAREER NOTES: Selected by New York Jets in first round (first pick overall) of 1996 NFL draft. ... Signed by Jets (August 6, 1996).
CHAMPIONSHIP GAME EXPERIENCE: Played in AFC championship game (1998 season).
HONORS: Named wide receiver on THE SPORTING NEWS college All-America first team (1995). ... Played in Pro Bowl (1998 season). ... Named co-Oustanding Player of Pro Bowl (1998 season).
PRO STATISTICS: 1998—Rushed twice for 60 yards and one touchdown.
SINGLE GAME HIGHS (regular season): Receptions—10 (November 22, 1998, vs. Tennessee); yards—126 (September 6, 1998, vs. San Francisco); and touchdown receptions—2 (September 6, 1998, vs. San Francisco).
STATISTICAL PLATEAUS: 100-yard receiving games: 1997 (1), 1998 (4). Total: 5.

				RECEIVING			TOTALS			
Year Team	G	GS	No.	Yds.	Avg.	TD	TD	2pt.	Pts.	Fum.
1996—New York Jets NFL	14	11	63	844	13.4	8	8	1	50	0
1997—New York Jets NFL	16	16	70	963	13.8	5	5	0	30	0
1998—New York Jets NFL	16	16	83	1131	13.6	10	11	0	66	0
Pro totals (3 years)	46	43	216	2938	13.6	23	24	1	146	0

JOHNSON, LEE — P — PATRIOTS

PERSONAL: Born November 27, 1961, in Dallas. ... 6-2/200.
HIGH SCHOOL: McCullough (The Woodlands, Texas).
COLLEGE: Brigham Young.
TRANSACTIONS/CAREER NOTES: Selected by Houston Gamblers in ninth round (125th pick overall) of 1985 USFL draft. ... Selected by Houston Oilers in fifth round (138th pick overall) of 1985 NFL draft. ... Signed by Oilers (June 25, 1985). ... Crossed picket line during players strike (October 14, 1987). ... Claimed on waivers by Buffalo Bills (December 2, 1987). ... Claimed on waivers by Cleveland Browns (December 10, 1987). ... Claimed on waivers by Cincinnati Bengals (September 23, 1988). ... Granted free agency (February 1, 1991). ... Re-signed by Bengals (1991). ... Granted unconditional free agency (March 1, 1993). ... Re-signed by Bengals (May 10, 1993). ... Released by Bengals (December 7, 1998). ... Signed by New England Patriots (February 18, 1999).
CHAMPIONSHIP GAME EXPERIENCE: Played in AFC championship game (1987 and 1988 seasons). ... Played in Super Bowl XXIII (1988 season).
POST SEASON RECORDS: Holds Super Bowl career record for longest punt—63 yards (January 22, 1989, vs. San Francisco).
PRO STATISTICS: 1985—Rushed once for no yards, fumbled twice and recovered one fumble in his own end zone for a safety. 1987—Had 32.8-yard net punting average. 1988—Had 33.4-yard net punting average. 1989—Rushed once for minus seven yards. 1990—Attempted one pass with a completion for four yards and a touchdown. 1991—Attempted one pass with a completion for three yards, rushed once for minus two yards and fumbled once. 1993—Attempted one pass without a completion. 1994—Attempted one pass with a completion for seven yards and one touchdown. 1995—Attempted one pass with a completion for five yards, rushed once for minus 16 yards and fumbled once. 1997—Rushed once for no yards and recovered two fumbles.

Year	Team	G	No.	Yds.	PUNTING Avg.	Net avg.	In. 20	Blk.	XPM	XPA	KICKING FGM	FGA	Lg.	50+	Pts.
1985	Houston NFL	16	83	3464	41.7	35.7	22	0	0	0	0	0	0	0-0	0
1986	Houston NFL	16	88	3623	41.2	35.7	26	0	0	0	0	0	0	0-0	0
1987	Houston NFL	9	25	1008	40.3	...	5	1	0	0	0	0	0	0-0	0
	—Cleveland NFL	3	9	317	35.2	32.2	3	0	0	0	0	0	0	0-0	0
1988	Cleveland NFL	3	31	1237	39.9	...	6	0	0	0	1	2	50	1-2	3
	—Cincinnati NFL	12	14	594	42.4	...	4	0	0	0	0	0	0	0-0	0
1989	Cincinnati NFL	16	61	2446	40.1	30.1	14	2	0	1	0	0	0	0-0	0
1990	Cincinnati NFL	16	64	2705	42.3	34.2	12	0	0	0	1	0	0	0-0	0
1991	Cincinnati NFL	16	64	2795	43.7	34.7	15	0	0	1	3	53	1-3	3
1992	Cincinnati NFL	16	76	3196	42.1	35.8	15	0	0	0	1	0	0	0-1	0
1993	Cincinnati NFL	16	▲90	3954	43.9	36.6	24	0	0	0	0	0	0	0-0	0
1994	Cincinnati NFL	16	79	3461	43.8	35.2	19	1	0	0	0	0	0	0-0	0
1995	Cincinnati NFL	16	68	2861	42.1	38.6	26	0	0	0	0	0	0	0-0	0
1996	Cincinnati NFL	16	80	3630	45.4	34.3	16	1	0	0	0	0	0	0-0	0
1997	Cincinnati NFL	16	81	3471	42.9	35.9	27	0	0	0	0	0	0	0-0	0
1998	Cincinnati NFL	13	69	3083	44.7	35.6	14	1	0	0	0	0	0	0-0	0
Pro totals (14 years)		216	982	41845	42.6	32.8	248	6	0	1	2	7	53	2-6	6

JOHNSON, LEON   RB/KR   JETS

PERSONAL: Born July 13, 1974, in Morganton, N.C.. ... 6-0/215. ... Full name: William Leon Johnson.
HIGH SCHOOL: Freedom (Morganton, N.C.).
COLLEGE: North Carolina.
TRANSACTIONS/CAREER NOTES: Selected by New York Jets in fourth round (104th pick overall) of 1997 NFL draft. ... Signed by Jets (July 17, 1997). ... On injured reserve with rib injury (December 16, 1998-remainder of season).
PRO STATISTICS: 1997—Attempted two passes without a completion and one interception, fumbled five times and recovered five fumbles. 1998—Fumbled three times and recovered three fumbles.
SINGLE GAME HIGHS (regular season): Attempts—13 (October 11, 1998, vs. St. Louis); yards—56 (October 11, 1998, vs. St. Louis); and rushing touchdowns—2 (September 20, 1998, vs Indianapolis).

Year Team	G	GS	RUSHING Att. Yds. Avg. TD	RECEIVING No. Yds. Avg. TD	PUNT RETURNS No. Yds. Avg. TD	KICKOFF RETURNS No. Yds. Avg. TD	TOTALS TD 2pt. Pts.
1997—N.Y. Jets NFL	16	1	48 158 3.3 2	16 142 8.9 0	§51 *619 12.1 1	12 319 26.6 ▲1	4 0 24
1998—N.Y. Jets NFL	12	2	41 185 4.5 2	13 222 17.1 2	29 203 7.0 0	16 366 22.9 0	4 0 24
Pro totals (2 years)	28	3	89 343 3.9 4	29 364 12.6 2	80 822 10.3 1	28 685 24.5 1	8 0 48

JOHNSON, LONNIE   TE   CHIEFS

PERSONAL: Born February 14, 1971, in Miami. ... 6-3/240. ... Full name: Lonnie Demetrius Johnson.
HIGH SCHOOL: Miami High.
COLLEGE: Florida State.
TRANSACTIONS/CAREER NOTES: Selected by Buffalo Bills in second round (61st pick overall) of 1994 NFL draft. ... Signed by Bills (July 15, 1994). ... Granted free agency (February 14, 1997). ... Re-signed by Bills (June 12, 1997). ... Granted unconditional free agency (February 13, 1998). ... Re-signed by Bills (March 30, 1998). ... Granted unconditional free agency (February 12, 1999). ... Signed by Kansas City Chiefs (April 12, 1999).
PRO STATISTICS: 1995—Recovered one fumble. 1996—Recovered four fumbles. 1997—Rushed once for six yards and recovered one fumble. 1998—Returned three kickoffs for 18 yards.
SINGLE GAME HIGHS (regular season): Receptions—7 (October 15, 1995, vs. Seattle); yards—90 (October 20, 1996, vs. New York Jets); and touchdown receptions—1 (December 27, 1998, vs. New Orleans).

Year Team	G	GS	RECEIVING No. Yds. Avg. TD	TOTALS TD 2pt. Pts. Fum.
1994—Buffalo NFL	10	1	3 42 14.0 0	0 0 0 0
1995—Buffalo NFL	16	16	49 504 10.3 1	1 0 6 0
1996—Buffalo NFL	16	15	46 457 9.9 0	0 0 0 1
1997—Buffalo NFL	16	16	41 340 8.3 2	2 0 12 2
1998—Buffalo NFL	16	16	14 146 10.4 2	2 0 12 1
Pro totals (5 years)	74	64	153 1489 9.7 5	5 0 30 4

JOHNSON, MELVIN   S   CHARGERS

PERSONAL: Born April 15, 1972, in Cincinnati. ... 6-0/205. ... Full name: Melvin Carlton Johnson III.
HIGH SCHOOL: St. Xavier (Cincinnati).
COLLEGE: Kentucky (degree in psychology).
TRANSACTIONS/CAREER NOTES: Selected by Tampa Bay Buccaneers in second round (43rd pick overall) of 1995 NFL draft. ... Signed by Buccaneers (May 10, 1995). ... Traded by Buccaneers to Kansas City Chiefs for conditional pick in 1999 draft (April 19, 1998). ... Released by Chiefs (October 28, 1998). ... Signed by Washington Redskins to practice squad (October 29, 1998). ... Granted free agency after 1998 season. ... Signed by San Diego Chargers (January 7, 1999).
PRO STATISTICS: 1996—Recovered one fumble. 1998—Credited with one sack.

Year Team	G	GS	INTERCEPTIONS No. Yds. Avg. TD
1995—Tampa Bay NFL	11	3	1 0 0.0 0
1996—Tampa Bay NFL	16	16	2 24 12.0 0
1997—Tampa Bay NFL	16	7	1 19 19.0 0
1998—Kansas City NFL	7	1	0 0 ... 0
Pro totals (4 years)	50	27	4 43 10.8 0

JOHNSON, NORM — K

PERSONAL: Born May 31, 1960, in Garden Grove, Calif. ... 6-2/202. ... Full name: Norm Douglas Johnson.
HIGH SCHOOL: Pacifica (Garden Grove, Calif.).
COLLEGE: UCLA.
TRANSACTIONS/CAREER NOTES: Signed as non-drafted free agent by Seattle Seahawks (May 4, 1982). ... Crossed picket line during players strike (October 14, 1987). ... Granted free agency (February 1, 1991). ... Re-signed by Seahawks (July 19, 1991). ... Released by Seahawks (August 26, 1991). ... Signed by Atlanta Falcons (September 9, 1991). ... Granted free agency (February 1, 1992). ... Re-signed by Falcons for 1992 season. ... Released by Falcons (July 20, 1995). ... Signed by Pittsburgh Steelers (August 22, 1995). ... Released by Steelers (July 9, 1997). ... Re-signed by Steelers (August 25, 1997). ... Granted unconditional free agency (February 12, 1999).
CHAMPIONSHIP GAME EXPERIENCE: Played in AFC championship game (1983, 1995 and 1997 seasons). ... Played in Super Bowl XXX (1995 season).
HONORS: Named kicker on THE SPORTING NEWS NFL All-Pro team (1984). ... Played in Pro Bowl (1984 and 1993 seasons).
RECORDS: Holds NFL career record for most consecutive points after touchdown made—276 (1991-present).
PRO STATISTICS: 1982—Attempted one pass with one completion for 27 yards. 1991—Punted once for 21 yards. 1992—Punted once for 37 yards.

				KICKING				
Year Team	G	XPM	XPA	FGM	FGA	Lg.	50+	Pts.
1982—Seattle NFL	9	13	14	10	14	48	0-1	43
1983—Seattle NFL	16	49	50	18	25	54	1-3	103
1984—Seattle NFL	16	50	51	20	24	50	1-3	110
1985—Seattle NFL	16	40	41	14	25	51	1-3	82
1986—Seattle NFL	16	42	42	22	35	54	5-7	108
1987—Seattle NFL	13	§40	§40	15	20	49	0-1	85
1988—Seattle NFL	16	39	39	22	28	47	0-0	105
1989—Seattle NFL	16	27	27	15	25	50	1-5	72
1990—Seattle NFL	16	33	34	23	32	51	1-3	102
1991—Atlanta NFL	14	38	39	19	23	50	1-2	95
1992—Atlanta NFL	16	39	39	18	22	†54	4-4	93
1993—Atlanta NFL	15	34	34	26	27	54	2-2	112
1994—Atlanta NFL	16	32	32	21	25	50	1-5	95
1995—Pittsburgh NFL	16	39	39	*34	*41	50	1-1	§141
1996—Pittsburgh NFL	16	37	37	23	30	49	0-1	106
1997—Pittsburgh NFL	16	40	40	22	25	52	1-2	106
1998—Pittsburgh NFL	15	21	21	26	31	49	0-2	99
Pro totals (17 years)	258	613	619	348	452	54	20-45	1657

JOHNSON, PATRICK — WR — RAVENS

PERSONAL: Born August 10, 1976, in Gainesville, Ga. ... 5-10/180. ... Full name: Patrick Jevon Johnson.
HIGH SCHOOL: Redlands (Calif.).
COLLEGE: Oregon.
TRANSACTIONS/CAREER NOTES: Selected by Baltimore Ravens in second round (42nd pick overall) of 1998 NFL draft. ... Signed by Ravens (June 24, 1998).
HONORS: Named kick returner on THE SPORTING NEWS college All-America second team (1997).
SINGLE GAME HIGHS (regular season): Receptions—3 (November 1, 1998, vs. Jacksonville); yards—42 (October 11, 1998, vs. Tennessee); and touchdown receptions—1 (November 1, 1998, vs. Jacksonville).

			RECEIVING				PUNT RETURNS			KICKOFF RETURNS				TOTALS		
Year Team	G	GS	No.	Yds.	Avg.	TD	No.	Yds.	Avg.	TD	No.	Yds.	Avg.	TD	TD	2pt.	Pts. Fum.
1998—Baltimore NFL	13	0	12	159	13.3	1	1	6	6.0	0	16	399	24.9	▲1	2	0	12 1

JOHNSON, PEPPER — LB

PERSONAL: Born July 29, 1964, in Detroit. ... 6-3/259. ... Full name: Thomas Johnson.
HIGH SCHOOL: MacKenzie (Detroit).
COLLEGE: Ohio State.
TRANSACTIONS/CAREER NOTES: Selected by New Jersey Generals in 1986 USFL territorial draft. ... Selected by New York Giants in second round (51st pick overall) of 1986 NFL draft. ... Signed by Giants (July 30, 1986). ... Granted free agency (February 1, 1989). ... Re-signed by Giants (September 14, 1989). ... Granted roster exemption (September 14-23, 1989). ... Granted free agency (February 1, 1991). ... Re-signed by Giants (August 14, 1991). ... Designated by Giants as transition player (February 25, 1993). ... Claimed on waivers by Cleveland Browns (September 1, 1993). ... Granted unconditional free agency (February 17, 1994). ... Re-signed by Browns (June 3, 1994). ... Browns franchise moved to Baltimore and renamed Ravens for 1996 season (March 11, 1996). ... Released by Ravens (July 9, 1996). ... Signed by Detroit Lions (August 21, 1996). ... Granted unconditional free agency (February 14, 1997). ... Signed by New York Jets (February 25, 1997). ... On injured reserve with leg injury (October 20, 1997-remainder of season). ... Granted unconditional free agency (February 12, 1999).
CHAMPIONSHIP GAME EXPERIENCE: Played in NFC championship game (1986 and 1990 seasons). ... Member of Super Bowl championship team (1986 and 1990 seasons). ... Played in AFC championship game (1998 season).
HONORS: Named inside linebacker on THE SPORTING NEWS NFL All-Pro team (1990). ... Played in Pro Bowl (1990 and 1994 seasons).
PRO STATISTICS: 1987—Recovered one fumble. 1988—Recovered one fumble. 1989—Recovered one fumble. 1990—Recovered one fumble. 1992—Fumbled once and recovered two fumbles. 1994—Recovered one fumble for 10 yards. 1998—Recovered one fumble.

				INTERCEPTIONS			SACKS
Year Team	G	GS	No.	Yds.	Avg.	TD	No.
1986—New York Giants NFL	16	0	1	13	13.0	0	2.0
1987—New York Giants NFL	12	12	0	0	...	0	1.0
1988—New York Giants NFL	16	15	1	33	33.0	1	4.0
1989—New York Giants NFL	14	4	3	60	20.0	∞1	1.0
1990—New York Giants NFL	16	14	1	0	0.0	0	3.5

Year Team	G	GS	INTERCEPTIONS No.	Yds.	Avg.	TD	SACKS No.
1991—New York Giants NFL	16	16	2	5	2.5	0	6.5
1992—New York Giants NFL	16	16	2	42	21.0	0	1.0
1993—Cleveland NFL	16	11	0	0	...	0	1.0
1994—Cleveland NFL	16	16	0	0	...	0	2.5
1995—Cleveland NFL	16	16	2	22	11.0	0	2.0
1996—Detroit NFL	15	12	0	0	...	0	0.0
1997—New York Jets NFL	8	8	1	13	13.0	0	0.0
1998—New York Jets NFL	16	16	1	0	0.0	0	1.0
Pro totals (13 years)	193	156	14	188	13.4	2	25.5

JOHNSON, RAYLEE — DE — CHARGERS

PERSONAL: Born June 1, 1970, in Chicago, Ill. ... 6-3/272. ... Full name: Raylee Terrell Johnson.
HIGH SCHOOL: Fordyce (Ark.).
COLLEGE: Arkansas.
TRANSACTIONS/CAREER NOTES: Selected by San Diego Chargers in fourth round (95th pick overall) of 1993 NFL draft. ... Signed by Chargers (July 15, 1993). ... Granted unconditional free agency (February 14, 1997). ... Re-signed by Chargers (March 11, 1997).
CHAMPIONSHIP GAME EXPERIENCE: Played in AFC championship game (1994 season). ... Played in Super Bowl XXIX (1994 season).

Year Team	G	GS	SACKS
1993—San Diego NFL	9	0	0.0
1994—San Diego NFL	15	0	1.5
1995—San Diego NFL	16	1	3.0
1996—San Diego NFL	16	1	3.0
1997—San Diego NFL	16	0	2.5
1998—San Diego NFL	16	3	5.5
Pro totals (6 years)	88	5	15.5

JOHNSON, ROB — QB — BILLS

PERSONAL: Born March 18, 1973, in Newport Beach, Calif. ... 6-4/214. ... Full name: Rob Garland Johnson. ... Brother of Bret Johnson, quarterback, Toronto Argonauts of CFL; and cousin of Bart Johnson, pitcher with Chicago White Sox (1969-1974, 1976 and 1977).
HIGH SCHOOL: El Toro (Calif.).
COLLEGE: Southern California.
TRANSACTIONS/CAREER NOTES: Selected by Jacksonville Jaguars in fourth round (99th pick overall) of 1995 NFL draft. ... Signed by Jaguars (June 1, 1995). ... Traded by Jaguars to Buffalo Bills for first- (RB Fred Taylor) and fourth-round (RB Tavian Banks) picks in 1998 draft (February 13, 1998).
CHAMPIONSHIP GAME EXPERIENCE: Member of Jaguars for AFC championship game (1996 season); did not play.
PRO STATISTICS: 1998—Fumbled twice and recovered one fumble for minus one yard.
SINGLE GAME HIGHS (regular season): Attempts—28 (September 20, 1998, vs. St. Louis); completions—20 (August 31, 1997, vs. Baltimore); yards—294 (August 31, 1997, vs. Baltimore); and touchdown passes—3 (December 27, 1998, vs. New Orleans).
MISCELLANEOUS: Selected by Minnesota Twins organization in 16th round of free-agent draft (June 4, 1991); did not sign. ... Regular-season record as starting NFL quarterback: 4-3 (.571).

Year Team	G	GS	Att.	Cmp.	Pct.	PASSING Yds.	TD	Int.	Avg.	Rat.	Att.	RUSHING Yds.	Avg.	TD	TD	TOTALS 2pt.	Pts.
1995—Jacksonville NFL	1	0	7	3	42.9	24	0	1	3.43	12.5	3	17	5.7	0	0	0	0
1996—Jacksonville NFL	2	0	0	0	...	0	0	0	...	...	0	0	...	0	0	0	0
1997—Jacksonville NFL	5	1	28	22	78.6	344	2	2	12.29	111.9	10	34	3.4	1	1	0	6
1998—Buffalo NFL	8	6	107	67	62.6	910	8	3	8.50	102.9	24	123	5.1	1	1	0	6
Pro totals (4 years)	16	7	142	92	64.8	1278	10	6	9.00	99.4	37	174	4.7	2	2	0	12

JOHNSON, TED — LB — PATRIOTS

PERSONAL: Born December 4, 1972, in Alameda, Calif. ... 6-3/240. ... Full name: Ted Curtis Johnson.
HIGH SCHOOL: Carlsbad (Calif.).
COLLEGE: Colorado.
TRANSACTIONS/CAREER NOTES: Selected by New England Patriots in second round (57th pick overall) of 1995 NFL draft. ... Signed by Patriots (July 18, 1995). ... On injured reserve with bicep injury (December 11, 1998-remainder of season).
CHAMPIONSHIP GAME EXPERIENCE: Played in AFC championship game (1996 season). ... Played in Super Bowl XXXI (1996 season).
HONORS: Named linebacker on THE SPORTING NEWS college All-America second team (1994).
PRO STATISTICS: 1995—Recovered two fumbles. 1996—Intercepted one pass for no yards and recovered one fumble.

Year Team	G	GS	SACKS
1995—New England NFL	12	11	0.5
1996—New England NFL	16	16	0.0
1997—New England NFL	16	16	4.0
1998—New England NFL	13	13	2.0
Pro totals (4 years)	57	56	6.5

JOHNSON, TONY — TE — SAINTS

PERSONAL: Born February 5, 1972, in Como, Miss. ... 6-5/255.
HIGH SCHOOL: North Panola (Sardis, Miss.).
COLLEGE: Alabama (degree in accounting).

TRANSACTIONS/CAREER NOTES: Selected by Philadelphia Eagles in sixth round (197th pick overall) of 1996 NFL draft. ... Signed by Eagles (July 15, 1996). ... Released by Eagles (August 20, 1996). ... Signed by New Orleans Saints to practice squad (September 18, 1996). ... Activated (October 19, 1996). ... Released by Saints (December 2, 1996). ... Re-signed by Saints (July 14, 1997). ... On injured reserve with groin injury (December 19, 1998-remainder of season). ... Granted free agency (February 12, 1999).
SINGLE GAME HIGHS (regular season): Receptions—4 (November 17, 1996, vs. Atlanta); yards—48 (November 17, 1996, vs. Atlanta); and touchdown receptions—1 (November 24, 1996, vs. Tampa Bay).
MISCELLANEOUS: Played tight end during 1996 and 1997 seasons.

			RECEIVING				TOTALS		
Year Team	G	GS	No.	Yds.	Avg.	TD	TD	2pt.	Pts.	Fum.
1996—New Orleans NFL	9	7	7	76	10.9	1	1	0	6	0
1997—New Orleans NFL	7	1	1	13	13.0	0	0	0	0	1
1998—New Orleans NFL	11	0	1	8	8.0	0	0	0	0	0
Pro totals (3 years)	27	8	9	97	10.8	1	1	0	6	1

JOHNSON, TRE' G REDSKINS

PERSONAL: Born August 30, 1971, in Manhattan, N.Y. ... 6-2/326. ... Full name: Edward Stanton Johnson III. ... Name pronounced TRAY.
HIGH SCHOOL: Peekskill (N.Y.).
COLLEGE: Temple (degree in social administration, 1993).
TRANSACTIONS/CAREER NOTES: Selected by Washington Redskins in second round (31st pick overall) of 1994 NFL draft. ... Signed by Redskins (July 22, 1994). ... On injured reserve with shoulder injury (December 16, 1997-remainder of season). ... Granted unconditional free agency (February 13, 1998). ... Re-signed by Redskins (February 13, 1998). ... On injured reserve with knee injury (November 24, 1998-remainder of season).
PLAYING EXPERIENCE: Washington NFL, 1994-1998. ... Games/Games started: 1994 (14/1), 1995 (10/9), 1996 (15/15), 1997 (11/10), 1998 (10/10). Total: 60/45.
PRO STATISTICS: 1994—Ran four yards with lateral from kickoff return. 1996—Recovered one fumble.

JOHNSTON, DARYL FB COWBOYS

PERSONAL: Born February 10, 1966, in Youngstown, N.Y. ... 6-2/242. ... Full name: Daryl Peter Johnston. ... Nickname: Moose.
HIGH SCHOOL: Lewiston-Porter Central (Youngstown, N.Y.).
COLLEGE: Syracuse (degree in economics, 1989).
TRANSACTIONS/CAREER NOTES: Selected by Dallas Cowboys in second round (39th pick overall) of 1989 NFL draft. ... Signed by Cowboys (July 24, 1989). ... Granted free agency (March 1, 1993). ... Re-signed by Cowboys (July 16, 1993). ... Granted unconditional free agency (February 17, 1994). ... Re-signed by Cowboys (April 7, 1994). ... Granted unconditional free agency (February 14, 1997). ... Re-signed by Cowboys (March 19, 1997).
CHAMPIONSHIP GAME EXPERIENCE: Played in NFC championship game (1992-1995 seasons). ... Member of Super Bowl championship team (1992, 1993 and 1995 seasons).
HONORS: Played in Pro Bowl (1993 and 1994 seasons).
PRO STATISTICS: 1990—Recovered one fumble. 1992—Recovered one fumble. 1993—Recovered one fumble. 1995—Recovered one fumble. 1996—Recovered one fumble.
SINGLE GAME HIGHS (regular season): Attempts—16 (December 24, 1989, vs. Green Bay); yards—60 (December 24, 1989, vs. Green Bay); and rushing touchdowns—1 (October 29, 1995, vs. Atlanta).

			RUSHING				RECEIVING				TOTALS			
Year Team	G	GS	Att.	Yds.	Avg.	TD	No.	Yds.	Avg.	TD	TD	2pt.	Pts.	Fum.
1989—Dallas NFL	16	10	67	212	3.2	0	16	133	8.3	3	3	...	18	3
1990—Dallas NFL	16	0	10	35	3.5	1	14	148	10.6	1	2	...	12	1
1991—Dallas NFL	16	14	17	54	3.2	0	28	244	8.7	1	1	0	6	0
1992—Dallas NFL	16	16	17	61	3.6	0	32	249	7.8	2	2	0	12	0
1993—Dallas NFL	16	16	24	74	3.1	3	50	372	7.4	1	4	0	24	1
1994—Dallas NFL	16	16	40	138	3.5	2	44	325	7.4	2	4	0	24	2
1995—Dallas NFL	16	16	25	111	4.4	2	30	248	8.3	1	3	0	18	1
1996—Dallas NFL	16	15	22	48	2.2	1	43	278	6.5	1	1	0	6	1
1997—Dallas NFL	6	6	2	3	1.5	0	18	166	9.2	1	1	0	6	1
1998—Dallas NFL	16	13	8	17	2.1	0	18	60	3.3	1	1	0	6	0
Pro totals (10 years)	150	122	232	753	3.2	8	293	2223	7.6	14	22	0	132	10

JOHNSTONE, LANCE DE RAIDERS

PERSONAL: Born June 11, 1973, in Philadelphia. ... 6-4/250.
HIGH SCHOOL: Germantown (Pa.).
COLLEGE: Temple.
TRANSACTIONS/CAREER NOTES: Selected by Oakland Raiders in second round (57th pick overall) of 1996 NFL draft. ... Signed by Raiders for 1996 season.
PRO STATISTICS: 1997—Recovered one fumble for two yards. 1998—Recovered one fumble for 40 yards and a touchdown.

Year Team	G	GS	SACKS
1996—Oakland NFL	16	10	1.0
1997—Oakland NFL	14	6	3.5
1998—Oakland NFL	16	15	11.0

Pro totals (3 years).. 46   31   15.5

JONES, BRIAN   LB

PERSONAL: Born January 22, 1968, in Iowa City, Iowa. ... 6-1/250. ... Full name: Brian Keith Jones.
HIGH SCHOOL: Dunbar (Lubbock, Texas).
COLLEGE: UCLA, then Texas.
TRANSACTIONS/CAREER NOTES: Selected by Los Angeles Raiders in eighth round (213th pick overall) of 1991 NFL draft. ... Released by Raiders (August 26, 1991). ... Signed by Indianapolis Colts to practice squad (September 9, 1991). ... Activated (October 4, 1991). ... Granted unconditional free agency (February 1, 1992). ... Signed by Miami Dolphins (April 1, 1992). ... Released by Dolphins (July 20, 1992). ... Signed by Raiders for 1994 season. ... Released by Raiders (August 30, 1994). ... Selected by Scottish Claymores in 33rd round (197th pick overall) of 1995 World League Draft. ... Signed by New Orleans Saints (July 31, 1995). ... Granted free agency (February 14, 1997). ... Re-signed by Saints (June 1, 1997). ... On injured reserve with knee injury (August 18, 1997-entire season). ... Released by Saints (September 8, 1998).
PLAYING EXPERIENCE: Indianapolis NFL, 1991; Scottish Claymores W.L., 1995; New Orleans NFL, 1995, 1996 and 1998. ... Games/Games started: 1991 (11/1), 1995 (W.L.- games played unavailable; NFL- 16/7), 1996 (16/1), 1998 (2/0). Total NFL: 45/9.
PRO STATISTICS: W.L.: 1995—Credited with 1 1/2 sacks. NFL: 1995—Credited with one sack and recovered one fumble. 1996—Recovered one fumble for 11 yards and a touchdown.

JONES, CEDRIC   DE   GIANTS

PERSONAL: Born April 30, 1974, in Houston. ... 6-4/275.
HIGH SCHOOL: Lamar (Houston).
COLLEGE: Oklahoma.
TRANSACTIONS/CAREER NOTES: Selected by New York Giants in first round (fifth pick overall) of 1996 NFL draft. ... Signed by Giants (July 27, 1996). ... On injured reserve with leg injury (December 11, 1997-remainder of season).
PLAYING EXPERIENCE: New York Giants NFL, 1996-1998. ... Games/Games started: 1996 (16/0), 1997 (9/2), 1998 (16/1). Total: 41/3.
HONORS: Named defensive lineman on THE SPORTING NEWS college All-America first team (1995).
PRO STATISTICS: 1998—Credited with four sacks and recovered one fumble.

JONES, CHARLIE   WR   CHARGERS

PERSONAL: Born December 1, 1972, in Hanford, Calif. ... 5-8/175. ... Full name: Charlie Edward Jones.
HIGH SCHOOL: Lemoore (Calif.).
COLLEGE: Fresno State.
TRANSACTIONS/CAREER NOTES: Selected by San Diego Chargers in fourth round (114th pick overall) of 1996 NFL draft. ... Signed by Chargers for 1996 season. ... Granted free agency (February 12, 1999). ... Re-signed by Chargers (April 2, 1999).
PRO STATISTICS: 1996—Returned one punt for 21 yards. 1997—Rushed four times for 42 yards. 1998—Rushed four times for 39 yards and returned two kickoffs for 25 yards.
SINGLE GAME HIGHS (regular season): Receptions—7 (October 27, 1996, vs. Seattle); yards—86 (November 16, 1997, vs. Oakland); and touchdown receptions—1 (November 22, 1998, vs. Kansas City).

			RECEIVING				TOTALS		
Year Team	G	GS	No.	Yds.	Avg.	TD	TD	2pt.	Pts.	Fum.
1996—San Diego NFL	14	4	41	524	12.8	4	4	0	24	0
1997—San Diego NFL	16	11	32	423	13.2	1	1	0	6	0
1998—San Diego NFL	16	11	46	699	15.2	3	3	0	18	1
Pro totals (3 years)	46	26	119	1646	13.8	8	8	0	48	1

JONES, CLARENCE   OT   PANTHERS

PERSONAL: Born May 6, 1968, in Brooklyn, N.Y. ... 6-6/300. ... Full name: Clarence Thomas Jones.
HIGH SCHOOL: Central Islip (N.Y.).
COLLEGE: Maryland.
TRANSACTIONS/CAREER NOTES: Selected by New York Giants in fourth round (111th pick overall) of 1991 NFL draft. ... On injured reserve with ankle injury (October 1991). ... Activated (November 1991). ... Granted free agency (February 17, 1994). ... Released by Giants (May 6, 1994). ... Signed by Los Angeles Rams (June 1, 1994). ... Rams franchise moved to St. Louis (April 12, 1995). ... Granted unconditional free agency (February 16, 1996). ... Signed by New Orleans Saints (February 20, 1996). ... Granted unconditional free agency (February 12, 1999). ... Signed by Carolina Panthers (March 26, 1999).
PLAYING EXPERIENCE: New York Giants NFL, 1991-1993; Los Angeles Rams NFL, 1994; St. Louis NFL, 1995; New Orleans NFL, 1996-1998. ... Games/Games started: 1991 (3/0), 1992 (3/0), 1993 (4/0), 1994 (16/16), 1995 (13/0), 1996 (16/16), 1997 (15/15), 1998 (14/14). Total: 84/61.
PRO STATISTICS: 1997—Recovered two fumbles. 1998—Recovered one fumble.

JONES, DAMON   TE   JAGUARS

PERSONAL: Born September 18, 1974, in Evanston, Ill. ... 6-5/265.
HIGH SCHOOL: Evanston (Ill.).
COLLEGE: Michigan, then Southern Illinois (degree in consumer ecnomics, 1997).
TRANSACTIONS/CAREER NOTES: Selected by Jacksonville Jaguars in fifth round (147th pick overall) of 1997 NFL draft. ... Signed by Jaguars (May 30, 1997).
PRO STATISTICS: 1998—Returned two kickoffs for minus one yard.
SINGLE GAME HIGHS (regular season): Receptions—2 (November 29, 1998, vs. Cincinnati); yards—34 (November 30, 1997, vs. Baltimore); and touchdown receptions—1 (November 29, 1998, vs. Cincinnati).

				RECEIVING			TOTALS			
Year Team	G	GS	No.	Yds.	Avg.	TD	TD	2pt.	Pts.	Fum.
1997—Jacksonville NFL	11	3	5	87	17.4	2	2	0	12	0
1998—Jacksonville NFL	16	7	8	90	11.3	4	4	0	24	1
Pro totals (2 years)	27	10	13	177	13.6	6	6	0	36	1

JONES, DONTA — LB — PANTHERS

PERSONAL: Born August 27, 1972, in Washington, D.C. ... 6-2/235. ... Full name: Markeysia Donta Jones. ... Name pronounced DON-tay.
HIGH SCHOOL: McDonough (Pomfret, Md.).
COLLEGE: Nebraska (degree in accounting and business administration, 1994).
TRANSACTIONS/CAREER NOTES: Selected by Pittsburgh Steelers in fourth round (125th pick overall) of 1995 NFL draft. ... Signed by Steelers (July 19, 1995). ... Granted free agency (February 13, 1998). ... Re-signed by Steelers (June 9, 1998). ... Granted unconditional free agency (February 12, 1999). ... Signed by Carolina Panthers (February 15, 1999).
PLAYING EXPERIENCE: Pittsburgh NFL, 1995-1998. ... Games/Games started: 1995 (16/0), 1996 (15/2), 1997 (16/4), 1998 (16/4). Total: 63/10.
CHAMPIONSHIP GAME EXPERIENCE: Played in AFC championship game (1995 and 1997 seasons). ... Played in Super Bowl XXX (1995 season).
PRO STATISTICS: 1996—Credited with one sack and returned one punt for three yards. 1997—Recovered one fumble for six yards. 1998—Credited with three sacks.

JONES, ERNEST — LB — PANTHERS

PERSONAL: Born April 1, 1971, in Utica, N.Y. ... 6-2/255. ... Full name: Ernest Lee Jones.
HIGH SCHOOL: Utica (N.Y.) Senior Academy.
COLLEGE: Oregon.
TRANSACTIONS/CAREER NOTES: Selected by Los Angeles Rams in third round (100th pick overall) of 1994 NFL draft. ... Signed by Rams (June 20, 1994). ... On injured reserve with knee injury (August 28, 1994-entire season). ... Released by Rams (August 21, 1995). ... Signed by New Orleans Saints to practice squad (August 28, 1995). ... Activated (October 21, 1995). ... Released by Saints (October 30, 1995). ... Re-signed by Saints to practice squad (November 1, 1995). ... Granted free agency (February 16, 1996). ... Signed by Denver Broncos (March 25, 1996). ... Granted free agency (February 13, 1998). ... Re-signed by Broncos (April 7, 1998). ... Claimed on waivers by New Orleans Saints (October 14, 1998). ... Inactive for three games with Saints (1998). ... Claimed on waivers by Carolina Panthers (November 5, 1998). ... Granted unconditional free agency (February 12, 1999). ... Re-signed by Panthers (March 17, 1999).
PLAYING EXPERIENCE: New Orleans NFL, 1995; Denver NFL, 1996 and 1997; Denver (1)-Carolina (7) NFL, 1998. ... Games/Games started: 1995 (1/0), 1996 (6/0), 1997 (1/0), 1998 (Den.-1/0; Car.-7/0; Total: 8/0). Total: 16/0.
CHAMPIONSHIP GAME EXPERIENCE: Member of Broncos for AFC championship game (1997 season); inactive. ... Member of Super Bowl championship team (1997 season); inactive.

JONES, FREDDIE — TE — CHARGERS

PERSONAL: Born September 16, 1974, in Cheverly, Md. ... 6-5/270. ... Full name: Freddie Ray Jones Jr.
HIGH SCHOOL: McKinley (Landover, Md.).
COLLEGE: North Carolina.
TRANSACTIONS/CAREER NOTES: Selected by San Diego Chargers in second round (45th pick overall) of 1997 NFL draft. ... Signed by Chargers (May 21, 1997). ... On injured reserve with leg injury (December 12, 1997-remainder of season).
SINGLE GAME HIGHS (regular season): Receptions—6 (October 25, 1998, vs. Seattle); yards—81 (October 25, 1998, vs. Seattle); and touchdown receptions—1 (December 6, 1998, vs. Washington).

				RECEIVING			TOTALS			
Year Team	G	GS	No.	Yds.	Avg.	TD	TD	2pt.	Pts.	Fum.
1997—San Diego NFL	13	8	41	505	12.3	2	2	0	12	0
1998—San Diego NFL	16	16	57	602	10.6	3	3	1	20	1
Pro totals (2 years)	29	24	98	1107	11.3	5	5	1	32	1

JONES, GEORGE — RB — JAGUARS

PERSONAL: Born December 31, 1973, in Greenville, S.C. ... 5-9/212. ... Full name: George Dee Jones.
HIGH SCHOOL: Eastside (Greenville, S.C.).
JUNIOR COLLEGE: Bakersfield (Calif.) College.
COLLEGE: San Diego State.
TRANSACTIONS/CAREER NOTES: Selected by Pittsburgh Steelers in fifth round (154th pick overall) of 1997 NFL draft. ... Signed by Steelers (July 15, 1997). ... Released by Steelers (August 25, 1998). ... Signed by Jacksonville Jaguars (September 22, 1998).
CHAMPIONSHIP GAME EXPERIENCE: Member of Steelers for AFC championship game (1997 season); inactive.
PRO STATISTICS: 1997—Recovered one fumble. 1998—Returned one kickoff for 21 yards.
SINGLE GAME HIGHS (regular season): Attempts—16 (December 21, 1997, vs. Tennessee); yards—64 (November 16, 1997, vs. Cincinnati); and rushing touchdowns—1 (November 9, 1997, vs. Baltimore).

			RUSHING				RECEIVING				TOTALS			
Year Team	G	GS	Att.	Yds.	Avg.	TD	No.	Yds.	Avg.	TD	TD	2pt.	Pts.	Fum.
1997—Pittsburgh NFL	16	1	72	235	3.3	1	16	96	6.0	1	2	0	12	3
1998—Jacksonville NFL	12	0	39	121	3.1	0	1	9	9.0	0	0	0	0	0
Pro totals (2 years)	28	1	111	356	3.2	1	17	105	6.2	1	2	0	12	3

JONES, GREG — LB — REDSKINS

PERSONAL: Born May 22, 1974, in Denver. ... 6-4/238. ... Full name: Greg Phillip Jones.
HIGH SCHOOL: John F. Kennedy (Denver).
COLLEGE: Colorado (degree in small business management, 1996).
TRANSACTIONS/CAREER NOTES: Selected by Washington Redskins in second round (51st pick overall) of 1997 NFL draft. ... Signed by Redskins (July 11, 1997).
PRO STATISTICS: 1997—Returned one kickoff for six yards. 1998—Intercepted one pass for nine yards.

Year Team	G	GS	SACKS
1997—Washington NFL	16	3	3.5
1998—Washington NFL	16	5	1.0
Pro totals (2 years)	32	8	4.5

JONES, HENRY — S — BILLS

PERSONAL: Born December 29, 1967, in St. Louis. ... 5-11/197.
HIGH SCHOOL: St. Louis University High.
COLLEGE: Illinois (degree in psychology, 1990).
TRANSACTIONS/CAREER NOTES: Selected by Buffalo Bills in first round (26th pick overall) of 1991 NFL draft. ... Signed by Bills (August 30, 1991). ... Activated (September 7, 1991). ... Designated by Bills as transition player (February 15, 1994). ... On injured reserve with broken leg (October 9, 1996-remainder of season).
CHAMPIONSHIP GAME EXPERIENCE: Played in AFC championship game (1991-1993 seasons). ... Played in Super Bowl XXVI (1991 season), Super Bowl XXVII (1992 season) and Super Bowl XXVIII (1993 season).
HONORS: Named strong safety on The Sporting News NFL All-Pro team (1992). ... Played in Pro Bowl (1992 season).
RECORDS: Shares NFL single-game record for most touchdowns scored by interception—2 (September 20, 1992, vs. Indianapolis).
PRO STATISTICS: 1991—Recovered one fumble. 1992—Recovered two fumbles. 1993—Credited with one safety and recovered two fumbles. 1994—Recovered one fumble. 1995—Recovered one fumble. 1997—Returned one punt for no yards, fumbled once and recovered one fumble.

			INTERCEPTIONS				SACKS
Year Team	G	GS	No.	Yds.	Avg.	TD	No.
1991—Buffalo NFL	15	0	0	0	...	0	0.0
1992—Buffalo NFL	16	16	†8	*263	32.9	▲2	0.0
1993—Buffalo NFL	16	16	2	92	46.0	▲1	2.0
1994—Buffalo NFL	16	16	2	45	22.5	0	1.0
1995—Buffalo NFL	13	13	1	10	10.0	0	0.0
1996—Buffalo NFL	5	5	0	0	...	0	0.0
1997—Buffalo NFL	15	15	0	0	...	0	2.0
1998—Buffalo NFL	16	16	3	0	0.0	0	0.0
Pro totals (8 years)	112	97	16	410	25.6	3	5.0

JONES, JAMES — DT — LIONS

PERSONAL: Born February 6, 1969, in Davenport, Iowa. ... 6-2/290. ... Full name: James Alfie Jones. ... Nickname: J.J.
HIGH SCHOOL: Davenport (Iowa) Central.
COLLEGE: Northern Iowa (degree in science, 1992).
TRANSACTIONS/CAREER NOTES: Selected by Cleveland Browns in third round (57th pick overall) of 1991 NFL draft. ... Signed by Browns (1991). ... Granted unconditional free agency (February 17, 1995). ... Signed by Denver Broncos (February 24, 1995). ... Released by Broncos (July 17, 1996). ... Signed by Baltimore Ravens (August 21, 1996). ... Granted unconditional free agency (February 12, 1999). ... Signed by Detroit Lions (February 17, 1999).
PRO STATISTICS: 1991—Credited with one safety, intercepted one pass for 20 yards and a touchdown and recovered three fumbles for 15 yards. 1992—Recovered one fumble. 1993—Rushed twice for two yards and one touchdown. 1994—Rushed once for no yards, caught one pass for one yard and recovered two fumbles. 1995—Recovered two fumbles. 1996—Caught one pass for two yards and a touchdown. 1997—Recovered one fumble. 1998—Recovered one fumble.

Year Team	G	GS	SACKS
1991—Cleveland NFL	16	16	1.0
1992—Cleveland NFL	16	16	4.0
1993—Cleveland NFL	16	12	5.5
1994—Cleveland NFL	16	5	3.0
1995—Denver NFL	16	16	1.0
1996—Baltimore NFL	16	11	1.0
1997—Baltimore NFL	16	16	6.0
1998—Baltimore NFL	16	16	5.5
Pro totals (8 years)	128	108	27.0

JONES, LENOY — LB — BROWNS

PERSONAL: Born September 25, 1974, in Marlin, Texas. ... 6-1/235.
HIGH SCHOOL: Groesbeck (Texas).
COLLEGE: Texas Christian.
TRANSACTIONS/CAREER NOTES: Signed as non-drafted free agent by Houston Oilers (April 23, 1996). ... Released by Oilers (August 20, 1996). ... Re-signed by Oilers to practice squad (August 26, 1996). ... Activated (October 9, 1996). ... Oilers franchise moved to Tennessee for 1997 season. ... Oilers franchise renamed Tennessee Titans for 1999 season (December 26, 1998). ... Selected by Cleveland Browns from Titans in NFL expansion draft (February 9, 1999). ... Granted free agency (February 12, 1999).
PLAYING EXPERIENCE: Houston NFL, 1996; Tennessee NFL, 1997 and 1998. ... Games/Games started: 1996 (11/0), 1997 (16/0), 1998 (9/0). Total: 36/0.
PRO STATISTICS: 1996—Recovered one fumble. 1997—Credited with one sack.

JONES, MARCUS   DT   BUCCANEERS

PERSONAL: Born August 15, 1973, in Jacksonville, N.C. ... 6-6/286. ... Full name: Marcus Edward Jones.
HIGH SCHOOL: Southwest Onslow (Jacksonville, N.C.).
COLLEGE: North Carolina.
TRANSACTIONS/CAREER NOTES: Selected by Tampa Bay Buccaneers in first round (22nd pick overall) of 1996 NFL draft. ... Signed by Buccaneers (July 21, 1996). ... On injured reserve with ankle injury (December 23, 1997-remainder of season).
PLAYING EXPERIENCE: Tampa Bay NFL, 1996-1998. ... Games/Games started: 1996 (16/3), 1997 (7/1), 1998 (15/0). Total: 38/4.
HONORS: Named defensive lineman on THE SPORTING NEWS college All-America second team (1995).
PRO STATISTICS: 1996—Credited with one sack. 1997—Recovered one fumble. 1998—Recovered one fumble.

JONES, MARVIN   LB   JETS

PERSONAL: Born June 28, 1972, in Miami. ... 6-2/250. ... Full name: Marvin Maurice Jones.
HIGH SCHOOL: Miami Northwestern.
COLLEGE: Florida State.
TRANSACTIONS/CAREER NOTES: Selected after junior season by New York Jets in first round (fourth pick overall) of 1993 NFL draft. ... Signed by Jets (August 5, 1993). ... On injured reserve with hip injury (November 16, 1993-remainder of season). ... On injured reserve with knee injury (July 29, 1998-entire season).
HONORS: Butkus Award winner (1992). ... Named College Football Player of the Year by THE SPORTING NEWS (1992). ... Named linebacker on THE SPORTING NEWS college All-America first team (1992).
PRO STATISTICS: 1993—Recovered one fumble. 1997—Recovered one fumble.

Year Team	G	GS	SACKS
1993—New York Jets NFL	9	0	0.0
1994—New York Jets NFL	15	11	0.5
1995—New York Jets NFL	10	10	1.5
1996—New York Jets NFL	12	12	1.0
1997—New York Jets NFL	16	16	3.0
1998—New York Jets NFL	Did not play.		
Pro totals (5 years)	62	49	6.0

JONES, MIKE A.   LB   RAMS

PERSONAL: Born April 15, 1969, in Kansas City, Mo. ... 6-1/240. ... Full name: Michael Anthony Jones.
HIGH SCHOOL: Southwest (Kansas City, Mo.).
COLLEGE: Missouri.
TRANSACTIONS/CAREER NOTES: Signed as non-drafted free agent by Los Angeles Raiders (April 1991). ... Assigned by Raiders to Sacramento Surge in 1992 World League enhancement allocation program (February 20, 1992). ... Raiders franchise moved to Oakland (July 21, 1995). ... Granted unconditional free agency (February 14, 1997). ... Signed by St. Louis Rams (March 18, 1997).
PLAYING EXPERIENCE: Los Angeles Raiders NFL, 1991-1994; Sacramento W.L., 1992; Oakland NFL, 1995 and 1996; St. Louis NFL, 1997 and 1998. ... Games/Games started: 1991 (16/0), 1992 (W.L.- 7/7; NFL -16/0; Total: 23/7), 1993 (16/2), 1994 (16/1), 1995 (16/16), 1996 (15/15), 1997 (16/16), 1998 (16/16). Total W.L.: 7/7. Total NFL: 127/66. Total Pro: 134/73.
PRO STATISTICS: W.L.: 1992—Credited with two sacks. NFL: 1995—Intercepted one pass for 23 yards, recovered two fumbles for 52 yards and a touchdown. 1996—Credited with one sack. 1997—Intercepted one pass for no yards and credited with two sacks. 1998—Intercepted two passes for 13 yards and credited with three sacks.

JONES, MIKE D.   DT/DE   TITANS

PERSONAL: Born August 25, 1969, in Columbia, S.C. ... 6-4/280. ... Full name: Michael David Jones.
HIGH SCHOOL: C.A. Johnson (Columbia, S.C.).
COLLEGE: North Carolina State.
TRANSACTIONS/CAREER NOTES: Selected by Phoenix Cardinals in second round (32nd pick overall) of 1991 NFL draft. ... Signed by Cardinals (July 15, 1991). ... Granted free agency (February 17, 1994). ... Signed by New England Patriots (June 7, 1994). ... Granted unconditional free agency (February 14, 1997). ... Re-signed by Patriots (March 10, 1997). ... Traded by Patriots to St. Louis Rams for fifth-round pick in 2000 draft (August 30, 1998). ... Granted unconditional free agency (February 12, 1999). ... Signed by Tennessee Titans (February 24, 1999).
CHAMPIONSHIP GAME EXPERIENCE: Played in Super Bowl XXXI (1996 season).
PRO STATISTICS: 1994—Recovered one fumble. 1996—Recovered one fumble for 31 yards. 1997—Recovered one fumble. 1998—Returned one kickoff for two yards and recovered two fumbles for 43 yards.

Year Team	G	GS	SACKS
1991—Phoenix NFL	16	1	0.0
1992—Phoenix NFL	15	15	6.0
1993—Phoenix NFL	16	2	3.0
1994—New England NFL	16	16	6.0
1995—New England NFL	13	3	3.0
1996—New England NFL	16	12	2.0
1997—New England NFL	16	7	4.0
1998—St. Louis NFL	16	15	2.5
Pro totals (8 years)	124	71	26.5

JONES, ROBERT — LB — DOLPHINS

PERSONAL: Born September 27, 1969, in Blackstone, Va. ... 6-3/250. ... Full name: Robert Lee Jones.
HIGH SCHOOL: Nottoway (Va.), then Fork Union (Va.) Military Academy.
COLLEGE: East Carolina.
TRANSACTIONS/CAREER NOTES: Selected by Dallas Cowboys in first round (24th pick overall) of 1992 NFL draft. ... Signed by Cowboys (April 26, 1992). ... Granted unconditional free agency (February 16, 1996). ... Signed by St. Louis Rams (March 5, 1996). ... Released by Rams (June 2, 1998). ... Signed by Miami Dolphins (June 10, 1998). ... Granted unconditional free agency (February 12, 1999). ... Re-signed by Dolphins (February 19, 1999).
PLAYING EXPERIENCE: Dallas NFL, 1992-1995; St. Louis NFL, 1996 and 1997; Miami NFL, 1998. ... Games/Games started: 1992 (15/13), 1993 (13/3), 1994 (16/16), 1995 (12/12), 1996 (16/13), 1997 (16/15), 1998 (16/16). Total: 104/88.
CHAMPIONSHIP GAME EXPERIENCE: Played in NFC championship game (1992-1995 seasons). ... Member of Super Bowl championship team (1992, 1993 and 1995 seasons).
HONORS: Named linebacker on THE SPORTING NEWS college All-America second team (1990). ... Named linebacker on THE SPORTING NEWS college All-America first team (1991).
PRO STATISTICS: 1992—Credited with one sack and recovered one fumble. 1993—Returned one kickoff for 12 yards. 1994—Returned one kickoff for eight yards and recovered one fumble. 1995—Credited with one sack. 1996—Intercepted one pass for no yards. 1997—Credited with one sack. 1998—Intercepted two passes for 14 yards and one touchdown and credited with five sacks.

JONES, ROD — OT — BENGALS

PERSONAL: Born January 11, 1974, in Detroit. ... 6-4/325. ... Full name: Rodrek E. Jones.
HIGH SCHOOL: Henry Ford (Detroit).
COLLEGE: Kansas (degree in human development/family living).
TRANSACTIONS/CAREER NOTES: Selected by Cincinnati Bengals in seventh round (219th pick overall) of 1996 NFL draft. ... Signed by Bengals (July 15, 1996). ... Granted free agency (February 12, 1999). ... Re-signed by Bengals (April 15, 1999).
PLAYING EXPERIENCE: Cincinnati NFL, 1996-1998. ... Games/Games started: 1996 (6/1), 1997 (13/8), 1998 (7/2). Total: 26/11.

JONES, TEBUCKY — CB — PATRIOTS

PERSONAL: Born October 6, 1974, in New Britain, Conn. ... 6-2/216. ... Full name: Tebucky Shermaine Jones.
HIGH SCHOOL: New Britain (Conn.).
COLLEGE: Syracuse.
TRANSACTIONS/CAREER NOTES: Selected by New England Patriots in first round (22nd pick overall) of 1998 NFL draft. ... Signed by Patriots (July 18, 1998).
PLAYING EXPERIENCE: New England NFL, 1998. ... Games/Games started: 16/0.
PRO STATISTICS: 1998—Recovered one fumble.

JONES, TONY — OT — BRONCOS

PERSONAL: Born May 24, 1966, in Royston, Ga. ... 6-5/291. ... Full name: Tony Edward Jones.
HIGH SCHOOL: Franklin County (Carnesville, Ga.).
COLLEGE: Western Carolina (degree in management, 1989).
TRANSACTIONS/CAREER NOTES: Signed as non-drafted free agent by Cleveland Browns (May 2, 1988). ... On injured reserve with toe injury (August 29-October 22, 1988). ... On injured reserve with toe injury (September 20-November 7, 1989). ... Granted free agency (February 1, 1992). ... Re-signed by Browns (July 29, 1992). ... Browns franchise moved to Baltimore and renamed Ravens for 1996 season (March 11, 1996). ... Traded by Ravens to Denver Broncos for second-round pick (S Kim Herring) in 1997 draft (February 14, 1997).
PLAYING EXPERIENCE: Cleveland NFL, 1988-1995; Baltimore NFL, 1996; Denver NFL, 1997 and 1998. ... Games/Games started: 1988 (4/0), 1989 (9/3), 1990 (16/16), 1991 (16/16), 1992 (16/16), 1993 (16/16), 1994 (16/16), 1995 (16/16), 1996 (15/15), 1997 (16/16), 1998 (16/16). Total: 156/146.
CHAMPIONSHIP GAME EXPERIENCE: Played in AFC championship game (1989, 1997 and 1998 seasons). ... Member of Super Bowl championship team (1997 and 1998 seasons).
HONORS: Played in Pro Bowl (1998 season).
PRO STATISTICS: 1989—Recovered one fumble. 1991—Recovered one fumble. 1994—Recovered one fumble. 1995—Recovered one fumble.

JONES, WALTER — OT — SEAHAWKS

PERSONAL: Born January 19, 1974, in Aliceville, Ala. ... 6-5/300.
HIGH SCHOOL: Aliceville (Ala.).
JUNIOR COLLEGE: Holmes Junior College (Miss.).
COLLEGE: Florida State.
TRANSACTIONS/CAREER NOTES: Selected by Seattle Seahawks in first round (sixth pick overall) of 1997 NFL draft. ... Signed by Seahawks (August 6, 1997).
PLAYING EXPERIENCE: Seattle NFL, 1997 and 1998. ... Games/Games started: 1997 (12/12), 1998 (16/16). Total: 28/28.

JORDAN, ANDREW — TE — EAGLES

PERSONAL: Born June 21, 1972, in Charlotte. ... 6-4/254. ... Full name: Andrew Jordan Jr.
HIGH SCHOOL: West Charlotte.
COLLEGE: North Greenville College (S.C.), then Western Carolina (degree in criminal justice, 1993).
TRANSACTIONS/CAREER NOTES: Selected by Minnesota Vikings in sixth round (179th pick overall) of 1994 NFL draft. ... Signed by Vikings (June 17, 1994). ... Released by Vikings (September 23, 1997). ... Signed by Tampa Bay Buccaneers (December 9, 1997). ... Released by

Buccaneers (August 25, 1998). ... Signed by Philadelphia Eagles (December 1, 1998). ... Granted unconditional free agency (February 12, 1999). ... Re-signed by Eagles (February 18, 1999).
PRO STATISTICS: 1994—Returned one kickoff for eight yards and recovered a fumble.
SINGLE GAME HIGHS (regular season): Receptions—5 (November 13, 1994, vs. New England); yards—57 (November 13, 1994, vs. New England); and touchdown receptions—1 (November 5, 1995, vs. Green Bay).

				RECEIVING				TOTALS			
Year Team	G	GS	No.	Yds.	Avg.	TD	TD	2pt.	Pts.	Fum.
1994—Minnesota NFL	16	12	35	336	9.6	0	0	1	2	1
1995—Minnesota NFL	13	7	27	185	6.9	2	2	0	12	1
1996—Minnesota NFL	13	9	19	128	6.7	0	0	1	2	0
1997—Minnesota NFL	2	0	0	0	...	0	0	0	0	0
—Tampa Bay NFL	2	0	1	0	0.0	0	0	0	0	0
1998—Philadelphia NFL	3	0	2	9	4.5	0	0	0	0	0
Pro totals (5 years)	49	28	84	658	7.8	2	2	2	16	2

JORDAN, ANTONY — LB — COLTS

PERSONAL: Born December 19, 1974, in Sewell, N.J. ... 6-2/234.
HIGH SCHOOL: Washington Township (Sewell, N.J.).
COLLEGE: Vanderbilt.
TRANSACTIONS/CAREER NOTES: Selected by Indianapolis Colts in fifth round (135th pick overall) of 1998 NFL draft. ... Signed by Colts (July 24, 1998).
PLAYING EXPERIENCE: Indianapolis NFL, 1998. ... Games/Games started: 15/3.

JORDAN, CHARLES — WR — SEAHAWKS

PERSONAL: Born October 9, 1969, in Los Angeles. ... 5-11/185. ... Full name: Charles Alexander Jordan.
HIGH SCHOOL: Morningside (Inglewood, Calif.).
COLLEGE: Long Beach (Calif.) City College.
TRANSACTIONS/CAREER NOTES: Signed as non-drafted free agent by Los Angeles Raiders (May 4, 1993). ... Inactive for six games (1993). ... On injured reserve with abdominal injury (October 27, 1993-remainder of season). ... Traded by Raiders to Green Bay Packers for fifth-round pick (traded to Washington) in 1995 draft (August 28, 1994). ... Granted free agency (February 16, 1996). ... Tendered offer sheet by Miami Dolphins (March 7, 1996). ... Packers declined to match offer (March 13, 1996). ... On injured reserve with groin injury (October 8, 1998-remainder of season). ... Granted unconditional free agency (February 12, 1999). ... Signed by Seattle Seahawks (June 4, 1999).
CHAMPIONSHIP GAME EXPERIENCE: Member of Packers for NFC championship game (1995 season); inactive.
PRO STATISTICS: 1994—Rushed once for five yards. 1995—Recovered one fumble. 1997—Rushed three times for 12 yards and recovered one fumble. 1998—Recovered one fumble.
SINGLE GAME HIGHS (regular season): Receptions—5 (December 7, 1997, vs. Detroit); yards—106 (November 30, 1997, vs. Oakland); and touchdown receptions—2 (November 30, 1997, vs. Oakland).
STATISTICAL PLATEAUS: 100-yard receiving games: 1997 (2).

			RECEIVING				PUNT RETURNS				KICKOFF RETURNS				TOTALS			
Year Team	G	GS	No.	Yds.	Avg.	TD	No.	Yds.	Avg.	TD	No.	Yds.	Avg.	TD	TD	2pt.	Pts.	Fum.
1993—L.A. Raiders NFL									Did not play.									
1994—Green Bay NFL	10	0	0	0	...	0	1	0	0.0	0	5	115	23.0	0	0	0	0	1
1995—Green Bay NFL	6	1	7	117	16.7	2	21	213	10.1	0	21	444	21.1	0	2	0	12	1
1996—Miami NFL	6	0	7	152	21.7	0	0	0	...	0	4	81	20.3	0	0	0	0	0
1997—Miami NFL	14	1	27	471	17.4	3	26	273	10.5	0	1	6	6.0	0	3	0	18	2
1998—Miami NFL	3	0	2	17	8.5	0	5	47	9.4	0	0	0	...	0	0	0	0	2
Pro totals (5 years)	39	2	43	757	17.6	5	53	533	10.1	0	31	646	20.8	0	5	0	30	6

JORDAN, RANDY — RB — RAIDERS

PERSONAL: Born June 6, 1970, in Henderson, N.C. ... 5-10/215. ... Full name: Randy Loment Jordan.
HIGH SCHOOL: Warren County (Warrenton, N.C.).
COLLEGE: North Carolina.
TRANSACTIONS/CAREER NOTES: Signed as non-drafted free agent by Los Angeles Raiders (May 1993). ... Released by Raiders (August 25, 1993). ... Re-signed by Raiders to practice squad (August 31, 1993). ... Activated (October 30, 1993). ... Released by Raiders (August 28, 1994). ... Signed by Jacksonville Jaguars (December 15, 1994). ... Granted free agency (February 14, 1997). ... Re-signed by Jaguars (May 5, 1997). ... Released by Jaguars (August 19, 1997). ... Re-signed by Jaguars (September 24, 1997). ... Granted unconditional free agency (February 13, 1998). ... Signed by Oakland Raiders (June 2, 1998).
CHAMPIONSHIP GAME EXPERIENCE: Played in AFC championship game (1996 season).
PRO STATISTICS: 1996—Recovered one fumble.
SINGLE GAME HIGHS (regular season): Attempts—24 (December 20, 1998, vs. San Diego); yards—82 (December 20, 1998, vs. San Diego); and rushing touchdowns—1 (December 26, 1998, vs. Kansas City).

			RUSHING				RECEIVING				KICKOFF RETURNS				TOTALS			
Year Team	G	GS	Att.	Yds.	Avg.	TD	No.	Yds.	Avg.	TD	No.	Yds.	Avg.	TD	TD	2pt.	Pts.	Fum.
1993—L.A. Raiders NFL	10	2	12	33	2.8	0	4	42	10.5	0	0	0	...	0	0	...	0	2
1994—Jacksonville NFL									Did not play.									
1995—Jacksonville NFL	12	2	21	62	3.0	0	5	89	17.8	1	2	41	20.5	0	1	0	6	0
1996—Jacksonville NFL	15	0	0	0	...	0	0	0	...	0	26	553	21.3	0	0	0	0	1
1997—Jacksonville NFL	7	0	1	2	2.0	0	0	0	...	0	0	0	...	0	0	0	0	0
1998—Oakland NFL	16	0	47	159	3.4	1	3	2	0.7	0	0	0	...	0	1	0	6	1
Pro totals (5 years)	60	4	81	256	3.2	1	12	133	11.1	1	28	594	21.2	0	2	0	12	4

JORDAN, RICHARD   LB   LIONS

PERSONAL: Born December 1, 1974, in Holdenville, Okla. ... 6-1/245. ... Full name: Richard Lamont Jordan.
HIGH SCHOOL: Vian (Okla.).
COLLEGE: Missouri Southern.
TRANSACTIONS/CAREER NOTES: Selected by Detroit Lions in seventh round (239th pick overall) of 1997 NFL draft. ... Signed by Lions (May 22, 1997). ... Released by Lions (August 25, 1997). ... Re-signed by Lions to practice squad (August 27, 1997). ... Activated (September 27, 1997).
PLAYING EXPERIENCE: Detroit NFL, 1997 and 1998. ... Games/Games started: 1997 (10/0), 1998 (16/3). Total: 26/3.
PRO STATISTICS: 1998—Intercepted one pass for four yards.

JOSEPH, KERRY   S   SEAHAWKS

PERSONAL: Born October 4, 1973, in New Iberia, La. ... 6-2/205.
HIGH SCHOOL: New Iberia (La.).
COLLEGE: McNeese State.
TRANSACTIONS/CAREER NOTES: Signed as non-drafted free agent by Cincinnati Bengals (April 22, 1996). ... Released by Bengals (May 6, 1997). ... Signed by Washington Redskins (May 16, 1997). ... Released by Redskins (August 25, 1997). ... Selected by Rhein Fire in 1998 NFL Europe draft (February 18, 1998). ... Signed by Seattle Seahawks (June 29, 1998).
PRO STATISTICS: NFLE: 1998—Intercepted four passes for 25 yards. NFL: 1998—Returned two kickoffs for 49 yards.

				PUNT RETURNS				TOTALS			
Year Team	G	GS	No.	Yds.	Avg.	TD	TD	2pt.	Pts.	Fum.
1996—Cincinnati NFL							Did not play.			
1997—							Did not play.			
1998—Rhein NFLE	...	...	4	43	10.8	0	0	0	0	0
—Seattle NFL	16	0	15	182	12.1	0	0	0	0	1
NFL Europe totals (1 year)	...	...	4	43	10.8	0	0	0	0	0
NFL totals (0 year)	16	0	15	182	12.1	0	0	0	0	1
Pro totals (1 years)	...	...	19	225	11.8	0	0	0	0	1

JOYCE, MATT   OL   CARDINALS

PERSONAL: Born March 30, 1972, in La Crosse, Wis. ... 6-7/313.
HIGH SCHOOL: New York Military Academy (Cornwall Hudson, N.Y.).
COLLEGE: Richmond (degree in health science, 1994).
TRANSACTIONS/CAREER NOTES: Signed as non-drafted free agent by Dallas Cowboys (May 2, 1994). ... Claimed on waivers by Cincinnati Bengals (August 28, 1994); released after failing physical. ... Signed by Cowboys to practice squad (September 5, 1994). ... Granted free agency after 1994 season. ... Signed by Seattle Seahawks (March 1, 1995). ... Released by Seahawks (August 25, 1996). ... Signed by Arizona Cardinals (December 3, 1996). ... Assigned by Cardinals to Scottish Claymores in 1997 World League enhancement allocation program (February 19, 1997). ... Granted free agency (February 12, 1999). ... Re-signed by Cardinals (April 1, 1999).
PLAYING EXPERIENCE: Seattle NFL, 1995; Scottish Claymores W.L., 1997; Arizona NFL, 1996-1998. ... Games/Games started: 1995 (16/13), 1996 (2/0), W.L. 1997 (games played unavailable), NFL 1997 (9/5), 1998 (11/0). Total: 38/19.
PRO STATISTICS: 1995—Recovered one fumble.

JOYNER, SETH   LB

PERSONAL: Born November 18, 1964, in Spring Valley, N.Y. ... 6-2/245.
HIGH SCHOOL: Spring Valley (N.Y.).
COLLEGE: Texas-El Paso.
TRANSACTIONS/CAREER NOTES: Selected by Philadelphia Eagles in eighth round (208th pick overall) of 1986 NFL draft. ... Signed by Eagles (July 17, 1986). ... Released by Eagles (September 1, 1986). ... Re-signed by Eagles (September 17, 1986). ... Granted free agency (February 1, 1991). ... Re-signed by Eagles (August 28, 1991). ... Activated (August 30, 1991). ... Designated by Eagles as transition player (February 25, 1993). ... Free agency status changed by Eagles from transitional to unconditional (February 17, 1994). ... Signed by Arizona Cardinals (April 17, 1994). ... Released by Cardinals (June 16, 1997). ... Signed by Green Bay Packers (July 16, 1997). ... Traded by Packers to Denver Broncos for past considerations (August 30, 1998). ... Granted unconditional free agency (February 12, 1999).
CHAMPIONSHIP GAME EXPERIENCE: Played in NFC championship game (1997 season). ... Played in Super Bowl XXXII (1997 season). ... Played in AFC championship game (1998 season). ... Member of Super Bowl championship team (1998 season).
HONORS: Played in Pro Bowl (1991, 1993 and 1994 seasons).
RECORDS: Shares NFL single-season records for most touchdowns by fumble recovery—2 (1991); and most touchdowns by recovery of opponents' fumbles—2 (1991).
PRO STATISTICS: 1987—Recovered two fumbles for 18 yards and one touchdown. 1988—Fumbled once and recovered one fumble. 1990—Fumbled once. 1991—Recovered four fumbles for 47 yards and two touchdowns. 1992—Recovered one fumble. 1995—Fumbled once and recovered three fumbles. 1996—Recovered one fumble.

			INTERCEPTIONS				SACKS
Year Team	G	GS	No.	Yds.	Avg.	TD	No.
1986—Philadelphia NFL	14	7	1	4	4.0	0	2.0
1987—Philadelphia NFL	12	12	2	42	21.0	0	4.0
1988—Philadelphia NFL	16	16	4	96	24.0	0	3.5
1989—Philadelphia NFL	14	14	1	0	0.0	0	4.5
1990—Philadelphia NFL	16	16	1	9	9.0	0	7.5
1991—Philadelphia NFL	16	16	3	41	13.7	0	6.5
1992—Philadelphia NFL	16	16	4	88	22.0	2	6.5
1993—Philadelphia NFL	16	16	1	6	6.0	0	2.0
1994—Arizona NFL	16	16	3	2	0.7	0	6.0
1995—Arizona NFL	16	16	3	9	3.0	0	1.0
1996—Arizona NFL	16	16	1	10	10.0	0	5.0
1997—Green Bay NFL	11	10	0	0	...	0	3.0
1998—Denver NFL	16	1	0	0	...	0	0.0
Pro totals (13 years)	195	172	24	307	12.8	2	51.5

JUNKIN, TREY — TE — CARDINALS

PERSONAL: Born January 23, 1961, in Conway, Ark. ... 6-2/258. ... Full name: Abner Kirk Junkin. ... Brother of Mike Junkin, linebacker with Cleveland Browns (1987 and 1988) and Kansas City Chiefs (1989).
HIGH SCHOOL: Northeast (North Little Rock, Ark.).
COLLEGE: Louisiana Tech.
TRANSACTIONS/CAREER NOTES: Selected by Buffalo Bills in fourth round (93rd pick overall) of 1983 NFL draft. ... Signed by Bills for 1983 season. ... Released by Bills (September 12, 1984). ... Signed by Washington Redskins (September 25, 1984). ... Rights relinquished by Redskins (February 1, 1985). ... Signed by Los Angeles Raiders (March 10, 1985). ... On injured reserve with knee injury (September 24, 1986-remainder of season). ... Released by Raiders (September 3, 1990). ... Signed by Seattle Seahawks (October 3, 1990). ... Granted unconditional free agency (February 1-April 1, 1991). ... Re-signed by Seahawks (July 9, 1991). ... Granted unconditional free agency (February 1-April 1, 1992). ... Re-signed by Seahawks for 1992 season. ... Granted unconditional free agency (March 1, 1993). ... Re-signed by Seahawks (March 11, 1993). ... Released by Seahawks (August 30, 1993). ... Re-signed by Seahawks (August 31, 1993). ... Granted unconditional free agency (February 17, 1994). ... Re-signed by Seahawks (May 31, 1994). ... Granted unconditional free agency (February 17, 1995). ... Re-signed by Seahawks (March 20, 1995). ... Granted unconditional free agency (February 16, 1996). ... Signed by Oakland Raiders (June 10, 1996). ... Claimed on waivers by Arizona Cardinals (October 14, 1996).
PRO STATISTICS: 1983—Recovered one fumble. 1984—Recovered one fumble. 1989—Returned one kickoff for no yards.
SINGLE GAME HIGHS (regular season): Receptions—2 (November 22, 1992, vs. Kansas City); yards—38 (September 21, 1986, vs. New York Giants); and touchdown receptions—1 (September 25, 1994, vs. Pittsburgh).

				RECEIVING				TOTALS		
Year Team	G	GS	No.	Yds.	Avg.	TD	TD	2pt.	Pts.	Fum.
1983—Buffalo NFL	16	0	0	0	...	0	0	...	0	0
1984—Buffalo NFL	2	0	0	0	...	0	0	...	0	0
—Washington NFL	12	0	0	0	...	0	0	...	0	0
1985—Los Angeles Raiders NFL	16	0	2	8	4.0	1	1	...	6	0
1986—Los Angeles Raiders NFL	3	0	2	38	19.0	0	0	...	0	0
1987—Los Angeles Raiders NFL	12	1	2	15	7.5	0	0	...	0	0
1988—Los Angeles Raiders NFL	16	1	4	25	6.3	2	2	...	12	0
1989—Los Angeles Raiders NFL	16	0	3	32	10.7	2	2	...	12	0
1990—Seattle NFL	12	0	0	0	...	0	0	...	0	0
1991—Seattle NFL	16	0	0	0	...	0	0	...	0	0
1992—Seattle NFL	16	1	3	25	8.3	1	1	...	6	0
1993—Seattle NFL	16	1	0	0	...	0	0	...	0	0
1994—Seattle NFL	16	0	1	1	1.0	1	1	0	6	0
1995—Seattle NFL	16	0	0	0	...	0	0	0	0	0
1996—Oakland NFL	6	0	0	0	...	0	0	0	0	0
—Arizona NFL	10	0	0	0	...	0	0	0	0	0
1997—Arizona NFL	16	0	0	0	...	0	0	0	0	0
1998—Arizona NFL	16	0	0	0	...	0	0	0	0	0
Pro totals (16 years)	**233**	**4**	**17**	**144**	**8.5**	**7**	**7**	**0**	**42**	**0**

JUREVICIUS, JOE — WR — GIANTS

PERSONAL: Born December 23, 1974, in Cleveland. ... 6-5/231. ... Full name: Joe Michael Jurevicius. ... Name pronounced jur-ih-VISH-us.
HIGH SCHOOL: Lake Catholic (Mentor, Ohio).
COLLEGE: Penn State.
TRANSACTIONS/CAREER NOTES: Selected by New York Giants in second round (55th pick overall) of 1998 NFL draft. ... Signed by Giants (July 28, 1998).
SINGLE GAME HIGHS (regular season): Receptions—3 (December 13, 1998, vs. Denver); yards—65 (November 22, 1998, vs. Philadelphia); and touchdown receptions—0.

			RECEIVING			
Year Team	G	GS	No.	Yds.	Avg.	TD
1998—New York Giants NFL	14	1	9	146	16.2	0

JURKOVIC, JOHN — DT — BROWNS

PERSONAL: Born August 18, 1967, in Friedrischafen, West Germany. ... 6-2/301. ... Full name: Ivan Jurkovic.
HIGH SCHOOL: Thornton Fractional North (Calumet City, Ill.).
COLLEGE: Eastern Illinois (degree in business).
TRANSACTIONS/CAREER NOTES: Signed as non-drafted free agent by Miami Dolphins (April 27, 1990). ... Released by Dolphins (August 28, 1990). ... Re-signed by Dolphins to practice squad (October 3, 1990). ... Granted free agency after 1990 season. ... Signed by Green Bay Packers (March 8, 1991). ... Released by Packers (August 26, 1991). ... Re-signed by Packers to practice squad (August 28, 1991). ... Activated (November 22, 1991). ... Granted unconditional free agency (February 1-April 1, 1992). ... Re-signed by Packers (April 2, 1992). ... Granted unconditional free agency (February 16, 1996). ... Signed by Jacksonville Jaguars (April 13, 1996). ... On injured reserve with leg injury (September 23, 1997-remainder of season). ... Granted unconditional free agency (February 12, 1999). ... Signed by Cleveland Browns (March 26, 1999).
CHAMPIONSHIP GAME EXPERIENCE: Played in NFC championship game (1995 season). ... Played in AFC championship game (1996 season).
PRO STATISTICS: 1992—Returned three kickoffs for 39 yards. 1993—Returned two kickoffs for 22 yards. 1994—Returned four kickoffs for 57 yards. 1995—Returned one kickoff for 17 yards. 1996—Recovered two fumbles.

Year Team	G	GS	SACKS
1990—Miami NFL		Did not play.	
1991—Green Bay NFL	5	0	0.0
1992—Green Bay NFL	16	12	2.0
1993—Green Bay NFL	16	12	5.5
1994—Green Bay NFL	16	15	0.0
1995—Green Bay NFL	16	14	0.0
1996—Jacksonville NFL	16	14	1.0
1997—Jacksonville NFL	3	3	0.0
1998—Jacksonville NFL	16	16	0.5
Pro totals (8 years)	**104**	**86**	**9.0**

JUSTIN, PAUL — QB

PERSONAL: Born May 19, 1968, in Schaumburg, Ill. ... 6-4/211. ... Full name: Paul Donald Justin.
HIGH SCHOOL: Schaumburg (Ill.).
COLLEGE: Arizona State.
TRANSACTIONS/CAREER NOTES: Selected by Chicago Bears in seventh round (190th pick overall) of 1991 NFL draft. ... Signed by Bears for 1991 season. ... Released by Bears (August 27, 1991). ... Re-signed by Bears to practice squad (August 28, 1991). ... Released by Bears (August 31, 1992). ... Signed by Indianapolis Colts (April 11, 1994). ... Released by Colts (August 25, 1994). ... Re-signed by Colts to practice squad (August 29, 1994). ... Assigned by Colts to Frankfurt Galaxy in 1995 World League enhancement allocation program (February 20, 1995). ... On injured reserve with knee injury (December 5, 1997-remainder of season). ... Granted free agency (February 13, 1998). ... Re-signed by Colts (March 26, 1998). ... Traded by Colts to Cincinnati Bengals for fifth-round pick (LB Antony Jordan) in 1998 draft (March 26, 1998). ... Released by Bengals (April 20, 1999).
CHAMPIONSHIP GAME EXPERIENCE: Member of Colts for AFC championship game (1995 season); inactive.
PRO STATISTICS: 1995—Fumbled once and recovered one fumble for minus one yard. 1996—Fumbled once and recovered one fumble. 1997—Fumbled once.
SINGLE GAME HIGHS (regular season): Attempts—40 (December 1, 1996, vs. Buffalo); completions—24 (November 16, 1997, vs. Green Bay); yards—340 (November 16, 1997, vs. Green Bay); and touchdown passes—2 (October 26, 1997, vs. San Diego).
STATISTICAL PLATEAUS: 300-yard passing games: 1997 (1).
MISCELLANEOUS: Regular-season record as starting NFL quarterback: 3-7 (.300).

				PASSING							RUSHING				TOTALS		
Year Team	G	GS	Att.	Cmp.	Pct.	Yds.	TD	Int.	Avg.	Rat.	Att.	Yds.	Avg.	TD	TD	2pt.	Pts.
1991—Chicago NFL...............						Did not play.											
1992—						Did not play.											
1993—						Did not play.											
1994—Indianapolis NFL.........						Did not play.											
1995—Frankfurt W.L..............	...	...	279	172	61.6	2394	17	12	8.58	91.6	14	50	3.6	0	0	0	0
—Indianapolis NFL.............	3	1	36	20	55.6	212	0	2	5.89	49.8	3	1	0.3	0	0	0	0
1996—Indianapolis NFL.........	8	2	127	74	58.3	839	2	0	6.61	83.4	2	7	3.5	0	0	0	0
1997—Indianapolis NFL.........	8	4	140	83	59.3	1046	5	5	7.47	79.6	6	2	0.3	0	0	0	0
1998—Cincinnati NFL............	5	3	63	34	54.0	426	1	3	6.76	60.7	1	2	2.0	0	0	1	2
W.L. totals (1 year)	...	...	279	172	61.6	2394	17	12	8.58	91.6	14	50	3.6	0	0	0	0
NFL totals (3 years)	24	10	366	211	57.7	2523	8	10	6.89	74.7	12	12	1.0	0	0	1	2
Pro totals (4 years)	...	...	645	383	59.4	4917	25	22	7.62	82.0	26	62	2.4	0	0	1	2

KAISER, JASON — S — CHIEFS

PERSONAL: Born November 9, 1973, in Denver. ... 6-0/190.
HIGH SCHOOL: Highlands Ranch (Colo.).
COLLEGE: Culver-Stockton College (Mo.).
TRANSACTIONS/CAREER NOTES: Signed by Hamilton Tiger-Cats of CFL (May 23, 1996). ... Released by Tiger-Cats (July 24, 1997). ... Signed as non-drafted free agent by Denver Broncos (April 23, 1998). ... Released by Broncos (August 25, 1998). ... Signed by Kansas City Chiefs to practice squad (November 3, 1998). ... Activated (December 17, 1998).
PLAYING EXPERIENCE: Hamilton Tiger-Cats CFL, 1996 and 1997; Kansas City NFL, 1998. ... Games/Games started: Hamilton, 1996 (8/games started unavailable), 1997 (2/games started unavailable), 1998 (1/0). Total CFL: (10/-). Total NFL: (1/0). Total Pro: (11/-).
PRO STATISTICS: CFL: 1996—Intercepted two passes for 25 yards, returned 10 punts for 81 yards and returned three kickoffs for 43 yards. 1997—Returned one kickoff for no yards.

KALU, NDUKWE — DE — REDSKINS

PERSONAL: Born August 3, 1975, in Baltimore. ... 6-3/246. ... Full name: Ndukwe Dike Kalu. ... Name pronounced EN-doo-kway ka-LOO.
HIGH SCHOOL: John Marshall (San Antonio).
COLLEGE: Rice.
TRANSACTIONS/CAREER NOTES: Selected by Philadelphia Eagles in fifth round (152nd pick overall) of 1997 NFL draft. ... Signed by Eagles (July 15, 1997). ... Released by Eagles (August 25, 1998). ... Signed by Washington Redskins (August 30, 1998).
PLAYING EXPERIENCE: Philadelphia NFL, 1997; Washington NFL, 1998. ... Games/Games started: 1997 (3/0), 1998 (13/1). Total: 16/1.
PRO STATISTICS: 1998—Credited with three sacks.

KANELL, DANNY — QB — FALCONS

PERSONAL: Born November 21, 1973, in Fort Lauderdale, Fla. ... 6-3/220. ... Son of Dan Kanell, team physician, Miami Dolphins and spring training physician, New York Yankees.
HIGH SCHOOL: Westminster Academy (Fort Lauderdale, Fla.).
COLLEGE: Florida State.
TRANSACTIONS/CAREER NOTES: Selected by New York Giants in fourth round (130th pick overall) of 1996 NFL draft. ... Signed by Giants (July 18, 1996). ... Released by Giants (February 19, 1999). ... Signed by Atlanta Falcons (March 5, 1999).
PRO STATISTICS: 1996—Fumbled twice for minus one yard. 1997—Fumbled six times for minus 10 yards. 1998—Fumbled six times and recovered one fumble.
SINGLE GAME HIGHS (regular season): Attempts—45 (September 21, 1998, vs. Dallas); completions—25 (September 21, 1998, vs. Dallas); yards—259 (October 18, 1998, vs. Arizona); and touchdown passes—3 (October 18, 1998, vs. Arizona).
MISCELLANEOUS: Selected by Milwaukee Brewers organization in 19th round of free-agent baseball draft (June 1, 1992); did not sign. ... Selected by New York Yankees organization in 25th round of free-agent baseball draft (June 1, 1995); did not sign. ... Regular-season record as starting NFL quarterback: 10-9-1 (.525). ... Postseason record as starting NFL quarterback: 0-1.

				PASSING						RUSHING			TOTALS		
Year Team	G	GS	Att.	Cmp.	Pct.	Yds.	TD	Int.	Avg.	Rat.	Att.	Yds.	Avg.	TD	TD	2pt.	Pts.
1996—N.Y. Giants NFL	4	0	60	23	38.3	227	1	1	3.78	48.4	7	6	0.9	0	0	0	0
1997—N.Y. Giants NFL	16	10	294	156	53.1	1740	11	9	5.92	70.7	15	2	0.1	0	0	0	0
1998—N.Y. Giants NFL	10	10	299	160	53.5	1603	11	10	5.36	67.3	15	36	2.4	0	0	0	0
Pro totals (3 years)	30	20	653	339	51.9	3570	23	20	5.47	67.1	37	44	1.2	0	0	0	0

KASAY, JOHN — K — PANTHERS

PERSONAL: Born October 27, 1969, in Athens, Ga. ... 5-10/198. ... Full name: John David Kasay. ... Name pronounced KAY-see.
HIGH SCHOOL: Clarke Central (Athens, Ga.).
COLLEGE: Georgia (degree in journalism, 1994).
TRANSACTIONS/CAREER NOTES: Selected by Seattle Seahawks in fourth round (98th pick overall) of 1991 NFL draft. ... Signed by Seahawks (July 19, 1991). ... Granted free agency (February 17, 1994). ... Re-signed by Seahawks (July 19, 1994). ... Granted unconditional free agency (February 17, 1995). ... Signed by Carolina Panthers (February 20, 1995).
CHAMPIONSHIP GAME EXPERIENCE: Played in NFC championship game (1996 season).
HONORS: Played in Pro Bowl (1996 season).
RECORDS: Holds NFL single-season record for most field goals made—37 (1996).
PRO STATISTICS: 1993—Recovered one fumble. 1995—Punted once for 32 yards. 1996—Punted once for 30 yards.

				KICKING				
Year Team	G	XPM	XPA	FGM	FGA	Lg.	50+	Pts.
1991—Seattle NFL	16	27	28	25	31	54	2-3	102
1992—Seattle NFL	16	14	14	14	22	43	0-0	56
1993—Seattle NFL	16	29	29	23	28	55	3-5	98
1994—Seattle NFL	16	25	26	20	24	50	1-2	85
1995—Carolina NFL	16	27	28	26	33	52	1-1	105
1996—Carolina NFL	16	34	35	*37	*45	53	3-7	*145
1997—Carolina NFL	16	25	25	22	26	54	3-6	91
1998—Carolina NFL	16	35	37	19	26	56	4-7	92
Pro totals (8 years)	128	216	222	186	235	56	17-31	774

KAUFMAN, NAPOLEON — RB — RAIDERS

PERSONAL: Born June 7, 1973, in Kansas City, Mo. ... 5-9/185.
HIGH SCHOOL: Lompoc (Calif.).
COLLEGE: Washington.
TRANSACTIONS/CAREER NOTES: Selected by Los Angeles Raiders in first round (18th pick overall) of 1995 NFL draft. ... Signed by Raiders (May 24, 1995). ... Raiders franchise moved to Oakland (July 21, 1995).
HONORS: Named running back on THE SPORTING NEWS college All-America second team (1994).
PRO STATISTICS: 1997—Attempted one pass without a completion and recovered one fumble. 1998—Recovered one fumble.
SINGLE GAME HIGHS (regular season): Attempts—31 (October 25, 1998, vs. Cincinnati); yards—227 (October 19, 1997, vs. Denver); and rushing touchdowns—2 (September 14, 1997, vs. Atlanta).
STATISTICAL PLATEAUS: 100-yard rushing games: 1996 (3), 1997 (6), 1998 (4). Total: 13. ... 100-yard receiving games: 1997 (1).

			RUSHING				RECEIVING				KICKOFF RETURNS			TOTALS			
Year Team	G	GS	Att.	Yds.	Avg.	TD	No.	Yds.	Avg.	TD	No.	Yds.	Avg.	TD	TD	2pt.	Pts.	Fum.
1995—Oakland NFL	16	1	108	490	4.5	1	9	62	6.9	0	22	572	26.0	1	2	0	12	0
1996—Oakland NFL	16	9	150	874	*5.8	1	22	143	6.5	1	25	548	21.9	0	2	0	12	3
1997—Oakland NFL	16	16	272	1294	4.8	6	40	403	10.1	2	0	0	...	0	8	0	48	7
1998—Oakland NFL	13	13	217	921	4.2	2	25	191	7.6	0	0	0	...	0	2	0	12	2
Pro totals (4 years)	61	39	747	3579	4.8	10	96	799	8.3	3	47	1120	23.8	1	14	0	84	12

KELLY, BRIAN — CB — BUCCANEERS

PERSONAL: Born January 14, 1976, in Las Vegas, Nev. ... 5-11/195.
HIGH SCHOOL: Overland (Aurora, Colo.).
COLLEGE: Southern California.
TRANSACTIONS/CAREER NOTES: Selected by Tampa Bay Buccaneers in second round (45th pick overall) of 1998 NFL draft. ... Signed by Buccaneers (July 19, 1998).
PLAYING EXPERIENCE: Tampa Bay NFL, 1998. ... Games/Games started: 16/3.
PRO STATISTICS: 1998—Intercepted one pass for four yards, fumbled once and recovered one fumble for 15 yards.

KELLY, ROB — S — SAINTS

PERSONAL: Born June 21, 1974, in Newark, Ohio. ... 6-0/199. ... Full name: Robert James Kelly.
HIGH SCHOOL: Newark Catholic (Ohio).
COLLEGE: Ohio State.
TRANSACTIONS/CAREER NOTES: Selected by New Orleans Saints in second round (33rd pick overall) of 1997 NFL draft. ... Signed by Saints (July 17, 1997).

			INTERCEPTIONS			
Year Team	G	GS	No.	Yds.	Avg.	TD
1997—New Orleans NFL	16	2	1	15	15.0	0
1998—New Orleans NFL	16	3	2	104	52.0	1
Pro totals (2 years)	32	5	3	119	39.7	1

KENDALL, PETE   G   SEAHAWKS

PERSONAL: Born July 9, 1973, in Quincy, Mass. ... 6-5/292. ... Full name: Peter Marcus Kendall.
HIGH SCHOOL: Archbishop Williams (Weymouth, Mass.).
COLLEGE: Boston College (degree in marketing, 1995).
TRANSACTIONS/CAREER NOTES: Selected by Seattle Seahawks in first round (21st pick overall) of 1996 NFL draft. ... Signed by Seahawks (July 21, 1996).
PLAYING EXPERIENCE: Seattle NFL, 1996-1998. ... Games/Games started: 1996 (12/11), 1997 (16/16), 1998 (16/16). Total: 44/43.

KENNEDY, CORTEZ   DT   SEAHAWKS

PERSONAL: Born August 23, 1968, in Osceola, Ark. ... 6-3/306.
HIGH SCHOOL: Rivercrest (Wilson, Ark.).
JUNIOR COLLEGE: Northwest Mississippi Community College.
COLLEGE: Miami, Fla. (degree in criminal justice).
TRANSACTIONS/CAREER NOTES: Selected by Seattle Seahawks in first round (third pick overall) of 1990 NFL draft. ... Signed by Seahawks (September 3, 1990). ... Granted roster exemption (September 3-9, 1990). ... On injured reserve with ankle injury (December 10, 1997-remainder of season).
HONORS: Named defensive tackle on THE SPORTING NEWS college All-America first team (1989). ... Played in Pro Bowl (1991-1996 and 1998 seasons). ... Named defensive tackle on THE SPORTING NEWS NFL All-Pro team (1992 and 1993).
PRO STATISTICS: 1990—Recovered one fumble. 1991—Recovered one fumble. 1992—Fumbled once and recovered one fumble for 19 yards. 1993—Recovered one fumble. 1994—Recovered one fumble. 1998—Recovered one fumble for 39 yards and a touchdown.

Year Team	G	GS	SACKS
1990—Seattle NFL	16	2	1.0
1991—Seattle NFL	16	16	6.5
1992—Seattle NFL	16	16	14.0
1993—Seattle NFL	16	16	6.5
1994—Seattle NFL	16	16	4.0
1995—Seattle NFL	16	16	6.5
1996—Seattle NFL	16	16	8.0
1997—Seattle NFL	8	8	2.0
1998—Seattle NFL	15	15	2.0
Pro totals (9 years)	**135**	**121**	**50.5**

KENNEDY, LINCOLN   G   RAIDERS

PERSONAL: Born February 12, 1971, in York, Pa. ... 6-6/335. ... Full name: Tamerlane Lincoln Kennedy.
HIGH SCHOOL: Samuel F. B. Morse (San Diego).
COLLEGE: Washington (degree in speech and drama, 1993).
TRANSACTIONS/CAREER NOTES: Selected by Atlanta Falcons in first round (ninth pick overall) of 1993 NFL draft. ... Signed by Falcons (August 2, 1993). ... Granted free agency (February 16, 1996). ... Traded by Falcons to Oakland Raiders for fifth-round pick (traded to Washington) in 1997 draft (May 13, 1996).
PLAYING EXPERIENCE: Atlanta NFL, 1993-1995; Oakland NFL, 1996-1998. ... Games/Games started: 1993 (16/16), 1994 (16/2), 1995 (16/4), 1996 (16/16), 1997 (16/16), 1998 (16/16). Total: 96/70.
HONORS: Named offensive tackle on THE SPORTING NEWS college All-America first team (1992).
PRO STATISTICS: 1993—Recovered one fumble. 1994—Recovered one fumble. 1996—Recovered one fumble. 1998—Recovered one fumble for 27 yards.

KENNISON, EDDIE   WR   SAINTS

PERSONAL: Born January 20, 1973, in Lake Charles, La. ... 6-0/195. ... Full name: Eddie Joseph Kennison III.
HIGH SCHOOL: Washington-Marion (Lake Charles, La.).
COLLEGE: Louisiana State.
TRANSACTIONS/CAREER NOTES: Selected after junior season by St. Louis Rams in first round (18th pick overall) of 1996 NFL draft. ... Signed by Rams (July 27, 1996). ... Traded by Rams to New Orleans Saints for second-round pick (DB Dre' Bly) in 1999 draft (February 18, 1999).
PRO STATISTICS: 1997—Rushed three times for 13 yards. 1998—Rushed twice for nine yards and recovered one fumble.
SINGLE GAME HIGHS (regular season): Receptions—8 (December 8, 1996, vs. Chicago); yards—226 (December 15, 1996, vs. Atlanta); and touchdown receptions—3 (December 15, 1996, vs. Atlanta).
STATISTICAL PLATEAUS: 100-yard receiving games: 1996 (2).

			RECEIVING				PUNT RETURNS				KICKOFF RETURNS				TOTALS		
Year Team	G	GS	No.	Yds.	Avg.	TD	No.	Yds.	Avg.	TD	No.	Yds.	Avg.	TD	TD	2pt.	Pts.	Fum.
1996—St. Louis NFL	15	14	54	924	17.1	9	29	423	14.6	2	23	454	19.7	0	11	0	66	5
1997—St. Louis NFL	14	9	25	404	16.2	0	34	247	7.3	0	1	14	14.0	0	0	0	0	2
1998—St. Louis NFL	16	13	17	234	13.8	1	40	415	10.4	1	0	0	...	0	2	0	12	4
Pro totals (3 years)	**45**	**36**	**96**	**1562**	**16.3**	**10**	**103**	**1085**	**10.5**	**3**	**24**	**468**	**19.5**	**0**	**13**	**0**	**78**	**11**

KENT, JOEY   WR   TITANS

PERSONAL: Born April 23, 1974, in Huntsville, Ala. ... 6-1/191. ... Full name: Joseph Edward Kent III.
HIGH SCHOOL: Johnson (Huntsville, Ala.).
COLLEGE: Tennessee (degree in marketing).

TRANSACTIONS/CAREER NOTES: Selected by Houston Oilers in second round (46th pick overall) of 1997 NFL draft. ... Oilers franchise moved to Tennessee for 1997 season. ... Signed by Oilers (July 17, 1997). ... Oilers franchise renamed Tennessee Titans for 1999 season (December 26, 1998).
HONORS: Named wide receiver on THE SPORTING NEWS college All-America second team (1996).
SINGLE GAME HIGHS (regular season): Receptions—2 (October 11, 1998, vs. Baltimore); yards—26 (October 11, 1998, vs. Baltimore); and touchdown receptions—1 (December 4, 1997, vs. Cincinnati).

			RECEIVING					TOTALS		
Year Team	G	GS	No.	Yds.	Avg.	TD	TD	2pt.	Pts.	Fum.
1997—Tennessee NFL	12	0	6	55	9.2	1	1	0	6	0
1998—Tennessee NFL	10	0	4	62	15.5	0	0	0	0	0
Pro totals (2 years)	22	0	10	117	11.7	1	1	0	6	0

KERNER, MARLON — CB

PERSONAL: Born March 18, 1973, in Columbus, Ohio. ... 5-10/187.
HIGH SCHOOL: Brookhaven (Columbus, Ohio).
COLLEGE: Ohio State.
TRANSACTIONS/CAREER NOTES: Selected by Buffalo Bills in third round (76th pick overall) of 1995 NFL draft. ... Signed by Bills (July 10, 1995). ... On injured reserve with knee injury (December 1, 1997-remainder of season). ... Granted free agency (February 13, 1998). ... Re-signed by Bills for 1998 season. ... On injured reserve with knee injury (September 9, 1998-remainder of season). ... Granted unconditional free agency (February 12, 1999).
PLAYING EXPERIENCE: Buffalo NFL, 1995-1998. ... Games/Games started: 1995 (14/5), 1996 (15/0), 1997 (13/2), 1998 (1/0). Total: 43/7.
PRO STATISTICS: 1996—Intercepted one pass for six yards and credited with one sack. 1997—Intercepted two passes for 20 yards and recovered one fumble.

KIDD, JOHN — P

PERSONAL: Born August 22, 1961, in Springfield, Ill. ... 6-3/214. ... Full name: Max John Kidd.
HIGH SCHOOL: Findlay (Ohio).
COLLEGE: Northwestern (degree in industrial engineering and management science, 1984).
TRANSACTIONS/CAREER NOTES: Selected by Chicago Blitz in 1984 USFL territorial draft. ... Selected by Buffalo Bills in fifth round (128th pick overall) of 1984 NFL draft. ... Signed by Bills (June 1, 1984). ... Granted unconditional free agency (February 1, 1990). ... Signed by San Diego Chargers (March 15, 1990). ... Granted free agency (February 1, 1992). ... Re-signed by Chargers (July 23, 1992). ... Granted unconditional free agency (March 1, 1993). ... Re-signed by Chargers (July 23, 1993). ... Granted unconditional free agency (February 17, 1994). ... Re-signed by Chargers (August 20, 1994). ... On injured reserve with hamstring injury (September 12-22, 1994). ... Released by Chargers (September 22, 1994). ... Signed by Miami Dolphins (November 30, 1994). ... Granted unconditional free agency (February 17, 1995). ... Re-signed by Dolphins (April 18, 1995). ... Released by Dolphins (October 3, 1997). ... Re-signed by Dolphins (October 7, 1997). ... Granted unconditional free agency (February 13, 1998). ... Re-signed by Dolphins (July 21, 1998). ... Released by Dolphins (August 25, 1998). ... Signed by Detroit Lions (October 1, 1998). ... Released by Lions (October 23, 1998). ... Signed by New York Jets (November 3, 1998). ... Released by Jets (March 10, 1999).
CHAMPIONSHIP GAME EXPERIENCE: Played in AFC championship game (1988 and 1998 seasons).
PRO STATISTICS: 1986—Rushed once for no yards and recovered one fumble. 1987—Attempted one pass without a completion. 1990—Fumbled once and recovered one fumble. 1992—Rushed twice for minus 13 yards, fumbled once and recovered one fumble for minus nine yards. 1993—Rushed three times for minus 13 yards and a touchdown. 1996—Rushed once for three yards. 1997—Rushed once for four yards.

				PUNTING			
Year Team	G	No.	Yds.	Avg.	Net avg.	In. 20	Blk.
1984—Buffalo NFL	16	88	3696	42.0	32.7	16	2
1985—Buffalo NFL	16	92	3818	41.5	35.8	*33	0
1986—Buffalo NFL	16	75	3031	40.4	34.5	14	0
1987—Buffalo NFL	12	64	2495	39.0	34.5	†20	0
1988—Buffalo NFL	16	62	2451	39.5	35.2	13	0
1989—Buffalo NFL	16	65	2564	39.4	32.2	15	2
1990—San Diego NFL	16	61	2442	40.0	36.6	14	1
1991—San Diego NFL	16	76	3064	40.3	34.7	22	1
1992—San Diego NFL	16	68	2899	42.6	36.3	22	0
1993—San Diego NFL	14	57	2431	42.6	35.8	16	0
1994—San Diego NFL	2	7	246	35.1	32.2	1	0
—Miami NFL	4	14	602	43.0	29.1	2	0
1995—Miami NFL	16	57	2433	42.7	36.2	15	0
1996—Miami NFL	16	78	3611	*46.3	38.7	26	0
1997—Miami NFL	13	52	2247	43.2	37.0	13	0
1998—Detroit NFL	2	13	520	40.0	34.9	1	0
—New York Jets NFL	8	28	1166	41.6	36.9	8	0
Pro totals (15 years)	213	957	39716	41.5	35.3	251	6

KILLENS, TERRY — LB — TITANS

PERSONAL: Born March 24, 1974, in Cincinnati. ... 6-1/235. ... Full name: Terry Deleon Killens.
HIGH SCHOOL: Purcell (Cincinnati).
COLLEGE: Penn State.
TRANSACTIONS/CAREER NOTES: Selected by Houston Oilers in third round (74th pick overall) of 1996 NFL draft. ... Signed by Oilers (July 20, 1996). ... Oilers franchise moved to Tennessee for 1997 season. ... Oilers franchise renamed Tennessee Titans for 1999 season (December 26, 1998). ... Granted free agency (February 12, 1999).
PLAYING EXPERIENCE: Houston NFL, 1996; Tennessee NFL, 1997 and 1998. ... Games/Games started: 1996 (14/0), 1997 (16/0), 1998 (16/1). Total: 46/1.

KINCHEN, BRIAN — TE — PANTHERS

PERSONAL: Born August 6, 1965, in Baton Rouge, La. ... 6-2/240. ... Full name: Brian Douglas Kinchen. ... Brother of Todd Kinchen, wide receiver/kick returner, Carolina Panthers.
HIGH SCHOOL: University (Baton Rouge, La.).
COLLEGE: Louisiana State.
TRANSACTIONS/CAREER NOTES: Selected by Miami Dolphins in 12th round (320th pick overall) of 1988 NFL draft. ... Signed by Dolphins (June 6, 1988). ... On injured reserve with hamstring injury (October 4, 1990-remainder of season). ... Granted unconditional free agency (February 1, 1991). ... Signed by Green Bay Packers (April 1, 1991). ... Released by Packers (August 26, 1991). ... Signed by Cleveland Browns (September 13, 1991). ... Granted unconditional free agency (February 1-April 1, 1992). ... Re-signed by Browns for 1992 season. ... Granted unconditional free agency (February 17, 1994). ... Re-signed by Browns (March 4, 1994). ... Granted unconditional free agency (February 16, 1996). ... Browns franchise moved to Baltimore and renamed Ravens for 1996 season (March 11, 1996). ... Re-signed by Ravens (April 3, 1996). ... Granted unconditional free agency (February 12, 1999). ... Signed by Carolina Panthers (March 8, 1999).
PRO STATISTICS: 1995—Recovered one fumble.
SINGLE GAME HIGHS (regular season): Receptions—9 (November 24, 1996, vs. Jacksonville); yards—87 (December 15, 1996, vs. Carolina); and touchdown receptions—1 (October 5, 1997, vs. Pittsburgh).

			RECEIVING				KICKOFF RETURNS				TOTALS			
Year Team	G	GS	No.	Yds.	Avg.	TD	No.	Yds.	Avg.	TD	TD	2pt.	Pts.	Fum.
1988—Miami NFL	16	0	1	3	3.0	0	0	0	...	0	0	...	0	0
1989—Miami NFL	16	0	1	12	12.0	0	2	26	13.0	0	0	...	0	2
1990—Miami NFL	4	0	0	0	...	0	1	16	16.0	0	0	...	0	0
1991—Cleveland NFL	14	0	0	0	...	0	0	0	...	0	0	...	0	1
1992—Cleveland NFL	16	0	0	0	...	0	0	0	...	0	0	...	0	0
1993—Cleveland NFL	16	15	29	347	12.0	2	1	0	0.0	0	2	...	12	1
1994—Cleveland NFL	16	11	24	232	9.7	1	3	38	12.7	0	1	0	6	1
1995—Cleveland NFL	13	12	20	216	10.8	0	0	0	...	0	0	0	0	1
1996—Baltimore NFL	16	16	55	581	10.6	1	1	19	19.0	0	1	0	6	1
1997—Baltimore NFL	16	6	11	95	8.6	1	0	0	...	0	1	0	6	0
1998—Baltimore NFL	16	5	13	110	8.5	0	2	33	16.5	0	0	0	0	0
Pro totals (11 years)	159	65	154	1596	10.4	5	10	132	13.2	0	5	0	30	7

KINCHEN, TODD — WR/KR — PANTHERS

PERSONAL: Born January 7, 1969, in Baton Rouge, La. ... 5-11/187. ... Full name: Todd Whittington Kinchen. ... Brother of Brian Kinchen, tight end, Carolina Panthers.
HIGH SCHOOL: Trafton Academy (Baton Rouge, La.).
COLLEGE: Louisiana State.
TRANSACTIONS/CAREER NOTES: Selected by Los Angeles Rams in third round (60th pick overall) of 1992 NFL draft. ... Signed by Rams (July 13, 1992). ... On injured reserve with knee injury (November 23, 1993-remainder of season). ... On physically unable to perform list with knee injury (July 22-28, 1994). ... Released by Rams (September 6, 1994). ... Re-signed by Rams (September 21, 1994). ... Granted free agency (February 17, 1995). ... Rams franchise moved to St. Louis (April 12, 1995). ... Re-signed by Rams (June 16, 1995). ... Traded by Rams to Denver Broncos for fifth-round pick (CB Taje Allen) in 1997 draft (August 27, 1996). ... Released by Broncos (February 25, 1997). ... Signed by Atlanta Falcons (April 11, 1997). ... Granted unconditional free agency (February 12, 1999). ... Signed by Carolina Panthers (April 7, 1999).
CHAMPIONSHIP GAME EXPERIENCE: Member of Falcons for NFC championship game (1998 season); inactive. ... Member of Falcons for Super Bowl XXXIII (1998 season); inactive.
RECORDS: Shares NFL single-game records for most touchdowns by punt return—2; and most touchdowns by combined kick return—2 (December 27, 1992, vs. Atlanta).
PRO STATISTICS: 1993—Fumbled once. 1994—Fumbled five times. 1995—Attempted one pass without a completion, fumbled eight times and recovered one fumble. 1996—Fumbled five times and recovered one fumble. 1997—Fumbled five times and recovered two fumbles. 1998—Fumbled twice.
SINGLE GAME HIGHS (regular season): Receptions—5 (December 4, 1994, vs. New Orleans); yards—85 (October 19, 1997, vs. San Francisco); and touchdown receptions—1 (November 22, 1998, vs. Chicago).

			RUSHING				RECEIVING				PUNT RETURNS				KICKOFF RETURNS				TOTALS		
Year Team	G	GS	Att.	Yds.	Avg.	TD	No.	Yds.	Avg.	TD	No.	Yds.	Avg.	TD	No.	Yds.	Avg.	TD	TD	2pt.	Pts.
1992—L.A. Rams NFL	14	0	0	0	...	0	0	0	...	0	4	103	25.8	†2	4	63	15.8	0	2	...	12
1993—L.A. Rams NFL	6	1	2	10	5.0	0	8	137	17.1	1	7	32	4.6	0	6	96	16.0	0	1	...	6
1994—L.A. Rams NFL	13	0	1	44	44.0	1	23	352	15.3	3	16	158	9.9	0	21	510	24.3	0	4	0	24
1995—St. Louis NFL	16	1	4	16	4.0	0	36	419	11.6	4	*53	416	7.8	0	35	743	21.2	0	4	0	24
1996—Denver NFL	7	0	0	0	...	0	1	27	27.0	0	26	300	11.5	0	0	0	...	0	0	0	0
1997—Atlanta NFL	16	0	0	0	...	0	16	266	16.6	1	*52	446	8.6	0	1	18	18.0	0	1	0	6
1998—Atlanta NFL	11	0	0	0	...	0	11	157	14.3	1	6	38	6.3	0	0	0	...	0	1	0	6
Pro totals (7 years)	83	2	7	70	10.0	1	95	1358	14.3	10	164	1493	9.1	2	67	1430	21.3	0	13	0	78

KING, CARLOS — FB — STEELERS

PERSONAL: Born November 27, 1973, in Booneville, N.C. ... 6-0/230. ... Full name: Carlos Jermaine King.
HIGH SCHOOL: Starmount (Booneville, N.C.), then Hargrave Military Academy (Chatham, Va.).
COLLEGE: North Carolina State.
TRANSACTIONS/CAREER NOTES: Selected by Pittsburgh Steelers in fourth round (123rd pick overall) of 1998 NFL draft. ... Signed by Steelers (July 6, 1998). ... Released by Steelers (October 6, 1998). ... Re-signed by Steelers to practice squad (October 7, 1998). ... Activated (November 25, 1998).
PLAYING EXPERIENCE: Pittsburgh NFL, 1998. ... Games/Games started: 1/0.

KING, SHAWN — DE — COLTS

PERSONAL: Born June 24, 1972, in West Monroe, La. ... 6-3/278.
HIGH SCHOOL: West Monroe (La.).

COLLEGE: Louisiana State, then Northeast Louisiana.
TRANSACTIONS/CAREER NOTES: Selected by Carolina Panthers in second round (36th pick overall) of 1995 NFL draft. ... Signed by Panthers (July 15, 1995). ... On reserve/suspended list for violating league substance abuse policy (August 24-October 17, 1997). ... On injured reserve with knee injury (December 15, 1997-remainder of season). ... On injured reserve with arm injury (August 24, 1998-entire season). ... Granted unconditional free agency (February 12, 1999). ... Signed by Indianapolis Colts (February 15, 1999).
PRO STATISTICS: 1996—Intercepted one pass for one yard and recovered one fumble for 12 yards and a touchdown.

Year Team	G	GS	SACKS
1995—Carolina NFL	13	0	2.0
1996—Carolina NFL	16	0	3.0
1997—Carolina NFL	9	2	2.0
1998—Carolina NFL	Did not play.		
Pro totals (3 years)	38	2	7.0

KINNEY, KELVIN   DE   REDSKINS

PERSONAL: Born December 31, 1972, in Montgomery, W.Va. ... 6-6/264.
HIGH SCHOOL: Montgomery (W.Va.).
COLLEGE: Virginia State.
TRANSACTIONS/CAREER NOTES: Selected by Washington Redskins in sixth round (174th pick overall) of 1996 NFL draft. ... Signed by Redskins (June 4, 1996). ... On injured reserve with foot injury (August 20, 1996-entire season). ... Granted free agency (February 12, 1999). ... Re-signed by Redskins (April 30, 1999).
PLAYING EXPERIENCE: Washington NFL, 1997 and 1998. ... Games/Games started: 1997 (4/1), 1998 (14/12). Total: 18/13.
PRO STATISTICS: 1998—Credited with one sack.

KIRBY, TERRY   RB   BROWNS

PERSONAL: Born January 20, 1970, in Hampton, Va. ... 6-1/213. ... Full name: Terry Gayle Kirby. ... Brother of Wayne Kirby, outfielder, Toronto Blue Jays organization; and cousin of Chris Slade, linebacker, New England Patriots.
HIGH SCHOOL: Tabb (Va.).
COLLEGE: Virginia (degree in psychology).
TRANSACTIONS/CAREER NOTES: Selected by Miami Dolphins in third round (78th pick overall) of 1993 NFL draft. ... Signed by Dolphins (July 19, 1993). ... On injured reserve with knee injury (September 26, 1994-remainder of season). ... Granted free agency (February 16, 1996). ... Traded by Dolphins to San Francisco 49ers for fourth-round pick (traded to Oakland) in 1997 draft (August 19, 1996). ... Released by 49ers (March 3, 1998). ... Re-signed by 49ers (September 23, 1998). ... Granted unconditional free agency (February 12, 1999). ... Signed by Cleveland Browns (March 9, 1999).
CHAMPIONSHIP GAME EXPERIENCE: Played in NFC championship game (1997 season).
PRO STATISTICS: 1993—Recovered four fumbles. 1995—Attempted one pass with a completion for 31 yards and a touchdown. 1996—Attempted two passes with one completion for 24 yards and a touchdown and returned one punt for three yards. 1997—Recovered two fumbles. 1998—Attempted one pass with a completion for 28 yards and a touchdown.
SINGLE GAME HIGHS (regular season): Attempts—19 (October 8, 1995, vs. Indianapolis); yards—105 (December 2, 1996, vs. Atlanta); and rushing touchdowns—2 (December 14, 1998, vs. Detroit).
STATISTICAL PLATEAUS: 100-yard rushing games: 1994 (1), 1996 (1). Total: 2. ... 100-yard receiving games: 1993 (2).

			RUSHING				RECEIVING				KICKOFF RETURNS				TOTALS		
Year Team	G	GS	Att.	Yds.	Avg.	TD	No.	Yds.	Avg.	TD	No.	Yds.	Avg.	TD	TD	2pt.	Pts.	Fum.
1993—Miami NFL	16	8	119	390	3.3	3	75	874	11.7	3	4	85	21.3	0	6	...	36	5
1994—Miami NFL	4	4	60	233	3.9	2	14	154	11.0	0	0	0	...	0	2	1	14	2
1995—Miami NFL	16	4	108	414	3.8	4	66	618	9.4	3	0	0	...	0	7	0	42	2
1996—San Francisco NFL	14	10	134	559	4.2	3	52	439	8.4	1	1	22	22.0	0	4	0	24	1
1997—San Francisco NFL	16	3	125	418	3.3	6	23	279	12.1	1	3	124	41.3	1	8	2	52	3
1998—San Francisco NFL	9	0	48	258	5.4	3	16	134	8.4	0	17	340	20.0	0	3	0	18	0
Pro totals (6 years)	75	29	594	2272	3.8	21	246	2498	10.2	8	25	571	22.8	1	30	3	186	13

KIRK, RANDY   LB

PERSONAL: Born December 27, 1964, in San Jose, Calif. ... 6-2/242. ... Full name: Randall Scott Kirk.
HIGH SCHOOL: Bellarmine College Prep (San Jose, Calif.).
JUNIOR COLLEGE: De Anza College (Calif.).
COLLEGE: San Diego State.
TRANSACTIONS/CAREER NOTES: Signed as non-drafted free agent by New York Giants (May 10, 1987). ... Released by Giants (August 31, 1987). ... Signed as replacement player by San Diego Chargers (September 24, 1987). ... Granted unconditional free agency (February 1, 1989). ... Signed by Phoenix Cardinals (March 31, 1989). ... On injured reserve with broken ankle (October 16, 1989-remainder of season). ... On injured reserve with foot injury (August 27-September 18, 1990). ... Released by Cardinals (September 18, 1990). ... Signed by Washington Redskins (November 7, 1990). ... Released by Redskins (November 13, 1990). ... Signed by Cleveland Browns (July 27, 1991). ... On injured reserve with back injury (September 13-November 19, 1991). ... Claimed on waivers by Chargers (November 19, 1991). ... Granted unconditional free agency (February 1, 1992). ... Signed by Cincinnati Bengals (March 3, 1992). ... Granted unconditional free agency (February 17, 1994). ... Signed by Cardinals (March 7, 1994). ... Cardinals franchise renamed Arizona Cardinals for 1994 season. ... Granted unconditional free agency (February 16, 1996). ... Signed by San Francisco 49ers (March 26, 1996). ... Released by 49ers (February 10, 1999).
PLAYING EXPERIENCE: San Diego NFL, 1987 and 1988; Phoenix NFL, 1989; Washington NFL, 1990; Cleveland (2)-San Diego (5) NFL, 1991; Cincinnati NFL, 1992 and 1993; Arizona NFL, 1994 and 1995; San Francisco NFL, 1996-1998. ... Games/Games started: 1987 (13/1), 1988 (16/0), 1989 (6/0), 1990 (1/0) (Cle.-2/0; S.D.-5/0; Total: 7/0), 1992 (15/0), 1993 (16/0), 1994 (16/0), 1995 (16/0), 1996 (16/0), 1997 (16/0), 1998 (16/0). Total: 154/1.
CHAMPIONSHIP GAME EXPERIENCE: Played in NFC championship game (1997 season).
PRO STATISTICS: 1987—Credited with one sack. 1988—Recovered one fumble. 1992—Recovered two fumbles for seven yards. 1998—Fumbled once for minus 18 yards.

KIRKLAND, LEVON — LB — STEELERS

PERSONAL: Born February 17, 1969, in Lamar, S.C. ... 6-1/270. ... Full name: Lorenzo Levon Kirkland. ... Name pronounced luh-VON.
HIGH SCHOOL: Lamar (S.C.).
COLLEGE: Clemson.
TRANSACTIONS/CAREER NOTES: Selected by Pittsburgh Steelers in second round (38th pick overall) of 1992 NFL draft. ... Signed by Steelers (July 25, 1992).
CHAMPIONSHIP GAME EXPERIENCE: Played in AFC championship game (1994, 1995 and 1997 seasons). ... Played in Super Bowl XXX (1995 season).
HONORS: Named linebacker on THE SPORTING NEWS college All-America first team (1991). ... Played in Pro Bowl (1996 and 1997 seasons). ... Named inside linebacker on THE SPORTING NEWS NFL All-Pro team (1997).
PRO STATISTICS: 1993—Recovered two fumbles for 24 yards and one touchdown. 1995—Recovered two fumbles. 1997—Recovered one fumble.

			INTERCEPTIONS				SACKS
Year Team	G	GS	No.	Yds.	Avg.	TD	No.
1992—Pittsburgh NFL	16	0	0	0	...	0	0.0
1993—Pittsburgh NFL	16	13	0	0	...	0	1.0
1994—Pittsburgh NFL	16	15	2	0	0.0	0	3.0
1995—Pittsburgh NFL	16	16	0	0	...	0	1.0
1996—Pittsburgh NFL	16	16	4	12	3.0	0	4.0
1997—Pittsburgh NFL	16	16	2	14	7.0	0	5.0
1998—Pittsburgh NFL	16	16	1	1	1.0	0	2.5
Pro totals (7 years)	112	92	9	27	3.0	0	16.5

KISELAK, MIKE — C/G — COWBOYS

PERSONAL: Born March 9, 1967, in North Tarrytown, N.Y. ... 6-3/295.
HIGH SCHOOL: Pine Bush (N.Y.).
COLLEGE: Maryland.
TRANSACTIONS/CAREER NOTES: Signed as non-drafted free agent by Kansas City Chiefs (May 1, 1990). ... Released by Chiefs (August 28, 1990). ... Signed by Houston Oilers (July 16, 1991). ... Released by Oilers (August 19, 1991). ... Signed by Green Bay Packers (June 2, 1992). ... Released by Packers (August 1992). ... Signed by New York Giants (August 1992). ... Released by Giants (August 24, 1992). ... Signed by Sacramento Gold Miners of CFL (March 1993). ... Granted free agency (February 1995). ... Signed by San Antonio Texans of CFL (April 1995). ... Selected by Saskatchewan Roughriders in tenth round of 1996 U.S. Team Dispersal Draft. ... Traded by Roughriders to Toronto Argonauts for OL John Terry (April 4, 1996). ... Granted free agency (February 16, 1998). ... Signed by Dallas Cowboys (March 9, 1998).
PLAYING EXPERIENCE: Sacramento CFL, 1993 and 1994; San Antonio CFL, 1995; Toronto CFL, 1996 and 1997; Dallas NFL, 1998. ... Games/Games started: 1993 (17/games started unavailable), 1994 (18/-), 1995 (18/-), 1996 (18/-), 1997 (18/-), 1998 (16/7). Total CFL: 89/-. Total NFL: 16/7. Total Pro: 105/-.
HONORS: Named to CFL All-Star team (1995-1997). ... Winner of CFL/Chrysler Most Outstanding Offensive Lineman Award (1996 and 1997 seasons).
PRO STATISTICS: 1994—Caught one pass for two yards. 1997—Caught one pass for minus three yards. 1998—Recovered one fumble.

KITNA, JON — QB — SEAHAWKS

PERSONAL: Born September 21, 1972, in Tacoma, Wash. ... 6-2/217.
HIGH SCHOOL: Lincoln (Tacoma, Wash.).
COLLEGE: Central Washington (degree in math education, 1995).
TRANSACTIONS/CAREER NOTES: Signed as non-drafted free agent by Seattle Seahawks (April 25, 1996). ... Released by Seahawks (August 19, 1996). ... Re-signed by Seahawks to practice squad (August 20, 1996). ... Assigned by Seahawks to Barcelona Dragons in 1997 World League enhancement allocation program (April 7, 1997).
PRO STATISTICS: 1997—Fumbled once and recovered one fumble for minus two yards. 1998—Fumbled six times and recovered four fumbles for minus 10 yards.
SINGLE GAME HIGHS (regular season): Attempts—39 (November 29, 1998, vs. Tennessee); completions—24 (November 29, 1998, vs. Tennessee); yards—298 (November 29, 1998, vs. Tennessee); and touchdown passes—2 (December 6, 1998, vs. New York Jets).
MISCELLANEOUS: Regular-season record as starting NFL quarterback: 4-2 (.667).

			PASSING							RUSHING				TOTALS		
Year Team	G	GS	Att.	Cmp.	Pct.	Yds.	TD	Int.	Avg.	Rat.	Att.	Yds.	Avg.	TD	TD	2pt.	Pts.
1997—Barcelona W.L.	...	...	317	171	53.9	2448	22	15	7.72	82.6	50	334	6.7	3	3	...	18
—Seattle NFL	3	1	45	31	68.9	371	1	2	8.24	82.7	10	9	0.9	1	1	0	6
1998—Seattle NFL	6	5	172	98	57.0	1177	7	8	6.84	72.3	20	67	3.4	1	1	0	6
W.L. totals (1 year)	...	...	317	171	53.9	2448	22	15	7.72	82.6	50	334	6.7	3	3	0	18
NFL totals (2 years)	9	6	217	129	59.4	1548	8	10	7.13	74.4	30	76	2.5	2	2	0	12
Pro totals (3 years)	...	...	534	300	56.2	3996	30	25	7.48	79.3	80	410	5.1	5	5	0	30

KITTS, JIM — FB — PACKERS

PERSONAL: Born December 28, 1972, in Portsmouth, Va. ... 6-1/245.
HIGH SCHOOL: Great Bridge (Chesapeake, Va.).
COLLEGE: Ferrum (Va.).
TRANSACTIONS/CAREER NOTES: Played with Albany Firebirds of Arena League (1995 and 1996). ... Signed as non-drafted free agent by Washington Redskins (June 12, 1996). ... Released by Redskins (August 20, 1996). ... Re-signed by Redskins (February 19, 1997). ... Assigned by Redskins to Frankfurt Galaxy in 1997 World League enhancement allocation program (February 19, 1997). ... Released by Redskins (August 18, 1997). ... Re-signed by Redskins to practice squad (August 26, 1997). ... Released by Redskins (September 22, 1997). ... Signed by Green Bay Packers to practice squad (September 23, 1997). ... Signed by Miami Dolphins off Packers practice squad (October

1, 1997). ... Released by Dolphins (September 8, 1998). ... Signed by Redskins (October 6, 1998). ... Released by Redskins (November 3, 1998). ... Signed by Green Bay Packers (December 16, 1998).
PLAYING EXPERIENCE: Frankfurt W.L., 1997; Miami NFL, 1997; Washington (3)-Green Bay (2) NFL, 1998. ... Games/Games started: 1997 (W.L.- games played unavailable; NFL- 10/0), 1998 (Was.-3/0; G.B.-2/0; Total: 5/0). Total NFL: 15/0.
PRO STATISTICS: W.L.: 1997- Rushed three times for 10 yards and caught 10 passes for 53 yards.

KNIGHT, SAMMY — S — SAINTS

PERSONAL: Born September 10, 1975, in Fontana, Calif. ... 6-0/205.
HIGH SCHOOL: Rubidoux (Riverside, Calif.).
COLLEGE: Southern California.
TRANSACTIONS/CAREER NOTES: Signed as non-drafted free agent by New Orleans Saints (April 25, 1997).
PRO STATISTICS: 1997—Recovered one fumble. 1998—Recovered two fumbles for three yards.

			INTERCEPTIONS				TOTALS		
Year Team	G	GS	No.	Yds.	Avg.	TD	TD	2pt.	Pts.	Fum.
1997—New Orleans NFL	16	12	5	75	15.0	0	0	0	0	0
1998—New Orleans NFL	14	13	6	171	28.5	2	2	0	12	0
Pro totals (2 years)	30	25	11	246	22.4	2	2	0	12	0

KNIGHT, TOM — CB — CARDINALS

PERSONAL: Born December 29, 1974, in Marlton, N.J. ... 5-11/196. ... Full name: Thomas Lorenzo Knight.
HIGH SCHOOL: Cherokee (Marlton, N.J.).
COLLEGE: Iowa.
TRANSACTIONS/CAREER NOTES: Selected by Arizona Cardinals in first round (ninth pick overall) of 1997 NFL draft. ... Signed by Cardinals (July 16, 1997).
PLAYING EXPERIENCE: Arizona NFL, 1997 and 1998. ... Games/Games Started: 1997 (15/14), 1998 (8/5). Total: 23/19.
PRO STATISTICS: 1998—Credited with one sack.

KOONCE, GEORGE — LB — PACKERS

PERSONAL: Born October 15, 1968, in New Bern, N.C. ... 6-1/245. ... Full name: George Earl Koonce Jr.
HIGH SCHOOL: West Craven (Vanceboro, N.C.).
COLLEGE: Chowan College (N.C.), then East Carolina.
TRANSACTIONS/CAREER NOTES: Signed as non-drafted free agent by Atlanta Falcons (April 30, 1991). ... Released by Falcons (August 26, 1991). ... Selected by Ohio Glory in 13th round (143rd pick overall) of 1992 World League draft. ... Signed by Green Bay Packers (June 2, 1992). ... On injured reserve with shoulder injury (January 3, 1994-entire 1993 playoffs). ... Granted free agency (February 17, 1995). ... Re-signed by Packers (June 2, 1995). ... On injured reserve with knee injury (January 10, 1997-remainder of 1996 playoffs). ... On physically unable to perform list with knee injury (August 19-November 18, 1997). ... Granted unconditional free agency (February 12, 1999). ... Re-signed by Packers (February 18, 1999).
CHAMPIONSHIP GAME EXPERIENCE: Played in NFC championship game (1995 and 1997 seasons). ... Member of Packers for NFC championship game (1996); inactive. ... Member of Super Bowl championship team (1996 season); inactive. ... Played in Super Bowl XXXII (1997 season).
PRO STATISTICS: W.L.: 1992—Recovered two fumbles for 35 yards. NFL: 1992—Recovered one fumble. 1993—Recovered one fumble. 1994—Recovered two fumbles. 1996—Recovered one fumble. 1998—Recovered one fumble for four yards.

			INTERCEPTIONS				SACKS
Year Team	G	GS	No.	Yds.	Avg.	TD	No.
1992—Ohio W.L.	10	9	0	0	...	0	2.5
—Green Bay NFL	16	10	0	0	...	0	1.5
1993—Green Bay NFL	15	15	0	0	...	0	3.0
1994—Green Bay NFL	16	16	0	0	...	0	1.0
1995—Green Bay NFL	16	16	1	12	12.0	0	1.0
1996—Green Bay NFL	16	16	3	84	28.0	1	0.0
1997—Green Bay NFL	4	0	0	0	...	0	0.0
1998—Green Bay NFL	14	14	0	0	...	0	1.0
W.L. totals (1 year)	10	9	0	0	...	0	2.5
NFL totals (7 years)	97	87	4	96	24.0	1	7.5
Pro totals (8 years)	107	96	4	96	24.0	1	10.0

KOPP, JEFF — LB — RAVENS

PERSONAL: Born July 8, 1971, in Danville, Calif. ... 6-3/244. ... Full name: Jeffery Blair Kopp.
HIGH SCHOOL: San Ramon (Danville, Calif.).
COLLEGE: Southern California (degree in communications, 1994).
TRANSACTIONS/CAREER NOTES: Selected by Miami Dolphins in sixth round (194th pick overall) of 1995 NFL draft. ... Signed by Dolphins for 1995 season. ... Released by Dolphins (August 25, 1996). ... Signed by Jacksonville Jaguars (September 24, 1996). ... Released by Jaguars (October 21, 1998). ... Signed by Baltimore Ravens (October 28, 1998). ... Granted unconditional free agency (February 12, 1999). ... Re-signed by Ravens (April 22, 1999).
PLAYING EXPERIENCE: Miami NFL, 1995; Jacksonville NFL, 1996 and 1997; Jacksonville (6)-Baltimore (7) NFL, 1998. ... Games/Games started: 1995 (16/0), 1996 (12/0) 1997 (16/3), 1998 (Jax.-6/0; Bal.-7/0; Total: 13/0). Total: 57/3.
CHAMPIONSHIP GAME EXPERIENCE: Played in AFC championship game (1996 season).
PRO STATISTICS: 1997—Intercepted one pass for nine yards and credited with one sack.

KOWALKOWSKI, SCOTT   LB   LIONS

PERSONAL: Born August 23, 1968, in Farmington Hills, Mich. ... 6-2/228. ... Full name: Scott Thomas Kowalkowski. ... Son of Bob Kowalkowski, guard with Detroit Lions (1966-76) and Green Bay Packers (1977). ... Name pronounced KO-wal-KOW-skee.
HIGH SCHOOL: St. Mary's Prep (Orchard Lake, Mich.).
COLLEGE: Notre Dame (degree in American studies).
TRANSACTIONS/CAREER NOTES: Selected by Philadelphia Eagles in eighth round (217th pick overall) of 1991 NFL draft. ... Signed by Eagles (July 10, 1991). ... On injured reserve with ankle injury (August 30-November 23, 1993). ... Released by Eagles (November 23, 1993). ... Signed by Detroit Lions (February 4, 1994). ... Granted unconditional free agency (February 17, 1995). ... Re-signed by Lions (March 24, 1995). ... Granted unconditional free agency (February 16, 1996). ... Re-signed by Lions (February 29, 1996). ... Granted unconditional free agency (February 14, 1997). ... Re-signed by Lions (March 18, 1997).
PLAYING EXPERIENCE: Philadelphia NFL, 1991 and 1992; Detroit NFL, 1994-1998. ... Games/Games started: 1991 (16/0), 1992 (16/0), 1994 (16/0), 1995 (16/0), 1996 (16/1), 1997 (16/0), 1998 (15/0). Total: 111/1.
PRO STATISTICS: 1991—Recovered one fumble. 1996—Recovered one fumble. 1998—Recovered one fumble.

KOZLOWSKI, BRIAN   TE   FALCONS

PERSONAL: Born October 4, 1970, in Rochester, N.Y. ... 6-3/250. ... Full name: Brian Scott Kozlowski.
HIGH SCHOOL: Webster (N.Y.).
COLLEGE: Connecticut.
TRANSACTIONS/CAREER NOTES: Signed as non-drafted free agent by New York Giants (May 1, 1993). ... Released by Giants (August 16, 1993). ... Re-signed by Giants to practice squad (December 8, 1993). ... Granted unconditional free agency (February 14, 1997). ... Signed by Atlanta Falcons (March 21, 1997). ... Granted unconditional free agency (February 13, 1998). ... Re-signed by Falcons (March 4, 1998).
CHAMPIONSHIP GAME EXPERIENCE: Played in NFC championship game (1998 season). ... Played in Super Bowl XXXIII (1998 season).
PRO STATISTICS: 1995—Recovered one fumble.
SINGLE GAME HIGHS (regular season): Receptions—2 (December 20, 1998, vs. Detroit); yards—41 (December 14, 1995, vs. Philadelphia); and touchdown receptions—1 (September 13, 1998, vs. Philadelphia).

				RECEIVING				KICKOFF RETURNS				TOTALS		
Year Team	G	GS	No.	Yds.	Avg.	TD	No.	Yds.	Avg.	TD	TD	2pt.	Pts.	Fum.
1993—New York Giants NFL								Did not play.						
1994—New York Giants NFL	16	2	1	5	5.0	0	2	21	10.5	0	0	0	0	0
1995—New York Giants NFL	16	0	2	17	8.5	0	5	75	15.0	0	0	0	0	1
1996—New York Giants NFL	5	0	1	4	4.0	1	1	16	16.0	0	1	0	6	0
1997—Atlanta NFL	16	5	7	99	14.1	1	2	49	24.5	0	1	0	6	0
1998—Atlanta NFL	16	4	10	103	10.3	1	1	12	12.0	0	1	0	6	0
Pro totals (5 years)	69	11	21	228	10.9	3	11	173	15.7	0	3	0	18	1

KRAMER, ERIK   QB   BEARS

PERSONAL: Born November 6, 1964, in Encino, Calif. ... 6-1/204. ... Full name: William Erik Kramer.
HIGH SCHOOL: Burroughs (Burbank, Calif.).
JUNIOR COLLEGE: Los Angeles Pierce Junior College.
COLLEGE: North Carolina State.
TRANSACTIONS/CAREER NOTES: Signed as non-drafted free agent by New Orleans Saints (May 6, 1987). ... Released by Saints (August 31, 1987). ... Signed as replacement player by Atlanta Falcons (September 24, 1987). ... Released by Falcons (September 1, 1988). ... Signed by Calgary Stampeders of CFL (September 28, 1988). ... Released by Stampeders (July 4, 1989). ... Signed by Detroit Lions (March 21, 1990). ... On injured reserve with shoulder injury (September 4-December 28, 1990). ... Released by Lions (December 28, 1990). ... Re-signed by Lions (March 6, 1991). ... Granted free agency (March 1, 1993). ... Tendered offer sheet by Dallas Cowboys (April 1993). ... Offer matched by Lions (April 23, 1993). ... Granted unconditional free agency (February 17, 1994). ... Signed by Chicago Bears (February 21, 1994). ... On injured reserve with neck injury (October 14, 1996-remainder of season). ... Granted unconditional free agency (February 14, 1997). ... Re-signed by Bears (March 11, 1997). ... Granted unconditional free agency (February 13, 1998). ... Re-signed by Bears (February 20, 1998). ... On injured reserve with shoulder and knee injuries (December 2, 1998-remainder of season).
CHAMPIONSHIP GAME EXPERIENCE: Played in NFC championship game (1991 season).
PRO STATISTICS: CFL: 1988—Fumbled seven times. NFL: 1991—Fumbled eight times and recovered four fumbles for minus five yards. 1992—Fumbled four times and recovered one fumble for minus one yard. 1993—Fumbled once. 1994—Fumbled three times and recovered two fumbles for minus five yards. 1995—Fumbled six times and recovered two fumbles for minus 13 yards. 1996—Fumbled once and recovered one fumble for minus one yard. 1997—Fumbled 11 times and recovered three fumbles for minus 14 yards. 1998—Fumbled three times.
SINGLE GAME HIGHS (regular season): Attempts—60 (November 16, 1997, vs. New York Jets); completions—32 (November 16, 1997, vs. New York Jets); yards—372 (September 27, 1998, vs. Minnesota); and touchdown passes—4 (September 27, 1998, vs. Minnesota).
STATISTICAL PLATEAUS: 300-yard passing games: 1987 (1), 1992 (1), 1994 (1), 1995 (3), 1997 (2), 1998 (1). Total: 9.
MISCELLANEOUS: Regular-season record as starting NFL quarterback: 29-34 (.460). ... Postseason record as starting NFL quarterback: 1-2 (.333).

					PASSING						RUSHING				TOTALS	
Year Team	G	GS	Att.	Cmp.	Pct.	Yds.	TD	Int.	Avg.	Rat.	Att.	Yds.	Avg.	TD	TD	2pt.	Pts.
1987—Atlanta NFL	3	2	92	45	48.9	559	4	5	6.08	60.0	2	10	5.0	0	0	...	0
1988—Calgary CFL	6	0	153	62	40.5	964	5	13	6.30	37.6	12	17	1.4	1	1	...	6
1989—							Did not play.										
1990—Detroit NFL							Did not play.										
1991—Detroit NFL	13	8	265	136	51.3	1635	11	8	6.17	71.8	35	26	0.7	1	1	...	6
1992—Detroit NFL	7	3	106	58	54.7	771	4	8	7.27	59.1	12	34	2.8	0	0	...	0
1993—Detroit NFL	5	4	138	87	63.0	1002	8	3	7.26	95.1	10	5	0.5	0	0	...	0
1994—Chicago NFL	6	5	158	99	62.7	1129	8	8	7.15	79.9	6	-2	-0.3	0	0	...	0
1995—Chicago NFL	16	16	522	315	60.3	3838	29	10	7.35	93.5	35	39	1.1	1	1	0	6
1996—Chicago NFL	4	4	150	73	48.7	781	3	6	5.21	54.3	8	4	0.5	0	0	0	0
1997—Chicago NFL	15	13	477	275	57.7	3011	14	14	6.31	74.0	27	83	3.1	2	2	0	12
1998—Chicago NFL	8	8	250	151	60.4	1823	9	7	7.29	83.1	13	17	1.3	1	1	0	6
CFL totals (1 year)	6	0	153	62	40.5	964	5	13	6.30	37.6	12	17	1.4	1	1	0	6
NFL totals (9 years)	77	63	2158	1239	57.4	14549	90	69	6.74	78.6	148	216	1.5	5	5	0	30
Pro totals (10 years)	83	63	2311	1301	56.3	15513	95	82	6.71	75.9	160	233	1.5	6	6	0	36

KRESSER, ERIC — QB — BENGALS

PERSONAL: Born February 6, 1973, in Cincinnati. ... 6-2/223. ... Full name: Eric Joel Kresser.
HIGH SCHOOL: Palm Beach Gardens (Fla.).
COLLEGE: Florida, then Marshall.
TRANSACTIONS/CAREER NOTES: Signed as non-drafted free agent by Cincinnati Bengals (April 25, 1997). ... Released by Bengals (August 24, 1997). ... Re-signed by Bengals to practice squad (October 21, 1997). ... Activated (November 17, 1997). ... Inactive for five games (1997). ... Released by Bengals (August 30, 1998). ... Re-signed by Bengals to practice squad (August 31, 1998). ... Activated (December 3, 1998).
SINGLE GAME HIGHS (regular season): Attempts—17 (December 27, 1998, vs. Tampa Bay); completions—7 (December 27, 1998, vs. Tampa Bay); yards—102 (December 27, 1998, vs. Tampa Bay); and touchdown passes—1 (December 13, 1998, vs. Indianapolis).

				PASSING						RUSHING				TOTALS	
Year Team	G	GS	Att.	Cmp.	Pct.	Yds.	TD	Int.	Avg.	Rat.	Att.	Yds.	Avg.	TD	TD	2pt.	Pts.
1997—Cincinnati NFL							Did not play.									
1998—Cincinnati NFL	2	0	21	10	47.6	164	1	2	7.81	50.6	1	-1	-1.0	0	0	0	0

KREUTZ, OLIN — C — BEARS

PERSONAL: Born June 9, 1977, in Honolulu. ... 6-2/300. ... Name pronounced KROOTZ.
HIGH SCHOOL: St. Louis (Honolulu).
COLLEGE: Washington.
TRANSACTIONS/CAREER NOTES: Selected after junior season by Chicago Bears in third round (64th pick overall) of 1998 NFL draft. ... Signed by Bears (July 20, 1998).
PLAYING EXPERIENCE: Chicago NFL, 1998. ... Games/Games started: 9/0.
HONORS: Named center on THE SPORTING NEWS college All-America first team (1997).

KRIEG, DAVE — QB

PERSONAL: Born October 20, 1958, in Iola, Wis. ... 6-1/202. ... Full name: David M. Krieg. ... Name pronounced CRAIG.
HIGH SCHOOL: D.C. Everest (Schofield, Wis.).
COLLEGE: Milton College, Wis. (degree in marketing management, 1980).
TRANSACTIONS/CAREER NOTES: Signed as non-drafted free agent by Seattle Seahawks (May 6, 1980). ... On injured reserve with separated shoulder (September 19-November 12, 1988). ... On injured reserve with thumb injury (September 3-October 18, 1991). ... Granted unconditional free agency (February 1, 1992). ... Signed by Kansas City Chiefs (March 19, 1992). ... Granted unconditional free agency (February 17, 1994). ... Signed by Detroit Lions (April 22, 1994). ... Granted unconditional free agency (February 17, 1995). ... Signed by Arizona Cardinals (March 11, 1995). ... Released by Cardinals (April 8, 1996). ... Signed by Chicago Bears (May 21, 1996). ... Granted unconditional free agency (February 14, 1997). ... Signed by Houston Oilers (May 5, 1997). ... Oilers franchise moved to Tennessee for 1997 season. ... Oilers franchise renamed Tennessee Titans for 1999 season (December 26, 1998). ... Granted unconditional free agency (February 12, 1999).
CHAMPIONSHIP GAME EXPERIENCE: Played in AFC championship game (1983 and 1993 seasons).
HONORS: Played in Pro Bowl (1984, 1988 and 1998 seasons).
RECORDS: Holds NFL single-season record for most own fumbles recovered—9 (1989). ... Shares NFL single-season record for most fumbles recovered, own and opponents'—9 (1989).
PRO STATISTICS: 1981—Fumbled four times. 1982—Fumbled five times and recovered two fumbles for minus 14 yards. 1983—Caught one pass for 11 yards, fumbled 10 times and recovered two fumbles. 1984—Fumbled 11 times and recovered three fumbles for minus 24 yards. 1985—Fumbled 11 times and recovered three fumbles for minus two yards. 1986—Fumbled 10 times and recovered one fumble for minus five yards. 1987—Led the AFC with 11 fumbles and recovered five fumbles for minus two yards. 1988—Fumbled six times. 1989—Led league with 18 fumbles and recovered nine fumbles for minus 20 yards. 1990—Caught one pass for minus six yards, fumbled 16 times and recovered two fumbles. 1991—Fumbled six times. 1992—Fumbled 10 times and recovered six fumbles for minus 15 yards. 1993—Fumbled six times and recovered one fumble. 1994—Fumbled four times and recovered two fumbles for minus one yard. 1995—Led league with 16 fumbles and recovered seven fumbles for minus 13 yards. 1996—Caught one pass for five yards, fumbled six times and recovered three fumbles for minus nine yards. 1998—Fumbled three times and recovered two fumbles for minus two yards.
SINGLE GAME HIGHS (regular season): Attempts—51 (October 13, 1985, vs. Atlanta); completions—33 (October 13, 1985, vs. Atlanta); yards—420 (November 20, 1983, vs. Denver); and touchdown passes—5 (November 28, 1988, vs. Los Angeles Raiders).
STATISTICAL PLATEAUS: 300-yard passing games: 1983 (1), 1984 (3), 1985 (2), 1986 (1), 1988 (1), 1989 (1), 1990 (1), 1991 (1), 1992 (2), 1994 (1), 1995 (4). Total: 18.
MISCELLANEOUS: Regular-season record as starting NFL quarterback: 98-77 (.560). ... Postseason record as starting NFL quarterback: 3-6 (.333). ... Holds Seattle Seahawks all-time records for most yards passing (26,132) and most touchdown passes (195).

					PASSING						RUSHING				TOTALS		
Year Team	G	GS	Att.	Cmp.	Pct.	Yds.	TD	Int.	Avg.	Rat.	Att.	Yds.	Avg.	TD	TD	2pt.	Pts.
1980—Seattle NFL	1	0	2	0	0.0	0	0	0	...	39.6	0	0	...	0	0	...	0
1981—Seattle NFL	7	3	112	64	57.1	843	7	5	7.53	83.3	11	56	5.1	1	1	...	6
1982—Seattle NFL	3	2	78	49	62.8	501	2	2	6.42	79.1	6	-3	-0.5	0	0	...	0
1983—Seattle NFL	9	8	243	147	60.5	2139	18	11	§8.80	95.0	16	55	3.4	2	2	...	12
1984—Seattle NFL	16	16	480	276	57.5	3671	32	*24	7.65	83.3	46	186	4.0	3	3	...	18
1985—Seattle NFL	16	16	532	285	53.6	3602	27	20	6.77	76.2	35	121	3.5	1	1	...	6
1986—Seattle NFL	15	14	375	225	60.0	2921	21	11	7.79	91.0	35	122	3.5	1	1	...	6
1987—Seattle NFL	12	12	294	178	60.5	2131	23	15	7.25	87.6	36	155	4.3	2	2	...	12
1988—Seattle NFL	9	9	228	134	58.8	1741	18	8	7.64	94.6	24	64	2.7	0	0	...	0
1989—Seattle NFL	15	14	499	286	57.3	3309	21	20	6.63	74.8	40	160	4.0	0	0	...	0
1990—Seattle NFL	16	16	448	265	59.2	3194	15	20	7.13	73.6	32	115	3.6	0	0	...	0
1991—Seattle NFL	10	9	285	187	*65.6	2080	11	12	7.30	82.5	13	59	4.5	0	0	...	0
1992—Kansas City NFL	16	16	413	230	55.7	3115	15	12	§7.54	79.9	37	74	2.0	2	2	...	12
1993—Kansas City NFL	12	5	189	105	55.6	1238	7	3	6.55	81.4	21	24	1.1	0	0	...	0
1994—Detroit NFL	14	7	212	131	61.8	1629	14	3	7.68	101.7	23	35	1.5	0	0	...	0
1995—Arizona NFL	16	16	521	304	58.3	3554	16	*21	6.82	72.6	19	29	1.5	0	0	...	0
1996—Chicago NFL	13	12	377	226	59.9	2278	14	12	6.04	76.3	16	12	0.8	1	1	...	6
1997—Tennessee NFL	8	0	2	1	50.0	2	0	1	1.00	56.3	4	-2	-0.5	0	0	...	0
1998—Tennessee NFL	5	0	21	12	57.1	199	0	0	9.48	89.2	3	-1	-0.3	0	0	...	0
Pro totals (19 years)	213	175	5311	3105	58.5	38147	261	199	7.18	81.5	417	1261	3.0	13	13	0	78

KUBERSKI, BOB   DT   FALCONS

PERSONAL: Born April 5, 1971, in Chester, Pa. ... 6-4/300. ... Full name: Robert Kenneth Kuberski Jr.
HIGH SCHOOL: Ridley (Folsom, Pa.).
COLLEGE: Navy (degree in political science).
TRANSACTIONS/CAREER NOTES: Selected by Green Bay Packers in seventh round (183rd pick overall) of 1993 NFL draft. ... Signed by Packers (June 7, 1993). ... On reserve/military list (August 23, 1993-April 19, 1995). ... Granted unconditional free agency (February 12, 1999). ... Signed by Atlanta Falcons (March 2, 1999).
PLAYING EXPERIENCE: Green Bay NFL, 1995-1998. ... Games/Games started: 1995 (9/0), 1996 (1/0), 1997 (11/3), 1998 (16/0). Total: 37/3.
CHAMPIONSHIP GAME EXPERIENCE: Played in NFC championship game (1995 and 1997 seasons). ... Member of Packers for NFC championship game (1996 season); inactive. ... Member of Super Bowl championship team (1996 season); inactive. ... Played in Super Bowl XXXII (1997 season).
PRO STATISTICS: 1995—Credited with two sacks.

KYLE, JASON   LB   BROWNS

PERSONAL: Born May 12, 1972, in Tempe, Ariz. ... 6-3/242. ... Full name: Jason C. Kyle.
HIGH SCHOOL: McClintock (Tempe, Ariz.).
COLLEGE: Arizona State.
TRANSACTIONS/CAREER NOTES: Selected by Seattle Seahawks in fourth round (126th pick overall) of 1995 NFL draft. ... Signed by Seahawks (July 16, 1995). ... On injured reserve with shoulder injury (August 18, 1997-entire season). ... Granted free agency (February 13, 1998). ... Re-signed by Seahawks (April 16, 1998). ... Selected by Cleveland Browns from Seahawks in NFL expansion draft (February 9, 1999).
PLAYING EXPERIENCE: Seattle NFL, 1995, 1996 and 1998. ... Games/Games started: 1995 (16/0), 1996 (16/0), 1998 (16/0). Total: 48/0.

LaBOUNTY, MATT   DE   SEAHAWKS

PERSONAL: Born January 3, 1969, in San Francisco. ... 6-4/275. ... Full name: Matthew James LaBounty.
HIGH SCHOOL: San Marin (Novato, Calif.).
COLLEGE: Oregon.
TRANSACTIONS/CAREER NOTES: Selected by San Francisco 49ers in 12th round (327th pick overall) of 1992 NFL draft. ... Signed by 49ers (July 13, 1992). ... Released by 49ers (August 31, 1992). ... Re-signed by 49ers to practice squad (September 1, 1992). ... Released by 49ers (October 17, 1993). ... Re-signed by 49ers to practice squad (October 20, 1993). ... Activated (December 2, 1993). ... Claimed on waivers by Green Bay Packers (December 8, 1993). ... On injured reserve with back injury (August 23, 1994-entire season). ... Traded by Packers to Seattle Seahawks for S Eugene Robinson (June 27, 1996). ... Granted unconditional free agency (February 13, 1998). ... Re-signed by Seahawks (February 11, 1998).
CHAMPIONSHIP GAME EXPERIENCE: Played in NFC championship game (1995 season).
PRO STATISTICS: 1998—Fumbled once and recovered one fumble for 13 yards.

Year Team	G	GS	SACKS
1992—San Francisco NFL	Did not play.		
1993—San Francisco NFL	6	0	0.0
1994—Green Bay NFL	Did not play.		
1995—Green Bay NFL	14	2	3.0
1996—Seattle NFL	3	0	0.0
1997—Seattle NFL	15	6	3.0
1998—Seattle NFL	16	1	6.0
Pro totals (5 years)	**54**	**9**	**12.0**

LACINA, CORBIN   G   PANTHERS

PERSONAL: Born November 2, 1970, in Mankato, Minn. ... 6-4/308.
HIGH SCHOOL: Cretin-Derham Hall (St. Paul, Minn.).
COLLEGE: Augustana (S.D.).
TRANSACTIONS/CAREER NOTES: Selected by Buffalo Bills in sixth round (167th pick overall) of 1993 NFL draft. ... Signed by Bills (July 12, 1993). ... Released by Bills (August 30, 1993). ... Re-signed by Bills to practice squad (September 1, 1993). ... Activated (December 3, 1993); did not play. ... On injured reserve with foot injury (December 22, 1994-remainder of season). ... On injured reserve with groin injury (November 30, 1996-remainder of season). ... Granted free agency (February 14, 1997). ... Re-signed by Bills (June 12, 1997). ... Granted unconditional free agency (February 13, 1998). ... Signed by Carolina Panthers (February 26, 1998).
PLAYING EXPERIENCE: Buffalo NFL, 1994-1997; Carolina NFL, 1998. ... Games/Games started: 1994 (11/10), 1995 (16/3), 1996 (12/2), 1997 (16/13), 1998 (10/10). Total: 65/38.
CHAMPIONSHIP GAME EXPERIENCE: Member of Bills for AFC championship game (1993 season); inactive. ... Member of Bills for Super Bowl XXVIII (1993 season); inactive.
PRO STATISTICS: 1997—Recovered one fumble. 1998—Recovered one fumble.

LADD, ANTHONY   WR   PATRIOTS

PERSONAL: Born December 23, 1973, in Homestead, Fla. ... 6-1/193.
HIGH SCHOOL: Homestead (Fla.).
COLLEGE: Cincinnati.
TRANSACTIONS/CAREER NOTES: Signed as non-drafted free agent by Atlanta Falcons (April 20, 1997). ... Claimed on waivers by Tampa Bay Buccaneers (August 4, 1997). ... Released by Buccaneers (August 25, 1997). ... Re-signed by Buccaneers to practice squad (August 26, 1997). ... Released by Buccaneers (September 16, 1997). ... Signed by New England Patriots to practice squad (December 2, 1997). ... Assigned by Patriots to Barcelona Dragons in 1998 NFL Europe enhancement allocation program (February 18, 1998). ... Released by Patriots (August 25, 1998). ... Re-signed by Patriots to practice squad (August 31, 1998). ... Activated (October 20, 1998). ... Released by Patriots (November 13, 1998). ... Re-signed by Patriots to practice squad (November 17, 1998). ... Activated (November 21, 1998).
PLAYING EXPERIENCE: Barcelona Dragons NFLE, 1998; New England NFL, 1998. ... Games/Games started: NFLE 1998 (games played unavailable), NFL 1998 (3/0).
PRO STATISTICS: NFLE: 1998—Caught eight passes for 139 yards.

LaFLEUR, DAVID — TE — COWBOYS

PERSONAL: Born January 29, 1974, in Lake Charles, La. ... 6-7/272. ... Full name: David Alan LaFleur.
HIGH SCHOOL: Westlake (La.).
COLLEGE: Louisiana State.
TRANSACTIONS/CAREER NOTES: Selected by Dallas Cowboys in first round (22nd pick overall) of 1997 NFL draft. ... Signed by Cowboys (July 17, 1997).
PRO STATISTICS: 1998—Returned one kickoff for 12 yards.
SINGLE GAME HIGHS (regular season): Receptions—4 (October 4, 1998, vs. Washington); yards—39 (November 22, 1998, vs. Seattle); and touchdown receptions—2 (December 14, 1997, vs. Cincinnati).

			RECEIVING				TOTALS		
Year Team	G	GS	No.	Yds.	Avg.	TD	TD	2pt.	Pts.	Fum.
1997—Dallas NFL	16	5	18	122	6.8	2	2	0	12	1
1998—Dallas NFL	13	13	20	176	8.8	2	2	0	12	1
Pro totals (2 years)	29	18	38	298	7.8	4	4	0	24	2

LAGEMAN, JEFF — DE

PERSONAL: Born July 18, 1967, in Fairfax, Va. ... 6-6/265. ... Full name: Jeffrey David Lageman. ... Name pronounced LOG-a-man.
HIGH SCHOOL: Park View (Sterling, Va.).
COLLEGE: Virginia (degree in economics, 1989).
TRANSACTIONS/CAREER NOTES: Selected by New York Jets in first round (14th pick overall) of 1989 NFL draft. ... Signed by Jets (August 24, 1989). ... On injured reserve with knee injury (September 15, 1992-remainder of season). ... Granted unconditional free agency (February 17, 1995). ... Signed by Jacksonville Jaguars (March 14, 1995). ... On injured reserve with foot injury (December 19, 1995-remainder of season). ... Granted unconditional free agency (February 13, 1998). ... Re-signed by Jaguars (February 18, 1998). ... On injured reserve with arm injury (September 9, 1998-remainder of season). ... Granted unconditional free agency (February 12, 1999). ... Announced retirement (June 6, 1999).
CHAMPIONSHIP GAME EXPERIENCE: Played in AFC championship game (1996 season).
PRO STATISTICS: 1989—Rushed once for minus five yards. 1993—Intercepted one pass for 15 yards. 1994—Recovered three fumbles. 1995—Recovered one fumble. 1997—Recovered one fumble.

Year Team	G	GS	SACKS
1989—New York Jets NFL	16	15	4.5
1990—New York Jets NFL	16	16	4.0
1991—New York Jets NFL	16	16	10.0
1992—New York Jets NFL	2	2	1.0
1993—New York Jets NFL	16	16	8.5
1994—New York Jets NFL	16	16	6.5
1995—Jacksonville NFL	11	11	3.0
1996—Jacksonville NFL	12	9	4.5
1997—Jacksonville NFL	16	16	5.0
1998—Jacksonville NFL	1	1	0.0
Pro totals (10 years)	122	118	47.0

LAKE, CARNELL — S — JAGUARS

PERSONAL: Born July 15, 1967, in Salt Lake City. ... 6-1/210. ... Full name: Carnell Augustino Lake.
HIGH SCHOOL: Culver City (Calif.).
COLLEGE: UCLA (degree in political science, 1993).
TRANSACTIONS/CAREER NOTES: Selected by Pittsburgh Steelers in second round (34th pick overall) of 1989 NFL draft. ... Signed by Steelers (July 23, 1989). ... Granted free agency (February 1, 1992). ... Re-signed by Steelers (August 21, 1992). ... Granted roster exemption (August 21-28, 1992). ... Designated by Steelers as franchise player (February 15, 1995). ... Granted unconditional free agency (February 12, 1999). ... Signed by Jacksonville Jaguars (February 15, 1999).
CHAMPIONSHIP GAME EXPERIENCE: Played in AFC championship game (1994, 1995 and 1997 seasons). ... Played in Super Bowl XXX (1995 season).
HONORS: Named linebacker on THE SPORTING NEWS college All-America second team (1987). ... Played in Pro Bowl (1994-1997 seasons). ... Named strong safety on THE SPORTING NEWS NFL All-Pro team (1997).
POST SEASON RECORDS: Shares NFL postseason single-game record for most safeties—1 (January 7, 1995, vs. Cleveland).
PRO STATISTICS: 1989—Recovered six fumbles for two yards. 1990—Recovered one fumble. 1992—Recovered one fumble for 12 yards. 1993—Recovered two fumbles. 1994—Recovered one fumble. 1995—Recovered one fumble. 1996—Recovered two fumbles for 85 yards and one touchdown. 1997—Recovered one fumble for 38 yards and a touchdown. 1998—Recovered one fumble for minus two yards.

			INTERCEPTIONS				SACKS
Year Team	G	GS	No.	Yds.	Avg.	TD	No.
1989—Pittsburgh NFL	15	15	1	0	0.0	0	1.0
1990—Pittsburgh NFL	16	16	1	0	0.0	0	1.0
1991—Pittsburgh NFL	16	16	0	0	...	0	1.0
1992—Pittsburgh NFL	16	16	0	0	...	0	2.0
1993—Pittsburgh NFL	14	14	4	31	7.8	0	5.0
1994—Pittsburgh NFL	16	16	1	2	2.0	0	1.0
1995—Pittsburgh NFL	16	16	1	32	32.0	▲1	1.5
1996—Pittsburgh NFL	13	13	1	47	47.0	1	2.0
1997—Pittsburgh NFL	16	16	3	16	5.3	0	6.0
1998—Pittsburgh NFL	16	16	4	33	8.3	1	1.0
Pro totals (10 years)	154	154	16	161	10.1	3	21.5

LANDETA, SEAN — P — EAGLES

PERSONAL: Born January 6, 1962, in Baltimore. ... 6-0/200. ... Full name: Sean Edward Landeta.
HIGH SCHOOL: Loch Raven (Baltimore).
COLLEGE: Towson State.
TRANSACTIONS/CAREER NOTES: Selected by Philadelphia Stars in 14th round (161st pick overall) of 1983 USFL draft. ... Signed by Stars (January 24, 1983). ... Stars franchise moved to Baltimore (November 1, 1984). ... Granted free agency (August 1, 1985). ... Signed by New York Giants (August 5, 1985). ... On injured reserve with back injury (September 7, 1988-remainder of season). ... Granted free agency (February 1, 1990). ... Re-signed by Giants (July 23, 1990). ... On injured reserve with knee injury (November 25, 1992-remainder of season). ... Granted unconditional free agency (March 1, 1993). ... Re-signed by Giants (March 18, 1993). ... Released by Giants (November 9, 1993). ... Signed by Los Angeles Rams (November 12, 1993). ... Granted unconditional free agency (February 17, 1994). ... Re-signed by Rams (May 10, 1994). ... Granted unconditional free agency (February 17, 1995). ... Rams franchise moved to St. Louis (April 12, 1995). ... Re-signed by Rams (May 8, 1995). ... Released by Rams (March 18, 1997). ... Signed by Tampa Bay Buccaneers (October 9, 1997). ... Granted unconditional free agency (February 13, 1998). ... Signed by Green Packers (February 26, 1998). ... Granted unconditional free agency (February 12, 1999). ... Signed by Philadelphia Eagles (March 26, 1999).
CHAMPIONSHIP GAME EXPERIENCE: Played in USFL championship game (1983-1985 seasons). ... Played in NFC championship game (1986 and 1990 seasons). ... Member of Super Bowl championship team (1986 and 1990 seasons).
HONORS: Named punter on THE SPORTING NEWS USFL All-Star team (1983 and 1984). ... Named punter on THE SPORTING NEWS NFL All-Pro team (1986, 1989 and 1990). ... Played in Pro Bowl (1986 and 1990 seasons).
PRO STATISTICS: USFL: 1983—Rushed once for minus five yards, fumbled once and recovered one fumble. 1984—Recovered one fumble. NFL: 1985—Attempted one pass without a completion. 1996—Rushed twice for no yards, fumbled once and recovered one fumble for minus 11 yards.

			PUNTING				
Year Team	G	No.	Yds.	Avg.	Net avg.	In. 20	Blk.
1983—Philadelphia USFL	18	86	3601	41.9	36.5	31	0
1984—Philadelphia USFL	18	53	2171	41.0	*38.1	18	0
1985—Baltimore USFL	18	65	2718	41.8	33.2	18	0
—New York Giants NFL	16	81	3472	42.9	36.3	20	0
1986—New York Giants NFL	16	79	3539	‡44.8	‡37.1	24	0
1987—New York Giants NFL	12	65	2773	42.7	31.0	13	1
1988—New York Giants NFL	1	6	222	37.0	35.7	1	0
1989—New York Giants NFL	16	70	3019	43.1	*37.7	19	0
1990—New York Giants NFL	16	75	3306	‡44.1	37.2	†24	0
1991—New York Giants NFL	15	64	2768	43.3	35.2	16	0
1992—New York Giants NFL	11	53	2317	43.7	31.5	13	*2
1993—New York Giants NFL	8	33	1390	42.1	35.0	11	1
—Los Angeles Rams NFL	8	42	1825	43.5	32.8	7	0
1994—Los Angeles Rams NFL	16	78	3494	*44.8	34.2	23	0
1995—St. Louis NFL	16	83	3679	‡44.3	36.7	23	0
1996—St. Louis NFL	16	78	3491	44.8	36.1	23	0
1997—Tampa Bay NFL	10	54	2274	42.1	34.1	15	1
1998—Green Bay NFL	16	65	2788	42.9	37.1	30	0
USFL totals (3 years)	54	204	8490	41.6	35.9	67	0
NFL totals (14 years)	193	926	40357	43.6	35.4	262	5
Pro totals (17 years)	247	1130	48847	43.2	35.5	329	5

LANE, FRED — RB — PANTHERS

PERSONAL: Born September 6, 1975, in Nashville. ... 5-10/205. ... Full name: Freddie Brown Lane Jr.
HIGH SCHOOL: Franklin (Tenn.).
COLLEGE: Lane (Tenn.).
TRANSACTIONS/CAREER NOTES: Signed as non-drafted free agent by Carolina Panthers (April 19, 1997).
PRO STATISTICS: 1997—Recovered two fumbles.
SINGLE GAME HIGHS (regular season): Attempts—35 (November 1, 1998, vs. New Orleans); yards—147 (November 2, 1997, vs. Oakland); and rushing touchdowns—3 (November 2, 1997, vs. Oakland).
STATISTICAL PLATEAUS: 100-yard rushing games: 1997 (4), 1998 (2). Total: 6.
MISCELLANEOUS: Holds Carolina Panthers all-time record for most rushing touchdowns (12).

			RUSHING				RECEIVING			TOTALS			
Year Team	G	GS	Att.	Yds.	Avg.	TD	No.	Yds.	Avg.	TD	TD	2pt.	Pts.	Fum.
1997—Carolina NFL	13	7	182	809	4.4	7	8	27	3.4	0	7	0	42	4
1998—Carolina NFL	14	11	205	717	3.5	5	12	85	7.1	0	5	0	30	4
Pro totals (2 years)	27	18	387	1526	3.9	12	20	112	5.6	0	12	0	72	8

LANE, MAX — G — PATRIOTS

PERSONAL: Born February 22, 1971, in Norborne, Mo. ... 6-6/305. ... Full name: Max Aaron Lane.
HIGH SCHOOL: Norborne (Mo.), then Naval Academy Preparatory (Newport, R.I.).
COLLEGE: Navy.
TRANSACTIONS/CAREER NOTES: Selected by New England Patriots in sixth round (168th pick overall) of 1994 NFL draft. ... Signed by Patriots (June 1, 1994). ... Granted free agency (February 14, 1997). ... Re-signed by Patriots (June 20, 1997).
PLAYING EXPERIENCE: New England NFL, 1994-1998. ... Games/Games started: 1994 (14/0), 1995 (16/16), 1996 (16/16), 1997 (16/16), 1998 (16/11). Total: 78/59.
CHAMPIONSHIP GAME EXPERIENCE: Played in AFC championship game (1996 season). ... Played in Super Bowl XXXI (1996 season).
PRO STATISTICS: 1995—Recovered one fumble. 1996—Recovered three fumbles. 1997—Recovered one fumble.

LANG, KENARD — DE — REDSKINS

PERSONAL: Born January 31, 1975, in Orlando. ... 6-4/277. ... Full name: Kenard Dushun Lang.
HIGH SCHOOL: Maynard Evans (Orlando).
COLLEGE: Miami (Fla.).
TRANSACTIONS/CAREER NOTES: Selected by Washington Redskins in first round (17th pick overall) of 1997 NFL draft. ... Signed by Redskins (July 28, 1997).
PRO STATISTICS: 1997—Recovered two fumbles.

Year Team	G	GS	SACKS
1997—Washington NFL	12	11	1.5
1998—Washington NFL	16	16	7.0
Pro totals (2 years)	28	27	8.5

LANGFORD, JEVON — DE — BENGALS

PERSONAL: Born February 16, 1974, in Washington, D.C. ... 6-3/290.
HIGH SCHOOL: Bishop Carroll (Washington, D.C.).
COLLEGE: Oklahoma State.
TRANSACTIONS/CAREER NOTES: Selected after junior season by Cincinnati Bengals in fourth round (108th pick overall) of 1996 NFL draft. ... Signed by Bengals (August 5, 1996). ... Granted free agency (February 12, 1999). ... Re-signed by Bengals (May 25, 1999).
PRO STATISTICS: 1996—Recovered one fumble.

Year Team	G	GS	SACKS
1996—Cincinnati NFL	12	3	2.0
1997—Cincinnati NFL	15	0	1.0
1998—Cincinnati NFL	14	1	0.5
Pro totals (3 years)	41	4	3.5

LANGHAM, ANTONIO — DB — BROWNS

PERSONAL: Born July 31, 1972, in Town Creek, Ala. ... 6-0/184. ... Full name: Collie Antonio Langham.
HIGH SCHOOL: Hazelwood (Town Creek, Ala.).
COLLEGE: Alabama.
TRANSACTIONS/CAREER NOTES: Selected by Cleveland Browns in first round (ninth pick overall) of 1994 NFL draft. ... Signed by Browns (August 4, 1994). ... Browns franchise moved to Baltimore and renamed Ravens for 1996 season (March 11, 1996). ... Granted unconditional free agency (February 13, 1998). ... Signed by San Francisco 49ers (March 9, 1998). ... Selected by Cleveland Browns from 49ers in NFL expansion draft (February 9, 1999).
HONORS: Jim Thorpe Award winner (1993). ... Named defensive back on THE SPORTING NEWS college All-America first team (1993).
PRO STATISTICS: 1994—Fumbled once. 1997—Credited with one sack.
MISCELLANEOUS: Holds Baltimore Ravens all-time record for most interceptions (8).

			INTERCEPTIONS			
Year Team	G	GS	No.	Yds.	Avg.	TD
1994—Cleveland NFL	16	16	2	2	1.0	0
1995—Cleveland NFL	16	16	2	29	14.5	0
1996—Baltimore NFL	15	14	5	59	11.8	0
1997—Baltimore NFL	16	15	3	40	13.3	1
1998—San Francisco NFL	11	6	1	0	0.0	0
Pro totals (5 years)	74	67	13	130	10.0	1

LASSITER, KWAMIE — S — CARDINALS

PERSONAL: Born December 3, 1969, in Hampton, Va. ... 6-0/202.
HIGH SCHOOL: Menchville (Newport News, Va.).
JUNIOR COLLEGE: Butler County Community College (Kan.).
COLLEGE: Kansas.
TRANSACTIONS/CAREER NOTES: Signed as non-drafted free agent by Arizona Cardinals (April 28, 1995). ... On injured reserve with ankle injury (October 5, 1995-remainder of season). ... Granted free agency (February 13, 1998). ... Re-signed by Cardinals (May 21, 1998). ... Granted unconditional free agency (February 12, 1999). ... Re-signed by Cardinals (March 10, 1999).
PRO STATISTICS: 1995—Rushed once for one yard. 1997—Credited with three sacks. 1998—Recovered one fumble.

			INTERCEPTIONS			
Year Team	G	GS	No.	Yds.	Avg.	TD
1995—Arizona NFL	5	0	0	0	...	0
1996—Arizona NFL	14	0	1	20	20.0	0
1997—Arizona NFL	16	1	1	10	10.0	0
1998—Arizona NFL	16	6	‡8	80	10.0	0
Pro totals (4 years)	51	7	10	110	11.0	0

LATHON, LAMAR — LB

PERSONAL: Born December 23, 1967, in Wharton, Texas. ... 6-3/260. ... Full name: Lamar Lavantha Lathon. ... Name pronounced LAY-thin.
HIGH SCHOOL: Wharton (Texas).
COLLEGE: Houston.
TRANSACTIONS/CAREER NOTES: Selected by Houston Oilers in first round (15th pick overall) of 1990 NFL draft. ... Signed by Oilers (July 18, 1990). ... On injured reserve with shoulder injury (September 19-October 19, 1990). ... On injured reserve with knee injury (November 24,

1992-January 2, 1993). ... Granted unconditional free agency (February 17, 1995). ... Signed by Carolina Panthers (March 1, 1995). ... On injured reserve with knee injury (September 21, 1998-remainder of season). ... Released by Panthers (February 10, 1999).
CHAMPIONSHIP GAME EXPERIENCE: Played in NFC championship game (1996 season).
HONORS: Named linebacker on THE SPORTING NEWS NFL All-Pro team (1996). ... Played in Pro Bowl (1996 season).
PRO STATISTICS: 1990—Recovered one fumble. 1993—Recovered one fumble. 1994—Credited with one safety and recovered one fumble. 1995—Recovered one fumble. 1996—Recovered two fumbles for four yards.

				INTERCEPTIONS			SACKS
Year Team	G	GS	No.	Yds.	Avg.	TD	No.
1990—Houston NFL	11	1	0	0	...	0	0.0
1991—Houston NFL	16	16	3	77	25.7	1	2.0
1992—Houston NFL	11	11	0	0	...	0	1.5
1993—Houston NFL	13	1	0	0	...	0	2.0
1994—Houston NFL	16	15	0	0	...	0	8.5
1995—Carolina NFL	15	15	0	0	...	0	8.0
1996—Carolina NFL	16	16	0	0	...	0	13.5
1997—Carolina NFL	15	15	1	1	1.0	0	2.0
1998—Carolina NFL	2	2	0	0	...	0	0.0
Pro totals (9 years)	115	92	4	78	19.5	1	37.5

LAW, TY — CB — PATRIOTS

PERSONAL: Born February 10, 1974, in Aliquippa, Pa. ... 5-11/200. ... Full name: Tajuan Law.
HIGH SCHOOL: Aliquippa (Pa.).
COLLEGE: Michigan.
TRANSACTIONS/CAREER NOTES: Selected after junior season by New England Patriots in first round (23rd pick overall) of 1995 NFL draft. ... Signed by Patriots (July 20, 1995).
CHAMPIONSHIP GAME EXPERIENCE: Played in AFC championship game (1996 season). ... Played in Super Bowl XXXI (1996 season).
HONORS: Named cornerback on THE SPORTING NEWS NFL All-Pro team (1998). ... Played in Pro Bowl (1998 season). ... Named co-Oustanding Player of Pro Bowl (1998 season).
PRO STATISTICS: 1995—Credited with one sack. 1997—Credited with 1/2 sack, fumbled once and recovered one fumble. 1998—Recovered one fumble for 17 yards.

			INTERCEPTIONS			
Year Team	G	GS	No.	Yds.	Avg.	TD
1995—New England NFL	14	7	3	47	15.7	0
1996—New England NFL	13	12	3	45	15.0	1
1997—New England NFL	16	16	3	70	23.3	0
1998—New England NFL	16	16	*9	133	14.8	1
Pro totals (4 years)	59	51	18	295	16.4	2

LAYMAN, JASON — G — TITANS

PERSONAL: Born July 29, 1973, in Sevierville, Tenn. ... 6-5/310. ... Full name: Jason Todd Layman.
HIGH SCHOOL: Sevier County (Sevierville, Tenn.).
COLLEGE: Tennessee.
TRANSACTIONS/CAREER NOTES: Selected by Houston Oilers in second round (48th pick overall) of 1996 NFL draft. ... Signed by Oilers (July 20, 1996). ... Oilers franchise moved to Tennessee for 1997 season. ... Oilers franchise renamed Tennessee Titans for 1999 season (December 26, 1998).
PLAYING EXPERIENCE: Houston NFL, 1996; Tennessee NFL, 1997 and 1998. ... Games/Games started: 1996 (16/0), 1997 (13/0), 1998 (16/15). Total: 45/15.
PRO STATISTICS: 1997—Returned one kickoff for five yards. 1998—Recovered one fumble.

LEAF, RYAN — QB — CHARGERS

PERSONAL: Born May 15, 1976, in Great Falls, Mont. ... 6-5/235. ... Full name: Ryan David Leaf.
HIGH SCHOOL: Russell (Great Falls, Mont.).
COLLEGE: Washington State.
TRANSACTIONS/CAREER NOTES: Selected after junior season by San Diego Chargers in first round (second pick overall) of 1998 NFL draft. ... Signed by Chargers (July 28, 1998).
HONORS: Named quarterback on THE SPORTING NEWS college All-America first team (1997).
PRO STATISTICS: 1998—Fumbled eight times and recovered two fumbles for minus 18 yards.
SINGLE GAME HIGHS (regular season): Attempts—52 (October 25, 1998, vs. Seattle); completions—25 (October 25, 1998, vs. Seattle); yards—281 (October 25, 1998, vs. Seattle); and touchdown passes—1 (October 25, 1998, vs. Seattle).
MISCELLANEOUS: Regular-season record as starting NFL quarterback: 3-6 (.333).

			PASSING							RUSHING			TOTALS		
Year Team	G	GS	Att.	Cmp.	Pct.	Yds.	TD	Int.	Avg.	Rat.	Att.	Yds.	Avg.	TD	TD	2pt.	Pts.
1998—San Diego NFL	10	9	245	111	45.3	1289	2	15	5.26	39.0	27	80	3.0	0	0	0	0

LE BEL, HARPER — TE

PERSONAL: Born July 14, 1963, in Granada Hills, Calif. ... 6-4/250. ... Full name: Brian Harper Le Bel.
HIGH SCHOOL: Notre Dame (Sherman Oaks, Calif.).
COLLEGE: Colorado State.

TRANSACTIONS/CAREER NOTES: Selected by Kansas City Chiefs in 12th round (321st pick overall) of 1985 NFL draft. ... Signed by Chiefs (July 18, 1985). ... Released by Chiefs (August 12, 1985). ... Signed by San Francisco 49ers (December 20, 1985). ... Released by 49ers after failing physical (April 7, 1986). ... Signed as replacement player by San Diego Chargers (September 29, 1987). ... Released by Chargers (October 20, 1987). ... Signed by Dallas Cowboys (April 27, 1988). ... Released by Cowboys (August 2, 1988). ... Signed by Tampa Bay Buccaneers (August 15, 1988). ... Released by Buccaneers (August 23, 1988). ... Signed by Seattle Seahawks (August 8, 1989). ... Granted unconditional free agency (February 1, 1990). ... Signed by Philadelphia Eagles (March 30, 1990). ... Granted unconditional free agency (February 1, 1991). ... Signed by Atlanta Falcons (April 1, 1991). ... On injured reserve with wrist injury (September 18, 1991-remainder of season). ... Granted unconditional free agency (February 1-April 1, 1992). ... Re-signed by Falcons for 1992 season. ... Granted free agency (March 1, 1993). ... Re-signed by Falcons (June 11, 1993). ... Granted unconditional free agency (February 17, 1994). ... Re-signed by Falcons (March 30, 1994). ... Granted unconditional free agency (February 17, 1995). ... Re-signed by Falcons (March 22, 1995). ... Granted unconditional free agency (February 14, 1997). ... Signed by Green Bay Packers (March 31, 1997). ... Released by Packers (August 24, 1997). ... Signed by Chicago Bears (August 27, 1997). ... Granted unconditional free agency (February 13, 1998). ... Signed by Baltimore Ravens (July 29, 1998). ... On injured reserve with elbow injury (October 1, 1998-remainder of season). ... Granted unconditional free agency (February 12, 1999).
PLAYING EXPERIENCE: Seattle NFL, 1989; Philadelphia NFL, 1990; Atlanta NFL, 1991-1996; Chicago NFL, 1997; Baltimore NFL, 1998. ... Games/Games started: 1989 (16/0), 1990 (16/0), 1991 (3/0), 1992 (16/2), 1993 (16/0), 1994 (16/0), 1995 (16/0), 1996 (16/0), 1997 (16/0), 1998 (5/0). Total: 136/2.
PRO STATISTICS: 1989—Fumbled once for minus 25 yards. 1990—Caught one pass for nine yards and fumbled once. 1992—Fumbled once for minus 37 yards. 1993—Fumbled once. 1995—Fumbled once for minus eight yards. 1996—Recovered one fumble. 1997—Rushed once for no yards, fumbled once and recovered one fumble. 1998—Fumbled once for minus 31 yards.
SINGLE GAME HIGHS (regular season): Receptions—1 (September 16, 1990, vs. Arizona); yards—9 (September 16, 1990, vs. Arizona); and touchdown receptions—0.

LEE, AMP   RB   RAMS

PERSONAL: Born October 1, 1971, in Chipley, Fla. ... 5-11/200. ... Full name: Anthonia Wayne Lee.
HIGH SCHOOL: Chipley (Fla.).
COLLEGE: Florida State.
TRANSACTIONS/CAREER NOTES: Selected after junior season by San Francisco 49ers in second round (45th pick overall) of 1992 NFL draft. ... Signed by 49ers (July 18, 1992). ... Released by 49ers (May 4, 1994). ... Signed by Minnesota Vikings (May 24, 1994). ... On physically unable to perform list (July 13-20, 1994). ... Granted unconditional free agency (February 14, 1997). ... Signed by St. Louis Rams (August 4, 1997). ... Granted unconditional free agency (February 13, 1998). ... Re-signed by Rams (February 24, 1998).
CHAMPIONSHIP GAME EXPERIENCE: Played in NFC championship game (1992 and 1993 seasons).
PRO STATISTICS: 1992—Fumbled once and recovered three fumbles. 1993—Fumbled once. 1994—Fumbled once and recovered one fumble. 1995—Fumbled three times and recovered two fumbles. 1996—Fumbled twice and recovered one fumble. 1998—Fumbled three times.
SINGLE GAME HIGHS (regular season): Attempts—23 (December 13, 1992, vs. Minnesota); yards—134 (December 13, 1992, vs. Minnesota); and rushing touchdowns—2 (October 11, 1998, vs. New York Jets).
STATISTICAL PLATEAUS: 100-yard rushing games: 1992 (1). ... 100-yard receiving games: 1997 (3).

				RUSHING				RECEIVING				PUNT RETURNS				KICKOFF RETURNS			TOTALS		
Year Team	G	GS	Att.	Yds.	Avg.	TD	No.	Yds.	Avg.	TD	No.	Yds.	Avg.	TD	No.	Yds.	Avg.	TD	TD	2pt.	Pts.
1992—San Fran. NFL	16	3	91	362	4.0	2	20	102	5.1	2	0	0	...	0	14	276	19.7	0	4	0	24
1993—San Fran. NFL	15	3	72	230	3.2	1	16	115	7.2	2	0	0	...	0	10	160	16.0	0	3	0	18
1994—Minnesota NFL	13	0	29	104	3.6	0	45	368	8.2	2	0	0	...	0	3	42	14.0	0	2	0	12
1995—Minnesota NFL	16	3	69	371	5.4	2	71	558	7.9	1	5	50	10.0	0	5	100	20.0	0	3	0	18
1996—Minnesota NFL	16	3	51	161	3.2	0	54	422	7.8	2	10	84	8.4	0	5	85	17.0	0	2	0	12
1997—St. Louis NFL	16	1	28	104	3.7	0	61	825	13.5	3	0	0	...	0	4	71	17.8	0	3	0	18
1998—St. Louis NFL	14	1	44	175	4.0	2	64	667	10.4	2	0	0	...	0	0	0	...	0	4	1	26
Pro totals (7 years)	106	14	384	1507	3.9	7	331	3057	9.2	14	15	134	8.9	0	41	734	17.9	0	21	1	128

LEE, LLOYD   S   CHARGERS

PERSONAL: Born August 8, 1976, in Minneapolis, Minn. ... 6-2/215.
HIGH SCHOOL: Thomas Jefferson (Bloomington, Minn.).
COLLEGE: Dartmouth.
TRANSACTIONS/CAREER NOTES: Signed as non-drafted free agent by San Diego Chargers (April 20, 1998). ... Released by Chargers (August 30, 1998). ... Re-signed by Chargers to practice squad (August 31, 1998). ... Activated (September 26, 1998). ... Released by Chargers (November 19, 1998). ... Re-signed by Chargers to practice squad (November 4, 1998). ... Activated (December 3, 1998).
PLAYING EXPERIENCE: San Diego NFL, 1998. ... Games/Games started: 8/0.

LEE, SHAWN   DT

PERSONAL: Born October 24, 1966, in Brooklyn, N.Y. ... 6-2/300. ... Full name: Shawn Swaboda Lee.
HIGH SCHOOL: Erasmus Hall (Brooklyn, N.Y.).
JUNIOR COLLEGE: Westchester Community College (Valhalla, N.Y.).
COLLEGE: North Alabama.
TRANSACTIONS/CAREER NOTES: Selected by Tampa Bay Buccaneers in sixth round (163rd pick overall) of 1988 NFL draft. ... Signed by Buccaneers (July 10, 1988). ... Granted unconditional free agency (February 1-April 1, 1990). ... Re-signed by Buccaneers (July 20, 1990). ... Claimed on waivers by Atlanta Falcons (August 29, 1990). ... Traded by Falcons to Miami Dolphins for conditional pick in 1991 draft (September 3, 1990). ... On injured reserve with ankle injury (September 29-October 27, 1990). ... Granted free agency (February 1, 1991). ... Re-signed by Dolphins (August 21, 1991). ... On injured reserve with knee injury (September 17, 1991-remainder of season). ... Granted free agency (February 1, 1992). ... Re-signed by Dolphins (July 22, 1992). ... Released by Dolphins (August 31, 1992). ... Signed by San Diego Chargers (October 28, 1992). ... Granted unconditional free agency (March 1, 1993). ... Re-signed by Chargers (April 23, 1993). ... Traded by Chargers to Chicago Bears for fifth-round pick (DE Adrian Dingle) in 1999 draft (June 8, 1998). ... Granted unconditional free agency (February 12, 1999).
CHAMPIONSHIP GAME EXPERIENCE: Member of Chargers for AFC championship game (1994 season); inactive. ... Played in Super Bowl XXIX (1994 season).

PRO STATISTICS: 1991—Intercepted one pass for 14 yards. 1992—Recovered one fumble. 1993—Recovered one fumble. 1994—Recovered one fumble. 1995—Recovered one fumble. 1996—Intercepted one pass for minus one yard. 1998—Recovered one fumble for 15 yards and a touchdown.

Year Team	G	GS	SACKS
1988—Tampa Bay NFL	15	0	2.0
1989—Tampa Bay NFL	15	3	1.0
1990—Miami NFL	13	10	1.5
1991—Miami NFL	3	2	0.0
1992—San Diego NFL	9	1	0.5
1993—San Diego NFL	16	15	3.0
1994—San Diego NFL	15	15	6.5
1995—San Diego NFL	16	15	8.0
1996—San Diego NFL	15	7	1.0
1997—San Diego NFL	16	15	3.0
1998—Chicago NFL	15	14	2.0
Pro totals (11 years)	**148**	**97**	**28.5**

LEEUWENBURG, JAY   C/G   COLTS

PERSONAL: Born June 18, 1969, in St. Louis. ... 6-3/290. ... Full name: Jay Robert Leeuwenburg. ... Son of Richard Leeuwenburg, tackle with Chicago Bears (1965).
HIGH SCHOOL: Kirkwood (Mo.).
COLLEGE: Colorado (degree in English).
TRANSACTIONS/CAREER NOTES: Selected by Kansas City Chiefs in ninth round (244th pick overall) of 1992 NFL draft. ... Signed by Chiefs (July 20, 1992). ... Claimed on waivers by Chicago Bears (September 2, 1992). ... Granted free agency (February 17, 1995). ... Re-signed by Bears (April 12, 1995). ... Granted unconditional free agency (February 16, 1996). ... Signed by Indianapolis Colts (February 21, 1996).
PLAYING EXPERIENCE: Chicago NFL, 1992-1995; Indianapolis NFL, 1996-1998. ... Games/Games started: 1992 (12/0), 1993 (16/16), 1994 (16/16), 1995 (16/16), 1996 (15/7), 1997 (16/16), 1998 (16/16). Total: 107/87.
HONORS: Named center on THE SPORTING NEWS college All-America first team (1991).
PRO STATISTICS: 1992—Returned one kickoff for 12 yards. 1995—Recovered one fumble. 1997—Fumbled once for minus 20 yards. 1998—Recovered one fumble.

LEGETTE, TYRONE   CB

PERSONAL: Born February 15, 1970, in Columbia, S.C. ... 5-9/179. ... Full name: Tyrone Christopher Legette. ... Name pronounced luh-GET.
HIGH SCHOOL: Spring Valley (Columbia, S.C.).
COLLEGE: Nebraska.
TRANSACTIONS/CAREER NOTES: Selected by New Orleans Saints in third round (72nd pick overall) of 1992 NFL draft. ... Signed by Saints (July 26, 1992). ... On injured reserve with hamstring injury (November 3, 1992-remainder of season). ... Granted free agency (February 17, 1995). ... Re-signed by Saints (July 23, 1995). ... Granted unconditional free agency (February 16, 1996). ... Signed by Tampa Bay Buccaneers (June 28, 1996). ... Granted unconditional free agency (February 14, 1997). ... Re-signed by Buccaneers (February 26, 1997). ... Released by Buccaneers (August 25, 1998). ... Signed by San Francisco 49ers (November 11, 1998). ... Released by 49ers (January 3, 1999).
PLAYING EXPERIENCE: New Orleans NFL, 1992-1995; Tampa Bay NFL, 1996 and 1997; San Francisco NFL, 1998. ... Games/Games started: 1992 (8/0), 1993 (14/1), 1994 (15/2), 1995 (16/1), 1996 (15/0), 1997 (16/1), 1998 (7/0). Total: 91/5.
PRO STATISTICS: 1994—Credited with one sack, returned one punt for no yards and fumbled once. 1995—Credited with one sack, intercepted one pass for 43 yards and returned one punt for six yards. 1997—Intercepted one pass for no yards.

LEPSIS, MATT   OT   BRONCOS

PERSONAL: Born January 13, 1974, in Conroe, Texas ... 6-4/290. ... Full name: Matthew Lepsis.
HIGH SCHOOL: Frisco (Texas).
COLLEGE: Colorado.
TRANSACTIONS/CAREER NOTES: Signed as non-drafted free agent by Denver Broncos (April 22, 1997). ... On reserve/non-football injury list with knee injury (July 16, 1997-entire season). ... Assigned by Broncos to Barcelona Dragons in 1998 NFL Europe enhancement allocation program (February 18, 1998).
PLAYING EXPERIENCE: Barcelona Dragons NFLE, 1998; Denver NFL, 1998. ... Games/Games started: NFLE 1998 (games played unavailable), NFL 1998 (16/0).
CHAMPIONSHIP GAME EXPERIENCE: Played in AFC championship game (1998 season). ... Member of Super Bowl championship team (1998 season).

LESTER, TIM   FB

PERSONAL: Born June 15, 1968, in Miami. ... 5-10/238. ... Full name: Timothy Lee Lester. ... Brother of Fred Lester, fullback with New York Jets (1994), Tampa Bay Buccaneers (1995-96) and Atlanta Falcons (1997).
HIGH SCHOOL: Miami Southridge.
COLLEGE: Eastern Kentucky.
TRANSACTIONS/CAREER NOTES: Selected by Los Angeles Rams in 10th round (255th pick overall) of 1992 NFL draft. ... Signed by Rams (July 13, 1992). ... Released by Rams (September 4, 1992). ... Re-signed by Rams to practice squad (September 7, 1992). ... Activated (October 7, 1992). ... Released by Rams (August 29, 1995). ... Signed by Pittsburgh Steelers (October 3, 1995). ... On physically unable to perform list with rotator cuff and knee injuries (August 25-October 17, 1998). ... Granted unconditional free agency (February 12, 1999).
CHAMPIONSHIP GAME EXPERIENCE: Played in AFC championship game (1995 and 1997 seasons). ... Played in Super Bowl XXX (1995 season).
PRO STATISTICS: 1994—Returned one kickoff for eight yards and recovered one fumble.
SINGLE GAME HIGHS (regular season): Attempts—5 (December 11, 1994, vs. Tampa Bay); yards—28 (October 14, 1993, vs. Atlanta); and rushing touchdowns—1 (November 25, 1996, vs. Miami).

Year	Team	G	GS	Rushing Att.	Yds.	Avg.	TD	Receiving No.	Yds.	Avg.	TD	Totals TD	2pt.	Pts.	Fum.
1992	Los Angeles Rams NFL	11	0	0	0	...	0	0	0	...	0	0	...	0	0
1993	Los Angeles Rams NFL	16	14	11	74	6.7	0	18	154	8.6	0	0	...	0	0
1994	Los Angeles Rams NFL	14	4	7	14	2.0	0	1	1	1.0	0	0	0	0	1
1995	Pittsburgh NFL	6	1	5	9	1.8	1	0	0	...	0	1	0	6	0
1996	Pittsburgh NFL	16	13	8	20	2.5	1	7	70	10.0	0	1	0	6	1
1997	Pittsburgh NFL	16	13	2	9	4.5	0	10	51	5.1	0	0	0	0	0
1998	Pittsburgh NFL	9	7	0	0	...	0	9	46	5.1	0	0	0	0	0
Pro totals (7 years)		88	52	33	126	3.8	2	45	322	7.2	0	2	0	12	2

LETT, LEON — DT — COWBOYS

PERSONAL: Born October 12, 1968, in Mobile, Ala. ... 6-6/290. ... Full name: Leon Lett Jr. ... Nickname: The Big Cat.
HIGH SCHOOL: Fairhope (Ala.).
JUNIOR COLLEGE: Hinds Community College (Miss.).
COLLEGE: Emporia (Kan.) State.
TRANSACTIONS/CAREER NOTES: Selected by Dallas Cowboys in seventh round (173rd pick overall) of 1991 NFL draft. ... Signed by Cowboys (July 14, 1991). ... On injured reserve with back injury (August 27-November 21, 1991). ... On suspended list for violating league substance abuse policy (November 3-24, 1995). ... On suspended list for violating league substance abuse policy (December 3, 1996-December 1, 1997).
CHAMPIONSHIP GAME EXPERIENCE: Played in NFC championship game (1992-1995 seasons). ... Member of Super Bowl championship team (1992, 1993 and 1995 seasons).
HONORS: Played in Pro Bowl (1994 and 1998 seasons).
POST SEASON RECORDS: Holds Super Bowl career record for most yards by fumble recovery—64. ... Holds Super Bowl single-game record for most yards by fumble recovery—64 (January 31, 1993).
PRO STATISTICS: 1992—Recovered one fumble. 1993—Fumbled once. 1995—Recovered two fumbles. 1996—Recovered two fumbles.

Year	Team	G	GS	SACKS
1991	Dallas NFL	5	0	0.0
1992	Dallas NFL	16	0	3.5
1993	Dallas NFL	11	6	0.0
1994	Dallas NFL	16	16	4.0
1995	Dallas NFL	12	12	3.0
1996	Dallas NFL	13	13	3.5
1997	Dallas NFL	3	3	0.5
1998	Dallas NFL	16	15	4.0
Pro totals (8 years)		92	65	18.5

LEVENS, DORSEY — RB — PACKERS

PERSONAL: Born May 21, 1970, in Syracuse, N.Y. ... 6-1/228. ... Full name: Herbert Dorsey Levens.
HIGH SCHOOL: Nottingham (Syracuse, N.Y.).
COLLEGE: Notre Dame, then Georgia Tech (degree in business management).
TRANSACTIONS/CAREER NOTES: Selected by Green Bay Packers in fifth round (149th pick overall) of 1994 NFL draft. ... Signed by Packers (June 9, 1994). ... Granted free agency (February 14, 1997). ... Re-signed by Packers (June 20, 1997). ... Designated by Packers as franchise player (February 13, 1998). ... Re-signed by Packers (August 30, 1998).
CHAMPIONSHIP GAME EXPERIENCE: Played in NFC championship game (1995-97 seasons). ... Member of Super Bowl championship team (1996 season). ... Played in Super Bowl XXXII (1997 season).
HONORS: Played in Pro Bowl (1997 season).
PRO STATISTICS: 1996—Recovered one fumble. 1997—Recovered one fumble for minus seven yards.
SINGLE GAME HIGHS (regular season): Attempts—33 (November 23, 1997, vs. Dallas); yards—190 (November 23, 1997, vs. Dallas); and rushing touchdowns—2 (December 1, 1997, vs. Minnesota).
STATISTICAL PLATEAUS: 100-yard rushing games: 1997 (6), 1998 (1). Total: 7.

Year	Team	G	GS	Rushing Att.	Yds.	Avg.	TD	Receiving No.	Yds.	Avg.	TD	Kickoff Returns No.	Yds.	Avg.	TD	Totals TD	2pt.	Pts.	Fum.
1994	Green Bay NFL	14	0	5	15	3.0	0	1	9	9.0	0	2	31	15.5	0	0	0	0	0
1995	Green Bay NFL	15	12	36	120	3.3	3	48	434	9.0	4	0	0	...	0	7	0	42	0
1996	Green Bay NFL	16	1	121	566	4.7	5	31	226	7.3	5	5	84	16.8	0	10	0	60	2
1997	Green Bay NFL	16	16	329	1435	4.4	7	53	370	7.0	5	0	0	...	0	12	1	74	5
1998	Green Bay NFL	7	4	115	378	3.3	1	27	162	6.0	0	0	0	...	0	1	0	6	0
Pro totals (5 years)		68	33	606	2514	4.1	16	160	1201	7.5	14	7	115	16.4	0	30	1	182	7

LEVY, CHUCK — RB — 49ERS

PERSONAL: Born January 7, 1972, in Torrance, Calif. ... 6-0/206. ... Full name: Charles Levy.
HIGH SCHOOL: Lynwood (Calif.).
COLLEGE: Arizona.
TRANSACTIONS/CAREER NOTES: Selected after junior season by Arizona Cardinals in second round (38th pick overall) of 1994 NFL draft. ... Signed by Cardinals (August 10, 1994). ... On suspended list for violating league substance abuse policy (August 25, 1995-July 18, 1996). ... Released by Cardinals (August 25, 1996). ... Signed by San Francisco 49ers (December 25, 1996).
CHAMPIONSHIP GAME EXPERIENCE: Played in NFC championship game (1997 season).
POST SEASON RECORDS: Shares NFL postseason single-game record for most touchdowns by kickoff return—1 (January 11, 1998, vs. Green Bay).
PRO STATISTICS: 1994—Recovered one fumble. 1997—Returned six punts for 109 yards and tied for NFC lead with one touchdown.
SINGLE GAME HIGHS (regular season): Attempts—8 (October 11, 1998, vs. New Orleans); yards—61 (December 21, 1997, vs. Seattle); and rushing touchdowns—1 (September 14, 1998, vs. Washington).

– 235 –

Year	Team	G	GS	Att. RUSHING Yds.	Avg.	TD	No. RECEIVING Yds.	Avg.	TD	No. KICKOFF RETURNS Yds.	Avg.	TD	TD TOTALS 2pt.	Pts.	Fum.
1994—Arizona NFL		11	0	3 15	5.0	0	4 35	8.8	0	26 513	19.7	0	0 0	0	0
1995—Arizona NFL							Did not play.								
1996—							Did not play.								
1997—San Francisco NFL		14	0	16 90	5.6	0	5 68	13.6	0	36 793	22.0	0	1 0	6	1
1998—San Francisco NFL		12	0	25 112	4.5	1	15 64	4.3	0	22 383	17.4	0	1 0	6	0
Pro totals (3 years)		37	0	44 217	4.9	1	24 167	7.0	0	84 1689	20.1	0	2 0	12	1

LEWIS, ALBERT — DB — RAIDERS

PERSONAL: Born October 6, 1960, in Mansfield, La. ... 6-2/205. ... Full name: Albert Ray Lewis.
HIGH SCHOOL: DeSoto (Mansfield, La.).
COLLEGE: Grambling State (degree in political science, 1983).
TRANSACTIONS/CAREER NOTES: Selected by Philadelphia Stars in 15th round (175th pick overall) of 1983 USFL draft. ... Selected by Kansas City Chiefs in third round (61st pick overall) of 1983 NFL draft. ... Signed by Chiefs (May 19, 1983). ... On injured reserve with knee injury (December 10, 1984-remainder of season). ... On reserve/did not report list (July 24-September 17, 1990). ... On injured reserve with knee injury (December 14, 1991-remainder of season). ... On injured reserve with forearm injury (November 11, 1992-remainder of season). ... On practice squad (December 16-23, 1992). ... Granted unconditional free agency (February 17, 1994). ... Signed by Los Angeles Raiders (March 15, 1994). ... Raiders franchise moved to Oakland (July 21, 1995).
CHAMPIONSHIP GAME EXPERIENCE: Played in AFC championship game (1993 season).
HONORS: Played in Pro Bowl (1987, 1989 and 1990 seasons). ... Named to play in Pro Bowl (1988 season); replaced by Eric Thomas due to injury. ... Named cornerback on THE SPORTING NEWS NFL All-Pro team (1989 and 1990).
PRO STATISTICS: 1983—Recovered two fumbles. 1985—Recovered one fumble in end zone for a touchdown. 1986—Recovered two fumbles. 1987—Recovered one fumble. 1988—Credited with one safety and recovered one fumble. 1990—Recovered three fumbles for one yard. 1993—Recovered blocked punt in end zone for a touchdown and recovered two fumbles. 1995—Recovered one fumble for 29 yards.

Year	Team	G	GS	INTERCEPTIONS No.	Yds.	Avg.	TD	SACKS No.
1983—Kansas City NFL		16	1	4	42	10.5	0	0.0
1984—Kansas City NFL		15	15	4	57	14.3	0	1.0
1985—Kansas City NFL		16	16	▲8	59	7.4	0	1.5
1986—Kansas City NFL		15	15	4	18	4.5	0	1.0
1987—Kansas City NFL		12	12	1	0	0.0	0	0.0
1988—Kansas City NFL		14	12	1	19	19.0	0	0.0
1989—Kansas City NFL		16	16	4	37	9.3	0	1.0
1990—Kansas City NFL		15	14	2	15	7.5	0	0.0
1991—Kansas City NFL		8	6	3	21	7.0	0	0.0
1992—Kansas City NFL		9	8	1	0	0.0	0	0.0
1993—Kansas City NFL		14	13	6	61	10.2	0	0.0
1994—Los Angeles Raiders NFL		14	9	0	0	...	0	1.0
1995—Oakland NFL		16	15	0	0	...	0	1.0
1996—Oakland NFL		16	13	2	0	0.0	0	3.0
1997—Oakland NFL		14	11	0	0	...	0	2.0
1998—Oakland NFL		15	12	2	74	37.0	1	1.0
Pro totals (16 years)		225	188	42	403	9.6	1	12.5

LEWIS, CHAD — TE — RAMS

PERSONAL: Born October 5, 1971, in Fort Dix, N.J. ... 6-6/252. ... Full name: Chad Wayne Lewis.
HIGH SCHOOL: Orem (Utah).
COLLEGE: Brigham Young (degrees in communications and Chinese).
TRANSACTIONS/CAREER NOTES: Signed as non-drafted free agent by Philadelphia Eagles (April 23, 1997). ... Released by Eagles (September 15, 1998). ... Signed by St. Louis Rams (December 9, 1998). ... Inactive for three games with Rams (1998).
PRO STATISTICS: 1997—Returned one kickoff for 11 yards.
SINGLE GAME HIGHS (regular season): Receptions—3 (August 31, 1997, vs. New York Giants); yards—34 (August 31, 1997, vs. New York Giants); and touchdown receptions—1 (November 30, 1997, vs. Cincinnati).

Year	Team	G	GS	RECEIVING No.	Yds.	Avg.	TD	TD TOTALS 2pt.	Pts.	Fum.
1997—Philadelphia NFL		16	3	12	94	7.8	4	4 0	24	0
1998—Philadelphia NFL		2	0	0	0	...	0	0 0	0	0
Pro totals (2 years)		18	3	12	94	7.8	4	4 0	24	0

LEWIS, DARRYLL — CB — TITANS

PERSONAL: Born December 16, 1968, in West Covina, Calif. ... 5-9/186. ... Full name: Darryll Lamont Lewis.
HIGH SCHOOL: Nogales (West Covina, Calif.).
COLLEGE: Arizona.
TRANSACTIONS/CAREER NOTES: Selected by Houston Oilers in second round (38th pick overall) of 1991 NFL draft. ... Signed by Oilers (July 19, 1991). ... On injured reserve with knee injury (October 25, 1993-remainder of season). ... Granted free agency (February 17, 1994). ... Re-signed by Oilers (July 17, 1994). ... Granted unconditional free agency (February 17, 1995). ... Re-signed by Oilers (March 9, 1995). ... Oilers franchise moved to Tennessee for 1997 season. ... Oilers franchise renamed Tennessee Titans for 1999 season (December 26, 1998).
HONORS: Jim Thorpe Award winner (1990). ... Named defensive back on THE SPORTING NEWS college All-America first team (1990). ... Played in Pro Bowl (1995 season).
PRO STATISTICS: 1991—Recovered one fumble. 1992—Returned eight kickoffs for 171 yards and recovered one fumble. 1997—Recovered three fumbles for 68 yards and fumbled once.

				INTERCEPTIONS			SACKS
Year Team	G	GS	No.	Yds.	Avg.	TD	No.
1991—Houston NFL	16	1	1	33	33.0	1	1.0
1992—Houston NFL	13	0	0	0	...	0	1.0
1993—Houston NFL	4	4	1	47	47.0	▲1	0.0
1994—Houston NFL	16	15	5	57	11.4	0	0.0
1995—Houston NFL	16	15	6	§145	24.2	▲1	1.0
1996—Houston NFL	16	16	5	103	20.6	1	0.0
1997—Tennessee NFL	16	14	5	115	23.0	1	0.0
1998—Tennessee NFL	16	15	4	40	10.0	0	1.0
Pro totals (8 years)	113	80	27	540	20.0	5	4.0

LEWIS, JERMAINE — WR/PR — RAVENS

PERSONAL: Born October 16, 1974, in Lanham, Md. ... 5-7/172. ... Full name: Jermaine Edward Lewis.
HIGH SCHOOL: Eleanor Roosevelt (Lanham, Md.).
COLLEGE: Maryland.
TRANSACTIONS/CAREER NOTES: Selected by Baltimore Ravens in fifth round (153rd pick overall) of 1996 NFL draft. ... Signed by Ravens (July 18, 1996).
HONORS: Named punt returner on THE SPORTING NEWS NFL All-Pro team (1998). ... Played in Pro Bowl (1998 season).
RECORDS: Shares NFL single-game records for most touchdowns by punt returns—2; and most touchdowns by combined kick return—2 (December 7, 1997, vs. Seattle).
PRO STATISTICS: 1996—Rushed once for minus three yards and recovered one fumble. 1997—Rushed three times for 35 yards and recovered two fumbles. 1998—Rushed five times for 20 yards and recovered three fumbles.
SINGLE GAME HIGHS (regular season): Receptions—8 (September 21, 1997, vs. Tennessee); yards—124 (September 21, 1997, vs. Tennessee); and touchdown receptions—2 (August 31, 1997, vs. Jacksonville).
STATISTICAL PLATEAUS: 100-yard receiving games: 1997 (2), 1998 (2). Total: 4.

			RECEIVING				PUNT RETURNS			KICKOFF RETURNS			TOTALS			
Year Team	G	GS	No.	Yds.	Avg.	TD	No.	Yds.	Avg.	TD	No.	Yds.	Avg.	TD	2pt.	Pts.	Fum.
1996—Baltimore NFL	16	1	5	78	15.6	1	36	339	9.4	0	41	883	21.5	0	1	0	6	4
1997—Baltimore NFL	14	7	42	648	15.4	6	28	437	*15.6	2	41	905	22.1	0	8	0	48	3
1998—Baltimore NFL	13	13	41	784	19.1	6	32	405	12.7	†2	6	145	24.2	0	8	0	48	3
Pro totals (3 years)	43	21	88	1510	17.2	13	96	1181	12.3	4	88	1933	22.0	0	17	0	102	10

LEWIS, MO — LB — JETS

PERSONAL: Born October 21, 1969, in Atlanta. ... 6-3/258. ... Full name: Morris C. Lewis.
HIGH SCHOOL: J.C. Murphy (Atlanta).
COLLEGE: Georgia.
TRANSACTIONS/CAREER NOTES: Selected by New York Jets in third round (62nd pick overall) of 1991 NFL draft. ... Signed by Jets (July 18, 1991).
CHAMPIONSHIP GAME EXPERIENCE: Played in AFC championship game (1998 season).
HONORS: Played in Pro Bowl (1998 season).
PRO STATISTICS: 1991—Recovered one fumble. 1992—Recovered four fumbles for 22 yards. 1994—Recovered one fumble for 11 yards. 1997—Recovered one fumble for 26 yards. 1998—Fumbled once and recovered one fumble.

				INTERCEPTIONS			SACKS
Year Team	G	GS	No.	Yds.	Avg.	TD	No.
1991—New York Jets NFL	16	16	0	0	...	0	2.0
1992—New York Jets NFL	16	16	1	1	1.0	0	2.0
1993—New York Jets NFL	16	16	2	4	2.0	0	4.0
1994—New York Jets NFL	16	16	4	106	26.5	2	6.0
1995—New York Jets NFL	16	16	2	22	11.0	▲1	5.0
1996—New York Jets NFL	9	9	0	0	...	0	0.5
1997—New York Jets NFL	16	16	1	43	43.0	1	8.0
1998—New York Jets NFL	16	16	1	11	11.0	0	7.0
Pro totals (8 years)	121	121	11	187	17.0	4	34.5

LEWIS, RAY — LB — RAVENS

PERSONAL: Born May 15, 1975, in Bartow, Fla. ... 6-1/240. ... Full name: Ray Anthony Lewis.
HIGH SCHOOL: Kathleen (Lakeland, Fla.).
COLLEGE: Miami (Fla.).
TRANSACTIONS/CAREER NOTES: Selected after junior season by Baltimore Ravens in first round (26th pick overall) of 1996 NFL draft. ... Signed by Ravens (July 15, 1996).
HONORS: Named linebacker on THE SPORTING NEWS college All-America second team (1995). ... Played in Pro Bowl (1997 and 1998 seasons). ... Named linebacker on THE SPORTING NEWS NFL All-Pro team (1998).
PRO STATISTICS: 1997—Recovered one fumble.

				INTERCEPTIONS			SACKS
Year Team	G	GS	No.	Yds.	Avg.	TD	No.
1996—Baltimore NFL	14	13	1	0	0.0	0	2.5
1997—Baltimore NFL	16	16	1	18	18.0	0	4.0
1998—Baltimore NFL	14	14	2	25	12.5	0	3.0
Pro totals (3 years)	44	43	4	43	10.8	0	9.5

LINCOLN, JEREMY — CB

PERSONAL: Born April 7, 1969, in Toledo, Ohio. ... 5-10/180. ... Full name: Jeremy Arlo Lincoln.
HIGH SCHOOL: DeVilbiss (Toledo, Ohio).
COLLEGE: Tennessee.
TRANSACTIONS/CAREER NOTES: Selected by Chicago Bears in third round (80th pick overall) of 1992 NFL draft. ... Signed by Bears (July 23, 1992). ... On injured reserve with knee injury (September 1, 1992-entire season). ... Granted free agency (February 17, 1995). ... Re-signed by Bears (July 17, 1995). ... Released by Bears (August 20, 1996). ... Signed by St. Louis Rams (September 5, 1996). ... Released by Rams (February 24, 1997). ... Signed by Seattle Seahawks (June 4, 1997). ... Granted unconditional free agency (February 13, 1998). ... Signed by New York Giants (June 15, 1998). ... Granted unconditional free agency (February 12, 1999).
PRO STATISTICS: 1995—Credited with one sack. 1996—Recovered one fumble. 1997—Recovered one fumble.

				INTERCEPTIONS		
Year Team	G	GS	No.	Yds.	Avg.	TD
1992—Chicago NFL				Did not play.		
1993—Chicago NFL	16	7	3	109	‡36.3	1
1994—Chicago NFL	15	14	1	5	5.0	0
1995—Chicago NFL	16	14	1	32	32.0	0
1996—St. Louis NFL	13	1	1	3	3.0	0
1997—Seattle NFL	13	3	0	0	...	0
1998—New York Giants NFL	16	1	1	0	0.0	0
Pro totals (6 years)	89	40	7	149	21.3	1

LINDSAY, EVERETT — OL — RAVENS

PERSONAL: Born September 18, 1970, in Burlington, Iowa. ... 6-4/302. ... Full name: Everett Eric Lindsay.
HIGH SCHOOL: Millbrook (Raleigh, N.C.).
COLLEGE: Mississippi (degree in general business, 1992).
TRANSACTIONS/CAREER NOTES: Selected by Minnesota Vikings in fifth round (133rd pick overall) of 1993 NFL draft. ... Signed by Vikings (July 14, 1993). ... On injured reserve with shoulder injury (December 22, 1993-remainder of season). ... On injured reserve with shoulder injury (August 23, 1994-entire season). ... On physically unable to perform list with knee injury (July 22-August 20, 1996). ... On reserve/non-football injury list with knee injury (August 20, 1996-entire season). ... Assigned by Vikings to Barcelona Dragons in 1997 World League enhancement allocation program (February 19, 1997). ... Granted unconditional free agency (February 13, 1998). ... Re-signed by Vikings (February 17, 1998). ... Traded by Vikings to Baltimore Ravens for sixth-round pick (DE Talance Sawyer) in 1999 draft (April 17, 1999).
PLAYING EXPERIENCE: Minnesota NFL, 1993, 1995, 1997 and 1998. ... Games/Games started: 1993 (12/12), 1995 (16/0), 1997 (16/3), 1998 (16/3). Total: 60/18.
CHAMPIONSHIP GAME EXPERIENCE: Played in NFC championship game (1998 season).
HONORS: Named offensive tackle on THE SPORTING NEWS college All-America second team (1992).

LINTON, JONATHAN — FB — BILLS

PERSONAL: Born October 7, 1974, in Allentown, Pa ... 6-0/248. ... Full name: Jonathan C. Linton.
HIGH SCHOOL: Catasauqua (Pa).
COLLEGE: North Carolina.
TRANSACTIONS/CAREER NOTES: Selected by Buffalo Bills in fifth round (131st pick overall) of 1998 NFL draft. ... Signed by Bills (June 8, 1998).
PRO STATISTICS: 1998—Recovered one fumble.
SINGLE GAME HIGHS (regular season): Attempts—13 (December 27, 1998, vs. New Orleans); yards—60 (December 27, 1998, vs. New Orleans); rushing touchdowns—1 (December 27, 1998, vs. New Orleans).

			RUSHING				RECEIVING			TOTALS			
Year Team	G	GS	Att.	Yds.	Avg.	TD	No.	Yds.	Avg.	TD	TD	2pt.	Pts.	Fum.
1998—Buffalo NFL	14	0	45	195	4.3	1	1	10	10.0	0	1	0	6	0

LITTLE, EARL — DB — SAINTS

PERSONAL: Born March 10, 1973, in Miami. ... 6-0/191. ... Full name: Earl Jerome Little.
HIGH SCHOOL: North Miami.
COLLEGE: Michigan, then Miami (Fla.).
TRANSACTIONS/CAREER NOTES: Signed as non-drafted free agent by Miami Dolphins (April 24, 1997). ... Released by Dolphins (August 24, 1997). ... Re-signed by Dolphins to practice squad (August 26, 1997). ... Released by Dolphins (August 29, 1997). ... Signed by New Orleans Saints to practice squad (October 1, 1997).
PLAYING EXPERIENCE: New Orleans NFL, 1998. ... Games/Games started: 16/0.
PRO STATISTICS: 1998—Returned four kickoffs for 64 yards.

LITTLE, LEONARD — LB

PERSONAL: Born October 19, 1974, in Asheville, N.C. ... 6-3/237. ... Full name: Leonard Antonio Little.
HIGH SCHOOL: Asheville (N.C.).
JUNIOR COLLEGE: Coffeyville (Kan.) Community College.
COLLEGE: Tennessee (degree in psychology, 1997).
TRANSACTIONS/CAREER NOTES: Selected by St. Louis Rams in third round (65th pick overall) of 1998 NFL draft. ... Signed by Rams (July 2, 1998). ... On non-football injury list for personal reasons (November 17, 1998-present).
PLAYING EXPERIENCE: St. Louis NFL, 1998. ... Games/Games started: 6/0.
PRO STATISTICS: 1998—Credited with ½ sack.

LIWIENSKI, CHRIS — OL — VIKINGS

PERSONAL: Born August 2, 1975, in Sterling Heights, Mich. ... 6-5/308.
HIGH SCHOOL: Stevenson (Sterling Heights, Mich.).
COLLEGE: Indiana.
TRANSACTIONS/CAREER NOTES: Selected by Detroit Lions in seventh round (207th pick overall) of 1998 NFL draft. ... Signed by Lions (July 15, 1998). ... Released by Lions (August 24, 1998). ... Signed by Minnesota Vikings to practice squad (August 31, 1998). ... Activated (November 18, 1998).
PLAYING EXPERIENCE: Minnesota NFL, 1998. ... Games/Games started: 1/0.
CHAMPIONSHIP GAME EXPERIENCE: Member of Vikings for NFC championship game (1998 season); inactive.

LLOYD, GREG — LB

PERSONAL: Born May 26, 1965, in Miami. ... 6-2/235. ... Full name: Gregory Lenard Lloyd.
HIGH SCHOOL: Peach County (Fort Valley, Ga.).
COLLEGE: Fort Valley (Ga.) State.
TRANSACTIONS/CAREER NOTES: Selected by Pittsburgh Steelers in sixth round (150th pick overall) of 1987 NFL draft. ... Signed by Steelers (May 19, 1987). ... On injured reserve with knee injury (August 31, 1987-entire season). ... On injured reserve with knee injury (August 30-October 22, 1988). ... On injured reserve with knee injury (September 10, 1996-remainder of season). ... Released by Steelers (July 14, 1998). ... Signed by Carolina Panthers (July 25, 1998). ... Granted unconditional free agency (February 12, 1999).
CHAMPIONSHIP GAME EXPERIENCE: Played in AFC championship game (1994 and 1995 seasons). ... Played in Super Bowl XXX (1995 season). ... Member of Steelers for AFC championship game (1997 season); inactive.
HONORS: Played in Pro Bowl (1991-1995 seasons). ... Named outside linebacker on THE SPORTING NEWS NFL All-Pro team (1994 and 1995).
PRO STATISTICS: 1988—Recovered one fumble. 1989—Fumbled once and recovered three fumbles. 1991—Fumbled once and recovered two fumbles. 1992—Fumbled once and recovered four fumbles. 1993—Recovered one fumble. 1994—Recovered one fumble. 1997—Fumbled once and recovered three fumbles for 61 yards. 1998—Recovered one fumble for six yards.

				INTERCEPTIONS			SACKS
Year Team	G	GS	No.	Yds.	Avg.	TD	No.
1987—Pittsburgh NFL				Did not play.			
1988—Pittsburgh NFL	9	4	0	0	...	0	0.5
1989—Pittsburgh NFL	16	16	3	49	16.3	0	7.0
1990—Pittsburgh NFL	15	14	1	9	9.0	0	4.5
1991—Pittsburgh NFL	16	16	1	0	0.0	0	8.0
1992—Pittsburgh NFL	16	16	1	35	35.0	0	6.5
1993—Pittsburgh NFL	15	15	0	0	...	0	6.0
1994—Pittsburgh NFL	15	15	1	8	8.0	0	10.0
1995—Pittsburgh NFL	16	16	3	85	28.3	0	6.5
1996—Pittsburgh NFL	1	1	0	0	...	0	1.0
1997—Pittsburgh NFL	12	12	0	0	...	0	3.5
1998—Carolina NFL	16	14	1	3	3.0	0	1.0
Pro totals (11 years)	147	139	11	189	17.2	0	54.5

LOCKETT, KEVIN — WR — CHIEFS

PERSONAL: Born September 8, 1974, in Tulsa, Okla. ... 6-0/188.
HIGH SCHOOL: Washington (Tulsa, Okla.).
COLLEGE: Kansas State (degree in accounting).
TRANSACTIONS/CAREER NOTES: Selected by Kansas City Chiefs in second round (47th pick overall) of 1997 NFL draft. ... Signed by Chiefs (July 25, 1997).
PRO STATISTICS: 1998—Recovered two fumbles.
SINGLE GAME HIGHS (regular season): Receptions—4 (September 27, 1998, vs. Philadelphia); yards—74 (September 27, 1998, vs. Philadelphia); and touchdown receptions—0.

			RECEIVING				PUNT RETURNS			TOTALS			
Year Team	G	GS	No.	Yds.	Avg.	TD	No.	Yds.	Avg.	TD	TD	2pt.	Pts.	Fum.
1997—Kansas City NFL	9	0	1	35	35.0	0	0	0	...	0	0	0	0	0
1998—Kansas City NFL	13	3	19	281	14.8	0	7	36	5.1	0	0	0	0	2
Pro totals (2 years)	22	3	20	316	15.8	0	7	36	5.1	0	0	0	0	2

LODISH, MIKE — DT — BRONCOS

PERSONAL: Born August 11, 1967, in Detroit. ... 6-3/270. ... Full name: Michael Timothy Lodish. ... Name pronounced LO-dish.
HIGH SCHOOL: Brother Rice (Birmingham, Mich.).
COLLEGE: UCLA (degree in history and business administration, 1990).
TRANSACTIONS/CAREER NOTES: Selected by Buffalo Bills in 10th round (265th pick overall) of 1990 NFL draft. ... Signed by Bills (July 26, 1990). ... Granted free agency (February 1, 1992). ... Re-signed by Bills (July 23, 1992). ... Granted unconditional free agency (February 17, 1995). ... Signed by Denver Broncos (April 4, 1995). ... Granted unconditional free agency (February 14, 1997). ... Re-signed by Broncos (August 6, 1997).
CHAMPIONSHIP GAME EXPERIENCE: Played in AFC championship game (1990-1993, 1997 and 1998 seasons). ... Played in Super Bowl XXV (1990 season), Super Bowl XXVI (1991 season), Super Bowl XXVII (1992 season) and Super Bowl XXVIII (1993 season). ... Member of Super Bowl championship team (1997 and 1998 seasons).
POST SEASON RECORDS: Holds Super Bowl career record for most games—6.
PRO STATISTICS: 1992—Recovered one fumble for 18 yards and a touchdown. 1993—Recovered one fumble. 1994—Recovered one fumble in end zone for a touchdown. 1997—Recovered one fumble.

Year Team	G	GS	SACKS
1990—Buffalo NFL	12	0	2.0
1991—Buffalo NFL	16	6	1.5
1992—Buffalo NFL	16	0	0.0
1993—Buffalo NFL	15	1	0.5
1994—Buffalo NFL	15	5	0.0
1995—Denver NFL	16	0	0.0
1996—Denver NFL	16	16	1.5
1997—Denver NFL	16	0	1.0
1998—Denver NFL	15	1	2.0
Pro totals (9 years)	137	29	8.5

LOFTON, STEVE CB PANTHERS

PERSONAL: Born November 26, 1968, in Jacksonville, Texas. ... 5-9/177. ... Full name: Steven Lynn Lofton.
HIGH SCHOOL: Alto (Texas).
COLLEGE: Texas A&M.
TRANSACTIONS/CAREER NOTES: Signed as non-drafted free agent by WLAF (January 31, 1991). ... Selected by Montreal Machine in third round (34th defensive back) of 1991 WLAF positional draft. ... Signed by Phoenix Cardinals (July 9, 1991). ... On injured reserve with hamstring injury (October 12-December 2, 1992). ... On practice squad (December 2, 1992-remainder of season). ... Cardinals franchise renamed Arizona Cardinals for 1994 season. ... Claimed on waivers by Cincinnati Bengals (August 4, 1994). ... Released by Bengals (August 7, 1994). ... Signed by Carolina Panthers (April 11, 1995). ... Granted unconditional free agency (February 14, 1997). ... Signed by New England Patriots (September 30, 1997). ... On injured reserve with hamstring injury (December 9, 1997-remainder of season). ... Claimed on waivers by Panthers (October 23, 1998). ... Granted unconditional free agency (February 12, 1999). ... Re-signed by Panthers (March 30, 1999).
CHAMPIONSHIP GAME EXPERIENCE: Member of Panthers for NFC championship game (1996 season); did not play.
PRO STATISTICS: W.L.: 1991—Recovered one fumble. NFL: 1993—Returned one kickoff for 18 yards.

			INTERCEPTIONS			
Year Team	G	GS	No.	Yds.	Avg.	TD
1991—Montreal W.L.	10	8	2	16	8.0	0
—Phoenix NFL	11	1	0	0	...	0
1992—Phoenix NFL	4	0	0	0	...	0
1993—Phoenix NFL	13	0	0	0	...	0
1994—			Did not play.			
1995—Carolina NFL	9	2	0	0	...	0
1996—Carolina NFL	11	3	1	42	42.0	0
1997—New England NFL	4	0	0	0	...	0
1998—New England NFL	6	0	0	0	...	0
—Carolina NFL	10	7	0	0	...	0
W.L. totals (1 year)	10	8	2	16	8.0	0
NFL totals (7 years)	68	13	1	42	42.0	0
Pro totals (8 years)	78	21	3	58	19.3	0

LOGAN, ERNIE DL JETS

PERSONAL: Born May 18, 1968, in Fort Bragg, N.C. ... 6-3/290. ... Full name: Ernest Edward Logan.
HIGH SCHOOL: Pine Forest (Fayetteville, N.C.).
COLLEGE: East Carolina.
TRANSACTIONS/CAREER NOTES: Selected by Atlanta Falcons in ninth round (226th pick overall) of 1991 NFL draft. ... Released by Falcons (August 19, 1991). ... Signed by Cleveland Browns (August 21, 1991). ... Released by Browns (September 8, 1993). ... Signed by Falcons (October 7, 1993). ... Granted free agency (February 17, 1994). ... Re-signed by Falcons (April 28, 1994). ... Released by Falcons (August 22, 1994). ... Signed by Jacksonville Jaguars (December 15, 1994). ... Granted unconditional free agency (February 14, 1997). ... Signed by New York Jets (March 20, 1997). ... On injured reserve with leg injury (December 15, 1997-remainder of season).
CHAMPIONSHIP GAME EXPERIENCE: Member of Jaguars for AFC championship game (1996 season); inactive. ... Played in AFC championship game (1998 season).
PRO STATISTICS: 1991—Recovered one fumble.

Year Team	G	GS	SACKS
1991—Cleveland NFL	15	5	0.5
1992—Cleveland NFL	16	0	1.0
1993—Atlanta NFL	8	1	1.0
1994—	Did not play.		
1995—Jacksonville NFL	15	1	3.0
1996—Jacksonville NFL	4	0	0.0
1997—New York Jets NFL	15	14	0.0
1998—New York Jets NFL	16	12	2.5
Pro totals (7 years)	89	33	8.0

LOGAN, JAMES LB SEAHAWKS

PERSONAL: Born December 6, 1972, in Opp, Ala. ... 6-2/225.
HIGH SCHOOL: Opp (Ala.).
JUNIOR COLLEGE: Jones County Junior College (Miss.).
COLLEGE: Memphis State.
TRANSACTIONS/CAREER NOTES: Signed as non-drafted free agent by Houston Oilers (May 3, 1995). ... Released by Oilers (August 27, 1995). ... Re-signed by Oilers to practice squad (August 30, 1995). ... Activated (September 15, 1995). ... Claimed on waivers by Cincinnati Bengals (October 18, 1995). ... Claimed on waivers by Seattle Seahawks (October 31, 1995). ... Assigned by Seahawks to Scottish Claymores in 1997 World League enhancement allocation program (February 19, 1997). ... On injured reserve with fractured leg (September 30, 1998-remainder of season). ... Granted unconditional free agency (February 12, 1999). ... Re-signed by Seahawks (March 23, 1999).

PLAYING EXPERIENCE: Houston (3)-Cincinnati (1)-Seattle (6) NFL, 1995; Seattle NFL, 1996; Scotland W.L., 1997; Seattle NFL, 1997 and 1998. ... Games/Games started: 1995 (Hou.-3/0; Cin.-1/0; Sea.-6/0; Total: 10/0), 1996 (6/0), 1997 (W.L.- games played unavailable; NFL- 14/1), 1998 (4/1). Total NFL: 34/2.
PRO STATISTICS: W.L.: 1997—Intercepted one pass for no yards, NFL: 1997—Recovered one fumble. 1998—Credited with one sack.

LOGAN, MIKE — S — JAGUARS

PERSONAL: Born September 15, 1974, in Pittsburgh. ... 6-0/206. ... Full name: Michael V. Logan.
HIGH SCHOOL: McKeesport (Pa.).
COLLEGE: West Virginia.
TRANSACTIONS/CAREER NOTES: Selected by Jacksonville Jaguars in second round (50th pick overall) of 1997 NFL draft. ... Signed by Jaguars (May 23, 1997).
PRO STATISTICS: 1998—Recovered one fumble for two yards.

			PUNT RETURNS				KICKOFF RETURNS				TOTALS		
Year Team	G	GS	No.	Yds.	Avg.	TD	No.	Yds.	Avg.	TD	TD	2pt.	Pts.	Fum.
1997—Jacksonville NFL	11	0	0	0	...	0	10	236	23.6	0	0	0	0	0
1998—Jacksonville NFL	15	0	2	26	13.0	0	18	414	23.0	0	0	0	0	1
Pro totals (2 years)	26	0	2	26	13.0	0	28	650	23.2	0	0	0	0	1

LONDON, ANTONIO — LB

PERSONAL: Born April 14, 1971, in Tullahoma, Tenn. ... 6-2/238. ... Full name: Antonio Monte London.
HIGH SCHOOL: Tullahoma (Tenn.).
COLLEGE: Alabama.
TRANSACTIONS/CAREER NOTES: Selected by Detroit Lions in third round (62nd pick overall) of 1993 NFL draft. ... Signed by Lions (July 17, 1993). ... Released by Lions (February 3, 1998). ... Signed by Green Bay Packers (February 24, 1998). ... On injured reserve with knee injury (September 17, 1998-remainder of season). ... Released by Packers (June 7, 1999).

Year Team	G	GS	SACKS
1993—Detroit NFL	14	0	1.0
1994—Detroit NFL	16	0	0.0
1995—Detroit NFL	15	0	7.0
1996—Detroit NFL	14	12	3.0
1997—Detroit NFL	16	6	2.0
1998—Green Bay NFL	1	0	0.0
Pro totals (6 years)	76	18	13.0

LONG, KEVIN — C — TITANS

PERSONAL: Born May 2, 1975, in Summerville, S.C. ... 6-5/295. ... Full name: Kevin Dale Long.
HIGH SCHOOL: Summerville (S.C.).
COLLEGE: Florida State.
TRANSACTIONS/CAREER NOTES: Selected by Tennessee Oilers in seventh round (229th pick overall) of 1998 NFL draft. ... Signed by Oilers (July 2, 1998). ... Oilers franchise renamed Tennessee Titans for 1999 season (December 26, 1998).
PLAYING EXPERIENCE: Tennessee NFL, 1998. ... Games/Games started: 16/2.

LONGWELL, RYAN — K — PACKERS

PERSONAL: Born August 16, 1974, in Seattle. ... 6-0/192. ... Full name: Ryan Walker Longwell.
HIGH SCHOOL: Bend (Ore.).
COLLEGE: California (degree in English).
TRANSACTIONS/CAREER NOTES: Signed as non-drafted free agent by San Francisco 49ers (April 28, 1997). ... Claimed on waivers by Green Bay Packers (July 10, 1997).
CHAMPIONSHIP GAME EXPERIENCE: Played in NFC championship game (1997 season). ... Played in Super Bowl XXXII (1997 season).

		KICKING						
Year Team	G	XPM	XPA	FGM	FGA	Lg.	50+	Pts.
1997—Green Bay NFL	16	*48	*48	24	30	50	1-1	120
1998—Green Bay NFL	16	41	43	29	33	45	0-1	128
Pro totals (2 years)	32	89	91	53	63	50	1-2	248

LOUD, KAMIL — WR — BILLS

PERSONAL: Born June 25, 1976, in Richmond, Calif. ... 6-0/190. ... Full name: Kamil Kassam Loud. ... Name pronounced KAY-meal.
HIGH SCHOOL: El Cerrito (Calif.).
COLLEGE: Cal Poly-SLO.
TRANSACTIONS/CAREER NOTES: Selected by Buffalo Bills in seventh round (238th pick overall) of 1998 NFL draft. ... Signed by Bills (June 8, 1998).
PLAYING EXPERIENCE: Buffalo NFL, 1998. ... Games/Games started: 5/0.
PRO STATISTICS: 1998—Recovered one fumble.

LOVE, CLARENCE — CB — EAGLES

PERSONAL: Born June 16, 1976, in Jackson, Mich. ... 5-10/181. ... Full name: Clarence Eugene Love.
HIGH SCHOOL: Jackson (Mich.).
COLLEGE: Toledo.
TRANSACTIONS/CAREER NOTES: Selected by Philadelphia Eagles in fourth round (116th pick overall) of 1998 NFL draft. ... Signed by Eagles (July 14, 1998). ... Assigned by Eagles to Frankfurt Galaxy in 1999 NFL Europe enhancement allocation program (February 22, 1999).
PLAYING EXPERIENCE: Philadelphia NFL, 1998. ... Games/Games started: 6/0.

LOVILLE, DEREK — RB — BRONCOS

PERSONAL: Born July 4, 1968, in San Francisco. ... 5-10/210. ... Full name: Derek Kevin Loville. ... Name pronounced luh-VILL.
HIGH SCHOOL: Riordan (San Francisco).
COLLEGE: Oregon (degree in American studies).
TRANSACTIONS/CAREER NOTES: Signed as non-drafted free agent by Seattle Seahawks (May 9, 1990). ... Granted unconditional free agency (February 1-April 1, 1991). ... Re-signed by Seahawks for 1991 season. ... Granted unconditional free agency (February 1, 1992). ... Signed by Los Angeles Rams (March 27, 1992). ... Released by Rams (August 31, 1992). ... Signed by San Francisco 49ers (March 22, 1993). ... On injured reserve with knee injury (August 30-November 10, 1993). ... Released by 49ers (November 10, 1993). ... Re-signed by 49ers (June 1, 1994). ... Granted unconditional free agency (February 17, 1995). ... Re-signed by 49ers (March 1, 1995). ... Released by 49ers (February 3, 1997). ... Signed by Denver Broncos (May 2, 1997). ... Granted unconditional free agency (February 13, 1998). ... Re-signed by Broncos (June 1, 1998).
CHAMPIONSHIP GAME EXPERIENCE: Played in NFC championship game (1994 season). ... Member of Super Bowl championship team (1994, 1997 and 1998 seasons). ... Played in AFC championship game (1997 and 1998 seasons).
PRO STATISTICS: 1991—Returned three punts for 16 yards and recovered one fumble.
SINGLE GAME HIGHS (regular season): Attempts—24 (December 3, 1995, vs. Buffalo); yards—88 (December 3, 1995, vs. Buffalo); and rushing touchdowns—1 (November 16, 1998, vs. Kansas City).

				RUSHING				RECEIVING				KICKOFF RETURNS				TOTALS		
Year Team	G	GS	Att.	Yds.	Avg.	TD	No.	Yds.	Avg.	TD	No.	Yds.	Avg.	TD	TD	2pt.	Pts.	Fum.
1990—Seattle NFL	11	1	7	12	1.7	0	0	0	...	0	18	359	19.9	0	0	...	0	1
1991—Seattle NFL	16	0	22	69	3.1	0	0	0	...	0	18	412	22.9	0	0	...	0	0
1992—									Did not play.									
1993—San Francisco NFL									Did not play.									
1994—San Francisco NFL	14	0	31	99	3.2	0	2	26	13.0	0	2	34	17.0	0	0	0	0	0
1995—San Francisco NFL	16	16	218	723	3.3	10	87	662	7.6	3	0	0	...	0	13	1	80	1
1996—San Francisco NFL	12	6	70	229	3.3	2	16	138	8.6	2	10	229	22.9	0	4	0	24	0
1997—Denver NFL	16	0	25	124	5.0	1	2	10	5.0	0	5	136	27.2	0	1	0	6	1
1998—Denver NFL	16	0	53	161	3.0	2	2	29	14.5	0	6	105	17.5	0	2	0	12	0
Pro totals (7 years)	101	23	426	1417	3.3	15	109	865	7.9	5	59	1275	21.6	0	20	1	122	3

LOWE, REGGIE — LB — JAGUARS

PERSONAL: Born June 14, 1975, in Phenix City, Ala. ... 6-2/240. ... Full name: Reginald James Lowe.
HIGH SCHOOL: Central High (Phenix City, Ala.).
COLLEGE: Troy State (degree in human services).
TRANSACTIONS/CAREER NOTES: Signed as non-drafted free agent by Seattle Seahawks (April 20, 1998). ... Released by Seahawks (August 30, 1998). ... Signed by Baltimore Ravens to practice squad (September 2, 1998). ... Released by Ravens (September 29, 1998). ... Signed by Jacksonville Jaguars to practice squad (October 1, 1998). ... Activated (November 24, 1998). ... Assigned by Jaguars to Rhein Fire in 1999 NFL Europe enhancement allocation program (February 22, 1999).
PLAYING EXPERIENCE: Jacksonville NFL, 1998. ... Games/Games started: 4/0.

LUCAS, RAY — QB — JETS

PERSONAL: Born August 6, 1972, in Harrison, N.J. ... 6-3/214.
HIGH SCHOOL: Harrison (N.J.).
COLLEGE: Rutgers.
TRANSACTIONS/CAREER NOTES: Signed as non-drafted free agent by New England Patriots (May 1, 1996). ... Released by Patriots (August 25, 1996). ... Re-signed by Patriots to practice squad (August 27, 1996). ... Activated (December 12, 1996). ... Claimed on waivers by New York Jets (August 19, 1997). ... Released by Jets (August 24, 1997). ... Re-signed by Jets to practice squad (August 26, 1997). ... Activated (November 22, 1997).
CHAMPIONSHIP GAME EXPERIENCE: Played in AFC championship game (1996 season). ... Played in Super Bowl XXXI (1996 season). ... Member of Jets for AFC championship game (1998 season); did not play.
SINGLE GAME HIGHS (regular season): Attempts—4 (December 21, 1997, vs. Detroit); completions—3 (December 21, 1997, vs. Detroit); yards—28 (December 21, 1997, vs. Detroit); and touchdown passes—0.

					PASSING						RUSHING				TOTALS	
Year Team	G	GS	Att.	Cmp.	Pct.	Yds.	TD	Int.	Avg.	Rat.	Att.	Yds.	Avg.	TD	TD	2pt.	Pts.
1996—New England NFL	2	0	0	0	...	0	0	0	...	...	0	0	...	0	0	0	0
1997—New York Jets NFL	5	0	4	3	75.0	28	0	1	7.00	54.2	6	55	9.2	0	0	0	0
1998—New York Jets NFL	15	0	3	1	33.3	27	0	0	9.00	67.4	5	23	4.6	0	0	0	0
Pro totals (3 years)	22	0	7	4	57.1	55	0	1	7.86	42.9	11	78	7.1	0	0	0	0

LUSK, HENRY — TE — REDSKINS

PERSONAL: Born May 8, 1972, in Seaside, Calif. ... 6-2/250. ... Full name: Hendrick H. Lusk.
HIGH SCHOOL: Monterey (Calif.).
COLLEGE: Utah (degree in sociology, 1995).
TRANSACTIONS/CAREER NOTES: Selected by New Orleans Saints in seventh round (246th pick overall) of 1996 NFL draft. ... Signed by Saints (July 12, 1996). ... Released by Saints (June 4, 1997). ... Signed by Green Bay Packers (June 19, 1997). ... Released by Packers (August 13, 1997). ... Signed by Washington Redskins (December 31, 1997). ... Claimed on waivers by Miami Dolphins (August 26, 1998). ... Released by Dolphins (March 25, 1999). ... Signed by Redskins (April 6, 1999).
PRO STATISTICS: 1996—Returned one kickoff for 16 yards. 1998—Rushed once for seven yards.
SINGLE GAME HIGHS (regular season): Receptions—4 (November 24, 1996, vs. Tampa Bay); yards—32 (October 6, 1996, vs. Jacksonville); and touchdown receptions—0.

				RECEIVING			TOTALS			
Year Team	G	GS	No.	Yds.	Avg.	TD	TD	2pt.	Pts.	Fum.
1996—New Orleans NFL	16	3	27	210	7.8	0	0	0	0	1
1997—						Did not play.				
1998—Miami NFL	3	1	0	0	...	0	0	0	0	0
Pro totals (2 years)	19	4	27	210	7.8	0	0	0	0	1

LYGHT, TODD — CB — RAMS

PERSONAL: Born February 9, 1969, in Kwajalein, Marshall Islands. ... 6-0/190. ... Full name: Todd William Lyght.
HIGH SCHOOL: Luke M. Powers Catholic (Flint, Mich.).
COLLEGE: Notre Dame.
TRANSACTIONS/CAREER NOTES: Selected by Los Angeles Rams in first round (fifth pick overall) of 1991 NFL draft. ... Signed by Rams (August 16, 1991). ... On injured reserve with shoulder injury (September 22-October 22, 1992). ... On injured reserve with knee injury (November 23, 1993-remainder of season). ... Designated by Rams as transition player (February 15, 1994). ... Rams franchise moved to St. Louis (April 12, 1995). ... Tendered offer sheet by Jacksonville Jaguars (April 12, 1996). ... Offer matched by Rams (April 15, 1996).
HONORS: Named defensive back on THE SPORTING NEWS college All-America first team (1989). ... Named defensive back on THE SPORTING NEWS college All-America second team (1990).
PRO STATISTICS: 1991—Fumbled once and recovered one fumble. 1993—Recovered one fumble for 13 yards. 1994—Returned one punt for 29 yards and recovered one fumble for 74 yards and a touchdown. 1995—Ran 16 yards with lateral from punt return. 1996—Fumbled once. 1997—Credited with one sack and recovered two fumbles. 1998—Credited with 1½ sacks.

			INTERCEPTIONS			
Year Team	G	GS	No.	Yds.	Avg.	TD
1991—Los Angeles Rams NFL	12	8	1	0	0.0	0
1992—Los Angeles Rams NFL	12	12	3	80	26.7	0
1993—Los Angeles Rams NFL	9	9	2	0	0.0	0
1994—Los Angeles Rams NFL	16	16	1	14	14.0	0
1995—St. Louis NFL	16	16	4	34	8.5	1
1996—St. Louis NFL	16	16	5	43	8.6	1
1997—St. Louis NFL	16	16	4	25	6.3	0
1998—St. Louis NFL	16	16	3	30	10.0	0
Pro totals (8 years)	113	109	23	226	9.8	2

LYLE, KEITH — S — RAMS

PERSONAL: Born April 17, 1972, in Washington, D.C. ... 6-2/210. ... Full name: Keith Allen Lyle. ... Son of Garry Lyle, free safety/running back with Chicago Bears (1968-74).
HIGH SCHOOL: Mendon (N.Y.), then George C. Marshall (Falls Church, Va.).
COLLEGE: Virginia (degree in psychology, 1993).
TRANSACTIONS/CAREER NOTES: Selected by Los Angeles Rams in third round (71st pick overall) of 1994 NFL draft. ... Signed by Rams (July 8, 1994). ... Rams franchise moved to St. Louis (April 12, 1995). ... Granted free agency (February 14, 1997). ... Re-signed by Rams (April 15, 1997).
PRO STATISTICS: 1995—Rushed once for four yards. 1996—Rushed three times for 39 yards and fumbled once. 1997—Credited with two sacks. 1998—Credited with one sack.

			INTERCEPTIONS			
Year Team	G	GS	No.	Yds.	Avg.	TD
1994—Los Angeles Rams NFL	16	0	2	1	0.5	0
1995—St. Louis NFL	16	16	3	42	14.0	0
1996—St. Louis NFL	16	16	†9	‡152	16.9	0
1997—St. Louis NFL	16	16	8	102	12.8	0
1998—St. Louis NFL	16	16	3	20	6.7	0
Pro totals (5 years)	80	64	25	317	12.7	0

LYLE, RICK — DL — JETS

PERSONAL: Born February 26, 1971, in Monroe, La. ... 6-5/290. ... Full name: Rick James Earl Lyle.
HIGH SCHOOL: Hickman Mills (Kansas City, Mo.).
COLLEGE: Missouri (degree in parks, recreation and tourism).
TRANSACTIONS/CAREER NOTES: Signed as non-drafted free agent by Cleveland Browns (May 2, 1994). ... On injured reserve with back injury (September 2, 1995-entire season). ... Browns franchise moved to Baltimore and renamed Ravens for 1996 season (March 11, 1996). ... Granted unconditional free agency (February 14, 1997). ... Signed by New York Jets (March 24, 1997).
PLAYING EXPERIENCE: Cleveland NFL, 1994; Baltimore NFL, 1996; New York Jets NFL, 1997 and 1998. ... Games/Games started: 1994 (3/0), 1996 (11/3), 1997 (16/16), 1998 (16/16). Total: 46/35.
CHAMPIONSHIP GAME EXPERIENCE: Played in AFC championship game (1998 season).
PRO STATISTICS: 1997—Credited with three sacks and recovered one fumble for two yards. 1998—Credited with 1½ sacks.

LYNCH, JOHN — S — BUCCANEERS

PERSONAL: Born September 25, 1971, in Hinsdale, Ill. ... 6-2/216. ... Full name: John Terrence Lynch. ... Son of John Lynch, linebacker with Pittsburgh Steelers (1969); brother-in-law of John Allred, tight end, Chicago Bears; and brother of Ryan Lynch, pitcher in San Diego Padres organization.
HIGH SCHOOL: Torrey Pines (Encinitas, Calif.).
COLLEGE: Stanford.
TRANSACTIONS/CAREER NOTES: Selected by Tampa Bay Buccaneers in third round (82nd pick overall) of 1993 NFL draft. ... Signed by Buccaneers (June 1, 1993). ... On injured reserve with knee injury (December 12, 1995-remainder of season). ... Granted free agency (February 16, 1996). ... Re-signed by Buccaneers (July 13, 1996).
HONORS: Played in Pro Bowl (1997 season).
PRO STATISTICS: 1996—Rushed once for 40 yards, credited with one sack, fumbled once and recovered one fumble. 1997—Recovered two fumbles. 1998—Credited with two sacks and recovered one fumble.

				INTERCEPTIONS		
Year Team	G	GS	No.	Yds.	Avg.	TD
1993—Tampa Bay NFL	15	4	0	0	...	0
1994—Tampa Bay NFL	16	0	0	0	...	0
1995—Tampa Bay NFL	9	6	3	3	1.0	0
1996—Tampa Bay NFL	16	14	3	26	8.7	0
1997—Tampa Bay NFL	16	16	2	28	14.0	0
1998—Tampa Bay NFL	15	15	2	29	14.5	0
Pro totals (6 years)	87	55	10	86	8.6	0

RECORD AS BASEBALL PLAYER

TRANSACTIONS/CAREER NOTES: Threw right, batted right. ... Selected by Florida Marlins organization in second round (66th pick overall) of free-agent draft (June 1, 1992).

PITCHING TOTALS

Year Team (League)	W	L	Pct.	ERA	G	GS	CG	ShO	Sv.	IP	H	R	ER	BB	SO
1992—Erie (N.Y.-Penn.)	0	3	.000	2.15	7	7	0	0	0	29 1/3	24	15	7	17	16
1993—Kane County (Midwest)	1	0	1.000	3.00	2	2	0	0	0	9	4	4	3	12	3
Totals (2 years)	1	3	.250	2.35	9	9	0	0	0	38 1/3	28	19	10	29	10

LYNN, ANTHONY — FB — BRONCOS

PERSONAL: Born December 21, 1968, in McKinney, Texas. ... 6-3/230. ... Full name: Anthony Ray Lynn.
HIGH SCHOOL: Celina (Texas).
COLLEGE: Texas Tech.
TRANSACTIONS/CAREER NOTES: Signed as non-drafted free agent by New York Giants (May 5, 1992). ... Released by Giants (August 31, 1992). ... Signed by Denver Broncos (April 21, 1993). ... Released by Broncos (August 23, 1994). ... Signed by San Francisco 49ers (March 28, 1995). ... Granted unconditional free agency (February 14, 1997). ... Signed by Broncos (March 4, 1997).
PLAYING EXPERIENCE: Denver NFL, 1993, 1997 and 1998; San Francisco NFL, 1995 and 1996. ... Games/Games started: 1993 (13/0), 1995 (6/0), 1996 (16/1), 1997 (16/0), 1998 (16/0). Total: 67/1.
CHAMPIONSHIP GAME EXPERIENCE: Played in AFC championship game (1997 and 1998 seasons). ... Member of Super Bowl championship team (1997 and 1998 seasons).
PRO STATISTICS: 1995—Rushed twice for 11 yards. 1996—Rushed 24 times for 164 yards and caught two passes for 14 yards. 1997—Caught one pass for 21 yards.
SINGLE GAME HIGHS (regular season): Attempts—2 (October 6, 1996, vs. St. Louis); yards—21 (November 9, 1997, vs. Carolina); and rushing touchdowns—0.

LYON, BILLY — DT — PACKERS

PERSONAL: Born December 10, 1973, in Ashland, Ky. ... 6-5/295. ... Full name: William Morton Lyon.
HIGH SCHOOL: Lloyd (Erlanger, Ky.).
COLLEGE: Marshall (degree in occupational safety).
TRANSACTIONS/CAREER NOTES: Signed as non-drafted free agent by Kansas City Chiefs (April 21, 1997). ... Released by Chiefs (August 15, 1997). ... Signed by Green Bay Packers to practice squad (November 20, 1997)
PLAYING EXPERIENCE: Green Bay NFL, 1998. ... Games/Games started: 4/0.
PRO STATISTICS: 1998—Credited with one sack.

LYONS, MITCH — TE — STEELERS

PERSONAL: Born May 13, 1970, in Grand Rapids, Mich. ... 6-5/268. ... Full name: Mitchell Warren Lyons.
HIGH SCHOOL: Forest Hills Northern (Grand Rapids, Mich.).
COLLEGE: Michigan State.
TRANSACTIONS/CAREER NOTES: Selected by Atlanta Falcons in sixth round (151st pick overall) of 1993 NFL draft. ... Signed by Falcons (May 26, 1993). ... Granted free agency (February 16, 1996). ... Re-signed by Falcons (June 12, 1996). ... Granted unconditional free agency (February 14, 1997). ... Signed by Pittsburgh Steelers (April 21, 1997). ... On injured reserve with knee injury (November 11, 1997-remainder of season). ... Released by Steelers (September 26, 1998). ... Re-signed by Steelers (September 28, 1998).
PRO STATISTICS: 1998—Rushed twice for minus four yards.
SINGLE GAME HIGHS (regular season): Receptions—4 (October 23, 1994, vs. Los Angeles Raiders); yards—34 (November 26, 1995, vs. Arizona); and touchdown receptions—1 (December 8, 1996, vs. New Orleans).

Year Team	G	GS	RECEIVING No.	Yds.	Avg.	TD	TOTALS TD	2pt.	Pts.	Fum.
1993—Atlanta NFL	16	8	8	63	7.9	0	0	...	0	0
1994—Atlanta NFL	7	2	7	54	7.7	0	0	0	0	0
1995—Atlanta NFL	13	5	5	83	16.6	0	0	0	0	0
1996—Atlanta NFL	14	4	4	16	4.0	1	1	0	6	0
1997—Pittsburgh NFL	10	3	4	29	7.3	0	0	0	0	0
1998—Pittsburgh NFL	15	0	3	19	6.3	0	0	0	0	0
Pro totals (6 years)	75	22	31	264	8.5	1	1	0	6	0

LYONS, PRATT — DT/DE — TITANS

PERSONAL: Born September 17, 1974, in Fort Worth, Texas. ... 6-5/295.
HIGH SCHOOL: Trimble (Fort Worth, Texas).
COLLEGE: Utah State, then Troy (Ala.) State.
TRANSACTIONS/CAREER NOTES: Selected by Houston Oilers in fourth round (107th pick overall) of 1997 NFL draft. ... Oilers franchise moved to Tennessee for 1997 season. ... Signed by Oilers (July 15, 1997). ... Oilers franchise renamed Tennessee Titans for 1999 season (December 26, 1998).

Year Team	G	GS	SACKS
1997—Tennessee NFL	16	0	2.5
1998—Tennessee NFL	16	12	2.0
Pro totals (2 years)	32	12	4.5

MACK, TREMAIN — S — BENGALS

PERSONAL: Born November 21, 1974, in Tyler, Texas. ... 6-0/193. ... Nephew of Phillip Epps, wide receiver with Green Bay Packers (1982-88) and New York Jets (1989).
HIGH SCHOOL: Chapel Hill (Tyler, Texas).
COLLEGE: Miami (Fla.).
TRANSACTIONS/CAREER NOTES: Selected by Cincinnati Bengals in fourth round (111th pick overall) of 1997 NFL draft. ... Signed by Bengals (June 5, 1997). ... On non-football injury list with illness (November 5-December 1, 1997). ... On exempt/left squad list (December 3, 1998-remainder of season).
PRO STATISTICS: 1998—Recovered one fumble.

Year Team	G	GS	INTERCEPTIONS No.	Yds.	Avg.	TD	KICKOFF RETURNS No.	Yds.	Avg.	TD	TOTALS TD	2pt.	Pts.	Fum.
1997—Cincinnati NFL	4	4	1	29	29.0	0	0	0	...	0	0	0	0	0
1998—Cincinnati NFL	12	0	0	0	...	0	45	1165	25.9	▲1	1	0	6	2
Pro totals (2 years)	16	4	1	29	29.0	0	45	1165	25.9	1	1	0	6	2

MADDOX, MARK — LB — CARDINALS

PERSONAL: Born March 23, 1968, in Milwaukee. ... 6-1/233. ... Full name: Mark Anthony Maddox.
HIGH SCHOOL: James Madison Memorial (Madison, Wis.).
COLLEGE: Northern Michigan.
TRANSACTIONS/CAREER NOTES: Selected by Buffalo Bills in ninth round (249th pick overall) of 1991 NFL draft. ... Signed by Bills (June 18, 1991). ... On injured reserve with knee injury (August 27, 1991-entire season). ... On injured reserve with knee injury (October 10, 1995-remainder of season). ... Granted unconditional free agency (February 16, 1996). ... Re-signed by Bills (March 4, 1996). ... Released by Bills (June 2, 1997). ... Re-signed by Bills (July 2, 1997). ... Released by Bills (August 12, 1997). ... Re-signed by Bills (October 28, 1997). ... Granted unconditional free agency (February 13, 1998). ... Signed by Arizona Cardinals (March 19, 1998). ... Granted unconditional free agency (February 12, 1999). ... Re-signed by Cardinals (April 2, 1999).
PLAYING EXPERIENCE: Buffalo NFL, 1992-1997; Arizona NFL, 1998. ... Games/Games started: 1992 (15/1), 1993 (11/8), 1994 (15/14), 1995 (4/4), 1996 (14/14), 1997 (8/1), 1998 (14/3). Total: 81/45.
CHAMPIONSHIP GAME EXPERIENCE: Played in AFC championship game (1992 and 1993 season). ... Played in Super Bowl XXVII (1992 season) and Super Bowl XXVIII (1993 season).
PRO STATISTICS: 1993—Recovered two fumbles. 1994—Intercepted one pass for 11 yards and recovered one fumble. 1997—Intercepted one pass for 25 yards. 1998—Credited with one sack and recovered one fumble.

MADISON, SAM — CB — DOLPHINS

PERSONAL: Born April 23, 1974, in Thomasville, Ga. ... 5-11/185. ... Full name: Samuel A. Madison Jr.
HIGH SCHOOL: Florida A&M High (Monticello, Fla.).
COLLEGE: Louisville.
TRANSACTIONS/CAREER NOTES: Selected by Miami Dolphins in second round (44th pick overall) of 1997 NFL draft. ... Signed by Dolphins (June 16, 1997).
PRO STATISTICS: 1998—Credited with one sack.

Year Team	G	GS	INTERCEPTIONS No.	Yds.	Avg.	TD
1997—Miami NFL	14	3	1	21	21.0	0
1998—Miami NFL	16	16	8	114	14.3	0
Pro totals (2 years)	30	19	9	135	15.0	0

MAMULA, MIKE — LB/DE — EAGLES

PERSONAL: Born August 14, 1973, in Lackawanna, N.Y. ... 6-4/252. ... Full name: Michael David Mamula. ... Name pronounced ma-MOO-lah.
HIGH SCHOOL: Lackawanna (N.Y.) Secondary.
COLLEGE: Boston College (degree in sociology, 1994).
TRANSACTIONS/CAREER NOTES: Selected after junior season by Philadelphia Eagles in first round (seventh pick overall) of 1995 NFL draft. ... Signed by Eagles (July 19, 1995). ... On injured reserve with knee injury (August 18, 1998-entire season). ... Granted unconditional free agency (February 12, 1999). ... Re-signed by Eagles (February 12, 1999).
PRO STATISTICS: 1995—Recovered one fumble for 25 yards. 1996—Recovered three fumbles for four yards and a touchdown.

Year Team	G	GS	SACKS
1995—Philadelphia NFL	14	13	5.5
1996—Philadelphia NFL	16	16	8.0
1997—Philadelphia NFL	16	16	4.0
1998—Philadelphia NFL	Did not play.		
Pro totals (3 years)	46	45	17.5

MANDARICH, TONY — G — COLTS

PERSONAL: Born September 23, 1966, in Oakville, Ont. ... 6-5/324. ... Full name: Tony Joseph Mandarich. ... Brother of John Mandarich, defensive tackle with Edmonton Eskimos (1984-89) and Ottawa Rough Riders of CFL (1990).
HIGH SCHOOL: White Oaks (Ont.), then Roosevelt (Kent, Ohio).
COLLEGE: Michigan State (degree in telecommunications, 1990).
TRANSACTIONS/CAREER NOTES: Selected by Green Bay Packers in first round (second pick overall) of 1989 NFL draft. ... Signed by Packers (September 5, 1989). ... Granted roster exemption (September 5-18, 1989). ... On reserve/non-football injury list with thyroid problem (September 1, 1992-entire season). ... Granted free agency (March 1, 1993). ... Out of pro football (1993-95). ... Signed by Indianapolis Colts (February 22, 1996). ... Granted free agency (February 13, 1998). ... Tendered offer sheet by Chicago Bears (March 12, 1998). ... Offer matched by Colts (March 18, 1998). ... On injured reserve with back injury (December 2, 1998-remainder of season).
PLAYING EXPERIENCE: Green Bay NFL, 1989-1991; Indianapolis NFL, 1996-1998. ... Games/Games started: 1989 (14/0), 1990 (16/16), 1991 (15/15), 1996 (15/6), 1997 (16/16), 1998 (10/10). Total: 86/63.
HONORS: Named offensive tackle on THE SPORTING NEWS college All-America second team (1987). ... Named offensive tackle on THE SPORTING NEWS college All-America first team (1988).
PRO STATISTICS: 1989—Returned one kickoff for no yards. 1990—Recovered one fumble. 1997—Recovered one fumble.

MANGUM, JOHN — S

PERSONAL: Born March 16, 1967, in Magee, Miss. ... 5-10/190. ... Full name: John Wayne Mangum Jr. ... Son of John Mangum, defensive tackle with Boston Patriots of AFL (1966 and 1967); brother of Kris Mangum, tight end, Carolina Panthers.
HIGH SCHOOL: Magee (Miss.).
COLLEGE: Alabama (degree in finance).
TRANSACTIONS/CAREER NOTES: Selected by Chicago Bears in sixth round (144th pick overall) of 1990 NFL draft. ... Signed by Bears (July 24, 1990). ... Released by Bears (September 3, 1990). ... Signed by Tampa Bay Buccaneers to practice squad (October 1, 1990). ... Signed by Bears off Buccaneers practice squad (October 23, 1990). ... On injured reserve with knee injury (October 8, 1992-remainder of season). ... Granted free agency (March 1, 1993). ... Re-signed by Bears (May 17, 1993). ... Granted unconditional free agency (February 17, 1995). ... Re-signed by Bears (March 2, 1995). ... Granted unconditional free agency (February 13, 1998). ... Re-signed by Bears (February 18, 1998). ... Announced retirement due to injury (September 30, 1998).
PRO STATISTICS: 1990—Recovered one fumble. 1991—Recovered two fumbles. 1993—Returned one kickoff for no yards. 1997—Recovered three fumbles.

			INTERCEPTIONS				SACKS
Year Team	G	GS	No.	Yds.	Avg.	TD	No.
1990—Chicago NFL	10	0	0	0	...	0	1.0
1991—Chicago NFL	16	1	1	5	5.0	0	1.0
1992—Chicago NFL	5	1	0	0	...	0	0.0
1993—Chicago NFL	12	1	1	0	0.0	0	0.0
1994—Chicago NFL	16	3	0	0	...	0	0.5
1995—Chicago NFL	11	1	1	2	2.0	0	1.0
1996—Chicago NFL	16	2	0	0	...	0	1.0
1997—Chicago NFL	16	16	2	4	2.0	0	1.0
1998—Chicago NFL	3	0	0	0	...	0	0.0
Pro totals (9 years)	105	25	5	11	2.2	0	5.5

MANGUM, KRIS — TE — PANTHERS

PERSONAL: Born August 15, 1973, in Magee, Miss. ... 6-4/249. ... Full name: Kris Thomas Mangum. ... Son of John Mangum, defensive tackle with Boston Patriots (1966 and 1967) of AFL; and brother of John Mangum, cornerback with Chicago Bears (1990-98).
HIGH SCHOOL: Magee (Miss.).
COLLEGE: Mississippi.
TRANSACTIONS/CAREER NOTES: Selected by Carolina Panthers in seventh round (228th pick overall) of 1997 NFL draft. ... Signed by Panthers (May 20, 1997). ... Released by Panthers (September 2, 1997). ... Re-signed by Panthers to practice squad (September 4, 1997). ... Activated (December 5, 1997).
PLAYING EXPERIENCE: Carolina NFL, 1997 and 1998. ... Games/Games started: 1997 (2/1), 1998 (6/0). Total: 8/1.
PRO STATISTICS: 1997—Caught four passes for 56 yards. 1998—Caught one pass for five yards.
SINGLE GAME HIGHS (regular season): Receptions—4 (December 20, 1997, vs. St. Louis); yards—56 (December 20, 1997, vs. St. Louis); and touchdown receptions—0.

MANIECKI, JASON — DT

PERSONAL: Born August 15, 1972, in Rabka, Poland. ... 6-4/291. ... Full name: Jason Zbiyniew Maniecki. ... Name pronounced muh-NECK-ee.
HIGH SCHOOL: Wisconsin Dells (Wis.).
COLLEGE: Wisconsin.
TRANSACTIONS/CAREER NOTES: Selected by Tampa Bay Buccaneers in fifth round (140th pick overall) of 1996 NFL draft. ... Signed by Buccaneers (July 16, 1996). ... On injured reserve with back injury (November 11, 1998-remainder of season). ... Released by Buccaneers (February 12, 1999).
PLAYING EXPERIENCE: Tampa Bay NFL, 1996-1998. ... Games/Games started: 1996 (5/0), 1997 (10/0), 1998 (3/0). Total: 18/0.
PRO STATISTICS: 1997—Credited with one sack and recovered one fumble.

MANNELLY, PATRICK — OT — BEARS

PERSONAL: Born April 18, 1975, in Atlanta. ... 6-5/285. ... Full name: James Patrick Mannelly.
HIGH SCHOOL: Marist (Atlanta).
COLLEGE: Duke.
TRANSACTIONS/CAREER NOTES: Selected by Chicago Bears in sixth round (189th pick overall) of 1998 NFL draft. ... Signed by Bears (June 11, 1998).
PLAYING EXPERIENCE: Chicago NFL, 1998. ... Games/Games started: 16/0.

MANNING, BRIAN — WR — PACKERS

PERSONAL: Born April 22, 1975, in Kansas City, Kan. ... 5-11/186. ... Full name: Brian Keith Manning.
HIGH SCHOOL: Ruskin (Kansas City, Mo.).
COLLEGE: Stanford.
TRANSACTIONS/CAREER NOTES: Selected by Miami Dolphins in sixth round (170th pick overall) of 1997 NFL draft. ... Signed by Dolphins (June 17, 1997). ... Released by Dolphins (August 30, 1998). ... Signed by Green Bay Packers to practice squad (September 2, 1998). ... Activated (December 8, 1998).
PLAYING EXPERIENCE: Miami NFL, 1997; Green Bay NFL, 1998. ... Games/Games started: 1997 (7/0), 1998 (3/0). Total: 10/0.
PRO STATISTICS: 1997—Caught seven passes for 85 yards and recovered one fumble for minus one yard.
SINGLE GAME HIGHS (regular season): Receptions—5 (November 23, 1997, vs. New England); yards—60 (November 23, 1997, vs. New England); and touchdown receptions—0.

MANNING, PEYTON — QB — COLTS

PERSONAL: Born March 24, 1976, in New Orleans. ... 6-5/230. ... Full name: Peyton Williams Manning. ... Son of Archie Manning, quarterback with New Orleans Saints (1971-82), Houston Oilers (1982-83) and Minnesota Vikings (1983-84).
HIGH SCHOOL: Isidore Newman (New Orleans).
COLLEGE: Tennessee (degree in speech communication).
TRANSACTIONS/CAREER NOTES: Selected by Indianapolis Colts in first round (first pick overall) of 1998 NFL draft. ... Signed by Colts (July 28, 1998).
HONORS: Davey O'Brien Award winner (1997). ... Named College Player of the Year by THE SPORTING NEWS (1997). ... Named quarterback on THE SPORTING NEWS college All-America second team (1997).
RECORDS: Holds NFL rookie-season records for most passes attempted—575 (1998); most passes completed—326 (1998); and most yards passing—3,739.
PRO STATISTICS: 1998—Fumbled three times.
SINGLE GAME HIGHS (regular season): Attempts—52 (November 1, 1998, vs. New England); completions—30 (November 1, 1998, vs. New England); yards—357 (November 29, 1998, vs. Baltimore); and touchdown passes—3 (December 13, 1998, vs. Cincinnati).
STATISTICAL PLATEAUS: 300-yard passing games: 1998 (4).
MISCELLANEOUS: Regular-season record as starting NFL quarterback: 3-13 (.188).

				PASSING						RUSHING				TOTALS		
Year Team	G	GS	Att.	Cmp.	Pct.	Yds.	TD	Int.	Avg.	Rat.	Att.	Yds.	Avg.	TD	TD	2pt.	Pts.
1998—Indianapolis NFL	16	16	*575	§326	56.7	§3739	26	*28	6.50	71.2	15	62	4.1	0	0	0	0

MANUEL, ROD — DE — BROWNS

PERSONAL: Born October 8, 1974, in Fort Worth, Texas. ... 6-5/295. ... Full name: Roderick Demond Manuel.
HIGH SCHOOL: Western Hills (Fort Worth, Texas).
COLLEGE: Oklahoma.
TRANSACTIONS/CAREER NOTES: Selected by Pittsburgh Steelers in sixth round (199th pick overall) of 1997 NFL draft. ... Signed by Steelers (June 17, 1997). ... Selected by Cleveland Browns from Steelers in NFL expansion draft (February 9, 1999).
PLAYING EXPERIENCE: Pittsburgh NFL, 1997 and 1998. ... Games/Games started: 1997 (1/0), 1998 (2/0). Total: 3/0.
CHAMPIONSHIP GAME EXPERIENCE: Member of Steelers for AFC championship game (1997); inactive.

MANUSKY, GREG — LB — CHIEFS

PERSONAL: Born August 12, 1966, in Wilkes-Barre, Pa. ... 6-1/234. ... Full name: Gregory Manusky.
HIGH SCHOOL: Dallas (Pa.).
COLLEGE: Colgate (degrees in education and geology, 1988).
TRANSACTIONS/CAREER NOTES: Signed as non-drafted free agent by Washington Redskins (May 3, 1988). ... On injured reserve with thigh injury (August 29-November 4, 1988). ... Granted unconditional free agency (February 1, 1991). ... Signed by Minnesota Vikings (March 27,

1991). ... On injured reserve with kidney injury (November 24-December 23, 1992). ... Granted unconditional free agency (March 1, 1993). ... Re-signed by Vikings for 1993 season. ... Released by Vikings (August 30, 1993). ... Re-signed by Vikings (August 31, 1993). ... Released by Vikings (August 22, 1994). ... Signed by Kansas City Chiefs (August 31, 1994). ... Granted unconditional free agency (February 16, 1996). ... Re-signed by Chiefs (April 9, 1996). ... Granted unconditional free agency (February 13, 1998). ... Re-signed by Chiefs (April 24, 1998).
PLAYING EXPERIENCE: Washington NFL, 1988-1990; Minnesota NFL, 1991-1993; Kansas City NFL, 1994-1998. ... Games/Games started: 1988 (7/0), 1989 (16/7), 1990 (16/8), 1991 (16/0), 1992 (11/0), 1993 (16/0), 1994 (16/2), 1995 (16/1), 1996 (16/1), 1997 (16/1), 1998 (16/1). Total: 162/21.
PRO STATISTICS: 1989—Recovered one fumble. 1994—Recovered two fumbles. 1996—Returned two kickoffs for 32 yards, fumbled once and recovered three fumbles. 1997—Returned one kickoff for 16 yards and recovered one fumble. 1998—Returned three kickoffs for 20 yards and recovered two fumbles for seven yards.

MARE, OLINDO   K   DOLPHINS

PERSONAL: Born June 6, 1973, in Hollywood, Fla. ... 5-10/190. ... Full name: Olindo Franco Mare. ... Name pronounced oh-LYNN-doe muh-RAY.
HIGH SCHOOL: Cooper City (Fla.).
JUNIOR COLLEGE: Valencia Community College (Fla.).
COLLEGE: Syracuse.
TRANSACTIONS/CAREER NOTES: Signed as non-drafted free agent by New York Giants (May 2, 1996). ... Released by Giants (August 25, 1996). ... Re-signed by Giants to practice squad (August 27, 1996). ... Granted free agency after 1996 season. ... Signed by Miami Dolphins (February 27, 1997).

			PUNTING					KICKING				
Year Team	G	No.	Yds.	Avg.	Net avg.	In. 20	Blk.	XPM	XPA	FGM	FGA	Lg.	50+	Pts.
1996—New York Giants NFL							Did not play.							
1997—Miami NFL	16	5	235	47.0	46.2	2	0	33	33	28	36	50	1-3	117
1998—Miami NFL	16	3	115	38.3	31.7	1	0	33	34	22	27	48	0-2	99
Pro totals (2 years)	32	8	350	43.8	40.8	3	0	66	67	50	63	50	1-5	216

MARINO, DAN   QB   DOLPHINS

PERSONAL: Born September 15, 1961, in Pittsburgh. ... 6-4/228. ... Full name: Daniel Constantine Marino Jr. ... Brother-in-law of Bill Maas, nose tackle with Kansas City Chiefs (1984-92) and Green Bay Packers (1993); and current NFL broadcaster, Fox Sports.
HIGH SCHOOL: Central Catholic (Pittsburgh).
COLLEGE: Pittsburgh (degree in communications).
TRANSACTIONS/CAREER NOTES: Selected by Los Angeles Express in first round (first pick overall) of 1983 USFL draft. ... Selected by Miami Dolphins in first round (27th pick overall) of 1983 NFL draft. ... Signed by Dolphins (July 9, 1983). ... Left Dolphins camp voluntarily (July 25-August 31, 1985). ... Granted roster exemption (September 1-5, 1985). ... On injured reserve with Achilles' tendon injury (October 13, 1993-remainder of season).
CHAMPIONSHIP GAME EXPERIENCE: Played in AFC championship game (1984, 1985 and 1992 seasons). ... Played in Super Bowl XIX (1984 season).
HONORS: Named quarterback on THE SPORTING NEWS college All-America first team (1981). ... Named NFL Rookie of the Year by THE SPORTING NEWS (1983). ... Named to play in Pro Bowl (1983 season); replaced by Bill Kenney due to injury. ... Named NFL Player of the Year by THE SPORTING NEWS (1984). ... Named quarterback on THE SPORTING NEWS NFL All-Pro team (1984-1986). ... Played in Pro Bowl (1984 and 1992 seasons). ... Named to play in Pro Bowl (1985 season); replaced by Ken O'Brien due to injury. ... Named to play in Pro Bowl (1986 season); replaced by Boomer Esiason due to injury. ... Named to play in Pro Bowl (1987 season); replaced by Jim Kelly due to injury. ... Named to play in Pro Bowl (1991 season); replaced by John Elway due to injury. Elway replaced by Ken O'Brien due to injury. ... Named to play in Pro Bowl (1994 season); replaced by Jeff Hostetler due to injury. ... Named to play in Pro Bowl (1995 season); replaced by Steve Bono due to injury.
RECORDS: Holds NFL career records for most touchdown passes—408; most yards passing—58,913; most passes attempted—7,989; most passes completed—4,763; most games with 400 or more yards passing—12; and most games with four or more touchdown passes—21. ... Holds NFL records for most seasons with 4,000 or more yards passing—6; most seasons with 3,000 or more yards passing—13; most consecutive seasons with 3,000 or more yards passing—9 (1984-1992); most games with 300 or more yards passing—60; most consecutive games with four or more touchdown passes—4 (November 26-December 17, 1984); most seasons leading league in pass attempts—5; and most seasons leading league in pass completions—6. ... Holds NFL single-season records for most yards passing—5,084 (1984); most touchdown passes—48 (1984); most games with 400 or more yards passing—4 (1984); most games with four or more touchdown passes—6 (1984); and most consecutive games with four or more touchdown passes—4 (1984). ... Holds NFL rookie-season records for highest pass completion percentage—58.45 (1983); and highest passer rating—96.0 (1983). ... Shares NFL records for most seasons leading league in yards passing—5; most consecutive seasons leading league in pass completions—3 (1984-1986); and most consecutive games with 400 or more yards passing—2 (December 2 and 9, 1984). ... Shares NFL single-season record for most games with 300 or more yards passing—9 (1984).
POST SEASON RECORDS: Holds NFL postseason career record for most consecutive games with one or more touchdown passes—13. ... Shares NFL postseason single-game record for pass attempts—64 (December 30, 1995, vs. Buffalo).
PRO STATISTICS: 1983—Fumbled five times and recovered two fumbles. 1984—Fumbled six times and recovered two fumbles for minus three yards. 1985—Fumbled nine times and recovered two fumbles for minus four yards. 1986—Fumbled eight times and recovered four fumbles for minus 12 yards. 1987—Fumbled five times and recovered four fumbles for minus 25 yards. 1988—Fumbled 10 times and recovered eight fumbles for minus 31 yards. 1989—Fumbled seven times. 1990—Fumbled three times and recovered two fumbles. 1991—Fumbled six times and recovered three fumbles for minus eight yards. 1992—Fumbled five times and recovered two fumbles for minus 12 yards. 1993—Fumbled four times and recovered two fumbles for minus 13 yards. 1994—Fumbled nine times and recovered three fumbles for minus four yards. 1995—Caught one pass for minus six yards, fumbled seven times and recovered three fumbles for minus 14 yards. 1996—Fumbled four times and recovered one fumble for minus three yards. 1997—Fumbled eight times and recovered three fumbles for minus 17 yards. 1998—Fumbled nine times and recovered five fumbles for minus nine yards.
SINGLE GAME HIGHS (regular season): Attempts—60 (November 23, 1997, vs. New England); completions—39 (November 16, 1986, vs. Buffalo); yards—521 (October 23, 1988, vs. New York Jets); and touchdown passes—6 (September 21, 1986, vs. New York Jets).
STATISTICAL PLATEAUS: 300-yard passing games: 1983 (1), 1984 (9), 1985 (6), 1986 (6), 1987 (4), 1988 (4), 1989 (5), 1990 (1), 1991 (3), 1992 (3), 1994 (5), 1995 (3), 1997 (4), 1998 (4). Total: 60.
MISCELLANEOUS: Selected by Kansas City Royals organization in fourth round of free-agent baseball draft (June 5, 1979); did not sign. ... Regular-season record as starting NFL quarterback: 142-87 (.620). ... Postseason record as starting NFL quarterback: 7-9 (.438). ... Active NFL leader for career passing yards (58,913) and touchdown passes (408). ... Holds Miami Dolphins all-time records for most yards passing (58,913) and most touchdown passes (408).

					PASSING					RUSHING				TOTALS		
Year	Team	G	GS	Att.	Cmp.	Pct.	Yds.	TD	Int.	Avg.	Rat.	Att.	Yds.	Avg.	TD	TD	2pt.	Pts.
1983—Miami NFL		11	9	296	173	58.4	2210	20	6	7.47	§96.0	28	45	1.6	2	2	...	12
1984—Miami NFL		16	16	*564	*362	§64.2	*5084	*48	17	*9.01	*108.9	28	-7	-0.3	0	0	...	0
1985—Miami NFL		16	16	567	*336	59.3	*4137	*30	21	7.30	84.1	26	-24	-0.9	0	0	...	0
1986—Miami NFL		16	16	*623	*378	60.7	*4746	*44	23	7.62	§92.5	12	-3	-0.3	0	0	...	0
1987—Miami NFL		12	12	§444	§263	59.2	3245	§26	13	7.31	89.2	12	-5	-0.4	1	1	...	6
1988—Miami NFL		16	16	*606	*354	58.4	*4434	▲28	§23	7.32	80.8	20	-17	-0.9	0	0	...	0
1989—Miami NFL		16	16	§550	§308	56.0	§3997	24	†22	7.27	76.9	14	-7	-0.5	2	2	...	12
1990—Miami NFL		16	16	531	306	57.6	3563	21	11	6.71	82.6	16	29	1.8	0	0	...	0
1991—Miami NFL		16	16	549	318	57.9	3970	25	13	7.23	85.8	27	32	1.2	1	1	...	6
1992—Miami NFL		16	16	*554	*330	59.6	*4116	§24	16	7.43	85.1	20	66	3.3	0	0	...	0
1993—Miami NFL		5	5	150	91	60.7	1218	8	3	8.12	95.9	9	-4	-0.4	1	1	...	6
1994—Miami NFL		16	16	615	385	62.6	4453	§30	17	7.24	§89.2	22	-6	-0.3	1	1	0	6
1995—Miami NFL		14	14	482	309	§64.1	3668	24	15	7.61	90.8	11	14	1.3	0	0	0	0
1996—Miami NFL		13	13	373	221	59.2	2795	17	9	7.49	87.8	11	-3	-0.3	0	0	0	0
1997—Miami NFL		16	16	*548	*319	58.2	3780	16	11	6.90	80.7	18	-14	-0.8	0	0	0	0
1998—Miami NFL		16	16	537	310	57.7	3497	23	15	6.51	80.0	21	-3	-0.1	1	1	0	6
Pro totals (16 years)		231	229	7989	4763	59.6	58913	408	235	7.37	87.3	295	93	0.3	9	9	0	54

MARION, BROCK   S   DOLPHINS

PERSONAL: Born June 11, 1970, in Bakersfield, Calif. ... 5-11/205. ... Full name: Brock Elliot Marion. ... Son of Jerry Marion, wide receiver with Pittsburgh Steelers (1967); and nephew of Brent McClanahan, running back with Minnesota Vikings (1973-79).
HIGH SCHOOL: West (Bakersfield, Calif.).
COLLEGE: Nevada.
TRANSACTIONS/CAREER NOTES: Selected by Dallas Cowboys in seventh round (196th overall) of 1993 NFL draft. ... Signed by Cowboys (July 14, 1993). ... Granted free agency (February 16, 1996). ... Re-signed by Cowboys (May 2, 1996). ... Granted unconditional free agency (February 14, 1997). ... Re-signed by Cowboys (April 7, 1997). ... Granted unconditional free agency (February 13, 1998). ... Signed by Miami Dolphins (March 3, 1998).
CHAMPIONSHIP GAME EXPERIENCE: Played in NFC championship game (1993-1995 seasons). ... Member of Super Bowl championship team (1993 and 1995 seasons).
PRO STATISTICS: 1993—Recovered one fumble. 1994—Credited with one sack and returned two kickoffs for 39 yards. 1995—Returned one kickoff for 16 yards. 1996—Returned three kickoffs for 68 yards, fumbled once and recovered one fumble for 45 yards. 1997—Returned 10 kickoffs for 311 yards and recovered one fumble for 13 yards. 1998—Returned six kickoffs for 109 yards and recovered one fumble for two yards.

			INTERCEPTIONS			
Year Team	G	GS	No.	Yds.	Avg.	TD
1993—Dallas NFL	15	0	1	2	2.0	0
1994—Dallas NFL	14	1	1	11	11.0	0
1995—Dallas NFL	16	16	6	40	6.7	1
1996—Dallas NFL	10	10	0	0	...	0
1997—Dallas NFL	16	16	0	0	...	0
1998—Miami NFL	16	16	0	0	...	0
Pro totals (6 years)	87	59	8	53	6.6	1

MARSHALL, ANTHONY   S

PERSONAL: Born September 16, 1970, in Mobile, Ala. ... 6-1/212. ... Full name: Anthony Dewayne Marshall.
HIGH SCHOOL: LeFlore (Mobile, Ala.).
COLLEGE: Louisiana State.
TRANSACTIONS/CAREER NOTES: Signed as non-drafted free agent by Chicago Bears (April 28, 1994). ... Released by Bears (August 28, 1994). ... Re-signed by Bears to practice squad (August 30, 1994). ... Activated (December 9, 1994). ... Claimed on waivers by New York Jets (December 17, 1997). ... Granted free agency (February 13, 1998). ... Re-signed by Jets (March 23, 1998). ... Released by Jets (August 8, 1998). ... Signed by Philadelphia Eagles (August 17, 1998). ... Granted unconditional free agency (February 12, 1999).
PRO STATISTICS: 1995—Returned one blocked punt 11 yards for a touchdown. 1996—Ran 75 yards with lateral from kickoff return. 1997—Ran three yards from lateral on a kickoff, credited with three sacks, fumbled once and recovered two fumbles for 10 yards. 1998—Recovered one fumble.

			INTERCEPTIONS			
Year Team	G	GS	No.	Yds.	Avg.	TD
1994—Chicago NFL	3	0	0	0	...	0
1995—Chicago NFL	16	2	1	0	0.0	0
1996—Chicago NFL	13	3	2	20	10.0	0
1997—Chicago NFL	14	1	2	0	0.0	0
1998—Philadelphia NFL	16	0	0	0	...	0
Pro totals (5 years)	62	6	5	20	4.0	0

MARTIN, CURTIS   RB   JETS

PERSONAL: Born May 1, 1973, in Pittsburgh. ... 5-11/210.
HIGH SCHOOL: Taylor-Allderdice (Pittsburgh).
COLLEGE: Pittsburgh.
TRANSACTIONS/CAREER NOTES: Selected after junior season by New England Patriots in third round (74th pick overall) of 1995 NFL draft. ... Signed by Patriots (July 18, 1995). ... Granted free agency (February 13, 1998). ... Tendered offer sheet by New York Jets (March 20, 1998). ... Patriots declined to match offer (March 25, 1998).
CHAMPIONSHIP GAME EXPERIENCE: Played in AFC championship game (1996 and 1998 seasons). ... Played in Super Bowl XXXI (1996 season).

HONORS: Named NFL Rookie of the Year by THE SPORTING NEWS (1995). ... Played in Pro Bowl (1995, 1996 and 1998 seasons).
PRO STATISTICS: 1995—Recovered three fumbles. 1996—Recovered one fumble. 1998—Recovered one fumble.
SINGLE GAME HIGHS (regular season): Attempts—40 (September 14, 1997, vs. New York Jets); yards—199 (September 14, 1997, vs. New York Jets); and rushing touchdowns—3 (November 3, 1996, vs. Miami).
STATISTICAL PLATEAUS: 100-yard rushing games: 1995 (9), 1996 (2), 1997 (3), 1998 (8). Total: 22.

				RUSHING				RECEIVING				TOTALS		
Year Team	G	GS	Att.	Yds.	Avg.	TD	No.	Yds.	Avg.	TD	TD	2pt.	Pts.	Fum.
1995—New England NFL	16	15	§368	§1487	4.0	14	30	261	8.7	1	15	1	92	5
1996—New England NFL	16	15	316	1152	3.6	§14	46	333	7.2	§3	§17	1	104	4
1997—New England NFL	13	13	274	1160	4.2	4	41	296	7.2	1	5	0	30	3
1998—New York Jets NFL	15	15	369	1287	3.5	8	43	365	8.5	1	9	0	54	5
Pro totals (4 years)	60	58	1327	5086	3.8	40	160	1255	7.8	6	46	2	280	17

MARTIN, JAMIE — QB

PERSONAL: Born February 8, 1970, in Orange, Calif. ... 6-2/210. ... Full name: Jamie Blane Martin.
HIGH SCHOOL: Arroyo Grande (Calif.).
COLLEGE: Weber State.
TRANSACTIONS/CAREER NOTES: Signed as non-drafted free agent by Los Angeles Rams (May 3, 1993). ... Released by Rams (August 24, 1993). ... Re-signed by Rams to practice squad (August 31, 1993). ... Activated (November 23, 1993). ... Inactive for five games (1993). ... Released by Rams (August 27, 1994). ... Re-signed by Rams (October 4, 1994). ... Released by Rams (October 12, 1994). ... Re-signed by Rams (November 15, 1994). ... Active for one game (1994); did not play. ... Assigned by Rams to Amsterdam Admirals of World Football League (1995). ... On physically unable to perform list with broken collarbone (June 3, 1995-entire season). ... Released by Rams (August 17, 1997). ... Signed by Washington Redskins (December 2, 1997). ... Granted free agency (February 13, 1998). ... Signed by Jacksonville Jaguars (March 6, 1998). ... On injured reserve with knee injury (December 15, 1998-remainder of season). ... Granted unconditional free agency (February 12, 1999).
HONORS: Walter Payton Award winner (1991).
PRO STATISTICS: 1996—Fumbled twice and recovered one fumble for minus two yards.
SINGLE GAME HIGHS (regular season): Attempts—23 (December 6, 1998, vs. Detroit); completions—15 (December 6, 1998, vs. Detroit); yards—228 (December 6, 1998, vs. Detroit); and touchdown passes—2 (December 6, 1998, vs. Detroit).
MISCELLANEOUS: Regular-season record as starting NFL quarterback: 0-1.

			PASSING							RUSHING				TOTALS	
Year Team	G	GS	Att.	Cmp.	Pct.	Yds.	TD	Int.	Avg.	Rat.	Att.	Yds.	Avg.	TD	TD	2pt.	Pts.
1993—L.A. Rams NFL						Did not play.										
1994—L.A. Rams NFL						Did not play.										
1995—Amsterdam W.L.	9	9	219	126	57.5	1433	11	6	6.54	82.6	...	...	...	...	0	...
1996—St. Louis NFL	6	0	34	23	67.6	241	3	2	7.09	92.9	7	14	2.0	0	0	0	0
1997—Washington NFL						Did not play.										
1998—Jacksonville NFL	4	1	45	27	60.0	355	2	0	7.89	99.8	5	8	1.6	0	0	0	0
W.L. totals (1 year)	9	9	219	126	57.5	1433	11	6	6.54	82.6	0	0	0	0	0	0
NFL totals (2 years)	10	1	79	50	63.3	596	5	2	7.54	96.8	12	22	1.8	0	0	0	0
Pro totals (3 years)	19	10	298	176	59.1	2029	16	8	6.81	86.4	12	22	1.8	0	0	0	0

MARTIN, MANNY — S — BILLS

PERSONAL: Born July 31, 1969, in Miami. ... 5-11/184. ... Full name: Emanuel C. Martin.
HIGH SCHOOL: Miami Central.
COLLEGE: Alabama State.
TRANSACTIONS/CAREER NOTES: Signed as non-drafted free agent by Houston Oilers (May 17, 1993). ... Released by Oilers (August 19, 1993). ... Re-signed by Oilers to practice squad (September 29, 1993). ... Activated (October 6, 1993). ... Released by Oilers (October 25, 1993). ... Re-signed by Oilers to practice squad (October 27, 1993). ... Released by Oilers (August 28, 1994). ... Signed by Ottawa Rough Riders of CFL for 1994 season. ... Granted free agency (February 16, 1996). ... Signed by Buffalo Bills (April 4, 1996). ... Granted free agency (February 12, 1999). ... Re-signed by Bills (April 26, 1999).
PRO STATISTICS: CFL: 1995: Returned one punt for 33 yards and a touchdown, credited with one sack and recovered one fumble.

			INTERCEPTIONS			
Year Team	G	GS	No.	Yds.	Avg.	TD
1993—Houston NFL	1	0	0	0	...	0
1994—Ottawa CFL	3	3	0	0	...	0
1995—Ottawa CFL	17	17	2	12	6.0	0
1996—Buffalo NFL	16	1	2	35	17.5	0
1997—Buffalo NFL	16	2	1	12	12.0	0
1998—Buffalo NFL	14	4	1	23	23.0	0
CFL totals (2 years)	20	20	2	12	6.0	0
NFL totals (4 years)	47	7	4	70	17.5	0
Pro totals (6 years)	67	27	6	82	13.7	0

MARTIN, STEVE — DT — EAGLES

PERSONAL: Born May 31, 1974, in St. Paul, Minn. ... 6-4/303. ... Full name: Steven Albert Martin.
HIGH SCHOOL: Jefferson City (Mo.).
COLLEGE: Missouri.
TRANSACTIONS/CAREER NOTES: Selected by Indianapolis Colts in fifth round (151st pick overall) of 1996 NFL draft. ... Signed by Colts (July 5, 1996). ... Claimed on waivers by Philadelphia Eagles (October 23, 1998). ... Granted free agency (February 12, 1999). ... Re-signed by Eagles (April 9, 1999).
PRO STATISTICS: 1996—Recovered one fumble.

Year Team	G	GS	SACKS
1996—Indianapolis NFL	14	5	1.0
1997—Indianapolis NFL	12	0	0.0
1998—Indianapolis NFL	4	0	0.0
—Philadelphia NFL	9	3	1.0
Pro totals (3 years)	**39**	**8**	**2.0**

MARTIN, TONY   WR   DOLPHINS

PERSONAL: Born September 5, 1965, in Miami. ... 6-1/181. ... Full name: Tony Derrick Martin.
HIGH SCHOOL: Miami Northwestern.
COLLEGE: Bishop (Texas), then Mesa State College (Colo.).
TRANSACTIONS/CAREER NOTES: Selected by New York Jets in fifth round (126th pick overall) of 1989 NFL draft. ... Signed by New York Jets for 1989 season. ... Released by Jets (September 4, 1989). ... Signed by Miami Dolphins to developmental squad (September 5, 1989). ... Activated (December 23, 1989); did not play. ... Granted free agency (February 1, 1992). ... Re-signed by Dolphins (March 10, 1992). ... Traded by Dolphins to San Diego Chargers for fourth-round pick (traded to Arizona) in 1994 draft (March 24, 1994). ... Designated by Chargers as franchise player (February 13, 1997). ... Re-signed by Chargers (May 1, 1997). ... Traded by Chargers to Atlanta Falcons for second-round pick (RB Jermaine Fazande) in 1999 draft (June 3, 1998). ... Released by Falcons (February 26, 1999). ... Signed by Dolphins (April 9, 1999).
CHAMPIONSHIP GAME EXPERIENCE: Played in AFC championship game (1992 and 1994 seasons). ... Played in Super Bowl XXIX (1994 season) and Super Bowl XXXIII (1998 season). ... Played in NFC championship game (1998 season).
HONORS: Played in Pro Bowl (1996 season).
RECORDS: Shares NFL record for longest pass reception (from Stan Humphries)—99 yards, touchdown (September 18, 1994, at Seattle).
PRO STATISTICS: 1990—Recovered two fumbles. 1992—Attempted one pass without a completion and recovered one fumble. 1994—Attempted one pass without a completion and returned eight kickoffs for 167 yards. 1995—Attempted one pass without a completion. 1998—Attempted one pass without a completion.
SINGLE GAME HIGHS (regular season): Receptions—13 (September 10, 1995, vs. Seattle); yards—172 (December 11, 1994, vs. San Francisco); and touchdown receptions—3 (September 28, 1997, vs. Baltimore).
STATISTICAL PLATEAUS: 100-yard receiving games: 1991 (2), 1993 (1), 1994 (2), 1995 (4), 1996 (4), 1997 (2), 1998 (5). Total: 20.

			RUSHING			RECEIVING				PUNT RETURNS				TOTALS		
Year Team	G	GS	Att.	Yds.	Avg.	TD	No.	Yds.	Avg.	TD	No.	Yds.	Avg.	TD	TD	2pt.	Pts.	Fum.
1990—Miami NFL	16	5	1	8	8.0	0	29	388	13.4	2	26	140	5.4	0	2	...	12	4
1991—Miami NFL	16	0	0	0	...	0	27	434	16.1	2	1	10	10.0	0	2	...	12	2
1992—Miami NFL	16	3	1	-2	-2.0	0	33	553	16.8	2	1	0	0.0	0	2	...	12	2
1993—Miami NFL	12	0	1	6	6.0	0	20	347	17.4	3	0	0	...	0	3	...	18	1
1994—San Diego NFL	16	1	2	-9	-4.5	0	50	885	17.7	7	0	0	...	0	7	0	42	2
1995—San Diego NFL	16	16	0	0	...	0	90	1224	13.6	6	0	0	...	0	6	0	36	3
1996—San Diego NFL	16	16	0	0	...	0	85	1171	13.8	14	0	0	...	0	14	0	84	0
1997—San Diego NFL	16	16	0	0	...	0	63	904	14.3	6	0	0	...	0	6	0	36	0
1998—Atlanta NFL	16	16	0	0	...	0	66	1181	17.9	6	0	0	...	0	6	0	36	0
Pro totals (9 years)	**140**	**73**	**5**	**3**	**0.6**	**0**	**463**	**7087**	**15.3**	**48**	**28**	**150**	**5.4**	**0**	**48**	**0**	**288**	**14**

MARTIN, WAYNE   DT   SAINTS

PERSONAL: Born October 26, 1965, in Forrest City, Ark. ... 6-5/275. ... Full name: Gerald Wayne Martin.
HIGH SCHOOL: Cross Country (Cherry Valley, Ark.).
COLLEGE: Arkansas (degree in criminal justice, 1990).
TRANSACTIONS/CAREER NOTES: Selected by New Orleans Saints in first round (19th pick overall) of 1989 NFL draft. ... Signed by Saints (August 10, 1989). ... On injured reserve with knee injury (December 19, 1990-remainder of season). ... Granted free agency (March 1, 1993). ... Tendered offer sheet by Washington Redskins (April 8, 1993). ... Offer matched by Saints (April 14, 1993).
HONORS: Named defensive lineman on THE SPORTING NEWS college All-America first team (1988). ... Played in Pro Bowl (1994 season).
PRO STATISTICS: 1989—Recovered two fumbles. 1991—Recovered one fumble. 1992—Recovered two fumbles. 1993—Recovered two fumbles for seven yards. 1995—Intercepted one pass for 12 yards and recovered one fumble. 1996—Recovered one fumble. 1997—Recovered one fumble. 1998—Credited with a safety and recovered one fumble.

Year Team	G	GS	SACKS
1989—New Orleans NFL	16	0	2.5
1990—New Orleans NFL	11	11	4.0
1991—New Orleans NFL	16	16	3.5
1992—New Orleans NFL	16	16	15.5
1993—New Orleans NFL	16	16	5.0
1994—New Orleans NFL	16	16	10.0
1995—New Orleans NFL	16	16	∞13.0
1996—New Orleans NFL	16	16	11.0
1997—New Orleans NFL	16	16	10.5
1998—New Orleans NFL	16	16	3.0
Pro totals (10 years)	**155**	**139**	**78.0**

MARTS, LONNIE   LB   TITANS

PERSONAL: Born November 10, 1968, in New Orleans. ... 6-2/250. ... Full name: Lonnie Marts Jr.
HIGH SCHOOL: St. Augustine (New Orleans).
COLLEGE: Tulane (degree in sociology).
TRANSACTIONS/CAREER NOTES: Signed as non-drafted free agent by Kansas City Chiefs (May 1, 1990). ... On injured reserve with ankle injury (September 8, 1990-entire season). ... Granted unconditional free agency (February 17, 1994). ... Signed by Tampa Bay Buccaneers (March 21, 1994). ... Granted unconditional free agency (February 14, 1997). ... Signed by Houston Oilers (April 3, 1997). ... Oilers franchise moved to Tennessee for 1997 season. ... Oilers franchise renamed Tennessee Titans for 1999 season (December 26, 1998).
CHAMPIONSHIP GAME EXPERIENCE: Played in AFC championship game (1993 season).

PRO STATISTICS: 1991—Recovered one fumble. 1992—Recovered one fumble for two yards. 1993—Returned one kickoff for no yards and recovered one fumble. 1994—Recovered two fumbles. 1995—Recovered one fumble. 1996—Recovered two fumbles. 1997—Recovered one fumble.

				INTERCEPTIONS				SACKS
Year Team		G	GS	No.	Yds.	Avg.	TD	No.
1990—Kansas City NFL					Did not play.			
1991—Kansas City NFL		16	2	0	0	...	0	1.0
1992—Kansas City NFL		15	3	1	36	36.0	1	0.0
1993—Kansas City NFL		16	15	1	20	20.0	0	2.0
1994—Tampa Bay NFL		16	14	0	0	...	0	0.0
1995—Tampa Bay NFL		15	13	1	8	8.0	0	0.0
1996—Tampa Bay NFL		16	13	0	0	...	0	7.0
1997—Tennessee NFL		14	14	0	0	...	0	1.0
1998—Tennessee NFL		16	15	1	27	27.0	1	4.0
Pro totals (8 years)		124	89	4	91	22.8	2	15.0

MARYLAND, RUSSELL   DT   RAIDERS

PERSONAL: Born March 22, 1969, in Chicago. ... 6-1/295.
HIGH SCHOOL: Whitney-Young (Chicago).
COLLEGE: Miami, Fla. (degree in psychology, 1990).
TRANSACTIONS/CAREER NOTES: Selected by Dallas Cowboys in first round (first pick overall) of 1991 NFL draft. ... Signed by Cowboys (April 22, 1991). ... Granted unconditional free agency (February 16, 1996). ... Signed by Oakland Raiders (February 22, 1996).
CHAMPIONSHIP GAME EXPERIENCE: Played in NFC championship game (1992-1995 seasons). ... Member of Super Bowl championship team (1992, 1993 and 1995 seasons).
HONORS: Named defensive tackle on THE SPORTING NEWS college All-America second team (1989). ... Outland Trophy winner (1990). ... Named defensive lineman on THE SPORTING NEWS college All-America first team (1990). ... Played in Pro Bowl (1993 season).
PRO STATISTICS: 1992—Recovered two fumbles for 26 yards and a touchdown. 1993—Recovered two fumbles. 1994—Recovered one fumble.

Year Team	G	GS	SACKS
1991—Dallas NFL	16	7	4.5
1992—Dallas NFL	14	13	2.5
1993—Dallas NFL	16	12	2.5
1994—Dallas NFL	16	16	3.0
1995—Dallas NFL	13	13	2.0
1996—Oakland NFL	16	16	2.0
1997—Oakland NFL	16	16	4.5
1998—Oakland NFL	15	15	2.0
Pro totals (8 years)	122	108	23.0

MASON, DERRICK   WR   TITANS

PERSONAL: Born January 17, 1974, in Detroit. ... 5-10/188. ... Full name: Derrick James Mason.
HIGH SCHOOL: Mumford (Detroit).
COLLEGE: Michigan State.
TRANSACTIONS/CAREER NOTES: Selected by Houston Oilers in fourth round (98th pick overall) of 1997 NFL draft. ... Oilers franchise moved to Tennessee for 1997 season. ... Signed by Oilers (July 19, 1997). ... Oilers franchise renamed Tennessee Titans for 1999 season (December 26, 1998).
PRO STATISTICS: 1997—Rushed once for minus seven yards. 1998—Recovered one fumble.
SINGLE GAME HIGHS (regular season): Receptions—4 (December 20, 1998, vs. Green Bay); yards—75 (December 26, 1998, vs. Minnesota); and touchdown receptions—2 (December 20, 1998, vs. Green Bay).

			RECEIVING			PUNT RETURNS			KICKOFF RETURNS			TOTALS			
Year Team	G	GS	No.	Yds.	Avg.	TD	No.	Yds.	Avg.	TD	No.	Yds.	Avg.	TD	TD 2pt. Pts. Fum.
1997—Tennessee NFL	16	2	14	186	13.3	0	13	95	7.3	0	26	551	21.2	0	0 0 0 5
1998—Tennessee NFL	16	0	25	333	13.3	3	31	228	7.4	0	8	154	19.3	0	3 0 18 1
Pro totals (2 years)	32	2	39	519	13.3	3	44	323	7.3	0	34	705	20.7	0	3 0 18 6

MASON, EDDIE   LB   JAGUARS

PERSONAL: Born January 9, 1972, in Siler City, N.C. ... 6-0/223. ... Full name: Eddie Lee Mason.
HIGH SCHOOL: Jordan-Matthews (Siler City, N.C.).
COLLEGE: North Carolina.
TRANSACTIONS/CAREER NOTES: Selected by New York Jets in sixth round (178th pick overall) of 1995 NFL draft. ... Signed by Jets (June 14, 1995). ... On injured reserve with knee injury (August 20, 1996-entire season). ... Granted unconditional free agency (February 14, 1997). ... Signed by Tampa Bay Buccaneers (April 21, 1997). ... Released by Buccaneers (August 17, 1997). ... Signed by Carolina Panthers (March 4, 1998). ... Released by Panthers (August 24, 1998). ... Signed by Jacksonville Jaguars (December 2, 1998).
PLAYING EXPERIENCE: New York Jets NFL, 1995; Jacksonville NFL, 1998. ... Games/Games started: 1995 (15/0), 1998 (4/0). Total: 19/0.

MASTON, Le'SHAI   FB

PERSONAL: Born October 7, 1970, in Dallas. ... 6-1/242. ... Full name: Le'Shai Edwoin Maston. ... Name pronounced le-SHAY.
HIGH SCHOOL: David W. Carter (Dallas).
COLLEGE: Baylor (degree in business management, 1992).
TRANSACTIONS/CAREER NOTES: Signed as non-drafted free agent by Houston Oilers (June 30, 1993). ... Released by Oilers (August 30, 1993). ... Re-signed by Oilers to practice squad (August 31, 1993). ... Activated (September 10, 1993). ... Selected by Jacksonville Jaguars

from Oilers in NFL expansion draft (February 15, 1995). ... Granted free agency (February 16, 1996). ... Re-signed by Jaguars for 1996 season. ... Released by Jaguars (August 24, 1997). ... Signed by Washington Redskins (February 11, 1998). ... Released by Redskins (August 25, 1998). ... Re-signed by Redskins (December 22, 1998). ... Granted unconditional free agency (February 12, 1999).
CHAMPIONSHIP GAME EXPERIENCE: Played in AFC championship game (1996 season).
PRO STATISTICS: 1995—Returned one kickoff for five yards and recovered one fumble for four yards.
SINGLE GAME HIGHS (regular season): Attempts—7 (December 17, 1995, vs. Detroit); yards—38 (September 17, 1995, vs. New York Jets); and rushing touchdowns—0.

			RUSHING				RECEIVING			TOTALS			
Year Team	G	GS	Att.	Yds.	Avg.	TD	No.	Yds.	Avg.	TD	TD	2pt.	Pts.	Fum.
1993—Houston NFL	10	0	1	10	10.0	0	1	14	14.0	0	0	...	0	1
1994—Houston NFL	5	1	0	0	...	0	2	12	6.0	0	0	0	0	0
1995—Jacksonville NFL	16	10	41	186	4.5	0	18	131	7.3	0	0	0	0	3
1996—Jacksonville NFL	15	7	8	22	2.8	0	6	54	9.0	0	0	0	0	0
1997—							Did not play.							
1998—Washington NFL	1	0	0	0	...	0	0	0	...	0	0	0	0	0
Pro totals (5 years)	47	18	50	218	4.4	0	27	211	7.8	0	0	0	0	4

MATHEWS, JASON   OT   TITANS

PERSONAL: Born February 9, 1971, in Orange, Texas. ... 6-5/304. ... Full name: Samuel Jason Mathews.
HIGH SCHOOL: Bridge City (Texas).
COLLEGE: Brigham Young, then Texas A&M.
TRANSACTIONS/CAREER NOTES: Selected by Indianapolis Colts in third round (67th pick overall) of 1994 NFL draft. ... Signed by Colts (July 23, 1994). ... Granted free agency (February 14, 1997). ... Re-signed by Colts (April 30, 1997). ... Granted unconditional free agency (February 13, 1998). ... Signed by Tampa Bay Buccaneers (May 7, 1998). ... Released by Buccaneers (August 30, 1998). ... Signed by Tennessee Oilers (September 1, 1998). ... Oilers franchise renamed Tennessee Titans for 1999 season (December 26, 1998).
PLAYING EXPERIENCE: Indianapolis NFL, 1994-1997; Tennessee NFL, 1998. ... Games/Games started: 1994 (10/0), 1995 (16/16), 1996 (16/15), 1997 (16/0), 1998 (3/0). Total: 61/31.
CHAMPIONSHIP GAME EXPERIENCE: Played in AFC championship game (1995 season).
PRO STATISTICS: 1996—Recovered one fumble.

MATHIAS, RIC   CB   BENGALS

PERSONAL: Born December 10, 1975, in Monroe, Wis. ... 5-10/180.
HIGH SCHOOL: Monroe (Wis.).
COLLEGE: Wisconsin-La Crosse.
TRANSACTIONS/CAREER NOTES: Signed as non-drafted free agent by Cincinnati Bengals (April 20, 1998). ... Released by Bengals (October 1, 1998). ... Signed by Indianapolis Colts (October 2, 1998). ... Inactive for three games with Colts (1998). ... Released by Colts (October 30, 1998). ... Signed by Bengals to practice squad (November 5, 1998).
PLAYING EXPERIENCE: Cincinnati NFL, 1998. ... Games/Games started: 3/0.

MATHIS, KEVIN   CB   COWBOYS

PERSONAL: Born April 9, 1974, in Gainesville, Texas. ... 5-9/179.
HIGH SCHOOL: Gainesville (Texas).
COLLEGE: East Texas State.
TRANSACTIONS/CAREER NOTES: Signed as non-drafted free agent by Dallas Cowboys (April 24, 1997).
PRO STATISTICS: 1997—Recovered two fumbles. 1998—Recovered four fumbles for six yards.

			PUNT RETURNS				TOTALS			
Year Team	G	GS	No.	Yds.	Avg.	TD	TD	2pt.	Pts.	Fum.
1997—Dallas NFL	16	3	11	91	8.3	0	0	0	0	2
1998—Dallas NFL	13	4	2	3	1.5	0	0	0	0	2
Pro totals (2 years)	29	7	13	94	7.2	0	0	0	0	4

MATHIS, TERANCE   WR   FALCONS

PERSONAL: Born June 7, 1967, in Detroit. ... 5-10/186. ... Cousin of Jason Ferguson, defensive tackle with New York Jets.
HIGH SCHOOL: Redan (Stone Mountain, Ga.).
COLLEGE: New Mexico.
TRANSACTIONS/CAREER NOTES: Selected by New York Jets in sixth round (140th pick overall) of 1990 NFL draft. ... Signed by Jets (July 12, 1990). ... Granted unconditional free agency (February 17, 1994). ... Signed by Atlanta Falcons (May 3, 1994). ... Granted unconditional free agency (February 16, 1996). ... Re-signed by Falcons (April 30, 1996).
CHAMPIONSHIP GAME EXPERIENCE: Played in NFC championship game (1998 season). ... Played in Super Bowl XXXIII (1998 season).
HONORS: Named wide receiver on THE SPORTING NEWS college All-America first team (1989). ... Played in Pro Bowl (1994 season).
RECORDS: Holds NFL career record for most two-point conversions—6.
PRO STATISTICS: 1990—Fumbled once. 1991—Fumbled four times and recovered one fumble. 1992—Fumbled twice and recovered one fumble. 1993—Fumbled five times and recovered one fumble. 1994—Recovered one fumble. 1995—Fumbled once. 1996—Recovered one fumble. 1998—Recovered two fumbles.
SINGLE GAME HIGHS (regular season): Receptions—13 (September 18, 1994, vs. Kansas City); yards—198 (December 13, 1998, vs. New Orleans); and touchdown receptions—3 (November 19, 1995, vs. St. Louis).
STATISTICAL PLATEAUS: 100-yard receiving games: 1992 (1), 1994 (5), 1995 (2), 1996 (2), 1997 (1), 1998 (3). Total: 14.

Year Team	G	GS	RUSHING Att.	Yds.	Avg.	TD	RECEIVING No.	Yds.	Avg.	TD	PUNT RETURNS No.	Yds.	Avg.	TD	KICKOFF RETURNS No.	Yds.	Avg.	TD	TOTALS TD	2pt.	Pts.
1990—N.Y. Jets NFL	16	1	2	9	4.5	0	19	245	12.9	0	11	165	15.0	†1	43	787	18.3	0	1	...	6
1991—N.Y. Jets NFL	16	0	1	19	19.0	0	28	329	11.8	1	23	157	6.8	0	29	599	20.7	0	1	...	6
1992—N.Y. Jets NFL	16	1	3	25	8.3	1	22	316	14.4	3	2	24	12.0	0	28	492	17.6	0	4	...	24
1993—N.Y. Jets NFL	16	3	2	20	10.0	1	24	352	14.7	0	14	99	7.1	0	7	102	14.6	0	1	...	6
1994—Atlanta NFL	16	16	0	0	...	0	111	1342	12.1	11	0	0	...	0	0	0	...	0	11	∞2	70
1995—Atlanta NFL	14	12	0	0	...	0	78	1039	13.3	9	0	0	...	0	0	0	...	0	9	*3	60
1996—Atlanta NFL	16	16	0	0	...	0	69	771	11.2	7	3	19	6.3	0	0	0	...	0	7	1	44
1997—Atlanta NFL	16	16	3	35	11.7	0	62	802	12.9	6	0	0	...	0	0	0	...	0	6	0	36
1998—Atlanta NFL	16	16	1	-6	-6.0	0	64	1136	17.8	11	1	0	0.0	0	0	0	...	0	11	0	66
Pro totals (9 years)	142	81	12	102	8.5	2	477	6332	13.3	48	54	464	8.6	1	107	1980	18.5	0	51	6	318

MATTHEWS, BRUCE   G/C   TITANS

PERSONAL: Born August 8, 1961, in Raleigh, N.C. ... 6-5/309. ... Full name: Bruce Rankin Matthews. ... Son of Clay Matthews Sr., defensive end/tackle with San Francisco 49ers (1950 and 1953-55); and brother of Clay Matthews Jr., linebacker with Cleveland Browns (1978-93) and Atlanta Falcons (1994-96).
HIGH SCHOOL: Arcadia (Calif.).
COLLEGE: Southern California (degree in industrial engineering, 1983).
TRANSACTIONS/CAREER NOTES: Selected by Los Angeles Express in 1983 USFL territorial draft. ... Selected by Houston Oilers in first round (ninth pick overall) of 1983 NFL draft. ... Signed by Oilers (July 24, 1983). ... Granted free agency (February 1, 1987). ... On reserve/unsigned list (August 31-November 3, 1987). ... Re-signed by Oilers (November 4, 1987). ... Granted roster exemption (November 4-7, 1987). ... Granted unconditional free agency (February 17, 1995). ... Re-signed by Oilers (August 8, 1995). ... Oilers franchise moved to Tennessee for 1997 season. ... Oilers franchise renamed Tennessee Titans for 1999 season (December 26, 1998). ... Granted unconditional free agency (February 12, 1999). ... Re-signed by Titans (May 13, 1999).
PLAYING EXPERIENCE: Houston NFL, 1983-1996; Tennessee NFL, 1997 and 1998. ... Games/Games started: 1983 (16/15), 1984 (16/16), 1985 (16/16), 1986 (16/16), 1987 (8/5), 1988 (16/16), 1989 (16/16), 1990 (16/16), 1991 (16/16), 1992 (16/16), 1993 (16/16), 1994 (16/16), 1995 (16/16), 1996 (16/16), 1997 (16/16), 1998 (16/16). Total: 248/244.
HONORS: Named guard on THE SPORTING NEWS college All-America first team (1982). ... Named guard on THE SPORTING NEWS NFL All-Pro team (1988-1990, 1992 and 1998). ... Played in Pro Bowl (1988-1994, 1996 and 1997 seasons). ... Named center on THE SPORTING NEWS NFL All-Pro team (1993). ... Named to play in Pro Bowl (1995 season); replaced by Will Shields due to injury. ... Named to play in Pro Bowl (1998 season); replaced by Mark Schlereth due to injury.
PRO STATISTICS: 1985—Recovered three fumbles. 1986—Recovered one fumble for seven yards. 1989—Fumbled twice and recovered one fumble for minus 29 yards. 1990—Recovered one fumble. 1991—Fumbled once and recovered one fumble for minus three yards. 1994—Fumbled twice. 1997—Recovered two fumbles. 1998—Recovered one fumble.

MATTHEWS, STEVE   QB   TITANS

PERSONAL: Born October 13, 1970, in Tullahoma, Tenn. ... 6-3/228. ... Full name: Steven Keith Matthews.
HIGH SCHOOL: Tullahoma (Tenn.).
COLLEGE: Memphis State.
TRANSACTIONS/CAREER NOTES: Selected by Kansas City Chiefs in seventh round (199th pick overall) of 1994 NFL draft. ... On reserve/non-football injury list with knee injury (July 18, 1994-entire season). ... On reserve/non-football injury list with knee injury (July 21, 1995-entire season). ... Assigned by Chiefs to Scottish Claymores in 1996 World League enhancement allocation program (February 19, 1996). ... Inactive for all 16 games (1996). ... Claimed on waivers by Jacksonville Jaguars (August 20, 1997). ... Claimed on waivers by Tennessee Oilers (August 26, 1998). ... Oilers franchise renamed Tennessee Titans for 1999 season (December 26, 1998). ... Granted free agency (February 12, 1999).
PRO STATISTICS: 1997—Fumbled once.
SINGLE GAME HIGHS (regular season): Attempts—35 (September 7, 1997, vs. New York Giants); completions—23 (September 7, 1997, vs. New York Giants); yards—252 (September 7, 1997, vs. New York Giants); and touchdown passes—0.
MISCELLANEOUS: Regular-season record as starting NFL quarterback: 1-0.

Year Team	G	GS	PASSING Att.	Cmp.	Pct.	Yds.	TD	Int.	Avg.	Rat.	RUSHING Att.	Yds.	Avg.	TD	TOTALS TD	2pt.	Pts.
1994—Kansas City NFL						Did not play.											
1995—Kansas City NFL						Did not play.											
1996—Scottish W.L.	...	...	205	115	56.1	1560	9	10	7.61	74.8	26	105	4.0	1	1	0	6
—Kansas City NFL						Did not play.											
1997—Jacksonville NFL	2	1	40	26	65.0	275	0	0	6.88	84.9	1	10	10.0	0	0	0	0
1998—Tennessee NFL	1	0	3	2	66.7	24	0	0	8.00	91.0	0	0	...	0	0	0	0
W.L. totals (1 year)	...	...	205	115	56.1	1560	9	10	7.61	74.8	26	105	4.0	1	1	0	6
NFL totals (3 years)	3	1	43	28	65.1	299	0	0	6.95	85.3	1	10	10.0	0	0	0	0
Pro totals (4 years)	...	...	248	143	57.7	1859	9	10	7.50	76.7	27	115	4.3	1	1	0	6

MAWAE, KEVIN   C   JETS

PERSONAL: Born January 23, 1971, in Savannah, Ga. ... 6-4/305. ... Full name: Kevin James Mawae. ... Name pronounced ma-WHY.
HIGH SCHOOL: Leesville (La.).
COLLEGE: Louisiana State (degree in general studies).
TRANSACTIONS/CAREER NOTES: Selected by Seattle Seahawks in second round (36th pick overall) of 1994 NFL draft. ... Signed by Seahawks (July 21, 1994). ... Granted free agency (February 14, 1997). ... Re-signed by Seahawks (May 5, 1997). ... Granted unconditional free agency (February 13, 1998). ... Signed by New York Jets (February 19, 1998).
PLAYING EXPERIENCE: Seattle NFL, 1994-1997; New York Jets NFL, 1998. ... Games/Games started: 1994 (14/11), 1995 (16/16), 1996 (16/16), 1997 (16/16), 1998 (16/16). Total: 78/75.
CHAMPIONSHIP GAME EXPERIENCE: Played in AFC championship game (1998 season).
PRO STATISTICS: 1994—Recovered one fumble. 1996—Recovered two fumbles. 1997—Recovered two fumbles.

MAY, DEEMS   TE   SEAHAWKS

PERSONAL: Born March 6, 1969, in Lexington, N.C. ... 6-4/263. ... Full name: Bert Deems May Jr.
HIGH SCHOOL: Lexington (N.C.) Senior.
COLLEGE: North Carolina (degree in political science, 1991).
TRANSACTIONS/CAREER NOTES: Selected by San Diego Chargers in seventh round (174th pick overall) of 1992 NFL draft. ... Signed by Chargers (July 16, 1992). ... On injured reserve with foot injury (November 2, 1994-remainder of season). ... Granted free agency (February 17, 1995). ... Re-signed by Chargers (May 19, 1995). ... On physically unable to perform list with foot injury (July 18-October 10, 1995). ... Granted unconditional free agency (February 14, 1997). ... Signed by Seattle Seahawks (May 7, 1997).
CHAMPIONSHIP GAME EXPERIENCE: Member of Chargers for Super Bowl XXIX (1994 season); inactive.
PRO STATISTICS: 1996—Recovered one fumble. 1997—Returned one kickoff for eight yards.
SINGLE GAME HIGHS (regular season): Receptions—4 (November 24, 1996, vs. Kansas City); yards—44 (November 17, 1996, vs. Tampa Bay); and touchdown receptions—1 (December 27, 1998, vs. Denver).

			RECEIVING				TOTALS		
Year Team	G	GS	No.	Yds.	Avg.	TD	TD	2pt.	Pts.	Fum.
1992—San Diego NFL	16	6	0	0	...	0	0	...	0	0
1993—San Diego NFL	15	1	0	0	...	0	0	...	0	0
1994—San Diego NFL	5	2	2	22	11.0	0	0	0	0	0
1995—San Diego NFL	5	0	0	0	...	0	0	0	0	0
1996—San Diego NFL	16	12	19	188	9.9	0	0	0	0	0
1997—Seattle NFL	16	0	2	21	10.5	0	0	0	0	0
1998—Seattle NFL	16	1	3	7	2.3	1	1	0	6	0
Pro totals (7 years)	89	22	26	238	9.2	1	1	0	6	0

MAYBERRY, JERMANE   G/OT   EAGLES

PERSONAL: Born August 29, 1973, in Floresville, Texas. ... 6-4/325. ... Full name: Jermane Timothy Mayberry.
HIGH SCHOOL: Floresville (Texas).
JUNIOR COLLEGE: Navarro College (Texas).
COLLEGE: Texas A&M-Kingsville.
TRANSACTIONS/CAREER NOTES: Selected by Philadelphia Eagles in first round (25th pick overall) of 1996 NFL draft. ... Signed by Eagles (June 13, 1996).
PLAYING EXPERIENCE: Philadelphia NFL, 1996-1998. ... Games/Games started: 1996 (3/1), 1997 (16/16), 1998 (15/10). Total: 34/27.
PRO STATISTICS: 1997—Recovered one fumble.

MAYBERRY, TONY   C   BUCCANEERS

PERSONAL: Born December 8, 1967, in Wurzburg, West Germany. ... 6-4/282. ... Full name: Eino Anthony Mayberry.
HIGH SCHOOL: Hayfield (Alexandria, Va.).
COLLEGE: Wake Forest (degree in sociology, 1989).
TRANSACTIONS/CAREER NOTES: Selected by Tampa Bay Buccaneers in fourth round (108th pick overall) of 1990 NFL draft. ... Signed by Buccaneers (July 19, 1990). ... Granted free agency (March 1, 1993). ... Tendered offer sheet by New England Patriots (March 11, 1993). ... Offer matched by Buccaneers (March 18, 1993). ... Granted unconditional free agency (February 16, 1996). ... Re-signed by Buccaneers (February 27, 1996).
PLAYING EXPERIENCE: Tampa Bay NFL, 1990-1998. ... Games/Games started: 1990 (16/1), 1991 (16/16), 1992 (16/16), 1993 (16/16), 1994 (16/16), 1995 (16/16), 1996 (16/16), 1997 (16/16), 1998 (16/16). Total: 144/129.
HONORS: Played in Pro Bowl (1997 and 1998 seasons).
PRO STATISTICS: 1991—Fumbled three times for minus 17 yards. 1993—Fumbled once and recovered one fumble for minus six yards. 1994—Recovered one fumble. 1996—Recovered one fumble.

MAYES, ALONZO   TE   BEARS

PERSONAL: Born June 4, 1975, in Oklahoma City. ... 6-4/259.
HIGH SCHOOL: Douglass (Oklahoma City).
JUNIOR COLLEGE: Rose State College (Okla.); did not play.
COLLEGE: Oklahoma State.
TRANSACTIONS/CAREER NOTES: Selected by Chicago Bears in fourth round (94th pick overall) of 1998 NFL draft. ... Signed by Bears (August 2, 1998).
HONORS: Named tight end on THE SPORTING NEWS college All-America first team (1997).
SINGLE GAME HIGHS (regular season): Receptions—4 (October 18, 1998, vs. Dallas); yards—57 (October 18, 1998, vs. Dallas); and touchdown receptions—0.

			RECEIVING				TOTALS		
Year Team	G	GS	No.	Yds.	Avg.	TD	TD	2pt.	Pts.	Fum.
1998—Chicago NFL	16	16	21	217	10.3	0	0	0	0	2

MAYES, DERRICK   WR   PACKERS

PERSONAL: Born January 28, 1974, in Indianapolis. ... 6-0/205. ... Full name: Derrick Binet Mayes.
HIGH SCHOOL: North Central (Indianapolis).
COLLEGE: Notre Dame (degree in communications).
TRANSACTIONS/CAREER NOTES: Selected by Green Bay Packers in second round (56th pick overall) of 1996 NFL draft. ... Signed by Packers (July 17, 1996). ... Granted free agency (February 12, 1999).

CHAMPIONSHIP GAME EXPERIENCE: Member of Packers for NFC championship game (1996 season); inactive. ... Member of Super Bowl championship team (1996 season); inactive. ... Played in NFC championship game (1997 season). ... Played in Super Bowl XXXII (1997 season).
PRO STATISTICS: 1997—Returned 14 punts for 141 yards. 1998—Returned one punt for nine yards.
SINGLE GAME HIGHS (regular season): Receptions—5 (December 13, 1998, vs. Chicago); yards—119 (November 16, 1997, vs. Indianapolis); and touchdown receptions—3 (September 27, 1998, vs. Carolina).
STATISTICAL PLATEAUS: 100-yard receiving games: 1997 (1).

				RECEIVING				TOTALS			
Year Team	G	GS	No.	Yds.	Avg.	TD	TD	2pt.	Pts.	Fum.
1996—Green Bay NFL	7	0	6	46	7.7	2	2	0	12	0
1997—Green Bay NFL	12	3	18	290	16.1	0	0	0	0	0
1998—Green Bay NFL	10	6	30	394	13.1	3	3	0	18	1
Pro totals (3 years)	29	9	54	730	13.5	5	5	0	30	1

MAYNARD, BRAD P GIANTS

PERSONAL: Born February 9, 1974, in Tipton, Ind. ... 6-1/190. ... Full name: Bradley Alan Maynard.
HIGH SCHOOL: Sheridan (Atlanta, Ind.).
COLLEGE: Ball State.
TRANSACTIONS/CAREER NOTES: Selected by New York Giants in third round (95th pick overall) of 1997 NFL draft. ... Signed by Giants (July 19, 1997).
HONORS: Named punter on THE SPORTING NEWS college All-America second team (1996).
PRO STATISTICS: 1998—Rushed once for minus five yards and attempted one pass without a completion.

		PUNTING					
Year Team	G	No.	Yds.	Avg.	Net avg.	In. 20	Blk.
1997—New York Giants NFL	16	*111	*4531	40.8	34.6	*33	1
1998—New York Giants NFL	16	101	*4566	45.2	37.8	∞33	0
Pro totals (2 years)	32	212	9097	42.9	36.1	66	1

MAYS, KIVUUSAMA LB VIKINGS

PERSONAL: Born January 7, 1975, in Anniston, Ala. ... 6-3/250. ... Name pronounced kih-vy-YOU-sa-ma.
HIGH SCHOOL: Cole (San Antonio), then Anniston (Ala.).
COLLEGE: North Carolina.
TRANSACTIONS/CAREER NOTES: Selected by Minnesota Vikings in fourth round (110th pick overall) of 1998 NFL draft. ... Signed by Vikings (June 26, 1998).
PLAYING EXPERIENCE: Minnesota NFL, 1998. ... Games/Games started: 16/0.
CHAMPIONSHIP GAME EXPERIENCE: Member of Vikings for NFC championship game (1998 season); inactive.
PRO STATISTICS: 1998—Recovered one fumble.

McAFEE, FRED RB

PERSONAL: Born June 20, 1968, in Philadelphia, Miss. ... 5-10/198. ... Full name: Fred Lee McAfee.
HIGH SCHOOL: Philadelphia (Miss.).
COLLEGE: Mississippi College (degree in mass communications, 1990).
TRANSACTIONS/CAREER NOTES: Selected by New Orleans Saints in sixth round (154th pick overall) of 1991 NFL draft. ... Signed by Saints (July 14, 1991). ... Released by Saints (August 26, 1991). ... Re-signed by Saints to practice squad (August 28, 1991). ... Activated (October 18, 1991). ... On injured reserve with shoulder injury (December 15, 1992-remainder of season). ... Granted free agency (February 17, 1994). ... Signed by Arizona Cardinals (August 2, 1994). ... Released by Cardinals (October 31, 1994). ... Signed by Pittsburgh Steelers (November 9, 1994). ... Granted unconditional free agency (February 16, 1996). ... Re-signed by Steelers (April 12, 1996). ... Granted unconditional free agency (February 12, 1999).
CHAMPIONSHIP GAME EXPERIENCE: Played in AFC championship game (1994, 1995 and 1997 seasons). ... Played in Super Bowl XXX (1995 season).
PRO STATISTICS: 1995—Recovered one fumble. 1998—Recovered a blocked punt in the end zone for a touchdown.
SINGLE GAME HIGHS (regular season): Attempts—28 (November 24, 1991, vs. Atlanta); yards—138 (November 24, 1991, vs. Atlanta); and rushing touchdowns—1 (September 10, 1995, vs. Houston).
STATISTICAL PLATEAUS: 100-yard rushing games: 1991 (1).

			RUSHING				RECEIVING				KICKOFF RETURNS			TOTALS			
Year Team	G	GS	Att.	Yds.	Avg.	TD	No.	Yds.	Avg.	TD	No.	Yds.	Avg.	TD	TD	2pt.	Pts. Fum.
1991—New Orleans NFL	9	0	109	494	4.5	2	1	8	8.0	0	1	14	14.0	0	2	...	12	2
1992—New Orleans NFL	14	1	39	114	2.9	1	1	16	16.0	0	19	393	20.7	0	1	...	6	0
1993—New Orleans NFL	15	4	51	160	3.1	1	1	3	3.0	0	28	580	20.7	0	1	...	6	3
1994—Arizona NFL	7	0	2	-5	-2.5	1	1	4	4.0	0	7	113	16.1	0	1	0	6	1
—Pittsburgh NFL	6	0	16	56	3.5	1	0	0	...	0	0	0	...	0	1	0	6	0
1995—Pittsburgh NFL	16	1	39	156	4.0	1	15	88	5.9	0	5	56	11.2	0	1	0	6	0
1996—Pittsburgh NFL	14	0	7	17	2.4	0	5	21	4.2	0	0	0	...	0	0	0	0	0
1997—Pittsburgh NFL	14	0	13	41	3.2	0	2	44	22.0	0	0	0	...	0	0	0	0	1
1998—Pittsburgh NFL	14	0	18	111	6.2	0	9	27	3.0	0	1	10	10.0	0	1	0	6	0
Pro totals (8 years)	109	6	294	1144	3.9	7	35	211	6.0	0	61	1166	19.1	0	8	0	48	7

– 256 –

McBURROWS, GERALD — S — FALCONS

PERSONAL: Born October 7, 1973, in Detroit. ... 5-11/205. ... Full name: Gerald Lance McBurrows.
HIGH SCHOOL: Martin Luther King (Detroit).
COLLEGE: Kansas.
TRANSACTIONS/CAREER NOTES: Selected by St. Louis Rams in seventh round (214th pick overall) of 1995 NFL draft. ... Signed by Rams (June 16, 1995). ... On injured reserve with knee injury (October 29, 1997-remainder of season). ... Granted free agency (February 13, 1998). ... Re-signed by Rams (April 24, 1998). ... On injured reserve with knee injury (November 17, 1998-remainder of season). ... Granted unconditional free agency (February 12, 1999). ... Signed by Atlanta Falcons (March 2, 1999).
PLAYING EXPERIENCE: St. Louis NFL, 1995-1998. ... Games/Games started: 1995 (14/3), 1996 (16/7), 1997 (8/3), 1998 (10/0). Total: 48/13.
PRO STATISTICS: 1995—Credited with one sack. 1996—Intercepted one pass for three yards. 1998—Recovered one fumble.

McCAFFREY, ED — WR — BRONCOS

PERSONAL: Born August 17, 1968, in Waynesboro, Pa. ... 6-5/215. ... Full name: Edward McCaffrey.
HIGH SCHOOL: Allentown (Pa.) Central Catholic.
COLLEGE: Stanford.
TRANSACTIONS/CAREER NOTES: Selected by New York Giants in third round (83rd pick overall) of 1991 NFL draft. ... Signed by Giants (July 23, 1991). ... Granted free agency (February 17, 1994). ... Signed by San Francisco 49ers (July 24, 1994). ... Granted unconditional free agency (February 17, 1995). ... Signed by Denver Broncos (March 7, 1995).
CHAMPIONSHIP GAME EXPERIENCE: Played in NFC championship game (1994 season). ... Member of Super Bowl championship team (1994, 1997 and 1998 seasons). ... Played in AFC championship game (1997 and 1998 seasons).
HONORS: Named wide receiver on THE SPORTING NEWS college All-America second team (1990). ... Played in Pro Bowl (1998 season).
PRO STATISTICS: 1995—Rushed once for minus one yard. 1997—Recovered two fumbles.
SINGLE GAME HIGHS (regular season): Receptions—9 (November 8, 1998, vs. San Diego); yards—133 (November 8, 1998, vs. San Diego); and touchdown receptions—3 (October 20, 1996, vs. Baltimore).
STATISTICAL PLATEAUS: 100-yard receiving games: 1992 (1), 1997 (1), 1998 (4). Total: 6.

				RECEIVING			TOTALS			
Year Team	G	GS	No.	Yds.	Avg.	TD	TD	2pt.	Pts.	Fum.
1991—New York Giants NFL	16	0	16	146	9.1	0	0	...	0	0
1992—New York Giants NFL	16	3	49	610	12.4	5	5	...	30	2
1993—New York Giants NFL	16	1	27	335	12.4	2	2	...	12	0
1994—San Francisco NFL	16	0	11	131	11.9	2	2	0	12	0
1995—Denver NFL	16	5	39	477	12.2	2	2	1	14	1
1996—Denver NFL	15	15	48	553	11.5	7	7	0	42	0
1997—Denver NFL	15	15	45	590	13.1	8	8	0	48	0
1998—Denver NFL	15	15	64	1053	16.5	10	10	1	62	1
Pro totals (8 years)	125	54	299	3895	13.0	36	36	2	220	4

McCARDELL, KEENAN — WR — JAGUARS

PERSONAL: Born January 6, 1970, in Houston. ... 6-1/184. ... Full name: Keenan Wayne McCardell.
HIGH SCHOOL: Waltrip (Houston).
COLLEGE: UNLV (degree in business management, 1991).
TRANSACTIONS/CAREER NOTES: Selected by Washington Redskins in 12th round (326th pick overall) of 1991 NFL draft. ... Signed by Redskins for 1991 season. ... On injured reserve with knee injury (August 20, 1991-entire season). ... Granted unconditional free agency (February 1, 1992). ... Signed by Cleveland Browns (March 24, 1992). ... Released by Browns (September 1, 1992). ... Re-signed by Browns to practice squad (September 3, 1992). ... Activated (October 6, 1992). ... Released by Browns (October 13, 1992). ... Re-signed by Browns to practice squad (October 14, 1992). ... Activated (November 14, 1992). ... Released by Browns (November 19, 1992). ... Re-signed by Browns to practice squad (November 20, 1992). ... Activated (December 26, 1992). ... Released by Browns (September 22, 1993). ... Signed by Chicago Bears to practice squad (November 2, 1993). ... Signed by Browns off Bears practice squad (November 24, 1993). ... Granted free agency (February 17, 1994). ... Re-signed by Browns (March 4, 1994). ... Granted unconditional free agency (February 16, 1996). ... Signed by Jacksonville Jaguars (March 2, 1996).
CHAMPIONSHIP GAME EXPERIENCE: Played in AFC championship game (1996 season).
HONORS: Played in Pro Bowl (1996 season).
PRO STATISTICS: 1995—Returned 13 punts for 93 yards and returned nine kickoffs for 161 yards. 1996—Returned one punt for two yards and recovered three fumbles. 1998—Returned one kickoff for 15 yards.
SINGLE GAME HIGHS (regular season): Receptions—16 (October 20, 1996, vs. St. Louis); yards—232 (October 20, 1996, vs. St. Louis); and touchdown receptions—2 (November 29, 1998, vs. Cincinnati).
STATISTICAL PLATEAUS: 100-yard receiving games: 1995 (1), 1996 (3), 1997 (4), 1998 (2). Total: 10.

				RECEIVING			TOTALS			
Year Team	G	GS	No.	Yds.	Avg.	TD	TD	2pt.	Pts.	Fum.
1991—Washington NFL					Did not play.					
1992—Cleveland NFL	2	0	1	8	8.0	0	0	...	0	0
1993—Cleveland NFL	6	3	13	234	18.0	4	4	...	24	0
1994—Cleveland NFL	13	3	10	182	18.2	0	0	0	0	0
1995—Cleveland NFL	16	5	56	709	12.7	4	4	0	24	0
1996—Jacksonville NFL	16	15	85	1129	13.3	3	3	2	22	1
1997—Jacksonville NFL	16	16	85	1164	13.7	5	5	0	30	0
1998—Jacksonville NFL	15	15	64	892	13.9	6	6	1	38	0
Pro totals (7 years)	84	57	314	4318	13.8	22	22	3	138	1

McCLEON, DEXTER — CB — RAMS

PERSONAL: Born October 9, 1973, in Meridian, Miss. ... 5-10/195. ... Full name: Dexter Keith McCleon.
HIGH SCHOOL: Meridian (Miss.).
COLLEGE: Clemson (degree in management, 1996).
TRANSACTIONS/CAREER NOTES: Selected by St. Louis Rams in second round (40th pick overall) of 1997 NFL draft. ... Signed by Rams (July 3, 1997).
PRO STATISTICS: 1997—Credited with one sack.
MISCELLANEOUS: Selected by Minnesota Twins organization in 13th round of free-agent baseball draft (June 3, 1993); did not sign.

			INTERCEPTIONS		
Year Team	G	GS	No.	Yds.	Avg.	TD
1997—St. Louis NFL	16	1	1	0	0.0	0
1998—St. Louis NFL	15	6	2	29	14.5	0
Pro totals (2 years)	31	7	3	29	9.7	0

McCLESKEY, J.J. — CB — CARDINALS

PERSONAL: Born April 10, 1970, in Knoxville, Tenn. ... 5-8/184. ... Full name: Tommy Joe McCleskey.
HIGH SCHOOL: Karns Comprehensive (Knoxville, Tenn.).
COLLEGE: Tennessee (degree in political science, 1993).
TRANSACTIONS/CAREER NOTES: Signed as non-drafted free agent by New Orleans Saints (May 7, 1993). ... Released by Saints (August 24, 1993). ... Re-signed by Saints to practice squad (August 31, 1993). ... Activated (December 23, 1993). ... Released by Saints (August 23, 1994). ... Re-signed by Saints (September 20, 1994). ... On injured reserve with hamstring injury (October 16-18, 1996). ... Claimed on waivers by Arizona Cardinals (October 18, 1996). ... Granted free agency (February 14, 1997). ... Re-signed by Cardinals for 1997 season. ... Granted unconditional free agency (February 13, 1998). ... Re-signed by Cardinals (February 23, 1998).
PLAYING EXPERIENCE: New Orleans NFL, 1994 and 1995; New Orleans (5)-Arizona (5) NFL, 1996; Arizona NFL, 1997 and 1998. ... Games/Games started: 1994 (13/0), 1995 (14/1), 1996 (N.O.-5/0; Ariz.-5/0; Total: 10/0), 1997 (13/0), 1998 (12/0). Total: 62/1.
PRO STATISTICS: 1994—Recovered one fumble. 1995—Intercepted one pass for no yards, returned one kickoff for no yards and recovered one fumble. 1997—Intercepted one pass for 15 yards and credited with one sack. 1998—Intercepted one pass for one yard.

McCLOUD, TYRUS — LB — RAVENS

PERSONAL: Born November 23, 1974, in Pompano Beach, Fla. ... 6-1/250. ... Full name: Tyrus Kamall McCloud.
HIGH SCHOOL: Nova (Fort Lauderdale, Fla.).
COLLEGE: Louisville.
TRANSACTIONS/CAREER NOTES: Selected by Baltimore Ravens in fourth round (118th pick overall) of 1997 NFL draft. ... Signed by Ravens (July 10, 1997). ... On injured reserve with knee injury (October 28, 1998-remainder of season).
PLAYING EXPERIENCE: Baltimore NFL, 1997 and 1998. ... Games/Games Started: 1997 (16/0), 1998 (7/2). Total: 23/2.
HONORS: Named inside linebacker on THE SPORTING NEWS college All-America second team (1996).
PRO STATISTICS: 1997—Fumbled once and recovered one fumble.

McCOLLUM, ANDY — G — RAMS

PERSONAL: Born June 2, 1970, in Akron, Ohio. ... 6-4/295. ... Full name: Andrew Jon McCollum.
HIGH SCHOOL: Revere (Richfield, Ohio).
COLLEGE: Toledo.
TRANSACTIONS/CAREER NOTES: Played in Arena League with Milwaukee Mustangs (1994). ... Signed as non-drafted free agent by Cleveland Browns (June 1994). ... Released by Browns (August 28, 1994). ... Re-signed by Browns to practice squad (August 30, 1994). ... Signed by New Orleans Saints off Browns practice squad (November 15, 1994). ... Inactive for five games (1994). ... Assigned by Saints to Barcelona Dragons in 1995 World League enhancement allocation program (February 20, 1995). ... Granted unconditional free agency (February 12, 1999). ... Signed by St. Louis Rams (April 19, 1999).
PLAYING EXPERIENCE: Barcelona W.L., 1995; New Orleans NFL, 1995-1998. ... Games/Games started: W.L. 1995 (games played unavailable); NFL 1995 (11/9), 1996 (16/16), 1997 (16/16), 1998 (16/5). Total NFL: 59/46.
PRO STATISTICS: 1996—Recovered one fumble. 1998—Recovered one fumble.

McCOMBS, TONY — LB — CARDINALS

PERSONAL: Born August 24, 1974, in Hopkinsville, Ky. ... 6-2/246. ... Full name: Antonias Orlando McCombs.
HIGH SCHOOL: Christian County (Hopkinsville, Ky.).
COLLEGE: Eastern Kentucky.
TRANSACTIONS/CAREER NOTES: Selected by Arizona Cardinals in sixth round (188th pick overall) of 1997 NFL draft. ... Signed by Cardinals (June 2, 1997).
PLAYING EXPERIENCE: Arizona NFL, 1997 and 1998. ... Games/Games started: 1997 (12/0), 1998 (14/13). Total: 26/13.
PRO STATISTICS: 1998—Intercepted one pass for 14 yards and recovered one fumble.

McCORMACK, HURVIN — DT — BROWNS

PERSONAL: Born April 6, 1972, in Brooklyn, N.Y. ... 6-5/275.
HIGH SCHOOL: New Dorp (Staten Island, N.Y.).
COLLEGE: Indiana.

TRANSACTIONS/CAREER NOTES: Signed as non-drafted free agent by Dallas Cowboys (April 28, 1994). ... Granted unconditional free agency (February 14, 1997). ... Re-signed by Cowboys (July 1997). ... Granted unconditional free agency (February 13, 1998). ... Re-signed by Cowboys (March 9, 1998). ... Selected by Cleveland Browns from Cowboys in NFL expansion draft (February 9, 1999).
PLAYING EXPERIENCE: Dallas NFL, 1994-1997. ... Games/Games started: 1994 (4/0), 1995 (14/2), 1996 (16/4), 1997 (13/0). Total: 47/6.
CHAMPIONSHIP GAME EXPERIENCE: Member of Cowboys for NFC championship game (1994 season); did not play. ... Played in NFC championship game (1995 season). ... Member of Super Bowl championship team (1995 season).
PRO STATISTICS: 1998—Recovered one fumble.

Year Team	G	GS	SACKS
1994—Dallas NFL	4	0	0.0
1995—Dallas NFL	14	2	2.0
1996—Dallas NFL	16	4	2.5
1997—Dallas NFL	13	0	0.5
1998—Dallas NFL	16	1	5.0
Pro totals (5 years)	63	7	10.0

McCOY, TONY DT COLTS

PERSONAL: Born June 10, 1969, in Orlando. ... 6-0/282. ... Full name: Anthony Bernard McCoy.
HIGH SCHOOL: Maynard Evans (Orlando).
COLLEGE: Florida.
TRANSACTIONS/CAREER NOTES: Selected by Indianapolis Colts in fourth round (105th pick overall) of 1992 NFL draft. ... Signed by Colts (July 17, 1992). ... Granted free agency (February 17, 1995). ... Re-signed by Colts (June 7, 1995).
CHAMPIONSHIP GAME EXPERIENCE: Played in AFC championship game (1995 season).
PRO STATISTICS: 1992—Recovered one fumble. 1994—Recovered one fumble. 1996—Recovered one fumble.

Year Team	G	GS	SACKS
1992—Indianapolis NFL	16	3	1.0
1993—Indianapolis NFL	6	0	0.0
1994—Indianapolis NFL	15	15	6.0
1995—Indianapolis NFL	16	16	2.5
1996—Indianapolis NFL	15	15	5.0
1997—Indianapolis NFL	16	11	2.5
1998—Indianapolis NFL	14	13	6.0
Pro totals (7 years)	98	73	23.0

McCRARY, MICHAEL DE RAVENS

PERSONAL: Born July 7, 1970, in Vienna, Va. ... 6-4/270. ... Full name: Michael Curtis McCrary.
HIGH SCHOOL: George C. Marshall (Falls Church, Va.).
COLLEGE: Wake Forest.
TRANSACTIONS/CAREER NOTES: Selected by Seattle Seahawks in seventh round (170th pick overall) of 1993 NFL draft. ... Signed by Seahawks (July 13, 1993). ... Granted free agency (February 16, 1996). ... Re-signed by Seahawks (June 6, 1996). ... Granted unconditional free agency (February 14, 1997). ... Signed by Baltimore Ravens (April 7, 1997).
HONORS: Named defensive end on THE SPORTING NEWS NFL All-Pro team (1998). ... Played in Pro Bowl (1998 season).
PRO STATISTICS: 1996—Recovered one fumble. 1997—Recovered two fumbles.
MISCELLANEOUS: Holds Baltimore Ravens all-time record for most sacks (23.5).

Year Team	G	GS	SACKS
1993—Seattle NFL	15	0	4.0
1994—Seattle NFL	16	0	1.5
1995—Seattle NFL	11	0	1.0
1996—Seattle NFL	16	13	▲13.5
1997—Baltimore NFL	15	15	9.0
1998—Baltimore NFL	16	16	14.5
Pro totals (6 years)	89	44	43.5

McCULLOUGH, GEORGE CB TITANS

PERSONAL: Born February 18, 1975, in Galveston, Texas. ... 5-10/187. ... Full name: George Wayne McCullough Jr.
HIGH SCHOOL: Ball (Galveston, Texas).
COLLEGE: Baylor.
TRANSACTIONS/CAREER NOTES: Selected by Houston Oilers in fifth round (143rd pick overall) of 1997 NFL draft. ... Oilers franchise moved to Tennessee for 1997 season. ... Signed by Oilers (July 19, 1997). ... Released by Oilers (August 25, 1997). ... Re-signed by Oilers to practice squad (August 26, 1997). ... Activated (December 5, 1997). ... Assigned by Oilers to Barcelona Dragons in 1998 NFL Europe enhancement allocation program (February 18, 1998). ... Oilers franchise renamed Tennessee Titans for 1999 season (December 26, 1998).
PLAYING EXPERIENCE: Tennessee NFL, 1997 and 1998; Barcelona Dragons NFLE, 1998. ... Games/Games started: 1997 (2/0), NFLE 1998 (games played unavailable), NFL 1998 (6/0). Total NFL: 8/0.
PRO STATISTICS: NFLE: 1998—Intercepted three passes for 89 yards and one touchdown and credited with two sacks.

McDANIEL, ED LB VIKINGS

PERSONAL: Born February 23, 1969, in Battesburg, S.C. ... 5-11/230.
HIGH SCHOOL: Battesburg (S.C.)-Leesville.
COLLEGE: Clemson (degree in human resources and development, 1991).

TRANSACTIONS/CAREER NOTES: Selected by Minnesota Vikings in fifth round (125th pick overall) of 1992 NFL draft. ... Signed by Vikings (July 20, 1992). ... Released by Vikings (August 31, 1992). ... Re-signed by Vikings to practice squad (September 1, 1992). ... Activated (November 5, 1992). ... On injured reserve with knee injury (August 25, 1996-entire season). ... Granted unconditional free agency (February 12, 1999). ... Re-signed by Vikings (February 18, 1999).
CHAMPIONSHIP GAME EXPERIENCE: Played in NFC championship game (1998 season).
HONORS: Named to play in Pro Bowl (1998 season); replaced by Hardy Nickerson due to injury.
PRO STATISTICS: 1995—Recovered one fumble. 1998—Recovered two fumbles for five yards.

				INTERCEPTIONS			SACKS
Year Team	G	GS	No.	Yds.	Avg.	TD	No.
1992—Minnesota NFL	8	0	0	0	...	0	0.0
1993—Minnesota NFL	7	1	0	0	...	0	0.0
1994—Minnesota NFL	16	16	1	0	0.0	0	1.5
1995—Minnesota NFL	16	16	1	3	3.0	0	4.5
1996—Minnesota NFL			Did not play.				
1997—Minnesota NFL	16	16	1	18	18.0	0	1.5
1998—Minnesota NFL	16	16	0	0	...	0	7.0
Pro totals (6 years)	79	65	3	21	7.0	0	14.5

McDANIEL, RANDALL — G — VIKINGS

PERSONAL: Born December 19, 1964, in Phoenix. ... 6-3/287. ... Full name: Randall Cornell McDaniel.
HIGH SCHOOL: Agua Fria Union (Avondale, Ariz.).
COLLEGE: Arizona State (degree in physical education, 1988).
TRANSACTIONS/CAREER NOTES: Selected by Minnesota Vikings in first round (19th pick overall) of 1988 NFL draft. ... Signed by Vikings (July 22, 1988). ... Granted free agency (February 1, 1991). ... Re-signed by Vikings (July 22, 1991). ... Designated by Vikings as transition player (February 25, 1993). ... Free agency status changed by Vikings from transitional to unconditional (February 17, 1994). ... Re-signed by Vikings (April 21, 1994). ... Designated by Vikings as franchise player (February 13, 1997). ... Re-signed by Vikings (February 21, 1997).
PLAYING EXPERIENCE: Minnesota NFL, 1988-1998. ... Games/Games started: 1988 (16/15), 1989 (14/13), 1990 (16/16), 1991 (16/16), 1992 (16/16), 1993 (16/16), 1994 (16/16), 1995 (16/16), 1996 (16/16), 1997 (16/16), 1998 (16/16). Total: 174/172.
CHAMPIONSHIP GAME EXPERIENCE: Played in NFC championship game (1998 season).
HONORS: Named guard on THE SPORTING NEWS college All-America second team (1987). ... Played in Pro Bowl (1989-1998 seasons). ... Named guard on THE SPORTING NEWS NFL All-Pro team (1991-1994 and 1996-1998).
PRO STATISTICS: 1991—Recovered one fumble. 1994—Recovered one fumble. 1996—Rushed twice for one yard.

McDANIEL, TERRY — CB

PERSONAL: Born February 8, 1965, in Saginaw, Mich. ... 5-10/180. ... Full name: Terence Lee McDaniel.
HIGH SCHOOL: Saginaw (Mich.).
COLLEGE: Tennessee.
TRANSACTIONS/CAREER NOTES: Selected by Los Angeles Raiders in first round (ninth pick overall) of 1988 NFL draft. ... Signed by Raiders (July 13, 1988). ... On injured reserve with broken leg (September 14, 1988-remainder of season). ... Granted free agency (February 1, 1992). ... Re-signed by Raiders (August 12, 1992). ... Designated by Raiders as transition player (February 25, 1993). ... Raiders franchise moved to Oakland (July 21, 1995). ... Granted unconditional free agency (February 14, 1997). ... Re-signed by Raiders (February 14, 1997). ... Released by Raiders (June 4, 1998). ... Signed by Green Bay Packers (July 20, 1998). ... Released by Packers (August 30, 1998). ... Signed by Seattle Seahawks (September 9, 1998). ... Granted unconditional free agency (February 12, 1999).
CHAMPIONSHIP GAME EXPERIENCE: Played in AFC championship game (1990 season).
HONORS: Named defensive back on THE SPORTING NEWS college All-America second team (1987). ... Played in Pro Bowl (1992-1996 seasons).
PRO STATISTICS: 1989—Credited with one sack. 1990—Credited with two sacks, recovered two fumbles for 44 yards and one touchdown. 1991—Recovered one fumble. 1992—Recovered one fumble for 40 yards. 1994—Recovered three fumbles for 48 yards and one touchdown. 1997—Fumbled once.

				INTERCEPTIONS		
Year Team	G	GS	No.	Yds.	Avg.	TD
1988—Los Angeles Raiders NFL	2	2	0	0	...	0
1989—Los Angeles Raiders NFL	16	15	3	21	7.0	0
1990—Los Angeles Raiders NFL	16	13	3	20	6.7	0
1991—Los Angeles Raiders NFL	16	16	0	0	...	0
1992—Los Angeles Raiders NFL	16	16	4	180	*45.0	0
1993—Los Angeles Raiders NFL	16	16	5	87	17.4	▲1
1994—Los Angeles Raiders NFL	16	16	7	103	14.7	2
1995—Oakland NFL	16	16	6	46	7.7	▲1
1996—Oakland NFL	16	15	5	150	30.0	1
1997—Oakland NFL	13	12	1	17	17.0	0
1998—Seattle NFL	9	0	1	43	43.0	1
Pro totals (11 years)	152	137	35	667	19.1	6

McDANIELS, PELLOM — DE — FALCONS

PERSONAL: Born February 21, 1968, in San Jose, Calif. ... 6-3/295. ... Full name: Pellom McDaniels III.
HIGH SCHOOL: Silver Creek (San Jose, Calif.).
COLLEGE: Oregon State (degree in communications and political science).

TRANSACTIONS/CAREER NOTES: Selected by Birmingham Fire in fifth round of 1991 World League draft. ... Signed as non-drafted free agent by Philadelphia Eagles (June 19, 1991). ... Released by Eagles (August 12, 1991). ... Signed by Kansas City Chiefs (June 5, 1992). ... Released by Chiefs (August 31, 1992). ... Re-signed by Chiefs to practice squad (September 2, 1992). ... Released by Chiefs (September 16, 1992). ... Re-signed by Chiefs for 1993 season. ... On injured reserve with shoulder injury (December 20, 1994-remainder of season). ... On injured reserve with ankle injury (December 17, 1998-remainder of season). ... Granted unconditional free agency (February 12, 1999). ... Signed by Atlanta Falcons (April 19, 1999).

CHAMPIONSHIP GAME EXPERIENCE: Played in AFC championship game (1993 season).

PRO STATISTICS: 1994—Recovered one fumble. 1995—Returned one kickoff for no yards. 1997—Recovered one fumble.

Year Team	G	GS	SACKS
1991—Birmingham W.L.	10	6	3.0
1992—Birmingham W.L.	10	10	3.5
1993—Kansas City NFL	10	0	0.0
1994—Kansas City NFL	12	3	2.0
1995—Kansas City NFL	16	2	2.0
1996—Kansas City NFL	9	1	0.0
1997—Kansas City NFL	16	6	3.5
1998—Kansas City NFL	11	2	0.0
W.L. totals (2 years)	20	16	6.5
NFL totals (6 years)	74	14	7.5
Pro totals (8 years)	94	30	14.0

McDONALD, RAMOS   CB   VIKINGS

PERSONAL: Born April 30, 1976, in Dallas. ... 5-11/194.
HIGH SCHOOL: Liberty Eylau (Texarkana, Texas).
JUNIOR COLLEGE: Navarro College (Texas).
COLLEGE: New Mexico.
TRANSACTIONS/CAREER NOTES: Selected by Minnesota Vikings in third round (80th pick overall) of 1998 NFL draft. ... Signed by Vikings (July 25, 1998).
PLAYING EXPERIENCE: Minnesota NFL, 1998. ... Games/Games started: 15/0.
CHAMPIONSHIP GAME EXPERIENCE: Played in NFC championship game (1998 season).

McDONALD, RICARDO   LB   BEARS

PERSONAL: Born November 8, 1969, in Kingston, Jamaica. ... 6-2/248. ... Full name: Ricardo Milton McDonald. ... Twin brother of Devon McDonald, linebacker with Indianapolis Colts (1993-95) and Arizona Cardinals (1996).
HIGH SCHOOL: Eastside (Paterson, N.J.).
COLLEGE: Pittsburgh.
TRANSACTIONS/CAREER NOTES: Selected by Cincinnati Bengals in fourth round (88th pick overall) of 1992 NFL draft. ... Signed by Bengals (July 24, 1992). ... On injured reserve with knee injury (December 24, 1993-remainder of season). ... Granted free agency (February 17, 1995). ... Re-signed by Bengals (March 6, 1995). ... Granted unconditional free agency (February 16, 1996). ... Re-signed by Bengals (March 8, 1996). ... Granted unconditional free agency (February 13, 1998). ... Signed by Chicago Bears (May 12, 1998). ... On injured reserve with hamstring injury (December 22, 1998-remainder of season).

PRO STATISTICS: 1992—Intercepted one pass for no yards and recovered one fumble for four yards. 1995—Recovered one fumble.

Year Team	G	GS	SACKS
1992—Cincinnati NFL	16	13	0.0
1993—Cincinnati NFL	14	12	1.0
1994—Cincinnati NFL	13	13	1.0
1995—Cincinnati NFL	16	15	5.0
1996—Cincinnati NFL	16	15	5.0
1997—Cincinnati NFL	13	12	1.0
1998—Chicago NFL	15	14	1.0
Pro totals (7 years)	103	94	14.0

McDONALD, TIM   S   49ERS

PERSONAL: Born January 6, 1965, in Fresno, Calif. ... 6-2/219. ... Full name: Timothy McDonald.
HIGH SCHOOL: Edison (Fresno, Calif.).
COLLEGE: Southern California.
TRANSACTIONS/CAREER NOTES: Selected by St. Louis Cardinals in second round (34th pick overall) of 1987 NFL draft. ... Signed by Cardinals (August 2, 1987). ... On injured reserve with broken ankle (September 1-December 12, 1987). ... Cardinals franchise moved to Phoenix (March 15, 1988). ... Granted free agency (February 1, 1990). ... Re-signed by Cardinals (August 21, 1990). ... On injured reserve with broken leg and ankle (December 3, 1991-remainder of season). ... Designated by Cardinals as franchise player (February 25, 1993). ... Signed by San Francisco 49ers (April 7, 1993); Cardinals received first-round pick (OT Ernest Dye) in 1993 draft as compensation.
CHAMPIONSHIP GAME EXPERIENCE: Played in NFC championship game (1993, 1994 and 1997 seasons). ... Member of Super Bowl championship team (1994 season).
HONORS: Named defensive back on THE SPORTING NEWS college All-America second team (1984). ... Named defensive back on THE SPORTING NEWS college All-America first team (1985). ... Played in Pro Bowl (1989 and 1992-1995 seasons). ... Named to play in Pro Bowl (1991 season); replaced by Shaun Gayle due to injury.
PRO STATISTICS: 1988—Recovered one fumble for nine yards. 1989—Recovered one fumble for one yard. 1990—Recovered one fumble. 1991—Recovered one fumble. 1992—Recovered three fumbles for two yards. 1993—Recovered one fumble for 15 yards. 1994—Recovered one fumble for 49 yards and a touchdown. 1996—Recovered one fumble. 1997—Recovered three fumbles. 1998—Recovered two fumbles.

Year Team	G	GS	INTERCEPTIONS No.	Yds.	Avg.	TD	SACKS No.
1987—St. Louis NFL	3	0	0	0	...	0	0.0
1988—Phoenix NFL	16	15	2	11	5.5	0	2.0
1989—Phoenix NFL	16	16	7	‡170	24.3	∞1	0.0
1990—Phoenix NFL	16	16	4	63	15.8	0	0.0
1991—Phoenix NFL	13	13	5	36	7.2	0	0.0
1992—Phoenix NFL	16	16	2	35	17.5	0	0.5
1993—San Francisco NFL	16	16	3	23	7.7	0	0.0
1994—San Francisco NFL	16	16	2	79	39.5	1	0.0
1995—San Francisco NFL	16	16	4	135	33.8	†2	0.0
1996—San Francisco NFL	16	16	2	14	7.0	0	1.0
1997—San Francisco NFL	15	15	3	34	11.3	0	0.0
1998—San Francisco NFL	16	16	4	22	5.5	0	4.0
Pro totals (12 years)	175	171	38	622	16.4	4	7.5

McDUFFIE, O.J. WR DOLPHINS

PERSONAL: Born December 2, 1969, in Marion, Ohio. ... 5-10/195. ... Full name: Otis James McDuffie.
HIGH SCHOOL: Hawken (Gates Mills, Ohio).
COLLEGE: Penn State (degree in labor and industrial relations).
TRANSACTIONS/CAREER NOTES: Selected by Miami Dolphins in first round (25th pick overall) of 1993 NFL draft. ... Signed by Dolphins (July 18, 1993).
HONORS: Named wide receiver on THE SPORTING NEWS college All-America second team (1992).
POST SEASON RECORDS: Shares NFL postseason career and single-game records for most two-point conversions—1 (December 30, 1995, vs. Buffalo).
PRO STATISTICS: 1993—Fumbled four times and recovered one fumble. 1994—Fumbled three times. 1995—Fumbled four times and recovered two fumbles. 1996—Fumbled six times and recovered three fumbles. 1997—Recovered two fumbles for three yards.
SINGLE GAME HIGHS (regular season): Receptions—11 (December 13, 1998, vs. New York Jets); yards—137 (October 27, 1997, vs. Chicago); and touchdown receptions—3 (November 29, 1998, vs. New Orleans).
STATISTICAL PLATEAUS: 100-yard receiving games: 1994 (1), 1996 (2), 1997 (3), 1998 (3). Total: 9.

			RUSHING				RECEIVING				PUNT RETURNS				KICKOFF RETURNS				TOTALS		
Year Team	G	GS	Att.	Yds.	Avg.	TD	No.	Yds.	Avg.	TD	No.	Yds.	Avg.	TD	No.	Yds.	Avg.	TD	TD	2pt.	Pts.
1993—Miami NFL	16	0	1	-4	-4.0	0	19	197	10.4	0	28	317	11.3	†2	32	755	23.6	0	2	...	12
1994—Miami NFL	15	3	5	32	6.4	0	37	488	13.2	3	32	228	7.1	0	36	767	21.3	0	3	0	18
1995—Miami NFL	16	16	3	6	2.0	0	62	819	13.2	8	24	163	6.8	0	23	564	24.5	0	8	1	50
1996—Miami NFL	16	16	2	7	3.5	0	74	918	12.4	8	22	212	9.6	0	0	0	...	0	8	0	48
1997—Miami NFL	16	16	0	0	...	0	76	943	12.4	1	2	4	2.0	0	0	0	...	0	1	0	6
1998—Miami NFL	16	16	3	11	3.7	0	*90	1050	11.7	7	12	141	11.8	0	0	0	...	0	7	0	42
Pro totals (6 years)	95	67	14	52	3.7	0	358	4415	12.3	27	120	1065	8.9	2	91	2086	22.9	0	29	1	176

McELMURRY, BLAINE S JAGUARS

PERSONAL: Born October 23, 1973, in Helena, Mont. ... 6-0/193. ... Full name: Blaine Richard McElmurry.
HIGH SCHOOL: Troy (Mont.).
COLLEGE: Montana (degree in microbiology).
TRANSACTIONS/CAREER NOTES: Signed as non-drafted free agent by Tennessee Oilers (May 2, 1997). ... Claimed on waivers by Philadelphia Eagles (August 24, 1997). ... Released by Eagles (August 29, 1997). ... Signed by Green Bay Packers to practice squad (September 3, 1997). ... Activated (November 25, 1997). ... Released by Packers (August 21, 1998). ... Signed by Tennessee Oilers to practice squad (November 4, 1998). ... Signed by Jacksonville Jaguars off Oilers practice squad (December 16, 1998).
PLAYING EXPERIENCE: Jacksonville NFL, 1998. ... Games/Games started: 2/0.
CHAMPIONSHIP GAME EXPERIENCE: Member of Packers for NFC championship team (1997 season); inactive. ... Member of Packers for Super Bowl XXXII (1997 season); inactive.

McELROY, RAY CB COLTS

PERSONAL: Born July 31, 1972, in Bellwood, Ill. ... 5-11/207. ... Full name: Raymond Edward McElroy.
HIGH SCHOOL: Proviso West (Hillside, Ill.).
COLLEGE: Eastern Illinois.
TRANSACTIONS/CAREER NOTES: Selected by Indianapolis Colts in fourth round (114th pick overall) of 1995 NFL draft. ... Signed by Colts (July 12, 1995). ... Granted free agency (February 13, 1998). ... Re-signed by Colts (February 24, 1998). ... Released by Colts (August 24, 1998). ... Re-signed by Colts (August 28, 1998). ... Granted unconditional free agency (February 12, 1999). ... Re-signed by Cotls (May 3, 1999).
PLAYING EXPERIENCE: Indianapolis NFL, 1995-1998. ... Games/Games started: 1995 (16/0), 1996 (16/5), 1997 (16/4), 1998 (16/0). Total: 64/9.
CHAMPIONSHIP GAME EXPERIENCE: Played in AFC championship game (1995 season).
PRO STATISTICS: 1997—Returned blocked field goal attempt 42 yards for a touchdown.

McENDOO, JASON C SEAHAWKS

PERSONAL: Born February 25, 1975, in San Diego. ... 6-5/315. ... Full name: Jason Howard McEndoo. ... Nephew of Jim Winn, pitcher with Pittsburgh Pirates (1983-86), Chicago White Sox (1987) and Minnesota Twins (1988).
HIGH SCHOOL: Aberdeen (Cosmopolis, Wash.).
COLLEGE: Washington State.

TRANSACTIONS/CAREER NOTES: Selected by Seattle Seahawks in seventh round (197th pick overall) of 1998 NFL draft. ... Signed by Seahawks (June 5, 1998). ... Released by Seahawks (August 24, 1998). ... Re-signed by Seahawks to practice squad (August 31, 1998). ... Activated (October 30, 1998). ... Released by Seahawks (November 10, 1998). ... Re-signed by Seahawks to practice squad (November 10, 1998). ... Activated (December 25, 1998). ... Assigned by Seahawks to Berlin Thunder in 1999 NFL Europe enhancement allocation program (February 22, 1999).
PLAYING EXPERIENCE: Seattle NFL, 1998. ... Games/Games started: 1/0.
PRO STATISTICS: 1998—Fumbled once for minus four yards.

McGARRAHAN, SCOTT S PACKERS

PERSONAL: Born February 12, 1974, in Arlington, Texas. ... 6-1/197. ... Full name: John Scott McGarrahan.
HIGH SCHOOL: Lamar (Arlington, Texas).
COLLEGE: New Mexico.
TRANSACTIONS/CAREER NOTES: Selected by Green Bay Packers in sixth round (156th pick overall) of 1998 NFL draft. ... Signed by Packers (July 17, 1998).
PLAYING EXPERIENCE: Green Bay NFL, 1998. ... Games/Games started: 15/0.

McGEE, DELL CB

PERSONAL: Born September 7, 1973, in Columbus, Ga. ... 5-8/185.
HIGH SCHOOL: Kendrick (Columbus, Ga.).
COLLEGE: Auburn.
TRANSACTIONS/CAREER NOTES: Selected by Arizona Cardinals in fifth round (162nd pick overall) of 1996 NFL draft. ... Signed by Cardinals (July 21, 1996). ... Released by Cardinals (August 25, 1996). ... Re-signed by Cardinals to practice squad (August 27, 1996). ... On injured reserve with shoulder injury (August 19, 1997-entire season). ... Released by Cardinals (August 30, 1998). ... Re-signed by Cardinals (October 2, 1998). ... Released by Cardinals (October 27, 1998). ... Selected by Rhein Fire in 1999 NFL Europe draft (February 23, 1999).
PLAYING EXPERIENCE: Arizona NFL, 1998. ... Games/Games started: 3/0.

McGEE, TONY TE BENGALS

PERSONAL: Born April 21, 1971, in Terre Haute, Ind. ... 6-3/250.
HIGH SCHOOL: Terre Haute (Ind.) South.
COLLEGE: Michigan (degree in communications).
TRANSACTIONS/CAREER NOTES: Selected by Cincinnati Bengals in second round (37th pick overall) of 1993 NFL draft. ... Signed by Bengals (July 20, 1993). ... Granted free agency (February 16, 1996). ... Re-signed by Bengals for 1996 season.
PRO STATISTICS: 1994—Returned one kickoff for four yards.
SINGLE GAME HIGHS (regular season): Receptions—8 (December 22, 1996, vs. Indianapolis); yards—118 (September 3, 1995, vs. Indianapolis); and touchdown receptions—2 (November 9, 1997, vs. Indianapolis).
STATISTICAL PLATEAUS: 100-yard receiving games: 1993 (1), 1995 (1). Total: 2.

			RECEIVING				TOTALS			
Year Team	G	GS	No.	Yds.	Avg.	TD	TD	2pt.	Pts.	Fum.
1993—Cincinnati NFL	15	15	44	525	11.9	0	0	...	0	1
1994—Cincinnati NFL	16	16	40	492	12.3	1	1	0	6	0
1995—Cincinnati NFL	16	16	55	754	13.7	4	4	0	24	2
1996—Cincinnati NFL	16	16	38	446	11.7	4	4	0	24	0
1997—Cincinnati NFL	16	16	34	414	12.2	6	6	1	38	0
1998—Cincinnati NFL	16	16	22	363	16.5	1	1	0	6	0
Pro totals (6 years)	95	95	233	2994	12.8	16	16	1	98	3

McGILL, LENNY CB SEAHAWKS

PERSONAL: Born May 31, 1971, in Long Beach, Calif. ... 6-1/202. ... Full name: Charles Leonard McGill.
HIGH SCHOOL: Orange Glen (Escondido, Calif.).
COLLEGE: Arizona State.
TRANSACTIONS/CAREER NOTES: Signed as non-drafted free agent by Green Bay Packers (May 2, 1994). ... On injured reserve with torn knee ligament (November 1, 1994-remainder of season). ... Traded by Packers to Atlanta Falcons for RB Robert Baldwin (June 6, 1996). ... Granted unconditional free agency (February 14, 1997). ... Re-signed by Falcons (April 1, 1997). ... Released by Falcons (August 24, 1997). ... Re-signed by Falcons (September 3, 1997). ... Granted unconditional free agency (February 13, 1998). ... Re-signed by Falcons (April 1, 1998). ... Released by Falcons (August 29, 1998). ... Signed by Carolina Panthers (October 14, 1998). ... Granted unconditional free agency (February 12, 1999). ... Signed by Seattle Seahawks (March 12, 1999).
CHAMPIONSHIP GAME EXPERIENCE: Played in NFC championship game (1995 season).
PRO STATISTICS: 1995—Recovered one fumble. 1996—Recovered one fumble. 1998—Credited with one sack.

			INTERCEPTIONS			
Year Team	G	GS	No.	Yds.	Avg.	TD
1994—Green Bay NFL	6	0	2	16	8.0	0
1995—Green Bay NFL	15	1	0	0	...	0
1996—Atlanta NFL	16	8	0	0	...	0
1997—Atlanta NFL	15	0	1	7	7.0	0
1998—Carolina NFL	10	0	1	6	6.0	0
Pro totals (5 years)	62	9	4	29	7.3	0

McGINEST, WILLIE   DE   PATRIOTS

PERSONAL: Born December 11, 1971, in Long Beach, Calif. ... 6-5/255. ... Full name: William Lee McGinest Jr.
HIGH SCHOOL: Polytechnic (Long Beach, Calif.).
COLLEGE: Southern California.
TRANSACTIONS/CAREER NOTES: Selected by New England Patriots in first round (fourth pick overall) of 1994 NFL draft. ... Signed by Patriots (May 17, 1994). ... Granted unconditional free agency (February 13, 1998). ... Re-signed by Patriots (February 12, 1998).
CHAMPIONSHIP GAME EXPERIENCE: Played in AFC championship game (1996 season). ... Played in Super Bowl XXXI (1996 season).
PRO STATISTICS: 1994—Recovered two fumbles. 1996—Intercepted one pass for 46 yards and a touchdown and recovered two fumbles (including one in end zone for a touchdown). 1997—Recovered three fumbles.

Year Team	G	GS	SACKS
1994—New England NFL	16	7	4.5
1995—New England NFL	16	16	11.0
1996—New England NFL	16	16	9.5
1997—New England NFL	11	11	2.0
1998—New England NFL	9	8	3.5
Pro totals (5 years)	68	58	30.5

McGLOCKTON, CHESTER   DT   CHIEFS

PERSONAL: Born September 16, 1969, in Whiteville, N.C. ... 6-4/320.
HIGH SCHOOL: Whiteville (N.C.).
COLLEGE: Clemson.
TRANSACTIONS/CAREER NOTES: Selected after junior season by Los Angeles Raiders in first round (16th pick overall) of 1992 NFL draft. ... Signed by Raiders for 1992 season. ... On injured reserve (January 11, 1994-remainder of 1993 playoffs). ... Raiders franchise moved to Oakland (July 21, 1995). ... Designated by Raiders as franchise player (February 12, 1998). ... Tendered offer sheet by Kansas City Chiefs (April 10, 1998). ... Raiders declined to match offer (April 17, 1998).
HONORS: Named defensive tackle on THE SPORTING NEWS NFL All-Pro team (1994). ... Played in Pro Bowl (1994-1997 seasons).
PRO STATISTICS: 1993—Intercepted one pass for 19 yards. 1994—Recovered one fumble. 1995—Recovered two fumbles. 1997—Recovered one fumble. 1998—Recovered one fumble.

Year Team	G	GS	SACKS
1992—Los Angeles Raiders NFL	10	0	3.0
1993—Los Angeles Raiders NFL	16	16	7.0
1994—Los Angeles Raiders NFL	16	16	9.5
1995—Oakland NFL	16	16	7.5
1996—Oakland NFL	16	16	8.0
1997—Oakland NFL	16	16	4.5
1998—Kansas City NFL	10	9	1.0
Pro totals (7 years)	100	89	40.5

McGUIRE, KAIPO   WR   COLTS

PERSONAL: Born January 16, 1974, in Honolulu. ... 5-10/174. ... Full name: Roy Kaiponohea McGuire.
HIGH SCHOOL: St. Louis (Honolulu).
COLLEGE: Brigham Young (degree in psychology, 1996).
TRANSACTIONS/CAREER NOTES: Signed as non-drafted free agent by Indianapolis Colts (May 5, 1997). ... Released by Colts (August 24, 1997). ... Re-signed by Colts to practice squad (August 25, 1997). ... Activated (September 13, 1997). ... Released by Colts (October 7, 1997). ... Re-signed by Colts (December 23, 1997). ... Released by Colts (August 26, 1998). ... Re-signed by Colts to practice squad (August 31, 1998). ... Released by Colts (September 7, 1998). ... Re-signed by Colts to practice squad (September 16, 1998). ... Activated (December 25, 1998).
PLAYING EXPERIENCE: Indianapolis NFL, 1997 and 1998. ... Games/Games started: 1997 (3/0), 1998 (1/0). Total: 4/0.
PRO STATISTICS: 1998—Returned two punts for four yards and returned four kickoffs for 75 yards.

McIVER, EVERETT   G   COWBOYS

PERSONAL: Born August 5, 1970, in Cumberland, N.C. ... 6-5/330. ... Full name: Everett Allen McIver.
HIGH SCHOOL: 71st Senior (Fayetteville, N.C.).
COLLEGE: Elizabeth City (N.C.) State.
TRANSACTIONS/CAREER NOTES: Signed as non-drafted free agent by San Diego Chargers (April 27, 1993). ... Claimed on waivers by Dallas Cowboys (July 27, 1993). ... Released by Cowboys (August 30, 1993). ... Re-signed by Cowboys to practice squad (August 31, 1993). ... Released by Cowboys (December 7, 1993). ... Signed by New York Jets to practice squad (December 10, 1993). ... Activated (January 2, 1994). ... Assigned by Jets to London Monarchs in 1996 World League enhancement allocation program (February 19, 1996). ... Released by Jets (August 7, 1996). ... Signed by Miami Dolphins (August 13, 1996). ... Released by Dolphins (September 2, 1996). ... Re-signed by Dolphins (October 7, 1996). ... Granted unconditional free agency (February 13, 1998). ... Signed by Cowboys (February 23, 1998). ... On injured reserve with knee injury (November 24, 1998-remainder of season).
PLAYING EXPERIENCE: New York Jets NFL, 1994 and 1995; London W.L., 1996; Miami NFL, 1996 and 1997; Dallas NFL, 1998. ... Games/Games started: 1994 (4/0), 1995 (14/4), 1996 (W.L.- games played unavailable; NFL-7/5.) 1997 (14/14), 1998 (6/6). Total NFL: 45/29.

McKENZIE, KEITH   DE   PACKERS

PERSONAL: Born October 17, 1973, in Detroit. ... 6-3/264. ... Full name: Keith Derrick McKenzie.
HIGH SCHOOL: Highland Park (Mich.).
COLLEGE: Ball State (degree in history).

TRANSACTIONS/CAREER NOTES: Selected by Green Bay Packers in seventh round (252nd pick overall) of 1996 NFL draft. ... Signed by Packers (July 15, 1996). ... Granted free agency (February 12, 1999).
CHAMPIONSHIP GAME EXPERIENCE: Member of Super Bowl championship team (1996 season). ... Played in NFC championship game (1996 and 1997 seasons). ... Played in Super Bowl XXXII (1997 season).
PRO STATISTICS: 1998—Intercepted one pass for 33 yards and a touchdown, returned one kickoff for 17 yards and recovered three fumbles for 88 yards and one touchdown.

Year Team	G	GS	SACKS
1996—Green Bay NFL	10	0	1.0
1997—Green Bay NFL	16	0	1.5
1998—Green Bay NFL	16	0	8.0
Pro totals (3 years)	42	0	10.5

McKENZIE, RALEIGH   G/C   PACKERS

PERSONAL: Born February 8, 1963, in Knoxville, Tenn. ... 6-2/285. ... Twin brother of Reggie McKenzie, linebacker with Los Angeles Raiders (1985-88), Montreal Machine of World League (1990) and San Francisco 49ers (1992).
HIGH SCHOOL: Austin-East (Knoxville, Tenn.).
COLLEGE: Tennessee.
TRANSACTIONS/CAREER NOTES: Selected by Washington Redskins in 11th round (290th pick overall) of 1985 NFL draft. ... Signed by Redskins (June 20, 1985). ... Granted free agency (February 1, 1992). ... Re-signed by Redskins for 1992 season. ... Granted unconditional free agency (February 17, 1995). ... Signed by Philadelphia Eagles (March 28, 1995). ... Granted unconditional free agency (February 14, 1997). ... Signed by San Diego Chargers (February 20, 1997). ... Granted unconditional free agency (February 12, 1999). ... Signed by Green Bay Packers (February 25, 1999).
PLAYING EXPERIENCE: Washington NFL, 1985-1994; Philadelphia NFL, 1995 and 1996; San Diego NFL, 1997 and 1998. ... Games/Games started: 1985 (6/0), 1986 (15/5), 1987 (12/12), 1988 (16/14), 1989 (15/8), 1990 (16/12), 1991 (16/14), 1992 (16/16), 1993 (16/16), 1994 (16/16), 1995 (16/16), 1996 (16/16), 1997 (16/16), 1998 (16/16). Total: 208/177.
CHAMPIONSHIP GAME EXPERIENCE: Played in NFC championship game (1986, 1987 and 1991 seasons). ... Member of Super Bowl championship team (1987 and 1991 seasons).
PRO STATISTICS: 1994—Recovered one fumble. 1995—Recovered one fumble. 1997—Recovered one fumble.

McKINNEY, STEVE   G   COLTS

PERSONAL: Born October 15, 1975, in Houston. ... 6-4/297. ... Full name: Stephen Michael McKinney.
HIGH SCHOOL: Clear Lake (Houston).
COLLEGE: Texas A&M.
TRANSACTIONS/CAREER NOTES: Selected by Indianapolis Colts in fourth round (93rd pick overall) of 1998 NFL draft. ... Signed by Colts (July 23, 1998).
PLAYING EXPERIENCE: Indianapolis NFL, 1998. ... Games/Games started: 16/16.

McKINNON, RONALD   LB   CARDINALS

PERSONAL: Born September 20, 1973, in Fort Rucker Army Base, Ala. ... 6-0/240.
HIGH SCHOOL: Elba (Ala.).
COLLEGE: North Alabama.
TRANSACTIONS/CAREER NOTES: Signed as non-drafted free agent by Arizona Cardinals (April 23, 1996). ... Granted free agency (February 12, 1999).
HONORS: Harlon Hill Trophy winner (1995).
PRO STATISTICS: 1996—Rushed once for minus four yards. 1997—Rushed once for three yards. 1998—Fumbled once and recovered two fumbles.

			INTERCEPTIONS				SACKS
Year Team	G	GS	No.	Yds.	Avg.	TD	No.
1996—Arizona NFL	16	0	0	0	...	0	0.0
1997—Arizona NFL	16	16	3	40	13.3	0	1.0
1998—Arizona NFL	13	13	5	25	5.0	0	2.0
Pro totals (3 years)	45	29	8	65	8.1	0	3.0

McKNIGHT, JAMES   WR   SEAHAWKS

PERSONAL: Born June 17, 1972, in Orlando. ... 6-1/198.
HIGH SCHOOL: Apopka (Fla.).
COLLEGE: Liberty (Va.).
TRANSACTIONS/CAREER NOTES: Signed as non-drafted free agent by Seattle Seahawks (April 29, 1994). ... Released by Seahawks (August 28, 1994). ... Re-signed by Seahawks to practice squad (August 29, 1994). ... Activated (November 19, 1994). ... Granted unconditional free agency (February 13, 1998). ... Re-signed by Seahawks (February 17, 1998).
PRO STATISTICS: 1995—Returned one kickoff for four yards and recovered one fumble. 1996—Returned three kickoffs for 86 yards and recovered one fumble. 1997—Returned one kickoff for 14 yards.
SINGLE GAME HIGHS (regular season): Receptions—5 (November 29, 1998, vs. Tennessee); yards—113 (November 29, 1998, vs. Tennessee); and touchdown receptions—1 (November 29, 1998, vs. Tennessee).
STATISTICAL PLATEAUS: 100-yard receiving games: 1997 (1), 1998 (1). Total: 2.

			RECEIVING				TOTALS			
Year Team	G	GS	No.	Yds.	Avg.	TD	TD	2pt.	Pts.	Fum.
1994—Seattle NFL	2	0	1	25	25.0	1	1	0	6	0
1995—Seattle NFL	16	0	6	91	15.2	0	0	0	0	1
1996—Seattle NFL	16	0	1	73	73.0	0	0	0	0	0
1997—Seattle NFL	12	5	34	637	*18.7	6	6	0	36	1
1998—Seattle NFL	14	2	21	346	16.5	2	2	0	12	0
Pro totals (5 years)	60	7	63	1172	18.6	9	9	0	54	2

McMANUS, TOM LB JAGUARS

PERSONAL: Born July 30, 1970, in Buffalo Grove, Ill. ... 6-2/255. ... Full name: Thomas Edward McManus.
HIGH SCHOOL: Wheeling (Ill.).
COLLEGE: Boston College (degree in marketing, 1992).
TRANSACTIONS/CAREER NOTES: Signed as non-drafted free agent by New Orleans Saints (May 7, 1993). ... Released by Saints (August 24, 1993). ... Signed by Jacksonville Jaguars (February 1, 1995). ... On injured reserve with knee injury (July 30, 1997-entire season). ... Granted free agency (February 13, 1998). ... Re-signed by Jaguars (June 3, 1998). ... Granted unconditional free agency (February 12, 1999). ... Re-signed by Jaguars (March 19, 1999).
PLAYING EXPERIENCE: Jacksonville NFL, 1995, 1996 and 1998. ... Games/Games started: 1995 (14/2), 1996 (16/11), 1998 (16/4). Total: 46/17.
CHAMPIONSHIP GAME EXPERIENCE: Played in AFC championship game (1996 season).

McMILLIAN, MARK CB 49ERS

PERSONAL: Born April 29, 1970, in Los Angeles. ... 5-7/148. ... Nephew of Gary Davis, running back with Miami Dolphins (1976-79) and Tampa Bay Buccaneers (1980-81). ... Name pronounced mik-MILL-en.
HIGH SCHOOL: John F. Kennedy (Granada Hills, Calif.).
JUNIOR COLLEGE: Glendale (Calif.) College.
COLLEGE: Alabama.
TRANSACTIONS/CAREER NOTES: Selected by Philadelphia Eagles in 10th round (272nd pick overall) of 1992 NFL draft. ... Signed by Eagles (July 20, 1992). ... Granted unconditional free agency (February 16, 1996). ... Signed by New Orleans Saints (February 29, 1996). ... Released by Saints (May 15, 1997). ... Signed by Kansas City Chiefs (June 16, 1997). ... Released by Chiefs (February 26, 1999). ... Signed by San Francisco 49ers (June 8, 1999).
PRO STATISTICS: 1993—Fumbled once and recovered one fumble. 1994—Recovered one fumble. 1995—Recovered two fumbles for minus one yard. 1996—Recovered one fumble for minus six yards.

			INTERCEPTIONS			
Year Team	G	GS	No.	Yds.	Avg.	TD
1992—Philadelphia NFL	16	3	1	0	0.0	0
1993—Philadelphia NFL	16	12	2	25	12.5	0
1994—Philadelphia NFL	16	16	2	2	1.0	0
1995—Philadelphia NFL	16	16	3	27	9.0	0
1996—New Orleans NFL	16	16	2	4	2.0	0
1997—Kansas City NFL	16	2	▲8	*274	*34.3	†3
1998—Kansas City NFL	16	10	3	48	16.0	0
Pro totals (7 years)	112	75	21	380	18.1	3

McNAIR, STEVE QB TITANS

PERSONAL: Born February 14, 1973, in Mount Olive, Miss. ... 6-2/225. ... Full name: Steve LaTreal McNair. ... Brother of Fred McNair, quarterback with Toronto Argonauts of CFL (1991) and London Monarchs of World League (1992).
HIGH SCHOOL: Mount Olive (Miss.).
COLLEGE: Alcorn State.
TRANSACTIONS/CAREER NOTES: Selected by Houston Oilers in first round (third pick overall) of 1995 NFL draft. ... Signed by Oilers (July 25, 1995). ... Oilers franchise moved to Tennessee for 1997 season. ... Oilers franchise renamed Tennessee Titans for 1999 season (December 26, 1998).
HONORS: Walter Payton Award winner (1994).
PRO STATISTICS: 1995—Fumbled three times and recovered two fumbles for minus two yards. 1996—Fumbled seven times and recovered four fumbles. 1997—Led NFL with 16 fumbles and recovered seven fumbles for minus two yards. 1998—Fumbled five times and recovered three fumbles for minus seven yards.
SINGLE GAME HIGHS (regular season): Attempts—49 (December 20, 1998, vs. Green Bay); completions—29 (December 20, 1998, vs. Green Bay); yards—308 (December 8, 1996, vs. Jacksonville); and touchdown passes—3 (December 20, 1998, vs. Green Bay).
STATISTICAL PLATEAUS: 300-yard passing games: 1996 (1).
MISCELLANEOUS: Regular-season record as starting NFL quarterback: 20-18 (.526).

				PASSING						RUSHING			TOTALS		
Year Team	G	GS	Att.	Cmp.	Pct.	Yds.	TD	Int.	Avg.	Rat.	Att.	Yds.	Avg.	TD	TD	2pt.	Pts.
1995—Houston NFL	6	2	80	41	51.3	569	3	1	7.11	81.7	11	38	3.5	0	0	0	0
1996—Houston NFL	9	4	143	88	61.5	1197	6	4	8.37	90.6	31	169	5.5	2	2	0	12
1997—Tennessee NFL	16	16	415	216	52.0	2665	14	13	6.42	70.4	101	674	*6.7	8	8	0	48
1998—Tennessee NFL	16	16	492	289	58.7	3228	15	10	6.56	80.1	77	559	7.3	4	4	0	24
Pro totals (4 years)	47	38	1130	634	56.1	7659	38	28	6.78	78.0	220	1440	6.5	14	14	0	84

McNEIL, RYAN — CB

PERSONAL: Born October 4, 1970, in Fort Pierce, Fla. ... 6-2/192. ... Full name: Ryan Darrell McNeil.
HIGH SCHOOL: Westwood (Fla.).
COLLEGE: Miami, Fla. (degree in psychology, 1992).
TRANSACTIONS/CAREER NOTES: Selected by Detroit Lions in second round (33rd pick overall) of 1993 NFL draft. ... Signed by Lions (August 25, 1993). ... Granted unconditional free agency (February 14, 1997). ... Signed by St. Louis Rams (July 7, 1997). ... Designated by Rams as franchise player (February 13, 1998). ... Re-signed by Rams (August 31, 1998). ... Granted unconditional free agency (February 12, 1999).
HONORS: Named defensive back on THE SPORTING NEWS college All-America second team (1992).
PRO STATISTICS: 1995—Recovered two fumbles. 1996—Recovered two fumbles. 1997—Fumbled once and recovered one fumble. 1998—Recovered one fumble.

				INTERCEPTIONS		
Year Team	G	GS	No.	Yds.	Avg.	TD
1993—Detroit NFL	16	2	2	19	9.5	0
1994—Detroit NFL	14	13	1	14	14.0	0
1995—Detroit NFL	16	16	2	26	13.0	0
1996—Detroit NFL	16	16	5	14	2.8	0
1997—St. Louis NFL	16	16	*9	127	14.1	1
1998—St. Louis NFL	16	12	1	37	37.0	1
Pro totals (6 years)	94	75	20	237	11.9	2

McPHAIL, JERRIS — RB — BROWNS

PERSONAL: Born June 26, 1972, in Clinton, N.C. ... 5-11/198. ... Full name: Jerris Cornelius McPhail.
HIGH SCHOOL: Clinton (N.C.).
COLLEGE: Mount Olive (N.C.) College, then East Carolina.
TRANSACTIONS/CAREER NOTES: Selected by Miami Dolphins in fifth round (134th pick overall) of 1996 NFL draft. ... Signed by Dolphins (July 15, 1996). ... On injured reserve with fractured left wrist (December 17, 1996-remainder of season). ... Released by Dolphins (August 25, 1998). ... Signed by Detroit Lions (August 29, 1998). ... Selected by Cleveland Browns from Lions in NFL expansion draft (February 9, 1999). ... Granted free agency (February 12, 1999). ... Re-signed by Browns (March 30, 1999).
PRO STATISTICS: 1996—Recovered one fumble.
SINGLE GAME HIGHS (regular season): Attempts—3 (December 14, 1997, vs. Indianapolis); yards—77 (October 27, 1997, vs. Chicago); and rushing touchdowns—1 (October 27, 1997, vs. Chicago).

			RUSHING				RECEIVING				KICKOFF RETURNS				TOTALS		
Year Team	G	GS	Att.	Yds.	Avg.	TD	No.	Yds.	Avg.	TD	No.	Yds.	Avg.	TD	TD	2pt.	Pts.	Fum.
1996—Miami NFL	9	1	6	28	4.7	0	20	282	14.1	0	15	335	22.3	0	0	0	0	2
1997—Miami NFL	14	1	17	146	8.6	1	34	262	7.7	1	15	314	20.9	0	2	0	12	1
1998—Detroit NFL	3	0	0	0	...	0	0	0	...	0	6	71	11.8	0	0	0	0	0
Pro totals (3 years)	26	2	23	174	7.6	1	54	544	10.1	1	36	720	20.0	0	2	0	12	3

McQUARTERS, R.W. — CB/KR — 49ERS

PERSONAL: Born December 21, 1976, in Tulsa, Okla. ... 5-9/198. ... Full name: Robert William McQuarters II.
HIGH SCHOOL: Washington (Tulsa, Okla.).
COLLEGE: Oklahoma State.
TRANSACTIONS/CAREER NOTES: Selected after junior season by San Francisco 49ers in first round (28th pick overall) of 1998 NFL draft. ... Signed by 49ers (July 28, 1998).
PRO STATISTICS: 1998—Recovered two fumbles.

			PUNT RETURNS				KICKOFF RETURNS				TOTALS			
Year Team	G	GS	No.	Yds.	Avg.	TD	No.	Yds.	Avg.	TD	TD	2pt.	Pts.	Fum.
1998—San Francisco NFL	16	7	*47	406	8.6	1	17	339	19.9	0	1	0	6	4

McTYER, TIM — DB — BROWNS

PERSONAL: Born December 14, 1975, in Los Angeles ... 5-11/181. ... Full name: Timothy Thomas McTyer.
HIGH SCHOOL: Washington (Los Angeles).
JUNIOR COLLEGE: Los Angeles Southwest Community College.
COLLEGE: Brigham Young.
TRANSACTIONS/CAREER NOTES: Signed as non-drafted free agent by Indianapolis Colts (April 25, 1997). ... Released by Colts (August 18, 1997). ... Signed by Philadelphia Eagles to practice squad (August 27, 1997). ... Released by Eagles (September 2, 1997). ... Re-signed by Eagles to practice squad (September 18, 1997). ... Activated (October 17, 1997). ... Selected by Cleveland Browns from Eagles in NFL expansion draft (February 9, 1999).
PLAYING EXPERIENCE: Philadelphia NFL, 1997 and 1998. ... Games/Games started: 1997 (10/0), 1998 (16/1). Total: 26/1.
PRO STATISTICS: 1998—Intercepted one pass for 18 yards, credited with $1/2$ sack and recovered one fumble.

McWILLIAMS, JOHNNY — TE — CARDINALS

PERSONAL: Born December 14, 1972, in Ontario, Calif. ... 6-4/271.
HIGH SCHOOL: Pomona (Calif.).
COLLEGE: Southern California.
TRANSACTIONS/CAREER NOTES: Selected by Arizona Cardinals in third round (64th pick overall) of 1996 NFL draft. ... Signed by Cardinals (August 28, 1996). ... On reserve/did not report list (August 25-September 9, 1996). ... Granted free agency (February 12, 1999).

SINGLE GAME HIGHS (regular season): Receptions—5 (November 10, 1996, vs. Washington); yards—54 (November 10, 1996, vs. Washington); and touchdown receptions—1 (November 22, 1998, vs. Washington).

Year Team	G	GS	RECEIVING No.	Yds.	Avg.	TD	TOTALS TD	2pt.	Pts.	Fum.
1996—Arizona NFL	12	0	7	80	11.4	1	1	0	6	0
1997—Arizona NFL	16	7	7	75	10.7	0	0	0	0	0
1998—Arizona NFL	16	15	26	284	10.9	4	4	0	24	0
Pro totals (3 years)	44	22	40	439	11.0	5	5	0	30	0

MEADOWS, ADAM OT COLTS

PERSONAL: Born January 25, 1974, in Powder Springs, Ga. ... 6-5/299. ... Full name: Adam Jonathan Meadows.
HIGH SCHOOL: McEachern (Powder Springs, Ga.).
COLLEGE: Georgia.
TRANSACTIONS/CAREER NOTES: Selected by Indianapolis Colts in second round (48th pick overall) of 1997 NFL draft. ... Signed by Colts (July 8, 1997).
PLAYING EXPERIENCE: Indianapolis NFL, 1997 and 1998. ... Games/Games started: 1997 (16/16), 1998 (14/14). Total: 30/30.

MEANS, NATRONE RB CHARGERS

PERSONAL: Born April 26, 1972, in Harrisburg, N.C. ... 5-10/245. ... Full name: Natrone Jermaine Means. ... Name pronounced NAY-trone.
HIGH SCHOOL: Central Cabarrus (Concord, N.C.).
COLLEGE: North Carolina.
TRANSACTIONS/CAREER NOTES: Selected after junior season by San Diego Chargers in second round (41st pick overall) of 1993 NFL draft. ... Signed by Chargers (July 18, 1993). ... Claimed on waivers by Jacksonville Jaguars (March 11, 1996). ... Granted unconditional free agency (February 13, 1998). ... Signed by Chargers (March 4, 1998). ... On injured reserve with foot injury (November 16, 1998-remainder of season).
CHAMPIONSHIP GAME EXPERIENCE: Played in AFC championship game (1994 and 1996 seasons). ... Played in Super Bowl XXIX (1994 season).
HONORS: Played in Pro Bowl (1994 season).
PRO STATISTICS: 1993—Attempted one pass without a completion, returned two kickoffs for 22 yards and recovered one fumble. 1994—Attempted one pass without a completion. 1996—Recovered one fumble. 1998—Recovered one fumble.
SINGLE GAME HIGHS (regular season): Attempts—37 (October 11, 1998, vs. Oakland); yards—165 (September 20, 1998, vs. Kansas City); and rushing touchdowns—3 (October 16, 1994, vs. New Orleans).
STATISTICAL PLATEAUS: 100-yard rushing games: 1993 (2), 1994 (6), 1995 (3), 1996 (1), 1998 (4). Total: 16.

Year Team	G	GS	RUSHING Att.	Yds.	Avg.	TD	RECEIVING No.	Yds.	Avg.	TD	TOTALS TD	2pt.	Pts.	Fum.
1993—San Diego NFL	16	0	160	645	4.0	8	10	59	5.9	0	8	...	48	1
1994—San Diego NFL	16	16	§343	1350	3.9	§12	39	235	6.0	0	▲12	0	72	5
1995—San Diego NFL	10	9	186	730	3.9	5	7	46	6.6	0	5	0	30	2
1996—Jacksonville NFL	14	4	152	507	3.3	2	7	45	6.4	1	3	0	18	3
1997—Jacksonville NFL	14	11	244	823	3.4	9	15	104	6.9	0	9	0	54	5
1998—San Diego NFL	10	10	212	883	4.2	5	16	91	5.7	0	5	0	30	2
Pro totals (6 years)	80	50	1297	4938	3.8	41	94	580	6.2	1	42	0	252	18

MEGGETT, DAVE RB/KR

PERSONAL: Born April 30, 1966, in Charleston, S.C. ... 5-7/190. ... Full name: David Lee Meggett.
HIGH SCHOOL: Bonds-Wilson (North Charleston, S.C.).
COLLEGE: Morgan State, then Towson State.
TRANSACTIONS/CAREER NOTES: Selected by New York Giants in fifth round (132nd pick overall) of 1989 NFL draft. ... Signed by Giants (July 24, 1989). ... Granted free agency (February 1, 1991). ... Re-signed by Giants (August 29, 1991). ... Granted free agency (March 1, 1993). ... Re-signed by Giants (July 28, 1993). ... Granted unconditional free agency (February 17, 1995). ... Signed by New England Patriots (March 3, 1995). ... Released by Patriots (May 29, 1998). ... Signed by New York Jets (December 15, 1998). ... Granted unconditional free agency (February 12, 1999).
CHAMPIONSHIP GAME EXPERIENCE: Played in NFC championship game (1990 season). ... Member of Super Bowl championship team (1990 season). ... Played in AFC championship game (1996 and 1998 seasons). ... Played in Super Bowl XXXI (1996 season).
HONORS: Walter Payton Award winner (1988). ... Played in Pro Bowl (1989 and 1996 seasons). ... Named punt returner on THE SPORTING NEWS NFL All-Pro team (1990).
RECORDS: Holds NFL career records for most punt returns—349; and most yards gained by punt return—3,708.
POST SEASON RECORDS: Shares Super Bowl single-game record for most fair catches—3 (January 27, 1991, vs. Buffalo). ... Holds NFL postseason career records for most punt returns—34; and most yards by punt return—312.
PRO STATISTICS: 1989—Fumbled eight times and recovered three fumbles. 1990—Fumbled three times and recovered two fumbles. 1991—Attempted one pass without a completion, fumbled eight times and recovered three fumbles. 1992—Fumbled five times and recovered three fumbles. 1993—Attempted two passes with two completions for 63 yards and two touchdowns, fumbled once and recovered one fumble. 1994—Attempted two passes with one completion for 16 yards and a touchdown, fumbled six times and recovered five fumbles. 1995—Attempted one pass without a completion and fumbled five times. 1996—Attempted one pass without a completion, fumbled seven times and recovered four fumbles. 1997—Attempted one pass with a completion for 35 yards and a touchdown, fumbled twice and recovered one fumble.
SINGLE GAME HIGHS (regular season): Attempts—26 (September 18, 1994, vs. Washington); yards—82 (September 18, 1994, vs. Washington); and rushing touchdowns—2 (September 18, 1994, vs. Washington).

Year	Team	G	GS	RUSHING Att.	Yds.	Avg.	TD	RECEIVING No.	Yds.	Avg.	TD	PUNT RETURNS No.	Yds.	Avg.	TD	KICKOFF RETURNS No.	Yds.	Avg.	TD	TOTALS TD	2pt.	Pts.
1989	N.Y. Giants NFL	16	2	28	117	4.2	0	34	531	15.6	4	‡46	*582	12.7	†1	27	577	21.4	0	5	...	30
1990	N.Y. Giants NFL	16	1	22	164	7.5	0	39	410	10.5	1	*43	*467	10.9	†1	21	492	‡23.4	0	2	...	12
1991	N.Y. Giants NFL	16	2	29	153	5.3	1	50	412	8.2	3	28	287	10.3	1	25	514	20.6	0	5	...	30
1992	N.Y. Giants NFL	16	0	32	167	5.2	0	38	229	6.0	2	27	240	8.9	0	20	455	22.8	1	3	...	18
1993	N.Y. Giants NFL	16	1	69	329	4.8	0	38	319	8.4	0	32	331	10.3	1	24	403	16.8	0	1	...	6
1994	N.Y. Giants NFL	16	3	91	298	3.3	4	32	293	9.2	0	26	323	12.4	†2	29	548	18.9	0	6	0	36
1995	New England NFL	16	0	60	250	4.2	2	52	334	6.4	0	45	383	8.5	0	38	964	25.4	0	2	▲2	16
1996	New England NFL	16	1	40	122	3.1	0	33	292	8.8	0	§52	§588	11.3	▲1	34	781	23.0	0	1	0	6
1997	New England NFL	16	2	20	60	3.0	1	19	203	10.7	1	45	467	10.4	0	33	816	24.7	0	2	0	12
1998	N.Y. Jets NFL	2	0	7	24	3.4	0	1	15	15.0	0	5	40	8.0	0	1	16	16.0	0	0	0	0
Pro totals (10 years)		146	12	398	1684	4.2	8	336	3038	9.0	11	349	3708	10.6	7	252	5566	22.1	1	27	2	166

METCALF, ERIC — WR

PERSONAL: Born January 23, 1968, in Seattle. ... 5-10/188. ... Full name: Eric Quinn Metcalf. ... Son of Terry Metcalf, running back with St. Louis Cardinals (1973-77), Toronto Argonauts of CFL (1978-80) and Washington Redskins (1981); and cousin of Ray Hall, defensive tackle with Jacksonville Jaguars (1995).
HIGH SCHOOL: Bishop Dennis J. O'Connell (Arlington, Va.).
COLLEGE: Texas (degree in liberal arts, 1990).
TRANSACTIONS/CAREER NOTES: Selected by Cleveland Browns in first round (13th pick overall) of 1989 NFL draft. ... Signed by Browns (August 20, 1989). ... Granted free agency (February 1, 1991). ... Re-signed by Browns for 1991 season. ... On injured reserve with shoulder injury (November 2, 1991-remainder of season). ... Granted free agency (February 1, 1992). ... Re-signed by Browns (August 30, 1992). ... Granted roster exemption (August 30-September 5, 1992). ... Traded by Browns with first-round pick (DB Devin Bush) in 1995 draft to Atlanta Falcons for first-round pick (traded to San Francisco) in 1995 draft (March 25, 1995). ... Granted unconditional free agency (February 14, 1997). ... Signed by San Diego Chargers (May 8, 1997). ... Traded by Chargers with first- (DE Andre Wadsworth) and second-round (CB Corey Chavous) picks in 1998 draft, first-round pick (WR David Boston) in 1999 draft and LB Patrick Sapp to Arizona Cardinals for first-round pick (QB Ryan Leaf) in 1998 draft (March 12, 1998). ... Granted unconditional free agency (February 12, 1999).
CHAMPIONSHIP GAME EXPERIENCE: Played in AFC championship game (1989 season).
HONORS: Named all-purpose player on THE SPORTING NEWS college All-America second team (1987). ... Named punt returner on THE SPORTING NEWS NFL All-Pro team (1993 and 1994). ... Played in Pro Bowl (1993, 1994 and 1997 seasons).
RECORDS: Holds NFL career record for most touchdowns by punt return—9. ... Shares NFL single-game records for most touchdowns by punt return—2; and most touchdowns by combined kick return—2 (October 24, 1993, vs. Pittsburgh and November 2, 1997, vs. Cincinnati).
POST SEASON RECORDS: Shares NFL postseason career record for most touchdowns by kickoff return—1 (January 6, 1990, vs. Buffalo).
PRO STATISTICS: 1989—Attempted two passes with one completion for 32 yards and a touchdown and fumbled five times. 1990—Fumbled eight times and recovered one fumble. 1991—Fumbled once. 1992—Attempted one pass without a completion, fumbled six times and recovered two fumbles. 1993—Fumbled five times. 1994—Attempted one pass without a completion and fumbled six times. 1995—Attempted one pass without a completion, fumbled four times and recovered two fumbles. 1996—Fumbled three times. 1997—Fumbled four times and recovered two fumbles. 1998—Fumbled five times and recovered two fumbles.
SINGLE GAME HIGHS (regular season): Receptions—11 (September 17, 1995, vs. New Orleans); yards—177 (September 20, 1992, vs. Los Angeles Raiders); and touchdown receptions—3 (September 20, 1992, vs. Los Angeles Raiders).
STATISTICAL PLATEAUS: 100-yard receiving games: 1992 (1), 1993 (1), 1995 (2), 1996 (1), 1997 (1). Total: 6.

Year	Team	G	GS	RUSHING Att.	Yds.	Avg.	TD	RECEIVING No.	Yds.	Avg.	TD	PUNT RETURNS No.	Yds.	Avg.	TD	KICKOFF RETURNS No.	Yds.	Avg.	TD	TOTALS TD	2pt.	Pts.
1989	Cleveland NFL	16	11	187	633	3.4	6	54	397	7.4	4	0	0	...	0	31	718	23.2	0	10	...	60
1990	Cleveland NFL	16	9	80	248	3.1	1	57	452	7.9	1	0	0	...	0	*52	*1052	20.2	*2	4	...	24
1991	Cleveland NFL	8	3	30	107	3.6	0	29	294	10.1	0	12	100	8.3	0	23	351	15.3	0	0	...	0
1992	Cleveland NFL	16	5	73	301	4.1	4	47	614	13.1	5	*44	§429	9.8	1	9	157	17.4	0	7	...	42
1993	Cleveland NFL	16	9	129	611	4.7	1	63	539	8.6	2	36	464§12.9		†2	15	318	21.2	0	5	...	30
1994	Cleveland NFL	16	8	93	329	3.5	2	47	436	9.3	0	35	348	9.9	†2	9	210	23.3	0	7	0	42
1995	Atlanta NFL	16	14	28	133	4.8	1	104	1189	11.4	8	39	383	9.8	†1	12	278	23.2	0	10	0	60
1996	Atlanta NFL	16	11	3	8	2.7	0	54	599	11.1	6	27	296	11.0	0	49	1034	21.1	0	6	0	36
1997	San Diego NFL	16	1	3	-5	-1.7	0	40	576	14.4	2	45	489	10.9	†3	16	355	22.2	0	5	0	30
1998	Arizona NFL	16	3	0	0	...	0	31	324	10.5	0	43	295	6.9	0	57	1218	21.4	0	0	0	0
Pro totals (10 years)		152	74	626	2365	3.8	12	526	5420	10.3	31	281	2804	10.0	9	273	5691	20.8	2	54	0	324

MICKENS, RAY — CB — JETS

PERSONAL: Born January 4, 1973, in Frankfurt, West Germany. ... 5-8/184.
HIGH SCHOOL: Andress (El Paso, Texas).
COLLEGE: Texas A&M.
TRANSACTIONS/CAREER NOTES: Selected by New York Jets in third round (62nd pick overall) of 1996 NFL draft. ... Signed by Jets (July 13, 1996). ... Granted free agency (February 12, 1999). ... Re-signed by Jets (April 9, 1999).
CHAMPIONSHIP GAME EXPERIENCE: Played in AFC championship game (1998 season).
HONORS: Named defensive back on THE SPORTING NEWS college All-America second team (1995).
PRO STATISTICS: 1997—Credited with one sack and returned blocked field goal attempt 72 yards for a touchdown. 1998—Recovered one fumble.

				INTERCEPTIONS			
Year	Team	G	GS	No.	Yds.	Avg.	TD
1996	New York Jets NFL	15	10	0	0	...	0
1997	New York Jets NFL	16	0	4	2	0.5	0
1998	New York Jets NFL	16	3	3	10	3.3	0
Pro totals (3 years)		47	13	7	12	1.7	0

MICKENS, TERRY   WR   RAIDERS

PERSONAL: Born February 21, 1971, in Tallahassee, Fla. ... 6-0/201. ... Full name: Terry KaJuan Mickens.
HIGH SCHOOL: Leon (Tallahassee, Fla.).
COLLEGE: Florida A&M.
TRANSACTIONS/CAREER NOTES: Selected by Green Bay Packers in fifth round (146th pick overall) of 1994 NFL draft. ... Signed by Packers (July 7, 1994). ... Granted unconditional free agency (February 13, 1998). ... Signed by Oakland Raiders (April 25, 1998). ... Granted unconditional free agency (February 12, 1999). ... Re-signed by Raiders (April 23, 1999).
CHAMPIONSHIP GAME EXPERIENCE: Played in NFC championship game (1995-97 seasons). ... Member of Super Bowl championship team (1996 season). ... Played in Super Bowl XXXII (1997 season).
PRO STATISTICS: 1995—Returned one kickoff for no yards. 1997—Returned one kickoff for no yards. 1998—Recovered two fumbles for three yards.
SINGLE GAME HIGHS (regular season): Receptions—7 (November 3, 1996, vs. Detroit); yards—86 (November 22, 1998, vs. Denver); and touchdown receptions—2 (November 3, 1996, vs. Detroit).

			RECEIVING				TOTALS			
Year Team	G	GS	No.	Yds.	Avg.	TD	TD	2pt.	Pts.	Fum.
1994—Green Bay NFL	12	0	4	31	7.8	0	0	0	0	0
1995—Green Bay NFL	16	0	3	50	16.7	0	0	0	0	0
1996—Green Bay NFL	8	5	18	161	8.9	2	2	0	12	1
1997—Green Bay NFL	11	0	1	2	2.0	1	1	0	6	0
1998—Oakland NFL	16	2	24	346	14.4	1	1	0	6	0
Pro totals (5 years)	63	7	50	590	11.8	4	4	0	24	1

MIDDLETON, FRANK   G   BUCCANEERS

PERSONAL: Born October 25, 1974, in Beaumont, Texas. ... 6-3/340. ... Full name: Frank Middleton Jr.
HIGH SCHOOL: West Brook (Beaumont, Texas).
JUNIOR COLLEGE: Fort Scott (Kan.) Community College.
COLLEGE: Arizona.
TRANSACTIONS/CAREER NOTES: Selected by Tampa Bay Buccaneers in third round (63rd pick overall) of 1997 NFL draft. ... Signed by Buccaneers (July 20, 1997).
PLAYING EXPERIENCE: Tampa Bay NFL, 1997 and 1998. ... Games/Games started: 1997 (15/2), 1998 (16/16). Total: 31/18.

MILBURN, GLYN   RB/KR   BEARS

PERSONAL: Born February 19, 1971, in Santa Monica, Calif. ... 5-8/174. ... Full name: Glyn Curt Milburn. ... Cousin of Rod Milburn, gold medalist in 110-meter high hurdles in 1972 Summer Olympics.
HIGH SCHOOL: Santa Monica (Calif.).
COLLEGE: Oklahoma, then Stanford (degree in public policy).
TRANSACTIONS/CAREER NOTES: Selected by Denver Broncos in second round (43rd pick overall) of 1993 NFL draft. ... Signed by Broncos (July 15, 1993). ... Traded by Broncos to Detroit Lions for second- (traded to Baltimore) and seventh-round (P Brian Gragert) picks in 1996 NFL draft (April 12, 1996). ... Traded by Lions to Green Bay Packers for seventh-round pick (traded to Miami) in 1999 draft (April 21, 1998). ... Traded by Packers to Chicago Bears for seventh-round pick (WR Donald Driver) in 1999 draft (August 30, 1998).
HONORS: Named kick returner for THE SPORTING NEWS NFL All-Pro team (1995). ... Played in Pro Bowl (1995 season).
RECORDS: Holds NFL single-season record for most combined kick returns—102. ... Holds NFL single-game record for most combined net yards gained—404 (December 10, 1995).
PRO STATISTICS: 1993—Fumbled nine times and recovered one fumble. 1994—Fumbled four times and recovered one fumble. 1995—Fumbled twice. 1997—Fumbled three times and recovered two fumbles. 1998—Fumbled once.
SINGLE GAME HIGHS (regular season): Attempts—18 (December 10, 1995, vs. Seattle); yards—131 (December 10, 1995, vs. Seattle); and rushing touchdowns—1 (December 17, 1994, vs. San Francisco). Receptions—9 (September 18, 1994 vs. Los Angeles Raiders); yards—85 (September 18, 1994 vs. Los Angeles Raiders); and touchdown receptions—1 (November 6, 1994 vs. Los Angeles Rams).
STATISTICAL PLATEAUS: 100-yard rushing games: 1995 (1).

			RUSHING				RECEIVING				PUNT RETURNS				KICKOFF RETURNS				TOTALS		
Year Team	G	GS	Att.	Yds.	Avg.	TD	No.	Yds.	Avg.	TD	No.	Yds.	Avg.	TD	No.	Yds.	Avg.	TD	TD	2pt.	Pts.
1993—Denver NFL	16	2	52	231	4.4	0	38	300	7.9	3	40	425	10.6	0	12	188	15.7	0	3	...	18
1994—Denver NFL	16	3	58	201	3.5	1	77	549	7.1	3	41	379	9.2	0	37	793	21.4	0	4	0	24
1995—Denver NFL	16	1	49	266	5.4	0	22	191	8.7	0	31	354	11.4	0	47	1269	27.0	0	0	0	0
1996—Detroit NFL	16	0	0	0	...	0	0	0	...	0	34	284	8.4	0	64	1627	25.4	0	0	0	0
1997—Detroit NFL	16	1	0	0	...	0	5	77	15.4	0	47	433	9.2	0	55	1315	23.9	0	0	0	0
1998—Chicago NFL	16	0	4	8	2.0	0	4	37	9.3	0	25	291	11.6	1	*62	*1550	25.0	†2	3	0	18
Pro totals (6 years)	96	7	163	706	4.3	1	146	1154	7.9	6	218	2166	9.9	1	277	6742	24.3	2	10	0	60

MILI, ITULA   TE   SEAHAWKS

PERSONAL: Born April 20, 1973, in Kahuku, Hawaii. ... 6-4/265. ... Name pronounced ee-TWO-la MEE-lee.
HIGH SCHOOL: Kahuku (Hawaii).
COLLEGE: Brigham Young.
TRANSACTIONS/CAREER NOTES: Selected by Seattle Seahawks in sixth round (174th pick overall) of 1997 NFL draft. ... Signed by Seahawks (June 11, 1997). ... On physically unable to perform list with knee injury (August 18, 1997-remainder of season). ... On injured reserve with knee injury (December 25, 1998-remainder of season).
PLAYING EXPERIENCE: Seattle NFL, 1998. ... Games/Games started: 7/0.
PRO STATISTICS: 1998—Caught one pass for 20 yards.
SINGLE GAME HIGHS (regular season): Receptions—1 (November 22, 1998, vs. Dallas); yards—20 (November 22, 1998, vs. Dallas); and touchdown receptions—0.

MILLER, BUBBA — C/G — EAGLES

PERSONAL: Born January 24, 1973, in Nashville. ... 6-1/305. ... Full name: Stephen DeJuan Miller.
HIGH SCHOOL: Brentwood Academy (Franklin, Tenn.).
COLLEGE: Tennessee.
TRANSACTIONS/CAREER NOTES: Signed as non-drafted free agent by Philadelphia Eagles (April 26, 1996). ... Inactive for all 16 games (1996). ... Granted free agency (February 12, 1999). ... Re-signed by Eagles (April 22, 1999).
PLAYING EXPERIENCE: Philadelphia NFL, 1997 and 1998. ... Games/Games started: 1997 (13/3), 1998 (15/4). Total: 28/7.
PRO STATISTICS: 1998—Caught one pass for 11 yards.

MILLER, CHRIS — QB — BRONCOS

PERSONAL: Born August 9, 1965, in Pomona, Calif. ... 6-2/212. ... Full name: Christopher James Miller.
HIGH SCHOOL: Sheldon (Eugene, Ore.).
COLLEGE: Oregon.
TRANSACTIONS/CAREER NOTES: Selected by Atlanta Falcons in first round (13th pick overall) of 1987 NFL draft. ... Signed by Falcons (October 30, 1987). ... Granted roster exemption (October 30-November 9, 1987). ... On injured reserve with broken collarbone (December 4, 1990-remainder of season). ... On injured reserve with knee injury (November 1, 1992-remainder of season). ... On injured reserve with knee injury (October 7, 1993-remainder of season). ... Granted unconditional free agency (February 17, 1994). ... Signed by Los Angeles Rams (March 7, 1994). ... Rams franchise moved to St. Louis (April 12, 1995). ... On injured reserve with concussion (December 14, 1995-remainder of season). ... Released by Rams (March 11, 1996). ... Out of pro football (1996-1998 seasons). ... Signed by Denver Broncos (April 26, 1999).
HONORS: Played in Pro Bowl (1991 season).
PRO STATISTICS: 1988—Fumbled twice and recovered one fumble. 1989—Successful on 25-yard field-goal attempt, fumbled 13 times and recovered five fumbles for minus three yards. 1990—Fumbled 11 times and recovered four fumbles for minus nine yards. 1991—Fumbled five times. 1992—Fumbled six times and recovered one fumble for minus one yard. 1993—Fumbled twice. 1994—Fumbled seven times and recovered three fumbles for minus five yards. 1995—Fumbled four times and recovered two fumbles for minus six yards.
STATISTICAL PLATEAUS: 300-yard passing games: 1989 (3), 1990 (2), 1991 (2), 1992 (1), 1994 (1), 1995 (2). Total: 11.
MISCELLANEOUS: Regular-season record as starting NFL quarterback: 32-57 (.360).

			PASSING							RUSHING				TOTALS		
Year Team	G	GS	Att.	Cmp.	Pct.	Yds.	TD	Int.	Avg.	Rat.	Att.	Yds.	Avg.	TD	TD	2pt.	Pts.
1987—Atlanta NFL	3	2	92	39	42.4	552	1	9	6.00	26.4	4	21	5.3	0	0	...	0
1988—Atlanta NFL	13	13	351	184	52.4	2133	11	12	6.08	67.3	31	138	4.5	1	1	...	6
1989—Atlanta NFL	15	15	526	280	53.2	3459	16	10	6.58	76.1	10	20	2.0	0	0	...	3
1990—Atlanta NFL	12	12	388	222	57.2	2735	17	14	7.05	78.7	26	99	3.8	1	1	...	6
1991—Atlanta NFL	15	14	413	220	53.3	3103	26	18	7.51	80.6	32	229	7.2	0	0	...	0
1992—Atlanta NFL	8	8	253	152	60.1	1739	15	6	6.87	90.7	23	89	3.9	0	0	...	0
1993—Atlanta NFL	3	2	66	32	48.5	345	1	3	5.23	50.4	2	11	5.5	0	0	...	0
1994—L.A. Rams NFL	13	10	317	173	54.6	2104	16	14	6.64	73.6	20	100	5.0	0	0	0	0
1995—St. Louis NFL	13	13	405	232	57.3	2623	18	15	6.48	76.2	22	67	3.0	0	0	0	0
1996—							Did not play.										
1997—							Did not play.										
1998—							Did not play.										
Pro totals (9 years)	95	89	2811	1534	54.6	18793	121	101	6.69	74.8	170	774	4.6	2	2	0	15

MILLER, COREY — LB — VIKINGS

PERSONAL: Born October 25, 1968, in Pageland, S.C. ... 6-2/252.
HIGH SCHOOL: Central (Pageland, S.C.).
COLLEGE: South Carolina.
TRANSACTIONS/CAREER NOTES: Selected by New York Giants in sixth round (167th pick overall) of 1991 NFL draft. ... Signed by Giants (July 15, 1991). ... Granted free agency (February 17, 1994). ... Re-signed by Giants (July 22, 1994). ... Granted unconditional free agency (February 17, 1995). ... Re-signed by Giants (March 9, 1995). ... On injured reserve with neck injury (August 25, 1998-entire season). ... Released by Giants (February 8, 1999). ... Signed by Minnesota Vikings (March 30, 1999).
PRO STATISTICS: 1991—Recovered one fumble. 1993—Recovered two fumbles and fumbled once. 1994—Recovered one fumble.

			INTERCEPTIONS				SACKS
Year Team	G	GS	No.	Yds.	Avg.	TD	No.
1991—New York Giants NFL	16	1	0	0	...	0	2.5
1992—New York Giants NFL	16	7	2	10	5.0	0	2.0
1993—New York Giants NFL	16	14	2	18	9.0	0	6.5
1994—New York Giants NFL	15	13	2	6	3.0	0	0.0
1995—New York Giants NFL	14	9	0	0	...	0	0.0
1996—New York Giants NFL	14	13	0	0	...	0	2.0
1997—New York Giants NFL	14	13	0	0	...	0	1.0
1998—New York Giants NFL					Did not play.		
Pro totals (7 years)	105	70	6	34	5.7	0	14.0

MILLER, FRED — OT — RAMS

PERSONAL: Born February 6, 1973, in Houston. ... 6-7/315. ... Full name: Fred Miller Jr.
HIGH SCHOOL: Aldine Eisenhower (Houston).
COLLEGE: Baylor (degree in sociology, 1995).
TRANSACTIONS/CAREER NOTES: Selected by St. Louis Rams in fifth round (141st pick overall) of 1996 NFL draft. ... Signed by Rams (July 15, 1996). ... Granted free agency (February 12, 1999).
PLAYING EXPERIENCE: St. Louis NFL, 1996-1998. ... Games/Games started: 1996 (14/0), 1997 (15/7), 1998 (15/15). Total: 44/22.

MILLER, JAMIR — LB — BROWNS

PERSONAL: Born November 19, 1973, in Philadelphia. ... 6-5/266. ... Full name: Jamir Malik Miller. ... Cousin of Mark Gunn, defensive lineman with New York Jets (1991-94), Philadelphia Eagles (1995-96) and New York Jets (1996).
HIGH SCHOOL: El Cerrito (Calif.).
COLLEGE: UCLA.
TRANSACTIONS/CAREER NOTES: Selected after junior season by Arizona Cardinals in first round (10th pick overall) of 1994 NFL draft. ... Signed by Cardinals (August 12, 1994). ... On suspended list for violating league substance abuse policy (September 4-October 3, 1995). ... Granted unconditional free agency (February 12, 1999). ... Signed by Cleveland Browns (May 11, 1999).
HONORS: Named linebacker on The Sporting News college All-America first team (1993).
PRO STATISTICS: 1995—Fumbled once and recovered two fumbles for 26 yards. 1996—Recovered one fumble for 26 yards and a touchdown. 1998—Recovered two fumbles.

Year—Team	G	GS	SACKS
1994—Arizona NFL	16	0	3.0
1995—Arizona NFL	11	8	1.0
1996—Arizona NFL	16	16	1.0
1997—Arizona NFL	16	16	5.5
1998—Arizona NFL	16	16	3.0
Pro totals (5 years)	75	56	13.5

MILLER, JOSH — P — STEELERS

PERSONAL: Born July 14, 1970, in Rockway, N.Y. ... 6-3/219.
HIGH SCHOOL: East Brunswick (N.J.).
JUNIOR COLLEGE: Scottsdale (Ariz.) Community College.
COLLEGE: Arizona (degree in communications, 1993).
TRANSACTIONS/CAREER NOTES: Signed as non-drafted free agent by Green Bay Packers (April 1993). ... Released by Packers before 1993 season. ... Signed by Baltimore Stallions of CFL (June 1994). ... Signed by Seattle Seahawks (May 29, 1996). ... Released by Seahawks (August 13, 1996). ... Signed by Pittsburgh Steelers (August 15, 1996).
CHAMPIONSHIP GAME EXPERIENCE: Played in Grey Cup (1994). ... Played in AFC championship game (1997 season).
HONORS: Named punter on The Sporting News college All-America first team (1992).
PRO STATISTICS: CFL: 1994—Fumbled once. NFL: 1997—Rushed once for minus seven yards.

Year—Team	G	No.	Yds.	Avg.	Net avg.	In. 20	Blk.
1994—Baltimore CFL	18	117	5024	42.9	36.9	...	...
1995—Baltimore CFL	18	118	5629	47.7	42.2	...	...
1996—Pittsburgh NFL	12	55	2256	41.0	33.6	18	0
1997—Pittsburgh NFL	16	64	2729	42.6	35.0	17	0
1998—Pittsburgh NFL	16	81	3530	43.6	36.8	*34	0
CFL totals (2 years)	36	235	10653	45.3	39.6	...	...
NFL totals (3 years)	44	200	8515	42.6	35.3	69	0
Pro totals (5 years)	80	435	19168	44.1	37.6	...	...

MILLER, LES — DE

PERSONAL: Born March 1, 1965, in Arkansas City, Kan. ... 6-7/305. ... Full name: Leslie Paul Miller.
HIGH SCHOOL: Arkansas City (Kan.).
COLLEGE: Kansas State, then Fort Hays State (Kan.).
TRANSACTIONS/CAREER NOTES: Signed as non-drafted free agent by New Orleans Saints (May 11, 1987). ... Released by Saints (September 7, 1987). ... Signed as replacement player by San Diego Chargers (September 24, 1987). ... On injured reserve with back injury (December 22, 1990-remainder of season). ... Granted unconditional free agency (February 1, 1991). ... Signed by Saints (April 1, 1991). ... Granted unconditional free agency (March 1, 1993). ... Re-signed by Saints (March 9, 1993). ... Released by Saints (October 25, 1994). ... Signed by Chargers (November 2, 1994). ... Granted unconditional free agency (February 17, 1995). ... Signed by Saints (August 16, 1995). ... Released by Saints (August 27, 1995). ... Signed by Carolina Panthers (February 7, 1996). ... Granted unconditional free agency (February 14, 1997). ... Re-signed by Panthers (June 13, 1997). ... Granted unconditional free agency (February 12, 1999).
CHAMPIONSHIP GAME EXPERIENCE: Member of Chargers for AFC championship game (1994 season); did not play. ... Played in Super Bowl XXIX (1994 season).
RECORDS: Shares NFL single-season records for most touchdowns by fumble recovery—2 (1990); and most touchdowns by recovery of opponents' fumbles—2 (1990).
PRO STATISTICS: 1987—Recovered two fumbles (including one in end zone for a touchdown). 1989—Recovered one fumble. 1990—Recovered three fumbles for one yard (including two in end zone for touchdowns). 1992—Recovered one fumble. 1996—Recovered one fumble for 14 yards. 1997—Recovered one fumble for three yards. 1998—Fumbled once and recovered three fumbles for eight yards.

Year—Team	G	GS	SACKS
1987—San Diego NFL	9	4	3.0
1988—San Diego NFL	13	0	0.0
1989—San Diego NFL	14	0	2.5
1990—San Diego NFL	14	9	1.0
1991—New Orleans NFL	16	0	1.0
1992—New Orleans NFL	16	2	1.0
1993—New Orleans NFL	13	11	2.5
1994—New Orleans NFL	8	5	0.0
—San Diego NFL	4	0	0.5
1995—	Did not play.		
1996—Carolina NFL	15	5	3.0
1997—Carolina NFL	16	11	5.5
1998—Carolina NFL	14	3	0.0
Pro totals (11 years)	152	50	20.0

MILLOY, LAWYER — S — PATRIOTS

PERSONAL: Born November 14, 1973, in St. Louis. ... 6-0/208.
HIGH SCHOOL: Lincoln (Tacoma, Wash.).
COLLEGE: Washington.
TRANSACTIONS/CAREER NOTES: Selected after junior season by New England Patriots in second round (36th pick overall) of 1996 NFL draft. ... Signed by Patriots (June 5, 1996).
CHAMPIONSHIP GAME EXPERIENCE: Played in AFC championship game (1996 season). ... Played in Super Bowl XXXI (1996 season).
HONORS: Named defensive back on THE SPORTING NEWS college All-America first team (1995). ... Played in Pro Bowl (1998 season).
PRO STATISTICS: 1996—Recovered one fumble. 1997—Recovered two fumbles. 1998—Recovered one fumble.

			INTERCEPTIONS				SACKS
Year Team	G	GS	No.	Yds.	Avg.	TD	No.
1996—New England NFL	16	10	2	14	7.0	0	1.0
1997—New England NFL	16	16	3	15	5.0	0	0.0
1998—New England NFL	16	16	6	54	9.0	1	1.0
Pro totals (3 years)	48	42	11	83	7.5	1	2.0

MILLS, ERNIE — WR — COWBOYS

PERSONAL: Born October 28, 1968, in Dunnellon, Fla. ... 5-11/196. ... Full name: Ernest Lee Mills III.
HIGH SCHOOL: Dunnellon (Fla.) Senior.
COLLEGE: Florida (degree in sports administration/exercise and sports science).
TRANSACTIONS/CAREER NOTES: Selected by Pittsburgh Steelers in third round (73rd pick overall) of 1991 NFL draft. ... Signed by Steelers (August 13, 1991). ... Granted free agency (February 17, 1994). ... Re-signed by Steelers (June 1, 1994). ... On physically unable to perform list with knee injury (August 24-October 25, 1996). ... Granted unconditional free agency (February 14, 1997). ... Signed by Carolina Panthers (March 5, 1997). ... Released by Panthers (February 9, 1998). ... Signed by Dallas Cowboys (February 27, 1998). ... On injured reserve with abdominal injury (December 2, 1998-remainder of season). ... Granted unconditional free agency (February 12, 1999). ... Re-signed by Cowboys (May 11, 1999).
CHAMPIONSHIP GAME EXPERIENCE: Played in AFC championship game (1994 and 1995 seasons). ... Played in Super Bowl XXX (1995 season).
PRO STATISTICS: 1991—Recovered punt return in end zone for a touchdown, returned one punt for no yards and recovered one fumble. 1995—Recovered one fumble. 1996—Recovered one fumble for five yards.
SINGLE GAME HIGHS (regular season): Receptions—6 (December 24, 1995, vs. Green Bay); yards—110 (October 11, 1998, vs. Carolina); and touchdown receptions—2 (December 10, 1995, vs. Oakland).
STATISTICAL PLATEAUS: 100-yard receiving games: 1998 (1).

			RUSHING				RECEIVING				KICKOFF RETURNS				TOTALS			
Year Team	G	GS	Att.	Yds.	Avg.	TD	No.	Yds.	Avg.	TD	No.	Yds.	Avg.	TD	TD	2pt.	Pts.	Fum.
1991—Pittsburgh NFL	16	2	0	0	...	0	3	79	26.3	1	11	284	25.8	0	2	...	12	0
1992—Pittsburgh NFL	16	5	1	20	20.0	0	30	383	12.8	3	1	11	11.0	0	3	...	18	2
1993—Pittsburgh NFL	14	5	3	12	4.0	0	29	386	13.3	1	0	0	...	0	1	0	6	0
1994—Pittsburgh NFL	15	6	3	18	6.0	0	19	384	20.2	1	2	6	3.0	0	1	0	6	1
1995—Pittsburgh NFL	16	4	5	39	7.8	0	39	679	17.4	8	54	1306	24.2	0	8	0	48	2
1996—Pittsburgh NFL	9	3	2	24	12.0	0	7	92	13.1	1	8	146	18.3	0	1	0	6	0
1997—Carolina NFL	10	5	0	0	...	0	11	127	11.5	1	4	65	16.3	0	1	0	6	0
1998—Dallas NFL	11	1	3	9	3.0	0	28	479	17.1	4	0	0	...	0	4	0	24	0
Pro totals (8 years)	107	31	17	122	7.2	0	166	2609	15.7	20	80	1818	22.7	0	21	0	126	5

MILLS, JOHN HENRY — TE — VIKINGS

PERSONAL: Born October 31, 1969, in Jacksonville. ... 6-0/235. ... Full name: John Henry Mills.
HIGH SCHOOL: Godby (Tallahassee, Fla.).
COLLEGE: Wake Forest (degree in speech communications, 1993).
TRANSACTIONS/CAREER NOTES: Selected by Houston Oilers in fifth round (131st pick overall) of 1993 NFL draft. ... Signed by Oilers (July 16, 1993). ... Released by Oilers (August 30, 1993). ... Re-signed by Oilers (August 31, 1993). ... Granted free agency (February 16, 1996). ... Re-signed by Oilers (July 20, 1996). ... Granted unconditional free agency (February 14, 1997). ... Signed by Oakland Raiders (June 6, 1997). ... Granted unconditional free agency (February 13, 1998). ... Re-signed by Raiders (February 23, 1998). ... On injured reserve with hamstring injury (November 4-18, 1998). ... Released by Raiders (November 18, 1998). ... Signed by Cleveland Browns (December 23, 1998). ... Released by Browns (April 29, 1999). ... Signed by Minnesota Vikings (May 10, 1999).
HONORS: Played in Pro Bowl (1996 season).
PRO STATISTICS: 1994—Caught one pass for four yards. 1996—Recovered two fumbles.

			KICKOFF RETURNS				TOTALS			
Year Team	G	GS	No.	Yds.	Avg.	TD	TD	2pt.	Pts.	Fum.
1993—Houston NFL	16	0	11	230	20.9	0	0	...	0	0
1994—Houston NFL	16	1	15	282	18.8	0	0	0	0	1
1995—Houston NFL	16	0	0	0	...	0	0	0	0	0
1996—Houston NFL	16	0	0	0	...	0	0	0	0	0
1997—Oakland NFL	16	0	0	0	...	0	0	0	0	0
1998—Oakland NFL	5	0	0	0	...	0	0	0	0	0
Pro totals (6 years)	85	1	26	512	19.7	0	0	0	0	1

MILNE, BRIAN — FB — BENGALS

PERSONAL: Born January 7, 1973, in Waterford, Pa. ... 6-3/254. ... Full name: Brian Fitzsimons Milne.
HIGH SCHOOL: Fort LeBoeuf (Pa.).

COLLEGE: Penn State (degree in labor and industrial relations).
TRANSACTIONS/CAREER NOTES: Selected by Indianapolis Colts in fourth round (115th pick overall) of 1996 NFL draft. ... Signed by Colts (July 5, 1996). ... Claimed on waivers by Cincinnati Bengals (August 21, 1996). ... Granted free agency (February 12, 1999). ... Re-signed by Bengals (May 20, 1999).
PRO STATISTICS: 1998—Recovered one fumble.
SINGLE GAME HIGHS (regular season): Attempts—3 (November 22, 1998, vs. Baltimore); yards—11 (November 29, 1998, vs. Jacksonville); and rushing touchdowns—1 (November 29, 1998, vs. Jacksonville).
MISCELLANEOUS: Won NCAA discus championship (1993).

				RUSHING				RECEIVING				TOTALS		
Year Team	G	GS	Att.	Yds.	Avg.	TD	No.	Yds.	Avg.	TD	TD	2pt.	Pts.	Fum.
1996—Cincinnati NFL	6	5	8	22	2.8	1	3	29	9.7	0	1	0	6	0
1997—Cincinnati NFL	16	16	13	32	2.5	2	23	138	6.0	0	2	0	12	0
1998—Cincinnati NFL	14	14	10	41	4.1	1	26	124	4.8	0	1	0	6	0
Pro totals (3 years)	36	35	31	95	3.1	4	52	291	5.6	0	4	0	24	0

MILSTEAD, ROD   G   REDSKINS

PERSONAL: Born November 10, 1969, in Washington, D.C. ... 6-2/290. ... Full name: Roderick Leon Milstead Jr.
HIGH SCHOOL: Lackey (Indian Head, Md.).
COLLEGE: Delaware State (degree in sociology and criminal justice).
TRANSACTIONS/CAREER NOTES: Selected by Dallas Cowboys in fifth round (121st pick overall) of 1992 NFL draft. ... Signed by Cowboys for 1992 season. ... Traded by Cowboys to Cleveland Browns for eighth-round pick (traded to Los Angeles Rams) in 1993 draft (August 24, 1992). ... On injured reserve with back injury (September 3, 1992-entire season). ... Released by Browns (August 30, 1993). ... Re-signed by Browns (October 6, 1993). ... Released by Browns (November 27, 1993). ... Re-signed by Browns (November 30, 1993). ... Inactive for 11 games (1993). ... Released by Browns (August 28, 1994). ... Signed by San Francisco 49ers (September 14, 1994). ... Granted unconditional free agency (February 14, 1997). ... Re-signed by 49ers (May 1, 1997). ... Released by 49ers (August 24, 1997). ... Re-signed by 49ers (October 22, 1997). ... Granted unconditional free agency (February 13, 1998). ... Signed by Washington Redskins (March 3, 1998). ... Granted unconditional free agency (February 12, 1999). ... Re-signed by Redskins (March 15, 1999).
PLAYING EXPERIENCE: San Francisco NFL, 1994-1997; Washington NFL, 1998. ... Games/Games started: 1994 (5/0), 1995 (16/12), 1996 (11/0), 1997 (4/0), 1998 (14/11). Total: 50/23.
CHAMPIONSHIP GAME EXPERIENCE: Member of 49ers for NFC championship game (1994 and 1997 seasons); inactive. ... Member of Super Bowl championship team (1994 season).

MIMS, CHRIS   DT   CHARGERS

PERSONAL: Born September 29, 1970, in Los Angeles. ... 6-5/300. ... Full name: Christopher Eddie Mims.
HIGH SCHOOL: Dorsey (Los Angeles).
JUNIOR COLLEGE: Los Angeles Pierce Junior College, then Los Angeles Southwest Community College.
COLLEGE: Tennessee.
TRANSACTIONS/CAREER NOTES: Selected by San Diego Chargers in first round (23rd pick overall) of 1992 NFL draft. ... Signed by Chargers (June 5, 1992). ... Released by Chargers (April 14, 1997). ... Signed by Washington Redskins (June 10, 1997). ... Granted unconditional free agency (February 13, 1998). ... Signed by Oakland Raiders (April 25, 1998). ... Released by Raiders (June 4, 1998). ... Signed by Chargers (June 10, 1998).
CHAMPIONSHIP GAME EXPERIENCE: Played in AFC championship game (1994 season). ... Played in Super Bowl XXIX (1994 season).
PRO STATISTICS: 1992—Credited with one safety and recovered one fumble. 1993—Recovered two fumbles. 1994—Recovered two fumbles. 1995—Recovered one fumble. 1996—Recovered two fumbles.

Year Team	G	GS	SACKS
1992—San Diego NFL	16	4	10.0
1993—San Diego NFL	16	7	7.0
1994—San Diego NFL	16	16	11.0
1995—San Diego NFL	15	15	2.0
1996—San Diego NFL	15	15	6.0
1997—Washington NFL	11	7	4.0
1998—San Diego NFL	6	0	2.0
Pro totals (7 years)	95	64	42.0

MINCY, CHARLES   DB   RAIDERS

PERSONAL: Born December 16, 1969, in Los Angeles. ... 6-0/195. ... Full name: Charles Anthony Mincy.
HIGH SCHOOL: Dorsey (Los Angeles).
JUNIOR COLLEGE: Pasadena (Calif.) City College.
COLLEGE: Washington.
TRANSACTIONS/CAREER NOTES: Selected by Kansas City Chiefs in fifth round (133rd pick overall) of 1991 NFL draft. ... Signed by Chiefs (July 17, 1991). ... On injured reserve with ankle/toe injury (August 30-December 25, 1991). ... Did not play during regular season (1991); played in two playoff games. ... Granted free agency (February 17, 1994). ... Re-signed by Chiefs (June 17, 1994). ... Granted unconditional free agency (February 17, 1995). ... Signed by Minnesota Vikings (March 6, 1995). ... Released by Vikings (February 9, 1996). ... Signed by Tampa Bay Buccaneers (October 2, 1996). ... Granted unconditional free agency (February 13, 1998). ... Re-signed by Buccaneers (March 30, 1998). ... Released by Buccaneers (February 11, 1999). ... Signed by Oakland Raiders (April 28, 1999).
CHAMPIONSHIP GAME EXPERIENCE: Played in AFC championship game (1993 season).
PRO STATISTICS: 1992—Recovered one fumble for 30 yards and a touchdown. 1993—Recovered two fumbles. 1995—Recovered two fumbles for 10 yards. 1997—Recovered one fumble.

Year Team	G	GS	INTERCEPTIONS No.	Yds.	Avg.	TD	PUNT RETURNS No.	Yds.	Avg.	TD	TOTALS TD	2pt.	Pts.	Fum.
1991—Kansas City NFL							Did not play.							
1992—Kansas City NFL	16	16	4	128	32.0	▲2	1	4	4.0	0	3	...	18	0
1993—Kansas City NFL	16	4	5	44	8.8	0	2	9	4.5	0	0	...	0	0
1994—Kansas City NFL	16	7	3	49	16.3	0	0	0	...	0	0	0	0	0
1995—Minnesota NFL	16	9	3	37	12.3	0	4	22	5.5	0	0	0	0	0
1996—Tampa Bay NFL	2	0	1	26	26.0	0	0	0	...	0	0	0	0	0
1997—Tampa Bay NFL	16	9	1	14	14.0	0	0	0	...	0	0	0	0	0
1998—Tampa Bay NFL	16	16	4	58	14.5	1	0	0	...	0	1	0	6	0
Pro totals (7 years)	98	61	21	356	17.0	3	7	35	5.0	0	4	0	24	0

MINTER, BARRY — LB — BEARS

PERSONAL: Born January 28, 1970, in Mt. Pleasant, Texas. ... 6-2/242. ... Full name: Barry Antoine Minter.
HIGH SCHOOL: Mt. Pleasant (Texas).
COLLEGE: Tulsa.
TRANSACTIONS/CAREER NOTES: Selected by Dallas Cowboys in sixth round (168th pick overall) of 1993 NFL draft. ... Signed by Cowboys (July 14, 1993). ... Traded by Cowboys with LB Vinson Smith and sixth-round pick (DE Carl Reeves) in 1995 draft to Chicago Bears for TE Kelly Blackwell, S Markus Paul and LB John Roper (August 17, 1993). ... Granted free agency (February 16, 1996). ... Re-signed by Bears (February 26, 1996). ... Granted unconditional free agency (February 13, 1998). ... Re-signed by Bears (February 20, 1998).
PLAYING EXPERIENCE: Chicago NFL, 1993-1998. ... Games/Games started: 1993 (2/0), 1994 (13/1), 1995 (16/3), 1996 (16/7), 1997 (16/16), 1998 (16/16). Total: 79/43.
PRO STATISTICS: 1994—Recovered one fumble. 1995—Intercepted one pass for two yards and a touchdown. 1996—Intercepted one pass for five yards and credited with one sack. 1997—Credited with six sacks and recovered three fumbles. 1998—Intercepted one pass for 17 yards, credited with one sack and recovered one fumble for 11 yards.

MINTER, MIKE — S — PANTHERS

PERSONAL: Born January 15, 1974, in Cleveland. ... 5-10/188. ... Full name: Michael Christopher Minter.
HIGH SCHOOL: Lawton (Okla.).
COLLEGE: Nebraska (degree in engineering, 1996).
TRANSACTIONS/CAREER NOTES: Selected by Carolina Panthers in second round (56th pick overall) of 1997 NFL draft. ... Signed by Panthers (June 12, 1997).
PLAYING EXPERIENCE: Carolina NFL, 1997 and 1998. ... Games/Games started: 1997 (16/11), 1998 (6/4). Total: 22/15.
PRO STATISTICS: 1997—Credited with 3 1/2 sacks and recovered two fumbles. 1998—Intercepted one pass for seven yards.

MIRER, RICK — QB — PACKERS

M

PERSONAL: Born March 19, 1970, in Goshen, Ind. ... 6-3/212. ... Full name: Rick F. Mirer.
HIGH SCHOOL: Goshen (Ind.).
COLLEGE: Notre Dame.
TRANSACTIONS/CAREER NOTES: Selected by Seattle Seahawks in first round (second pick overall) of 1993 NFL draft. ... Signed by Seahawks (August 2, 1993). ... On injured reserve with thumb injury (December 20, 1994-remainder of season). ... Traded by Seahawks with fourth-round pick (RB Darnell Autry) in 1997 draft to Chicago Bears for first-round pick (traded to Atlanta) in 1997 draft (February 18, 1997). ... Released by Bears (August 30, 1998). ... Signed by Green Bay Packers (September 2, 1998). ... Active for four games (1998); did not play.
PRO STATISTICS: 1993—Fumbled 13 times and recovered five fumbles for minus 14 yards. 1994—Fumbled twice and recovered one fumble for minus seven yards. 1995—Fumbled five times and recovered one fumble for minus one yard. 1996—Fumbled four times. 1997—Fumbled three times and recovered one fumble for minus four yards.
SINGLE GAME HIGHS (regular season): Attempts—43 (October 24, 1993, vs. New England); completions—25 (October 3, 1993, vs. San Diego); yards—287 (December 5, 1993, vs. Kansas City); and touchdown passes—3 (September 11, 1994, vs. Los Angeles Raiders).
MISCELLANEOUS: Regular-season record as starting NFL quarterback: 20-34 (.370).

Year Team	G	GS	PASSING Att.	Cmp.	Pct.	Yds.	TD	Int.	Avg.	Rat.	RUSHING Att.	Yds.	Avg.	TD	TOTALS TD	2pt.	Pts.
1993—Seattle NFL	16	16	486	274	56.4	2833	12	17	5.83	67.0	68	343	5.0	3	3	...	18
1994—Seattle NFL	13	13	381	195	51.2	2151	11	7	5.65	70.2	34	153	4.5	0	0	0	0
1995—Seattle NFL	15	13	391	209	53.5	2564	13	§20	6.56	63.7	43	193	4.5	1	1	0	6
1996—Seattle NFL	11	9	265	136	51.3	1546	5	12	5.83	56.6	33	191	5.8	2	2	0	12
1997—Chicago NFL	7	3	103	53	51.5	420	0	6	4.08	37.7	20	78	3.9	1	1	0	8
1998—Green Bay NFL							Did not play.										
Pro totals (5 years)	62	54	1626	867	53.3	9514	41	62	5.85	63.4	198	958	4.8	7	7	0	44

MITCHELL, BRANDON — DT — PATRIOTS

PERSONAL: Born June 19, 1975, in Abbeville, La. ... 6-3/289. ... Full name: Brandon Pete Mitchell.
HIGH SCHOOL: Abbeville (La.).
COLLEGE: Texas A&M.
TRANSACTIONS/CAREER NOTES: Selected by New England Patriots in second round (59th pick overall) of 1997 NFL draft. ... Signed by Patriots (June 6, 1997). ... On injured reserve with ankle injury (October 30, 1998-remainder of season).
PLAYING EXPERIENCE: New England NFL, 1997 and 1998. ... Games/Games started: 1997 (11/0), 1998 (7/1). Total: 18/1.
PRO STATISTICS: 1998—Credited with two sacks.

MITCHELL, BRIAN   RB   REDSKINS

PERSONAL: Born August 18, 1968, in Fort Polk, La. ... 5-10/221. ... Full name: Brian Keith Mitchell.
HIGH SCHOOL: Plaquemine (La.).
COLLEGE: Southwestern Louisiana.
TRANSACTIONS/CAREER NOTES: Selected by Washington Redskins in fifth round (130th pick overall) of 1990 NFL draft. ... Signed by Redskins (July 22, 1990). ... Granted free agency (February 1, 1992). ... Re-signed by Redskins for 1992 season. ... Granted unconditional free agency (February 17, 1994). ... Re-signed by Redskins (May 24, 1994). ... Granted free agency (February 17, 1995). ... Re-signed by Redskins (March 27, 1995). ... Granted unconditional free agency (February 13, 1998). ... Re-signed by Redskins (February 12, 1998).
CHAMPIONSHIP GAME EXPERIENCE: Played in NFC championship game (1991 season). ... Member of Super Bowl championship team (1991 season).
HONORS: Named punt returner on THE SPORTING NEWS NFL All-Pro team (1995). ... Played in Pro Bowl (1995 season).
RECORDS: Holds NFL single-season record for most yards by combined kick return—1,930 (1994).
PRO STATISTICS: 1990—Attempted six passes with three completions for 40 yards and fumbled twice. 1991—Fumbled eight times and recovered one fumble. 1992—Attempted one pass without a completion, fumbled four times and recovered two fumbles. 1993—Attempted two passes with one completion for 50 yards and an interception, fumbled three times and recovered one fumble. 1994—Had only pass attempt intercepted and fumbled four times. 1995—Fumbled twice and recovered one fumble. 1996—Attempted one pass without a completion, fumbled once and recovered two fumbles. 1997—Fumbled three times. 1998—Attempted two passes with one completion for no yards and fumbled three times.
SINGLE GAME HIGHS (regular season): Attempts—21 (September 6, 1993, vs. Dallas); yards—116 (September 6, 1993, vs. Dallas); and rushing touchdowns—2 (September 6, 1993, vs. Dallas).
STATISTICAL PLATEAUS: 100-yard rushing games: 1993 (1).

				RUSHING				RECEIVING				PUNT RETURNS				KICKOFF RETURNS				TOTALS	
Year Team	G	GS	Att.	Yds.	Avg.	TD	No.	Yds.	Avg.	TD	No.	Yds.	Avg.	TD	No.	Yds.	Avg.	TD	TD	2pt.	Pts.
1990—Washington NFL	15	0	15	81	5.4	1	2	5	2.5	0	12	107	8.9	0	18	365	20.3	0	1	...	6
1991—Washington NFL	16	0	3	14	4.7	0	0	0	...	0	45	*600	13.3	*2	29	583	20.1	0	2	...	12
1992—Washington NFL	16	0	6	70	11.7	0	3	30	10.0	0	29	271	9.3	1	23	492	21.4	0	1	...	6
1993—Washington NFL	16	4	63	246	3.9	3	20	157	7.9	0	29	193	6.7	0	33	678	20.5	0	3	...	18
1994—Washington NFL	16	7	78	311	4.0	0	26	236	9.1	1	32	‡452	*14.1	†2	58	1478	25.5	0	3	1	20
1995—Washington NFL	16	1	46	301	6.5	1	38	324	8.5	1	25	315	12.6	†1	55	1408	‡25.6	0	3	0	18
1996—Washington NFL	16	2	39	193	4.9	0	32	286	8.9	0	23	258	11.2	0	56	1258	22.5	0	0	0	0
1997—Washington NFL	16	1	23	107	4.7	1	36	438	12.2	1	38	442	11.6	∞1	47	1094	23.3	1	4	0	24
1998—Washington NFL	16	0	39	208	5.3	2	44	306	7.0	0	44	‡506	11.5	0	59	1337	22.7	1	3	0	18
Pro totals (9 years)	143	15	312	1531	4.9	8	201	1782	8.9	3	277	3144	11.4	7	378	8693	23.0	2	20	1	122

MITCHELL, JEFF   C   RAVENS

PERSONAL: Born January 29, 1974, in Dallas. ... 6-4/300. ... Full name: Jeffrey Clay Mitchell.
HIGH SCHOOL: Countryside (Clearwater, Fla.).
COLLEGE: Florida.
TRANSACTIONS/CAREER NOTES: Selected by Baltimore Ravens in fifth round (134th pick overall) of 1997 NFL draft. ... Signed by Ravens (July 10, 1997). ... On injured reserve with knee injury (August 18, 1997-entire season).
PLAYING EXPERIENCE: Baltimore NFL, 1998. ... Games/Games started: 11/10.
PRO STATISTICS: 1998—Fumbled once for minus 11 yards.

MITCHELL, KEITH   LB   SAINTS

PERSONAL: Born July 24, 1974, in Garland, Texas ... 6-2/245. ... Full name: Clarence Marquis Mitchell.
HIGH SCHOOL: Lakeview (Garland, Texas).
COLLEGE: Texas A&M.
TRANSACTIONS/CAREER NOTES: Signed as non-drafted free agent by New Orleans Saints (April 25, 1997).
HONORS: Named outside linebacker on THE SPORTING NEWS college All-America second team (1996).
PRO STATISTICS: 1998—Recovered three fumbles for 63 yards and one touchdown.

Year Team	G	GS	SACKS
1997—New Orleans NFL	16	2	4.0
1998—New Orleans NFL	16	15	2.5
Pro totals (2 years)	32	17	6.5

MITCHELL, KEVIN   LB   SAINTS

PERSONAL: Born January 1, 1971, in Harrisburg, Pa. ... 6-1/250. ... Full name: Kevin Danyelle Mitchell. ... Cousin of Troy Drayton, tight end, Miami Dolphins.
HIGH SCHOOL: Harrisburg (Pa.).
COLLEGE: Syracuse (degree in sociology).
TRANSACTIONS/CAREER NOTES: Selected by San Francisco 49ers in second round (53rd pick overall) of 1994 NFL draft. ... Signed by 49ers (July 20, 1994). ... Granted free agency (February 14, 1997). ... Re-signed by 49ers (April 24, 1997). ... Granted free agency (February 13, 1998). ... Signed by New Orleans Saints (February 19, 1998).
PLAYING EXPERIENCE: San Francisco NFL, 1994-1997; New Orleans NFL, 1998. ... Games/Games started: 1994 (16/0), 1995 (15/0), 1996 (12/3), 1997 (16/0), 1998 (8/8). Total: 67/11.
CHAMPIONSHIP GAME EXPERIENCE: Played in NFC championship game (1994 and 1997 seasons). ... Member of Super Bowl championship team (1994 season).
HONORS: Named defensive lineman on THE SPORTING NEWS college All-America second team (1992 and 1993).
PRO STATISTICS: 1996—Credited with one sack and recovered one fumble. 1998—Credited with 2$\frac{1}{2}$ sacks.

MITCHELL, PETE — TE — GIANTS

PERSONAL: Born October 9, 1971, in Royal Oak, Mich. ... 6-2/240. ... Full name: Peter Clark Mitchell.
HIGH SCHOOL: Brother Rice (Bloomfield Hills, Mich.).
COLLEGE: Boston College (degree in communications, 1994).
TRANSACTIONS/CAREER NOTES: Selected by Miami Dolphins in fourth round (122nd pick overall) of 1995 NFL draft. ... Signed by Dolphins (July 14, 1995). ... Traded by Dolphins to Jacksonville Jaguars for WR Mike Williams (August 27, 1995). ... Granted free agency (February 13, 1998). ... Re-signed by Jaguars (April 13, 1998). ... Designated by Jaguars as transition player (February 12, 1999). ... Signed by New York Giants (March 24, 1999).
CHAMPIONSHIP GAME EXPERIENCE: Played in AFC championship game (1996 season).
HONORS: Named tight end on THE SPORTING NEWS college All-America first team (1993 and 1994).
PRO STATISTICS: 1997—Returned two kickoffs for 17 yards and recovered one fumble. 1998—Returned two kickoffs for 27 yards and recovered one fumble.
SINGLE GAME HIGHS (regular season): Receptions—10 (November 19, 1995, vs. Tampa Bay); yards—161 (November 19, 1995, vs. Tampa Bay); and touchdown receptions—1 (December 20, 1998, vs. Minnesota).
STATISTICAL PLATEAUS: 100-yard receiving games: 1995 (1).

			RECEIVING				TOTALS		
Year Team	G	GS	No.	Yds.	Avg.	TD	TD	2pt.	Pts.	Fum.
1995—Jacksonville NFL	16	4	41	527	12.9	2	2	0	12	0
1996—Jacksonville NFL	16	7	52	575	11.1	1	1	0	6	1
1997—Jacksonville NFL	16	12	35	380	10.9	4	4	0	24	0
1998—Jacksonville NFL	16	16	38	363	9.6	2	2	0	12	0
Pro totals (4 years)	64	39	166	1845	11.1	9	9	0	54	1

MITCHELL, SCOTT — QB — RAVENS

PERSONAL: Born January 2, 1968, in Salt Lake City. ... 6-6/230. ... Full name: William Scott Mitchell.
HIGH SCHOOL: Springville (Utah).
COLLEGE: Utah.
TRANSACTIONS/CAREER NOTES: Selected after junior season by Miami Dolphins in fourth round (93rd pick overall) of 1990 NFL draft. ... Signed by Dolphins (July 20, 1990). ... Inactive for 16 games (1990). ... Granted free agency (February 1, 1992). ... Assigned by Dolphins to Orlando Thunder in 1992 World League enhancement allocation program (February 20, 1992). ... Re-signed by Dolphins (February 21, 1992). ... Granted unconditional free agency (February 17, 1994). ... Signed by Detroit Lions (March 6, 1994). ... On injured reserve with wrist injury (November 8, 1994-remainder of season). ... Traded by Lions to Baltimore Ravens for third-round pick (traded to Miami) in 1999 draft and conditional fourth- or fifth-round pick in 2000 draft (March 16, 1999).
CHAMPIONSHIP GAME EXPERIENCE: Played in AFC championship game (1992 season).
PRO STATISTICS: W.L.: 1992—Fumbled six times and recovered two fumbles for minus 19 yards. NFL: 1993—Fumbled once and recovered one fumble for minus four yards. 1994—Fumbled eight times and recovered two fumbles for minus five yards. 1995—Fumbled eight times and recovered one fumble. 1996—Fumbled nine times and recovered five fumbles for minus three yards. 1997—Tied for NFC lead with 15 fumbles and recovered four fumbles for minus 15 yards. 1998—Fumbled once for minus nine yards.
SINGLE GAME HIGHS (regular season): Attempts—50 (September 7, 1997, vs. Tampa Bay); completions—31 (October 13, 1996, vs. Oakland); yards—410 (November 23, 1995, vs. Minnesota); and touchdown passes—4 (September 22, 1996, vs. Chicago).
STATISTICAL PLATEAUS: 300-yard passing games: 1993 (1), 1995 (5), 1996 (2), 1997 (1). Total: 9.
MISCELLANEOUS: Regular-season record as starting NFL quarterback: 30-34 (.469). ... Postseason record as starting NFL quarterback: 0-2.

			PASSING							RUSHING				TOTALS		
Year Team	G	GS	Att.	Cmp.	Pct.	Yds.	TD	Int.	Avg.	Rat.	Att.	Yds.	Avg.	TD	TD	2pt.	Pts.
1990—Miami NFL							Did not play.										
1991—Miami NFL	2	0	0	0	...	0	0	0	...	...	0	0	...	0	0	...	0
1992—Orlando W.L.	10	10	*361	*201	55.7	2213	12	7	6.13	77.0	21	45	2.1	1	1	...	6
—Miami NFL	16	0	8	2	25.0	32	0	1	4.00	4.2	8	10	1.3	0	0	...	0
1993—Miami NFL	13	7	233	133	57.1	1773	12	8	7.61	84.2	21	89	4.2	0	0	...	0
1994—Detroit NFL	9	9	246	119	48.4	1456	10	11	5.92	62.0	15	24	1.6	1	1	0	6
1995—Detroit NFL	16	16	583	346	59.3	4338	32	12	7.44	92.3	36	104	2.9	4	4	0	24
1996—Detroit NFL	14	14	437	253	57.9	2917	17	17	6.68	74.9	37	83	2.2	4	4	0	24
1997—Detroit NFL	16	16	509	293	57.6	3484	19	14	6.84	79.6	37	83	2.2	1	1	0	6
1998—Detroit NFL	2	2	75	38	50.7	452	1	3	6.03	57.2	7	30	4.3	0	0	0	0
W.L. totals (1 year)	10	10	361	201	55.7	2213	12	7	6.13	77.0	21	45	2.1	1	1	0	6
NFL totals (8 years)	88	64	2091	1184	56.6	14452	91	66	6.91	79.4	161	423	2.6	10	10	0	60
Pro totals (9 years)	98	74	2452	1385	56.5	16665	103	73	6.80	79.1	182	468	2.6	11	11	0	66

MIXON, KENNY — DE — DOLPHINS

PERSONAL: Born May 31, 1975, in Sun Valley, Calif. ... 6-4/273. ... Full name: Kenneth Jermaine Mixon.
HIGH SCHOOL: Pineville (La.).
COLLEGE: Louisiana State.
TRANSACTIONS/CAREER NOTES: Selected by Miami Dolphins in second round (49th pick overall) of 1998 NFL draft. ... Signed by Dolphins (July 21, 1998).

Year Team	G	GS	SACKS
1998—Miami NFL	16	16	2.0

MOBLEY, JOHN — LB — BRONCOS

PERSONAL: Born October 10, 1973, in Chester, Pa. ... 6-1/236. ... Full name: John Ulysses Mobley.
HIGH SCHOOL: Chichester (Chester, Pa.).
COLLEGE: Kutztown (Pa.) University.
TRANSACTIONS/CAREER NOTES: Selected by Denver Broncos in first round (15th pick overall) of 1996 NFL draft. ... Signed by Broncos (July 23, 1996).
CHAMPIONSHIP GAME EXPERIENCE: Played in AFC championship game (1997 and 1998 seasons). ... Member of Super Bowl championship team (1997 and 1998 seasons).
HONORS: Named outside linebacker on THE SPORTING NEWS NFL All-Pro team (1997).
PRO STATISTICS: 1997—Recovered one fumble. 1998—Recovered one fumble.

				INTERCEPTIONS			SACKS
Year Team	G	GS	No.	Yds.	Avg.	TD	No.
1996—Denver NFL	16	16	1	8	8.0	0	1.5
1997—Denver NFL	16	16	1	13	13.0	1	4.0
1998—Denver NFL	16	15	1	-2	-2.0	0	1.0
Pro totals (3 years)	48	47	3	19	6.3	1	6.5

MOBLEY, SINGOR — S — COWBOYS

PERSONAL: Born October 12, 1972, in Tacoma, Wash. ... 5-11/195. ... Full name: Singor A. Mobley.
HIGH SCHOOL: Curtis (Tacoma, Wash.).
COLLEGE: Washington State.
TRANSACTIONS/CAREER NOTES: Signed by Edmonton Eskimos of CFL (April 1995). ... Signed as non-drafted free agent by Dallas Cowboys (February 12, 1997).
PLAYING EXPERIENCE: Edmonton CFL, 1995 and 1996; Dallas NFL, 1997 and 1998. ... Games/Games started: 1995 (17/games started unavailable), 1996 (16/games started unavailable); 1997 (12/0), 1998 (16/0). Total CFL: 33/-. Total NFL: 28/0. Total Pro: 61/-.
PRO STATISTICS: CFL: 1995—Intercepted one pass for four yards, credited with one sack and recovered three fumbles for 129 yards and one touchdown. 1996—Credited with five sacks and recovered one fumble. NFL: 1998—Recovered one fumble.

MOHR, CHRIS — P — BILLS

PERSONAL: Born May 11, 1966, in Atlanta. ... 6-5/215. ... Full name: Christopher Garrett Mohr. ... Name pronounced MORE.
HIGH SCHOOL: Briarwood Academy (Thomson, Ga.).
COLLEGE: Alabama (degree in criminal justice).
TRANSACTIONS/CAREER NOTES: Selected by Tampa Bay Buccaneers in sixth round (146th pick overall) of 1989 NFL draft. ... Signed by Buccaneers (July 15, 1989). ... Released by Buccaneers (September 2, 1990). ... Signed by WLAF (January 31, 1991). ... Selected by Montreal Machine in first round (eighth punter) of 1991 WLAF positional draft. ... Signed by Buffalo Bills (June 6, 1991). ... Granted unconditional free agency (February 17, 1994). ... Re-signed by Bills (March 3, 1994). ... Granted unconditional free agency (February 14, 1997). ... Re-signed by Bills (March 4, 1997).
CHAMPIONSHIP GAME EXPERIENCE: Played in AFC championship game (1991-1993 seasons). ... Played in Super Bowl XXVI (1991 season), Super Bowl XXVII (1992 season) and Super Bowl XXVIII (1993 season).
HONORS: Named punter on All-World League team (1991).
PRO STATISTICS: NFL: 1989—Converted one extra point. 1991—Attempted one pass with a completion for minus nine yards. 1992—Rushed once for 11 yards and recovered one fumble. 1993—Fumbled once and recovered one fumble. 1994—Rushed once for minus nine yards. 1997—Rushed once for no yards, attempted one pass with a completion for 29 yards, fumbled once and recovered one fumble for minus 10 yards. W.L.: 1991—Had only pass attempt intercepted and rushed three times for minus four yards.

			PUNTING				
Year Team	G	No.	Yds.	Avg.	Net avg.	In. 20	Blk.
1989—Tampa Bay NFL	16	∞84	3311	39.4	32.1	10	2
1990—				Did not play.			
1991—Montreal W.L.	10	57	2436	42.7	34.0	13	2
—Buffalo NFL	16	54	2085	38.6	36.1	12	0
1992—Buffalo NFL	15	60	2531	42.2	36.7	12	0
1993—Buffalo NFL	16	74	2991	40.4	36.0	19	0
1994—Buffalo NFL	16	67	2799	41.8	36.0	13	0
1995—Buffalo NFL	16	86	3473	40.4	36.2	23	0
1996—Buffalo NFL	16	§101	§4194	41.5	36.5	§27	0
1997—Buffalo NFL	16	90	3764	41.8	36.0	24	1
1998—Buffalo NFL	16	69	2882	41.8	33.2	18	0
W.L. totals (1 year)	10	57	2436	42.7	34.0	13	2
NFL totals (9 years)	143	685	28030	40.9	35.4	158	3
Pro totals (10 years)	153	742	30466	41.1	35.3	171	5

MOHRING, MICHAEL — DT — CHARGERS

PERSONAL: Born March 22, 1974, in Glen Cove, N.Y. ... 6-5/295. ... Full name: Michael Joseph Mohring. ... Cousin of John Mohring, linebacker with Detroit Lions (1980) and Cleveland Browns (1980).
HIGH SCHOOL: West Chester (Pa.) East.
COLLEGE: Pittsburgh.
TRANSACTIONS/CAREER NOTES: Signed as non-drafted free agent by Miami Dolphins (April 24, 1997). ... Released by Dolphins (August 18, 1997). ... Signed by San Diego Chargers to practice squad (August 25, 1997). ... Activated (December 12, 1997).
PLAYING EXPERIENCE: San Diego NFL, 1997 and 1998. ... Games/Games started: 1997 (2/0), 1998 (10/0). Total: 12/0.
PRO STATISTICS: 1998—Credited with one sack.

MOLDEN, ALEX — CB — SAINTS

PERSONAL: Born August 4, 1973, in Detroit. ... 5-10/190. ... Full name: Alex M. Molden.
HIGH SCHOOL: Sierra (Colorado Springs, Colo.).
COLLEGE: Oregon.
TRANSACTIONS/CAREER NOTES: Selected by New Orleans Saints in first round (11th pick overall) of 1996 NFL draft. ... Signed by Saints (July 21, 1996).
HONORS: Named defensive back on THE SPORTING NEWS college All-America second team (1995).
PRO STATISTICS: 1997—Recovered two fumbles.

			INTERCEPTIONS				SACKS
Year Team	G	GS	No.	Yds.	Avg.	TD	No.
1996—New Orleans NFL	14	2	2	2	1.0	0	2.0
1997—New Orleans NFL	16	15	0	0	...	0	4.0
1998—New Orleans NFL	16	15	2	35	17.5	0	0.0
Pro totals (3 years)	46	32	4	37	9.3	0	6.0

MONTGOMERY, MONTY — DB — COLTS

PERSONAL: Born December 8, 1973, in Dallas. ... 5-11/197. ... Full name: Delmonico Montgomery.
HIGH SCHOOL: Gladewater (Texas).
COLLEGE: Houston.
TRANSACTIONS/CAREER NOTES: Selected by Indianapolis Colts in fourth round (117th pick overall) of 1997 NFL draft. ... Signed by Colts (July 7, 1997).
PRO STATISTICS: 1998—Intercepted one pass for 22 yards and recovered two fumbles for 14 yards.

Year Team	G	GS	SACKS
1997—Indianapolis NFL	16	3	1.0
1998—Indianapolis NFL	16	5	2.0
Pro totals (2 years)	32	8	3.0

MONTY, PETE — LB — GIANTS

PERSONAL: Born July 13, 1974, in Fort Collins, Colo. ... 6-2/250. ... Full name: Peter Monty.
HIGH SCHOOL: Fort Collins (Colo.).
COLLEGE: Wisconsin.
TRANSACTIONS/CAREER NOTES: Selected by New York Giants in fourth round (103rd pick overall) of 1997 NFL draft. ... Signed by Giants (July 19, 1997). ... On injured reserve with knee injury (September 30, 1997-remainder of season).
PLAYING EXPERIENCE: New York Giants NFL, 1997 and 1998. ... Games/Games started: 1997 (3/0), 1998 (11/0). Total: 14/0.

MOON, WARREN — QB — CHIEFS

PERSONAL: Born November 18, 1956, in Los Angeles. ... 6-3/213. ... Full name: Harold Warren Moon.
HIGH SCHOOL: Hamilton (Los Angeles).
JUNIOR COLLEGE: West Los Angeles Junior College.
COLLEGE: Washington.
TRANSACTIONS/CAREER NOTES: Signed by Edmonton Eskimos of CFL (March 1978). ... USFL rights traded by Memphis Showboats to Los Angeles Express for future draft pick (August 30, 1983). ... Granted free agency (March 1, 1984). ... Signed by Houston Oilers (March 1, 1984). ... On injured reserve with fractured scapula (September 5-October 15, 1988). ... Traded by Oilers to Minnesota Vikings for third-round pick (WR Malcolm Seabron) in 1994 draft and third-round pick (RB Rodney Thomas) in 1995 draft (April 14, 1994). ... Released by Vikings (February 21, 1997). ... Signed by Seattle Seahawks (March 7, 1997). ... Released by Seahawks (February 11, 1999). ... Signed by Kansas City Chiefs (April 26, 1999).
CHAMPIONSHIP GAME EXPERIENCE: Played in Grey Cup, CFL championship game (1978-1982 seasons).
HONORS: Played in Pro Bowl (1988-1995 and 1997 seasons). ... Named quarterback on THE SPORTING NEWS NFL All-Pro team (1990). ... Named Outstanding Player of Pro Bowl (1997 season).
RECORDS: Holds NFL career records for most fumbles—160; most own and opponents' fumbles recovered—55; and most own fumbles recovered—55. ... Holds NFL single-season record for most passes completed—404 (1991). ... Shares NFL single-game record for most games with 300 or more yards passing—9 (1990). ... Shares NFL single-game record for most times sacked—12 (September 29, 1985, vs. Dallas).
POST SEASON RECORDS: Holds NFL postseason career records for most fumbles—16; and most own fumbles recovered—8. ... Holds NFL postseason single-game records for most passes completed—36 (January 3, 1993, OT, at Buffalo); and most fumbles—5 (January 16, 1994, vs. Kansas City).
PRO STATISTICS: CFL: 1978—Fumbled once. 1979—Fumbled once. 1981—Fumbled once. 1982—Fumbled once and recovered one fumble. 1983—Fumbled seven times. NFL: 1984—Led league with 17 fumbles and recovered seven fumbles for minus one yard. 1985—Fumbled 12 times and recovered five fumbles for minus eight yards. 1986—Fumbled 11 times and recovered three fumbles for minus four yards. 1987—Fumbled eight times and recovered six fumbles for minus seven yards. 1988—Fumbled eight times and recovered four fumbles for minus 12 yards. 1989—Fumbled 11 times and recovered six fumbles for minus 13 yards. 1990—Led league with 18 fumbles and recovered four fumbles. 1991—Fumbled 11 times and recovered four fumbles for minus three yards. 1992—Fumbled seven times. 1993—Fumbled 13 times and recovered five fumbles for minus seven yards. 1994—Fumbled nine times and recovered two fumbles for minus five yards. 1995—Fumbled 13 times and recovered five fumbles for minus 12 yards. 1996—Fumbled seven times and recovered two fumbles. 1997—Fumbled seven times and recovered one fumble for minus two yards. 1998—Fumbled eight times and recovered one fumble for minus 12 yards.
SINGLE GAME HIGHS (regular season): Attempts—57 (November 6, 1994, vs. New Orleans); completions—41 (November 10, 1991, vs. Dallas); yards—527 (December 16, 1990, vs. Kansas City); and touchdown passes—5 (October 26, 1997, vs. Oakland).
STATISTICAL PLATEAUS: 300-yard passing games: 1984 (4), 1985 (3), 1986 (3), 1987 (2), 1989 (4), 1990 (9), 1991 (6), 1992 (4), 1993 (3), 1994 (6), 1995 (4), 1997 (1). Total: 49.
MISCELLANEOUS: Regular-season record as starting NFL quarterback: 102-100 (.505). ... Postseason record as starting NFL quarterback: 3-7 (.300). ... Holds Oilers franchise all-time records for most yards passing (33,685) and most touchdown passes (196).

Year Team	G	GS	Att.	Cmp.	Pct.	PASSING Yds.	TD	Int.	Avg.	Rat.	Att.	RUSHING Yds.	Avg.	TD	TD	TOTALS 2pt.	Pts.
1978—Edmonton CFL	16	...	173	89	51.4	1112	5	7	6.43	64.5	30	114	3.8	1	1	...	6
1979—Edmonton CFL	16	...	274	149	54.4	2382	20	12	8.69	89.7	56	150	2.7	2	2	...	12
1980—Edmonton CFL	16	...	331	181	54.7	3127	25	11	9.45	98.3	55	352	6.4	3	3	...	18
1981—Edmonton CFL	15	9	378	237	62.7	3959	27	12	10.47	108.6	50	298	6.0	3	3	...	18
1982—Edmonton CFL	16	16	562	333	59.3	5000	36	16	8.90	98.0	54	259	4.8	4	4	...	24
1983—Edmonton CFL	16	16	664	380	57.2	5648	31	19	8.51	88.9	85	527	6.2	3	3	...	18
1984—Houston NFL	16	16	450	259	57.6	3338	12	14	7.42	76.9	58	211	3.6	1	1	...	6
1985—Houston NFL	14	14	377	200	53.1	2709	15	19	7.19	68.5	39	130	3.3	0	0	...	0
1986—Houston NFL	15	15	488	256	52.5	3489	13	*26	7.15	62.3	42	157	3.7	2	2	...	12
1987—Houston NFL	12	12	368	184	50.0	2806	21	18	7.63	74.2	34	112	3.3	3	3	...	18
1988—Houston NFL	11	11	294	160	54.4	2327	17	8	7.91	88.4	33	88	2.7	5	5	...	30
1989—Houston NFL	16	16	464	280	60.3	3631	23	14	7.83	88.9	70	268	3.8	4	4	...	24
1990—Houston NFL	15	15	*584	*362	62.0	*4689	*33	18	8.03	96.8	55	215	3.9	2	2	...	12
1991—Houston NFL	16	16	*655	*404	61.7	*4690	23	*21	7.16	81.7	33	68	2.1	2	2	...	12
1992—Houston NFL	11	10	346	224	64.7	2521	18	12	7.29	§89.2	27	147	5.4	1	1	...	6
1993—Houston NFL	16	14	520	303	58.3	3485	21	§21	6.70	75.2	48	145	3.0	1	1	...	6
1994—Minnesota NFL	15	15	‡601	‡371	61.7	‡4264	18	‡19	7.09	79.9	27	55	2.0	0	0	0	0
1995—Minnesota NFL	16	16	‡606	*377	62.2	4228	33	14	6.98	91.5	33	82	2.5	0	0	0	0
1996—Minnesota NFL	8	8	247	134	54.3	1610	7	9	6.52	68.7	9	6	0.7	0	0	0	0
1997—Seattle NFL	15	14	528	313	59.3	3678	25	16	6.97	83.7	17	40	2.4	1	1	0	6
1998—Seattle NFL	10	10	258	145	56.2	1632	11	8	6.33	76.6	16	10	0.6	0	0	0	0
CFL totals (6 years)	95	...	2382	1369	57.5	21228	144	77	8.91	93.8	330	1700	5.2	16	16	0	96
NFL totals (15 years)	205	202	6786	3972	58.5	49097	290	232	7.24	81.0	541	1734	3.2	22	22	0	132
Pro totals (21 years)	300	...	9168	5341	58.3	70325	434	309	7.67	84.3	871	3434	3.9	38	38	0	228

MOORE, DAVE — TE — BUCCANEERS

PERSONAL: Born November 11, 1969, in Morristown, N.J. ... 6-2/245. ... Full name: David Edward Moore.
HIGH SCHOOL: Roxbury (Succasunna, N.J.).
COLLEGE: Pittsburgh (degree in justice administration, 1991).
TRANSACTIONS/CAREER NOTES: Selected by Miami Dolphins in seventh round (191st pick overall) of 1992 NFL draft. ... Signed by Dolphins (July 15, 1992). ... Released by Dolphins (August 31, 1992). ... Re-signed by Dolphins to practice squad (September 1, 1992). ... Released by Dolphins (September 16, 1992). ... Re-signed by Dolphins to practice squad (October 21, 1992). ... Activated (October 24, 1992). ... Released by Dolphins (October 28, 1992). ... Re-signed by Dolphins to practice squad (October 28, 1992). ... Released by Dolphins (November 18, 1992). ... Signed by Tampa Bay Buccaneers to practice squad (November 24, 1992). ... Activated (December 4, 1992). ... Granted free agency (February 16, 1996). ... Re-signed by Buccaneers (May 31, 1996). ... Granted unconditional free agency (February 14, 1997). ... Re-signed by Buccaneers (February 18, 1997).
PRO STATISTICS: 1993—Attempted one pass without a completion and recovered one fumble. 1995—Rushed once for four yards.
SINGLE GAME HIGHS (regular season): Receptions—6 (November 2, 1997, vs. Indianapolis); yards—62 (November 3, 1996, vs. Chicago); and touchdown receptions—1 (December 19, 1998, vs. Washington).

Year Team	G	GS	RECEIVING No.	Yds.	Avg.	TD	TD	TOTALS 2pt.	Pts.	Fum.
1992—Miami NFL	1	0	0	0	...	0	0	...	0	0
—Tampa Bay NFL	4	2	1	10	10.0	0	0	...	0	0
1993—Tampa Bay NFL	15	1	4	47	11.8	1	1	0	6	0
1994—Tampa Bay NFL	15	5	4	57	14.3	0	0	0	0	0
1995—Tampa Bay NFL	16	9	13	102	7.8	0	0	0	0	0
1996—Tampa Bay NFL	16	8	27	237	8.8	3	3	0	18	0
1997—Tampa Bay NFL	16	7	19	217	11.4	4	4	0	24	0
1998—Tampa Bay NFL	16	16	24	255	10.6	4	4	0	24	1
Pro totals (7 years)	99	48	92	925	10.1	12	12	0	72	1

MOORE, HERMAN — WR — LIONS

PERSONAL: Born October 20, 1969, in Danville, Va. ... 6-4/210. ... Full name: Herman Joseph Moore.
HIGH SCHOOL: George Washington (Danville, Va.).
COLLEGE: Virginia (degree in rhetoric and communication studies, 1991).
TRANSACTIONS/CAREER NOTES: Selected after junior season by Detroit Lions in first round (10th pick overall) of 1991 NFL draft. ... Signed by Lions (July 19, 1991). ... On injured reserve with quadricep injury (September 11-October 9, 1992). ... On practice squad (October 9-14, 1992). ... Designated by Lions as transition player (February 25, 1993).
CHAMPIONSHIP GAME EXPERIENCE: Played in NFC championship game (1991 season).
HONORS: Named wide receiver on THE SPORTING NEWS college All-America first team (1990). ... Played in Pro Bowl (1994-1997 seasons). ... Named wide receiver on THE SPORTING NEWS NFL All-Pro team (1995-1997).
RECORDS: Holds NFL single-season record for most pass receptions—123 (1995).
POST SEASON RECORDS: Shares NFL postseason career and single-game records for most two-point conversions—1 (December 30, 1995, vs. Philadelphia).
SINGLE GAME HIGHS (regular season): Receptions—14 (December 4, 1995, vs. Chicago); yards—183 (December 4, 1995, vs. Chicago); and touchdown receptions—3 (October 29, 1995, vs. Green Bay).
STATISTICAL PLATEAUS: 100-yard receiving games: 1992 (3), 1993 (3), 1994 (3), 1995 (10), 1996 (5), 1997 (6), 1998 (4). Total: 34.
MISCELLANEOUS: Holds Detroit Lions all-time records for most yards receiving (8,467), most receptions (610) and most touchdown receptions (57).

Year	Team	G	GS	RECEIVING No.	Yds.	Avg.	TD	TOTALS TD	2pt.	Pts.	Fum.
1991—Detroit NFL		13	1	11	135	12.3	0	0	...	0	0
1992—Detroit NFL		12	11	51	966	‡18.9	4	4	...	24	0
1993—Detroit NFL		15	15	61	935	15.3	6	6	...	36	2
1994—Detroit NFL		16	16	72	1173	16.3	11	11	0	66	1
1995—Detroit NFL		16	16	*123	1686	13.7	14	14	0	84	2
1996—Detroit NFL		16	16	106	1296	12.2	9	9	1	56	0
1997—Detroit NFL		16	16	†104	1293	12.4	8	8	1	50	0
1998—Detroit NFL		15	15	82	983	12.0	5	5	0	30	0
Pro totals (8 years)		119	106	610	8467	13.9	57	57	2	346	5

MOORE, JERALD   FB

PERSONAL: Born November 20, 1974, in Houston. ... 5-9/225. ... Full name: Jerald Christopher Moore.
HIGH SCHOOL: Jack Yates (Houston).
COLLEGE: Oklahoma.
TRANSACTIONS/CAREER NOTES: Selected after junior season by St. Louis Rams in third round (83rd pick overall) of 1996 NFL draft. ... Signed by Rams (July 15, 1996). ... Granted free agency (February 12, 1999).
PRO STATISTICS: 1997—Recovered two fumbles. 1998—Recovered two fumbles.
SINGLE GAME HIGHS (regular season): Attempts—27 (December 20, 1997, vs. Carolina); yards—113 (December 20, 1997, vs. Carolina); and rushing touchdowns—1 (November 22, 1998, vs. Carolina).
STATISTICAL PLATEAUS: 100-yard rushing games: 1997 (1).

Year	Team	G	GS	RUSHING Att.	Yds.	Avg.	TD	RECEIVING No.	Yds.	Avg.	TD	TOTALS TD	2pt.	Pts.	Fum.
1996—St. Louis NFL		11	4	11	32	2.9	0	3	13	4.3	0	0	0	0	0
1997—St. Louis NFL		9	5	104	380	3.7	3	8	69	8.6	0	3	0	18	4
1998—St. Louis NFL		11	4	55	137	2.5	2	9	60	6.7	0	2	0	12	3
NFL totals (3 years)		31	13	170	549	3.2	5	20	142	7.1	0	5	0	30	7

MOORE, KELVIN   S   BENGALS

PERSONAL: Born March 7, 1975, in Los Angeles. ... 6-0/203.
HIGH SCHOOL: Hamilton (Calif.).
JUNIOR COLLEGE: Santa Monica (Calif.) College.
COLLEGE: Iowa State, then Morgan State.
TRANSACTIONS/CAREER NOTES: Signed as non-drafted free agent by Cincinnati Bengals (April 21, 1998). ... Released by Bengals (August 25, 1998). ... Re-signed by Bengals to practice squad (September 24, 1998). ... Activated (December 3, 1998).
PLAYING EXPERIENCE: Cincinnati NFL, 1998. ... Games/Games started: 4/0.

MOORE, LARRY   G   COLTS

PERSONAL: Born June 1, 1975, in San Diego. ... 6-3/301.
HIGH SCHOOL: Monte Vista (Spring Valley, Calif.).
JUNIOR COLLEGE: Grossmont College (Calif.).
COLLEGE: Brigham Young.
TRANSACTIONS/CAREER NOTES: Signed as non-drafted free agent by Seattle Seahawks (April 25, 1997). ... Released by Seahawks (August 17, 1997). ... Signed by Washington Redskins to practice squad (August 26, 1997). ... Released by Redskins (September 3, 1997). ... Signed by Indianapolis Colts (January 29, 1998).
PLAYING EXPERIENCE: Indianapolis NFL, 1998. ... Games/Games started: 6/5.

MOORE, MARTY   LB   PATRIOTS

PERSONAL: Born March 19, 1971, in Phoenix. ... 6-1/244. ... Full name: Martin Neff Moore.
HIGH SCHOOL: Highlands (Fort Thomas, Ky.).
COLLEGE: Kentucky.
TRANSACTIONS/CAREER NOTES: Selected by New England Patriots in seventh round (222nd pick overall) of 1994 NFL draft. ... Signed by Patriots (June 1, 1994). ... Granted free agency (February 14, 1997). ... Re-signed by Patriots (June 6, 1997). ... Granted unconditional free agency (February 13, 1998). ... Re-signed by Patriots (April 3, 1998).
PLAYING EXPERIENCE: New England NFL, 1994-1998. ... Games/Games started: 1994 (16/4), 1995 (16/3), 1996 (16/0), 1997 (16/0), 1998 (14/2). Total: 78/9.
CHAMPIONSHIP GAME EXPERIENCE: Played in AFC championship game (1996 season). ... Played in Super Bowl XXXI (1996 season).
PRO STATISTICS: 1997—Intercepted two passes for seven yards. 1998—Recovered one fumble.

MOORE, ROB — WR — CARDINALS

PERSONAL: Born September 27, 1968, in New York. ... 6-3/203. ... Full name: Robert S. Moore.
HIGH SCHOOL: Hempstead (N.Y.).
COLLEGE: Syracuse (degree in sociology, 1990).
TRANSACTIONS/CAREER NOTES: Selected by New York Jets in first round of 1990 NFL supplemental draft. ... Signed by Jets (July 22, 1990). ... Designated by Jets as transition player (February 25, 1993). ... Free agency status changed by Jets from transitional to restricted (February 17, 1994). ... Re-signed by Jets (July 12, 1994). ... Designated by Jets as franchise player (February 15, 1995). ... Traded by Jets to Arizona Cardinals for RB Ronald Moore and first- (DE Hugh Douglas) and fourth-round (OT Melvin Hayes) picks in 1995 draft (April 21, 1995). ... Designated by Cardinals as franchise player (February 12, 1999).
HONORS: Named wide receiver on THE SPORTING NEWS college All-America first team (1989). ... Played in Pro Bowl (1994 and 1997 seasons).
PRO STATISTICS: 1990—Rushed twice for minus four yards. 1992—Rushed once for 21 yards. 1993—Rushed once for minus six yards. 1994—Rushed once for minus three yards and recovered one fumble. 1995—Attempted two passes with one completion for 33 yards and an interception.
SINGLE GAME HIGHS (regular season): Receptions—9 (December 20, 1998, vs. New Orleans); yards—188 (November 30, 1997, vs. Pittsburgh); and touchdown receptions—3 (December 7, 1997, vs. Washington).
STATISTICAL PLATEAUS: 100-yard receiving games: 1990 (1), 1993 (2), 1994 (2), 1995 (3), 1996 (3), 1997 (8), 1998 (2). Total: 21.

				RECEIVING				TOTALS			
Year Team	G	GS	No.	Yds.	Avg.	TD	TD	2pt.	Pts.	Fum.	
1990—New York Jets NFL	15	14	44	692	15.7	6	6	...	36	1	
1991—New York Jets NFL	16	16	70	987	14.1	5	5	...	30	2	
1992—New York Jets NFL	16	15	50	726	14.5	4	4	...	24	0	
1993—New York Jets NFL	13	13	64	843	13.2	1	1	...	6	2	
1994—New York Jets NFL	16	16	78	1010	12.9	6	6	2	40	0	
1995—Arizona NFL	15	15	63	907	14.4	5	5	1	32	0	
1996—Arizona NFL	16	16	58	1016	17.5	4	4	1	26	0	
1997—Arizona NFL	16	16	97	*1584	16.3	8	8	1	50	0	
1998—Arizona NFL	16	16	67	982	14.7	5	5	0	30	0	
Pro totals (9 years)	139	137	591	8747	14.8	44	44	5	274	5	

MOORE, RON — RB — BROWNS

PERSONAL: Born January 26, 1970, in Spencer, Okla. ... 5-10/220. ... Full name: Ronald L. Moore.
HIGH SCHOOL: Star Spencer (Okla.).
COLLEGE: Pittsburg (Kan.) State.
TRANSACTIONS/CAREER NOTES: Selected by Phoenix Cardinals in fourth round (87th pick overall) of 1993 NFL draft. ... Signed by Cardinals (July 22, 1993). ... Cardinals franchise renamed Arizona Cardinals for 1994 season. ... Traded by Cardinals with first- (DE Hugh Douglas) and fourth-round (OT Melvin Hayes) picks in 1995 draft to New York Jets for WR Rob Moore (April 21, 1995). ... Granted unconditional free agency (February 14, 1997). ... Signed by St. Louis Rams (March 5, 1997). ... Released by Rams (October 29, 1997). ... Signed by Cardinals (November 3, 1997). ... Released by Cardinals (August 25, 1998). ... Signed by Miami Dolphins (September 30, 1998). ... Selected by Cleveland Browns from Dolphins in NFL expansion draft (February 9, 1999).
HONORS: Harlon Hill Trophy winner (1992).
PRO STATISTICS: 1993—Returned one kickoff for nine yards and recovered one fumble. 1994—Attempted one pass without a completion and recovered one fumble. 1995—Recovered one fumble.
SINGLE GAME HIGHS (regular season): Attempts—36 (November 7, 1993, vs. Philadelphia); yards—160 (November 7, 1993, vs. Philadelphia); and rushing touchdowns—4 (December 5, 1993, vs. Los Angeles Rams).
STATISTICAL PLATEAUS: 100-yard rushing games: 1993 (3), 1994 (1). Total: 4.

			RUSHING				RECEIVING				KICKOFF RETURNS				TOTALS		
Year Team	G	GS	Att.	Yds.	Avg.	TD	No.	Yds.	Avg.	TD	No.	Yds.	Avg.	TD	TD	2pt.	Pts. Fum.
1993—Phoenix NFL	16	11	263	1018	3.9	9	3	16	5.3	0	1	9	9.0	0	9	...	54 3
1994—Arizona NFL	16	16	232	780	3.4	4	8	52	6.5	1	0	0	...	0	5	1	32 2
1995—New York Jets NFL	15	3	43	121	2.8	0	8	50	6.3	0	8	166	20.8	0	0	0	0 3
1996—New York Jets NFL	16	0	1	1	1.0	0	0	0	...	0	8	118	14.8	0	0	0	0 0
1997—St. Louis NFL	7	2	24	103	4.3	1	4	34	8.5	0	1	17	17.0	0	1	0	6 0
—Arizona NFL	6	2	57	175	3.1	0	0	0	...	0	0	0	...	0	0	0	0 0
1998—Miami NFL	1	1	4	12	3.0	0	1	1	1.0	0	0	0	...	0	0	0	0 1
Pro totals (6 years)	77	35	624	2210	3.5	14	24	153	6.4	1	18	310	17.2	0	15	1	92 9

MOORE, STEVON — S — RAVENS

PERSONAL: Born February 9, 1967, in Wiggins, Miss. ... 5-11/210. ... Full name: Stevon Nathaniel Moore. ... Name pronounced stee-VON.
HIGH SCHOOL: Stone County (Wiggins, Miss.).
COLLEGE: Mississippi.
TRANSACTIONS/CAREER NOTES: Selected by New York Jets in seventh round (181st pick overall) of 1989 NFL draft. ... Signed by Jets (July 22, 1989). ... On injured reserve with knee injury (August 28, 1989-entire season). ... Granted unconditional free agency (February 1, 1990). ... Signed by Miami Dolphins (March 30, 1990). ... On physically unable to perform list with knee injury (July 21-August 27, 1990). ... On physically unable to perform list with knee injury (August 28-October 18, 1990). ... On injured reserve with hamstring injury (November 8-December 8, 1990). ... On injured reserve with knee injury (August 27, 1991-entire season). ... Granted unconditional free agency (February 1, 1992). ... Signed by Cleveland Browns (March 25, 1992). ... On injured reserve with separated shoulder (December 15, 1992-remainder of season). ... Browns franchise moved to Baltimore and renamed Ravens for 1996 season (March 11, 1996). ... Granted unconditional free agency (February 14, 1997). ... Re-signed by Ravens (April 2, 1997).
PRO STATISTICS: 1990—Recovered one fumble. 1992—Recovered three fumbles for 115 yards and one touchdown. 1993—Recovered one fumble for 22 yards and a touchdown. 1994—Recovered five fumbles for three yards. 1996—Recovered one fumble.

– 282 –

Year	Team	G	GS	No.	Yds.	Avg.	TD	No.
1989—New York Jets NFL					Did not play.			
1990—Miami NFL		7	0	0	0	...	0	0.0
1991—Miami NFL					Did not play.			
1992—Cleveland NFL		14	4	0	0	...	0	2.0
1993—Cleveland NFL		16	16	0	0	...	0	0.0
1994—Cleveland NFL		16	16	0	0	...	0	0.0
1995—Cleveland NFL		16	16	5	55	11.0	0	1.0
1996—Baltimore NFL		16	16	1	10	10.0	0	0.0
1997—Baltimore NFL		13	12	4	56	14.0	0	0.0
1998—Baltimore NFL		16	16	0	0	...	0	0.0
Pro totals (8 years)		114	96	10	121	12.1	0	3.0

MOORE, WILL — WR — JAGUARS

PERSONAL: Born February 21, 1970, in Dallas. ... 6-1/186. ... Full name: Will Henry Moore III.
HIGH SCHOOL: David D. Carter (Dallas).
COLLEGE: Texas Southern (degree in business, 1992).
TRANSACTIONS/CAREER NOTES: Signed by Calgary Stampeders of CFL (April 1992). ... Granted free agency (February 1995). ... Signed as non-drafted free agent by New England Patriots (April 3, 1995). ... Released by Patriots (September 10, 1996). ... Signed by Jacksonville Jaguars (January 9, 1997). ... Granted free agency (February 12, 1999). ... Re-signed by Jaguars (March 24, 1999).
PRO STATISTICS: CFL: 1994—Attempted two passes with two completions for 52 yards and returned two kickoffs for two yards. NFL: 1997—Returned one kickoff for 36 yards. 1998—Ran 10 yards with lateral from kickoff return.
SINGLE GAME HIGHS (regular season): Receptions—8 (September 10, 1995, vs. Miami); yards—112 (September 10, 1995, vs. Miami); and touchdown receptions—1 (October 15, 1995, vs. Kansas City).

					RECEIVING			TOTALS			
Year	Team	G	GS	No.	Yds.	Avg.	TD	TD	2pt.	Pts.	Fum.
1992—Calgary CFL	1	...	3	38	12.7	0	0	...	0	0
1993—Calgary CFL	18	...	73	1083	14.8	12	12	...	72	2
1994—Calgary CFL	18	...	44	792	18.0	11	11	0	66	0
1995—New England NFL	14	13	43	502	11.7	1	1	0	6	0
1996—New England NFL	2	1	3	37	12.3	0	0	0	0	0
1997—Jacksonville NFL	11	0	1	10	10.0	0	0	0	0	0
1998—Jacksonville NFL	16	0	1	9	9.0	0	0	0	0	0
CFL totals (3 years)	37	...	120	1913	15.9	23	23	0	138	2
NFL totals (4 years)	43	14	48	558	11.6	1	1	0	6	0
Pro totals (7 years)	80	...	168	2471	14.7	24	24	0	144	2

MORABITO, TIM — NT — PANTHERS

PERSONAL: Born October 12, 1973, in Garnerville, N.Y. ... 6-3/296. ... Full name: Timothy Robert Morabito.
HIGH SCHOOL: St. Joseph's Regional.
COLLEGE: Boston College (degree in sociology).
TRANSACTIONS/CAREER NOTES: Signed as non-drafted free agent by Cincinnati Bengals (April 23, 1996). ... Released by Bengals (September 11, 1996). ... Re-signed by Bengals to practice squad (September 12, 1996). ... Activated (November 5, 1996). ... Claimed on waivers by Carolina Panthers (August 26, 1997). ... Granted free agency (February 12, 1999).
PLAYING EXPERIENCE: Cincinnati NFL, 1996; Carolina NFL, 1997 and 1998. ... Games/Games started: 1996 (7/1); 1997 (8/0); 1998 (8/8). Total: 23/9.
PRO STATISTICS: 1997—Recovered one fumble.

MORAN, SEAN — DE — BILLS

PERSONAL: Born June 5, 1973, in Denver. ... 6-3/275. ... Full name: Sean Farrell Moran.
HIGH SCHOOL: Overland (Aurora, Colo.).
COLLEGE: Colorado State.
TRANSACTIONS/CAREER NOTES: Selected by Buffalo Bills in fourth round (120th pick overall) of 1996 NFL draft. ... Signed by Bills (July 9, 1996). ... Granted free agency (February 1, 1999). ... Re-signed by Bills (April 1, 1999).
PLAYING EXPERIENCE: Buffalo NFL, 1996-1998. ... Games/Games started: 1996 (16/0), 1997 (16/7), 1998 (10/2). Total: 42/9.
PRO STATISTICS: 1997—Intercepted two passes for 12 yards, credited with 4$^{1}/_{2}$ sacks and recovered one fumble.

MORENO, MOSES — QB — BEARS

PERSONAL: Born September 5, 1975, in Chula Vista, Calif. ... 6-1/205. ... Full name: Moses Nathaniel Moreno.
HIGH SCHOOL: Castle Park (Chula Vista, Calif.).
COLLEGE: Colorado State.
TRANSACTIONS/CAREER NOTES: Selected by Chicago Bears in seventh round (232nd pick overall) of 1998 NFL draft. ... Signed by Bears (June 20, 1998). ... On injured reserve with ankle injury (December 15, 1998-remainder of season).
PRO STATISTICS: 1998—Fumbled twice for minus four yards.
SINGLE GAME HIGHS (regular season): Attempts—41 (November 29, 1998, vs. Tampa Bay); completions—18 (November 29, 1998, vs. Tampa Bay); yards—153 (November 29, 1998, vs. Tampa Bay); and touchdown passes—1 (November 29, 1998, vs. Tampa Bay).
MISCELLANEOUS: Regular-season record as starting NFL quarterback: 0-1.

				PASSING						RUSHING				TOTALS		
Year	Team	G	GS	Att.	Cmp.	Pct.	Yds.	TD	Int.	Avg.	Rat.	Att.	Yds.	Avg.	TD	TD	2pt.	Pts.
1998—Chicago NFL	2	1	43	19	44.2	166	1	0	3.86	62.7	4	9	2.3	0	0	0	0

MORRIS, BAM — RB — CHIEFS

PERSONAL: Born January 13, 1972, in Cooper, Texas. ... 6-0/248. ... Full name: Byron Morris. ... Brother of Ron Morris, wide receiver with Chicago Bears (1987-92); and cousin of Terry Norris, former World Boxing Council junior middleweight champion.
HIGH SCHOOL: Cooper (Texas).
COLLEGE: Texas Tech.
TRANSACTIONS/CAREER NOTES: Selected after junior season by Pittsburgh Steelers in third round (91st pick overall) of 1994 NFL draft. ... Signed by Steelers (July 15, 1994). ... Released by Steelers (July 10, 1996). ... On suspended list for violating league substance abuse policy (September 1-22, 1996). ... Signed by Baltimore Ravens (September 24, 1996). ... On suspended list for violating league substance abuse policy (August 31-September 22, 1997). ... Granted unconditional free agency (February 13, 1998). ... Signed by Chicago Bears (August 4, 1998). ... Traded by Bears to Kansas City Chiefs for fifth-round pick (RB Jerry Azumah) in 1999 draft (October 13, 1998).
CHAMPIONSHIP GAME EXPERIENCE: Played in AFC championship game (1994 and 1995 seasons). ... Played in Super Bowl XXX (1995 season).
HONORS: Doak Walker Award winner (1993). ... Named running back on THE SPORTING NEWS college All-America second team (1993).
PRO STATISTICS: 1994—Recovered one fumble. 1997—Recovered four fumbles. 1998—Recovered one fumble.
SINGLE GAME HIGHS (regular season): Attempts—36 (October 26, 1997, vs. Washington); yards—176 (October 26, 1997, vs. Washington); and rushing touchdowns—3 (November 22, 1998, vs. San Diego).
STATISTICAL PLATEAUS: 100-yard rushing games: 1994 (2), 1995 (2), 1996 (3), 1997 (2), 1998 (1). Total: 10.
MISCELLANEOUS: Holds Baltimore Ravens all-time record for most yards rushing (1,511) and most rushing touchdowns (8).

				RUSHING				RECEIVING				KICKOFF RETURNS				TOTALS		
Year Team	G	GS	Att.	Yds.	Avg.	TD	No.	Yds.	Avg.	TD	No.	Yds.	Avg.	TD	TD	2pt.	Pts.	Fum.
1994—Pittsburgh NFL	15	6	198	836	4.2	7	22	204	9.3	0	4	114	28.5	0	7	0	42	3
1995—Pittsburgh NFL	13	4	148	559	3.8	9	8	36	4.5	0	0	0	...	0	9	0	54	3
1996—Baltimore NFL	11	7	172	737	4.3	4	25	242	9.7	1	1	3	3.0	0	5	0	30	0
1997—Baltimore NFL	11	8	204	774	3.8	4	29	176	6.1	0	1	23	23.0	0	4	0	24	4
1998—Chicago NFL	2	0	3	8	2.7	0	0	0	...	0	0	0	...	0	0	0	0	0
—Kansas City NFL	10	5	129	481	3.7	8	12	95	7.9	0	0	0	...	0	8	0	48	3
Pro totals (5 years)	62	30	854	3395	4.0	32	96	753	7.8	1	6	140	23.3	0	33	0	198	13

MORRIS, MIKE — C — VIKINGS

PERSONAL: Born February 22, 1961, in Centerville, Iowa. ... 6-5/272. ... Full name: Michael Stephen Morris.
HIGH SCHOOL: Centerville (Iowa).
COLLEGE: Northeast Missouri State (degree in psychology and physical education, 1982).
TRANSACTIONS/CAREER NOTES: Signed as non-drafted free agent by Arizona Outlaws of USFL (November 1, 1984). ... Released by Outlaws (February 11, 1985). ... Signed by Denver Broncos (May 8, 1986). ... Released by Broncos (July 21, 1986). ... Signed by St. Louis Cardinals (May 20, 1987). ... Crossed picket line during players strike (October 7, 1987). ... Cardinals franchise moved to Phoenix (March 15, 1988). ... On injured reserve with knee injury (August 23, 1988-entire season). ... Granted unconditional free agency (February 1, 1989). ... Signed by Washington Redskins (March 20, 1989). ... Claimed on waivers by Kansas City Chiefs (August 30, 1989). ... Released by Chiefs (October 11, 1989). ... Signed by New England Patriots (October 13, 1989). ... Granted unconditional free agency (February 1, 1990). ... Signed by Chiefs (April 1, 1990). ... Released by Chiefs (July 28, 1990). ... Signed by Seattle Seahawks (August 1990). ... Released by Seahawks (October 4, 1990). ... Signed by Cleveland Browns (October 16, 1990). ... Granted unconditional free agency (February 1-April 1, 1991). ... Re-signed by Browns for 1991 season. ... Released by Browns (July 22, 1991). ... Signed by Minnesota Vikings (August 10, 1991). ... Released by Vikings (August 26, 1991). ... Re-signed by Vikings (August 29, 1991). ... Granted unconditional free agency (February 1-April 1, 1992). ... Re-signed by Vikings for 1992 season. ... Granted unconditional free agency (February 17, 1994). ... Re-signed by Vikings (May 17, 1994). ... Granted unconditional free agency (February 1, 1995). ... Re-signed by Vikings (March 27, 1995). ... Granted unconditional free agency (February 12, 1999). ... Re-signed by Vikings (March 12, 1999).
PLAYING EXPERIENCE: St. Louis NFL, 1987; Kansas City (5)-New England (11) NFL, 1989; Seattle (4)-Cleveland (10) NFL, 1990; Minnesota NFL, 1991-1998. ... Games/Games started: 1987 (14/0), 1989 (K.C.-5/0; N.E.-11/0; Total: 16/0), 1990 (Sea.-4/0; Clev.-10/0; Total: 14/0), 1991 (16/0), 1992 (16/0), 1993 (16/0), 1994 (16/0), 1995 (16/0), 1996 (16/0), 1997 (16/0), 1998 (16/0). Total: 172/0.
CHAMPIONSHIP GAME EXPERIENCE: Played in NFC championship game (1998 season).
PRO STATISTICS: 1990—Fumbled once for minus 23 yards.

MORRISON, STEVE — LB

PERSONAL: Born December 28, 1971, in Farmington, Mich. ... 6-3/246. ... Full name: Steven Craig Morrison.
HIGH SCHOOL: Brother Rice (Bloomfield Hills, Mich.).
COLLEGE: Michigan (degree in sports management and communcations).
TRANSACTIONS/CAREER NOTES: Signed as non-drafted free agent by Indianapolis Colts (April 27, 1995). ... Granted free agency (February 13, 1998). ... Re-signed by Colts (March 12, 1998). ... Granted unconditional free agency (February 12, 1999).
PLAYING EXPERIENCE: Indianapolis NFL, 1995-1998. ... Games/Games started: 1995 (10/0), 1996 (16/8), 1997 (16/9), 1998 (16/12). Total: 58/29.
CHAMPIONSHIP GAME EXPERIENCE: Member of Colts for AFC championship game (1995 season); inactive.
PRO STATISTICS: 1995—Returned two kickoffs for six yards. 1996—Intercepted one pass for 20 yards and recovered two fumbles. 1997—Intercepted one pass for two yards, credited with one sack and recovered two fumbles for 27 yards. 1998—Returned one kickoff for two yards and credited with one sack.

MORROW, HAROLD — FB — VIKINGS

PERSONAL: Born February 24, 1973, in Maplesville, Ala. ... 5-11/217. ... Full name: Harold Morrow Jr. ... Cousin of Tommie Agee, fullback with Seattle Seahawks (1988), Kansas City Chiefs (1989) and Dallas Cowboys (1990-94).
HIGH SCHOOL: Maplesville (Ala.).
COLLEGE: Auburn.
TRANSACTIONS/CAREER NOTES: Signed as non-drafted free agent by Dallas Cowboys (April 25, 1996). ... Claimed on waivers by Minnesota Vikings (August 26, 1996). ... Granted free agency (February 12, 1999). ... Re-signed by Vikings (April 23, 1999).
PLAYING EXPERIENCE: Minnesota NFL, 1996-1998. ... Games/Games started: 1996 (8/0), 1997 (16/0), 1998 (11/0). Total: 35/0.

CHAMPIONSHIP GAME EXPERIENCE: Played in NFC championship game (1998 season).
PRO STATISTICS: 1996—Returned six kickoffs for 117 yards. 1997—Returned five kickoffs for 99 yards. 1998—Rushed three times for seven yards and recovered one fumble.
SINGLE GAME HIGHS (regular season): Attempts—3 (December 20, 1998, vs. Jacksonville); yards—7 (December 20, 1998, vs. Jacksonville); and rushing touchdowns—0.

MORTON, JOHNNIE — WR — LIONS

PERSONAL: Born October 7, 1971, in Inglewood, Calif. ... 6-0/190. ... Full name: Johnnie James Morton.
HIGH SCHOOL: South Torrance (Calif.).
COLLEGE: Southern California (degree in communications).
TRANSACTIONS/CAREER NOTES: Selected by Detroit Lions in first round (21st pick overall) of 1994 NFL draft. ... Signed by Lions (July 18, 1994).
HONORS: Named wide receiver on THE SPORTING NEWS college All-America first team (1993).
PRO STATISTICS: 1994—Recovered one fumble. 1995—Returned seven punts for 48 yards.
SINGLE GAME HIGHS (regular season): Receptions—9 (September 6, 1998, vs. Green Bay); yards—174 (September 22, 1996, vs. Chicago); and touchdown receptions—2 (September 22, 1996, vs. Chicago).
STATISTICAL PLATEAUS: 100-yard receiving games: 1995 (1), 1996 (2), 1997 (3), 1998 (3). Total: 9.

			RUSHING				RECEIVING				KICKOFF RETURNS				TOTALS			
Year Team	G	GS	Att.	Yds.	Avg.	TD	No.	Yds.	Avg.	TD	No.	Yds.	Avg.	TD	TD	2pt.	Pts.	Fum.
1994—Detroit NFL	14	0	0	0	...	0	3	39	13.0	1	4	143	35.8	1	2	0	12	1
1995—Detroit NFL	16	14	3	33	11.0	0	44	590	13.4	8	18	390	21.7	0	8	0	48	1
1996—Detroit NFL	16	15	9	35	3.9	0	55	714	13.0	6	0	0	...	0	6	0	36	1
1997—Detroit NFL	16	16	3	33	11.0	0	80	1057	13.2	6	0	0	...	0	6	0	36	2
1998—Detroit NFL	16	16	1	11	11.0	0	69	1028	14.9	2	0	0	...	0	2	0	12	0
Pro totals (5 years)	78	61	16	112	7.0	0	251	3428	13.7	23	22	533	24.2	1	24	0	144	5

MORTON, MIKE — LB — PACKERS

PERSONAL: Born March 28, 1972, in Kannapolis, N.C. ... 6-4/235. ... Full name: Michael Anthony Morton Jr.
HIGH SCHOOL: A.L. Brown (Kannapolis, N.C.).
COLLEGE: North Carolina.
TRANSACTIONS/CAREER NOTES: Selected by Los Angeles Raiders in fourth round (118th pick overall) of 1995 NFL draft. ... Signed by Raiders (July 21, 1995). ... Raiders franchise moved to Oakland (July 21, 1995). ... Granted unconditional free agency (February 12, 1999). ... Signed by Green Bay Packers (April 30, 1999).
PLAYING EXPERIENCE: Oakland NFL, 1995-1998. ... Games/Games started: 1995 (12/0), 1996 (16/6), 1997 (11/11), 1998 (16/0). Total: 55/17.
PRO STATISTICS: 1995—Recovered one fumble. 1996—Intercepted two passes for 13 yards and credited with one sack. 1997—Returned one kickoff for 14 yards and recovered one fumble. 1998—Returned one kickoff for three yards and recovered two fumbles.

MOSS, RANDY — WR — VIKINGS

PERSONAL: Born February 13, 1977, in Rand, W.Va. ... 6-4/202. ... Half brother of Eric Moss, guard, Minnesota Vikings.
HIGH SCHOOL: DuPont (Rand, W.Va.).
COLLEGE: Florida State (did not play), then Marshall.
TRANSACTIONS/CAREER NOTES: Selected after sophomore season by Minnesota Vikings in first round (21st pick overall) of 1998 NFL draft. ... Signed by Minnesota Vikings (July 26, 1998).
CHAMPIONSHIP GAME EXPERIENCE: Played in NFC championship game (1998 season).
HONORS: Fred Biletnikoff Award winner (1997). ... Named wide receiver on THE SPORTING NEWS college All-America first team (1997). ... Named NFL Rookie of the Year by THE SPORTING NEWS (1998). ... Named wide receiver on THE SPORTING NEWS NFL All-Pro team (1998). ... Played in Pro Bowl (1998 season).
RECORDS: Holds NFL rookie-season record for most touchdowns—17 (1998).
PRO STATISTICS: 1998—Rushed once for four yards and returned one punt for no yards.
SINGLE GAME HIGHS (regular season): Receptions—8 (December 6, 1998, vs. Chicago); yards—190 (October 5, 1998, vs. Green Bay); and touchdown receptions—3 (December 6, 1998, vs. Chicago).
STATISTICAL PLATEAUS: 100-yard receiving games: 1998 (4).

			RECEIVING				TOTALS			
Year Team	G	GS	No.	Yds.	Avg.	TD	TD	2pt.	Pts.	Fum.
1998—Minnesota NFL	16	11	69	1313	‡19.0	17	‡17	2	106	2

MOSS, ZEFROSS — OT — PATRIOTS

PERSONAL: Born August 17, 1966, in Holt, Ala. ... 6-6/325.
HIGH SCHOOL: Holt (Ala.).
COLLEGE: Alabama State.
TRANSACTIONS/CAREER NOTES: Signed as non-drafted free agent by Dallas Cowboys (April 29, 1988). ... Released by Cowboys (August 24, 1988). ... Re-signed by Cowboys (December 8, 1988). ... Traded by Cowboys to Indianapolis Colts for 10th-round pick (traded to Minnesota) in 1990 draft (August 22, 1989). ... On injured reserve with ankle injury (December 20, 1991-remainder of season). ... Granted unconditional free agency (February 17, 1995). ... Signed by Detroit Lions (April 28, 1995). ... Granted unconditional free agency (February 14, 1997). ... Signed by New England Patriots (March 31, 1997).
PLAYING EXPERIENCE: Indianapolis NFL, 1989-1994; Detroit NFL, 1995 and 1996; New England NFL, 1997 and 1998. ... Games/Games started: 1989 (16/0), 1990 (16/16), 1991 (11/10), 1992 (13/13), 1993 (16/16), 1994 (11/11), 1995 (14/14), 1996 (15/15), 1997 (15/15), 1998 (14/14). Total: 141/124.

MOTEN, MIKE — DT — CARDINALS

PERSONAL: Born March 12, 1974, in Daytona Beach, Fla. ... 6-5/266. ... Full name: Michael Edward Moten.
HIGH SCHOOL: Mainland (Daytona Beach, Fla.).
COLLEGE: Florida (degree in leisure service management, 1998).
TRANSACTIONS/CAREER NOTES: Signed as non-drafted free agent by Arizona Cardinals (June 5, 1998). ... Released by Cardinals (August 1998). ... Re-signed by Cardinals to practice squad (October 27, 1998) ... Activated (December 11, 1998).
PLAYING EXPERIENCE: Arizona NFL, 1998. ... Games/Games started: 1/0.

MOULDS, ERIC — WR — BILLS

PERSONAL: Born July 17, 1973, in Lucedale, Miss. ... 6-0/204. ... Full name: Eric Shannon Moulds.
HIGH SCHOOL: George County (Miss.).
COLLEGE: Mississippi State.
TRANSACTIONS/CAREER NOTES: Selected by Buffalo Bills in first round (24th pick overall) of 1996 NFL draft. ... Signed by Bills (July 16, 1996).
HONORS: Played in Pro Bowl (1998 season).
POST SEASON RECORDS: Holds NFL postseason single-game record for most yards receiving—240 (January 2, 1999, vs. Miami).
PRO STATISTICS: 1997—Returned two punts for 20 yards and recovered one fumble.
SINGLE GAME HIGHS (regular season): Receptions—8 (November 29, 1998, vs. New England); yards—196 (December 6, 1998, vs. Cincinnati); and touchdown receptions—2 (December 6, 1998, vs. Cincinnati).
STATISTICAL PLATEAUS: 100-yard receiving games: 1998 (4).

				RUSHING			RECEIVING				KICKOFF RETURNS				TOTALS			
Year Team	G	GS	Att.	Yds.	Avg.	TD	No.	Yds.	Avg.	TD	No.	Yds.	Avg.	TD	TD	2pt.	Pts.	Fum.
1996—Buffalo NFL	16	5	12	44	3.7	0	20	279	14.0	2	52	1205	23.2	▲1	3	0	18	1
1997—Buffalo NFL	16	8	4	59	14.8	0	29	294	10.1	0	43	921	21.4	0	0	1	2	3
1998—Buffalo NFL	16	15	0	0	...	0	67	§1368	20.4	9	0	0	...	0	9	0	54	0
Pro totals (3 years)	48	28	16	103	6.4	0	116	1941	16.7	11	95	2126	22.4	1	12	1	74	4

MUHAMMAD, MUHSIN — WR — PANTHERS

PERSONAL: Born May 5, 1973, in Lansing, Mich. ... 6-2/217. ... Full name: Muhsin Muhammad II. ... Name pronounced moo-SEEN moo-HAH-med.
HIGH SCHOOL: Waverly (Lansing, Mich.).
COLLEGE: Michigan State.
TRANSACTIONS/CAREER NOTES: Selected by Carolina Panthers in second round (43rd pick overall) of 1996 NFL draft. ... Signed by Panthers (July 23, 1996).
CHAMPIONSHIP GAME EXPERIENCE: Played in NFC championship game (1996 season).
PRO STATISTICS: 1996—Rushed once for minus one yard. 1998—Recovered one fumble.
SINGLE GAME HIGHS (regular season): Receptions—9 (September 13, 1998, vs. New Orleans); yards—192 (September 13, 1998, vs. New Orleans); and touchdown receptions—1 (December 20, 1998, vs. St. Louis).
STATISTICAL PLATEAUS: 100-yard receiving games: 1998 (3).

			RECEIVING				TOTALS			
Year Team	G	GS	No.	Yds.	Avg.	TD	TD	2pt.	Pts.	Fum.
1996—Carolina NFL	9	5	25	407	16.3	1	1	0	6	0
1997—Carolina NFL	13	5	27	317	11.7	0	0	1	2	0
1998—Carolina NFL	16	16	68	941	13.8	6	6	1	38	2
Pro totals (3 years)	38	26	120	1665	13.9	7	7	2	46	2

MULLEN, RODERICK — DB — PANTHERS

PERSONAL: Born December 5, 1972, in St. Francisville, La. ... 6-1/204. ... Full name: Roderick Louis Mullen.
HIGH SCHOOL: West Feleciana (St. Francisville, La.).
COLLEGE: Grambling State (degree in criminal justice).
TRANSACTIONS/CAREER NOTES: Selected by New York Giants in fifth round (153rd pick overall) of 1995 NFL draft. ... Signed by Giants (July 23, 1995). ... Released by Giants (August 29, 1995). ... Signed by Green Bay Packers (October 18, 1995). ... On injured reserve with shoulder injury (August 6, 1998-entire season). ... Granted unconditional free agency (February 12, 1999). ... Signed by Carolina Panthers (March 8, 1999).
PLAYING EXPERIENCE: Green Bay NFL, 1995-1997. ... Games/Games started: 1995 (8/0), 1996 (14/0), 1997 (16/1). Total: 38/1.
CHAMPIONSHIP GAME EXPERIENCE: Played in NFC championship game (1995-97 seasons). ... Member of Super Bowl championship team (1996 season). ... Played in Super Bowl XXXII (1997 season).
PRO STATISTICS: 1997—Intercepted one pass for 17 yards and recovered one fumble for one yard.

MURRELL, ADRIAN — RB — CARDINALS

PERSONAL: Born October 16, 1970, in Fayetteville, N.C. ... 5-11/214. ... Full name: Adrian Bryan Murrell.
HIGH SCHOOL: Leilehua (Wahiawa, Hawaii).
COLLEGE: West Virginia.
TRANSACTIONS/CAREER NOTES: Selected by New York Jets in fifth round (120th pick overall) of 1993 NFL draft. ... Signed by Jets (July 22, 1993). ... Granted free agency (February 16, 1996). ... Re-signed by Jets (April 21, 1996). ... Traded by Jets with seventh-round pick (DE Jomo Cousins) in 1998 draft to Arizona Cardinals for third-round pick (traded to St. Louis) in 1998 draft (April 7, 1998).
PRO STATISTICS: 1993—Recovered two fumbles. 1995—Recovered two fumbles. 1996—Recovered two fumbles for minus 16 yards. 1997—Recovered two fumbles. 1998—Recovered one fumble.

SINGLE GAME HIGHS (regular season): Attempts—40 (September 28, 1997, vs. Cincinnati); yards—199 (October 27, 1996, vs. Arizona); and rushing touchdowns—2 (November 10, 1996, vs. New England).
STATISTICAL PLATEAUS: 100-yard rushing games: 1995 (1), 1996 (5), 1997 (3), 1998 (3). Total: 12.

			RUSHING				RECEIVING				KICKOFF RETURNS				TOTALS		
Year Team	G	GS	Att.	Yds.	Avg.	TD	No.	Yds.	Avg.	TD	No.	Yds.	Avg.	TD	TD	2pt.	Pts. Fum.
1993—New York Jets NFL	16	0	34	157	4.6	1	5	12	2.4	0	23	342	14.9	0	1	0	6 4
1994—New York Jets NFL	10	1	33	160	4.8	0	7	76	10.9	0	14	268	19.1	0	0	0	0 1
1995—New York Jets NFL	15	9	192	795	4.1	1	71	465	6.5	2	1	5	5.0	0	3	0	18 2
1996—New York Jets NFL	16	16	301	1249	4.1	6	17	81	4.8	1	0	0	...	0	7	0	42 6
1997—New York Jets NFL	16	15	300	1086	3.6	7	27	106	3.9	0	0	0	...	0	7	0	42 4
1998—Arizona NFL	15	14	274	1042	3.8	8	18	169	9.4	2	0	0	...	0	10	0	60 6
Pro totals (6 years)	88	55	1134	4489	4.0	23	145	909	6.3	5	38	615	16.2	0	28	0	168 23

MYERS, GREG   S   BENGALS

PERSONAL: Born September 30, 1972, in Tampa. ... 6-1/202. ... Full name: Gregory Jay Myers.
HIGH SCHOOL: Windsor (Colo.).
COLLEGE: Colorado State.
TRANSACTIONS/CAREER NOTES: Selected by Cincinnati Bengals in fifth round (144th pick overall) of 1996 NFL draft. ... Signed by Bengals (July 2, 1996). ... Granted free agency (February 12, 1999). ... Re-signed by Bengals (May 6, 1999).
HONORS: Named defensive back on THE SPORTING NEWS college All-America first team (1994 and 1995). ... Jim Thorpe Award winner (1995).
PRO STATISTICS: 1996—Fumbled once. 1997—Recovered two fumbles. 1998—Recovered one fumble.

			INTERCEPTIONS				PUNT RETURNS				TOTALS		
Year Team	G	GS	No.	Yds.	Avg.	TD	No.	Yds.	Avg.	TD	TD	2pt.	Pts. Fum.
1996—Cincinnati NFL	14	0	2	10	5.0	0	9	51	5.7	0	0	0	0 1
1997—Cincinnati NFL	16	14	1	25	25.0	0	26	201	7.7	0	0	0	0 3
1998—Cincinnati NFL	16	16	0	0	...	0	0	0	...	0	0	0	0 0
Pro totals (3 years)	46	30	3	35	11.7	0	35	252	7.2	0	0	0	0 4

MYERS, MICHAEL   DL   COWBOYS

PERSONAL: Born January 20, 1976, in Vicksburg, Miss. ... 6-2/275.
HIGH SCHOOL: Vicksburg (Miss.).
JUNIOR COLLEGE: Hinds Community College (Miss.).
COLLEGE: Alabama.
TRANSACTIONS/CAREER NOTES: Selected by Dallas Cowboys in fourth round (100th pick overall) of 1998 NFL draft. ... Signed by Cowboys (July 10, 1998).
HONORS: Named defensive tackle on THE SPORTING NEWS college All-America first team (1996).

Year Team	G	GS	SACKS
1998—Dallas NFL	16	1	3.0

MYLES, DESHONE   LB   SEAHAWKS

PERSONAL: Born October 31, 1974, in Las Vegas, Nev. ... 6-2/235. ... Name pronounced de-SHAWN.
HIGH SCHOOL: Cheyenne (Las Vegas, Nev.).
COLLEGE: Nevada.
TRANSACTIONS/CAREER NOTES: Selected by Seattle Seahawks in fourth round (108th pick overall) of 1998 NFL draft. ... Signed by Seahawks (July 15, 1998).
PLAYING EXPERIENCE: Seattle NFL, 1998. ... Games/Games started: 12/7.
PRO STATISTICS: 1998—Recovered one fumble.

MYSLINSKI, TOM   OL   COLTS

PERSONAL: Born December 7, 1968, in Rome, N.Y. ... 6-3/293. ... Full name: Thomas Joseph Myslinski.
HIGH SCHOOL: Free Academy (Rome, N.Y.).
COLLEGE: Tennessee (degree in exercise physiology).
TRANSACTIONS/CAREER NOTES: Selected by Dallas Cowboys in fourth round (109th pick overall) of 1992 NFL draft. ... Signed by Cowboys (July 15, 1992). ... Released by Cowboys (August 31, 1992). ... Re-signed by Cowboys to practice squad (September 1, 1992). ... Signed by Cleveland Browns off Cowboys practice squad (September 8, 1992). ... Inactive for three games with Browns (1992). ... Released by Browns (October 9, 1992). ... Re-signed by Browns to practice squad (October 14, 1992). ... Released by Browns (October 17, 1992). ... Signed by Washington Redskins to practice squad (October 21, 1992). ... Activated (November 11, 1992). ... Released by Redskins (November 28, 1992). ... Signed by Buffalo Bills (April 6, 1993). ... Released by Bills (August 30, 1993). ... Re-signed by Bills (August 31, 1993). ... Released by Bills (November 15, 1993). ... Signed by Chicago Bears (November 30, 1993). ... Selected by Jacksonville Jaguars from Bears in NFL expansion draft (February 15, 1995). ... Granted free agency (February 17, 1995). ... Re-signed by Jaguars (April 19, 1995). ... Granted free agency (February 16, 1996). ... Signed by Pittsburgh Steelers (April 24, 1996). ... Released by Steelers (August 24, 1996). ... Re-signed by Steelers (August 27, 1996). ... Granted unconditional free agency (February 13, 1998). ... Signed by Indianapolis Colts (February 19, 1998).
PLAYING EXPERIENCE: Washington NFL, 1992; Buffalo (1)-Chicago (1) NFL, 1993; Chicago NFL, 1994; Jacksonville NFL, 1995; Pittsburgh NFL, 1996 and 1997; Indianapolis NFL, 1998. ... Games/Games started: 1992 (1/0), 1993 (Buf.-1/0; Chi.-1/0; Total: 2/0), 1994 (4/0), 1995 (9/9), 1996 (8/6), 1997 (16/7), 1998 (1/0). Total: 41/22.
CHAMPIONSHIP GAME EXPERIENCE: Played in AFC championship game (1997 season).

NAEOLE, CHRIS — G — SAINTS

PERSONAL: Born December 25, 1974, in Kailua, Hawaii. ... 6-3/313. ... Full name: Chris Kealoha Naeole. ... Name pronounced nay-OH-lee.
HIGH SCHOOL: Kahuka (Kaaava, Hawaii).
COLLEGE: Colorado.
TRANSACTIONS/CAREER NOTES: Selected by New Orleans Saints in first round (10th pick overall) of 1997 NFL draft. ... Signed by Saints (July 17, 1997). ... On injured reserve with ankle injury (October 17, 1997-remainder of season).
PLAYING EXPERIENCE: New Orleans NFL, 1997 and 1998. ... Games/Games started: 1997 (4/0), 1998 (16/16). Total: 20/16.
HONORS: Named guard on THE SPORTING NEWS college All-America second team (1996).
PRO STATISTICS: 1998—Recovered one fumble.

NAILS, JAMIE — OT — BILLS

PERSONAL: Born June 3, 1975, in Baxley, Ga. ... 6-6/354. ... Full name: Jamie Marcellus Nails.
HIGH SCHOOL: Appling County (Baxley, Ga.).
COLLEGE: Florida A&M.
TRANSACTIONS/CAREER NOTES: Selected by Buffalo Bills in fourth round (120th pick overall) of 1997 NFL draft. ... Signed by Bills (July 2, 1997).
PLAYING EXPERIENCE: Buffalo NFL, 1997 and 1998. ... Games/Games started: 1997 (2/0), 1998 (15/3). Total: 17/3.

NALEN, TOM — C — BRONCOS

PERSONAL: Born May 13, 1971, in Foxboro, Mass. ... 6-2/286. ... Full name: Thomas Andrew Nalen.
HIGH SCHOOL: Foxboro (Mass.).
COLLEGE: Boston College.
TRANSACTIONS/CAREER NOTES: Selected by Denver Broncos in seventh round (218th pick overall) of 1994 NFL draft. ... Signed by Broncos (July 15, 1994). ... Released by Broncos (September 2, 1994). ... Re-signed by Broncos to practice squad (September 6, 1994). ... Activated (October 7, 1994).
PLAYING EXPERIENCE: Denver NFL, 1994-1998. ... Games/Games started: 1994 (7/1), 1995 (15/15), 1996 (16/16), 1997 (16/16), 1998 (16/16). Total: 70/64.
CHAMPIONSHIP GAME EXPERIENCE: Played in AFC championship game (1997 and 1998 seasons). ... Member of Super Bowl championship team (1997 and 1998 seasons).
HONORS: Played in Pro Bowl (1997 and 1998 seasons).
PRO STATISTICS: 1997—Caught one pass for minus one yard.

NASH, MARCUS — WR — BRONCOS

PERSONAL: Born February 1, 1976, in Tulsa, Okla. ... 6-3/195. ... Full name: Marcus DeLando Nash.
HIGH SCHOOL: Edmond Memorial (Tulsa, Okla.).
COLLEGE: Tennessee.
TRANSACTIONS/CAREER NOTES: Selected by Denver Broncos in first round (30th pick overall) of 1998 NFL draft. ... Signed by Broncos (July 26, 1998).
CHAMPIONSHIP GAME EXPERIENCE: Played in AFC championship game (1998 season). ... Member of Super Bowl championship team (1998 season).
SINGLE GAME HIGHS (regular season): Receptions—2 (November 16, 1998, vs. Kansas City); yards—36 (November 16, 1998, vs. Kansas City); and touchdown receptions—0.

			RECEIVING			
Year Team	G	GS	No.	Yds.	Avg.	TD
1998—Denver NFL	8	0	4	76	19.0	0

NEAL, LORENZO — FB — TITANS

PERSONAL: Born December 27, 1970, in Hanford, Calif. ... 5-11/240. ... Full name: Lorenzo LaVonne Neal.
HIGH SCHOOL: Lemoore (Calif.).
COLLEGE: Fresno State.
TRANSACTIONS/CAREER NOTES: Selected by New Orleans Saints in fourth round (89th pick overall) of 1993 NFL draft. ... Signed by Saints (July 15, 1993). ... On injured reserve with ankle injury (September 15, 1993-remainder of season). ... Granted free agency (February 16, 1996). ... Re-signed by Saints (July 1, 1996). ... Granted unconditional free agency (February 14, 1997). ... Signed by New York Jets (March 31, 1997). ... Traded by Jets to Tampa Bay Buccaneers for fifth-round pick (TE Blake Spence) in 1998 draft (March 12, 1998). ... Released by Buccaneers (February 11, 1999). ... Signed by Tennessee Titans (March 2, 1999).
PRO STATISTICS: 1994—Returned one kickoff for 17 yards. 1995—Returned four kickoffs for 28 yards. 1996—Recovered two fumbles. 1997—Returned two kickoffs for 22 yards.
SINGLE GAME HIGHS (regular season): Attempts—14 (October 9, 1994, vs. Chicago); yards—89 (September 5, 1993, vs. Houston); and rushing touchdowns—1 (December 15, 1996, vs. New York Giants).

			RUSHING				RECEIVING				TOTALS		
Year Team	G	GS	Att.	Yds.	Avg.	TD	No.	Yds.	Avg.	TD	TD	2pt.	Pts.	Fum.
1993—New Orleans NFL	2	2	21	175	8.3	1	0	0	...	0	1	...	6	1
1994—New Orleans NFL	16	7	30	90	3.0	1	2	9	4.5	0	1	0	6	1
1995—New Orleans NFL	16	7	5	3	0.6	0	12	123	10.3	1	1	0	6	2
1996—New Orleans NFL	16	11	21	58	2.8	1	31	194	6.3	1	2	0	12	1
1997—New York Jets NFL	16	3	10	28	2.8	0	8	40	5.0	1	1	0	6	0
1998—Tampa Bay NFL	16	1	5	25	5.0	0	5	14	2.8	1	1	0	6	0
Pro totals (6 years)	82	31	92	379	4.1	3	58	380	6.6	4	7	0	42	5

NEAL, RANDY — LB

PERSONAL: Born December 29, 1972, in Hackensack, N.J. ... 6-3/245. ... Full name: Randy Peter Neal.
HIGH SCHOOL: Hackensack (N.J.).
COLLEGE: Virginia.
TRANSACTIONS/CAREER NOTES: Signed as non-drafted free agent by Cleveland Browns (May 2, 1995). ... Released by Browns (August 18, 1995). ... Signed by Green Bay Packers to practice squad (August 29, 1995). ... Signed by Cincinnati Bengals off Packers practice squad (November 22, 1995). ... Released by Bengals (August 25, 1996). ... Re-signed by Bengals to practice squad (August 26, 1996). ... Activated (December 2, 1996). ... Released by Bengals (August 18, 1997). ... Selected by England Monarchs in 1998 NFL Europe draft (February 18, 1998). ... Signed by San Francisco 49ers (July 20, 1998). ... Released by 49ers (September 22, 1998). ... Signed by Cleveland Browns (January 8, 1999). ... Released by Browns (June 3, 1999).
PLAYING EXPERIENCE: Cincinnati NFL, 1995 and 1996; England Monarchs NFLE, 1998; San Francisco NFL, 1998. ... Games/Games started: 1995 (2/0), 1996 (1/0), NFLE 1998 (games played unavailable), NFL 1998 (1/0). Total NFL: 4/0.
PRO STATISTICS: NFLE: 1998—Credited with one sack.

NEDNEY, JOE — K — CARDINALS

PERSONAL: Born March 22, 1973, in San Jose, Calif. ... 6-4/215. ... Full name: Joseph Thomas Nedney.
HIGH SCHOOL: Santa Teresa (San Jose, Calif.).
COLLEGE: San Jose State (degree in recreation administration, 1998).
TRANSACTIONS/CAREER NOTES: Signed as non-drafted free agent by Green Bay Packers (April 1995). ... Released by Packers (August 27, 1995). ... Signed by Oakland Raiders (August 29, 1995). ... Released by Raiders (September 6, 1995). ... Signed by Miami Dolphins to practice squad (September 21, 1995). ... Claimed on waivers by New York Jets (August 12, 1997). ... Released by Jets (August 25, 1997). ... Signed by Dolphins (October 3, 1997). ... Released by Dolphins (October 6, 1997). ... Signed by Arizona Cardinals (October 15, 1997). ... On injured reserve with knee injury (December 1, 1998-remainder of season). ... Released by Cardinals (February 12, 1999). ... Re-signed by Cardinals (March 30, 1999).

				KICKING				
Year Team	G	XPM	XPA	FGM	FGA	Lg.	50+	Pts.
1995—Miami NFL				Did not play.				
1996—Miami NFL	16	35	36	18	29	44	0-2	89
1997—Arizona NFL	10	19	19	11	17	45	0-2	52
1998—Arizona NFL	12	30	30	13	19	53	1-4	69
Pro totals (3 years)	38	84	85	42	65	53	1-8	210

NEIL, DAN — G — BRONCOS

PERSONAL: Born October 21, 1973, in Houston. ... 6-2/281.
HIGH SCHOOL: Cypress Creek (Houston).
COLLEGE: Texas.
TRANSACTIONS/CAREER NOTES: Selected by Denver Broncos in third round (67th pick overall) of 1997 NFL draft. ... Signed by Broncos (July 17, 1997).
PLAYING EXPERIENCE: Denver NFL, 1997 and 1998. ... Games/Games started: 1997 (3/0), 1998 (16/16). Total: 19/16.
CHAMPIONSHIP GAME EXPERIENCE: Member of Broncos for AFC championship game (1997 season); inactive. ... Member of Super Bowl championship team (1997 season); inactive. ... Played in AFC championship game (1998 season). ... Member of Super Bowl championship team (1998 season).
HONORS: Named guard on THE SPORTING NEWS college All-America first team (1996).

NEUJAHR, QUENTIN — C — JAGUARS

PERSONAL: Born January 30, 1971, in Seward, Neb. ... 6-4/297. ... Full name: Quentin Troy Neujahr. ... Name pronounced NEW-year.
HIGH SCHOOL: Centennial (Ulysses, Neb.).
COLLEGE: Kansas State.
TRANSACTIONS/CAREER NOTES: Signed as non-drafted free agent by Los Angeles Raiders (May 3, 1994). ... Released by Raiders (August 23, 1994). ... Signed by Cleveland Browns to practice squad (December 27, 1994). ... Active for one game (1995); did not play. ... Browns franchise moved to Baltimore and renamed Ravens for 1996 season (March 11, 1996). ... Granted free agency (February 13, 1998). ... Tendered offer sheet by Jacksonville Jaguars (February 24, 1998). ... Ravens declined to match offer (March 3, 1998).
PLAYING EXPERIENCE: Baltimore NFL, 1996 and 1997; Jacksonville NFL, 1998. ... Games/Games started: 1996 (5/0), 1997 (9/7), 1998 (16/16). Total: 30/23.
PRO STATISTICS: 1996—Recovered one fumble.

NEWMAN, ANTHONY — DB — RAIDERS

PERSONAL: Born November 21, 1965, in Bellingham, Wash. ... 6-0/215. ... Full name: Anthony Q. Newman.
HIGH SCHOOL: Beaverton (Ore.).
COLLEGE: Oregon.
TRANSACTIONS/CAREER NOTES: Selected by Los Angeles Rams in second round (35th pick overall) of 1988 NFL draft. ... Signed by Rams (July 11, 1988). ... On injured reserve with fractured elbow (December 21, 1989-remainder of season). ... Granted free agency (February 1, 1992). ... Re-signed by Rams (July 21, 1992). ... Rams franchise moved to St. Louis (April 12, 1995). ... Released by Rams (August 27, 1995). ... Signed by New Orleans Saints (August 28, 1995). ... Granted unconditional free agency (February 16, 1996). ... Re-signed by Saints (March 6, 1996). ... Granted unconditional free agency (February 13, 1998). ... Signed by Oakland Raiders (March 26, 1998).
PRO STATISTICS: 1988—Recovered one fumble. 1990—Recovered one fumble. 1991—Credited with a sack and recovered one fumble for 17 yards and a touchdown. 1992—Recovered three fumbles. 1994—Recovered one fumble. 1995—Caught one pass for 18 yards. 1996—Recovered two fumbles. 1997—Recovered one fumble.

MISCELLANEOUS: Selected by Toronto Blue Jays organization in 26th round of free-agent baseball draft (June 4, 1984); did not sign. ... Selected by Cleveland Indians organization in secondary phase of free-agent baseball draft (January 9, 1985); did not sign. ... Selected by Texas Rangers organization in secondary phase of free-agent baseball draft (June 3, 1985); did not sign.

				INTERCEPTIONS		
Year Team	G	GS	No.	Yds.	Avg.	TD
1988—Los Angeles Rams NFL	16	0	2	27	13.5	0
1989—Los Angeles Rams NFL	15	1	0	0	...	0
1990—Los Angeles Rams NFL	16	6	2	0	0.0	0
1991—Los Angeles Rams NFL	16	1	1	58	58.0	0
1992—Los Angeles Rams NFL	16	16	4	33	8.3	0
1993—Los Angeles Rams NFL	16	16	0	0	...	0
1994—Los Angeles Rams NFL	16	14	2	46	23.0	1
1995—New Orleans NFL	13	1	0	0	...	0
1996—New Orleans NFL	16	16	3	40	13.3	0
1997—New Orleans NFL	12	12	3	19	6.3	0
1998—Oakland NFL	11	11	2	17	8.5	0
Pro totals (11 years)	163	94	19	240	12.6	1

NEWSOME, CRAIG — CB — PACKERS

PERSONAL: Born August 10, 1971, in San Bernardino, Calif. ... 6-0/190.
HIGH SCHOOL: Eisenhower (Rialto, Calif.).
JUNIOR COLLEGE: San Bernardino (Calif.) Valley.
COLLEGE: Arizona State.
TRANSACTIONS/CAREER NOTES: Selected by Green Bay Packers in first round (32nd pick overall) of 1995 NFL draft. ... Signed by Packers (May 23, 1995). ... On injured reserve with knee injury (September 3, 1997-remainder of season).
CHAMPIONSHIP GAME EXPERIENCE: Played in NFC championship game (1995 and 1996 seasons). ... Member of Super Bowl championship team (1996 season).
PRO STATISTICS: 1996—Recovered one fumble.

				INTERCEPTIONS		
Year Team	G	GS	No.	Yds.	Avg.	TD
1995—Green Bay NFL	16	16	1	3	3.0	0
1996—Green Bay NFL	16	16	2	22	11.0	0
1997—Green Bay NFL	1	1	0	0	...	0
1998—Green Bay NFL	13	13	1	26	26.0	0
Pro totals (4 years)	46	46	4	51	12.8	0

NEWTON, NATE — G

PERSONAL: Born December 20, 1961, in Orlando. ... 6-3/318. ... Full name: Nathaniel Newton Jr. ... Brother of Tim Newton, defensive tackle with Minnesota Vikings (1985-89), Tampa Bay Buccaneers (1990-91) and Kansas City Chiefs (1993).
HIGH SCHOOL: Jones (Orlando).
COLLEGE: Florida A&M.
TRANSACTIONS/CAREER NOTES: Selected by Tampa Bay Bandits in 1983 USFL territorial draft. ... Signed as non-drafted free agent by Washington Redskins (May 5, 1983). ... Released by Redskins (August 29, 1983). ... Signed by Bandits (November 6, 1983). ... Granted free agency when USFL suspended operations (August 7, 1986). ... Signed by Dallas Cowboys (August 14, 1986). ... Granted roster exemption (August 14-21, 1986). ... Crossed picket line during players strike (October 24, 1987). ... Granted unconditional free agency (February 17, 1994). ... Re-signed by Cowboys (April 7, 1994). ... Granted unconditional free agency (February 12, 1999).
PLAYING EXPERIENCE: Tampa Bay USFL, 1984 and 1985; Dallas NFL, 1986-1998. ... Games/Games started: 1984 (18/18), 1985 (18/18), 1986 (11/0), 1987 (11/11), 1988 (15/15), 1989 (16/16), 1990 (16/16), 1991 (14/14), 1992 (15/15), 1993 (16/16), 1994 (16/16), 1995 (16/16), 1996 (16/16), 1997 (13/13), 1998 (16/16). Total USFL: 36/36. Total NFL: 191/180. Total Pro: 227/216.
CHAMPIONSHIP GAME EXPERIENCE: Played in NFC championship game (1992-1995 seasons). ... Member of Super Bowl championship team (1992, 1993 and 1995 seasons).
HONORS: Played in Pro Bowl (1992-1996 and 1998 seasons). ... Named guard on THE SPORTING NEWS NFL All-Pro team (1995).
PRO STATISTICS: 1988—Caught one pass for two yards. 1990—Recovered two fumbles. 1991—Recovered one fumble. 1992—Recovered one fumble. 1997—Recovered one fumble.

NICKERSON, HARDY — LB — BUCCANEERS

PERSONAL: Born September 1, 1965, in Compton, Calif. ... 6-2/225. ... Full name: Hardy Otto Nickerson.
HIGH SCHOOL: Verbum Dei (Los Angeles).
COLLEGE: California (degree in sociology, 1986).
TRANSACTIONS/CAREER NOTES: Selected by Pittsburgh Steelers in fifth round (122nd pick overall) of 1987 NFL draft. ... Signed by Steelers (July 26, 1987). ... On injured reserve with ankle and knee injuries (November 3-December 16, 1989). ... Granted free agency (February 1, 1992). ... Re-signed by Steelers (June 15, 1992). ... Granted unconditional free agency (March 1, 1993). ... Signed by Tampa Bay Buccaneers (March 18, 1993). ... Granted unconditional free agency (February 16, 1996). ... Re-signed by Buccaneers (February 22, 1996). ... On injured reserve with heart problems (November 25, 1998-remainder of season).
HONORS: Named linebacker on THE SPORTING NEWS college All-America second team (1985). ... Named inside linebacker on THE SPORTING NEWS NFL All-Pro team (1993). ... Played in Pro Bowl (1993 and 1996-1998 seasons).
PRO STATISTICS: 1987—Recovered one fumble. 1988—Intercepted one pass for no yards and recovered one fumble. 1992—Recovered two fumbles for 44 yards. 1993—Intercepted one pass for six yards and recovered one fumble. 1994—Intercepted two passes for nine yards. 1995—Recovered three fumbles. 1996—Intercepted two passes for 24 yards and recovered two fumbles. 1997—Recovered two fumbles. 1998—Recovered one fumble.

Year—Team	G	GS	SACKS
1987—Pittsburgh NFL	12	0	0.0
1988—Pittsburgh NFL	15	10	3.5
1989—Pittsburgh NFL	10	8	1.0
1990—Pittsburgh NFL	16	14	2.0
1991—Pittsburgh NFL	16	14	1.0
1992—Pittsburgh NFL	15	15	2.0
1993—Tampa Bay NFL	16	16	1.0
1994—Tampa Bay NFL	14	14	1.0
1995—Tampa Bay NFL	16	16	1.5
1996—Tampa Bay NFL	16	16	3.0
1997—Tampa Bay NFL	16	16	1.0
1998—Tampa Bay NFL	10	10	1.0
Pro totals (12 years)	172	149	18.0

NORGARD, ERIK G JETS

PERSONAL: Born November 4, 1965, in Bellevue, Wash. ... 6-1/290. ... Full name: Erik Christian Norgard.
HIGH SCHOOL: Arlington (Wash.).
COLLEGE: Western Washington, then Colorado (degree in communications, 1989).
TRANSACTIONS/CAREER NOTES: Signed as non-drafted free agent by Houston Oilers (May 12, 1989). ... Released by Oilers (August 30, 1989). ... Re-signed by Oilers to developmental squad (September 6, 1989). ... Released by Oilers (January 2, 1990). ... Re-signed by Oilers (March 8, 1990). ... Re-signed by Oilers (August 26, 1991). ... Re-signed by Oilers (August 27, 1991). ... On injured reserve with shoulder injury (August 29, 1991-entire season). ... Granted unconditional free agency (February 1-April 1, 1992). ... Assigned by Oilers to San Antonio Riders in 1992 World League enhancement allocation program. ... Re-signed by Oilers for 1992 season. ... Released by Oilers (August 31, 1992). ... Re-signed by Oilers (September 11, 1992). ... Granted unconditional free agency (February 17, 1994). ... Re-signed by Oilers (March 9, 1994). ... Released by Oilers (July 14, 1995). ... Signed by Atlanta Falcons (August 2, 1995); released after failing physical. ... Signed by Oilers (August 8, 1995). ... Oilers franchise moved to Tennessee for 1997 season. ... On injured reserve with shoulder injury (September 9, 1998-remainder of season). ... Released by Oilers (February 12, 1999). ... Signed by New York Jets (March 29, 1999).
PLAYING EXPERIENCE: Houston NFL, 1990 and 1992-1996; San Antonio W.L., 1992; Tennessee NFL, 1997 and 1998. ... Games/Games started: 1990 (16/0), 1992 (W.L.-10/10; NFL-15/0; Total: 25/10), 1993 (16/4), 1994 (16/7), 1995 (15/0), 1996 (13/0), 1997 (15/0), 1998 (1/1). W.L.:10/10. Total NFL: 107/12. Total Pro: 117/22.
PRO STATISTICS: NFL: 1990—Returned two kickoffs for no yards. 1993—Caught one pass for 13 yards and recovered one fumble. 1996—Caught one pass for one yard and a touchdown. 1997—Recovered one fumble. W.L.: 1992—Caught two passes for 22 yards.

NORTHERN, GABE LB BILLS

PERSONAL: Born June 8, 1974, in Baton Rouge, La. ... 6-2/240. ... Full name: Gabriel O'Kara Northern.
HIGH SCHOOL: Southern University Lab (Baton Rouge, La.), then Glen Oaks (Baton Rouge, La.).
COLLEGE: Louisiana State.
TRANSACTIONS/CAREER NOTES: Selected by Buffalo Bills in second round (53rd pick overall) of 1996 NFL draft. ... Signed by Bills (July 17, 1996).
PRO STATISTICS: 1996—Returned blocked punt 18 yards for a touchdown. 1998—Intercepted one pass for 40 yards and a touchdown.

Year—Team	G	GS	SACKS
1996—Buffalo NFL	16	2	5.0
1997—Buffalo NFL	16	1	0.0
1998—Buffalo NFL	16	16	2.0
Pro totals (3 years)	48	19	7.0

NORTON, KEN LB 49ERS

PERSONAL: Born September 29, 1966, in Lincoln, Ill. ... 6-2/254. ... Full name: Kenneth Howard Norton Jr. ... Son of Ken Norton Sr., former world heavyweight boxing champion.
HIGH SCHOOL: Westchester (Los Angeles).
COLLEGE: UCLA (degree in sociology, 1998).
TRANSACTIONS/CAREER NOTES: Selected by Dallas Cowboys in second round (41st pick overall) of 1988 NFL draft. ... Signed by Cowboys (July 13, 1988). ... On injured reserve with broken arm (August 23-December 3, 1988). ... On injured reserve with knee injury (December 24, 1990-remainder of season). ... Granted free agency (February 1, 1992). ... Re-signed by Cowboys (August 12, 1992). ... Granted unconditional free agency (February 17, 1994). ... Signed by San Francisco 49ers (April 20, 1994).
CHAMPIONSHIP GAME EXPERIENCE: Played in NFC championship game (1992-1994 and 1997 seasons). ... Member of Super Bowl championship team (1992-1994 seasons).
HONORS: Named linebacker on THE SPORTING NEWS college All-America first team (1987). ... Played in Pro Bowl (1993, 1995 and 1997 seasons).
POST SEASON RECORDS: Shares Super Bowl career record for most touchdowns by fumble recovery—1 (January 31, 1993, vs. Buffalo).
PRO STATISTICS: 1988—Recovered one fumble. 1990—Recovered two fumbles. 1992—Recovered two fumbles. 1993—Recovered one fumble for three yards. 1996—Recovered one fumble for 21 yards. 1997—Recovered two fumbles. 1998—Recovered three fumbles for 12 yards.

			INTERCEPTIONS			SACKS
Year—Team	G	GS	No.	Yds.	Avg.	TD	No.
1988—Dallas NFL	3	0	0	0	...	0	0.0
1989—Dallas NFL	13	13	0	0	...	0	2.5
1990—Dallas NFL	15	15	0	0	...	0	2.5
1991—Dallas NFL	16	16	0	0	...	0	0.0
1992—Dallas NFL	16	16	0	0	...	0	0.0
1993—Dallas NFL	16	16	1	25	25.0	0	2.0
1994—San Francisco NFL	16	16	1	0	0.0	0	0.0
1995—San Francisco NFL	16	16	3	102	‡34.0	†2	1.0
1996—San Francisco NFL	16	16	0	0	...	0	0.0
1997—San Francisco NFL	16	16	0	0	...	0	1.5
1998—San Francisco NFL	16	16	0	0	...	0	2.0
Pro totals (11 years)	159	156	5	127	25.4	2	11.5

NOVAK, JEFF — G/OT

PERSONAL: Born July 27, 1967, in Arlington Heights, Ill. ... 6-6/292. ... Full name: Jeff Ladd Novak.
HIGH SCHOOL: Clear Lake (Houston).
COLLEGE: Southwest Texas State (degree in hospital administration, 1990).
TRANSACTIONS/CAREER NOTES: Selected by San Diego Chargers in seventh round (172nd pick overall) of 1990 NFL draft. ... Signed by Chargers for 1990 season. ... Released by Chargers (August 30, 1990). ... Selected by Montreal Machine in first round of 1991 World League draft. ... Signed by New York Giants (June 1, 1992). ... Released by Giants (August 31, 1992). ... Re-signed by Giants to practice squad (September 2, 1992). ... On injured reserve with hand injury (October 12, 1992-remainder of season). ... Released by Giants (August 30, 1993). ... Re-signed by Giants to practice squad (August 31, 1993). ... Signed by Miami Dolphins off Giants practice squad (December 15, 1993). ... Selected by Jacksonville Jaguars from Dolphins in NFL expansion draft (February 15, 1995). ... On injured reserve with back injury (November 30, 1998-remainder of season). ... Granted unconditional free agency (February 12, 1999).
PLAYING EXPERIENCE: Montreal W.L., 1991 and 1992; Miami NFL, 1994; Jacksonville NFL, 1995-1998. ... Games/Games started: 1991 (9/9), 1992 (10/10), 1994 (6/0), 1995 (16/13), 1996 (5/0), 1997 (7/2), 1998 (4/0). Total W.L.: 19/19. Total NFL: 38/15. Total Pro: 57/34.
CHAMPIONSHIP GAME EXPERIENCE: Member of Jaguars for AFC championship game (1996 season); did not play.

NUTTEN, TOM — G — RAMS

PERSONAL: Born June 8, 1971, in Magog, Quebec. ... 6-5/300. ... Full name: Thomas Nutten. ... Name pronounced NEW-ton.
HIGH SCHOOL: Champlain Regional (Lennoxville, Quebec).
COLLEGE: Western Michigan (degree in marketing, 1994).
TRANSACTIONS/CAREER NOTES: Selected by Hamilton Tiger-Cats in first round (first pick overall) of 1995 CFL draft. ... Selected by Buffalo Bills in seventh round (221st pick overall) of 1995 NFL draft. ... Signed by Bills (June 12, 1995). ... Released by Bills (August 27, 1995). ... Re-signed by Bills to practice squad (August 29, 1995). ... Activated (October 10, 1995). ... Waived by Bills (August 26, 1996). ... Signed by Denver Broncos (January 14, 1997). ... Released by Broncos (July 16, 1997). ... Signed by Hamilton Tiger-Cats of CFL (July 28, 1997). ... Signed by St. Louis Rams (January 16, 1998). ... Assigned by Rams to Amsterdam Admirals in 1998 NFL Europe enhancement allocation program (February 18, 1998). ... On injured reserve with neck injury (November 17, 1998-remainder of season).
PLAYING EXPERIENCE: Buffalo NFL, 1995; Hamilton CFL, 1997; Amsterdam Admirals NFLE, 1998; St. Louis NFL, 1998. ... Games/Games started: 1995 (1/0), 1997 (13/games started unavailable), NFLE 1998 (games played unavailable), NFL 1998 (4/2). Total NFL: 5/2. Total CFL: 13/-. Total Pro: 18/-.
PRO STATISTICS: 1997—Recovered one fumble.

OBEN, ROMAN — OT — GIANTS

PERSONAL: Born October 9, 1972, in Cameroon, West Africa. ... 6-4/310.
HIGH SCHOOL: Gonzaga (Washington, D.C.), then Fork Union (Va.) Military Academy.
COLLEGE: Louisville (degree in economics).
TRANSACTIONS/CAREER NOTES: Selected by New York Giants in third round (66th pick overall) of 1996 NFL draft. ... Signed by Giants (July 20, 1996). ... Granted free agency (February 12, 1999).
PLAYING EXPERIENCE: New York Giants NFL, 1996-1998. ... Games/Games started: 1996 (2/0), 1997 (16/16), 1998 (16/16). Total: 34/32.

ODOM, JASON — OT — BUCCANEERS

PERSONAL: Born March 31, 1974, in Winter Haven, Fla. ... 6-6/308. ... Full name: Jason Brian Odom.
HIGH SCHOOL: Bartow (Fla.).
COLLEGE: Florida (degree in sports management, 1995).
TRANSACTIONS/CAREER NOTES: Selected by Tampa Bay Buccaneers in fourth round (96th pick overall) of 1996 NFL draft. ... Signed by Buccaneers (July 16, 1996). ... Granted free agency (February 12, 1999).
PLAYING EXPERIENCE: Tampa Bay NFL, 1996-1998. ... Games/Games started: 1996 (12/7), 1997 (16/16), 1998 (15/15). Total: 43/38.
HONORS: Named offensive lineman on THE SPORTING NEWS college All-America first team (1995).
PRO STATISTICS: 1996—Recovered one fumble.

O'DONNELL, NEIL — QB

PERSONAL: Born July 3, 1966, in Morristown, N.J. ... 6-3/228. ... Full name: Neil Kennedy O'Donnell.
HIGH SCHOOL: Madison (N.J.)-Boro.
COLLEGE: Maryland (degree in economics, 1990).
TRANSACTIONS/CAREER NOTES: Selected by Pittsburgh Steelers in third round (70th pick overall) of 1990 NFL draft. ... Signed by Steelers (August 8, 1990). ... Active for three games (1990); did not play. ... Granted free agency (March 1, 1993). ... Tendered offer sheet by Tampa Bay Buccaneers (April 2, 1993). ... Offer matched by Steelers (April 12, 1993). ... Granted unconditional free agency (February 16, 1996). ... Signed by New York Jets (February 29, 1996). ... Released by Jets (June 24, 1998). ... Signed by Cincinnati Bengals (July 7, 1998). ... On injured reserve with hand injury (December 9, 1998-remainder of season). ... Released by Bengals (April 19, 1999).
CHAMPIONSHIP GAME EXPERIENCE: Played in AFC championship game (1994 and 1995 seasons). ... Played in Super Bowl XXX (1995 season).
HONORS: Played in Pro Bowl (1992 season).
RECORDS: Holds NFL career record for lowest interception percentage—1.99.
POST SEASON RECORDS: Holds NFL postseason single-game record for most passes attempted without an interception—54 (January 15, 1995, vs. San Diego).
PRO STATISTICS: 1991—Fumbled 11 times and recovered two fumbles for minus three yards. 1992—Fumbled six times and recovered four fumbles for minus 20 yards. 1993—Fumbled five times. 1994—Fumbled four times and recovered one fumble. 1995—Fumbled twice and recovered one fumble. 1996—Fumbled twice. 1997—Fumbled nine times and recovered two fumbles for minus one yard. 1998—Fumbled six times and recovered one fumble for minus two yards.
SINGLE GAME HIGHS (regular season): Attempts—55 (December 24, 1995, vs. Green Bay); completions—34 (November 5, 1995, vs. Chicago); yards—377 (November 19, 1995, vs. Cincinnati); and touchdown passes—5 (August 31, 1997, vs. Seattle).

STATISTICAL PLATEAUS: 300-yard passing games: 1991 (1), 1993 (1), 1995 (4), 1996 (2), 1997 (1), 1998 (1). Total: 10.
MISCELLANEOUS: Regular-season record as starting NFL quarterback: 49-43 (.533). ... Postseason record as starting NFL quarterback: 3-4 (.429).

				PASSING							RUSHING			TOTALS		
Year Team	G	GS	Att.	Cmp.	Pct.	Yds.	TD	Int.	Avg.	Rat.	Att.	Yds.	Avg.	TD	TD	2pt.	Pts.
1990—Pittsburgh NFL								Did not play.									
1991—Pittsburgh NFL	12	8	286	156	54.5	1963	11	7	6.86	78.8	18	82	4.6	1	1	...	6
1992—Pittsburgh NFL	12	12	313	185	59.1	2283	13	9	7.29	83.6	27	5	0.2	1	1	...	6
1993—Pittsburgh NFL	16	15	486	270	55.6	3208	14	14	6.60	79.5	26	111	4.3	0	0	...	0
1994—Pittsburgh NFL	14	14	370	212	57.3	2443	13	9	6.60	78.9	31	80	2.6	1	1	0	6
1995—Pittsburgh NFL	12	12	416	246	59.1	2970	17	7	7.14	87.7	24	45	1.9	0	0	0	0
1996—New York Jets NFL	6	6	188	110	58.5	1147	4	7	6.10	67.8	6	30	5.0	0	0	0	0
1997—New York Jets NFL	15	14	460	259	56.3	2796	17	7	6.08	80.5	32	36	1.1	1	1	0	6
1998—Cincinnati NFL	13	11	343	212	§61.8	2216	15	4	6.46	90.2	13	34	2.6	0	0	0	0
Pro totals (8 years)	100	92	2862	1650	57.7	19026	104	57	6.65	81.6	177	423	2.4	4	4	0	24

O'DWYER, MATT — G

PERSONAL: Born September 1, 1972, in Lincolnshire, Ill. ... 6-5/300. ... Full name: Matthew Phillip O'Dwyer.
HIGH SCHOOL: Adlai E. Stevenson (Prairie View, Ill.).
COLLEGE: Northwestern.
TRANSACTIONS/CAREER NOTES: Selected by New York Jets in second round (33rd pick overall) of 1995 NFL draft. ... Signed by Jets (July 20, 1995). ... Granted unconditional free agency (February 12, 1999).
PLAYING EXPERIENCE: New York Jets NFL, 1995-1998. ... Games/Games started: 1995 (12/2), 1996 (16/16), 1997 (16/16), 1998 (16/16). Total: 60/50.
CHAMPIONSHIP GAME EXPERIENCE: Played in AFC championship game (1998 season).

OFODILE, A.J. — TE — RAVENS

PERSONAL: Born October 9, 1973, in Detroit. ... 6-6/260. ... Full name: Anselm Ofodile Jr. ... Name pronounced oh-FAH-duh-lay.
HIGH SCHOOL: Cass Technical (Detroit).
COLLEGE: Missouri.
TRANSACTIONS/CAREER NOTES: Selected after junior season by Buffalo Bills in fifth round (158th pick overall) of 1994 NFL draft. ... Signed by Bills (July 15, 1994). ... On physically unable to perform list with knee injury (August 23, 1994-entire season). ... Released by Bills (August 22, 1995). ... Signed by Pittsburgh Steelers to practice squad (August 29, 1995). ... Released by Steelers (August 19, 1996). ... Signed by Baltimore Ravens (February 12, 1997). ... Assigned by Ravens to Rhein Fire in 1997 World League enhancement allocation program (February 19, 1997). ... Released by Ravens (August 30, 1998). ... Re-signed by Ravens (September 3, 1998). ... Granted free agency (February 12, 1999). ... Re-signed by Ravens (May 19, 1999).
PLAYING EXPERIENCE: Rhein W.L. 1997; Baltimore NFL, 1997 and 1998. ... Games/Games started: W.L. 1997 (games played unavailable), NFL 1997 (12/0), 1998 (5/0). Total NFL: 17/0.
PRO STATISTICS: W.L.: 1997—Caught 10 passes for 146 yards and one touchdown.

OGBOGU, ERIC — DE — JETS

PERSONAL: Born July 18, 1975, in Irvington, N.Y. ... 6-4/280.
HIGH SCHOOL: Archbishop Stepinac (White Plains, N.Y.).
COLLEGE: Maryland.
TRANSACTIONS/CAREER NOTES: Selected by New York Jets in sixth round (163rd pick overall) of 1998 NFL draft. ... Signed by Jets (July 2, 1998).
PLAYING EXPERIENCE: New York Jets NFL, 1998. ... Games/Games started: 12/0.
CHAMPIONSHIP GAME EXPERIENCE: Played in AFC championship game (1998 season).

OGDEN, JEFF — WR — COWBOYS

PERSONAL: Born February 2, 1975, in Snohomish, Wash. ... 6-0/190. ... Full name: Jeffery Ogden.
HIGH SCHOOL: Snohomish (Wash.).
COLLEGE: Eastern Washington.
TRANSACTIONS/CAREER NOTES: Signed as non-drafted free agent by Dallas Cowboys (April 21, 1998).
PRO STATISTICS: 1998—Rushed once for 12 yards and returned three kickoffs for 65 yards.
SINGLE GAME HIGHS (regular season): Receptions—4 (November 22, 1998, vs. Seattle); yards—26 (November 22, 1998, vs. Seattle); and touchdown receptions—0.

			RECEIVING				TOTALS		
Year Team	G	GS	No.	Yds.	Avg.	TD	TD	2pt.	Pts.	Fum.
1998—Dallas NFL	16	0	8	63	7.9	0	0	0	0	1

OGDEN, JONATHAN — OL — RAVENS

PERSONAL: Born July 31, 1974, in Washington, D.C. ... 6-8/318. ... Full name: Jonathan Phillip Ogden.
HIGH SCHOOL: St. Alban's (Washington, D.C.).
COLLEGE: UCLA.
TRANSACTIONS/CAREER NOTES: Selected by Baltimore Ravens in first round (fourth pick overall) of 1996 NFL draft. ... Signed by Ravens (July 15, 1996).
PLAYING EXPERIENCE: Baltimore NFL, 1996-1998. ... Games/Games started: 1996 (16/16), 1997 (16/16), 1998 (13/13). Total: 45/45.
HONORS: Outland Trophy winner (1995). ... Named offensive lineman on THE SPORTING NEWS college All-America first team (1995). ... Named offensive tackle on the THE SPORTING NEWS NFL All-Pro team (1997). ... Played in Pro Bowl (1997 and 1998 seasons).
PRO STATISTICS: 1996—Caught one pass for one yard and a touchdown.

– 293 –

OLDHAM, CHRIS   S   STEELERS

PERSONAL: Born October 26, 1968, in Sacramento. ... 5-9/200. ... Full name: Christopher Martin Oldham. ... Name pronounced OLD-um.
HIGH SCHOOL: O. Perry Walker (New Orleans).
COLLEGE: Oregon (degree in communications).
TRANSACTIONS/CAREER NOTES: Selected by Detroit Lions in fourth round (105th pick overall) of 1990 NFL draft. ... Signed by Lions (July 19, 1990). ... Released by Lions (August 26, 1991). ... Signed by Buffalo Bills (September 25, 1991). ... Released by Bills (October 8, 1991). ... Signed by Phoenix Cardinals (October 15, 1991). ... Released by Cardinals (November 13, 1991). ... Signed by San Diego Chargers (February 15, 1992). ... Assigned by Chargers to San Antonio Riders in 1992 World League enhancement allocation program (February 20, 1992). ... Released by Chargers (August 25, 1992). ... Signed by Cardinals (December 22, 1992). ... Granted unconditional free agency (February 17, 1994). ... Cardinals franchise renamed Arizona Cardinals for 1994 season. ... Re-signed by Cardinals (June 7, 1994). ... Granted unconditional free agency (February 17, 1995). ... Signed by Pittsburgh Steelers (April 12, 1995).
CHAMPIONSHIP GAME EXPERIENCE: Played in AFC championship game (1995 and 1997 seasons). ... Played in Super Bowl XXX (1995 season).
PRO STATISTICS: NFL: 1990—Returned 13 kickoffs for 234 yards and fumbled twice. 1995—Recovered one fumble for 23 yards and a touchdown. 1998—Recovered five fumbles for 79 yards and one touchdown. W.L.: 1992—Returned one kickoff for 11 yards, credited with one sack and recovered one fumble.

			INTERCEPTIONS				SACKS
Year Team	G	GS	No.	Yds.	Avg.	TD	No.
1990—Detroit NFL	16	0	1	28	28.0	0	0.0
1991—Buffalo NFL	2	0	0	0	...	0	0.0
—Phoenix NFL	2	0	0	0	...	0	0.0
1992—San Antonio W.L.	9	9	3	52	17.3	*1	0.0
—Phoenix NFL	1	0	0	0	...	0	0.0
1993—Phoenix NFL	16	6	1	0	0.0	0	1.0
1994—Arizona NFL	11	1	0	0	...	0	0.0
1995—Pittsburgh NFL	15	0	1	12	12.0	0	0.0
1996—Pittsburgh NFL	16	0	0	0	...	0	2.0
1997—Pittsburgh NFL	16	0	2	16	8.0	0	4.0
1998—Pittsburgh NFL	16	1	1	14	14.0	0	0.5
W.L. totals (1 year)	9	9	3	52	17.3	1	0.0
NFL totals (9 years)	111	8	6	70	11.7	0	7.5
Pro totals (10 years)	120	17	9	122	13.6	1	7.5

OLIVER, WINSLOW   PR   PANTHERS

PERSONAL: Born March 3, 1973, in Houston. ... 5-7/180. ... Full name: Winslow Paul Oliver.
HIGH SCHOOL: Clements (Sugar Land, Texas), then Kempner (Sugar Land, Texas).
COLLEGE: New Mexico.
TRANSACTIONS/CAREER NOTES: Selected by Carolina Panthers in third round (73rd pick overall) of 1996 NFL draft. ... Signed by Panthers (July 20, 1996).
CHAMPIONSHIP GAME EXPERIENCE: Played in NFC championship game (1996 season).
PRO STATISTICS: 1996—Fumbled four times. 1997—Fumbled twice. 1998—Fumbled once.
SINGLE GAME HIGHS (regular season): Attempts—8 (November 10, 1996, vs. New York Giants); yards—37 (September 1, 1996, vs. Atlanta); and rushing touchdowns—0.

			RUSHING			RECEIVING				PUNT RETURNS				KICKOFF RETURNS				TOTALS		
Year Team	G	GS	Att.	Yds.	Avg.	TD	No.	Yds.	Avg.	TD	No.	Yds.	Avg.	TD	No.	Yds.	Avg.	TD	TD	2pt.	Pts.
1996—Carolina NFL	16	0	47	183	3.9	0	15	144	9.6	0	52	598	11.5	1	7	160	22.9	0	1	0	6
1997—Carolina NFL	6	0	1	0	0.0	0	6	47	7.8	0	14	111	7.9	0	0	0	...	0	0	0	0
1998—Carolina NFL	16	0	0	0	...	0	0	0	...	0	44	464	10.5	0	2	43	21.5	0	0	0	0
Pro totals (3 years)	38	0	48	183	3.8	0	21	191	9.1	0	110	1173	10.7	1	9	203	22.6	0	1	0	6

OLIVO, BROCK   FB   LIONS

PERSONAL: Born June 24, 1976, in St. Louis. ... 6-0/226.
HIGH SCHOOL: St. Francis Borgia (Washington, Mo.).
COLLEGE: Missouri.
TRANSACTIONS/CAREER NOTES: Signed as non-drafted free agent by San Francisco 49ers (April 24, 1998). ... Released by 49ers (August 30, 1998). ... Re-signed by 49ers to practice squad (September 1, 1998). ... Signed by Detroit Lions off 49ers practice squad (September 23, 1998). ... Released by Lions (December 8, 1998). ... Re-signed by Lions to practice squad (December 9, 1998).
PLAYING EXPERIENCE: Detroit NFL, 1998. ... Games/Games started: 1/0.

OLSAVSKY, JERRY   LB

PERSONAL: Born March 29, 1967, in Youngstown, Ohio. ... 6-1/224. ... Full name: Jerome Donald Olsavsky. ... Name pronounced ol-SAV-skee.
HIGH SCHOOL: Chaney (Youngstown, Ohio).
COLLEGE: Pittsburgh (degree in information science).
TRANSACTIONS/CAREER NOTES: Selected by Pittsburgh Steelers in 10th round (258th pick overall) of 1989 NFL draft. ... Signed by Steelers (July 18, 1989). ... On injured reserve with foot injury (November 6-December 27, 1992); on practice squad (December 2-27, 1992). ... On injured reserve with knee injury (October 26, 1993-remainder of season). ... Released by Steelers (February 17, 1994). ... Re-signed by Steelers (November 16, 1994). ... Granted unconditional free agency (February 16, 1996). ... Re-signed by Steelers (April 21, 1996). ... Released by Steelers (February 2, 1998). ... Signed by Cincinnati Bengals (March 3, 1998). ... Released by Bengals (August 13, 1998). ... Signed by Baltimore Ravens (October 28, 1998). ... Granted unconditional free agency (February 12, 1999).
PLAYING EXPERIENCE: Pittsburgh NFL, 1989-1997; Baltimore NFL, 1998. ... Games/Games started: 1989 (16/8), 1990 (15/0), 1991 (16/4), 1992 (7/0), 1993 (7/7), 1994 (1/0), 1995 (15/5), 1996 (15/13), 1997 (16/0), 1998 (9/0). Total: 117/37.

CHAMPIONSHIP GAME EXPERIENCE: Member of Steelers for AFC championship game (1994 season); inactive. ... Played in AFC championship game (1995 and 1997 seasons). ... Played in Super Bowl XXX (1995 season).
PRO STATISTICS: 1989—Credited with one sack. 1995—Credited with one sack. 1996—Intercepted one pass for five yards and recovered one fumble for six yards.

OLSON, BENJI   G   TITANS

PERSONAL: Born June 5, 1975, in Bremerton, Wash. ... 6-3/315. ... Full name: Benji Dempsey Olson.
HIGH SCHOOL: South Kitsap (Port Orchard, Wash.).
COLLEGE: Washington.
TRANSACTIONS/CAREER NOTES: Selected after junior season by Tennessee Oilers in fifth round (139th pick overall) of 1998 NFL draft. ... Signed by Oilers (June 29, 1998). ... Oilers franchise renamed Tennessee Titans for 1999 season (December 26, 1998).
PLAYING EXPERIENCE: Tennessee NFL, 1998. ... Games/Games started: 13/1.
HONORS: Named guard on THE SPORTING NEWS college All-America first team (1996).

O'NEAL, LESLIE   DE   CHIEFS

PERSONAL: Born May 7, 1964, in Little Rock, Ark. ... 6-4/275. ... Full name: Leslie Cornelius O'Neal.
HIGH SCHOOL: Hall (Little Rock, Ark.).
COLLEGE: Oklahoma State.
TRANSACTIONS/CAREER NOTES: Selected by New Jersey Generals in 1986 USFL territorial draft. ... Selected by San Diego Chargers in first round (eighth pick overall) of 1986 NFL draft. ... Signed by Chargers (August 5, 1986). ... On injured reserve with knee injury (December 4, 1986-remainder of season). ... On physically unable to perform list with knee injury (August 30, 1987-entire season). ... On physically unable to perform list with knee injury (July 23-August 21, 1988). ... On physically unable to perform list with knee injury (August 22-October 15, 1988). ... Granted free agency (February 1, 1990). ... Re-signed by Chargers (August 21, 1990). ... Granted free agency (February 1, 1992). ... Re-signed by Chargers (July 23, 1992). ... Designated by Chargers as franchise player (February 25, 1993). ... Free agency status changed by Chargers from franchise player to restricted free agent (June 15, 1993). ... Re-signed by Chargers (August 19, 1993). ... Granted unconditional free agency (February 16, 1996). ... Signed by St. Louis Rams (March 1, 1996). ... Released by Rams (February 23, 1998). ... Signed by Kansas City Chiefs (April 17, 1998).
CHAMPIONSHIP GAME EXPERIENCE: Played in AFC championship game (1994 season). ... Played in Super Bowl XXIX (1994 season).
HONORS: Named defensive lineman on THE SPORTING NEWS college All-America first team (1984 and 1985). ... Played in Pro Bowl (1989, 1990 and 1992-1995 seasons).
RECORDS: Shares NFL rookie-season record for most sacks—12.5 (1986).
PRO STATISTICS: 1986—Intercepted two passes for 22 yards and one touchdown and recovered two fumbles. 1989—Recovered two fumbles for 10 yards. 1990—Fumbled once and recovered two fumbles for 10 yards. 1992—Recovered one fumble. 1993—Recovered one fumble for 13 yards. 1994—Recovered one fumble. 1996—Recovered three fumbles. 1997—Intercepted one pass for five yards and recovered two fumbles for 66 yards and one touchdown. 1998—Recovered two fumbles.
MISCELLANEOUS: Holds San Diego Chargers all-time record for most sacks (105.5).

Year Team	G	GS	SACKS
1986—San Diego NFL	13	13	12.5
1987—San Diego NFL	Did not play.		
1988—San Diego NFL	9	1	4.0
1989—San Diego NFL	16	16	12.5
1990—San Diego NFL	16	16	13.5
1991—San Diego NFL	16	16	9.0
1992—San Diego NFL	15	15	§17.0
1993—San Diego NFL	16	16	12.0
1994—San Diego NFL	16	16	12.5
1995—San Diego NFL	16	16	12.5
1996—St. Louis NFL	16	16	7.0
1997—St. Louis NFL	15	14	10.0
1998—Kansas City NFL	16	13	4.5
Pro totals (12 years)	180	168	127.0

O'NEILL, KEVIN   LB   LIONS

PERSONAL: Born April 14, 1975, in Twinsburg, Ohio. ... 6-2/239.
HIGH SCHOOL: Walsh Jesuit (Twinsburg, Ohio).
COLLEGE: Bowling Green State.
TRANSACTIONS/CAREER NOTES: Signed as non-drafted free agent by Detroit Lions (April 24, 1998).
PLAYING EXPERIENCE: Detroit NFL, 1998. ... Games/Games started: 11/0.

ORLANDO, BO   S

PERSONAL: Born April 3, 1966, in Berwick, Pa. ... 5-10/180. ... Full name: Joseph John Orlando.
HIGH SCHOOL: Berwick (Pa.) Area Senior.
COLLEGE: West Virginia.
TRANSACTIONS/CAREER NOTES: Selected by Houston Oilers in sixth round (157th pick overall) of 1989 NFL draft. ... Signed by Oilers (July 26, 1989). ... Released by Oilers (September 5, 1989). ... Re-signed by Oilers to developmental squad (September 8, 1989). ... Released by Oilers (January 2, 1990). ... Re-signed by Oilers (April 17, 1990). ... Granted free agency (February 1, 1992). ... Re-signed by Oilers (August 11, 1992). ... On injured reserve with knee injury (September 11-November 24, 1992). ... Granted unconditional free agency (February 17, 1995). ... Signed by San Diego Chargers (April 18, 1995). ... Granted unconditional free agency (February 16, 1996). ... Signed by Cincinnati Bengals (March 5, 1996). ... Released by Bengals (April 20, 1998). ... Signed by Pittsburgh Steelers (June 12, 1998). ... Released by Steelers (April 5, 1999).

PRO STATISTICS: 1991—Recovered two fumbles. 1995—Ran 37 yards with lateral from interception return. 1996—Credited with one sack and recovered one fumble. 1997—Credited with one sack and recovered one fumble.

					INTERCEPTIONS		
Year Team		G	GS	No.	Yds.	Avg.	TD
1989—Houston NFL				Did not play.			
1990—Houston NFL		16	0	0	0	...	0
1991—Houston NFL		16	16	4	18	4.5	0
1992—Houston NFL		6	1	0	0	...	0
1993—Houston NFL		16	3	3	68	22.7	▲1
1994—Houston NFL		16	0	0	0	...	0
1995—San Diego NFL		16	16	0	37	...	0
1996—Cincinnati NFL		16	16	2	0	0.0	0
1997—Cincinnati NFL		16	2	1	3	3.0	0
1998—Pittsburgh NFL		11	1	0	0	...	0
Pro totals (9 years)		129	55	10	126	12.6	1

OSBORNE, CHUCK   DT   RAIDERS

PERSONAL: Born November 2, 1973, in Los Angeles. ... 6-2/290. ... Full name: Charles Wayne Osborne.
HIGH SCHOOL: Country (Calif.).
COLLEGE: Arizona.
TRANSACTIONS/CAREER NOTES: Selected by St. Louis Rams in seventh round (222nd pick overall) of 1996 NFL draft. ... Signed by Rams (June 27, 1996). ... Released by Rams (August 19, 1997). ... Selected by Amsterdam Admirals in 1998 NFL Europe draft (February 18, 1998). ... Signed by Oakland Raiders (June 24, 1998). ... On injured reserve with knee injury (October 21, 1998-remainder of season).
PLAYING EXPERIENCE: St. Louis NFL, 1996; Amsterdam Admirals NFLE, 1998; Oakland NFL, 1998. ... Games/Games started: 1996 (15/1), NFLE 1998 (games played unavailable), NFL 1998 (6/0). Total NFL: 21/1.
PRO STATISTICS: 1996—Credited with one sack. NFLE: 1998—Credited with eight sacks.

OSTROSKI, JERRY   G   BILLS

PERSONAL: Born July 12, 1970, in Collegeville, Pa. ... 6-4/310. ... Full name: Gerald Ostroski Jr.
HIGH SCHOOL: Owen J. Roberts (Pottstown, Pa.).
COLLEGE: Tulsa.
TRANSACTIONS/CAREER NOTES: Selected by Kansas City Chiefs in 10th round (271st pick overall) of 1992 NFL draft. ... Signed by Chiefs (July 21, 1992). ... Released by Chiefs (August 25, 1992). ... Signed by Atlanta Falcons (May 7, 1993). ... Released by Falcons (August 24, 1993). ... Signed by Buffalo Bills to practice squad (November 18, 1993). ... Released by Bills (August 28, 1994). ... Re-signed by Bills to practice squad (August 29, 1994). ... Activated (November 30, 1994). ... Granted free agency (February 13, 1998). ... Re-signed by Bills (April 8, 1998). ... Granted unconditional free agency (February 12, 1999). ... Re-signed by Bills (February 17, 1999).
PLAYING EXPERIENCE: Buffalo NFL, 1994-1998. ... Games/Games started: 1994 (4/3), 1995 (16/13), 1996 (16/16), 1997 (16/16), 1998 (16/16). Total: 68/64.
PRO STATISTICS: 1997—Recovered three fumbles.

OWENS, DAN   DT   LIONS

PERSONAL: Born March 16, 1967, in Whittier, Calif. ... 6-3/290. ... Full name: Daniel William Owens.
HIGH SCHOOL: La Habra (Calif.).
COLLEGE: Southern California.
TRANSACTIONS/CAREER NOTES: Selected by Detroit Lions in second round (35th pick overall) of 1990 NFL draft. ... Signed by Lions (July 26, 1990). ... Granted free agency (March 1, 1993). ... Re-signed by Lions (August 14, 1993). ... Granted unconditional free agency (February 17, 1995). ... Re-signed by Lions (March 13, 1995). ... Granted unconditional free agency (February 16, 1996). ... Signed by Atlanta Falcons (March 26, 1996). ... Granted unconditional free agency (February 13, 1998). ... Signed by Lions (February 18, 1998). ... On injured reserve with knee injury (November 23, 1998-remainder of season).
CHAMPIONSHIP GAME EXPERIENCE: Played in NFC championship game (1991 season).
PRO STATISTICS: 1991—Recovered two fumbles. 1992—Recovered one fumble. 1993—Intercepted one pass for one yard and recovered two fumbles for 17 yards. 1995—Returned one kickoff for nine yards. 1996—Recovered one fumble. 1997—Intercepted one pass for 14 yards, returned one kickoff for nine yards, fumbled once and recovered one fumble for two yards.

Year Team	G	GS	SACKS
1990—Detroit NFL	16	12	3.0
1991—Detroit NFL	16	16	5.5
1992—Detroit NFL	16	4	2.0
1993—Detroit NFL	15	11	3.0
1994—Detroit NFL	16	8	3.0
1995—Detroit NFL	16	0	0.0
1996—Atlanta NFL	16	9	5.5
1997—Atlanta NFL	15	15	8.0
1998—Detroit NFL	11	11	2.5
Pro totals (9 years)	137	86	32.5

OWENS, RICH   DE   DOLPHINS

PERSONAL: Born May 22, 1972, in Philadelphia. ... 6-6/281.
HIGH SCHOOL: Lincoln (Philadelphia).
COLLEGE: Lehigh.
TRANSACTIONS/CAREER NOTES: Selected by Washington Redskins in fifth round (152nd pick overall) of 1995 NFL draft. ... Signed by Redskins (May 23, 1995). ... Granted free agency (February 13, 1998). ... Re-signed by Redskins (May 7, 1998). ... On injured reserve with

knee injury (August 25, 1998-entire season). ... Granted unconditional free agency (February 12, 1999). ... Signed by Miami Dolphins (March 16, 1999).

PRO STATISTICS: 1997—Recovered one fumble.

Year Team	G	GS	SACKS
1995—Washington NFL	10	3	3.0
1996—Washington NFL	16	16	11.0
1997—Washington NFL	16	15	2.5
1998—Washington NFL		Did not play.	
Pro totals (3 years)	42	34	16.5

OWENS, TERRELL   WR   49ERS

PERSONAL: Born December 7, 1973, in Alexander City, Ala. ... 6-3/217. ... Full name: Terrell Eldorado Owens. ... Name pronounced TARE-el.
HIGH SCHOOL: Benjamin Russell (Alexander City, Ala.).
COLLEGE: Tennessee-Chattanooga.
TRANSACTIONS/CAREER NOTES: Selected by San Francisco 49ers in third round (89th pick overall) of 1996 NFL draft. ... Signed by 49ers (July 18, 1996). ... On physically unable to perform list with foot injury (July 17-August 11, 1997). ... Designated by 49ers as franchise player (February 12, 1999).
CHAMPIONSHIP GAME EXPERIENCE: Played in NFC championship game (1997 season).
PRO STATISTICS: 1996—Returned three kickoffs for 47 yards. 1997—Returned two kickoffs for 31 yards and recovered one fumble. 1998—Rushed four times for 53 yards and one touchdown and recovered one fumble for 13 yards.
SINGLE GAME HIGHS (regular season): Receptions—7 (October 18, 1998, vs. Indianapolis); yards—140 (November 30, 1998, vs. New York Giants); and touchdown receptions—2 (November 22, 1998, vs. New Orleans).
STATISTICAL PLATEAUS: 100-yard receiving games: 1996 (1), 1998 (2). Total: 3.

			RECEIVING				TOTALS			
Year Team	G	GS	No.	Yds.	Avg.	TD	TD	2pt.	Pts.	Fum.
1996—San Francisco NFL	16	10	35	520	14.9	4	4	0	24	1
1997—San Francisco NFL	16	15	60	936	15.6	8	8	0	48	1
1998—San Francisco NFL	16	8	67	1097	16.4	14	15	1	92	1
Pro totals (3 years)	48	33	162	2553	15.8	26	27	1	164	3

OXENDINE, KEN   RB   FALCONS

PERSONAL: Born October 4, 1975, in Richmond, Va. ... 6-0/230. ... Full name: Ken Qwarious Oxendine.
HIGH SCHOOL: Thomas Dale (Chester, Va.).
COLLEGE: Virginia Tech.
TRANSACTIONS/CAREER NOTES: Selected by Atlanta Falcons in seventh round (201st pick overall) of 1998 NFL draft. ... Signed by Falcons (May 27, 1998).
CHAMPIONSHIP GAME EXPERIENCE: Played in NFC championship game (1998 season).
SINGLE GAME HIGHS (regular season): Attempts—6 (October 4, 1998, vs. Carolina); yards—32 (December 27, 1998, vs. Miami); and rushing touchdowns—0.

			RUSHING				RECEIVING			TOTALS			
Year Team	G	GS	Att.	Yds.	Avg.	TD	No.	Yds.	Avg.	TD	TD	2pt.	Pts.	Fum.
1998—Atlanta NFL	9	0	18	50	2.8	0	1	11	11.0	0	0	0	0	1

PACE, ORLANDO   OT   RAMS

PERSONAL: Born November 4, 1975, in Sandusky, Ohio. ... 6-7/320. ... Full name: Orlando Lamar Pace.
HIGH SCHOOL: Sandusky (Ohio).
COLLEGE: Ohio State.
TRANSACTIONS/CAREER NOTES: Selected after junior season by St. Louis Rams in first round (first pick overall) of 1997 NFL draft. ... Signed by Rams (August 16, 1997).
PLAYING EXPERIENCE: St. Louis NFL, 1997 and 1998. ... Games/Games started: 1997 (13/9), 1998 (16/16). Total: 29/25.
HONORS: Lombardi Award winner (1995 and 1996). ... Named offensive tackle on THE SPORTING NEWS college All-America first team (1995 and 1996). ... Outland Trophy winner (1996).
PRO STATISTICS: 1997—Recovered one fumble. 1998—Recovered one fumble.

PALELEI, LONNIE   G   EAGLES

PERSONAL: Born October 15, 1970, in Nu'uuli, American Samoa. ... 6-3/315. ... Full name: Si'ulagi Jack Palelei. ... Name pronounced SEE-oo-lon-nee pah-le-LAY.
HIGH SCHOOL: Blue Springs (Mo.).
COLLEGE: Purdue, then UNLV.
TRANSACTIONS/CAREER NOTES: Selected by Pittsburgh Steelers in fifth round (135th pick overall) of 1993 NFL draft. ... Signed by Steelers (July 9, 1993). ... Inactive for all 16 games (1994). ... On reserve/non-football injury list with knee injury (August 21-November 3, 1995). ... Claimed on waivers by Cleveland Browns (November 28, 1995). ... Browns franchise moved to Baltimore and renamed Ravens for 1996 season (March 11, 1996). ... Released by Ravens (August 25, 1996). ... Signed by New York Jets (March 3, 1997). ... Released by Jets (August 25, 1998). ... Signed by New York Giants (August 27, 1998). ... On injured reserve with heart problems (December 3, 1998-remainder of season). ... Granted unconditional free agency (February 12, 1999). ... Signed by Philadelphia Eagles (May 20, 1999).
PLAYING EXPERIENCE: Pittsburgh NFL, 1993 and 1995; New York Jets NFL, 1997; New York Giants NFL, 1998. ... Games/Games started: 1993 (3/0), 1995 (1/0), 1997 (15/14), 1998 (9/0). Total: 28/14.
CHAMPIONSHIP GAME EXPERIENCE: Member of Steelers for AFC championship game (1994 season); inactive.
PRO STATISTICS: 1997—Recovered one fumble. 1998—Returned three kickoffs for 14 yards and fumbled once.

PALMER, DAVID   RB/KR   VIKINGS

PERSONAL: Born November 19, 1972, in Birmingham, Ala. ... 5-8/173. ... Full name: David L. Palmer.
HIGH SCHOOL: Jackson-Olin (Birmingham, Ala.).
COLLEGE: Alabama.
TRANSACTIONS/CAREER NOTES: Selected after junior season by Minnesota Vikings in second round (40th pick overall) of 1994 NFL draft. ... Signed by Vikings (July 19, 1994). ... Granted free agency (February 14, 1997). ... Re-signed by Vikings (May 7, 1997). ... Granted unconditional free agency (February 12, 1999). ... Re-signed by Vikings (March 3, 1999).
CHAMPIONSHIP GAME EXPERIENCE: Played in NFC championship game (1998 season).
HONORS: Named kick returner on THE SPORTING NEWS college All-America first team (1993).
PRO STATISTICS: 1994—Fumbled twice. 1995—Fumbled once. 1996—Fumbled three times and recovered one fumble. 1997—Fumbled twice. 1998—Fumbled twice and recovered one fumble.
SINGLE GAME HIGHS (regular season): Attempts—4 (November 16, 1997, vs. Detroit); yards—15 (September 20, 1998, vs. Detroit); and rushing touchdowns—1 (November 9, 1997, vs. Chicago).

				RUSHING				RECEIVING				PUNT RETURNS				KICKOFF RETURNS				TOTALS		
Year Team	G	GS	Att.	Yds.	Avg.	TD	No.	Yds.	Avg.	TD	No.	Yds.	Avg.	TD	No.	Yds.	Avg.	TD	TD	2pt.	Pts.
1994—Minnesota NFL	13	1	1	1	1.0	0	6	90	15.0	0	30	193	6.4	0	0	0	...	0	0	0	0
1995—Minnesota NFL	14	0	7	15	2.1	0	12	100	8.3	0	26	342*13.2		†1	17	354	20.8	0	1	0	6
1996—Minnesota NFL	11	1	2	9	4.5	0	6	40	6.7	0	22	216	9.8	1	13	292	22.5	0	1	0	6
1997—Minnesota NFL	16	0	11	36	3.3	0	26	193	7.4	1	34	444‡13.1		0	32	711	22.2	0	2	0	12
1998—Minnesota NFL	16	0	10	52	5.2	0	18	185	10.3	0	28	289	10.3	0	50	1176	23.5	1	1	0	6
Pro totals (5 years)	70	2	31	113	3.6	1	68	608	8.9	1	140	1484	10.6	2	112	2533	22.6	1	5	0	30

PALMER, MITCH   LB   BUCCANEERS

PERSONAL: Born September 2, 1973, in San Diego. ... 6-4/250. ... Full name: Richard Mitchell Palmer.
HIGH SCHOOL: Poway (San Diego).
COLLEGE: Colorado State.
TRANSACTIONS/CAREER NOTES: Signed as non-drafted free agent by Carolina Panthers (April 28, 1997). ... Released by Panthers (August 17, 1997). ... Signed by Tampa Bay Buccaneers (April 28, 1998).
PLAYING EXPERIENCE: Tampa Bay NFL, 1998. ... Games/Games started: 16/0.

PANOS, JOE   G   BILLS

PERSONAL: Born January 24, 1971, in Brookfield, Wis. ... 6-2/293. ... Full name: Zois Panagiotopoulos.
HIGH SCHOOL: Brookfield (Wis.) East.
COLLEGE: Wisconsin.
TRANSACTIONS/CAREER NOTES: Selected by Philadelphia Eagles in third round (77th pick overall) of 1994 NFL draft. ... Signed by Eagles (July 11, 1994). ... On injured reserve with shoulder injury (November 12, 1995-remainder of season). ... Granted free agency (February 14, 1997). ... Re-signed by Eagles (July 19, 1997). ... Granted unconditional free agency (February 13, 1998). ... Signed by Buffalo Bills (February 20, 1998).
PLAYING EXPERIENCE: Philadelphia NFL, 1994-1997; Buffalo NFL, 1998. ... Games/Games started: 1994 (16/2), 1995 (9/9), 1996 (16/16), 1997 (13/13), 1998 (16/16). Total: 70/56.
PRO STATISTICS: 1997—Recovered one fumble.

PARKER, ANTHONY   CB

PERSONAL: Born February 11, 1966, in Sylacauga, Ala. ... 5-10/181. ... Full name: Will Anthony Parker. ... Son of Billy Parker, second baseman/third baseman with California Angels (1971-73).
HIGH SCHOOL: McClintock (Tempe, Ariz.).
COLLEGE: Arizona State (degree in physical education, 1989).
TRANSACTIONS/CAREER NOTES: Signed as non-drafted free agent by Indianapolis Colts (April 21, 1989). ... On injured reserve with hamstring injury (September 5-November 17, 1989). ... Granted unconditional free agency (February 1, 1990). ... Signed by New York Jets (March 31, 1990). ... Released by Jets (September 4, 1990). ... Signed by WLAF (January 31, 1991). ... Selected by New York/New Jersey Knights in first round (second defensive back) of 1991 WLAF positional draft. ... Signed by Phoenix Cardinals (July 9, 1991). ... Released by Cardinals (August 13, 1991). ... Signed by Kansas City Chiefs to practice squad (September 11, 1991). ... Activated (September 15, 1991). ... Released by Chiefs (September 25, 1991). ... Re-signed by Chiefs to practice squad (October 1, 1991). ... Activated (December 14, 1991). ... Granted unconditional free agency (February 1, 1992). ... Signed by Minnesota Vikings (March 26, 1992). ... Granted free agency (February 17, 1995). ... Re-signed by Vikings (May 7, 1994). ... Granted unconditional free agency (February 17, 1995). ... Signed by Los Angeles Rams (April 4, 1995). ... Rams franchise moved to St. Louis (April 12, 1995). ... Released by Rams (July 15, 1997). ... Signed by Tampa Bay Buccaneers (July 20, 1997). ... Released by Buccaneers (February 11, 1999).
HONORS: Named cornerback on All-World League team (1991).
PRO STATISTICS: 1992—Returned two kickoffs for 30 yards and recovered two fumbles for 58 yards and a touchdown. 1994—Recovered one fumble for 23 yards and a touchdown. 1995—Recovered four fumbles for 35 yards and a touchdown. 1996—Recovered one fumble. 1997—Credited with one sack. 1998—Credited with one sack.
MISCELLANEOUS: Only player in NFL history to score a defensive touchdown in three consecutive games (1994).

Year	Team	G	GS	INTERCEPTIONS No.	Yds.	Avg.	TD	PUNT RETURNS No.	Yds.	Avg.	TD	TOTALS TD	2pt.	Pts.	Fum.
1989	Indianapolis NFL	1	0	0	0	...	0	0	0	...	0	0	...	0	0
1990								Did not play.							
1991	New York/New Jersey W.L.	10	10	*11	*270	24.5	*2	0	0	...	0	2	...	12	0
	Kansas City NFL	2	0	0	0	...	0	0	0	...	0	0	...	0	0
1992	Minnesota NFL	16	3	3	23	7.7	0	33	336	10.2	0	1	...	6	2
1993	Minnesota NFL	14	0	1	1	1.0	0	9	64	7.1	0	0	...	0	0
1994	Minnesota NFL	15	15	4	99	24.8	2	4	31	7.8	0	3	0	18	1
1995	St. Louis NFL	16	16	2	-5	-2.5	0	0	0	...	0	1	0	6	0
1996	St. Louis NFL	14	14	4	128	32.0	†2	0	0	...	0	2	0	12	0
1997	Tampa Bay NFL	15	14	1	5	5.0	0	0	0	...	0	0	0	0	1
1998	Tampa Bay NFL	11	7	0	0	...	0	0	0	...	0	0	0	0	0
W.L. totals (1 year)		10	10	11	270	24.5	2	0	0	...	0	2	0	12	0
NFL totals (9 years)		104	69	15	251	16.7	4	46	431	9.4	0	7	0	42	4
Pro totals (10 years)		114	79	26	521	20.0	6	46	431	9.4	0	9	0	54	4

PARKER, GLENN — G/OT — CHIEFS

PERSONAL: Born April 22, 1966, in Westminster, Calif. ... 6-5/305. ... Full name: Glenn Andrew Parker.
HIGH SCHOOL: Edison (Huntington Beach, Calif.).
JUNIOR COLLEGE: Golden West Junior College (Calif.).
COLLEGE: Arizona.
TRANSACTIONS/CAREER NOTES: Selected by Buffalo Bills in third round (69th pick overall) of 1990 NFL draft. ... Signed by Bills (July 26, 1990). ... Granted free agency (March 1, 1993). ... Re-signed by Bills (March 11, 1993). ... Released by Bills (August 24, 1997). ... Signed by Kansas City Chiefs (August 28, 1997).
PLAYING EXPERIENCE: Buffalo NFL, 1990-1996; Kansas City NFL, 1997 and 1998. ... Games/Games started: 1990 (16/3), 1991 (16/5), 1992 (13/13), 1993 (16/9), 1994 (16/16), 1995 (13/13), 1996 (14/13), 1997 (15/15), 1998 (15/15). Total: 134/102.
CHAMPIONSHIP GAME EXPERIENCE: Played in AFC championship game (1990, 1992 and 1993 seasons). ... Member of Bills for AFC championship game (1991 season); inactive. ... Played in Super Bowl XXV (1990 season), Super Bowl XXVI (1991 season), Super Bowl XXVII (1992 season) and Super Bowl XXVIII (1993 season).
PRO STATISTICS: 1992—Recovered one fumble. 1995—Recovered one fumble. 1996—Recovered two fumbles. 1998—Recovered one fumble.

PARKER, RIDDICK — DT — SEAHAWKS

PERSONAL: Born November 20, 1972, in Emporia, Va. ... 6-3/274.
HIGH SCHOOL: Southampton (Courtland, Va.).
COLLEGE: North Carolina.
TRANSACTIONS/CAREER NOTES: Signed as non-drafted free agent by San Diego Chargers (April 28, 1995). ... Released by Chargers (August 22, 1995). ... Signed by Seattle Seahawks (July 8, 1996). ... Released by Seahawks (August 24, 1996). ... Re-signed by Seahawks to practice squad (August 26, 1996).
PLAYING EXPERIENCE: Seattle NFL, 1997 and 1998. ... Games/Games started: 1997 (11/0), 1998 (8/0). Total: 19/0.
PRO STATISTICS: 1998—Credited with one sack.

PARKER, VAUGHN — OT — CHARGERS

PERSONAL: Born June 5, 1971, in Buffalo. ... 6-3/300. ... Full name: Vaughn Antoine Parker.
HIGH SCHOOL: Saint Joseph's Collegiate Institute (Buffalo).
COLLEGE: UCLA.
TRANSACTIONS/CAREER NOTES: Selected by San Diego Chargers in second round (63rd pick overall) of 1994 NFL draft. ... Signed by Chargers (July 12, 1994). ... Granted free agency (February 14, 1997). ... Re-signed by Chargers (June 6, 1997). ... On injured reserve with leg injury (December 12, 1998-remainder of season).
PLAYING EXPERIENCE: San Diego NFL, 1994-1998. ... Games/Games started: 1994 (6/0), 1995 (14/7), 1996 (16/16), 1997 (16/16), 1998 (6/6). Total: 58/45.
CHAMPIONSHIP GAME EXPERIENCE: Played in AFC championship game (1994 season). ... Played in Super Bowl XXIX (1994 season).
PRO STATISTICS: 1994—Returned one kickoff for one yard. 1996—Recovered one fumble. 1997—Recovered two fumbles.

PARMALEE, BERNIE — RB — DOLPHINS

PERSONAL: Born September 16, 1967, in Jersey City, N.J. ... 5-11/210. ... Full name: Bernard Parmalee.
HIGH SCHOOL: Lincoln (Jersey City, N.J.).
COLLEGE: Ball State (degree in business administration).
TRANSACTIONS/CAREER NOTES: Signed as non-drafted free agent by Miami Dolphins (May 1, 1992). ... Released by Dolphins (August 31, 1992). ... Re-signed by Dolphins to practice squad (September 1, 1992). ... Activated (October 21, 1992). ... Deactivated for remainder of 1992 playoffs (January 16, 1993). ... Granted free agency (February 17, 1995). ... Re-signed by Dolphins (March 31, 1995). ... Granted unconditional free agency (February 14, 1997). ... Re-signed by Dolphins (April 17, 1997). ... Granted unconditional free agency (February 13, 1998). ... Re-signed by Dolphins (March 2, 1998).
PRO STATISTICS: 1994—Recovered three fumbles for 20 yards. 1998—Recovered two fumbles.
SINGLE GAME HIGHS (regular season): Attempts—30 (October 16, 1994, vs. Los Angeles Raiders); yards—150 (October 16, 1994, vs. Los Angeles Raiders); and rushing touchdowns—3 (December 25, 1994, vs. Detroit).
STATISTICAL PLATEAUS: 100-yard rushing games: 1994 (3), 1995 (3). Total: 6.

Year Team	G	GS	RUSHING Att.	Yds.	Avg.	TD	RECEIVING No.	Yds.	Avg.	TD	KICKOFF RETURNS No.	Yds.	Avg.	TD	TOTALS TD	2pt	Pts.	Fum.
1992—Miami NFL	10	0	6	38	6.3	0	0	0	...	0	14	289	20.6	0	0	...	0	3
1993—Miami NFL	16	0	4	16	4.0	0	1	1	1.0	0	0	0	...	0	0	...	0	0
1994—Miami NFL	15	10	216	868	4.0	6	34	249	7.3	1	2	0	0.0	0	7	1	44	5
1995—Miami NFL	16	12	236	878	3.7	9	39	345	8.8	1	0	0	...	0	10	0	60	5
1996—Miami NFL	16	0	25	80	3.2	0	21	189	9.0	0	0	0	...	0	0	0	0	1
1997—Miami NFL	16	4	18	59	3.3	0	28	301	10.8	1	0	0	...	0	1	0	6	1
1998—Miami NFL	15	0	8	20	2.5	0	21	221	10.5	0	0	0	...	0	0	0	0	2
Pro totals (7 years)	104	26	513	1959	3.8	15	144	1306	9.1	3	16	289	18.1	0	18	1	110	17

PARRELLA, JOHN — DT — CHARGERS

PERSONAL: Born November 22, 1969, in Topeka, Kan. ... 6-3/300. ... Full name: John Lorin Parrella.
HIGH SCHOOL: Grand Island (Neb.) Central Catholic.
COLLEGE: Nebraska.
TRANSACTIONS/CAREER NOTES: Selected by Buffalo Bills in second round (55th pick overall) of 1993 NFL draft. ... Signed by Bills (July 12, 1993). ... Released by Bills (August 28, 1994). ... Signed by San Diego Chargers (September 12, 1994). ... Granted free agency (February 16, 1996). ... Re-signed by Chargers (June 14, 1996).
CHAMPIONSHIP GAME EXPERIENCE: Member of Bills for AFC championship game (1993 season); inactive. ... Member of Bills for Super Bowl XXVIII (1993 season); inactive. ... Played in AFC championship game (1994 season). ... Played in Super Bowl XXIX (1994 season).
PRO STATISTICS: 1997—Recovered one fumble. 1998—Recovered one fumble.

Year Team	G	GS	SACKS
1993—Buffalo NFL	10	0	1.0
1994—San Diego NFL	13	1	1.0
1995—San Diego NFL	16	1	2.0
1996—San Diego NFL	16	9	2.0
1997—San Diego NFL	16	16	3.5
1998—San Diego NFL	16	16	1.5
Pro totals (6 years)	87	43	11.0

PARRISH, TONY — S — BEARS

PERSONAL: Born November 23, 1975, in Huntington Beach, Calif. ... 5-10/205.
HIGH SCHOOL: Marina (Huntington Beach, Calif.).
COLLEGE: Washington.
TRANSACTIONS/CAREER NOTES: Selected by Chicago Bears in second round (35th pick overall) of 1998 NFL draft. ... Signed by Bears (July 20, 1998).
PRO STATISTICS: 1998—Intercepted one pass for eight yards, credited with one sack, fumbled once and recovered two fumbles for minus two yards.

PARTEN, TY — DT — CHIEFS

PERSONAL: Born October 13, 1969, in Washington, D.C. ... 6-5/295. ... Full name: Ty Daniel Parten.
HIGH SCHOOL: Horizon (Scottsdale, Ariz.).
COLLEGE: Arizona.
TRANSACTIONS/CAREER NOTES: Selected by Cincinnati Bengals in third round (63rd pick overall) of 1993 draft. ... Signed by Bengals (July 19, 1993). ... On injured reserve with left thumb injury (November 29, 1993-remainder of season). ... Released by Bengals (September 20, 1995). ... Selected by Scottish Claymores in 1996 World League draft (February 22, 1996). ... Signed by St. Louis Rams (April 2, 1997). ... Released by Rams (August 24, 1997). ... Signed by Kansas City Chiefs (December 10, 1997). ... Granted free agency (February 12, 1999).
PLAYING EXPERIENCE: Cincinnati NFL, 1993-1995; Kansas City NFL, 1997 and 1998. ... Games/Games started: 1993 (11/1), 1994 (14/4), 1995 (1/1), 1997 (2/0), 1998 (16/6). Total: 44/12.
PRO STATISTICS: 1998—Returned two kickoffs for 22 yards and recovered one fumble.

PATHON, JEROME — WR — COLTS

PERSONAL: Born December 16, 1975, in Capetown, South Africa. ... 6-0/187. ... Name pronounced PAY-thon.
HIGH SCHOOL: Carson Graham Secondary School (North Vancouver).
COLLEGE: Acadia (Nova Scotia), then Washington.
TRANSACTIONS/CAREER NOTES: Selected by Indianapolis Colts in second round (32nd pick overall) of 1998 NFL draft. ... Signed by Colts (July 26, 1998).
HONORS: Named wide receiver on THE SPORTING NEWS college All-America second team (1997).
PRO STATISTICS: 1998—Rushed three times for minus two yards.
SINGLE GAME HIGHS (regular season): Receptions—7 (November 1, 1998, vs. New England); yards—66 (December 20, 1998, vs. Seattle); and touchdown receptions—1 (November 29, 1998, vs. Baltimore).

Year Team	G	GS	RECEIVING No.	Yds.	Avg.	TD	TOTALS TD	2pt.	Pts.	Fum.
1998—Indianapolis NFL	16	15	50	511	10.2	1	1	0	6	0

PATTEN, DAVID — WR/KR — GIANTS

PERSONAL: Born August 19, 1974, in Hopkins, S.C. ... 5-9/180.
HIGH SCHOOL: Lower Richland (Columbia, S.C.).

COLLEGE: Western Carolina.
TRANSACTIONS/CAREER NOTES: Played in Arena League with Albany Firebirds (1996). ... Signed as non-drafted free agent by New York Giants (March 24, 1997). ... Released by Giants (August 24, 1997). ... Re-signed by Giants to practice squad (August 25, 1997). ... Activated (August 27, 1997). ... On injured reserve with knee injury (December 16, 1998-remainder of season).
PRO STATISTICS: 1997—Rushed once for two yards and recovered one fumble.
SINGLE GAME HIGHS (regular season): Receptions—3 (October 18, 1998, vs. Arizona); yards—66 (October 12, 1997, vs. Arizona); and touchdown receptions—1 (October 11, 1998, vs. Atlanta).

			RECEIVING			KICKOFF RETURNS				TOTALS			
Year Team	G	GS	No.	Yds.	Avg.	TD	No.	Yds.	Avg.	TD	TD	2pt.	Pts.	Fum.
1997—New York Giants NFL	16	3	13	226	17.4	2	8	123	15.4	0	2	0	12	2
1998—New York Giants NFL	12	0	11	119	10.8	1	43	928	21.6	1	2	0	12	0
Pro totals (2 years)	28	3	24	345	14.4	3	51	1051	20.6	1	4	0	24	2

PATTON, JOE — OT — REDSKINS

PERSONAL: Born January 5, 1972, in Birmingham, Ala. ... 6-5/306. ... Full name: Joseph Patton.
HIGH SCHOOL: Jones Valley (Birmingham, Ala.).
COLLEGE: Alabama A&M.
TRANSACTIONS/CAREER NOTES: Selected by Washington Redskins in third round (97th pick overall) of 1994 NFL draft. ... Signed by Redskins (July 19, 1994). ... Granted free agency (February 14, 1997). ... Re-signed by Redskins (June 2, 1997). ... Granted unconditional free agency (February 13, 1998). ... Re-signed by Redskins (February 19, 1998).
PLAYING EXPERIENCE: Washington NFL, 1994-1998. ... Games/Games started: 1994 (2/0), 1995 (16/13), 1996 (16/15), 1997 (16/16), 1998 (11/10). Total: 61/54.
PRO STATISTICS: 1995—Recovered one fumble. 1996—Recovered one fumble. 1997—Recovered one fumble.

PATTON, MARVCUS — LB — CHIEFS

PERSONAL: Born May 1, 1967, in Los Angeles. ... 6-2/236. ... Full name: Marvcus Raymond Patton.
HIGH SCHOOL: Leuzinger (Lawndale, Calif.).
COLLEGE: UCLA (degree in political science, 1990).
TRANSACTIONS/CAREER NOTES: Selected by Buffalo Bills in eighth round (208th pick overall) of 1990 NFL draft. ... Signed by Bills (July 27, 1990). ... On injured reserve with broken leg (January 26, 1991-remainder of 1990 playoffs). ... Granted free agency (February 1, 1992). ... Re-signed by Bills (July 23, 1992). ... Granted unconditional free agency (February 17, 1995). ... Signed by Washington Redskins (February 22, 1995). ... Granted unconditional free agency (February 12, 1999). ... Signed by Kansas City Chiefs (April 27, 1999).
CHAMPIONSHIP GAME EXPERIENCE: Played in AFC championship game (1991-1993 seasons). ... Played in Super Bowl XXVI (1991 season), Super Bowl XXVII (1992 season) and Super Bowl XXVIII (1993 season).
PRO STATISTICS: 1993—Recovered three fumbles for five yards. 1994—Recovered one fumble and fumbled once. 1995—Recovered one fumble. 1997—Returned one kickoff for 10 yards and recovered one fumble.

			INTERCEPTIONS				SACKS
Year Team	G	GS	No.	Yds.	Avg.	TD	No.
1990—Buffalo NFL	16	0	0	0	...	0	0.5
1991—Buffalo NFL	16	2	0	0	...	0	0.0
1992—Buffalo NFL	16	4	0	0	...	0	2.0
1993—Buffalo NFL	16	16	2	0	0.0	0	1.0
1994—Buffalo NFL	16	16	2	8	4.0	0	0.0
1995—Washington NFL	16	16	2	7	3.5	0	2.0
1996—Washington NFL	16	16	2	26	13.0	0	2.0
1997—Washington NFL	16	16	2	5	2.5	0	4.5
1998—Washington NFL	16	16	0	0	...	0	3.0
Pro totals (9 years)	144	102	10	46	4.6	0	15.0

PAUL, TITO — CB — BRONCOS

PERSONAL: Born December 7, 1971, in Kissimmee, Fla. ... 6-0/195. ... Cousin of Markus Paul, safety with Chicago Bears (1989-93) and Tampa Bay Buccaneers (1993).
HIGH SCHOOL: Osceola (Fla.).
COLLEGE: Ohio State.
TRANSACTIONS/CAREER NOTES: Selected by Arizona Cardinals in fifth round (167th pick overall) of 1995 NFL draft. ... Signed by Cardinals (July 20, 1995). ... Released by Cardinals (September 1, 1997). ... Signed by Cincinnati Bengals (September 9, 1997). ... Released by Bengals (April 20, 1998). ... Signed by Denver Broncos (May 7, 1998).
PLAYING EXPERIENCE: Arizona NFL, 1995 and 1996; Arizona (1)-Cincinnati (14) NFL, 1997; Denver NFL, 1998. ... Games/Games started: 1995 (14/4), 1996 (16/3), 1997 (Ari.-1/0; Cin.-14/5; Total: 15/5), 1998 (16/0). Total: 61/12.
CHAMPIONSHIP GAME EXPERIENCE: Played in AFC championship game (1998 season). ... Member of Super Bowl championship team (1998 season).
PRO STATISTICS: 1994—Intercepted one pass for four yards. 1996—Recovered one fumble. 1997—Recovered one fumble. 1998—Returned one punt for no yards, fumbled once and recovered one fumble.

PAUP, BRYCE — LB — JAGUARS

PERSONAL: Born February 29, 1968, in Jefferson, Iowa. ... 6-5/247. ... Full name: Bryce Eric Paup.
HIGH SCHOOL: Scranton (Iowa).
COLLEGE: Northern Iowa (degree in business).
TRANSACTIONS/CAREER NOTES: Selected by Green Bay Packers in sixth round (159th pick overall) of 1990 NFL draft. ... Signed by Packers (July 22, 1990). ... On injured reserve with hand injury (September 4-November 17, 1990). ... On injured reserve with calf injury (December

12, 1991-remainder of season). ... Granted free agency (February 1, 1992). ... Re-signed by Packers (August 13, 1992). ... Granted unconditional free agency (February 17, 1995). ... Signed by Buffalo Bills (March 9, 1995). ... Granted unconditional free agency (February 13, 1998). ... Signed by Jacksonville Jaguars (February 16, 1998).

HONORS: Played in Pro Bowl (1994-1997 seasons). ... Named linebacker on THE SPORTING NEWS NFL All-Pro team (1995).

PRO STATISTICS: 1991—Credited with a safety. 1992—Recovered two fumbles. 1994—Recovered two fumbles. 1995—Recovered one fumble. 1997—Recovered one fumble.

				INTERCEPTIONS				SACKS
Year Team		G	GS	No.	Yds.	Avg.	TD	No.
1990—Green Bay NFL		5	0	0	0	...	0	0.0
1991—Green Bay NFL		12	1	0	0	...	0	7.5
1992—Green Bay NFL		16	10	0	0	...	0	6.5
1993—Green Bay NFL		15	14	1	8	8.0	0	11.0
1994—Green Bay NFL		16	16	3	47	15.7	1	7.5
1995—Buffalo NFL		15	15	2	0	0.0	0	*17.5
1996—Buffalo NFL		12	11	0	0	...	0	6.0
1997—Buffalo NFL		16	16	0	0	...	0	9.5
1998—Jacksonville NFL		16	16	0	0	...	0	6.5
Pro totals (9 years)		123	99	6	55	9.2	1	72.0

PAYNE, ROD — C — BENGALS

PERSONAL: Born June 14, 1974, in Miami. ... 6-4/305. ... Full name: Reginald Gerald Payne.
HIGH SCHOOL: Killian (Miami).
COLLEGE: Michigan.
TRANSACTIONS/CAREER NOTES: Selected by Cincinnati Bengals in third round (76th pick overall) of 1997 NFL draft. ... Signed by Bengals (July 17, 1997). ... Inactive for all 16 games (1997).
PLAYING EXPERIENCE: Cincinnati NFL, 1998. ... Games/Games started: 5/0.

PAYNE, SETH — DT — JAGUARS

PERSONAL: Born February 12, 1975, in Clifton Springs, N.Y. ... 6-4/292. ... Full name: Seth Copeland Payne.
HIGH SCHOOL: Victor (N.Y.) Central.
COLLEGE: Cornell.
TRANSACTIONS/CAREER NOTES: Selected by Jacksonville Jaguars in fourth round (114th pick overall) of 1997 NFL draft. ... Signed by Jaguars (May 23, 1997). ... On injured reserve with shoulder injury (November 17, 1998-remainder of season).
PLAYING EXPERIENCE: Jacksonville NFL, 1997 and 1998. ... Games/Games started: 1997 (12/5), 1998 (6/1). Total: 18/6.

PEDERSON, DOUG — QB — EAGLES

PERSONAL: Born January 31, 1968, in Bellingham, Wash. ... 6-3/216. ... Full name: Douglas Irvin Pederson.
HIGH SCHOOL: Ferndale (Wash.).
COLLEGE: Northeast Louisiana (degree in business management).
TRANSACTIONS/CAREER NOTES: Signed as non-drafted free agent by Miami Dolphins (April 30, 1991). ... Released by Dolphins (August 16, 1991). ... Selected by New York/New Jersey Knights in fifth round (49th pick overall) of 1992 World League draft. ... Re-signed by Dolphins (June 1, 1992). ... Released by Dolphins (August 31, 1992). ... Re-signed by Dolphins to practice squad (September 1, 1992). ... Released by Dolphins (October 7, 1992). ... Re-signed by Dolphins (March 3, 1993). ... Released by Dolphins (August 30, 1993). ... Re-signed by Dolphins to practice squad (August 31, 1993). ... Activated (October 22, 1993). ... Released by Dolphins (December 15, 1993). ... Re-signed by Dolphins (April 15, 1994). ... Inactive for all 16 games (1994). ... Selected by Carolina Panthers from Dolphins in NFL expansion draft (February 15, 1995). ... Released by Panthers (May 22, 1995). ... Signed by Dolphins (July 11, 1995). ... Released by Dolphins (August 21, 1995). ... Re-signed by Dolphins (October 10, 1995). ... Inactive for two games with Dolphins (1995). ... Released by Dolphins (October 25, 1995). ... Signed by Green Bay Packers (November 22, 1995). ... Inactive for five games with Packers (1995). ... Granted unconditional free agency (February 14, 1997). ... Re-signed by Packers (February 20, 1997). ... Granted unconditional free agency (February 12, 1999). ... Signed by Philadelphia Eagles (February 18, 1999).
CHAMPIONSHIP GAME EXPERIENCE: Member of Packers for NFC championship game (1995-97 seasons); inactive. ... Member of Super Bowl championship team (1996 season); inactive. ... Member of Packers for Super Bowl XXXII (1997 season); inactive.
PRO STATISTICS: 1993—Recovered one fumble for minus one yard. 1998—Fumbled once for minus two yards.
SINGLE GAME HIGHS (regular season): Attempts—16 (October 5, 1998, vs. Minnesota); completions—10 (October 5, 1998, vs. Minnesota); yards—103 (October 5, 1998, vs. Minnesota); and touchdown passes—2 (October 5, 1998, vs. Minnesota).

			PASSING							RUSHING			TOTALS		
Year Team	G	GS	Att.	Cmp.	Pct.	Yds.	TD	Int.	Avg.	Rat.	Att.	Yds.	Avg.	TD	TD	2pt.	Pts.
1992—N.Y./New Jersey W.L.	7	1	128	70	54.7	1077	8	3	8.41	93.7	15	46	3.1	0	0	...	0
1993—Miami NFL	7	0	8	4	50.0	41	0	0	5.13	65.1	2	-1	-0.5	0	0	...	0
1994—Miami NFL						Did not play.											
1995—Miami NFL						Did not play.											
—Green Bay NFL						Did not play.											
1996—Green Bay NFL	1	0	0	0	...	0	0	...	...	...	0	0	...	0	0	0	0
1997—Green Bay NFL	1	0	0	0	...	0	0	...	...	...	3	-4	-1.3	0	0	0	0
1998—Green Bay NFL	12	0	24	14	58.3	128	2	0	5.33	100.7	8	-4	-0.5	0	0	0	0
W.L. totals (1 year)	7	1	128	70	54.7	1077	8	3	8.41	93.7	15	46	3.1	0	0	0	0
NFL totals (4 years)	21	0	32	18	56.3	169	2	0	5.28	91.8	13	-9	-0.7	0	0	0	0
Pro totals (5 years)	28	1	160	88	55.0	1246	10	3	7.79	93.4	28	37	1.3	0	0	0	0

PEETE, RODNEY — QB — REDSKINS

PERSONAL: Born March 16, 1966, in Mesa, Ariz. ... 6-0/225. ... Son of Willie Peete, former running backs coach and scout with Chicago Bears; and cousin of Calvin Peete, professional golfer.
HIGH SCHOOL: Sahuaro (Tucson, Ariz.), then Shawnee Mission South (Overland Park, Kan.).
COLLEGE: Southern California (degree in communications, 1989).
TRANSACTIONS/CAREER NOTES: Selected by Detroit Lions in sixth round (141st pick overall) of 1989 NFL draft. ... Signed by Lions (July 13, 1989). ... On injured reserve with Achilles' tendon injury (October 30, 1991-remainder of season). ... Granted free agency (February 1, 1992). ... Re-signed by Lions (July 30, 1992). ... Granted unconditional free agency (February 17, 1994). ... Signed by Dallas Cowboys (May 4, 1994). ... Granted unconditional free agency (February 17, 1995). ... Signed by Philadelphia Eagles (April 22, 1995). ... Granted unconditional free agency (February 16, 1996). ... Re-signed by Eagles (March 14, 1996). ... On injured reserve with knee injury (October 3, 1996-remainder of season). ... Granted unconditional free agency (February 14, 1997). ... Re-signed by Eagles (April 1, 1997). ... Traded by Eagles to Washington Redskins for sixth-round pick in 2000 draft (April 28, 1999).
CHAMPIONSHIP GAME EXPERIENCE: Member of Cowboys for NFC championship game (1994 season); did not play.
HONORS: Named quarterback on THE SPORTING NEWS college All-America second team (1988).
PRO STATISTICS: 1989—Fumbled nine times and recovered three fumbles. 1990—Fumbled nine times and recovered one fumble. 1991—Fumbled twice and recovered one fumble for minus one yard. 1992—Fumbled six times and recovered two fumbles for minus seven yards. 1993—Fumbled 11 times and recovered four fumbles for minus eight yards. 1994—Fumbled three times and recovered two fumbles for minus one yard. 1995—Fumbled 13 times and recovered five fumbles. 1996—Fumbled twice and recovered one fumble. 1997—Fumbled five times and recovered two fumbles for minus two yards. 1998—Fumbled once.
SINGLE GAME HIGHS (regular season): Attempts—45 (October 8, 1995, vs. Washington); completions—30 (October 8, 1995, vs. Washington); yards—323 (September 27, 1992, vs. Tampa Bay); and touchdown passes—4 (December 16, 1990, vs. Chicago).
STATISTICAL PLATEAUS: 300-yard passing games: 1990 (1), 1992 (1). Total: 2.
MISCELLANEOUS: Selected by Toronto Blue Jays organization in 30th round of free-agent baseball draft (June 4, 1984); did not sign. ... Selected by Oakland Athletics organization in 14th round of free-agent baseball draft (June 1, 1988); did not sign. ... Selected by Athletics organization in 13th round of free-agent baseball draft (June 5, 1989); did not sign. ... Regular-season record as starting NFL quarterback: 37-35 (.514). ... Postseason record as starting NFL quarterback: 1-1 (.500).

				PASSING							RUSHING				TOTALS		
Year Team	G	GS	Att.	Cmp.	Pct.	Yds.	TD	Int.	Avg.	Rat.	Att.	Yds.	Avg.	TD	TD	2pt.	Pts.
1989—Detroit NFL	8	8	195	103	52.8	1479	5	9	7.58	67.0	33	148	4.5	4	4	...	24
1990—Detroit NFL	11	11	271	142	52.4	1974	13	8	7.28	79.8	47	363	7.7	6	6	...	36
1991—Detroit NFL	8	8	194	116	59.8	1339	5	9	6.90	69.9	25	125	5.0	2	2	...	12
1992—Detroit NFL	10	10	213	123	57.7	1702	9	9	7.99	80.0	21	83	4.0	0	0	...	0
1993—Detroit NFL	10	10	252	157	62.3	1670	6	14	6.63	66.4	45	165	3.7	1	1	...	6
1994—Dallas NFL	7	1	56	33	58.9	470	4	1	8.39	102.5	9	-2	-0.2	0	0	...	0
1995—Philadelphia NFL	15	12	375	215	57.3	2326	8	14	6.20	67.3	32	147	4.6	1	1	0	6
1996—Philadelphia NFL	5	5	134	80	59.7	992	3	5	7.40	74.6	20	31	1.6	0	1	0	6
1997—Philadelphia NFL	5	3	118	68	57.6	869	4	4	7.36	78.0	8	37	4.6	0	0	0	0
1998—Philadelphia NFL	5	4	129	71	55.0	758	2	4	5.88	64.7	5	30	6.0	1	1	0	6
Pro totals (10 years)	84	72	1937	1108	57.2	13579	59	77	7.01	72.6	245	1127	4.6	16	16	0	96

PELFREY, DOUG — K — BENGALS

PERSONAL: Born September 25, 1970, in Fort Thomas, Ky. ... 5-11/185. ... Full name: William Douglas Pelfrey.
HIGH SCHOOL: Scott (Covington, Ky.).
COLLEGE: Kentucky (degree in biology, 1993).
TRANSACTIONS/CAREER NOTES: Selected by Cincinnati Bengals in eighth round (202nd pick overall) of 1993 NFL draft. ... Signed by Bengals (July 19, 1993). ... Granted free agency (February 16, 1996). ... Re-signed by Bengals (June 8, 1996).
PRO STATISTICS: 1995—Punted twice for 52 yards. 1996—Punted once for four yards. 1998—Attempted one pass without a completion.

				KICKING				
Year Team	G	XPM	XPA	FGM	FGA	Lg.	50+	Pts.
1993—Cincinnati NFL	15	13	16	24	31	53	2-3	85
1994—Cincinnati NFL	16	24	25	28	33	54	2-4	108
1995—Cincinnati NFL	16	34	34	29	36	51	1-2	121
1996—Cincinnati NFL	16	41	41	23	28	49	0-0	110
1997—Cincinnati NFL	16	41	43	12	16	46	0-2	77
1998—Cincinnati NFL	16	21	21	19	27	51	2-5	78
Pro totals (6 years)	95	174	180	135	171	54	7-16	579

PENN, CHRIS — WR — BEARS

PERSONAL: Born April 20, 1971, in Lenapah, Okla. ... 6-0/198. ... Full name: Christopher Anthony Penn.
HIGH SCHOOL: Lenapah (Okla.).
COLLEGE: Northwestern Oklahoma A&M, then Tulsa.
TRANSACTIONS/CAREER NOTES: Selected by Kansas City Chiefs in third round (96th pick overall) of 1994 NFL draft. ... Signed by Chiefs (June 2, 1994). ... Granted free agency (February 14, 1997). ... Re-signed by Chiefs (July 18, 1997). ... Traded by Chiefs to Chicago Bears for fifth-round pick (DB Robert Williams) in 1998 draft (August 24, 1997).
PRO STATISTICS: 1997—Rushed once for minus one yard.
SINGLE GAME HIGHS (regular season): Receptions—7 (November 16, 1997, vs. New York Jets); yards—106 (October 4, 1998, vs. Detroit); and touchdown receptions—2 (September 15, 1996, vs. Seattle).
STATISTICAL PLATEAUS: 100-yard receiving games: 1998 (1).

			RECEIVING				PUNT RETURNS				KICKOFF RETURNS				TOTALS		
Year Team	G	GS	No.	Yds.	Avg.	TD	No.	Yds.	Avg.	TD	No.	Yds.	Avg.	TD	TD	2pt.	Pts. Fum.
1994—Kansas City NFL	8	0	3	24	8.0	0	0	0	...	0	9	194	21.6	0	0	0	0 0
1995—Kansas City NFL	2	0	1	12	12.0	0	4	12	3.0	0	2	26	13.0	0	0	0	0 0
1996—Kansas City NFL	16	16	49	628	12.8	5	14	148	10.6	0	0	0	...	0	5	0	30 3
1997—Chicago NFL	14	4	47	576	12.3	3	0	0	...	0	0	0	...	0	3	0	18 1
1998—Chicago NFL	14	1	31	448	14.5	3	0	0	...	0	0	0	...	0	3	1	20 1
Pro totals (5 years)	54	21	131	1688	12.9	11	18	160	8.9	0	11	220	20.0	0	11	1	68 5

PERRY, DARREN — S — CHARGERS

PERSONAL: Born December 29, 1968, in Chesapeake, Va. ... 5-11/199.
HIGH SCHOOL: Deep Creek (Chesapeake, Va.).
COLLEGE: Penn State (degree in business administration/management, 1991).
TRANSACTIONS/CAREER NOTES: Selected by Pittsburgh Steelers in eighth round (203rd pick overall) of 1992 NFL draft. ... Signed by Steelers (July 16, 1992). ... Granted free agency (February 17, 1995). ... Re-signed by Steelers (June 15, 1995). ... Granted unconditional free agency (February 12, 1999). ... Signed by San Diego Chargers (March 19, 1999).
CHAMPIONSHIP GAME EXPERIENCE: Played in AFC championship game (1994, 1995 and 1997 seasons). ... Played in Super Bowl XXX (1995 season).
HONORS: Named defensive back on THE SPORTING NEWS college All-America second team (1991).
PRO STATISTICS: 1992—Recovered one fumble. 1994—Recovered two fumbles. 1995—Fumbled once and recovered two fumbles. 1996—Returned one kickoff for eight yards, fumbled once and recovered two fumbles. 1997—Credited with one sack. 1998—Credited with 1/2 sack, fumbled once and recovered one fumble.

			INTERCEPTIONS			
Year Team	G	GS	No.	Yds.	Avg.	TD
1992—Pittsburgh NFL	16	16	6	69	11.5	0
1993—Pittsburgh NFL	16	16	4	61	15.3	0
1994—Pittsburgh NFL	16	16	7	112	16.0	0
1995—Pittsburgh NFL	16	16	4	71	17.8	0
1996—Pittsburgh NFL	16	16	5	115	23.0	1
1997—Pittsburgh NFL	16	16	4	77	19.3	0
1998—Pittsburgh NFL	14	14	2	69	34.5	0
Pro totals (7 years)	110	110	32	574	17.9	1

PERRY, ED — TE — DOLPHINS

PERSONAL: Born September 1, 1974, in Richmond, Va. ... 6-4/255. ... Full name: Edward Lewis Perry.
HIGH SCHOOL: Highlands Springs (Richmond, Va.).
COLLEGE: James Madison.
TRANSACTIONS/CAREER NOTES: Selected by Miami Dolphins in sixth round (177th pick overall) of 1997 NFL draft. ... Signed by Dolphins (June 13, 1997).
PRO STATISTICS: 1997—Returned one kickoff for seven yards and recovered one fumble.
SINGLE GAME HIGHS (regular season): Receptions—4 (September 13, 1998, vs. Buffalo); yards—59 (November 23, 1998, vs. New England); and touchdown receptions—1 (November 17, 1997, vs. Buffalo).

			RECEIVING				TOTALS			
Year Team	G	GS	No.	Yds.	Avg.	TD	TD	2pt.	Pts.	Fum.
1997—Miami NFL	16	4	11	45	4.1	1	1	0	6	0
1998—Miami NFL	14	5	25	255	10.2	0	0	0	0	0
Pro totals (2 years)	30	9	36	300	8.3	1	1	0	6	0

PERRY, MARLO — LB — BILLS

PERSONAL: Born August 25, 1972, in Forest, Miss. ... 6-4/250. ... Full name: Malcolm Marlo Perry.
HIGH SCHOOL: Central (Forest, Miss.).
COLLEGE: Jackson State.
TRANSACTIONS/CAREER NOTES: Selected by Buffalo Bills in third round (81st pick overall) of 1994 NFL draft. ... Signed by Bills (July 18, 1994). ... Granted free agency (February 14, 1997). ... Re-signed by Bills (June 12, 1997). ... Granted unconditional free agency (February 13, 1998). ... Re-signed by Bills for 1998 season.
PLAYING EXPERIENCE: Buffalo NFL, 1994-1998. ... Games/Games started: 1994 (2/0), 1995 (16/11), 1996 (13/0), 1997 (13/0), 1998 (16/1). Total: 60/12.
PRO STATISTICS: 1996—Intercepted one pass for six yards. 1997—Intercepted one pass for four yards and recovered one fumble.

PERRY, TODD — G — BEARS

PERSONAL: Born November 28, 1970, in Elizabethtown, Ky. ... 6-5/308. ... Full name: Todd Joseph Perry.
HIGH SCHOOL: North Hardin (Elizabethtown, Ky.).
COLLEGE: Kentucky.
TRANSACTIONS/CAREER NOTES: Selected by Chicago Bears in fourth round (97th pick overall) of 1993 NFL draft. ... Signed by Bears (June 16, 1993). ... On injured reserve with back injury (December 19, 1997-remainder of season).
PLAYING EXPERIENCE: Chicago NFL, 1993-1998. ... Games/Games started: 1993 (13/3), 1994 (15/4), 1995 (15/15), 1996 (16/16), 1997 (11/11), 1998 (16/16). Total: 86/65.
PRO STATISTICS: 1996—Recovered one fumble.

PERRY, WILMONT — RB — SAINTS

PERSONAL: Born February 24, 1975, in Franklinton, N.C. ... 6-1/235. ... Full name: Wilmont Darnell Perry.
HIGH SCHOOL: Garner (Franklinton, N.C.).
COLLEGE: Barber-Scotia, N.C. (did not play), then Livingstone (N.C.).
TRANSACTIONS/CAREER NOTES: Selected by New Orleans Saints in fifth round (132nd pick overall) of 1998 NFL draft. ... Signed by Saints (June 11, 1998).
SINGLE GAME HIGHS (regular season): Attempts—12 (December 6, 1998, vs. Dallas); yards—45 (December 27, 1998, vs. Buffalo); and rushing touchdowns—0.

			RUSHING				RECEIVING				TOTALS		
Year Team	G	GS	Att.	Yds.	Avg.	TD	No.	Yds.	Avg.	TD	TD	2pt.	Pts.	Fum.
1998—New Orleans NFL	6	2	30	122	4.1	0	1	2	2.0	0	0	0	0	1

PETER, CHRISTIAN — DT — GIANTS

PERSONAL: Born October 5, 1972, in Locust, N.J. ... 6-3/300. ... Brother of Jason Peter, defensive end, Carolina Panthers.
HIGH SCHOOL: Middletown South (Middleton, N.J.), then Milford (Conn.) Academy.
COLLEGE: Nebraska.
TRANSACTIONS/CAREER NOTES: Selected by New England Patriots in fifth round (149th pick overall) of 1996 NFL draft. ... Patriots released rights (April 24, 1996). ... Signed by New York Giants (January 22, 1997).

Year Team	G	GS	SACKS
1997—New York Giants NFL	7	0	0.5
1998—New York Giants NFL	16	6	1.0
Pro totals (2 years)	23	6	1.5

PETER, JASON — DE — PANTHERS

PERSONAL: Born September 13, 1974, in Locust, N.J. ... 6-4/295. ... Full name: Jason Michael Peter. ... Brother of Christian Peter, defensive tackle, New York Giants.
HIGH SCHOOL: Middletown South (Middleton, N.J.), then Milford (Conn.) Academy.
COLLEGE: Nebraska (degree in communication studies, 1997).
TRANSACTIONS/CAREER NOTES: Selected by Carolina Panthers in first round (14th pick overall) of 1998 NFL draft. ... Signed by Panthers (August 31, 1998).
HONORS: Named defensive tackle on THE SPORTING NEWS college All-America first team (1997).
PRO STATISTICS: 1998—Recovered one fumble.

Year Team	G	GS	SACKS
1998—Carolina NFL	14	11	1.0

PETERS, TYRELL — LB — RAVENS

PERSONAL: Born August 4, 1974, in Oklahoma City. ... 6-0/230.
HIGH SCHOOL: Norman (Okla.).
COLLEGE: Oklahoma.
TRANSACTIONS/CAREER NOTES: Signed as non-drafted free agent by Seattle Seahawks (April 25, 1997). ... Released by Seahawks (August 18, 1997). ... Signed by Baltimore Ravens (August 25, 1997). ... Released by Ravens (October 14, 1997). ... Re-signed by Ravens to practice squad (October 16, 1997). ... Activated (December 19, 1997).
PLAYING EXPERIENCE: Baltimore NFL, 1997 and 1998. ... Games/Games started: 1997 (4/0), 1998 (10/0). Total: 14/0.

PETERSON, ANTHONY — LB — 49ERS

PERSONAL: Born January 23, 1972, in Cleveland. ... 6-1/232. ... Full name: Anthony Wayne Peterson.
HIGH SCHOOL: Ringgold (Monongahela, Pa.).
COLLEGE: Notre Dame.
TRANSACTIONS/CAREER NOTES: Selected by San Francisco 49ers in fifth round (153rd pick overall) of 1994 NFL draft. ... Signed by 49ers (July 20, 1994). ... On injured reserve with hamstring injury (January 18, 1995-remainder of 1994 playoffs). ... Granted unconditional free agency (February 14, 1997). ... Signed by Chicago Bears (March 7, 1997). ... Traded by Bears to 49ers for seventh-round pick (OT Chad Overhauser) in 1998 draft (April 15, 1998).
PLAYING EXPERIENCE: San Francisco NFL, 1994-1996; Chicago NFL, 1997; San Francisco NFL, 1998. ... Games/Games started: 1994 (15/0), 1995 (15/0), 1996 (13/0), 1997 (16/0), 1998 (16/1). Total: 75/1.
CHAMPIONSHIP GAME EXPERIENCE: Member of 49ers for NFC championship game (1994 season); inactive.
PRO STATISTICS: 1997—Recovered one fumble. 1998—Credited with one sack.

PETERSON, TODD — K — SEAHAWKS

PERSONAL: Born February 4, 1970, in Washington, D.C. ... 5-10/171. ... Full name: Joseph Todd Peterson.
HIGH SCHOOL: Valdosta (Ga.).
COLLEGE: Navy, then Georgia (degree in finance, 1992).
TRANSACTIONS/CAREER NOTES: Selected by New York Giants in seventh round (177th pick overall) of 1993 NFL draft. ... Signed by Giants (July 19, 1993). ... Released by Giants (August 24, 1993). ... Signed by New England Patriots to practice squad (November 30, 1993). ... Released by Patriots (December 6, 1993). ... Signed by Atlanta Falcons (May 3, 1994). ... Released by Falcons (August 29, 1994). ... Signed by Arizona Cardinals (October 12, 1994). ... Released by Cardinals (October 24, 1994). ... Signed by Seattle Seahawks (January 17, 1995). ... Granted free agency (February 13, 1998). ... Re-signed by Seahawks for 1998 season. ... Granted unconditional free agency (February 12, 1999). ... Re-signed by Seahawks (March 2, 1999).

				KICKING				
Year Team	G	XPM	XPA	FGM	FGA	Lg.	50+	Pts.
1993—New England NFL					Did not play.			
1994—Arizona NFL	2	4	4	2	4	35	0-0	10
1995—Seattle NFL	16	§40	§40	23	28	49	0-2	109
1996—Seattle NFL	16	27	27	28	34	54	2-3	111
1997—Seattle NFL	16	37	37	22	28	52	1-2	103
1998—Seattle NFL	16	41	41	19	24	51	3-7	98
Pro totals (5 years)	66	149	149	94	118	54	6-14	431

PHENIX, PERRY — S — TITANS

PERSONAL: Born November 14, 1974, in Dallas. ... 5-11/210.
HIGH SCHOOL: Hillcrest (Dallas).
JUNIOR COLLEGE: Trinity Valley Community College (Texas).
COLLEGE: Southern Mississippi.
TRANSACTIONS/CAREER NOTES: Signed as non-drafted free agent by Tennessee Oilers (April 20, 1998).
PLAYING EXPERIENCE: Tennessee NFL, 1998. ... Games/Games started: 15/3.
PRO STATISTICS: 1998—Recovered one fumble for 18 yards.

PHIFER, ROMAN — LB — JETS

PERSONAL: Born March 5, 1968, in Plattsburgh, N.Y. ... 6-2/240. ... Full name: Roman Zubinsky Phifer.
HIGH SCHOOL: South Mecklenburg (Pineville, N.C.).
COLLEGE: UCLA.
TRANSACTIONS/CAREER NOTES: Selected by Los Angeles Rams in second round (31st pick overall) of 1991 NFL draft. ... Signed by Rams (July 19, 1991). ... On injured reserve with broken leg (November 26, 1991-remainder of season). ... Granted unconditional free agency (February 17, 1995). ... Re-signed by Rams (March 22, 1995). ... Rams franchise moved to St. Louis (April 12, 1995). ... Granted unconditional free agency (February 12, 1999). ... Signed by New York Jets (March 9, 1999).
PRO STATISTICS: 1992—Recovered two fumbles. 1993—Recovered two fumbles for 10 yards. 1995—Fumbled once. 1998—Fumbled once.

Year Team	G	GS	No.	Yds.	Avg.	TD	Sacks No.
1991—Los Angeles Rams NFL	12	5	0	0	...	0	2.0
1992—Los Angeles Rams NFL	16	14	1	3	3.0	0	0.0
1993—Los Angeles Rams NFL	16	16	0	0	...	0	0.0
1994—Los Angeles Rams NFL	16	15	2	7	3.5	0	1.5
1995—St. Louis NFL	16	16	3	52	17.3	0	3.0
1996—St. Louis NFL	15	15	0	0	...	0	1.5
1997—St. Louis NFL	16	15	0	0	...	0	2.0
1998—St. Louis NFL	13	13	1	41	41.0	0	6.5
Pro totals (8 years)	120	109	7	103	14.7	0	16.5

PHILLIPS, ANTHONY — CB

PERSONAL: Born October 5, 1970, in Galveston, Texas. ... 6-2/209. ... Full name: Anthony Dwayne Phillips.
HIGH SCHOOL: Ball (Galveston, Texas).
JUNIOR COLLEGE: Trinity Valley Community College (Texas).
COLLEGE: Texas A&M-Kingsville.
TRANSACTIONS/CAREER NOTES: Selected by Atlanta Falcons in third round (72nd pick overall) of 1994 NFL draft. ... Signed by Falcons (July 19, 1994). ... On suspended list (August 11-12, 1995). ... On injured reserve with broken leg (November 17, 1995-remainder of season). ... Granted free agency (February 14, 1997). ... Re-signed by Falcons (April 21, 1997). ... Released by Falcons (August 24, 1997). ... Signed by Minnesota Vikings (March 24, 1998). ... On physically unable to perform list with knee injury (July 27-October 30, 1998). ... On injured reserve with knee injury (December 3, 1998-remainder of season). ... Granted unconditional free agency (February 12, 1999).
PLAYING EXPERIENCE: Atlanta NFL, 1994-1996; Minnesota NFL, 1998. ... Games/Games started: 1994 (5/0), 1995 (6/4), 1996 (7/5), 1998 (2/0). Total: 20/9.
PRO STATISTICS: 1994—Intercepted one pass for no yards. 1995—Intercepted one pass for 43 yards.

PHILLIPS, JOE — DT

PERSONAL: Born July 15, 1963, in Portland, Ore. ... 6-5/305. ... Full name: Joseph Gordon Phillips.
HIGH SCHOOL: Columbia River (Vancouver, Wash.).
JUNIOR COLLEGE: Chemeketa Community College (Ore.).
COLLEGE: Oregon State, then Southern Methodist (degree in psychology, 1985).
TRANSACTIONS/CAREER NOTES: Selected by Minnesota Vikings in fourth round (93rd pick overall) of 1986 NFL draft. ... Signed by Vikings (July 28, 1986). ... Released by Vikings (September 7, 1987). ... Signed as replacement player by San Diego Chargers (September 24, 1987). ... Granted free agency (February 1, 1988). ... Re-signed by Chargers (August 29, 1988). ... On reserve/non-football injury list with head injuries (September 26, 1990-remainder of season). ... Granted free agency (February 1, 1992). ... Rights relinquished by Chargers (September 21, 1992). ... Signed by Kansas City Chiefs (September 30, 1992). ... Granted unconditional free agency (February 17, 1994). ... Re-signed by Chiefs (March 29, 1994). ... Released by Chiefs (February 13, 1998). ... Signed by St. Louis Rams (April 24, 1998). ... Released by Rams (February 18, 1999).
CHAMPIONSHIP GAME EXPERIENCE: Played in AFC championship game (1993 season).
PRO STATISTICS: 1986—Recovered one fumble. 1991—Recovered one fumble. 1992—Recovered one fumble. 1994—Recovered one fumble. 1995—Intercepted one pass for two yards and recovered one fumble. 1997—Recovered one fumble and credited with a safety.

Year Team	G	GS	SACKS
1986—Minnesota NFL	16	1	0.0
1987—San Diego NFL	13	7	5.0
1988—San Diego NFL	16	16	2.0
1989—San Diego NFL	16	15	1.0
1990—San Diego NFL	3	3	0.5
1991—San Diego NFL	16	15	1.0
1992—Kansas City NFL	12	10	2.5
1993—Kansas City NFL	16	16	1.5
1994—Kansas City NFL	16	16	3.0
1995—Kansas City NFL	16	16	4.5
1996—Kansas City NFL	16	16	2.0
1997—Kansas City NFL	15	15	0.5
1998—St. Louis NFL	13	4	0.0
Pro totals (13 years)	184	150	23.5

PHILLIPS, RYAN — LB — GIANTS

PERSONAL: Born February 7, 1974, in Renton, Wash. ... 6-4/252.
HIGH SCHOOL: Auburn (Wash.).
COLLEGE: Idaho.
TRANSACTIONS/CAREER NOTES: Selected by New York Giants in third round (68th pick overall) of 1997 NFL draft. ... Signed by Giants (July 19, 1997).
PLAYING EXPERIENCE: New York Giants NFL, 1997 and 1998. ... Games/Games started: 1997 (10/0), 1998 (16/3). Total: 26/3.
PRO STATISTICS: 1997—Credited with one sack.

PICKENS, CARL — WR — BENGALS

PERSONAL: Born March 23, 1970, in Murphy, N.C. ... 6-2/206. ... Full name: Carl McNally Pickens.
HIGH SCHOOL: Murphy (N.C.).
COLLEGE: Tennessee.
TRANSACTIONS/CAREER NOTES: Selected after junior season by Cincinnati Bengals in second round (31st pick overall) of 1992 NFL draft. ... Signed by Bengals (August 4, 1992). ... Granted free agency (February 17, 1995). ... Tendered offer sheet by Arizona Cardinals (March 17, 1995). ... Offer matched by Bengals (March 24, 1995). ... On injured reserve with groin injury (December 15, 1997-remainder of season). ... Designated by Bengals as franchise player (February 12, 1999).
HONORS: Named wide receiver on THE SPORTING NEWS college All-America first team (1991). ... Played in Pro Bowl (1995 and 1996 seasons).
PRO STATISTICS: 1992—Recovered two fumbles. 1993—Attempted one pass without a completion. 1994—Recovered one fumble. 1995—Rushed once for six yards. 1996—Rushed twice for two yards and attempted one pass with a completion for 12 yards. 1998—Rushed twice for four yards.
SINGLE GAME HIGHS (regular season): Receptions—13 (October 11, 1998, vs. Pittsburgh); yards—204 (October 11, 1998, vs. Pittsburgh); and touchdown receptions—3 (December 1, 1996, vs. Jacksonville).
STATISTICAL PLATEAUS: 100-yard receiving games: 1993 (1), 1994 (5), 1995 (5), 1996 (2), 1997 (1), 1998 (2). Total: 16.
MISCELLANEOUS: Holds Cincinnati Bengals all-time records for most receptions (473) and most touchdown receptions (57).

			RECEIVING				PUNT RETURNS				TOTALS			
Year Team	G	GS	No.	Yds.	Avg.	TD	No.	Yds.	Avg.	TD	TD	2pt.	Pts.	Fum.
1992—Cincinnati NFL	16	10	26	326	12.5	1	18	229	12.7	1	2	...	12	3
1993—Cincinnati NFL	13	12	43	565	13.1	6	4	16	4.0	0	6	...	36	1
1994—Cincinnati NFL	15	15	71	1127	15.9	§11	9	62	6.9	0	11	0	66	1
1995—Cincinnati NFL	16	15	§99	1234	12.5	†17	5	-2	-0.4	0	§17	0	102	1
1996—Cincinnati NFL	16	16	§100	1180	11.8	12	1	2	2.0	0	12	1	74	0
1997—Cincinnati NFL	12	12	52	695	13.4	5	0	0	...	0	5	0	30	1
1998—Cincinnati NFL	16	16	82	1023	12.5	5	0	0	...	0	5	1	32	2
Pro totals (7 years)	104	96	473	6150	13.0	57	37	307	8.3	1	58	2	352	9

PIERSON, PETE — OT — BUCCANEERS

PERSONAL: Born February 4, 1971, in Portland, Ore. ... 6-5/315. ... Full name: Peter Samuel Pierson.
HIGH SCHOOL: David Douglas (Portland, Ore.).
COLLEGE: Washington (degree in political science, 1994).
TRANSACTIONS/CAREER NOTES: Selected by Tampa Bay Buccaneers in fifth round (136th pick overall) of 1994 NFL draft. ... Signed by Buccaneers (July 6, 1994). ... Released by Buccaneers (August 28, 1994). ... Re-signed by Buccaneers to practice squad (September 2, 1994). ... Activated (November 22, 1994). ... Released by Buccaneers (August 18, 1996). ... Re-signed by Buccaneers (September 10, 1996). ... Granted free agency (February 13, 1998). ... Re-signed by Buccaneers (June 11, 1998).
PLAYING EXPERIENCE: Tampa Bay NFL, 1995-1998. ... Games/Games started: 1995 (12/4), 1996 (11/2), 1997 (15/0), 1998 (16/0). Total: 54/6.
PRO STATISTICS: 1995—Recovered one fumble.

PIKE, MARK — DE

PERSONAL: Born December 27, 1963, in Elizabethtown, Ky. ... 6-4/272. ... Full name: Mark Harold Pike.
HIGH SCHOOL: Dixie Heights (Edgewood, Ky.).
COLLEGE: Georgia Tech.
TRANSACTIONS/CAREER NOTES: Selected by Jacksonville Bulls in 1986 USFL territorial draft. ... Selected by Buffalo Bills in seventh round (178th pick overall) of 1986 NFL draft. ... Signed by Bills (July 20, 1986). ... On injured reserve with shoulder injury (August 26, 1986-entire season). ... On injured reserve with leg injury (September 16-November 14, 1987). ... On injured reserve with foot injury (December 8, 1987-remainder of season). ... Granted free agency (February 1, 1991). ... Re-signed by Bills for 1991 season. ... Granted unconditional free agency (February 1-April 1, 1992). ... Re-signed by Bills for 1992 season. ... Granted unconditional free agency (March 1, 1993). ... Re-signed by Bills (May 26, 1993). ... Granted unconditional free agency (February 17, 1995). ... Re-signed by Bills (March 14, 1995). ... Granted unconditional free agency (February 13, 1998). ... Re-signed by Bills (June 1, 1998). ... Announced retirement (January 2, 1999).
PLAYING EXPERIENCE: Buffalo NFL, 1987-1998. ... Games/Games started: 1987 (3/0), 1988 (16/0), 1989 (16/0), 1990 (16/0), 1991 (16/0), 1992 (16/0), 1993 (14/0), 1994 (16/0), 1995 (16/0), 1996 (16/0), 1997 (15/0), 1998 (13/0). Total: 173/0.
CHAMPIONSHIP GAME EXPERIENCE: Played in AFC championship game (1988 and 1990-1993 seasons). ... Played in Super Bowl XXV (1990 season), Super Bowl XXVI (1991 season), Super Bowl XXVII (1992 season) and Super Bowl XXVIII (1993 season).
PRO STATISTICS: 1988—Returned one kickoff for five yards. 1989—Recovered one fumble. 1992—Credited with one sack. 1994—Returned two kickoffs for nine yards. 1995—Returned one kickoff for 20 yards. 1997—Returned one kickoff for 11 yards.

PILGRIM, EVAN G TITANS

PERSONAL: Born August 14, 1972, in Pittsburgh, Calif. ... 6-4/305.
HIGH SCHOOL: Antioch (Calif.).
COLLEGE: Brigham Young.
TRANSACTIONS/CAREER NOTES: Selected by Chicago Bears in third round (87th pick overall) of 1995 NFL draft. ... Signed by Bears (July 19, 1995). ... Inactive for all 16 games (1995). ... Released by Bears (December 9, 1997). ... Signed by Tennessee Oilers (May 14, 1998). ... Released by Oilers (August 30, 1998). ... Re-signed by Oilers (September 9, 1998). ... Released by Oilers (November 4, 1998). ... Re-signed by Oilers (December 16, 1998). ... Oilers franchise renamed Tennessee Titans for 1999 season (December 26, 1998).
PLAYING EXPERIENCE: Chicago NFL, 1996 and 1997; Tennessee NFL, 1998. ... Games/Games started: 1996 (6/0), 1997 (13/6), 1998 (2/0). Total: 21/6.
PRO STATISTICS: 1997—Recovered one fumble.

PITTMAN, JULIAN DT SAINTS

PERSONAL: Born April 22, 1975, in Niceville, Fla. ... 6-4/294.
HIGH SCHOOL: Niceville (Fla.).
COLLEGE: Florida State.
TRANSACTIONS/CAREER NOTES: Selected by New Orleans Saints in fourth round (99th pick overall) of 1998 NFL draft. ... Signed by Saints (July 28, 1998). ... On roster/exempt list (October 30-November 30, 1998).
PLAYING EXPERIENCE: New Orleans NFL, 1998. ... Games/Games started: 2/0.

PITTMAN, KAVIKA DE COWBOYS

PERSONAL: Born October 9, 1974, in Frankfurt, West Germany. ... 6-6/267. ... Name pronounced kah-VEEK-ah.
HIGH SCHOOL: Leesville (La.).
COLLEGE: McNeese State.
TRANSACTIONS/CAREER NOTES: Selected by Dallas Cowboys in second round (37th pick overall) of 1996 NFL draft. ... Signed by Cowboys (July 16, 1996).
PRO STATISTICS: 1997—Returned one kickoff for no yards. 1998—Recovered two fumbles for seven yards.

Year—Team	G	GS	SACKS
1996—Dallas NFL	15	0	0.0
1997—Dallas NFL	15	0	1.0
1998—Dallas NFL	15	15	6.0
Pro totals (3 years)	45	15	7.0

PITTMAN, MICHAEL RB CARDINALS

PERSONAL: Born August 14, 1975, in New Orleans. ... 6-0/214.
HIGH SCHOOL: Mira Mesa (San Diego).
COLLEGE: Fresno State.
TRANSACTIONS/CAREER NOTES: Selected by Arizona Cardinals in fourth round (95th pick overall) of 1998 NFL draft. ... Signed by Cardinals (May 20, 1998).
PRO STATISTICS: 1998—Recovered one fumble.
SINGLE GAME HIGHS (regular season): Attempts—17 (October 11, 1998, vs. Chicago); yards—56 (October 11, 1998, vs. Chicago); and rushing touchdowns—0.

| | | | RUSHING |||| KICKOFF RETURNS |||| TOTALS ||||
Year Team	G	GS	Att.	Yds.	Avg.	TD	No.	Yds.	Avg.	TD	TD	2pt.	Pts.	Fum.
1998—Arizona NFL	15	0	29	91	3.1	0	4	84	21.0	0	0	0	0	1

PLAYER, SCOTT P CARDINALS

PERSONAL: Born December 17, 1969, in St. Augustine, Fla. ... 6-0/220.
HIGH SCHOOL: St. Augustine (Fla.).
JUNIOR COLLEGE: Florida Community College.
COLLEGE: Flagler College (Fla.), then Florida State (degree in education).
TRANSACTIONS/CAREER NOTES: Played with Birmingham Barracudas of CFL (1995). ... Granted free agency (March 7, 1996). ... Signed as non-drafted free agent by Arizona Cardinals (April 23, 1996). ... Released by Cardinals (August 19, 1996). ... Signed by New York Giants (February 14, 1997). ... Assigned by Giants to Frankfurt Galaxy in 1997 World League enhancement allocation program (February 18, 1997). ... Released by Giants (August 24, 1997). ... Signed by New York Jets to practice squad (August 26, 1997). ... Released by Jets (August 28, 1997). ... Re-signed by Cardinals (March 3, 1998).
PRO STATISTICS: 1995—Attempted two passes with one completion for 52 yards.

| | | PUNTING ||||||
Year Team	G	No.	Yds.	Avg.	Net avg.	In. 20	Blk.
1995—Birmingham CFL	18	143	6247	43.7	36.5	...	...
1996—			Did not play.				
1997—Frankfurt W.L.	...	60	2617	43.6	34.3	17	1
1998—Arizona NFL	16	81	3378	41.7	35.9	12	∞1
W.L. totals (1 year)	...	60	2617	43.6	34.3	17	1
CFL totals (1 year)	18	143	6247	43.7	36.5	...	...
NFL totals (1 year)	16	81	3378	41.7	35.9	12	1
Pro totals (3 years)	...	284	12242	43.1	35.9	29	2

PLEASANT, ANTHONY — DE — JETS

PERSONAL: Born January 27, 1968, in Century, Fla. ... 6-5/280. ... Full name: Anthony Devon Pleasant.
HIGH SCHOOL: Century (Fla.).
COLLEGE: Tennessee State.
TRANSACTIONS/CAREER NOTES: Selected by Cleveland Browns in third round (73rd pick overall) of 1990 NFL draft. ... Signed by Browns (July 22, 1990). ... Browns franchise moved to Baltimore and renamed Ravens for 1996 season (March 11, 1996). ... Granted unconditional free agency (February 14, 1997). ... Signed by Atlanta Falcons (June 21, 1997). ... Released by Falcons (February 11, 1998). ... Signed by New York Jets (March 12, 1998).
CHAMPIONSHIP GAME EXPERIENCE: Played in AFC championship game (1998 season).
PRO STATISTICS: 1991—Recovered one fumble for four yards. 1993—Credited with one safety. 1996—Recovered one fumble for 36 yards.

Year Team	G	GS	SACKS
1990—Cleveland NFL	16	7	3.5
1991—Cleveland NFL	16	7	2.5
1992—Cleveland NFL	16	14	4.0
1993—Cleveland NFL	16	13	11.0
1994—Cleveland NFL	14	14	4.5
1995—Cleveland NFL	16	16	8.0
1996—Baltimore NFL	12	12	4.0
1997—Atlanta NFL	11	0	0.5
1998—New York Jets NFL	16	15	6.0
Pro totals (9 years)	133	98	44.0

PLUMMER, JAKE — QB — CARDINALS

PERSONAL: Born December 19, 1974, in Boise, Idaho. ... 6-2/197. ... Full name: Jason Steven Plummer.
HIGH SCHOOL: Capital (Boise, Idaho).
COLLEGE: Arizona State.
TRANSACTIONS/CAREER NOTES: Selected by Arizona Cardinals in second round (42nd pick overall) of 1997 NFL draft. ... Signed by Cardinals (July 14, 1997).
HONORS: Named quarterback on The Sporting News college All-America second team (1996).
PRO STATISTICS: 1997—Caught one pass for two yards, fumbled six times and recovered one fumble for minus one yard. 1998—Fumbled 12 times and recovered three fumbles for minus two yards.
SINGLE GAME HIGHS (regular season): Attempts—56 (November 15, 1998, vs. Dallas); completions—32 (December 20, 1998, vs. New Orleans); yards—465 (November 15, 1998, vs. Dallas); and touchdown passes—4 (December 7, 1997, vs. Washington).
STATISTICAL PLATEAUS: 300-yard passing games: 1997 (2), 1998 (2). Total: 4.
MISCELLANEOUS: Regular-season record as starting NFL quarterback: 12-13 (.480). ... Postseason record as starting NFL quarterback: 1-1 (.500).

			PASSING							RUSHING				TOTALS		
Year Team	G	GS	Att.	Cmp.	Pct.	Yds.	TD	Int.	Avg.	Rat.	Att.	Yds.	Avg.	TD	TD	2pt.	Pts.
1997—Arizona NFL	10	9	296	157	53.0	2203	15	15	7.44	73.1	39	216	5.5	2	2	1	14
1998—Arizona NFL	16	16	547	324	59.2	3737	17	20	6.83	75.0	51	217	4.3	4	4	0	24
Pro totals (2 years)	26	25	843	481	57.1	5940	32	35	7.05	74.3	90	433	4.8	6	6	1	38

POLLARD, MARCUS — TE — COLTS

PERSONAL: Born February 8, 1972, in Valley, Ala. ... 6-4/257. ... Full name: Marcus LaJuan Pollard.
HIGH SCHOOL: Valley (Ala.).
JUNIOR COLLEGE: Seward County Community College, Kan. (did not play football).
COLLEGE: Bradley (did not play football).
TRANSACTIONS/CAREER NOTES: Signed as non-drafted free agent by Indianapolis Colts (January 24, 1995). ... Released by Colts (August 22, 1995). ... Re-signed by Colts to practice squad (August 28, 1995). ... Activated (October 10, 1995). ... Granted free agency (February 13, 1998). ... Tendered offer sheet by Philadelphia Eagles (March 4, 1998). ... Offer matched by Colts (March 9, 1998).
CHAMPIONSHIP GAME EXPERIENCE: Played in AFC championship game (1995 season).
PRO STATISTICS: 1996—Recovered one fumble. 1998—Returned one kickoff for four yards.
SINGLE GAME HIGHS (regular season): Receptions—6 (September 13, 1998, vs. New England); yards—65 (December 27, 1998, vs. Carolina); and touchdown receptions—1 (December 27, 1998, vs. Carolina).
MISCELLANEOUS: Played basketball during college.

			RECEIVING				TOTALS			
Year Team	G	GS	No.	Yds.	Avg.	TD	TD	2pt.	Pts.	Fum.
1995—Indianapolis NFL	8	0	0	0	...	0	0	0	0	0
1996—Indianapolis NFL	16	4	6	86	14.3	1	1	0	6	0
1997—Indianapolis NFL	16	5	10	116	11.6	0	0	1	2	0
1998—Indianapolis NFL	16	11	24	309	12.9	4	4	†2	28	0
Pro totals (4 years)	56	20	40	511	12.8	5	5	3	36	0

PONDS, ANTWUANE — LB — REDSKINS

PERSONAL: Born June 29, 1975, in Harrisburg, Pa. ... 6-2/239.
HIGH SCHOOL: Paxon (Jacksonville).
COLLEGE: Syracuse.
TRANSACTIONS/CAREER NOTES: Selected by Washington Redskins in seventh round (206th pick overall) of 1998 NFL draft. ... Signed by Redskins (June 3, 1998). ... On injured reserve with knee injury (November 25, 1998-remainder of season).
PLAYING EXPERIENCE: Washington NFL, 1998. ... Games/Games started: 3/0.

POOLE, KEITH — WR — SAINTS

PERSONAL: Born June 18, 1974, in San Jose, Calif. ... 6-0/193. ... Full name: Keith Robert Strohmaier Poole.
HIGH SCHOOL: Clovis (Calif.).
COLLEGE: Arizona State.
TRANSACTIONS/CAREER NOTES: Selected by New Orleans Saints in fourth round (116th pick overall) of 1997 NFL draft. ... Signed by Saints (June 10, 1997).
SINGLE GAME HIGHS (regular season): Receptions—5 (November 1, 1998, vs. Carolina); yards—154 (October 18, 1998, vs. Atlanta); and touchdown receptions—2 (October 18, 1998, vs. Atlanta).
STATISTICAL PLATEAUS: 100-yard receiving games: 1998 (1).

				RECEIVING				TOTALS			
Year Team	G	GS	No.	Yds.	Avg.	TD	TD	2pt.	Pts.	Fum.
1997—New Orleans NFL	3	0	4	98	24.5	2	2	0	12	0
1998—New Orleans NFL	15	4	24	509	21.2	2	2	0	12	0
Pro totals (2 years)	18	4	28	607	21.7	4	4	0	24	0

POOLE, TYRONE — DB — COLTS

PERSONAL: Born February 3, 1972, in LaGrange, Ga. ... 5-8/188.
HIGH SCHOOL: LaGrange (Ga.).
COLLEGE: Fort Valley (Ga.) State.
TRANSACTIONS/CAREER NOTES: Selected by Carolina Panthers in first round (22nd pick overall) of 1995 NFL draft. ... Signed by Panthers (July 15, 1995). ... Traded by Panthers to Indianapolis Colts for second-round pick (OT Chris Terry) in 1999 draft (July 22, 1998).
CHAMPIONSHIP GAME EXPERIENCE: Played in NFC championship game (1996 season).
PRO STATISTICS: 1996—Recovered one fumble. 1997—Returned one kickoff for five yards and recovered three fumbles for 11 yards.

			INTERCEPTIONS				SACKS	PUNT RETURNS				TOTALS			
Year Team	G	GS	No.	Yds.	Avg.	TD	No.	No.	Yds.	Avg.	TD	TD	2pt.	Pts.	Fum.
1995—Carolina NFL	16	13	2	8	4.0	0	2.0	0	0	...	0	0	0	0	0
1996—Carolina NFL	15	15	1	35	35.0	0	0.0	3	26	8.7	0	0	0	0	0
1997—Carolina NFL	16	16	2	0	0.0	0	1.0	26	191	7.3	0	0	0	0	3
1998—Indianapolis NFL	15	15	1	0	0.0	0	0.0	12	107	8.9	0	0	0	0	0
Pro totals (4 years)	62	59	6	43	7.2	0	3.0	41	324	7.9	0	0	0	0	3

POPE, MARQUEZ — DB — BROWNS

PERSONAL: Born October 29, 1970, in Nashville. ... 5-11/193. ... Full name: Marquez Phillips Pope. ... Name pronounced Mar-KEZ.
HIGH SCHOOL: Long Beach (Calif.) Polytechnic.
COLLEGE: Fresno State (degree in speech and mass communication, 1998).
TRANSACTIONS/CAREER NOTES: Selected by San Diego Chargers in second round (33rd pick overall) of 1992 NFL draft. ... Signed by Chargers (July 16, 1992). ... On reserve non-football illness list with virus (September 1-28, 1992). ... On practice squad (September 28-November 7, 1992). ... Traded by Chargers to Los Angeles Rams for sixth-round pick (G Troy Sienkiewicz) in 1995 draft (April 11, 1994). ... Granted free agency (February 17, 1995). ... Tendered offer sheet by San Francisco 49ers (April 9, 1995). ... Rams declined to match offer (April 12, 1995); received second-round pick (OL Jesse James) in 1995 draft as compensation. ... Granted unconditional free agency (February 12, 1999). ... Signed by Cleveland Browns (March 8, 1999).
CHAMPIONSHIP GAME EXPERIENCE: Played in NFC championship game (1997 season).
PRO STATISTICS: 1993—Credited with $1/2$ sack. 1996—Recovered one fumble for four yards.

			INTERCEPTIONS			
Year Team	G	GS	No.	Yds.	Avg.	TD
1992—San Diego NFL	7	0	0	0	...	0
1993—San Diego NFL	16	1	2	14	7.0	0
1994—Los Angeles Rams NFL	16	16	3	66	22.0	0
1995—San Francisco NFL	16	16	1	-7	-7.0	0
1996—San Francisco NFL	16	16	6	98	16.3	1
1997—San Francisco NFL	5	5	1	7	7.0	0
1998—San Francisco NFL	6	3	1	0	0.0	0
Pro totals (7 years)	82	57	14	178	12.7	1

POPSON, TED — TE — CHIEFS

PERSONAL: Born September 10, 1966, in Granada Hills, Calif. ... 6-4/245. ... Full name: Theodore Paul Popson.
HIGH SCHOOL: Tahoe Truckee (Truckee, Calif.).
JUNIOR COLLEGE: Marin Community College (Calif.).
COLLEGE: Portland State.
TRANSACTIONS/CAREER NOTES: Selected by New York Giants in 11th round (306th pick overall) of 1991 NFL draft. ... Signed by Giants for 1991 season. ... Selected by London Monarchs in 1992 World League draft. ... Released by Giants (August 31, 1992). ... Re-signed by Giants to practice squad (September 2, 1992). ... Released by Giants (October 7, 1992). ... Signed by San Francisco 49ers (April 30, 1993). ... Released by 49ers (August 27, 1993). ... Re-signed by 49ers to practice squad (August 31, 1993). ... Released by 49ers (February 15, 1996). ... Re-signed by 49ers (June 13, 1996). ... Granted unconditional free agency (February 14, 1997). ... Signed by Kansas City Chiefs (June 17, 1997). ... On injured reserve with head injury (December 17, 1998-remainder of season).
CHAMPIONSHIP GAME EXPERIENCE: Played in NFC championship game (1994 season). ... Member of Super Bowl championship team (1994 season).
PRO STATISTICS: W.L.: 1992—Returned three kickoffs for 31 yards. NFL: 1995—Fumbled once. 1996—Recovered one fumble.

SINGLE GAME HIGHS (regular season): Receptions—8 (October 20, 1996, vs. Cincinnati); yards—116 (October 20, 1996, vs. Cincinnati); and touchdown receptions—2 (October 20, 1996, vs. Cincinnati).
STATISTICAL PLATEAUS: 100-yard receiving games: 1996 (1).

			RECEIVING				TOTALS			
Year Team	G	GS	No.	Yds.	Avg.	TD	TD	2pt.	Pts.	Fum.
1991—New York Giants NFL						Did not play.				
1992—London W.L.	10	5	4	24	6.0	0	0	...	0	0
1993—San Francisco NFL						Did not play.				
1994—San Francisco NFL	16	1	13	141	10.8	0	0	0	0	0
1995—San Francisco NFL	12	0	16	128	8.0	0	0	0	0	1
1996—San Francisco NFL	15	6	26	301	11.6	6	6	0	36	0
1997—Kansas City NFL	13	12	35	320	9.1	2	2	0	12	0
1998—Kansas City NFL	12	1	13	90	6.9	0	0	0	0	0
W.L. totals (1 year)	10	5	4	24	6.0	0	0	0	0	0
NFL totals (5 years)	68	20	103	980	9.5	8	8	0	48	1
Pro totals (6 years)	78	25	107	1004	9.4	8	8	0	48	1

PORCHER, ROBERT — DE — LIONS

PERSONAL: Born July 30, 1969, in Wando, S.C. ... 6-3/270. ... Full name: Robert Porcher III. ... Name pronounced por-SHAY.
HIGH SCHOOL: Cainhoy (Huger, S.C.).
COLLEGE: Tennessee State, then South Carolina State (degree in criminal justice).
TRANSACTIONS/CAREER NOTES: Selected by Detroit Lions in first round (26th pick overall) of 1992 NFL draft. ... Signed by Lions (July 25, 1992). ... Granted unconditional free agency (February 16, 1996). ... Re-signed by Lions (March 29, 1996). ... Granted unconditional free agency (February 14, 1997). ... Re-signed by Lions (March 4, 1997).
PRO STATISTICS: 1994—Recovered one fumble. 1996—Recovered two fumbles.

Year Team	G	GS	SACKS
1992—Detroit NFL	16	1	1.0
1993—Detroit NFL	16	4	8.5
1994—Detroit NFL	15	15	3.0
1995—Detroit NFL	16	16	5.0
1996—Detroit NFL	16	16	10.0
1997—Detroit NFL	16	15	12.5
1998—Detroit NFL	16	16	11.5
Pro totals (7 years)	111	83	51.5

PORTER, DARYL — CB — BILLS

PERSONAL: Born January 16, 1974, in Fort Lauderdale, Fla. ... 5-9/190. ... Full name: Daryl Maurice Porter. ... Cousin of Bennie Blades, cornerback with Detroit Lions (1988-96) and Seattle Seahawks (1997); and cousin of Brian Blades, wide receiver, Seattle Seahawks.
HIGH SCHOOL: St. Thomas Aquinas (Fort Lauderdale, Fla.).
COLLEGE: Boston College.
TRANSACTIONS/CAREER NOTES: Selected by Pittsburgh Steelers in sixth round (186th pick overall) of 1997 NFL draft. ... Signed by Steelers (June 6, 1997). ... Released by Steelers (August 19, 1997). ... Re-signed by Steelers to practice squad (August 26, 1997). ... Released by Steelers (October 20, 1997). ... Signed by Detroit Lions (October 21, 1997). ... Released by Lions (August 24, 1998). ... Signed by Steelers to practice squad (September 1, 1998). ... Signed by Buffalo Bills off Steelers practice squad (December 16, 1998).
PLAYING EXPERIENCE: Detroit NFL, 1997; Buffalo NFL, 1998. ... Games/Games started: 1997 (7/0), 1998 (2/0). Total: 9/0.

PORTILLA, JOSE — OT — FALCONS

PERSONAL: Born September 11, 1972, in Houston. ... 6-6/315. ... Full name: Jose Casiano Portilla.
HIGH SCHOOL: MacArthur (Houston).
JUNIOR COLLEGE: Ricks College (Idaho).
COLLEGE: Arizona.
TRANSACTIONS/CAREER NOTES: Signed as non-drafted free agent by Atlanta Falcons (April 20, 1998).
PLAYING EXPERIENCE: Atlanta NFL, 1998. ... Games/Games started: 16/0.
CHAMPIONSHIP GAME EXPERIENCE: Played in NFC championship game (1998 season). ... Played in Super Bowl XXXIII (1998 season).
PRO STATISTICS: 1998—Recovered one fumble.

POSEY, JEFF — DE — 49ERS

PERSONAL: Born August 14, 1975, in Bassfield, Miss. ... 6-4/240.
HIGH SCHOOL: Greenville (Miss.).
JUNIOR COLLEGE: Pearl River Community College (Miss.).
COLLEGE: Southern Mississippi.
TRANSACTIONS/CAREER NOTES: Signed as non-drafted free agent by San Francisco 49ers (May 2, 1997) ... Released by 49ers (August 19, 1997). ... Re-signed by 49ers to practice squad (August 25, 1997).
PLAYING EXPERIENCE: San Francisco NFL, 1998. ... Games/Games started: 16/0.
PRO STATISTICS: 1998—Credited with $1/2$ sack.

POTTS, ROOSEVELT — FB — DOLPHINS

PERSONAL: Born January 8, 1971, in Rayville, La. ... 6-0/250. ... Full name: Roosevelt Bernard Potts. ... Cousin of Reggie Burnette, linebacker with Tampa Bay Buccaneers (1991-93).
HIGH SCHOOL: Rayville (La.).
COLLEGE: Northeast Louisiana.
TRANSACTIONS/CAREER NOTES: Selected by Indianapolis Colts in second round (49th pick overall) of 1993 NFL draft. ... Signed by Colts (July 20, 1993). ... On injured reserve with knee injury (December 19, 1995-remainder of season). ... Granted free agency (February 16, 1996). ... Suspended by NFL for violating league substance abuse policy (August 19, 1996-July 15, 1997). ... Re-signed by Colts (August 11, 1997). ... Released by Colts (November 4, 1997). ... Signed by Miami Dolphins (November 10, 1997). ... Granted unconditional free agency (February 13, 1998). ... Signed by Baltimore Ravens (March 4, 1998). ... Granted unconditional free agency (February 12, 1999). ... Signed by Dolphins (March 29, 1999).
PRO STATISTICS: 1993—Recovered two fumbles. 1994—Recovered one fumble. 1997—Returned one kickoff for 16 yards. 1998—Returned one kickoff for three yards and recovered two fumbles.
SINGLE GAME HIGHS (regular season): Attempts—23 (October 31, 1991, vs. New England); yards—113 (October 10, 1993, vs. Dallas); and rushing touchdowns—1 (September 11, 1994, vs. Tampa Bay).
STATISTICAL PLATEAUS: 100-yard rushing games: 1993 (2).

				RUSHING				RECEIVING				TOTALS			
Year Team	G	GS	Att.	Yds.	Avg.	TD	No.	Yds.	Avg.	TD	TD	2pt.	Pts.	Fum.
1993—Indianapolis NFL	16	15	179	711	4.0	0	26	189	7.3	0	0	...	0	8
1994—Indianapolis NFL	16	15	77	336	4.4	1	26	251	9.7	1	2	0	12	5
1995—Indianapolis NFL	15	15	65	309	4.8	0	21	228	10.9	1	1	0	6	0
1996—Indianapolis NFL								Did not play.						
1997—Indianapolis NFL	1	0	1	1	1.0	0	0	0	...	0	0	0	0	0
—Miami NFL	6	1	1	3	3.0	0	3	27	9.0	0	0	0	0	0
1998—Baltimore NFL	16	15	36	115	3.2	0	30	168	5.6	2	2	0	12	4
Pro totals (5 years)	70	61	359	1475	4.1	1	106	863	8.1	4	5	0	30	17

POUNDS, DARRYL — CB — REDSKINS

PERSONAL: Born July 21, 1972, in Fort Worth, Texas. ... 5-10/189.
HIGH SCHOOL: South Pike (Magnolia, Miss.).
COLLEGE: Nicholls State.
TRANSACTIONS/CAREER NOTES: Selected by Washington Redskins in third round (68th pick overall) of 1995 NFL draft. ... Signed by Redskins (May 26, 1995). ... On physically unable to perform list with back injury (August 22-October 17, 1995). ... Granted free agency (February 13, 1998). ... Re-signed by Redskins (April 9, 1998).
PRO STATISTICS: 1995—Fumbled once. 1996—Recovered one fumble. 1997—Credited with two sacks and recovered three fumbles for 18 yards and one touchdown. 1998—Credited with ½ sack and recovered one fumble.

			INTERCEPTIONS			
Year Team	G	GS	No.	Yds.	Avg.	TD
1995—Washington NFL	9	0	1	26	26.0	0
1996—Washington NFL	12	1	2	11	5.5	0
1997—Washington NFL	16	0	3	42	14.0	1
1998—Washington NFL	16	3	0	0	...	0
Pro totals (4 years)	53	4	6	79	13.2	1

POURDANESH, SHAR — OT — REDSKINS

PERSONAL: Born July 19, 1970, in Tehran, Iran. ... 6-6/312. ... Full name: Shahriar Pourdanesh. ... Name pronounced Shar-E-are PORE-donish.
HIGH SCHOOL: University (Irvine, Calif.).
COLLEGE: Nevada-Reno.
TRANSACTIONS/CAREER NOTES: Signed as non-drafted free agent by Cleveland Browns (April 1993). ... Released by Browns before 1993 season. ... Signed by Baltimore of CFL (1994). ... Signed by Washington Redskins (March 20, 1995).
PLAYING EXPERIENCE: Baltimore CFL, 1994 and 1995; Washington NFL, 1996-1998. ... Games/Games started: 1994 (18/18), 1995 (14/14), 1996 (16/8), 1997 (16/14), 1998 (16/15). Total CFL: 32/32. Total NFL: 48/37. Total Pro: 80/69.
CHAMPIONSHIP GAME EXPERIENCE: Played in Grey Cup (1994).
HONORS: Named tackle on CFL All-Star team (1994). ... Named CFL Most Outstanding Offensive Lineman (1994).
PRO STATISTICS: 1998—Fumbled once and recovered one fumble for minus four yards.

POWELL, CRAIG — LB

PERSONAL: Born November 13, 1971, in Youngstown, Ohio. ... 6-4/235. ... Full name: Craig Steven Powell.
HIGH SCHOOL: Rayen (Youngstown, Ohio).
COLLEGE: Ohio State.
TRANSACTIONS/CAREER NOTES: Selected after junior season by Cleveland Browns in first round (30th pick overall) of 1995 NFL draft. ... Signed by Browns (July 31, 1995). ... On injured reserve with knee injury (October 4, 1995-remainder of season). ... Browns franchise moved to Baltimore and renamed Ravens for 1996 season (March 11, 1996). ... Released by Ravens (June 2, 1997). ... Signed by New York Jets (October 14, 1998). ... On injured reserve with knee injury (October 27, 1998-remainder of season). ... Released by Jets after 1998 season.
PLAYING EXPERIENCE: Cleveland NFL, 1995; Baltimore NFL, 1996; New York Jets NFL, 1998. ... Games/Games started: 1995 (3/0), 1996 (9/0), 1998 (2/0). Total: 14/0.

PRESTON, ROELL   WR/KR

PERSONAL: Born June 23, 1972, in Miami. ... 5-10/185. ... Name pronounced ROW-ell.
HIGH SCHOOL: Hialeah (Fla.).
JUNIOR COLLEGE: Northwest Mississippi Community College.
COLLEGE: Mississippi.
TRANSACTIONS/CAREER NOTES: Selected by Atlanta Falcons in fifth round (145th pick overall) of 1995 NFL draft. ... Signed by Falcons (July 13, 1995). ... Released by Falcons (August 24, 1997). ... Signed by Green Bay Packers (November 12, 1997). ... Released by Packers (November 18, 1997). ... Signed by Washington Redskins (December 3, 1997). ... Inactive for one game with Redskins (1997). ... Released by Redskins (December 9, 1997). ... Signed by Packers (February 26, 1998). ... Granted free agency (February 12, 1999).
HONORS: Played in Pro Bowl (1998 season).
PRO STATISTICS: 1995—Fumbled once. 1997—Returned one punt for no yards. 1998—Recovered one fumble.
SINGLE GAME HIGHS (regular season): Receptions—9 (October 13, 1996, vs. Houston); yards—79 (November 26, 1995, vs. Arizona); and touchdown receptions—1 (September 29, 1996, vs. San Francisco).

			RECEIVING				PUNT RETURNS				KICKOFF RETURNS				TOTALS			
Year Team	G	GS	No.	Yds.	Avg.	TD	No.	Yds.	Avg.	TD	No.	Yds.	Avg.	TD	TD	2pt.	Pts.	Fum.
1995—Atlanta NFL	14	0	7	129	18.4	1	0	0	...	0	30	627	20.9	0	1	0	6	1
1996—Atlanta NFL	15	2	21	208	9.9	1	0	0	...	0	32	681	21.3	0	1	0	6	0
1997—Green Bay NFL	1	0	0	0	...	0	1	0	0.0	0	7	211	30.1	0	0	0	0	0
1998—Green Bay NFL	16	0	2	23	11.5	0	44	398	9.0	1	57	1497	26.3	†2	3	0	18	7
Pro totals (4 years)	46	2	30	360	12.0	2	45	398	8.8	1	126	3016	23.9	2	5	0	30	8

PRICE, MARCUS   G/OT   CHARGERS

PERSONAL: Born March 3, 1972, in Port Arthur, Texas. ... 6-6/321. ... Full name: Marcus Raymond Price.
HIGH SCHOOL: Lincoln (Port Arthur, Texas).
COLLEGE: Louisiana State.
TRANSACTIONS/CAREER NOTES: Selected by Jacksonville Jaguars in sixth round (172nd pick overall) of 1995 NFL draft. ... Signed by Jaguars (June 1, 1995). ... On injured reserve with ankle injury (August 19, 1995-entire season). ... Released by Jaguars (August 25, 1996). ... Signed by Denver Broncos to practice squad (December 3, 1996). ... Released by Broncos (December 30, 1996). ... Signed by Jaguars (January 31, 1997). ... Released by Jaguars (August 19, 1997). ... Re-signed by Jaguars to practice squad (October 28, 1997). ... Signed by San Diego Chargers off Jaguars practice squad (November 26, 1997).
PLAYING EXPERIENCE: San Diego NFL, 1997 and 1998. ... Games/Games started: 1997 (2/0), 1998 (10/0). Total: 12/0.

PRICE, SHAWN   DE   BILLS

PERSONAL: Born March 28, 1970, in Van Nuys, Calif. ... 6-5/285. ... Full name: Shawn Sterling Price.
HIGH SCHOOL: North Tahoe (Nev.).
JUNIOR COLLEGE: Sierra College (Calif.).
COLLEGE: Pacific.
TRANSACTIONS/CAREER NOTES: Signed as non-drafted free agent by Tampa Bay Buccaneers (April 29, 1993). ... Released by Buccaneers (August 30, 1993). ... Re-signed by Buccaneers to practice squad (August 31, 1993). ... Activated (November 5, 1993). ... Selected by Carolina Panthers in NFL expansion draft (February 15, 1995). ... Granted unconditional free agency (February 16, 1996). ... Signed by Buffalo Bills (April 12, 1996). ... Granted unconditional free agency (February 13, 1998). ... Re-signed by Bills (March 9, 1998).

Year Team	G	GS	SACKS
1993—Tampa Bay NFL	9	6	3.0
1994—Tampa Bay NFL	6	0	0.0
1995—Carolina NFL	16	0	1.0
1996—Buffalo NFL	15	0	0.0
1997—Buffalo NFL	10	0	0.0
1998—Buffalo NFL	14	2	5.0
Pro totals (6 years)	70	8	9.0

PRIOR, ANTHONY   CB

PERSONAL: Born March 27, 1970, in Mira Loma, Calif. ... 5-11/186. ... Full name: Anthony Eugene Prior.
HIGH SCHOOL: Rubidoux (Riverside, Calif.).
COLLEGE: Washington State.
TRANSACTIONS/CAREER NOTES: Selected by New York Giants in ninth round (238th pick overall) of 1992 NFL draft. ... Signed by Giants (July 21, 1992). ... Released by Giants (August 25, 1992). ... Signed by New York Jets to practice squad (September 9, 1992). ... Released by Jets (September 29, 1992). ... Re-signed by Jets for 1993 season. ... Released by Jets (March 1, 1996). ... Signed by Cincinnati Bengals (March 12, 1996). ... Released by Bengals (July 15, 1996). ... Signed by San Francisco 49ers (July 19, 1996). ... Released by 49ers (August 20, 1996). ... Signed by Minnesota Vikings (December 4, 1996). ... Granted unconditional free agency (February 14, 1997). ... Re-signed by Vikings (April 9, 1997). ... On injured reserve with groin injury (November 29, 1997-remainder of season). ... Released by Vikings (February 2, 1998). ... Signed by Kansas City Chiefs (April 6, 1998). ... Released by Chiefs (August 25, 1998). ... Signed by Oakland Raiders (November 4, 1998). ... Released by Raiders (December 2, 1998).
PRO STATISTICS: 1993—Recovered one fumble. 1998—Returned one punt for no yards and fumbled once.

			KICKOFF RETURNS				TOTALS			
Year Team	G	GS	No.	Yds.	Avg.	TD	TD	2pt.	Pts.	Fum.
1992—New York Jets NFL						Did not play.				
1993—New York Jets NFL	16	0	9	126	14.0	0	0	...	0	0
1994—New York Jets NFL	13	0	16	316	19.8	0	0	0	0	0
1995—New York Jets NFL	11	0	0	0	...	0	0	0	0	0
1996—Minnesota NFL	3	0	0	0	...	0	0	0	0	0
1997—Minnesota NFL	12	0	0	0	...	0	0	0	0	0
1998—Oakland NFL	4	0	0	0	...	0	0	0	0	1
Pro totals (6 years)	59	0	25	442	17.7	0	0	0	0	1

PRIOR, MIKE — S

PERSONAL: Born November 14, 1963, in Chicago Heights, Ill. ... 6-0/208. ... Full name: Michael Robert Prior.
HIGH SCHOOL: Marian Catholic (Chicago Heights, Ill.).
COLLEGE: Illinois State (degree in business administration, 1985).
TRANSACTIONS/CAREER NOTES: Selected by Memphis Showboats in fourth round (60th pick overall) of 1985 USFL draft. ... Selected by Tampa Bay Buccaneers in seventh round (176th pick overall) of 1985 NFL draft. ... Signed by Buccaneers (June 10, 1985). ... On injured reserve with fractured wrist (August 25-September 28, 1986). ... Released by Buccaneers (September 29, 1986). ... Signed by Indianapolis Colts (May 11, 1987). ... Released by Colts (August 31, 1987). ... Re-signed as replacement player by Colts (September 23, 1987). ... On injured reserve with abdomen injury (October 11-December 6, 1991). ... Granted unconditional free agency (March 1, 1993). ... Signed by Green Bay Packers (April 16, 1993). ... Released by Packers (July 27, 1994). ... Re-signed by Packers (July 27, 1994). ... Granted unconditional free agency (February 17, 1995). ... Re-signed by Packers (April 28, 1995). ... Granted unconditional free agency (February 14, 1997). ... Re-signed by Packers (April 2, 1997). ... Released by Packers (February 27, 1998). ... Re-signed by Packers (April 24, 1998). ... Granted unconditional free agency (February 12, 1999).
CHAMPIONSHIP GAME EXPERIENCE: Played in NFC championship game (1995-97 seasons). ... Member of Super Bowl championship team (1996 season). ... Played in Super Bowl XXXII (1997 season).
PRO STATISTICS: 1985—Recovered three fumbles. 1987—Credited with one sack and recovered three fumbles. 1988—Credited with one sack and recovered one fumble for 12 yards. 1989—Recovered one fumble for 10 yards. 1990—Caught one pass for 40 yards and recovered two fumbles for six yards. 1991—Recovered one fumble. 1992—Caught one pass for 17 yards and recovered one fumble. 1993—Recovered two fumbles. 1994—Recovered two fumbles. 1995—Credited with 1$^{1}/_{2}$ sacks and recovered one fumble.
MISCELLANEOUS: Selected by Baltimore Orioles organization in 18th round of free-agent baseball draft (June 4, 1984); did not sign. ... Selected by Los Angeles Dodgers organization in fourth round of free-agent baseball draft (June 3, 1985); did not sign.

				INTERCEPTIONS				PUNT RETURNS				KICKOFF RETURNS				TOTALS		
Year Team	G	GS	No.	Yds.	Avg.	TD	No.	Yds.	Avg.	TD	No.	Yds.	Avg.	TD	TD	2pt.	Pts.	Fum.
1985—Tampa Bay NFL	16	0	0	0	...	0	13	105	8.1	0	10	131	13.1	0	0	...	0	4
1986—									Did not play.									
1987—Indianapolis NFL	13	7	▲6	57	9.5	0	0	0	...	0	3	47	15.7	0	0	...	0	0
1988—Indianapolis NFL	16	16	3	46	15.3	0	1	0	0.0	0	0	0	...	0	0	...	0	1
1989—Indianapolis NFL	16	16	6	88	14.7	1	0	0	...	0	0	0	...	0	1	...	6	0
1990—Indianapolis NFL	16	16	3	66	22.0	0	2	0	0.0	0	0	0	...	0	0	...	0	1
1991—Indianapolis NFL	9	7	3	50	16.7	0	0	0	...	0	0	0	...	0	0	...	0	0
1992—Indianapolis NFL	16	16	6	44	7.3	0	1	7	7.0	0	0	0	...	0	0	...	0	0
1993—Green Bay NFL	16	4	1	1	1.0	0	17	194	11.4	0	0	0	...	0	0	...	0	3
1994—Green Bay NFL	16	0	0	0	...	0	8	62	7.8	0	0	0	...	0	0	...	0	3
1995—Green Bay NFL	16	2	1	9	9.0	0	1	10	10.0	0	0	0	...	0	0	...	0	0
1996—Green Bay NFL	16	0	1	7	7.0	0	0	0	...	0	0	0	...	0	0	...	0	0
1997—Green Bay NFL	16	0	4	72	18.0	0	1	0	0.0	0	0	0	...	0	0	...	0	1
1998—Green Bay NFL	16	1	0	0	0.0	0	1	0	0.0	0	0	0	...	0	0	...	0	1
Pro totals (13 years)	198	85	35	440	12.6	1	45	378	8.4	0	13	178	13.7	0	1	0	6	14

PRITCHARD, MIKE — WR — SEAHAWKS

PERSONAL: Born October 26, 1969, in Shaw AFB, S.C. ... 5-10/193. ... Full name: Michael Robert Pritchard.
HIGH SCHOOL: Rancho (North Las Vegas, Nev.).
COLLEGE: Colorado (degree in economics, 1998).
TRANSACTIONS/CAREER NOTES: Selected by Atlanta Falcons in first round (13th pick overall) of 1991 NFL draft. ... Signed by Falcons (July 24, 1991). ... Traded by Falcons with seventh-round pick (WR Byron Chamberlain) in 1995 draft to Denver Broncos for first-round pick (traded to Minnesota) in 1995 draft (April 24, 1994). ... On injured reserve with kidney injury (November 2, 1994-remainder of season). ... Released by Broncos (June 3, 1996). ... Signed by Seattle Seahawks (June 19, 1996).
PRO STATISTICS: 1991—Returned one kickoff for 18 yards.
SINGLE GAME HIGHS (regular season): Receptions—10 (September 5, 1993, vs. Detroit); yards—119 (September 4, 1994, vs. San Diego); and touchdown receptions—2 (November 21, 1993, vs. Dallas).
STATISTICAL PLATEAUS: 100-yard receiving games: 1992 (1), 1994 (2). Total: 3.

			RUSHING				RECEIVING				TOTALS			
Year Team	G	GS	Att.	Yds.	Avg.	TD	No.	Yds.	Avg.	TD	TD	2pt.	Pts.	Fum.
1991—Atlanta NFL	16	11	0	0	...	0	50	624	12.5	2	2	...	12	2
1992—Atlanta NFL	16	15	5	37	7.4	0	77	827	10.7	5	5	...	30	3
1993—Atlanta NFL	15	14	2	4	2.0	0	74	736	9.9	7	7	...	42	1
1994—Denver NFL	3	0	0	0	...	0	19	271	14.3	1	1	0	6	1
1995—Denver NFL	15	13	6	17	2.8	0	33	441	13.4	3	3	0	18	1
1996—Seattle NFL	16	5	2	13	6.5	0	21	328	15.6	1	1	0	6	0
1997—Seattle NFL	16	15	1	14	14.0	0	64	843	13.2	2	2	0	12	2
1998—Seattle NFL	16	16	1	17	17.0	0	58	742	12.8	3	3	1	20	1
Pro totals (8 years)	113	89	17	102	6.0	0	396	4812	12.2	24	24	1	146	11

PRITCHETT, KELVIN — DT — LIONS

PERSONAL: Born October 24, 1969, in Atlanta. ... 6-3/301. ... Full name: Kelvin Bratodd Pritchett.
HIGH SCHOOL: Therrell (Atlanta).
COLLEGE: Mississippi.
TRANSACTIONS/CAREER NOTES: Selected by Dallas Cowboys in first round (20th pick overall) of 1991 NFL draft. ... Rights traded by Cowboys to Detroit Lions for second- (LB Dixon Edwards), third- (G James Richards) and fourth-round (DE Tony Hill) picks in 1991 draft (April 21, 1991). ... Granted free agency (February 17, 1994). ... Re-signed by Lions (August 12, 1994). ... Granted unconditional free agency (February 17, 1995). ... Signed by Jacksonville Jaguars (March 11, 1995). ... On injured reserve with knee injury (November 4, 1997-remainder of season). ... Granted unconditional free agency (February 12, 1999). ... Signed by Lions (April 27, 1999).
CHAMPIONSHIP GAME EXPERIENCE: Played in NFC championship game (1991 season). ... Played in AFC championship game (1996 season).
PRO STATISTICS: 1994—Recovered one fumble. 1996—Recovered two fumbles. 1997—Recovered one fumble.

Year Team	G	GS	SACKS
1991—Detroit NFL	16	0	1.5
1992—Detroit NFL	16	15	6.5
1993—Detroit NFL	16	5	4.0
1994—Detroit NFL	16	15	5.5
1995—Jacksonville NFL	16	16	1.5
1996—Jacksonville NFL	13	4	2.0
1997—Jacksonville NFL	8	5	3.0
1998—Jacksonville NFL	15	9	3.0
Pro totals (8 years)	116	69	27.0

PRITCHETT, STANLEY   FB   DOLPHINS

PERSONAL: Born December 12, 1973, in Atlanta. ... 6-1/242. ... Full name: Stanley Jerome Pritchett.
HIGH SCHOOL: Frederick Douglass (College Park, Ga.).
COLLEGE: South Carolina.
TRANSACTIONS/CAREER NOTES: Selected by Miami Dolphins in fourth round (118th pick overall) of 1996 NFL draft. ... Signed by Dolphins (July 10, 1996). ... Granted free agency (February 12, 1999). ... Re-signed by Dolphins (April 13, 1999).
PRO STATISTICS: 1996—Recovered one fumble. 1998—Recovered one fumble.
SINGLE GAME HIGHS (regular season): Attempts—2 (December 13, 1998, vs. New York Jets); yards—16 (October 13, 1996, vs. Buffalo); and rushing touchdowns—1 (December 13, 1998, vs. New York Jets).

			RUSHING				RECEIVING				TOTALS			
Year Team	G	GS	Att.	Yds.	Avg.	TD	No.	Yds.	Avg.	TD	TD	2pt.	Pts.	Fum.
1996—Miami NFL	16	16	7	27	3.9	0	33	354	10.7	2	2	0	12	3
1997—Miami NFL	6	5	3	7	2.3	0	5	35	7.0	0	0	0	0	0
1998—Miami NFL	16	12	6	19	3.2	1	17	97	5.7	0	1	0	6	0
Pro totals (3 years)	38	33	16	53	3.3	1	55	486	8.8	2	3	0	18	3

PROEHL, RICKY   WR   RAMS

PERSONAL: Born March 7, 1968, in Bronx, N.Y. ... 6-0/190. ... Full name: Richard Scott Proehl.
HIGH SCHOOL: Hillsborough (N.J.).
COLLEGE: Wake Forest.
TRANSACTIONS/CAREER NOTES: Selected by Phoenix Cardinals in third round (58th pick overall) of 1990 NFL draft. ... Signed by Cardinals (July 23, 1990). ... Granted free agency (March 1, 1993). ... Tendered offer sheet by New England Patriots (April 13, 1993). ... Offer matched by Cardinals (April 19, 1993). ... Cardinals franchise renamed Arizona Cardinals for 1994 season. ... Traded by Cardinals to Seattle Seahawks for fourth-round pick (traded to New York Jets) in 1995 draft (April 3, 1995). ... Released by Seahawks (March 7, 1997). ... Signed by Chicago Bears (April 10, 1997). ... Granted unconditional free agency (February 13, 1998). ... Signed by St. Louis Rams (February 25, 1998).
PRO STATISTICS: 1990—Returned one punt for two yards and returned four kickoffs for 53 yards. 1991—Returned four punts for 26 yards and recovered one fumble. 1992—Had only pass attempt intercepted and fumbled five times. 1993—Fumbled once. 1994—Fumbled twice and recovered two fumbles. 1997—Returned eight punts for 59 yards.
SINGLE GAME HIGHS (regular season): Receptions—11 (November 16, 1997, vs. New York Jets); yards—164 (November 27, 1997, vs. Detroit); and touchdown receptions—2 (December 27, 1998, vs. San Francisco).
STATISTICAL PLATEAUS: 100-yard receiving games: 1990 (2), 1991 (1), 1992 (3), 1993 (1), 1997 (3), 1998 (1). Total: 11.

			RUSHING				RECEIVING				TOTALS			
Year Team	G	GS	Att.	Yds.	Avg.	TD	No.	Yds.	Avg.	TD	TD	2pt.	Pts.	Fum.
1990—Phoenix NFL	16	2	1	4	4.0	0	56	802	14.3	4	4	...	24	0
1991—Phoenix NFL	16	16	3	21	7.0	0	55	766	13.9	2	2	...	12	0
1992—Phoenix NFL	16	15	3	23	7.7	0	60	744	12.4	3	3	...	18	5
1993—Phoenix NFL	16	16	8	47	5.9	0	65	877	13.5	7	7	...	42	1
1994—Arizona NFL	16	16	0	0	...	0	51	651	12.8	5	5	0	30	2
1995—Seattle NFL	8	0	0	0	...	0	5	29	5.8	0	0	0	0	0
1996—Seattle NFL	16	7	0	0	...	0	23	309	13.4	2	2	0	12	0
1997—Chicago NFL	15	10	0	0	...	0	58	753	13.0	7	7	1	44	2
1998—St. Louis NFL	16	10	1	14	14.0	0	60	771	12.9	3	3	1	20	0
Pro totals (9 years)	135	92	16	109	6.8	0	433	5702	13.2	33	33	2	202	10

PRYCE, TREVOR   DT   BRONCOS

PERSONAL: Born August 3, 1975, in Brooklyn, N.Y. ... 6-5/295.
HIGH SCHOOL: Lake Howell (Casselberry, Fla.).
COLLEGE: Clemson.
TRANSACTIONS/CAREER NOTES: Selected by Denver Broncos in first round (28th pick overall) of 1997 NFL draft. ... Signed by Broncos (July 24, 1997).
CHAMPIONSHIP GAME EXPERIENCE: Played in AFC championship game (1997 and 1998 seasons). ... Member of Super Bowl championship team (1997 and 1998 seasons).
PRO STATISTICS: 1998—Intercepted one pass for one yard.

Year Team	G	GS	SACKS
1997—Denver NFL	8	3	2.0
1998—Denver NFL	16	15	8.5
Pro totals (2 years)	24	18	10.5

PUPUNU, AL — TE — CHARGERS

PERSONAL: Born October 17, 1969, in Tonga. ... 6-2/260. ... Full name: Alfred Sione Pupunu. ... Name pronounced puh-POO-noo.
HIGH SCHOOL: Salt Lake City South.
JUNIOR COLLEGE: Dixie College (Utah).
COLLEGE: Weber State.
TRANSACTIONS/CAREER NOTES: Signed as non-drafted free agent by Kansas City Chiefs (May 2, 1992). ... Claimed on waivers by San Diego Chargers (September 1, 1992). ... Granted unconditional free agency (February 16, 1996). ... Re-signed by Chargers (March 5, 1996). ... Released by Chargers (November 4, 1997). ... Signed by Chiefs (November 11, 1997). ... Released by Chiefs (November 25, 1997). ... Signed by New York Giants (December 22, 1997). ... On injured reserve with knee injury (November 17, 1998-remainder of season). ... Granted unconditional free agency (February 12, 1999). ... Signed by Chargers (April 7, 1999).
CHAMPIONSHIP GAME EXPERIENCE: Played in AFC championship game (1994 season). ... Played in Super Bowl XXIX (1994 season).
POST SEASON RECORDS: Shares Super Bowl and NFL postseason career and single-game records for most two-point conversions—1 (January 29, 1995, vs. San Francisco).
PRO STATISTICS: 1993—Recovered one fumble. 1995—Fumbled once. 1996—Returned one kickoff for 15 yards and recovered two fumbles. 1997—Recovered one fumble.
SINGLE GAME HIGHS (regular season): Receptions—6 (December 19, 1993, vs. Kansas City); yards—83 (September 29, 1996, vs. Kansas City); and touchdown receptions—1 (November 11, 1996, vs. Detroit).

			RECEIVING				TOTALS			
Year Team	G	GS	No.	Yds.	Avg.	TD	TD	2pt.	Pts.	Fum.
1992—San Diego NFL	15	2	0	0	...	0	0	...	0	0
1993—San Diego NFL	16	7	13	142	10.9	0	0	0	0	0
1994—San Diego NFL	13	10	21	214	10.2	2	2	0	12	0
1995—San Diego NFL	15	14	35	315	9.0	0	0	0	0	1
1996—San Diego NFL	9	8	24	271	11.3	1	1	0	6	0
1997—San Diego NFL	8	1	1	7	7.0	0	0	0	0	0
—Kansas City NFL	1	0	0	0	...	0	0	0	0	0
1998—New York Giants NFL	9	0	1	2	2.0	0	0	0	0	0
Pro totals (7 years)	86	42	95	951	10.0	3	3	0	18	2

PURNELL, LOVETT — TE — RAVENS

PERSONAL: Born April 7, 1972, in Seaford, Del. ... 6-3/245. ... Full name: Lovett S. Purnell.
HIGH SCHOOL: Seaford (Del.).
COLLEGE: West Virginia.
TRANSACTIONS/CAREER NOTES: Selected by New England Patriots in seventh round (216th pick overall) of 1996 NFL draft. ... Signed by Patriots (July 11, 1996). ... Released by Patriots (October 9, 1996). ... Re-signed by Patriots to practice squad (October 11, 1996). ... Activated (December 10, 1996). ... Granted free agency (February 12, 1999). ... Re-signed by Patriots (March 30, 1999). ... Traded by Patriots to Baltimore Ravens for sixth-round pick (DB Marcus Washington) in 1999 draft (March 31, 1999).
CHAMPIONSHIP GAME EXPERIENCE: Member of Patriots for AFC championship game (1996 season); inactive. ... Member of Patriots for Super Bowl XXXI (1996 season); inactive.
PRO STATISTICS: 1997—Recovered one fumble.
SINGLE GAME HIGHS (regular season): Receptions—4 (December 13, 1998, vs. St. Louis); yards—37 (December 13, 1998, vs. St. Louis); and touchdown receptions—1 (December 13, 1998, vs. St. Louis).

			RECEIVING				TOTALS			
Year Team	G	GS	No.	Yds.	Avg.	TD	TD	2pt.	Pts.	Fum.
1996—New England NFL	2	0	0	0	...	0	0	0	0	0
1997—New England NFL	16	2	5	57	11.4	3	3	0	18	0
1998—New England NFL	16	5	12	92	7.7	2	2	0	12	0
Pro totals (3 years)	34	7	17	149	8.8	5	5	0	30	0

PURVIS, ANDRE — DE — BENGALS

PERSONAL: Born July 14, 1973, in Jacksonville. ... 6-4/310. ... Full name: Andre Lamont Purvis.
HIGH SCHOOL: White Oak (Jacksonville), then Swansboro (N.C.).
COLLEGE: North Carolina.
TRANSACTIONS/CAREER NOTES: Selected by Cincinnati Bengals in fifth round (144th pick overall) of 1997 NFL draft. ... Signed by Bengals (June 5, 1997).
PLAYING EXPERIENCE: Cincinnati NFL, 1997 and 1998. ... Games/Games started: 1997 (7/1), 1998 (9/0). Total: 16/1.
PRO STATISTICS: 1998—Credited with one sack.

PYNE, JIM — C — BROWNS

PERSONAL: Born November 23, 1971, in Milford, Conn. ... 6-2/297. ... Full name: James M. Pyne. ... Son of George Pyne III, tackle with Boston Patriots of AFL (1965); and grandson of George Pyne Jr., tackle with Providence Steamrollers of NFL (1931).
HIGH SCHOOL: Choate Prep (Wallingford, Conn.), then Milford (Mass.).
COLLEGE: Virginia Tech.
TRANSACTIONS/CAREER NOTES: Selected by Tampa Bay Buccaneers in seventh round (200th pick overall) of 1994 NFL draft. ... Signed by Buccaneers (July 14, 1994). ... On injured reserve with broken leg (December 17, 1996-remainder of season). ... Granted free agency (February 14, 1997). ... Re-signed by Buccaneers (April 18, 1997). ... Granted unconditional free agency (February 13, 1998). ... Signed by Detroit Lions (February 21, 1998). ... Selected by Cleveland Browns from Lions in NFL expansion draft (February 9, 1999).
PLAYING EXPERIENCE: Tampa Bay NFL, 1995-1997; Detroit NFL, 1998. ... Games/Games started: 1995 (15/13), 1996 (12/11), 1997 (15/14), 1998 (16/16). Total: 58/54.
HONORS: Named offensive lineman on THE SPORTING NEWS college All-America first team (1993).
PRO STATISTICS: 1995—Recovered one fumble. 1997—Fumbled once for minus five yards.

QUARLES, SHELTON   LB   BUCCANEERS

PERSONAL: Born September 11, 1971, in Nashville. ... 6-1/223. ... Full name: Shelton Eugene Quarles.
HIGH SCHOOL: Whites Creek (Tenn.).
COLLEGE: Vanderbilt (degree in human and organized development).
TRANSACTIONS/CAREER NOTES: Signed as non-drafted free agent by Miami Dolphins (April 29, 1994). ... Released by Dolphins (August 15, 1994). ... Signed by B.C. Lions of CFL (December 1, 1994). ... Granted free agency (February 16, 1997). ... Signed by Tampa Bay Buccaneers (March 21, 1997).
PLAYING EXPERIENCE: B.C. CFL, 1995 and 1996; Tampa Bay NFL, 1997 and 1998. ... Games/Games started: 1995 (16/games started unavailable), 1996 (16/-), 1997 (16/0), 1998 (16/0). Total CFL: 32/-. Total NFL: 32/0. Total Pro: 64/-.
PRO STATISTICS: 1995—Intercepted one pass for no yards and recovered one fumble for 14 yards. 1996—Credited with 10 sacks and intercepted one pass for 22 yards. 1997—Recovered two fumbles. 1998—Credited with one sack.

QUINN, JONATHON   QB   JAGUARS

PERSONAL: Born February 27, 1975, in Turlock, Calif. ... 6-5/245. ... Full name: Jonathon Ryan Quinn.
HIGH SCHOOL: McGavock (Nashville).
COLLEGE: Tulane, then Middle Tennessee State (degree in business administration, 1997).
TRANSACTIONS/CAREER NOTES: Selected by Jacksonville Jaguars in third round (86th pick overall) of 1998 NFL draft. ... Signed by Jaguars (May 19, 1998).
PRO STATISTICS: 1998—Fumbled three times.
SINGLE GAME HIGHS (regular season): Attempts—27 (December 20, 1998, vs. Minnesota); completions—12 (December 20, 1998, vs. Minnesota); yards—192 (December 28, 1998, vs. Pittsburgh); and touchdown passes—1 (December 28, 1998, vs. Pittsburgh).
MISCELLANEOUS: Regular-season record as starting NFL quarterback: 1-1 (.500).

				PASSING						RUSHING				TOTALS	
Year Team	G	GS	Att.	Cmp.	Pct.	Yds.	TD	Int.	Avg.	Rat.	Att.	Yds.	Avg.	TD	TD	2pt.	Pts.
1998—Jacksonville NFL	4	2	64	34	53.1	387	2	3	6.05	62.4	11	77	7.0	1	1	0	6

QUINN, MIKE   QB   COWBOYS

PERSONAL: Born April 15, 1974, in Houston. ... 6-4/217. ... Full name: Michael Patrick Quinn.
HIGH SCHOOL: Robert E. Lee (Houston).
COLLEGE: Stephen F. Austin State.
TRANSACTIONS/CAREER NOTES: Signed as non-drafted free agent by Pittsburgh Steelers (April 21, 1997). ... Assigned by Steelers to Rhein Fire in 1998 NFL Europe enhancement allocation program (February 18, 1998). ... Claimed on waivers by Indianapolis Colts (August 31, 1998). ... Inactive for one game with Colts (1998). ... Claimed on waivers by Dallas Cowboys (September 9, 1998).
CHAMPIONSHIP GAME EXPERIENCE: Member of Steelers for AFC championship game (1997 season); inactive.
SINGLE GAME HIGHS (regular season): Attempts—2 (November 9, 1997, vs. Baltimore); completions—1 (November 2, 1998, vs. Philadelphia); yards—10 (November 2, 1998, vs. Philadelphia); and touchdown passes—0.

				PASSING						RUSHING				TOTALS	
Year Team	G	GS	Att.	Cmp.	Pct.	Yds.	TD	Int.	Avg.	Rat.	Att.	Yds.	Avg.	TD	TD	2pt.	Pts.
1997—Pittsburgh NFL	1	0	2	1	50.0	10	0	0	5.00	64.6	0	0	...	0	0	0	0
1998—Rhein NFLE	...	...	264	133	50.4	1997	13	3	7.56	87.3	29	122	4.2	0	0	0	0
—Dallas NFL	3	0	1	1	100.0	10	0	0	10.00	108.3	5	-6	-1.2	0	0	0	0
NFL Europe totals (1 year)	...	...	264	133	50.4	1997	13	3	7.56	87.3	29	122	4.2	0	0	0	0
NFL totals (2 years)	4	0	3	2	66.7	20	0	0	6.67	85.4	5	-6	-1.2	0	0	0	0
Pro totals (3 years)	...	...	267	135	50.6	2017	13	3	7.55	87.2	34	116	3.4	0	0	0	0

RAAB, MARC   C

PERSONAL: Born January 26, 1969, in San Diego. ... 6-3/265.
HIGH SCHOOL: Helix (La Mesa, Calif.).
COLLEGE: Southern California.
TRANSACTIONS/CAREER NOTES: Signed as non-drafted free agent by Washington Redskins (December 21, 1993). ... Released by Redskins (April 14, 1994). ... Out of pro football (1994-97). ... Signed by San Diego Chargers (December 12, 1998). ... Released by Chargers (December 14, 1998).
PLAYING EXPERIENCE: Washington NFL, 1993; San Diego NFL, 1998. ... Games/Games started: 1993 (2/0), 1998 (1/0). Total: 3/0.

RACHAL, LATARIO   WR/KR

PERSONAL: Born January 31, 1973, in Lynwood, Calif. ... 5-11/183. ... Full name: Latario Deshawn Rachal.
HIGH SCHOOL: Carson (Calif.).
JUNIOR COLLEGE: El Camino (Torrance, Calif.).
COLLEGE: Fresno State.
TRANSACTIONS/CAREER NOTES: Signed as non-drafted free agent by San Diego Chargers (February 27, 1997). ... Assigned by Chargers to Amsterdam Admirals in 1997 World League enhancement allocation program (February 27, 1997). ... Released by Chargers (November 24, 1998).
PRO STATISTICS: W.L.: 1997—Caught 14 passes for 141 yards and one touchdown. NFL: 1997—Recovered one fumble. 1998—Recovered one fumble.

Year Team	G	GS	PUNT RETURNS No.	Yds.	Avg.	TD	KICKOFF RETURNS No.	Yds.	Avg.	TD	TOTALS TD	2pt.	Pts.	Fum.
1997—Amsterdam W.L.	...	...	0	0	...	0	1	37	37.0	0	1	...	6	...
—San Diego NFL	14	0	0	0	...	0	15	336	22.4	0	0	0	0	1
1998—San Diego NFL	11	0	32	387	12.1	0	11	192	17.5	0	0	0	0	4
W.L. totals (1 year)	...	...	0	0		0	1	37	37.0	0	1	...	6	...
NFL totals (2 years)	25	0	32	387	12.1	0	26	528	20.3	0	0	0	0	5
Pro totals (3 years)	...	...	32	387	12.1	0	27	565	20.9	0	1	...	6	...

RAMIREZ, TONY   OT   LIONS

PERSONAL: Born January 26, 1973, in Lincoln, Neb. ... 6-6/296.
HIGH SCHOOL: Northglenn (Denver), then Lincoln (Neb.).
COLLEGE: Northern Colorado.
TRANSACTIONS/CAREER NOTES: Selected by Detroit Lions in sixth round (168th pick overall) of 1997 NFL draft. ... Signed by Lions (July 11, 1997).
PLAYING EXPERIENCE: Detroit NFL, 1997 and 1998. ... Games/Games started: 1997 (2/0), 1998 (16/7). Total: 18/7.

RANDLE, JOHN   DT   VIKINGS

PERSONAL: Born December 12, 1967, in Hearne, Texas. ... 6-1/283. ... Brother of Ervin Randle, linebacker with Tampa Bay Buccaneers (1985-90) and Kansas City Chiefs (1991-92).
HIGH SCHOOL: Hearne (Texas).
JUNIOR COLLEGE: Trinity Valley Community College (Texas).
COLLEGE: Texas A&I.
TRANSACTIONS/CAREER NOTES: Signed as non-drafted free agent by Minnesota Vikings (May 4, 1990). ... Designated by Vikings as transition player (January 15, 1994). ... Designated by Vikings as transition player (February 13, 1998). ... Tendered offer sheet by Miami Dolphins (February 16, 1998). ... Offer matched by Vikings (February 18, 1998).
CHAMPIONSHIP GAME EXPERIENCE: Played in NFC championship game (1998 season).
HONORS: Played in Pro Bowl (1993-1998 seasons). ... Named defensive tackle on THE SPORTING NEWS NFL All-Pro team (1994-1998).
PRO STATISTICS: 1992—Recovered one fumble. 1994—Recovered two fumbles. 1997—Recovered two fumbles for five yards. 1998—Recovered one fumble.

Year Team	G	GS	SACKS
1990—Minnesota NFL	16	0	1.0
1991—Minnesota NFL	16	8	9.5
1992—Minnesota NFL	16	14	11.5
1993—Minnesota NFL	16	16	12.5
1994—Minnesota NFL	16	16	∞13.5
1995—Minnesota NFL	16	16	10.5
1996—Minnesota NFL	16	16	11.5
1997—Minnesota NFL	16	16	*15.5
1998—Minnesota NFL	16	16	10.5
Pro totals (9 years)	144	118	96.0

RANDOLPH, THOMAS   CB   BENGALS

PERSONAL: Born October 5, 1970, in Norfolk, Va. ... 5-9/185. ... Full name: Thomas C. Randolph.
HIGH SCHOOL: Manhattan (Kan.).
COLLEGE: Kansas State.
TRANSACTIONS/CAREER NOTES: Selected by New York Giants in second round (47th pick overall) of 1994 NFL draft. ... Signed by Giants (July 17, 1994). ... Granted unconditional free agency (February 13, 1998). ... Signed by Cincinnati Bengals (March 4, 1998).
PRO STATISTICS: 1995—Recovered one fumble. 1996—Recovered one fumble for 17 yards.

Year Team	G	GS	INTERCEPTIONS No.	Yds.	Avg.	TD
1994—New York Giants NFL	16	10	1	0	0.0	0
1995—New York Giants NFL	16	16	2	15	7.5	0
1996—New York Giants NFL	16	2	0	0	...	0
1997—New York Giants NFL	16	4	1	1	1.0	0
1998—Cincinnati NFL	16	1	1	0	0.0	0
Pro totals (5 years)	80	33	5	16	3.2	0

RANSOM, DERRICK   DT   CHIEFS

PERSONAL: Born September 13, 1976, in Indianapolis. ... 6-3/291. ... Full name: Derrick Wayne Ransom Jr.
HIGH SCHOOL: Lawrence Central (Indianapolis).
COLLEGE: Cincinnati (degree in finance).
TRANSACTIONS/CAREER NOTES: Selected by Kansas City Chiefs in sixth round (181st pick overall) of 1998 NFL draft. ... Signed by Chiefs (June 3, 1998).
PLAYING EXPERIENCE: Kansas City NFL, 1998. ... Games/Games started: 7/0.
PRO STATISTICS: 1998—Returned one kickoff for no yards.

RASBY, WALTER   TE   LIONS

PERSONAL: Born September 7, 1972, in Washington, D.C. ... 6-3/247. ... Full name: Walter Herbert Rasby.
HIGH SCHOOL: Washington (N.C.).
COLLEGE: Wake Forest.
TRANSACTIONS/CAREER NOTES: Signed as non-drafted free agent by Pittsburgh Steelers (April 29, 1994). ... Released by Steelers (August 27, 1995). ... Signed by Carolina Panthers (October 17, 1995). ... Granted free agency (February 14, 1997). ... Re-signed by Panthers (June 3, 1997). ... On injured reserve with knee injury (December 10, 1997-remainder of season). ... Granted unconditional free agency (February 13, 1998). ... Signed by Detroit Lions (April 13, 1998).
CHAMPIONSHIP GAME EXPERIENCE: Played in AFC championship game (1994 season). ... Played in NFC championship game (1996 season).
PRO STATISTICS: 1996—Recovered one fumble. 1997—Returned three kickoffs for 32 yards.
SINGLE GAME HIGHS (regular season): Receptions—5 (October 4, 1998, vs. Chicago); yards—39 (October 4, 1998, vs. Chicago); and touchdown receptions—1 (November 22, 1998, vs. Tampa Bay).

			RECEIVING				TOTALS		
Year Team	G	GS	No.	Yds.	Avg.	TD	TD	2pt.	Pts.	Fum.
1994—Pittsburgh NFL	2	0	0	0	...	0	0	0	0	0
1995—Carolina NFL	9	2	5	47	9.4	0	0	1	2	0
1996—Carolina NFL	16	1	0	0	...	0	0	0	0	0
1997—Carolina NFL	14	2	1	1	1.0	0	0	0	0	0
1998—Detroit NFL	16	16	15	119	7.9	1	1	0	6	0
Pro totals (5 years)	57	21	21	167	8.0	1	1	1	8	0

RAYMER, CORY   C   REDSKINS

PERSONAL: Born March 3, 1973, in Fond du Lac, Wis. ... 6-2/289.
HIGH SCHOOL: Goodrich (Fond du Lac, Wis.).
COLLEGE: Wisconsin.
TRANSACTIONS/CAREER NOTES: Selected by Washington Redskins in second round (37th pick overall) of 1995 NFL draft. ... Signed by Redskins (July 24, 1995). ... On injured reserve with back injury (November 25, 1996-remainder of season). ... Granted unconditional free agency (February 12, 1999). ... Re-signed by Redskins (March 15, 1999).
PLAYING EXPERIENCE: Washington NFL, 1995-1998. ... Games/Games started: 1995 (3/2), 1996 (6/5), 1997 (6/3), 1998 (16/16). Total: 31/26.
HONORS: Named offensive lineman on THE SPORTING NEWS college All-America first team (1994).
PRO STATISTICS: 1996—Recovered one fumble. 1998—Recovered one fumble.

REDMON, ANTHONY   G   PANTHERS

PERSONAL: Born April 9, 1971, in Brewton, Ala. ... 6-5/308. ... Full name: Kendrick Anthony Redmon.
HIGH SCHOOL: T. R. Miller (Brewton, Ala.).
COLLEGE: Auburn.
TRANSACTIONS/CAREER NOTES: Selected by Arizona Cardinals in fifth round (139th pick overall) of 1994 NFL draft. ... Signed by Cardinals (June 13, 1994). ... Granted free agency (February 14, 1997). ... Re-signed by Cardinals (June 13, 1997). ... Granted unconditional free agency (February 13, 1998). ... Signed by Miami Dolphins (July 24, 1998). ... Released by Dolphins (August 30, 1998). ... Signed by Carolina Panthers (October 14, 1998). ... Granted unconditional free agency (February 12, 1999). ... Re-signed by Panthers (February 12, 1999).
PLAYING EXPERIENCE: Arizona NFL, 1994-1997; Carolina NFL, 1998. ... Games/Games started: 1994 (6/5), 1995 (12/9), 1996 (16/16), 1997 (16/16), 1998 (10/4). Total: 60/50.
PRO STATISTICS: 1996—Recovered one fumble.

REECE, TRAVIS   FB   LIONS

PERSONAL: Born April 3, 1975, in Detroit. ... 6-3/252.
HIGH SCHOOL: Denby (Detroit).
COLLEGE: Michigan State.
TRANSACTIONS/CAREER NOTES: Signed as non-drafted free agent by Detroit Lions (April 24, 1998). ... Released by Lions (August 30, 1998). ... Re-signed by Lions to practice squad (September 1, 1998). ... Activated (September 18, 1998). ... Released by Lions (October 5, 1998). ... Re-signed by Lions to practice squad (October 7, 1998). ... Activated (December 23, 1998).
PLAYING EXPERIENCE: Detroit NFL, 1998. ... Games/Games started: 3/0.

REED, ANDRE   WR   BILLS

PERSONAL: Born January 29, 1964, in Allentown, Pa. ... 6-2/190. ... Full name: Andre Darnell Reed.
HIGH SCHOOL: Louis E. Dieruff (Allentown, Pa.).
COLLEGE: Kutztown (Pa.) University.
TRANSACTIONS/CAREER NOTES: Selected by Orlando Renegades in third round (39th pick overall) of 1985 USFL draft. ... Selected by Buffalo Bills in fourth round (86th pick overall) of 1985 NFL draft. ... Signed by Bills (July 19, 1985). ... Granted unconditional free agency (February 16, 1996). ... Re-signed by Bills (May 7, 1996). ... On injured reserve with shoulder injury (December 18, 1997-remainder of season).
CHAMPIONSHIP GAME EXPERIENCE: Played in AFC championship game (1988 and 1990-1993 seasons). ... Played in Super Bowl XXV (1990 season), Super Bowl XXVI (1991 season), Super Bowl XXVII (1992 season) and Super Bowl XXVIII (1993 season).
HONORS: Played in Pro Bowl (1988-1990, 1992 and 1994 seasons). ... Member of Pro Bowl squad (1991 season); did not play. ... Named to play in Pro Bowl (1993 season); replaced by Haywood Jeffires due to injury.
RECORDS: Shares NFL record for most seasons with 50 or more receptions—12.
POST SEASON RECORDS: Shares NFL postseason single-game record for most touchdown receptions—3 (January 3, 1993, OT, vs. Houston).

PRO STATISTICS: 1985—Returned five punts for 12 yards and recovered two fumbles. 1986—Recovered two fumbles for two yards. 1990—Recovered one fumble. 1994—Attempted one pass with a completion for 32 yards and recovered two fumbles.
SINGLE GAME HIGHS (regular season): Receptions—15 (November 20, 1994, vs. Green Bay); yards—191 (November 20, 1994, vs. Green Bay); and touchdown receptions—3 (September 5, 1993, vs. New England).
STATISTICAL PLATEAUS: 100-yard receiving games: 1985 (1), 1987 (2), 1988 (3), 1989 (6), 1990 (2), 1991 (4), 1992 (2), 1993 (2), 1994 (5), 1996 (5), 1997 (2), 1998 (1). Total: 35.
MISCELLANEOUS: Active AFC leader for career receptions (889), receiving yards (12,559) and touchdown receptions (85). ... Shares active AFC lead in touchdowns (86). ... Holds Buffalo Bills all-time record for most receptions (889), most yards receiving (12,559) and most touchdown receptions (85). ... Shares Buffalo Bills all-time record for most touchdowns (86).

				RUSHING				RECEIVING				TOTALS		
Year Team	G	GS	Att.	Yds.	Avg.	TD	No.	Yds.	Avg.	TD	TD	2pt.	Pts.	Fum.
1985—Buffalo NFL	16	15	3	-1	-0.3	1	48	637	13.3	4	5	...	30	1
1986—Buffalo NFL	15	15	3	-8	-2.7	0	53	739	13.9	7	7	...	42	2
1987—Buffalo NFL	12	12	1	1	1.0	0	57	752	13.2	5	5	...	30	0
1988—Buffalo NFL	15	14	6	64	10.7	0	71	968	13.6	6	6	...	36	1
1989—Buffalo NFL	16	16	2	31	15.5	0	§88	§1312	14.9	9	9	...	54	4
1990—Buffalo NFL	16	16	3	23	7.7	0	71	945	13.3	8	8	...	48	1
1991—Buffalo NFL	16	16	12	136	11.3	0	81	1113	13.7	10	10	...	60	1
1992—Buffalo NFL	16	16	8	65	8.1	0	65	913	14.0	3	3	...	18	4
1993—Buffalo NFL	15	15	9	21	2.3	0	52	854	16.4	6	6	...	36	3
1994—Buffalo NFL	16	16	10	87	8.7	0	90	1303	14.5	8	8	0	48	3
1995—Buffalo NFL	6	6	7	48	6.9	0	24	312	13.0	3	3	0	18	2
1996—Buffalo NFL	16	16	8	22	2.8	0	66	1036	15.7	6	6	0	36	1
1997—Buffalo NFL	15	15	3	11	3.7	0	60	880	14.7	5	5	0	30	1
1998—Buffalo NFL	15	13	0	0	...	0	63	795	12.6	5	5	0	30	0
Pro totals (14 years)	205	201	75	500	6.7	1	889	12559	14.1	85	86	0	516	24

REED, JAKE — WR — VIKINGS

PERSONAL: Born September 28, 1967, in Covington, Ga. ... 6-3/216. ... Full name: Willis Reed. ... Brother of Dale Carter, cornerback, Denver Broncos.
HIGH SCHOOL: Newton County (Covington, Ga.).
COLLEGE: Grambling State (degree in criminal justice, 1990).
TRANSACTIONS/CAREER NOTES: Selected by Minnesota Vikings in third round (68th pick overall) of 1991 NFL draft. ... Signed by Vikings (July 22, 1991). ... On injured reserve with ankle injury (November 2, 1991-remainder of season). ... Granted free agency (February 17, 1994). ... Re-signed by Vikings (May 6, 1994). ... Granted unconditional free agency (February 17, 1995). ... Re-signed by Vikings (February 28, 1995).
CHAMPIONSHIP GAME EXPERIENCE: Member of Vikings for NFC championship game (1998 season); inactive.
PRO STATISTICS: 1992—Returned one kickoff for one yard. 1995—Recovered one fumble.
SINGLE GAME HIGHS (regular season): Receptions—12 (September 7, 1997, vs. Chicago); yards—157 (November 6, 1994, vs. New Orleans); and touchdown receptions—2 (November 1, 1998, vs. Tampa Bay).
STATISTICAL PLATEAUS: 100-yard receiving games: 1994 (3), 1995 (3), 1996 (3), 1997 (5), 1998 (1). Total: 15.

			RECEIVING				TOTALS			
Year Team	G	GS	No.	Yds.	Avg.	TD	TD	2pt.	Pts.	Fum.
1991—Minnesota NFL	1	0	0	0	...	0	0	...	0	0
1992—Minnesota NFL	16	0	6	142	23.7	0	0	...	0	0
1993—Minnesota NFL	10	1	5	65	13.0	0	0	...	0	0
1994—Minnesota NFL	16	16	85	1175	13.8	4	4	0	24	3
1995—Minnesota NFL	16	16	72	1167	16.2	9	9	0	54	1
1996—Minnesota NFL	16	15	72	1320	18.3	7	7	0	42	0
1997—Minnesota NFL	16	16	68	1138	16.7	6	6	0	36	0
1998—Minnesota NFL	11	11	34	474	13.9	4	4	0	24	0
Pro totals (8 years)	102	75	342	5481	16.0	30	30	0	180	4

REED, MIKE — FB — EAGLES

PERSONAL: Born January 6, 1975, in Great Britain. ... 6-0/215.
HIGH SCHOOL: Woodbridge American (Great Britain), then Clover Park (Tacoma, Wash.).
COLLEGE: Washington.
TRANSACTIONS/CAREER NOTES: Signed as non-drafted free agent by Philadelphia Eagles (April 21, 1998). ... Released by Eagles (August 30, 1998). ... Re-signed by Eagles to practice squad (September 1, 1998). ... Activated (October 5, 1998). ... Released by Eagles (November 27, 1998). ... Re-signed by Eagles to practice squad (December 1, 1998). ... Activated (December 10, 1998).
PLAYING EXPERIENCE: Philadelphia NFL, 1998. ... Games/Games started: 4/0.

REESE, IKE — LB — EAGLES

PERSONAL: Born October 16, 1973, in Jacksonville, N.C. ... 6-2/222. ... Full name: Isaiah Reese.
HIGH SCHOOL: Woodard (Cincinnati), then Aiken (Cincinnati).
COLLEGE: Michigan State.
TRANSACTIONS/CAREER NOTES: Selected by Philadelphia Eagles in fifth round (142nd pick overall) of 1998 NFL draft. ... Signed by Eagles (July 14, 1998).
PLAYING EXPERIENCE: Philadelphia NFL, 1998. ... Games/Games started: 16/0.

REESE, IZELL — S — COWBOYS

PERSONAL: Born May 7, 1974, in Dothan, Ala. ... 6-2/196.
HIGH SCHOOL: Northview (Dothan, Ala.).
COLLEGE: Alabama-Birmingham.
TRANSACTIONS/CAREER NOTES: Selected by Dallas Cowboys in sixth round (188th pick overall) of 1998 NFL draft. ... Signed by Cowboys (July 15, 1998).
PLAYING EXPERIENCE: Dallas NFL, 1998. ... Games/Games started: 16/0.
PRO STATISTICS: 1998—Intercepted one pass for six yards.

REEVES, CARL — DE — BRONCOS

PERSONAL: Born December 17, 1971, in Durham, N.C. ... 6-4/270.
HIGH SCHOOL: Northern Durham (N.C.).
COLLEGE: North Carolina State.
TRANSACTIONS/CAREER NOTES: Selected by Chicago Bears in sixth round (198th pick overall) of 1995 NFL draft. ... Signed by Bears (June 27, 1995). ... On injured reserve with back injury (August 22, 1995-entire season). ... Assigned by Bears to Barcelona Dragons in 1997 World League enhancement allocation program (February 19, 1997). ... Granted unconditional free agency (February 12, 1999). ... Signed by Denver Broncos (April 12, 1999).
PLAYING EXPERIENCE: Chicago NFL, 1996-1998; Barcelona W.L., 1997. ... Games/Games started: 1996 (5/0), W.L. 1997 (games played unavailable), NFL 1997 (15/11), 1998 (11/0). Total NFL: 31/11.
PRO STATISTICS: 1997—Credited with $\frac{1}{2}$ sack and recovered one fumble. 1998—Credited with one sack.

REHBERG, SCOTT — OT — BROWNS

PERSONAL: Born November 17, 1973, in Kalamazoo, Mich. ... 6-8/330. ... Full name: Scott Joseph Rehberg. ... Name pronounced RAY-berg.
HIGH SCHOOL: Central (Kalamazoo, Mich.).
COLLEGE: Central Michigan.
TRANSACTIONS/CAREER NOTES: Selected by New England Patriots in seventh round (230th pick overall) of 1997 NFL draft. ... Signed by Patriots (June 19, 1997). ... Selected by Cleveland Browns from Patriots in NFL expansion draft (February 9, 1999).
PLAYING EXPERIENCE: New England NFL, 1997 and 1998. ... Games/Games started: 1997 (6/0), 1998 (2/0). Total: 8/0.

REICH, FRANK — QB

PERSONAL: Born December 4, 1961, in Freeport, N.Y. ... 6-4/210. ... Full name: Frank Michael Reich. ... Name pronounced RIKE.
HIGH SCHOOL: Cedar Crest (Lebanon, Pa.).
COLLEGE: Maryland (degree in finance, 1984).
TRANSACTIONS/CAREER NOTES: Selected by Tampa Bay Bandits in 1985 USFL territorial draft. ... Selected by Buffalo Bills in third round (57th pick overall) of 1985 NFL draft. ... Signed by Bills (August 1, 1985). ... On injured reserve with Achilles' tendon injury (September 3-December 6, 1985). ... Active for 12 games with Bills (1987); did not play. ... Granted unconditional free agency (February 17, 1995). ... Signed by Carolina Panthers (March 27, 1995). ... Granted unconditional free agency (February 16, 1996). ... Signed by New York Jets (April 11, 1996). ... Released by Jets (March 3, 1997). ... Signed by Detroit Lions (March 6, 1997). ... Granted unconditional free agency (February 12, 1999).
CHAMPIONSHIP GAME EXPERIENCE: Member of Bills for AFC championship game (1988 season); did not play. ... Played in AFC championship game (1990-1993 seasons). ... Played in Super Bowl XXV (1990 season), Super Bowl XXVI (1991 season), Super Bowl XXVII (1992 season) and Super Bowl XXVIII (1993 season).
POST SEASON RECORDS: Shares Super Bowl single-game record for most fumbles—3 (January 31, 1993, vs. Dallas).
PRO STATISTICS: 1986—Fumbled once. 1989—Fumbled twice. 1990—Fumbled once. 1992—Fumbled three times and recovered two fumbles for minus four yards. 1994—Fumbled once and recovered one fumble. 1995—Fumbled three times and recovered one fumble. 1996—Fumbled nine times and recovered one fumble for minus 70 yards. 1998—Fumbled twice and recovered one fumble.
SINGLE GAME HIGHS (regular season): Attempts—50 (November 24, 1996, vs. Buffalo); completions—26 (December 24, 1994, vs. Indianapolis); yards—352 (November 17, 1996, vs. Indianapolis); and touchdown passes—3 (November 17, 1996, vs. Indianapolis).
STATISTICAL PLATEAUS: 300-yard passing games: 1995 (1), 1996 (1). Total: 2.
MISCELLANEOUS: Regular-season record as starting NFL quarterback: 5-15 (.250). ... Postseason record as starting NFL quarterback: 2-0.

				PASSING							RUSHING				TOTALS	
Year Team	G	GS	Att.	Cmp.	Pct.	Yds.	TD	Int.	Avg.	Rat.	Att.	Yds.	Avg.	TD	TD	2pt.	Pts.
1985—Buffalo NFL	1	0	1	1	100.0	19	0	0	19.00	118.8	0	0	...	0	0	...	0
1986—Buffalo NFL	3	0	19	9	47.4	104	0	2	5.47	24.8	1	0	0.0	0	0	...	0
1987—Buffalo NFL							Did not play.										
1988—Buffalo NFL	3	0	0	0	...	0	0	0	...	...	3	-3	-1.0	0	0	...	0
1989—Buffalo NFL	7	3	87	53	60.9	701	7	2	8.06	103.7	9	30	3.3	0	0	...	0
1990—Buffalo NFL	16	2	63	36	57.1	469	2	0	7.44	91.3	15	24	1.6	0	0	...	0
1991—Buffalo NFL	16	1	41	27	65.9	305	6	2	7.44	107.2	13	6	0.5	0	0	...	0
1992—Buffalo NFL	16	0	47	24	51.1	221	0	2	4.70	46.5	9	-9	-1.0	0	0	...	0
1993—Buffalo NFL	15	0	26	16	61.5	153	2	0	5.88	103.5	6	-6	-1.0	0	0	...	0
1994—Buffalo NFL	16	2	93	56	60.2	568	1	4	6.11	63.4	6	3	0.5	0	0	0	0
1995—Carolina NFL	3	3	84	37	44.0	441	2	5	5.25	58.7	1	3	3.0	0	0	0	0
1996—New York Jets NFL	10	7	331	175	52.9	2205	15	16	6.66	68.9	18	31	1.7	0	0	0	0
1997—Detroit NFL	6	0	30	11	36.7	121	0	2	4.03	21.7	4	-4	-1.0	0	0	0	0
1998—Detroit NFL	6	2	110	63	57.3	768	5	4	6.98	78.9	6	3	0.5	0	0	0	0
Pro totals (13 years)	118	20	932	508	54.5	6075	40	36	6.52	72.9	91	78	0.9	0	0	0	0

– 321 –

REID, SPENCER — LB — PANTHERS

PERSONAL: Born February 8, 1976, in Pago Pago, American Samoa. ... 6-1/247. ... Full name: Spencer Eldon Karene Reid.
HIGH SCHOOL: Leone (American Samoa).
COLLEGE: Brigham Young.
TRANSACTIONS/CAREER NOTES: Signed as non-drafted free agent by Carolina Panthers (April 18, 1998).
PLAYING EXPERIENCE: Carolina NFL, 1998. ... Games/Games started: 16/0.

REYNOLDS, JERRY — OT

PERSONAL: Born April 2, 1970, in Fort Thomas, Ky. ... 6-6/325. ... Full name: Jerry Bradford Reynolds.
HIGH SCHOOL: Highlands (Fort Thomas, Ky.).
COLLEGE: UNLV.
TRANSACTIONS/CAREER NOTES: Selected by Cincinnati Bengals in sixth round (184th pick overall) of 1994 NFL draft. ... Signed by Bengals for 1994 season. ... Released by Bengals (August 25, 1994). ... Re-signed by Bengals to practice squad (August 30, 1994). ... Signed by Dallas Cowboys off Bengals practice squad (November 2, 1994). ... Active for one game (1994); did not play. ... Released by Cowboys (August 27, 1995). ... Signed by New York Giants (August 31, 1995). ... Active for four games (1995); did not play. ... Granted free agency (February 14, 1997). ... Re-signed by Giants for 1997 season. ... Granted unconditional free agency (February 13, 1998). ... Re-signed by Giants (March 10, 1998). ... Released by Giants (February 11, 1999).
PLAYING EXPERIENCE: New York Giants NFL, 1996-1998. ... Games/Games started: 1996 (8/0), 1997 (5/0), 1998 (12/2). Total: 25/2.
CHAMPIONSHIP GAME EXPERIENCE: Member of Cowboys for NFC championship game (1994 season); inactive.

RHEAMS, LEONTA — DT — PATRIOTS

PERSONAL: Born August 1, 1976, in Tyler, Texas. ... 6-2/280. ... Full name: Leonta DeMarkel Rheams.
HIGH SCHOOL: Robert E. Lee (Tyler, Texas).
COLLEGE: Houston.
TRANSACTIONS/CAREER NOTES: Selected by New England Patriots in fourth round (115th pick overall) of 1998 NFL draft. ... Signed by Patriots (June 30, 1998). ... Released by Patriots (August 30, 1998). ... Re-signed by Patriots to practice squad (August 31, 1998). ... Activated (November 4, 1998).
PLAYING EXPERIENCE: New England NFL, 1998. ... Games/Games started: 6/0.

RHETT, ERRICT — RB — RAVENS

PERSONAL: Born December 11, 1970, in Pembroke Pines, Fla. ... 5-11/210. ... Full name: Errict Undra Rhett.
HIGH SCHOOL: McArthur (Hollywood, Fla.).
COLLEGE: Florida (degree in commercial management).
TRANSACTIONS/CAREER NOTES: Selected by Tampa Bay Buccaneers in second round (34th pick overall) of 1994 NFL draft. ... Signed by Buccaneers (August 9, 1994). ... Granted free agency (February 13, 1998). ... Re-signed by Buccaneers (February 18, 1998). ... Traded by Buccaneers to Baltimore Ravens for third-round pick (traded back to Baltimore) in 1999 draft (February 18, 1998). ... Granted unconditional free agency (February 12, 1999). ... Re-signed by Ravens (April 26, 1999).
HONORS: Named running back on THE SPORTING NEWS college All-America second team (1993).
PRO STATISTICS: 1994—Recovered one fumble. 1995—Recovered one fumble. 1996—Recovered one fumble. 1997—Returned one kickoff for 16 yards.
SINGLE GAME HIGHS (regular season): Attempts—40 (December 4, 1994, vs. Washington); yards—192 (December 4, 1994, vs. Washington); and rushing touchdowns—2 (November 19, 1995, vs. Jacksonville).
STATISTICAL PLATEAUS: 100-yard rushing games: 1994 (4), 1995 (4). Total: 8.

				RUSHING				RECEIVING				TOTALS		
Year Team	G	GS	Att.	Yds.	Avg.	TD	No.	Yds.	Avg.	TD	TD	2pt.	Pts.	Fum.
1994—Tampa Bay NFL	16	8	284	1011	3.6	7	22	119	5.4	0	7	1	44	2
1995—Tampa Bay NFL	16	16	332	1207	3.6	11	14	110	7.9	0	11	0	66	2
1996—Tampa Bay NFL	9	7	176	539	3.1	3	4	11	2.8	1	4	0	24	3
1997—Tampa Bay NFL	11	0	31	96	3.1	3	0	0	...	0	3	0	18	0
1998—Baltimore NFL	13	1	44	180	4.1	0	11	65	5.9	0	0	0	0	0
Pro totals (5 years)	65	32	867	3033	3.5	24	51	305	6.0	1	25	1	152	7

RICE, JERRY — WR — 49ERS

PERSONAL: Born October 13, 1962, in Starkville, Miss. ... 6-2/196. ... Full name: Jerry Lee Rice.
HIGH SCHOOL: Crawford MS Moor (Crawford, Miss.).
COLLEGE: Mississippi Valley State.
TRANSACTIONS/CAREER NOTES: Selected by Birmingham Stallions in first round (first pick overall) of 1985 USFL draft. ... Selected by San Francisco 49ers in first round (16th pick overall) of 1985 NFL draft. ... Signed by 49ers (July 23, 1985). ... Granted free agency (February 1, 1992). ... Re-signed by 49ers (August 25, 1992). ... On injured reserve with knee injury (December 23, 1997-remainder of season).
CHAMPIONSHIP GAME EXPERIENCE: Played in NFC championship game (1988-1990 and 1992-1994 seasons). ... Member of Super Bowl championship team (1988, 1989 and 1994 seasons).
HONORS: Named wide receiver on THE SPORTING NEWS college All-America first team (1984). ... Named wide receiver on THE SPORTING NEWS NFL All-Pro team (1986-1996). ... Played in Pro Bowl (1986, 1987, 1989-1993, 1995 and 1998 seasons). ... Named NFL Player of the Year by THE SPORTING NEWS (1987 and 1990). ... Named Most Valuable Player of Super Bowl XXIII (1988 season). ... Named to play in Pro Bowl (1988 season); replaced by J.T. Smith due to injury. ... Named to play in Pro Bowl (1994 season); replaced by Herman Moore due to injury. ... Named Outstanding Player of Pro Bowl (1995 season). ... Named to play in Pro Bowl (1996 season); replaced by Irving Fryar due to injury.
RECORDS: Holds NFL career records for most touchdowns—175; most touchdown receptions—164; most receiving yards—17,612; most pass receptions—1,139; most seasons with 1,000 or more yards receiving—12; most games with 100 or more yards receiving—64; most

consecutive games with one or more reception—193 (December 9, 1985-present); and most consecutive games with one or more touchdown reception—13 (December 19, 1986-December 27, 1987). ... Holds NFL single-season record for most yards receiving—1,848 (1995); and most touchdown receptions—22 (1987). ... Shares NFL record for most seasons with 50 or more receptions—12. ... Shares NFL single-game record for most touchdown receptions—5 (October 14, 1990, at Atlanta).
POST SEASON RECORDS: Holds Super Bowl career records for most points—42; most touchdowns—7; most touchdown receptions—7; most receptions—28; most combined yards—527; and most yards receiving—512. ... Holds Super Bowl single-game records for most touchdowns receptions—3 (January 28, 1990, vs. Denver and January 29, 1995, vs. San Diego); and most yards receiving—215 (January 22, 1989, vs. Cincinnati). ... Shares Super Bowl single-game records for most points—18; most touchdowns—3 (January 28, 1990, vs. Denver and January 29, 1995, vs. San Diego); and most receptions—11 (January 22, 1989, vs. Cincinnati). ... Holds NFL postseason career records for most touchdowns—19; most touchdown receptions—19; most receptions—124; most yards receiving—1,811; and most games with 100 or more yards receiving—7. ... Holds NFL postseason record for most consecutive games with one or more receptions—23 (1985-present). ... Shares NFL postseason career record for most consecutive games with 100 or more yards receiving—3 (1988-89). ... Shares NFL postseason single-game record for most touchdown receptions—3 (January 28, 1990, vs. Denver; January 1, 1989, vs. Minnesota; and January 29, 1995, vs. San Diego).
PRO STATISTICS: 1985—Returned one kickoff for six yards. 1986—Attempted two passes with one completion for 16 yards and recovered three fumbles. 1987—Recovered one fumble. 1988—Attempted three passes with one completion for 14 yards and one interception and recovered one fumble. 1993—Recovered one fumble. 1995—Attempted one pass with a completion for 41 yards and a touchdown and recovered one fumble in end zone for a touchdown. 1996—Attempted one pass without a completion.
SINGLE GAME HIGHS (regular season): Receptions—16 (November 20, 1994, vs. Los Angeles Rams); yards—289 (December 18, 1995, vs. Minnesota); and touchdowns—5 (October 14, 1990, vs. Atlanta).
STATISTICAL PLATEAUS: 100-yard receiving games: 1985 (2), 1986 (6), 1987 (4), 1988 (5), 1989 (8), 1990 (7), 1991 (4), 1992 (5), 1993 (5), 1994 (5), 1995 (9), 1996 (3), 1998 (3). Total: 64.
MISCELLANEOUS: Active NFL leader for career receptions (1,139), receiving yards (17,612), touchdown receptions (164), and touchdowns (175). ... Holds San Francisco 49ers all-time records for most yards receiving (17,612), most touchdowns (175), most receptions (1,139) and most touchdown receptions (164).

				RUSHING				RECEIVING				TOTALS		
Year Team	G	GS	Att.	Yds.	Avg.	TD	No.	Yds.	Avg.	TD	TD	2pt.	Pts.	Fum.
1985—San Francisco NFL	16	4	6	26	4.3	1	49	927	18.9	3	4	...	24	1
1986—San Francisco NFL	16	15	10	72	7.2	1	‡86	*1570	18.3	*15	16	...	96	2
1987—San Francisco NFL	12	12	8	51	6.4	1	65	1078	16.6	*22	*23	...	*138	2
1988—San Francisco NFL	16	16	13	107	8.2	1	64	1306	20.4	9	10	...	60	2
1989—San Francisco NFL	16	16	5	33	6.6	0	82	*1483	18.1	*17	17	...	102	0
1990—San Francisco NFL	16	16	2	0	0.0	0	*100	*1502	15.0	*13	13	...	78	1
1991—San Francisco NFL	16	16	1	2	2.0	0	80	1206	15.1	*14	14	...	84	1
1992—San Francisco NFL	16	16	9	58	6.4	1	84	1201	14.3	10	11	...	66	2
1993—San Francisco NFL	16	16	3	69	23.0	1	98	*1503	15.3	†15	*16	...	96	3
1994—San Francisco NFL	16	16	7	93	13.3	2	112	*1499	13.4	13	15	1	92	1
1995—San Francisco NFL	16	16	5	36	7.2	1	122	*1848	15.1	15	17	1	104	3
1996—San Francisco NFL	16	16	11	77	7.0	1	*108	1254	11.6	8	9	0	54	0
1997—San Francisco NFL	2	1	1	-10	-10.0	0	7	78	11.1	1	1	0	6	0
1998—San Francisco NFL	16	16	0	0	...	0	82	1157	14.1	9	9	†2	58	2
Pro totals (14 years)	206	192	81	614	7.6	10	1139	17612	15.5	164	175	4	1058	20

RICE, RON S

PERSONAL: Born November 9, 1972, in Detroit. ... 6-1/206. ... Full name: Ronald Wilson Rice.
HIGH SCHOOL: University of Detroit Jesuit.
COLLEGE: Eastern Michigan (degree in criminal justice).
TRANSACTIONS/CAREER NOTES: Signed as non-drafted free agent by Detroit Lions (April 24, 1995). ... Released by Lions (August 18, 1995). ... Re-signed by Lions to practice squad (August 29, 1995). ... Activated (November 1, 1995); did not play. ... Granted free agency (February 13, 1998). ... Re-signed by Lions (June 25, 1998). ... Granted unconditional free agency (February 12, 1999).
PLAYING EXPERIENCE: Detroit NFL, 1996-1998. ... Games/Games started: 1996 (13/2), 1997 (12/8), 1998 (16/16). Total: 41/26.
PRO STATISTICS: 1997—Intercepted one pass for 18 yards and credited with one sack. 1998—Intercepted three passes for 25 yards and credited with 3 1/2 sacks.

RICE, SIMEON DE CARDINALS

PERSONAL: Born February 24, 1974, in Chicago. ... 6-5/260.
HIGH SCHOOL: Mount Carmel (Chicago).
COLLEGE: Illinois (degree in speech communications, 1996).
TRANSACTIONS/CAREER NOTES: Selected by Arizona Cardinals in first round (third pick overall) of 1996 NFL draft. ... Signed by Cardinals (August 19, 1996).
HONORS: Named linebacker on THE SPORTING NEWS college All-America second team (1995).
RECORDS: Shares NFL rookie-season record for most sacks—12.5 (1996).
PRO STATISTICS: 1996—Recovered one fumble. 1997—Intercepted one pass for no yards. 1998—Recovered four fumbles for 39 yards.

Year Team	G	GS	SACKS
1996—Arizona NFL	16	15	12.5
1997—Arizona NFL	16	15	5.0
1998—Arizona NFL	16	16	10.0
Pro totals (3 years)	48	46	27.5

RICHARD, STANLEY S

PERSONAL: Born October 21, 1967, in Miniola, Texas. ... 6-2/198. ... Full name: Stanley Palmer Richard.
HIGH SCHOOL: Hawkins (Texas).
COLLEGE: Texas.

TRANSACTIONS/CAREER NOTES: Selected by San Diego Chargers in first round (ninth pick overall) of 1991 NFL draft. ... Signed by Chargers (August 5, 1991). ... Granted free agency (February 17, 1994). ... Re-signed by Chargers (May 2, 1994). ... Granted unconditional free agency (February 17, 1995). ... Signed by Washington Redskins (March 10, 1995). ... Granted unconditional free agency (February 12, 1999).
CHAMPIONSHIP GAME EXPERIENCE: Played in AFC championship game (1994 season). ... Played in Super Bowl XXIX (1994 season).
PRO STATISTICS: 1992—Recovered one fumble. 1993—Credited with two sacks and recovered one fumble. 1995—Recovered one fumble. 1997—Recovered one fumble. 1998—Recovered one fumble.

				INTERCEPTIONS		
Year Team	G	GS	No.	Yds.	Avg.	TD
1991—San Diego NFL	15	14	2	5	2.5	0
1992—San Diego NFL	14	14	3	26	8.7	0
1993—San Diego NFL	16	16	1	-2	-2.0	0
1994—San Diego NFL	16	16	4	§224	56.0	2
1995—Washington NFL	16	16	3	24	8.0	0
1996—Washington NFL	16	15	3	47	15.7	0
1997—Washington NFL	16	16	4	28	7.0	0
1998—Washington NFL	15	15	1	0	0.0	0
Pro totals (8 years)	124	122	21	352	16.8	2

RICHARDSON, DAMIEN   S   PANTHERS

PERSONAL: Born April 3, 1976, in Los Angeles. ... 6-1/210. ... Full name: Damien A. Richardson.
HIGH SCHOOL: Clovis West (Fresno, Calif.).
COLLEGE: Arizona State.
TRANSACTIONS/CAREER NOTES: Selected by Carolina Panthers in sixth round (165th pick overall) of 1998 NFL draft. ... Signed by Panthers (July 24, 1998).
PLAYING EXPERIENCE: Carolina NFL, 1998. ... Games/Games started: 14/7.
PRO STATISTICS: 1998—Recovered one fumble.

RICHARDSON, KYLE   P   RAVENS

PERSONAL: Born March 2, 1973, in Farmington, Mo. ... 6-2/190. ... Full name: Kyle Davis Richardson.
HIGH SCHOOL: Farmington (Mo.).
COLLEGE: Arkansas State.
TRANSACTIONS/CAREER NOTES: Signed as non-drafted free agent by Miami Dolphins (September 3, 1997). ... Released by Dolphins (September 8, 1997). ... Re-signed by Dolphins (September 18, 1997). ... Released by Dolphins (October 7, 1997). ... Signed by Seattle Seahawks (November 12, 1997). ... Released by Seahawks (November 25, 1997). ... Signed by Baltimore Ravens (March 25, 1998).
PRO STATISTICS: 1997—Rushed once for no yards and fumbled once for minus 13 yards. 1998—Rushed once for no yards and recovered one fumble.

			PUNTING			
Year Team	G	No.	Yds.	Avg.	Net avg.	In. 20	Blk.
1997—Miami NFL	3	11	480	43.6	33.1	0	0
—Seattle NFL	2	8	324	40.5	23.8	2	†2
1998—Baltimore NFL	16	90	3948	43.9	38.3	25	*2
Pro totals (2 years)	21	109	4752	43.6	36.7	27	4

RICHARDSON, TONY   FB   CHIEFS

PERSONAL: Born December 17, 1971, in Frankfurt, West Germany. ... 6-1/230. ... Full name: Antonio Richardson.
HIGH SCHOOL: Daleville (Ala.).
COLLEGE: Auburn.
TRANSACTIONS/CAREER NOTES: Signed as non-drafted free agent by Dallas Cowboys (April 28, 1994). ... Released by Cowboys (August 28, 1994). ... Re-signed by Cowboys to practice squad (August 30, 1994). ... Granted free agency after 1994 season. ... Signed by Kansas City Chiefs (February 28, 1995). ... On injured reserve with wrist injury (December 11, 1996-remainder of season).
PRO STATISTICS: 1996—Recovered one fumble. 1998—Returned one kickoff for no yards and recovered one fumble.
SINGLE GAME HIGHS (regular season): Attempts—4 (November 1, 1998, vs. New York Jets); yards—13 (November 1, 1998, vs. New Yrok Jets); and rushing touchdowns—1 (November 1, 1998, vs. New York Jets).

			RUSHING				RECEIVING			TOTALS			
Year Team	G	GS	Att.	Yds.	Avg.	TD	No.	Yds.	Avg.	TD	2pt.	Pts.	Fum.
1995—Kansas City NFL	14	1	8	18	2.3	0	0	0	...	0	0	0	0
1996—Kansas City NFL	13	0	4	10	2.5	0	2	18	9.0	1	1	6	0
1997—Kansas City NFL	14	0	2	11	5.5	0	3	6	2.0	3	0	18	0
1998—Kansas City NFL	14	1	20	45	2.3	2	2	13	6.5	0	2	12	0
Pro totals (4 years)	55	2	34	84	2.5	2	7	37	5.3	4	6	36	0

RICHARDSON, WALLY   QB   RAVENS

PERSONAL: Born February 11, 1974, in Sumter, S.C. ... 6-4/225. ... Full name: Wallace Herman Richardson.
HIGH SCHOOL: Sumter (S.C.).
COLLEGE: Penn State.
TRANSACTIONS/CAREER NOTES: Selected by Baltimore Ravens in seventh round (234th pick overall) of 1997 NFL draft. ... Signed by Ravens (July 10, 1997). ... Active for 16 games (1997); did not play. ... Assigned by Ravens to England Monarchs in 1998 NFL Europe enhancement allocation program (February 18, 1998).
SINGLE GAME HIGHS (regular season): Attempts—2 (December 27, 1998, vs. Detroit); completions—1 (December 27, 1998, vs. Detroit); yards—1 (December 27, 1998, vs. Detroit); and touchdown passes—0.

				PASSING						RUSHING				TOTALS		
Year Team	G	GS	Att.	Cmp.	Pct.	Yds.	TD	Int.	Avg.	Rat.	Att.	Yds.	Avg.	TD	TD	2pt.	Pts.
1997—Baltimore NFL						Did not play.											
1998—England NFLE	...	...	43	19	44.2	194	2	2	4.51	53.8	4	9	2.3	0	0	...	0
—Baltimore NFL	1	0	2	1	50.0	1	0	0	0.50	56.3	1	0	0.0	0	0	0	0
NFL Europe totals (1 year)	...	...	43	19	44.2	194	2	2	4.51	53.8	4	9	2.3	0	0	...	0
NFL totals (0 years)	1	0	2	1	50.0	1	0	0	0.50	56.3	1	0	0.0	0	0	0	0
Pro totals (1 years)	...	...	45	20	44.4	195	2	2	4.33	53.5	5	9	1.8	0	0	...	0

RICHEY, WADE — K — 49ERS

PERSONAL: Born May 19, 1976, in Lafayette, La. ... 6-4/200. ... Full name: Wade Edward Richey.
HIGH SCHOOL: Carencro (Lafayette, La.).
COLLEGE: Louisiana State.
TRANSACTIONS/CAREER NOTES: Signed as non-drafted free agent by Seattle Seahawks (April 21, 1998). ... Claimed on waivers by San Francisco 49ers (August 26, 1998).

		KICKING					
Year Team	G	XPM	XPA	FGM	FGA	Lg.	50+	Pts.
1998—San Francisco NFL	16	49	51	18	27	46	0-0	103

RICHIE, DAVID — DT — 49ERS

PERSONAL: Born September 26, 1973, in Orange, Calif. ... 6-4/280.
HIGH SCHOOL: Kelso (Wash.).
COLLEGE: Washington.
TRANSACTIONS/CAREER NOTES: Signed as non-drafted free agent by Denver Broncos (April 28, 1997). ... Traded by Broncos with C Steve Gordon to San Francisco 49ers for past considerations (August 25, 1998). ... Released by 49ers (November 7, 1998). ... Re-signed by 49ers to practice squad (November 17, 1998). ... Activated (December 2, 1998).
PLAYING EXPERIENCE: Denver NFL, 1997; San Francisco NFL, 1998. ... Games/Games started: 1997 (2/0), 1998 (8/0). Total: 10/0.
CHAMPIONSHIP GAME EXPERIENCE: Member of Broncos for AFC championship game (1997 season); inactive. ... Member of Super Bowl championship team (1997 season); inactive.
PRO STATISTICS: 1997—Credited with 1/2 sack. 1998—Returned one kickoff for 11 yards.

RICKS, MIKHAEL — WR — CHARGERS

PERSONAL: Born November 14, 1974, in Galveston, Texas. ... 6-5/237. ... Full name: Mikhael Roy Ricks. ... Name pronounced MICHAEL.
HIGH SCHOOL: Anahuac (Texas).
COLLEGE: Stephen F. Austin State.
TRANSACTIONS/CAREER NOTES: Selected by San Diego Chargers in second round (59th pick overall) of 1998 NFL draft. ... Signed by Chargers (July 23, 1998).
SINGLE GAME HIGHS (regular season): Receptions—5 (October 25, 1998, vs. Seattle); yards—76 (December 6, 1998, vs. Washington); and touchdown receptions—1 (December 20, 1998, vs. Oakland).

			RECEIVING				TOTALS		
Year Team	G	GS	No.	Yds.	Avg.	TD	TD	2pt.	Pts.	Fum.
1998—San Diego NFL	16	9	30	450	15.0	2	2	0	12	1

RIDDICK, LOUIS — S

PERSONAL: Born March 15, 1969, in Quakertown, Pa. ... 6-2/215. ... Full name: Louis Angelo Riddick. ... Brother of Robb Riddick, running back with Buffalo Bills (1981, 1983, 1984 and 1986-88); and cousin of Tim Lewis, defensive back//kick returner with Green Bay Packers (1983-86).
HIGH SCHOOL: Pennridge (Perkasie, Pa.).
COLLEGE: Pittsburgh (degree in economics, 1991).
TRANSACTIONS/CAREER NOTES: Selected by San Francisco 49ers in ninth round (248th pick overall) of 1991 NFL draft. ... Signed by 49ers (July 11, 1991). ... Released by 49ers (August 20, 1991). ... Selected by Sacramento Surge in 19th round (200th pick overall) of 1992 World League draft. ... Signed by Atlanta Falcons (June 25, 1992). ... Released by Falcons (August 31, 1993). ... Signed by Cleveland Browns (September 8, 1993). ... Granted free agency (February 17, 1995). ... Re-signed by Browns (March 31, 1995). ... Granted unconditional free agency (February 16, 1996). ... Signed by Falcons (April 11, 1996). ... Granted unconditional free agency (February 14, 1997). ... Signed by Oakland Raiders (May 5, 1998). ... Granted unconditional free agency (February 12, 1999).
PRO STATISTICS: W.L.: 1992—Intercepted one pass for three yards and recovered one fumble. NFL: 1993—Credited with one safety. 1995—Caught one pass for 25 yards. 1998—Recovered one fumble.

Year Team	G	GS	SACKS
1992—Sacramento W.L.	10	10	1.0
—Atlanta NFL	16	4	1.0
1993—Cleveland NFL	15	0	0.0
1994—Cleveland NFL	16	0	0.0
1995—Cleveland NFL	16	0	0.0
1996—Atlanta NFL	16	1	1.0
1997—	Did not play.		
1998—Oakland NFL	15	3	0.0
W.L. totals (1 year)	10	10	1.0
NFL totals (6 years)	94	8	2.0
Pro totals (7 years)	104	18	3.0

RIEMERSMA, JAY — TE — BILLS

PERSONAL: Born May 17, 1973, in Evansville, Ind. ... 6-5/254. ... Full name: Allen Jay Riemersma. ... Name pronounced REE-mers-muh.
HIGH SCHOOL: Zeeland (Mich.).
COLLEGE: Michigan.
TRANSACTIONS/CAREER NOTES: Selected by Buffalo Bills in seventh round (244th pick overall) of 1996 NFL draft. ... Signed by Bills (July 9, 1996). ... Released by Bills (August 25, 1996). ... Re-signed by Bills to practice squad (August 26, 1996). ... Activated (October 15, 1996); did not play. ... Granted free agency (February 12, 1999). ... Re-signed by Bills (April 26, 1999).
PRO STATISTICS: 1998—Returned one kickoff for nine yards and recovered one fumble.
SINGLE GAME HIGHS (regular season): Receptions—5 (November 23, 1997, vs. Tennessee); yards—54 (August 31, 1997, vs. Minnesota); and touchdown receptions—2 (November 1, 1998, vs. Miami).

				RECEIVING				TOTALS		
Year Team	G	GS	No.	Yds.	Avg.	TD	TD	2pt.	Pts.	Fum.
1996—Buffalo NFL						Did not play.				
1997—Buffalo NFL	16	8	26	208	8.0	2	2	1	14	1
1998—Buffalo NFL	16	3	25	288	11.5	6	6	0	36	0
Pro totals (2 years)	32	11	51	496	9.7	8	8	1	50	1

RILEY, VICTOR — OT — CHIEFS

PERSONAL: Born November 4, 1974, in Swansea, S.C. ... 6-5/321. ... Full name: Victor Allan Riley.
HIGH SCHOOL: Swansea (S.C.).
COLLEGE: Auburn.
TRANSACTIONS/CAREER NOTES: Selected by Kansas City Chiefs in first round (27th pick overall) of 1998 NFL draft. ... Signed by Chiefs (July 2, 1998).
PLAYING EXPERIENCE: Kansas City NFL, 1998. ... Games/Games started: 16/15.
PRO STATISTICS: 1998—Recovered one fumble.

RISON, ANDRE — WR — CHIEFS

PERSONAL: Born March 18, 1967, in Flint, Mich. ... 6-1/195. ... Full name: Andre Previn Rison. ... Name pronounced RYE-zun.
HIGH SCHOOL: Northwestern (Flint, Mich.).
COLLEGE: Michigan State.
TRANSACTIONS/CAREER NOTES: Selected by Indianapolis Colts in first round (22nd pick overall) of 1989 NFL draft. ... Signed by Colts (May 2, 1989). ... Traded by Colts with OT Chris Hinton, fifth-round pick (OT Reggie Redding) in 1990 draft and first-round pick (WR Mike Pritchard) in 1991 draft to Atlanta Falcons for first- (QB Jeff George) and fourth-round (WR Stacey Simmons) picks in 1990 draft (April 20, 1990). ... Granted roster exemption for one game (September 1992). ... Designated by Falcons as transition player (February 25, 1993). ... On reserve/did not report list (July 23-August 20, 1993). ... Granted roster exemption (August 20-26, 1993). ... On suspended list (November 21-22, 1994). ... Free agency status changed by Falcons from transitional to unconditional (February 17, 1995). ... Signed by Cleveland Browns (March 24, 1995). ... Browns franchise moved to Baltimore and renamed Ravens for 1996 season (March 11, 1996). ... Released by Ravens (July 9, 1996). ... Signed by Jacksonville Jaguars (July 17, 1996). ... Released by Jaguars (November 18, 1996). ... Claimed on waivers by Green Bay Packers (November 19, 1996). ... Released by Packers (March 25, 1997). ... Signed by Kansas City Chiefs (June 18, 1997).
CHAMPIONSHIP GAME EXPERIENCE: Played in NFC championship game (1996 season). ... Member of Super Bowl championship team (1996 season).
HONORS: Named wide receiver on THE SPORTING NEWS NFL All-Pro team (1990). ... Played in Pro Bowl (1990-1993 and 1997 seasons). ... Named Outstanding Player of Pro Bowl (1993 season).
PRO STATISTICS: 1989—Rushed three times for 18 yards and returned two punts for 20 yards. 1990—Returned two punts for 10 yards. 1991—Rushed once for minus nine yards. 1995—Rushed twice for no yards and recovered one fumble. 1997—Rushed once for two yards. 1998—Rushed twice for 12 yards and recovered one fumble.
SINGLE GAME HIGHS (regular season): Receptions—14 (September 4, 1994, vs. Detroit); yards—193 (September 4, 1994, vs. Detroit); and touchdown receptions—3 (September 19, 1993, vs. San Francisco).
STATISTICAL PLATEAUS: 100-yard receiving games: 1989 (3), 1990 (5), 1991 (1), 1992 (2), 1993 (4), 1994 (3), 1995 (2), 1996 (1), 1997 (2). Total: 23.
MISCELLANEOUS: Holds Atlanta Falcons all-time records for most receptions (423), most touchdowns (56) and most touchdown receptions (56).

				RECEIVING				KICKOFF RETURNS			TOTALS		
Year Team	G	GS	No.	Yds.	Avg.	TD	No.	Yds.	Avg.	TD	TD	2pt.	Pts.	Fum.
1989—Indianapolis NFL	16	13	52	820	15.8	4	8	150	18.8	0	4	...	24	1
1990—Atlanta NFL	16	15	82	1208	14.7	10	0	0	...	0	10	...	60	2
1991—Atlanta NFL	16	15	81	976	12.0	12	0	0	...	0	12	...	72	1
1992—Atlanta NFL	15	13	93	1119	12.0	11	0	0	...	0	11	...	66	2
1993—Atlanta NFL	16	16	86	1242	14.4	15	0	0	...	0	15	...	90	2
1994—Atlanta NFL	15	14	81	1088	13.4	8	0	0	...	0	8	1	50	1
1995—Cleveland NFL	16	14	47	701	14.9	3	0	0	...	0	3	0	18	1
1996—Jacksonville NFL	10	9	34	458	13.5	2	0	0	...	0	2	0	12	0
—Green Bay NFL	5	4	13	135	10.4	1	0	0	...	0	1	0	6	1
1997—Kansas City NFL	16	16	72	1092	15.2	7	0	0	...	0	7	0	42	0
1998—Kansas City NFL	14	13	40	542	13.6	5	0	0	...	0	5	0	30	1
Pro totals (10 years)	155	142	681	9381	13.8	78	8	150	18.8	0	78	1	470	12

RITCHIE, JON — RB — RAIDERS

PERSONAL: Born September 4, 1974, in Mechanicsburgh, Pa. ... 6-1/250.
HIGH SCHOOL: Cumberland Valley (Pa.).
COLLEGE: Michigan, then Stanford.
TRANSACTIONS/CAREER NOTES: Selected by Oakland Raiders in third round (63rd pick overall) of 1998 NFL draft. ... Signed by Raiders (July 18, 1998).

SINGLE GAME HIGHS (regular season): Attempts—2 (December 6, 1998, vs. Miami); yards—14 (November 15, 1998, vs. Seattle); and rushing touchdowns—0.

				RUSHING				RECEIVING				TOTALS		
Year Team	G	GS	Att.	Yds.	Avg.	TD	No.	Yds.	Avg.	TD	TD	2pt.	Pts.	Fum.
1998—Oakland NFL	15	10	9	23	2.6	0	29	225	7.8	0	0	0	0	2

RIVERA, MARCO   G   PACKERS

PERSONAL: Born April 26, 1972, in Brooklyn, N.Y. ... 6-4/305. ... Full name: Marco Anthony Rivera.
HIGH SCHOOL: Elmont (N.Y.) Memorial.
COLLEGE: Penn State (degree in administration of justice).
TRANSACTIONS/CAREER NOTES: Selected by Green Bay Packers in sixth round (208th pick overall) of 1996 NFL draft. ... Signed by Packers (July 15, 1996). ... Inactive for all 16 games (1996). ... Assigned by Packers to Scottish Claymores in 1997 World League enhancement allocation program (February 19, 1997). ... Granted free agency (February 12, 1999). ... Re-signed by Packers (March 24, 1999).
PLAYING EXPERIENCE: Scottish W.L., 1997; Green Bay NFL, 1997 and 1998. ... Games/Games started: W.L. 1997 (10/10), NFL 1997 (14/0), 1998 (15/15). Total W.L.: 10/10. Total NFL: 29/15. Total Pro: 39/25.
CHAMPIONSHIP GAME EXPERIENCE: Member of Packers for NFC championship game (1996 season); inactive. ... Member of Super Bowl championship team (1996 season); inactive. ... Played in NFC championship game (1997 season). ... Played in Super Bowl XXXII (1997 season).

RIVERS, RON   RB   LIONS

PERSONAL: Born November 13, 1971, in Elizabeth City, N.J. ... 5-8/205. ... Full name: Ronald Leroy Rivers.
HIGH SCHOOL: San Gorgonio (San Bernardino, Calif.).
COLLEGE: Fresno State.
TRANSACTIONS/CAREER NOTES: Signed as non-drafted free agent by San Diego Chargers (April 28, 1994). ... Released by Chargers (August 29, 1994). ... Signed by Detroit Lions to practice squad (September 21, 1994). ... Activated (December 22, 1994); did not play. ... Granted free agency (February 13, 1998). ... Re-signed by Lions (April 29, 1998).
POST SEASON RECORDS: Shares NFL postseason career and single-game records for most two-point conversions—1 (December 30, 1995, vs. Philadelphia).
PRO STATISTICS: 1995—Caught one pass for five yards and recovered one fumble. 1997—Recovered one fumble.
SINGLE GAME HIGHS (regular season): Attempts—11 (December 17, 1995, vs. Jacksonville); yards—59 (December 17, 1995, vs. Jacksonville); and rushing touchdowns—1 (November 27, 1997, vs. Chicago).

			RUSHING				RECEIVING				KICKOFF RETURNS				TOTALS			
Year Team	G	GS	Att.	Yds.	Avg.	TD	No.	Yds.	Avg.	TD	No.	Yds.	Avg.	TD	TD	2pt.	Pts.	Fum.
1994—Detroit NFL								Did not play.										
1995—Detroit NFL	16	0	18	73	4.1	1	1	5	5.0	0	19	420	22.1	0	1	0	6	2
1996—Detroit NFL	15	0	19	86	4.5	0	2	28	14.0	0	1	8	8.0	0	0	0	0	0
1997—Detroit NFL	16	0	29	166	5.7	1	0	0	...	0	2	34	17.0	0	1	0	6	0
1998—Detroit NFL	15	0	19	102	5.4	1	3	58	19.3	0	2	15	7.5	0	1	0	6	0
Pro totals (4 years)	62	0	85	427	5.0	3	6	91	15.2	0	24	477	19.9	0	3	0	18	2

ROAF, WILLIE   OT   SAINTS

PERSONAL: Born April 18, 1970, in Pine Bluff, Ark. ... 6-5/312. ... Full name: William Layton Roaf.
HIGH SCHOOL: Pine Bluff (Ark.).
COLLEGE: Louisiana Tech.
TRANSACTIONS/CAREER NOTES: Selected by New Orleans Saints in first round (eighth pick overall) of 1993 NFL draft. ... Signed by Saints (July 15, 1993). ... Designated by Saints as transition player (February 15, 1994).
PLAYING EXPERIENCE: New Orleans NFL, 1993-1998. ... Games/Games started: 1993 (16/16), 1994 (16/16), 1995 (16/16), 1996 (13/13), 1997 (16/16), 1998 (15/15). Total: 92/92.
HONORS: Named offensive tackle on THE SPORTING NEWS college All-America second team (1992). ... Named offensive tackle on THE SPORTING NEWS NFL All-Pro team (1994-1996). ... Played in Pro Bowl (1994-1997 seasons). ... Named to play in Pro Bowl (1998 season); replaced by Bob Whitfield due to injury.
PRO STATISTICS: 1994—Recovered one fumble. 1996—Recovered one fumble.

ROAN, MICHAEL   TE/RB   TITANS

PERSONAL: Born August 29, 1972, in Iowa City, Iowa. ... 6-3/250. ... Full name: Michael Phillip Roan.
HIGH SCHOOL: Iowa City (Iowa) High.
COLLEGE: Wisconsin.
TRANSACTIONS/CAREER NOTES: Selected by Houston Oilers in fourth round (101st pick overall) of 1995 NFL draft. ... Signed by Oilers (July 10, 1995). ... Oilers franchise moved to Tennessee for 1997 season. ... Oilers franchise renamed Tennessee Titans for 1999 season (December 26, 1998).
PRO STATISTICS: 1995—Recovered one fumble. 1996—Returned one kickoff for 13 yards. 1997—Returned two kickoffs for 20 yards. 1998—Returned one kickoff for four yards and recovered one fumble in end zone for a touchdown.
SINGLE GAME HIGHS (regular season): Receptions—4 (December 6, 1998, vs. Baltimore); yards—51 (November 2, 1997, vs. Jacksonville); and touchdown receptions—0.

			RECEIVING				TOTALS			
Year Team	G	GS	No.	Yds.	Avg.	TD	TD	2pt.	Pts.	Fum.
1995—Houston NFL	5	2	8	46	5.8	0	0	0	0	1
1996—Houston NFL	15	1	0	0	...	0	0	0	0	0
1997—Tennessee NFL	14	13	12	159	13.3	0	0	0	0	0
1998—Tennessee NFL	16	1	13	93	7.2	0	1	0	6	1
Pro totals (4 years)	50	17	33	298	9.0	0	1	0	6	2

ROBBINS, AUSTIN — DT — SAINTS

PERSONAL: Born March 1, 1971, in Washington, D.C. ... 6-6/290. ... Full name: Austin Dion Robbins.
HIGH SCHOOL: Howard D. Woodson (Washington, D.C.).
COLLEGE: North Carolina.
TRANSACTIONS/CAREER NOTES: Selected by Los Angeles Raiders in fourth round (120th pick overall) of 1994 NFL draft. ... Signed by Raiders (July 14, 1994). ... Raiders franchise moved to Oakland (July 21, 1995). ... Traded by Raiders to New Orleans Saints for undisclosed pick in 1997 draft (August 25, 1996). ... Granted free agency (February 14, 1997). ... Re-signed by Saints (June 7, 1997). ... Granted unconditional free agency (February 13, 1998). ... Re-signed by Saints (March 6, 1998).
PRO STATISTICS: 1995—Recovered two fumbles for six yards and one touchdown. 1998—Recovered one fumble in end zone for a touchdown.

Year Team	G	GS	SACKS
1994—Los Angeles Raiders NFL	2	0	0.0
1995—Oakland NFL	16	0	2.0
1996—New Orleans NFL	15	7	1.0
1997—New Orleans NFL	12	0	0.0
1998—New Orleans NFL	16	1	1.0
Pro totals (5 years)	61	8	4.0

ROBBINS, BARRET — C — RAIDERS

PERSONAL: Born August 26, 1973, in Houston. ... 6-3/315.
HIGH SCHOOL: Sharpstown (Houston).
COLLEGE: Texas Christian.
TRANSACTIONS/CAREER NOTES: Selected by Los Angeles Raiders in second round (49th pick overall) of 1995 NFL draft. ... Signed by Raiders (June 20, 1995). ... Raiders franchise moved to Oakland (July 21, 1995).
PLAYING EXPERIENCE: Oakland NFL, 1995-1998. ... Games/Games started: 1995 (16/0), 1996 (14/14), 1997 (16/16), 1998 (16/16). Total: 62/46.
PRO STATISTICS: 1996—Recovered one fumble.

ROBERSON, JAMES — DE — TITANS

PERSONAL: Born May 3, 1971, in Bartow, Fla. ... 6-3/275. ... Full name: James Earl Roberson.
HIGH SCHOOL: Lake Wales (Fla.).
COLLEGE: Florida State.
TRANSACTIONS/CAREER NOTES: Signed as non-drafted free agent by New Orleans Saints (April 27, 1995). ... Claimed on waivers by Green Bay Packers (July 27, 1995). ... Released by Packers (August 21, 1995). ... Signed by Rhein Fire of World League (February 1996). ... Signed by Houston Oilers (July 20, 1996). ... Released by Oilers (August 25, 1996). ... Re-signed by Oilers to practice squad (August 26, 1996). ... Activated (September 6, 1996). ... Oilers franchise moved to Tennessee for 1997 season. ... Oilers franchise renamed Tennessee Titans for 1999 season (December 26, 1998). ... Granted free agency (February 12, 1999). ... Re-signed by Titans (May 3, 1999).
PRO STATISTICS: 1996—Recovered one fumble for four yards. 1997—Recovered one fumble.

Year Team	G	GS	SACKS
1996—Rhein W.L.	...	...	3.0
—Houston NFL	15	5	3.0
1997—Tennessee NFL	15	11	2.0
1998—Tennessee NFL	10	5	0.0
W.L. totals (1 year)	...	...	3.0
NFL totals (3 years)	40	21	5.0
Pro totals (4 years)	...	...	8.0

ROBERTS, RAY — OT — LIONS

PERSONAL: Born June 3, 1969, in Asheville, N.C. ... 6-6/308. ... Full name: Richard Ray Roberts Jr.
HIGH SCHOOL: Asheville (N.C.).
COLLEGE: Virginia (degree in communication studies, 1991).
TRANSACTIONS/CAREER NOTES: Selected by Seattle Seahawks in first round (10th pick overall) of 1992 NFL draft. ... Signed by Seahawks (August 1, 1992). ... Designated by Seahawks as transition player (February 15, 1994). ... On injured reserve with ankle injury (December 11, 1994-remainder of season). ... Free agency status changed by Seahawks from transitional to unconditional (February 16, 1996). ... Signed by Detroit Lions (March 11, 1996). ... Granted unconditional free agency (February 13, 1998). ... Re-signed by Lions (February 19, 1998).
PLAYING EXPERIENCE: Seattle NFL, 1992-1995; Detroit NFL, 1996-1998. ... Games/Games started: 1992 (16/16), 1993 (16/16), 1994 (14/14), 1995 (11/0), 1996 (16/16), 1997 (14/14), 1998 (16/16). Total: 103/92.
HONORS: Named offensive tackle on THE SPORTING NEWS college All-America second team (1991).
PRO STATISTICS: 1993—Caught one pass for four yards. 1996—Ran five yards with lateral from reception and recovered two fumbles. 1997—Recovered two fumbles for four yards.

ROBERTSON, MARCUS — S — TITANS

PERSONAL: Born October 2, 1969, in Pasadena, Calif. ... 5-11/205. ... Full name: Marcus Aaron Robertson.
HIGH SCHOOL: John Muir (Pasadena, Calif.).
COLLEGE: Iowa State.
TRANSACTIONS/CAREER NOTES: Selected by Houston Oilers in fourth round (102nd pick overall) of 1991 NFL draft. ... Signed by Oilers (July 16, 1991). ... On injured reserve with knee injury (December 30, 1993-remainder of season). ... Granted free agency (February 17, 1994). ... Re-signed by Oilers (July 11, 1994). ... On injured reserve with knee injury (November 30, 1995-remainder of season). ... Oilers franchise moved to Tennessee for 1997 season. ... Oilers franchise renamed Tennessee Titans for 1999 season (December 26, 1998).

HONORS: Named free safety on THE SPORTING NEWS NFL All-Pro team (1993).
PRO STATISTICS: 1991—Credited with one sack, returned one punt for no yards and fumbled once. 1993—Recovered three fumbles for 107 yards and one touchdown. 1994—Returned one punt for no yards, fumbled once and recovered one fumble. 1996—Recovered one fumble for five yards. 1997—Returned one punt for no yards and recovered three fumbles for 67 yards and two touchdowns.

				INTERCEPTIONS		
Year Team	G	GS	No.	Yds.	Avg.	TD
1991—Houston NFL	16	0	0	0	...	0
1992—Houston NFL	16	14	1	27	27.0	0
1993—Houston NFL	13	13	7	137	19.6	0
1994—Houston NFL	16	16	3	90	30.0	0
1995—Houston NFL	2	2	0	0	...	0
1996—Houston NFL	16	16	4	44	11.0	0
1997—Tennessee NFL	14	14	5	127	25.4	0
1998—Tennessee NFL	12	12	1	0	0.0	0
Pro totals (8 years)	105	87	21	425	20.2	0

ROBINSON, BRYAN — DL — BEARS

PERSONAL: Born June 22, 1974, in Toledo, Ohio. ... 6-4/283. ... Full name: Bryan Keith Robinson.
HIGH SCHOOL: Woodward (Toledo, Ohio).
JUNIOR COLLEGE: College of the Desert (Palm Desert, Calif.).
COLLEGE: Fresno State.
TRANSACTIONS/CAREER NOTES: Signed as non-drafted free agent by St. Louis Rams (April 29, 1997). ... Claimed on waivers by Chicago Bears (August 31, 1998).
PLAYING EXPERIENCE: St. Louis NFL, 1997; Chicago NFL, 1998. ... Games/Games started: 1997 (11/0), 1998 (10/5). Total: 21/5.
PRO STATISTICS: 1997—Credited with one sack. 1998—Credited with 1/2 sack.

ROBINSON, DAMIEN — S — BUCCANEERS

PERSONAL: Born December 22, 1973, in Dallas. ... 6-2/205. ... Full name: Damien Dion Robinson.
HIGH SCHOOL: Hillcrest (Dallas).
COLLEGE: Iowa.
TRANSACTIONS/CAREER NOTES: Selected by Philadelphia Eagles in fourth round (119th pick overall) of 1997 NFL draft. ... Signed by Eagles (June 4, 1997). ... Released by Eagles (August 25, 1997). ... Re-signed by Eagles to practice squad (August 27, 1997). ... Signed by Tampa Bay Buccaneers off Eagles practice squad (September 17, 1997). ... Inactive for 13 games (1997). ... On injured reserve with arm injury (October 27, 1998-remainder of season).
PLAYING EXPERIENCE: Tampa Bay NFL, 1998. ... Games/Games started: 7/0.

ROBINSON, EDDIE — LB — TITANS

PERSONAL: Born April 13, 1970, in New Orleans. ... 6-1/243. ... Full name: Eddie Joseph Robinson Jr.
HIGH SCHOOL: Brother Martin (New Orleans).
COLLEGE: Alabama State (degree in chemistry, 1993).
TRANSACTIONS/CAREER NOTES: Selected by Houston Oilers in second round (50th pick overall) of 1992 NFL draft. ... Signed by Oilers (July 16, 1992). ... Granted free agency (February 17, 1995). ... Re-signed by Oilers (July 1995). ... Granted unconditional free agency (February 16, 1996). ... Signed by Jacksonville Jaguars (March 1, 1996). ... Released by Jaguars (August 30, 1998). ... Signed by Tennessee Oilers (September 1, 1998). ... Oilers franchise renamed Tennessee Titans for 1999 season (December 26, 1998). ... Granted unconditional free agency (February 12, 1999). ... Re-signed by Titans (March 1, 1999).
CHAMPIONSHIP GAME EXPERIENCE: Played in AFC championship game (1996 season).
PRO STATISTICS: 1995—Intercepted one pass for 49 yards and a touchdown and recovered one fumble. 1996—Recovered one fumble. 1997—Intercepted one pass for no yards and recovered two fumbles. 1998—Intercepted one pass for 11 yards.

Year Team	G	GS	SACKS
1992—Houston NFL	16	11	1.0
1993—Houston NFL	16	15	1.0
1994—Houston NFL	15	15	0.0
1995—Houston NFL	16	16	3.5
1996—Jacksonville NFL	16	15	1.0
1997—Jacksonville NFL	16	14	2.0
1998—Tennessee NFL	16	16	3.5
Pro totals (7 years)	111	102	12.0

ROBINSON, EUGENE — S — FALCONS

PERSONAL: Born May 28, 1963, in Hartford, Conn. ... 6-1/200. ... Full name: Eugene Keefe Robinson.
HIGH SCHOOL: Weaver (Hartford, Conn.).
COLLEGE: Colgate.
TRANSACTIONS/CAREER NOTES: Selected by New Jersey Generals in 1985 USFL territorial draft. ... Signed as non-drafted free agent by Seattle Seahawks (May 15, 1985). ... On injured reserve with Achilles' tendon injury (December 11, 1994-remainder of season). ... Traded by Seahawks to Green Bay Packers for LB Matt LaBounty (June 27, 1996). ... Granted unconditional free agency (February 13, 1998). ... Signed by Atlanta Falcons (March 6, 1998).
CHAMPIONSHIP GAME EXPERIENCE: Played in NFC championship game (1996-98 seasons). ... Member of Super Bowl championship team (1996 season). ... Played in Super Bowl XXXII (1997 season) and Super Bowl XXXIII (1998 season).
HONORS: Played in Pro Bowl (1992, 1993 and 1998 seasons).

PRO STATISTICS: 1985—Returned one kickoff for 10 yards. 1986—Recovered three fumbles for six yards. 1987—Returned blocked punt eight yards for a touchdown and recovered one fumble. 1989—Fumbled once and recovered one fumble. 1990—Recovered four fumbles for 16 yards and a touchdown. 1991—Recovered one fumble. 1992—Recovered one fumble. 1993—Recovered two fumbles for seven yards. 1994—Recovered one fumble. 1995—Returned one punt for one yard and recovered one fumble. 1997—Fumbled once and recovered two fumbles. 1998—Recovered two fumbles for 16 yards.
MISCELLANEOUS: Active NFL leader for career interceptions (53).

				INTERCEPTIONS				SACKS
Year	Team	G	GS	No.	Yds.	Avg.	TD	No.
1985—Seattle NFL		16	0	2	47	23.5	0	0.0
1986—Seattle NFL		16	16	3	39	13.0	0	0.0
1987—Seattle NFL		12	12	3	75	25.0	0	0.0
1988—Seattle NFL		16	16	1	0	0.0	0	1.0
1989—Seattle NFL		16	14	5	24	4.8	0	0.0
1990—Seattle NFL		16	16	3	89	29.7	0	0.0
1991—Seattle NFL		16	16	5	56	11.2	0	1.0
1992—Seattle NFL		16	16	7	126	18.0	0	0.0
1993—Seattle NFL		16	16	†9	80	8.9	0	2.0
1994—Seattle NFL		14	14	3	18	6.0	0	1.0
1995—Seattle NFL		16	16	1	32	32.0	0	0.0
1996—Green Bay NFL		16	16	6	107	17.8	0	0.0
1997—Green Bay NFL		16	16	1	26	26.0	0	2.5
1998—Atlanta NFL		16	16	4	36	9.0	1	0.0
Pro totals (14 years)		218	200	53	755	14.2	1	7.5

ROBINSON, JEFF   DE   RAMS

PERSONAL: Born February 20, 1970, in Kennewick, Wash. ... 6-4/275. ... Full name: Jeffrey William Robinson.
HIGH SCHOOL: Joel E. Ferris (Spokane, Wash.).
COLLEGE: Idaho (degree in finance, 1992).
TRANSACTIONS/CAREER NOTES: Selected by Denver Broncos in fourth round (98th pick overall) of 1993 NFL draft. ... Signed by Broncos (July 13, 1993). ... Granted free agency (February 16, 1996). ... Re-signed by Broncos (March 28, 1996). ... Granted unconditional free agency (February 14, 1997). ... Signed by St. Louis Rams (March 14, 1997).
PRO STATISTICS: 1993—Recovered one fumble for minus 10 yards. 1995—Returned one kickoff for 14 yards and recovered one fumble. 1996—Recovered one fumble. 1998—Caught one pass for four yards and a touchdown.

Year	Team	G	GS	SACKS
1993—Denver NFL		16	0	3.5
1994—Denver NFL		16	0	1.0
1995—Denver NFL		16	0	1.0
1996—Denver NFL		16	0	0.5
1997—St. Louis NFL		16	0	0.5
1998—St. Louis NFL		16	0	0.0
Pro totals (6 years)		96	0	6.5

ROBINSON, MARCUS   WR   BEARS

PERSONAL: Born February 27, 1975, in Fort Valley, Ga. ... 6-3/215.
HIGH SCHOOL: Peach County (Fort Valley, Ga.).
COLLEGE: South Carolina.
TRANSACTIONS/CAREER NOTES: Selected by Chicago Bears in fourth round (108th pick overall) of 1997 NFL draft. ... Signed by Bears (July 11, 1997). ... Inactive for four games (1997). ... On injured reserve with thumb injury (September 24, 1997-remainder of season). ... Assigned by Bears to Rhein Fire in 1998 NFL Europe enhancement allocation program (February 18, 1998).
PLAYING EXPERIENCE: Rhein Fire NFLE, 1998; Chicago NFL, 1998. ... Games/Games started: NFLE 1998 (games played unavailable), NFL 1998 (3/0).
PRO STATISTICS: NFLE: 1998—Caught 39 passes for 811 yards and five touchdowns. NFL: 1998—Caught four passes for 44 yards and one touchdown.
SINGLE GAME HIGHS (regular season): Receptions—2 (October 4, 1998, vs. Detroit); yards—33 (October 4, 1998, vs. Detroit); and touchdown receptions—1 (October 4, 1998, vs. Detroit).

ROBY, REGGIE   P

PERSONAL: Born July 30, 1961, in Waterloo, Iowa. ... 6-2/258. ... Full name: Reginald Henry Roby. ... Brother of Mike Roby, first baseman/outfielder with San Francisco Giants organization (1967-68).
HIGH SCHOOL: East (Waterloo, Iowa).
COLLEGE: Iowa.
TRANSACTIONS/CAREER NOTES: Selected by Chicago Blitz in 16th round (187th pick overall) of 1983 USFL draft. ... Selected by Miami Dolphins in sixth round (167th pick overall) of 1983 NFL draft. ... Signed by Dolphins (July 9, 1983). ... On injured reserve with knee, ankle and groin injuries (September 16-October 31, 1987). ... Crossed picket line during players strike (October 14, 1987). ... On injured reserve with knee injury (September 18-November 4, 1992). ... Released by Dolphins (August 30, 1993). ... Signed by Washington Redskins (September 7, 1993). ... Granted unconditional free agency (February 17, 1995). ... Signed by Tampa Bay Buccaneers (February 20, 1995). ... Released by Buccaneers (May 13, 1996). ... Signed by Houston Oilers (June 13, 1996). ... Oilers franchise moved to Tennessee for 1997 season. ... Released by Oilers (February 14, 1998). ... Signed by San Francisco 49ers (September 22, 1998). ... Granted unconditional free agency (February 12, 1999).
CHAMPIONSHIP GAME EXPERIENCE: Played in AFC championship game (1984, 1985 and 1992 seasons). ... Played in Super Bowl XIX (1984 season).
HONORS: Named punter on THE SPORTING NEWS NFL All-Pro team (1984 and 1994). ... Played in Pro Bowl (1984, 1989 and 1994 seasons).
PRO STATISTICS: 1986—Rushed twice for minus eight yards, fumbled twice and recovered two fumbles for minus 11 yards. 1987—Rushed once for no yards and recovered one fumble. 1989—Rushed twice for no yards and recovered two fumbles. 1993—Rushed once for no yards

...and recovered one fumble. 1994—Fumbled once and recovered one fumble. 1995—Rushed once for no yards, attempted one pass with a completion for 48 yards. 1997—Rushed once for 12 yards. 1998—Rushed once for no yards.

				PUNTING			
Year Team	G	No.	Yds.	Avg.	Net avg.	In. 20	Blk.
1983—Miami NFL	16	74	3189	43.1	36.5	§26	1
1984—Miami NFL	16	51	2281	44.7	*38.1	15	0
1985—Miami NFL	16	59	2576	43.7	34.7	19	0
1986—Miami NFL	15	56	2476	44.2	*37.3	13	0
1987—Miami NFL	10	32	1371	42.8	38.2	8	0
1988—Miami NFL	15	64	2754	43.0	35.2	18	0
1989—Miami NFL	16	58	2458	42.4	35.2	18	1
1990—Miami NFL	16	72	3022	42.0	35.6	20	0
1991—Miami NFL	16	54	2466	*45.7	36.3	17	1
1992—Miami NFL	9	35	1443	41.2	34.2	11	0
1993—Washington NFL	15	78	3447	44.2	37.2	25	0
1994—Washington NFL	16	82	3639	44.4	36.1	21	0
1995—Tampa Bay NFL	16	77	3296	42.8	36.2	23	1
1996—Houston NFL	16	67	2973	44.4	38.0	25	1
1997—Tennessee NFL	16	73	3049	41.8	35.6	25	0
1998—San Francisco NFL	14	60	2511	41.9	34.3	14	0
Pro totals (16 years)	238	992	42951	43.3	36.2	298	5

ROCHE, BRIAN   TE   CHIEFS

PERSONAL: Born May 5, 1973, in Downey, Calif. ... 6-5/255. ... Full name: Brian Matthew Roche.
HIGH SCHOOL: Damien (LaVerne, Calif.).
COLLEGE: Cal Poly-SLO, then San Jose State (degree in communications, 1995).
TRANSACTIONS/CAREER NOTES: Selected by San Diego Chargers in third round (81st pick overall) of 1996 NFL draft. ... Signed by Chargers (July 14, 1996). ... On injured reserve with knee injury (November 26, 1997-remainder of season). ... Released by Chargers (September 1, 1998). ... Signed by Kansas City Chiefs (September 8, 1998). ... Released by Chiefs (October 13, 1998). ... Re-signed by Chiefs (December 9, 1998). ... Granted free agency (February 12, 1999). ... Re-signed by Chiefs (April 9, 1999).
PLAYING EXPERIENCE: San Diego NFL, 1996 and 1997; Kansas City NFL, 1998. ... Games/Games started: 1996 (13/0), 1997 (5/0), 1998 (4/1). Total: 22/1.
PRO STATISTICS: 1996—Caught 13 passes for 111 yards.
SINGLE GAME HIGHS (regular season): Receptions—3 (December 22, 1996, vs. Denver); yards—23 (December 22, 1996, vs. Denver); and touchdown receptions—0.

RODENHAUSER, MARK   C

PERSONAL: Born June 1, 1961, in Elmhurst, Ill. ... 6-5/280. ... Full name: Mark Todd Rodenhauser. ... Name pronounced RO-den-how-ser.
HIGH SCHOOL: Addison (Ill.) Trail.
COLLEGE: Illinois State (degree in industrial technology).
TRANSACTIONS/CAREER NOTES: Signed as non-drafted free agent by Michigan Panthers of USFL (January 15, 1984). ... Released by Panthers (February 13, 1984). ... Signed by Memphis Showboats of USFL (December 3, 1984). ... Released by Showboats (January 22, 1985). ... Signed by Chicago Bruisers of Arena Football League (June 29, 1987). ... Granted free agency (August 15, 1987). ... Signed as replacement player by Chicago Bears (September 24, 1987). ... Left camp voluntarily (August 16, 1988). ... Released by Bears (August 17, 1988). ... Signed by Minnesota Vikings (March 16, 1989). ... Granted unconditional free agency (February 1, 1990). ... Signed by San Diego Chargers (March 1, 1990). ... Granted unconditional free agency (February 1-April 1, 1991). ... Re-signed by Chargers (April 5, 1991). ... On injured reserve with foot injury (November 13, 1991-remainder of season). ... Granted unconditional free agency (February 1, 1992). ... Signed by Bears (March 6, 1992). ... Released by Bears (December 18, 1992). ... Signed by Detroit Lions (April 30, 1993). ... Granted unconditional free agency (February 17, 1994). ... Re-signed by Lions (August 15, 1994). ... Selected by Carolina Panthers from Lions in NFL expansion draft (February 15, 1995). ... Granted unconditional free agency (February 16, 1996). ... Re-signed by Panthers (March 15, 1996). ... Granted unconditional free agency (February 14, 1997). ... Re-signed by Panthers (February 25, 1997). ... Granted unconditional free agency (February 13, 1998). ... Re-signed by Panthers (March 24, 1998). ... Released by Panthers (August 30, 1998). ... Signed by Pittsburgh Steelers (September 1, 1998). ... Released by Steelers (April 19, 1999).
PLAYING EXPERIENCE: Chicago Bruisers Arena Football, 1987; Chicago NFL, 1987 and 1992; Minnesota NFL, 1989; San Diego NFL, 1990 and 1991; Detroit NFL, 1993 and 1994; Carolina NFL, 1995-1997; Pittsburgh NFL, 1998. ... Games/Games started: 1987 Arena Football (4/4), 1987 NFL (9/3), 1988 (16/0), 1990 (16/0), 1992 (13/0), 1993 (16/0), 1994 (16/0), 1995 (16/0), 1996 (16/0), 1997 (16/0), 1998 (16/0). Total Arena League: 4/4. Total NFL: 160/3. Total Pro: 164/7.
CHAMPIONSHIP GAME EXPERIENCE: Played in NFC championship game (1996 season).

RODGERS, DERRICK   LB   DOLPHINS

PERSONAL: Born October 14, 1971, in Memphis, Tenn. ... 6-1/227. ... Full name: Derrick Andre Rodgers.
HIGH SCHOOL: St. Augustine (New Orleans).
JUNIOR COLLEGE: Riverside (Calif.) Community College.
COLLEGE: Arizona State.
TRANSACTIONS/CAREER NOTES: Selected by Miami Dolphins in third round (92nd pick overall) of 1997 NFL draft. ... Signed by Dolphins (July 8, 1997).
PRO STATISTICS: 1997—Recovered one fumble.

Year Team	G	GS	SACKS
1997—Miami NFL	15	14	5.0
1998—Miami NFL	16	16	2.5
Pro totals (2 years)	31	30	7.5

ROE, JAMES — WR — RAVENS

PERSONAL: Born August 23, 1973, in Richmond, Va. ... 6-1/187. ... Full name: James Edward Roe II.
HIGH SCHOOL: Henrico (Richmond, Va.).
COLLEGE: Norfolk State.
TRANSACTIONS/CAREER NOTES: Selected by Baltimore Ravens in sixth round (186th pick overall) of 1996 NFL draft. ... Signed by Ravens for 1996 season. ... Granted free agency (February 12, 1999). ... Re-signed by Ravens (April 9, 1999).
PRO STATISTICS: 1997—Recovered one fumble.
SINGLE GAME HIGHS (regular season): Receptions—4 (November 29, 1998, vs. Indianapolis); yards—80 (November 30, 1997, vs. Jacksonville); and touchdown receptions—1 (November 29, 1998, vs. Indianapolis).

				RECEIVING			PUNT RETURNS				KICKOFF RETURNS				TOTALS			
Year Team	G	GS	No.	Yds.	Avg.	TD	No.	Yds.	Avg.	TD	No.	Yds.	Avg.	TD	TD	2pt.	Pts.	Fum.
1996—Baltimore NFL	1	0	0	0	...	0	0	0	...	0	0	0	...	0	0	0	0	0
1997—Baltimore NFL	12	4	7	124	17.7	0	8	72	9.0	0	9	189	21.0	0	0	0	0	1
1998—Baltimore NFL	10	3	8	115	14.4	1	9	87	9.7	0	2	40	20.0	0	1	0	6	0
Pro totals (3 years)	23	7	15	239	15.9	1	17	159	9.4	0	11	229	20.8	0	1	0	6	1

ROGERS, SAM — LB — BILLS

PERSONAL: Born May 30, 1970, in Pontiac, Mich. ... 6-3/245. ... Full name: Sammy Lee Rogers.
HIGH SCHOOL: Saint Mary's Preparatory (Pontiac, Mich.).
JUNIOR COLLEGE: West Hills College (Calif.), then West Los Angeles College.
COLLEGE: Colorado.
TRANSACTIONS/CAREER NOTES: Selected by Buffalo Bills in second round (64th pick overall) of 1994 NFL draft. ... Signed by Bills (July 12, 1994). ... Granted free agency (February 14, 1997). ... Re-signed by Bills (June 12, 1997). ... Granted unconditional free agency (February 13, 1998). ... Re-signed by Bills (February 15, 1998).
PRO STATISTICS: 1995—Recovered one fumble. 1996—Recovered two fumbles.

Year Team	G	GS	SACKS
1994—Buffalo NFL	14	0	0.0
1995—Buffalo NFL	16	8	2.0
1996—Buffalo NFL	14	14	3.5
1997—Buffalo NFL	15	15	3.5
1998—Buffalo NFL	15	15	4.5
Pro totals (5 years)	74	52	13.5

ROLLE, SAMARI — CB — TITANS

PERSONAL: Born August 10, 1976, in Miami. ... 6-0/175. ... Name pronounced suh-MAHR-ree ROLL.
HIGH SCHOOL: Miami Beach.
COLLEGE: Florida State.
TRANSACTIONS/CAREER NOTES: Selected by Tennessee Oilers in second round (46th pick overall) of 1998 NFL draft. ... Signed by Oilers (July 24, 1998). ... Oilers franchise renamed Tennessee Titans for 1999 season (December 26, 1998).
PLAYING EXPERIENCE: Tennessee NFL, 1998. ... Games/Games started: 15/1.
PRO STATISTICS: 1998—Credited with two sacks.

ROMANOWSKI, BILL — LB — BRONCOS

PERSONAL: Born April 2, 1966, in Vernon, Conn. ... 6-4/245. ... Full name: William Thomas Romanowski.
HIGH SCHOOL: Rockville (Vernon, Conn.).
COLLEGE: Boston College (degree in general management, 1988).
TRANSACTIONS/CAREER NOTES: Selected by San Francisco 49ers in third round (80th pick overall) of 1988 NFL draft. ... Signed by 49ers (July 15, 1988). ... Granted free agency (February 1, 1991). ... Re-signed by 49ers (July 17, 1991). ... Granted unconditional free agency (March 1, 1993). ... Re-signed by 49ers (March 23, 1993). ... Traded by 49ers to Philadelphia Eagles for third- (traded to Los Angeles Rams) and sixth-round (traded to Green Bay) picks in 1994 draft (April 24, 1994). ... Granted unconditional free agency (February 16, 1996). ... Signed by Denver Broncos (February 23, 1996).
CHAMPIONSHIP GAME EXPERIENCE: Played in NFC championship game (1988-1990, 1992 and 1993 seasons). ... Member of Super Bowl championship team (1988, 1989, 1997 and 1998 seasons). ... Played in AFC championship game (1997 and 1998 seasons).
HONORS: Played in Pro Bowl (1996 and 1998 seasons).
PRO STATISTICS: 1988—Recovered one fumble. 1989—Returned one punt for no yards, fumbled once and recovered two fumbles. 1991—Recovered two fumbles. 1992—Recovered one fumble. 1993—Recovered one fumble. 1994—Recovered one fumble. 1995—Recovered one fumble. 1996—Recovered three fumbles. 1998—Recovered three fumbles.

			INTERCEPTIONS				SACKS
Year Team	G	GS	No.	Yds.	Avg.	TD	No.
1988—San Francisco NFL	16	8	0	0	...	0	0.0
1989—San Francisco NFL	16	4	1	13	13.0	∞1	1.0
1990—San Francisco NFL	16	16	0	0	...	0	1.0
1991—San Francisco NFL	16	16	1	7	7.0	0	1.0
1992—San Francisco NFL	16	16	0	0	...	0	1.0
1993—San Francisco NFL	16	16	0	0	...	0	3.0
1994—Philadelphia NFL	16	15	2	8	4.0	0	2.5
1995—Philadelphia NFL	16	16	2	5	2.5	0	1.0
1996—Denver NFL	16	16	3	1	0.3	0	3.0
1997—Denver NFL	16	16	1	7	7.0	0	2.0
1998—Denver NFL	16	16	2	22	11.0	0	7.5
Pro totals (11 years)	176	155	12	63	5.3	1	23.0

ROQUE, JUAN OT LIONS

PERSONAL: Born February 6, 1974, in San Diego. ... 6-8/333. ... Full name: Juan Armando Roque. ... Name pronounced row-KAY.
HIGH SCHOOL: Ontario (Calif.).
COLLEGE: Arizona State (degree in Latin American history).
TRANSACTIONS/CAREER NOTES: Selected by Detroit Lions in second round (35th pick overall) of 1997 NFL draft. ... Signed by Lions (July 13, 1997). ... On injured reserve with knee injury (December 2, 1997-remainder of season). ... On injured reserve with knee injury (August 31, 1998-entire season).
PLAYING EXPERIENCE: Detroit NFL, 1997. ... Games/Games started: 13/1.
HONORS: Named offensive tackle on THE SPORTING NEWS college All-America second team (1996).

ROSS, ADRIAN LB BENGALS

PERSONAL: Born February 19, 1975, in Santa Clara, Calif. ... 6-2/244. ... Full name: Adrian Lamont Ross.
HIGH SCHOOL: Elk Grove (Calif.).
COLLEGE: Colorado State.
TRANSACTIONS/CAREER NOTES: Signed as non-drafted free agent by Cincinnati Bengals (April 21, 1998).
PLAYING EXPERIENCE: Cincinnati NFL, 1998. ... Games/Games started: 14/1.
PRO STATISTICS: 1998—Intercepted one pass for 11 yards.

ROSS, OLIVER OT COWBOYS

PERSONAL: Born September 27, 1974, in Culver City, Calif. ... 6-4/300.
HIGH SCHOOL: Washington (Los Angeles).
JUNIOR COLLEGE: Southwestern College (Calif.).
COLLEGE: Iowa State.
TRANSACTIONS/CAREER NOTES: Selected by Dallas Cowboys in fifth round (138th pick overall) of 1998 NFL draft. ... Signed by Cowboys (July 16, 1998). ... Assigned by Cowboys to Rhein Fire in 1999 NFL Europe enhancement allocation program (February 22, 1999).
PLAYING EXPERIENCE: Dallas NFL, 1998. ... Games/Games started: 2/0.

ROSSUM, ALLEN CB/KR EAGLES

PERSONAL: Born October 22, 1975, in Dallas. ... 5-8/178. ... Name pronounced ROSS-um.
HIGH SCHOOL: Skyline (Dallas).
COLLEGE: Notre Dame.
TRANSACTIONS/CAREER NOTES: Selected by Philadelphia Eagles in third round (85th pick overall) of 1998 NFL draft. ... Signed by Eagles (July 14, 1998).
PRO STATISTICS: 1998—Credited with one sack and recovered three fumbles.

			PUNT RETURNS				KICKOFF RETURNS				TOTALS			
Year Team	G	GS	No.	Yds.	Avg.	TD	No.	Yds.	Avg.	TD	TD	2pt.	Pts.	Fum.
1998—Philadelphia NFL	15	2	22	187	8.5	0	44	1080	24.5	0	0	0	0	4

ROUEN, TOM P BRONCOS

PERSONAL: Born June 9, 1968, in Hinsdale, Ill. ... 6-3/225. ... Full name: Thomas Francis Rouen Jr. ... Name pronounced RUIN.
HIGH SCHOOL: Heritage (Littleton, Colo.).
COLLEGE: Colorado State, then Colorado.
TRANSACTIONS/CAREER NOTES: Signed as non-drafted free agent by New York Giants (April 29, 1991). ... Released by Giants (August 19, 1991). ... Selected by Ohio Glory in fourth round (44th pick overall) of 1992 World League draft. ... Signed by Los Angeles Rams (July 1992). ... Released by Rams (August 24, 1992). ... Signed by Denver Broncos (April 29, 1993). ... Granted unconditional free agency (February 14, 1997). ... Re-signed by Broncos (March 6, 1997).
CHAMPIONSHIP GAME EXPERIENCE: Played in AFC championship game (1997 and 1998 seasons). ... Member of Super Bowl championship team (1997 and 1998 seasons).
HONORS: Named punter on THE SPORTING NEWS college All-America second team (1989).
PRO STATISTICS: 1993—Rushed once for no yards. 1998—Rushed once for no yards, missed one extra-point attempt and fumbled once for minus 15 yards.

		PUNTING					
Year Team	G	No.	Yds.	Avg.	Net avg.	In. 20	Blk.
1992—Ohio W.L.	10	48	1992	41.5	36.1	14	1
1993—Denver NFL	16	67	3017	45.0	37.1	17	1
1994—Denver NFL	16	76	3258	42.9	*37.1	23	0
1995—Denver NFL	16	52	2192	42.2	37.6	22	1
1996—Denver NFL	16	65	2714	41.8	36.2	16	0
1997—Denver NFL	16	60	2598	43.3	38.1	22	0
1998—Denver NFL	16	66	3097	46.9	37.6	14	1
W.L. totals (1 year)	10	48	1992	41.5	36.1	14	1
NFL totals (6 years)	96	386	16876	43.7	37.3	114	3
Pro totals (7 years)	106	434	18868	43.5	37.1	128	4

ROUNDTREE, RALEIGH   OT   CHARGERS

PERSONAL: Born August 31, 1975, in Augusta, Ga. ... 6-4/295. ... Full name: Raleigh Cito Roundtree.
HIGH SCHOOL: Josey (Augusta, Ga.).
COLLEGE: South Carolina State.
TRANSACTIONS/CAREER NOTES: Selected by San Diego Chargers in fourth round (109th pick overall) of 1997 NFL draft. ... Signed by Chargers (July 14, 1997). ... Inactive for all 16 games (1997).
PLAYING EXPERIENCE: San Diego NFL, 1998. ... Games/Games started: 15/5.
PRO STATISTICS: 1998—Recovered one fumble.

ROYAL, ANDRE   LB   COLTS

PERSONAL: Born December 1, 1972, in North Port, Ala. ... 6-1/220. ... Full name: Andre Tierre Royal.
HIGH SCHOOL: Tuscaloosa County (North Port, Ala.).
COLLEGE: Alabama.
TRANSACTIONS/CAREER NOTES: Signed as non-drafted free agent by Cleveland Browns (May 2, 1995). ... Released by Browns (August 21, 1995). ... Signed by Carolina Panthers to practice squad (August 30, 1995). ... Activated (September 26, 1995). ... Granted free agency (February 13, 1998). ... Tendered offer sheet by New Orleans Saints (March 19, 1998). ... Panthers declined to match offer (March 25, 1998). ... Traded by Saints to Indianapolis Colts for TE Scott Slutzker (August 30, 1998). ... On injured reserve with knee injury (December 24, 1998-remainder of season).
PLAYING EXPERIENCE: Carolina NFL, 1995-1997; Indianapolis NFL, 1998. ... Games/Games started: 1995 (12/0), 1996 (16/0), 1997 (16/13), 1998 (13/9). Total: 57/22.
CHAMPIONSHIP GAME EXPERIENCE: Played in NFC championship game (1996 season).
PRO STATISTICS: 1996—Recovered one fumble. 1997—Credited with five sacks and recovered one fumble.

ROYALS, MARK   P   SAINTS

PERSONAL: Born June 22, 1964, in Hampton, Va. ... 6-5/220. ... Full name: Mark Alan Royals.
HIGH SCHOOL: Mathews (Va.).
JUNIOR COLLEGE: Chowan College (N.C.).
COLLEGE: Appalachian State (degree in political science).
TRANSACTIONS/CAREER NOTES: Signed as non-drafted free agent by Dallas Cowboys (June 6, 1986). ... Released by Cowboys (August 8, 1986). ... Signed as replacement player by St. Louis Cardinals (September 30, 1987). ... Released by Cardinals (October 7, 1987). ... Signed as replacement player by Philadelphia Eagles (October 14, 1987). ... Released by Eagles (November 1987). ... Signed by Cardinals (December 12, 1987). ... Released by Cardinals (July 27, 1988). ... Signed by Miami Dolphins (May 2, 1989). ... Released by Dolphins (August 28, 1989). ... Signed by Tampa Bay Buccaneers (April 24, 1990). ... Granted unconditional free agency (February 1, 1992). ... Signed by Pittsburgh Steelers (March 15, 1992). ... Granted unconditional free agency (February 17, 1995). ... Signed by Detroit Lions (April 26, 1995). ... Granted free agency (February 16, 1996). ... Re-signed by Lions (June 19, 1996). ... Granted unconditional free agency (February 14, 1997). ... Signed by New Orleans Saints (April 25, 1997).
CHAMPIONSHIP GAME EXPERIENCE: Played in AFC championship game (1994 season).
PRO STATISTICS: 1987—Had 23.3-yard net punting average. 1992—Attempted one pass with a completion for 44 yards. 1994—Rushed once for minus 13 yards. 1995—Rushed once for minus seven yards. 1996—Attempted one pass with a completion for minus eight yards and recovered one fumble.

				PUNTING			
Year Team	G	No.	Yds.	Avg.	Net avg.	In. 20	Blk.
1987—St. Louis NFL	1	6	222	37.0	...	2	0
—Philadelphia NFL	1	5	209	41.8	...	1	0
1988—				Did not play.			
1989—				Did not play.			
1990—Tampa Bay NFL	16	72	2902	40.3	34.0	8	0
1991—Tampa Bay NFL	16	84	3389	40.3	32.2	22	0
1992—Pittsburgh NFL	16	73	3119	42.7	35.6	22	1
1993—Pittsburgh NFL	16	89	3781	42.5	34.2	§28	0
1994—Pittsburgh NFL	16	§97	3849	39.7	35.7	†35	0
1995—Detroit NFL	16	57	2393	42.0	31.0	15	2
1996—Detroit NFL	16	69	3020	43.8	33.3	11	1
1997—New Orleans NFL	16	88	4038	*45.9	34.9	21	0
1998—New Orleans NFL	16	88	4017	45.6	36.0	26	0
Pro totals (10 years)	146	728	30939	42.5	33.7	191	4

ROYE, ORPHEUS   DE   STEELERS

PERSONAL: Born January 21, 1974, in Miami. ... 6-4/288. ... Full name: Orpheus Michael Roye. ... Name pronounced OR-fee-us Roy.
HIGH SCHOOL: Miami Springs.
JUNIOR COLLEGE: Jones County Junior College (Miss.).
COLLEGE: Florida State.
TRANSACTIONS/CAREER NOTES: Selected by Pittsburgh Steelers in sixth round (200th pick overall) of 1996 NFL draft. ... Signed by Steelers (July 16, 1996). ... Granted free agency (February 12, 1999). ... Re-signed by Steelers (April 28, 1999).
PLAYING EXPERIENCE: Pittsburgh NFL, 1996-1998. ... Games/Games started: 1996 (13/1), 1997 (16/0), 1998 (16/9). Total: 45/10.
CHAMPIONSHIP GAME EXPERIENCE: Played in AFC championship game (1997 season).
PRO STATISTICS: 1996—Recovered one fumble. 1997—Credited with one sack. 1998—Returned one kickoff for no yards and credited with 3½ sacks.

RUCCI, TODD   G   PATRIOTS

PERSONAL: Born July 14, 1970, in Upper Darby, Pa. ... 6-5/296. ... Full name: Todd L. Rucci.
HIGH SCHOOL: Upper Darby (Pa.).
COLLEGE: Penn State.
TRANSACTIONS/CAREER NOTES: Selected by New England Patriots in second round (51st pick overall) of 1993 NFL draft. ... Signed by Patriots (July 22, 1993). ... On injured reserve with pectoral muscle injury (September 19, 1993-remainder of season). ... Granted unconditional free agency (February 13, 1998). ... Re-signed by Patriots (February 24, 1998).
PLAYING EXPERIENCE: New England NFL, 1993-1998. ... Games/Games started: 1993 (2/1), 1994 (13/10), 1995 (6/5), 1996 (16/12), 1997 (16/16), 1998 (16/16). Total: 69/60.
CHAMPIONSHIP GAME EXPERIENCE: Played in AFC championship game (1996 season). ... Played in Super Bowl XXXI (1996 season).

RUDD, DWAYNE   LB   VIKINGS

PERSONAL: Born February 3, 1976, in Batesville, Miss. ... 6-2/238. ... Full name: Dwayne Dupree Rudd.
HIGH SCHOOL: South Panola (Miss.).
COLLEGE: Alabama.
TRANSACTIONS/CAREER NOTES: Selected by Minnesota Vikings in first round (20th pick overall) of 1997 NFL draft. ... Signed by Vikings (July 18, 1997).
CHAMPIONSHIP GAME EXPERIENCE: Played in NFC championship game (1998 season).
RECORDS: Shares NFL single-season records for most touchdowns by fumble recovery—2 (1998); most touchdowns by recovery of opponents' fumbles—2 (1998).
PRO STATISTICS: 1998—Recovered three fumbles for 157 yards and two touchdowns.

Year Team	G	GS	SACKS
1997—Minnesota NFL	16	2	5.0
1998—Minnesota NFL	15	15	2.0
Pro totals (2 years)	**31**	**17**	**7.0**

RUDDY, TIM   C   DOLPHINS

PERSONAL: Born April 27, 1972, in Scranton, Pa. ... 6-3/300. ... Full name: Timothy Daniel Ruddy.
HIGH SCHOOL: Dunmore (Pa.).
COLLEGE: Notre Dame (degree in mechanical engineering).
TRANSACTIONS/CAREER NOTES: Selected by Miami Dolphins in second round (65th pick overall) of 1994 NFL draft. ... Signed by Dolphins (July 18, 1994).
PLAYING EXPERIENCE: Miami NFL, 1994-1998. ... Games/Games started: 1994 (16/0), 1995 (16/16), 1996 (16/16), 1997 (15/15), 1998 (16/16). Total: 79/63.
PRO STATISTICS: 1995—Fumbled once. 1996—Fumbled once for minus 14 yards. 1998—Fumbled once for minus three yards.

RUHMAN, CHRIS   OT   49ERS

PERSONAL: Born December 19, 1974, in Houston. ... 6-5/321. ... Full name: Christopher Aamon Ruhman. ... Name pronounced RU-man.
HIGH SCHOOL: Nimitz (Irving, Texas).
COLLEGE: Texas A&M.
TRANSACTIONS/CAREER NOTES: Selected by San Francisco 49ers in third round (89th pick overall) of 1998 NFL draft. ... Signed by 49ers (July 18, 1998).
PLAYING EXPERIENCE: San Francisco NFL, 1998. ... Games/Games started: 6/0.
PRO STATISTICS: 1998—Recovered one fumble.

RUNYAN, JON   OT   TITANS

PERSONAL: Born November 27, 1973, in Flint, Mich. ... 6-7/320. ... Full name: Jon Daniel Runyan.
HIGH SCHOOL: Carman-Ainsworth (Flint, Mich.).
COLLEGE: Michigan.
TRANSACTIONS/CAREER NOTES: Selected after junior season by Houston Oilers in fourth round (109th pick overall) of 1996 NFL draft. ... Signed by Oilers (July 20, 1996). ... Oilers franchise moved to Tennessee for 1997 season. ... Oilers franchise renamed Tennessee Titans for 1999 season (December 26, 1998). ... Granted free agency (February 12, 1999).
PLAYING EXPERIENCE: Houston NFL, 1996; Tennessee NFL, 1997 and 1998. ... Games/Games started: 1996 (10/0), 1997 (16/16), 1998 (16/16). Total: 42/32.
HONORS: Named offensive lineman on THE SPORTING NEWS college All-America second team (1995).

RUSS, BERNARD   LB   PATRIOTS

PERSONAL: Born November 4, 1973, in Utica, N.Y. ... 6-1/238. ... Full name: Bernard Dion Russ.
HIGH SCHOOL: Collinwood (Cleveland).
JUNIOR COLLEGE: Arizona Western College.
COLLEGE: West Virginia.
TRANSACTIONS/CAREER NOTES: Signed as non-drafted free agent by Baltimore Ravens (April 25, 1997). ... Released by Ravens (August 24, 1997). ... Signed by New England Patriots to practice squad (August 27, 1997). ... Activated (December 9, 1997). ... On injured reserve with jaw injury (October 20, 1998-remainder of season). ... Assigned by Patriots to Scottish Claymores in 1999 NFL Europe enhancement allocation program (February 22, 1999).
PLAYING EXPERIENCE: New England NFL, 1997 and 1998. ... Games/Games started: 1997 (2/0), 1998 (1/0). Total: 3/0.

RUSSELL, DARRELL   DT   RAIDERS

PERSONAL: Born May 27, 1976, in Pensacola, Fla. ... 6-5/320.
HIGH SCHOOL: St. Augustine (San Diego).
COLLEGE: Southern California.
TRANSACTIONS/CAREER NOTES: Selected by Oakland Raiders in first round (second pick overall) of 1997 NFL draft. ... Signed by Raiders (July 23, 1997).
HONORS: Played in Pro Bowl (1998 season).
PRO STATISTICS: 1998—Recovered one fumble.

Year Team	G	GS	SACKS
1997—Oakland NFL	16	10	3.5
1998—Oakland NFL	16	16	10.0
Pro totals (2 years)	32	26	13.5

RUSSELL, MATT   LB   LIONS

PERSONAL: Born July 5, 1973, in Tokyo. ... 6-2/245. ... Full name: Matthew Jason Russell.
HIGH SCHOOL: Belleville (Ill.) East.
COLLEGE: Colorado.
TRANSACTIONS/CAREER NOTES: Selected by Detroit Lions in fourth round (130th pick overall) of 1997 NFL draft. ... Signed by Lions (July 13, 1997). ... On injured reserve with knee injury (August 11, 1998-entire season).
PLAYING EXPERIENCE: Detroit NFL, 1997. ... Games/Games started: 14/0.
HONORS: Butkus Award winner (1996). ... Named inside linebacker on THE SPORTING NEWS college All-America first team (1996).
PRO STATISTICS: 1997—Returned one kickoff for no yards and recovered one fumble.

RUSSELL, TWAN   LB   REDSKINS

PERSONAL: Born April 25, 1974, in Fort Lauderdale, Fla. ... 6-1/219. ... Full name: Twan Sanchez Russell.
HIGH SCHOOL: St. Thomas Aquinas (Fort Lauderdale, Fla.).
COLLEGE: Miami, Fla. (degree in broadcasting, 1996).
TRANSACTIONS/CAREER NOTES: Selected by Washington Redskins in fifth round (148th pick overall) of 1997 NFL draft. ... Signed by Redskins (May 9, 1997). ... On injured reserve with foot and knee injuries (September 23, 1998-remainder of season).
PLAYING EXPERIENCE: Washington NFL, 1997 and 1998. ... Games/Games started: 1997 (14/0), 1998 (3/0). Total: 17/0.

RUTLEDGE, ROD   TE   PATRIOTS

PERSONAL: Born August 12, 1975, in Birmingham, Ala. ... 6-5/262. ... Full name: Rodrick Almar Rutledge.
HIGH SCHOOL: Erwin (Birmingham, Ala.).
COLLEGE: Alabama.
TRANSACTIONS/CAREER NOTES: Selected by New England Patriots in second round (54th pick overall) of 1998 NFL draft. ... Signed by Patriots (June 15, 1998).
PLAYING EXPERIENCE: New England NFL, 1998. ... Games/Games started: 16/4.

SADOWSKI, TROY   TE   REDSKINS

PERSONAL: Born December 8, 1965, in Atlanta. ... 6-5/252. ... Full name: Troy Robert Sadowski.
HIGH SCHOOL: Chamblee (Ga.).
COLLEGE: Georgia.
TRANSACTIONS/CAREER NOTES: Selected by Atlanta Falcons in sixth round (145th pick overall) of 1989 NFL draft. ... Signed by Falcons for 1989 season. ... Released by Falcons (August 30, 1989). ... Re-signed by Falcons to developmental squad (December 6, 1989). ... Released by Falcons (January 9, 1990). ... Re-signed by Falcons (February 20, 1990). ... Released by Falcons (September 3, 1990). ... Re-signed by Falcons (September 4, 1990). ... Granted unconditional free agency (February 1, 1991). ... Signed by Kansas City Chiefs (April 2, 1991). ... Released by Chiefs (December 17, 1991). ... Signed by New York Jets (March 23, 1992). ... Released by Jets (October 25, 1992). ... Re-signed by Jets (April 20, 1993). ... Released by Jets (August 24, 1993). ... Re-signed by Jets (September 28, 1993). ... Granted unconditional free agency (February 17, 1994). ... Signed by Cincinnati Bengals (April 26, 1994). ... Released by Bengals (August 18, 1997). ... Signed by Pittsburgh Steelers (November 11, 1997). ... On injured reserve with shoulder injury (August 30-October 20, 1998). ... Released by Steelers (October 20, 1998). ... Signed by Jacksonville Jaguars (November 17, 1998). ... Granted unconditional free agency (February 12, 1999). ... Signed by Washington Redskins (April 21, 1999).
CHAMPIONSHIP GAME EXPERIENCE: Played in AFC championship game (1997 season).
PRO STATISTICS: 1993—Returned one kickoff for no yards. 1994—Recovered one fumble. 1995—Recovered one fumble. 1996—Returned two kickoffs for seven yards. 1998—Returned one kickoff for no yards.
SINGLE GAME HIGHS (regular season): Receptions—3 (November 6, 1994, vs. Seattle); yards—20 (September 6, 1992, vs. Atlanta); and touchdown receptions—0.

			RECEIVING				TOTALS		
Year Team	G	GS	No.	Yds.	Avg.	TD	TD	2pt.	Pts.	Fum.
1990—Atlanta NFL	13	1	0	0	...	0	0	...	0	0
1991—Kansas City NFL	14	1	0	0	...	0	0	...	0	0
1992—New York Jets NFL	6	2	1	20	20.0	0	0	...	0	0
1993—New York Jets NFL	13	1	2	14	7.0	0	0	...	0	0
1994—Cincinnati NFL	15	1	11	54	4.9	0	0	0	0	0
1995—Cincinnati NFL	12	1	5	37	7.4	0	0	0	0	0
1996—Cincinnati NFL	16	0	3	15	5.0	0	0	0	0	0
1997—Pittsburgh NFL	5	0	1	12	12.0	0	0	0	0	0
1998—Jacksonville NFL	5	0	0	0	...	0	0	0	0	0
Pro totals (9 years)	99	7	23	152	6.6	0	0	0	0	0

SAGAPOLUTELE, PIO — DT — SAINTS

PERSONAL: Born November 28, 1969, in American Samoa. ... 6-6/302. ... Full name: Pio Alika Sagapolutele. ... Name pronounced PEE-o Saang-a-POO-la-tel-lee.
HIGH SCHOOL: Maryknoll (Honolulu).
COLLEGE: San Diego State (degree in criminal justice, 1991).
TRANSACTIONS/CAREER NOTES: Selected by Cleveland Browns in fourth round (85th pick overall) of 1991 NFL draft. ... Signed by Browns for 1991 season. ... Granted free agency (February 17, 1994). ... Re-signed by Browns (May 11, 1994). ... Granted unconditional free agency (February 17, 1995). ... Re-signed by Browns (April 17, 1995). ... Granted unconditional free agency (February 16, 1996). ... Signed by New England Patriots (March 20, 1996). ... Released by Patriots (June 12, 1997). ... Signed by New Orleans Saints (July 21, 1997). ... On injured reserve with arm injury (August 25, 1998-entire season).
CHAMPIONSHIP GAME EXPERIENCE: Played in AFC championship game (1996 season). ... Played in Super Bowl XXXI (1996 season).

Year Team	G	GS	SACKS
1991—Cleveland NFL	15	8	1.5
1992—Cleveland NFL	14	0	0.0
1993—Cleveland NFL	8	0	0.0
1994—Cleveland NFL	11	0	0.0
1995—Cleveland NFL	15	3	0.5
1996—New England NFL	15	10	3.0
1997—New Orleans NFL	15	13	2.0
1998—New Orleans NFL	Did not play.		
Pro totals (7 years)	93	34	7.0

SALAAM, EPHRAIM — OT — FALCONS

PERSONAL: Born June 19, 1976, in Chicago. ... 6-7/310. ... Full name: Ephraim Mateen Salaam. ... Name pronounced EE-frum sah-LAHM.
HIGH SCHOOL: Florin (Sacramento).
COLLEGE: San Diego State.
TRANSACTIONS/CAREER NOTES: Selected by Atlanta Falcons in seventh round (199th pick overall) of 1998 NFL draft. ... Signed by Falcons (June 3, 1998).
PLAYING EXPERIENCE: Atlanta NFL, 1998. ... Games/Games started: 16/16.
CHAMPIONSHIP GAME EXPERIENCE: Played in NFC championship game (1998 season). ... Played in Super Bowl XXXIII (1998 season).

SALAVE'A, JOE — DT — TITANS

PERSONAL: Born March 23, 1975, in Leone, American Samoa. ... 6-3/290. ... Full name: Joe Fagaone Salave'a. ... Name pronounced sal-ah-VAY-ah.
HIGH SCHOOL: Oceanside (Calif.).
COLLEGE: Arizona (degree in sociology, 1997).
TRANSACTIONS/CAREER NOTES: Selected by Tennessee Oilers in fourth round (107th pick overall) of 1998 NFL draft. ... Signed by Oilers (June 30, 1998). ... Oilers franchise renamed Tennessee Titans for 1999 season (December 26, 1998).
PLAYING EXPERIENCE: Tennessee NFL, 1998. ... Games/Games started: 13/0.
HONORS: Named defensive tackle on THE SPORTING NEWS college All-America third team (1997).
PRO STATISTICS: 1998—Credited with one sack.

SALEAUMUA, DAN — DT

PERSONAL: Born November 25, 1964, in San Diego. ... 6-0/315. ... Full name: Raymond Daniel Saleaumua. ... Name pronounced SOL-ee-uh-MOO-uh.
HIGH SCHOOL: Sweetwater (National City, Calif.).
COLLEGE: Arizona State.
TRANSACTIONS/CAREER NOTES: Selected by Detroit Lions in seventh round (175th pick overall) of 1987 NFL draft. ... Signed by Lions (July 25, 1987). ... On injured reserve with hamstring injury (September 7-October 31, 1987). ... Granted unconditional free agency (February 1, 1989). ... Signed by Kansas City Chiefs (March 20, 1989). ... Designated by Chiefs as transition player (February 25, 1993). ... Free agency status changed by Chiefs from transitional to unconditional (February 17, 1994). ... Re-signed by Chiefs (August 23, 1994). ... Released by Chiefs (July 28, 1997). ... Signed by Seattle Seahawks (August 6, 1997). ... Released by Seahawks (February 10, 1999).
CHAMPIONSHIP GAME EXPERIENCE: Played in AFC championship game (1993 season).
HONORS: Played in Pro Bowl (1995 season).
PRO STATISTICS: 1987—Returned three kickoffs for 57 yards. 1988—Returned one kickoff for no yards and fumbled once. 1989—Intercepted one pass for 21 yards, returned kickoff for eight yards and recovered five fumbles for two yards. 1990—Recovered six fumbles (including one in end zone for a touchdown). 1991—Credited with one safety and recovered two fumbles. 1992—Recovered one fumble. 1993—Intercepted one pass for 13 yards and recovered one fumble for 16 yards and a touchdown. 1994—Recovered one fumble. 1995—Intercepted one pass for no yards and recovered one fumble. 1997—Recovered one fumble and credited with a safety.

Year Team	G	GS	SACKS
1987—Detroit NFL	9	0	2.0
1988—Detroit NFL	16	0	2.0
1989—Kansas City NFL	16	8	2.0
1990—Kansas City NFL	16	16	7.0
1991—Kansas City NFL	16	16	1.5
1992—Kansas City NFL	16	16	6.0
1993—Kansas City NFL	16	16	3.5
1994—Kansas City NFL	14	14	1.0
1995—Kansas City NFL	16	16	7.0
1996—Kansas City NFL	15	14	0.0
1997—Seattle NFL	16	8	3.5
1998—Seattle NFL	11	6	0.0
Pro totals (12 years)	177	130	35.5

SALEH, TAREK   LB   BROWNS

PERSONAL: Born November 7, 1974, in Woodbridge, Conn. ... 6-0/240. ... Full name: Tarek Muhammad Saleh. ... Name pronounced TAR-ick SAH-luh.
HIGH SCHOOL: Notre Dame (Woodbridge, Conn.).
COLLEGE: Wisconsin.
TRANSACTIONS/CAREER NOTES: Selected by Carolina Panthers in fourth round (122nd pick overall) of 1997 NFL draft. ... Signed by Panthers for 1997 season. ... Selected by Cleveland Browns from Panthers in NFL expansion draft (February 9, 1999).
PLAYING EXPERIENCE: Carolina NFL, 1997 and 1998. ... Games/Games started: 1997 (3/0), 1998 (11/1). Total: 14/1.
PRO STATISTICS: 1997—Credited with one sack. 1998—Returned one kickoff for eight yards.

SANDERS, BARRY   RB   LIONS

PERSONAL: Born July 16, 1968, in Wichita, Kan. ... 5-8/200.
HIGH SCHOOL: North (Wichita, Kan.).
COLLEGE: Oklahoma State.
TRANSACTIONS/CAREER NOTES: Selected after junior season by Detroit Lions in first round (third pick overall) of 1989 NFL draft. ... Signed by Lions (September 7, 1989).
CHAMPIONSHIP GAME EXPERIENCE: Played in NFC championship game (1991 season).
HONORS: Named kick returner on THE SPORTING NEWS college All-America first team (1987). ... Heisman Trophy winner (1988). ... Named College Football Player of the Year by THE SPORTING NEWS (1988). ... Maxwell Award winner (1988). ... Named running back on THE SPORTING NEWS college All-America first team (1988). ... Named NFL Rookie of the Year by THE SPORTING NEWS (1989). ... Named running back on THE SPORTING NEWS NFL All-Pro team (1989-1991 and 1993-1997). ... Played in Pro Bowl (1989-1992 and 1994-1998 seasons). ... Named to play in Pro Bowl (1993 season); replaced by Ricky Watters due to injury. ... Named NFL Player of the Year by THE SPORTING NEWS (1997).
RECORDS: Holds NFL record for most consecutive seasons with 1,000 or more yards rushing—10 (1989-1998); and most consecutive games with 100 or more yards rushing—14 (September 14-December 21, 1997). ... Shares NFL record for most seasons with 1,000 or more yards rushing—10 (1989-98). ... Holds NFL single-season record for most games with 100 or more yards rushing—14 (1997); and most consecutive games with 100 or more yards rushing—14 (September 14-December 21, 1997).
PRO STATISTICS: 1989—Returned five kickoffs for 118 yards. 1990—Recovered two fumbles. 1991—Recovered one fumble. 1992—Attempted one pass without a completion and recovered two fumbles. 1993—Recovered three fumbles. 1995—Attempted two passes with one completion for 11 yards and recovered one fumble. 1996—Attempted one pass without a completion and an interception and recovered two fumbles. 1997—Recovered one fumble. 1998—Recovered one fumble.
SINGLE GAME HIGHS (regular season): Attempts—40 (September 19, 1994, vs. Dallas); yards—237 (November 13, 1994, vs. Tampa Bay); and rushing touchdowns—4 (November 24, 1991, vs. Minnesota).
STATISTICAL PLATEAUS: 100-yard rushing games: 1989 (7), 1990 (4), 1991 (8), 1992 (7), 1993 (4), 1994 (10), 1995 (7), 1996 (7), 1997 (14), 1998 (8). Total: 76. ... 100-yard receiving games: 1990 (1), 1997 (1). Total: 2.
MISCELLANEOUS: Active NFL leader for career rushing yards (15,269). ... Holds Detroit Lions all-time records for most yards rushing (15,269), most touchdowns (109) and most rushing touchdowns (99).

				RUSHING				RECEIVING				TOTALS		
Year Team	G	GS	Att.	Yds.	Avg.	TD	No.	Yds.	Avg.	TD	TD	2pt.	Pts.	Fum.
1989—Detroit NFL	15	13	280	‡1470	5.3	14	24	282	11.8	0	14	...	84	10
1990—Detroit NFL	16	16	255	*1304	5.1	13	36	480	13.3	3	*16	...	96	4
1991—Detroit NFL	15	15	342	1548	4.5	*16	41	307	7.5	1	*17	...	102	5
1992—Detroit NFL	16	16	312	1352	4.3	9	29	225	7.8	1	10	...	60	6
1993—Detroit NFL	11	11	243	1115	4.6	3	36	205	5.7	0	3	...	18	3
1994—Detroit NFL	16	16	331	*1883	*5.7	7	44	283	6.4	1	8	0	48	0
1995—Detroit NFL	16	16	314	1500	4.8	11	48	398	8.3	1	12	0	72	3
1996—Detroit NFL	16	16	307	*1553	‡5.1	11	24	147	6.1	0	11	0	66	4
1997—Detroit NFL	16	16	‡335	*2053	‡6.1	‡11	33	305	9.2	3	‡14	0	84	3
1998—Detroit NFL	16	16	343	1491	4.3	4	37	289	7.8	0	4	0	24	3
Pro totals (10 years)	153	151	3062	15269	5.0	99	352	2921	8.3	10	109	0	654	41

SANDERS, BRANDON   DB   BROWNS

PERSONAL: Born June 10, 1973, in San Diego. ... 5-9/185. ... Full name: Brandon Christopher Sanders.
HIGH SCHOOL: Helix (La Mesa, Calif.).
COLLEGE: Arizona.
TRANSACTIONS/CAREER NOTES: Signed as non-drafted free agent by Kansas City Chiefs (April 27, 1996). ... Released by Chiefs (August 20, 1996). ... Signed by New York Giants (March 10, 1997). ... Selected by Cleveland Browns from Giants in NFL expansion draft (February 9, 1999).
PLAYING EXPERIENCE: New York Giants NFL, 1997 and 1998. ... Games/Games started: 1997 (12/0), 1998 (13/0). Total: 25/0.

SANDERS, CHRIS   WR   TITANS

PERSONAL: Born May 8, 1972, in Denver. ... 6-1/188. ... Full name: Christopher Dwayne Sanders.
HIGH SCHOOL: Montbello (Denver).
COLLEGE: Ohio State.
TRANSACTIONS/CAREER NOTES: Selected by Houston Oilers in third round (67th pick overall) of 1995 NFL draft. ... Signed by Oilers (July 20, 1995). ... Oilers franchise moved to Tennessee for 1997 season. ... Oilers franchise renamed Tennessee Titans for 1999 season (December 26, 1998).
PRO STATISTICS: 1995—Rushed twice for minus 19 yards. 1997—Rushed once for minus eight yards. 1998—Rushed once for minus nine yards.

SINGLE GAME HIGHS (regular season): Receptions—7 (December 14, 1997, vs. Baltimore); yards—147 (November 26, 1995, vs. Denver); and touchdown receptions—2 (October 26, 1997, vs. Arizona).
STATISTICAL PLATEAUS: 100-yard receiving games: 1995 (1), 1996 (3), 1997 (1), 1998 (1). Total: 6.

				RECEIVING				TOTALS			
Year Team	G	GS	No.	Yds.	Avg.	TD	TD	2pt.	Pts.	Fum.
1995—Houston NFL	16	10	35	823	*23.5	9	9	0	54	0
1996—Houston NFL	16	15	48	882	§18.4	4	4	0	24	0
1997—Tennessee NFL	15	14	31	498	16.1	3	3	0	18	1
1998—Tennessee NFL	14	1	5	136	27.2	0	0	0	0	1
Pro totals (4 years)	61	40	119	2339	19.7	16	16	0	96	2

SANDERS, DEION °CB/WR COWBOYS

PERSONAL: Born August 9, 1967, in Fort Myers, Fla. ... 6-1/195. ... Full name: Deion Luwynn Sanders. ... Nickname: Prime Time.
HIGH SCHOOL: North Fort Myers (Fla.).
COLLEGE: Florida State.
TRANSACTIONS/CAREER NOTES: Selected by Atlanta Falcons in first round (fifth pick overall) of 1989 NFL draft. ... Signed by Falcons (September 7, 1989). ... On reserve/did not report list (July 27-August 13, 1990). ... Granted roster exemption for one game (September 1992). ... On reserve/did not report list (July 23-October 14, 1993). ... Designated by Falcons as transition player (February 15, 1994). ... Free agency status changed by Falcons from transitional to unconditional (April 28, 1994). ... Signed by San Francisco 49ers (September 15, 1994). ... Granted unconditional free agency (February 17, 1995). ... Signed by Dallas Cowboys (September 9, 1995). ... On reserve/did not report list (July 16-August 29, 1997).
CHAMPIONSHIP GAME EXPERIENCE: Played in NFC championship game (1994 and 1995 seasons). ... Member of Super Bowl championship team (1994 and 1995 seasons).
HONORS: Named defensive back on THE SPORTING NEWS college All-America first team (1986-1988). ... Jim Thorpe Award winner (1988). ... Named cornerback on THE SPORTING NEWS NFL All-Pro team (1991-1998). ... Played in Pro Bowl (1991-1994 and 1998 seasons). ... Named kick returner on THE SPORTING NEWS NFL All-Pro team (1992). ... Named to play in Pro Bowl (1996 season); replaced by Darrell Green due to injury. ... Named to play in Pro Bowl (1997 season); replaced by Cris Dishman due to injury.
PRO STATISTICS: 1989—Fumbled twice and recovered one fumble. 1990—Fumbled four times and recovered two fumbles. 1991—Credited with a sack, fumbled once and recovered one fumble. 1992—Rushed once for minus four yards, fumbled three times and recovered two fumbles. 1993—Attempted one pass without a completion. 1994—Recovered one fumble. 1995—Rushed twice for nine yards. 1996—Rushed three times for two yards, fumbled twice and recovered three fumbles for 15 yards and one touchdown. 1997—Rushed once for minus 11 yards and fumbled once. 1998—Fumbled once and recovered one fumble.
MISCELLANEOUS: Only person in history to play in both the World Series (1992) and Super Bowl (1994 and 1995 seasons).

			INTERCEPTIONS				RECEIVING				PUNT RETURNS				KICKOFF RETURNS				TOTALS		
Year Team	G	GS	No.	Yds.	Avg.	TD	No.	Yds.	Avg.	TD	No.	Yds.	Avg.	TD	No.	Yds.	Avg.	TD	TD	2pt.	Pts.
1989—Atlanta NFL	15	10	5	52	10.4	0	1	-8	-8.0	0	28	307	11.0	†1	35	725	20.7	0	1	...	6
1990—Atlanta NFL	16	16	3	153	*51.0	2	0	0	...	0	29	250	8.6	†1	39	851	21.8	0	3	...	18
1991—Atlanta NFL	15	15	∞6	119	19.8	∞1	1	17	17.0	0	21	170	8.1	0	26	576	22.2	†1	2	...	12
1992—Atlanta NFL	13	12	3	105	‡35.0	0	3	45	15.0	1	13	41	3.2	0	40	*1067	‡26.7	*2	3	...	18
1993—Atlanta NFL	11	10	‡7	91	13.0	0	6	106	17.7	1	2	21	10.5	0	7	169	24.1	0	1	...	6
1994—San Fran. NFL	14	12	6	*303	*50.5	‡3	0	0	...	0	0	0	...	0	0	0	...	0	3	0	18
1995—Dallas NFL	9	9	2	34	17.0	0	2	25	12.5	0	1	54	54.0	0	1	15	15.0	0	0	0	0
1996—Dallas NFL	16	16	2	3	1.5	0	36	475	13.2	1	1	4	4.0	0	0	0	...	0	2	0	12
1997—Dallas NFL	13	12	2	81	40.5	1	0	0	...	0	33	407	12.3	∞1	1	18	18.0	0	2	0	12
1998—Dallas NFL	11	11	5	153	30.6	1	7	100	14.3	0	24	375	*15.6	†2	1	16	16.0	0	3	0	18
Pro totals (10 years)	133	122	41	1094	26.7	8	56	760	13.6	3	152	1629	10.7	5	150	3437	22.9	3	20	0	120

RECORD AS BASEBALL PLAYER

TRANSACTIONS/CAREER NOTES: Selected by Kansas City Royals organization in sixth round of free-agent draft (June 3, 1985); did not sign. ... Selected by New York Yankees organization in 30th round of free-agent draft (June 1, 1988). ... On disqualified list (August 1-September 24, 1990). ... Released by Yankees organization (September 24, 1990). ... Signed by Atlanta Braves (January 29, 1991). ... Placed on Richmond temporarily inactive list (August 1, 1991). ... On disqualified list (April 29-May 21, 1993). ... On disabled list (August 22-September 6, 1993). ... Traded by Braves to Cincinnati Reds for OF Roberto Kelly and P Roger Etheridge (May 29, 1994). ... On Cincinnati disabled list (June 1-July 16, 1995); included rehabilitation assignment to Chattanooga (July 12-14). ... Traded by Reds with P John Roper, P Ricky Pickett, P Scott Service and IF Dave McCarty to San Francisco Giants for OF Darren Lewis, P Mark Portugal and P Dave Burba (July 21, 1995). ... Granted free agency (December 21, 1995). ... Did not play baseball during 1996 season. ... Granted free agency (November 5, 1996). ... Re-signed by Reds (February 17, 1997). ... Granted free agency after 1997 season. ... Re-signed by Reds organization (January 8, 1998). ... Did not play baseball during 1998 season.
STATISTICAL NOTES: Led N.L. in caught stealing with 16 in 1994.

			BATTING										FIELDING			
Year Team (League)	Pos.	G	AB	R	H	2B	3B	HR	RBI	Avg.	BB	SO	SB	PO	A	E	Avg.
1988—GC Yankees (GCL)	OF	17	75	7	21	4	2	0	6	.280	2	10	11	33	1	2	.944
—Fort Lauderdale (FSL)	OF	6	21	5	9	2	0	0	2	.429	1	3	2	22	2	0	1.000
—Columbus (Int'l)	OF	5	20	3	3	1	0	0	0	.150	1	4	1	13	0	0	1.000
1989—Alb./Colon. (Eastern)	OF	33	119	28	34	2	2	1	6	.286	11	20	17	79	3	0	1.000
—New York (A.L.)	OF	14	47	7	11	2	0	2	7	.234	3	8	1	30	1	1	.969
—Columbus (Int'l)	OF	70	259	38	72	12	7	5	30	.278	22	46	16	165	0	4	.976
1990—New York (A.L.)	OF-DH	57	133	24	21	2	2	3	9	.158	13	27	8	69	2	2	.973
—Columbus (Int'l)	OF	22	84	21	27	7	1	2	10	.321	17	15	9	49	1	0	1.000
1991—Atlanta (N.L.)■	OF	54	110	16	21	1	2	4	13	.191	12	23	11	57	3	3	.952
—Richmond (Int'l)	OF	29	130	20	34	6	3	5	16	.262	10	28	12	73	1	1	.987
1992—Atlanta (N.L.)	OF	97	303	54	92	6	*14	8	28	.304	18	52	26	174	4	3	.983
1993—Atlanta (N.L.)	OF	95	272	42	75	18	6	6	28	.276	16	42	19	137	1	2	.986
1994—Atlanta (N.L.)	OF	46	191	32	55	10	0	4	21	.288	16	28	19	99	0	2	.980
—Cincinnati (N.L.)■	OF	46	184	26	51	7	4	0	7	.277	16	35	19	110	2	0	1.000
1995—Cincinnati (N.L.)	OF	33	129	19	31	2	3	1	10	.240	9	18	16	88	2	3	.968
—Chattanooga (Sou.)	OF	2	7	1	4	0	0	1	2	.571	0	1	1	3	1	0	1.000

Year	Team (League)	Pos.	G	AB	R	H	2B	3B	HR	RBI	Avg.	BB	SO	SB	PO	A	E	Avg.
—San Fran. (N.L.)■		OF	52	214	29	61	9	5	5	18	.285	18	42	8	127	0	2	.984
1996—								Did not play.										
1997—Cincinnati (N.L.)■		OF	115	465	53	127	13	7	5	23	.273	34	67	56	236	3	4	.984
1998—Cincinnati (N.L.)								Did not play.										
American League totals (2 years)			71	180	31	32	4	2	5	16	.178	16	35	9	99	3	3	.971
National League totals (6 years)			538	1868	271	513	66	41	33	148	.275	139	307	174	1028	15	19	.982
Major league totals (8 years)			609	2048	302	545	70	43	38	164	.266	155	342	183	1127	18	22	.981

CHAMPIONSHIP SERIES RECORD

Year	Team (League)	Pos.	G	AB	R	H	2B	3B	HR	RBI	Avg.	BB	SO	SB	PO	A	E	Avg.
1992—Atlanta (N.L.)		OF-PH	4	5	0	0	0	0	0	0	.000	0	3	0	1	0	0	1.000
1993—Atlanta (N.L.)		PH-OF-PR	5	3	0	0	0	0	0	0	.000	0	1	0	0	0	0	...
Championship series totals (2 years)			9	8	0	0	0	0	0	0	.000	0	4	0	1	0	0	1.000

WORLD SERIES RECORD

Year	Team (League)	Pos.	G	AB	R	H	2B	3B	HR	RBI	Avg.	BB	SO	SB	PO	A	E	Avg.
1992—Atlanta (N.L.)		OF	4	15	4	8	2	0	0	1	.533	2	1	5	5	1	0	1.000

SANDERS, FRANK — WR — CARDINALS

PERSONAL: Born February 17, 1973, in Fort Lauderdale, Fla.. ... 6-2/197. ... Full name: Frank Vondel Sanders.
HIGH SCHOOL: Dillard (Fort Lauderdale, Fla.).
COLLEGE: Auburn.
TRANSACTIONS/CAREER NOTES: Selected by Arizona Cardinals in second round (47th pick overall) of 1995 NFL draft. ... Signed by Cardinals (July 17, 1995). ... Granted free agency (February 13, 1998). ... Re-signed by Cardinals (March 13, 1998).
HONORS: Named wide receiver on THE SPORTING NEWS college All-America second team (1994).
PRO STATISTICS: 1995—Rushed once for one yard. 1996—Rushed twice for minus four yards and recovered one fumble. 1997—Attempted one pass with a completion for 26 yards and rushed once for five yards. 1998—Rushed four times for no yards and recovered two fumbles.
SINGLE GAME HIGHS (regular season): Receptions—11 (November 15, 1998, vs. Dallas); yards—190 (November 15, 1998, vs. Dallas); and touchdown receptions—2 (October 8, 1995, vs. New York Giants).
STATISTICAL PLATEAUS: 100-yard receiving games: 1995 (2), 1997 (2), 1998 (5). Total: 9.

			RECEIVING				TOTALS			
Year Team	G	GS	No.	Yds.	Avg.	TD	TD	2pt.	Pts.	Fum.
1995—Arizona NFL	16	15	52	883	17.0	2	2	2	16	0
1996—Arizona NFL	16	16	69	813	11.8	4	4	0	24	1
1997—Arizona NFL	16	16	75	1017	13.6	4	4	1	26	3
1998—Arizona NFL	16	16	‡89	1145	12.9	3	3	0	18	3
Pro totals (4 years)	64	63	285	3858	13.5	13	13	3	84	7

SANDERSON, SCOTT — OT — TITANS

PERSONAL: Born July 25, 1974, in Walnut Creek, Calif. ... 6-6/295. ... Full name: Scott Michael Sanderson.
HIGH SCHOOL: Clayton Valley (Calif.).
COLLEGE: Washington State.
TRANSACTIONS/CAREER NOTES: Selected by Houston Oilers in third round (81st pick overall) of 1997 NFL draft. ... Oilers franchise moved to Tennessee for 1997 season. ... Signed by Oilers (July 17, 1997). ... Oilers franchise renamed Tennessee Titans for 1999 season (December 26, 1998).
PLAYING EXPERIENCE: Tennessee NFL, 1997 and 1998. ... Games/Games started: 1997 (10/0), 1998 (15/3). Total: 25/3.
HONORS: Named offensive tackle on THE SPORTING NEWS college All-America first team (1996).

SANTIAGO, O.J. — TE — FALCONS

PERSONAL: Born April 4, 1974, in Whitby, Ont. ... 6-7/264. ... Full name: Otis Jason Santiago.
HIGH SCHOOL: St. Michael's (Toronto).
COLLEGE: Kent.
TRANSACTIONS/CAREER NOTES: Selected by Atlanta Falcons in third round (70th pick overall) of 1997 NFL draft. ... Signed by Falcons (July 11, 1997). ... On injured reserved with leg injury (November 20, 1997-remainder of season).
CHAMPIONSHIP GAME EXPERIENCE: Played in NFC championship game (1998 season). ... Played in Super Bowl XXXIII (1998 season).
PRO STATISTICS: 1998—Recovered one fumble.
SINGLE GAME HIGHS (regular season): Reception—5 (September 14, 1997, vs. Oakland); yards—65 (December 27, 1998, vs. Miami); and touchdown receptions—2 (December 27, 1998, vs. Miami).

			RECEIVING				TOTALS			
Year Team	G	GS	No.	Yds.	Avg.	TD	TD	2pt.	Pts.	Fum.
1997—Atlanta NFL	11	11	17	217	12.8	2	2	0	12	1
1998—Atlanta NFL	16	16	27	428	15.9	5	5	0	30	1
Pro totals (2 years)	27	27	44	645	14.7	7	7	0	42	2

SAPP, PATRICK   LB   CARDINALS

PERSONAL: Born May 11, 1973, in Jacksonville. ... 6-4/258. ... Full name: Patrick Zolley Sapp.
HIGH SCHOOL: Raines (Jacksonville).
COLLEGE: Clemson.
TRANSACTIONS/CAREER NOTES: Selected by San Diego Chargers in second round (50th pick overall) of 1996 NFL draft. ... Signed by Chargers for 1996 season. ... Traded by Chargers with first- (DE Andre Wadsworth) and second-round (CB Corey Chavous) picks in 1998 draft, first-round pick (WR David Boston) in 1999 draft and KR Eric Metcalf to Arizona Cardinals for first-round pick (QB Ryan Leaf) in 1998 draft (March 12, 1998). ... Granted free agency (February 12, 1999).
PLAYING EXPERIENCE: San Diego NFL, 1996 and 1997; Arizona NFL, 1998. ... Games/Games started: 1996 (16/0), 1997 (16/9), 1998 (16/1). Total: 48/10.
PRO STATISTICS: 1998—Credited with one sack.

SAPP, WARREN   DT   BUCCANEERS

PERSONAL: Born December 19, 1972, in Orlando. ... 6-2/291. ... Full name: Warren Carlos Sapp.
HIGH SCHOOL: Apopka (Fla.).
COLLEGE: Miami (Fla.).
TRANSACTIONS/CAREER NOTES: Selected after junior season by Tampa Bay Buccaneers in first round (12th pick overall) of 1995 NFL draft. ... Signed by Buccaneers (April 27, 1995).
HONORS: Lombardi Award winner (1994). ... Named defensive lineman on THE SPORTING NEWS college All-America first team (1994). ... Played in Pro Bowl (1997 and 1998 seasons).
PRO STATISTICS: 1995—Intercepted one pass for five yards and a touchdown. 1996—Recovered one fumble. 1997—Recovered one fumble for 23 yards. 1998—Recovered one fumble.

Year Team	G	GS	SACKS
1995—Tampa Bay NFL	16	8	3.0
1996—Tampa Bay NFL	15	14	9.0
1997—Tampa Bay NFL	15	15	10.5
1998—Tampa Bay NFL	16	16	7.0
Pro totals (4 years)	62	53	29.5

SARGENT, KEVIN   OT   BENGALS

PERSONAL: Born March 31, 1969, in Bremerton, Wash. ... 6-6/300.
HIGH SCHOOL: Bremerton (Wash.).
COLLEGE: Eastern Washington.
TRANSACTIONS/CAREER NOTES: Signed as non-drafted free agent by Cincinnati Bengals (April 1992). ... On injured reserve with fractured forearm (December 3, 1993-remainder of season). ... On injured reserve with neck injury (August 14, 1996-entire season). ... Granted unconditional free agency (February 14, 1997). ... Re-signed by Bengals (March 13, 1997). ... On physically unable to perform list with neck injury (August 24-October 18, 1997).
PLAYING EXPERIENCE: Cincinnati NFL, 1992-1995, 1997 and 1998. ... Games/Games started: 1992 (16/8), 1993 (1/1), 1994 (16/15), 1995 (15/15), 1997 (10/8), 1998 (16/16). Total: 74/63.
PRO STATISTICS: 1992—Recovered two fumbles. 1995—Recovered one fumble.

SASA, DON   DT

PERSONAL: Born September 16, 1972, in American Samoa. ... 6-3/303. ... Name pronounced SAW-sa.
HIGH SCHOOL: Polytechnic (Long Beach, Calif.).
JUNIOR COLLEGE: Long Beach (Calif.) City College.
COLLEGE: Washington State.
TRANSACTIONS/CAREER NOTES: Selected by San Diego Chargers in third round (93rd pick overall) of 1995 NFL draft. ... Signed by Chargers (July 17, 1995). ... On injured reserve with knee injury (October 17, 1995-remainder of season). ... Released by Chargers (August 24, 1997). ... Signed by Washington Redskins (October 9, 1997). ... Released by Redskins (October 31, 1997). ... Signed by Carolina Panthers (December 16, 1997). ... Inactive for one game with Panthers (1997). ... Released by Panthers (September 28, 1998). ... Re-signed by Panthers to practice squad (September 30, 1998). ... Signed by Detroit Lions off Panthers practice squad (December 8, 1998). ... Released by Lions (February 12, 1999).
PLAYING EXPERIENCE: San Diego NFL, 1995 and 1996; Washington NFL, 1997; Carolina (2)-Detroit (2) NFL, 1998. ... Games/Games started: 1995 (5/0), 1996 (4/1), 1997 (1/0), 1998 (Car.-2/0; Det.-2/0; Total: 4/0). Total: 14/1.

SAUER, CRAIG   LB   FALCONS

PERSONAL: Born December 13, 1972, in Sartell, Minn. ... 6-1/235.
HIGH SCHOOL: Sartell (Minn.).
COLLEGE: Minnesota.
TRANSACTIONS/CAREER NOTES: Selected by Atlanta Falcons in sixth round (188th pick overall) of 1996 NFL draft. ... Signed by Falcons (June 6, 1996).
PLAYING EXPERIENCE: Atlanta NFL, 1996-1998. ... Games/Games started: 1996 (16/1), 1997 (16/1), 1998 (16/6). Total: 48/8.
CHAMPIONSHIP GAME EXPERIENCE: Played in NFC championship game (1998 season). ... Played in Super Bowl XXXIII (1998 season).
PRO STATISTICS: 1997—Recovered one fumble. 1998—Intercepted one pass for no yards.

SAUERBRUN, TODD — P — BEARS

PERSONAL: Born January 4, 1973, in Setauket, N.Y. ... 5-10/209. ... Name pronounced SOW-er-bruhn.
HIGH SCHOOL: Ward Melville (Setauket, N.Y.).
COLLEGE: West Virginia.
TRANSACTIONS/CAREER NOTES: Selected by Chicago Bears in second round (56th pick overall) of 1995 NFL draft. ... Signed by Bears (July 20, 1995). ... Granted free agency (February 13, 1998). ... Re-signed by Bears (May 19, 1998). ... On injured reserve with knee injury (September 23, 1998-remainder of season).
HONORS: Named punter on THE SPORTING NEWS college All-America first team (1994).
PRO STATISTICS: 1996—Rushed once for three yards, attempted two passes with two completions for 63 yards. 1997—Rushed twice for eight yards and fumbled once for minus nine yards.

			PUNTING				
Year Team	G	No.	Yds.	Avg.	Net avg.	In. 20	Blk.
1995—Chicago NFL	15	55	2080	37.8	31.1	16	0
1996—Chicago NFL	16	78	3491	44.8	34.8	15	0
1997—Chicago NFL	16	95	4059	42.7	32.8	26	0
1998—Chicago NFL	3	15	741	49.4	42.1	6	0
Pro totals (4 years)	50	243	10371	42.7	33.6	63	0

SAWYER, COREY — CB — BENGALS

PERSONAL: Born October 4, 1971, in Key West, Fla. ... 5-11/177. ... Full name: Corey F. Sawyer.
HIGH SCHOOL: Key West (Fla.).
COLLEGE: Florida State.
TRANSACTIONS/CAREER NOTES: Selected after junior season by Cincinnati Bengals in fourth round (104th pick overall) of 1994 NFL draft. ... Signed by Bengals (July 22, 1994). ... On injured reserve with knee injury (September 23, 1998-remainder of season). ... Granted unconditional free agency (February 12, 1999). ... Re-signed by Bengals (May 11, 1999).
HONORS: Named defensive back on THE SPORTING NEWS college All-America first team (1993).
PRO STATISTICS: 1994—Recovered one fumble. 1996—Recovered one fumble.

			INTERCEPTIONS			SACKS	PUNT RETURNS				KICKOFF RETURNS				TOTALS			
Year Team	G	GS	No.	Yds.	Avg.	TD	No.	No.	Yds.	Avg.	TD	No.	Yds.	Avg.	TD	TD	2pt.	Pts.	Fum.
1994—Cincinnati NFL	15	0	2	0	0.0	0	0.0	26	307	11.8	1	1	14	14.0	0	1	0	6	2
1995—Cincinnati NFL	12	8	2	61	30.5	0	2.0	9	58	6.4	0	2	50	25.0	0	0	0	0	1
1996—Cincinnati NFL	15	2	2	0	0.0	0	1.5	15	117	7.8	0	12	241	20.1	0	0	0	0	2
1997—Cincinnati NFL	15	2	4	44	11.0	0	0.0	0	0	...	0	0	0	...	0	0	0	0	0
1998—Cincinnati NFL	3	0	1	58	58.0	1	0.0	0	0	...	0	0	0	...	0	1	0	6	0
Pro totals (5 years)	60	12	11	163	14.8	1	3.5	50	482	9.6	1	15	305	20.3	0	2	0	12	5

SCHLERETH, MARK — G — BRONCOS

PERSONAL: Born January 25, 1966, in Anchorage, Alaska. ... 6-3/287. ... Name pronounced SHLARE-eth.
HIGH SCHOOL: Robert Service (Anchorage, Alaska).
COLLEGE: Idaho.
TRANSACTIONS/CAREER NOTES: Selected by Washington Redskins in 10th round (263rd pick overall) of 1989 NFL draft. ... Signed by Redskins (July 23, 1989). ... On injured reserve with knee injury (September 5-November 11, 1989). ... On injured reserve with a nerve condition known as Guillain-Barre Syndrome (November 16, 1993-remainder of season). ... Released by Redskins (September 2, 1994). ... Re-signed by Redskins (September 3, 1994). ... Granted unconditional free agency (February 17, 1995). ... Signed by Denver Broncos (March 27, 1995). ... Released by Broncos (February 14, 1997). ... Re-signed by Broncos (April 11, 1997). ... Granted unconditional free agency (February 13, 1998). ... Re-signed by Broncos (February 24, 1998).
PLAYING EXPERIENCE: Washington NFL, 1989-1994; Denver NFL, 1995-1998. ... Games/Games started: 1989 (6/6), 1990 (12/7), 1991 (16/16), 1992 (16/16), 1993 (9/8), 1994 (16/6), 1995 (16/16), 1996 (14/14), 1997 (11/11), 1998 (16/16). Total: 132/116.
CHAMPIONSHIP GAME EXPERIENCE: Played in NFC championship game (1991 season). ... Member of Super Bowl championship team (1991, 1997 and 1998 seasons). ... Played in AFC championship game (1997 and 1998 seasons).
HONORS: Played in Pro Bowl (1991 and 1998 seasons).
PRO STATISTICS: 1989—Recovered one fumble. 1993—Recovered one fumble. 1997—Recovered one fumble.

SCHLESINGER, CORY — FB — LIONS

PERSONAL: Born June 23, 1972, in Columbus, Neb. ... 6-0/240.
HIGH SCHOOL: Columbus (Neb.).
COLLEGE: Nebraska (degree in indusrial technology education).
TRANSACTIONS/CAREER NOTES: Selected by Detroit Lions in sixth round (192nd pick overall) of 1995 NFL draft. ... Signed by Lions (July 19, 1995).
PRO STATISTICS: 1995—Recovered one fumble for 11 yards.
SINGLE GAME HIGHS (regular season): Attempts—4 (November 27, 1997, vs. Chicago); yards—9 (November 27, 1997, vs. Chicago); and rushing touchdowns—0.

			RUSHING				RECEIVING				TOTALS			
Year Team	G	GS	Att.	Yds.	Avg.	TD	No.	Yds.	Avg.	TD	TD	2pt.	Pts.	Fum.
1995—Detroit NFL	16	1	1	1	1.0	0	1	2	2.0	0	0	0	0	0
1996—Detroit NFL	16	1	0	0	...	0	0	0	...	0	0	0	0	0
1997—Detroit NFL	16	2	7	11	1.6	0	5	69	13.8	1	1	0	6	0
1998—Detroit NFL	15	2	5	17	3.4	0	3	16	5.3	1	1	0	6	0
Pro totals (4 years)	63	6	13	29	2.2	0	9	87	9.7	2	2	0	12	0

SCHREIBER, ADAM   C/G   FALCONS

PERSONAL: Born February 20, 1962, in Galveston, Texas. ... 6-4/295. ... Full name: Adam Blayne Schreiber.
HIGH SCHOOL: Butler (Huntsville, Ala.).
COLLEGE: Texas.
TRANSACTIONS/CAREER NOTES: Selected by Seattle Seahawks in ninth round (243rd pick overall) of 1984 NFL draft. ... Signed by Seahawks (June 20, 1984). ... Released by Seahawks (August 27, 1984). ... Re-signed by Seahawks (October 10, 1984). ... Released by Seahawks (August 29, 1985). ... Signed by New Orleans Saints (November 20, 1985). ... Released by Saints (September 1, 1986). ... Signed by Philadelphia Eagles (October 16, 1986). ... Claimed on waivers by New York Jets (October 19, 1988). ... Granted unconditional free agency (February 1, 1990). ... Signed by Minnesota Vikings (March 21, 1990). ... Granted unconditional free agency (February 1-April 1, 1992). ... Re-signed by Vikings for 1992 season. ... Granted unconditional free agency (March 1, 1993). ... Re-signed by Vikings (May 7, 1993). ... Released by Vikings (July 12, 1994). ... Signed by New York Giants (August 16, 1994). ... Granted unconditional free agency (February 17, 1995). ... Re-signed by Giants (May 8, 1995). ... Granted unconditional free agency (February 14, 1997). ... Signed by Atlanta Falcons (August 5, 1997). ... Granted unconditional free agency (February 12, 1999). ... Re-signed by Falcons (April 21, 1999).
PLAYING EXPERIENCE: Seattle NFL, 1984; New Orleans NFL, 1985; Philadelphia NFL, 1986 and 1987; Philadelphia (6)-New York Jets (7) NFL, 1988; New York Jets NFL, 1989; Minnesota NFL, 1990-1993; New York Giants NFL, 1994-1996; Atlanta NFL, 1997 and 1998. ... Games/Games started: 1984 (6/0), 1985 (1/0), 1986 (9/0), 1987 (12/12), 1988 (Phi.-6/0; N.Y. Jets-7/0; Total: 13/0), 1989 (16/0), 1990 (16/0), 1991 (15/0), 1992 (16/1), 1993 (16/16), 1994 (16/2), 1995 (16/0), 1996 (15/2), 1997 (16/0), 1998 (16/0). Total: 199/33.
CHAMPIONSHIP GAME EXPERIENCE: Played in NFC championship game (1998 season). ... Played in Super Bowl XXXIII (1998 season).
PRO STATISTICS: 1990—Returned one kickoff for five yards. 1992—Recovered one fumble.

SCHROEDER, BILL   WR   PACKERS

PERSONAL: Born January 9, 1971, in Eau Claire, Wis. ... 6-3/200. ... Full name: William Fredrich Schroeder.
HIGH SCHOOL: Sheboygan (Wis.) South.
COLLEGE: Wisconsin-La Crosse (degree in physical education/teaching).
TRANSACTIONS/CAREER NOTES: Selected by Green Bay Packers in sixth round (181st pick overall) of 1994 NFL draft. ... Signed by Packers (May 10, 1994). ... Released by Packers (August 28, 1994). ... Re-signed by Packers to practice squad (August 30, 1994). ... Activated (December 29, 1994). ... Traded by Packers with TE Jeff Wilner to New England Patriots for C Mike Arthur (August 11, 1995). ... On injured reserve with foot injury (August 27, 1995-entire season). ... Released by Patriots (August 14, 1996). ... Signed by Packers to practice squad (August 28, 1996). ... Assigned by Packers to Rhein Fire in 1997 World League enhancement allocation program (February 19, 1997). ... On injured reserve with broken collarbone (December 9, 1998-remainder of season).
CHAMPIONSHIP GAME EXPERIENCE: Member of Packers for NFC championship game (1997 season); inactive. ... Member of Packers for Super Bowl XXXII (1997 season); inactive.
PRO STATISTICS: W.L.: 1997—Rushed twice for 18 yards. NFL: 1997—Recovered one fumble.
SINGLE GAME HIGHS (regular season): Receptions—7 (November 22, 1998, vs. Minnesota); yards—128 (November 29, 1998, vs. Philadelphia); and touchdown receptions—1 (October 5, 1998, vs. Minnesota).
STATISTICAL PLATEAUS: 100-yard receiving games: 1998 (1).

			RECEIVING				PUNT RETURNS				KICKOFF RETURNS				TOTALS		
Year Team	G	GS	No.	Yds.	Avg.	TD	No.	Yds.	Avg.	TD	No.	Yds.	Avg.	TD	TD	2pt.	Pts.	Fum.
1994—Green Bay NFL								Did not play.										
1995—New England NFL								Did not play.										
1996—Green Bay NFL								Did not play.										
1997—Rhein W.L.	...	...	43	702	16.3	6	0	0	0	0	1	20	20.0	0	6	0	36	...
—Green Bay NFL	15	1	2	15	7.5	1	33	342	10.4	0	24	562	23.4	0	1	0	6	4
1998—Green Bay NFL	13	3	31	452	14.6	1	2	5	2.5	0	0	0	...	0	1	0	6	1
W.L. totals (1 year)	...	...	43	702	16.3	6	0	0	0	0	1	20	20.0	0	6	0	36	0
NFL totals (2 years)	28	4	33	467	14.2	2	35	347	9.9	0	24	562	23.4	0	2	0	12	5
Pro totals (3 years)	...	...	76	1169	15.4	8	35	347	9.9	0	25	582	23.3	0	8	0	48	5

SCHULTERS, LANCE   S   49ERS

PERSONAL: Born May 27, 1975, in Brooklyn, N.Y. ... 6-2/195. ... Name pronounced SHUL-ters.
HIGH SCHOOL: Canarsie (Brooklyn, N.Y.).
JUNIOR COLLEGE: Nassau Community College (N.Y.).
COLLEGE: Hofstra.
TRANSACTIONS/CAREER NOTES: Selected by San Francisco 49ers in fourth round (119th pick overall) of 1998 NFL draft. ... Signed by 49ers (July 18, 1998).
PLAYING EXPERIENCE: San Francisco NFL, 1998. ... Games/Games started: 15/0.

SCHULZ, KURT   S   BILLS

PERSONAL: Born December 12, 1968, in Wenatchee, Wash. ... 6-1/208. ... Full name: Kurt Erich Schulz.
HIGH SCHOOL: Eisenhower (Yakima, Wash.).
COLLEGE: Eastern Washington.
TRANSACTIONS/CAREER NOTES: Selected by Buffalo Bills in seventh round (195th pick overall) of 1992 NFL draft. ... Signed by Bills (July 22, 1992). ... On injured reserve with knee injury (October 26-December 19, 1992).
CHAMPIONSHIP GAME EXPERIENCE: Played in AFC championship game (1993 season). ... Member of Bills for Super Bowl XXVII (1992 season); inactive. ... Played in Super Bowl XXVIII (1993 season).
PRO STATISTICS: 1992—Recovered two fumbles. 1998—Recovered one fumble for nine yards.

				INTERCEPTIONS		
Year Team	G	GS	No.	Yds.	Avg.	TD
1992—Buffalo NFL	8	1	0	0	...	0
1993—Buffalo NFL	12	0	0	0	...	0
1994—Buffalo NFL	16	0	0	0	...	0
1995—Buffalo NFL	13	13	6	48	8.0	▲1
1996—Buffalo NFL	15	15	4	24	6.0	0
1997—Buffalo NFL	15	14	2	23	11.5	0
1998—Buffalo NFL	12	12	6	48	8.0	0
Pro totals (7 years)	91	55	18	143	7.9	1

SCHWANTZ, JIM LB BEARS

PERSONAL: Born January 23, 1970, in Arlington, Ill. ... 6-2/240. ... Full name: James William Schwantz.
HIGH SCHOOL: William Fremd (Palatine, Ill).
COLLEGE: Purdue.
TRANSACTIONS/CAREER NOTES: Signed as non-drafted free agent by Chicago Bears (April 1992). ... Released by Bears (August 31, 1992). ... Re-signed by Bears to practice squad (September 2, 1992). ... Activated (December 26, 1992). ... Released by Bears (August 30, 1993). ... Re-signed by Bears to practice squad (August 31, 1993). ... Traded by Bears to Dallas Cowboys for sixth-round pick (traded to St. Louis) in 1996 draft (August 28, 1994). ... Granted free agency (February 14, 1997). ... Signed by San Francisco 49ers (May 2, 1997). ... Released by 49ers (August 25, 1998). ... Signed by Bears (August 29, 1998).
PLAYING EXPERIENCE: Chicago NFL, 1992 and 1998; Dallas NFL, 1994-1996; San Francisco NFL, 1997. ... Games/Games started: 1992 (1/0), 1994 (7/0), 1995 (16/0), 1996 (16/0), 1997 (16/0), 1998 (16/0). Totals: 72/10.
CHAMPIONSHIP GAME EXPERIENCE: Member of Cowboys for NFC championship game (1994 season); inactive. ... Played in NFC championship game (1995 and 1997 seasons). ... Member of Super Bowl championship team (1995 season).
HONORS: Played in Pro Bowl (1996 season).
PRO STATISTICS: 1995—Returned one kickoff for nine yards. 1998—Recovered one fumble.

SCHWARTZ, BRYAN LB JAGUARS

PERSONAL: Born December 5, 1971, in St. Lawrence, S.D. ... 6-4/256. ... Full name: Bryan Lee Schwartz.
HIGH SCHOOL: Miller (S.D.).
COLLEGE: Augustana, S.D. (degree in biology, 1995).
TRANSACTIONS/CAREER NOTES: Selected by Jacksonville Jaguars in second round (64th pick overall) of 1995 NFL draft. ... Signed by Jaguars (June 1, 1995). ... On injured reserve with knee injury (September 24, 1996-remainder of season). ... Granted free agency (February 13, 1998). ... Re-signed by Jaguars (May 15, 1998). ... Granted unconditional free agency (February 12, 1999). ... Re-signed by Jaguars (April 20, 1999).
PLAYING EXPERIENCE: Jacksonville NFL, 1995-1998. ... Games/Games started: 1995 (14/9), 1996 (4/3), 1997 (16/16), 1998 (13/12). Total: 47/40.
PRO STATISTICS: 1995—Recovered one fumble. 1997—Credited with $^1/_2$ sack and recovered one fumble. 1998—Recovered four fumbles.

SCIFRES, STEVE OT SAINTS

PERSONAL: Born January 22, 1972, in Colorado Springs, Colo. ... 6-4/300. ... Full name: Steve William Scifres. ... Name pronounced SCI-ferz.
HIGH SCHOOL: Mitchell (Colorado Springs, Colo.).
COLLEGE: Wyoming.
TRANSACTIONS/CAREER NOTES: Selected by Dallas Cowboys in third round (83rd pick overall) of 1997 NFL draft. ... Signed by Cowboys (July 14, 1997). ... Released by Cowboys (September 1, 1998). ... Signed by Carolina Panthers (September 30, 1998). ... Released by Panthers (November 5, 1998). ... Signed by Miami Dolphins (November 25, 1998). ... Active for one game with Dolphins (1998); did not play. ... Released by Dolphins (December 14, 1998). ... Signed by New Orleans Saints (February 22, 1999). ... Assigned by Saints to Frankfurt Galaxy in 1999 NFL Europe enhancement allocation program (February 22, 1999).
PLAYING EXPERIENCE: Dallas NFL, 1997; Carolina NFL, 1998. ... Games/Games started: 1997 (5/0), 1998 (1/0). Total: 6/0.

SCOTT, CHAD DB STEELERS

PERSONAL: Born September 6, 1974, in Washington, D.C. ... 6-1/192. ... Full name: Chad Oliver Scott.
HIGH SCHOOL: Suitland (Capitol Heights, Md.).
COLLEGE: Towson State, then Maryland.
TRANSACTIONS/CAREER NOTES: Selected by Pittsburgh Steelers in first round (24th pick overall) of 1997 NFL draft. ... Signed by Steelers (July 16, 1997). ... On injured reserve with knee injury (July 20, 1998-entire season).
CHAMPIONSHIP GAME EXPERIENCE: Played in AFC championship game (1997 season).

				INTERCEPTIONS		
Year Team	G	GS	No.	Yds.	Avg.	TD
1997—Pittsburgh NFL	13	9	2	-4	-2.0	0
1998—Pittsburgh NFL				Did not play.		

SCOTT, DARNAY WR BENGALS

PERSONAL: Born July 7, 1972, in St. Louis. ... 6-1/205.
HIGH SCHOOL: Kearny (San Diego).
COLLEGE: San Diego State.

TRANSACTIONS/CAREER NOTES: Selected after junior season by Cincinnati Bengals in second round (30th pick overall) of 1994 NFL draft. ... Signed by Bengals (July 18, 1994). ... Granted free agency (February 14, 1997). ... Re-signed by Bengals (June 16, 1997).
PRO STATISTICS: 1994—Attempted one pass with a completion for 53 yards.
SINGLE GAME HIGHS (regular season): Receptions—8 (December 8, 1996, vs. Baltimore); yards—157 (November 6, 1994, vs. Seattle); and touchdown receptions—2 (October 11, 1998, vs. Pittsburgh).
STATISTICAL PLATEAUS: 100-yard receiving games: 1994 (2), 1995 (1), 1996 (1), 1997 (2), 1998 (2). Total: 8.

				RUSHING			RECEIVING				KICKOFF RETURNS				TOTALS		
Year Team	G	GS	Att.	Yds.	Avg.	TD	No.	Yds.	Avg.	TD	No.	Yds.	Avg.	TD	TD	2pt.	Pts.	Fum.
1994—Cincinnati NFL	16	12	10	106	10.6	0	46	866	§18.8	5	15	342	22.8	0	5	0	30	0
1995—Cincinnati NFL	16	16	5	11	2.2	0	52	821	15.8	5	0	0	...	0	5	0	30	0
1996—Cincinnati NFL	16	16	3	4	1.3	0	58	833	14.4	5	0	0	...	0	5	0	30	0
1997—Cincinnati NFL	16	15	1	6	6.0	0	54	797	14.8	5	0	0	...	0	5	0	30	0
1998—Cincinnati NFL	13	13	2	10	5.0	0	51	817	16.0	7	0	0	...	0	7	0	42	0
Pro totals (5 years)	77	72	21	137	6.5	0	261	4134	15.8	27	15	342	22.8	0	27	0	162	0

SCOTT, FREDDIE — WR — LIONS

PERSONAL: Born August 26, 1974, in Southfield, Mich. ... 5-10/189. ... Full name: Freddie Lee Scott Jr. ... Son of Freddie Scott Sr., wide receiver with Baltimore Colts (1974-77), Detroit Lions (1978-83) and Los Angeles Express of USFL (1984).
HIGH SCHOOL: Detroit Country Day (Beverly Hills, Mich.).
COLLEGE: Penn State.
TRANSACTIONS/CAREER NOTES: Signed as non-drafted free agent by Atlanta Falcons (April 24, 1996). ... Released by Falcons (October 27, 1997). ... Signed by Indianapolis Colts (April 8, 1998). ... Released by Colts (September 11, 1998). ... Signed by Detroit Lions (April 12, 1999).
PLAYING EXPERIENCE: Atlanta NFL, 1996 and 1997; Indianapolis NFL, 1998. ... Games/Games started: 1996 (10/0), 1997 (2/0), 1998 (1/0). Total: 13/0.
PRO STATISTICS: 1996—Caught seven passes for 80 yards.
SINGLE GAME HIGHS (regular season): Receptions—4 (October 13, 1996, vs. Houston); yards—32 (October 13, 1996, vs. Houston); and touchdown receptions—0.

SCOTT, LANCE — C — GIANTS

PERSONAL: Born February 15, 1972, in Salt Lake City. ... 6-3/285.
HIGH SCHOOL: Taylorsville (Salt Lake City).
COLLEGE: Utah (degree in exercise and sports science).
TRANSACTIONS/CAREER NOTES: Selected by Arizona Cardinals in fifth round (165th pick overall) of 1995 NFL draft. ... Signed by Cardinals (July 24, 1995). ... Released by Cardinals (August 27, 1995). ... Re-signed by Cardinals to practice squad (October 2, 1995). ... Activated (November 14, 1995); did not play. ... Inactive for one game (1996). ... On injured reserve with shoulder injury (October 16, 1996-remainder of season). ... Released by Cardinals (August 19, 1997). ... Signed by New York Giants (August 25, 1997). ... Granted free agency (February 13, 1998). ... Re-signed by Giants (April 8, 1998). ... Granted unconditional free agency (February 12, 1999). ... Re-signed by Giants (May 11, 1999).
PLAYING EXPERIENCE: New York Giants NFL, 1997 and 1998. ... Games/Games started: 1997 (16/11), 1998 (16/16). Total: 32/27.
PRO STATISTICS: 1998—Fumbled once and recovered one fumble for minus one yard.

SCRAFFORD, KIRK — OT

PERSONAL: Born March 15, 1967, in Billings, Mont. ... 6-6/275. ... Full name: Kirk Tippet Scrafford.
HIGH SCHOOL: Billings (Mont.) West.
COLLEGE: Montana.
TRANSACTIONS/CAREER NOTES: Signed as non-drafted free agent by Cincinnati Bengals (May 1990). ... On injured reserve with knee injury (September 4-November 23, 1990). ... On practice squad (November 23-December 22, 1990). ... On injured reserve with knee injury (August 27-October 15, 1991). ... Claimed on waivers by Seattle Seahawks (November 16, 1992). ... Released by Seahawks after failing physical (November 17, 1992). ... Signed by Bengals (November 1992). ... Claimed on waivers by Denver Broncos (August 17, 1993). ... Granted unconditional free agency (February 17, 1995). ... Signed by San Francisco 49ers (March 29, 1995). ... Announced retirement (April 14, 1998). ... Came out of retirement to re-sign with 49ers (October 29, 1998). ... Announced retirement (February 3, 1999).
PLAYING EXPERIENCE: Cincinnati NFL, 1990-1992; Denver NFL, 1993 and 1994; San Francisco NFL, 1995-1998. ... Games/Games started: 1990 (2/0), 1991 (9/5), 1992 (8/4), 1993 (16/0), 1994 (16/7), 1995 (16/11), 1996 (7/1), 1997 (16/16), 1998 (9/8). Total: 99/52.
CHAMPIONSHIP GAME EXPERIENCE: Played in NFC championship game (1997 season).
PRO STATISTICS: 1994—Recovered one fumble.

SCROGGINS, TRACY — DE — LIONS

PERSONAL: Born September 11, 1969, in Checotah, Okla. ... 6-2/255.
HIGH SCHOOL: Checotah (Okla.).
JUNIOR COLLEGE: Coffeyville (Kan.) Community College.
COLLEGE: Tulsa.
TRANSACTIONS/CAREER NOTES: Selected by Detroit Lions in second round (53rd pick overall) of 1992 NFL draft. ... Signed by Lions (July 23, 1992). ... Granted free agency (February 17, 1995). ... Re-signed by Lions (May 17, 1995).
PRO STATISTICS: 1993—Intercepted one pass for no yards and recovered one fumble. 1994—Recovered one fumble. 1995—Recovered one fumble for 81 yards and a touchdown. 1996—Recovered one fumble. 1997—Recovered one fumble for 17 yards and a touchdown and credited with a safety.

Year Team	G	GS	SACKS
1992—Detroit NFL	16	7	7.5
1993—Detroit NFL	16	0	8.0
1994—Detroit NFL	16	9	2.5
1995—Detroit NFL	16	16	9.5
1996—Detroit NFL	6	6	2.0
1997—Detroit NFL	15	6	7.5
1998—Detroit NFL	11	3	6.5
Pro totals (7 years)	96	47	43.5

SCURLOCK, MIKE   S   PANTHERS

PERSONAL: Born February 26, 1972, in Tucson, Ariz ... 5-10/200. ... Full name: Michael Lee Scurlock Jr. ... Cousin of Randy Robbins, safety with Denver Broncos (1984-91) and New England Patriots (1992). ... Name pronounced SKER-lock.
HIGH SCHOOL: Sunnyside (Tucson, Ariz.), then Cholla (Tucson, Ariz.).
COLLEGE: Arizona.
TRANSACTIONS/CAREER NOTES: Selected by St. Louis Rams in fifth round (140th pick overall) of 1995 NFL draft. ... Signed by Rams (June 20, 1995). ... On injured reserve with sprained left knee (December 20, 1995-remainder of season). ... Released by Rams (August 24, 1997). ... Re-signed by Rams (November 4, 1997). ... Granted free agency (February 13, 1998). ... Re-signed by Rams (April 21, 1998). ... Granted unconditional free agency (February 12, 1999). ... Signed by Carolina Panthers (March 17, 1999).
PLAYING EXPERIENCE: St. Louis NFL, 1995-1998. ... Games/Games started: 1995 (14/1), 1996 (16/0), 1997 (5/0), 1998 (16/0). Total: 51/1.
PRO STATISTICS: 1995—Intercepted one pass for 13 yards and recovered one fumble.

SEARCY, LEON   OT   JAGUARS

PERSONAL: Born December 21, 1969, in Washington, D.C. ... 6-4/322. ... Full name: Leon Searcy Jr. ... Name pronounced SEER-see.
HIGH SCHOOL: Maynard Evans (Orlando).
COLLEGE: Miami, Fla. (degree in sociology, 1992).
TRANSACTIONS/CAREER NOTES: Selected by Pittsburgh Steelers in first round (11th pick overall) of 1992 NFL draft. ... Signed by Steelers (August 3, 1992). ... Granted unconditional free agency (February 16, 1996). ... Signed by Jacksonville Jaguars (February 18, 1996).
PLAYING EXPERIENCE: Pittsburgh NFL, 1992-1995; Jacksonville NFL, 1996-1998. ... Games/Games started: 1992 (15/0), 1993 (16/16), 1994 (16/16), 1995 (16/16), 1996 (16/16), 1997 (16/16), 1998 (15/15). Total: 110/95.
CHAMPIONSHIP GAME EXPERIENCE: Played in AFC championship game (1994-1996 seasons). ... Played in Super Bowl XXX (1995 season).
HONORS: Named offensive tackle on THE SPORTING NEWS college All-America second team (1991).
PRO STATISTICS: 1993—Recovered one fumble. 1995—Recovered one fumble. 1996—Recovered one fumble.

SEARS, COREY   DT   RAMS

PERSONAL: Born April 15, 1973, in San Antonio. ... 6-2/293. ... Full name: Corey Alexander Sears.
HIGH SCHOOL: Converse Judson (Converse, Texas).
JUNIOR COLLEGE: Navarro College (Texas).
COLLEGE: Mississippi State.
TRANSACTIONS/CAREER NOTES: Signed as non-drafted free agent by Baltimore Ravens (April 29, 1996). ... On injured reserve (August 20-November 6, 1996). ... Released by Ravens (November 6, 1996). ... Signed by St. Louis Rams (April 24, 1998). ... Claimed on waivers by San Francisco 49ers (August 26, 1998). ... Released by 49ers (August 28, 1998). ... Re-signed by Rams to practice squad (September 1, 1998). ... Activated (November 30, 1998).
PLAYING EXPERIENCE: St. Louis NFL, 1998. ... Games/Games started: 4/0.

SEAU, JUNIOR   LB   CHARGERS

PERSONAL: Born January 19, 1969, in San Diego. ... 6-3/250. ... Full name: Tiaina Seau Jr. ... Name pronounced SAY-ow.
HIGH SCHOOL: Oceanside (Calif.).
COLLEGE: Southern California.
TRANSACTIONS/CAREER NOTES: Selected after junior season by San Diego Chargers in first round (fifth pick overall) of 1990 NFL draft. ... Signed by Chargers (August 27, 1990).
CHAMPIONSHIP GAME EXPERIENCE: Played in AFC championship game (1994 season). ... Played in Super Bowl XXIX (1994 season).
HONORS: Named linebacker on THE SPORTING NEWS college All-America first team (1989). ... Played in Pro Bowl (1991-1998 seasons). ... Named inside linebacker on THE SPORTING NEWS NFL All-Pro team (1992-1996 and 1998).
PRO STATISTICS: 1992—Recovered one fumble for 10 yards. 1993—Recovered one fumble for 21 yards. 1994—Recovered three fumbles. 1995—Recovered three fumbles for 30 yards and one touchdown. 1996—Recovered three fumbles. 1997—Fumbled once and recovered two fumbles for five yards. 1998—Recovered two fumbles.

			INTERCEPTIONS				SACKS
Year Team	G	GS	No.	Yds.	Avg.	TD	No.
1990—San Diego NFL	16	15	0	0	...	0	1.0
1991—San Diego NFL	16	16	0	0	...	0	7.0
1992—San Diego NFL	15	15	2	51	25.5	0	4.5
1993—San Diego NFL	16	16	2	58	29.0	0	0.0
1994—San Diego NFL	16	16	0	0	...	0	5.5
1995—San Diego NFL	16	16	2	5	2.5	0	2.0
1996—San Diego NFL	15	15	2	18	9.0	0	7.0
1997—San Diego NFL	15	15	2	33	16.5	0	7.0
1998—San Diego NFL	16	16	0	0	...	0	3.5
Pro totals (9 years)	141	140	10	165	16.5	0	37.5

SEHORN, JASON — CB — GIANTS

PERSONAL: Born April 15, 1971, in Sacramento. ... 6-2/210. ... Name pronounced SEE-horn.
HIGH SCHOOL: Mt. Shasta (Calif.).
JUNIOR COLLEGE: Shasta College (Calif.).
COLLEGE: Southern California.
TRANSACTIONS/CAREER NOTES: Selected by New York Giants in second round (59th pick overall) of 1994 NFL draft. ... Signed by Giants (July 17, 1994). ... Granted free agency (February 14, 1997). ... Re-signed by Giants (August 9, 1997). ... On injured reserve with knee injury (August 25, 1998-entire season).
PRO STATISTICS: 1996—Credited with three sacks, returned one punt for no yards, fumbled once and recovered one fumble. 1997—Credited with 1½ sacks and recovered one fumble for two yards.

				INTERCEPTIONS			
Year Team	G	GS	No.	Yds.	Avg.	TD
1994—New York Giants NFL	8	0	0	0	...	0
1995—New York Giants NFL	14	0	0	0	...	0
1996—New York Giants NFL	16	15	5	61	12.2	1
1997—New York Giants NFL	16	16	6	74	12.3	1
1998—New York Giants NFL			Did not play.			
Pro totals (4 years)	54	31	11	135	12.3	2

RECORD AS BASEBALL PLAYER

TRANSACTIONS/CAREER NOTES: Threw right, batted right. ... Signed as non-drafted free agent by Chicago Cubs organization (July 24, 1989). ... Released by Cubs organization (April 4, 1991).

					BATTING								FIELDING		
Year Team (League)	Pos.	G	AB	R	H	2B	3B	HR	RBI	Avg.	BB	SO	SB	PO	A	E	Avg.
1990—Huntington (Appal.)	OF	49	125	21	23	3	1	1	10	.184	8	52	9	82	3	5	.944

SELLERS, MIKE — FB — REDSKINS

PERSONAL: Born July 21, 1975, in Frankfurt, West Germany ... 6-3/260.
HIGH SCHOOL: North Thurston (Lacey, Wash.).
JUNIOR COLLEGE: Walla Walla (Wash.) Community College.
TRANSACTIONS/CAREER NOTES: Signed by Edmonton Eskimos of CFL (March 21, 1995). ... Tranferred by Eskimos to reserve list (August 23, 1995). ... Transferred by Eskimos to injured list (October 12, 1995). ... Transferred by Eskimos to active roster (December 18, 1995). ... Signed by Washington Redskins (February 11, 1998).
PLAYING EXPERIENCE: Edmonton CFL, 1996 and 1997; Washington NFL, 1998. ... Games/Games started: 1996 (17/games started unavailable), 1997 (16/-), 1998 (14/1).
PRO STATISTICS: CFL: 1997— Rushed 40 times for 133 yards, caught five passes for 57 yards, returned one kickoff for 14 yards and recovered one fumble for 43 yards. 1998—Caught three passes for 18 yards, returned two kickoffs for 33 yards and recovered one fumble.
SINGLE GAME HIGHS (regular season): Receptions—3 (December 27, 1998, vs. Dallas); yards—18 (December 27, 1998, vs. Dallas); and touchdown receptions—0.

SEMPLE, TONY — G — LIONS

PERSONAL: Born December 20, 1970, in Springfield, Ill. ... 6-5/305. ... Full name: Anthony Lee Semple.
HIGH SCHOOL: Lincoln (Ill.) Community.
COLLEGE: Memphis State (degree in sports administration).
TRANSACTIONS/CAREER NOTES: Selected by Detroit Lions in fifth round (154th pick overall) of 1994 NFL draft. ... Signed by Lions (July 21, 1994). ... On injured reserve with knee injury (August 19, 1994-entire season). ... Granted free agency (February 14, 1997). ... Re-signed by Lions (June 13, 1997). ... Granted unconditional free agency (February 13, 1998). ... Re-signed by Lions (February 21, 1998).
PLAYING EXPERIENCE: Detroit NFL, 1995-1998. ... Games/Games started: 1995 (16/0), 1996 (15/1), 1997 (16/1), 1998 (16/3). Total: 63/5.

SETTLES, TAWAMBI — S

PERSONAL: Born January 19, 1976, in Chattanooga, Tenn. ... 6-1/191.
HIGH SCHOOL: McCallie (Chattanooga, Tenn.).
COLLEGE: Duke.
TRANSACTIONS/CAREER NOTES: Signed as non-drafted free agent by Detroit Lions (April 24, 1998). ... Released by Lions (August 24, 1998). ... Signed by Green Bay Packers to practice squad (September 1, 1998). ... Released by Packers (October 27, 1998). ... Signed by Jacksonville Jaguars (October 28, 1998). ... On injured reserve with knee injury (December 15, 1998-remainder of season). ... Granted free agency after 1998 season.
PLAYING EXPERIENCE: Jacksonville NFL, 1998. ... Games/Games started: 7/0.

SHADE, SAM — S — REDSKINS

PERSONAL: Born June 14, 1973, in Birmingham, Ala. ... 6-1/201.
HIGH SCHOOL: Wenonah (Birmingham, Ala.).
COLLEGE: Alabama.

TRANSACTIONS/CAREER NOTES: Selected by Cincinnati Bengals in fourth round (102nd pick overall) of 1995 NFL draft. ... Signed by Bengals (July 18, 1995). ... Granted free agency (February 13, 1998). ... Re-signed by Bengals (June 15, 1998). ... Granted unconditional free agency (February 12, 1999). ... Signed by Washington Redskins (February 19, 1999).
PLAYING EXPERIENCE: Cincinnati NFL, 1995-1998. ... Games/Games started: 1995 (16/2), 1996 (12/0), 1997 (16/12), 1998 (16/14). Total: 60/28.
PRO STATISTICS: 1997—Intercepted one pass for 21 yards, credited with four sacks, fumbled once and recovered one fumble. 1998—Intercepted three passes for 33 yards, credited with one sack and recovered two fumbles for 55 yards and one touchdown.

SHARPE, SHANNON TE BRONCOS

PERSONAL: Born June 26, 1968, in Chicago. ... 6-2/230. ... Brother of Sterling Sharpe, wide receiver with Green Bay Packers (1988-94).
HIGH SCHOOL: Glennville (Ga.).
COLLEGE: Savannah (Ga.) State.
TRANSACTIONS/CAREER NOTES: Selected by Denver Broncos in seventh round (192nd pick overall) of 1990 NFL draft. ... Signed by Broncos (July 1990). ... Granted free agency (February 1, 1992). ... Re-signed by Broncos (July 31, 1992). ... Designated by Broncos as transition player (February 15, 1994).
CHAMPIONSHIP GAME EXPERIENCE: Played in AFC championship game (1991, 1997 and 1998 seasons). ... Member of Super Bowl championship team (1997 and 1998 seasons).
HONORS: Played in Pro Bowl (1992, 1993 and 1995-1997 seasons). ... Named tight end on THE SPORTING NEWS NFL All-Pro team (1993 and 1996-1998). ... Named to play in Pro Bowl (1994 season); replaced by Eric Green due to injury. ... Named to play in Pro Bowl (1998 season); replaced by Frank Wycheck due to injury.
POST SEASON RECORDS: Shares NFL postseason single-game record for most receptions—13 (January 9, 1994, vs. Los Angeles Raiders).
PRO STATISTICS: 1991—Rushed once for 15 yards and recovered one fumble. 1992—Rushed twice for minus six yards. 1993—Returned one kickoff for no yards. 1995—Recovered one fumble.
SINGLE GAME HIGHS (regular season): Receptions—13 (October 6, 1996, vs. San Diego); yards—180 (September 3, 1995, vs. Buffalo); and touchdown receptions—3 (October 6, 1996, vs. San Diego).
STATISTICAL PLATEAUS: 100-yard receiving games: 1992 (2), 1993 (2), 1994 (1), 1995 (2), 1996 (3), 1997 (4). Total: 14.
MISCELLANEOUS: Shares Denver Broncos all-time record for most touchdown receptions (44).

				RECEIVING				TOTALS			
Year Team	G	GS	No.	Yds.	Avg.	TD	TD	2pt.	Pts.	Fum.
1990—Denver NFL	16	2	7	99	14.1	1	1	...	6	1
1991—Denver NFL	16	9	22	322	14.6	1	1	...	6	0
1992—Denver NFL	16	11	53	640	12.1	2	2	...	12	1
1993—Denver NFL	16	12	81	995	12.3	§9	9	...	54	1
1994—Denver NFL	15	13	87	1010	11.6	4	4	2	28	1
1995—Denver NFL	13	12	63	756	12.0	4	4	0	24	1
1996—Denver NFL	15	15	80	1062	13.3	10	10	0	60	1
1997—Denver NFL	16	16	72	1107	15.4	3	3	1	20	1
1998—Denver NFL	16	16	64	768	12.0	10	10	0	60	0
Pro totals (9 years)	139	106	529	6759	12.8	44	44	3	270	7

SHARPER, DARREN S PACKERS

PERSONAL: Born November 3, 1975, in Richmond, Va. ... 6-2/210. ... Full name: Darren Mallory Sharper. ... Brother of Jamie Sharper, linebacker, Baltimore Ravens.
HIGH SCHOOL: Hermitage (Richmond, Va.).
COLLEGE: William & Mary.
TRANSACTIONS/CAREER NOTES: Selected by Green Bay Packers in second round (60th pick overall) of 1997 NFL draft. ... Signed by Packers (July 11, 1997).
CHAMPIONSHIP GAME EXPERIENCE: Played in NFC championship game (1997 season). ... Played in Super Bowl XXXII (1997 season).
PRO STATISTICS: 1997—Returned one kickoff for three yards and recovered one fumble for 34 yards and a touchdown.

			INTERCEPTIONS				PUNT RETURNS				TOTALS		
Year Team	G	GS	No.	Yds.	Avg.	TD	No.	Yds.	Avg.	TD	2pt.	Pts.	Fum.
1997—Green Bay NFL	14	0	2	70	35.0	∞2	7	32	4.6	0	3	0	18	1
1998—Green Bay NFL	16	16	0	0	...	0	0	0	...	0	0	0	0	0
Pro totals (2 years)	30	16	2	70	35.0	2	7	32	4.6	0	3	0	18	1

SHARPER, JAMIE LB RAVENS

PERSONAL: Born November 23, 1974, in Richmond, Va. ... 6-3/240. ... Full name: Harry Jamie Sharper Jr. ... Brother of Darren Sharper, defensive back, Green Bay Packers.
HIGH SCHOOL: Hermitage (Glen Allen, Va.).
COLLEGE: Virginia (degree in psychology, 1996).
TRANSACTIONS/CAREER NOTES: Selected by Baltimore Ravens in second round (34th pick overall) of 1997 NFL draft. ... Signed by Ravens (July 23, 1997).
PRO STATISTICS: 1997—Fumbled once.

			INTERCEPTIONS				SACKS
Year Team	G	GS	No.	Yds.	Avg.	TD	No.
1997—Baltimore NFL	16	15	1	4	4.0	0	3.0
1998—Baltimore NFL	16	16	0	0	...	0	1.0
Pro totals (2 years)	32	31	1	4	4.0	0	4.0

SHAW, BOBBY　　　　　　　　WR　　　　　　　　STEELERS

PERSONAL: Born April 23, 1975, in San Francisco. ... 6-0/186.
HIGH SCHOOL: Galileo (San Francisco).
COLLEGE: California.
TRANSACTIONS/CAREER NOTES: Selected by Seattle Seahawks in sixth round (169th pick overall) of 1998 NFL draft. ... Signed by Seahawks (June 5, 1998). ... Released by Seahawks (August 30, 1998). ... Re-signed by Seahawks to practice squad (August 31, 1998). ... Activated (November 4, 1998). ... Released by Seahawks (November 18, 1998). ... Signed by Pittsburgh Steelers (November 20, 1998).
PLAYING EXPERIENCE: Seattle NFL, 1998. ... Games/Games started: 1/1.
HONORS: Named wide receiver on THE SPORTING NEWS college All-America first team (1997).

SHAW, HAROLD　　　　　　　　RB　　　　　　　　PATRIOTS

PERSONAL: Born September 3, 1974, in Magee, Miss. ... 6-0/228. ... Full name: Harold Lamar Shaw.
HIGH SCHOOL: Magee (Miss.).
COLLEGE: Southern Mississippi.
TRANSACTIONS/CAREER NOTES: Selected by New England Patriots in sixth round (176th pick overall) of 1998 NFL draft. ... Signed by Patriots (July 16, 1998).
PLAYING EXPERIENCE: New England NFL, 1998. ... Games/Games started: 11/0.

SHAW, SCOTT　　　　　　　　G　　　　　　　　BENGALS

PERSONAL: Born June 2, 1974, in Detroit. ... 6-3/303. ... Full name: Scott Harold Shaw.
HIGH SCHOOL: Henry Ford II (Sterling Heights, Mich.).
COLLEGE: Michigan State.
TRANSACTIONS/CAREER NOTES: Selected by Miami Dolphins in fifth round (143rd pick overall) of 1998 NFL draft. ... Signed by Dolphins (July 17, 1998). ... Released by Dolphins (August 25, 1998). ... Signed by Cincinnati Bengals (August 30, 1998).
PLAYING EXPERIENCE: Cincinnati NFL, 1998. ... Games/Games started: 1/0.

SHAW, SEDRICK　　　　　　　　RB　　　　　　　　BROWNS

PERSONAL: Born November 16, 1973, in Austin, Texas. ... 6-0/214.
HIGH SCHOOL: Lyndon B. Johnson (Austin, Texas).
COLLEGE: Iowa.
TRANSACTIONS/CAREER NOTES: Selected by New England Patriots in third round (61st pick overall) of 1997 NFL draft. ... Signed by Patriots (July 15, 1997). ... Traded by Patriots to Cleveland Browns for past considerations (April 22, 1999).
PRO STATISTICS: 1998—Returned one kickoff for 16 yards and recovered one fumble for minus seven yards.
SINGLE GAME HIGHS (regular season): Attempts—19 (October 11, 1998, vs. Kansas City); yards—81 (December 27, 1998, vs. New York Jets); and rushing touchdowns—0.

			RUSHING				RECEIVING			TOTALS		
Year Team	G	GS	Att.	Yds.	Avg.	TD	No.	Yds.	Avg.	TD	TD	2pt.	Pts.	Fum.
1997—New England NFL	1	0	0	0	...	0	0	0	...	0	0	0	0	0
1998—New England NFL	13	1	48	236	4.9	0	6	30	5.0	0	0	0	0	2
Pro totals (2 years)	14	1	48	236	4.9	0	6	30	5.0	0	0	0	0	2

SHAW, TERRANCE　　　　　　　　CB　　　　　　　　CHARGERS

PERSONAL: Born November 11, 1973, in Marshall, Texas. ... 5-11/190. ... Full name: Terrance Bernard Shaw.
HIGH SCHOOL: Marshall (Texas).
COLLEGE: Stephen F. Austin State.
TRANSACTIONS/CAREER NOTES: Selected by San Diego Chargers in second round (34th pick overall) of 1995 NFL draft. ... Signed by Chargers (June 15, 1995).
PRO STATISTICS: 1997—Recovered one fumble.

			INTERCEPTIONS			
Year Team	G	GS	No.	Yds.	Avg.	TD
1995—San Diego NFL	16	14	1	31	31.0	0
1996—San Diego NFL	16	16	3	78	26.0	0
1997—San Diego NFL	16	16	1	11	11.0	0
1998—San Diego NFL	13	13	2	0	0.0	0
Pro totals (4 years)	61	59	7	120	17.1	0

SHEDD, KENNY　　　　　　　　WR　　　　　　　　RAIDERS

PERSONAL: Born February 14, 1971, in Davenport, Iowa. ... 5-10/164.
HIGH SCHOOL: West (Davenport, Iowa).
COLLEGE: Northern Iowa.
TRANSACTIONS/CAREER NOTES: Selected by New York Jets in fifth round (129th pick overall) of 1993 NFL draft. ... Signed by Jets (July 13, 1993). ... Released by Jets (August 24, 1993). ... Re-signed by Jets to practice squad (September 1, 1993). ... Activated (December 31, 1993); did not play. ... Released by Jets (September 17, 1994). ... Re-signed by Jets to practice squad (September 21, 1994). ... Signed by Chicago Bears off Jets practice squad (October 25, 1994). ... Inactive for nine games (1994). ... Released by Bears (August 27, 1995). ... Selected by

London Monarchs in 1996 World League draft (February 22, 1996). ... Signed by Barcelona Dragons of World League (May 23, 1996). ... Signed by Oakland Raiders (June 1996).
PRO STATISTICS: NFL: 1996—Credited with a safety and returned three kickoffs for 51 yards. 1997—Returned two kickoffs for 38 yards and recovered two fumbles for 25 yards and one touchdown. 1998—Returned two kickoffs for 32 yards and recovered two fumbles for four yards.
SINGLE GAME HIGHS (regular season): Receptions—3 (September 21, 1997, vs. New York Jets); yards—51 (December 22, 1996, vs. Seattle); and touchdown receptions—1 (September 22, 1996, vs. San Diego).

				RECEIVING				TOTALS		
Year Team	G	GS	No.	Yds.	Avg.	TD	TD	2pt.	Pts.	Fum.
1996—Barcelona W.L.	...	...	14	328	23.4	1	1	0	6	...
—Oakland NFL	16	1	3	87	29.0	1	1	0	8	0
1997—Oakland NFL	16	0	10	115	11.5	0	1	0	6	0
1998—Oakland NFL	15	0	3	50	16.7	0	0	0	0	0
W.L. totals (1 year)	...	...	14	328	23.4	1	1	0	6	0
NFL totals (3 years)	47	1	16	252	15.8	1	2	0	14	0
Pro totals (4 years)	...	...	30	580	19.3	2	3	0	20	0

SHEHEE, RASHAAN   RB   CHIEFS

PERSONAL: Born June 20, 1975, in Bakersfield, Calif. ... 5-10/205. ... Name pronounced ruh-SHAHN.
HIGH SCHOOL: Foothill (Bakersfield, Calif.).
COLLEGE: Washington.
TRANSACTIONS/CAREER NOTES: Selected by Kansas City Chiefs in third round (88th pick overall) of 1998 NFL draft. ... Signed by Chiefs (July 17, 1998).
SINGLE GAME HIGHS (regular season): Attempts—11 (October 4, 1998, vs. Seattle); yards—28 (October 28, 1998, vs. Seattle); and rushing touchdowns—0.

			RUSHING				RECEIVING				KICKOFF RETURNS				TOTALS			
Year Team	G	GS	Att.	Yds.	Avg.	TD	No.	Yds.	Avg.	TD	No.	Yds.	Avg.	TD	TD	2pt.	Pts.	Fum.
1998—Kansas City NFL	16	0	22	57	2.6	0	10	73	7.3	0	4	72	18.0	0	0	0	0	2

SHELDON, MIKE   OT   DOLPHINS

PERSONAL: Born June 8, 1973, in Hinsdale, Ill. ... 6-4/305. ... Full name: Michael Joseph Sheldon.
HIGH SCHOOL: Willowbrook (Villa Park, Ill.).
COLLEGE: Grand Valley State (Mich.).
TRANSACTIONS/CAREER NOTES: Signed as non-drafted free agent by Buffalo Bills (April 1995). ... Released by Bills (August 27, 1995). ... Re-signed by Bills to practice squad (August 29, 1995). ... Released by Bills (August 20, 1996). ... Signed by Miami Dolphins to practice squad (August 27, 1996). ... Assigned by Dolphins to Rhein Fire in 1997 World League enhancement allocation program (February 17, 1997).
PLAYING EXPERIENCE: Rhein W.L., 1997; Miami NFL, 1997 and 1998. ... Games/Games started: W.L. 1997 (10/10), NFL 1997 (11/0), 1998 (9/2). Total W.L.: 10/10. Total NFL: 20/2. Total Pro: 30/12.

SHELLO, KENDEL   DT   RAIDERS

PERSONAL: Born November 24, 1973, in New Iberia, La. ... 6-3/301.
HIGH SCHOOL: New Iberia (La.).
COLLEGE: Southern.
TRANSACTIONS/CAREER NOTES: Signed as non-drafted free agent by Indianapolis Colts (April 26, 1996). ... Released by Colts (August 25, 1996). ... Re-signed by Colts to practice squad (August 27, 1996). ... Activated (September 22, 1996); did not play. ... On injured reserve with back injury (December 24, 1998-remainder of season). ... Granted free agency (February 12, 1999). ... Signed by Oakland Raiders (April 28, 1999).
PLAYING EXPERIENCE: Indianapolis NFL, 1997 and 1998. ... Games/Games started: 1997 (6/0), 1998 (6/1). Total: 12/1.
PRO STATISTICS: 1997—Credited with one sack. 1998—Credited with one sack and recovered one fumble.

SHELTON, DAIMON   FB   JAGUARS

PERSONAL: Born September 15, 1972, in Duarte, Calif. ... 6-0/251.
HIGH SCHOOL: Duarte (Calif.).
JUNIOR COLLEGE: Fresno (Calif.) City College.
COLLEGE: Cal State Sacramento.
TRANSACTIONS/CAREER NOTES: Selected by Jacksonville Jaguars in sixth round (184th pick overall) of 1997 NFL draft. ... Signed by Jaguars (May 23, 1997).
SINGLE GAME HIGHS (regular season): Attempts—13 (October 18, 1998, vs. Buffalo); yards —44 (October 18, 1998, vs. Buffalo); and rushing touchdowns—1 (November 1, 1998, vs. Baltimore).

			RUSHING				RECEIVING				TOTALS			
Year Team	G	GS	Att.	Yds.	Avg.	TD	No.	Yds.	Avg.	TD	TD	2pt.	Pts.	Fum.
1997—Jacksonville NFL	13	0	6	4	0.7	0	0	0	...	0	0	0	0	1
1998—Jacksonville NFL	14	8	30	95	3.2	1	10	79	7.9	0	1	0	6	0
Pro totals (2 years)	27	8	36	99	2.8	1	10	79	7.9	0	1	0	6	1

SHEPHERD, LESLIE   WR   BROWNS

PERSONAL: Born November 3, 1969, in Washington, D.C. ... 5-11/186. ... Full name: Leslie Glenard Shepherd.

HIGH SCHOOL: Forestville (Md.).
COLLEGE: Temple.
TRANSACTIONS/CAREER NOTES: Signed as non-drafted free agent by Tampa Bay Buccaneers (May 2, 1992). ... Released by Buccaneers (August 31, 1992). ... Signed by Pittsburgh Steelers (March 17, 1993). ... Released by Steelers (August 24, 1993). ... Re-signed by Steelers to practice squad (August 31, 1993). ... Claimed on waivers by Washington Redskins (September 4, 1994). ... Released by Redskins (September 16, 1994). ... Re-signed by Redskins to practice squad (September 20, 1994). ... Activated (December 2, 1994). ... On injured reserve with elbow and wrist injuries (November 19, 1997-remainder of season). ... Granted unconditional free agency (February 12, 1999). ... Signed by Cleveland Browns (April 7, 1999).
PRO STATISTICS: 1995—Returned three kickoffs for 85 yards and recovered one fumble. 1996—Recovered one fumble.
SINGLE GAME HIGHS (regular season): Receptions—7 (November 22, 1998, vs. Arizona); yards—135 (October 29, 1995, vs. New York Giants); and touchdown receptions—2 (September 28, 1997, vs. Jacksonville).
STATISTICAL PLATEAUS: 100-yard receiving games: 1995 (1), 1998 (1). Total: 2.

				RUSHING				RECEIVING				TOTALS		
Year Team	G	GS	Att.	Yds.	Avg.	TD	No.	Yds.	Avg.	TD	TD	2pt.	Pts.	Fum.
1994—Washington NFL	3	0	0	0	...	0	1	8	8.0	0	0	0	0	0
1995—Washington NFL	14	4	7	63	9.0	1	29	486	16.8	2	3	0	18	0
1996—Washington NFL	12	6	6	96	16.0	2	23	344	15.0	3	5	0	30	0
1997—Washington NFL	11	9	4	27	6.8	0	29	562	19.4	5	5	0	30	0
1998—Washington NFL	16	16	6	91	15.2	1	43	712	16.6	8	9	1	56	0
Pro totals (5 years)	56	35	23	277	12.0	4	125	2112	16.9	18	22	1	134	0

SHIELDS, WILL   G   CHIEFS

PERSONAL: Born September 15, 1971, in Fort Riley, Kan. ... 6-3/310. ... Full name: Will Herthie Shields.
HIGH SCHOOL: Lawton (Okla.).
COLLEGE: Nebraska (degree in communications).
TRANSACTIONS/CAREER NOTES: Selected by Kansas City Chiefs in the third round (74th pick overall) of 1993 NFL draft. ... Signed by Chiefs (May 3, 1993).
PLAYING EXPERIENCE: Kansas City NFL, 1993-1998. ... Games/Games started: 1993 (16/15), 1994 (16/16), 1995 (16/16), 1996 (16/16), 1997 (16/16), 1998 (16/16). Total: 96/95.
CHAMPIONSHIP GAME EXPERIENCE: Played in AFC championship game (1993 season).
HONORS: Named guard on THE SPORTING NEWS college All-America second team (1991). ... Named guard on THE SPORTING NEWS college All-America first team (1992). ... Played in Pro Bowl (1995-1998 seasons).
PRO STATISTICS: 1993—Recovered two fumbles. 1994—Recovered one fumble. 1995—Recovered one fumble. 1998—Caught one pass for four yards and recovered one fumble.

SHIVER, CLAY   C   BRONCOS

PERSONAL: Born December 7, 1972, in Tifton, Ga. ... 6-2/283.
HIGH SCHOOL: Tift County (Tifton, Ga.).
COLLEGE: Florida State.
TRANSACTIONS/CAREER NOTES: Selected by Dallas Cowboys in third round (67th pick overall) of 1996 NFL draft. ... Signed by Cowboys (July 16, 1996). ... Granted free agency (February 12, 1999). ... Signed by Denver Broncos (June 8, 1999).
PLAYING EXPERIENCE: Dallas NFL, 1996-1998. ... Games/Games started: 1996 (14/0), 1997 (16/16), 1998 (13/9). Total: 43/25.
HONORS: Named offensive lineman on THE SPORTING NEWS college All-America first team (1995).
PRO STATISTICS: 1997—Fumbled twice and recovered one fumble.

SHULER, HEATH   QB   RAIDERS

PERSONAL: Born December 31, 1971, in Bryson City, N.C. ... 6-2/216. ... Full name: Joseph Heath Shuler.
HIGH SCHOOL: Swain County (Bryson City, N.C.).
COLLEGE: Tennessee.
TRANSACTIONS/CAREER NOTES: Selected after junior season by Washington Redskins in first round (third pick overall) of 1994 NFL draft. ... Signed by Redskins (August 3, 1994). ... Granted free agency (February 14, 1997). ... Traded by Redskins to New Orleans Saints for fifth-round pick (S Jamel Williams) in 1997 draft and third-round pick (RB Skip Hicks) in 1998 draft (April 16, 1997). ... On injured reserve with foot injury (November 19, 1997-remainder of season). ... Inactive for eight games (1998). ... On injured reserve with foot injury (November 4, 1998-remainder of season). ... Released by Saints (February 22, 1999). ... Signed by Oakland Raiders (April 22, 1999).
HONORS: Named quarterback on THE SPORTING NEWS college All-America second team (1993).
PRO STATISTICS: 1994—Fumbled three times. 1995—Fumbled once and recovered one fumble. 1996—Fumbled once for minus 14 yards. 1997—Fumbled eight times and recovered three fumbles for minus 20 yards.
SINGLE GAME HIGHS (regular season): Attempts—38 (September 27, 1997, vs. San Diego); completions—21 (November 9, 1997, vs. Oakland); yards—286 (December 11, 1994, vs. Arizona); and touchdown passes—2 (December 18, 1994, vs. Tampa Bay).
MISCELLANEOUS: Regular-season record as starting NFL quarterback: 8-14 (.364).

			PASSING								RUSHING			TOTALS		
Year Team	G	GS	Att.	Cmp.	Pct.	Yds.	TD	Int.	Avg.	Rat.	Att.	Yds.	Avg.	TD	TD	2pt.	Pts.
1994—Washington NFL	11	8	265	120	45.3	1658	10	12	6.26	59.6	26	103	4.0	0	0	0	0
1995—Washington NFL	7	5	125	66	52.8	745	3	7	5.96	55.6	18	57	3.2	0	0	0	0
1996—Washington NFL	1	0	0	0	...	0	0	0	...	...	1	0	0.0	0	0	0	0
1997—New Orleans NFL	10	9	203	106	52.2	1288	2	14	6.34	46.7	22	38	1.7	1	1	0	6
1998—New Orleans NFL							Did not play.										
Pro totals (4 years)	29	22	593	292	49.2	3691	15	33	6.22	54.3	67	198	3.0	1	1	0	6

SIDNEY, DAINON   CB   TITANS

PERSONAL: Born May 30, 1975, in Atlanta. ... 6-0/188. ... Full name: Dainon Tarquinius Sidney. ... Name pronounced DAY-none.
HIGH SCHOOL: Riverdale (Ga.).
COLLEGE: East Tennessee State, then Alabama-Birmingham.
TRANSACTIONS/CAREER NOTES: Selected by Tennessee Oilers in third round (77th pick overall) of 1998 NFL draft. ... Signed by Oilers (July 21, 1998). ... Oilers franchise renamed Tennessee Titans for 1999 season (December 26, 1998).
PLAYING EXPERIENCE: Tennessee NFL, 1998. ... Games/Games started: 16/1.

SIENKIEWICZ, TROY   DT   CHARGERS

PERSONAL: Born May 27, 1972, in Charleston, S.C. ... 6-5/300. ... Full name: Troy Allen Sienkiewicz. ... Name pronounced sen-KEV-itch.
HIGH SCHOOL: Alamogordo (N.M.).
COLLEGE: New Mexico State.
TRANSACTIONS/CAREER NOTES: Selected by San Diego Chargers in sixth round (177th pick overall) of 1995 NFL draft. ... Signed by Chargers (July 14, 1995). ... Inactive for all 16 games (1995). ... On injured reserve with neck injury (October 25, 1996-remainder of season). ... Granted free agency (February 13, 1998). ... Re-signed by Chargers (June 11, 1998). ... Granted unconditional free agency (February 12, 1999). ... Re-signed by Chargers (April 2, 1999).
PLAYING EXPERIENCE: San Diego NFL, 1996-1998. ... Games/Games started: 1996 (7/0), 1997 (14/6), 1998 (7/0). Total: 28/6.
PRO STATISTICS: 1997—Recovered two fumbles for seven yards.

SIGLAR, RICKY   OT

PERSONAL: Born June 14, 1966, in Albuquerque, N.M. ... 6-7/308. ... Full name: Ricky Allan Siglar.
HIGH SCHOOL: Manzano (Albuquerque, N.M.).
JUNIOR COLLEGE: Arizona Western College.
COLLEGE: San Jose State.
TRANSACTIONS/CAREER NOTES: Signed as non-drafted free agent by Dallas Cowboys (March 24, 1989). ... Released by Cowboys (September 5, 1989). ... Signed by San Francisco 49ers to developmental squad (September 20, 1989). ... Released by 49ers (January 29, 1990). ... Re-signed by 49ers (February 5, 1990). ... Released by 49ers (August 20, 1991). ... Re-signed by 49ers (February 4, 1992). ... Released by 49ers (August 31, 1992). ... Signed by Kansas City Chiefs (April 1993). ... Granted free agency (February 17, 1995). ... Tendered offer sheet by Jacksonville Jaguars (March 3, 1995). ... Offer matched by Chiefs (March 10, 1995). ... Granted unconditional free agency (February 14, 1997). ... Signed by New Orleans Saints (June 13, 1997). ... Released by Saints (August 30, 1998). ... Signed by Carolina Panthers (October 14, 1998). ... Released by Panthers (October 27, 1998). ... Signed by Saints (October 30, 1998). ... Released by Saints (November 30, 1998). ... Signed by Kansas City Chiefs (December 2, 1998). ... Granted unconditional free agency (February 12, 1999).
PLAYING EXPERIENCE: San Francisco NFL, 1990; Kansas City NFL, 1993-1996; New Orleans NFL, 1997; Carolina (1)-New Orleans (1)-Kansas City (4) NFL, 1998. ... Games/Games started: 1990 (15/0), 1993 (14/14), 1994 (16/8), 1995 (16/12), 1996 (16/16), 1997 (16/1), 1998 (Car.-1/0; N.O.-1/0; K.C.-4/0; Total: 6/0). Total: 99/51.
CHAMPIONSHIP GAME EXPERIENCE: Played in NFC championship game (1990 season). ... Played in AFC championship game (1993 season).

SIMMONS, ANTHONY   LB   SEAHAWKS

PERSONAL: Born June 20, 1976, in Spartanburg, S.C. ... 6-0/230.
HIGH SCHOOL: Spartanburg (S.C.).
COLLEGE: Clemson (degree in marketing, 1998).
TRANSACTIONS/CAREER NOTES: Selected after junior season by Seattle Seahawks in first round (15th pick overall) of 1998 NFL draft. ... Signed by Seahawks (July 18, 1998).
PLAYING EXPERIENCE: Seattle NFL, 1998. ... Games/Games started: 12/4.
HONORS: Named inside linebacker on THE SPORTING NEWS college All-America first team (1996 and 1997).
PRO STATISTICS: 1998—Intercepted one pass for 36 yards and a touchdown.

SIMMONS, BRIAN   LB   BENGALS

PERSONAL: Born June 21, 1975, in New Bern, N.C. ... 6-3/233. ... Full name: Brian Eugene Simmons.
HIGH SCHOOL: New Bern (N.C.).
COLLEGE: North Carolina.
TRANSACTIONS/CAREER NOTES: Selected by Cincinnati Bengals in first round (17th pick overall) of 1998 NFL draft. ... Signed by Bengals (July 27, 1998).
HONORS: Named outside linebacker on THE SPORTING NEWS college All-America second team (1996). ... Named outside linebacker on THE SPORTING NEWS college All-America third team (1997).
PRO STATISTICS: 1998—Recovered one fumble for 22 yards.

			INTERCEPTIONS				SACKS
Year Team	G	GS	No.	Yds.	Avg.	TD	No.
1998—Cincinnati NFL	14	12	1	18	18.0	0	3.0

SIMMONS, CLYDE   DE   BEARS

PERSONAL: Born August 4, 1964, in Lanes, S.C. ... 6-5/287. ... Full name: Clyde Simmons Jr.
HIGH SCHOOL: New Hanover (Wilmington, N.C.).
COLLEGE: Western Carolina (degree in industrial distribution).

TRANSACTIONS/CAREER NOTES: Selected by Philadelphia Eagles in ninth round (233rd pick overall) of 1986 NFL draft. ... Signed by Eagles (July 3, 1986). ... Granted free agency (February 1, 1991). ... Re-signed by Eagles (August 28, 1991). ... Designated by Eagles as transition player (February 15, 1994). ... Signed by Phoenix Cardinals (March 17, 1994); Eagles received second-round pick (DB Brian Dawkins) in 1996 draft as compensation. ... Cardinals franchise renamed Arizona Cardinals for 1994 season. ... Released by Cardinals (August 19, 1996). ... Signed by Jacksonville Jaguars (August 23, 1996). ... Released by Jaguars (March 6, 1998). ... Signed by Cincinnati Bengals (May 13, 1998). ... Granted unconditional free agency (February 12, 1999). ... Signed by Chicago Bears (February 25, 1999).
CHAMPIONSHIP GAME EXPERIENCE: Played in AFC championship game (1996 season).
HONORS: Played in Pro Bowl (1991 and 1992 seasons). ... Named defensive end on THE SPORTING NEWS NFL All-Pro team (1991).
PRO STATISTICS: 1986—Returned one kickoff for no yards. 1987—Recovered one fumble. 1988—Credited with one safety, ran 15 yards with blocked field-goal attempt and recovered three fumbles. 1989—Intercepted one pass for 60 yards and a touchdown. 1990—Recovered two fumbles for 28 yards and one touchdown. 1991—Recovered three fumbles (including one in end zone for a touchdown). 1992—Recovered one fumble. 1993—Intercepted one pass for no yards. 1995—Intercepted one pass for 25 yards and a touchdown and recovered one fumble. 1996—Recovered one fumble.

Year—Team	G	GS	SACKS
1986—Philadelphia NFL	16	0	2.0
1987—Philadelphia NFL	12	12	6.0
1988—Philadelphia NFL	16	16	8.0
1989—Philadelphia NFL	16	16	15.5
1990—Philadelphia NFL	16	16	7.5
1991—Philadelphia NFL	16	16	13.0
1992—Philadelphia NFL	16	16	*19.0
1993—Philadelphia NFL	16	16	5.0
1994—Arizona NFL	16	16	6.0
1995—Arizona NFL	16	16	11.0
1996—Jacksonville NFL	16	14	7.5
1997—Jacksonville NFL	16	13	8.5
1998—Cincinnati NFL	16	16	5.0
Pro totals (13 years)	**204**	**183**	**114.0**

SIMMONS, JASON CB STEELERS

PERSONAL: Born March 30, 1976, in Inglewood, Calif. ... 5-8/186. ... Full name: Jason Lawrence Simmons.
HIGH SCHOOL: Leuzinger (Lawndale, Calif.).
COLLEGE: Arizona State.
TRANSACTIONS/CAREER NOTES: Selected by Pittsburgh Steelers in fifth round (137th pick overall) of 1998 NFL draft. ... Signed by Steelers (July 14, 1998).
PLAYING EXPERIENCE: Pittsburgh NFL, 1998. ... Games/Games started: 6/0.

SIMMONS, TONY WR PATRIOTS

PERSONAL: Born December 8, 1974, in Gallipolis, Ohio. ... 6-1/206. ... Full name: Tony Angelo Simmons.
HIGH SCHOOL: St. Rita (Chicago).
COLLEGE: Wisconsin (degree in construction administration).
TRANSACTIONS/CAREER NOTES: Selected by New England Patriots in second round (52nd pick overall) of 1998 NFL draft. ... Signed by Patriots (July 18, 1998).
SINGLE GAME HIGHS (regular season): Receptions—5 (December 20, 1998, vs. San Francisco); yards—109 (November 1, 1998, vs. Indianapolis); and touchdown receptions—1 (December 27, 1998, vs. New York Jets).
STATISTICAL PLATEAUS: 100-yard receiving games: 1998 (1).

			RECEIVING				TOTALS			
Year—Team	G	GS	No.	Yds.	Avg.	TD	TD	2pt.	Pts.	Fum.
1998—New England NFL	11	6	23	474	20.6	3	3	0	18	0

SIMMONS, WAYNE LB

PERSONAL: Born December 15, 1969, in Beauford, S.C. ... 6-2/250. ... Full name: Wayne General Simmons.
HIGH SCHOOL: Hilton Head (S.C.).
COLLEGE: Clemson (degree in finance).
TRANSACTIONS/CAREER NOTES: Selected by Green Bay Packers in first round (15th pick overall) of 1993 NFL draft. ... Signed by Packers (July 1, 1993). ... Granted unconditional free agency (February 14, 1997). ... Re-signed by Packers (May 25, 1997). ... Traded by Packers to Kansas City Chiefs for fifth-round pick (WR Corey Bradford) in 1998 draft (October 7, 1997). ... Claimed on waivers by Buffalo Bills (November 19, 1998). ... Released by Bills (February 10, 1999).
CHAMPIONSHIP GAME EXPERIENCE: Played in NFC championship game (1995 and 1996 seasons). ... Member of Super Bowl championship team (1996 season).
PRO STATISTICS: 1993—Recovered one fumble. 1995—Recovered one fumble. 1998—Recovered two fumbles for 17 yards.

			INTERCEPTIONS				SACKS
Year—Team	G	GS	No.	Yds.	Avg.	TD	No.
1993—Green Bay NFL	14	8	2	21	10.5	0	1.0
1994—Green Bay NFL	12	1	0	0	...	0	0.0
1995—Green Bay NFL	16	16	0	0	...	0	4.0
1996—Green Bay NFL	16	16	1	0	0.0	0	2.5
1997—Green Bay NFL	6	6	0	0	...	0	0.0
—Kansas City NFL	10	8	0	0	...	0	3.5
1998—Kansas City NFL	10	10	0	0	...	0	0.0
—Buffalo NFL	6	0	0	0	...	0	0.5
Pro totals (6 years)	**90**	**65**	**3**	**21**	**7.0**	**0**	**11.5**

SIMPSON, CARL — DE — CARDINALS

PERSONAL: Born April 18, 1970, in Baxley, Ga. ... 6-2/292. ... Full name: Carl Wilhelm Simpson.
HIGH SCHOOL: Appling County (Baxley, Ga.).
COLLEGE: Florida State (degree in criminology).
TRANSACTIONS/CAREER NOTES: Selected by Chicago Bears in second round (35th pick overall) of 1993 NFL draft. ... Signed by Bears (July 17, 1993). ... Released by Bears (August 30, 1998). ... Signed by Arizona Cardinals (September 11, 1998). ... Granted unconditional free agency (February 12, 1999). ... Re-signed by Cardinals (April 19, 1999).
PRO STATISTICS: 1995—Recovered two fumbles. 1996—Recovered two fumbles for two yards.

Year Team	G	GS	SACKS
1993—Chicago NFL	11	0	0.5
1994—Chicago NFL	15	8	0.0
1995—Chicago NFL	16	8	1.0
1996—Chicago NFL	16	16	1.5
1997—Chicago NFL	16	16	4.5
1998—Arizona NFL	13	1	0.0
Pro totals (6 years)	87	49	7.5

SIMS, KEITH — G — REDSKINS

PERSONAL: Born June 17, 1967, in Baltimore. ... 6-3/318. ... Full name: Keith Alexander Sims.
HIGH SCHOOL: Watchung Hills Regional (Warren, N.J.).
COLLEGE: Iowa State (degree in industrial technology, 1989).
TRANSACTIONS/CAREER NOTES: Selected by Miami Dolphins in second round (39th pick overall) of 1990 NFL draft. ... Signed by Dolphins (July 30, 1990). ... On injured reserve with knee injury (October 12-November 18, 1991). ... Granted free agency (March 1, 1993). ... Re-signed by Dolphins (July 16, 1993). ... Granted unconditional free agency (February 16, 1996). ... Re-signed by Dolphins (March 8, 1996). ... Released by Dolphins (December 9, 1997). ... Signed by Washington Redskins (December 11, 1997). ... Inactive for two games with Redskins (1997). ... Granted unconditional free agency (February 13, 1998). ... Signed by Philadelphia Eagles (March 2, 1998). ... Released by Eagles (August 30, 1998). ... Signed by Washington Redskins (November 24, 1998). ... Granted unconditional free agency (February 12, 1999). ... Re-signed by Redskins (March 15, 1999).
PLAYING EXPERIENCE: Miami NFL, 1990-1997; Washington NFL, 1998. ... Games/Games started: 1990 (14/13), 1991 (12/12), 1992 (16/16), 1993 (16/16), 1994 (16/16), 1995 (16/16), 1996 (15/15), 1997 (8/4), 1998 (4/0). Total: 117/108.
CHAMPIONSHIP GAME EXPERIENCE: Played in AFC championship game (1992 season).
HONORS: Played in Pro Bowl (1993-1995 seasons).
PRO STATISTICS: 1990—Returned one kickoff for nine yards and recovered one fumble. 1991—Caught one pass for nine yards. 1993—Recovered one fumble. 1994—Recovered two fumbles. 1995—Recovered one fumble.

SINCENO, KASEEM — TE — EAGLES

PERSONAL: Born March 26, 1976, in Bronx, N.Y. ... 6-4/259.
HIGH SCHOOL: Liberty (N.Y.).
COLLEGE: Syracuse.
TRANSACTIONS/CAREER NOTES: Signed as non-drafted free agent by Phiadelphia Eagles (April 21, 1998). ... Released by Eagles (August 30, 1998). ... Re-signed by Eagles to practice squad (September 1, 1998). ... Activated (September 17, 1998). ... On injured reserve with ankle injury (December 1, 1998-remainder of season).
PLAYING EXPERIENCE: Philadelphia NFL, 1998. ... Games/Games started: 10/0.
PRO STATISTICS: 1998—Caught three passes for 42 yards and one touchdown and fumbled once.
SINGLE GAME HIGHS (regular season): Receptions—1 (November 15, 1998, vs. Washington); yards—28 (September 27, 1998, vs. Kansas City); and touchdown receptions—1 (October 11, 1998, vs. Washington).

SINCLAIR, MICHAEL — DE — SEAHAWKS

PERSONAL: Born January 31, 1968, in Galveston, Texas. ... 6-4/267. ... Full name: Michael Glenn Sinclair.
HIGH SCHOOL: Charlton-Pollard (Beaumont, Texas).
COLLEGE: Eastern New Mexico (degree in physical education).
TRANSACTIONS/CAREER NOTES: Selected by Seattle Seahawks in sixth round (155th pick overall) of 1991 NFL draft. ... Signed by Seahawks (July 18, 1991). ... Released by Seahawks (August 26, 1991). ... Re-signed by Seahawks to practice squad (August 28, 1991). ... Activated (November 30, 1991). ... On injured reserve with back injury (December 14, 1991-remainder of season). ... Active for two games (1991); did not play. ... Assigned by Seahawks to Sacramento Surge in 1992 World League enhancement allocation program (February 20, 1992). ... On injured reserve with ankle injury (September 1-October 3, 1992). ... On injured reserve with thumb injury (November 10, 1993-remainder of season). ... Granted free agency (February 17, 1995). ... Re-signed by Seahawks (May 24, 1995). ... Granted unconditional free agency (February 16, 1996). ... Re-signed by Seahawks (February 17, 1996).
PLAYING EXPERIENCE: Played for the Sacramento Surge of the World League (1992).
HONORS: Named defensive end on All-World League team (1992). ... Played in Pro Bowl (1996-1998 seasons).
PRO STATISTICS: W.L.: 1992—Recovered one fumble. NFL: 1995—Recovered two fumbles. 1997—Recovered one fumble in end zone for a touchdown.

Year Team	G	GS	SACKS
1991—Seattle NFL	Did not play.		
1992—Sacramento W.L.	10	10	10.0
—Seattle NFL	12	1	1.0
1993—Seattle NFL	9	1	8.0
1994—Seattle NFL	12	2	4.5
1995—Seattle NFL	16	15	5.5
1996—Seattle NFL	16	16	13.0
1997—Seattle NFL	16	16	12.0
1998—Seattle NFL	16	16	*16.5
W.L. totals (1 year)	10	10	10.0
NFL totals (6 years)	97	67	60.5
Pro totals (7 years)	107	77	70.5

SINGLETON, ALSHERMOND   LB   BUCCANEERS

PERSONAL: Born August 7, 1975, in Newark, N.J. ... 6-2/213. ... Full name: Alshermond Glendale Singleton.
HIGH SCHOOL: Irvington (N.J.).
COLLEGE: Temple (degree in sports recreation management).
TRANSACTIONS/CAREER NOTES: Selected by Tampa Bay Buccaneers in fourth round (128th pick overall) of 1997 NFL draft. ... Signed by Buccaneers (July 17, 1997).
PLAYING EXPERIENCE: Tampa Bay NFL, 1997 and 1998. ... Games/Games started: 1997 (12/0), 1998 (15/0). Total: 27/0.
PRO STATISTICS: 1997—Returned blocked punt 28 yards for a touchdown.

SIRAGUSA, TONY   DT   RAVENS

PERSONAL: Born May 14, 1967, in Kenilworth, N.J. ... 6-3/320. ... Full name: Anthony Siragusa.
HIGH SCHOOL: David Brearley Regional (Kenilworth, N.J.).
COLLEGE: Pittsburgh.
TRANSACTIONS/CAREER NOTES: Signed as non-drafted free agent by Indianapolis Colts (April 30, 1990). ... Granted unconditional free agency (February 14, 1997). ... Signed by Baltimore Ravens (April 24, 1997).
CHAMPIONSHIP GAME EXPERIENCE: Played in AFC championship game (1995 season).
PRO STATISTICS: 1990—Recovered one fumble. 1991—Recovered one fumble for five yards. 1992—Recovered one fumble. 1994—Recovered one fumble. 1996—Recovered one fumble. 1997—Recovered one fumble for seven yards. 1998—Recovered one fumble.

Year Team	G	GS	SACKS
1990—Indianapolis NFL	13	6	1.0
1991—Indianapolis NFL	13	6	2.0
1992—Indianapolis NFL	16	12	3.0
1993—Indianapolis NFL	14	14	1.5
1994—Indianapolis NFL	16	16	5.0
1995—Indianapolis NFL	14	14	2.0
1996—Indianapolis NFL	10	10	2.0
1997—Baltimore NFL	14	13	0.0
1998—Baltimore NFL	15	15	0.0
Pro totals (9 years)	125	106	16.5

SLADE, CHRIS   LB   PATRIOTS

PERSONAL: Born January 30, 1971, in Newport News, Va. ... 6-5/245. ... Full name: Christopher Carroll Slade. ... Cousin of Terry Kirby, running back, Cleveland Browns; and cousin of Wayne Kirby, outfielder, Toronto Blue Jays organization.
HIGH SCHOOL: Tabb (Va.).
COLLEGE: Virginia.
TRANSACTIONS/CAREER NOTES: Selected by New England Patriots in second round (31st pick overall) of 1993 NFL draft. ... Signed by Patriots (July 24, 1993). ... Granted free agency (February 16, 1996). ... Re-signed by Patriots (May 28, 1996).
CHAMPIONSHIP GAME EXPERIENCE: Played in AFC championship game (1996 season). ... Played in Super Bowl XXXI (1996 season).
HONORS: Named defensive lineman on THE SPORTING NEWS college All-America first team (1992). ... Played in Pro Bowl (1997 season).
PRO STATISTICS: 1993—Recovered one fumble. 1995—Recovered two fumbles for 38 yards and one touchdown. 1996—Intercepted one pass for two yards and fumbled once. 1997—Intercepted one pass for one yard and a touchdown.

Year Team	G	GS	SACKS
1993—New England NFL	16	5	9.0
1994—New England NFL	16	16	9.5
1995—New England NFL	16	16	4.0
1996—New England NFL	16	9	7.0
1997—New England NFL	16	16	9.0
1998—New England NFL	15	15	4.0
Pro totals (6 years)	95	77	42.5

SLAUGHTER, WEBSTER   WR   RAVENS

PERSONAL: Born October 19, 1964, in Stockton, Calif. ... 6-1/175. ... Full name: Webster M. Slaughter.
HIGH SCHOOL: Franklin (Stockton, Calif.).
JUNIOR COLLEGE: Delta College (Calif.).
COLLEGE: San Diego State.

TRANSACTIONS/CAREER NOTES: Selected by Cleveland Browns in second round (43rd pick overall) of 1986 NFL draft. ... Signed by Browns (July 24, 1986). ... On injured reserve with broken arm (October 21-December 12, 1988). ... Granted free agency (February 1, 1992). ... Granted unconditional free agency (September 24, 1992). ... Signed by Houston Oilers (September 29, 1992). ... On injured reserve with knee injury (December 30, 1993-remainder of season). ... Released by Oilers (July 20, 1995). ... Signed by Kansas City Chiefs (August 9, 1995). ... Released by Chiefs (February 15, 1996). ... Signed by New York Jets (July 23, 1996). ... Granted unconditional free agency (February 14, 1997). ... Signed by San Diego Chargers (April 21, 1998). ... On injured reserve with finger injury (November 25, 1998-remainder of season). ... Granted unconditional free agency (February 12, 1999). ... Signed by Baltimore Ravens (June 7, 1999).
CHAMPIONSHIP GAME EXPERIENCE: Played in AFC championship game (1986, 1987 and 1989 seasons).
HONORS: Played in Pro Bowl (1989 season). ... Named to play in Pro Bowl (1993 season); did not play due to injury.
PRO STATISTICS: 1986—Recovered one fumble in end zone for a touchdown. 1992—Returned one kickoff for 21 yards and recovered two fumbles. 1994—Recovered one fumble.
SINGLE GAME HIGHS (regular season): Receptions—11 (December 22, 1991, vs. Pittsburgh); yards—186 (October 23, 1989, vs. Chicago); and touchdown receptions—2 (October 17, 1993, vs. New England).
STATISTICAL PLATEAUS: 100-yard receiving games: 1986 (1), 1987 (2), 1988 (1), 1989 (4), 1990 (3), 1991 (3), 1993 (2), 1994 (2). Total: 18.

				RUSHING				RECEIVING				PUNT RETURNS				TOTALS		
Year Team	G	GS	Att.	Yds.	Avg.	TD	No.	Yds.	Avg.	TD	No.	Yds.	Avg.	TD	TD	2pt.	Pts.	Fum.
1986—Cleveland NFL	16	16	1	1	1.0	0	40	577	14.4	4	1	2	2.0	0	5	...	30	1
1987—Cleveland NFL	12	12	0	0	...	0	47	806	17.1	7	0	0	...	0	7	...	42	1
1988—Cleveland NFL	8	8	0	0	...	0	30	462	15.4	3	0	0	...	0	3	...	18	1
1989—Cleveland NFL	16	16	0	0	...	0	65	1236	§19.0	6	0	0	...	0	6	...	36	2
1990—Cleveland NFL	16	16	5	29	5.8	0	59	847	14.4	4	0	0	...	0	4	...	24	2
1991—Cleveland NFL	16	16	0	0	...	0	64	906	14.2	3	17	112	6.6	0	3	...	18	1
1992—Houston NFL	12	9	3	20	6.7	0	39	486	12.5	4	20	142	7.1	0	4	...	24	3
1993—Houston NFL	14	14	0	0	...	0	77	904	11.7	5	0	0	...	0	5	...	30	0
1994—Houston NFL	16	12	0	0	...	0	68	846	12.4	2	0	0	...	0	2	0	12	2
1995—Kansas City NFL	16	7	0	0	...	0	34	514	15.1	4	0	0	...	0	4	0	24	0
1996—New York Jets NFL	10	1	0	0	...	0	32	434	13.6	2	0	0	...	0	2	0	12	0
1997—								Did not play.										
1998—San Diego NFL	10	0	0	0	...	0	8	93	11.6	0	0	0	...	0	0	0	0	0
Pro totals (12 years)	162	127	9	50	5.6	0	563	8111	14.4	44	38	256	6.7	0	45	0	270	17

SLAY, HENRY DT EAGLES

PERSONAL: Born April 28, 1975, in Elyria, Ohio. ... 6-2/290.
HIGH SCHOOL: Elyria (Ohio) West.
COLLEGE: West Virginia.
TRANSACTIONS/CAREER NOTES: Selected by Atlanta Falcons in seventh round (203rd pick overall) of 1998 NFL draft. ... Signed by Falcons (June 1, 1998). ... Released by Falcons (August 24, 1998). ... Signed by Philadelphia Eagles to practice squad (September 17, 1998). ... Released by Eagles (November 11, 1998). ... Re-signed by Eagles to practice squad (November 18, 1998). ... Activated (December 2, 1998). ... Assigned by Eagles to Berlin Thunder in 1999 NFL Europe enhancement allocation program (February 22, 1999).
PLAYING EXPERIENCE: Philadelphia NFL, 1998. ... Games/Games started: 3/0.

SLOAN, DAVID TE LIONS

PERSONAL: Born June 8, 1972, in Fresno, Calif. ... 6-6/254. ... Full name: David Lyle Sloan.
HIGH SCHOOL: Sierra Joint Union (Tollhouse, Calif.).
JUNIOR COLLEGE: Fresno (Calif.) City College.
COLLEGE: New Mexico.
TRANSACTIONS/CAREER NOTES: Selected by Detroit Lions in third round (70th pick overall) of 1995 NFL draft. ... Signed by Lions (July 20, 1995). ... Granted free agency (February 13, 1998). ... Re-signed by Lions (June 10, 1998). ... On physically unable to perform list with knee injury (August 25-October 23, 1998). ... Granted unconditional free agency (February 12, 1999). ... Re-signed by Lions (March 31, 1999).
PRO STATISTICS: 1995—Returned one kickoff for 14 yards. 1996—Recovered one fumble.
SINGLE GAME HIGHS (regular season): Receptions—7 (September 7, 1997, vs. Tampa Bay); yards—49 (September 7, 1997, vs. Tampa Bay); and touchdown receptions—1 (December 14, 1998, vs. San Francisco).

			RECEIVING				TOTALS		
Year Team	G	GS	No.	Yds.	Avg.	TD	TD	2pt.	Pts.	Fum.
1995—Detroit NFL	16	8	17	184	10.8	1	1	0	6	0
1996—Detroit NFL	4	4	7	51	7.3	0	0	0	0	0
1997—Detroit NFL	14	12	29	264	9.1	0	0	0	0	0
1998—Detroit NFL	10	2	11	146	13.3	1	1	0	6	0
Pro totals (4 years)	44	26	64	645	10.1	2	2	0	12	0

SLUTZKER, SCOTT TE SAINTS

PERSONAL: Born December 20, 1972, in Hasbrouck Heights, N.J. ... 6-4/240.
HIGH SCHOOL: Hasbrouck Heights (N.J.).
COLLEGE: Iowa.
TRANSACTIONS/CAREER NOTES: Selected by Indianapolis Colts in third round (82nd pick overall) of 1996 NFL draft. ... Signed by Colts (July 11, 1996). ... On injured reserve with ankle injury (November 27, 1997-remainder of season). ... Traded by Colts to New Orleans Saints for LB Andre Royal (August 30, 1998). ... Granted free agency (February 12, 1999). ... Re-signed by Saints (April 14, 1999).
PLAYING EXPERIENCE: Indianapolis NFL, 1996 and 1997; New Orleans NFL, 1998. ... Games/Games started: 1996 (15/0), 1997 (12/2), 1998 (3/0). Total: 30/2.
PRO STATISTICS: 1997—Caught three passes for 22 yards and recovered two fumbles. 1998—Caught one pass for 10 yards.
SINGLE GAME HIGHS (regular season): Receptions—2 (October 5, 1997, vs. New York Jets); yards—16 (October 5, 1997, vs. New York Jets); and touchdown receptions—0.

SMALL, TORRANCE — WR — EAGLES

PERSONAL: Born September 4, 1970, in Tampa. ... 6-3/209. ... Full name: Torrance Ramon Small.
HIGH SCHOOL: Thomas Jefferson (Tampa).
COLLEGE: Alcorn State.
TRANSACTIONS/CAREER NOTES: Selected by New Orleans Saints in fifth round (138th pick overall) of 1992 NFL draft. ... Signed by Saints (July 15, 1992). ... Released by Saints (September 3, 1992). ... Re-signed by Saints to practice squad (September 4, 1992). ... Activated (September 19, 1992). ... Granted free agency (February 17, 1995). ... Tendered offer sheet by Seattle Seahawks (March 8, 1995). ... Offer matched by Saints (March 15, 1995). ... Released by Saints (May 28, 1997). ... Signed by St. Louis Rams (June 7, 1997). ... Granted unconditional free agency (February 13, 1998). ... Signed by Indianapolis Colts (April 15, 1998). ... Granted unconditional free agency (February 12, 1999). ... Signed by Philadelphia Eagles (February 16, 1999).
PRO STATISTICS: 1994—Recovered one fumble. 1995—Rushed six times for 75 yards and one touchdown and recovered one fumble. 1996—Rushed four times for 51 yards and one touchdown. 1998—Rushed once for two yards and attempted one pass without a completion.
SINGLE GAME HIGHS (regular season): Receptions—9 (November 29, 1998, vs. Baltimore); yards—200 (December 24, 1994, vs. Denver); and touchdown receptions—2 (December 13, 1998, vs. Cincinnati).
STATISTICAL PLATEAUS: 100-yard receiving games: 1994 (1), 1998 (2). Total: 3.

			RECEIVING				TOTALS			
Year Team	G	GS	No.	Yds.	Avg.	TD	TD	2pt.	Pts.	Fum.
1992—New Orleans NFL	13	2	23	278	12.1	3	3	...	18	0
1993—New Orleans NFL	11	0	16	164	10.3	1	1	...	6	0
1994—New Orleans NFL	16	0	49	719	14.7	5	5	1	32	0
1995—New Orleans NFL	16	1	38	461	12.1	5	6	0	36	0
1996—New Orleans NFL	16	13	50	558	11.2	2	3	0	18	1
1997—St. Louis NFL	13	7	32	488	15.3	1	1	0	6	0
1998—Indianapolis NFL	16	4	45	681	15.1	7	7	0	42	0
Pro totals (7 years)	101	27	253	3349	13.2	24	26	1	158	1

SMEDLEY, ERIC — DB — BILLS

PERSONAL: Born July 23, 1973, in Charleston, W.Va. ... 5-11/199. ... Full name: Eric Alan Smedley.
HIGH SCHOOL: Capital (Chesterton, W.Va.).
COLLEGE: Indiana.
TRANSACTIONS/CAREER NOTES: Selected by Buffalo Bills in seventh round (249th pick overall) of 1996 NFL draft. ... Signed by Bills (July 2, 1996). ... Granted free agency (February 12, 1999). ... Re-signed by Bills (April 19, 1999).
PLAYING EXPERIENCE: Buffalo NFL, 1996-1998. ... Games/Games started: 1996 (6/0), 1997 (13/1), 1998 (16/0). Total: 35/1.
PRO STATISTICS: 1998—Credited with two sacks.

SMEENGE, JOEL — DE — JAGUARS

PERSONAL: Born April 1, 1968, in Holland, Mich. ... 6-6/270. ... Full name: Joel Andrew Smeenge. ... Name pronounced SMEN-ghee.
HIGH SCHOOL: Hudsonville (Mich.).
COLLEGE: Western Michigan.
TRANSACTIONS/CAREER NOTES: Selected by New Orleans Saints in third round (70th pick overall) of 1990 NFL draft. ... Signed by Saints (July 17, 1990). ... Granted free agency (March 1, 1993). ... Re-signed by Saints (July 9, 1993). ... Granted unconditional free agency (February 17, 1995). ... Signed by Jacksonville Jaguars (February 28, 1995). ... On injured reserve with broken jaw (November 12, 1996-remainder of season).
PRO STATISTICS: 1991—Recovered one fumble. 1992—Recovered one fumble. 1995—Intercepted one pass for 12 yards and fumbled once. 1997—Recovered two fumbles for one yard. 1998—Recovered one fumble.
MISCELLANEOUS: Holds Jacksonville Jaguars all-time record for most sacks (23.0).

Year Team	G	GS	SACKS
1990—New Orleans NFL	15	0	0.0
1991—New Orleans NFL	14	0	0.0
1992—New Orleans NFL	11	0	0.5
1993—New Orleans NFL	16	2	1.0
1994—New Orleans NFL	16	2	0.0
1995—Jacksonville NFL	15	15	4.0
1996—Jacksonville NFL	10	10	5.0
1997—Jacksonville NFL	16	0	6.5
1998—Jacksonville NFL	16	14	7.5
Pro totals (9 years)	129	43	24.5

SMITH, ANTOWAIN — RB — BILLS

PERSONAL: Born March 14, 1972, in Montgomery, Ala ... 6-2/224. ... Full name: Antowain Drurell Smith. ... Name pronounced an-TWAN.
HIGH SCHOOL: Elmore (Ala.).
JUNIOR COLLEGE: East Mississippi Junior College.
COLLEGE: Houston.
TRANSACTIONS/CAREER NOTES: Selected by Buffalo Bills in first round (23rd pick overall) of 1997 NFL draft. ... Signed by Bills (July 11, 1997).
PRO STATISTICS: 1998—Recovered two fumbles.
SINGLE GAME HIGHS (regular season): Attempts—31 (October 11, 1998, vs. Indianapolis); yards—130 (October 11, 1998, vs. Indianapolis); and rushing touchdowns—3 (September 21, 1997, vs. Indianapolis).
STATISTICAL PLATEAUS: 100-yard rushing games: 1997 (1), 1998 (3). Total: 4.

| | | | | RUSHING | | | | RECEIVING | | | | TOTALS | | | |
|Year Team| |G |GS |Att.|Yds.|Avg.|TD|No.|Yds.|Avg.|TD|TD|2pt.|Pts.|Fum.|
|1997—Buffalo NFL| |16|0 |194|840|4.3|8 |28|177|6.3|0 |8 |0|48|4|
|1998—Buffalo NFL| |16|14|300|1124|3.7|8|5 |11 |2.2|0 |8 |0|48|5|
|Pro totals (2 years)| |32|14|494|1964|4.0|16|33|188|5.7|0|16|0|96|9|

SMITH, ARTIE — DT — CHIEFS

PERSONAL: Born May 15, 1970, in Wayne, Mich. ... 6-5/305. ... Full name: Artie Enlow Smith.
HIGH SCHOOL: Stillwater (Okla.).
COLLEGE: Louisiana Tech.
TRANSACTIONS/CAREER NOTES: Selected by San Francisco 49ers in fifth round (116th pick overall) of 1993 NFL draft. ... Signed by 49ers (July 14, 1993). ... Claimed on waivers by Cincinnati Bengals (September 16, 1994). ... Granted free agency (February 16, 1996). ... Re-signed by Bengals (May 4, 1996). ... Released by Bengals (August 5, 1997). ... Selected by Rhein Fire in 1998 NFL Europe draft (February 18, 1998). ... Signed by New England Patriots (March 12, 1998). ... Traded by Patriots to Dallas Cowboys for future considerations (August 25, 1998). ... Granted unconditional free agency (February 12, 1999). ... Signed by Kansas City Chiefs (April 20, 1999).
CHAMPIONSHIP GAME EXPERIENCE: Played in NFC championship game (1993 season).
PRO STATISTICS: 1996—Recovered one fumble.

Year Team		G	GS	SACKS
1993—San Francisco NFL		16	6	1.5
1994—San Francisco NFL		2	0	0.0
—Cincinnati NFL		7	0	0.0
1995—Cincinnati NFL		16	16	2.0
1996—Cincinnati NFL		16	12	1.0
1997—		Did not play.		
1998—Dallas NFL		16	0	0.0
Pro totals (5 years)		73	34	4.5

SMITH, BRADY — DE — SAINTS

PERSONAL: Born June 5, 1973, in Royal Oak, Mich. ... 6-5/260. ... Full name: Brady McKay Smith. ... Son of Steve Smith, offensive tackle for four NFL teams (1966-74).
HIGH SCHOOL: Barrington (Ill.).
COLLEGE: Colorado State (degree in liberal arts).
TRANSACTIONS/CAREER NOTES: Selected by New Orleans Saints in third round (70th pick overall) of 1996 NFL draft. ... Signed by Saints (July 12, 1996). ... Granted free agency (February 12, 1999). ... Re-signed by Saints (April 14, 1999).
PRO STATISTICS: 1996—Returned two kickoffs for 14 yards.

Year Team		G	GS	SACKS
1996—New Orleans NFL		16	4	2.0
1997—New Orleans NFL		16	2	5.0
1998—New Orleans NFL		14	5	0.0
Pro totals (3 years)		46	11	7.0

SMITH, BRENT — G — DOLPHINS

PERSONAL: Born November 21, 1973, in Dallas. ... 6-5/315. ... Full name: Gary Brent Smith.
HIGH SCHOOL: Pontotoc (Miss.).
COLLEGE: Mississippi State.
TRANSACTIONS/CAREER NOTES: Selected by Miami Dolphins in third round (96th pick overall) of 1997 NFL draft. ... Signed by Dolphins (July 8, 1997). ... Active for two games (1997); did not play.
PLAYING EXPERIENCE: Miami NFL, 1998. ... Games/Games started: 8/7.

SMITH, BRUCE — DE — BILLS

PERSONAL: Born June 18, 1963, in Norfolk, Va. ... 6-4/273. ... Full name: Bruce Bernard Smith.
HIGH SCHOOL: Booker T. Washington (Norfolk, Va.).
COLLEGE: Virginia Tech.
TRANSACTIONS/CAREER NOTES: Selected by Baltimore Stars in 1985 USFL territorial draft. ... Signed by Buffalo Bills (February 28, 1985). ... Selected officially by Bills in first round (first pick overall) of 1985 NFL draft. ... On non-football injury list with substance abuse problem (September 2-28, 1988). ... Granted free agency (February 1, 1989). ... Tendered offer sheet by Denver Broncos (March 23, 1989). ... Offer matched by Bills (March 29, 1989). ... On injured reserve with knee injury (October 12-November 30, 1991).
CHAMPIONSHIP GAME EXPERIENCE: Played in AFC championship game (1988 and 1990-1993 seasons). ... Played in Super Bowl XXV (1990 season), Super Bowl XXVI (1991 season), Super Bowl XXVII (1992 season) and Super Bowl XXVIII (1993 season).
HONORS: Named defensive lineman on THE SPORTING NEWS college All-America second team (1983 and 1984). ... Outland Trophy winner (1984). ... Named defensive end on THE SPORTING NEWS NFL All-Pro team (1987, 1988, 1990 and 1992-1997). ... Played in Pro Bowl (1987-1990, 1994, 1995, 1997 and 1998 seasons). ... Named Outstanding Player of Pro Bowl (1987 season). ... Named to play in Pro Bowl (1992 season); replaced by Howie Long due to injury. ... Named to play in Pro Bowl (1993 season); replaced by Sean Jones due to injury. ... Named to play in Pro Bowl (1996 season); replaced by Willie McGinest due to injury.
POST SEASON RECORDS: Shares Super Bowl single-game record for most safeties—1 (January 27, 1991, vs. New York Giants). ... Shares NFL postseason career record for most sacks—12. ... Shares NFL postseason single-game record for most safeties—1 (January 27, 1991, vs. New York Giants).
PRO STATISTICS: 1985—Rushed once for no yards and recovered four fumbles. 1987—Recovered two fumbles for 15 yards and one touchdown. 1988—Credited with one safety. 1993—Intercepted one pass for no yards and recovered one fumble. 1994—Intercepted one pass

– 358 –

for no yards and recovered two fumbles. 1995—Recovered one fumble. 1996—Recovered one fumble. 1998—Recovered two fumbles for 18 yards.
MISCELLANEOUS: Active AFC leader for career sacks (164). ... Holds Buffalo Bills all-time record for most sacks (164).

Year Team	G	GS	SACKS
1985—Buffalo NFL	16	13	6.5
1986—Buffalo NFL	16	15	15.0
1987—Buffalo NFL	12	12	12.0
1988—Buffalo NFL	12	12	11.0
1989—Buffalo NFL	16	16	13.0
1990—Buffalo NFL	16	16	19.0
1991—Buffalo NFL	5	5	1.5
1992—Buffalo NFL	15	15	14.0
1993—Buffalo NFL	16	16	14.0
1994—Buffalo NFL	15	15	10.0
1995—Buffalo NFL	15	15	10.5
1996—Buffalo NFL	16	16	▲13.5
1997—Buffalo NFL	16	16	§14.0
1998—Buffalo NFL	15	15	10.0
Pro totals (14 years)	**201**	**197**	**164.0**

SMITH, CHUCK — DE — FALCONS

PERSONAL: Born December 21, 1969, in Athens, Ga. ... 6-2/262. ... Full name: Charles Henry Smith III.
HIGH SCHOOL: Clarke Central (Athens, Ga.).
COLLEGE: Northeastern Oklahoma A&M, then Tennessee.
TRANSACTIONS/CAREER NOTES: Selected by Atlanta Falcons in second round (51st pick overall) of 1992 NFL draft. ... Signed by Falcons (July 27, 1992). ... On suspended list (July 25-August 15, 1994). ... On injured reserve with knee injury (December 21, 1994-remainder of season). ... Granted free agency (February 17, 1995). ... Re-signed by Falcons (July 14, 1995). ... Granted unconditional free agency (February 16, 1996). ... Re-signed by Falcons (February 27, 1996).
CHAMPIONSHIP GAME EXPERIENCE: Played in NFC championship game (1998 season). ... Played in Super Bowl XXXIII (1998 season).
PRO STATISTICS: 1993—Recovered two fumbles. 1994—Intercepted one pass for 36 yards and a touchdown and recovered two fumbles. 1995—Recovered two fumbles. 1996—Intercepted one pass for 21 yards and recovered one fumble. 1997—Intercepted one pass for four yards. 1998—Recovered four fumbles for 71 yards and one touchdown.

Year Team	G	GS	SACKS
1992—Atlanta NFL	16	0	2.0
1993—Atlanta NFL	15	1	3.5
1994—Atlanta NFL	15	10	11.0
1995—Atlanta NFL	14	13	5.5
1996—Atlanta NFL	15	15	6.0
1997—Atlanta NFL	16	15	12.0
1998—Atlanta NFL	16	16	8.5
Pro totals (7 years)	**107**	**70**	**48.5**

SMITH, DARRIN — LB — SEAHAWKS

PERSONAL: Born April 15, 1970, in Miami. ... 6-1/230. ... Full name: Darrin Andrew Smith.
HIGH SCHOOL: Norland (Miami).
COLLEGE: Miami, Fla. (degree in business management, 1991; master's degree in business administration, 1993).
TRANSACTIONS/CAREER NOTES: Selected by Dallas Cowboys in second round (54th pick overall) of 1993 NFL draft. ... Signed by Cowboys (July 21, 1993). ... On reserve/did not report list (July 20-October 14, 1995). ... Granted free agency (February 16, 1996). ... Re-signed by Cowboys (June 17, 1996). ... Granted unconditional free agency (February 14, 1997). ... Signed by Philadelphia Eagles (April 19, 1997). ... On injured reserve with ankle injury (November 19, 1997-remainder of season). ... Granted unconditional free agency (February 13, 1998). ... Signed by Seattle Seahawks (February 19, 1998).
CHAMPIONSHIP GAME EXPERIENCE: Played in NFC championship game (1993 and 1995 seasons). ... Member of Super Bowl championship team (1993 and 1995 seasons).
PRO STATISTICS: 1993—Recovered one fumble. 1994—Recovered two fumbles for 11 yards. 1995—Recovered one fumble for 63 yards. 1997—Recovered one fumble. 1998—Recovered two fumbles.

			INTERCEPTIONS				SACKS
Year Team	G	GS	No.	Yds.	Avg.	TD	No.
1993—Dallas NFL	16	13	0	0	...	0	1.0
1994—Dallas NFL	16	16	2	13	6.5	1	4.0
1995—Dallas NFL	9	9	0	0	...	0	3.0
1996—Dallas NFL	16	16	0	0	...	0	1.0
1997—Philadelphia NFL	7	7	0	0	...	0	1.0
1998—Seattle NFL	13	12	3	56	18.7	▲2	5.0
Pro totals (6 years)	**77**	**73**	**5**	**69**	**13.8**	**3**	**15.0**

SMITH, DEREK — LB — REDSKINS

PERSONAL: Born January 18, 1975, in American Fork, Utah. ... 6-2/239. ... Full name: Derek Mecham Smith.
HIGH SCHOOL: American Fork (Utah).
JUNIOR COLLEGE: Snow College (Utah).
COLLEGE: Arizona State.

TRANSACTIONS/CAREER NOTES: Selected by Washington Redskins in third round (80th pick overall) of 1997 NFL draft. ... Signed by Redskins (July 11, 1997).
PRO STATISTICS: 1997—Recovered two fumbles for five yards. 1998—Recovered one fumble.

Year Team	G	GS	SACKS
1997—Washington NFL	16	16	2.0
1998—Washington NFL	16	15	0.5
Pro totals (2 years)	**32**	**31**	**2.5**

SMITH, DETRON FB BRONCOS

PERSONAL: Born February 25, 1974, in Dallas. ... 5-9/230. ... Full name: Detron Negil Smith.
HIGH SCHOOL: Lake Highlands (Dallas).
COLLEGE: Texas A&M.
TRANSACTIONS/CAREER NOTES: Selected by Denver Broncos in third round (65th pick overall) of 1996 NFL draft. ... Signed by Broncos (July 20, 1996).
PLAYING EXPERIENCE: Denver NFL, 1996-1998. ... Games/Games started: 1996 (13/0), 1997 (16/0), 1998 (15/2). Total: 44/2.
CHAMPIONSHIP GAME EXPERIENCE: Played in AFC championship game (1997 and 1998 seasons). ... Member of Super Bowl championship team (1997 and 1998 seasons).
PRO STATISTICS: 1997—Rushed four times for 10 yards, caught four passes for 41 yards and one touchdown and returned one kickoff for no yards. 1998—Caught three passes for 24 yards and returned three kickoffs for 51 yards.
SINGLE GAME HIGHS (regular season): Attempts—2 (December 21, 1997, vs. San Diego); yards—11 (December 21, 1997, vs. San Diego); and rushing touchdowns—0.

SMITH, ED TE

PERSONAL: Born June 5, 1969, in Trenton, N.J. ... 6-4/253. ... Full name: Ed Martin Smith. ... Brother of Irv Smith, tight end, Cleveland Browns.
HIGH SCHOOL: Pemberton (N.J.).
COLLEGE: None.
TRANSACTIONS/CAREER NOTES: Played for Frankfurt Galaxy of World League (1996). ... Signed as non-drafted free agent by St. Louis Rams (July 6, 1996). ... Released by Rams (August 20, 1996). ... Signed by Washington Redskins to practice squad (August 26, 1996). ... Granted free agency after 1996 season. ... Signed by Atlanta Falcons (March 3, 1997). ... Released by Falcons (August 24, 1997). ... Re-signed by Falcons to practice squad (August 26, 1997). ... Activated (November 20, 1997). ... Claimed on waivers by Cleveland Browns (April 23, 1999). ... Released by Browns (June 3, 1999).
PLAYING EXPERIENCE: Atlanta NFL, 1997 and 1998. ... Games/Games started: 1997 (5/1), 1998 (15/0). Total: 20/1.
CHAMPIONSHIP GAME EXPERIENCE: Played in NFC championship game (1998 season). ... Played in Super Bowl XXXIII (1998 season).
PRO STATISTICS: 1997—Caught one pass for two yards.
SINGLE GAME HIGHS (regular season): Receptions—1 (November 30, 1997, vs. Seattle); yards—2 (November 30, 1997, vs. Seattle); and touchdown receptions—0.

RECORD AS BASEBALL PLAYER
TRANSACTIONS/CAREER NOTES: Batted right, threw right. ... Selected by Chicago White Sox organization in seventh round of free-agent draft (June 2, 1987). ... Traded by White Sox organization to Milwaukee Brewers organization for P Mike Hooper (June 13, 1991). ... Granted free agency after 1993 season. ... Signed by Chicago Cubs organization (November 5, 1993). ... Granted free agency after 1994 season. ... Signed by Cleveland Indians organization (December 9, 1994).
STATISTICAL NOTES: Led Gulf Coast League third basemen with nine double plays in 1987. ... Led Midwest League third basemen with 37 double plays in 1988. ... Led Midwest League third basemen with 40 errors in 1989.

							BATTING							FIELDING		
Year Team (League)	Pos.	G	AB	R	H	2B	3B	HR	RBI	Avg.	BB	SO	SB	PO	A	E	Avg.
1987—GC Whi. Sox (GCL)	3B	32	114	10	27	3	0	2	18	.237	6	28	3	31	73	12	.897
1988—South Bend (Mid.)	3B	130	462	51	107	14	1	3	46	.232	51	87	5	110	272	37	.912
1989—South Bend (Mid.)	3B-1B	115	382	52	94	20	2	8	49	.246	43	84	7	180	140	43	.882
1990—Sarasota (Fla. St.)	3B-1B	63	239	22	46	10	3	4	23	.192	11	61	0	91	97	17	.917
—Birmingham (Sou.)	3B-1B	72	247	22	61	14	3	1	23	.247	22	49	2	103	138	15	.941
1991—Sarasota (FSL)	1B-3B	54	198	27	43	7	0	3	27	.217	15	52	4	248	45	2	.993
—Beloit (Midwest)■	3B-1B	61	218	31	57	13	2	4	37	.261	21	41	5	64	112	10	.946
1992—Stockton (California)	3B-1B	99	355	57	93	21	4	11	57	.262	49	72	6	108	90	20	.908
—El Paso (Texas)	3B-1B	22	86	11	25	5	0	2	15	.291	8	20	0	104	43	7	.955
1993—El Paso (Texas)	1B-OF-3B	118	419	64	123	23	6	8	69	.294	38	97	13	505	63	14	.976
1994—Orlando (South.)■	3B-1B	115	401	51	104	17	5	16	60	.259	37	75	4	167	199	21	.946
1995—Buffalo (A.A.)■	3B-1B	13	31	4	10	0	1	3	9	.323	3	5	0	108	164	14	.951
—Cant./Akr. (Eastern)	OF-3B-1B	103	365	41	88	18	2	11	52	.241	36	93	0	13	1	3	.824

SMITH, EMMITT RB COWBOYS

PERSONAL: Born May 15, 1969, in Pensacola, Fla. ... 5-9/214. ... Full name: Emmitt J. Smith III.
HIGH SCHOOL: Escambia (Pensacola, Fla.).
COLLEGE: Florida (degree in public recreation, 1996).
TRANSACTIONS/CAREER NOTES: Selected after junior season by Dallas Cowboys in first round (17th pick overall) of 1990 NFL draft. ... Signed by Cowboys (September 4, 1990). ... Granted roster exemption (September 4-8, 1990). ... Granted free agency (March 1, 1993). ... Re-signed by Cowboys (September 16, 1993).
CHAMPIONSHIP GAME EXPERIENCE: Played in NFC championship game (1992-1995 seasons). ... Member of Super Bowl championship team (1992, 1993 and 1995 seasons).
HONORS: Named running back on THE SPORTING NEWS college All-America first team (1989). ... Played in Pro Bowl (1990-1992, 1995 and 1998 seasons). ... Named running back on THE SPORTING NEWS NFL All-Pro team (1992-1995). ... Named NFL Player of the Year by THE SPORTING NEWS (1993). ... Named Most Valuable Player of Super Bowl XXVIII (1993 season). ... Named to play in Pro Bowl (1993 season); replaced by Rodney

Hampton due to injury. ... Named Sportsman of the Year by THE SPORTING NEWS (1994). ... Named to play in Pro Bowl (1994 season); replaced by Ricky Watters due to injury.
RECORDS: Holds NFL career record for most rushing touchdowns—125. ... Holds NFL single-season records for most touchdowns—25 (1995); and most rushing touchdowns—25 (1995).
POST SEASON RECORDS: Holds Super Bowl career record for most rushing touchdowns—5. ... Holds NFL postseason career record for most rushing touchdowns—18. ... Shares NFL postseason career record for most games with 100 or more yards rushing—7.
PRO STATISTICS: 1991—Recovered one fumble. 1992—Recovered one fumble. 1993—Recovered three fumbles. 1996—Recovered one fumble. 1997—Recovered one fumble. 1998—Recovered one fumble.
SINGLE GAME HIGHS (regular season): Attempts—35 (November 7, 1994, vs. New York Giants); yards—237 (October 31, 1993, vs. Philadelphia); and rushing touchdowns—4 (September 4, 1995, vs. New York Giants).
STATISTICAL PLATEAUS: 100-yard rushing games: 1990 (3), 1991 (8), 1992 (7), 1993 (7), 1994 (6), 1995 (11), 1996 (4), 1997 (2), 1998 (7). Total: 55. ... 100-yard receiving games: 1990 (1), 1993 (1). Total: 2.
MISCELLANEOUS: Active NFL leader for career rushing touchdowns (125). ... Holds Dallas Cowboys all-time records for most yards rushing (12,566), most touchdowns (134) and most rushing touchdowns (125).

			RUSHING				RECEIVING				TOTALS		
Year Team	G	GS	Att.	Yds.	Avg.	TD	No.	Yds.	Avg.	TD	TD	2pt.	Pts.	Fum.
1990—Dallas NFL	16	15	241	937	3.9	11	24	228	9.5	0	11	...	66	7
1991—Dallas NFL	16	16	*365	*1563	4.3	12	49	258	5.3	1	13	...	78	8
1992—Dallas NFL	16	16	‡373 ▲1713		4.6	*18	59	335	5.7	*1	*19	...	114	4
1993—Dallas NFL	14	13	283	*1486	*5.3	9	57	414	7.3	1	10	...	60	4
1994—Dallas NFL	15	15	*368	1484	4.0	*21	50	341	6.8	*1	*22	0	132	1
1995—Dallas NFL	16	16	*377	*1773	4.7	*25	62	375	6.0	*0	*25	0	*150	7
1996—Dallas NFL	15	15	327	1204	3.7	12	47	249	5.3	3	15	0	90	5
1997—Dallas NFL	16	16	261	1074	4.1	4	40	234	5.9	0	4	1	26	1
1998—Dallas NFL	16	16	319	1332	4.2	13	27	175	6.5	2	15	0	90	3
Pro totals (9 years)	140	138	2914	12566	4.3	125	415	2609	6.3	9	134	1	806	40

SMITH, FERNANDO   DE   RAVENS

PERSONAL: Born August 2, 1971, in Flint, Mich. ... 6-6/277. ... Full name: Fernando Dewitt Smith.
HIGH SCHOOL: Northwestern Community (Flint, Mich.).
COLLEGE: Jackson State.
TRANSACTIONS/CAREER NOTES: Selected by Minnesota Vikings in second round (55th pick overall) of 1994 NFL draft. ... Signed by Vikings (July 15, 1994). ... Granted free agency (February 14, 1997). ... Re-signed by Vikings (February 20, 1997). ... Released by Vikings (July 28, 1998). ... Signed by Jacksonville Jaguars (August 13, 1998). ... Granted unconditional free agency (February 12, 1999). ... Signed by Baltimore Ravens (March 19, 1999).
PRO STATISTICS: 1996—Recovered two fumbles for four yards. 1997—Recovered one fumble for six yards. 1998—Recovered one fumble.

Year Team	G	GS	SACKS
1994—Minnesota NFL	7	0	0.0
1995—Minnesota NFL	12	1	2.5
1996—Minnesota NFL	16	16	9.5
1997—Minnesota NFL	12	11	4.0
1998—Jacksonville NFL	14	0	2.0
Pro totals (5 years)	61	28	18.0

SMITH, FRANKIE   CB   BEARS

PERSONAL: Born October 8, 1968, in Groesbeck, Texas. ... 5-9/182. ... Full name: Frankie L. Smith.
HIGH SCHOOL: Groesbeck (Texas).
COLLEGE: Baylor.
TRANSACTIONS/CAREER NOTES: Selected by Atlanta Falcons in fourth round (104th pick overall) of 1992 NFL draft. ... Signed by Falcons (July 7, 1992). ... Released by Falcons (August 25, 1992). ... Signed by Miami Dolphins (March 17, 1993). ... Released by Dolphins (October 22, 1993). ... Re-signed by Dolphins to practice squad (October 23, 1993). ... Activated (November 29, 1993). ... Claimed on waivers by New England Patriots (February 27, 1996). ... Released by Patriots (August 17, 1996). ... Signed by San Francisco 49ers (September 12, 1996). ... Granted unconditional free agency (February 14, 1997). ... Re-signed by 49ers (March 26, 1997). ... Granted unconditional free agency (February 13, 1998). ... Signed by Chicago Bears (August 5, 1998). ... Granted unconditional free agency (February 12, 1999). ... Re-signed by Bears (March 26, 1999).
PLAYING EXPERIENCE: Miami NFL, 1993-1995; San Francisco NFL, 1996 and 1997; Chicago NFL, 1998. ... Games/Games started: 1993 (5/1), 1994 (13/2), 1995 (11/1), 1996 (14/0), 1997 (16/0), 1998 (15/0). Total: 74/4.
CHAMPIONSHIP GAME EXPERIENCE: Played in NFC championship game (1997 season).
PRO STATISTICS: 1994—Credited with one sack. 1997—Recovered one fumble.

SMITH, IRV   TE   BROWNS

PERSONAL: Born October 13, 1971, in Trenton, N.J. ... 6-3/262. ... Full name: Irvin Martin Smith. ... Brother of Ed Smith, offensive tackle, Cleveland Browns.
HIGH SCHOOL: Pemberton (N.J.).
COLLEGE: Notre Dame (degree in marketing).
TRANSACTIONS/CAREER NOTES: Selected by New Orleans Saints in first round (20th pick overall) of 1993 NFL draft. ... Signed by Saints (July 25, 1993). ... On physically unable to perform list with knee injury (July 14-29, 1996). ... On inactive list for six games (1996). ... On injured reserve with knee injury (December 14, 1996-remainder of season). ... Granted unconditional free agency (February 13, 1998). ... Signed by San Francisco 49ers (February 26, 1998). ... Traded by 49ers with DE Roy Barker to Cleveland Browns for past considerations (February 12, 1999).

PRO STATISTICS: 1993—Recovered one fumble. 1994—Returned two kickoffs for 10 yards. 1995—Returned one kickoff for six yards. 1998—Returned two kickoffs for 35 yards.
SINGLE GAME HIGHS (regular season): Receptions—9 (November 12, 1995, vs. Indianapolis); yards—83 (November 12, 1995, vs. Indianapolis); and touchdown receptions—2 (December 10, 1995, vs. Atlanta).

				RECEIVING				TOTALS			
Year Team	G	GS	No.	Yds.	Avg.	TD	TD	2pt.	Pts.	Fum.
1993—New Orleans NFL	16	8	16	180	11.3	2	2	...	12	1
1994—New Orleans NFL	16	16	41	330	8.0	3	3	0	18	0
1995—New Orleans NFL	16	16	45	466	10.4	3	3	1	20	1
1996—New Orleans NFL	7	7	15	144	9.6	0	0	0	0	0
1997—New Orleans NFL	11	8	17	180	10.6	1	1	0	6	1
1998—San Francisco NFL	16	8	25	266	10.6	5	5	0	30	0
Pro totals (6 years)	82	63	159	1566	9.8	14	14	1	86	3

SMITH, JEFF — C/G — CHIEFS

PERSONAL: Born May 25, 1973, in Decatur, Tenn. ... 6-3/322. ... Full name: Jeffery Lee Smith.
HIGH SCHOOL: Meigs County (Decatur, Tenn.).
COLLEGE: Tennessee.
TRANSACTIONS/CAREER NOTES: Selected by Kansas City Chiefs in seventh round (241st pick overall) of 1996 NFL draft. ... Signed by Chiefs (July 24, 1996). ... Active for one game (1996); did not play. ... Assigned by Chiefs to Scottish Claymores in 1997 World League enhancement allocation program (February 19, 1997). ... Granted free agency (February 12, 1999).
PLAYING EXPERIENCE: Scottish Claymores W.L., 1997. Kansas City NFL, 1997 and 1998. ... Games/Games started: W.L. 1997 (10/games started unavailable), NFL 1997 (3/0), 1998 (11/3). Total NFL: 14/3.

SMITH, JIMMY — WR — JAGUARS

PERSONAL: Born February 9, 1969, in Detroit. ... 6-1/207. ... Full name: Jimmy Lee Smith Jr.
HIGH SCHOOL: Callaway (Jackson, Miss.).
COLLEGE: Jackson State (degree in business management, 1992).
TRANSACTIONS/CAREER NOTES: Selected by Dallas Cowboys in second round (36th pick overall) of 1992 NFL draft. ... Signed by Cowboys (April 26, 1992). ... On injured reserve with fibula injury (September 2-October 7, 1992); on practice squad (September 28-October 7, 1992). ... On non-football injury list with appendicitis (September 2, 1993-remainder of season). ... Released by Cowboys (July 11, 1994). ... Signed by Philadelphia Eagles (July 19, 1994). ... Released by Eagles (August 29, 1994). ... Signed by Jacksonville Jaguars (February 28, 1995). ... Granted free agency (February 16, 1996). ... Re-signed by Jaguars (May 28, 1996).
CHAMPIONSHIP GAME EXPERIENCE: Played in NFC championship game (1992 season). ... Member of Super Bowl championship team (1992 season). ... Played in AFC championship game (1996 season).
HONORS: Played in Pro Bowl (1997 and 1998 seasons).
PRO STATISTICS: 1995—Recovered blocked punt in end zone for a touchdown and recovered one fumble. 1997—Recovered one fumble. 1998—Recovered two fumbles.
SINGLE GAME HIGHS (regular season): Receptions—10 (September 22, 1997, vs. Pittsburgh); yards—164 (September 22, 1997, vs. Pittsburgh); and touchdown receptions—2 (August 31, 1997, vs. Baltimore).
STATISTICAL PLATEAUS: 100-yard receiving games: 1996 (4), 1997 (6), 1998 (5). Total: 15.
MISCELLANEOUS: Holds Jacksonville Jaguars all-time record for most receptions (265), most yards receiving (4,038), most touchdowns (24) and most touchdown receptions (22).

			RECEIVING				KICKOFF RETURNS			TOTALS			
Year Team	G	GS	No.	Yds.	Avg.	TD	No.	Yds.	Avg.	TD	TD	2pt.	Pts.	Fum.
1992—Dallas NFL	7	0	0	0	...	0	0	0	...	0	0	...	0	0
1993—Dallas NFL							Did not play.							
1994—							Did not play.							
1995—Jacksonville NFL	16	4	22	288	13.1	3	24	540	22.5	1	5	0	30	2
1996—Jacksonville NFL	16	9	83	§1244	15.0	7	2	49	24.5	0	7	0	42	1
1997—Jacksonville NFL	16	16	82	1324	16.1	4	0	0	...	0	4	0	24	1
1998—Jacksonville NFL	16	15	78	1182	15.2	8	0	0	...	0	8	0	48	2
Pro totals (5 years)	71	44	265	4038	15.2	22	26	589	22.7	1	24	0	144	6

SMITH, KEVIN — CB — COWBOYS

PERSONAL: Born April 7, 1970, in Orange, Texas. ... 5-11/190. ... Full name: Kevin Rey Smith.
HIGH SCHOOL: West Orange-Stark (Orange, Texas).
COLLEGE: Texas A&M.
TRANSACTIONS/CAREER NOTES: Selected by Dallas Cowboys in first round (17th pick overall) of 1992 NFL draft. ... Signed by Cowboys (April 26, 1992). ... On injured reserve with Achilles' tendon injury (September 22, 1995-remainder of season).
CHAMPIONSHIP GAME EXPERIENCE: Played in NFC championship game (1992-1994 seasons). ... Member of Super Bowl championship team (1992, 1993 and 1995 seasons).
HONORS: Named defensive back on THE SPORTING NEWS college All-America first team (1991).
PRO STATISTICS: 1992—Returned one punt for 17 yards and returned one kickoff for nine yards. 1993—Returned one kickoff for 33 yards and recovered one fumble for 14 yards. 1998—Returned one punt for 11 yards.

Year Team	G	GS	INTERCEPTIONS No.	Yds.	Avg.	TD
1992—Dallas NFL	16	6	2	10	5.0	0
1993—Dallas NFL	16	16	6	56	9.3	1
1994—Dallas NFL	16	16	2	11	5.5	0
1995—Dallas NFL	1	1	0	0	...	0
1996—Dallas NFL	16	16	5	45	9.0	0
1997—Dallas NFL	16	16	1	21	21.0	0
1998—Dallas NFL	14	14	2	31	15.5	0
Pro totals (7 years)	95	85	18	174	9.7	1

SMITH, LAMAR   RB   SAINTS

PERSONAL: Born November 29, 1970, in Fort Wayne, Ind. ... 5-11/225.
HIGH SCHOOL: South Side (Fort Wayne, Ind.).
COLLEGE: Houston.
TRANSACTIONS/CAREER NOTES: Selected by Seattle Seahawks in third round (73rd pick overall) of 1994 NFL draft. ... Signed by Seahawks (July 19, 1994). ... On non-football injury list with back injury (December 13, 1994-remainder of season). ... Granted free agency (February 14, 1997). ... Re-signed by Seahawks (February 1997). ... Granted unconditional free agency (February 13, 1998). ... Signed by New Orleans Saints (February 28, 1998).
PRO STATISTICS: 1995—Returned one kickoff for 20 yards. 1996—Recovered one fumble. 1997—Returned one kickoff for 14 yards. 1998—Attempted two passes with one completion for 20 yards and a touchdown.
SINGLE GAME HIGHS (regular season): Attempts—33 (November 17, 1996, vs. Detroit); yards—157 (September 27, 1998, vs. Indianapolis); and rushing touchdowns—2 (December 22, 1996, vs. Oakland).
STATISTICAL PLATEAUS: 100-yard rushing games: 1996 (1), 1998 (1). Total: 2.

Year Team	G	GS	RUSHING Att.	Yds.	Avg.	TD	RECEIVING No.	Yds.	Avg.	TD	TOTALS TD	2pt.	Pts.	Fum.
1994—Seattle NFL	2	0	2	-1	-0.5	0	0	0	...	0	0	0	0	0
1995—Seattle NFL	13	0	36	215	6.0	0	1	10	10.0	0	0	0	0	1
1996—Seattle NFL	16	2	153	680	4.4	8	9	58	6.4	0	8	*3	54	4
1997—Seattle NFL	12	2	91	392	4.3	2	23	183	8.0	0	2	1	14	0
1998—New Orleans NFL	14	9	138	457	3.3	1	24	249	10.4	2	3	0	18	4
Pro totals (5 years)	57	13	420	1743	4.2	11	57	500	8.8	2	13	4	86	9

SMITH, MARK   DT   CARDINALS

PERSONAL: Born August 28, 1974, in Vicksburg, Miss. ... 6-4/290. ... Full name: Mark Anthony Smith.
HIGH SCHOOL: Vicksburg (Miss.).
JUNIOR COLLEGE: Navarro College (Texas), then Hinds Community College (Miss.).
COLLEGE: Auburn.
TRANSACTIONS/CAREER NOTES: Selected by Arizona Cardinals in seventh round (212th pick overall) of 1997 NFL draft. ... Signed by Cardinals (May 5, 1997).
PRO STATISTICS: 1998—Recovered one fumble.

Year Team	G	GS	SACKS
1997—Arizona NFL	16	4	6.0
1998—Arizona NFL	14	13	9.0
Pro totals (2 years)	30	17	15.0

SMITH, MYRON   LB   COWBOYS

PERSONAL: Born March 28, 1975, in Corsicana, Texas ... 6-1/225.
HIGH SCHOOL: Corsicana (Texas).
COLLEGE: Louisiana Tech.
TRANSACTIONS/CAREER NOTES: Signed as non-drafted free agent by Oakland Raiders (February 1998). ... Released by Raiders (August 30, 1998). ... Re-signed by Raiders to practice squad (August 31, 1998). ... Signed by Dallas Cowboys off Raiders practice squad (September 30, 1998). ... Released by Cowboys (December 3, 1998). ... Re-signed by Cowboys to practice squad (December 7, 1998).
PLAYING EXPERIENCE: Dallas NFL, 1998. ... Games/Games started: 1/0.

SMITH, NEIL   DE   BRONCOS

PERSONAL: Born April 10, 1966, in New Orleans. ... 6-4/270.
HIGH SCHOOL: McDonogh 35 (New Orleans).
COLLEGE: Nebraska.
TRANSACTIONS/CAREER NOTES: Selected by Kansas City Chiefs in first round (second pick overall) of 1988 NFL draft. ... Signed by Chiefs (July 19, 1988). ... Designated by Chiefs as franchise player (February 25, 1993). ... Granted unconditional free agency (February 14, 1997). ... Signed by Denver Broncos (April 14, 1997). ... Granted unconditional free agency (February 13, 1998). ... Re-signed by Broncos (March 11, 1998).
CHAMPIONSHIP GAME EXPERIENCE: Played in AFC championship game (1993, 1997 and 1998 seasons). ... Member of Super Bowl championship team (1997 and 1998 season).
HONORS: Named defensive lineman on THE SPORTING NEWS college All-America first team (1987). ... Played in Pro Bowl (1991-1993, 1995 and 1997 seasons). ... Named to play in Pro Bowl (1994 season); replaced by Rob Burnett due to injury.

PRO STATISTICS: 1989—Recovered two fumbles for three yards and one touchdown. 1990—Recovered one fumble. 1991—Recovered two fumbles for 10 yards. 1992—Intercepted one pass for 22 yards and a touchdown and recovered two fumbles. 1993—Intercepted one pass for three yards and recovered three fumbles. 1994—Intercepted one pass for 41 yards and recovered one fumble for six yards. 1995—Recovered one fumble. 1998—Intercepted one pass for two yards.

Year Team	G	GS	SACKS
1988—Kansas City NFL	13	7	2.5
1989—Kansas City NFL	15	15	6.5
1990—Kansas City NFL	16	15	9.5
1991—Kansas City NFL	16	16	8.0
1992—Kansas City NFL	16	16	14.5
1993—Kansas City NFL	16	15	*15.0
1994—Kansas City NFL	14	13	11.5
1995—Kansas City NFL	16	14	12.0
1996—Kansas City NFL	16	16	6.0
1997—Denver NFL	14	13	8.5
1998—Denver NFL	14	14	4.0
Pro totals (11 years)	166	154	98.0

SMITH, OTIS   CB   JETS

PERSONAL: Born October 22, 1965, in New Orleans. ... 5-11/195. ... Full name: Otis Smith III.
HIGH SCHOOL: East Jefferson (Metairie, La.).
JUNIOR COLLEGE: Taft (Calif.) College.
COLLEGE: Missouri.
TRANSACTIONS/CAREER NOTES: Signed as non-drafted free agent by Philadelphia Eagles (April 25, 1990). ... On physically unable to perform list with appendectomy (August 2, 1990-entire season). ... Granted free agency (February 1, 1992). ... Re-signed by Eagles (August 11, 1992). ... Granted unconditional free agency (February 17, 1994). ... Re-signed by Eagles (April 25, 1994). ... Released by Eagles (March 22, 1995). ... Signed by New York Jets (April 13, 1995). ... Released by Jets (September 24, 1996). ... Signed by New England Patriots (October 9, 1996). ... Granted unconditional free agency (February 14, 1997). ... Re-signed by Jets (May 20, 1997). ... Granted unconditional free agency (February 13, 1998). ... Re-signed by Jets (April 9, 1998).
CHAMPIONSHIP GAME EXPERIENCE: Played in AFC championship game (1996 and 1998 seasons). ... Played in Super Bowl XXXI (1996 season).
PRO STATISTICS: 1991—Recovered one fumble. 1994—Credited with one sack and returned one kickoff for 14 yards. 1995—Returned one kickoff for six yards. 1996—Credited with one sack. 1997—Recovered two fumbles for 40 yards.

				INTERCEPTIONS		
Year Team	G	GS	No.	Yds.	Avg.	TD
1990—Philadelphia NFL				Did not play.		
1991—Philadelphia NFL	15	1	2	74	37.0	∞1
1992—Philadelphia NFL	16	1	1	0	0.0	0
1993—Philadelphia NFL	15	0	1	0	0.0	0
1994—Philadelphia NFL	16	2	0	0	...	0
1995—New York Jets NFL	11	10	6	101	16.8	▲1
1996—New York Jets NFL	2	0	0	0	...	0
—New England NFL	11	6	2	20	10.0	...
1997—New York Jets NFL	16	16	6	158	26.3	†3
1998—New York Jets NFL	16	16	2	34	17.0	0
Pro totals (8 years)	118	52	20	387	19.4	5

SMITH, ROBERT   RB   VIKINGS

PERSONAL: Born March 4, 1972, in Euclid, Ohio. ... 6-2/212. ... Full name: Robert Scott Smith.
HIGH SCHOOL: Euclid (Ohio).
COLLEGE: Ohio State.
TRANSACTIONS/CAREER NOTES: Selected after sophomore season by Minnesota Vikings in first round (21st pick overall) of 1993 NFL draft. ... Signed by Vikings (July 16, 1993). ... On injured reserve with knee injury (December 7, 1993-remainder of season). ... On physically unable to perform list with knee injury (July 13-19, 1994). ... Granted free agency (February 16, 1996). ... Re-signed by Vikings (August 10, 1996). ... On injured reserve with knee injury (November 15, 1996-remainder of season). ... Granted unconditional free agency (February 14, 1997). ... Re-signed by Vikings (April 18, 1997). ... Designated by Vikings as franchise player (February 13, 1998). ... Free agency status changed from franchise to transitional (February 25, 1998). ... Re-signed by Vikings (March 4, 1998).
CHAMPIONSHIP GAME EXPERIENCE: Played in NFC championship game (1998 season).
PRO STATISTICS: 1993—Returned one punt for four yards. 1996—Recovered one fumble. 1997—Recovered one fumble.
SINGLE GAME HIGHS (regular season): Attempts—30 (September 8, 1996, vs. Atlanta); yards—179 (September 13, 1998, vs. St. Louis); and rushing touchdowns—2 (September 13, 1998, vs. St. Louis).
STATISTICAL PLATEAUS: 100-yard rushing games: 1993 (1), 1995 (2), 1996 (3), 1997 (6), 1998 (5). Total: 17.

			RUSHING				RECEIVING				KICKOFF RETURNS				TOTALS		
Year Team	G	GS	Att.	Yds.	Avg.	TD	No.	Yds.	Avg.	TD	No.	Yds.	Avg.	TD	TD	2pt.	Pts. Fum.
1993—Minnesota NFL	10	2	82	399	4.9	2	24	111	4.6	0	3	41	13.7	0	2	...	12 0
1994—Minnesota NFL	14	0	31	106	3.4	1	15	105	7.0	0	16	419	26.2	0	1	0	6 0
1995—Minnesota NFL	9	7	139	632	4.5	5	7	35	5.0	0	0	0	...	0	5	1	32 5
1996—Minnesota NFL	8	7	162	692	4.3	3	7	39	5.6	0	0	0	...	0	3	0	18 2
1997—Minnesota NFL	14	14	232	1266	5.5	6	37	197	5.3	1	0	0	...	0	7	0	42 0
1998—Minnesota NFL	14	14	249	1187	4.8	6	28	291	10.4	2	0	0	...	0	8	0	48 1
Pro totals (6 years)	69	44	895	4282	4.8	23	118	778	6.6	3	19	460	24.2	0	26	1	158 4

SMITH, ROD   CB

PERSONAL: Born March 12, 1970, in St. Paul, Minn. ... 5-11/187. ... Full name: Rodney Marc Smith.
HIGH SCHOOL: Roseville (Minn.).
COLLEGE: Notre Dame (degree in economics).
TRANSACTIONS/CAREER NOTES: Selected by New England Patriots in second round (35th pick overall) of 1992 NFL draft. ... Signed by Patriots (August 3, 1992). ... Selected by Carolina Panthers from Patriots in NFL expansion draft (February 15, 1995). ... Granted free agency (February 17, 1995). ... Re-signed by Panthers (May 5, 1995). ... Granted unconditional free agency (February 16, 1996). ... Signed by Minnesota Vikings (May 3, 1996). ... Inactive for seven games with Vikings (1996). ... Released by Vikings (October 9, 1996). ... Signed by Panthers (October 22, 1996). ... Granted unconditional free agency (February 14, 1997). ... Re-signed by Panthers (February 26, 1997). ... Claimed on waivers by Green Bay Packers (October 26, 1998). ... Granted unconditional free agency (February 12, 1999).
CHAMPIONSHIP GAME EXPERIENCE: Played in NFC championship game (1996 season).
PRO STATISTICS: 1993—Returned one punt for no yards. 1994—Credited with 1/2 sack. 1996—Credited with one sack. 1998—Recovered one fumble for 35 yards.

			INTERCEPTIONS			
Year Team	G	GS	No.	Yds.	Avg.	TD
1992—New England NFL	16	1	1	0	0.0	0
1993—New England NFL	16	9	0	0	...	0
1994—New England NFL	16	7	2	10	5.0	0
1995—Carolina NFL	16	5	0	0	...	0
1996—Carolina NFL	8	1	0	0	...	0
1997—Carolina NFL	16	2	0	0	...	0
1998—Carolina NFL	6	2	1	43	43.0	0
—Green Bay NFL	8	0	1	0	0.0	0
Pro totals (7 years)	102	27	5	53	10.6	0

SMITH, ROD   WR   BRONCOS

PERSONAL: Born May 15, 1970, in Texarkana, Ark. ... 6-0/200.
HIGH SCHOOL: Arkansas (Texarkana, Ark.).
COLLEGE: Missouri Southern.
TRANSACTIONS/CAREER NOTES: Signed as non-drafted free agent by Denver Broncos (March 23, 1995).
CHAMPIONSHIP GAME EXPERIENCE: Played in AFC championship game (1997 and 1998 seasons). ... Member of Super Bowl championship team (1997 and 1998 seasons).
PRO STATISTICS: 1996—Rushed once for one yard. 1997—Rushed five times for 16 yards and recovered one fumble. 1998—Rushed six times for 63 yards, attempted one pass with a completion for 14 yards and recovered two fumbles for 11 yards and one touchdown.
SINGLE GAME HIGHS (regular season): Receptions—9 (December 27, 1998, vs. Seattle); yards—165 (December 6, 1998, vs. Kansas City); and touchdown receptions—2 (October 4, 1998, vs. Philadelphia).
STATISTICAL PLATEAUS: 100-yard receiving games: 1997 (6), 1998 (4). Total: 10.

			RECEIVING				PUNT RETURNS				KICKOFF RETURNS				TOTALS		
Year Team	G	GS	No.	Yds.	Avg.	TD	No.	Yds.	Avg.	TD	No.	Yds.	Avg.	TD	TD	2pt.	Pts.	Fum.
1995—Denver NFL	16	1	6	152	25.3	1	0	0	...	0	4	54	13.5	0	1	0	6	0
1996—Denver NFL	10	1	16	237	14.8	2	23	283	12.3	0	1	29	29.0	0	2	0	12	1
1997—Denver NFL	16	16	70	1180	16.9▲12	1	12	12.0	0	0	0	...	0	12	0	72	3
1998—Denver NFL	16	16	86	1222	14.2	6	0	0	...	0	0	0	...	0	7	0	42	0
Pro totals (4 years)	58	34	178	2791	15.7	21	24	295	12.3	0	5	83	16.6	0	22	0	132	4

SMITH, SHEVIN   S   BUCCANEERS

PERSONAL: Born June 17, 1975, in Miami. ... 5-11/195. ... Full name: Shevin Jamar Smith. ... Cousin of Derrick Thomas, linebacker, Kansas City Chiefs; and cousin of Winston Moss, linebacker with Tampa Bay Buccaneers (1987-90), Los Angeles Raiders (1991-94) and Seattle Seahawks (1995-97).
HIGH SCHOOL: Southridge (Miami).
COLLEGE: Florida State (degree in finance, 1998).
TRANSACTIONS/CAREER NOTES: Selected by Tampa Bay Buccaneers in sixth round (184th pick overall) of 1998 NFL draft. ... Signed by Buccaneers (June 4, 1998). ... Released by Buccaneers (August 25, 1998). ... Re-signed by Buccaneers to practice squad (August 31, 1998). ... Activated (November 11, 1998).
PLAYING EXPERIENCE: Tampa Bay NFL, 1998. ... Games/Games started: 3/0.

SMITH, THOMAS   CB   BILLS

PERSONAL: Born December 5, 1970, in Gates, N.C. ... 5-11/188. ... Full name: Thomas Lee Smith Jr. ... Cousin of Sam Perkins, forward/center, Indiana Pacers.
HIGH SCHOOL: Gates County (Gatesville, N.C.).
COLLEGE: North Carolina.
TRANSACTIONS/CAREER NOTES: Selected by Buffalo Bills in first round (28th pick overall) of 1993 NFL draft. ... Signed by Bills (July 16, 1993). ... Granted free agency (February 16, 1996). ... Re-signed by Bills (February 27, 1996).
PRO STATISTICS: 1993—Recovered one fumble. 1997—Fumbled once and recovered one fumble for one yard. 1998—Recovered one fumble.

Year Team	G	GS	INTERCEPTIONS No.	Yds.	Avg.	TD
1993—Buffalo NFL	16	1	0	0	...	0
1994—Buffalo NFL	16	16	1	4	4.0	0
1995—Buffalo NFL	16	16	2	23	11.5	0
1996—Buffalo NFL	16	16	1	0	0.0	0
1997—Buffalo NFL	16	16	0	0	...	0
1998—Buffalo NFL	14	14	1	0	0.0	0
Pro totals (6 years)	94	79	5	27	5.4	0

SMITH, TRAVIAN — LB — RAIDERS

PERSONAL: Born August 26, 1975, in Good Shepard, Texas. ... 6-4/238.
HIGH SCHOOL: Tatum (Texas).
COLLEGE: Oklahoma.
TRANSACTIONS/CAREER NOTES: Selected by Oakland Raiders in fifth round (152nd pick overall) of 1998 NFL draft. ... Signed by Raiders (July 6, 1998). ... Released by Raiders (August 26, 1998). ... Re-signed by Raiders to practice squad (August 31, 1998). ... Activated (December 15, 1998).
PLAYING EXPERIENCE: Oakland NFL, 1998. ... Games/Games started: 2/0.

SMITH, VINSON — LB — SAINTS

PERSONAL: Born July 3, 1965, in Statesville, N.C. ... 6-2/247. ... Full name: Vinson Robert Smith.
HIGH SCHOOL: Statesville (N.C.).
COLLEGE: East Carolina (degree in communications, 1989).
TRANSACTIONS/CAREER NOTES: Signed as non-drafted free agent by Atlanta Falcons (May 2, 1988). ... On injured reserve with elbow injury (August 29-November 4, 1988). ... On injured reserve with knee injury (December 10, 1988-remainder of season). ... Granted unconditional free agency (February 1, 1989). ... Signed by Pittsburgh Steelers (February 28, 1989). ... On injured reserve with broken foot (August 29, 1989-entire season). ... Granted unconditional free agency (February 1, 1990). ... Signed by Dallas Cowboys (March 3, 1990). ... Granted free agency (February 1, 1992). ... Re-signed by Cowboys (August 4, 1992). ... Traded by Cowboys with LB Barry Minter and sixth-round pick (DE Carl Reeves) in 1995 draft to Chicago Bears for TE Kelly Blackwell, S Markus Paul and LB John Roper (August 17, 1993). ... Granted unconditional free agency (February 17, 1995). ... Re-signed by Bears (March 2, 1995). ... Granted unconditional free agency (February 14, 1997). ... Signed by Cowboys (July 19, 1997). ... Granted unconditional free agency (February 13, 1998). ... Signed by New Orleans Saints (September 9, 1998). ... Granted unconditional free agency (February 12, 1999). ... Re-signed by Saints (February 25, 1999).
CHAMPIONSHIP GAME EXPERIENCE: Played in NFC championship game (1992 season). ... Member of Super Bowl championship team (1992 season).
PRO STATISTICS: 1990—Recovered two fumbles. 1992—Recovered two fumbles. 1995—Fumbled once for two yards and recovered one fumble. 1996—Recovered two fumbles for 34 yards.

Year Team	G	GS	SACKS
1988—Atlanta NFL	3	0	0.0
1989—Pittsburgh NFL	Did not play.		
1990—Dallas NFL	16	1	0.0
1991—Dallas NFL	13	12	0.0
1992—Dallas NFL	16	13	1.0
1993—Chicago NFL	16	13	0.0
1994—Chicago NFL	12	10	1.0
1995—Chicago NFL	16	13	4.0
1996—Chicago NFL	15	12	1.0
1997—Dallas NFL	14	3	1.0
1998—New Orleans NFL	15	0	0.0
Pro totals (10 years)	136	77	8.0

SOLOMON, FREDDIE — WR

PERSONAL: Born August 15, 1972, in Gainesville, Fla. ... 5-10/180. ... Full name: Freddie Lee Solomon Jr.
HIGH SCHOOL: Santa Fe (N.M.).
COLLEGE: South Carolina State.
TRANSACTIONS/CAREER NOTES: Signed as non-drafted free agent by Philadelphia Eagles (April 26, 1995). ... Released by Eagles (August 27, 1995). ... Re-signed by Eagles to practice squad (September 6, 1995). ... Activated (December 22, 1995); did not play. ... Released by Eagles (August 19, 1997). ... Re-signed by Eagles (September 1, 1997). ... Selected by Cleveland Browns from Eagles in NFL expansion draft (February 1, 1999). ... Granted free agency (February 12, 1999).
PRO STATISTICS: 1997—Recovered one fumble.
SINGLE GAME HIGHS (regular season): Receptions—4 (December 3, 1998, vs. St. Louis); yards—77 (November 2, 1997, vs. Arizona); and touchdown receptions—1 (December 3, 1998, vs. St. Louis).

Year Team	G	GS	RECEIVING No.	Yds.	Avg.	TD	PUNT RETURNS No.	Yds.	Avg.	TD	TOTALS TD	2pt.	Pts.	Fum.
1995—Philadelphia NFL			Did not play.											
1996—Philadelphia NFL	12	0	8	125	15.6	0	5	27	5.4	0	0	0	0	0
1997—Philadelphia NFL	15	5	29	455	15.7	3	10	55	5.5	0	3	1	20	3
1998—Philadelphia NFL	16	1	21	193	9.2	1	11	100	9.1	0	1	0	6	0
Pro totals (3 years)	43	6	58	773	13.3	4	26	182	7.0	0	4	1	26	3

SOWELL, JERALD — FB — JETS

PERSONAL: Born January 21, 1974, in Baton Rouge, La. ... 6-0/248. ... Full name: Jerald Monye Sowell.
HIGH SCHOOL: Baker (La.).
COLLEGE: Tulane (degree in exercise science/kinesiology).
TRANSACTIONS/CAREER NOTES: Selected by Green Bay Packers in seventh round (231st pick overall) of 1997 NFL draft. ... Signed by Packers (July 10, 1997). ... Claimed on waivers by New York Jets (August 25, 1997).
CHAMPIONSHIP GAME EXPERIENCE: Member of Jets for AFC championship game (1998 season); inactive.
SINGLE GAME HIGHS (regular season): Attempts—14 (November 8, 1998, vs. Buffalo); yards—82 (September 20, 1998, vs. Indianapolis); and rushing touchdowns—0.

				RUSHING				RECEIVING				TOTALS		
Year Team	G	GS	Att.	Yds.	Avg.	TD	No.	Yds.	Avg.	TD	TD	2pt.	Pts.	Fum.
1997—New York Jets NFL	9	0	7	35	5.0	0	1	8	8.0	0	0	0	0	0
1998—New York Jets NFL	16	2	40	164	4.1	0	10	59	5.9	0	0	0	0	2
Pro totals (2 years)	25	2	47	199	4.2	0	11	67	6.1	0	0	0	0	2

SPARKS, PHILLIPPI — CB — GIANTS

PERSONAL: Born April 15, 1969, in Oklahoma City. ... 5-11/195. ... Full name: Phillippi Dwaine Sparks.
HIGH SCHOOL: Maryvale (Phoenix).
JUNIOR COLLEGE: Glendale (Ariz.) Community College.
COLLEGE: Arizona State.
TRANSACTIONS/CAREER NOTES: Selected by New York Giants in second round (41st pick overall) of 1992 NFL draft. ... Signed by Giants (July 21, 1992). ... Granted free agency (February 17, 1995). ... Re-signed by Giants (May 8, 1995).
PRO STATISTICS: 1992—Returned two kickoffs for 23 yards. 1997—Returned one kickoff for eight yards and credited with one sack.

			INTERCEPTIONS			
Year Team	G	GS	No.	Yds.	Avg.	TD
1992—New York Giants NFL	16	2	1	0	0.0	0
1993—New York Giants NFL	5	3	0	0	...	0
1994—New York Giants NFL	11	11	3	4	1.3	0
1995—New York Giants NFL	16	16	5	11	2.2	0
1996—New York Giants NFL	14	14	3	23	7.7	0
1997—New York Giants NFL	13	13	5	72	14.4	0
1998—New York Giants NFL	13	13	4	25	6.3	0
Pro totals (7 years)	88	72	21	135	6.4	0

SPEARS, MARCUS — OT — CHIEFS

PERSONAL: Born September 28, 1971, in Baton Rouge, La. ... 6-4/320. ... Full name: Marcus DeWayne Spears.
HIGH SCHOOL: Belaire (Baton Rouge, La.).
COLLEGE: Northwestern (La.) State.
TRANSACTIONS/CAREER NOTES: Selected by Chicago Bears in second round (39th pick overall) of 1994 NFL draft. ... Signed by Bears (July 16, 1994). ... Assigned by Bears to Amsterdam Admirals in 1996 World League enhancement allocation program (February 19, 1996). ... Granted unconditional free agency (February 14, 1997). ... Signed by Green Bay Packers (March 12, 1997). ... Released by Packers (August 19, 1997). ... Signed by Kansas City Chiefs (September 16, 1997). ... On injured reserve with hand injury (December 9, 1998-remainder of season). ... Granted unconditional free agency (February 12, 1999). ... Re-signed by Chiefs (February 16, 1999).
PLAYING EXPERIENCE: Amsterdam W.L., 1996; Chicago NFL, 1996; Kansas City NFL, 1997 and 1998. ... Games/Games started: W.L.1996 (games played unavailable), NFL 1996 (9/0), 1997 (3/0), 1998 (12/0). Total: 24/0.
HONORS: Named offensive lineman on THE SPORTING NEWS college All-America second team (1993).
PRO STATISTICS: 1996—Caught one pass for one yard and a touchdown.

SPENCE, BLAKE — TE — JETS

PERSONAL: Born June 20, 1975, in Garden Grove, Calif. ... 6-4/249. ... Full name: Blake Andrew Spence.
HIGH SCHOOL: Capistrano Valley (San Juan Capistrano, Calif.).
COLLEGE: Oregon.
TRANSACTIONS/CAREER NOTES: Selected by New York Jets in fifth round (146th pick overall) of 1998 NFL draft. ... Signed by Jets (June 23, 1998).
PLAYING EXPERIENCE: New York Jets NFL, 1998. ... Games/Games started: 5/0.
CHAMPIONSHIP GAME EXPERIENCE: Played in AFC championship game (1998 season).
PRO STATISTICS: 1998—Caught one pass for five yards.
SINGLE GAME HIGHS (regular season): Receptions—1 (October 25, 1998, vs. Atlanta); yards—5 (October 25, 1998, vs. Atlanta); and touchdown receptions—0.

SPENCER, JIMMY — CB — CHARGERS

PERSONAL: Born March 29, 1969, in Manning, S.C. ... 5-10/185. ... Full name: James Arthur Spencer Jr.
HIGH SCHOOL: Glades Central (Belle Glade, Fla.).
COLLEGE: Florida.

TRANSACTIONS/CAREER NOTES: Selected by Washington Redskins in eighth round (215th pick overall) of 1991 NFL draft. ... Signed by Redskins for 1991 season. ... Released by Redskins (August 26, 1991). ... Signed by New Orleans Saints (April 2, 1992). ... Granted unconditional free agency (February 16, 1996). ... Signed by Cincinnati Bengals (March 21, 1996). ... Released by Bengals (August 25, 1998). ... Signed by San Diego Chargers (September 1, 1998). ... Granted unconditional free agency (February 12, 1999). ... Re-signed by Chargers (April 7, 1999).

PRO STATISTICS: 1992—Recovered one fumble. 1993—Recovered three fumbles for 53 yards. 1994—Recovered one fumble. 1996—Recovered one fumble for 59 yards.

				INTERCEPTIONS		
Year Team	G	GS	No.	Yds.	Avg.	TD
1992—New Orleans NFL	16	4	0	0	...	0
1993—New Orleans NFL	16	3	0	0	...	0
1994—New Orleans NFL	16	16	5	24	4.8	0
1995—New Orleans NFL	16	15	4	11	2.8	0
1996—Cincinnati NFL	15	14	5	48	9.6	0
1997—Cincinnati NFL	16	9	1	-2	-2.0	0
1998—San Diego NFL	15	4	1	0	0.0	0
Pro totals (7 years)	110	65	16	81	5.1	0

SPIELMAN, CHRIS   LB   BROWNS

PERSONAL: Born October 11, 1965, in Massillon, Ohio. ... 6-0/247. ... Full name: Charles Christopher Spielman.
HIGH SCHOOL: Washington (Massillon, Ohio).
COLLEGE: Ohio State.
TRANSACTIONS/CAREER NOTES: Selected by Detroit Lions in second round (29th pick overall) of 1988 NFL draft. ... Signed by Lions (July 15, 1988). ... On injured reserve with separated shoulder (September 19-October 26, 1990). ... Granted unconditional free agency (February 16, 1996). ... Signed by Buffalo Bills (March 19, 1996). ... On injured reserve with neck injury (October 28, 1997-remainder of season). ... Sat out 1998 season for personal reasons. ... Traded by Bills to Cleveland Browns for past considerations (February 16, 1999).
CHAMPIONSHIP GAME EXPERIENCE: Played in NFC championship game (1991 season).
HONORS: Named linebacker on THE SPORTING NEWS college All-America first team (1986 and 1987). ... Lombardi Award winner (1987). ... Played in Pro Bowl (1989-1991 and 1994 seasons). ... Named inside linebacker on THE SPORTING NEWS NFL All-Pro team (1994).
PRO STATISTICS: 1988—Recovered one fumble. 1989—Recovered two fumbles for 31 yards. 1990—Recovered two fumbles. 1991—Recovered three fumbles. 1992—Recovered one fumble. 1993—Recovered two fumbles. 1994—Recovered three fumbles for 25 yards and a touchdown. 1995—Recovered three fumbles for eight yards. 1996—Recovered two fumbles.

				INTERCEPTIONS			SACKS
Year Team	G	GS	No.	Yds.	Avg.	TD	No.
1988—Detroit NFL	16	16	0	0	...	0	0.0
1989—Detroit NFL	16	16	0	0	...	0	5.0
1990—Detroit NFL	12	12	1	12	12.0	0	2.0
1991—Detroit NFL	16	16	0	0	...	0	1.0
1992—Detroit NFL	16	16	0	0	...	0	1.0
1993—Detroit NFL	16	16	2	-2	-1.0	0	0.5
1994—Detroit NFL	16	16	0	0	...	0	0.0
1995—Detroit NFL	16	16	1	4	4.0	0	1.0
1996—Buffalo NFL	16	16	1	14	14.0	0	0.0
1997—Buffalo NFL	8	8	1	8	8.0	0	0.0
1998—Buffalo NFL			Did not play.				
Pro totals (10 years)	148	148	6	36	6.0	0	10.5

SPIKES, TAKEO   LB   BENGALS

PERSONAL: Born December 17, 1976, in Sandersville, Ga. ... 6-2/230. ... Full name: Takeo Gerard Spikes. ... Name pronounced tuh-KEY-oh.
HIGH SCHOOL: Washington County (Sandersville, Ga.).
COLLEGE: Auburn.
TRANSACTIONS/CAREER NOTES: Selected after junior season by Cincinnati Bengals in first round (13th pick overall) of 1998 NFL draft. ... Signed by Bengals (July 25, 1998).
PLAYING EXPERIENCE: Cincinnati NFL, 1998. ... Games/Games started: 16/16.
HONORS: Named inside linebacker on THE SPORTING NEWS college All-America first team (1997).
PRO STATISTICS: 1998—Credited with two sacks.

SPINDLER, MARC   DE/DT

PERSONAL: Born November 28, 1969, in West Scranton, Pa. ... 6-5/290. ... Full name: Marc Rudolph Spindler.
HIGH SCHOOL: West Scranton (Pa.).
COLLEGE: Pittsburgh.
TRANSACTIONS/CAREER NOTES: Selected after junior season by Detroit Lions in third round (62nd pick overall) of 1990 NFL draft. ... Signed by Lions (July 24, 1990). ... On injured reserve with knee injury (September 27, 1990-remainder of season). ... On injured reserve with hamstring injury (September 18-October 14, 1992). ... Granted free agency (March 1, 1993). ... Re-signed by Lions (August 2, 1993). ... Granted unconditional free agency (February 17, 1995). ... Signed by Tampa Bay Buccaneers (April 25, 1995). ... Traded by Buccaneers with WR Charles Wilson to New York Jets for fourth-round pick (OT Jason Odom) in 1996 draft (August 27, 1995). ... Released by Jets (February 13, 1997). ... Signed by Seattle Seahawks (June 2, 1997). ... Released by Seahawks (August 6, 1997). ... Signed by Chicago Bears (August 12, 1997). ... Released by Bears (August 24, 1997). ... Signed by Lions (August 26, 1997). ... Released by Lions (September 27, 1997). ... Re-signed by Lions (September 30, 1997). ... Granted unconditional free agency (February 13, 1998). ... Re-signed by Lions (March 6, 1998). ... Released by Lions (February 10, 1999).
CHAMPIONSHIP GAME EXPERIENCE: Played in NFC championship game (1991 season).

HONORS: Named defensive tackle on THE SPORTING NEWS college All-America first team (1989).
PRO STATISTICS: 1991—Recovered one fumble. 1993—Recovered two fumbles. 1996—Recovered one fumble.

Year Team	G	GS	SACKS
1990—Detroit NFL	3	2	1.0
1991—Detroit NFL	16	16	3.5
1992—Detroit NFL	13	13	2.5
1993—Detroit NFL	16	16	2.0
1994—Detroit NFL	9	8	0.0
1995—New York Jets NFL	10	4	0.0
1996—New York Jets NFL	15	5	0.5
1997—Detroit NFL	10	0	0.0
1998—Detroit NFL	15	1	0.0
Pro totals (9 years)	107	65	9.5

SPIRES, GREG — DE — PATRIOTS

PERSONAL: Born August 12, 1974, in Mariana, Fla. ... 6-1/260. ... Full name: Greg Tyrone Spires.
HIGH SCHOOL: Mariner (Cape Coral, Fla.).
COLLEGE: Florida State.
TRANSACTIONS/CAREER NOTES: Selected by New England Patriots in third round (83rd pick overall) of 1998 NFL draft. ... Signed by Patriots (July 16, 1998).

Year Team	G	GS	SACKS
1998—New England NFL	15	1	3.0

SPRIGGS, MARCUS — OT — BILLS

PERSONAL: Born May 17, 1974, in Hattiesburg, Miss. ... 6-3/295. ... Full name: Thomas Marcus Spriggs.
HIGH SCHOOL: Byram (Jackson, Miss.).
JUNIOR COLLEGE: Hinds Community College (Miss.).
COLLEGE: Houston.
TRANSACTIONS/CAREER NOTES: Selected by Buffalo Bills in sixth round (185th pick overall) of 1997 NFL draft. ... Signed by Bills (June 13, 1997).
PLAYING EXPERIENCE: Buffalo NFL, 1997 and 1998. ... Games/Games started: 1997 (2/0), 1998 (1/0). Total: 3/0.

SPRINGS, SHAWN — CB — SEAHAWKS

PERSONAL: Born March 11, 1975, in Williamsburg, W.Va. ... 6-0/195. ... Son of Ron Springs, running back with Dallas Cowboys (1979-84) and Tampa Bay Buccaneers (1985-86).
HIGH SCHOOL: Springbrook (Silver Spring, Md.).
COLLEGE: Ohio State.
TRANSACTIONS/CAREER NOTES: Selected by Seattle Seahawks in first round (third pick overall) of 1997 NFL draft. ... Signed by Seahawks (August 4, 1997).
HONORS: Named cornerback on THE SPORTING NEWS college All-America second team (1996). ... Played in Pro Bowl (1998 season).
PRO STATISTICS: 1998—Recovered two fumbles for 14 yards and one touchdown.

			INTERCEPTIONS				TOTALS			
Year Team	G	GS	No.	Yds.	Avg.	TD	TD	2pt.	Pts.	Fum.
1997—Seattle NFL	10	10	1	0	0.0	0	0	0	0	0
1998—Seattle NFL	16	16	7	142	20.3	▲2	3	0	18	0
Pro totals (2 years)	26	26	8	142	17.8	2	3	0	18	0

SPROTTE, JIMMY — LB — BENGALS

PERSONAL: Born October 2, 1974, in Olathe, Kan. ... 6-3/235. ... Full name: John Wild Sprotte. ... Name pronounced SPRAHT.
HIGH SCHOOL: Blue Ridge (Lakeside, Ariz.).
COLLEGE: Arizona.
TRANSACTIONS/CAREER NOTES: Selected by Tennessee Oilers in seventh round (205th pick overall) of 1998 NFL draft. ... Signed by Oilers (July 7, 1998). ... Released by Oilers (August 25, 1998). ... Re-signed by Oilers to practice squad (September 1, 1998). ... Signed by Cincinnati Bengals off Oilers practice squad (October 1, 1998).
PLAYING EXPERIENCE: Cincinnati NFL, 1998. ... Games/Games started: 5/0.

STAAT, JEREMY — DE — STEELERS

PERSONAL: Born October 10, 1976, in Bakersfield, Calif. ... 6-5/300. ... Full name: Jeremy Ray Staat. ... Name pronounced STOUGHT.
HIGH SCHOOL: Bakersfield (Calif.).
JUNIOR COLLEGE: Bakersfield (Calif.) College.
COLLEGE: Arizona State.
TRANSACTIONS/CAREER NOTES: Selected by Pittsburgh Steelers in second round (41st pick overall) of 1998 NFL draft. ... Signed by Steelers (June 19, 1998).
PLAYING EXPERIENCE: Pittsburgh NFL, 1998. ... Games/Games started: 5/0.
HONORS: Named defensive tackle on THE SPORTING NEWS college All-America second team (1997).

STABLEIN, BRIAN — WR — LIONS

PERSONAL: Born April 14, 1970, in Erie, Pa. ... 6-1/193. ... Full name: Brian Patrick Stablein.
HIGH SCHOOL: McDowell (Erie, Pa.).
COLLEGE: Ohio State.
TRANSACTIONS/CAREER NOTES: Selected by Denver Broncos in eighth round (210nd pick overall) of 1993 NFL draft. ... Signed by Broncos (June 7, 1993). ... Released by Broncos (August 24, 1993). ... Signed by Indianapolis Colts to practice squad (September 7, 1993). ... Active for two games (1994); did not play. ... Granted free agency (February 14, 1997). ... Re-signed by Colts (June 10, 1997). ... Granted unconditional free agency (February 13, 1998). ... Signed by New England Patriots (March 19, 1998). ... Released by Patriots (August 30, 1998). ... Signed by Detroit Lions (September 1, 1998). ... Granted unconditional free agency (February 12, 1999). ... Re-signed by Lions (April 6, 1999).
CHAMPIONSHIP GAME EXPERIENCE: Played in AFC championship game (1995 season).
PRO STATISTICS: 1996—Returned six punts for 56 yards. 1997—Returned 17 punts for 133 yards.
SINGLE GAME HIGHS (regular season): Receptions—5 (November 24, 1996, vs. New England); yards—47 (October 5, 1997, vs. New York Jets); and touchdown receptions—1 (October 12, 1997, vs. Pittsburgh).

			RECEIVING				TOTALS			
Year Team	G	GS	No.	Yds.	Avg.	TD	татого TD	2pt.	Pts.	Fum.
1993—Indianapolis NFL						Did not play.				
1994—Indianapolis NFL						Did not play.				
1995—Indianapolis NFL	15	0	8	95	11.9	0	0	0	0	0
1996—Indianapolis NFL	16	0	18	192	10.7	1	1	0	6	0
1997—Indianapolis NFL	16	0	25	253	10.1	1	1	1	8	0
1998—Detroit NFL	10	0	7	80	11.4	0	0	0	0	0
Pro totals (4 years)	57	0	58	620	10.7	2	2	1	14	0

STAI, BRENDEN — G — STEELERS

PERSONAL: Born March 30, 1972, in Phoenix. ... 6-4/310. ... Full name: Brenden Michael Stai. ... Name pronounced STY.
HIGH SCHOOL: Anaheim (Calif.) Esperanza.
COLLEGE: Nebraska.
TRANSACTIONS/CAREER NOTES: Selected by Pittsburgh Steelers in third round (91st pick overall) of 1995 NFL draft. ... Signed by Steelers (July 18, 1995). ... Granted free agency (February 13, 1998). ... Re-signed by Steelers (June 9, 1998).
PLAYING EXPERIENCE: Pittsburgh NFL, 1995-1998. ... Games/Games started: 1995 (16/9), 1996 (9/9), 1997 (10/9), 1998 (16/16). Total: 51/43.
CHAMPIONSHIP GAME EXPERIENCE: Played in AFC championship game (1995 and 1997 seasons). ... Played in Super Bowl XXX (1995 season).
HONORS: Named offensive lineman on THE SPORTING NEWS college All-America second team (1994).

STALEY, DUCE — RB — EAGLES

PERSONAL: Born February 27, 1975, in Columbia, S.C. ... 5-11/220. ... Name pronounced DEUCE.
HIGH SCHOOL: Airport (Columbia, S.C.).
JUNIOR COLLEGE: Itawamba Junior College (Miss.).
COLLEGE: South Carolina.
TRANSACTIONS/CAREER NOTES: Selected by Philadelphia Eagles in third round (71st pick overall) of 1997 NFL draft. ... Signed by Eagles (June 12, 1997).
PRO STATISTICS: 1997—Recovered one fumble. 1998—Recovered two fumbles.
SINGLE GAME HIGHS (regular season): Attempts—30 (December 13, 1998, vs. Arizona); yards—141 (December 13, 1998, vs. Arizona); and rushing touchdowns—2 (September 27, 1998, vs. St. Louis).
STATISTICAL PLATEAUS: 100-yard rushing games: 1998 (1).

			RUSHING				RECEIVING				KICKOFF RETURNS				TOTALS			
Year Team	G	GS	Att.	Yds.	Avg.	TD	No.	Yds.	Avg.	TD	No.	Yds.	Avg.	TD	TD	2pt.	Pts.	Fum.
1997—Philadelphia NFL	16	0	7	29	4.1	0	2	22	11.0	0	47	1139	24.2	0	0	0	0	0
1998—Philadelphia NFL	16	13	258	1065	4.1	5	57	432	7.6	1	1	19	19.0	0	6	0	36	2
Pro totals (2 years)	32	13	265	1094	4.1	5	59	454	7.7	1	48	1158	24.1	0	6	0	36	2

STALLINGS, DENNIS — LB — TITANS

PERSONAL: Born May 25, 1974, in East St. Louis, Ill. ... 6-0/240. ... Full name: Dennis Dawon Stallings.
HIGH SCHOOL: East St. Louis (Ill.) Senior.
COLLEGE: Illinois.
TRANSACTIONS/CAREER NOTES: Selected by Houston Oilers in sixth round (181st pick overall) of 1997 NFL draft. ... Oilers franchise moved to Tennessee for 1997 season. ... Signed by Oilers (July 19, 1997). ... Oilers franchise renamed Tennessee Titans for 1999 season (December 26, 1998).
PLAYING EXPERIENCE: Tennessee NFL, 1997 and 1998. ... Games/ Games started: 1997 (13/0), 1998 (15/0). Total: 28/0.

STARKS, DUANE — CB — RAVENS

PERSONAL: Born May 23, 1974, in Miami. ... 5-10/170. ... Full name: Duane Lonell Starks.
HIGH SCHOOL: Miami Beach Senior.
JUNIOR COLLEGE: Holmes Junior College (Miss.).
COLLEGE: Miami (Fla.).

TRANSACTIONS/CAREER NOTES: Selected by Baltimore Ravens in first round (10th pick overall) of 1998 NFL draft. ... Signed by Ravens (August 5, 1998).

Year Team	G	GS	INTERCEPTIONS No.	Yds.	Avg.	TD
1998—Baltimore NFL	16	8	5	3	0.6	0

STATEN, RALPH S

PERSONAL: Born December 3, 1974, in Mobile, Ala. ... 6-3/205. ... Full name: Ralph Lahquan Staten.
HIGH SCHOOL: Montgomery (Semmes, Ala.).
COLLEGE: Alabama.
TRANSACTIONS/CAREER NOTES: Selected by Baltimore Ravens in seventh round (236th pick overall) of 1997 NFL draft. ... Signed by Ravens (July 14, 1997). ... Released by Ravens (April 26, 1999).
PRO STATISTICS: 1998—Fumbled once.

Year Team	G	GS	INTERCEPTIONS No.	Yds.	Avg.	TD	SACKS No.
1997—Baltimore NFL	10	3	2	12	6.0	0	0.0
1998—Baltimore NFL	15	3	3	25	8.3	0	1.0
Pro totals (2 years)	25	6	5	37	7.4	0	1.0

STEED, JOEL NT STEELERS

PERSONAL: Born February 17, 1969, in Frankfurt, West Germany. ... 6-2/308. ... Full name: Joel Edward Steed.
HIGH SCHOOL: W.C. Hinkley (Aurora, Colo.).
COLLEGE: Colorado (degree in sociology, 1991).
TRANSACTIONS/CAREER NOTES: Selected by Pittsburgh Steelers in third round (67th pick overall) of 1992 NFL draft. ... Signed by Steelers (July 27, 1992). ... On suspended list for anabolic steroid use (October 23-November 20, 1995). ... Granted unconditional free agency (February 13, 1998). ... Re-signed by Steelers (February 18, 1998).
CHAMPIONSHIP GAME EXPERIENCE: Played in AFC championship game (1994, 1995 and 1997 seasons). ... Played in Super Bowl XXX (1995 season).
HONORS: Named defensive lineman on THE SPORTING NEWS college All-America second team (1991). ... Played in Pro Bowl (1997 season).
PRO STATISTICS: 1993—Recovered one fumble. 1996—Recovered one fumble. 1997—Recovered one fumble.

Year Team	G	GS	SACKS
1992—Pittsburgh NFL	11	4	0.0
1993—Pittsburgh NFL	14	12	1.5
1994—Pittsburgh NFL	16	16	2.0
1995—Pittsburgh NFL	12	11	1.0
1996—Pittsburgh NFL	16	14	0.0
1997—Pittsburgh NFL	16	16	1.0
1998—Pittsburgh NFL	16	16	1.0
Pro totals (7 years)	101	89	6.5

STEELE, GLEN DE BENGALS

PERSONAL: Born October 4, 1974, in Ligonier, Ind. ... 6-4/295. ... Full name: James Lendale Steele Jr.
HIGH SCHOOL: West Noble (Ligonier, Ind.).
COLLEGE: Michigan.
TRANSACTIONS/CAREER NOTES: Selected by Cincinnati Bengals in fourth round (105th pick overall) of 1998 NFL draft. ... Signed by Bengals (July 14, 1998). ... On injured reserve with ankle injury (December 15, 1998-remainder of season).
PLAYING EXPERIENCE: Cincinnati NFL, 1998. ... Games/Games started: 10/0.

STENSTROM, STEVE QB

PERSONAL: Born December 23, 1971, in El Toro, Calif. ... 6-2/202.
HIGH SCHOOL: El Toro (Calif.).
COLLEGE: Stanford (degree in public policy, 1994).
TRANSACTIONS/CAREER NOTES: Selected by Kansas City Chiefs in fourth round (134th pick overall) of 1995 NFL draft. ... Signed by Chiefs (September 11, 1995). ... Claimed on waivers by Chicago Bears (September 13, 1995). ... Activated (September 25, 1995). ... Active for 12 games during the 1995 season; did not play. ... Granted free agency (February 13, 1998). ... Re-signed by Bears (June 25, 1998). ... Granted unconditional free agency (February 12, 1999).
PRO STATISTICS: 1997—Fumbled once. 1998—Fumbled six times and recovered one fumble for minus nine yards.
SINGLE GAME HIGHS (regular season): Attempts—42 (December 6, 1998, vs. Minnesota); completions—25 (December 6, 1998, vs. Minnesota); yards—303 (December 6, 1998, vs. Minnesota); and touchdown passes—1 (December 27, 1998, vs. Green Bay).
STATISTICAL PLATEAUS: 300-yard passing games: 1998 (1).
MISCELLANEOUS: Regular-season record as starting NFL quarterback: 1-6 (.143).

			PASSING						RUSHING				TOTALS		
Year Team	G	GS	Att.	Cmp.	Pct.	Yds.	TD	Int.	Avg.	Rat.	Att.	Yds.	Avg.	TD	TD	2pt.	Pts.
1995—Chicago NFL						Did not play.											
1996—Chicago NFL	1	0	4	3	75.0	37	0	0	9.25	103.1	0	0	...	0	0	0	0
1997—Chicago NFL	3	0	14	8	57.1	70	0	2	5.00	31.0	1	6	6.0	0	0	0	0
1998—Chicago NFL	7	7	196	112	57.1	1252	4	6	6.39	70.4	18	79	4.4	2	2	0	12
Pro totals (4 years)	13	7	214	123	57.5	1359	4	8	6.35	67.1	19	85	4.5	2	2	0	12

STEPHENS, JAMAIN   OT   STEELERS

PERSONAL: Born January 9, 1974, in Lumberton, N.C. ... 6-6/330.
HIGH SCHOOL: Lumberton (N.C.).
COLLEGE: North Carolina A&T.
TRANSACTIONS/CAREER NOTES: Selected by Pittsburgh Steelers in first round (29th pick overall) of 1996 NFL draft. ... Signed by Steelers (July 17, 1996). ... Inactive for all 16 games (1996).
PLAYING EXPERIENCE: Pittsburgh NFL, 1997 and 1998. ... Games/Games started: 1997 (7/1), 1998 (11/10). Total: 18/11.
CHAMPIONSHIP GAME EXPERIENCE: Member of Steelers for AFC championship game (1997 season); inactive.

STEPHENS, TREMAYNE   RB   CHARGERS

PERSONAL: Born April 16, 1976, in Greenville, S.C. ... 5-11/206. ... Full name: Tremayne Raphael Stephens.
HIGH SCHOOL: Greer Riverside (S.C.).
COLLEGE: North Carolina State.
TRANSACTIONS/CAREER NOTES: Signed as non-drafted free agent by San Diego Chargers (April 20, 1998).
SINGLE GAME HIGHS (regular season): Attempts—10 (December 27, 1998, vs. Arizona); yards—42 (December 27, 1998, vs. Arizona; and rushing touchdowns—1 (November 22, 1998, vs. Kansas City).

				RUSHING				RECEIVING				KICKOFF RETURNS				TOTALS		
Year Team	G	GS	Att.	Yds.	Avg.	TD	No.	Yds.	Avg.	TD	No.	Yds.	Avg.	TD	TD	2pt.	Pts.	Fum.
1998—San Diego NFL	13	1	35	122	3.5	1	2	9	4.5	0	16	349	21.8	0	1	0	6	1

STEPNOSKI, MARK   C   COWBOYS

PERSONAL: Born January 20, 1967, in Erie, Pa. ... 6-2/265. ... Full name: Mark Matthew Stepnoski.
HIGH SCHOOL: Cathedral Prep (Erie, Pa.).
COLLEGE: Pittsburgh (degree in communications).
TRANSACTIONS/CAREER NOTES: Selected by Dallas Cowboys in third round (57th pick overall) of 1989 NFL draft. ... Signed by Cowboys (July 23, 1989). ... Granted free agency (February 1, 1992). ... Re-signed by Cowboys (September 5, 1992). ... Granted roster exemption (September 5-14, 1992). ... On injured reserve with knee injury (December 22, 1993-remainder of season). ... Granted unconditional free agency (February 17, 1994). ... Re-signed by Cowboys (June 29, 1994). ... Granted unconditional free agency (February 17, 1995). ... Signed by Houston Oilers (March 11, 1995). ... Oilers franchise moved to Tennessee for 1997 season. ... Granted unconditional free agency (February 12, 1999). ... Signed by Cowboys (April 13, 1999).
PLAYING EXPERIENCE: Dallas NFL, 1989-1994; Houston NFL, 1995 and 1996; Tennessee NFL, 1997 and 1998. ... Games/Games started: 1989 (16/4), 1990 (16/16), 1991 (16/16), 1992 (14/14), 1993 (13/13), 1994 (16/16), 1995 (16/16), 1996 (16/16), 1997 (16/16), 1998 (13/13). Total: 152/140.
CHAMPIONSHIP GAME EXPERIENCE: Played in NFC championship game (1992 and 1994 seasons). ... Member of Super Bowl championship team (1992 season).
HONORS: Named guard on THE SPORTING NEWS college All-America first team (1988). ... Played in Pro Bowl (1992 and 1994-1996 seasons).
PRO STATISTICS: 1989—Recovered three fumbles. 1990—Returned one kickoff for 15 yards. 1992—Recovered one fumble. 1993—Fumbled once. 1994—Fumbled four times for minus three yards. 1997—Fumbled twice and recovered one fumble for minus seven yards. 1998—Rushed once for no yards, fumbled twice and recovered one fumble for minus six yards.

STEUSSIE, TODD   OT   VIKINGS

PERSONAL: Born December 1, 1970, in Canoga Park, Calif. ... 6-6/316. ... Full name: Todd Edward Steussie.
HIGH SCHOOL: Agoura (Calif.).
COLLEGE: California.
TRANSACTIONS/CAREER NOTES: Selected by Minnesota Vikings in first round (19th pick overall) of 1994 NFL draft. ... Signed by Vikings (July 13, 1994).
PLAYING EXPERIENCE: Minnesota NFL, 1994-1998. ... Games/Games started: 1994 (16/16), 1995 (16/16), 1996 (16/16), 1997 (16/16), 1998 (15/15). Total: 79/79.
CHAMPIONSHIP GAME EXPERIENCE: Played in NFC championship game (1998 season).
HONORS: Named offensive lineman on THE SPORTING NEWS college All-America second team (1993). ... Played in Pro Bowl (1997 and 1998 seasons).
PRO STATISTICS: 1994—Recovered one fumble. 1996—Recovered one fumble.

STEVENS, MATT   S   REDSKINS

PERSONAL: Born June 15, 1973, in Chapel Hill, N.C. ... 6-0/206. ... Full name: Matthew Brian Stevens.
HIGH SCHOOL: Chapel Hill (N.C.).
COLLEGE: Appalachian State.
TRANSACTIONS/CAREER NOTES: Selected by Buffalo Bills in third round (87th pick overall) of 1996 NFL draft. ... Signed by Bills (July 15, 1996). ... Claimed on waivers by Philadelphia Eagles (August 25, 1997). ... On suspended list for anabolic steroid use (August 27-September 29, 1997). ... Claimed on waivers by Washington Redskins (December 8, 1998). ... Granted free agency (February 12, 1999). ... Re-signed by Redskins (April 23, 1999).
PRO STATISTICS: 1996—Recovered one fumble. 1997—Recovered one fumble.

				INTERCEPTIONS			
Year Team	G	GS	No.	Yds.	Avg.	TD
1996—Buffalo NFL	13	11	2	0	0.0	0
1997—Philadelphia NFL	11	0	1	0	0.0	0
1998—Philadelphia NFL	7	1	0	0	...	0
—Washington NFL	3	0	0	0	...	0
Pro totals (3 years)	34	12	3	0	0.0	0

STEWART, JAMES — RB — JAGUARS

PERSONAL: Born December 27, 1971, in Morristown, Tenn. ... 6-1/224. ... Full name: James Ottis Stewart III.
HIGH SCHOOL: Morristown (Tenn.)-Hamblen West.
COLLEGE: Tennessee.
TRANSACTIONS/CAREER NOTES: Selected by Jacksonville Jaguars in first round (19th pick overall) of 1995 NFL draft. ... Signed by Jaguars (June 1, 1995). ... On injured reserve with knee injury (September 22, 1998-remainder of season).
CHAMPIONSHIP GAME EXPERIENCE: Played in AFC championship game (1996 season).
PRO STATISTICS: 1996—Recovered one fumble.
SINGLE GAME HIGHS (regular season): Attempts—29 (October 20, 1996, vs. St. Louis Rams); yards—115 (September 6, 1998, vs. Chicago); and rushing touchdowns—5 (October 12, 1997, vs. Philadelphia).
STATISTICAL PLATEAUS: 100-yard rushing games: 1996 (1), 1997 (1), 1998 (2). Total: 4.
MISCELLANEOUS: Holds Jacksonville Jaguars all-time record for most yards rushing (2,020) and most rushing touchdowns (20).

			RUSHING				RECEIVING				TOTALS			
Year Team	G	GS	Att.	Yds.	Avg.	TD	No.	Yds.	Avg.	TD	TD	2pt.	Pts.	Fum.
1995—Jacksonville NFL	14	7	137	525	3.8	2	21	190	9.0	1	3	0	18	1
1996—Jacksonville NFL	13	11	190	723	3.8	8	30	177	5.9	2	10	0	60	2
1997—Jacksonville NFL	16	5	136	555	4.1	8	41	336	8.2	1	9	0	54	0
1998—Jacksonville NFL	3	3	53	217	4.1	2	6	42	7.0	1	3	0	18	2
Pro totals (4 years)	46	26	516	2020	3.9	20	98	745	7.6	5	25	0	150	5

STEWART, KORDELL — QB — STEELERS

PERSONAL: Born October 16, 1972, in New Orleans. ... 6-1/211.
HIGH SCHOOL: John Ehret (Marrero, La.).
COLLEGE: Colorado.
TRANSACTIONS/CAREER NOTES: Selected by Pittsburgh Steelers in second round (60th pick overall) of 1995 NFL draft. ... Signed by Steelers (July 17, 1995).
CHAMPIONSHIP GAME EXPERIENCE: Played in AFC championship game (1995 and 1997 seasons). ... Played in Super Bowl XXX (1995 season).
PRO STATISTICS: 1995—Compiled a quarterback rating of 136.9. 1996—Compiled a quarterback rating of 18.8 and fumbled once. 1997—Compiled a quarterback rating of 75.2, fumbled six times and recovered one fumble for minus one yard. 1998—Compiled a quarterback rating of 62.9, punted once for 35 yards, fumbled three times and recovered two fumbles.
SINGLE GAME HIGHS (regular season): Attempts—48 (December 13, 1997, vs. New England); completions—26 (December 13, 1997, vs. New England); yards—317 (October 26, 1997, vs. Jacksonville); and touchdown passes—3 (December 7, 1997, vs. Denver).
STATISTICAL PLATEAUS: 300-yard passing games: 1997 (2). ... 100-yard rushing games: 1996 (1), 1998 (1). Total: 2.
MISCELLANEOUS: Started two games at wide receiver (1995). ... Started two games at wide receiver (1996). ... Regular-season record as starting NFL quarterback: 18-14 (.563). ... Postseason record as starting NFL quarterback: 1-1 (.500).

			PASSING							RUSHING				RECEIVING				TOTALS		
Year Team	G	GS	Att.	Cmp.	Pct.	Yds.	TD	Int.	Avg.	Att.	Yds.	Avg.	TD	No.	Yds.	Avg.	TD	TD	2pt.	Pts.
1995—Pittsburgh NFL	10	2	7	5	71.4	60	1	0	8.57	15	86	5.7	1	14	235	16.8	1	2	0	12
1996—Pittsburgh NFL	16	2	30	11	36.7	100	0	2	3.33	39	171	4.4	5	17	293	17.2	3	8	0	48
1997—Pittsburgh NFL	16	16	440	236	53.6	3020	21	§17	6.86	88	476	5.4	11	0	...	...	0	11	0	66
1998—Pittsburgh NFL	16	16	458	252	55.0	2560	11	18	5.59	81	406	5.0	2	1	17	17.0	0	2	0	12
Pro totals (4 years)	58	36	935	504	53.9	5740	33	37	6.14	223	1139	5.1	19	32	545	17.0	4	23	0	138

STEWART, RAYNA — S — DOLPHINS

PERSONAL: Born June 18, 1973, in Oklahoma City. ... 5-10/200. ... Full name: Rayna Cottrell Stewart II. ... Name pronounced ruh-NAY.
HIGH SCHOOL: Chatsworth (Calif.).
COLLEGE: Northern Arizona (degree in advertising, 1995).
TRANSACTIONS/CAREER NOTES: Selected by Houston Oilers in fifth round (143rd pick overall) of 1996 NFL draft. ... Signed by Oilers (June 27, 1996). ... Oilers franchise moved to Tennessee for 1997 season. ... Released by Oilers (August 30, 1998). ... Signed by Miami Dolphins (September 15, 1998).
PLAYING EXPERIENCE: Houston NFL, 1996; Tennessee NFL, 1997; Miami NFL, 1998. ... Games/Games started: 1996 (15/0), 1997 (16/5), 1998 (14/0). Total: 45/5.
PRO STATISTICS: 1997—Credited with $1/2$ sack and recovered one fumble.

STEWART, RYAN — S — LIONS

PERSONAL: Born September 30, 1973, in Moncks Corner, S.C. ... 6-1/207.
HIGH SCHOOL: Berkeley (Moncks Corner, S.C.).
COLLEGE: Georgia Tech (degree in business management).

STILL, BRYAN   WR   CHARGERS

PERSONAL: Born June 3, 1974, in Newport News, Va. ... 5-11/174. ... Full name: Bryan Andrei Still.
HIGH SCHOOL: Huguenot (Richmond, Va.).
COLLEGE: Virginia Tech.
TRANSACTIONS/CAREER NOTES: Selected by San Diego Chargers in second round (41st pick overall) of 1996 NFL draft. ... Signed by Chargers (June 25, 1996). ... Granted free agency (February 12, 1999).
PRO STATISTICS: 1996—Returned one punt for one yard.
SINGLE GAME HIGHS (regular season): Receptions—8 (September 27, 1998, vs. New York Giants); yards—128 (September 6, 1998, vs. Buffalo); and touchdown receptions—1 (November 29, 1998, vs. Denver).
STATISTICAL PLATEAUS: 100-yard receiving games: 1998 (2).

			RECEIVING				KICKOFF RETURNS				TOTALS		
Year Team	G	GS	No.	Yds.	Avg.	TD	No.	Yds.	Avg.	TD	TD	2pt.	Pts.	Fum.
1996—San Diego NFL	16	0	6	142	23.7	0	4	113	28.3	0	0	0	0	2
1997—San Diego NFL	15	4	24	324	13.5	0	0	0	...	0	0	0	0	0
1998—San Diego NFL	14	9	43	605	14.1	2	0	0	...	0	2	0	12	0
Pro totals (3 years)	45	13	73	1071	14.7	2	4	113	28.3	0	2	0	12	2

STOKES, BARRY   OT   DOLPHINS

PERSONAL: Born December 20, 1973, in Flint, Mich. ... 6-4/315. ... Full name: Barry Wade Stokes.
HIGH SCHOOL: Davison (Flint, Mich.).
COLLEGE: Eastern Michigan.
TRANSACTIONS/CAREER NOTES: Signed as non-drafted free agent by Detroit Lions (April 26, 1996). ... Released by Lions (August 14, 1996). ... Signed by Jacksonville Jaguars to practice squad (October 25, 1996). ... Granted free agency after 1996 season. ... Signed by Atlanta Falcons (January 30, 1997). ... Released by Falcons (August 1997). ... Signed by St. Louis Rams to practice squad (August 27, 1997). ... Released by Rams (October 6, 1997). ... Signed by Miami Dolphins to practice squad (November 26, 1997). ... Assigned by Dolphins to Scottish Claymores in 1998 NFL Europe enhancement allocation program (February 18, 1998). ... Released by Dolphins (August 25, 1998). ... Re-signed by Dolphins (November 4, 1998). ... Assigned by Dolphins to Scottish Claymores in 1999 NFL Europe enhancement allocation program (February 22, 1999).
PLAYING EXPERIENCE: Scottish Claymores NFLE, 1998; Miami NFL, 1998. ... Games/Games started: NFLE 1998 (10/10), NFL 1998 (3/0). Total Pro: 13/10.

STOKES, ERIC   DB   BROWNS

PERSONAL: Born December 18, 1973, in Heabron, Neb. ... 5-11/200.
HIGH SCHOOL: Lincoln (Neb.) East.
COLLEGE: Nebraska (degree in sociology, 1996).
TRANSACTIONS/CAREER NOTES: Selected by Seattle Seahawks in fifth round (142nd pick overall) of 1997 NFL draft. ... Signed by Seahawks (July 11, 1997). ... Released by Seahawks (August 24, 1997). ... Re-signed by Seahawks to practice squad (August 27, 1997). ... Activated (October 27, 1997). ... Selected by Cleveland Browns from Seahawks in NFL expansion draft (February 9, 1999).
PLAYING EXPERIENCE: Seattle NFL, 1997 and 1998. ... Games/ Games started: 1997 (7/0), 1998 (4/0). Total: 11/0.

STOKES, J.J.   WR   49ERS

PERSONAL: Born October 6, 1972, in San Diego. ... 6-4/223. ... Full name: Jerel Jamal Stokes.
HIGH SCHOOL: Point Loma (San Diego).
COLLEGE: UCLA (degree in sociology, 1994).
TRANSACTIONS/CAREER NOTES: Selected by San Francisco 49ers in first round (10th pick overall) of 1995 NFL draft. ... Signed by 49ers (July 27, 1995). ... On injured reserve with wrist injury (October 26, 1996-remainder of season). ... Granted unconditional free agency (February 12, 1999). ... Re-signed by 49ers (March 8, 1999).
CHAMPIONSHIP GAME EXPERIENCE: Played in NFC championship game (1997 season).
HONORS: Named wide receiver on THE SPORTING NEWS college All-America first team (1993).
PRO STATISTICS: 1997—Recovered two fumbles.
SINGLE GAME HIGHS (regular season): Receptions—9 (October 18, 1998, vs. Indianapolis); yards—111 (September 6, 1998, vs. New York Jets); and touchdown receptions—2 (December 6, 1998, vs. Carolina).
STATISTICAL PLATEAUS: 100-yard receiving games: 1995 (1), 1998 (2). Total: 3.

			RECEIVING				TOTALS			
Year Team	G	GS	No.	Yds.	Avg.	TD	TD	2pt.	Pts.	Fum.
1995—San Francisco NFL	12	2	38	517	13.6	4	4	0	24	0
1996—San Francisco NFL	6	6	18	249	13.8	0	0	0	0	0
1997—San Francisco NFL	16	16	58	733	12.6	4	4	0	24	1
1998—San Francisco NFL	16	13	63	770	12.2	8	8	0	48	0
Pro totals (4 years)	50	37	177	2269	12.8	16	16	0	96	1

STOLTENBERG, BRYAN — C — PANTHERS

PERSONAL: Born August 25, 1972, in Kearney, Neb. ... 6-1/300. ... Full name: Bryan Douglas Stoltenberg.
HIGH SCHOOL: Clements (Sugar Land, Texas).
COLLEGE: Colorado (degree in marketing).
TRANSACTIONS/CAREER NOTES: Selected by San Diego Chargers in sixth round (192nd pick overall) of 1996 NFL draft. ... Signed by Chargers (July 2, 1996). ... Released by Chargers (August 25, 1996). ... Re-signed by Chargers to practice squad (August 26, 1996). ... Activated (October 9, 1996). ... Released by Chargers (August 18, 1997). ... Signed by New York Giants (September 30, 1997). ... Granted free agency (February 13, 1998). ... Re-signed by Giants (May 4, 1998). ... Released by Giants (August 30, 1998). ... Signed by Carolina Panthers (September 2, 1998). ... Granted free agency (February 12, 1999). ... Re-signed by Panthers (April 7, 1999).
PLAYING EXPERIENCE: San Diego NFL, 1996; New York Giants NFL, 1997; Carolina NFL, 1998. ... Games/Games started: 1996 (9/0), 1997 (3/0), 1998 (14/10). Total: 26/10.
HONORS: Named offensive lineman on THE SPORTING NEWS college All-America second team (1995).
PRO STATISTICS: 1997—Fumbled once.

STONE, DWIGHT — WR/KR

PERSONAL: Born January 28, 1964, in Florala, Ala. ... 6-0/195.
HIGH SCHOOL: Florala (Ala.).
JUNIOR COLLEGE: Marion (Ala.) Military Academy.
COLLEGE: Middle Tennessee State (degree in social work).
TRANSACTIONS/CAREER NOTES: Signed as non-drafted free agent by Pittsburgh Steelers (May 19, 1987). ... Crossed picket line during players strike (October 7, 1987). ... Granted free agency (February 1, 1992). ... Re-signed by Steelers (May 15, 1992). ... Released by Steelers (August 30, 1993). ... Re-signed by Steelers (August 31, 1993). ... Granted unconditional free agency (February 17, 1995). ... Signed by Carolina Panthers (May 16, 1995). ... Granted unconditional free agency (February 16, 1996). ... Re-signed by Panthers (March 19, 1996). ... Granted unconditional free agency (February 14, 1997). ... Re-signed by Panthers (July 17, 1997). ... Granted unconditional free agency (February 13, 1998). ... Re-signed by Panthers (March 24, 1998). ... Granted unconditional free agency (February 12, 1999).
CHAMPIONSHIP GAME EXPERIENCE: Played in AFC championship game (1994 season). ... Played in NFC championship game (1996 season).
PRO STATISTICS: 1987—Recovered one fumble. 1989—Recovered one fumble. 1990—Recovered two fumbles. 1993—Recovered one fumble. 1997—Recovered one fumble and credited with a safety. 1998—Recovered a blocked punt in the end zone for a touchdown.
SINGLE GAME HIGHS (regular season): Receptions—6 (October 19, 1992, vs. Cincinnati); yards—124 (September 1, 1991, vs. San Diego); and touchdown receptions—2 (October 19, 1992, vs. Cincinnati).
STATISTICAL PLATEAUS: 100-yard receiving games: 1991 (1), 1992 (1), 1993 (1). Total: 3.

			RUSHING				RECEIVING				KICKOFF RETURNS				TOTALS		
Year Team	G	GS	Att.	Yds.	Avg.	TD	No.	Yds.	Avg.	TD	No.	Yds.	Avg.	TD	TD	2pt.	Pts.	Fum.
1987—Pittsburgh NFL	14	0	17	135	7.9	0	1	22	22.0	0	28	568	20.3	0	0	...	0	0
1988—Pittsburgh NFL	16	6	40	127	3.2	0	11	196	17.8	1	29	610	21.0	†1	2	...	12	5
1989—Pittsburgh NFL	16	8	10	53	5.3	0	7	92	13.1	0	7	173	24.7	0	0	...	0	2
1990—Pittsburgh NFL	16	2	2	-6	-3.0	0	19	332	17.5	1	5	91	18.2	0	1	...	6	1
1991—Pittsburgh NFL	16	8	1	2	2.0	0	32	649	§20.3	5	6	75	12.5	0	5	...	30	0
1992—Pittsburgh NFL	15	12	12	118	9.8	0	34	501	14.7	3	12	219	18.3	0	3	...	18	0
1993—Pittsburgh NFL	16	15	12	121	10.1	1	41	587	14.3	2	11	168	15.3	0	3	...	18	2
1994—Pittsburgh NFL	15	1	2	7	3.5	0	7	81	11.6	0	11	182	16.5	0	0	1	2	0
1995—Carolina NFL	16	1	1	3	3.0	0	0	0	...	0	12	269	22.4	0	0	0	0	0
1996—Carolina NFL	16	0	1	6	6.0	0	1	11	11.0	0	0	0	...	0	0	0	0	0
1997—Carolina NFL	16	0	0	0	...	0	0	0	...	0	3	76	25.3	0	0	0	2	0
1998—Carolina NFL	16	0	0	0	...	0	1	7	7.0	0	9	252	28.0	0	1	0	6	0
Pro totals (12 years)	188	52	98	566	5.8	1	154	2478	16.1	12	133	2683	20.2	1	15	1	94	10

STONE, RON — G — GIANTS

PERSONAL: Born July 20, 1971, in West Roxbury, Mass. ... 6-5/325.
HIGH SCHOOL: West Roxbury (Mass.).
COLLEGE: Boston College.
TRANSACTIONS/CAREER NOTES: Selected by Dallas Cowboys in fourth round (96th pick overall) of 1993 NFL draft. ... Signed by Cowboys (July 16, 1993). ... Active for four games with Cowboys (1993); did not play. ... Granted free agency (February 16, 1996). ... Tendered offer sheet by New York Giants (March 1, 1996). ... Cowboys declined to match offer (March 7, 1996).
PLAYING EXPERIENCE: Dallas NFL, 1994 and 1995; New York Giants NFL, 1996-1998. ... Games/Games started: 1994 (16/0), 1995 (16/1), 1996 (16/16), 1997 (16/16), 1998 (14/14). Total: 78/47.
CHAMPIONSHIP GAME EXPERIENCE: Member of Cowboys for NFC championship game (1993 season); inactive. ... Member of Super Bowl championship team (1993 and 1995 seasons). ... Played in NFC championship game (1994 and 1995 seasons).
PRO STATISTICS: 1994—Recovered one fumble. 1997—Recovered one fumble.

STORZ, ERIK — LB — JAGUARS

PERSONAL: Born June 24, 1975, in Rockaway, N.J. ... 6-2/234. ... Full name: Erik Erwin Storz.
HIGH SCHOOL: Morris Catholic (Rockaway, N.J.).
COLLEGE: Boston College (degree in marketing).
TRANSACTIONS/CAREER NOTES: Signed as non-drafted free agent by Cincinnati Bengals (April 21, 1998). ... Released by Bengals (July 25, 1998). ... Signed by Jacksonville Jaguars (August 19, 1998). ... Released by Jaguars (August 25, 1998). ... Re-signed by Jaguars to practice squad (November 25, 1998). ... Activated (December 25, 1998).
PLAYING EXPERIENCE: Jacksonville NFL, 1998. ... Games/Games started: 1/0.

STOUTMIRE, OMAR S COWBOYS

PERSONAL: Born July 9, 1974, in Pensacola, Fla. ... 5-11/201.
HIGH SCHOOL: Polytechnic (Long Beach, Calif.).
COLLEGE: Fresno State.
TRANSACTIONS/CAREER NOTES: Selected by Dallas Cowboys in seventh round (224th pick overall) of 1997 NFL draft. ... Signed by Cowboys (July 14, 1997).
PRO STATISTICS: 1997—Recovered one fumble. 1998—Recovered one fumble.

			INTERCEPTIONS				SACKS
Year Team	G	GS	No.	Yds.	Avg.	TD	No.
1997—Dallas NFL	16	2	2	8	4.0	0	2.0
1998—Dallas NFL	16	12	0	0	...	0	1.0
Pro totals (2 years)	32	14	2	8	4.0	0	3.0

STOVER, MATT K RAVENS

PERSONAL: Born January 27, 1968, in Dallas. ... 5-11/178. ... Full name: John Matthew Stover.
HIGH SCHOOL: Lake Highlands (Dallas).
COLLEGE: Louisiana Tech (degree in marketing, 1991).
TRANSACTIONS/CAREER NOTES: Selected by New York Giants in 12th round (329th pick overall) of 1990 NFL draft. ... Signed by Giants (July 23, 1990). ... On injured reserve with leg injury (September 4, 1990-entire season). ... Granted unconditional free agency (February 1, 1991). ... Signed by Cleveland Browns (March 15, 1991). ... Granted free agency (March 1, 1993). ... Re-signed by Browns (July 24, 1993). ... Released by Browns (August 30, 1993). ... Re-signed by Browns (August 31, 1993). ... Granted unconditional free agency (February 17, 1994). ... Re-signed by Browns (March 4, 1994). ... Browns franchise moved to Baltimore and renamed Ravens for 1996 season (March 11, 1996).
PRO STATISTICS: 1992—Had only pass attempt intercepted.

				KICKING				
Year Team	G	XPM	XPA	FGM	FGA	Lg.	50+	Pts.
1990—New York Giants NFL				Did not play.				
1991—Cleveland NFL	16	33	34	16	22	‡55	2-2	81
1992—Cleveland NFL	16	29	30	21	29	51	1-3	92
1993—Cleveland NFL	16	36	36	16	22	53	1-4	84
1994—Cleveland NFL	16	32	32	26	28	45	0-1	110
1995—Cleveland NFL	16	26	26	29	33	47	0-1	113
1996—Baltimore NFL	16	34	35	19	25	50	1-1	91
1997—Baltimore NFL	16	32	32	26	34	49	0-2	110
1998—Baltimore NFL	16	24	24	21	28	48	0-0	87
Pro totals (8 years)	128	246	249	174	221	55	5-14	768

STOYANOVICH, PETE K CHIEFS

PERSONAL: Born April 28, 1967, in Dearborn Heights, Mich. ... 5-11/191. ... Full name: Peter Stoyanovich. ... Name pronounced sto-YAWN-o-vich.
HIGH SCHOOL: Crestwood (Dearborn Heights, Mich.).
COLLEGE: Indiana (degree in public affairs, 1989).
TRANSACTIONS/CAREER NOTES: Selected by Miami Dolphins in eighth round (203rd pick overall) of 1989 NFL draft. ... Signed by Dolphins (July 27, 1989). ... Granted free agency (February 1, 1991). ... Re-signed by Dolphins (September 6, 1991). ... Activated (September 13, 1991). ... Granted unconditional free agency (February 17, 1994). ... Re-signed by Dolphins (February 21, 1994). ... Traded by Dolphins to Kansas City Chiefs for fifth-round pick (DT Barron Tanner) in 1997 draft (August 21, 1996).
CHAMPIONSHIP GAME EXPERIENCE: Played in AFC championship game (1992 season).
HONORS: Named kicker on THE SPORTING NEWS college All-America second team (1988). ... Named kicker on THE SPORTING NEWS NFL All-Pro team (1992).
POST SEASON RECORDS: Holds NFL postseason record for longest field goal—58 yards (January 5, 1991, vs. Kansas City).

		PUNTING						KICKING					
Year Team	G	No.	Yds.	Avg.	Net avg.	In. 20	Blk.	XPM	XPA	FGM	FGA	Lg.	50+	Pts.
1989—Miami NFL	16	0	0	...	...	0	0	38	39	19	26	*59	1-3	95
1990—Miami NFL	16	0	0	...	...	0	0	37	37	21	25	53	2-3	100
1991—Miami NFL	14	2	85	42.5	38.5	1	0	28	29	*31	▲37	53	3-5	§121
1992—Miami NFL	16	2	90	45.0	45.0	0	0	34	36	†30	§37	53	3-8	*124
1993—Miami NFL	16	0	0	...	...	0	0	37	37	24	32	52	2-2	109
1994—Miami NFL	16	0	0	...	...	0	0	35	35	24	31	50	1-2	107
1995—Miami NFL	16	0	0	...	...	0	0	37	37	27	34	51	2-5	118
1996—Kansas City NFL	16	0	0	...	...	0	0	34	34	17	24	45	0-1	85
1997—Kansas City NFL	16	1	24	24.0	24.0	1	0	35	36	26	27	54	2-2	113
1998—Kansas City NFL	16	1	29	29.0	29.0	1	0	34	34	27	32	53	2-2	115
Pro totals (10 years)	158	6	228	38.0	36.7	3	0	349	354	246	305	59	18-33	1087

STRAHAN, MICHAEL DE GIANTS

PERSONAL: Born November 21, 1971, in Houston. ... 6-4/280. ... Full name: Michael Anthony Strahan. ... Nephew of Art Strahan, defensive tackle with Atlanta Falcons (1968).
HIGH SCHOOL: Westbury (Houston), then Mannheim (West Germany) American.
COLLEGE: Texas Southern.

TRANSACTIONS/CAREER NOTES: Selected by New York Giants in second round (40th pick overall) of 1993 NFL draft. ... Signed by Giants (July 25, 1993). ... On injured reserve with foot injury (January 13, 1994-remainder of 1993 playoffs). ... Granted free agency (February 16, 1996). ... Re-signed by Giants (July 8, 1996).
HONORS: Named defensive end on THE SPORTING NEWS NFL All-Pro team (1997). ... Played in Pro Bowl (1997 and 1998 seasons).
PRO STATISTICS: 1995—Intercepted two passes for 56 yards. 1997—Recovered one fumble. 1998—Intercepted one pass for 24 yards and a touchdown.

Year Team	G	GS	SACKS
1993—New York Giants NFL	9	0	1.0
1994—New York Giants NFL	15	15	4.5
1995—New York Giants NFL	15	15	7.5
1996—New York Giants NFL	16	16	5.0
1997—New York Giants NFL	16	16	14.0
1998—New York Giants NFL	16	15	15.0
Pro totals (6 years)	87	77	47.0

STRICKLAND, FRED LB REDSKINS

PERSONAL: Born August 15, 1966, in Buffalo. ... 6-2/251. ... Full name: Fredrick William Strickland Jr.
HIGH SCHOOL: Lakeland Regional (Wanaque, N.J.).
COLLEGE: Purdue.
TRANSACTIONS/CAREER NOTES: Selected by Los Angeles Rams in second round (47th pick overall) of 1988 NFL draft. ... Signed by Rams (July 10, 1988). ... On injured reserve with foot injury (October 16, 1990-remainder of season). ... Granted free agency (February 1, 1991). ... Re-signed by Rams (August 13, 1991). ... Granted unconditional free agency (March 1, 1993). ... Signed by Minnesota Vikings (May 7, 1993). ... Granted unconditional free agency (February 17, 1994). ... Signed by Green Bay Packers (June 24, 1994). ... Granted unconditional free agency (February 16, 1996). ... Signed by Dallas Cowboys (March 11, 1996). ... Released by Cowboys (February 11, 1999). ... Signed by Washington Redskins (March 26, 1999).
CHAMPIONSHIP GAME EXPERIENCE: Played in NFC championship game (1989 and 1995 seasons).
PRO STATISTICS: 1988—Recovered two fumbles. 1989—Recovered one fumble for minus three yards. 1993—Recovered four fumbles for four yards. 1994—Recovered one fumble. 1996—Recovered one fumble. 1997—Recovered two fumbles.

			INTERCEPTIONS				SACKS
Year Team	G	GS	No.	Yds.	Avg.	TD	No.
1988—Los Angeles Rams NFL	16	0	0	0	...	0	4.0
1989—Los Angeles Rams NFL	12	12	2	56	28.0	0	2.0
1990—Los Angeles Rams NFL	5	5	0	0	...	0	0.0
1991—Los Angeles Rams NFL	14	10	0	0	...	0	1.0
1992—Los Angeles Rams NFL	16	0	0	0	...	0	0.0
1993—Minnesota NFL	16	15	0	0	...	0	0.0
1994—Green Bay NFL	16	14	1	7	7.0	0	0.0
1995—Green Bay NFL	14	10	0	0	...	0	0.0
1996—Dallas NFL	16	16	1	0	0.0	0	1.0
1997—Dallas NFL	15	14	0	0	...	0	0.5
1998—Dallas NFL	16	15	0	0	...	0	0.0
Pro totals (11 years)	156	111	4	63	15.8	0	8.5

STRINGER, KOREY OT VIKINGS

PERSONAL: Born May 8, 1974, in Warren, Ohio. ... 6-4/335.
HIGH SCHOOL: Harding (Warren, Ohio).
COLLEGE: Ohio State.
TRANSACTIONS/CAREER NOTES: Selected after junior season by Minnesota Vikings in first round (24th pick overall) of 1995 NFL draft. ... Signed by Vikings (July 22, 1995).
PLAYING EXPERIENCE: Minnesota NFL, 1995-1998. ... Games/Games started: 1995 (16/15), 1996 (16/15), 1997 (15/15), 1998 (14/14). Total: 61/59.
CHAMPIONSHIP GAME EXPERIENCE: Played in NFC championship game (1998 season).
HONORS: Named offensive lineman on THE SPORTING NEWS college All-America second team (1993). ... Named offensive lineman on THE SPORTING NEWS college All-America first team (1994).
PRO STATISTICS: 1995—Caught one pass for minus one yard and recovered two fumbles.

STRONG, MACK FB SEAHAWKS

PERSONAL: Born September 11, 1971, in Fort Benning, Ga. ... 6-0/235.
HIGH SCHOOL: Brookstone (Columbus, Ga.).
COLLEGE: Georgia.
TRANSACTIONS/CAREER NOTES: Signed as non-drafted free agent by Seattle Seahawks (April 28, 1993). ... Released by Seahawks (September 4, 1993). ... Re-signed by Seahawks to practice squad (September 6, 1993).
PRO STATISTICS: 1995—Returned four kickoffs for 65 yards and recovered one fumble. 1996—Recovered one fumble. 1997—Returned one kickoff for 16 yards and recovered one fumble. 1998—Recovered one fumble.
SINGLE GAME HIGHS (regular season): Attempts—10 (December 11, 1994, vs. Houston); yards—44 (December 11, 1994, vs. Houston); rushing touchdowns—1 (November 12, 1995, vs. Jacksonville).

				RUSHING				RECEIVING				TOTALS			
Year	Team	G	GS	Att.	Yds.	Avg.	TD	No.	Yds.	Avg.	TD	TD	2pt.	Pts.	Fum.
1993	—Seattle NFL							Did not play.							
1994	—Seattle NFL	8	1	27	114	4.2	2	3	3	1.0	0	2	0	12	1
1995	—Seattle NFL	16	1	8	23	2.9	1	12	117	9.8	3	4	0	24	2
1996	—Seattle NFL	14	8	5	8	1.6	0	9	78	8.7	0	0	0	0	0
1997	—Seattle NFL	16	10	4	8	2.0	0	13	91	7.0	2	2	0	12	0
1998	—Seattle NFL	16	5	15	47	3.1	0	8	48	6.0	2	2	0	12	2
Pro totals (5 years)		70	25	59	200	3.4	3	45	337	7.5	7	10	0	60	5

STRYZINSKI, DAN — P — FALCONS

PERSONAL: Born May 15, 1965, in Indianapolis. ... 6-2/200. ... Full name: Daniel Thomas Stryzinski. ... Name pronounced stri-ZIN-skee.
HIGH SCHOOL: Lincoln (Vincennes, Ind.).
COLLEGE: Indiana (bachelor of science degree in public finance and management, 1988).
TRANSACTIONS/CAREER NOTES: Signed as non-drafted free agent by Indianapolis Colts (July 1988). ... Released by Colts (August 23, 1988). ... Signed by Cleveland Browns (August 25, 1988). ... Released by Browns (August 30, 1988). ... Re-signed by Browns for 1989 season. ... Released by Browns (August 30, 1989). ... Signed by New Orleans Saints to developmental squad (October 11, 1989). ... Granted free agency after 1989 season. ... Signed by Pittsburgh Steelers (March 14, 1990). ... Granted unconditional free agency (February 1, 1992). ... Signed by Tampa Bay Buccaneers (February 21, 1992). ... Granted unconditional free agency (February 17, 1995). ... Signed by Atlanta Falcons (February 20, 1995).
CHAMPIONSHIP GAME EXPERIENCE: Played in NFC championship game (1998 season). ... Played in Super Bowl XXXIII (1998 season).
PRO STATISTICS: 1990—Rushed three times for 17 yards and recovered one fumble. 1991—Rushed four times for minus 11 yards, fumbled once and recovered two fumbles. 1992—Attempted two passes with two completions for 14 yards and rushed once for seven yards. 1994—Attempted one pass with a completion for 21 yards. 1995—Rushed once for no yards.

				PUNTING				
Year	Team	G	No.	Yds.	Avg.	Net avg.	In. 20	Blk.
1990	—Pittsburgh NFL	16	65	2454	37.8	34.1	18	1
1991	—Pittsburgh NFL	16	74	2996	40.5	36.2	10	1
1992	—Tampa Bay NFL	16	74	3015	40.7	36.2	15	0
1993	—Tampa Bay NFL	16	*93	3772	40.6	35.2	24	1
1994	—Tampa Bay NFL	16	72	2800	38.9	35.8	20	0
1995	—Atlanta NFL	16	67	2759	41.2	36.2	21	0
1996	—Atlanta NFL	16	75	3152	42.0	35.5	22	0
1997	—Atlanta NFL	16	89	3498	39.3	36.7	20	0
1998	—Atlanta NFL	16	74	2963	40.0	36.6	25	0
Pro totals (9 years)		144	683	27409	40.1	35.9	175	3

STRZELCZYK, JUSTIN — G/OT — STEELERS

PERSONAL: Born August 18, 1968, in Seneca, N.Y. ... 6-6/309. ... Full name: Justin Conrad Strzelczyk. ... Name pronounced STREL-zik.
HIGH SCHOOL: West Seneca (N.Y.) West.
COLLEGE: Maine.
TRANSACTIONS/CAREER NOTES: Selected by Pittsburgh Steelers in 11th round (293rd pick overall) of 1990 NFL draft. ... Signed by Steelers (July 18, 1990). ... On injured reserve with leg injury (October 28, 1998-remainder of season).
PLAYING EXPERIENCE: Pittsburgh NFL, 1990-1998. ... Games/Games started: 1990 (16/0), 1991 (16/0), 1992 (16/7), 1993 (16/12), 1994 (16/5), 1995 (16/14), 1996 (16/16), 1997 (14/14), 1998 (7/7). Total: 133/75.
CHAMPIONSHIP GAME EXPERIENCE: Played in AFC championship game (1994, 1995 and 1997 seasons). ... Played in Super Bowl XXX (1995 season).
PRO STATISTICS: 1993—Recovered one fumble.

STUBBLEFIELD, DANA — DT — REDSKINS

PERSONAL: Born November 14, 1970, in Cleves, Ohio. ... 6-2/315. ... Full name: Dana William Stubblefield.
HIGH SCHOOL: Taylor (Cleves, Ohio).
COLLEGE: Kansas.
TRANSACTIONS/CAREER NOTES: Selected by San Francisco 49ers in first round (26th pick overall) of 1993 NFL draft. ... Signed by 49ers (July 14, 1993). ... Granted unconditional free agency (February 13, 1998). ... Signed by Washington Redskins (February 23, 1998).
CHAMPIONSHIP GAME EXPERIENCE: Played in NFC championship game (1993, 1994 and 1997 seasons). ... Member of Super Bowl championship team (1994 season).
HONORS: Played in Pro Bowl (1994, 1995 and 1997 seasons). ... Named defensive tackle on THE SPORTING NEWS NFL All-Pro team (1997).
PRO STATISTICS: 1995—Intercepted one pass for 12 yards. 1996—Intercepted one pass for 15 yards and recovered one fumble.

Year	Team	G	GS	SACKS
1993	—San Francisco NFL	16	14	10.5
1994	—San Francisco NFL	14	14	8.5
1995	—San Francisco NFL	16	16	4.5
1996	—San Francisco NFL	15	15	1.0
1997	—San Francisco NFL	16	16	15.0
1998	—Washington NFL	7	7	1.5
Pro totals (6 years)		84	82	41.0

STUBBS, DANIEL   DE

PERSONAL: Born January 3, 1965, in Long Branch, N.J. ... 6-4/270. ... Full name: Daniel Stubbs II.
HIGH SCHOOL: Red Bank Regional (Little Silver, N.J.).
COLLEGE: Miami, Fla. (degree in criminal justice, 1988).
TRANSACTIONS/CAREER NOTES: Selected by San Francisco 49ers in second round (33rd pick overall) of 1988 NFL draft. ... Signed by 49ers (July 19, 1988). ... Traded by 49ers with RB Terrence Flagler and third- (traded to Pittsburgh) and 11th-round (traded to Los Angeles Raiders) picks in 1990 draft to Dallas Cowboys for second- (DL Dennis Brown) and third-round (WR Ronald Lewis) picks in 1990 draft (April 19, 1990). ... Granted free agency (February 1, 1991). ... Re-signed by Cowboys (August 10, 1991). ... Claimed on waivers by Cincinnati Bengals (November 6, 1991). ... Granted unconditional free agency (February 17, 1994). ... Re-signed by Bengals (June 14, 1994). ... Released by Bengals (August 16, 1994). ... Signed by Philadelphia Eagles (April 7, 1995). ... Granted unconditional free agency (February 16, 1996). ... Signed by Miami Dolphins (April 4, 1996). ... Granted unconditional free agency (February 14, 1997). ... Re-signed by Dolphins (March 18, 1997). ... On injured reserve with knee injury (September 3, 1997-remainder of season). ... Granted unconditional free agency (February 12, 1999).
CHAMPIONSHIP GAME EXPERIENCE: Played in NFC championship game (1988 season). ... Member of Super Bowl championship team (1988 season).
HONORS: Named defensive lineman on THE SPORTING NEWS college All-America second team (1986). ... Named defensive lineman on THE SPORTING NEWS college All-America first team (1987).
PRO STATISTICS: 1988—Recovered one fumble. 1990—Recovered two fumbles. 1991—Recovered one fumble. 1992—Recovered one fumble. 1993—Recovered one fumble. 1995—Recovered one fumble.

Year Team	G	GS	SACKS
1988—San Francisco NFL	16	1	6.0
1989—San Francisco NFL	16	0	4.5
1990—Dallas NFL	16	15	7.5
1991—Dallas NFL	9	0	1.0
—Cincinnati NFL	7	0	3.0
1992—Cincinnati NFL	16	12	9.0
1993—Cincinnati NFL	16	0	5.0
1994—	Did not play.		
1995—Philadelphia NFL	16	5	5.5
1996—Miami NFL	16	15	9.0
1997—Miami NFL	1	0	1.0
1998—Miami NFL	5	1	0.0
Pro totals (10 years)	134	49	51.5

STUCKEY, SHAWN   LB   PATRIOTS

PERSONAL: Born October 22, 1975, in Daleville, Ala. ... 6-0/229.
HIGH SCHOOL: Daleville (Ala.).
COLLEGE: Troy (Ala.) State.
TRANSACTIONS/CAREER NOTES: Signed as non-drafted free agent by Minnesota Vikings (April 22, 1998). ... Released by Vikings (August 24, 1998). ... Signed by New England Patriots to practice squad (September 10, 1998). ... Released by Patriots (October 15, 1998). ... Re-signed by Patriots to practice squad (November 4, 1998). ... Activated (November 13, 1998).
PLAYING EXPERIENCE: New England NFL, 1998. ... Games/Games started: 6/0.
PRO STATISTICS: 1998—Recovered one fumble.

STYLES, LORENZO   LB   RAMS

PERSONAL: Born January 31, 1974, in Sharon, Pa, ... 6-1/245.
HIGH SCHOOL: Independence (Columbus, Ohio), then Farrell (Pa.).
COLLEGE: Ohio State.
TRANSACTIONS/CAREER NOTES: Selected after junior season by Atlanta Falcons in third round (77th pick overall) of 1995 NFL draft. ... Signed by Falcons (July 21, 1995). ... Released by Falcons (August 26, 1997). ... Signed by St. Louis Rams (November 4, 1997). ... On injured reserve with shoulder injury (December 9, 1997-remainder of season). ... Granted free agency (February 13, 1998). ... Re-signed by Rams (March 25, 1998). ... On injured reserve with shoulder injury (November 30, 1998-remainder of season).
PLAYING EXPERIENCE: Atlanta NFL, 1995 and 1996; St. Louis NFL, 1997 and 1998. ... Games/Games started: 1995 (12/0), 1996 (16/0), 1997 (3/0), 1998 (7/3). Total: 38/3.
PRO STATISTICS: 1996—Returned one kickoff for 12 yards.

SUALUA, NICKY   FB   COWBOYS

PERSONAL: Born April 15, 1975, in Santa Ana, Calif. ... 5-11/260.
HIGH SCHOOL: Mater Dei (Santa Ana, Calif.).
COLLEGE: Ohio State.
TRANSACTIONS/CAREER NOTES: Selected by Dallas Cowboys in fourth round (129th pick overall) of 1997 NFL draft. ... Signed by Cowboys (July 14, 1997).
PLAYING EXPERIENCE: Dallas NFL, 1997 and 1998. ... Games/ Games started: 1997 (10/1), 1998 (16/0). Total: 26/1.

SULLIVAN, CHRIS — DE — PATRIOTS

PERSONAL: Born March 14, 1973, in North Attleboro, Mass. ... 6-4/279. ... Full name: Christopher Patrick Sullivan.
HIGH SCHOOL: North Attleboro (Mass.).
COLLEGE: Boston College (degree in sociology, 1995).
TRANSACTIONS/CAREER NOTES: Selected by New England Patriots in fourth round (119th pick overall) of 1996 NFL draft. ... Signd by Patriots (July 12, 1996). ... Granted free agency (February 12, 1999).
PLAYING EXPERIENCE: New England NFL, 1996-1998. ... Games/Games started: 1996 (16/0), 1997 (16/10), 1998 (15/10). Total: 47/20.
CHAMPIONSHIP GAME EXPERIENCE: Played in AFC championship game (1996 season). ... Played in Super Bowl XXXI (1996 season).
PRO STATISTICS: 1996—Recovered one fumble. 1998—Returned two kickoffs for 14 yards and credited with two sacks.

SUPERNAW, KYWIN — S — LIONS

PERSONAL: Born June 2, 1975, in Claremore, Okla. ... 6-1/206.
HIGH SCHOOL: Skiatook (Okla.).
COLLEGE: Northeastern Oklahoma A&M, then Indiana.
TRANSACTIONS/CAREER NOTES: Signed as non-drafted free agent by Detroit Lions (April 24, 1998). ... Released by Lions (August 30, 1998). ... Re-signed by Lions to practice squad (September 1, 1998). ... Activated (December 1, 1998).
PLAYING EXPERIENCE: Detroit NFL, 1998. ... Games/Games started: 2/0.

SURTAIN, PATRICK — CB — DOLPHINS

PERSONAL: Born June 19, 1976, in New Orleans, La. ... 5-11/197. ... Full name: Patrick Frank Surtain.
HIGH SCHOOL: Edna Karr (New Orleans).
COLLEGE: Southern Mississippi.
TRANSACTIONS/CAREER NOTES: Selected by Miami Dolphins in second round (44th pick overall) of 1998 NFL draft. ... Signed by Dolphins (July 21, 1998).
HONORS: Named cornerback on The Sporting News college All-America second team (1997).

			INTERCEPTIONS		
Year Team	G	GS	No.	Yds.	Avg.	TD
1998—Miami NFL	16	0	2	1	0.5	0

SUTTER, RYAN — S — PANTHERS

PERSONAL: Born September 14, 1974, in Fort Collins, Colo. ... 6-1/203. ... Full name: Ryan Allen Sutter.
HIGH SCHOOL: Fort Collins (Colo.).
COLLEGE: Colorado.
TRANSACTIONS/CAREER NOTES: Selected by Baltimore Ravens in fifth round (133rd pick overall) of 1998 NFL draft. ... Signed by Ravens for 1998 season. ... Released by Ravens (August 25, 1998). ... Signed by Carolina Panthers to practice squad (September 1, 1998). ... Activated (November 28, 1998). ... On injured reserve with shoulder injury (December 5, 1998-remainder of season).
PLAYING EXPERIENCE: Carolina NFL, 1998. ... Games/Games started: 1/0.

SUTTON, MIKE — DE — TITANS

PERSONAL: Born April 21, 1975, in Jacksonville, N.C. ... 6-4/265.
HIGH SCHOOL: Salmen (Slidell, La.).
COLLEGE: Louisiana State.
TRANSACTIONS/CAREER NOTES: Signed as non-drafted free agent by Tennessee Oilers (April 20, 1998). ... Released by Oilers (August 26, 1998). ... Re-signed by Oilers to practice squad (September 1, 1998). ... Activated (December 12, 1998). ... Oilers franchise renamed Tennessee Titans for 1999 season (December 26, 1998). ... Assigned by Titans to Rhein Fire in 1999 NFL Europe enhancement allocation program (February 22, 1999).
PLAYING EXPERIENCE: Tennessee NFL, 1998. ... Games/Games started: 1/0.

SWANN, ERIC — DT — CARDINALS

PERSONAL: Born August 16, 1970, in Pinehurst, N.C. ... 6-5/313. ... Full name: Eric Jerrod Swann.
HIGH SCHOOL: Western Harnett (Lillington, N.C.).
COLLEGE: Wake Technical College, N.C. (did not play football).
TRANSACTIONS/CAREER NOTES: Played with Bay State Titans of Minor League Football System (1990). ... Selected by Phoenix Cardinals in first round (sixth pick overall) of 1991 NFL draft. ... Signed by Cardinals (April 24, 1991). ... On injured reserve with knee injury (August 27-September 27, 1991). ... On injured reserve with knee injury (November 17, 1993-remainder of season). ... Cardinals franchise renamed Arizona Cardinals for 1994 season. ... Designated by Cardinals as franchise player (February 16, 1996). ... On injured reserve with dislocated finger (December 17, 1997-remainder of season). ... On injured reserve with knee injury (December 10, 1998-remainder of season).
HONORS: Named defensive tackle on The Sporting News NFL All-Pro team (1995). ... Played in Pro Bowl (1995 and 1996 seasons).
PRO STATISTICS: 1992—Credited with one safety. 1993—Credited with one safety and recovered one fumble. 1994—Credited with one safety and recovered one fumble for 10 yards. 1995—Recovered two fumbles. 1996—Recovered three fumbles for 11 yards. 1997—Rushed once for no yards, fumbled once and recovered one fumble.

Year Team	G	GS	SACKS
1991—Phoenix NFL	12	3	4.0
1992—Phoenix NFL	16	11	2.0
1993—Phoenix NFL	9	9	3.5
1994—Arizona NFL	16	16	7.0
1995—Arizona NFL	13	12	8.5
1996—Arizona NFL	16	15	5.0
1997—Arizona NFL	13	13	7.5
1998—Arizona NFL	7	5	4.0
Pro totals (8 years)	102	84	41.5

SWAYDA, SHAWN — DE — FALCONS

PERSONAL: Born September 4, 1974, in Phoenix. ... 6-5/297. ... Full name: Shawn Gerald Swayda.
HIGH SCHOOL: Brophy Prep (Phoenix).
COLLEGE: Arizona State.
TRANSACTIONS/CAREER NOTES: Selected by Chicago Bears in sixth round (196th pick overall) of 1997 NFL draft. ... Signed by Bears (July 10, 1997). ... Released by Bears (August 18, 1997). ... Signed by Dallas Cowboys to practice squad (October 9, 1997). ... Released by Cowboys (November 4, 1997). ... Signed by Detroit Lions to practice squad (November 24, 1997). ... Granted free agency after 1997 season. ... Signed by Atlanta Falcons (March 24, 1998).
PLAYING EXPERIENCE: Atlanta NFL, 1998. ... Games/Games started: 5/0.
CHAMPIONSHIP GAME EXPERIENCE: Member of Falcons for NFC championship game (1998 season); inactive. ... Member of Falcons for Super Bowl XXXIII (1998 season); inactive.

SWAYNE, HARRY — OT — RAVENS

PERSONAL: Born February 2, 1965, in Philadelphia. ... 6-5/295. ... Full name: Harry Vonray Swayne.
HIGH SCHOOL: Cardinal Dougherty (Philadelphia).
COLLEGE: Rutgers.
TRANSACTIONS/CAREER NOTES: Selected by Tampa Bay Buccaneers in seventh round (190th pick overall) of 1987 NFL draft. ... Signed by Buccaneers (July 18, 1987). ... On injured reserve with fractured hand (September 8-October 31, 1987). ... On injured reserve with neck injury (November 18, 1988-remainder of season). ... Granted free agency (February 1, 1990). ... Re-signed by Buccaneers (July 19, 1990). ... Granted unconditional free agency (February 1, 1991). ... Signed by San Diego Chargers (April 1, 1991). ... On injured reserve with fractured leg (November 26, 1991-remainder of season). ... Designated by Chargers as transition player (February 25, 1993). ... Tendered offer sheet by Phoenix Cardinals (April 9, 1993). ... Offer matched by Chargers (April 15, 1993). ... On physically unable to perform list (July 24-August 21, 1995). ... Free agency status changed by Chargers from transitional to unconditional (February 16, 1996). ... Re-signed by Chargers (July 24, 1996). ... Granted unconditional free agency (February 14, 1997). ... Signed by Denver Broncos (April 17, 1997). ... Granted unconditional free agency (February 12, 1999). ... Signed by Baltimore Ravens (February 26, 1999).
PLAYING EXPERIENCE: Tampa Bay NFL, 1987-1990; San Diego NFL, 1991-1996; Denver NFL, 1997 and 1998. ... Games/Games started: 1987 (8/2), 1988 (10/1), 1989 (16/0), 1990 (10/0), 1991 (12/12), 1992 (16/16), 1993 (11/11), 1994 (16/16), 1995 (16/16), 1996 (16/3), 1997 (7/0), 1998 (16/16). Total: 154/93.
CHAMPIONSHIP GAME EXPERIENCE: Played in AFC championship game (1994, 1997 and 1998 seasons). ... Played in Super Bowl XXIX (1994 season). ... Member of Super Bowl championship team (1997 and 1998 seasons).
PRO STATISTICS: 1998—Recovered one fumble.

SWEENEY, JIM — C/G — STEELERS

PERSONAL: Born August 8, 1962, in Pittsburgh. ... 6-4/297. ... Full name: James Joseph Sweeney.
HIGH SCHOOL: Seton-LaSalle (Pittsburgh).
COLLEGE: Pittsburgh (degree in administration of justice).
TRANSACTIONS/CAREER NOTES: Selected by Pittsburgh Maulers in 1984 USFL territorial draft. ... Selected by New York Jets in second round (37th pick overall) of 1984 NFL draft. ... Signed by Jets (July 12, 1984). ... Granted free agency (February 1, 1990). ... Re-signed by Jets (August 27, 1990). ... Released by Jets (August 30, 1993). ... Re-signed by Jets (August 31, 1993). ... Granted unconditional free agency (February 17, 1994). ... Re-signed by Jets (May 2, 1994). ... Granted unconditional free agency (February 17, 1995). ... Signed by Seattle Seahawks (March 23, 1995). ... Released by Seahawks (July 19, 1996). ... Signed by Pittsburgh Steelers (August 19, 1996).
PLAYING EXPERIENCE: New York Jets NFL, 1984-1994; Seattle NFL, 1995; Pittsburgh NFL, 1996-1998. ... Games/Games started: 1984 (10/2), 1985 (16/16), 1986 (16/16), 1987 (12/12), 1988 (16/16), 1989 (16/16), 1990 (16/16), 1991 (16/16), 1992 (16/16), 1993 (16/16), 1994 (16/16), 1995 (16/16), 1996 (16/0), 1997 (16/1), 1998 (8/1). Total: 222/176.
CHAMPIONSHIP GAME EXPERIENCE: Played in AFC championship game (1997 season).
HONORS: Named guard on THE SPORTING NEWS college All-America second team (1983).
PRO STATISTICS: 1990—Recovered one fumble. 1994—Recovered one fumble.

SWILLING, PAT — DE/LB

PERSONAL: Born October 25, 1964, in Toccoa, Ga. ... 6-3/245. ... Full name: Patrick Travis Swilling.
HIGH SCHOOL: Stephens County (Toccoa, Ga.).
COLLEGE: Georgia Tech.
TRANSACTIONS/CAREER NOTES: Selected by Jacksonville Bulls in 1986 USFL territorial draft. ... Selected by New Orleans Saints in third round (60th pick overall) of 1986 NFL draft. ... Signed by Saints (July 21, 1986). ... Granted free agency (February 1, 1990). ... Re-signed by Saints (September 1, 1990). ... Granted free agency (February 1, 1992). ... Tendered offer sheet by Detroit Lions (March 23, 1992). ... Offer matched by Saints (March 30, 1992). ... Traded by Saints to Detroit Lions for first- (OT Willie Roaf) and fourth-round (RB Lorenzo Neal) picks in 1993 draft (April 25, 1993). ... Granted unconditional free agency (February 17, 1995). ... Signed by Los Angeles Raiders (April 11, 1995).

... Raiders franchise moved to Oakland (July 21, 1995). ... Released by Raiders following 1996 season. ... Re-signed by Raiders (May 29, 1998). ... Granted unconditional free agency (February 12, 1999).
HONORS: Named defensive lineman on THE SPORTING NEWS college All-America second team (1985). ... Played in Pro Bowl (1990-1993 seasons). ... Named outside linebacker on THE SPORTING NEWS NFL All-Pro team (1991 and 1992).
PRO STATISTICS: 1987—Recovered three fumbles for one yard. 1988—Recovered one fumble. 1989—Recovered one fumble. 1991—Recovered one fumble for five yards. 1992—Recovered one fumble. 1993—Recovered one fumble. 1994—Recovered one fumble for five yards. 1996—Recovered one fumble for 49 yards. 1998—Recovered one fumble.

				INTERCEPTIONS				SACKS
Year Team		G	GS	No.	Yds.	Avg.	TD	No.
1986—New Orleans NFL		16	0	0	0	...	0	4.0
1987—New Orleans NFL		12	12	1	10	10.0	0	10.5
1988—New Orleans NFL		15	14	0	0	...	0	7.0
1989—New Orleans NFL		16	15	1	14	14.0	0	16.5
1990—New Orleans NFL		16	16	0	0	...	0	11.0
1991—New Orleans NFL		16	16	1	39	39.0	∞1	17.0
1992—New Orleans NFL		16	16	0	0	...	0	10.5
1993—Detroit NFL		14	14	3	16	5.3	0	6.5
1994—Detroit NFL		16	7	0	0	...	0	3.5
1995—Oakland NFL		16	16	0	0	...	0	13.0
1996—Oakland NFL		16	16	0	0	...	0	6.0
1997—					Did not play.			
1998—Oakland NFL		16	0	0	0	...	0	2.0
Pro totals (12 years)		185	142	6	79	13.2	1	107.5

SWINGER, RASHOD   DT   CARDINALS

PERSONAL: Born November 27, 1974, in Paterson, N.J. ... 6-2/286. ... Full name: Rashod Alexander Swinger.
HIGH SCHOOL: Manalapan (N.J.).
COLLEGE: Rutgers (degree in communications).
TRANSACTIONS/CAREER NOTES: Signed as non-drafted free agent by San Diego Chargers (April 21, 1997). ... Released by Chargers (August 25, 1997). ... Re-signed by Chargers to practice squad (August 26, 1997). ... Released by Chargers (September 2, 1997). ... Signed by Arizona Cardinals to practice squad (September 8, 1997). ... Activated (December 17, 1997).
PLAYING EXPERIENCE: Arizona NFL, 1997 and 1998. ... Games/Games started: 1997 (1/0), 1998 (16/11). Total: 17/11.

SZOTT, DAVE   G   CHIEFS

PERSONAL: Born December 12, 1967, in Passaic, N.J. ... 6-4/293. ... Full name: David Andrew Szott. ... Name pronounced ZOT.
HIGH SCHOOL: Clifton (N.J.).
COLLEGE: Penn State (degree in political science).
TRANSACTIONS/CAREER NOTES: Selected by Kansas City Chiefs in seventh round (180th pick overall) of 1990 NFL draft. ... Signed by Chiefs (July 25, 1990). ... Granted free agency (March 1, 1993). ... Re-signed by Chiefs for 1993 season. ... On injured reserve with arm injury (December 2, 1998-remainder of season).
PLAYING EXPERIENCE: Kansas City NFL, 1990-1998. ... Games/Games started: 1990 (16/11), 1991 (16/16), 1992 (16/16), 1993 (14/13), 1994 (16/16), 1995 (16/16), 1996 (16/16), 1997 (16/16), 1998 (1/1). Total: 127/121.
CHAMPIONSHIP GAME EXPERIENCE: Played in AFC championship game (1993 season).
PRO STATISTICS: 1990—Recovered one fumble. 1991—Recovered one fumble. 1997—Recovered one fumble.

TALLEY, BEN   LB   FALCONS

PERSONAL: Born July 14, 1972, in Griffin, Ga. ... 6-3/245. ... Full name: Benjamin Jermaine Talley.
HIGH SCHOOL: Griffin (Ga.).
COLLEGE: Tennessee.
TRANSACTIONS/CAREER NOTES: Selected by New York Giants in fourth round (133rd pick overall) of 1995 NFL draft. ... Signed by Giants (July 23, 1995). ... On injured reserve with knee injury (August 12, 1996-entire season). ... Released by Giants (July 18, 1997). ... Signed by Atlanta Falcons (March 13, 1998). ... Granted free agency (February 12, 1999). ... Re-signed by Falcons (May 21, 1999).
PLAYING EXPERIENCE: New York Giants NFL, 1995; Atlanta NFL, 1998. ... Games/ Games started: 1995 (4/0), 1998 (8/0). Total: 12/0.
CHAMPIONSHIP GAME EXPERIENCE: Member of Falcons for NFC championship game (1998 season); did not play. ... Played in Super Bowl XXXIII (1998 season).
PRO STATISTICS: 1998—Recovered one fumble.

TAMM, RALPH   G/C

PERSONAL: Born March 11, 1966, in Philadelphia. ... 6-4/280. ... Full name: Ralph Earl Tamm.
HIGH SCHOOL: Bensalem (Pa.).
COLLEGE: West Chester (Pa.).
TRANSACTIONS/CAREER NOTES: Selected by New York Jets in ninth round (230th pick overall) of 1988 NFL draft. ... Signed by Jets for 1988 season. ... On injured reserve (August 29, 1988-entire season). ... Granted unconditional free agency (February 1, 1989). ... Signed by Washington Redskins for 1989 season. ... On injured reserve with shoulder injury (September 1, 1989-entire season). ... Granted unconditional free agency (February 1, 1990). ... Signed by Cleveland Browns (March 21, 1990). ... Released by Browns (September 5, 1991). ... Signed by Redskins (September 11, 1991). ... Released by Redskins (November 1991). ... Signed by Cincinnati Bengals (December 9, 1991). ... Granted unconditional free agency (February 1, 1992). ... Signed by San Francisco 49ers (March 29, 1992). ... On injured reserve with knee injury (December 15, 1992-January 16, 1993). ... Released by 49ers (May 5, 1995). ... Signed by Denver Broncos (June 7, 1995). ... Granted unconditional free agency (February 14, 1997). ... Signed by Kansas City Chiefs (June 9, 1997). ... Granted unconditional free agency (February 12, 1999).

PLAYING EXPERIENCE: Cleveland NFL, 1990; Cleveland (1)-Washington (2)-Cincinnati (1) NFL, 1991; San Francisco NFL, 1992-1994; Denver NFL, 1995 and 1996; Kansas City NFL, 1997 and 1998. ... Games/Games started: 1990 (16/12), 1991 (Clev.-1/0; Wash.-2/0; Cin.-1/0; Total: 4/0), 1992 (14/1), 1993 (16/16), 1994 (1/1), 1995 (13/1), 1996 (9/0), 1997 (16/0), 1998 (16/0). Total: 105/31.
CHAMPIONSHIP GAME EXPERIENCE: Played in NFC championship game (1992-1994 seasons). ... Member of Super Bowl championship team (1994 season).
PRO STATISTICS: 1993—Recovered one fumble in end zone for a touchdown. 1995—Recovered one fumble.

TANNER, BARRON   DT   DOLPHINS

PERSONAL: Born September 14, 1973, in Athens, Texas. ... 6-3/312. ... Full name: Barron Keith Tanner.
HIGH SCHOOL: Athens (Texas).
COLLEGE: Oklahoma.
TRANSACTIONS/CAREER NOTES: Selected by Miami Dolphins in fifth round (149th pick overall) of 1997 NFL draft. ... Signed by Dolphins (July 8, 1997).
PLAYING EXPERIENCE: Miami NFL, 1997 and 1998. ... Games/ Games started: 1997 (16/0), 1998 (13/0). Total: 29/0.

TANUVASA, MAA   DT   BRONCOS

PERSONAL: Born November 6, 1970, in America Samoa. ... 6-2/270. ... Full name: Maa Junior Tanuvasa. ... Name pronounced MAW-aw TAW-new-VA-suh.
HIGH SCHOOL: Mililani (Hawaii).
COLLEGE: Hawaii.
TRANSACTIONS/CAREER NOTES: Selected by Los Angeles Rams in eighth round (209th pick overall) of 1993 NFL draft. ... Signed by Rams for 1993 season. ... On injured reserve with knee injury (August 21, 1993- entire season). ... Released by Rams (August 23, 1994). ... Signed by Steelers to practice squad (December 1, 1994). ... Granted free agency after 1994 season. ... Signed by Denver Broncos (February 22, 1995). ... Released by Broncos (August 27, 1995). ... Re-signed by Broncos to practice squad (August 28, 1995). ... Activated (October 24, 1995). ... Granted free agency (February 14, 1997). ... Re-signed by Broncos (February 14, 1997).
CHAMPIONSHIP GAME EXPERIENCE: Played in AFC championship game (1997 and 1998 seasons). ... Member of Super Bowl championship team (1997 and 1998 seasons).
PRO STATISTICS: 1996—Recovered one fumble. 1998—Returned one kickoff for 13 yards and recovered two fumbles for minus one yard.

Year Team	G	GS	SACKS
1993—Los Angeles Rams NFL	Did not play.		
1994—Pittsburgh NFL	Did not play.		
1995—Denver NFL	1	0	0.0
1996—Denver NFL	16	1	5.0
1997—Denver NFL	15	5	8.5
1998—Denver NFL	16	16	8.5
Pro totals (4 years)	**48**	**22**	**22.0**

TATE, ROBERT   WR/KR   VIKINGS

PERSONAL: Born October 19, 1973, in Harrisburg, Pa. ... 5-10/186.
HIGH SCHOOL: John Harris (Harrisburg, Pa.), then Milford (Conn.) Academy.
COLLEGE: Cincinnati.
TRANSACTIONS/CAREER NOTES: Selected by Minnesota Vikings in sixth round (183rd pick overall) of 1997 NFL draft. ... Signed by Vikings (June 17, 1997). ... On injured reserve with ankle injury (October 8, 1997-remainder of season).
CHAMPIONSHIP GAME EXPERIENCE: Member of Vikings for NFC championship game (1998 season); inactive.
PRO STATISTICS: 1998—Caught one pass for 17 yards.
SINGLE GAME HIGHS (regular season): Receptions—1 (November 22, 1998, vs. Green Bay); yards—17 (November 22, 1998, vs Green Bay); and touchdown receptions—0.

			KICKOFF RETURNS			TOTALS			
Year Team	G	GS	No.	Yds.	Avg.	TD	TD	2pt.	Pts.	Fum.
1997—Minnesota NFL	4	0	10	196	19.6	0	0	0	0	0
1998—Minnesota NFL	15	1	2	43	21.5	0	0	0	0	0
Pro totals (2 years)	**19**	**1**	**12**	**239**	**19.9**	**0**	**0**	**0**	**0**	**0**

TATE, WILLY   TE

PERSONAL: Born September 7, 1972, in Fontana, Calif. ... 6-3/243. ... Full name: William R. Tate.
HIGH SCHOOL: Elk Grove (Calif.).
COLLEGE: Oregon.
TRANSACTIONS/CAREER NOTES: Signed by Kansas City Chiefs as a non-drafted free agent (May 1, 1995). ... Released by Chiefs (August 22, 1995). ... Re-signed by Chiefs to practice squad (August 29, 1995). ... Played for Scottish Claymores of World League (1996). ... Released by Chiefs (August 20, 1996). ... Signed by Tampa Bay Buccaneers (August 27, 1996). ... Released by Buccaneers (August 17, 1997). ... Played for Scottish Claymores of NFL Europe League (1998). ... Signed by Chiefs (June 23, 1998). ... Released by Chiefs (September 8, 1998).
PLAYING EXPERIENCE: Scottish Claymores W.L., 1996; Tampa Bay NFL, 1996; Scottish NFLE, 1998; Kansas City NFL, 1998. ... Games/Games started: W.L. 1996 (games played unavailable); NFL 1996 (13/0), NFLE 1998 (games played unavailable), NFL 1998 (1/0). Total NFL: 14/0.
PRO STATISTICS: W.L.: 1996—Caught 19 passes for 262 yards and returned one kickoff for no yards. NFLE: 1998—Caught 15 passes for 174 yards and two touchdowns.

TATUM, KINNON — LB — PANTHERS

PERSONAL: Born July 19, 1975, in Fayetteville, N.C. ... 6-0/222. ... Full name: Kinnon Ray Tatum.
HIGH SCHOOL: Douglas Byrd (Fayetteville, N.C.).
COLLEGE: Notre Dame.
TRANSACTIONS/CAREER NOTES: Selected by Carolina Panthers in third round (87th pick overall) of 1997 NFL draft. ... Signed by Panthers for 1997 season.
PLAYING EXPERIENCE: Carolina NFL, 1997 and 1998. ... Games/ Games started: 1997 (16/0), 1998 (15/0). Total: 31/0.
PRO STATISTICS: 1998—Recovered one fumble.

TAYLOR, AARON — G — CHARGERS

PERSONAL: Born November 14, 1972, in San Francisco. ... 6-4/305. ... Full name: Aaron Matthew Taylor.
HIGH SCHOOL: De La Salle Catholic (Concord, Calif.).
COLLEGE: Notre Dame (degree in sociology, 1994).
TRANSACTIONS/CAREER NOTES: Selected by Green Bay Packers in first round (16th pick overall) of 1994 NFL draft . ... Signed by Packers (July 26, 1994). ... On physically unable to perform list with knee injury (August 25, 1994-entire season). ... On injured reserve with knee injury (January 11, 1996-remainder of 1995 playoffs). ... Granted unconditional free agency (February 13, 1998). ... Signed by San Diego Chargers (March 6, 1998).
PLAYING EXPERIENCE: Green Bay NFL, 1995-1997; San Diego NFL, 1998. ... Games/Games started: 1995 (16/16), 1996 (16/16), 1997 (14/14), 1998 (15/15). Total: 61/61.
CHAMPIONSHIP GAME EXPERIENCE: Played in NFC championship game (1996 and 1997 seasons). ... Member of Super Bowl championship team (1996 season). ... Played in Super Bowl XXXII (1997 season).
HONORS: Named offensive lineman on The Sporting News college All-America first team (1992 and 1993). ... Outland Award winner (1993). ... Lombardi Award winner (1993).
PRO STATISTICS: 1995—Recovered two fumbles. 1996—Recovered one fumble. 1998—Recovered one fumble.

TAYLOR, BOBBY — CB — EAGLES

PERSONAL: Born December 28, 1973, in Houston. ... 6-3/216. ... Full name: Robert Taylor. ... Son of Robert Taylor, silver medalist in 100-meter dash and member of gold-medal winning 400-meter relay team at 1972 Summer Olympics.
HIGH SCHOOL: Longview (Texas).
COLLEGE: Notre Dame.
TRANSACTIONS/CAREER NOTES: Selected after junior season by Philadelphia Eagles in second round (49th pick overall) of 1995 NFL draft. ... Signed by Eagles (July 19, 1995). ... On injured reserve with knee injury (October 17, 1997-remainder of season). ... Granted free agency (February 13, 1998). ... Re-signed by Eagles (June 11, 1998).
HONORS: Named defensive back on The Sporting News college All-America first team (1993 and 1994).
PRO STATISTICS: 1996—Credited with one sack, fumbled once and recovered two fumbles for nine yards. 1997—Credited with two sacks.

			INTERCEPTIONS		
Year Team	G	GS	No.	Yds.	Avg.	TD
1995—Philadelphia NFL	16	12	2	52	26.0	0
1996—Philadelphia NFL	16	16	3	-1	-0.3	0
1997—Philadelphia NFL	6	5	0	0	...	0
1998—Philadelphia NFL	11	10	0	0	...	0
Pro totals (4 years)	49	43	5	51	10.2	0

TAYLOR, CORDELL — CB — JAGUARS

PERSONAL: Born December 22, 1973, in Norfolk, Va. ... 5-11/187. ... Full name: Cordell Jerome Taylor.
HIGH SCHOOL: Booker T. Washington (Norfolk, Va.).
COLLEGE: Hampton (Va.).
TRANSACTIONS/CAREER NOTES: Selected by Jacksonville Jaguars in second round (57th pick overall) of 1998 NFL draft. ... Signed by Jaguars (May 26, 1998).
PLAYING EXPERIENCE: Jacksonville NFL, 1998. ... Games/Games started: 10/0.

TAYLOR, FRED — RB — JAGUARS

PERSONAL: Born June 27, 1976, in Pahokee, Fla. ... 6-0/226. ... Full name: Frederick Antwon Taylor.
HIGH SCHOOL: Glades Central (Belle Glade, Fla.).
COLLEGE: Florida.
TRANSACTIONS/CAREER NOTES: Selected by Jacksonville Jaguars in first round (ninth pick overall) of 1998 NFL draft. ... Signed by Jaguars (July 6, 1998).
HONORS: Named running back on The Sporting News college All-America third team (1997).
PRO STATISTICS: 1998—Recovered one fumble for nine yards.
SINGLE GAME HIGHS (regular season): Attempts—32 (December 6, 1998, vs. Detroit); yards—183 (December 6, 1998, vs. Detroit); and rushing touchdowns—3 (November 15, 1998, vs. Tampa Bay).
STATISTICAL PLATEAUS: 100-yard rushing games: 1998 (6).

Year Team	G	GS	RUSHING Att.	Yds.	Avg.	TD	RECEIVING No.	Yds.	Avg.	TD	TOTALS TD	2pt.	Pts.	Fum.
1998—Jacksonville NFL	15	12	264	1223	4.6	14	44	421	9.6	3	17	0	102	3

TAYLOR, HENRY — DT — LIONS

PERSONAL: Born November 29, 1975, in Broward County, Fla. ... 6-2/295.
HIGH SCHOOL: Barnwell (S.C.).
COLLEGE: South Carolina.
TRANSACTIONS/CAREER NOTES: Signed as non-drafted free agent by San Diego Chargers (April 20, 1998). ... Released by Chargers (July 23, 1998). ... Re-signed by Chargers (July 31, 1998). ... Released by Chargers (August 25, 1998). ... Signed by Detroit Lions to practice squad (September 2, 1998). ... Activated (October 8, 1998); did not play. ... Released by Lions (October 19, 1998). ... Re-signed by Lions to practice squad (October 21, 1998). ... Activated (November 23, 1998). ... On injured reserve with groin injury (December 19, 1998-remainder of season). ... Assigned by Lions to Amsterdam Admirals in 1999 NFL Europe enhancement allocation program (February 22, 1999).
PLAYING EXPERIENCE: Detroit NFL, 1998. ... Games/Games started: 1/0.

TAYLOR, JASON — DE — DOLPHINS

PERSONAL: Born September 1, 1974, in Pittsburgh. ... 6-6/260. ... Full name: Jason Paul Taylor.
HIGH SCHOOL: Woodland Hills (Pa.).
COLLEGE: Akron.
TRANSACTIONS/CAREER NOTES: Selected by Miami Dolphins in third round (73rd pick overall) of 1997 NFL draft. ... Signed by Dolphins (July 9, 1997). ... On injured reserve with broken collarbone (December 29, 1998-remainder of 1998 playoffs).
PRO STATISTICS: 1997—Recovered two fumbles.

Year Team	G	GS	SACKS
1997—Miami NFL	13	11	5.0
1998—Miami NFL	16	15	9.0
Pro totals (2 years)	29	26	14.0

TEAGUE, GEORGE — S — COWBOYS

PERSONAL: Born February 18, 1971, in Lansing, Mich. ... 6-1/206. ... Full name: George Theo Teague. ... Name pronounced TEEG.
HIGH SCHOOL: Jefferson Davis (Montgomery, Ala.).
COLLEGE: Alabama.
TRANSACTIONS/CAREER NOTES: Selected by Green Bay Packers in first round (29th pick overall) of 1993 NFL draft. ... Signed by Packers (July 9, 1993). ... Granted free agency (February 16, 1996). ... Re-signed by Packers (April 12, 1996). ... Traded by Packers to Atlanta Falcons for conditional draft pick (July 16, 1996). ... Released by Falcons (August 17, 1996). ... Signed by Dallas Cowboys (August 23, 1996). ... Granted unconditional free agency (February 14, 1997). ... Signed by Miami Dolphins (March 20, 1997). ... Traded by Dolphins to Cowboys (May 6, 1998), as compensation for Dolphins signing free agent S Brock Marion (March 3, 1998).
CHAMPIONSHIP GAME EXPERIENCE: Played in NFC championship game (1995 season).
POST SEASON RECORDS: Holds NFL postseason single-game record for longest interception return—101 yards, touchdown (January 8, 1994, at Detroit).
PRO STATISTICS: 1993—Returned one punt for minus one yard and recovered two fumbles. 1995—Recovered one fumble for four yards. 1998—Credited with two sacks.

Year Team	G	GS	INTERCEPTIONS No.	Yds.	Avg.	TD
1993—Green Bay NFL	16	12	1	22	22.0	0
1994—Green Bay NFL	16	16	3	33	11.0	0
1995—Green Bay NFL	15	15	2	100	50.0	0
1996—Dallas NFL	16	8	4	47	11.8	0
1997—Miami NFL	15	6	2	25	12.5	0
1998—Dallas NFL	16	5	0	0	...	0
Pro totals (6 years)	94	62	12	227	18.9	0

TERRELL, PAT — S

PERSONAL: Born March 18, 1968, in Memphis, Tenn. ... 6-1/210. ... Full name: Patrick Christopher Terrell. ... Name pronounced TAIR-el.
HIGH SCHOOL: Lakewood Senior (St. Petersburg, Fla.).
COLLEGE: Notre Dame (degree in business administration).
TRANSACTIONS/CAREER NOTES: Selected by Los Angeles Rams in second round (49th pick overall) of 1990 NFL draft. ... Signed by Rams (August 1, 1990). ... Granted unconditional free agency (February 17, 1994). ... Signed by New York Jets (May 19, 1994). ... Released by Jets (August 21, 1995). ... Signed by Carolina Panthers (August 23, 1995). ... Granted unconditional free agency (February 16, 1996). ... Re-signed by Panthers (February 26, 1996). ... Granted unconditional free agency (February 13, 1998). ... Signed by Green Bay Packers (April 1, 1998). ... Released by Packers (March 18, 1999).
CHAMPIONSHIP GAME EXPERIENCE: Played in NFC championship game (1996 season).
PRO STATISTICS: 1990—Recovered one fumble. 1991—Recovered one fumble. 1995—Recovered one fumble. 1997—Recovered one fumble. 1998—Credited with one sack and recovered one fumble for six yards.

					INTERCEPTIONS			
Year	Team	G	GS	No.	Yds.	Avg.	TD	
1990—Los Angeles Rams NFL		15	1	1	6	6.0	0	
1991—Los Angeles Rams NFL		16	16	1	4	4.0	0	
1992—Los Angeles Rams NFL		15	11	0	0	...	0	
1993—Los Angeles Rams NFL		13	3	2	1	0.5	0	
1994—New York Jets NFL		16	2	0	0	...	0	
1995—Carolina NFL		16	13	3	33	11.0	0	
1996—Carolina NFL		16	16	3	6	2.0	0	
1997—Carolina NFL		16	5	0	0	...	0	
1998—Green Bay NFL		16	3	1	9	9.0	0	
Pro totals (9 years)		139	70	11	59	5.4	0	

TERRY, RICK — DE — PANTHERS

PERSONAL: Born April 5, 1974, in Lexington, N.C. ... 6-4/300. ... Full name: Richard Ross Terry Jr.
HIGH SCHOOL: Lexington (N.C.).
COLLEGE: North Carolina.
TRANSACTIONS/CAREER NOTES: Selected by New York Jets in second round (31st pick overall) of 1997 NFL draft. ... Signed by Jets (July 14, 1997). ... Inactive for four games with Jets (1998). ... Claimed on waivers by Carolina Panthers (October 7, 1998).

Year	Team	G	GS	SACKS
1997—New York Jets NFL		14	0	2.0
1998—Carolina NFL		7	3	2.0
Pro totals (2 years)		21	3	4.0

TESTAVERDE, VINNY — QB — JETS

PERSONAL: Born November 13, 1963, in Brooklyn, N.Y. ... 6-5/238. ... Full name: Vincent Frank Testaverde. ... Name pronounced TESS-tuh-VER-dee.
HIGH SCHOOL: Sewanhaka (Floral Park, N.Y.), then Fork Union (Va.) Military Academy.
COLLEGE: Miami (Fla.).
TRANSACTIONS/CAREER NOTES: Signed by Tampa Bay Buccaneers (April 3, 1987). ... Selected officially by Buccaneers in first round (first pick overall) of 1987 NFL draft. ... On injured reserve with ankle injury (December 20, 1989-remainder of season). ... Granted unconditional free agency (March 1, 1993). ... Signed by Cleveland Browns (March 31, 1993). ... Browns franchise moved to Baltimore and renamed Ravens for 1996 season (March 11, 1996). ... Released by Ravens (June 2, 1998). ... Signed by New York Jets (June 24, 1998). ... Granted free agency (February 12, 1999). ... Re-signed by Jets (March 1, 1999).
CHAMPIONSHIP GAME EXPERIENCE: Played in AFC championship game (1998 season).
HONORS: Named quarterback on THE SPORTING NEWS college All-America second team (1985). ... Heisman Trophy winner (1986). ... Named College Football Player of the Year by THE SPORTING NEWS (1986). ... Maxwell Award winner (1986). ... Davey O'Brien Award winner (1986). ... Named quarterback on THE SPORTING NEWS college All-America first team (1986). ... Played in Pro Bowl (1996 and 1998 seasons).
PRO STATISTICS: 1987—Fumbled seven times and recovered four fumbles for minus three yards. 1988—Fumbled eight times and recovered two fumbles. 1989—Fumbled four times and recovered two fumbles. 1990—Caught one pass for three yards, fumbled 10 times and recovered three fumbles. 1991—Fumbled five times and recovered three fumbles. 1992—Fumbled four times and recovered four fumbles for minus eight yards. 1993—Fumbled four times. 1994—Fumbled three times and recovered two fumbles for two yards. 1995—Caught one pass for seven yards and fumbled four times for minus four yards. 1996—Fumbled nine times and recovered 11 fumbles for minus 11 yards. 1997—Caught one pass for minus four yards, fumbled 11 times and recovered five fumbles for minus nine yards. 1998—Fumbled seven times and recovered three fumbles for minus six yards.
SINGLE GAME HIGHS (regular season): Attempts—63 (December 6, 1998, vs. Seattle); completions—42 (December 6, 1998, vs. Seattle); yards—469 (October 15, 1989, vs. Indianapolis); and touchdown passes—4 (December 27, 1998, vs. New England).
STATISTICAL PLATEAUS: 300-yard passing games: 1987 (1), 1988 (4), 1989 (4), 1991 (1), 1992 (1), 1993 (1), 1995 (2), 1996 (5), 1997 (3), 1998 (1). Total: 23. ... 100-yard rushing games: 1990 (1).
MISCELLANEOUS: Regular-season record as starting NFL quarterback: 60-84-1 (.417). ... Postseason record as starting NFL quarterback: 2-2 (.500). ... Holds Tampa Bay Buccaneers all-time records for most yards passing (14,820) and most touchdown passes (77). ... Holds Baltimore Ravens all-time records for most yards passing (7,148) and most touchdown passes (51).

				PASSING							RUSHING				TOTALS		
Year	Team	G	GS	Att.	Cmp.	Pct.	Yds.	TD	Int.	Avg.	Rat.	Att.	Yds.	Avg.	TD	TD	2pt.	Pts.
1987—Tampa Bay NFL		6	4	165	71	43.0	1081	5	6	6.55	60.2	13	50	3.8	1	1	...	6
1988—Tampa Bay NFL		15	15	466	222	47.6	3240	13	*35	6.95	48.8	28	138	4.9	1	1	...	6
1989—Tampa Bay NFL		14	14	480	258	53.8	3133	20	†22	6.53	68.9	25	139	5.6	0	0	...	0
1990—Tampa Bay NFL		14	13	365	203	55.6	2818	17	∞18	‡7.72	75.6	38	280	7.4	1	1	...	6
1991—Tampa Bay NFL		13	12	326	166	50.9	1994	8	15	6.12	59.0	32	101	3.2	0	0	...	0
1992—Tampa Bay NFL		14	14	358	206	57.5	2554	14	16	7.13	74.2	36	197	5.5	2	2	...	12
1993—Cleveland NFL		10	6	230	130	56.5	1797	14	9	‡7.81	85.7	18	74	4.1	0	0	...	0
1994—Cleveland NFL		14	13	376	207	55.1	2575	16	18	6.85	70.7	21	37	1.8	2	2	0	12
1995—Cleveland NFL		13	12	392	241	61.5	2883	17	10	7.35	87.8	18	62	3.4	2	2	0	12
1996—Baltimore NFL		16	16	549	325	59.2	4177	§33	19	7.61	88.7	34	188	5.5	2	2	1	14
1997—Baltimore NFL		13	13	470	271	57.7	2971	18	15	6.32	75.9	34	138	4.1	0	0	0	0
1998—New York Jets NFL		14	13	421	259	61.5	3256	§29	7	7.73	§101.6	24	104	4.3	1	1	0	6
Pro totals (12 years)		156	145	4598	2559	55.7	32479	204	190	7.06	75.7	321	1508	4.7	12	12	1	74

THARPE, LARRY — OT

PERSONAL: Born November 19, 1970, in Macon, Ga. ... 6-4/300.
HIGH SCHOOL: Southwest (Macon, Ga.).

COLLEGE: Tennessee State.
TRANSACTIONS/CAREER NOTES: Selected by Detroit Lions in sixth round (145th pick overall) of 1992 NFL draft. ... Signed by Lions (July 23, 1992). ... On injured reserve with back and knee injuries (September 4-October 14, 1992). ... Inactive for 15 games (1994). ... Granted free agency (February 17, 1995). ... Signed by Arizona Cardinals (March 25, 1995); Lions received sixth-round pick (TE Kevin Hickman) in 1995 draft as compensation. ... Granted unconditional free agency (February 16, 1996). ... Signed by New England Patriots (April 29, 1996). ... Active for one game with Patriots (1996); did not play. ... Released by Patriots (October 23, 1996). ... Signed by Lions (February 21, 1997). ... Granted unconditional free agency (February 13, 1998). ... Re-signed by Lions (June 10, 1998). ... Granted unconditional free agency (February 12, 1999).
PLAYING EXPERIENCE: Detroit NFL, 1992, 1993, 1997 and 1998; Arizona NFL, 1995. ... Games/Games started: 1992 (11/0), 1993 (5/3), 1995 (16/16), 1997 (16/15), 1998 (16/9). Total: 64/43.

THELWELL, RYAN — WR — CHARGERS

PERSONAL: Born April 6, 1973, in London, Ont. ... 6-2/188.
HIGH SCHOOL: Catholic Central (London, Ont.).
COLLEGE: Minnesota.
TRANSACTIONS/CAREER NOTES: Selected by San Francisco 49ers in seventh round (215th pick overall) of 1998 NFL draft. ... Signed by 49ers (July 18, 1998). ... Released by 49ers (August 25, 1998). ... Signed by San Diego Chargers to practice squad (September 2, 1998). ... Activated (October 21, 1998).
SINGLE GAME HIGHS (regular season): Receptions—5 (December 27, 1998, vs. Arizona); yards—84 (December 27, 1998, vs. Arizona); and touchdown receptions—1 (December 27, 1998, vs. Arizona).

			RECEIVING			
Year Team	G	GS	No.	Yds.	Avg.	TD
1998—San Diego NFL	6	3	16	268	16.8	1

THIERRY, JOHN — LB — BROWNS

PERSONAL: Born September 4, 1971, in Opelousas, La. ... 6-4/265. ... Full name: John Fitzgerald Thierry.
HIGH SCHOOL: Plaisance (Opelousas, La.).
COLLEGE: Alcorn State.
TRANSACTIONS/CAREER NOTES: Selected by Chicago Bears in first round (11th pick overall) of 1994 NFL draft. ... Signed by Bears (June 21, 1994). ... On injured reserve with knee injury (November 5, 1997-remainder of season). ... Granted unconditional free agency (February 12, 1999). ... Signed by Cleveland Browns (February 26, 1999).
PRO STATISTICS: 1994—Returned one kickoff for no yards. 1995—Recovered four fumbles. 1998—Intercepted one pass for 14 yards and credited with a safety.

Year Team	G	GS	SACKS
1994—Chicago NFL	16	1	0.0
1995—Chicago NFL	16	7	4.0
1996—Chicago NFL	16	2	2.0
1997—Chicago NFL	9	9	3.0
1998—Chicago NFL	16	9	3.5
Pro totals (5 years)	73	28	12.5

THIGPEN, YANCEY — WR — TITANS

PERSONAL: Born August 15, 1969, in Tarboro, N.C. ... 6-1/203. ... Full name: Yancey Dirk Thigpen.
HIGH SCHOOL: Southwest Edgecombe (Tarboro, N.C.).
COLLEGE: Winston-Salem (N.C.) State.
TRANSACTIONS/CAREER NOTES: Selected by San Diego Chargers in fourth round (90th pick overall) of 1991 NFL draft. ... Signed by Chargers (July 15, 1991). ... Released by Chargers (August 26, 1991). ... Re-signed by Chargers to practice squad (August 28, 1991). ... Activated (September 20, 1991). ... Released by Chargers (September 26, 1991). ... Re-signed by Chargers to practice squad (September 28, 1991). ... Activated (December 7, 1991). ... Released by Chargers (August 31, 1992). ... Signed by Pittsburgh Steelers (October 5, 1992). ... On injured reserve with foot injury (January 3, 1997-remainder of 1996 playoffs). ... Granted unconditional free agency (February 13, 1998). ... Signed by Tennessee Oilers (February 14, 1998). ... Oilers franchise renamed Tennessee Titans for 1999 season (December 26, 1998).
CHAMPIONSHIP GAME EXPERIENCE: Played in AFC championship game (1994, 1995 and 1997 seasons). ... Played in Super Bowl XXX (1995 season).
HONORS: Played in Pro Bowl (1995 and 1997 seasons).
PRO STATISTICS: 1995—Rushed once for one yard. 1997—Rushed once for three yards and recovered one fumble.
SINGLE GAME HIGHS (regular season): Receptions—11 (October 26, 1997, vs. Jacksonville); yards—196 (October 26, 1997, vs. Jacksonville); and touchdown receptions—3 (December 7, 1997, vs. Denver).
STATISTICAL PLATEAUS: 100-yard receiving games: 1995 (4), 1997 (6), 1998 (1). Total: 11.

			RECEIVING				KICKOFF RETURNS				TOTALS			
Year Team	G	GS	No.	Yds.	Avg.	TD	No.	Yds.	Avg.	TD	TD	2pt.	Pts.	Fum.
1991—San Diego NFL	4	1	0	0	...	0	0	0	...	0	0	...	0	0
1992—Pittsburgh NFL	12	0	1	2	2.0	0	2	44	22.0	0	0	...	0	0
1993—Pittsburgh NFL	12	0	9	154	17.1	3	1	23	23.0	0	3	...	18	0
1994—Pittsburgh NFL	15	6	36	546	15.2	4	5	121	24.2	0	4	0	24	0
1995—Pittsburgh NFL	16	15	85	1307	15.4	5	0	0	...	0	5	0	30	1
1996—Pittsburgh NFL	6	2	12	244	20.3	2	0	0	...	0	2	0	12	0
1997—Pittsburgh NFL	16	15	79	1398	17.7	7	0	0	...	0	7	1	44	1
1998—Tennessee NFL	9	8	38	493	13.0	3	0	0	...	0	3	0	18	0
Pro totals (8 years)	90	47	260	4144	15.9	24	8	188	23.5	0	24	1	146	2

THOMAS, BRODERICK — DE/LB

PERSONAL: Born February 20, 1967, in Houston. ... 6-4/254. ... Nephew of Mike Singletary, Hall of Fame linebacker with Chicago Bears (1981-92).
HIGH SCHOOL: James Madison (Houston).
COLLEGE: Nebraska.
TRANSACTIONS/CAREER NOTES: Selected by Tampa Bay Buccaneers in first round (sixth pick overall) of 1989 NFL draft. ... Signed by Buccaneers (August 29, 1989). ... Released by Buccaneers (June 30, 1994). ... Signed by Detroit Lions (July 15, 1994). ... Granted unconditional free agency (February 17, 1995). ... Signed by Minnesota Vikings (March 9, 1995). ... Released by Vikings (February 9, 1996). ... Signed by Dallas Cowboys (March 22, 1996). ... Granted unconditional free agency (February 14, 1997). ... Re-signed by Cowboys (March 24, 1997). ... Granted free agency (February 13, 1998). ... Re-signed by Cowboys (March 16, 1998). ... On injured reserve with knee injury (August 4, 1998-entire season). ... Granted unconditional free agency (February 12, 1999).
HONORS: Named defensive lineman on The Sporting News college All-America second team (1987). ... Named linebacker on The Sporting News college All-America first team (1988).
PRO STATISTICS: 1990—Recovered two fumbles. 1991—Recovered two fumbles for 12 yards. 1992—Intercepted two passes for 81 yards and one touchdown and recovered three fumbles for minus one yard. 1993—Recovered one fumble. 1994—Recovered two fumbles for 11 yards. 1995—Recovered one fumble. 1996—Recovered three fumbles for 23 yards. 1997—Recovered one fumble.

Year — Team	G	GS	SACKS
1989—Tampa Bay NFL	16	0	2.0
1990—Tampa Bay NFL	16	15	7.5
1991—Tampa Bay NFL	16	16	11.0
1992—Tampa Bay NFL	16	16	5.0
1993—Tampa Bay NFL	16	8	1.0
1994—Detroit NFL	16	16	7.0
1995—Minnesota NFL	16	16	6.0
1996—Dallas NFL	16	9	4.5
1997—Dallas NFL	16	0	3.5
1998—Dallas NFL	Did not play.		
Pro totals (9 years)	**144**	**96**	**47.5**

THOMAS, CHRIS — WR — REDSKINS

PERSONAL: Born July 16, 1971, in Ventura, Calif. ... 6-2/190. ... Full name: Chris Eric Thomas.
HIGH SCHOOL: Ventura (Calif.).
COLLEGE: Cal Poly-SLO (degree in English, 1994).
TRANSACTIONS/CAREER NOTES: Signed as non-drafted free agent by San Diego Chargers (May 6, 1993). ... Released by Chargers (August 30, 1993). ... Re-signed by Chargers to practice squad (September 1, 1993). ... Granted free agency after 1993 season. ... Signed by San Francisco 49ers (May 16, 1995). ... Released by 49ers (May 15, 1996). ... Re-signed by 49ers (May 15, 1996). ... Released by 49ers (August 20, 1996). ... Selected by Rhein Fire in 1997 World League draft (February 17, 1997). ... Signed by Washington Redskins (February 25, 1997). ... Released by Redskins (August 19, 1997). ... Re-signed by Redskins (August 21, 1997). ... Released by Redskins (August 23, 1997). ... Re-signed by Redskins (September 22, 1997). ... Granted free agency (February 12, 1999). ... Re-signed by Redskins (April 23, 1999).
PRO STATISTICS: 1995—Returned one punt for 25 yards and returned three kickoffs for 49 yards. 1998—Recovered one fumble.
SINGLE GAME HIGHS (regular season): Receptions—4 (December 6, 1998, vs. San Diego); yards—62 (December 6, 1998, vs. San Diego); and touchdown receptions—0.

			RECEIVING				TOTALS			
Year — Team	G	GS	No.	Yds.	Avg.	TD	TD	2pt.	Pts.	Fum.
1995—San Francisco NFL	14	0	6	73	12.2	0	0	0	0	0
1996—				Did not play.						
1997—Washington NFL	13	0	11	93	8.5	0	0	0	0	0
1998—Washington NFL	14	0	14	173	12.4	0	0	0	0	0
Pro totals (3 years)	**41**	**0**	**31**	**339**	**10.9**	**0**	**0**	**0**	**0**	**0**

THOMAS, COREY — WR — LIONS

PERSONAL: Born June 6, 1975, in Wilson, N.C. ... 6-0/174.
HIGH SCHOOL: Beddingfield (N.C.).
COLLEGE: Duke.
TRANSACTIONS/CAREER NOTES: Signed as non-drafted free agent by Detroit Lions (April 24, 1998). ... Released by Lions (August 24, 1998). ... Re-signed by Lions to practice squad (September 1, 1998). ... Activated (December 24, 1998).
PLAYING EXPERIENCE: Detroit NFL, 1998. ... Games/Games started: 1/0.

THOMAS, DAVE — CB — JAGUARS

PERSONAL: Born August 25, 1968, in Miami. ... 6-3/213. ... Full name: Dave G. Thomas.
HIGH SCHOOL: Miami Beach.
JUNIOR COLLEGE: Butler Community College (Kan.).
COLLEGE: Tennessee.
TRANSACTIONS/CAREER NOTES: Selected by Dallas Cowboys in eighth round (203rd pick overall) of 1993 NFL draft. ... Signed by Cowboys (July 15, 1993). ... Selected by Jacksonville Jaguars from Cowboys in NFL expansion draft (February 15, 1995). ... Granted free agency (February 16, 1996). ... Re-signed by Jaguars (June 3, 1996). ... On injured reserve with broken leg (October 29, 1996-remainder of season). ... Granted unconditional free agency (February 14, 1997). ... Re-signed by Jaguars (March 3, 1997).
CHAMPIONSHIP GAME EXPERIENCE: Played in NFC championship game (1993 and 1994 seasons). ... Member of Super Bowl championship team (1993 season).

PRO STATISTICS: 1995—Recovered one fumble. 1996—Returned one punt for one yard and fumbled once. 1997—Recovered one fumble. 1998—Recovered one fumble.

				INTERCEPTIONS		
Year Team	G	GS	No.	Yds.	Avg.	TD
1993—Dallas NFL	12	0	0	0	...	0
1994—Dallas NFL	16	0	0	0	...	0
1995—Jacksonville NFL	15	2	0	0	...	0
1996—Jacksonville NFL	9	5	2	7	3.5	0
1997—Jacksonville NFL	16	15	2	34	17.0	0
1998—Jacksonville NFL	14	13	1	0	0.0	0
Pro totals (6 years)	72	35	5	41	8.2	0

THOMAS, DERRICK — LB — CHIEFS

PERSONAL: Born January 1, 1967, in Miami. ... 6-3/247. ... Full name: Derrick Vincent Thomas. ... Cousin of Shevin Smith, safety, Tampa Bay Buccaneers.
HIGH SCHOOL: South (Miami).
COLLEGE: Alabama.
TRANSACTIONS/CAREER NOTES: Selected by Kansas City Chiefs in first round (fourth pick overall) of 1989 NFL draft. ... Signed by Chiefs (August 24, 1989). ... Granted free agency (March 1, 1993). ... Re-signed by Chiefs (May 21, 1993). ... Granted unconditional free agency (February 14, 1997). ... Re-signed by Chiefs (March 26, 1997).
CHAMPIONSHIP GAME EXPERIENCE: Played in AFC championship game (1993 season).
HONORS: Named linebacker on THE SPORTING NEWS college All-America second team (1987). ... Butkus Award winner (1988). ... Named linebacker on THE SPORTING NEWS college All-America first team (1988). ... Played in Pro Bowl (1989-1997 seasons). ... Named outside linebacker on THE SPORTING NEWS NFL All-Pro team (1990-1992).
RECORDS: Holds NFL single-game record for most sacks—7 (November 11, 1990, vs. Seattle).
PRO STATISTICS: 1989—Recovered one fumble. 1990—Recovered two fumbles for 14 yards. 1991—Recovered four fumbles for 23 yards and one touchdown. 1992—Recovered three fumbles (including one in end zone for a touchdown). 1993—Recovered one fumble for 86 yards and a touchdown. 1994—Credited with one safety and recovered three fumbles for 11 yards. 1995—Recovered one fumble. 1996—Recovered one fumble. 1997—Credited with a safety. 1998—Recovered two fumbles for 27 yards and one touchdown and credited with a safety.
MISCELLANEOUS: Holds Kansas City Chiefs all-time record for most sacks (119.5).

Year Team	G	GS	SACKS
1989—Kansas City NFL	16	16	10.0
1990—Kansas City NFL	15	15	*20.0
1991—Kansas City NFL	16	15	13.5
1992—Kansas City NFL	16	16	14.5
1993—Kansas City NFL	16	15	8.0
1994—Kansas City NFL	16	15	11.0
1995—Kansas City NFL	15	15	8.0
1996—Kansas City NFL	16	13	13.0
1997—Kansas City NFL	12	10	9.5
1998—Kansas City NFL	15	10	12.0
Pro totals (10 years)	153	140	119.5

THOMAS, FRED — CB — SEAHAWKS

PERSONAL: Born September 11, 1973, in Bruce, Miss. ... 5-9/172.
HIGH SCHOOL: Bruce (Miss.).
JUNIOR COLLEGE: Northwest Mississippi Community College.
COLLEGE: Mississippi Valley State (did not play football), then Mississippi, then Tennessee-Martin.
TRANSACTIONS/CAREER NOTES: Selected by Seattle Seahawks in second round (47th pick overall) of 1996 NFL draft. ... Signed by Seahawks (July 19, 1996). ... Granted free agency (February 12, 1999).
PLAYING EXPERIENCE: Seattle NFL, 1996-1998. ... Games/Games started: 1996 (15/0), 1997 (16/3), 1998 (15/2). Total: 46/5.
PRO STATISTICS: 1998—Recovered one fumble.

THOMAS, HENRY — DL — PATRIOTS

PERSONAL: Born January 12, 1965, in Houston. ... 6-2/277. ... Full name: Henry Lee Thomas Jr.
HIGH SCHOOL: Dwight D. Eisenhower (Houston).
COLLEGE: Louisiana Tech.
TRANSACTIONS/CAREER NOTES: Selected by Minnesota Vikings in third round (72nd pick overall) of 1987 NFL draft. ... Signed by Vikings (July 14, 1987). ... Designated by Vikings as transition player (February 25, 1993). ... Designated by Vikings as franchise player (February 15, 1994). ... Free agency status changed by Vikings from franchise to unconditional (February 15, 1995). ... Signed by Detroit Lions (February 27, 1995). ... Released by Lions (April 23, 1997). ... Signed by New England Patriots (June 12, 1997). ... Granted unconditional free agency (February 12, 1999). ... Re-signed by Patriots (February 22, 1999).
CHAMPIONSHIP GAME EXPERIENCE: Played in NFC championship game (1987 season).
HONORS: Named defensive lineman on THE SPORTING NEWS college All-America second team (1986). ... Played in Pro Bowl (1991 and 1992 seasons).

PRO STATISTICS: 1987—Intercepted one pass for no yards and recovered one fumble. 1988—Intercepted one pass for seven yards and recovered one fumble for two yards and a touchdown. 1989—Recovered three fumbles for 37 yards and one touchdown. 1990—Recovered one fumble. 1991—Recovered one fumble. 1993—Credited with one safety. 1994—Recovered one fumble. 1995—Recovered two fumbles. 1996—Recovered one fumble. 1997—Recovered one fumble. 1998—Intercepted one pass for 24 yards and a touchdown and recovered one fumble.

Year—Team	G	GS	SACKS
1987—Minnesota NFL	12	12	2.5
1988—Minnesota NFL	15	15	6.0
1989—Minnesota NFL	14	14	9.0
1990—Minnesota NFL	16	16	8.5
1991—Minnesota NFL	16	15	8.0
1992—Minnesota NFL	16	16	6.0
1993—Minnesota NFL	13	13	9.0
1994—Minnesota NFL	16	16	7.0
1995—Detroit NFL	16	16	10.5
1996—Detroit NFL	15	15	6.0
1997—New England NFL	16	16	7.0
1998—New England NFL	16	15	6.5
Pro totals (12 years)	181	179	86.0

THOMAS, HOLLIS   DT   EAGLES

PERSONAL: Born January 10, 1974, in Abilene, Texas. ... 6-0/306.
HIGH SCHOOL: Sumner (St. Louis).
COLLEGE: Northern Illinois.
TRANSACTIONS/CAREER NOTES: Signed as non-drafted free agent by Philadelphia Eagles (April 26, 1996). ... On injured reserve with arm/shoulder injury (December 2, 1998-remainder of season).
PRO STATISTICS: 1997—Recovered one fumble. 1998—Recovered one fumble.

Year—Team	G	GS	SACKS
1996—Philadelphia NFL	16	5	1.0
1997—Philadelphia NFL	16	16	2.5
1998—Philadelphia NFL	12	12	5.0
Pro totals (3 years)	44	33	8.5

THOMAS, J.T.   WR

PERSONAL: Born July 11, 1971, in San Bernardino, Calif. ... 5-10/180. ... Full name: Johnny Le'Mon Thomas.
HIGH SCHOOL: San Bernardino (Calif.).
JUNIOR COLLEGE: San Bernardino (Calif.) Valley.
COLLEGE: Arizona State.
TRANSACTIONS/CAREER NOTES: Selected after junior season by St. Louis Rams in seventh round (240th pick overall) of 1995 NFL draft. ... Signed by Rams (June 16, 1995). ... Granted free agency (February 13, 1998). ... Re-signed by Rams (May 6, 1998). ... Granted unconditional free agency (February 12, 1999).
PRO STATISTICS: 1995—Ran 61 yards with lateral from punt return, fumbled once and recovered one fumble for five yards. 1996—Rushed once for minus one yard.
SINGLE GAME HIGHS (regular season): Receptions—4 (December 3, 1998, vs. Philadelphia); yards—79 (December 3, 1998, vs. Phialdelphia); and touchdown receptions—0.

			RECEIVING				KICKOFF RETURNS				TOTALS			
Year—Team	G	GS	No.	Yds.	Avg.	TD	No.	Yds.	Avg.	TD	TD	2pt.	Pts.	Fum.
1995—St. Louis NFL	15	1	5	42	8.4	0	32	752	23.5	0	0	0	0	1
1996—St. Louis NFL	16	1	7	46	6.6	0	30	643	21.4	0	0	0	0	1
1997—St. Louis NFL	5	0	2	25	12.5	0	5	97	19.4	0	0	0	0	0
1998—St. Louis NFL	16	1	20	287	14.4	0	4	79	19.8	0	0	0	0	0
Pro totals (4 years)	52	3	34	400	11.8	0	71	1571	22.1	0	0	0	0	2

THOMAS, LAMAR   WR   DOLPHINS

PERSONAL: Born February 12, 1970, in Ocala, Fla. ... 6-1/175. ... Full name: Lamar Nathaniel Thomas.
HIGH SCHOOL: Buchholz (Gainesville, Fla.).
COLLEGE: Miami, Fla. (degree in sociology).
TRANSACTIONS/CAREER NOTES: Selected by Tampa Bay Buccaneers in third round (60th pick overall) of 1993 NFL draft. ... Signed by Buccaneers (July 14, 1993). ... Granted free agency (February 16, 1996). ... Re-signed by Buccaneers (May 16, 1996). ... Released by Buccaneers (July 17, 1996). ... Signed by Miami Dolphins (July 27, 1996). ... Granted unconditional free agency (February 14, 1997). ... Re-signed by Dolphins (March 11, 1997).
HONORS: Named wide receiver on THE SPORTING NEWS college All-America second team (1992).
PRO STATISTICS: 1995—Rushed once for five yards.
SINGLE GAME HIGHS (regular season): Receptions—6 (December 21, 1998, vs. Denver); yards—136 (December 21, 1998, vs. Denver); and touchdown receptions—3 (December 21, 1998, vs. Denver).
STATISTICAL PLATEAUS: 100-yard receiving games: 1998 (1).

				RECEIVING					TOTALS		
Year	Team	G	GS	No.	Yds.	Avg.	TD	TD	2pt.	Pts.	Fum.
1993	Tampa Bay NFL	14	2	8	186	23.3	2	2	...	12	0
1994	Tampa Bay NFL	11	0	7	94	13.4	0	0	0	0	0
1995	Tampa Bay NFL	11	0	10	107	10.7	0	0	0	0	0
1996	Miami NFL	9	3	10	166	16.6	1	1	0	6	0
1997	Miami NFL	12	6	28	402	14.4	2	2	0	12	1
1998	Miami NFL	16	2	43	603	14.0	5	5	0	30	0
Pro totals (6 years)		73	13	106	1558	14.7	10	10	0	60	1

THOMAS, MARK — DE — COLTS

PERSONAL: Born May 6, 1969, in Lilburn, Ga. ... 6-5/272. ... Full name: Mark Andrew Thomas.
HIGH SCHOOL: Lilburn (Ga.).
COLLEGE: North Carolina State.
TRANSACTIONS/CAREER NOTES: Selected by San Francisco 49ers in fourth round (89th pick overall) of 1992 NFL draft. ... Signed by 49ers (July 16, 1992). ... On injured reserve with ankle injury (September 1-October 7, 1992). ... On practice squad (October 7-November 11, 1992). ... On injured reserve (November 11, 1992-remainder of season). ... Selected by Carolina Panthers from 49ers in NFL expansion draft (February 15, 1995). ... Granted free agency (February 17, 1995). ... On injured reserve with thumb injury (November 27, 1995-remainder of season). ... Granted unconditional free agency (February 16, 1996). ... Re-signed by Panthers (February 20, 1996). ... Granted unconditional free agency (February 14, 1997). ... Signed by Chicago Bears (March 30, 1997). ... Claimed on waivers by Indianapolis Colts (December 2, 1998). ... Granted unconditional free agency (February 12, 1999). ... Re-signed by Colts (February 17, 1999).
CHAMPIONSHIP GAME EXPERIENCE: Member of 49ers for NFC championship game (1993 and 1994 seasons); inactive. ... Member of Super Bowl championship team (1994 season). ... Played in NFC championship game (1996 season).
PRO STATISTICS: 1993—Recovered one fumble. 1996—Recovered one fumble for 18 yards. 1997—Recovered one fumble.

Year	Team	G	GS	SACKS
1992—San Francisco NFL		Did not play.		
1993—San Francisco NFL		11	1	0.5
1994—San Francisco NFL		9	0	1.0
1995—Carolina NFL		10	0	2.0
1996—Carolina NFL		12	0	4.0
1997—Chicago NFL		16	7	4.5
1998—Chicago NFL		10	4	4.5
—Indianapolis NFL		4	1	1.0
Pro totals (6 years)		72	13	17.5

THOMAS, MARVIN — DE — BRONCOS

PERSONAL: Born October 19, 1973, in Bay Minette, Ala. ... 6-5/264.
HIGH SCHOOL: Baldwin (Ala.).
COLLEGE: Memphis.
TRANSACTIONS/CAREER NOTES: Selected by Chicago Bears in seventh round (233rd pick overall) of 1997 NFL draft. ... Signed by Bears (July 10, 1997). ... Released by Bears (August 18, 1997). ... Signed by Detroit Lions to practice squad (August 26, 1997). ... Activated (November 24, 1997); did not play. ... Released by Lions (October 8, 1998). ... Signed by Denver Broncos to practice squad (October 19, 1998). ... Assigned by Broncos to Barcelona Dragons in 1999 NFL Europe enhancement allocation program (February 22, 1999).
PLAYING EXPERIENCE: Detroit NFL, 1998. ... Games/Games started: 4/0.

THOMAS, ORLANDO — S — VIKINGS

PERSONAL: Born October 21, 1972, in Crowley, La. ... 6-1/214.
HIGH SCHOOL: Crowley (La.).
COLLEGE: Southwestern Louisiana.
TRANSACTIONS/CAREER NOTES: Selected by Minnesota Vikings in second round (42nd pick overall) of 1995 NFL draft. ... Signed by Vikings (July 25, 1995). ... Granted unconditional free agency (February 12, 1999). ... Re-signed by Vikings (February 22, 1999).
CHAMPIONSHIP GAME EXPERIENCE: Played in NFC championship game (1998 season).
PRO STATISTICS: 1995—Fumbled once and recovered four fumbles for 19 yards and one touchdown. 1996—Recovered one fumble. 1997—Fumbled once and recovered two fumbles for 26 yards and one touchdown. 1998—Credited with $1/2$ sack.

				INTERCEPTIONS			
Year	Team	G	GS	No.	Yds.	Avg.	TD
1995—Minnesota NFL		16	11	*9	108	12.0	1
1996—Minnesota NFL		16	16	5	57	11.4	0
1997—Minnesota NFL		15	13	2	1	0.5	0
1998—Minnesota NFL		16	16	2	27	13.5	0
Pro totals (4 years)		63	56	18	193	10.7	1

THOMAS, RATCLIFF — LB — COLTS

PERSONAL: Born January 2, 1974, in Alexandria, Va. ... 6-1/238.
HIGH SCHOOL: T.C. Williams (Alexandria, Va.).
COLLEGE: Maryland.
TRANSACTIONS/CAREER NOTES: Selected by Amsterdam Admirals in 1998 NFL Europe draft (February 18, 1998). ... Signed as non-drafted free agent by Indianapolis Colts (August 5, 1998). ... Released by Colts (September 9, 1998). ... Re-signed by Colts (September 29, 1998). ... Released by Colts (October 5, 1998). ... Re-signed by Colts (October 6, 1998). ... Released by Colts (November 25, 1998). ... Re-signed by Colts (January 19, 1999).
PLAYING EXPERIENCE: Indianapolis NFL, 1998. ... Games/Games started: 5/0.

THOMAS, ROBB — WR

PERSONAL: Born March 29, 1966, in Portland, Ore. ... 5-11/178. ... Full name: Robb Douglas Thomas. ... Son of Aaron Thomas, tight end/wide receiver with San Francisco 49ers (1961-62) and New York Giants (1962-70).
HIGH SCHOOL: Corvallis (Ore.).
COLLEGE: Oregon State.
TRANSACTIONS/CAREER NOTES: Selected by Kansas City Chiefs in sixth round (143rd pick overall) of 1989 NFL draft. ... Signed by Chiefs (May 30, 1989). ... On injured reserve with dislocated shoulder (October 24-December 4, 1989). ... On developmental squad (December 5-23, 1989). ... Released by Chiefs (August 31, 1992). ... Signed by Seattle Seahawks (September 8, 1992). ... Granted free agency (March 1, 1993). ... Re-signed by Seahawks (July 2, 1993). ... Released by Seahawks (August 30, 1993). ... Re-signed by Seahawks (August 31, 1993). ... Granted unconditional free agency (February 17, 1994). ... Re-signed by Seahawks (July 13, 1994). ... Granted unconditional free agency (February 17, 1996). ... Signed by Tampa Bay Buccaneers (August 27, 1996). ... Re-signed by Buccaneers (December 9, 1996). ... Released by Buccaneers (August 25, 1998). ... Re-signed by Buccaneers (September 17, 1998). ... Granted unconditional free agency (February 12, 1999).
PRO STATISTICS: 1992—Rushed once for minus one yard.
SINGLE GAME HIGHS (regular season): Receptions—7 (November 17, 1991, vs. Denver); yards—89 (November 17, 1991, vs. Denver); and touchdown receptions—2 (October 13, 1996, vs. Minnesota).

				RECEIVING				TOTALS			
Year Team	G	GS	No.	Yds.	Avg.	TD	TD	2pt.	Pts.	Fum.
1989—Kansas City NFL	8	1	8	58	7.3	2	2	...	12	1
1990—Kansas City NFL	16	12	41	545	13.3	4	4	...	24	0
1991—Kansas City NFL	15	12	43	495	11.5	1	1	...	6	0
1992—Seattle NFL	15	0	11	136	12.4	0	0	...	0	1
1993—Seattle NFL	16	0	7	67	9.6	0	0	...	0	0
1994—Seattle NFL	16	1	4	70	17.5	0	0	0	0	0
1995—Seattle NFL	15	2	12	239	19.9	1	1	0	6	0
1996—Tampa Bay NFL	12	8	33	427	12.9	2	2	0	12	0
1997—Tampa Bay NFL	16	1	13	129	9.9	0	0	0	0	0
1998—Tampa Bay NFL	7	0	2	63	31.5	1	1	0	6	0
Pro totals (10 years)	136	37	174	2229	12.8	11	11	0	66	2

THOMAS, ROBERT — LB — COWBOYS

PERSONAL: Born December 1, 1974, in Jacksonville, Ark. ... 6-1/260.
HIGH SCHOOL: Jacksonville (Ark.).
COLLEGE: Henderson State (Ark.).
TRANSACTIONS/CAREER NOTES: Signed as non-drafted free agent by Dallas Cowboys (February 24, 1998). ... Assigned by Cowboys to Rhein Fire in 1999 NFL Europe enhancement allocation program (February 22, 1999).
PLAYING EXPERIENCE: Dallas NFL, 1998. ... Games/Games started: 16/0.

THOMAS, RODNEY — RB — TITANS

PERSONAL: Born March 30, 1973, in Trinity, Texas. ... 5-10/210. ... Full name: Rodney Dejuane Thomas.
HIGH SCHOOL: Groveton (Texas).
COLLEGE: Texas A&M.
TRANSACTIONS/CAREER NOTES: Selected by Houston Oilers in third round (89th pick overall) of 1995 NFL draft. ... Signed by Oilers (August 1, 1995). ... Oilers franchise moved to Tennessee for 1997 season. ... Granted free agency (February 13, 1998). ... Re-signed by Oilers for 1998 season. ... Oilers franchise renamed Tennessee Titans for 1999 season (December 26, 1998).
SINGLE GAME HIGHS (regular season): Attempts—25 (November 19, 1995 vs. Kansas City); yards—108 (November 5, 1995, vs. Cleveland); and rushing touchdowns—2 (December 24, 1995, vs. Buffalo).
STATISTICAL PLATEAUS: 100-yard rushing games: 1995 (2).

			RUSHING				RECEIVING				KICKOFF RETURNS				TOTALS			
Year Team	G	GS	Att.	Yds.	Avg.	TD	No.	Yds.	Avg.	TD	No.	Yds.	Avg.	TD	TD	2pt.	Pts.	Fum.
1995—Houston NFL	16	10	251	947	3.8	5	39	204	5.2	2	3	48	16.0	0	7	1	44	8
1996—Houston NFL	16	0	49	151	3.1	1	13	128	9.8	0	5	80	16.0	0	1	0	6	0
1997—Tennessee NFL	16	1	67	310	4.6	3	14	111	7.9	0	17	346	20.4	0	3	0	18	1
1998—Tennessee NFL	11	0	24	100	4.2	2	6	55	9.2	0	3	64	21.3	0	2	0	12	0
Pro totals (4 years)	59	11	391	1508	3.9	11	72	498	6.9	2	28	538	19.2	0	13	1	80	9

THOMAS, THURMAN — RB — BILLS

PERSONAL: Born May 16, 1966, in Houston. ... 5-10/198. ... Full name: Thurman Lee Thomas.
HIGH SCHOOL: Willow Ridge (Missouri City, Texas).
COLLEGE: Oklahoma State.
TRANSACTIONS/CAREER NOTES: Selected by Buffalo Bills in second round (40th pick overall) of 1988 NFL draft. ... Signed by Bills (July 14, 1988).
CHAMPIONSHIP GAME EXPERIENCE: Played in AFC championship game (1988 and 1990-1993 seasons). ... Played in Super Bowl XXV (1990 season), Super Bowl XXVI (1991 season), Super Bowl XXVII (1992 season) and Super Bowl XXVIII (1993 season).
HONORS: Named running back on THE SPORTING NEWS college All-America second team (1985). ... Played in Pro Bowl (1989-1991 and 1993 seasons). ... Named to play in Pro Bowl (1992 season); replaced by Ronnie Harmon due to injury. ... Named running back on THE SPORTING NEWS NFL All-Pro team (1990 and 1991). ... Named NFL Player of the Year by THE SPORTING NEWS (1991).

POST SEASON RECORDS: Holds NFL postseason career records for most points scored—126; most touchdowns—21; and most yards gained—2,114. ... Holds NFL postseason record for most consecutive games with one or more touchdowns—9 (1992-present). ... Shares NFL postseason single-game record for most receptions—13 (January 6, 1990, at Cleveland).
PRO STATISTICS: 1988—Recovered one fumble. 1989—Recovered two fumbles. 1990—Recovered two fumbles. 1992—Recovered one fumble. 1993—Attempted one pass without a completion and recovered one fumble. 1994—Recovered two fumbles. 1996—Recovered one fumble.
SINGLE GAME HIGHS (regular season): Attempts—37 (November 8, 1992, vs. Pittsburgh); yards—214 (September 24, 1990, vs. New York Jets); and rushing touchdowns—3 (September 6, 1992, vs. Los Angeles).
STATISTICAL PLATEAUS: 100-yard rushing games: 1988 (2), 1989 (5), 1990 (5), 1991 (8), 1992 (9), 1993 (7), 1994 (4), 1995 (3), 1996 (2), 1997 (1). Total: 46. ... 100-yard receiving games: 1991 (2), 1996 (1). Total: 3.
MISCELLANEOUS: Active AFC leader for career rushing yards (11,786) and rushing touchdowns (65). ... Shares active AFC lead in touchdowns (86). ... Holds Buffalo Bills all-time record for most yards rushing (11,786) and most rushing touchdowns (65). ... Shares Buffalo Bills all-time record for most touchdowns (86).

				RUSHING				RECEIVING			TOTALS		
Year Team	G	GS	Att.	Yds.	Avg.	TD	No.	Yds.	Avg.	TD	TD	2pt.	Pts.	Fum.
1988—Buffalo NFL	15	15	207	881	4.3	2	18	208	11.6	0	2	...	12	9
1989—Buffalo NFL	16	16	298	1244	4.2	6	60	669	11.2	6	▲12	...	72	7
1990—Buffalo NFL	16	16	271	§1297	4.8	11	49	532	10.9	2	13	...	78	6
1991—Buffalo NFL	15	15	§288	§1407	*4.9	7	62	631	10.2	5	▲12	...	72	5
1992—Buffalo NFL	16	16	312	1487	§4.8	9	58	626	10.8	3	§12	...	72	6
1993—Buffalo NFL	16	16	*355	§1315	3.7	6	48	387	8.1	0	6	...	36	6
1994—Buffalo NFL	15	15	287	1093	3.8	7	50	349	7.0	2	9	0	54	1
1995—Buffalo NFL	14	14	267	1005	3.8	6	26	220	8.5	2	8	0	48	6
1996—Buffalo NFL	15	15	281	1033	3.7	8	26	254	9.8	0	8	0	48	1
1997—Buffalo NFL	16	16	154	643	4.2	1	30	208	6.9	0	1	0	6	2
1998—Buffalo NFL	14	3	93	381	4.1	2	26	220	8.5	1	3	0	18	0
Pro totals (11 years)	168	157	2813	11786	4.2	65	453	4304	9.5	21	86	0	516	49

THOMAS, TRA — OT — EAGLES

PERSONAL: Born November 20, 1974, in DeLand, Fla. ... 6-7/349. ... Full name: William Thomas III. ... Name pronounced TRAY.
HIGH SCHOOL: DeLand (Fla.).
COLLEGE: Florida State.
TRANSACTIONS/CAREER NOTES: Selected by Philadelphia Eagles in first round (11th pick overall) of 1998 NFL draft. ... Signed by Eagles (June 19, 1998).
PLAYING EXPERIENCE: Philadelphia NFL, 1998. ... Games/Games started: 16/16.
PRO STATISTICS: 1998—Recovered one fumble.

THOMAS, WILLIAM — LB — EAGLES

PERSONAL: Born August 13, 1968, in Amarillo, Texas. ... 6-2/223. ... Full name: William Harrison Thomas Jr.
HIGH SCHOOL: Palo Duro (Amarillo, Texas).
COLLEGE: Texas A&M.
TRANSACTIONS/CAREER NOTES: Selected by Philadelphia Eagles in fourth round (105th pick overall) of 1991 NFL draft. ... Signed by Eagles (July 17, 1991). ... Granted free agency (February 17, 1994). ... Re-signed by Eagles (July 1994).
HONORS: Played in Pro Bowl (1995 and 1996 seasons).
POST SEASON RECORDS: Shares NFL postseason record for most touchdowns by interception return—1 (December 30, 1995, vs. Detroit).
PRO STATISTICS: 1991—Recovered one fumble. 1992—Recovered two fumbles for two yards. 1993—Recovered three fumbles. 1995—Recovered one fumble. 1996—Recovered one fumble for 23 yards and a touchdown. 1997—Recovered one fumble for 37 yards and a touchdown. 1998—Blocked a punt out of end zone for a safety.

			INTERCEPTIONS				SACKS
Year Team	G	GS	No.	Yds.	Avg.	TD	No.
1991—Philadelphia NFL	16	7	0	0	...	0	2.0
1992—Philadelphia NFL	16	15	2	4	2.0	0	1.5
1993—Philadelphia NFL	16	16	2	39	19.5	0	6.5
1994—Philadelphia NFL	16	16	1	7	7.0	0	6.0
1995—Philadelphia NFL	16	16	7	104	14.9	1	2.0
1996—Philadelphia NFL	16	16	3	47	15.7	0	5.5
1997—Philadelphia NFL	14	14	2	11	5.5	0	5.0
1998—Philadelphia NFL	16	16	1	21	21.0	0	2.0
Pro totals (8 years)	126	116	18	233	12.9	1	30.5

THOMAS, ZACH — LB — DOLPHINS

PERSONAL: Born September 1, 1973, in Pampa, Texas. ... 5-11/235. ... Full name: Zach Michael Thomas.
HIGH SCHOOL: White Deer (Texas), then Pampa (Texas).
COLLEGE: Texas Tech.
TRANSACTIONS/CAREER NOTES: Selected by Miami Dolphins in fifth round (154th pick overall) of 1996 NFL draft. ... Signed by Dolphins (July 10, 1996). ... Granted free agency (February 12, 1999). ... Re-signed by Dolphins (February 12, 1999).
HONORS: Named linebacker on THE SPORTING NEWS college All-America second team (1994). ... Named linebacker on THE SPORTING NEWS college All-America first team (1995).
PRO STATISTICS: 1996—Returned one kickoff for 17 yards and recovered two fumbles for seven yards.

Year Team	G	GS	INTERCEPTIONS No.	Yds.	Avg.	TD	SACKS No.
1996—Miami NFL	16	16	3	64	21.3	1	2.0
1997—Miami NFL	15	15	1	10	10.0	0	0.5
1998—Miami NFL	16	16	3	21	7.0	▲2	2.0
Pro totals (3 years)	47	47	7	95	13.6	3	4.5

THOMASON, JEFF   TE   PACKERS

PERSONAL: Born December 30, 1969, in San Diego. ... 6-5/255. ... Full name: Jeffrey David Thomason.
HIGH SCHOOL: Corona Del Mar (Newport Beach, Calif.).
COLLEGE: Oregon (degree in psychology).
TRANSACTIONS/CAREER NOTES: Signed as non-drafted free agent by Cincinnati Bengals (April 29, 1992). ... On injured reserve with sprained knee (September 1-December 5, 1992). ... Released by Bengals (August 30, 1993). ... Re-signed by Bengals (September 15, 1993). ... Claimed on waivers by Green Bay Packers (August 2, 1994). ... Released by Packers (August 21, 1994). ... Re-signed by Packers (January 20, 1995). ... Granted unconditional free agency (February 13, 1998). ... Re-signed by Packers (March 17, 1998).
CHAMPIONSHIP GAME EXPERIENCE: Played in NFC championship game (1995-97 seasons). ... Member of Super Bowl championship team (1996 season). ... Played in Super Bowl XXXII (1997 season).
PRO STATISTICS: 1995—Returned one kickoff for 16 yards and recovered one fumble. 1996—Returned one kickoff for 20 yards.
SINGLE GAME HIGHS (regular season): Receptions—5 (September 1, 1997, vs. Chicago); yards—58 (September 1, 1997, vs. Chicago); and touchdown receptions—1 (September 1, 1997, vs. Chicago).

Year Team	G	GS	RECEIVING No.	Yds.	Avg.	TD	TOTALS TD	2pt.	Pts.	Fum.
1992—Cincinnati NFL	4	0	2	14	7.0	0	0	...	0	0
1993—Cincinnati NFL	3	0	2	8	4.0	0	0	...	0	0
1994—						Did not play.				
1995—Green Bay NFL	16	1	3	32	10.7	0	0	0	0	0
1996—Green Bay NFL	16	1	3	45	15.0	0	0	0	0	0
1997—Green Bay NFL	13	1	9	115	12.8	1	1	0	6	1
1998—Green Bay NFL	16	2	9	89	9.9	0	0	0	0	0
Pro totals (6 years)	68	5	28	303	10.8	1	1	0	6	1

THOMPSON, BENNIE   S   RAVENS

PERSONAL: Born February 10, 1963, in New Orleans. ... 6-0/214.
HIGH SCHOOL: John McDonogh (New Orleans).
COLLEGE: Grambling State.
TRANSACTIONS/CAREER NOTES: Signed as non-drafted free agent by Kansas City Chiefs (May 9, 1985). ... Released by Chiefs (August 5, 1985). ... Signed by Winnipeg Blue Bombers of CFL (April 21, 1986). ... Granted free agency (March 1, 1989). ... Signed by New Orleans Saints (April 12, 1989). ... Released by Saints (September 5, 1989). ... Re-signed by Saints to practice squad (September 6, 1989). ... Activated (December 15, 1989). ... Granted unconditional free agency (February 1-April 1, 1991). ... Re-signed by Saints for 1991 season. ... Granted unconditional free agency (February 1, 1992). ... Signed by Chiefs (March 28, 1992). ... Granted unconditional free agency (February 17, 1994). ... Rights relinquished by Chiefs (April 29, 1994). ... Signed by Cleveland Browns (July 19, 1994). ... Browns franchise moved to Baltimore and renamed Ravens for 1996 season (March 11, 1996). ... Granted unconditional free agency (February 13, 1998). ... Re-signed by Ravens (March 10, 1998).
CHAMPIONSHIP GAME EXPERIENCE: Played in AFC championship game (1993 season).
HONORS: Played in Pro Bowl (1991 and 1998 seasons).
PRO STATISTICS: CFL: 1987—Recovered one fumble. 1988—Fumbled once and recovered two fumbles for two yards. NFL: 1991— Recovered two fumbles. 1994—Recovered one fumble. 1997—Recovered two fumbles. 1998—Returned one punt for 43 yards.

Year Team	G	GS	INTERCEPTIONS No.	Yds.	Avg.	TD	SACKS No.
1986—Winnipeg CFL	9	...	2	49	24.5	0	0.0
1987—Winnipeg CFL	8	...	1	0	0.0	0	0.0
1988—Winnipeg CFL	18	...	4	58	14.5	0	0.0
1989—New Orleans NFL	2	0	0	0	...	0	0.0
1990—New Orleans NFL	16	2	2	0	0.0	0	0.0
1991—New Orleans NFL	16	0	1	14	14.0	0	0.0
1992—Kansas City NFL	16	0	4	26	6.5	0	1.5
1993—Kansas City NFL	16	0	0	0	...	0	0.5
1994—Cleveland NFL	16	0	0	0	...	0	1.0
1995—Cleveland NFL	13	0	0	0	...	0	0.0
1996—Baltimore NFL	16	0	0	0	...	0	3.0
1997—Baltimore NFL	16	1	0	0	...	0	0.0
1998—Baltimore NFL	16	0	0	0	...	0	0.0
CFL totals (3 years)	35	...	7	107	15.3	0	0.0
NFL totals (10 years)	143	3	7	40	5.7	0	6.0
Pro totals (13 years)	178	...	14	147	10.5	0	6.0

THOMPSON, DAVID   RB   RAMS

PERSONAL: Born January 13, 1975, in Okmulgee, Okla. ... 5-8/200. ... Full name: David Farrod Thompson.
HIGH SCHOOL: Okmulgee (Okla.).
COLLEGE: Oklahoma State (degree in speech communications, 1997).

TRANSACTIONS/CAREER NOTES: Signed as non-drafted free agent by Jacksonville Jaguars (April 20, 1997). ... Released by Jaguars (August 19, 1997). ... Signed by St. Louis Rams to practice squad (August 25, 1997). ... Activated (October 9, 1997). ... Released by Rams (August 30, 1998). ... Re-signed by Rams (September 29, 1998). ... Assigned by Rams to Amsterdam Admirals in 1999 NFL Europe enhancement allocation program (February 22, 1999).
PRO STATISTICS: 1997—Recovered one fumble.
SINGLE GAME HIGHS (regular season): Attempts—9 (December 7, 1997, vs. New Orleans); yards—18 (December 7, 1997, vs. New Orleans); and rushing touchdowns—1 (December 20, 1997, vs. Carolina).

				RUSHING				KICKOFF RETURNS			TOTALS			
Year Team	G	GS	Att.	Yds.	Avg.	TD	No.	Yds.	Avg.	TD	TD	2pt.	Pts.	Fum.
1997—St. Louis NFL	11	0	16	30	1.9	1	49	1110	22.7	0	1	0	6	2
1998—St. Louis NFL	1	0	0	0	...	0	0	0	...	0	0	0	0	0
Pro totals (2 years)	12	0	16	30	1.9	1	49	1110	22.7	0	1	0	6	2

THOMPSON, MIKE — DT — BROWNS

PERSONAL: Born December 22, 1971, in Portage, Wis. ... 6-4/295. ... Full name: Michael John Thompson.
HIGH SCHOOL: Portage (Wis.).
COLLEGE: Wisconsin.
TRANSACTIONS/CAREER NOTES: Selected by Jacksonville Jaguars in fourth round (123rd pick overall) of 1995 NFL draft. ... Signed by Jaguars (June 1, 1995). ... Released by Jaguars (August 25, 1996). ... Signed by Green Bay Packers (January 2, 1997). ... Released by Packers (August 18, 1997). ... Signed by Kansas City Chiefs (August 21, 1997). ... Released by Chiefs (August 28, 1997). ... Signed by Cincinnati Bengals (December 15, 1997). ... Inactive for one game (1997). ... Selected by Cleveland Browns from Bengals in NFL expansion draft (February 9, 1999).
PLAYING EXPERIENCE: Jacksonville NFL, 1995; Cincinnati NFL, 1998. ... Games/Games started: 1995 (2/0), 1998 (9/0). Total: 11/0.
PRO STATISTICS: 1998—Credited with $1/2$ sack.

THRASH, JAMES — WR — REDSKINS

PERSONAL: Born April 28, 1975, in Denver. ... 6-0/200.
HIGH SCHOOL: Wewoka (Okla.).
COLLEGE: Missouri Southern.
TRANSACTIONS/CAREER NOTES: Signed as non-drafted free agent by Philadelphia Eagles (April 22, 1997). ... Released by Eagles (July 8, 1997). ... Signed by Washington Redskins (July 11, 1997). ... On injured reserve with shoulder injury (December 8, 1998-remainder of season).
PRO STATISTICS: 1998—Returned six kickoffs for 129 yards.
SINGLE GAME HIGHS (regular season): Receptions—4 (December 6, 1998, vs. San Diego); yards—66 (December 6, 1998, vs. San Diego); and touchdown receptions—1 (December 6, 1998, vs. San Diego).

			RECEIVING				TOTALS			
Year Team	G	GS	No.	Yds.	Avg.	TD	TD	2pt.	Pts.	Fum.
1997—Washington NFL	4	0	2	24	12.0	0	0	0	0	0
1998—Washington NFL	10	1	10	163	16.3	1	1	0	6	0
Pro totals (2 years)	14	1	12	187	15.6	1	1	0	6	0

THREATS, JABBAR — DE — JAGUARS

PERSONAL: Born April 26, 1975, in Springfield, Ohio. ... 6-5/256. ... Full name: Anthayus Jabbar Threats.
HIGH SCHOOL: Springfield (Ohio) North.
JUNIOR COLLEGE: Garden City (Kan.) Community College.
COLLEGE: Michigan State.
TRANSACTIONS/CAREER NOTES: Signed as non-drafted free agent by Jacksonville Jaguars (July 15, 1997). ... On injured reserve with knee injury (October 1, 1998-remainder of season).
PLAYING EXPERIENCE: Jacksonville NFL, 1997 and 1998. ... Games/Games started: 1997 (1/0), 1998 (2/0). Total: 3/0.

TILLMAN, PAT — S — CARDINALS

PERSONAL: Born November 6, 1976, in Fremont, Calif. ... 5-11/204. ... Full name: Patrick Daniel Tillman.
HIGH SCHOOL: Leland (San Jose, Calif.).
COLLEGE: Arizona State (degree in marketing, 1997).
TRANSACTIONS/CAREER NOTES: Selected by Arizona Cardinals in seventh round (226th pick overall) of 1998 NFL draft. ... Signed by Cardinals for 1998 season.
PLAYING EXPERIENCE: Arizona NFL, 1998. ... Games/Games started: 16/10.
HONORS: Named outside linebacker on THE SPORTING NEWS college All-America first team (1997).
PRO STATISTICS: 1998—Credited with one sack.

TIMMERMAN, ADAM — C — RAMS

PERSONAL: Born August 14, 1971, in Cherokee, Iowa. ... 6-4/300. ... Full name: Adam Larry Timmerman.
HIGH SCHOOL: Washington (Cherokee, Iowa).
COLLEGE: South Dakota State (degree in agriculture business).

TRANSACTIONS/CAREER NOTES: Selected by Green Bay Packers in seventh round (230th pick overall) of 1995 NFL draft. ... Signed by Packers (June 2, 1995). ... Granted free agency (February 13, 1998). ... Re-signed by Packers (April 15, 1998). ... Granted unconditional free agency (February 12, 1999). ... Signed by St. Louis Rams (February 16, 1999).
PLAYING EXPERIENCE: Green Bay NFL, 1995-1998. ... Games/Games started: 1995 (13/0), 1996 (16/16), 1997 (16/16), 1998 (16/16). Total: 61/48.
CHAMPIONSHIP GAME EXPERIENCE: Played in NFC championship game (1995-97 seasons). ... Member of Super Bowl championship team (1996 season). ... Played in Super Bowl XXXII (1997 season).

TOBECK, ROBBIE   C/G   FALCONS

PERSONAL: Born March 6, 1970, in Tarpon Springs, Fla. ... 6-4/298. ... Full name: Robert L. Tobeck.
HIGH SCHOOL: New Port Richey (Fla.).
COLLEGE: Washington State.
TRANSACTIONS/CAREER NOTES: Signed as non-drafted free agent by Atlanta Falcons (May 7, 1993). ... Released by Falcons (August 30, 1993). ... Re-signed by Falcons to practice squad (August 31, 1993). ... Activated (January 1, 1994).
PLAYING EXPERIENCE: Atlanta NFL, 1994-1998. ... Games/Games started: 1994 (5/0), 1995 (16/16), 1996 (16/16), 1997 (16/15), 1998 (16/16). Total: 69/63.
CHAMPIONSHIP GAME EXPERIENCE: Played in NFC championship game (1998 season). ... Played in Super Bowl XXXIII (1998 season).
PRO STATISTICS: 1996—Caught two passes for 15 yards and a touchdown. 1997—Recovered one fumble. 1998—Recovered one fumble for one yard.

TOLLIVER, BILLY JOE   QB   SAINTS

PERSONAL: Born February 7, 1966, in Dallas. ... 6-1/217.
HIGH SCHOOL: Boyd (Texas).
COLLEGE: Texas Tech.
TRANSACTIONS/CAREER NOTES: Selected by San Diego Chargers in second round (51st pick overall) of 1989 NFL draft. ... Signed by Chargers (July 30, 1989). ... On injured reserve with broken collarbone (September 5-October 18, 1989). ... On developmental squad (October 19-20, 1989). ... Traded by Chargers to Atlanta Falcons for fifth-round pick (LB Kevin Little) in 1992 draft (August 28, 1991). ... Granted free agency (March 1, 1993). ... Re-signed by Falcons (August 9, 1993). ... Granted unconditional free agency (February 17, 1994). ... Signed by Houston Oilers (September 7, 1994). ... Granted unconditional free agency (February 17, 1995). ... Signed by Falcons (October 23, 1996). ... Inactive for nine games (1996). ... Granted unconditional free agency (February 14, 1997). ... Re-signed by Falcons (March 19, 1997). ... Released by Falcons (October 27, 1997). ... Signed by Kansas City Chiefs (November 5, 1997). ... Released by Chiefs (August 25, 1998). ... Signed by New Orleans Saints (September 9, 1998).
PRO STATISTICS: 1989—Fumbled four times and recovered one fumble for minus six yards. 1990—Fumbled six times and recovered two fumbles. 1991—Fumbled three times. 1992—Fumbled five times. 1994—Fumbled seven times. 1997—Fumbled seven times and recovered two fumbles for minus one yard. 1998—Fumbled three times for minus 13 yards.
SINGLE GAME HIGHS (regular season): Attempts—51 (December 16, 1990, vs. Denver); completions—26 (December 16, 1990, vs. Denver); yards—350 (December 10, 1989, vs. Washington); and touchdown passes—3 (December 27, 1998, vs. Buffalo).
STATISTICAL PLATEAUS: 300-yard passing games: 1989 (2), 1990 (1), 1998 (1). Total: 4.
MISCELLANEOUS: Regular-season record as starting NFL quarterback: 14-26 (.350).

				PASSING								RUSHING				TOTALS		
Year Team	G	GS	Att.	Cmp.	Pct.	Yds.	TD	Int.	Avg.	Rat.	Att.	Yds.	Avg.	TD	TD	2pt.	Pts.
1989—San Diego NFL	5	5	185	89	48.1	1097	5	8	5.93	57.9	7	0	0.0	0	0	...	0
1990—San Diego NFL	15	14	410	216	52.7	2574	16	16	6.28	68.9	14	22	1.6	0	0	...	0
1991—Atlanta NFL	7	2	82	40	48.8	531	4	2	6.48	75.8	9	6	0.7	0	0	...	0
1992—Atlanta NFL	9	5	131	73	55.7	787	5	5	6.01	70.4	4	15	3.8	0	0	...	0
1993—Atlanta NFL	7	2	76	39	51.3	464	3	5	6.11	56.0	7	48	6.9	0	0	...	0
1994—Houston NFL	10	7	240	121	50.4	1287	6	7	5.36	62.6	12	37	3.1	2	2	0	12
1995—								Did not play.									
1996—Atlanta NFL								Did not play.									
1997—Atlanta NFL	6	1	115	63	54.8	685	5	1	5.96	83.4	7	8	1.1	0	0	0	0
—Kansas City NFL	3	0	1	1	100.0	-8	0	0	-8.00	79.2	2	-1	-0.5	0	0	0	0
1998—New Orleans NFL	7	4	199	110	55.3	1427	8	4	7.17	83.1	11	43	3.9	0	0	0	0
Pro totals (8 years)	69	40	1439	752	52.3	8844	52	48	6.15	69.4	73	178	2.4	2	2	0	12

TOMCZAK, MIKE   QB   STEELERS

PERSONAL: Born October 23, 1962, in Chicago. ... 6-1/210. ... Full name: Michael John Tomczak. ... Name pronounced TOM-zak.
HIGH SCHOOL: Thornton Fractional North (Calumet City, Ill.).
COLLEGE: Ohio State (degree in communications).
TRANSACTIONS/CAREER NOTES: Selected by New Jersey Generals in 1985 USFL territorial draft. ... Signed as non-drafted free agent by Chicago Bears (May 9, 1985). ... Granted free agency (February 1, 1990). ... Re-signed by Bears (July 25, 1990). ... Granted unconditional free agency (February 1, 1991). ... Signed by Green Bay Packers (March 30, 1991). ... Granted free agency (February 1, 1992). ... Re-signed by Packers (August 19, 1992). ... Released by Packers (August 31, 1992). ... Signed by Cleveland Browns (September 16, 1992). ... Granted unconditional free agency (March 1, 1993). ... Signed by Pittsburgh Steelers (April 6, 1993). ... Granted unconditional free agency (February 14, 1997). ... Re-signed by Steelers (March 6, 1997).
CHAMPIONSHIP GAME EXPERIENCE: Member of Bears for NFC championship game (1985 season); did not play. ... Member of Super Bowl championship team (1985 season). ... Played in NFC championship game (1988 season). ... Member of Steelers for AFC championship game (1994 and 1995 seasons); did not play. ... Member of Steelers for Super Bowl XXX (1995 season); did not play. ... Played in AFC championship game (1997 season).

PRO STATISTICS: 1985—Fumbled once and recovered one fumble for minus 13 yards. 1986—Fumbled twice. 1987—Fumbled six times and recovered one fumble. 1988—Fumbled once. 1989—Fumbled twice. 1990—Caught one pass for five yards and fumbled twice. 1991—Fumbled five times and recovered two fumbles for minus one yard. 1992—Fumbled five times. 1993—Fumbled twice and recovered one fumble. 1994—Fumbled twice. 1995—Fumbled twice and recovered one fumble. 1996—Fumbled seven times and recovered two fumbles. 1998—Fumbled twice.

SINGLE GAME HIGHS (regular season): Attempts—43 (December 15, 1996, vs. San Francisco); completions—26 (November 20, 1994, vs. Miami); yards—343 (November 20, 1994, vs. Miami); and touchdown passes—3 (December 1, 1991, vs. Atlanta).

STATISTICAL PLATEAUS: 300-yard passing games: 1989 (1), 1991 (1), 1992 (1), 1994 (1), 1996 (1). Total: 5.

MISCELLANEOUS: Regular-season record as starting NFL quarterback: 41-27 (.603). Postseason record as starting NFL quarterback: 3-2 (.600).

				PASSING						RUSHING				TOTALS	
Year Team	G	GS	Att.	Cmp.	Pct.	Yds.	TD	Int.	Avg.	Rat.	Att.	Yds.	Avg.	TD	TD 2pt. Pts.
1985—Chicago NFL	6	0	6	2	33.3	33	0	0	5.50	52.8	2	3	1.5	0	0 ... 0
1986—Chicago NFL	13	7	151	74	49.0	1105	2	10	7.32	50.2	23	117	5.1	3	3 ... 18
1987—Chicago NFL	12	6	178	97	54.5	1220	5	10	6.85	62.0	18	54	3.0	1	1 ... 6
1988—Chicago NFL	14	5	170	86	50.6	1310	7	6	7.71	75.4	13	40	3.1	0	1 ... 6
1989—Chicago NFL	16	11	306	156	51.0	2058	16	16	6.73	68.2	24	71	3.0	0	1 ... 6
1990—Chicago NFL	16	2	104	39	37.5	521	3	5	5.01	43.8	12	41	3.4	2	2 ... 12
1991—Green Bay NFL	12	7	238	128	53.8	1490	11	9	6.26	72.6	17	93	5.5	1	1 ... 6
1992—Cleveland NFL	12	8	211	120	56.9	1693	7	7	8.02	80.1	24	39	1.6	0	0 ... 0
1993—Pittsburgh NFL	7	1	54	29	53.7	398	2	5	7.37	51.3	5	-4	-0.8	0	0 ... 0
1994—Pittsburgh NFL	6	2	93	54	58.1	804	4	0	8.65	100.8	4	22	5.5	0	0 0 0
1995—Pittsburgh NFL	7	4	113	65	57.5	666	1	9	5.89	44.3	11	25	2.3	0	0 0 0
1996—Pittsburgh NFL	16	15	401	222	55.4	2767	15	17	6.90	71.8	22	-7	-0.3	0	0 0 0
1997—Pittsburgh NFL	16	0	24	16	66.7	185	1	2	7.71	68.9	7	13	1.9	0	0 0 0
1998—Pittsburgh NFL	16	0	30	21	70.0	204	2	2	6.80	83.2	0	0	...	0	0 0 0
Pro totals (14 years)	169	68	2079	1109	53.3	14454	76	98	6.95	68.0	182	507	2.8	9	9 0 54

TOMICH, JARED — DE — SAINTS

PERSONAL: Born April 24, 1974, in St. John, Ind. ... 6-2/272. ... Full name: Jared James Tomich.
HIGH SCHOOL: Lake Central (St. John, Ind.).
COLLEGE: Nebraska.
TRANSACTIONS/CAREER NOTES: Selected by New Orleans Saints in second round (39th pick overall) of 1997 NFL draft. ... Signed by Saints (July 17, 1997).
PRO STATISTICS: 1997—Returned one kickoff for no yards, fumbled once and recovered one fumble. 1998—Returned one kickoff for no yards and recovered one fumble.

Year Team	G	GS	SACKS
1997—New Orleans NFL	16	1	1.0
1998—New Orleans NFL	16	11	6.0
Pro totals (2 years)	32	12	7.0

TONGUE, REGGIE — S — CHIEFS

PERSONAL: Born April 11, 1973, in Baltimore. ... 6-0/205. ... Full name: Reginald Clinton Tongue. ... Name pronounced TONG.
HIGH SCHOOL: Lathrop (Fairbanks, Alaska).
COLLEGE: Oregon State.
TRANSACTIONS/CAREER NOTES: Selected by Kansas City Chiefs in second round (58th pick overall) of 1996 NFL draft. ... Signed by Chiefs (July 26, 1996).
PLAYING EXPERIENCE: Kansas City NFL, 1996-1998. ... Games/Games started: 1996 (16/0), 1997 (16/16), 1998 (15/15). Total: 47/31.
PRO STATISTICS: 1997—Intercepted one pass for no yards and credited with 2$\frac{1}{2}$ sacks. 1998—Credited with two sacks and recovered one fumble.

TOOMER, AMANI — WR/KR — GIANTS

PERSONAL: Born September 8, 1974, in Berkely, Calif. ... 6-3/202. ... Name pronounced ah-MAH-nee.
HIGH SCHOOL: De La Salle Catholic (Concord, Calif.).
COLLEGE: Michigan.
TRANSACTIONS/CAREER NOTES: Selected by New York Giants in second round (34th pick overall) of 1996 NFL draft. ... Signed by Giants (July 21, 1996). ... On injured reserve with knee injury (October 31, 1996-remainder of season). ... Granted free agency (February 12, 1999).
PRO STATISTICS: 1996—Recovered two fumbles. 1998—Attempted one pass without a completion.
SINGLE GAME HIGHS (regular season): Receptions—4 (December 20, 1998, vs. Kansas City); yards—64 (November 16, 1997, vs. Arizona); and touchdown receptions—1 (December 20, 1998, vs. Kansas City).

			RECEIVING				PUNT RETURNS				KICKOFF RETURNS				TOTALS		
Year Team	G	GS	No.	Yds.	Avg.	TD	No.	Yds.	Avg.	TD	No.	Yds.	Avg.	TD	TD 2pt.	Pts.	Fum.
1996—New York Giants NFL	7	1	1	12	12.0	0	18	298	16.6	2	11	191	17.4	0	2 0	12	1
1997—New York Giants NFL	16	0	16	263	16.4	1	47	455	9.7	∞1	0	0	...	0	2 0	12	0
1998—New York Giants NFL	16	0	27	360	13.3	5	35	252	7.2	0	4	66	16.5	0	5 0	30	0
Pro totals (3 years)	39	1	44	635	14.4	6	100	1005	10.1	3	15	257	17.1	0	9 0	54	1

TOVAR, STEVE   LB   PANTHERS

PERSONAL: Born April 25, 1970, in Elyria, Ohio. ... 6-3/244. ... Full name: Steven Eric Tovar.
HIGH SCHOOL: West (Elyria, Ohio).
COLLEGE: Ohio State.
TRANSACTIONS/CAREER NOTES: Selected by the Cincinnati Bengals in third round (59th pick overall) of 1993 NFL draft. ... Signed by Bengals (July 19, 1993). ... Granted free agency (February 16, 1996). ... Re-signed by Bengals (April 15, 1996). ... On injured reserve with knee injury (December 2, 1996-remainder of season). ... Released by Bengals (August 21, 1998). ... Signed by San Diego Chargers (August 25, 1998). ... Granted unconditional free agency (February 12, 1999). ... Signed by Carolina Panthers (February 15, 1999).
PRO STATISTICS: 1993—Recovered one fumble. 1994—Returned one kickoff for eight yards and recovered two fumbles. 1996—Fumbled once.

			INTERCEPTIONS				SACKS
Year Team	G	GS	No.	Yds.	Avg.	TD	No.
1993—Cincinnati NFL	16	9	1	0	0.0	0	0.0
1994—Cincinnati NFL	16	16	1	14	14.0	0	3.0
1995—Cincinnati NFL	14	13	1	13	13.0	0	1.0
1996—Cincinnati NFL	13	13	4	42	10.5	0	3.0
1997—Cincinnati NFL	14	5	0	0	...	0	0.0
1998—San Diego NFL	16	2	0	0	...	0	1.0
Pro totals (6 years)	89	58	7	69	9.9	0	8.0

TOWNSEND, DESHEA   CB   STEELERS

PERSONAL: Born September 8, 1975, in Batesville, Miss. ... 5-10/175. ... Full name: Trevor Deshea Townsend.
HIGH SCHOOL: South Panola (Batesville, Miss.).
COLLEGE: Alabama.
TRANSACTIONS/CAREER NOTES: Selected by Pittsburgh Steelers in fourth round (117th pick overall) of 1998 NFL draft. ... Signed by Steelers (July 6, 1998).
PLAYING EXPERIENCE: Pittsburgh NFL, 1998. ... Games/Games started: 12/0.

TRAPP, JAMES   CB   RAVENS

PERSONAL: Born December 28, 1969, in Greenville, S.C. ... 6-0/195. ... Full name: James Harold Trapp.
HIGH SCHOOL: Lawton (Okla.).
COLLEGE: Clemson.
TRANSACTIONS/CAREER NOTES: Selected by Los Angeles Raiders in third round (72nd pick overall) of 1993 NFL draft. ... Signed by Raiders (July 13, 1993). ... Raiders franchise moved to Oakland (July 21, 1995). ... Granted free agency (February 16, 1996). ... Re-signed by Raiders (March 30, 1996). ... Granted unconditional free agency (February 12, 1999). ... Signed by Baltimore Ravens (April 23, 1999).
PLAYING EXPERIENCE: Los Angeles Raiders NFL, 1993 and 1994; Oakland NFL, 1995-1998. ... Games/Games started: 1993 (14/2), 1994 (16/2), 1995 (14/2), 1996 (12/4), 1997 (16/16), 1998 (16/0). Total: 88/26.
PRO STATISTICS: 1993—Intercepted one pass for seven yards. 1994—Credited with one sack. 1995—Recovered one fumble. 1996—Intercepted one pass for 23 yards. 1997—Intercepted two passes for 24 yards and recovered two fumbles.

TRAYLOR, KEITH   DT   BRONCOS

PERSONAL: Born September 3, 1969, in Little Rock, Ark. ... 6-2/304. ... Full name: Byron Keith Traylor. ... Cousin of Isaac Davis, guard, Oakland Raiders.
HIGH SCHOOL: Malvern (Ark.).
JUNIOR COLLEGE: Coffeyville (Kan.) Community College.
COLLEGE: Oklahoma, then Central Oklahoma.
TRANSACTIONS/CAREER NOTES: Selected by Denver Broncos in third round (61st pick overall) of 1991 NFL draft. ... Signed by Broncos for 1991 season. ... Released by Broncos (June 7, 1993). ... Signed by Los Angeles Raiders (June 1993). ... Released by Raiders (August 30, 1993). ... Signed by Green Bay Packers (September 14, 1993). ... Released by Packers (November 9, 1993). ... Signed by Kansas City Chiefs (January 7, 1994). ... Released by Chiefs (January 14, 1994). ... Re-signed by Chiefs (May 18, 1994). ... Released by Chiefs (August 28, 1994). ... Re-signed by Chiefs (February 28, 1995). ... Granted unconditional free agency (February 14, 1997). ... Signed by Broncos (March 10, 1997).
CHAMPIONSHIP GAME EXPERIENCE: Played in AFC championship game (1991, 1997 and 1998 seasons). ... Member of Super Bowl championship team (1997 and 1998 seasons).
PRO STATISTICS: 1992—Returned one kickoff for 13 yards. 1995—Recovered one fumble. 1997—Intercepted one pass for 62 yards and a touchdown. 1998—Recovered one fumble.

Year Team	G	GS	SACKS
1991—Denver NFL	16	2	0.0
1992—Denver NFL	16	3	1.0
1993—Green Bay NFL	5	0	0.0
1994—	Did not play.		
1995—Barcelona W.L.	8	3	0.0
—Kansas City NFL	16	0	1.5
1996—Kansas City NFL	15	2	1.0
1997—Denver NFL	16	16	2.0
1998—Denver NFL	15	14	2.0
W.L. totals (1 year)	8	3	0.0
NFL totals (7 years)	99	37	7.5
Pro totals (8 years)	107	40	7.5

TREU, ADAM — OT — RAIDERS

PERSONAL: Born June 24, 1974, in Lincoln, Neb. ... 6-5/300. ... Name pronounced TRUE.
HIGH SCHOOL: Pius X (Lincoln, Neb.).
COLLEGE: Nebraska.
TRANSACTIONS/CAREER NOTES: Selected by Oakland Raiders in third round (72nd pick overall) of 1997 NFL draft. ... Signed by Raiders for 1997 season.
PLAYING EXPERIENCE: Oakland NFL, 1997 and 1998. ... Games/Games started: 1997 (16/0), 1998 (16/0). Total: 32/0.

TROTTER, JEREMIAH — LB — EAGLES

PERSONAL: Born January 20, 1977, in Hooks, Texas. ... 6-0/261.
HIGH SCHOOL: Hooks (Texas).
COLLEGE: Stephen F. Austin State.
TRANSACTIONS/CAREER NOTES: Selected after junior season by Philadelphia Eagles in third round (72nd pick overall) of 1998 NFL draft. ... Signed by Eagles (July 14, 1998).
PLAYING EXPERIENCE: Philadelphia NFL, 1998. ... Games/Games started: 8/0.

TRUITT, GREG — C — BENGALS

PERSONAL: Born December 8, 1965, in Sarasota, Fla. ... 6-0/235.
HIGH SCHOOL: Riverview (Sarasota, Fla.).
COLLEGE: Penn State (degree in criminology).
TRANSACTIONS/CAREER NOTES: Signed as non-drafted free agent by Cincinnati Bengals (April 6, 1994).
PLAYING EXPERIENCE: Cincinnati NFL, 1994-1998. ... Games/Games started: 1994 (16/0), 1995 (16/0), 1996 (16/0), 1997 (16/0), 1998 (11/0). Total: 75/0.
PRO STATISTICS: 1997—Fumbled twice for minus 11 yards. 1998—Fumbled once for minus 12 yards.

TUAOLO, ESERA — DT

PERSONAL: Born July 11, 1968, in Honolulu. ... 6-3/276. ... Full name: Esera Tavai Tuaolo. ... Name pronounced ess-ER-uh TOO-ah-OH-lo.
HIGH SCHOOL: Don Antonio Lugo (Chino, Calif.).
COLLEGE: Oregon State.
TRANSACTIONS/CAREER NOTES: Selected by Green Bay Packers in second round (35th pick overall) of 1991 NFL draft. ... Signed by Packers (July 19, 1991). ... Released by Packers (October 1, 1992). ... Signed by Minnesota Vikings (November 24, 1992). ... Granted free agency (February 17, 1994). ... Re-signed by Vikings (July 18, 1994). ... Granted unconditional free agency (February 17, 1995). ... Re-signed by Vikings (March 7, 1995). ... On physically unable to perform list with Achilles' tendon injury (July 22-August 26, 1996). ... Released by Vikings (February 27, 1997). ... Signed by Buffalo Bills (June 25, 1997). ... Released by Bills (August 18, 1997). ... Signed by Jacksonville Jaguars (November 4, 1997). ... Granted unconditional free agency (February 13, 1998). ... Signed by Atlanta Falcons (May 14, 1998). ... Granted unconditional free agency (February 12, 1999).
CHAMPIONSHIP GAME EXPERIENCE: Played in NFC championship game (1998 season). ... Played in Super Bowl XXXIII (1998 season).
PRO STATISTICS: 1991—Intercepted one pass for 23 yards. 1995—Recovered two fumbles. 1998—Recovered one fumble.

Year Team	G	GS	SACKS
1991—Green Bay NFL	16	16	3.5
1992—Green Bay NFL	4	0	1.0
—Minnesota NFL	3	0	0.0
1993—Minnesota NFL	11	3	0.0
1994—Minnesota NFL	16	0	0.0
1995—Minnesota NFL	16	16	3.0
1996—Minnesota NFL	14	9	2.5
1997—Jacksonville NFL	6	1	1.0
1998—Atlanta NFL	13	1	0.0
Pro totals (8 years)	**99**	**46**	**11.0**

TUBBS, WINFRED — LB — 49ERS

PERSONAL: Born September 24, 1970, in Fairfield, Texas. ... 6-4/260. ... Full name: Winfred O'Neal Tubbs.
HIGH SCHOOL: Fairfield (Texas).
COLLEGE: Texas (degree in psychology, 1993).
TRANSACTIONS/CAREER NOTES: Selected by New Orleans Saints in third round (79th pick overall) of 1994 NFL draft. ... Signed by Saints (July 20, 1994). ... On injured reserve with knee injury (December 22, 1995-remainder of season). ... Granted free agency (February 14, 1997). ... Re-signed by Saints (July 17, 1997). ... Granted unconditional free agency (February 13, 1998). ... Signed by San Francisco 49ers (February 18, 1998).
HONORS: Played in Pro Bowl (1998 season).
PRO STATISTICS: 1995—Recovered one fumble. 1996—Recovered one fumble. 1997—Recovered two fumbles. 1998—Recovered one fumble.

			INTERCEPTIONS				SACKS
Year Team	G	GS	No.	Yds.	Avg.	TD	No.
1994—New Orleans NFL	13	7	1	0	0.0	0	1.0
1995—New Orleans NFL	7	6	1	6	6.0	0	1.0
1996—New Orleans NFL	16	13	1	11	11.0	0	1.0
1997—New Orleans NFL	16	16	2	21	10.5	0	2.5
1998—San Francisco NFL	16	16	1	7	7.0	0	1.0
Pro totals (5 years)	**68**	**58**	**6**	**45**	**7.5**	**0**	**6.5**

TUCKER, RYAN   C   RAMS

PERSONAL: Born June 12, 1975, in Midland, Texas. ... 6-5/305. ... Full name: Ryan Huey Tucker. ... Brother of Rex Tucker, offensive lineman, Chicago Bears.
HIGH SCHOOL: Robert E. Lee (Midland, Texas).
COLLEGE: Texas Christian.
TRANSACTIONS/CAREER NOTES: Selected by St. Louis Rams in fourth round (112th pick overall) of 1997 NFL draft. ... Signed by Rams (July 3, 1997). ... On physically unable to perform list with knee injury (August 19-October 29, 1997).
PLAYING EXPERIENCE: St. Louis NFL, 1997 and 1998. ... Games/Games started: 1997 (7/0), 1998 (4/0). Total: 11/0.

TUGGLE, JESSIE   LB   FALCONS

PERSONAL: Born April 4, 1965, in Spalding County, Ga. ... 5-11/230. ... Full name: Jessie Lloyd Tuggle Jr.
HIGH SCHOOL: Griffin (Ga.).
COLLEGE: Valdosta (Ga.) State.
TRANSACTIONS/CAREER NOTES: Signed as non-drafted free agent by Atlanta Falcons (May 2, 1987). ... Granted free agency (February 1, 1991). ... Re-signed by Falcons (August 7, 1991). ... On reserve/did not report list (July 23-August 30, 1993). ... Granted roster exemption (August 30-September 3, 1993).
CHAMPIONSHIP GAME EXPERIENCE: Played in NFC championship game (1998 season). ... Played in Super Bowl XXXIII (1998 season).
HONORS: Played in Pro Bowl (1992, 1994, 1995, 1997 and 1998 seasons).
RECORDS: Holds NFL career record for most touchdowns by recovery of opponents' fumbles—5; and most touchdowns by fumble recovery—5.
PRO STATISTICS: 1988—Recovered one fumble for two yards and one touchdown. 1989—Recovered one fumble. 1990—Recovered two fumbles for 65 yards and one touchdown. 1991—Recovered two fumbles for 18 yards and one touchdown. 1992—Recovered one fumble for 69 yards and a touchdown. 1993—Recovered one fumble. 1994—Recovered one fumble. 1998—Recovered one fumble for one yard and a touchdown.

			INTERCEPTIONS				SACKS
Year Team	G	GS	No.	Yds.	Avg.	TD	No.
1987—Atlanta NFL	12	4	0	0	...	0	1.0
1988—Atlanta NFL	16	8	0	0	...	0	0.0
1989—Atlanta NFL	16	16	0	0	...	0	1.0
1990—Atlanta NFL	16	14	0	0	...	0	5.0
1991—Atlanta NFL	16	16	1	21	21.0	0	1.0
1992—Atlanta NFL	15	15	1	1	1.0	0	1.0
1993—Atlanta NFL	16	16	0	0	...	0	2.0
1994—Atlanta NFL	16	16	1	0	0.0	0	0.0
1995—Atlanta NFL	16	16	3	84	28.0	1	1.0
1996—Atlanta NFL	16	16	0	0	...	0	1.0
1997—Atlanta NFL	16	15	0	0	...	0	1.5
1998—Atlanta NFL	16	16	0	0	...	0	3.0
Pro totals (12 years)	187	168	6	106	17.7	1	17.5

TUINEI, VAN   DL   COLTS

PERSONAL: Born February 16, 1971, in Garden Grove, Calif. ... 6-3/290. ... Full name: Vaega Van Tuinei. ... Name pronounced Two-uh-NAY.
HIGH SCHOOL: Westminster (Calif.).
JUNIOR COLLEGE: Golden West College (Calif.).
COLLEGE: Arizona.
TRANSACTIONS/CAREER NOTES: Signed as non-drafted free agent by San Diego Chargers (April 21, 1997). ... Released by Chargers (August 25, 1998). ... Re-signed by Chargers (August 27, 1998). ... Released by Chargers (August 30, 1998). ... Signed by Indianapolis Colts (September 16, 1998).
PLAYING EXPERIENCE: San Diego NFL, 1997; Indianapolis NFL, 1998. ... Games/Games started: 1997 (3/0), 1998 (12/0). Total: 15/0.
PRO STATISTICS: 1998—Credited with two sacks and recovered one fumble.

TUMULTY, TOM   LB   BENGALS

PERSONAL: Born February 11, 1973, in Penn Hills, Pa. ... 6-3/247. ... Full name: Thomas Patrick Tumulty.
HIGH SCHOOL: Penn Hills (Pa.).
COLLEGE: Pittsburgh.
TRANSACTIONS/CAREER NOTES: Selected by Cincinnati Bengals in sixth round (178th pick overall) of 1996 NFL draft. ... Signed by Bengals (July 15, 1996). ... On injured reserve with foot injury (December 1, 1997-remainder of season). ... On injured reserve with knee injury (October 1, 1998-remainder of season).
PLAYING EXPERIENCE: Cincinnati NFL, 1996-1998. ... Games/Games started: 1996 (16/3), 1997 (11/11), 1998 (4/4). Total: 31/18.
PRO STATISTICS: 1997—Credited with one sack. 1998—Credited with ½ sack.

TUPA, TOM   P   JETS

PERSONAL: Born February 6, 1966, in Cleveland. ... 6-4/220. ... Full name: Thomas Joseph Tupa Jr.
HIGH SCHOOL: Brecksville (Broadview Heights, Ohio).
COLLEGE: Ohio State.

TRANSACTIONS/CAREER NOTES: Selected by Phoenix Cardinals in third round (68th pick overall) of 1988 NFL draft. ... Signed by Cardinals (July 12, 1988). ... Granted free agency (February 1, 1991). ... Re-signed by Cardinals (July 17, 1991). ... Granted unconditional free agency (February 1, 1992). ... Signed by Indianapolis Colts (March 31, 1992). ... Released by Colts (August 30, 1993). ... Signed by Cleveland Browns (November 9, 1993). ... Released by Browns (November 24, 1993). ... Re-signed by Browns (March 30, 1994). ... Granted unconditional free agency (February 16, 1996). ... Signed by New England Patriots (March 15, 1996). ... Granted unconditional free agency (February 12, 1999). ... Signed by New York Jets (February 15, 1999).

CHAMPIONSHIP GAME EXPERIENCE: Played in AFC championship game (1996 season). ... Played in Super Bowl XXXI (1996 season).

PRO STATISTICS: 1988—Attempted six passes with four completions for 49 yards. 1989—Rushed 15 times for 75 yards, attempted 134 passes with 65 completions for 973 yards (three touchdowns and nine interceptions), fumbled twice and recovered one fumble for minus six yards. 1990—Rushed once for no yards and fumbled once for minus seven yards. 1991—Rushed 28 times for 97 yards and a touchdown, attempted 315 passes with 165 completions for 2,053 yards (six touchdowns and 13 interceptions), fumbled eight times and recovered two fumbles. 1992—Rushed three times for nine yards, attempted 33 passes with 17 completions for 156 yards (one touchdwon and two interceptions), fumbled once and recovered one fumble for minus one yard. 1995—Rushed once for nine yards, attempted one pass with a completion for 25 yards. 1996—Attempted two passes without a completion. 1998—Rushed twice for minus two yards.

STATISTICAL PLATEAUS: 300-yard passing games: 1991 (1).
MISCELLANEOUS: Regular-season starting record as starting NFL quarterback: 4-9 (.308).

					PUNTING			
Year	Team	G	No.	Yds.	Avg.	Net avg.	In. 20	Blk.
1988—Phoenix NFL		2	0	0	...	...	0	0
1989—Phoenix NFL		14	6	280	46.7	39.7	2	0
1990—Phoenix NFL		15	0	0	...	...	0	0
1991—Phoenix NFL		11	0	0	...	...	0	0
1992—Indianapolis NFL		3	0	0	...	...	0	0
1993—Cleveland NFL					Did not play.			
1994—Cleveland NFL		16	80	3211	40.1	35.3	27	0
1995—Cleveland NFL		16	65	2831	43.6	36.2	18	0
1996—New England NFL		16	63	2739	43.5	36.0	14	0
1997—New England NFL		16	78	3569	45.8	36.1	24	1
1998—New England NFL		16	74	3294	44.5	35.4	13	0
Pro totals (10 years)		125	366	15924	43.5	35.8	98	1

TURK, DAN　　　C　　　REDSKINS

PERSONAL: Born June 25, 1962, in Milwaukee. ... 6-4/290. ... Full name: Daniel Anthony Turk. ... Brother of Matt Turk, punter, Washington Redskins.
HIGH SCHOOL: James Madison (Milwaukee).
COLLEGE: Drake, then Wisconsin.
TRANSACTIONS/CAREER NOTES: Selected by Jacksonville Bulls in USFL territorial draft. ... USFL rights traded by Bulls with rights to RB Marck Harrison and TE Ken Whisenhunt to Tampa Bay Bandits for rights to RB Cedric Jones, K Bobby Raymond and DB Eric Riley (January 3, 1985). ... Selected by Pittsburgh Steelers in fourth round (101st pick overall) of 1985 NFL draft. ... Signed by Steelers (July 19, 1985). ... On injured reserve with broken wrist (September 16, 1985-remainder of season). ... Traded by Steelers to Tampa Bay Buccaneers for sixth-round pick (DE Tim Johnson) in 1987 draft (April 18, 1987). ... Crossed picket line during players strike (October 14, 1987). ... On injured reserve with knee injury (October 18-November 18, 1988). ... Granted free agency (February 1, 1989). ... Rights relinquished by Buccaneers (June 6, 1989). ... Signed by Los Angeles Raiders (June 21, 1989). ... Granted free agency (February 1, 1991). ... Re-signed by Raiders (July 12, 1991). ... Granted unconditional free agency (February 17, 1994). ... Re-signed by Raiders (February 23, 1994). ... Raiders franchise moved to Oakland (July 21, 1995). ... Granted unconditional free agency (February 14, 1997). ... Signed by Washington Redskins (July 10, 1997). ... Granted unconditional free agency (February 12, 1999). ... Re-signed by Redskins (June 2, 1999).
PLAYING EXPERIENCE: Pittsburgh NFL, 1985 and 1986; Tampa Bay NFL, 1987 and 1988; Los Angeles Raiders NFL, 1989-1994; Oakland NFL, 1995 and 1996; Washington NFL, 1997 and 1998. ... Games/Games started: 1985 (1/0), 1986 (16/4), 1987 (13/3), 1988 (12/10), 1989 (16/5), 1990 (16/0), 1991 (16/0), 1992 (16/0), 1993 (16/0), 1994 (16/0), 1995 (16/0), 1996 (16/2), 1997 (16/0), 1998 (16/0). Total: 202/40.
CHAMPIONSHIP GAME EXPERIENCE: Played in AFC championship game (1990 season).
PRO STATISTICS: 1988—Fumbled once and recovered one fumble for minus 19 yards. 1989—Returned one kickoff for two yards and fumbled once for minus eight yards. 1990—Returned one kickoff for seven yards. 1991—Returned one kickoff for no yards. 1992—Returned one kickoff for three yards. 1993—Returned one kickoff for no yards and recovered one fumble. 1996—Fumbled once and recovered one fumble for minus 29 yards. 1998—Fumbled once for minus four yards.

TURK, MATT　　　P　　　REDSKINS

PERSONAL: Born June 16, 1968, in Greenfield, Wis. ... 6-5/237. ... Brother of Dan Turk, center with five NFL teams (1985-98).
HIGH SCHOOL: Greenfield (Wis.).
COLLEGE: Wisconsin-Whitewater.
TRANSACTIONS/CAREER NOTES: Signed as non-drafted free agent by Green Bay Packers (July 13, 1993). ... Released by Packers (August 4, 1993). ... Signed by Los Angeles Rams (April 1994). ... Released by Rams (August 22, 1994). ... Signed by Washington Redskins (April 5, 1995).
HONORS: Played in Pro Bowl (1996-1998 seasons). ... Named punter on THE SPORTING NEWS NFL All-Pro team (1997).
PRO STATISTICS: 1996—Rushed once for no yards and fumbled once. 1997—Rushed once for no yards and fumbled once for minus 16 yards. 1998—Rushed twice for minus 12 yards and fumbled once.

					PUNTING			
Year	Team	G	No.	Yds.	Avg.	Net avg.	In. 20	Blk.
1995—Washington NFL		16	74	3140	42.4	37.7	†29	0
1996—Washington NFL		16	75	3386	*45.1	*39.2	25	0
1997—Washington NFL		16	84	3788	45.1	*39.2	32	1
1998—Washington NFL		16	93	4103	44.1	‡39.0	∞33	∞1
Pro totals (4 years)		64	326	14417	44.2	38.8	119	2

– 401 –

TURLEY, KYLE — OT — SAINTS

PERSONAL: Born September 24, 1975, in Provo, Utah. ... 6-5/300. ... Full name: Kyle John Turley.
HIGH SCHOOL: Valley View (Moreno Valley, Calif.).
COLLEGE: San Diego State.
TRANSACTIONS/CAREER NOTES: Selected by New Orleans Saints in first round (seventh pick overall) of 1998 NFL draft. ... Signed by Saints (July 23, 1998).
PLAYING EXPERIENCE: New Orleans NFL, 1998. ... Games/Games started: 15/15.
HONORS: Named offensive tackle on THE SPORTING NEWS college All-America first team (1997).

TURNER, ERIC — DB — RAIDERS

PERSONAL: Born September 20, 1968, in Ventura, Calif. ... 6-1/215. ... Full name: Eric Ray Turner.
HIGH SCHOOL: Ventura (Calif.).
COLLEGE: UCLA (degree in history, 1992).
TRANSACTIONS/CAREER NOTES: Selected by Cleveland Browns in first round (second pick overall) of 1991 NFL draft. ... Signed by Browns (July 14, 1991). ... On injured reserve with stress fracture in leg (August 28-November 2, 1991). ... Designated by Browns as transition player (February 25, 1993). ... Free agency status changed by Browns from transitional to franchise player (February 15, 1995). ... On injured reserve with back injury (December 15, 1995-remainder of season). ... Browns franchise moved to Baltimore and renamed Ravens for 1996 season (March 11, 1996). ... Released by Ravens (February 28, 1997). ... Signed by Oakland Raiders (April 24, 1997).
HONORS: Played in Pro Bowl (1994 and 1996 seasons).
PRO STATISTICS: 1991—Recovered one fumble. 1992—Credited with one sack and recovered two fumbles. 1994—Credited with one sack, returned one punt for no yards and recovered one fumble. 1997—Fumbled once and recovered three fumbles for 65 yards and one touchdown. 1998—Credited with one sack.

				INTERCEPTIONS		
Year Team	G	GS	No.	Yds.	Avg.	TD
1991—Cleveland NFL	8	7	2	42	21.0	1
1992—Cleveland NFL	15	13	1	6	6.0	0
1993—Cleveland NFL	16	16	5	25	5.0	0
1994—Cleveland NFL	16	16	†9	199	22.1	1
1995—Cleveland NFL	8	8	0	0	...	0
1996—Baltimore NFL	14	14	5	1	0.2	0
1997—Oakland NFL	16	15	2	45	22.5	0
1998—Oakland NFL	6	6	3	108	*36.0	1
Pro totals (8 years)	99	95	27	426	15.8	3

TURNER, FLOYD — WR — RAVENS

PERSONAL: Born May 29, 1966, in Shreveport, La. ... 5-11/199. ... Full name: Floyd Turner Jr.
HIGH SCHOOL: Mansfield (La.).
COLLEGE: Northwestern (La.) State (degree in education).
TRANSACTIONS/CAREER NOTES: Selected by New Orleans Saints in sixth round (159th pick overall) of 1989 NFL draft. ... Signed by Saints (July 22, 1989). ... On injured reserve with broken arm (December 6, 1989-remainder of season). ... Granted free agency (February 1, 1991). ... Re-signed by Saints (July 17, 1991). ... On injured reserve with leg injury (September 14, 1992-remainder of season). ... Granted free agency (March 1, 1993). ... Re-signed by Saints (July 23, 1993). ... Granted unconditional free agency (February 17, 1994). ... Signed by Indianapolis Colts (May 5, 1994). ... Granted unconditional free agency (February 16, 1996). ... Signed by Baltimore Ravens (July 9, 1996). ... Granted unconditional free agency (February 14, 1997). ... Re-signed by Ravens (July 24, 1998). ... Granted unconditional free agency (February 12, 1999). ... Re-signed by Ravens (February 26, 1999).
CHAMPIONSHIP GAME EXPERIENCE: Played in AFC championship game (1995 season).
PRO STATISTICS: 1989—Rushed twice for eight yards, returned one punt for seven yards and recovered three fumbles. 1992—Returned three punts for 10 yards. 1994—Rushed three times for minus three yards and recovered one fumble. 1996—Rushed twice for 12 yards.
SINGLE GAME HIGHS (regular season): Receptions—10 (December 13, 1998, vs. Minnesota); yards—179 (October 27, 1991, vs. Chicago); and touchdown receptions—2 (December 6, 1998, vs. Tennessee).
STATISTICAL PLATEAUS: 100-yard receiving games: 1991 (3), 1996 (2), 1998 (2). Total: 7.

			RECEIVING				TOTALS			
Year Team	G	GS	No.	Yds.	Avg.	TD	TD	2pt.	Pts.	Fum.
1989—New Orleans NFL	13	0	22	279	12.7	1	1	...	6	1
1990—New Orleans NFL	16	0	21	396	18.9	4	4	...	24	0
1991—New Orleans NFL	16	4	64	927	14.5	8	8	...	48	1
1992—New Orleans NFL	2	2	5	43	8.6	0	0	...	0	2
1993—New Orleans NFL	10	2	12	163	13.6	1	1	...	6	0
1994—Indianapolis NFL	16	16	52	593	11.4	6	6	0	36	1
1995—Indianapolis NFL	14	12	35	431	12.3	4	4	▲2	28	0
1996—Baltimore NFL	11	6	38	461	12.1	2	2	0	12	0
1997—						Did not play.				
1998—Baltimore NFL	16	3	32	512	16.0	5	5	†2	34	0
Pro totals (9 years)	114	45	281	3805	13.5	31	31	4	194	5

TURNER, KEVIN — FB — EAGLES

PERSONAL: Born June 12, 1969, in Prattville, Ala. ... 6-1/231. ... Full name: Paul Kevin Turner.
HIGH SCHOOL: Prattville (Ala.).

COLLEGE: Alabama.
TRANSACTIONS/CAREER NOTES: Selected by New England Patriots in third round (71st pick overall) of 1992 NFL draft. ... Signed by Patriots (July 21, 1992). ... Granted free agency (February 17, 1995). ... Tendered offer sheet by Philadelphia Eagles (February 26, 1995). ... Patriots declined to match offer (March 2, 1995). ... On injured reserve with knee injury (September 15, 1995-remainder of season).
PRO STATISTICS: 1992—Returned one kickoff for 11 yards and recovered two fumbles. 1993—Attempted one pass without a completion and recovered two fumbles for six yards. 1994—Recovered two fumbles for minus three yards. 1997—Returned three kickoffs for 48 yards. 1998—Returned one kickoff for 15 yards.
SINGLE GAME HIGHS (regular season): Attempts—12 (October 24, 1993 vs. Seattle); yards—63 (December 19, 1993, vs. Cleveland); and rushing touchdowns—1 (September 4, 1994, vs. Miami).

			RUSHING				RECEIVING				TOTALS			
Year Team	G	GS	Att.	Yds.	Avg.	TD	No.	Yds.	Avg.	TD	TD	2pt.	Pts.	Fum.
1992—New England NFL	16	1	10	40	4.0	0	7	52	7.4	2	2	...	12	2
1993—New England NFL	16	9	50	231	4.6	0	39	333	8.5	2	2	...	12	1
1994—New England NFL	16	9	36	111	3.1	1	52	471	9.1	2	3	0	18	4
1995—Philadelphia NFL	2	2	2	9	4.5	0	4	29	7.3	0	0	0	0	0
1996—Philadelphia NFL	16	12	18	39	2.2	0	43	409	9.5	1	1	0	6	1
1997—Philadelphia NFL	16	10	18	96	5.3	0	48	443	9.2	3	3	0	18	1
1998—Philadelphia NFL	16	15	20	94	4.7	0	34	232	6.8	0	0	0	0	1
Pro totals (7 years)	98	58	154	620	4.0	1	227	1969	8.7	10	11	0	66	10

TURNER, SCOTT   CB   CHARGERS

PERSONAL: Born February 26, 1972, in Richardson, Texas. ... 5-10/180.
HIGH SCHOOL: J.J. Pearce (Richardson, Texas).
COLLEGE: Illinois (degree in speech communications, 1994).
TRANSACTIONS/CAREER NOTES: Selected by Washington Redskins in seventh round (226th pick overall) of 1995 NFL draft. ... Signed by Redskins (July 18, 1995). ... On injured reserve with ankle injury (December 11, 1997-remainder of season). ... Granted free agency (February 13, 1998). ... Re-signed by Redskins (April 30,1998). ... Claimed on waivers by San Diego Chargers (August 31, 1998).
PRO STATISTICS: 1995—Returned one punt for no yards, credited with one sack, fumbled once and recovered one fumble. 1996—Recovered one fumble in end zone for a touchdown. 1998—Credited with one sack.

			INTERCEPTIONS			
Year Team	G	GS	No.	Yds.	Avg.	TD
1995—Washington NFL	16	0	1	0	0.0	0
1996—Washington NFL	16	0	2	16	8.0	0
1997—Washington NFL	9	0	0	0	...	0
1998—San Diego NFL	16	1	1	0	0.0	0
Pro totals (4 years)	57	1	4	16	4.0	0

TUTEN, RICK   P   RAMS

PERSONAL: Born January 5, 1965, in Perry, Fla. ... 6-2/221. ... Full name: Richard Lamar Tuten. ... Name pronounced TOOT-en.
HIGH SCHOOL: Forest (Ocala, Fla.).
COLLEGE: Miami (Fla.), then Florida State (degree in economics, 1986).
TRANSACTIONS/CAREER NOTES: Signed as non-drafted free agent by San Diego Chargers (May 10, 1988). ... Released by Chargers (August 23, 1988). ... Signed by Washington Redskins (June 2, 1989). ... Released by Redskins (August 27, 1989). ... Signed by Philadelphia Eagles (December 13, 1989). ... Granted unconditional free agency (February 1, 1990). ... Signed by Buffalo Bills (March 28, 1990). ... Released by Bills (August 15, 1990). ... Re-signed by Bills (September 19, 1990). ... Granted unconditional free agency (February 1-April 1, 1991). ... Re-signed by Bills for 1991 season. ... Released by Bills (August 20, 1991). ... Signed by Green Bay Packers (August 27, 1991). ... Released by Packers (August 30, 1991). ... Signed by Seattle Seahawks (October 9, 1991). ... Granted unconditional free agency (February 1-April 1, 1992). ... Re-signed by Seahawks for 1992 season. ... Granted unconditional free agency (February 16, 1996). ... Re-signed by Seahawks (August 12, 1996). ... On injured reserve with pelvis injury (December 5, 1997-remainder of season). ... Granted unconditional free agency (February 13, 1998). ... Signed by St. Louis Rams (March 10, 1998).
CHAMPIONSHIP GAME EXPERIENCE: Played in AFC championship game (1990 season). ... Played in Super Bowl XXV (1990 season).
HONORS: Played in Pro Bowl (1994 season).
PRO STATISTICS: 1992—Attempted one pass without a completion, rushed once for no yards, fumbled twice and recovered two fumbles for minus nine yards. 1993—Attempted one pass without a completion. 1994—Credited with one two-point conversion and attempted one pass without a completion. 1998—Attempted one pass without a completion.

				PUNTING			
Year Team	G	No.	Yds.	Avg.	Net avg.	In. 20	Blk.
1989—Philadelphia NFL	2	7	256	36.6	33.6	1	0
1990—Buffalo NFL	14	53	2107	39.8	34.2	12	0
1991—Seattle NFL	10	49	2106	43.0	36.8	8	0
1992—Seattle NFL	16	*108	*4760	44.1	38.7	*29	0
1993—Seattle NFL	16	▲90	*4007	44.5	37.2	21	1
1994—Seattle NFL	16	91	3905	42.9	36.7	33	0
1995—Seattle NFL	16	83	3735	*45.0	36.5	21	0
1996—Seattle NFL	16	85	3746	44.1	34.5	20	1
1997—Seattle NFL	11	48	2007	41.8	36.4	15	0
1998—St. Louis NFL	16	95	4202	44.2	35.3	16	0
Pro totals (10 years)	133	709	30831	43.5	36.4	176	2

TYLSKI, RICH — G/C — JAGUARS

PERSONAL: Born February 27, 1971, in San Diego. ... 6-5/306. ... Full name: Richard Lee Tylski. ... Name pronounced TILL-skee.
HIGH SCHOOL: Madison (San Diego).
COLLEGE: Utah State (degree in sociology, 1994).
TRANSACTIONS/CAREER NOTES: Signed as non-drafted free agent by New England Patriots (April 25, 1994). ... Released by Patriots (August 20, 1994). ... Re-signed by Patriots to practice squad (August 30, 1994). ... Claimed on waivers by Jacksonville Jaguars (July 26, 1995). ... Released by Jaguars (August 27, 1995). ... Re-signed by Jaguars to practice squad (August 28, 1995). ... Granted free agency (February 12, 1999). ... Re-signed by Jaguars (May 5, 1999).
PLAYING EXPERIENCE: Jacksonville NFL, 1996-1998. ... Games/Games started: 1996 (16/7), 1997 (13/13), 1998 (11/8). Total: 40/28.

UNUTOA, MORRIS — C — EAGLES

PERSONAL: Born March 10, 1971, in Torrance, Calif. ... 6-1/284. ... Full name: Morris Taua Unutoa. ... Name pronounced oo-nuh-TOE-uh.
HIGH SCHOOL: Carson (Calif.).
COLLEGE: Brigham Young.
TRANSACTIONS/CAREER NOTES: Signed as non-drafted free agent by Philadelphia Eagles (April 26, 1996). ... Granted free agency (February 12, 1999). ... Re-signed by Eagles (March 24, 1999).
PLAYING EXPERIENCE: Philadelphia NFL, 1996-1998. ... Games/Games started: 1996 (16/0), 1997 (16/0), 1998 (16/0). Total: 48/0.
PRO STATISTICS: 1996—Fumbled once.

UPSHAW, REGAN — DE — BUCCANEERS

PERSONAL: Born August 12, 1975, in Barrien Springs, Mich. ... 6-4/261. ... Full name: Regan Charles Upshaw.
HIGH SCHOOL: Pittsburg (Calif.).
COLLEGE: California.
TRANSACTIONS/CAREER NOTES: Selected after junior season by Tampa Bay Buccaneers in first round (12th pick overall) of 1996 NFL draft. ... Signed by Buccaneers (July 21, 1996).
PRO STATISTICS: 1996—Recovered one fumble. 1997—Recovered one fumble. 1998—Intercepted one pass for 26 yards.

Year Team	G	GS	SACKS
1996—Tampa Bay NFL	16	16	4.0
1997—Tampa Bay NFL	15	15	7.5
1998—Tampa Bay NFL	16	16	7.0
Pro totals (3 years)	47	47	18.5

UWAEZUOKE, IHEANYI — WR — PANTHERS

PERSONAL: Born July 24, 1973, in Lagos, Nigeria ... 6-2/198. ... Name pronounced E-hahn-E ooh-Way-zo-kay.
HIGH SCHOOL: Harvard (North Hollywood, Calif.).
COLLEGE: California (degree in political science, 1995).
TRANSACTIONS/CAREER NOTES: Selected by San Francisco 49ers in fifth round (160th pick overall) of 1996 NFL draft. ... Signed by 49ers (July 18, 1996). ... Claimed on waivers by Miami Dolphins (November 9, 1998). ... Granted free agency (February 12, 1999). ... Signed by Carolina Panthers (April 7, 1999).
CHAMPIONSHIP GAME EXPERIENCE: Played in NFC championship game (1997 season).
PRO STATISTICS: 1997—Recovered two fumbles.
SINGLE GAME HIGHS (regular season): Receptions—3 (November 2, 1997, vs. Dallas); yards—41 (September 21, 1997, vs. Atlanta); and touchdown receptions—1 (November 10, 1996, vs. Dallas).

			RECEIVING				PUNT RETURNS				KICKOFF RETURNS				TOTALS			
Year Team	G	GS	No.	Yds.	Avg.	TD	No.	Yds.	Avg.	TD	No.	Yds.	Avg.	TD	TD	2pt.	Pts.	Fum.
1996—San Francisco NFL	14	0	7	91	13.0	1	0	0	...	0	1	21	21.0	0	1	0	6	0
1997—San Francisco NFL	14	0	14	165	11.8	0	34	373	11.0	0	6	131	21.8	0	0	0	0	4
1998—San Francisco NFL	7	0	3	67	22.3	0	0	0	...	0	0	0	...	0	0	0	0	0
—Miami NFL	4	0	0	0	...	0	0	0	...	0	0	0	...	0	0	0	0	0
Pro totals (3 years)	39	0	24	323	13.5	1	34	373	11.0	0	7	152	21.7	0	1	0	6	4

VAN DYKE, ALEX — WR — STEELERS

PERSONAL: Born July 24, 1974, in Sacramento. ... 6-0/205. ... Full name: Franklin Alexander Van Dyke.
HIGH SCHOOL: Luther Burbank (Sacramento).
JUNIOR COLLEGE: Sacramento City College.
COLLEGE: Nevada.
TRANSACTIONS/CAREER NOTES: Selected by New York Jets in second round (31st pick overall) of 1996 NFL draft. ... Signed by Jets (July 15, 1996). ... Traded by Jets to Pittsburgh Steelers for sixth-round pick (LB Marc Megna) in 1999 draft (March 25, 1999).
CHAMPIONSHIP GAME EXPERIENCE: Played in AFC championship game (1998 season).
HONORS: Named wide receiver on THE SPORTING NEWS college All-America second team (1995).
SINGLE GAME HIGHS (regular season): Receptions—4 (October 13, 1996, vs. Jacksonville); yards—35 (December 7, 1997, vs. Indianapolis); and touchdown receptions—2 (December 7, 1997, vs. Indianapolis).

				RECEIVING			KICKOFF RETURNS			TOTALS			
Year Team	G	GS	No.	Yds.	Avg.	TD	No.	Yds.	Avg.	TD	TD	2pt.	Pts.	Fum.
1996—New York Jets NFL	15	1	17	118	6.9	1	15	289	19.3	0	1	0	6	0
1997—New York Jets NFL	5	0	3	53	17.7	2	6	138	23.0	0	2	0	12	0
1998—New York Jets NFL	16	0	5	40	8.0	0	0	0	...	0	0	0	0	0
Pro totals (3 years)	36	1	25	211	8.4	3	21	427	20.3	0	3	0	18	0

VAN PELT, ALEX — QB — BILLS

PERSONAL: Born May 1, 1970, in Pittsburgh. ... 6-0/220. ... Full name: Gregory Alexander Van Pelt.
HIGH SCHOOL: Grafton (W.Va.), then Winston Churchill (San Antonio).
COLLEGE: Pittsburgh.
TRANSACTIONS/CAREER NOTES: Selected by Pittsburgh Steelers in eighth round (216th pick overall) of 1993 NFL draft. ... Signed by Steelers for 1993 season. ... Released by Steelers (August 30, 1993). ... Signed by Kansas City Chiefs to practice squad (November 3, 1993). ... Activated (November 8, 1993); did not play. ... Released by Chiefs (November 17, 1993). ... Re-signed by Chiefs (May 18, 1994). ... Released by Chiefs (August 23, 1994). ... Signed by Buffalo Bills to practice squad (December 14, 1994). ... Activated (December 17, 1994); did not play.
PRO STATISTICS: 1997—Fumbled three times and recovered three fumbles for minus seven yards.
SINGLE GAME HIGHS (regular season): Attempts—44 (December 20, 1997, vs. Green Bay); completions—23 (December 20, 1997, vs. Green Bay); yards—255 (December 20, 1997, vs. Green Bay); and touchdown passes—2 (October 26, 1997, vs. Denver).
MISCELLANEOUS: Regular-season record as starting NFL quarterback: 1-2 (.333).

			PASSING								RUSHING				TOTALS	
Year Team	G	GS	Att.	Cmp.	Pct.	Yds.	TD	Int.	Avg.	Rat.	Att.	Yds.	Avg.	TD	TD	2pt.	Pts.
1993—Kansas City NFL						Did not play.											
1993—Buffalo NFL						Did not play.											
1995—Buffalo NFL	1	0	18	10	55.6	106	2	0	5.89	110.0	0	0	...	0	0	0	0
1996—Buffalo NFL	1	0	5	2	40.0	9	0	0	1.80	47.9	3	-5	-1.7	0	0	0	0
1997—Buffalo NFL	6	3	124	60	48.4	684	2	10	5.52	37.2	11	33	3.0	1	1	0	6
1998—Buffalo NFL	1	0	0	0	...	0	0	0	...	...	1	-1	-1.0	0	0	0	0
Pro totals (4 years)	9	3	147	72	49.0	799	4	10	5.44	46.3	15	27	1.8	1	1	0	6

VANCE, ERIC — S — BUCCANEERS

PERSONAL: Born July 14, 1975, in Tampa. ... 6-2/215.
HIGH SCHOOL: L.D. Bell (Hurst, Texas).
COLLEGE: Vanderbilt.
TRANSACTIONS/CAREER NOTES: Signed as non-drafted free agent by Carolina Panthers (April 25, 1997). ... Released by Panthers (September 1, 1997). ... Signed by San Diego Chargers to practice squad (December 3, 1997). ... Granted free agency after 1997 season. ... Signed by Tampa Bay Buccaneers (December 30, 1997). ... Released by Buccaneers (August 25, 1998). ... Signed by Indianapolis Colts to practice squad (August 31, 1998). ... Signed by Buccaneers off Colts practice squad (October 28, 1998).
PLAYING EXPERIENCE: Tampa Bay NFL, 1998. ... Games/Games started: 3/1.

VANDERJAGT, MIKE — K — COLTS

PERSONAL: Born March 24, 1970, in Oakville, Ont. ... 6-5/210.
HIGH SCHOOL: White Oaks (Ont.).
JUNIOR COLLEGE: Allan Hancock College (Calif.).
COLLEGE: West Virginia.
TRANSACTIONS/CAREER NOTES: Signed by Saskatchewan Roughriders prior to 1993 season. ... Signed by Toronto Argonauts of CFL (February 15, 1994). ... Released by Argonauts (June 13, 1994). ... Signed by Hamilton Tiger-Cats of CFL (June 24, 1994). ... Released by Tiger-Cats (July 11, 1994). ... Signed by Argonauts of CFL (March 16, 1995). ... Released by Argonauts (June 25, 1995). ... Re-signed by Argonauts of CFL (May 10, 1996). ... Signed as non-drafted free agent by Indianapolis Colts (March 4, 1998).
HONORS: Named Most Outstanding Canadian Player in Grey Cup (1996). ... Named to CFL All-Star team (1997).
PRO STATISTICS: CFL: 1996—Attempted two passes with one completion for 28 yards. 1997—Attempted one pass without a completion, rushed twice for 25 yards and fumbled once.

			PUNTING					KICKING					
Year Team	G	No.	Yds.	Avg.	Net avg.	In. 20	Blk.	XPM	XPA	FGM	FGA	Lg.	50+	Pts.
1993—Saskatchewan CFL	2	17	672	39.5	32.1	...	...	0	0	0	0	0	0-0	0
1994—								Did not play.						
1995—								Did not play.						
1996—Toronto CFL	18	103	4459	43.3	35.1	...	...	59	59	40	56	51	0-0	179
1997—Toronto CFL	18	118	5303	44.9	37.4	...	...	77	77	33	43	51	0-0	176
1998—Indianapolis NFL	14	0	0	...	...	0	0	23	23	27	31	53	6-9	104
CFL totals (3 years)	38	238	10434	43.8	36.0	0	0	136	136	73	99	51	0-0	355
NFL totals (1 year)	14	0	0	...	...	0	0	23	23	27	31	53	6-9	104
Pro totals (4 years)	52	238	10434	43.8	36.0	0	0	159	159	100	130	53	6-0	459

VANOVER, TAMARICK — WR — CHIEFS

PERSONAL: Born February 25, 1974, in Tallahassee, Fla. ... 5-11/220. ... Name pronounced tom-ARE-ik.
HIGH SCHOOL: Leon (Tallahassee, Fla.).
COLLEGE: Florida State.

– 405 –

TRANSACTIONS/CAREER NOTES: Signed after sophomore season with Las Vegas Posse of CFL (February 13, 1994). ... Selected by Kansas City Chiefs in third round (81st pick overall) of 1995 NFL draft. ... Signed by Chiefs for 1995 season.
HONORS: Named kick returner on THE SPORTING NEWS college All-America first team (1992). ... Named kick returner on THE SPORTING NEWS college All-America second team (1993).
PRO STATISTICS: CFL: 1994—Returned four unsuccessful field-goals for 31 yards, fumbled three times and recovered one fumble. NFL: 1996—Fumbled once. 1997—Fumbled six times and recovered one fumble. 1998—Fumbled twice.
SINGLE GAME HIGHS (regular season): Receptions—7 (September 1, 1996, vs. Houston); yards—85 (November 23, 1995, vs. Dallas); and touchdown receptions—1 (September 1, 1996, vs. Houston).

				RUSHING				RECEIVING				PUNT RETURNS				KICKOFF RETURNS				TOTALS		
Year Team	G	GS	Att.	Yds.	Avg.	TD	No.	Yds.	Avg.	TD	No.	Yds.	Avg.	TD	No.	Yds.	Avg.	TD	TD	2pt.	Pts.
1994—Las Vegas CFL	15	...	1	6	6.0	0	23	385	16.7	3	36	341	9.5	1	31	718	23.2	1	5	1	32
1995—Kansas City NFL	15	0	6	31	5.2	0	11	231	21.0	2	§51	*540	10.6	†1	43	1095	25.5	†2	5	0	30
1996—Kansas City NFL	13	6	4	6	1.5	0	21	241	11.5	1	17	116	6.8	0	33	854	§25.9	▲1	2	0	12
1997—Kansas City NFL	16	0	5	50	10.0	0	7	92	13.1	0	35	383	10.9	1	51	1308	25.6	▲1	2	1	14
1998—Kansas City NFL	12	0	2	1	0.5	0	0	0	...	0	27	264	9.8	0	41	956	23.3	0	0	0	0
CFL totals (1 year)	15	...	1	6	6.0	0	23	385	16.7	3	36	341	9.5	1	31	718	23.2	1	5	1	32
NFL totals (4 years)	56	6	17	88	5.2	0	39	564	14.5	3	130	1303	10.0	2	168	4213	25.1	4	9	1	56
Pro totals (5 years)	71	...	18	94	5.2	0	62	949	15.3	6	166	1644	9.9	3	199	4931	24.8	5	14	2	88

VARDELL, TOMMY   FB   49ERS

PERSONAL: Born February 20, 1969, in El Cajon, Calif. ... 6-2/234. ... Full name: Thomas Arthur Vardell.
HIGH SCHOOL: Granite Hills (El Cajon, Calif.).
COLLEGE: Stanford (degree in industrial engineering, 1992).
TRANSACTIONS/CAREER NOTES: Selected by Cleveland Browns in first round (ninth pick overall) of 1992 NFL draft. ... Signed by Browns (July 26, 1992). ... On injured reserve with calf injury (December 26, 1992-remainder of season). ... On injured reserve with knee injury (October 5, 1994-remainder of season). ... On physically unable to perform list with knee injury (July 17-23, 1995). ... Granted unconditional free agency (February 16, 1996). ... Signed by San Francisco 49ers (March 25, 1996). ... Released by 49ers (February 13, 1997). ... Signed by Detroit Lions (April 23, 1997). ... Granted unconditional free agency (February 12, 1999). ... Signed by 49ers (April 23, 1999).
PRO STATISTICS: 1992—Returned two kickoffs for 14 yards. 1993—Returned four kickoffs for 58 yards. 1997—Returned one kickoff for 15 yards and recovered one fumble. 1998—Returned one kickoff for 23 yards.
SINGLE GAME HIGHS (regular season): Attempts—25 (October 17, 1993, vs. Cincinnati); yards—104 (September 19, 1993, vs. Los Angeles Raiders); and rushing touchdowns—3 (November 16, 1997, vs. Minnesota).
STATISTICAL PLATEAUS: 100-yard rushing games: 1993 (1).

			RUSHING				RECEIVING				TOTALS			
Year Team	G	GS	Att.	Yds.	Avg.	TD	No.	Yds.	Avg.	TD	TD	2pt.	Pts.	Fum.
1992—Cleveland NFL	14	10	99	369	3.7	0	13	128	9.8	0	0	...	0	0
1993—Cleveland NFL	16	12	171	644	3.8	3	19	151	7.9	1	4	...	24	3
1994—Cleveland NFL	5	5	15	48	3.2	0	16	137	8.6	1	1	0	6	0
1995—Cleveland NFL	5	0	4	9	2.3	0	6	18	3.0	0	0	0	0	0
1996—San Francisco NFL	11	7	58	192	3.3	2	28	179	6.4	0	2	0	12	0
1997—Detroit NFL	16	10	32	122	3.8	6	16	218	13.6	0	6	0	36	1
1998—Detroit NFL	14	9	18	37	2.1	0	14	143	10.2	1	7	0	42	1
Pro totals (7 years)	81	53	397	1421	3.6	17	112	974	8.7	3	20	0	120	5

VELAND, TONY   S

PERSONAL: Born March 11, 1973, in Omaha, Neb. ... 6-1/209.
HIGH SCHOOL: Benson (Omaha, Neb.).
COLLEGE: Nebraska.
TRANSACTIONS/CAREER NOTES: Selected by Denver Broncos in sixth round (181st pick overall) of 1996 NFL draft. ... Signed by Broncos (July 16, 1996). ... Released by Broncos (August 25, 1996). ... Re-signed by Broncos to practice squad (August 27, 1996). ... Claimed on waivers by Carolina Panthers (August 31, 1998). ... Released by Panthers (March 18, 1999).
PLAYING EXPERIENCE: Denver NFL, 1997; Carolina NFL, 1998. ... Games/Games started: 1997 (12/0), 1998 (15/5). Total: 27/5.
CHAMPIONSHIP GAME EXPERIENCE: Played in AFC championship game (1997 season). ... Member of Super Bowl championship team (1997 season).
PRO STATISTICS: 1997—Recovered one fumble. 1998—Intercepted one pass for 24 yards.

VERBA, ROSS   OT   PACKERS

PERSONAL: Born October 31, 1973, in Des Moines, Iowa. ... 6-4/302. ... Full name: Ross Robert Verba.
HIGH SCHOOL: Dowling (West Des Moines, Iowa).
COLLEGE: Iowa.
TRANSACTIONS/CAREER NOTES: Selected by Green Bay Packers in first round (30th pick overall) of 1997 NFL draft. ... Signed by Packers (July 31, 1997).
PLAYING EXPERIENCE: Green Bay NFL, 1997 and 1998. ... Games/Games started: 1997 (16/11), 1998 (16/16). Total: 32/27.
CHAMPIONSHIP GAME EXPERIENCE: Played in NFC championship game (1997 season). ... Played in Super Bowl XXXII (1997 season).

VILLA, DANNY   G

PERSONAL: Born September 21, 1964, in Nogales, Ariz. ... 6-5/308. ... Full name: Daniel Villa. ... Name pronounced VEE-uh.

HIGH SCHOOL: Nogales (Ariz.).
COLLEGE: Arizona State.
TRANSACTIONS/CAREER NOTES: Selected by New England Patriots in fifth round (113th pick overall) of 1987 NFL draft. ... Signed by Patriots (July 25, 1987). ... On injured reserve with ankle injury (October 4-November 8, 1991). ... On injured reserve with ankle injury (December 11, 1991-remainder of season). ... Traded by Patriots to Phoenix Cardinals for sixth-round pick (traded to Detroit) in 1992 draft (January 30, 1992). ... Granted unconditional free agency (March 1, 1993). ... Signed by Kansas City Chiefs (April 19, 1993). ... Granted unconditional free agency (February 14, 1997). ... Signed by Oakland Raiders (April 1, 1997). ... Released by Raiders (August 24, 1997). ... Signed by Patriots (November 6, 1997). ... Granted unconditional free agency (February 13, 1998). ... Signed by Raiders (July 24, 1998). ... Released by Raiders (August 25, 1998). ... Signed by Carolina Panthers (November 10, 1998). ... Granted unconditional free agency (February 12, 1999).
PLAYING EXPERIENCE: New England NFL, 1987-1991 and 1997; Phoenix NFL, 1992; Kansas City NFL, 1993-1996; Carolina NFL, 1998. ... Games/Games started: 1987 (11/7), 1988 (16/14), 1989 (15/15), 1990 (16/16), 1991 (10/10), 1992 (16/12), 1993 (13/3), 1994 (14/0), 1995 (16/0), 1996 (16/0), 1997 (7/0), 1998 (7/0). Total: 157/77.
CHAMPIONSHIP GAME EXPERIENCE: Played in AFC championship game (1993 season).
PRO STATISTICS: 1987—Fumbled once for minus 13 yards. 1988—Fumbled once for minus 39 yards. 1990—Recovered one fumble. 1991—Recovered two fumbles.

VILLARRIAL, CHRIS — C — BEARS

PERSONAL: Born June 9, 1973, in Hummelstown, Pa. ... 6-4/310. ... Name pronounced vill-uh-ree-AL.
HIGH SCHOOL: Hershey (Pa.).
COLLEGE: Indiana University of Pennsylvania.
TRANSACTIONS/CAREER NOTES: Selected by Chicago Bears in fifth round (152nd pick overall) of 1996 NFL draft. ... Signed by Bears (July 11, 1996). ... Granted free agency (February 12, 1999). ... Re-signed by Bears (April 16, 1999).
PLAYING EXPERIENCE: Chicago NFL, 1996-1998. ... Games/Games started: 1996 (14/8), 1997 (11/11), 1998 (16/16). Total: 41/35.
PRO STATISTICS: 1998—Recovered one fumble.

VINATIERI, ADAM — K — PATRIOTS

PERSONAL: Born December 28, 1972, in Yunkton, S.D. ... 6-0/200. ... Full name: Adam Matthew Vinatieri.
HIGH SCHOOL: Rapid City (S.D.) Central.
COLLEGE: South Dakota State (degree in fitness and wellness).
TRANSACTIONS/CAREER NOTES: Signed by Amsterdam Admirals of World League for 1996 season. ... Signed by New England Patriots (June 28, 1996). ... Granted free agency (February 12, 1999). ... Re-signed by Patriots (March 12, 1999).
CHAMPIONSHIP GAME EXPERIENCE: Played in AFC championship game (1996 season). ... Played in Super Bowl XXXI (1996 season).
PRO STATISTICS: 1996—Punted once for 27 yards. 1998—Credited with one two-point conversion.

				KICKING				
Year Team	G	XPM	XPA	FGM	FGA	Lg.	50+	Pts.
1996—Amsterdam W.L.	10	4	4	9	10	43	0-0	31
—New England NFL	16	39	42	27	35	50	1-2	120
1997—New England NFL	16	40	40	25	29	52	1-1	115
1998—New England NFL	16	32	32	31	39	55	2-2	127
W.L. totals (1 year)	10	4	4	9	10	43	0-0	31
NFL totals (3 years)	48	111	114	83	103	55	4-5	362
Pro totals (4 years)	58	115	118	92	113	55	4-0	393

VINCENT, TROY — CB — EAGLES

PERSONAL: Born June 8, 1970, in Trenton, N.J. ... 6-0/194. ... Full name: Troy D. Vincent. ... Nephew of Steve Luke, safety with Green Bay Packers (1975-80).
HIGH SCHOOL: Pennsbury (Fairless Hills, Pa.).
COLLEGE: Wisconsin.
TRANSACTIONS/CAREER NOTES: Selected by Miami Dolphins in first round (seventh pick overall) of 1992 NFL draft. ... Signed by Dolphins (August 8, 1992). ... Designated by Dolphins as transition player (February 25, 1993). ... On injured reserve with knee injury (December 15, 1993-remainder of season). ... Tendered offer sheet by Philadelphia Eagles (February 24, 1996). ... Dolphins declined to match offer (March 3, 1996).
CHAMPIONSHIP GAME EXPERIENCE: Played in AFC championship game (1992 season).
HONORS: Named defensive back on The Sporting News college All-America first team (1991).
RECORDS: Holds NFL record for longest interception return for a touchdown—104 yards (November 3, 1996; with lateral from LB James Willis).
PRO STATISTICS: 1992—Returned five punts for 16 yards and recovered two fumbles. 1993—Recovered one fumble. 1994—Ran 58 yards with lateral from interception for a touchdown. 1996—Ran minus two yards with lateral from punt return. 1997—Returned one punt for minus eight yards, fumbled once and recovered two fumbles for five yards. 1998—Credited with one sack.

			INTERCEPTIONS			
Year Team	G	GS	No.	Yds.	Avg.	TD
1992—Miami NFL	15	14	2	47	23.5	0
1993—Miami NFL	13	13	2	29	14.5	0
1994—Miami NFL	13	12	5	113	22.6	1
1995—Miami NFL	16	16	5	95	19.0	▲1
1996—Philadelphia NFL	16	16	3	144	*48.0	1
1997—Philadelphia NFL	16	16	3	14	4.7	0
1998—Philadelphia NFL	13	13	2	29	14.5	0
Pro totals (7 years)	102	100	22	471	21.4	3

VON OELHOFFEN, KIMO — NT — BENGALS

PERSONAL: Born January 30, 1971, in Kaunakakai, Hawaii. ... 6-4/305. ... Full name: Kimo K. von Oelhoffen.
HIGH SCHOOL: Malokai (Hoolehua, Hawaii).
JUNIOR COLLEGE: Walla Walla (Wash.) Community College.
COLLEGE: Hawaii, then Boise State.
TRANSACTIONS/CAREER NOTES: Selected by Cincinnati Bengals in sixth round (162nd pick overall) of 1994 NFL draft. ... Signed by Bengals (May 9, 1994).
PLAYING EXPERIENCE: Cincinnati NFL, 1994-1998. ... Games/Games started: 1994 (7/0), 1995 (16/0), 1996 (11/1), 1997 (13/12), 1998 (16/16). Total: 63/29.
PRO STATISTICS: 1995—Returned one kickoff for 10 yards. 1996—Credited with one sack.

VRABEL, MIKE — LB — STEELERS

PERSONAL: Born August 14, 1975, in Akron, Ohio. ... 6-4/250. ... Full name: Michael George Vrabel. ... Name pronounced VRAY-bull.
HIGH SCHOOL: Walsh Jesuit (Stow, Ohio).
COLLEGE: Ohio State.
TRANSACTIONS/CAREER NOTES: Selected by Pittsburgh Steelers in third round (91st pick overall) of 1997 NFL draft. ... Signed by Steelers (July 15, 1997).
CHAMPIONSHIP GAME EXPERIENCE: Played in AFC championship game (1997 season).
PRO STATISTICS: 1997—Returned one kickoff for no yards and recovered one fumble.

Year Team	G	GS	SACKS
1997—Pittsburgh NFL	15	0	1.5
1998—Pittsburgh NFL	11	0	2.5
Pro totals (2 years)	26	0	4.0

WADDY, JUDE — LB — PACKERS

PERSONAL: Born September 12, 1975, in Washington, D.C. ... 6-2/220. ... Full name: Jude Michael Waddy.
HIGH SCHOOL: Suitland (Md.).
COLLEGE: William and Mary (degree in kinesiology).
TRANSACTIONS/CAREER NOTES: Signed as non-drafted free agent by Green Bay Packers (April 24, 1998). ... Suspended by NFL for four games for violation of league substance abuse policy (December 23, 1998).
PLAYING EXPERIENCE: Green Bay NFL, 1998. ... Games/Games started: 13/0.
PRO STATISTICS: 1998—Credited with one sack.

WADE, JOHN — C/G — JAGUARS

PERSONAL: Born January 25, 1975, in Harrisonburg, Va. ... 6-5/293. ... Full name: John Robert Wade.
HIGH SCHOOL: Harrisonburg (Va.).
COLLEGE: Marshall (degree in business management, 1997).
TRANSACTIONS/CAREER NOTES: Selected by Jacksonville Jaguars in fifth round (148th pick overall) of 1998 NFL draft. ... Signed by Jaguars (June 1, 1998).
PLAYING EXPERIENCE: Jacksonville NFL, 1998. ... Games/Games started: 4/0.

WADSWORTH, ANDRE — DE — CARDINALS

PERSONAL: Born October 19, 1974, in St. Croix, Virgin Islands (U.S.) ... 6-4/278.
HIGH SCHOOL: Florida Christian (Miami).
COLLEGE: Florida State (degree in marketing, 1997).
TRANSACTIONS/CAREER NOTES: Selected by Arizona Cardinals in first round (third pick overall) of 1998 NFL draft. ... Signed by Cardinals (September 5, 1998).
HONORS: Named defensive end on THE SPORTING NEWS college All-America first team (1997).
PRO STATISTICS: 1998—Recovered three fumbles.

Year Team	G	GS	SACKS
1998—Arizona NFL	16	15	5.0

WAHLE, MIKE — OT — PACKERS

PERSONAL: Born March 29, 1977, in Portland, Ore. ... 6-6/306. ... Full name: Michael James Wahle.
HIGH SCHOOL: Rim of the World (Lake Arrowhead, Calif.).
COLLEGE: Navy.
TRANSACTIONS/CAREER NOTES: Selected by Green Bay Packers in second round of 1998 supplemental draft (July 9, 1998). ... Signed by Packers (August 6, 1998).
PLAYING EXPERIENCE: Green Bay NFL, 1998. ... Games/Games started: 1/0.

WAINRIGHT, FRANK — TE — RAVENS

PERSONAL: Born October 10, 1967, in Peoria, Ill. ... 6-3/250. ... Full name: Frank Wesley Wainright.
HIGH SCHOOL: Pomona (Arvada, Colo.).
COLLEGE: Northern Colorado.
TRANSACTIONS/CAREER NOTES: Selected by New Orleans Saints in eighth round (210th pick overall) of 1991 NFL draft. ... Signed by Saints (July 14, 1991). ... Released by Saints (August 26, 1991). ... Re-signed by Saints to practice squad (August 28, 1991). ... Activated (September 14, 1991). ... Granted unconditional free agency (February 1-April 1, 1992). ... Re-signed by Saints for 1992 season. ... On injured reserve with foot injury (August 23, 1994-entire season). ... Granted unconditional free agency (February 17, 1995). ... Signed by Denver Broncos (April 17, 1995). ... Released by Broncos (August 22, 1995). ... Signed by Philadelphia Eagles (August 29, 1995). ... Released by Eagles (October 25, 1995). ... Signed by Miami Dolphins (November 15, 1995). ... Granted unconditional free agency (February 16, 1996). ... Re-signed by Dolphins (March 5, 1996). ... Granted unconditional free agency (February 14, 1997). ... Re-signed by Dolphins (February 27, 1997). ... On injured reserve with chest injury (December 9, 1997-remainder of season). ... Granted unconditional free agency (February 12, 1999). ... Signed by Baltimore Ravens (February 25, 1999).
PRO STATISTICS: 1995—Recovered one fumble. 1996—Returned one kickoff for 10 yards.
SINGLE GAME HIGHS (regular season): Receptions—2 (December 3, 1992, vs. Atlanta); yards—42 (December 3, 1992, vs. Atlanta); and touchdown receptions—1 (September 15, 1996, vs. New York Jets).

				RECEIVING			TOTALS			
Year Team	G	GS	No.	Yds.	Avg.	TD	TD	2pt.	Pts.	Fum.
1991—New Orleans NFL	14	2	1	3	3.0	0	0	...	0	0
1992—New Orleans NFL	13	4	9	143	15.9	0	0	...	0	0
1993—New Orleans NFL	16	2	0	0	...	0	0	...	0	0
1994—New Orleans NFL						Did not play.				
1995—Philadelphia NFL	7	0	0	0	...	0	0	...	0	0
—Miami NFL	6	0	0	0	...	0	0	...	0	0
1996—Miami NFL	16	0	1	2	2.0	1	1	0	6	0
1997—Miami NFL	9	0	0	0	...	0	0	0	0	0
1998—Miami NFL	16	1	0	0	...	0	0	0	0	0
Pro totals (7 years)	97	9	11	148	13.5	1	1	0	6	0

WALDROUP, KERWIN — DT

PERSONAL: Born August 1, 1974, in Country Club Hills, Ill. ... 6-3/260.
HIGH SCHOOL: Rich Central (Olympia Fields, Ill.).
COLLEGE: Michigan, then Central State (Ohio).
TRANSACTIONS/CAREER NOTES: Selected by Detroit Lions in fifth round (158th pick overall) of 1996 NFL draft. ... Signed by Lions (July 15, 1996). ... On injured reserve with knee injury (November 24, 1997-remainder of season). ... Granted free agency (February 12, 1999).
PRO STATISTICS: 1997—Recovered one fumble. 1998—Recovered one fumble.

Year Team	G	GS	SACKS
1996—Detroit NFL	16	10	2.5
1997—Detroit NFL	11	11	1.0
1998—Detroit NFL	13	13	1.5
Pro totals (3 years)	40	34	5.0

WALKER, BRACEY — S — CHIEFS

PERSONAL: Born June 11, 1970, in Spring Lake, N.C. ... 6-0/204. ... Full name: Bracey Wordell Walker.
HIGH SCHOOL: Pine Forest (Fayetteville, N.C.).
COLLEGE: North Carolina.
TRANSACTIONS/CAREER NOTES: Selected by Kansas City Chiefs in fourth round (127th pick overall) of 1994 NFL draft. ... Signed by Chiefs (July 20, 1994). ... Claimed on waivers by Cincinnati Bengals (October 12, 1994). ... Granted free agency (February 14, 1997). ... Re-signed by Bengals (April 18, 1997). ... Claimed on waivers by Miami Dolphins (August 20, 1997). ... On injured reserve with leg injury (December 2, 1997-remainder of season). ... Granted unconditional free agency (February 13, 1998). ... Re-signed by Dolphins (April 27, 1998). ... Released by Dolphins (August 19, 1998). ... Signed by Chiefs (November 3, 1998).
HONORS: Named defensive back on THE SPORTING NEWS college All-America second team (1993).
PRO STATISTICS: 1995—Recovered two fumbles. 1997—Recovered one fumble.

			INTERCEPTIONS			
Year Team	G	GS	No.	Yds.	Avg.	TD
1994—Kansas City NFL	2	0	0	0	...	0
—Cincinnati NFL	7	0	0	0	...	0
1995—Cincinnati NFL	14	14	4	56	14.0	0
1996—Cincinnati NFL	16	16	2	35	17.5	0
1997—Miami NFL	12	0	0	0	...	0
1998—Kansas City NFL	8	0	0	0	...	0
Pro totals (5 years)	59	30	6	91	15.2	0

WALKER, BRIAN — S — DOLPHINS

PERSONAL: Born May 31, 1972, in Colorado Springs, Colo. ... 6-1/198.
HIGH SCHOOL: Widefield (Colorado Springs, Colo.).
JUNIOR COLLEGE: Snow College (Utah).
COLLEGE: Washington State.
TRANSACTIONS/CAREER NOTES: Signed as non-drafted free agent by Washington Redskins (May 1, 1996). ... Released by Redskins (October 9, 1997). ... Signed by Miami Dolphins (December 9, 1997). ... Active for two games with Dolphins (1997); did not play.
PLAYING EXPERIENCE: Washington NFL, 1996 and 1997; Miami NFL, 1998. ... Games/Games started: 1996 (16/4), 1997 (5/0), 1998 (16/0). Total: 37/4.
PRO STATISTICS: 1996—Credited with one sack. 1998—Intercepted four passes for 12 yards.

WALKER, COREY   RB   EAGLES

PERSONAL: Born June 4, 1973, in Memphis, Tenn. ... 5-10/188.
HIGH SCHOOL: Hillcrest (Memphis, Tenn.).
COLLEGE: Arkansas State.
TRANSACTIONS/CAREER NOTES: Signed as non-drafted free agent by Philadelphia Eagles (April 22, 1997). ... On injured reserve with knee injury (August 19, 1997-entire season).
SINGLE GAME HIGHS (regular season): Attempts—5 (December 27, 1998, vs. New York Giants); yards—40 (December 20, 1998, vs. Dallas); and rushing touchdowns—0.

			RUSHING				RECEIVING			KICKOFF RETURNS				TOTALS		
Year Team	G	GS	Att.	Yds.	Avg.	TD	No.	Yds.	Avg.	TD	No.	Yds.	Avg.	TD	TD	2pt.	Pts. Fum.
1997—Philadelphia NFL									Did not play.								
1998—Philadelphia NFL	14	0	12	55	4.6	0	2	35	17.5	0	8	150	18.8	0	0	0	0	0

WALKER, DARNELL   CB   49ERS

PERSONAL: Born January 17, 1970, in St. Louis. ... 5-8/168. ... Full name: Darnell Robert Walker. ... Brother of Marquis Walker, defensive back, Oakland Raiders.
HIGH SCHOOL: Sumner (St. Louis).
JUNIOR COLLEGE: Coffeyville (Kan.) Community College.
COLLEGE: Oklahoma.
TRANSACTIONS/CAREER NOTES: Selected by Atlanta Falcons in seventh round (178th pick overall) of 1993 NFL draft. ... Signed by Falcons (July 14, 1993). ... Granted free agency (February 16, 1996). ... Re-signed by Falcons (June 12, 1996). ... Granted unconditional free agency (February 14, 1997). ... Signed by San Francisco 49ers (March 28, 1997).
CHAMPIONSHIP GAME EXPERIENCE: Played in NFC championship game (1997 season).
PRO STATISTICS: 1994—Credited with one sack. 1996—Recovered one fumble. 1997—Credited with one sack.

			INTERCEPTIONS			
Year Team	G	GS	No.	Yds.	Avg.	TD
1993—Atlanta NFL	15	8	3	7	2.3	0
1994—Atlanta NFL	16	5	3	105	35.0	1
1995—Atlanta NFL	16	7	0	0	...	0
1996—Atlanta NFL	15	9	1	0	0.0	0
1997—San Francisco NFL	16	11	3	49	16.3	0
1998—San Francisco NFL	16	16	4	78	19.5	0
Pro totals (6 years)	94	56	14	239	17.1	1

WALKER, DENARD   CB   TITANS

PERSONAL: Born August 9, 1973, in Dallas. ... 6-1/190. ... Full name: Denard Antuan Walker.
HIGH SCHOOL: South Garland (Texas), than Harlingen (Texas) Military Institute.
COLLEGE: Louisiana State.
TRANSACTIONS/CAREER NOTES: Selected by Houston Oilers in third round (75th pick overall) of 1997 NFL draft. ... Oilers franchise moved to Tennessee for 1997 season. ... Signed by Oilers (July 18, 1997). ... Oilers franchise renamed Tennessee Titans for 1999 season (December 26, 1998).

			INTERCEPTIONS			
Year Team	G	GS	No.	Yds.	Avg.	TD
1997—Tennessee NFL	15	11	2	53	26.5	1
1998—Tennessee NFL	16	16	2	6	3.0	0
Pro totals (2 years)	31	27	4	59	14.8	1

WALKER, GARY   DT   JAGUARS

PERSONAL: Born February 28, 1973, in Royston, Ga. ... 6-2/295. ... Full name: Gary Lamar Walker.
HIGH SCHOOL: Franklin County (Lavonia, Ga.).
JUNIOR COLLEGE: Hinds Community College (Miss.).
COLLEGE: Auburn.
TRANSACTIONS/CAREER NOTES: Selected by Houston Oilers in fifth round (159th pick overall) of 1995 NFL draft. ... Signed by Oilers (July 10, 1995). ... Oilers franchise moved to Tennessee for 1997 season. ... Granted free agency (February 13, 1998). ... Re-signed by Oilers (July 15, 1998). ... Granted unconditional free agency (February 12, 1999). ... Signed by Jacksonville Jaguars (February 15, 1999).
PRO STATISTICS: 1996—Recovered one fumble.

Year Team	G	GS	SACKS
1995—Houston NFL	15	9	2.5
1996—Houston NFL	16	16	5.5
1997—Tennessee NFL	15	15	7.0
1998—Tennessee NFL	16	16	1.0
Pro totals (4 years)	62	56	16.0

WALKER, MARQUIS   DB   RAIDERS

PERSONAL: Born July 6, 1972, in St. Louis. ... 5-10/175. ... Full name: Marquis Roshe Walker. ... Brother of Darnell Walker, cornerback, San Francisco 49ers.
HIGH SCHOOL: Berkeley (St. Louis).
JUNIOR COLLEGE: Blinn College (Texas), then Cisco (Texas) Junior College.
COLLEGE: Southeast Missouri State.

TRANSACTIONS/CAREER NOTES: Signed as non-drafted free agent by St. Louis Rams (April 24, 1996). ... Released by Rams (September 4, 1996). ... Signed by Washington Redskins to practice squad (September 4, 1996). ... Signed by Rams off Redskins practice squad (November 6, 1996). ... Released by Rams (November 19, 1997). ... Selected by Frankfurt Galaxy in 1998 NFL Europe draft (February 18, 1998). ... Signed by Oakland Raiders (May 5, 1998). ... Granted free agency (February 12, 1999). ... Re-signed by Raiders (March 5, 1999).
PLAYING EXPERIENCE: St. Louis (8)-Washington (1) NFL, 1996; St. Louis NFL, 1997; Oakland NFL, 1998. ... Games/Games started: 1996 (St.L-8/4; Wash.-1/0; Total: 9/4), 1997 (10/0), 1998 (16/7). Total: 35/11.
PRO STATISTICS: 1997—Recovered one fumble. 1998—Intercepted two passes for 28 yards and recovered one fumble for three yards.

WALLACE, AARON LB

PERSONAL: Born April 17, 1967, in Paris, Texas. ... 6-3/240.
HIGH SCHOOL: Franklin D. Roosevelt (Dallas).
COLLEGE: Texas A&M.
TRANSACTIONS/CAREER NOTES: Selected by Los Angeles Raiders in second round (37th pick overall) of 1990 NFL draft. ... Signed by Raiders (July 16, 1990). ... Granted free agency (March 1, 1993). ... Re-signed by Raiders (July 21, 1993). ... Raiders franchise moved to Oakland (July 21, 1995). ... Granted unconditional free agency (February 16, 1996). ... Signed by Denver Broncos (May 14, 1996). ... Released by Broncos (July 24, 1996). ... Signed by Raiders (June 19, 1997). ... Released by Raiders (August 19, 1997). ... Re-signed by Raiders (October 15, 1997). ... Granted unconditional free agency (February 13, 1998). ... Re-signed by Raiders (February 17, 1998). ... Released by Raiders (October 6, 1998).
CHAMPIONSHIP GAME EXPERIENCE: Played in AFC championship game (1990 season).
HONORS: Named linebacker on THE SPORTING NEWS college All-America second team (1988).
PRO STATISTICS: 1992—Recovered two fumbles. 1993—Recovered two fumbles. 1995—Recovered one fumble. 1998—Recovered one fumble.

Year Team	G	GS	SACKS
1990—Los Angeles Raiders NFL	16	0	9.0
1991—Los Angeles Raiders NFL	16	0	2.0
1992—Los Angeles Raiders NFL	16	16	4.0
1993—Los Angeles Raiders NFL	16	14	2.0
1994—Los Angeles Raiders NFL	16	5	2.0
1995—Oakland NFL	13	0	2.0
1996—	Did not play.		
1997—Oakland NFL	5	0	0.0
1998—Oakland NFL	4	0	0.0
Pro totals (8 years)	**102**	**35**	**21.0**

WALLACE, AL DE EAGLES

PERSONAL: Born March 25, 1974, in Delray Beach, Fla. ... 6-5/258. ... Full name: Alonzo Dwight Wallace.
HIGH SCHOOL: Spanish River (Delray Beach, Fla.).
COLLEGE: Maryland (degree in health education, 1997).
TRANSACTIONS/CAREER NOTES: Signed as non-drafted free agent by Jacksonville Jaguars (April 21, 1997). ... Released by Jaguars (August 19, 1997). ... Re-signed by Jaguars to practice squad (August 25, 1997). ... Signed by Philadelphia Eagles off Jaguars practice squad (December 2, 1997).
PLAYING EXPERIENCE: Philadelphia NFL, 1997 and 1998. ... Games/Games started: 1997 (1/0), 1998 (15/0). Total: 16/0.
PRO STATISTICS: 1998—Credited with six sacks.

WALLS, WESLEY TE PANTHERS

PERSONAL: Born February 26, 1966, in Pontotoc, Miss. ... 6-5/250. ... Full name: Charles Wesley Walls.
HIGH SCHOOL: Pontotoc (Miss.).
COLLEGE: Mississippi.
TRANSACTIONS/CAREER NOTES: Selected by San Francisco 49ers in second round (56th pick overall) of 1989 NFL draft. ... Signed by 49ers (July 26, 1989). ... Granted free agency (February 1, 1992). ... Re-signed by 49ers (July 18, 1992). ... On injured reserve with shoulder injury (September 1, 1992-January 16, 1993). ... On injured reserve with shoulder injury (October 27, 1993-remainder of season). ... Granted unconditional free agency (February 17, 1994). ... Signed by New Orleans Saints (April 27, 1994). ... Granted unconditional free agency (February 16, 1996). ... Signed by Carolina Panthers (February 21, 1996).
CHAMPIONSHIP GAME EXPERIENCE: Played in NFC championship game (1989, 1990 and 1996 seasons). ... Member of Super Bowl championship team (1989 season).
HONORS: Named tight end on THE SPORTING NEWS college All-America second team (1988). ... Played in Pro Bowl (1996-1998 seasons).
PRO STATISTICS: 1989—Recovered one fumble. 1990—Returned one kickoff for 16 yards. 1993—Recovered one fumble. 1995—Returned one kickoff for six yards, fumbled once and recovered one fumble.
SINGLE GAME HIGHS (regular season): Receptions—8 (November 15, 1998, vs. Miami); yards—147 (September 7, 1997, vs. Atlanta); and touchdown receptions—2 (November 22, 1998, vs. St. Louis).
STATISTICAL PLATEAUS: 100-yard receiving games: 1997 (2).
MISCELLANEOUS: Holds Carolina Panthers all-time records for most touchdown receptions (21) and most touchdowns (21).

			RECEIVING				TOTALS			
Year Team	G	GS	No.	Yds.	Avg.	TD	TD	2pt.	Pts.	Fum.
1989—San Francisco NFL	16	0	4	16	4.0	1	1	...	6	1
1990—San Francisco NFL	16	0	5	27	5.4	0	0	...	0	0
1991—San Francisco NFL	15	0	2	24	12.0	0	0	...	0	0
1992—San Francisco NFL					Did not play.					
1993—San Francisco NFL	6	0	0	0	...	0	0	...	0	0
1994—New Orleans NFL	15	7	38	406	10.7	4	4	1	26	0
1995—New Orleans NFL	16	10	57	694	12.2	4	4	1	26	1
1996—Carolina NFL	16	15	61	713	11.7	10	10	0	60	0
1997—Carolina NFL	15	15	58	746	12.9	6	6	0	36	0
1998—Carolina NFL	14	14	49	506	10.3	5	5	0	30	0
Pro totals (9 years)	**129**	**61**	**274**	**3132**	**11.4**	**30**	**30**	**2**	**184**	**2**

WALSH, CHRIS — WR — VIKINGS

PERSONAL: Born December 12, 1968, in Cleveland. ... 6-1/199. ... Full name: Christopher Lee Walsh.
HIGH SCHOOL: Ygnacio Valley (Concord, Calif.).
COLLEGE: Stanford (degree in quantitative economics, 1991).
TRANSACTIONS/CAREER NOTES: Selected by Buffalo Bills in ninth round (251st pick overall) of 1992 NFL draft. ... Signed by Bills (July 22, 1992). ... Released by Bills (August 31, 1992). ... Re-signed by Bills to practice squad (September 1, 1992). ... Activated (September 19, 1992). ... Released by Bills (October 2, 1992). ... Re-signed by Bills to practice squad (October 2, 1992). ... Released by Bills (March 10, 1994). ... Signed by Minnesota Vikings (May 6, 1994). ... Granted unconditional free agency (February 16, 1996). ... Re-signed by Vikings (March 4, 1996). ... Granted unconditional free agency (February 13, 1998). ... Re-signed by Vikings (March 4, 1998).
CHAMPIONSHIP GAME EXPERIENCE: Member of Bills for AFC championship game (1993 season); inactive. ... Member of Bills for Super Bowl XXVIII (1993 season); inactive. ... Played in NFC championship game (1998 season).
PRO STATISTICS: 1994—Returned one kickoff for six yards. 1995—Returned three kickoffs for 42 yards. 1996—Attempted one pass without a completion and credited with one two-point conversion. 1997—Returned one kickoff for 10 yards.
SINGLE GAME HIGHS (regular season): Receptions—4 (October 22, 1995, vs. Green Bay); yards—31 (October 22, 1995, vs. Green Bay); and touchdown receptions—1 (September 7, 1997, vs. Chicago).

				RECEIVING				TOTALS		
Year Team	G	GS	No.	Yds.	Avg.	TD	TD	2pt.	Pts.	Fum.
1992—Buffalo NFL	2	0	0	0	...	0	0	...	0	0
1993—Buffalo NFL	3	0	0	0	...	0	0	...	0	0
1994—Minnesota NFL	10	0	0	0	...	0	0	0	0	0
1995—Minnesota NFL	16	0	7	66	9.4	0	0	0	0	0
1996—Minnesota NFL	15	0	4	39	9.8	0	1	1	8	0
1997—Minnesota NFL	14	0	11	114	10.4	1	1	0	6	0
1998—Minnesota NFL	15	0	2	46	23.0	0	0	0	0	0
Pro totals (7 years)	75	0	24	265	11.0	2	2	1	14	0

WALSH, STEVE — QB

PERSONAL: Born December 1, 1966, in St. Paul, Minn. ... 6-3/215. ... Full name: Stephen John Walsh.
HIGH SCHOOL: Cretin-Derham Hall (St. Paul, Minn.).
COLLEGE: Miami, Fla. (degree in finance).
TRANSACTIONS/CAREER NOTES: Selected by Dallas Cowboys in first round of 1989 NFL supplemental draft (July 7, 1989). ... Signed by Cowboys (July 29, 1989). ... Traded by Cowboys to New Orleans Saints for first- (traded to New England) and third-round (OT Erik Williams) picks in 1991 draft and second-round pick (traded to Cleveland) in 1992 draft (September 25, 1990). ... Active for two games (1992); did not play. ... Granted free agency (March 1, 1993). ... Re-signed by Saints (July 15, 1993). ... Released by Saints (April 23, 1994). ... Signed by Chicago Bears (April 26, 1994). ... Granted unconditional free agency (February 17, 1995). ... Re-signed by Bears (April 17, 1995). ... Granted unconditional free agency (February 16, 1996). ... Signed by St. Louis Rams (April 10, 1996). ... Granted unconditional free agency (February 14, 1997). ... Signed by Tampa Bay Buccaneers (April 16, 1997). ... Granted unconditional free agency (February 12, 1999).
PRO STATISTICS: 1989—Fumbled three times and recovered two fumbles for minus 14 yards. 1990—Fumbled six times and recovered two fumbles. 1991—Fumbled three times and recovered one fumble for minus 20 yards. 1994—Fumbled seven times and recovered three fumbles for minus eight yards. 1996—Fumbled once and recovered one fumble. 1997—Fumbled once and recovered two fumbles.
SINGLE GAME HIGHS (regular season): Attempts—49 (October 29, 1989, vs. Phoenix); completions—26 (December 8, 1991, vs. Dallas); yards—317 (December 1, 1991, vs. San Francisco); and touchdown passes—3 (October 14, 1990, vs. Cleveland).
STATISTICAL PLATEAUS: 300-yard passing games: 1991 (1).
MISCELLANEOUS: Regular-season record as starting NFL quarterback: 20-18 (.526). ... Postseason record as starting NFL quarterback: 1-2 (.333).

			PASSING								RUSHING				TOTALS		
Year Team	G	GS	Att.	Cmp.	Pct.	Yds.	TD	Int.	Avg.	Rat.	Att.	Yds.	Avg.	TD	TD	2pt.	Pts.
1989—Dallas NFL	8	5	219	110	50.2	1371	5	9	6.26	60.5	6	16	2.7	0	0	...	0
1990—Dallas NFL	1	0	9	4	44.4	40	0	0	4.44	57.6	1	0	0.0	0	0	...	0
—New Orleans NFL	12	11	327	175	53.5	1970	12	13	6.02	67.5	19	25	1.3	0	0	...	0
1991—New Orleans NFL	8	7	255	141	55.3	1638	11	6	6.42	79.5	8	0	0.0	0	0	...	0
1992—New Orleans NFL						Did not play.											
1993—New Orleans NFL	2	1	38	20	52.6	271	2	3	7.13	60.3	4	-4	-1.0	0	0	...	0
1994—Chicago NFL	12	11	343	208	60.6	2078	10	8	6.06	77.9	30	4	0.1	1	1	0	6
1995—Chicago NFL	1	0	0	0	...	0	0	0	...	...	0	0	...	0	0	...	0
1996—St. Louis NFL	3	3	77	33	42.9	344	0	5	4.47	29.4	6	10	1.7	0	0	0	0
1997—Tampa Bay NFL	13	0	17	6	35.3	58	0	1	3.41	21.2	6	-4	-0.7	0	0	0	0
1998—Tampa Bay NFL	5	0	19	9	47.4	58	0	3	3.05	14.7	0	0	...	0	0	0	0
Pro totals (9 years)	65	38	1304	706	54.1	7828	40	48	6.00	67.1	80	47	0.6	1	1	0	6

WALTER, KEN — P — PANTHERS

PERSONAL: Born August 15, 1972, in Cleveland. ... 6-1/195. ... Full name: Kenneth Matthew Walter Jr.
HIGH SCHOOL: Euclid (Ohio).
COLLEGE: Kent.
TRANSACTIONS/CAREER NOTES: Signed as non-drafted free agent by Carolina Panthers (April 14, 1997).
PRO STATISTICS: 1997—Rushed once for minus five yards. 1998—Rushed three times for no yards, attempted one pass without a completion, fumbled twice and recovered two fumbles for minus 20 yards.

		PUNTING					
Year Team	G	No.	Yds.	Avg.	Net avg.	In. 20	Blk.
1997—Carolina NFL	16	85	3604	42.4	36.4	29	0
1998—Carolina NFL	16	77	3131	40.7	38.1	20	0
Pro totals (2 years)	32	162	6735	41.6	37.2	49	0

WALZ, ZACK   LB   CARDINALS

PERSONAL: Born February 13, 1976, in Mountain View, Calif. ... 6-4/228. ... Full name: Zachary Christian Walz.
HIGH SCHOOL: Saint Francis (San Jose, Calif.).
COLLEGE: Dartmouth (degree in government and economics, 1998).
TRANSACTIONS/CAREER NOTES: Selected by Arizona Cardinals in sixth round (158th pick overall) of 1998 NFL draft. ... Signed by Cardinals (June 4, 1998).
PLAYING EXPERIENCE: Arizona NFL, 1998. ... Games/Games started: 16/0.
PRO STATISTICS: 1998—Recovered one fumble.

WARD, DEDRIC   WR/KR   JETS

PERSONAL: Born September 29, 1974, in Cedar Rapids, Iowa. ... 5-9/184. ... Full name: Dedric Lamar Ward.
HIGH SCHOOL: Washington (Cedar Rapids, Iowa).
COLLEGE: Northern Iowa (degree in psychology).
TRANSACTIONS/CAREER NOTES: Selected by New York Jets in third round (88th pick overall) of 1997 NFL draft. ... Signed by Jets (July 17, 1997).
CHAMPIONSHIP GAME EXPERIENCE: Played in AFC championship game (1998 season).
PRO STATISTICS: 1997—Rushed twice for 25 yards. 1998—Rushed twice for seven yards.
SINGLE GAME HIGHS (regular season): Receptions—6 (November 9, 1997, vs. Miami); yards—108 (November 9, 1997, vs. Miami); and touchdown receptions—1 (December 27, 1998, vs. New England).
STATISTICAL PLATEAUS: 100-yard receiving games: 1997 (1).

			RECEIVING				PUNT RETURNS				KICKOFF RETURNS				TOTALS		
Year Team	G	GS	No.	Yds.	Avg.	TD	No.	Yds.	Avg.	TD	No.	Yds.	Avg.	TD	TD	2pt.	Pts.	Fum.
1997—New York Jets NFL	11	1	18	212	11.8	1	8	55	6.9	0	2	10	5.0	0	1	0	6	1
1998—New York Jets NFL	16	2	25	477	19.1	4	8	72	9.0	0	3	60	20.0	0	4	0	24	0
Pro totals (2 years)	27	3	43	689	16.0	5	16	127	7.9	0	5	70	14.0	0	5	0	30	1

WARD, HINES   WR   STEELERS

PERSONAL: Born March 8, 1976, in Rex, Ga. ... 6-0/197. ... Full name: Hines Ward Jr.
HIGH SCHOOL: Forest Park (Ga.).
COLLEGE: Georgia.
TRANSACTIONS/CAREER NOTES: Selected by Pittsburgh Steelers in third round (92nd pick overall) of 1998 NFL draft. ... Signed by Steelers (July 20, 1998).
PRO STATISTICS: 1998—Rushed once for 13 yards and attempted one pass with a completion for 17 yards.
SINGLE GAME HIGHS (regular season): Receptions—2 (December 6, 1998, vs. New England); yards—56 (November 9, 1998, vs. Green Bay); and touchdown receptions—0.

			RECEIVING			
Year Team	G	GS	No.	Yds.	Avg.	TD
1998—Pittsburgh NFL	16	0	15	246	16.4	0

WARD, PHILLIP   LB   RAMS

PERSONAL: Born November 11, 1974, in Gardena, Calif. ... 6-3/235.
HIGH SCHOOL: Pius X (Downey, Calif.).
COLLEGE: UCLA.
TRANSACTIONS/CAREER NOTES: Signed as non-drafted free agent by Indianapolis Colts (April 25, 1997). ... On injured reserve with leg injury (August 5-November 4, 1997). ... Released by Colts (November 4, 1997). ... Signed by Detroit Lions (March 26, 1998). ... Released by Lions (August 30, 1998). ... Signed by St. Louis Rams to practice squad (November 12, 1998). ... Activated (November 30, 1998). ... Assigned by Rams to Berlin Thunder in 1999 NFL Europe enhancement allocation program (February 22, 1999).
PLAYING EXPERIENCE: St. Louis NFL, 1998. ... Games/Games started: 2/0.

WARFIELD, ERIC   CB   CHIEFS

PERSONAL: Born March 3, 1976, in Vicksburg, Miss. ... 6-0/192. ... Full name: Eric Andrew Warfield.
HIGH SCHOOL: Arkansas (Texarkana, Ark.).
COLLEGE: Nebraska.
TRANSACTIONS/CAREER NOTES: Selected by Kansas City Chiefs in seventh round (216th pick overall) of 1998 NFL draft. ... Signed by Chiefs (May 27, 1998).
PLAYING EXPERIENCE: Kansas City NFL, 1998. ... Games/Games started: 12/0.

WARNER, KURT   QB   RAMS

PERSONAL: Born June 22, 1971, in Burlington, Iowa. ... 6-2/220. ... Full name: Kurtis Warner.
HIGH SCHOOL: Regis (Cedar Rapids, Iowa).
COLLEGE: Northern Iowa (degree in communications).
TRANSACTIONS/CAREER NOTES: Played for Iowa Barnstormers of Arena Football League (1995-97). ... Signed as non-drafted free agent by St. Louis Rams (December 26, 1997). ... Assigned by Rams to Amsterdam Admirals in 1998 NFL Europe enhancement allocation program (February 18, 1998).

SINGLE GAME HIGHS (regular season): Attempts—11 (December 27, 1998, vs. San Francisco); completions—4 (December 27, 1998, vs. San Francisco); yards—39 (December 27, 1998, vs. San Francisco); and touchdown passes—0.

				PASSING						RUSHING				TOTALS		
Year Team	G	GS	Att.	Cmp.	Pct.	Yds.	TD	Int.	Avg.	Rat.	Att.	Yds.	Avg.	TD	TD	2pt.	Pts.
1998—Amsterdam	...	...	326	165	50.6	2101	15	6	6.44	78.8	19	17	0.9	1	1	...	6
—St. Louis NFL	1	0	11	4	36.4	39	0	0	3.55	47.2	0	0	...	0	0	0	0
NFL Europe totals (1 year)	...	...	326	165	50.6	2101	15	6	6.44	78.8	19	17	0.9	1	1	0	6
NFL totals (1 year)	1	0	11	4	36.4	39	0	0	3.55	47.2	0	0		0	0	0	0
Pro totals (2 years)	...	...	337	169	50.1	2140	15	6	6.35	77.8	19	17	0.9	1	1	0	6

WARNER, RON   LB   SAINTS

PERSONAL: Born September 26, 1975, in Independence, Kan. ... 6-2/252.
HIGH SCHOOL: Independence (Kan.).
JUNIOR COLLEGE: Independence (Kan.) Community College.
COLLEGE: Kansas.
TRANSACTIONS/CAREER NOTES: Selected by New Orleans Saints in seventh round (239th pick overall) of 1998 NFL draft. ... Signed by Saints (July 23, 1998). ... On non-football injury list with knee injury (August 25-November 4, 1998).
PLAYING EXPERIENCE: New Orleans NFL, 1998. ... Games/Games started: 1/0.
HONORS: Named outside linebacker on THE SPORTING NEWS college All-America second team (1997).

WARREN, CHRIS   RB   COWBOYS

PERSONAL: Born January 24, 1968, in Silver Spring, Md. ... 6-2/236. ... Full name: Christopher Collins Warren Jr.
HIGH SCHOOL: Robinson Secondary (Fairfax, Va.).
COLLEGE: Virginia, then Ferrum, Va. (degree in psychology).
TRANSACTIONS/CAREER NOTES: Selected by Seattle Seahawks in fourth round (89th pick overall) of 1990 NFL draft. ... Signed by Seahawks (July 24, 1990). ... Granted free agency (March 1, 1993). ... Tendered offer sheet by New York Jets (April 23, 1993). ... Offer matched by Seahawks (April 23, 1993). ... Released by Seahawks (March 13, 1998). ... Signed by Dallas Cowboys (April 13, 1998).
HONORS: Played in Pro Bowl (1993-1995 seasons).
PRO STATISTICS: 1990—Fumbled three times and recovered one fumble. 1991—Fumbled three times and recovered one fumble. 1992—Fumbled twice and recovered two fumbles. 1993—Fumbled three times. 1994—Fumbled five times and recovered two fumbles. 1995—Fumbled five times and recovered two fumbles. 1996—Fumbled three times and recovered two fumbles for four yards. 1997—Fumbled twice. 1998—Recovered one fumble.
SINGLE GAME HIGHS (regular season): Attempts—36 (September 19, 1993, vs. New England); yards—185 (December 11, 1994, vs. Houston); and rushing touchdowns—3 (December 17, 1995, vs. Oakland).
STATISTICAL PLATEAUS: 100-yard rushing games: 1992 (3), 1993 (3), 1994 (7), 1995 (8), 1996 (3), 1998 (1). Total: 25.
MISCELLANEOUS: Holds Seattle Seahawks all-time record for most yards rushing (6,706).

			RUSHING				RECEIVING				PUNT RETURNS				KICKOFF RETURNS				TOTALS		
Year Team	G	GS	Att.	Yds.	Avg.	TD	No.	Yds.	Avg.	TD	No.	Yds.	Avg.	TD	No.	Yds.	Avg.	TD	TD	2pt.	Pts.
1990—Seattle NFL	16	0	6	11	1.8	1	0	0	...	0	28	269	9.6	0	23	478	20.8	0	1	...	6
1991—Seattle NFL	16	1	11	13	1.2	0	2	9	4.5	0	§32	298	9.3	▲1	32	792	24.8	0	1	...	6
1992—Seattle NFL	16	16	223	1017	4.6	3	16	134	8.4	0	34	252	7.4	0	28	524	18.7	0	3	...	18
1993—Seattle NFL	14	14	273	1072	3.9	7	15	99	6.6	0	0	0	...	0	0	0	...	0	7	...	42
1994—Seattle NFL	16	15	333	§1545	§4.6	9	41	323	7.9	2	0	0	...	0	0	0	...	0	11	1	68
1995—Seattle NFL	16	16	310	1346	4.3	§15	35	247	7.1	1	0	0	...	0	0	0	...	0	16	0	96
1996—Seattle NFL	14	14	203	855	4.2	5	40	273	6.8	0	0	0	...	0	0	0	...	0	5	1	32
1997—Seattle NFL	15	13	200	847	4.2	4	45	257	5.7	0	0	0	...	0	0	0	...	0	4	0	24
1998—Dallas NFL	9	0	59	291	4.9	4	13	66	5.1	1	2	11	5.5	0	5	90	18.0	0	5	0	30
Pro totals (9 years)	132	89	1618	6997	4.3	48	207	1408	6.8	4	96	830	8.6	1	88	1884	21.4	0	53	2	322

WARREN, LAMONT   RB   PATRIOTS

PERSONAL: Born January 4, 1973, in Indianapolis. ... 5-11/202. ... Full name: Lamont Allen Warren.
HIGH SCHOOL: Dorsey (Los Angeles).
COLLEGE: Colorado.
TRANSACTIONS/CAREER NOTES: Selected after junior season by Indianapolis Colts in sixth round (164th pick overall) of 1994 NFL draft. ... Signed by Colts (July 13, 1994). ... Released by Colts (April 12, 1999). ... Signed by New England Patriots (April 25, 1999).
CHAMPIONSHIP GAME EXPERIENCE: Played in AFC championship game (1995 season).
PRO STATISTICS: 1994—Attempted one pass without a completion. 1996—Recovered one fumble. 1997—Attempted one pass without a completion and recovered one fumble.
SINGLE GAME HIGHS (regular season): Attempts—22 (December 23, 1995, vs. New England); yards—90 (December 23, 1995, vs. New England); and rushing touchdowns—1 (December 20, 1998, vs. Seattle).

			RUSHING				RECEIVING				KICKOFF RETURNS				TOTALS			
Year Team	G	GS	Att.	Yds.	Avg.	TD	No.	Yds.	Avg.	TD	No.	Yds.	Avg.	TD	TD	2pt.	Pts.	Fum.
1994—Indianapolis NFL	11	0	18	80	4.4	0	3	47	15.7	0	2	56	28.0	0	0	0	0	0
1995—Indianapolis NFL	12	1	47	152	3.2	1	17	159	9.4	0	15	315	21.0	0	1	0	6	1
1996—Indianapolis NFL	13	3	67	230	3.4	1	22	174	7.9	0	3	54	18.0	0	1	0	6	2
1997—Indianapolis NFL	13	0	28	80	2.9	2	20	192	9.6	0	1	19	19.0	0	2	0	12	0
1998—Indianapolis NFL	12	2	25	61	2.4	1	11	44	4.0	1	8	152	19.0	0	2	0	12	0
Pro totals (5 years)	61	6	185	603	3.3	5	73	616	8.4	1	29	596	20.6	0	6	0	36	4

WASHINGTON, DEWAYNE — CB — STEELERS

PERSONAL: Born December 27, 1972, in Durham, N.C. ... 6-0/193. ... Full name: Dewayne Neron Washington.
HIGH SCHOOL: Northern (Durham, N.C.).
COLLEGE: North Carolina State.
TRANSACTIONS/CAREER NOTES: Selected by Minnesota Vikings in first round (18th pick overall) of 1994 NFL draft. ... Signed by Vikings (July 14, 1994). ... Granted unconditional free agency (February 13, 1998). ... Signed by Pittsburgh Steelers (February 25, 1998).
HONORS: Was a high school All-America selection by The Sporting News (1989).
PRO STATISTICS: 1994—Recovered two fumbles for 17 yards and one touchdown. 1998—Recovered two fumbles.

			INTERCEPTIONS			
Year Team	G	GS	No.	Yds.	Avg.	TD
1994—Minnesota NFL	16	16	3	135	45.0	2
1995—Minnesota NFL	15	15	1	25	25.0	0
1996—Minnesota NFL	16	16	2	27	13.5	1
1997—Minnesota NFL	16	16	4	71	17.8	0
1998—Pittsburgh NFL	16	16	5	§178	35.6	▲2
Pro totals (5 years)	79	79	15	436	29.1	5

WASHINGTON, KEITH — DE — RAVENS

PERSONAL: Born December 18, 1972, in Dallas. ... 6-4/270. ... Full name: Keith L. Washington.
HIGH SCHOOL: Wilmer-Hutchins (Dallas).
COLLEGE: UNLV.
TRANSACTIONS/CAREER NOTES: Signed as non-drafted free agent by Minnesota Vikings (April 9, 1995). ... Released by Vikings (August 27, 1995). ... Re-signed by Vikings to practice squad (August 28, 1995). ... Activated (October 9, 1995); did not play. ... On injured reserve with ankle injury (November 15, 1995-remainder of season). ... Released by Vikings (August 25, 1996). ... Signed by Detroit Lions (August 26, 1996). ... Released by Lions (August 26, 1997). ... Signed by Baltimore Ravens (October 15, 1997). ... Granted free agency (February 13, 1998). ... Re-signed by Ravens (April 14, 1998).
PLAYING EXPERIENCE: Detroit NFL, 1996; Baltimore NFL, 1997 and 1998. ... Games/Games started: 1996 (12/0), 1997 (10/1), 1998 (16/0). Total: 38/1.
PRO STATISTICS: 1996—Returned one kickoff for 14 yards. 1997—Credited with two sacks. 1998—Credited with one sack.

WASHINGTON, MARVIN — DE — 49ERS

PERSONAL: Born October 22, 1965, in Denver. ... 6-6/285. ... Full name: Marvin Andrew Washington. ... Cousin of Andrew Lang, center, Chicago Bulls.
HIGH SCHOOL: Justin F. Kimball (Dallas).
JUNIOR COLLEGE: Hinds Community College (Miss.).
COLLEGE: Texas-El Paso, then Idaho.
TRANSACTIONS/CAREER NOTES: Selected by New York Jets in sixth round (151st pick overall) of 1989 NFL draft. ... Signed by Jets (July 21, 1989). ... Granted free agency (February 1, 1991). ... Re-signed by Jets (May 5, 1991). ... Granted free agency (March 1, 1993). ... Tendered offer sheet by Seattle Seahawks (March 25, 1993). ... Offer matched by Jets (March 31, 1993). ... Released by Jets (August 11, 1997). ... Signed by San Francisco 49ers (August 21, 1997). ... On injured reserve with ankle injury (November 12, 1997-remainder of season). ... Granted unconditional free agency (February 13, 1998). ... Signed by Denver Broncos (March 2, 1998). ... Granted unconditional free agency (February 12, 1999). ... Signed by 49ers (April 1, 1999).
CHAMPIONSHIP GAME EXPERIENCE: Played in AFC championship game (1998 season). ... Member of Super Bowl championship team (1998 season).
PRO STATISTICS: 1989—Returned one kickoff for 11 yards and recovered one fumble. 1992—Credited with one safety. 1994—Intercepted one pass for seven yards, fumbled once and recovered one fumble. 1997—Recovered one fumble.

Year Team	G	GS	SACKS
1989—New York Jets NFL	16	0	1.5
1990—New York Jets NFL	16	0	4.5
1991—New York Jets NFL	15	15	6.0
1992—New York Jets NFL	16	14	8.5
1993—New York Jets NFL	16	16	5.5
1994—New York Jets NFL	15	15	3.0
1995—New York Jets NFL	16	16	6.0
1996—New York Jets NFL	14	14	2.5
1997—San Francisco NFL	10	1	1.0
1998—Denver NFL	16	0	2.0
Pro totals (10 years)	150	91	40.5

WASHINGTON, TED — NT — BILLS

PERSONAL: Born April 13, 1968, in Tampa. ... 6-4/325. ... Full name: Theodore Washington. ... Son of Ted Washington, linebacker with New York Jets (1973) and Houston Oilers (1974-82).
HIGH SCHOOL: Tampa Bay Vocational Tech Senior.
COLLEGE: Louisville.
TRANSACTIONS/CAREER NOTES: Selected by San Francisco 49ers in first round (25th pick overall) of 1991 NFL draft. ... Signed by 49ers (July 10, 1991). ... Traded by 49ers to Denver Broncos for fifth-round pick (traded to Green Bay) in 1994 draft (April 19, 1994). ... Granted unconditional free agency (February 17, 1995). ... Signed by Buffalo Bills (February 25, 1995). ... Designated by Bills as franchise player (February 13, 1998). ... Free agency status changed from franchise to transitional (February 27, 1998). ... Re-signed by Bills (March 2, 1998).
CHAMPIONSHIP GAME EXPERIENCE: Played in NFC championship game (1992 and 1993 seasons).
HONORS: Played in Pro Bowl (1997 and 1998 seasons).

PRO STATISTICS: 1993—Recovered one fumble. 1994—Intercepted one pass for five yards. 1997—Recovered one fumble. 1998—Intercepted one pass for no yards and credited with a safety.

Year Team	G	GS	SACKS
1991—San Francisco NFL	16	0	1.0
1992—San Francisco NFL	16	6	2.0
1993—San Francisco NFL	12	12	3.0
1994—Denver NFL	15	15	2.5
1995—Buffalo NFL	16	15	2.5
1996—Buffalo NFL	16	16	3.5
1997—Buffalo NFL	16	16	4.0
1998—Buffalo NFL	16	16	4.5
Pro totals (8 years)	123	96	23.0

WASHINGTON, TODD   C/G   BUCCANEERS

PERSONAL: Born July 19, 1976, in Nassawadox, Va. ... 6-3/325. ... Full name: Todd Page Washington.
HIGH SCHOOL: Nandua (Melfa, Va.).
COLLEGE: Virginia Tech (degree in physical education and health, 1998).
TRANSACTIONS/CAREER NOTES: Selected by Tampa Bay Buccaneers in fourth round (104th pick overall) of 1998 NFL draft. ... Signed by Buccaneers (June 11, 1998).
PLAYING EXPERIENCE: Tampa Bay NFL, 1998. ... Games/Games started: 4/0.

WATTERS, RICKY   RB   SEAHAWKS

PERSONAL: Born April 7, 1969, in Harrisburg, Pa. ... 6-1/217. ... Full name: Richard James Watters.
HIGH SCHOOL: Bishop McDevitt (Harrisburg, Pa.).
COLLEGE: Notre Dame (degree in design, 1990).
TRANSACTIONS/CAREER NOTES: Selected by San Francisco 49ers in second round (45th pick overall) of 1991 NFL draft. ... Signed by 49ers (July 11, 1991). ... On injured reserve with foot injury (August 27, 1991-entire season). ... Designated by 49ers as transition player (February 15, 1994). ... Tendered offer sheet by Philadelphia Eagles (March 18, 1995). ... 49ers declined to match offer (March 25, 1995). ... Granted unconditional free agency (February 13, 1998). ... Signed by Seattle Seahawks (March 4, 1998).
CHAMPIONSHIP GAME EXPERIENCE: Played in NFC championship game (1992-1994 seasons). ... Member of Super Bowl championship team (1994 season).
HONORS: Played in Pro Bowl (1992-1996 seasons).
POST SEASON RECORDS: Shares Super Bowl single-game records for most points—18; and most touchdowns—3 (January 29, 1995, vs. San Diego). ... Holds NFL postseason single-game records for most points—30; most touchdowns—5; and most rushing touchdowns—5 (January 15, 1994, vs. New York Giants).
PRO STATISTICS: 1992—Attempted one pass without a completion and recovered one fumble. 1993—Recovered one fumble. 1994—Recovered two fumbles. 1997—Recovered one fumble. 1998—Attempted one pass with a completion for one yard and a touchdown and recovered one fumble.
SINGLE GAME HIGHS (regular season): Attempts—33 (December 10, 1995, vs. Dallas); yards—178 (December 20, 1998, vs. Indianapolis); rushing touchdowns—3 (December 5, 1993, vs. Cincinnati).
STATISTICAL PLATEAUS: 100-yard rushing games: 1992 (4), 1993 (3), 1994 (2), 1995 (4), 1996 (6), 1997 (2), 1998 (4). Total: 25. ... 100-yard receiving games: 1994 (1).

			RUSHING				RECEIVING				TOTALS			
Year Team	G	GS	Att.	Yds.	Avg.	TD	No.	Yds.	Avg.	TD	TD	2pt.	Pts.	Fum.
1991—San Francisco NFL							Did not play.							
1992—San Francisco NFL	14	13	206	1013	4.9	9	43	405	9.4	2	11	...	66	2
1993—San Francisco NFL	13	13	208	950	4.6	‡10	31	326	10.5	‡1	11	...	66	5
1994—San Francisco NFL	16	16	239	877	3.7	6	66	719	10.9	5	11	0	66	8
1995—Philadelphia NFL	16	16	337	1273	3.8	11	62	434	7.0	1	12	0	72	6
1996—Philadelphia NFL	16	16	*353	1411	4.0	13	51	444	8.7	0	13	0	78	5
1997—Philadelphia NFL	16	16	285	1110	3.9	7	48	440	9.2	0	7	0	42	3
1998—Seattle NFL	16	16	319	1239	3.9	9	52	373	7.2	0	9	1	56	4
Pro totals (7 years)	107	106	1947	7873	4.0	65	353	3141	8.9	9	74	1	446	33

WAY, CHARLES   FB   GIANTS

PERSONAL: Born December 27, 1972, in Philadelphia. ... 6-0/250. ... Full name: Charles Christopher Way.
HIGH SCHOOL: Northeast (Philadelphia).
COLLEGE: Virginia.
TRANSACTIONS/CAREER NOTES: Selected by New York Giants in sixth round (206th pick overall) of 1995 NFL draft. ... Signed by Giants (July 23, 1995).
PRO STATISTICS: 1995—Returned one kickoff for eight yards. 1996—Returned two kickoffs for 19 yards and recovered three fumbles. 1997—Returned two kickoffs for 46 yards and recovered five fumbles. 1998—Recovered two fumbles.
SINGLE GAME HIGHS (regular season): Attempts—20 (October 26, 1997, vs. Cincinnati); yards—114 (November 16, 1997, vs. Arizona); rushing touchdowns—2 (October 26, 1997, vs. Cincinnati).
STATISTICAL PLATEAUS: 100-yard rushing games: 1997 (1).

			RUSHING				RECEIVING				TOTALS			
Year Team	G	GS	Att.	Yds.	Avg.	TD	No.	Yds.	Avg.	TD	TD	2pt.	Pts.	Fum.
1995—New York Giants NFL	16	4	2	6	3.0	0	7	76	10.9	1	1	0	6	0
1996—New York Giants NFL	16	12	22	79	3.6	1	32	328	10.3	1	2	0	12	0
1997—New York Giants NFL	16	16	151	698	4.6	4	37	304	8.2	1	5	0	30	3
1998—New York Giants NFL	16	15	113	432	3.8	3	31	131	4.2	1	4	0	24	0
Pro totals (4 years)	64	47	288	1215	4.2	8	107	839	7.8	4	12	0	72	3

WAYNE, NATE — LB — BRONCOS

PERSONAL: Born January 12, 1975, in Macon, Miss. ... 6-0/230.
HIGH SCHOOL: Noxubee County (Macon, Miss.).
COLLEGE: Mississippi.
TRANSACTIONS/CAREER NOTES: Selected by Denver Broncos in seventh round (219th pick overall) of 1998 NFL draft. ... Signed by Broncos (June 9, 1998). ... Assigned by Broncos to Barcelona Dragons in 1999 NFL Europe enhancement allocation program (February 22, 1999).
PLAYING EXPERIENCE: Denver NFL, 1998. ... Games/Games started: 1/0.
CHAMPIONSHIP GAME EXPERIENCE: Member of Broncos for AFC championship game (1998 season); inactive. ... Member of Super Bowl championship team (1998 season); inactive.

WEARY, FRED — CB — SAINTS

PERSONAL: Born April 12, 1974, in Jacksonville. ... 5-10/181. ... Full name: Joseph Fredrick Weary.
HIGH SCHOOL: Mandarin (Jacksonville).
COLLEGE: Florida.
TRANSACTIONS/CAREER NOTES: Selected by New Orleans Saints in fourth round (97th pick overall) of 1998 NFL draft. ... Signed by Saints (July 10, 1998).
HONORS: Named cornerback on THE SPORTING NEWS college All-America first team (1997).

			INTERCEPTIONS			
Year Team	G	GS	No.	Yds.	Avg.	TD
1998—New Orleans NFL	14	1	2	64	32.0	1

WEBB, RICHMOND — OT — DOLPHINS

PERSONAL: Born January 11, 1967, in Dallas. ... 6-6/320. ... Full name: Richmond Jewel Webb Jr.
HIGH SCHOOL: Franklin D. Roosevelt (Dallas).
COLLEGE: Texas A&M (degree in industrial distribution).
TRANSACTIONS/CAREER NOTES: Selected by Miami Dolphins in first round (ninth pick overall) of 1990 NFL draft. ... Signed by Dolphins (July 27, 1990). ... Designated by Dolphins as franchise player (February 12, 1999).
PLAYING EXPERIENCE: Miami NFL, 1990-1998. ... Games/Games started: 1990 (16/16), 1991 (14/14), 1992 (16/16), 1993 (16/16), 1994 (16/16), 1995 (16/16), 1996 (16/16), 1997 (16/16), 1998 (9/9). Total: 135/135.
CHAMPIONSHIP GAME EXPERIENCE: Played in AFC championship game (1992 season).
HONORS: Named NFL Rookie of the Year by THE SPORTING NEWS (1990). ... Played in Pro Bowl (1990-1996 seasons). ... Named offensive tackle on THE SPORTING NEWS NFL All-Pro team (1992 and 1994).
PRO STATISTICS: 1995—Recovered one fumble.

WEBSTER, LARRY — DL — RAVENS

PERSONAL: Born January 18, 1969, in Elkton, Md. ... 6-5/288. ... Full name: Larry Melvin Webster Jr.
HIGH SCHOOL: Elkton (Md.).
COLLEGE: Maryland.
TRANSACTIONS/CAREER NOTES: Selected by Miami Dolphins in third round (70th pick overall) of 1992 NFL draft. ... Signed by Dolphins (July 10, 1992). ... Granted free agency (February 17, 1995). ... Signed by Cleveland Browns (May 4, 1995). ... On suspended list for violating league substance abuse policy (September 4-26, 1995). ... Browns franchise moved to Baltimore and renamed Ravens for 1996 season (March 11, 1996). ... Suspended by NFL for violating league substance abuse policy (August 20, 1996-July 13, 1997). ... Granted unconditional free agency (February 13, 1998). ... Re-signed by Ravens (February 16, 1998).
PLAYING EXPERIENCE: Miami NFL, 1992-1994; Cleveland NFL, 1995; Baltimore NFL, 1997 and 1998. ... Games/Games started: 1992 (16/0), 1993 (13/9), 1994 (16/7), 1995 (10/0), 1997 (16/3), 1998 (15/0). Total: 86/19.
CHAMPIONSHIP GAME EXPERIENCE: Played in AFC championship game (1992 season).
PRO STATISTICS: 1992—Credited with 1 1/2 sacks. 1993—Recovered one fumble.

WEINER, TODD — OT — SEAHAWKS

PERSONAL: Born September 16, 1975, in Bristol, Pa. ... 6-4/300.
HIGH SCHOOL: Taravella (Coral Springs, Fla.).
COLLEGE: Kansas State.
TRANSACTIONS/CAREER NOTES: Selected by Seattle Seahawks in second round (47th pick overall) of 1998 NFL draft. ... Signed by Seahawks (July 15, 1998).
PLAYING EXPERIENCE: Seattle NFL, 1998. ... Games/Games started: 6/0.
HONORS: Named offensive tackle on THE SPORTING NEWS college All-America second team (1997).

WELLS, DEAN — LB — PANTHERS

PERSONAL: Born July 20, 1970, in Louisville, Ky. ... 6-3/248. ... Full name: Donald Dean Wells.
HIGH SCHOOL: Holy Cross (Louisville, Ky.).
COLLEGE: Kentucky (degree in marketing, 1992).
TRANSACTIONS/CAREER NOTES: Selected by Seattle Seahawks in fourth round (85th pick overall) of 1993 NFL draft. ... Signed by Seahawks (July 13, 1993). ... Granted unconditional free agency (February 12, 1999). ... Signed by Carolina Panthers (April 7, 1999).
PLAYING EXPERIENCE: Seattle NFL, 1993-1998. ... Games/Games started: 1993 (14/1), 1994 (15/0), 1995 (14/10), 1996 (16/15), 1997 (16/16), 1998 (9/8). Total: 84/50.
PRO STATISTICS: 1995—Recovered one fumble. 1996—Credited with one sack and recovered two fumbles. 1997—Credited with one sack and recovered one fumble. 1998—Intercepted one pass for 25 yards.

WELLS, MIKE — DT — BEARS

PERSONAL: Born January 6, 1971, in Arnold, Mo. ... 6-3/310. ... Full name: Mike Allan Wells.
HIGH SCHOOL: Fox (Arnold, Mo.).
COLLEGE: Iowa (degree in communication studies, 1994).
TRANSACTIONS/CAREER NOTES: Selected by Minnesota Vikings in fourth round (125th pick overall) of 1994 NFL draft. ... Signed by Vikings (June 24, 1994). ... Released by Vikings (August 28, 1994). ... Signed by Detroit Lions (August 29, 1994). ... Granted free agency (February 14, 1997). ... Re-signed by Lions (June 2, 1997). ... Granted unconditional free agency (February 13, 1998). ... Signed by Chicago Bears (February 17, 1998).
PLAYING EXPERIENCE: Detroit NFL, 1994-1997; Chicago NFL, 1998. ... Games/Games started: 1994 (4/0), 1995 (15/0), 1996 (16/1), 1997 (16/16), 1998 (16/16). Total: 67/33.
PRO STATISTICS: 1994—Credited with 1/2 sack. 1996—Recovered one fumble in end zone for a touchdown. 1997—Credited with one sack and recovered one fumble. 1998—Credited with three sacks.

WESTBROOK, BRYANT — CB — LIONS

PERSONAL: Born December 19, 1974, in Charlotte. ... 6-0/199. ... Full name: Bryant Antoine Westbrook.
HIGH SCHOOL: El Camino (Oceanside, Calif.).
COLLEGE: Texas.
TRANSACTIONS/CAREER NOTES: Selected by Detroit Lions in first round (fifth pick overall) of 1997 NFL draft. ... Signed by Lions (August 9, 1997).

			INTERCEPTIONS		
Year Team	G	GS	No.	Yds.	Avg.	TD
1997—Detroit NFL	15	14	2	64	32.0	1
1998—Detroit NFL	16	16	3	49	16.3	1
Pro totals (2 years)	31	30	5	113	22.6	2

WESTBROOK, MICHAEL — WR — REDSKINS

PERSONAL: Born July 7, 1972, in Detroit. ... 6-3/220.
HIGH SCHOOL: Chadsey (Detroit).
COLLEGE: Colorado.
TRANSACTIONS/CAREER NOTES: Selected by Washington Redskins in first round (fourth pick overall) of 1995 NFL draft. ... Signed by Redskins (August 14, 1995). ... On injured reserve with neck injury (December 8, 1998-remainder of season).
HONORS: Named wide receiver on THE SPORTING NEWS college All-America first team (1994).
SINGLE GAME HIGHS (regular season): Receptions—10 (November 22, 1998, vs. Arizona); yards—135 (November 22, 1998, vs. Arizona); and touchdown receptions—3 (November 22, 1998, vs. Arizona).
STATISTICAL PLATEAUS: 100-yard receiving games: 1996 (1), 1997 (1), 1998 (4). Total: 6.

			RUSHING				RECEIVING			TOTALS			
Year Team	G	GS	Att.	Yds.	Avg.	TD	No.	Yds.	Avg.	TD	TD	2pt.	Pts.	Fum.
1995—Washington NFL	11	9	6	114	19.0	1	34	522	15.4	1	2	0	12	0
1996—Washington NFL	11	6	2	2	1.0	0	34	505	14.9	1	1	0	6	0
1997—Washington NFL	13	9	3	-11	-3.7	0	34	559	16.4	3	3	0	18	0
1998—Washington NFL	11	10	1	11	11.0	0	44	736	16.7	6	6	0	36	0
Pro totals (4 years)	46	34	12	116	9.7	1	146	2322	15.9	11	12	0	72	0

WETNIGHT, RYAN — TE — BEARS

PERSONAL: Born November 5, 1970, in Fresno, Calif. ... 6-2/236. ... Full name: Ryan Scott Wetnight.
HIGH SCHOOL: Hoover (Fresno, Calif.).
JUNIOR COLLEGE: Fresno (Calif.) City College.
COLLEGE: Stanford.
TRANSACTIONS/CAREER NOTES: Signed as non-drafted free agent by Chicago Bears (April 29, 1993). ... Released by Bears (October 10, 1993). ... Re-signed by Bears to practice squad (October 11, 1993). ... Activated (October 29, 1993). ... Released by Bears (October 7, 1994). ... Re-signed by Bears (October 10, 1994). ... On injured reserve with knee injury (December 7, 1995-remainder of season). ... Granted unconditional free agency (February 14, 1997). ... Re-signed by Bears (April 2, 1997). ... Granted unconditional free agency (February 13, 1998). ... Re-signed by Bears (February 23, 1998).
PRO STATISTICS: 1997—Returned one kickoff for nine yards.
SINGLE GAME HIGHS (regular season): Receptions—6 (October 27, 1997, vs. Miami); yards—70 (December 7, 1997, vs. Buffalo); and touchdown receptions—1 (November 29, 1998, vs. Tampa Bay).

			RECEIVING				TOTALS			
Year Team	G	GS	No.	Yds.	Avg.	TD	TD	2pt.	Pts.	Fum.
1993—Chicago NFL	10	1	9	93	10.3	1	1	...	6	0
1994—Chicago NFL	11	0	11	104	9.5	1	1	0	6	0
1995—Chicago NFL	12	2	24	193	8.0	2	2	0	12	0
1996—Chicago NFL	11	5	21	223	10.6	1	1	0	6	0
1997—Chicago NFL	16	3	46	464	10.1	1	1	0	6	1
1998—Chicago NFL	15	3	23	168	7.3	2	2	0	12	1
Pro totals (6 years)	75	14	134	1245	9.3	8	8	0	48	2

WHEATLEY, TYRONE — RB — DOLPHINS

PERSONAL: Born January 19, 1972, in Inkster, Mich. ... 6-0/235.

HIGH SCHOOL: Robichaud (Dearborn Heights, Mich.).
COLLEGE: Michigan.
TRANSACTIONS/CAREER NOTES: Selected by New York Giants in first round (17th pick overall) of 1995 NFL draft. ... Signed by Giants (August 9, 1995). ... Traded by Giants to Miami Dolphins for seventh-round pick (LB O.J. Childress) in 1999 draft (February 12, 1999).
PRO STATISTICS: 1996—Attempted one pass with a completion for 24 yards and a touchdown and recovered one fumble for minus 18 yards. 1997—Recovered three fumbles.
SINGLE GAME HIGHS (regular season): Attempts—22 (October 12, 1997, vs. Arizona); yards—103 (October 12, 1997, vs. Arizona); and rushing touchdowns—2 (October 26, 1997, vs. Cincinnati).
STATISTICAL PLATEAUS: 100-yard rushing games: 1997 (1).

				RUSHING				RECEIVING			KICKOFF RETURNS				TOTALS		
Year Team	G	GS	Att.	Yds.	Avg.	TD	No.	Yds.	Avg.	TD	No.	Yds.	Avg.	TD	TD	2pt.	Pts.	Fum.
1995—New York Giants NFL..	13	1	78	245	3.1	3	5	27	5.4	0	10	186	18.6	0	3	0	18	2
1996—New York Giants NFL..	14	0	112	400	3.6	1	12	51	4.3	2	23	503	21.9	0	3	0	18	6
1997—New York Giants NFL..	14	7	152	583	3.8	4	16	140	8.8	0	0	0	...	0	4	0	24	3
1998—New York Giants NFL..	5	0	14	52	3.7	0	0	0	...	0	1	16	16.0	0	0	0	0	0
Pro totals (4 years)	46	8	356	1280	3.6	8	33	218	6.6	2	34	705	20.7	0	10	0	60	11

WHEATON, KENNY S COWBOYS

PERSONAL: Born March 8, 1975, in Phoenix. ... 5-10/195. ... Full name: Kenneth Tyrone Wheaton.
HIGH SCHOOL: McClintock (Tempe, Ariz.).
COLLEGE: Oregon.
TRANSACTIONS/CAREER NOTES: Selected by Dallas Cowboys in third round (94th pick overall) of 1997 NFL draft. ... Signed by Cowboys (July 14, 1997).
PLAYING EXPERIENCE: Dallas NFL, 1997 and 1998. ... Games/Games started: 1997 (2/0), 1998 (15/1). Total: 17/1.
PRO STATISTICS: 1998—Intercepted one pass for 41 yards, credited with a safety and recovered two fumbles for 15 yards and one touchdown.

WHEELER, LEONARD CB PANTHERS

PERSONAL: Born January 15, 1969, in Taccoa, Ga. ... 6-0/196. ... Full name: Leonard Tyrone Wheeler.
HIGH SCHOOL: Stephens County (Taccoa, Ga.).
JUNIOR COLLEGE: Northwest Mississippi Community College (did not play football).
COLLEGE: Lees-McRae Junior College (N.C.), then Mississippi (did not play football), then Troy (Ala.) State.
TRANSACTIONS/CAREER NOTES: Selected by Cincinnati Bengals in third round (84th pick overall) of 1992 NFL draft. ... Signed by Bengals (July 25, 1992). ... On injured reserve with wrist injury (August 28, 1994-entire season). ... Granted free agency (February 17, 1995). ... Re-signed by Bengals (April 13, 1995). ... Granted unconditional free agency (February 16, 1996). ... Re-signed by Bengals (April 26, 1996). ... Granted free agency (February 14, 1997). ... Signed by Minnesota Vikings (July 17, 1997). ... Granted unconditional free agency (February 13, 1998). ... Signed by Carolina Panthers (February 27, 1998).
PLAYING EXPERIENCE: Cincinnati NFL, 1992, 1993, 1995 and 1996; Minnesota NFL, 1997; Carolina NFL, 1998. ... Games/Games started: 1992 (16/2), 1993 (16/2), 1995 (16/1), 1996 (13/0), 1997 (15/0), 1998 (16/0). Total: 92/5.
PRO STATISTICS: 1992—Intercepted one pass for 12 yards. 1993—Recovered one fumble. 1997—Credited with two sacks and recovered one fumble. 1998—Recovered one fumble.

WHEELER, MARK DT EAGLES

PERSONAL: Born April 1, 1970, in San Marcos, Texas. ... 6-3/285. ... Full name: Mark Anthony Wheeler.
HIGH SCHOOL: San Marcos (Texas).
JUNIOR COLLEGE: Navarro College (Texas).
COLLEGE: Texas A&M.
TRANSACTIONS/CAREER NOTES: Selected by Tampa Bay Buccaneers in third round (59th pick overall) of 1992 NFL draft. ... Signed by Buccaneers (July 9, 1992). ... Granted unconditional free agency (February 16, 1996). ... Signed by New England Patriots (March 21, 1996). ... Granted unconditional free agency (February 12, 1999). ... Signed by Philadelphia Eagles (March 4, 1999).
CHAMPIONSHIP GAME EXPERIENCE: Played in AFC championship game (1996 season). ... Played in Super Bowl XXXI (1996 season).
PRO STATISTICS: 1996—Recovered one fumble.

Year Team	G	GS	SACKS
1992—Tampa Bay NFL	16	16	5.0
1993—Tampa Bay NFL	10	10	2.0
1994—Tampa Bay NFL	15	8	3.0
1995—Tampa Bay NFL	14	12	1.0
1996—New England NFL	16	15	1.0
1997—New England NFL	14	14	4.0
1998—New England NFL	10	2	0.0
Pro totals (7 years)	95	77	16.0

WHELIHAN, CRAIG QB CHARGERS

PERSONAL: Born April 15, 1971, in Santa Clara, Calif. ... 6-5/220. ... Full name: Craig Dominic Whelihan.
HIGH SCHOOL: Santa Teresa (San Jose, Calif.).
COLLEGE: Oregon State, then Pacific.
TRANSACTIONS/CAREER NOTES: Selected by San Diego Chargers in sixth round (197th pick overall) of 1995 NFL draft. ... Signed by Chargers (July 6, 1995). ... Inactive for 16 games (1995). ... Active for three games (1996); did not play.
PRO STATISTICS: 1997—Fumbled seven times and recovered two fumbles for minus 11 yards. 1998—Fumbled nine times and recovered three fumbles for minus 21 yards.

SINGLE GAME HIGHS (regular season): Attempts—53 (November 29, 1998, vs. Denver); completions—30 (November 29, 1998; vs. Denver); yards—304 (November 29, 1998, vs. Denver); and touchdown passes—2 (November 22, 1998, vs. Kansas City).
STATISTICAL PLATEAUS: 300-yard passing games: 1998 (1).
MISCELLANEOUS: Regular-season record as starting NFL quarterback: 2-12 (.143).

				PASSING							RUSHING				TOTALS		
Year Team	G	GS	Att.	Cmp.	Pct.	Yds.	TD	Int.	Avg.	Rat.	Att.	Yds.	Avg.	TD	TD	2pt.	Pts.
1995—San Diego NFL								Did not play.									
1996—San Diego NFL								Did not play.									
1997—San Diego NFL	9	7	237	118	49.8	1357	6	10	5.73	58.3	13	29	2.2	0	0	0	0
1998—San Diego NFL	11	7	320	149	46.6	1803	8	19	5.63	48.0	18	38	2.1	0	0	1	2
Pro totals (2 years)	20	14	557	267	47.9	3160	14	29	5.67	52.4	31	67	2.2	0	0	1	2

WHIGHAM, LARRY   S   PATRIOTS

PERSONAL: Born June 23, 1972, in Hattiesburg, Miss. ... 6-2/205. ... Full name: Larry Jerome Whigham.
HIGH SCHOOL: Hattiesburg (Miss.).
COLLEGE: Northeast Louisiana (degree in criminal justice).
TRANSACTIONS/CAREER NOTES: Selected by Seattle Seahawks in fourth round (110th pick overall) of 1994 NFL draft. ... Signed by Seahawks (June 9, 1994). ... Released by Seahawks (August 28, 1994). ... Re-signed by Seahawks to practice squad (August 29, 1994). ... Signed by New England Patriots off Seahawks practice squad (September 13, 1994). ... Granted free agency (February 14, 1997). ... Re-signed by Patriots (May 1, 1997). ... Granted unconditional free agency (February 12, 1999). ... Re-signed by Patriots (April 16, 1999).
CHAMPIONSHIP GAME EXPERIENCE: Played in AFC championship game (1996 season). ... Played in Super Bowl XXXI (1996 season).
HONORS: Played in Pro Bowl (1997 season).
PRO STATISTICS: 1994—Fumbled once. 1995—Recovered one fumble. 1996—Recovered one fumble. 1997—Credited with two sacks. 1998—Returned one kickoff for no yards.

			INTERCEPTIONS			
Year Team	G	GS	No.	Yds.	Avg.	TD
1994—New England NFL	12	0	1	21	21.0	0
1995—New England NFL	16	0	0	0	...	0
1996—New England NFL	16	1	0	0	...	0
1997—New England NFL	16	0	2	60	30.0	1
1998—New England NFL	16	0	1	0	0.0	0
Pro totals (5 years)	76	1	4	81	20.3	1

WHITE, JOSE   DT

PERSONAL: Born March 2, 1973, in Washington, D.C. ... 6-3/274. ... Full name: Jose C. White.
HIGH SCHOOL: Howard D. Woodson (Washington, D.C.).
COLLEGE: Howard.
TRANSACTIONS/CAREER NOTES: Selected by Minnesota Vikings in seventh round (232nd pick overall) of 1995 NFL draft. ... Signed by Vikings (July 22, 1995). ... Released by Vikings (September 21, 1995). ... Re-signed by Vikings to practice squad (September 22, 1995). ... Released by Vikings (August 20, 1996). ... Signed by New York Jets to practice squad (September 11, 1996). ... Released by Jets (October 1, 1996). ... Signed by New Orleans Saints to practice squad (October 31, 1996). ... Signed by Jacksonville Jaguars from Saints practice squad (December 3, 1996). ... Inactive for four games (1996). ... Re-signed by Jaguars (August 19, 1997). ... Re-signed by Jaguars (November 11, 1997). ... Released by Jaguars (April 22, 1999).
PLAYING EXPERIENCE: Jacksonville NFL, 1997 and 1998. ... Games/Games started: 1997 (3/0), 1998 (15/0). Total: 18/0.
CHAMPIONSHIP GAME EXPERIENCE: Member of Jaguars for AFC championship game (1996 season); inactive.
PRO STATISTICS: 1998—Credited with three sacks.

WHITE, REGGIE   DE

PERSONAL: Born December 19, 1961, in Chattanooga, Tenn. ... 6-5/304. ... Full name: Reginald Howard White.
HIGH SCHOOL: Howard (Chattanooga, Tenn.).
COLLEGE: Tennessee.
TRANSACTIONS/CAREER NOTES: Selected by Memphis Showboats in 1984 USFL territorial draft. ... Signed by Showboats (January 15, 1984). ... On developmental squad (March 9-24, 1984). ... Selected by Philadelphia Eagles in first round (fourth pick overall) of 1984 NFL supplemental draft. ... Released by Showboats (September 19, 1985). ... Signed by Eagles (September 21, 1985). ... Granted roster exemption (September 21-27, 1985). ... On reserve/did not report list (July 28-August 23, 1989). ... Designated by Eagles as franchise player (February 25, 1993). ... Signed by Green Bay Packers (April 6, 1993); Eagles received first-round pick (G Lester Holmes) in 1993 draft and first-round pick (traded to Cleveland) in 1994 draft as compensation. ... Announced retirement (April 19, 1998); decided to return for 1998 season. ... Announced retirement (January 6, 1999).
CHAMPIONSHIP GAME EXPERIENCE: Played in NFC championship game (1995-97 seasons). ... Member of Super Bowl championship team (1996 season). ... Played in Super Bowl XXXII (1997 season).
HONORS: Named defensive end on THE SPORTING NEWS college All-America first team (1983). ... Named defensive end on THE SPORTING NEWS USFL All-Star team (1985). ... Played in Pro Bowl (1986-1993, 1995-1998 seasons). ... Named Outstanding Player of Pro Bowl (1986 season). ... Named defensive end on THE SPORTING NEWS NFL All-Pro team (1987, 1988, 1991, 1993, 1995 and 1998). ... Named to play in Pro Bowl (1994 season); replaced by Wayne Martin due to injury.
RECORDS: Holds NFL career records for most sacks—192.5; and most seasons with 10 or more sacks—12.
POST SEASON RECORDS: Holds Super Bowl single-game record for most sacks (since 1982)—3 (January 26, 1997, vs. New England). ... Shares NFL postseason career record for most sacks—12. ... Shares NFL postseason single-game record for most safeties—1 (January 3, 1993, at New Orleans).
PRO STATISTICS: USFL: 1984—Recovered one fumble. 1985—Credited with one safety and recovered one fumble for 20 yards and a touchdown. NFL: 1985—Recovered two fumbles. 1987—Recovered one fumble for 70 yards and a touchdown. 1988—Recovered two fumbles. 1989—Recovered one fumble for 10 yards. 1990—Intercepted one pass for 33 yards and recovered one fumble. 1991—Intercepted one pass for no yards and recovered three fumbles for eight yards. 1992—Recovered one fumble for 37 yards and a touchdown. 1993—Recovered

two fumbles for 10 yards. 1994—Recovered one fumble. 1996—Intercepted one pass for 46 yards, fumbled twice and recovered three fumbles for two yards. 1997—Recovered two fumbles.
MISCELLANEOUS: Active NFL leader for career sacks (192.5). ... Holds Philadelphia Eagles all-time record for most sacks (124). ... Holds Green Bay Packers all-time record for most sacks (68.5).

Year Team	G	GS	SACKS
1984—Memphis USFL	16	16	12.0
1985—Memphis USFL	18	18	11.5
—Philadelphia NFL	13	12	13.0
1986—Philadelphia NFL	16	16	18.0
1987—Philadelphia NFL	12	12	*21.0
1988—Philadelphia NFL	16	16	*18.0
1989—Philadelphia NFL	16	16	11.0
1990—Philadelphia NFL	16	16	14.0
1991—Philadelphia NFL	16	16	15.0
1992—Philadelphia NFL	16	16	14.0
1993—Green Bay NFL	16	16	∞13.0
1994—Green Bay NFL	16	15	8.0
1995—Green Bay NFL	15	13	12.0
1996—Green Bay NFL	16	16	8.5
1997—Green Bay NFL	16	16	11.0
1998—Green Bay NFL	16	16	‡16.0
USFL totals (2 years)	34	34	23.5
NFL totals (14 years)	216	212	192.5
Pro totals (16 years)	250	246	216.0

WHITE, STEVE　　DE　　BUCCANEERS

PERSONAL: Born October 25, 1973, in Memphis, Tenn. ... 6-2/281. ... Full name: Stephen Gregory White.
HIGH SCHOOL: Westwood (Memphis, Tenn.).
COLLEGE: Tennessee (degree in psychology, 1996).
TRANSACTIONS/CAREER NOTES: Selected by Philadelphia Eagles in sixth round (194th pick overall) of 1996 NFL draft. ... Signed by Eagles (July 17, 1996). ... Released by Eagles (August 20, 1996). ... Signed by Tampa Bay Buccaneers to practice squad (August 27, 1996). ... Activated (October 15, 1996). ... Released by Buccaneers (November 9, 1996). ... Re-signed by Buccaneers (November 12, 1996).
PLAYING EXPERIENCE: Tampa Bay NFL, 1996-1998. ... Games/Games started: 1996 (4/0), 1997 (15/1), 1998 (16/0). Total: 35/1.
PRO STATISTICS: 1997—Returned one kickoff for no yards. 1998—Credited with two sacks and recovered one fumble.

WHITE, WILLIAM　　S

PERSONAL: Born February 19, 1966, in Lima, Ohio. ... 5-10/205. ... Full name: William Eugene White.
HIGH SCHOOL: Lima (Ohio).
COLLEGE: Ohio State.
TRANSACTIONS/CAREER NOTES: Selected by Detroit Lions in fourth round (85th pick overall) of 1988 NFL draft. ... Signed by Lions (July 11, 1988). ... Granted unconditional free agency (March 1, 1993). ... Re-signed by Lions (April 6, 1993). ... Traded by Lions to Kansas City Chiefs for conditional pick in 1995 draft (July 13, 1994). ... Granted unconditional free agency (February 14, 1997). ... Signed by Atlanta Falcons (March 13, 1997). ... Granted unconditional free agency (February 12, 1999).
CHAMPIONSHIP GAME EXPERIENCE: Played in NFC championship game (1991 and 1998 seasons). ... Played in Super Bowl XXXIII (1998 season).
PRO STATISTICS: 1988—Recovered one fumble. 1989—Recovered one fumble for 20 yards and a touchdown. 1991—Returned blocked field-goal attempt 55 yards for a touchdown. 1992—Fumbled once. 1998—Recovered one fumble for 18 yards and a touchdown.

			INTERCEPTIONS				SACKS
Year Team	G	GS	No.	Yds.	Avg.	TD	No.
1988—Detroit NFL	16	0	0	0	...	0	0.0
1989—Detroit NFL	15	15	1	0	0.0	0	1.0
1990—Detroit NFL	16	16	5	120	24.0	1	0.0
1991—Detroit NFL	16	16	2	35	17.5	0	0.0
1992—Detroit NFL	16	16	4	54	13.5	0	0.0
1993—Detroit NFL	16	16	1	5	5.0	0	1.5
1994—Kansas City NFL	15	14	2	0	0.0	0	0.0
1995—Kansas City NFL	16	5	2	48	24.0	0	1.0
1996—Kansas City NFL	12	2	0	0	...	0	0.0
1997—Atlanta NFL	16	16	1	11	11.0	0	0.0
1998—Atlanta NFL	16	16	2	36	18.0	0	0.0
Pro totals (11 years)	170	132	20	309	15.5	1	3.5

WHITFIELD, BOB　　OT　　FALCONS

PERSONAL: Born October 18, 1971, in Carson, Calif. ... 6-5/315. ... Full name: Bob Whitfield Jr.
HIGH SCHOOL: Banning (Los Angeles).
COLLEGE: Stanford.
TRANSACTIONS/CAREER NOTES: Selected after junior season by Atlanta Falcons in first round (eighth pick overall) of 1992 NFL draft. ... Signed by Falcons (September 4, 1992). ... Granted roster exemption for one game (September 1992).
PLAYING EXPERIENCE: Atlanta NFL, 1992-1998. ... Games/Games started: 1992 (11/0), 1993 (16/16), 1994 (16/16), 1995 (16/16), 1996 (16/16), 1997 (16/16), 1998 (16/16). Total: 107/96.
CHAMPIONSHIP GAME EXPERIENCE: Played in NFC championship game (1998 season). ... Played in Super Bowl XXXIII (1998 season).
HONORS: Named offensive tackle on THE SPORTING NEWS college All-America first team (1991). ... Played in Pro Bowl (1998 season).
PRO STATISTICS: 1993—Recovered two fumbles. 1996—Recovered one fumble.

WHITING, BRANDON — DT — EAGLES

PERSONAL: Born July 30, 1976, in Sante Rosa, Calif. ... 6-3/278. ... Name pronounced WHITE-ing.
HIGH SCHOOL: Long Beach (Calif.) Polytechnic.
COLLEGE: California.
TRANSACTIONS/CAREER NOTES: Selected by Philadelphia Eagles in fourth round (112th pick overall) of 1998 NFL draft. ... Signed by Eagles (July 14, 1998).
PRO STATISTICS: 1998—Recovered one fumble for 24 yards.

Year Team	G	GS	SACKS
1998—Philadelphia NFL	16	5	1.5

WHITTED, ALVIS — WR — JAGUARS

PERSONAL: Born September 4, 1974, in Durham, N.C. ... 5-11/179. ... Full name: Alvis James Whitted. ... Name pronounced WIH-ted.
HIGH SCHOOL: Orange (Hillsborough, N.C.).
COLLEGE: North Carolina State.
TRANSACTIONS/CAREER NOTES: Selected by Jacksonville Jaguars in seventh round (192nd pick overall) of 1998 NFL draft. ... Signed by Jaguars (May 19, 1998).
PRO STATISTICS: 1998—Returned a blocked punt 24 yards for a touchdown.
SINGLE GAME HIGHS (regular season): Receptions—1 (November 22, 1998, vs. Pittsburgh); yards—55 (November 8, 1998, vs. Cincinnati); and touchdown receptions—0.

			RUSHING				RECEIVING				TOTALS		
Year Team	G	GS	Att.	Yds.	Avg.	TD	No.	Yds.	Avg.	TD	TD	2pt.	Pts.	Fum.
1998—Jacksonville NFL	16	0	3	13	4.3	0	2	61	30.5	0	1	0	6	0

WHITTINGTON, BERNARD — DE — COLTS

PERSONAL: Born August 20, 1971, in St. Louis. ... 6-6/280. ... Full name: Bernard Maurice Whittington.
HIGH SCHOOL: Hazelwood East (St. Louis).
COLLEGE: Indiana (degree in sports management).
TRANSACTIONS/CAREER NOTES: Signed as non-drafted free agent by Indianapolis Colts (May 5, 1994). ... Granted free agency (February 14, 1997). ... Re-signed by Colts (June 13, 1997).
CHAMPIONSHIP GAME EXPERIENCE: Played in AFC championship game (1995 season).
PRO STATISTICS: 1995—Recovered one fumble. 1998—Recovered two fumbles.

Year Team	G	GS	SACKS
1994—Indianapolis NFL	13	8	0.0
1995—Indianapolis NFL	16	13	2.0
1996—Indianapolis NFL	16	14	3.0
1997—Indianapolis NFL	15	6	0.0
1998—Indianapolis NFL	15	11	4.0
Pro totals (5 years)	75	52	9.0

WHITTLE, JASON — G — GIANTS

PERSONAL: Born March 7, 1975, in Springfield, Mo. ... 6-6/300.
HIGH SCHOOL: Camdenton (Mo.).
COLLEGE: Southwest Missouri State.
TRANSACTIONS/CAREER NOTES: Signed as non-drafted free agent by New York Giants (April 24, 1998). ... Released by Giants (August 30, 1998). ... Re-signed by Giants to practice squad (September 1, 1998). ... Activated (December 16, 1998).
PLAYING EXPERIENCE: New York Giants NFL, 1998. ... Games/Games started: 1/0.

WIDELL, DAVE — C

PERSONAL: Born May 14, 1965, in Hartford, Conn. ... 6-7/312. ... Full name: David Harold Widell. ... Brother of Doug Widell, guard with four NFL teams (1989-97). ... Name pronounced WY-dell.
HIGH SCHOOL: South Catholic (Hartford, Conn.).
COLLEGE: Boston College (degree in finance, 1988).
TRANSACTIONS/CAREER NOTES: Selected by Dallas Cowboys in fourth round (94th pick overall) of 1988 NFL draft. ... Signed by Cowboys (July 12, 1988). ... Traded by Cowboys to Denver Broncos for seventh-round pick (DT Leon Lett) in 1991 draft and eighth-round pick (traded to Cleveland) in 1992 draft (August 24, 1990). ... Granted unconditional free agency (February 17, 1994). ... Re-signed by Broncos for 1994 season. ... Granted unconditional free agency (February 17, 1995). ... Signed by Jacksonville Jaguars (March 15, 1995). ... Granted unconditional free agency (February 13, 1998). ... Signed by Atlanta Falcons (May 13, 1998). ... Released by Falcons (February 17, 1999).
PLAYING EXPERIENCE: Dallas NFL, 1988 and 1989; Denver NFL, 1990-1994; Jacksonville NFL, 1995-1997; Atlanta NFL, 1998. ... Games/Games started: 1988 (14/9), 1989 (15/2), 1990 (16/5), 1991 (16/2), 1992 (16/1), 1993 (15/15), 1994 (16/16), 1995 (16/16), 1996 (15/14), 1997 (16/12), 1998 (1/0). Total: 156/92.
CHAMPIONSHIP GAME EXPERIENCE: Played in AFC championship game (1991 and 1996 seasons). ... Member of Falcons for NFC championship game (1998 season); inactive. ... Member of Falcons for Super Bowl XXXIII (1998 season); inactive.
PRO STATISTICS: 1988—Recovered one fumble. 1991—Fumbled once for minus 15 yards. 1994—Fumbled once. 1997—Recovered one fumble.

WIDMER, COREY — LB — GIANTS

PERSONAL: Born December 25, 1968, in Alexandria, Va. ... 6-3/255. ... Full name: Corey Edward Widmer.
HIGH SCHOOL: Bozeman (Mont.).
COLLEGE: Montana State.

TRANSACTIONS/CAREER NOTES: Selected by New York Giants in seventh round (180th pick overall) of 1992 NFL draft. ... Signed by Giants (July 21, 1992). ... On injured reserve with back injury (September 5-30, 1992). ... On practice squad (September 30-November 15, 1992). ... Granted free agency (February 17, 1995). ... Re-signed by Giants (April 18, 1995). ... Granted unconditional free agency (February 12, 1999). ... Re-signed by Giants (February 17, 1999).
PLAYING EXPERIENCE: New York Giants NFL, 1992-1998. ... Games/Games started: 1992 (8/0), 1993 (11/0), 1994 (16/5), 1995 (16/0), 1996 (16/16), 1997 (16/15), 1998 (16/15). Total: 99/51.
PRO STATISTICS: 1994—Credited with one sack. 1995—Returned one kickoff for no yards. 1996—Intercepted two passes for eight yards, credited with two sacks, fumbled once and recovered one fumble. 1997—Intercepted two passes for no yards and credited with 1 1/2 sacks. 1998—Recovered one fumble for four yards.

WIEGERT, ZACH — OT — JAGUARS

PERSONAL: Born August 16, 1972, in Fremont, Neb. ... 6-4/310. ... Full name: Zach Allen Wiegert. ... Name pronounced WEE-gert.
HIGH SCHOOL: Bergan (Fremont, Neb.).
COLLEGE: Nebraska.
TRANSACTIONS/CAREER NOTES: Selected by St. Louis Rams in second round (38th pick overall) of 1995 NFL draft. ... Signed by Rams (July 18, 1995). ... Granted free agency (February 13, 1998). ... Re-signed by Rams (June 17, 1998). ... Designated by Rams as transition player (February 12, 1999). ... Re-signed by Rams (March 24, 1999). ... Released by Rams (April 29, 1999). ... Signed by Jacksonville Jaguars (May 5, 1999).
PLAYING EXPERIENCE: St. Louis NFL, 1995-1998. ... Games/Games started: 1995 (5/2), 1996 (16/16), 1997 (15/15), 1998 (13/13). Total: 49/46.
HONORS: Outland Trophy Award winner (1994). ... Named offensive lineman on THE SPORTING NEWS college All-America first team (1994).
PRO STATISTICS: 1996—Recovered two fumbles. 1997—Caught one pass for one yard and recovered four fumbles for no yards and one touchdown. 1998—Recovered one fumble.

WIEGMANN, CASEY — C — BEARS

PERSONAL: Born July 20, 1973, in Parkersburg, Iowa. ... 6-3/295.
HIGH SCHOOL: Parkersburg (Iowa).
COLLEGE: Iowa.
TRANSACTIONS/CAREER NOTES: Signed as non-drafted free agent by Indianapolis Colts (April 26, 1996). ... Released by Colts (August 25, 1996). ... Re-signed by Colts to practice squad (August 27, 1996). ... Activated (September 10, 1996); did not play. ... Released by Colts (September 22, 1996). ... Re-signed by Colts to practice squad (September 23, 1996). ... Activated (October 15, 1996); did not play. ... Claimed on waivers by New York Jets (October 29, 1996). ... Released by Jets (September 21, 1997). ... Signed by Chicago Bears (September 24, 1997). ... Granted free agency (February 12, 1999). ... Tendered offer sheet by Miami Dolphins (April 5, 1999). ... Offer matched by Bears (April 9, 1999).
PLAYING EXPERIENCE: New York Jets (3)-Chicago (1) NFL, 1997; Chicago NFL, 1998. ... Games/Games started: 1997 (NYJ-3/0; Chi.-1/0; Total: 4/0), 1998 (16/16). Total: 20/16.
PRO STATISTICS: 1998—Returned one kickoff for eight yards, fumbled once and recovered one fumble for minus three yards.

WIGGINS, PAUL — OT — BROWNS

PERSONAL: Born August 17, 1973, in Portland, Ore. ... 6-3/305. ... Full name: Paul Anthony Wiggins.
HIGH SCHOOL: Benson (Portland, Ore.).
COLLEGE: Oregon.
TRANSACTIONS/CAREER NOTES: Selected by Pittsburgh Steelers in third round (82nd pick overall) of 1997 NFL draft. ... Signed by Steelers (July 14, 1997). ... On suspended list for violating league substance abuse policy (August 31-October 6, 1998). ... Released by Steelers (October 17, 1998). ... Signed by Washington Redskins (October 20, 1998). ... Selected by Cleveland Browns from Redskins in NFL expansion draft (February 9, 1999).
PLAYING EXPERIENCE: Pittsburgh NFL, 1997; Washington NFL, 1998. ... Games/Games started: 1997 (1/0), 1998 (1/0). Total: 2/0.
CHAMPIONSHIP GAME EXPERIENCE: Member of Steelers for AFC championship game (1997 season); inactive.

WILCOX, JOSH — FB — SAINTS

PERSONAL: Born June 5, 1974, in Junction City, Ore. ... 6-3/255.
HIGH SCHOOL: Junction City (Ore.).
COLLEGE: Oregon.
TRANSACTIONS/CAREER NOTES: Played for Amsterdam Admirals of World League (1997). ... Played for Amsterdam Admirals of NFL Europe (1998). ... Signed as non-drafted free agent by New Orleans Saints (July 24, 1998). ... Released by Saints (August 31, 1998). ... Re-signed by Saints to practice squad (September 1, 1998). ... Activated (December 9, 1998).
PLAYING EXPERIENCE: Amsterdam Admirals W.L., 1997; Amsterdam NFLE, 1998; New Orleans NFL, 1998. ... Games/Games started: 1997 (games played unavailable), NFLE 1998 (-), NFL 1998 (3/1).
PRO STATISTICS: 1998—Caught one pass for 10 yards.
SINGLE GAME HIGHS (regular season): Receptions—1 (December 27, 1998, vs. Buffalo); yards—10 (December 27, 1998, vs. Buffalo); and touchdown receptions—0.

				RECEIVING				KICKOFF RETURNS				TOTALS		
Year Team	G	GS	No.	Yds.	Avg.	TD	No.	Yds.	Avg.	TD	TD	2pt.	Pts.	Fum.
1997—Amsterdam W.L.	...	...			Statistics unavailable.									
1998—Amsterdam NFLE	...	...	9	151	16.8	0	1	11	11.0	0	0	...	0	0
—New Orleans NFL	3	1	1	10	10.0	0	0	0	...	0	0	0	0	0
NFL Europe totals (1 year)	...	...	9	151	16.8	0	1	11	11.0	0	0	0	0	0
NFL totals (1 year)	3	1	1	10	10.0	0	0	0		0	0	0	0	0
Pro totals (2 years)	...	...	10	161	16.1	0	1	11	11.0	0	0	0	0	0

WILEY, MARCELLUS — DE — BILLS

PERSONAL: Born November 30, 1974, in Compton, Calif. ... 6-5/271. ... Full name: Marcellus Vernon Wiley.
HIGH SCHOOL: Saint Monica (Los Angeles).
COLLEGE: Columbia (degree in sociology, 1997).
TRANSACTIONS/CAREER NOTES: Selected by Buffalo Bills in second round (52nd pick overall) of 1997 NFL draft. ... Signed by Bills (June 20, 1997).
PLAYING EXPERIENCE: Buffalo NFL, 1997 and 1998. ... Games/Games started: 1997 (16/0), 1998 (16/3). Total: 32/3.
PRO STATISTICS: 1997—Returned one kickoff for 12 yards, fumbled once and recovered two fumbles for 40 yards. 1998—Credited with $3^{1}/_{2}$ sacks and recovered one fumble for 15 yards.

WILKINS, GABE — DE — 49ERS

PERSONAL: Born September 1, 1971, in Cowpens, S.C. ... 6-5/315. ... Full name: Gabriel Nicholas Wilkins.
HIGH SCHOOL: Gettis D. Broome (Spartanburg, S.C.).
COLLEGE: Gardner-Webb (N.C.).
TRANSACTIONS/CAREER NOTES: Selected by Green Bay Packers in fourth round (126th pick overall) of 1994 NFL draft. ... Signed by Packers (June 17, 1994). ... Granted free agency (February 14, 1997). ... Re-signed by Packers (April 28, 1997). ... Granted unconditional free agency (February 13, 1998). ... Signed by San Francisco 49ers (February 26, 1998). ... On physically unable to perform list with knee injury (July 18-November 7, 1998).
CHAMPIONSHIP GAME EXPERIENCE: Played in NFC championship game (1995-97 season). ... Member of Super Bowl championship team (1996 season). ... Played in Super Bowl XXXII (1997 season).
PRO STATISTICS: 1997—Intercepted one pass for 77 yards and a touchdown and recovered three fumbles for one yard and one touchdown.

Year Team	G	GS	SACKS
1994—Green Bay NFL	15	0	1.0
1995—Green Bay NFL	13	8	3.0
1996—Green Bay NFL	16	1	3.0
1997—Green Bay NFL	16	16	5.5
1998—San Francisco NFL	8	4	0.0
Pro totals (5 years)	**68**	**29**	**12.5**

WILKINS, JEFF — K — RAMS

PERSONAL: Born April 19, 1972, in Youngstown, Ohio. ... 6-2/205. ... Full name: Jeff Allen Wilkins.
HIGH SCHOOL: Austintown Fitch (Youngstown, Ohio).
COLLEGE: Youngstown State (degree in communications, 1993).
TRANSACTIONS/CAREER NOTES: Signed as non-drafted free agent by Dallas Cowboys (April 28, 1994). ... Released by Cowboys (July 18, 1994). ... Signed by Philadelphia Eagles (November 14, 1994). ... Released by Eagles (August 14, 1995). ... Signed by San Francisco 49ers (November 8, 1995). ... Granted unconditional free agency (February 14, 1997). ... Signed by St. Louis Rams (March 6, 1997).

				KICKING				
Year Team	G	XPM	XPA	FGM	FGA	Lg.	50+	Pts.
1994—Philadelphia NFL	6	0	0	0	0	...	0-0	0
1995—San Francisco NFL	7	27	29	12	13	40	0-0	63
1996—San Francisco NFL	16	40	40	30	34	49	0-0	130
1997—St. Louis NFL	16	32	32	25	∞37	52	2-2	107
1998—St. Louis NFL	16	25	26	20	26	57	3-6	85
Pro totals (5 years)	**61**	**124**	**127**	**87**	**110**	**57**	**5-8**	**385**

WILKINSON, DAN — DT — REDSKINS

PERSONAL: Born March 13, 1973, in Dayton, Ohio. ... 6-5/313. ... Nickname: Big Daddy.
HIGH SCHOOL: Paul L. Dunbar (Dayton, Ohio).
COLLEGE: Ohio State.
TRANSACTIONS/CAREER NOTES: Selected after sophomore season by Cincinnati Bengals in first round (first pick overall) of 1994 NFL draft. ... Signed by Bengals (May 5, 1994). ... Designated by Bengals as franchise player (February 11, 1998). ... Tendered offer sheet by Washington Redskins (February 25, 1998). ... Bengals declined to match offer (February 26, 1998); Bengals received first- (LB Brian Simmons) and third-round (G Mike Goff) picks in 1998 draft as compensation.
HONORS: Named defensive lineman on THE SPORTING NEWS college All-America first team (1993).
PRO STATISTICS: 1996—Intercepted one pass for seven yards, fumbled once and recovered one fumble. 1998—Intercepted one pass for four yards and recovered one fumble.

Year Team	G	GS	SACKS
1994—Cincinnati NFL	16	14	5.5
1995—Cincinnati NFL	14	14	8.0
1996—Cincinnati NFL	16	16	6.5
1997—Cincinnati NFL	15	15	5.0
1998—Washington NFL	16	16	7.5
Pro totals (5 years)	**77**	**75**	**32.5**

WILLARD, JERROTT — LB

PERSONAL: Born July 11, 1972, in Fullerton, Calif. ... 6-1/233.
HIGH SCHOOL: Corona del Mar (Newport Beach, Calif.).
COLLEGE: California.

TRANSACTIONS/CAREER NOTES: Selected by Kansas City Chiefs in fifth round (164th pick overall) of 1995 NFL draft. ... Signed by Chiefs for 1995 season. ... Announced retirement (July 26, 1996). ... Out of pro football (1996-97). ... Signed by Chiefs to practice squad (November 6, 1998). ... Activated (November 29, 1998).
PLAYING EXPERIENCE: Kansas City NFL, 1998. ... Games/Games started: 1/0.

WILLIAMS, AENEAS   CB   CARDINALS

PERSONAL: Born January 29, 1968, in New Orleans. ... 5-11/202. ... Full name: Aeneas Demetrius Williams.
HIGH SCHOOL: Fortier (New Orleans).
COLLEGE: Southern (degree in accounting, 1990).
TRANSACTIONS/CAREER NOTES: Selected by Phoenix Cardinals in third round (59th pick overall) of 1991 NFL draft. ... Signed by Cardinals (July 26, 1991). ... Granted free agency (February 17, 1994). ... Cardinals franchise renamed Arizona Cardinals for 1994 season. ... Re-signed by Cardinals (June 1, 1994). ... Granted unconditional free agency (February 16, 1996). ... Re-signed by Cardinals (February 27, 1996).
HONORS: Played in Pro Bowl (1994-1998 seasons). ... Named cornerback on THE SPORTING NEWS NFL All-Pro team (1995 and 1997).
PRO STATISTICS: 1991—Fumbled once and recovered two fumbles for 10 yards. 1992—Recovered one fumble for 39 yards. 1993—Recovered two fumbles for 20 yards and a touchdown. 1994—Recovered one fumble. 1995—Fumbled once and recovered three fumbles. 1996—Credited with one sack and recovered one fumble. 1998—Credited with one sack.

				INTERCEPTIONS			
Year Team	G	GS	No.	Yds.	Avg.	TD
1991—Phoenix NFL	16	15	∞6	60	10.0	0
1992—Phoenix NFL	16	16	3	25	8.3	0
1993—Phoenix NFL	16	16	2	87	43.5	1
1994—Arizona NFL	16	16	†9	89	9.9	0
1995—Arizona NFL	16	16	6	86	14.3	†2
1996—Arizona NFL	16	16	6	89	14.8	1
1997—Arizona NFL	16	16	6	95	15.8	∞2
1998—Arizona NFL	16	16	1	15	15.0	0
Pro totals (8 years)	128	127	39	546	14.0	6

WILLIAMS, ALFRED   DE   BRONCOS

PERSONAL: Born November 6, 1968, in Houston. ... 6-6/265. ... Full name: Alfred Hamilton Williams.
HIGH SCHOOL: Jesse H. Jones Senior (Houston).
COLLEGE: Colorado.
TRANSACTIONS/CAREER NOTES: Selected by Cincinnati Bengals in first round (18th pick overall) of 1991 NFL draft. ... Signed by Bengals (July 18, 1991). ... Granted free agency (February 17, 1994). ... Re-signed by Bengals (June 15, 1994). ... Granted unconditional free agency (February 17, 1995). ... Signed by San Francisco 49ers (July 15, 1995). ... Granted unconditional free agency (February 16, 1996). ... Signed by Denver Broncos (February 27, 1996). ... On physically unable to perform list with tricep injury (August 25-October 23, 1998).
CHAMPIONSHIP GAME EXPERIENCE: Played in AFC championship game (1997 and 1998 seasons). ... Member of Super Bowl championship team (1997 and 1998 seasons).
HONORS: Named defensive end on THE SPORTING NEWS college All-America second team (1989). ... Butkus Award winner (1990). ... Named linebacker on THE SPORTING NEWS college All-America first team (1990). ... Named defensive end on THE SPORTING NEWS NFL All-Pro team (1996). ... Played in Pro Bowl (1996 season).
PRO STATISTICS: 1991—Recovered two fumbles for 24 yards. 1993—Credited with one safety. 1994—Credited with one safety and recovered one fumble. 1995—Recovered one fumble. 1996—Recovered one fumble. 1997—Recovered one fumble for 51 yards and a touchdown.

Year Team	G	GS	SACKS
1991—Cincinnati NFL	16	15	3.0
1992—Cincinnati NFL	15	6	10.0
1993—Cincinnati NFL	16	16	4.0
1994—Cincinnati NFL	16	16	9.5
1995—San Francisco NFL	16	0	4.5
1996—Denver NFL	16	16	13.0
1997—Denver NFL	16	16	8.5
1998—Denver NFL	10	0	3.0
Pro totals (8 years)	121	85	55.5

WILLIAMS, BEN   DE   VIKINGS

PERSONAL: Born May 28, 1970, in Belzoni, Miss. ... 6-2/287.
HIGH SCHOOL: Humphreys County (Belzoni, Miss.).
COLLEGE: Minnesota.
TRANSACTIONS/CAREER NOTES: Signed by Shreveport Pirates of CFL (May 1994). ... Signed as non-drafted free agent by Tampa Bay Buccaneers (July 30, 1996). ... Released by Buccaneers (August 18, 1996). ... Selected by England Monarchs in 1997 World League draft (February 1997). ... Signed by Arizona Cardinals (July 23, 1997). ... Released by Cardinals (August 19, 1997). ... Signed by Minnesota Vikings (June 15, 1998). ... Released by Vikings (August 30, 1998). ... Re-signed by Vikings to practice squad (August 31, 1998). ... Activated (December 8, 1998).
PLAYING EXPERIENCE: Shreveport Pirates CFL, 1994 and 1995; England Monarchs W.L., 1997; England NFLE, 1998; Minnesota NFL, 1998. ... Games/Games started: 1994 (16/games started unavailable), 1995 (18/-), 1997 (games played unavailable), NFLE 1998 (-), NFL 1998 (1/0).
CHAMPIONSHIP GAME EXPERIENCE: Member of Vikings for NFC championship game (1998 season); inactive.
PRO STATISTICS: CFL: 1994—Credited with seven sacks and recovered one fumble. 1995—Credited with eight sacks and recovered two fumbles. W.L.: 1997—Credited with 3$^1/_2$ sacks. NFLE: 1998—Credited with 5$^1/_2$ sacks.

WILLIAMS, BRIAN — LB — PACKERS

PERSONAL: Born December 17, 1972, in Dallas. ... 6-1/245. ... Full name: Brian Marcee Williams.
HIGH SCHOOL: Bishop Dunne (Dallas).
COLLEGE: Southern California (degree in public administration).
TRANSACTIONS/CAREER NOTES: Selected by Green Bay Packers in third round (73rd pick overall) of 1995 NFL draft. ... Signed by Packers (May 9, 1995). ... Granted free agency (February 13, 1998). ... Re-signed by Packers (February 17, 1998).
PLAYING EXPERIENCE: Green Bay NFL, 1995-1998. ... Games/Games started: 1995 (13/0), 1996 (16/16), 1997 (16/16), 1998 (16/15). Total: 61/47.
CHAMPIONSHIP GAME EXPERIENCE: Played in NFC championship game (1995-97 seasons). ... Member of Super Bowl championship team (1996 season). ... Played in Super Bowl XXXII (1997 season).
PRO STATISTICS: 1996—Credited with $1/2$ sack and recovered three fumbles. 1997—Intercepted two passes for 30 yards, credited with one sack and recovered one fumble. 1998—Credited with two sacks.

WILLIAMS, CHARLIE — DB — COWBOYS

PERSONAL: Born February 2, 1972, in Detroit. ... 6-0/207.
HIGH SCHOOL: Henry Ford (Detroit).
COLLEGE: Bowling Green State.
TRANSACTIONS/CAREER NOTES: Selected by Dallas Cowboys in third round (92nd pick overall) of 1995 NFL draft. ... Signed by Cowboys (July 18, 1995). ... On physically unable to perform list with knee injury (July 18-November 8, 1996). ... Granted free agency (February 13, 1998). ... Re-signed by Cowboys (April 16, 1998).
PLAYING EXPERIENCE: Dallas NFL, 1995-1998. ... Games/Games started: 1995 (16/0), 1996 (7/0), 1997 (16/0), 1998 (15/3). Total: 54/3.
CHAMPIONSHIP GAME EXPERIENCE: Played in NFC championship game (1995 season). ... Member of Super Bowl championship team (1995 season).
PRO STATISTICS: 1996—Returned two kickoffs for 21 yards and fumbled once. 1997—Credited with two sacks.

WILLIAMS, DAN — DE — CHIEFS

PERSONAL: Born December 15, 1969, in Ypsilanti, Mich. ... 6-4/290. ... Full name: Daniel Williams II. ... Brother of Lamanzer Williams, defensive end, Jacksonville Jaguars.
HIGH SCHOOL: Willow Run (Ypsilanti, Mich.).
COLLEGE: Tennessee State, then Toledo.
TRANSACTIONS/CAREER NOTES: Selected by Denver Broncos in first round (11th pick overall) of 1993 NFL draft. ... Signed by Broncos (July 19, 1993). ... On injured reserve with knee injury (December 19, 1995-remainder of season). ... Released by Broncos (July 18, 1997). ... Signed by Kansas City Chiefs (July 24, 1997). ... Designated by Chiefs as franchise player (February 13, 1998). ... Did not play 1998 season due to contract dispute. ... Granted unconditional free agency (February 12, 1999). ... Re-signed by Chiefs (February 16, 1999).
PRO STATISTICS: 1993—Recovered one fumble. 1994—Intercepted one pass for minus three yards. 1996—Recovered one fumble. 1997—Recovered two fumbles for two yards.

Year Team	G	GS	SACKS
1993—Denver NFL	13	11	1.0
1994—Denver NFL	12	7	0.0
1995—Denver NFL	6	6	2.0
1996—Denver NFL	15	15	1.0
1997—Kansas City NFL	15	6	10.5
1998—Kansas City NFL	Did not play.		
Pro totals (5 years)	61	45	14.5

WILLIAMS, DARRYL — S — SEAHAWKS

PERSONAL: Born January 8, 1970, in Miami. ... 6-0/202. ... Full name: Darryl Edwin Williams.
HIGH SCHOOL: American (Hialeah, Fla.).
COLLEGE: Miami (Fla.).
TRANSACTIONS/CAREER NOTES: Selected after junior season by Cincinnati Bengals in first round (28th pick overall) of 1992 NFL draft. ... Signed by Bengals (July 25, 1992). ... Designated by Bengals as transition player (February 15, 1994). ... Free agency status changed by Bengals from transitional to unconditional (February 16, 1996). ... Signed by Seattle Seahawks (February 21, 1996).
HONORS: Named defensive back on THE SPORTING NEWS college All-America second team (1991). ... Played in Pro Bowl (1997 season).
RECORDS: Shares NFL single-game record for most opponents' fumbles recovered—3 (October 4, 1998, vs. Kansas City).
PRO STATISTICS: 1992—Recovered one fumble. 1993—Recovered two fumbles. 1994—Returned one punt for four yards and recovered two fumbles. 1995—Recovered three fumbles. 1996—Recovered one fumble for two yards. 1997—Recovered one fumble. 1998—Recovered three fumbles.

			INTERCEPTIONS				SACKS
Year Team	G	GS	No.	Yds.	Avg.	TD	No.
1992—Cincinnati NFL	16	12	4	65	16.3	0	2.0
1993—Cincinnati NFL	16	16	2	126	63.0	▲1	2.0
1994—Cincinnati NFL	16	16	2	45	22.5	0	1.0
1995—Cincinnati NFL	16	16	1	1	1.0	0	1.0
1996—Seattle NFL	16	16	5	148	29.6	1	0.0
1997—Seattle NFL	16	16	▲8	172	21.5	1	0.0
1998—Seattle NFL	16	16	3	41	13.7	0	0.0
Pro totals (7 years)	112	108	25	598	23.9	3	6.0

WILLIAMS, ELIJAH   CB   FALCONS

PERSONAL: Born August 20, 1975, in Milton, Fla. ... 5-10/182. ... Full name: Elijah Elgebra Williams.
HIGH SCHOOL: Milton (Fla.).
COLLEGE: Florida.
TRANSACTIONS/CAREER NOTES: Selected by Atlanta Falcons in sixth round (166th pick overall) of 1998 NFL draft. ... Signed by Falcons (June 11, 1998).
PLAYING EXPERIENCE: Atlanta NFL, 1998. ... Games/Games started: 15/0.
CHAMPIONSHIP GAME EXPERIENCE: Played in NFC championship game (1998 season). ... Played in Super Bowl XXXIII (1998 season).
PRO STATISTICS: 1998—Rushed twice for minus two yards and returned seven kickoffs for 132 yards.

WILLIAMS, ERIK   OT   COWBOYS

PERSONAL: Born September 7, 1968, in Philadelphia. ... 6-6/328. ... Full name: Erik George Williams.
HIGH SCHOOL: John Bartram (Philadelphia).
COLLEGE: Central State (Ohio).
TRANSACTIONS/CAREER NOTES: Selected by Dallas Cowboys in third round (70th pick overall) of 1991 NFL draft. ... Signed by Cowboys (July 14, 1991). ... Designated by Cowboys as transition player (February 15, 1994). ... On reserve/non-football injury list with knee injury suffered in automobile accident (November 21, 1994-remainder of season).
PLAYING EXPERIENCE: Dallas NFL, 1991-1998. ... Games/Games started: 1991 (11/3), 1992 (16/16), 1993 (16/16), 1994 (7/7), 1995 (15/15), 1996 (16/16), 1997 (15/15), 1998 (15/15). Total: 111/103.
CHAMPIONSHIP GAME EXPERIENCE: Played in NFC championship game (1992, 1993 and 1995 seasons). ... Member of Super Bowl championship team (1992, 1993 and 1995 seasons).
HONORS: Named offensive tackle on The Sporting News NFL All-Pro team (1993 and 1995). ... Played in Pro Bowl (1993, 1996 and 1997 seasons).
PRO STATISTICS: 1991—Recovered one fumble.

WILLIAMS, GENE   G   FALCONS

PERSONAL: Born October 14, 1968, in Blair, Neb. ... 6-2/320. ... Full name: Eugene Williams.
HIGH SCHOOL: Creighton Preparatory (Omaha, Neb.).
COLLEGE: Iowa State (degree in speech communications, 1991).
TRANSACTIONS/CAREER NOTES: Selected by Miami Dolphins in fifth round (121st pick overall) of 1991 NFL draft. ... Signed by Dolphins (July 11, 1991). ... Traded by Dolphins to Cleveland Browns for fourth-round pick (LB Ronnie Woolfork) in 1994 draft (July 12, 1993). ... Granted free agency (February 17, 1994). ... Re-signed by Browns for 1994 season. ... Traded by Browns to Atlanta Falcons for fifth-round pick (WR Jermaine Lewis) in 1996 draft (August 28, 1995).
PLAYING EXPERIENCE: Miami NFL, 1991 and 1992; Cleveland NFL, 1993 and 1994; Atlanta NFL, 1995-1998. ... Games/Games started: 1991 (10/0), 1992 (5/0), 1993 (16/14), 1994 (15/9), 1995 (12/3), 1996 (10/0), 1997 (15/15), 1998 (16/16). Total: 99/57.
CHAMPIONSHIP GAME EXPERIENCE: Played in NFC championship game (1998 season). ... Played in Super Bowl XXXIII (1998 season).
PRO STATISTICS: 1997—Recovered two fumbles. 1998—Recovered one fumble.

WILLIAMS, GEORGE   DT   GIANTS

PERSONAL: Born December 8, 1975, in Roseboro, N.C. ... 6-3/295.
HIGH SCHOOL: Rosewood (Goldsboro, N.C.).
COLLEGE: North Carolina State.
TRANSACTIONS/CAREER NOTES: Signed as non-drafted free agent by New York Giants (April 24, 1998).
PLAYING EXPERIENCE: New York Giants NFL, 1998. ... Games/Games started: 2/0.

WILLIAMS, GEROME   DB   BROWNS

PERSONAL: Born July 9, 1973, in Houston. ... 6-2/210. ... Full name: Meltrix Gerome Williams.
HIGH SCHOOL: Kempner (Sugar Land, Texas).
COLLEGE: Houston.
TRANSACTIONS/CAREER NOTES: Signed as non-drafted free agent by San Diego Chargers (April 24, 1997). ... Released by Chargers (August 24, 1997). ... Re-signed by Chargers to practice squad (August 25, 1997). ... Activated (November 15, 1997). ... Selected by Cleveland Browns from Chargers in NFL expansion draft (February 9, 1999).
PLAYING EXPERIENCE: San Diego NFL, 1997 and 1998. ... Games/Games started: 1997 (6/0), 1998 (16/0). Total: 22/0.
PRO STATISTICS: 1998—Recovered one fumble.

WILLIAMS, GRANT   OT   SEAHAWKS

PERSONAL: Born May 10, 1974, in Hattiesburg, Miss. ... 6-7/323.
HIGH SCHOOL: Clinton (Miss.).
JUNIOR COLLEGE: Hinds Community College (Miss.).
COLLEGE: Louisiana Tech (degree in biology, 1995).
TRANSACTIONS/CAREER NOTES: Signed as non-drafted free agent by Seattle Seahawks (April 22, 1996).
PLAYING EXPERIENCE: Seattle NFL, 1996-1998. ... Games/Games started: 1996 (8/0), 1997 (16/8), 1998 (16/0). Total: 40/8.
PRO STATISTICS: 1997—Recovered two fumbles.

WILLIAMS, HARVEY   RB   RAIDERS

PERSONAL: Born April 22, 1967, in Hempstead, Texas. ... 6-2/220. ... Full name: Harvey Lavance Williams.
HIGH SCHOOL: Hempstead (Texas).
COLLEGE: Louisiana State.
TRANSACTIONS/CAREER NOTES: Selected by Kansas City Chiefs in first round (21st pick overall) of 1991 NFL draft. ... Signed by Chiefs (August 7, 1991). ... Released by Chiefs (April 6, 1994). ... Signed by Los Angeles Raiders (April 28, 1994). ... Granted unconditional free agency (February 17, 1995). ... Re-signed by Raiders (March 3, 1995). ... Raiders franchise moved to Oakland (July 21, 1995). ... On injured reserve with knee injury (December 15, 1997-remainder of season).
CHAMPIONSHIP GAME EXPERIENCE: Member of Chiefs for AFC championship game (1993 season); inactive.
PRO STATISTICS: 1991—Attempted one pass without a completion. 1994—Recovered two fumbles. 1995—Attempted one pass with a completion for 13 yards and a touchdown and recovered one fumble. 1996—Attempted two passes with one completion for 18 yards and a touchdown. 1998—Attempted one pass with a completion for 27 yards and recovered one fumble.
SINGLE GAME HIGHS (regular season): Attempts—29 (October 30, 1994, vs. Houston); yards—160 (October 8, 1995, vs. Seattle); rushing touchdowns—2 (November 16, 1997, vs. San Diego).
STATISTICAL PLATEAUS: 100-yard rushing games: 1991 (1), 1994 (2), 1995 (3). Total: 6.

			RUSHING				RECEIVING				KICKOFF RETURNS				TOTALS		
Year Team	G	GS	Att.	Yds.	Avg.	TD	No.	Yds.	Avg.	TD	No.	Yds.	Avg.	TD	TD	2pt.	Pts.	Fum.
1991—Kansas City NFL.........	14	1	97	447	4.6	1	16	147	9.2	2	24	524	21.8	0	3	...	18	1
1992—Kansas City NFL.........	14	0	78	262	3.4	1	5	24	4.8	0	21	405	19.3	0	1	...	6	1
1993—Kansas City NFL.........	7	6	42	149	3.5	0	7	42	6.0	0	3	53	17.7	0	0	...	0	3
1994—L.A. Raiders NFL.........	16	10	282	983	3.5	4	47	391	8.3	3	8	153	19.1	0	7	1	44	4
1995—Oakland NFL.................	16	16	255	1114	4.4	9	54	375	6.9	0	0	0	...	0	9	0	54	5
1996—Oakland NFL.................	13	5	121	431	3.6	0	22	143	6.5	0	0	0	...	0	0	0	0	3
1997—Oakland NFL.................	14	6	18	70	3.9	3	16	147	9.2	2	0	0	...	0	5	1	32	0
1998—Oakland NFL.................	16	3	128	496	3.9	2	26	173	6.7	0	0	0	...	0	2	0	12	3
Pro totals (8 years)	110	47	1021	3952	3.9	20	193	1442	7.5	7	56	1785	20.3	0	27	2	166	20

WILLIAMS, JAMAL   DT   CHARGERS

PERSONAL: Born April 28, 1976, in Washington, D.C. ... 6-3/305.
HIGH SCHOOL: Archbishop Carroll (Washington, D.C.).
COLLEGE: Oklahoma State.
TRANSACTIONS/CAREER NOTES: Selected by San Diego Chargers in second round of 1998 supplemental draft (July 9, 1998). ... Signed by Chargers (August 7, 1998).
PLAYING EXPERIENCE: San Diego NFL, 1998. ... Games/Games started: 9/0.
PRO STATISTICS: 1998—Intercepted one pass for 14 yards and a touchdown.

WILLIAMS, JAMEL   S   REDSKINS

PERSONAL: Born December 22, 1973, in Gary, Ind. ... 5-11/205. ... Full name: Jamel Ishmael Williams. ... Name pronounced ja-MELL.
HIGH SCHOOL: Merrillville (Indiana).
COLLEGE: Nebraska.
TRANSACTIONS/CAREER NOTES: Selected by Washington Redskins in fifth round (132nd pick overall) of 1997 NFL draft. ... Signed by Redskins (June 2, 1997).
PLAYING EXPERIENCE: Washington NFL, 1997 and 1998. ... Games/Games started: 1997 (16/0), 1998 (16/0). Total: 32/0.

WILLIAMS, JAMES   OT   BEARS

PERSONAL: Born March 29, 1968, in Pittsburgh. ... 6-7/340. ... Full name: James Otis Williams.
HIGH SCHOOL: Allderdice (Pittsburgh).
COLLEGE: Cheyney (Pa.) State.
TRANSACTIONS/CAREER NOTES: Signed as non-drafted free agent by Chicago Bears (April 25, 1991). ... Granted free agency (February 16, 1996). ... Re-signed by Bears (March 15, 1996).
PLAYING EXPERIENCE: Chicago NFL, 1991-1998. ... Games/Games started: 1991 (14/0), 1992 (5/0), 1993 (3/0), 1994 (16/15), 1995 (16/16), 1996 (16/16), 1997 (16/16), 1998 (16/16). Total: 102/79.
PRO STATISTICS: 1991—Credited with one sack. 1996—Recovered two fumbles.
MISCELLANEOUS: Switched from defensive line to offensive line during the 1992 season.

WILLIAMS, JAMES   LB   BROWNS

PERSONAL: Born October 10, 1968, in Natchez, Miss. ... 6-0/246. ... Full name: James Edward Williams.
HIGH SCHOOL: Natchez (Miss.).
COLLEGE: Mississippi State.
TRANSACTIONS/CAREER NOTES: Selected by New Orleans Saints in sixth round (158th pick overall) of 1990 NFL draft. ... Signed by Saints (May 9, 1990). ... Granted unconditional free agency (February 1-April 1, 1991). ... Re-signed by Saints for 1991 season. ... Granted unconditional free agency (February 17, 1994). ... Re-signed by Saints (March 18, 1994). ... Selected by Jacksonville Jaguars from Saints in NFL expansion draft (February 15, 1995). ... Released by Jaguars (December 5, 1995). ... Played with Amsterdam Admirals of World League (1996). ... Signed by Atlanta Falcons (May 6, 1996). ... On injured reserve with hamstring injury (August 20-22, 1996). ... Released by Falcons (August 22, 1996). ... Signed by New England Patriots (March 6, 1997). ... Released by Patriots (August 19, 1997). ... Signed by San Francisco 49ers (August 20, 1997). ... Granted unconditional free agency (February 13, 1998). ... Re-signed by 49ers (March 20, 1998). ... Selected by Cleveland Browns from 49ers in NFL expansion draft (February 9, 1999).

CHAMPIONSHIP GAME EXPERIENCE: Played in NFC championship game (1997 season).
PRO STATISTICS: 1991—Recovered one fumble. 1994—Intercepted two passes for 42 yards and one touchdown. 1995—Intercepted two passes for 19 yards. 1997—Recovered one fumble.

Year — Team	G	GS	SACKS
1990—New Orleans NFL	14	0	0.0
1991—New Orleans NFL	16	4	1.0
1992—New Orleans NFL	16	0	0.0
1993—New Orleans NFL	16	9	2.0
1994—New Orleans NFL	16	7	0.0
1995—Jacksonville NFL	12	6	0.0
1996—Amsterdam W.L.	...	...	1.0
1997—San Francisco NFL	16	0	0.0
1998—San Francisco NFL	15	0	0.0
W.L. totals (1 year)	...	...	1.0
NFL totals (8 years)	121	26	3.0
Pro totals (9 years)	...	...	4.0

WILLIAMS, JAY — DT — RAMS

PERSONAL: Born October 13, 1971, in Washington, D.C. ... 6-3/280. ... Full name: Jay Omar Williams.
HIGH SCHOOL: St. John's (Washington, D.C.).
COLLEGE: Wake Forest.
TRANSACTIONS/CAREER NOTES: Signed as non-drafted free agent by Miami Dolphins (April 28, 1994). ... Released by Dolphins (August 28, 1994). ... Signed by Los Angeles Rams to practice squad (September 27, 1994). ... Activated (December 7, 1994); did not play. ... Rams franchise moved from Los Angeles to St. Louis (April 12, 1995). ... On physically unable to perform list with forearm injury (July 31-November 18, 1996). ... Released by Rams (November 20, 1996). ... Re-signed by Rams (Devember 11, 1996). ... Granted free agency (February 12, 1999). ... Re-signed by Rams (May 4, 1999).
PLAYING EXPERIENCE: St. Louis NFL, 1996-1998. ... Games/Games started: 1996 (2/0), 1997 (16/2), 1998 (16/1). Total: 34/3.
PRO STATISTICS: 1997—Returned one kickoff for 10 yards and credited with one sack. 1998—Credited with one sack.

WILLIAMS, JERMAINE — RB — RAIDERS

PERSONAL: Born July 3, 1972, in Greenville, N.C. ... 6-0/228.
HIGH SCHOOL: J.H. Rose (N.C.).
JUNIOR COLLEGE: Butler County Community College (Kansas).
COLLEGE: Houston.
TRANSACTIONS/CAREER NOTES: Signed as non-drafted free agent by Tampa Bay Buccaneers (April 25, 1997). ... Released by Buccaneers (August 4, 1997). ... Signed by Oakland Raiders (April 25, 1998). ... Released by Raiders (September 1, 1998). ... Re-signed by Raiders to practice squad (September 2, 1998). ... Activated (October 24, 1998).
PLAYING EXPERIENCE: Oakland NFL, 1998. ... Games/Games started: 10/0.

WILLIAMS, JOHN — DB — RAVENS

PERSONAL: Born July 26, 1974, in Hammond, La. ... 5-7/180. ... Full name: John Wesley Williams. ... Nephew of David Williams, running back/kick returner with San Francisco 49ers (1977 and 1978) and Chicago Bears (1979-81); and nephew of Clyde Williams, offensive guard/tackle with St. Louis Cardinals (1967-71).
HIGH SCHOOL: Hammond (La.).
COLLEGE: Southern.
TRANSACTIONS/CAREER NOTES: Signed as non-drafted free agent by Baltimore Ravens (April 25, 1997). ... Released by Ravens (August 24, 1997). ... Re-signed by Ravens to practice squad (August 26, 1997). ... Activated (November 26, 1997). ... Assigned by Ravens to Berlin Thunder in 1999 NFL Europe enhancement allocation program (February 22, 1999).
PLAYING EXPERIENCE: Baltimore NFL, 1997 and 1998. ... Games/Games started: 1997 (4/0), 1998 (16/0). Total: 20/0.
PRO STATISTICS: 1998—Recovered one fumble.

WILLIAMS, KARL — WR — BUCCANEERS

PERSONAL: Born April 10, 1971, in Albion, Mich. ... 5-10/179.
HIGH SCHOOL: Garland (Texas).
COLLEGE: Texas A&M-Kingsville.
TRANSACTIONS/CAREER NOTES: Signed as non-drafted free agent by Tampa Bay Buccaneers (April 23, 1996).
PRO STATISTICS: 1996—Rushed once for minus three yards and recovered one fumble. 1997—Rushed once for five yards and recovered one fumble.
SINGLE GAME HIGHS (regular season): Receptions—6 (September 13, 1998, vs. Green Bay); yards—87 (December 7, 1997, vs. Green Bay); and touchdown receptions—2 (November 2, 1997, vs. Indianapolis).

			RECEIVING				PUNT RETURNS				KICKOFF RETURNS				TOTALS			
Year — Team	G	GS	No.	Yds.	Avg.	TD	No.	Yds.	Avg.	TD	No.	Yds.	Avg.	TD	TD	2pt.	Pts.	Fum.
1996—Tampa Bay NFL	16	0	22	246	11.2	0	13	274	21.1	1	14	383	27.4	0	2	0	12	2
1997—Tampa Bay NFL	16	8	33	486	14.7	4	46	‡597	13.0	∞1	15	277	18.5	0	5	0	30	5
1998—Tampa Bay NFL	13	6	21	252	12.0	1	10	83	8.3	0	0	0	...	0	1	0	6	0
Pro totals (3 years)	45	14	76	984	12.9	5	69	954	13.8	2	29	660	22.8	0	8	0	48	7

WILLIAMS, KEVIN   WR/KR   BILLS

PERSONAL: Born January 25, 1971, in Dallas. ... 5-9/195. ... Full name: Kevin Ray Williams.
HIGH SCHOOL: Franklin D. Roosevelt (Dallas).
COLLEGE: Miami (Fla.).
TRANSACTIONS/CAREER NOTES: Selected after junior season by Dallas Cowboys in second round (46th overall) of 1993 NFL draft. ... Signed by Cowboys (April 29, 1993). ... Granted unconditional free agency (February 14, 1997). ... Signed by Arizona Cardinals (July 15, 1997). ... Granted unconditional free agency (February 13, 1998). ... Signed by Buffalo Bills (February 17, 1998).
CHAMPIONSHIP GAME EXPERIENCE: Played in NFC championship game (1993-1995 seasons). ... Member of Super Bowl championship team (1993 and 1995 seasons).
PRO STATISTICS: 1993—Fumbled eight times and recovered four fumbles. 1994—Fumbled four times and recovered three fumbles. 1995—Fumbled three times. 1997—Fumbled three times and recovered one fumble. 1998—Fumbled three times and recovered two fumbles.
SINGLE GAME HIGHS (regular season): Receptions—9 (December 25, 1995, vs. Arizona); yards—203 (December 25, 1995, vs. Arizona); and touchdown receptions—2 (December 25, 1995, vs. Arizona).
STATISTICAL PLATEAUS: 100-yard receiving games: 1995 (1).

				RUSHING			RECEIVING				PUNT RETURNS				KICKOFF RETURNS				TOTALS		
Year Team	G	GS	Att.	Yds.	Avg.	TD	No.	Yds.	Avg.	TD	No.	Yds.	Avg.	TD	No.	Yds.	Avg.	TD	TD	2pt.	Pts.
1993—Dallas NFL	16	1	7	26	3.7	2	20	151	7.6	2	36	381	10.6	†2	31	689	22.2	0	6	...	36
1994—Dallas NFL	15	2	6	20	3.3	0	13	181	13.9	0	39	349	8.9	1	43	1148	26.7	1	2	0	12
1995—Dallas NFL	16	16	10	53	5.3	0	38	613	16.1	2	18	166	9.2	0	49	1108	22.6	0	2	0	12
1996—Dallas NFL	10	9	4	11	2.8	0	27	323	12.0	1	2	17	8.5	0	21	471	22.4	0	1	0	6
1997—Arizona NFL	16	0	1	-2	-2.0	0	20	273	13.7	1	40	462	11.6	0	‡59	*1458	24.7	0	1	0	6
1998—Buffalo NFL	16	0	5	46	9.2	0	29	392	13.5	1	37	369	10.0	0	47	1059	22.5	0	1	0	6
Pro totals (6 years)	89	28	33	154	4.7	2	147	1933	13.1	7	172	1744	10.1	3	250	5933	23.7	1	13	0	78

WILLIAMS, KEVIN   DB   JETS

PERSONAL: Born August 4, 1975, in Pine Bluff, Ark. ... 6-0/190.
HIGH SCHOOL: Watson Chapel (Pine Bluff, Ark.).
COLLEGE: Oklahoma State.
TRANSACTIONS/CAREER NOTES: Selected by New York Jets in third round (87th pick overall) of 1998 NFL draft. ... Signed by Jets (July 20, 1998).
CHAMPIONSHIP GAME EXPERIENCE: Played in AFC championship game (1998 season).

			INTERCEPTIONS				KICKOFF RETURNS				TOTALS		
Year Team	G	GS	No.	Yds.	Avg.	TD	No.	Yds.	Avg.	TD	TD	2pt.	Pts. Fum.
1998—New York Jets NFL	15	6	1	34	34.0	0	11	230	20.9	0	0	0	0 0

WILLIAMS, LAMANZER   DE   JAGUARS

PERSONAL: Born November 17, 1974, in Greensboro, Ala. ... 6-4/267. ... Full name: Lamanzer Deshan Williams. ... Brother of Dan Williams, defensive end, Kansas City Chiefs.
HIGH SCHOOL: Willow Run (Ypsilanti, Mich.).
COLLEGE: Minnesota.
TRANSACTIONS/CAREER NOTES: Selected by Jacksonville Jaguars in sixth round (179th pick overall) of 1998 NFL draft. ... Signed by Jaguars (May 19, 1998). ... Released by Jaguars (August 30, 1998). ... Re-signed by Jaguars to practice squad (August 31, 1998). ... Activated (September 19, 1998). ... Released by Jaguars (September 21, 1998). ... Re-signed by Jaguars to practice squad (September 22, 1998). ... Activated (October 1, 1998).
PLAYING EXPERIENCE: Jacksonville NFL, 1998. ... Games/Games started: 1/0.
HONORS: Named defensive end on THE SPORTING NEWS college All-America third team (1997).

WILLIAMS, MOE   RB   VIKINGS

PERSONAL: Born July 26, 1974, in Columbus, Ga. ... 6-1/200. ... Full name: Maurice Jabari Williams.
HIGH SCHOOL: Spencer (Columbus, Ga.).
COLLEGE: Kentucky.
TRANSACTIONS/CAREER NOTES: Selected after junior season by Minnesota Vikings in third round (75th pick overall) of 1996 NFL draft. ... Signed by Vikings (July 22, 1996). ... On injured reserve with foot injury (December 8, 1998-remainder of season). ... Granted free agency (February 12, 1999). ... Re-signed by Vikings (April 30, 1999).
PRO STATISTICS: 1998—Recovered one fumble.
SINGLE GAME HIGHS (regular season): Attempts—19 (November 2, 1997, vs. New England); yards—43 (November 2, 1997, vs. New England); and rushing touchdowns—1 (November 2, 1997, vs. New England).

			RUSHING				RECEIVING				KICKOFF RETURNS				TOTALS			
Year Team	G	GS	Att.	Yds.	Avg.	TD	No.	Yds.	Avg.	TD	No.	Yds.	Avg.	TD	TD	2pt.	Pts.	Fum.
1996—Minnesota NFL	9	0	0	0	...	0	0	0	...	0	0	0	...	0	0	0	0	0
1997—Minnesota NFL	14	0	22	59	2.7	1	4	14	3.5	0	16	388	24.3	0	1	0	6	0
1998—Minnesota NFL	12	1	0	0	...	0	1	64	64.0	0	2	19	9.5	0	...	0	...	1
Pro totals (3 years)	35	1	22	59	2.7	1	5	78	15.6	0	18	407	22.6	0	1	0	6	1

WILLIAMS, PAT   DT   BILLS

PERSONAL: Born October 24, 1972, in Monroe, La. ... 6-3/270. ... Full name: Patrick Williams.
HIGH SCHOOL: Wossman (Monroe, La.).
JUNIOR COLLEGE: Navarro College (Texas).

COLLEGE: Northeast Oklahoma, then Texas A&M.
TRANSACTIONS/CAREER NOTES: Signed as non-drafted free agent by Buffalo Bills (April 25, 1997).
PLAYING EXPERIENCE: Buffalo NFL, 1997 and 1998. ... Games/Games started: 1997 (1/0), 1998 (14/0). Total: 15/0.
PRO STATISTICS: 1998—Credited with 3½ sacks.

WILLIAMS, POOH BEAR — FB — BROWNS

PERSONAL: Born January 20, 1975, in Crescent City, Fla. ... 6-1/286. ... Full name: Clarence Williams.
HIGH SCHOOL: Crescent City (Fla.).
COLLEGE: Florida State.
TRANSACTIONS/CAREER NOTES: Signed as non-drafted free agent by Buffalo Bills (April 23, 1998). ... Selected by Cleveland Browns from Bills in NFL expansion draft (February 9, 1999).
PLAYING EXPERIENCE: Buffalo NFL, 1998. ... Games/Games started: 2/0.
PRO STATISTICS: 1998—Rushed twice for five yards.
SINGLE GAME HIGHS (regular season): Attempts—2 (December 27, 1998, vs. New Orleans); yards—5 (December 27, 1998, vs. New Orleans); and rushing touchdowns—0.

WILLIAMS, ROBERT — CB — CHIEFS

PERSONAL: Born May 29, 1977, in Shelby, N.C. ... 5-10/177. ... Full name: Robert M. Williams.
HIGH SCHOOL: Shelby (N.C.).
COLLEGE: North Carolina.
TRANSACTIONS/CAREER NOTES: Selected after junior season by Kansas City Chiefs in fifth round (128th pick overall) of 1998 NFL draft. ... Signed by Chiefs (July 17, 1998).
PLAYING EXPERIENCE: Kansas City NFL, 1998. ... Games/Games started: 16/1.
PRO STATISTICS: 1998—Credited with ½ sack.

WILLIAMS, RODNEY — WR — RAIDERS

PERSONAL: Born August 15, 1973, in Los Angeles. ... 6-0/185.
HIGH SCHOOL: Palmdale (Cailf.).
COLLEGE: Pierce College (Calif.), then Arizona.
TRANSACTIONS/CAREER NOTES: Signed as non-drafted free agent by Oakland Raiders (April 25, 1998).
PLAYING EXPERIENCE: Oakland NFL, 1998. ... Games/Games started: 1/0.
PRO STATISTICS: 1998—Returned four kickoffs for 63 yards and fumbled once.

RECORD AS BASEBALL PLAYER
TRANSACTIONS/CAREER NOTES: Threw right, batted right. ... Selected by Kansas City Royals in 37th round of free-agent draft (June 3, 1991).

Year — Team (League)	Pos.	G	AB	R	H	2B	3B	HR	RBI	Avg.	BB	SO	SB	PO	A	E	Avg.
1991—GC Royals (GCL)	OF	29	57	7	12	1	0	0	4	.211	6	20	4	13	4	1	.944
1992—Lethbridge (Pio.)	OF	34	114	7	19	1	0	0	5	.167	3	27	0	48	1	2	.961

WILLIAMS, ROLAND — TE — RAMS

PERSONAL: Born April 27, 1975, in Rochester, N.Y. ... 6-5/269. ... Full name: Roland Lamar Williams.
HIGH SCHOOL: East (Rochester, N.Y.).
COLLEGE: Syracuse (degree in speech communications, 1997).
TRANSACTIONS/CAREER NOTES: Selected by St. Louis Rams in fourth round (98th pick overall) of 1998 NFL draft. ... Signed by Rams (July 13, 1998).
SINGLE GAME HIGHS (regular season): Receptions—3 (November 1, 1998, vs. Atlanta); yards—43 (December 13, 1998, vs. New England); and touchdown receptions—1 (November 1, 1998, vs. Atlanta).

			RECEIVING			
Year — Team	G	GS	No.	Yds.	Avg.	TD
1998—St. Louis NFL	13	9	15	144	9.6	1

WILLIAMS, SHAUN — S — GIANTS

PERSONAL: Born October 10, 1976, in Los Angeles. ... 6-2/215. ... Full name: Shaun LeJon Williams.
HIGH SCHOOL: Crespi (Encino, Calif.).
COLLEGE: UCLA.
TRANSACTIONS/CAREER NOTES: Selected by New York Giants in first round (24th pick overall) of 1998 NFL draft. ... Signed by Giants (July 24, 1998).
HONORS: Named free safety on THE SPORTING NEWS college All-America second team (1997).

			INTERCEPTIONS			
Year — Team	G	GS	No.	Yds.	Avg.	TD
1998—New York Giants NFL	13	0	2	6	3.0	0

WILLIAMS, SHERMAN — RB

PERSONAL: Born August 13, 1973, in Mobile, Ala. ... 5-8/202.
HIGH SCHOOL: M.T. Blount (Prichard, Ala.).
COLLEGE: Alabama.
TRANSACTIONS/CAREER NOTES: Selected by Dallas Cowboys in second round (46th pick overall) of 1995 NFL draft. ... Signed by Cowboys (July 21, 1995). ... Released by Cowboys (July 10, 1998). ... Re-signed by Cowboys (September 1, 1998). ... Granted unconditional free agency (February 12, 1999).
CHAMPIONSHIP GAME EXPERIENCE: Played in NFC championship game (1995 season). ... Member of Super Bowl championship team (1995 season).
HONORS: Named running back on THE SPORTING NEWS college All-America second team (1994).
PRO STATISTICS: 1996—Attempted one pass without a completion. 1997—Recovered one fumble. 1998—Returned four kickoffs for 103 yards.
SINGLE GAME HIGHS (regular season): Attempts—23 (December 27, 1998, vs. Washington); yards—90 (December 27, 1998, vs. Washington); rushing touchdowns—1 (September 27, 1998, vs. New York Giants).

			RUSHING				RECEIVING				TOTALS		
Year Team	G	GS	Att.	Yds.	Avg.	TD	No.	Yds.	Avg.	TD	TD	2pt.	Pts.	Fum.
1995—Dallas NFL	11	0	48	205	4.3	1	3	28	9.3	0	1	0	6	2
1996—Dallas NFL	16	1	69	269	3.9	0	5	41	8.2	0	0	0	0	2
1997—Dallas NFL	16	0	121	468	3.9	2	21	159	7.6	0	2	0	12	5
1998—Dallas NFL	16	2	64	220	3.4	1	11	104	9.5	0	1	0	6	0
Pro totals (4 years)	59	3	302	1162	3.8	4	40	332	8.3	0	4	0	24	9

WILLIAMS, STEPFRET — WR — BENGALS

PERSONAL: Born June 14, 1973, in Minden, La. ... 6-0/170.
HIGH SCHOOL: Minden (La.).
COLLEGE: Northeast Louisiana.
TRANSACTIONS/CAREER NOTES: Selected by Dallas Cowboys in third round (94th pick overall) of 1996 NFL draft. ... Signed by Cowboys (July 18, 1996). ... Claimed on waivers by Cincinnati Bengals (September 2, 1998). ... Granted free agency (February 12, 1999). ... Re-signed by Bengals (April 15, 1999).
PRO STATISTICS: 1997—Returned two punts for 14 yards. 1998—Returned two punts for 16 yards and returned one kickoff for 20 yards.
SINGLE GAME HIGHS (regular season): Receptions—5 (November 2, 1997, vs. San Francisco); yards—53 (September 7, 1997, vs. Arizona); and touchdown receptions—1 (December 13, 1998, vs. Indianapolis).

			RECEIVING				TOTALS		
Year Team	G	GS	No.	Yds.	Avg.	TD	TD	2pt.	Pts.	Fum.
1996—Dallas NFL	5	0	1	32	32.0	0	0	0	0	0
1997—Dallas NFL	16	0	30	308	10.3	1	1	0	6	0
1998—Cincinnati NFL	5	0	6	81	13.5	1	1	0	6	0
Pro totals (3 years)	26	0	37	421	11.4	2	2	0	12	0

WILLIAMS, TONY — DT — VIKINGS

PERSONAL: Born July 9, 1975, in Germantown, Tenn. ... 6-1/285. ... Full name: Anthony Demetric Williams.
HIGH SCHOOL: Oakhaven (Memphis, Tenn.), then Germantown (Tenn.).
COLLEGE: Memphis.
TRANSACTIONS/CAREER NOTES: Selected by Minnesota Vikings in fifth round (151st pick overall) of 1997 NFL draft. ... Signed by Vikings (June 17, 1997).
PLAYING EXPERIENCE: Minnesota NFL, 1997 and 1998. ... Games/Games started: 1997 (6/2), 1998 (14/9). Total: 20/11.
CHAMPIONSHIP GAME EXPERIENCE: Played in NFC championship game (1998 season).
PRO STATISTICS: 1998—Credited with one sack and recovered one fumble for six yards.

WILLIAMS, TYRONE — CB — PACKERS

PERSONAL: Born May 31, 1973, in Bradenton, Fla. ... 5-11/192. ... Full name: Upton Tyrone Williams.
HIGH SCHOOL: Manatee (Bradenton, Fla.).
COLLEGE: Nebraska.
TRANSACTIONS/CAREER NOTES: Selected by Green Bay Packers in third round (93rd pick overall) of 1996 NFL draft. ... Signed by Packers (May 15, 1996). ... Granted free agency (February 12, 1999). ... Re-signed by Packers (May 17, 1999).
CHAMPIONSHIP GAME EXPERIENCE: Played in NFC championship game (1996 and 1997 seasons). ... Member of Super Bowl championship team (1996 season). ... Played in Super Bowl XXXII (1997 season).
PRO STATISTICS: 1996—Recovered one fumble.

			INTERCEPTIONS			
Year Team	G	GS	No.	Yds.	Avg.	TD
1996—Green Bay NFL	16	0	0	0	...	0
1997—Green Bay NFL	16	15	1	0	0.0	0
1998—Green Bay NFL	16	16	5	40	8.0	0
Pro totals (3 years)	48	31	6	40	6.7	0

WILLIAMS, WALLY — G/C — SAINTS

PERSONAL: Born February 19, 1971, in Tallahassee, Fla. ... 6-2/321. ... Full name: Wally James Williams Jr.
HIGH SCHOOL: James S. Rickards (Tallahassee, Fla.).
COLLEGE: Florida A&M.

TRANSACTIONS/CAREER NOTES: Signed as non-drafted free agent by Cleveland Browns (April 27, 1993). ... Browns franchise moved to Baltimore and renamed Ravens for 1996 season (March 11, 1996). ... Designated by Ravens as franchise player (February 13, 1998). ... Re-signed by Ravens (August 18, 1998). ... Granted unconditional free agency (February 12, 1999). ... Signed by New Orleans Saints (February 15, 1999).
PLAYING EXPERIENCE: Cleveland NFL, 1993-1995; Baltimore NFL, 1996-1998. ... Games/Games started: 1993 (2/0), 1994 (11/7), 1995 (16/16), 1996 (15/13), 1997 (10/10), 1998 (13/13). Total: 67/59.
PRO STATISTICS: 1994—Recovered one fumble. 1998—Recovered one fumble.

WILLIAMS, WILLIE   CB   SEAHAWKS

PERSONAL: Born December 26, 1970, in Columbia, S.C. ... 5-9/180. ... Full name: Willie James Williams Jr.
HIGH SCHOOL: Spring Valley (Columbia, S.C.).
COLLEGE: Western Carolina.
TRANSACTIONS/CAREER NOTES: Selected by Pittsburgh Steelers in sixth round (162nd pick overall) of 1993 NFL draft. ... Signed by Steelers (July 9, 1993). ... Granted free agency (February 16, 1996). ... Re-signed by Steelers (June 12, 1996). ... Granted unconditional free agency (February 14, 1997). ... Signed by Seattle Seahawks (February 18, 1997).
CHAMPIONSHIP GAME EXPERIENCE: Played in AFC championship game (1994 and 1995 seasons). ... Played in Super Bowl XXX (1995 season).
PRO STATISTICS: 1993—Returned one kickoff for 19 yards. 1996—Credited with one sack and recovered one fumble. 1998—Recovered one fumble.

			INTERCEPTIONS		
Year Team	G	GS	No.	Yds.	Avg.	TD
1993—Pittsburgh NFL	16	0	0	0	...	0
1994—Pittsburgh NFL	16	1	0	0	...	0
1995—Pittsburgh NFL	16	15	§7	122	17.4	▲1
1996—Pittsburgh NFL	15	14	1	1	1.0	0
1997—Seattle NFL	16	16	1	0	0.0	0
1998—Seattle NFL	14	14	2	36	18.0	1
Pro totals (6 years)	93	60	11	159	14.5	2

WILLIG, MATT   OT

PERSONAL: Born January 21, 1969, in La Mirada, Calif. ... 6-8/317. ... Full name: Matthew Joseph Willig.
HIGH SCHOOL: St. Paul (Santa Fe Springs, Calif.).
COLLEGE: Southern California.
TRANSACTIONS/CAREER NOTES: Signed as non-drafted free agent by New York Jets (May 5, 1992). ... Released by Jets (August 24, 1992). ... Re-signed by Jets to practice squad (September 2, 1992). ... Activated (December 24, 1992). ... Active for one game (1992); did not play. ... Signed by Jets (February 14, 1995). ... Released by Jets (April 23, 1996). ... Signed by Atlanta Falcons (May 2, 1996). ... Granted unconditional free agency (February 13, 1998). ... Signed by Green Bay Packers (May 5, 1998). ... Released by Packers (February 24, 1999).
PLAYING EXPERIENCE: New York Jets NFL, 1993-1995; Atlanta NFL, 1996 and 1997; Green Bay NFL, 1998. ... Games/Games started: 1993 (3/0), 1994 (16/3), 1995 (15/12), 1996 (12/0), 1997 (16/13), 1998 (16/0). Total: 78/28.
PRO STATISTICS: 1998—Recovered one fumble.

WILLIS, JAMES   LB

PERSONAL: Born September 2, 1972, in Huntsville, Ala. ... 6-2/237. ... Full name: James Edward Willis III.
HIGH SCHOOL: J.O. Johnson (Huntsville, Ala.).
COLLEGE: Auburn.
TRANSACTIONS/CAREER NOTES: Selected after junior season by Green Bay Packers in fifth round (119th pick overall) of 1993 NFL draft. ... Signed by Packers (May 21, 1993). ... On injured reserve with knee injury (December 23, 1993-remainder of season). ... Released by Packers (October 25, 1995). ... Signed by Philadelphia Eagles (October 31, 1995). ... Granted free agency (February 16, 1996). ... Re-signed by Eagles (March 1, 1996). ... Released by Eagles (June 8, 1999).
PRO STATISTICS: 1993—Recovered one fumble. 1994—Fumbled once and recovered one fumble. 1997—Credited with two sacks and recovered two fumbles. 1998—Recovered one fumble.

			INTERCEPTIONS		
Year Team	G	GS	No.	Yds.	Avg.	TD
1993—Green Bay NFL	13	0	0	0	...	0
1994—Green Bay NFL	12	0	2	20	10.0	0
1995—Philadelphia NFL	5	0	0	0	...	0
1996—Philadelphia NFL	16	13	1	14	14.0	0
1997—Philadelphia NFL	15	15	1	0	0.0	0
1998—Philadelphia NFL	16	16	0	0	...	0
Pro totals (6 years)	77	44	4	34	8.5	0

WILMSMEYER, KLAUS   P   PANTHERS

PERSONAL: Born December 4, 1967, in Mississauga, Ont. ... 6-2/205. ... Full name: Klaus Wilmsmeyer Jr.
HIGH SCHOOL: Lorne Park Secondary (Mississauga, Ont.).
COLLEGE: Louisville.
TRANSACTIONS/CAREER NOTES: Selected by Tampa Bay Buccaneers in 12th round (311th pick overall) of 1992 NFL draft. ... Signed by Buccaneers (June 9, 1992). ... Released by Buccaneers (August 24, 1992). ... Signed by San Francisco 49ers to practice squad (September 2, 1992). ... Activated (September 4, 1992). ... Granted unconditional free agency (February 17, 1995). ... Signed by New Orleans Saints (March 7, 1995). ... Granted unconditional free agency (February 14, 1997). ... Signed by Miami Dolphins (February 23, 1998). ... Granted unconditional free agency (February 12, 1999). ... Signed by Carolina Panthers (April 1, 1999).

CHAMPIONSHIP GAME EXPERIENCE: Played in NFC championship game (1992-1994 seasons). ... Member of Super Bowl championship team (1994 season).

PRO STATISTICS: 1992—Rushed twice for no yards, fumbled once and recovered one fumble. 1993—Rushed twice for no yards, fumbled twice and recovered one fumble for minus 10 yards. 1995—Attempted one pass with a completion for 18 yards. 1996—Credited with one two-point conversion.

			PUNTING				
Year Team	G	No.	Yds.	Avg.	Net avg.	In. 20	Blk.
1992—San Francisco NFL	15	49	1918	39.1	34.7	19	0
1993—San Francisco NFL	15	42	1718	40.9	34.5	11	0
1994—San Francisco NFL	16	54	2235	41.4	35.7	18	0
1995—New Orleans NFL	16	73	2965	40.6	35.6	21	1
1996—New Orleans NFL	16	87	3551	40.8	32.5	16	0
1997—				Did not play.			
1998—Miami NFL	16	93	3949	42.5	35.6	23	1
Pro totals (6 years)	94	398	16336	41.0	34.7	108	2

WILSON, BERNARD DT CARDINALS

PERSONAL: Born August 17, 1970, in Nashville. ... 6-3/318.
HIGH SCHOOL: Maplewood (Nashville).
COLLEGE: Tennessee State.
TRANSACTIONS/CAREER NOTES: Signed as non-drafted free agent by Detroit Lions (May 1, 1992). ... Released by Lions (August 31, 1992). ... Re-signed by Lions to practice squad (September 1, 1992). ... Released by Lions (September 6, 1993). ... Re-signed by Lions to practice squad (September 8, 1993). ... Signed by Tampa Bay Buccaneers off Lions practice squad (September 16, 1993). ... Claimed on waivers by Arizona Cardinals (September 7, 1994). ... Granted unconditional free agency (February 14, 1997). ... Re-signed by Cardinals (February 19, 1997). ... Granted unconditional free agency (February 12, 1999). ... Re-signed by Cardinals (April 28, 1999).
PRO STATISTICS: 1996—Recovered one fumble. 1997—Intercepted one pass for 66 yards and a touchdown.

Year Team	G	GS	SACKS
1992—Detroit NFL		Did not play.	
1993—Tampa Bay NFL	13	2	0.0
1994—Tampa Bay NFL	1	0	0.0
—Arizona NFL	13	12	1.0
1995—Arizona NFL	16	14	1.0
1996—Arizona NFL	16	16	1.0
1997—Arizona NFL	16	14	0.0
1998—Arizona NFL	16	3	1.0
Pro totals (6 years)	91	61	4.0

WILSON, JERRY CB DOLPHINS

PERSONAL: Born July 17, 1973, in Alexandria, La. ... 5-10/187. ... Full name: Jerry Lee Wilson Jr.
HIGH SCHOOL: LaGrange (Lake Charles, La.).
COLLEGE: Southern (degree in rehabilitation counseling).
TRANSACTIONS/CAREER NOTES: Selected by Tampa Bay Buccaneers in fourth round (105th pick overall) of 1995 NFL draft. ... Signed by Buccaneers (May 9, 1995). ... On injured reserve with knee injury (August 31, 1995-entire season). ... Released by Buccaneers (August 20, 1996). ... Signed by Miami Dolphins to practice squad (October 29, 1996). ... Activated (November 5, 1996).
PLAYING EXPERIENCE: Miami NFL, 1996-1998. ... Games/Games started: 1996 (2/0), 1997 (16/0), 1998 (16/0). Total: 34/0.
PRO STATISTICS: 1997—Credited with two sacks and recovered one fumble. 1998—Intercepted one pass for no yards.

WILSON, REINARD LB BENGALS

PERSONAL: Born December 17, 1973, in Lake City, Fla. ... 6-2/261.
HIGH SCHOOL: Columbia (Lake City, Fla.).
COLLEGE: Florida State.
TRANSACTIONS/CAREER NOTES: Selected by Cincinnati Bengals in first round (14th pick overall) of 1997 NFL draft. ... Signed by Bengals (July 18, 1997).
HONORS: Named defensive end on THE SPORTING NEWS college All-America second team (1996).

Year Team	G	GS	SACKS
1997—Cincinnati NFL	16	4	3.0
1998—Cincinnati NFL	16	15	6.0
Pro totals (2 years)	32	19	9.0

WILSON, ROBERT WR SEAHAWKS

PERSONAL: Born June 23, 1974, in Tallahassee, Fla. ... 5-11/176.
HIGH SCHOOL: Jefferson County (Monticello, Fla.).
COLLEGE: Florida A&M.
TRANSACTIONS/CAREER NOTES: Signed as non-drafted free agent by Seattle Seahawks (April 25, 1997). ... Released by Seahawks (August 18, 1997). ... Re-signed by Seahawks to practice squad (August 19, 1997). ... Activated (December 17, 1997). ... Inactive for one game (1997).
PLAYING EXPERIENCE: Seattle NFL, 1998. ... Games/Games started: 16/0.
PRO STATISTICS: 1998—Returned one kickoff for 16 yards.

WILSON, TROY — DE — SAINTS

PERSONAL: Born November 22, 1970, in Topeka, Kan. ... 6-4/257. ... Full name: Troy Ethan Wilson.
HIGH SCHOOL: Shawnee Heights (Tecumseh, Kan.).
COLLEGE: Pittsburg (Kan.) State (degree in business management, 1992).
TRANSACTIONS/CAREER NOTES: Selected by San Francisco 49ers in seventh round (194th pick overall) of 1993 NFL draft. ... Signed by 49ers (May 12, 1993). ... On non-football injury list with back injury (August 24-October 16, 1993). ... Released by 49ers (August 27, 1995). ... Signed by Denver Broncos (September 28, 1995). ... Released by Broncos (October 30, 1995). ... Signed by Kansas City Chiefs (April 1996). ... Released by Chiefs (August 20, 1996). ... Signed by St. Louis Rams (February 6, 1997). ... Released by Rams (August 19, 1997). ... Signed by 49ers (May 26, 1998). ... Claimed on waivers by New Orleans Saints (September 1, 1998). ... Granted free agency (February 12, 1999). ... Re-signed by Saints (May 17, 1999).
CHAMPIONSHIP GAME EXPERIENCE: Played in NFC championship game (1993 and 1994 seasons). ... Member of Super Bowl championship team (1994 season).

Year Team	G	GS	SACKS
1993—San Francisco NFL	10	0	5.5
1994—San Francisco NFL	11	0	2.0
1995—Denver NFL	3	0	0.5
1996—	Did not play.		
1997—	Did not play.		
1998—New Orleans NFL	15	0	1.0
Pro totals (4 years)	**39**	**0**	**9.0**

WILSON, WADE — QB — RAIDERS

PERSONAL: Born February 1, 1959, in Commerce, Texas. ... 6-3/210. ... Full name: Charles Wade Wilson.
HIGH SCHOOL: Commerce (Texas).
COLLEGE: East Texas State.
TRANSACTIONS/CAREER NOTES: Selected by Minnesota Vikings in eighth round (210th pick overall) of 1981 NFL draft. ... Signed by Vikings for 1981 season. ... On inactive list (September 12, 1982). ... On commissioner's exempt list (November 20-December 8, 1982). ... Active for four games with Vikings (1982); did not play. ... On injured reserve with broken thumb (September 26-November 24, 1990). ... On injured reserve with separated shoulder (December 26, 1990-remainder of season). ... Released by Vikings (July 9, 1992). ... Signed by Atlanta Falcons (July 15, 1992). ... Granted unconditional free agency (March 1, 1993). ... Signed by New Orleans Saints (April 12, 1993). ... Released by Saints (March 18, 1994). ... Re-signed by Saints (April 13, 1994). ... Released by Saints (March 20, 1995). ... Signed by Dallas Cowboys (May 22, 1995). ... Released by Cowboys (February 24, 1998). ... Signed by Oakland Raiders (July 6, 1998). ... Granted unconditional free agency (February 12, 1999). ... Re-signed by Raiders (February 16, 1999).
CHAMPIONSHIP GAME EXPERIENCE: Played in NFC championship game (1987 season). ... Member of Cowboys for NFC championship game (1995 season); did not play. ... Member of Super Bowl championship team (1995 season).
HONORS: Played in Pro Bowl (1988 season).
PRO STATISTICS: 1981—Fumbled twice and recovered one fumble. 1983—Fumbled once. 1984—Fumbled twice. 1986—Punted twice for 76 yards (38.0-yard avg.) with one punt blocked, fumbled three times and recovered one fumble for minus two yards. 1987—Fumbled three times. 1988—Fumbled four times and recovered four fumbles for minus nine yards. 1989—Fumbled five times and recovered two fumbles for minus seven yards. 1990—Fumbled three times and recovered one fumble for minus two yards. 1991—Fumbled three times and recovered one fumble for minus three yards. 1993—Fumbled nine times and recovered four fumbles for minus three yards. 1994—Fumbled once. 1995—Fumbled once and recovered one fumble. 1998—Fumbled once.
SINGLE GAME HIGHS (regular season): Attempts—47 (December 27, 1992, vs. Los Angeles Rams); completions—31 (December 27, 1992, vs. Los Angeles Rams); yards—391 (November 6, 1988, vs. Detroit); and touchdown passes—5 (December 13, 1992, vs. Tampa Bay).
STATISTICAL PLATEAUS: 300-yard passing games: 1986 (2), 1988 (2), 1989 (2), 1990 (1), 1992 (3), 1993 (1). Total: 11.
MISCELLANEOUS: Regular-season record as starting NFL quarterback: 36-33 (.522). ... Postseason record as starting NFL quarterback: 2-3 (.400).

					PASSING					RUSHING				TOTALS		
Year Team	G	GS	Att.	Cmp.	Pct.	Yds.	TD	Int.	Avg.	Rat.	Att.	Yds.	Avg.	TD	TD	2pt.	Pts.
1981—Minnesota NFL	3	0	13	6	46.2	48	0	2	3.69	16.3	0	0	...	0	0	...	0
1982—Minnesota NFL						Did not play.											
1983—Minnesota NFL	1	1	28	16	57.1	124	1	2	4.43	50.3	3	-3	-1.0	0	0	...	0
1984—Minnesota NFL	8	5	195	102	52.3	1019	5	11	5.23	52.5	9	30	3.3	0	0	...	0
1985—Minnesota NFL	4	1	60	33	55.0	404	3	3	6.73	71.8	0	0	...	0	0	...	0
1986—Minnesota NFL	9	3	143	80	55.9	1165	7	5	8.15	84.4	13	9	0.7	1	1	...	6
1987—Minnesota NFL	12	7	264	140	53.0	2106	14	13	*7.98	76.7	41	263	6.4	5	5	...	30
1988—Minnesota NFL	14	10	332	204	*61.4	2746	15	9	‡8.27	‡91.5	36	136	3.8	2	2	...	12
1989—Minnesota NFL	14	12	362	194	53.6	2543	9	12	7.02	70.5	32	132	4.1	1	1	...	6
1990—Minnesota NFL	6	4	146	82	56.2	1155	9	8	7.91	79.6	12	79	6.6	0	0	...	0
1991—Minnesota NFL	5	5	122	72	59.0	825	3	10	6.76	53.5	13	33	2.5	0	0	...	0
1992—Atlanta NFL	9	3	163	111	68.1	1366	13	4	8.38	110.1	15	62	4.1	0	0	...	0
1993—New Orleans NFL	14	14	388	221	57.0	2457	12	15	6.33	70.1	31	230	7.4	0	0	...	0
1994—New Orleans NFL	4	0	28	20	71.4	172	0	2	6.14	87.2	7	15	2.1	0	0	...	0
1995—Dallas NFL	7	0	57	38	66.7	391	1	3	6.86	70.1	10	12	1.2	0	0	...	0
1996—Dallas NFL	3	1	18	8	44.4	79	0	1	4.39	34.3	4	5	1.3	0	0	...	0
1997—Dallas NFL	7	0	21	12	57.1	115	0	5	5.48	72.5	6	-2	-0.3	0	0	...	0
1998—Oakland NFL	5	3	88	52	59.1	568	7	4	6.45	85.8	7	24	3.4	0	0	...	0
Pro totals (17 years)	**125**	**69**	**2428**	**1391**	**57.3**	**17283**	**99**	**102**	**7.12**	**75.6**	**239**	**1025**	**4.3**	**9**	**9**	**0**	**54**

WINTERS, FRANK — C — PACKERS

PERSONAL: Born January 23, 1964, in Hoboken, N.J. ... 6-3/300. ... Full name: Frank Mitchell Winters.
HIGH SCHOOL: Emerson (Union City, N.J.).
JUNIOR COLLEGE: College of Eastern Utah.
COLLEGE: Western Illinois (degree in political science administration, 1987).

TRANSACTIONS/CAREER NOTES: Selected by Cleveland Browns in 10th round (276th pick overall) of 1987 NFL draft. ... Signed by Browns (July 25, 1987). ... Granted unconditional free agency (February 1, 1989). ... Signed by New York Giants (March 17, 1989). ... Granted unconditional free agency (February 1, 1990). ... Signed by Kansas City Chiefs (March 26, 1990). ... Granted unconditional free agency (February 1, 1992). ... Signed by Green Bay Packers (March 17, 1992). ... Granted unconditional free agency (February 17, 1994). ... Re-signed by Packers (April 1, 1994). ... Granted unconditional free agency (February 14, 1997). ... Re-signed by Packers (March 26, 1997). ... On injured reserve with leg injury (December 16, 1998-remainder of season).
PLAYING EXPERIENCE: Cleveland NFL, 1987 and 1988; New York Giants NFL, 1989; Kansas City NFL, 1990 and 1991; Green Bay NFL, 1992-1998. ... Games/Games started: 1987 (12/0), 1988 (16/0), 1989 (15/0), 1990 (16/6), 1991 (16/0), 1992 (16/11), 1993 (16/16), 1994 (16/16), 1995 (16/16), 1996 (16/16), 1997 (13/13), 1998 (13/13). Total: 181/107.
CHAMPIONSHIP GAME EXPERIENCE: Played in AFC championship game (1987 season). ... Played in NFC championship game (1995-97 seasons). ... Member of Super Bowl championship team (1996 season). ... Played in Super Bowl XXXII (1997 season).
HONORS: Played in Pro Bowl (1996 season).
PRO STATISTICS: 1987—Fumbled once. 1990—Recovered two fumbles. 1992—Fumbled once. 1994—Fumbled once and recovered one fumble for minus two yards. 1996—Recovered one fumble.

WISNIEWSKI, STEVE   G   RAIDERS

PERSONAL: Born April 7, 1967, in Rutland, Vt. ... 6-4/305. ... Full name: Stephen Adam Wisniewski. ... Brother of Leo Wisniewski, nose tackle with Baltimore/Indianapolis Colts (1982-84). ... Name pronounced wiz-NEWS-ki.
HIGH SCHOOL: Westfield (Houston).
COLLEGE: Penn State.
TRANSACTIONS/CAREER NOTES: Selected by Dallas Cowboys in second round (29th pick overall) of 1989 NFL draft. ... Draft rights traded by Cowboys with sixth-round pick (LB Jeff Francis) in 1989 draft to Los Angeles Raiders for second-(RB Darryl Johnston), third-(DE Rhondy Weston) and fifth-round (LB Willis Crockett) picks in 1989 draft (April 23, 1989). ... Signed by Raiders (July 22, 1989). ... Granted free agency (March 1, 1993). ... Re-signed by Raiders for 1993 season. ... Raiders franchise moved to Oakland (July 21, 1995).
PLAYING EXPERIENCE: Los Angeles Raiders NFL, 1989-1994; Oakland NFL, 1995-1998. ... Games/Games started: 1989 (15/15), 1990 (16/16), 1991 (15/15), 1992 (16/16), 1993 (16/16), 1994 (16/16), 1995 (16/16), 1996 (16/16), 1997 (16/16), 1998 (16/16). Total: 158/158.
CHAMPIONSHIP GAME EXPERIENCE: Played in AFC championship game (1990 season).
HONORS: Named guard on The Sporting News college All-America first team (1987 and 1988). ... Named guard on The Sporting News NFL All-Pro team (1990-1994). ... Played in Pro Bowl (1990, 1991, 1993 and 1995 seasons). ... Named to play in Pro Bowl (1992 season); replaced by Jim Ritcher due to injury.
PRO STATISTICS: 1989—Recovered three fumbles. 1995—Recovered one fumble.

WISTROM, GRANT   DE   RAMS

PERSONAL: Born July 3, 1976, in Webb City, Mo. ... 6-4/267. ... Full name: Grant Alden Wistrom.
HIGH SCHOOL: Webb City (Mo.).
COLLEGE: Nebraska.
TRANSACTIONS/CAREER NOTES: Selected by St. Louis Rams in first round (sixth pick overall) of 1998 NFL draft. ... Signed by Rams (July 18, 1998).
HONORS: Named defensive end on The Sporting News college All-America first team (1996 and 1997).
PRO STATISTICS: 1998—Recovered one fumble for four yards.

Year Team	G	GS	SACKS
1998—St. Louis NFL	13	0	3.0

WITMAN, JON   FB   STEELERS

PERSONAL: Born June 1, 1972, in Wrightsville, Pa. ... 6-1/240. ... Full name: Jon Doyle Witman.
HIGH SCHOOL: Eastern York (Wrightsville, Pa.).
COLLEGE: Penn State.
TRANSACTIONS/CAREER NOTES: Selected by Pittsburgh Steelers in third round (92nd pick overall) of 1996 NFL draft. ... Signed by Steelers (July 16, 1996). ... Granted free agency (February 12, 1999). ... Re-signed by Steelers (March 10, 1999).
CHAMPIONSHIP GAME EXPERIENCE: Played in AFC championship game (1997).
PRO STATISTICS: 1996—Returned one kickoff for 20 yards.
SINGLE GAME HIGHS (regular season): Attempts—7 (November 3, 1996, vs. St. Louis); yards—33 (November 3, 1996, vs. St. Louis); and rushing touchdowns—0.

			RUSHING				RECEIVING				TOTALS		
Year Team	G	GS	Att.	Yds.	Avg.	TD	No.	Yds.	Avg.	TD	TD	2pt.	Pts.	Fum.
1996—Pittsburgh NFL	16	4	17	69	4.1	0	2	15	7.5	0	0	0	0	0
1997—Pittsburgh NFL	16	2	5	11	2.2	0	1	3	3.0	0	0	0	0	0
1998—Pittsburgh NFL	16	8	1	2	2.0	0	13	74	5.7	0	0	0	0	0
Pro totals (3 years)	48	14	23	82	3.6	0	16	92	5.8	0	0	0	0	0

WOHLABAUGH, DAVE   C   BROWNS

PERSONAL: Born April 13, 1972, in Hamburg, N.Y. ... 6-3/292. ... Full name: David Vincent Wohlabaugh. ... Name pronounced WOOL-uh-buh.
HIGH SCHOOL: Frontier (Hamburg, N.Y.).
COLLEGE: Syracuse.
TRANSACTIONS/CAREER NOTES: Selected by New England Patriots in fourth round (112th pick overall) of 1995 NFL draft. ... Signed by Patriots (June 26, 1995). ... Granted free agency (February 13, 1998). ... Re-signed by Patriots (May 28, 1998). ... Granted unconditional free agency (February 12, 1999). ... Signed by Cleveland Browns (February 16, 1999).
PLAYING EXPERIENCE: New England NFL, 1995-1998. ... Games/Games started: 1995 (11/11), 1996 (16/16), 1997 (14/14), 1998 (16/16). Total: 57/57.
CHAMPIONSHIP GAME EXPERIENCE: Played in AFC championship game (1996 season). ... Played in Super Bowl XXXI (1996 season).
PRO STATISTICS: 1995—Recovered one fumble. 1996—Recovered two fumbles for one yard.

WOLFORD, WILL — OT

PERSONAL: Born May 18, 1964, in Louisville, Ky. ... 6-5/300. ... Full name: William Charles Wolford. ... Name pronounced WOOL-ford.
HIGH SCHOOL: St. Xavier (Louisville, Ky.).
COLLEGE: Vanderbilt (degree in sociology, 1986).
TRANSACTIONS/CAREER NOTES: Selected by Memphis Showboats in 1986 USFL territorial draft. ... Selected by Buffalo Bills in first round (20th pick overall) of 1986 NFL draft. ... Signed by Bills (August 12, 1986). ... Granted roster exemption (August 12-22, 1986). ... Granted free agency (February 1, 1990). ... Re-signed by Bills (August 28, 1990). ... Granted roster exemption (August 28-September 9, 1990). ... Designated by Bills as transition player (February 25, 1993). ... Tendered offer sheet by Indianapolis Colts (March 28, 1993). ... Bills declined to match offer (April 23, 1993). ... On injured reserve with shoulder injury (December 10, 1993-remainder of season). ... Designated by Colts as transition player (February 15, 1994). ... Free agency status changed by Colts from transitional to unconditional (February 29, 1996). ... Signed by Pittsburgh Steelers (March 1, 1996). ... On non-football injury list with torn chest muscle (July 24-August 1998). ... Released by Steelers (April 7, 1999).
PLAYING EXPERIENCE: Buffalo NFL, 1986-1992; Indianapolis NFL, 1993-1995; Pittsburgh NFL, 1996-1998. ... Games/Games started: 1986 (16/16), 1987 (9/9), 1988 (16/16), 1989 (16/16), 1990 (14/14), 1991 (15/15), 1992 (16/16), 1993 (12/12), 1994 (16/16), 1995 (16/16), 1996 (16/16), 1997 (16/16), 1998 (13/13). Total: 191/191.
CHAMPIONSHIP GAME EXPERIENCE: Played in AFC championship game (1988, 1990-1992, 1995 and 1997 seasons). ... Played in Super Bowl XXV (1990 season), Super Bowl XXVI (1991 season) and Super Bowl XXVII (1992 season).
HONORS: Played in Pro Bowl (1990 and 1995 seasons). ... Named to play in Pro Bowl (1992 season); replaced by John Alt due to injury.
PRO STATISTICS: 1988—Recovered one fumble. 1994—Recovered one fumble. 1998—Recovered one fumble.

WONG, KAILEE — LB — VIKINGS

PERSONAL: Born May 23, 1976, in Eugene, Ore. ... 6-2/257. ... Name pronounced KI-lee.
HIGH SCHOOL: North Eugene (Ore.).
COLLEGE: Stanford.
TRANSACTIONS/CAREER NOTES: Selected by Minnesota Vikings in second round (51st pick overall) of 1998 NFL draft. ... Signed by Vikings (July 25, 1998). ... On injured reserve with leg injury (December 31, 1998-remainder of season).
PLAYING EXPERIENCE: Minnesota NFL, 1998. ... Games/Games started: 15/0.
PRO STATISTICS: 1998—Credited with $1^{1}/_{2}$ sacks.

WOODALL, LEE — LB — 49ERS

PERSONAL: Born October 31, 1969, in Carlisle, Pa. ... 6-1/224. ... Full name: Lee Artis Woodall.
HIGH SCHOOL: Carlisle (Pa.).
COLLEGE: West Chester (Pa.) University.
TRANSACTIONS/CAREER NOTES: Selected by San Francisco 49ers in sixth round (182nd pick overall) of 1994 NFL draft. ... Signed by 49ers (July 20, 1994).
CHAMPIONSHIP GAME EXPERIENCE: Played in NFC championship game (1994 and 1997 seasons). ... Member of Super Bowl championship team (1994 season).
HONORS: Played in Pro Bowl (1995 and 1997 seasons).
PRO STATISTICS: 1994—Recovered one fumble. 1995—Recovered two fumbles for 98 yards and one touchdown.

			INTERCEPTIONS				SACKS
Year Team	G	GS	No.	Yds.	Avg.	TD	No.
1994—San Francisco NFL	15	13	0	0	...	0	1.0
1995—San Francisco NFL	16	16	2	0	0.0	0	3.0
1996—San Francisco NFL	16	13	0	0	...	0	2.5
1997—San Francisco NFL	16	16	2	55	27.5	0	0.0
1998—San Francisco NFL	15	15	1	4	4.0	0	0.0
Pro totals (5 years)	78	73	5	59	11.8	0	6.5

WOODEN, SHAWN — S — DOLPHINS

PERSONAL: Born October 23, 1973, in Philadelphia. ... 5-11/205. ... Full name: Shawn Anthony Wooden.
HIGH SCHOOL: Abington (Pa.).
COLLEGE: Notre Dame (degree in computer science).
TRANSACTIONS/CAREER NOTES: Selected by Miami Dolphins in sixth round (189th pick overall) of 1996 NFL draft. ... Signed by Dolphins (July 10, 1996). ... On injured reserve with knee injury (September 15, 1998-remainder of season). ... Granted free agency (February 12, 1999). ... Re-signed by Dolphins (April 23, 1999).
PRO STATISTICS: 1996—Recovered two fumbles. 1997—Fumbled once and recovered two fumbles.

			INTERCEPTIONS			
Year Team	G	GS	No.	Yds.	Avg.	TD
1996—Miami NFL	16	11	2	15	7.5	0
1997—Miami NFL	16	15	2	10	5.0	0
1998—Miami NFL	2	1	0	0	...	0
Pro totals (3 years)	34	27	4	25	6.3	0

WOODEN, TERRY — LB

PERSONAL: Born January 14, 1967, in Hartford, Conn. ... 6-3/239. ... Full name: Terrence Tylon Wooden.
HIGH SCHOOL: Farmington (Conn.).
COLLEGE: Syracuse (degree in sociology).

TRANSACTIONS/CAREER NOTES: Selected by Seattle Seahawks in second round (29th pick overall) of 1990 NFL draft. ... Signed by Seahawks (July 27, 1990). ... On injured reserve with knee injury (November 10, 1990-remainder of season). ... On injured reserve with knee injury (October 28, 1992-remainder of season). ... Granted free agency (March 1, 1993). ... Re-signed by Seahawks (August 25, 1993). ... Granted unconditional free agency (February 14, 1997). ... Signed by Kansas City Chiefs (April 21, 1997). ... Released by Chiefs (August 30, 1998). ... Signed by Oakland Raiders (September 1, 1998). ... Released by Raiders (February 17, 1999).

PRO STATISTICS: 1991—Recovered four fumbles for five yards. 1993—Recovered one fumble. 1994—Recovered two fumbles. 1995—Recovered one fumble for 20 yards. 1996—Recovered two fumbles. 1997—Recovered one fumble. 1998—Recovered one fumble.

				INTERCEPTIONS				SACKS
Year Team		G	GS	No.	Yds.	Avg.	TD	No.
1990—Seattle NFL		8	8	0	0	...	0	0.0
1991—Seattle NFL		16	15	0	0	...	0	2.0
1992—Seattle NFL		8	8	1	3	3.0	0	0.0
1993—Seattle NFL		16	16	0	0	...	0	2.5
1994—Seattle NFL		16	15	3	78	26.0	1	1.5
1995—Seattle NFL		16	16	1	9	9.0	0	0.0
1996—Seattle NFL		9	9	1	13	13.0	0	0.0
1997—Kansas City NFL		15	8	0	0	...	0	2.0
1998—Oakland NFL		16	10	1	14	14.0	0	2.0
Pro totals (9 years)		120	105	7	117	16.7	1	10.0

WOODS, JEROME — S — CHIEFS

PERSONAL: Born March 17, 1973, in Memphis, Tenn. ... 6-2/207.
HIGH SCHOOL: Melrose (Memphis, Tenn.).
JUNIOR COLLEGE: Northeast Mississippi Community College.
COLLEGE: Memphis.
TRANSACTIONS/CAREER NOTES: Selected by Kansas City Chiefs in first round (28th pick overall) of 1996 NFL draft. ... Signed by Chiefs (August 12, 1996).
PRO STATISTICS: 1996—Fumbled once and recovered one fumble. 1997—Credited with one sack and recovered two fumbles for 13 yards.

				INTERCEPTIONS			
Year Team		G	GS	No.	Yds.	Avg.	TD
1996—Kansas City NFL		16	0	0	0	...	0
1997—Kansas City NFL		16	16	4	57	14.3	0
1998—Kansas City NFL		16	16	2	47	23.5	0
Pro totals (3 years)		48	32	6	104	17.3	0

WOODSON, CHARLES — DB — RAIDERS

PERSONAL: Born October 7, 1976, in Fremont, Ohio ... 6-0/200.
HIGH SCHOOL: Ross (Fremont, Ohio).
COLLEGE: Michigan.
TRANSACTIONS/CAREER NOTES: Selected after junior season by Oakland Raiders in first round (fourth pick overall) of 1998 NFL draft. ... Signed by Raiders (July 20, 1998).
HONORS: Named cornerback on THE SPORTING NEWS college All-America second team (1996). ... Heisman Trophy winner (1997). ... Jim Thorpe Award winner (1997). ... Maxwell Award winner (1997). ... Named College Football Player of the Year by The Sporting News (1997). ... Named cornerback on THE SPORTING NEWS college All-America first team (1997). ... Played in Pro Bowl (1998 season).

				INTERCEPTIONS			
Year Team		G	GS	No.	Yds.	Avg.	TD
1998—Oakland NFL		16	16	5	118	23.6	1

WOODSON, DARREN — S — COWBOYS

PERSONAL: Born April 25, 1969, in Phoenix. ... 6-1/219. ... Full name: Darren Ray Woodson.
HIGH SCHOOL: Maryvale (Phoenix).
COLLEGE: Arizona State (degree in criminal justice).
TRANSACTIONS/CAREER NOTES: Selected by Dallas Cowboys in second round (37th pick overall) of 1992 NFL draft. ... Signed by Cowboys (April 26, 1992).
CHAMPIONSHIP GAME EXPERIENCE: Played in NFC championship game (1992-1995 seasons). ... Member of Super Bowl championship team (1992, 1993 and 1995 seasons).
HONORS: Named strong safety on THE SPORTING NEWS NFL All-Pro team (1994-1996 and 1998). ... Played in Pro Bowl (1994-1996 and 1998 seasons). ... Named to play in Pro Bowl (1997 season); replaced by John Lynch due to injury.
PRO STATISTICS: 1993—Recovered three fumbles for three yards. 1994—Recovered one fumble. 1996—Fumbled once and recovered one fumble. 1997—Fumbled once and recovered two fumbles.

				INTERCEPTIONS				SACKS
Year Team		G	GS	No.	Yds.	Avg.	TD	No.
1992—Dallas NFL		16	2	0	0	...	0	1.0
1993—Dallas NFL		16	15	0	0	...	0	0.0
1994—Dallas NFL		16	16	5	140	28.0	1	0.0
1995—Dallas NFL		16	16	2	46	23.0	1	0.0
1996—Dallas NFL		16	16	5	43	8.6	0	3.0
1997—Dallas NFL		14	14	1	14	14.0	0	2.0
1998—Dallas NFL		16	15	1	1	1.0	0	3.0
Pro totals (7 years)		110	94	14	244	17.4	2	9.0

WOODSON, ROD — CB — RAVENS

PERSONAL: Born March 10, 1965, in Fort Wayne, Ind. ... 6-0/200. ... Full name: Roderick Kevin Woodson.
HIGH SCHOOL: R. Nelson Snider (Fort Wayne, Ind.).
COLLEGE: Purdue.
TRANSACTIONS/CAREER NOTES: Selected by Pittsburgh Steelers in first round (10th pick overall) of 1987 NFL draft. ... On reserve/unsigned list (August 31-October 27, 1987). ... Signed by Steelers (October 28, 1987). ... Granted roster exemption (October 28-November 7, 1987). ... Granted free agency (February 1, 1991). ... Re-signed by Steelers (August 22, 1991). ... Granted unconditional free agency (February 14, 1997). ... Signed by San Francisco 49ers (July 17, 1997). ... Released by 49ers (February 9, 1998). ... Signed by Baltimore Ravens (February 20, 1998).
CHAMPIONSHIP GAME EXPERIENCE: Played in AFC championship game (1994 season). ... Member of Steelers for AFC championship game (1995 season); inactive. ... Played in Super Bowl XXX (1995 season). ... Played in NFC championship game (1997 season).
HONORS: Named defensive back on The Sporting News college All-America second team (1985). ... Named kick returner on The Sporting News college All-America first team (1986). ... Named kick returner on The Sporting News NFL All-Pro team (1989). ... Played in Pro Bowl (1989-1994 and 1996 seasons). ... Named cornerback on The Sporting News NFL All-Pro team (1990 and 1992-1994).
PRO STATISTICS: 1987—Recovered two fumbles. 1988— Recovered three fumbles for two yards. 1989— Recovered four fumbles for one yard. 1990— Recovered three fumbles. 1991— Recovered three fumbles for 15 yards. 1992—Recovered one fumble for nine yards. 1993— Rushed once for no yards and recovered one fumble. 1994—Recovered one fumble. 1996—Recovered three fumbles for 42 yards and a touchdown. 1997—Recovered one fumble.
MISCELLANEOUS: Active AFC leader for career interceptions (47).

			INTERCEPTIONS				SACKS	PUNT RETURNS				KICKOFF RETURNS				TOTALS			
Year Team	G	GS	No.	Yds.	Avg.	TD	No.	No.	Yds.	Avg.	TD	No.	Yds.	Avg.	TD	TD	2pt.	Pts.	Fum.
1987—Pittsburgh NFL	8	0	1	45	45.0	1	0.0	16	135	8.4	0	13	290	22.3	0	1	...	6	3
1988—Pittsburgh NFL	16	16	4	98	24.5	0	0.5	33	281	8.5	0	37	850	23.0	†1	1	...	6	3
1989—Pittsburgh NFL	15	14	3	39	13.0	0	0.0	29	207	7.1	0	§36	§982	*27.3	†1	1	...	6	3
1990—Pittsburgh NFL	16	16	5	67	13.4	0	0.0	§38	§398	10.5	†1	35	764	21.8	0	1	...	6	3
1991—Pittsburgh NFL	15	15	3	72	24.0	0	1.0	28	320	§11.4	0	*44	§880	20.0	0	0	...	0	3
1992—Pittsburgh NFL	16	16	4	90	22.5	0	6.0	32	364	§11.4	1	25	469	18.8	0	1	...	6	2
1993—Pittsburgh NFL	16	16	8	§138	17.3	▲1	2.0	42	338	8.0	0	15	294	19.6	0	1	...	6	2
1994—Pittsburgh NFL	15	15	4	109	27.3	0	3.0	39	319	8.2	0	15	365	24.3	0	2	0	12	2
1995—Pittsburgh NFL	1	1	0	0	...	0	0.0	0	0	...	0	0	0	...	0	0	0	0	0
1996—Pittsburgh NFL	16	16	6	121	20.2	1	1.0	0	0	...	0	0	0	...	0	2	0	12	1
1997—San Francisco NFL	14	14	3	81	27.0	0	0.0	1	0	0.0	0	0	0	...	0	0	0	0	0
1998—Baltimore NFL	16	16	6	108	18.0	▲2	0.0	0	0	...	0	0	0	...	0	2	0	12	0
Pro totals (12 years)	164	155	47	968	20.6	7	13.5	258	2362	9.2	2	220	4894	22.2	2	12	0	72	22

WOOTEN, TITO — S — GIANTS

PERSONAL: Born December 12, 1971, in Goldsboro, N.C. ... 6-0/195.
HIGH SCHOOL: Goldsboro (N.C.).
COLLEGE: North Carolina, then Northeast Louisiana.
TRANSACTIONS/CAREER NOTES: Selected by New York Giants in fourth round of 1994 NFL supplemental draft. ... Signed by Giants (July 22, 1994). ... Granted free agency (February 14, 1997). ... Re-signed by Giants for 1997 season. ... Granted unconditional free agency (February 13, 1998). ... Re-signed by Giants (February 13, 1998).
PRO STATISTICS: 1995—Recovered one fumble for one yard and a touchdown. 1996—Credited with a safety and recovered one fumble for 54 yards and a touchdown. 1997—Fumbled once and recovered one fumble. 1998—Credited with three sacks.

			INTERCEPTIONS			
Year Team	G	GS	No.	Yds.	Avg.	TD
1994—New York Giants NFL	16	2	0	0	...	0
1995—New York Giants NFL	16	3	1	38	38.0	0
1996—New York Giants NFL	13	12	1	35	35.0	0
1997—New York Giants NFL	16	16	5	‡146	‡29.2	1
1998—New York Giants NFL	14	13	0	0	...	0
Pro totals (5 years)	75	46	7	219	31.3	1

WORTHAM, BARRON — LB — TITANS

PERSONAL: Born November 1, 1969, in Fort Worth, Texas. ... 5-11/245. ... Full name: Barron Winfred Wortham.
HIGH SCHOOL: Everman (Texas).
COLLEGE: Texas-El Paso.
TRANSACTIONS/CAREER NOTES: Selected by Houston Oilers in sixth round (194th pick overall) of 1994 NFL draft. ... Signed by Oilers (July 12, 1994). ... Granted free agency (February 14, 1997). ... Oilers franchise moved to Tennessee for 1997 season. ... Re-signed by Oilers (July 9, 1997). ... Granted unconditional free agency (February 13, 1998). ... Re-signed by Oilers (February 23, 1998). ... Oilers franchise renamed Tennessee Titans for 1999 season (December 26, 1998).
HONORS: Named linebacker on The Sporting News college All-America second team (1993).
PRO STATISTICS: 1994—Recovered one fumble. 1995—Returned one kickoff for minus three yards. 1996—Recovered two fumbles.

Year Team	G	GS	SACKS
1994—Houston NFL	16	1	0.0
1995—Houston NFL	16	5	1.0
1996—Houston NFL	15	14	2.0
1997—Tennessee NFL	16	16	0.0
1998—Tennessee NFL	13	0	0.0
Pro totals (5 years)	76	36	3.0

W

WRIGHT, TOBY — S — RAMS

PERSONAL: Born November 19, 1970, in Phoenix. ... 5-11/212. ... Full name: Toby Lin Wright. ... Brother of Terry Wright, defensive back with Indianapolis Colts (1987-88) and Hamilton Tiger-Cats of CFL (1991-95).
HIGH SCHOOL: Dobson (Mesa, Ariz.).
JUNIOR COLLEGE: Phoenix College.
COLLEGE: Nebraska.
TRANSACTIONS/CAREER NOTES: Selected by Los Angeles Rams in second round (49th pick overall) of 1994 NFL draft. ... Signed by Rams (May 18, 1994). ... Rams franchise moved to St. Louis (April 12, 1995). ... On injured reserve with knee injury (November 30, 1998-remainder of season).
PRO STATISTICS: 1994—Recovered one fumble for 98 yards and a touchdown. 1995—Rushed once for nine yards, recovered one fumble for 73 yards and a touchdown. 1997—Recovered one fumble for 34 yards. 1998—Credited with one sack.

Year — Team	G	GS	No.	Yds.	Avg.	TD
1994—Los Angeles Rams NFL	16	2	0	0	...	0
1995—St. Louis NFL	16	16	6	79	13.2	0
1996—St. Louis NFL	12	12	1	19	19.0	1
1997—St. Louis NFL	11	11	0	0	...	0
1998—St. Louis NFL	3	3	0	0	...	0
Pro totals (5 years)	58	44	7	98	14.0	1

WUERFFEL, DANNY — QB — SAINTS

PERSONAL: Born May 27, 1974, in Fort Walton, Fla. ... 6-1/208. ... Full name: Daniel Carl Wuerffel.
HIGH SCHOOL: Fort Walton Beach (Fla.).
COLLEGE: Florida.
TRANSACTIONS/CAREER NOTES: Selected by New Orleans Saints in fourth round (99th pick overall) of 1997 NFL draft. ... Signed by Saints (July 17, 1997).
HONORS: Davey O'Brien Award winner (1995 and 1996). ... Heisman Trophy winner (1996). ... Named College Player of the Year by THE SPORTING NEWS (1996). ... Named quarterback on THE SPORTING NEWS college All-America first team (1996).
PRO STATISTICS: 1997—Fumbled twice and recovered two fumbles. 1998—Fumbled once and recovered one fumble.
SINGLE GAME HIGHS (regular season): Attempts—47 (October 4, 1998, vs. New England); completions—25 (October 4, 1998, vs. New England); yards—278 (October 4, 1998, vs. New England); and touchdown passes—2 (October 4, 1998, vs. New England).
MISCELLANEOUS: Regular-season record as starting NFL quarterback: 2-4 (.333).

			PASSING							RUSHING				TOTALS		
Year — Team	G	GS	Att.	Cmp.	Pct.	Yds.	TD	Int.	Avg.	Rat.	Att.	Yds.	Avg.	TD	TD	2pt.	Pts.
1997—New Orleans NFL	7	2	91	42	46.2	518	4	8	5.69	42.3	6	26	4.3	0	0	0	0
1998—New Orleans NFL	5	4	119	62	52.1	695	5	5	5.84	66.3	11	60	5.5	0	0	0	0
Pro totals (2 years)	12	6	210	104	49.5	1213	9	13	5.78	55.7	17	86	5.1	0	0	0	0

WUNSCH, JERRY — OT — BUCCANEERS

PERSONAL: Born January 21, 1974, in Eau Claire, Wis. ... 6-6/334. ... Full name: Gerald Wunsch. ... Name pronounced WUNCH.
HIGH SCHOOL: West (Wausau, Wis.).
COLLEGE: Wisconsin (degree in history).
TRANSACTIONS/CAREER NOTES: Selected by Tampa Bay Buccaneers in second round (37th pick overall) of 1997 NFL draft. ... Signed by Buccaneers (July 18, 1997).
PLAYING EXPERIENCE: Tampa Bay NFL, 1997 and 1998. ... Games/Games started: 1997 (16/0), 1998 (16/1). Total: 32/1.
PRO STATISTICS: 1997—Recovered one fumble.

WYCHECK, FRANK — TE/RB — TITANS

PERSONAL: Born October 14, 1971, in Philadelphia. ... 6-3/250. ... Name pronounced WHY-check.
HIGH SCHOOL: Archbishop Ryan (Philadelphia).
COLLEGE: Maryland.
TRANSACTIONS/CAREER NOTES: Selected after junior season by Washington Redskins in sixth round (160th pick overall) of 1993 NFL draft. ... Signed by Redskins (July 15, 1993). ... On suspended list for anabolic steroid use (November 29, 1994-remainder of season). ... Released by Redskins (August 17, 1995). ... Signed by Houston Oilers (August 18, 1995). ... Granted free agency (February 16, 1996). ... Re-signed by Oilers (June 28, 1996). ... Oilers franchise moved to Tennessee for 1997 season. ... Oilers franchise renamed Tennessee Titans for 1999 season (December 26, 1998).
HONORS: Played in Pro Bowl (1998 season).
PRO STATISTICS: 1993—Recovered one fumble. 1995—Rushed once for one yard and a touchdown and recovered one fumble. 1996—Rushed twice for three yards. 1997—Recovered one fumble. 1998—Recovered two fumbles.
SINGLE GAME HIGHS (regular season): Receptions—10 (December 20, 1998, vs. Green Bay); yards—84 (October 18, 1998, vs. Cincinnati); and touchdown receptions—1 (November 1, 1998, vs. Pittsburgh).

			RECEIVING				KICKOFF RETURNS				TOTALS		
Year — Team	G	GS	No.	Yds.	Avg.	TD	No.	Yds.	Avg.	TD	2pt.	Pts.	Fum.
1993—Washington NFL	9	7	16	113	7.1	0	0	0	...	0	0	0	1
1994—Washington NFL	9	1	7	55	7.9	1	4	84	21.0	0	1	0	6	0
1995—Houston NFL	16	11	40	471	11.8	1	0	0	...	0	2	0	12	0
1996—Houston NFL	16	16	53	511	9.6	6	2	5	2.5	0	6	0	36	2
1997—Tennessee NFL	16	16	63	748	11.9	4	1	3	3.0	0	4	1	26	0
1998—Tennessee NFL	16	16	70	768	11.0	2	1	10	10.0	0	2	0	12	2
Pro totals (6 years)	82	67	249	2666	10.7	14	8	102	12.8	0	15	1	92	5

WYNN, RENALDO — DT/DE — JAGUARS

PERSONAL: Born September 3, 1974, in Chicago. ... 6-3/290. ... Full name: Renaldo Levalle Wynn.
HIGH SCHOOL: De La Salle Institute (Chicago).
COLLEGE: Notre Dame (degree in sociology, 1996).
TRANSACTIONS/CAREER NOTES: Selected by Jacksonville Jaguars in first round (21st pick overall) of 1997 NFL draft. ... Signed by Jaguars (July 21, 1997). ... On injured reserve with groin injury (December 25, 1998-remainder of season).
PRO STATISTICS: 1997—Recovered one fumble. 1998—Recovered one fumble.

Year Team	G	GS	SACKS
1997—Jacksonville NFL	16	8	2.5
1998—Jacksonville NFL	15	15	1.0
Pro totals (2 years)	31	23	3.5

YARBOROUGH, RYAN — WR

PERSONAL: Born April 26, 1971, in Baltimore. ... 6-2/195. ... Full name: Ryan Kenneth Yarborough.
HIGH SCHOOL: Rich East (Park Forest, Ill.).
COLLEGE: Wyoming.
TRANSACTIONS/CAREER NOTES: Selected by New York Jets in second round (41st pick overall) of 1994 NFL draft. ... Signed by Jets (June 21, 1994). ... Traded by Jets to Green Bay Packers for conditional pick in 1997 draft (July 26, 1996). ... Claimed on waivers by Baltimore Ravens (July 15, 1997). ... Released by Ravens (November 2, 1998).
HONORS: Named wide receiver on THE SPORTING NEWS college All-America second team (1993).
SINGLE GAME HIGHS (regular season): Receptions—6 (December 10, 1995, vs. New England); yards—105 (December 10, 1995, vs. New England); and touchdown receptions—2 (December 10, 1995, vs. New England).
STATISTICAL PLATEAUS: 100-yard receiving games: 1995 (1).

			RECEIVING				TOTALS			
Year Team	G	GS	No.	Yds.	Avg.	TD	TD	2pt.	Pts.	Fum.
1994—New York Jets NFL	13	0	6	42	7.0	1	1	0	6	0
1995—New York Jets NFL	16	2	18	230	12.8	2	2	0	12	0
1997—Baltimore NFL	16	3	16	183	11.4	0	0	0	0	3
1998—Baltimore NFL	6	1	4	39	9.8	0	0	0	0	0
Pro totals (4 years)	51	6	44	494	11.2	3	3	0	18	3

YOUNG, BRYANT — DT — 49ERS

PERSONAL: Born January 27, 1972, in Chicago Heights, Ill. ... 6-3/291. ... Full name: Bryant Colby Young.
HIGH SCHOOL: Bloom (Chicago Heights, Ill.).
COLLEGE: Notre Dame.
TRANSACTIONS/CAREER NOTES: Selected by San Francisco 49ers in first round (seventh pick overall) of 1994 NFL draft. ... Signed by 49ers (July 26, 1994). ... On injured reserve with broken leg (December 2, 1998-remainder of season).
CHAMPIONSHIP GAME EXPERIENCE: Played in NFC championship game (1994 and 1997 seasons). ... Member of Super Bowl championship team (1994 season).
HONORS: Named defensive tackle on THE SPORTING NEWS NFL All-Pro team (1996 and 1998). ... Played in Pro Bowl (1996 season).
PRO STATISTICS: 1994—Recovered one fumble. 1995—Recovered two fumbles. 1996—Recovered one fumble for 43 yards. 1998—Recovered one fumble.

Year Team	G	GS	SACKS
1994—San Francisco NFL	16	16	6.0
1995—San Francisco NFL	12	12	6.0
1996—San Francisco NFL	16	16	11.5
1997—San Francisco NFL	12	12	4.0
1998—San Francisco NFL	12	12	9.5
Pro totals (5 years)	68	68	37.0

YOUNG, DUANE — TE

PERSONAL: Born May 29, 1968, in Kalamazoo, Mich. ... 6-3/270. ... Full name: Curtis Duane Young.
HIGH SCHOOL: Kalamazoo (Mich.) Central.
COLLEGE: Michigan State (degree in elementary education).
TRANSACTIONS/CAREER NOTES: Selected by San Diego Chargers in fifth round (123rd pick overall) of 1991 NFL draft. ... Signed by Chargers (July 15, 1991). ... On injured reserve with ankle injury (August 27-November 9, 1991). ... Granted free agency (February 17, 1994). ... Re-signed by Chargers (April 7, 1994). ... Released by Chargers (February 29, 1996). ... Signed by Arizona Cardinals (August 7, 1996). ... Released by Cardinals (August 25, 1996). ... Out of pro football (1996-97). ... Signed by Buffalo Bills (March 30, 1998). ... Released by Bills (December 16, 1998).
CHAMPIONSHIP GAME EXPERIENCE: Played in AFC championship game (1994 season). ... Played in Super Bowl XXIX (1994 season).
SINGLE GAME HIGHS (regular season): Receptions—4 (November 20, 1994, vs. New England); yards—69 (November 20, 1994, vs. New England); and touchdown receptions—1 (November 13, 1994, vs. Kansas City).

			RECEIVING				TOTALS			
Year Team	G	GS	No.	Yds.	Avg.	TD	TD	2pt.	Pts.	Fum.
1991—San Diego NFL	7	5	2	12	6.0	0	0	...	0	0
1992—San Diego NFL	16	14	4	45	11.3	0	0	...	0	0
1993—San Diego NFL	16	15	6	41	6.8	2	2	...	12	0
1994—San Diego NFL	14	14	17	217	12.8	1	1	0	6	0
1995—San Diego NFL	16	16	9	90	10.0	0	0	0	0	0
1996—						Did not play.				
1997—						Did not play.				
1998—Buffalo NFL	4	0	0	0	...	0	0	0	0	0
Pro totals (4 years)	73	64	38	405	10.7	3	3	0	18	0

YOUNG, FLOYD   CB   BUCCANEERS

PERSONAL: Born November 23, 1975, in New Orleans. ... 6-0/178. ... Full name: Floyd Alexander Young.
HIGH SCHOOL: Clark (New Orleans).
JUNIOR COLLEGE: Scottsdale (Ariz.) Community College.
COLLEGE: Texas A&M-Kingsville.
TRANSACTIONS/CAREER NOTES: Signed as non-drafted free agent by Tampa Bay Buccaneers (May 5, 1997). ... Released by Buccaneers (July 18, 1997). ... Re-signed by Buccaneers (July 22, 1997). ... Released by Buccaneers (August 17, 1997). ... Re-signed by Buccaneers to practice squad (August 26, 1997). ... Activated (September 27, 1997).
PLAYING EXPERIENCE: Tampa Bay NFL, 1997 and 1998. ... Games/Games started: 1997 (12/1), 1998 (11/0). Total: 23/1.
PRO STATISTICS: 1998—Recovered one fumble.

YOUNG, RODNEY   S

PERSONAL: Born January 25, 1973, in Grambling, La. ... 6-1/210. ... Full name: Rodney Menard Young. ... Son of Willie Young, offensive tackle with New York Giants (1966-75).
HIGH SCHOOL: Ruston (La.).
COLLEGE: Louisiana State.
TRANSACTIONS/CAREER NOTES: Selected by New York Giants in third round (85th pick overall) of 1995 NFL draft. ... Signed by Giants (July 25, 1995). ... Granted free agency (February 13, 1998). ... Re-signed by Giants (March 11, 1998). ... Released by Giants (August 30, 1998). ... Re-signed by Giants (September 30, 1998). ... On injured reserve with back injury (November 13, 1998-remainder of season). ... Granted unconditional free agency (February 12, 1999).
PLAYING EXPERIENCE: New York Giants NFL, 1995-1998. ... Games/Games started: 1995 (10/0), 1996 (12/0), 1997 (9/0), 1998 (2/0). Total: 33/0.
PRO STATISTICS: 1995—Returned one punt for no yards and fumbled once.

YOUNG, STEVE   QB   49ERS

PERSONAL: Born October 11, 1961, in Salt Lake City. ... 6-2/205. ... Full name: Jon Steven Young.
HIGH SCHOOL: Greenwich (Conn.).
COLLEGE: Brigham Young (degree in law, 1994).
TRANSACTIONS/CAREER NOTES: Selected by Los Angeles Express in first round (10th pick overall) of 1984 USFL draft. ... Signed by Express (March 5, 1984). ... Granted roster exemption (March 5-30, 1984). ... Selected by Tampa Bay Buccaneers in first round (first pick overall) of 1984 NFL supplemental draft. ... On developmental squad (March 31-April 16, 1985). ... Released by Express (September 9, 1985). ... Signed by Buccaneers (September 10, 1985). ... Granted roster exemption (September 10-23, 1985). ... Traded by Buccaneers to San Francisco 49ers for second-round (LB Winston Moss) and fourth-round (WR Bruce Hill) picks in 1987 draft and cash (April 24, 1987). ... Granted free agency (February 1, 1991). ... Re-signed by 49ers (May 3, 1991). ... Designated by 49ers as franchise player (February 25, 1993).
CHAMPIONSHIP GAME EXPERIENCE: Played in NFC championship game (1988-1990, 1992-1994 and 1997 seasons). ... Member of 49ers for Super Bowl XXIII (1988 season); did not play. ... Member of Super Bowl championship team (1989 and 1994 seasons).
HONORS: Davey O'Brien Award winner (1983). ... Named quarterback on THE SPORTING NEWS college All-America first team (1983). ... Named NFL Player of the Year by THE SPORTING NEWS (1992 and 1994). ... Named quarterback on THE SPORTING NEWS NFL All-Pro team (1992, 1994 and 1998). ... Played in Pro Bowl (1992-1995, 1997 and 1998 seasons). ... Named Most Valuable Player of Super Bowl XXIX (1994 season). ... Named to play in Pro Bowl (1996 season); replaced by Kerry Collins due to injury.
RECORDS: Holds NFL career records for highest completion percentage—64.5; highest passer rating—97.6; most seasons leading league in touchdown passes—4; and most consecutive seasons leading league in passer rating—4 (1991-1994). ... Holds NFL record for most consecutive games with 300 or more yards passing—6 (September 6-October 18, 1998). ... Holds NFL single-season record for highest passer rating—112.8 (1994).
POST SEASON RECORDS: Holds Super Bowl single-game record for most touchdown passes—6 (January 29, 1995, vs. San Diego). ... Shares Super Bowl single-game record for most passes attempted without an interception—36 (January 29, 1995, vs. San Diego). ... Shares NFL postseason single-game record for most touchdown passes—6 (January 29, 1995, vs. San Diego).
PRO STATISTICS: USFL: 1984—Fumbled seven times and recovered four fumbles. 1985—Fumbled seven times and recovered one fumble for minus 11 yards. NFL: 1985—Fumbled four times and recovered one fumble for minus one yard. 1986—Fumbled 11 times and recovered four fumbles for minus 24 yards. 1988—Fumbled five times and recovered two fumbles for minus 10 yards. 1989—Fumbled twice and recovered one fumble. 1990—Fumbled once. 1991—Fumbled three times and recovered one fumble for minus six yards. 1992—Fumbled nine times and recovered three fumbles for minus 13 yards. 1993—Caught two passes for two yards, fumbled eight times and recovered two fumbles for minus four yards. 1994—Fumbled four times and recovered one fumble for minus four yards. 1995—Fumbled three times. 1996—Fumbled three times and recovered one fumble. 1997—Fumbled four times and recovered two fumbles for minus 11 yards. 1998—Fumbled nine times and recovered one fumble.
SINGLE GAME HIGHS (regular season): Attempts—51 (October 18, 1998, vs. Indianapolis); completions—33 (October 18, 1998, vs. Indianapolis); yards—462 (November 28, 1993, vs. Los Angeles Rams); and touchdown passes—4 (November 22, 1998, vs. New Orleans).
STATISTICAL PLATEAUS: USFL: 300-yard passing games: 1984 (2). ... 100-yard rushing games: 1984 (1), 1985 (1). Total: 2. ... NFL: 300-yard passing games: 1991 (3), 1992 (3), 1993 (3), 1994 (5), 1995 (5). Total: 19. ... 100-yard rushing games: 1990 (1).
MISCELLANEOUS: Active NFC leader for career passing yards (32,678); and career touchdown passes (229). ... Regular-season record as starting NFL quarterback: 92-48 (.657). ... Postseason record as starting NFL quarterback: 8-6 (.571).

				PASSING							RUSHING				TOTALS		
Year Team	G	GS	Att.	Cmp.	Pct.	Yds.	TD	Int.	Avg.	Rat.	Att.	Yds.	Avg.	TD	TD	2pt.	Pts.
1984—Los Angeles USFL	12	12	310	179	57.7	2361	10	9	7.62	80.6	79	515	6.5	7	7	3	48
1985—Los Angeles USFL	13	...	250	137	54.8	1741	6	13	6.96	63.1	56	368	6.6	2	2	0	12
—Tampa Bay NFL	5	5	138	72	52.2	935	3	8	6.78	56.9	40	233	5.8	1	1	...	6
1986—Tampa Bay NFL	14	14	363	195	53.7	2282	8	13	6.29	65.7	74	425	5.7	5	5	...	30
1987—San Francisco NFL	8	3	69	37	53.6	570	10	0	8.26	120.8	26	190	7.3	1	1	...	6
1988—San Francisco NFL	11	3	101	54	53.5	680	3	3	6.73	72.2	27	184	6.8	1	1	...	6
1989—San Francisco NFL	10	3	92	64	69.6	1001	8	3	10.88	120.8	38	126	3.3	2	2	...	12
1990—San Francisco NFL	6	1	62	38	61.3	427	2	0	6.88	92.6	15	159	10.6	0	0	...	0
1991—San Francisco NFL	11	10	279	180	64.5	2517	17	8	*9.02	*101.8	66	415	6.3	4	4	...	24
1992—San Francisco NFL	16	16	402	268	*66.7	‡3465	*25	7	*8.62	*107.0	76	537	7.1	4	4	...	24
1993—San Francisco NFL	16	16	462	314	68.0	‡4023	*29	16	*8.71	*101.5	69	407	5.9	2	2	...	12

Year	Team	G	GS	Att.	Cmp.	Pct.	Yds.	TD	Int.	Avg.	Rat.	Att.	Yds.	Avg.	TD	TD	2pt.	Pts.
1994	San Francisco NFL	16	16	461	324	*70.3	3969	*35	10	*8.61	*112.8	58	293	5.1	7	7	0	42
1995	San Francisco NFL	11	11	447	299	*66.9	3200	20	11	7.16	92.3	50	250	5.0	3	3	0	18
1996	San Francisco NFL	12	12	316	214	*67.7	2410	14	6	‡7.63	*97.2	52	310	6.0	4	4	1	26
1997	San Francisco NFL	15	15	356	241	*67.7	3029	19	6	*8.51	*104.7	50	199	4.0	3	3	0	18
1998	San Francisco NFL	15	15	517	322	62.3	4170	*36	12	8.07	101.1	70	454	6.5	6	6	0	36
USFL totals (2 years)		25	...	560	316	56.4	4102	16	22	7.33	72.8	135	883	6.5	9	9	3	60
NFL totals (14 years)		166	140	4065	2622	64.5	32678	229	103	8.04	97.6	711	4182	5.9	43	43	1	260
Pro totals (16 years)		191	...	4625	2938	63.5	36780	245	125	7.95	94.6	846	5065	6.0	52	52	4	320

ZEIER, ERIC — QB — BUCCANEERS

PERSONAL: Born September 6, 1972, in Pensacola, Fla. ... 6-1/205. ... Full name: Eric Royce Zeier. ... Name pronounced ZY-er.
HIGH SCHOOL: Heidelberg (West Germany), then Marietta (Ga.).
COLLEGE: Georgia.
TRANSACTIONS/CAREER NOTES: Selected by Cleveland Browns in third round (84th pick overall) of 1995 NFL draft. ... Signed by Browns (July 14, 1995). ... Browns franchise moved to Baltimore and renamed Ravens for 1996 season (March 11, 1996). ... Granted free agency (February 13, 1998). ... Tendered offer sheet by Atlanta Falcons (March 5, 1998). ... Offer matched by Ravens (March 10, 1998). ... Traded by Ravens to Tampa Bay Buccaneers for sixth-round pick (traded to Minnesota) in 1999 draft (April 17, 1999).
HONORS: Named quarterback on THE SPORTING NEWS college All-America second team (1994).
PRO STATISTICS: 1995—Fumbled three times. 1996—Fumbled twice and recovered one fumble. 1997—Fumbled three times for minus 14 yards. 1998—Fumbled twice and recovered one fumble.
SINGLE GAME HIGHS (regular season): Attempts—54 (November 5, 1995, vs. Houston); completions—28 (December 21, 1997, vs. Cincinnati); yards—349 (December 21, 1997, vs. Cincinnati); and touchdown passes—3 (December 14, 1997, vs. Tennessee).
STATISTICAL PLATEAUS: 300-yard passing games: 1995 (1), 1997 (2). Total: 3.
MISCELLANEOUS: Regular-season record as starting NFL quarterback: 4-7 (.364).

Year	Team	G	GS	Att.	Cmp.	Pct.	Yds.	TD	Int.	Avg.	Rat.	Att.	Yds.	Avg.	TD	TD	2pt.	Pts.
1995	Cleveland NFL	7	4	161	82	50.9	864	4	9	5.37	51.9	15	80	5.3	0	0	1	2
1996	Baltimore NFL	1	0	21	10	47.6	97	1	1	4.62	57.0	2	8	4.0	0	0	0	0
1997	Baltimore NFL	5	3	116	67	57.8	958	7	1	8.26	101.1	10	17	1.7	0	0	0	0
1998	Baltimore NFL	10	4	181	107	59.1	1312	4	3	7.25	82.0	11	17	1.5	0	0	0	0
Pro totals (4 years)		23	11	479	266	55.5	3231	16	14	6.75	75.4	38	122	3.2	0	0	1	2

ZEIGLER, DUSTY — C/G — BILLS

PERSONAL: Born September 27, 1973, in Savannah, Ga. ... 6-5/298. ... Full name: Curtis Dustin Zeigler.
HIGH SCHOOL: Effingham County (Springfield, Ga.).
COLLEGE: Notre Dame.
TRANSACTIONS/CAREER NOTES: Selected by Buffalo Bills in sixth round (202nd pick overall) of 1996 NFL draft. ... Signed by Bills (June 25, 1996). ... Granted free agency (February 12, 1999). ... Re-signed by Bills (April 15, 1999).
PLAYING EXPERIENCE: Buffalo NFL, 1996-1998. ... Games/Games started: 1996 (2/0), 1997 (13/13), 1998 (16/16). Total: 31/29.
PRO STATISTICS: 1997—Fumbled once and recovered one fumble for minus 12 yards. 1998—Fumbled three times for minus 19 yards.

ZELLARS, RAY — RB

PERSONAL: Born March 25, 1973, in Pittsburgh. ... 5-11/233. ... Full name: Raymond Mark Zellars.
HIGH SCHOOL: David B. Oliver (Pittsburgh).
COLLEGE: Notre Dame (degree in management).
TRANSACTIONS/CAREER NOTES: Selected by New Orleans Saints in second round (44th pick overall) of 1995 NFL draft. ... Signed by Saints (July 19, 1995). ... On injured reserve with neck injury (December 19, 1996-remainder of season). ... On physically unable to perform list with hamstring injury (July 18-August 1997). ... Claimed on waivers by Cincinnati Bengals (December 9, 1998). ... Active for two games with Bengals (1998); did not play. ... Granted unconditional free agency (February 12, 1999).
PRO STATISTICS: 1997—Recovered two fumbles.
SINGLE GAME HIGHS (regular season): Attempts—20 (November 3, 1996, vs. San Francisco); yards—174 (October 13, 1996, vs. Chicago); rushing touchdowns—2 (November 16, 1997, vs. Seattle).
STATISTICAL PLATEAUS: 100-yard rushing games: 1996 (1).

Year	Team	G	GS	Att.	Yds.	Avg.	TD	No.	Yds.	Avg.	TD	TD	2pt.	Pts.	Fum.
1995	New Orleans NFL	12	0	50	162	3.2	2	7	33	4.7	0	2	0	12	1
1996	New Orleans NFL	9	6	120	475	4.0	4	9	45	5.0	0	4	0	24	2
1997	New Orleans NFL	16	16	156	552	3.5	4	31	263	8.5	0	4	0	24	6
1998	New Orleans NFL	11	7	56	162	2.9	1	10	50	5.0	0	1	0	6	2
Pro totals (4 years)		48	29	382	1351	3.5	11	57	391	6.9	0	11	0	66	11

ZGONINA, JEFF — DT — RAMS

PERSONAL: Born May 24, 1970, in Chicago. ... 6-2/300. ... Full name: Jeffrey Marc Zgonina. ... Name pronounced skah-NEE-nah.
HIGH SCHOOL: Mt. Carmel (Chicago).
COLLEGE: Purdue (degree in community health promotion, 1992).
TRANSACTIONS/CAREER NOTES: Selected by Pittsburgh Steelers in seventh round (185th pick overall) of 1993 NFL draft. ... Signed by Steelers (July 16, 1993). ... Claimed on waivers by Carolina Panthers (August 28, 1995). ... Granted free agency (February 16, 1996). ... Re-signed by Panthers (April 11, 1996). ... Released by Panthers (August 19, 1996). ... Signed by Atlanta Falcons (October 8, 1996). ... Granted

– 443 –

unconditional free agency (February 14, 1997). ... Signed by St. Louis Rams (March 17, 1997). ... Released by Rams (August 30, 1998). ... Signed by Oakland Raiders (October 13, 1998). ... Released by Raiders (October 18, 1998). ... Signed by Indianapolis Colts (November 25, 1998). ... Granted unconditional free agency (February 12, 1999). ... Signed by Rams (April 5, 1999).
PLAYING EXPERIENCE: Pittsburgh NFL, 1993 and 1994; Carolina NFL, 1995; Atlanta NFL, 1996; St. Louis NFL, 1997; Indianapolis NFL, 1998. ... Games/Games started: 1993 (5/0), 1994 (16/0), 1995 (2/0), 1996 (8/0), 1997 (15/0), 1998 (2/0). Total: 48/0.
CHAMPIONSHIP GAME EXPERIENCE: Played in AFC championship game (1994 season).
PRO STATISTICS: 1993—Recovered one fumble. 1994—Returned two kickoffs for eight yards, fumbled once and recovered one fumble. 1996—Credited with one sack and recovered one fumble. 1997—Returned one kickoff for five yards and credited with two sacks.

ZOLAK, SCOTT   QB   JETS

PERSONAL: Born December 13, 1967, in Pittsburgh. ... 6-5/230. ... Full name: Scott David Zolak.
HIGH SCHOOL: Ringgold (Monongahela, Pa.).
COLLEGE: Maryland (degree in business administration).
TRANSACTIONS/CAREER NOTES: Selected by New England Patriots in fourth round (84th pick overall) of 1991 NFL draft. ... Inactive for all 16 games (1991). ... On injured reserve with ankle injury (December 18, 1992-remainder of season). ... Granted free agency (February 17, 1994). ... Re-signed by Patriots (April 2, 1994). ... Granted unconditional free agency (February 12, 1999). ... Signed by New York Jets (April 27, 1999).
CHAMPIONSHIP GAME EXPERIENCE: Member of Patriots for AFC championship game (1996 season); inactive. ... Member of Patriots for Super Bowl XXXI (1996 season); inactive.
PRO STATISTICS: 1992—Fumbled five times and recovered three fumbles for minus 21 yards. 1995—Fumbled four times and recovered one fumble for minus two yards. 1998—Fumbled once.
SINGLE GAME HIGHS (regular season): Attempts—45 (October 1, 1995, vs. Atlanta); completions—24 (October 1, 1995, vs. Atlanta); yards—261 (November 15, 1992, vs. Indianapolis); and touchdown passes—2 (December 20, 1998, vs. San Francisco).
MISCELLANEOUS: Regular-season record as starting NFL quarterback: 3-4 (.429). ... Postseason record as starting NFL quarterback: 0-1.

				PASSING						RUSHING				TOTALS		
Year Team	G	GS	Att.	Cmp.	Pct.	Yds.	TD	Int.	Avg.	Rat.	Att.	Yds.	Avg.	TD	TD	2pt.	Pts.
1991—New England NFL							Did not play.										
1992—New England NFL	6	4	100	52	52.0	561	2	4	5.61	58.8	18	71	3.9	0	0	...	0
1993—New England NFL	3	0	2	0	0.0	0	0	0	...	39.6	1	0	0.0	0	0	...	0
1994—New England NFL	16	0	8	5	62.5	28	0	0	3.50	68.8	1	-1	-1.0	0	0	0	0
1995—New England NFL	16	1	49	28	57.1	282	1	0	5.76	80.5	4	19	4.8	0	0	0	0
1996—New England NFL	3	0	1	1	100.0	5	0	0	5.00	87.5	4	-3	-0.8	0	0	0	0
1997—New England NFL	4	0	9	6	66.7	67	2	0	7.44	128.2	3	-3	-1.0	0	0	0	0
1998—New England NFL	6	2	75	32	42.7	371	3	3	4.95	54.9	5	0	0.0	0	0	0	0
Pro totals (7 years)	54	7	244	124	50.8	1314	8	7	5.39	65.8	36	83	2.3	0	0	0	0

ZORDICH, MICHAEL   S

PERSONAL: Born October 12, 1963, in Youngstown, Ohio ... 6-1/212. ... Full name: Michael Edward Zordich.
HIGH SCHOOL: Chaney (Youngstown, Ohio).
COLLEGE: Penn State (degree in hotel, restaurant and institutional management, 1986).
TRANSACTIONS/CAREER NOTES: Selected by Baltimore Stars in 1986 USFL territorial draft. ... Selected by San Diego Chargers in ninth round (235th pick overall) of 1986 NFL draft. ... Signed by Chargers (June 24, 1986). ... Released by Chargers (August 22, 1986). ... Signed by New York Jets (April 9, 1987). ... Released by Jets (September 6, 1987). ... Re-signed by Jets (September 14, 1987). ... Granted unconditional free agency (February 1, 1989). ... Signed by Phoenix Cardinals (March 2, 1989). ... Granted free agency (February 1, 1991). ... Re-signed by Cardinals (July 22, 1991). ... Granted unconditional free agency (March 1, 1993). ... Re-signed by Cardinals (July 23, 1993). ... Granted unconditional free agency (February 17, 1994). ... Signed by Philadelphia Eagles (June 28, 1994). ... Granted unconditional free agency (February 12, 1999).
PRO STATISTICS: 1990—Recovered one fumble. 1991—Recovered three fumbles for 19 yards. 1994—Returned one kickoff for no yards and recovered three fumbles for five yards. 1995—Recovered two fumbles for 58 yards and one touchdown. 1997—Recovered one fumble for minus one yard. 1998—Recovered one fumble.

			INTERCEPTIONS				SACKS
Year Team	G	GS	No.	Yds.	Avg.	TD	No.
1987—New York Jets NFL	10	0	0	0	...	0	1.0
1988—New York Jets NFL	16	0	1	35	35.0	1	0.0
1989—Phoenix NFL	16	6	1	16	16.0	∞1	1.0
1990—Phoenix NFL	16	1	1	25	25.0	0	0.0
1991—Phoenix NFL	16	16	1	27	27.0	0	0.0
1992—Phoenix NFL	16	16	3	37	12.3	0	0.0
1993—Phoenix NFL	16	9	1	0	0.0	0	0.0
1994—Philadelphia NFL	16	16	4	39	9.8	1	1.0
1995—Philadelphia NFL	15	15	1	10	10.0	0	1.0
1996—Philadelphia NFL	16	16	4	54	13.5	0	0.0
1997—Philadelphia NFL	16	16	1	21	21.0	0	2.0
1998—Philadelphia NFL	16	16	2	18	9.0	0	0.0
Pro totals (12 years)	185	127	20	282	14.1	3	6.0

1999 DRAFT PICKS

ABDULLAH, RAHIM — LB — BROWNS

PERSONAL: Born March 22, 1976, in Jacksonville. ... 6-5/233. ... Full name: Rahim Fahim Abdullah.
HIGH SCHOOL: Fletcher (Jacksonville).
COLLEGE: Clemson.
TRANSACTIONS/CAREER NOTES: Selected after junior season by Cleveland Browns in second round (45th pick overall) of 1999 NFL draft.
COLLEGE NOTES: Recovered one fumble for 74 yards and a touchdown (1997).

			INTERCEPTIONS			SACKS
Year Team	G	No.	Yds.	Avg.	TD	No.
1995—Clemson			Redshirted.			
1996—Clemson	11	1	4	4.0	1	6.0
1997—Clemson	12	1	63	63.0	1	3.0
1998—Clemson	11	0	0	...	0	7.5
College totals (3 years)	34	2	67	33.5	2	16.5

AKINS, CHRIS — S — PACKERS

PERSONAL: Born November 29, 1976, in Little Rock, Ark. ... 5-11/194.
HIGH SCHOOL: Little Rock (Ark.) Hall.
COLLEGE: Arkansas, then Arkansas-Pine Bluff.
TRANSACTIONS/CAREER NOTES: Selected by Green Bay Packers in seventh round (212th pick overall) of 1999 NFL draft.

		INTERCEPTIONS				KICKOFF RETURNS				TOTALS	
Year Team	G	No.	Yds.	Avg.	TD	No.	Yds.	Avg.	TD	TD	Pts.
1995—Arkansas	9	0	0	...	0	0	0	...	0	0	0
1996—Arkansas	8	1	30	30.0	0	0	0	...	0	0	0
1997—Arkansas-Pine Bluff	11	6	57	9.5	1	9	188	20.9	0	1	6
1998—Arkansas-Pine Bluff	11	5	150	30.0	2	1	19	19.0	0	2	12
College totals (4 years)	39	12	237	19.8	3	10	207	20.7	0	3	18

ALEXANDER, TIM — WR — REDSKINS

PERSONAL: Born October 14, 1974, in Elberton, Fla. ... 6-0/186. ... Full name: Timothy Roland Alexander.
HIGH SCHOOL: Riverview (Sarasota, Fla.).
COLLEGE: Oregon State.
TRANSACTIONS/CAREER NOTES: Selected by Washington Redskins in seventh round (217th pick overall) of 1999 NFL draft.
COLLEGE NOTES: Granted medical redshirt after two games (1994). ... Played quarterback (1994-97). ... Attempted four passes with two completions for 27 yards (1994); attempted 76 passes with 25 completions for 400 yards and four interceptions (1995); attempted 94 passes with 34 completions for 328 yards, two touchdowns and three interceptions (1996); attempted 327 passes with 157 completions for 1,745 yards, six touchdowns and 14 interceptions (1997); and attempted one pass without a completion (1998).

		RUSHING				RECEIVING				TOTALS	
Year Team	G	Att.	Yds.	Avg.	TD	No.	Yds.	Avg.	TD	TD	Pts.
1994—Oregon State	2	18	112	6.2	1	0	0	...	0	1	6
1995—Oregon State	8	109	439	4.0	3	0	0	...	0	3	18
1996—Oregon State	7	82	566	6.9	4	0	0	...	0	4	24
1997—Oregon State	11	127	288	2.3	2	3	45	15.0	0	2	12
1998—Oregon State	11	4	3	0.8	0	52	620	11.9	2	2	12
College totals (5 years)	39	340	1408	4.1	10	55	665	12.1	2	12	72

ARMOUR, JO JUAN — LB — RAIDERS

PERSONAL: Born July 10, 1976, in Toledo, Ohio. ... 5-11/219.
HIGH SCHOOL: Central Catholic (Toledo, Ohio).
COLLEGE: Miami (Ohio).
TRANSACTIONS/CAREER NOTES: Selected by Oakland Raiders in seventh round (224th pick overall) of 1999 NFL draft.
HONORS: Named outside linebacker on THE SPORTING NEWS college All-America second team (1997).
COLLEGE NOTES: Recovered one fumble for 14 yards and a touchdown (1997).

			INTERCEPTIONS			SACKS
Year Team	G	No.	Yds.	Avg.	TD	No.
1995—Miami of Ohio	5	2	3	1.5	0	7.0
1996—Miami of Ohio	11	0	0	0.0	0	7.0
1997—Miami of Ohio	11	2	7	3.5	0	7.0
1998—Miami of Ohio	11	0	0	0.0	0	4.0
College totals (4 years)	38	4	10	2.5	0	25.0

ATKINS, LARRY — S — CHIEFS

PERSONAL: Born July 21, 1975, in Santa Monica, Calif. ... 6-3/215. ... Full name: Larry Tabay Atkins III.
HIGH SCHOOL: Venice (Calif.).
COLLEGE: UCLA.

TRANSACTIONS/CAREER NOTES: Selected by Kansas City Chiefs in third round (84th pick overall) of 1999 NFL draft.
HONORS: Named free safety on THE SPORTING NEWS college All-America second team (1998).

Year Team	G	INTERCEPTIONS No.	Yds.	Avg.	TD	SACKS No.
1994—UCLA		Redshirted.				
1995—UCLA	10	0	0	...	0	1.0
1996—UCLA	11	0	0	...	0	1.0
1997—UCLA	12	6	154	25.7	0	4.0
1998—UCLA	12	4	77	19.3	0	0.0
College totals (4 years)	45	10	231	23.1	0	6.0

AZUMAH, JERRY — RB — BEARS

PERSONAL: Born September 1, 1977, in Worcester, Mass. ... 5-10/195.
HIGH SCHOOL: St. Peter-Marian (Worcester, Mass.).
COLLEGE: New Hampshire.
TRANSACTIONS/CAREER NOTES: Selected by Chicago Bears in fifth round (147th pick overall) of 1999 NFL draft.
HONORS: Walter Payton Award winner (1998).

		RUSHING				RECEIVING				KICKOFF RETURNS				TOTALS	
Year Team	G	Att.	Yds.	Avg.	TD	No.	Yds.	Avg.	TD	No.	Yds.	Avg.	TD	TD	Pts.
1995—New Hampshire	8	186	1105	5.9	8	15	116	7.7	0	6	86	14.3	0	8	48
1996—New Hampshire	11	245	1308	5.3	17	45	521	11.6	4	12	280	23.3	0	21	126
1997—New Hampshire	11	271	1585	5.8	13	26	298	11.5	3	12	351	29.3	1	17	102
1998—New Hampshire	11	343	2195	6.4	22	20	218	10.9	0	27	529	19.6	1	23	138
College totals (4 years)	41	1045	6193	5.9	60	106	1153	10.9	7	57	1246	21.9	2	69	414

BAILEY, CHAMP — CB — REDSKINS

PERSONAL: Born June 22, 1978 ... 6-1/184. ... Full name: Roland Champ Bailey.
HIGH SCHOOL: Charlton County (Folkson, Ga.).
COLLEGE: Georgia.
TRANSACTIONS/CAREER NOTES: Selected after junior season by Washington Redskins in first round (seventh pick overall) of 1999 NFL draft.
HONORS: Named cornerback on THE SPORTING NEWS college All-America second team (1998).

		INTERCEPTIONS				RECEIVING				PUNT RETURNS				KICKOFF RETURNS				TOTALS	
Year Team	G	No.	Yds.	Avg.	TD	No.	Yds.	Avg.	TD	No.	Yds.	Avg.	TD	No.	Yds.	Avg.	TD	TD	Pts.
1996—Georgia	11	2	0	0.0	0	0	0	...	0	0	0	...	0	0	0	...	0	0	0
1997—Georgia	11	3	47	15.7	1	12	234	19.5	0	0	0	...	0	11	250	22.7	0	1	6
1998—Georgia	11	3	20	6.7	0	47	744	15.8	5	4	49	12.3	0	12	261	21.8	0	5	30
College totals (3 years)	33	8	67	8.4	1	59	978	16.6	5	4	49	12.3	0	23	511	22.2	0	6	36

BAILEY, KARSTEN — WR — SEAHAWKS

PERSONAL: Born April 26, 1977, in Newnan, Ga. ... 5-10/201. ... Full name: Karsten Mario Bailey.
HIGH SCHOOL: East Coweta (Sharpsburg, Ga.).
COLLEGE: Auburn.
TRANSACTIONS/CAREER NOTES: Selected by Seattle Seahawks in third round (82nd pick overall) of 1999 NFL draft.

		RECEIVING			
Year Team	G	No.	Yds.	Avg.	TD
1995—Auburn	8	9	91	10.1	0
1996—Auburn	12	45	592	13.2	3
1997—Auburn	13	53	840	15.8	7
1998—Auburn	11	43	651	15.1	7
College totals (4 years)	44	150	2174	14.5	17

BAKER, EUGENE — WR — FALCONS

PERSONAL: Born March 18, 1976, in Monroeville, Pa. ... 6-0/165.
HIGH SCHOOL: Shady Side (Pa.) Academy.
COLLEGE: Kent.
TRANSACTIONS/CAREER NOTES: Selected by Atlanta Falcons in fifth round (164th pick overall) of 1999 NFL draft.
COLLEGE NOTES: Rushed twice for 15 yards (1998).

		RECEIVING				PUNT RETURNS				TOTALS	
Year Team	G	No.	Yds.	Avg.	TD	No.	Yds.	Avg.	TD	TD	Pts.
1994—Kent						Redshirted.					
1995—Kent	11	8	64	8.0	0	0	0	...	0	0	0
1996—Kent	11	69	1215	17.6	13	3	29	9.7	0	13	78
1997—Kent	11	103	1549	15.0	18	5	8	1.6	0	18	108
1998—Kent	6	49	685	14.0	4	0	0	...	0	4	24
College totals (4 years)	39	180	2828	15.7	35	8	37	4.6	0	35	210

BARNES, LIONEL — DL — RAMS

PERSONAL: Born April 19, 1976, in New Orleans. ... 6-4/264.
HIGH SCHOOL: Lakenheath American (Suffolk, England.).

JUNIOR COLLEGE: Barton County Community College, Kan. (did not play football).
COLLEGE: Northeast Louisiana.
TRANSACTIONS/CAREER NOTES: Selected by St. Louis Rams in sixth round (176th pick overall) of 1999 NFL draft.

Year Team	G	SACKS
1998—Northeast Louisiana	11	8.0

BARTHOLOMEW, BRENT — P — DOLPHINS

PERSONAL: Born October 22, 1976, in Apopka, Fla. ... 6-2/210.
HIGH SCHOOL: Apopka (Fla.).
COLLEGE: Ohio State.
TRANSACTIONS/CAREER NOTES: Selected by Miami Dolphins in sixth round (192nd pick overall) of 1999 NFL draft.

				PUNTING			
Year Team	G	No.	Yds.	Avg.	Net avg.	In. 20	Blk.
1995—Ohio State	11	49	1885	38.5	...	14	0
1996—Ohio State	12	58	2455	42.3	...	19	1
1997—Ohio State	13	72	3252	45.2	...	20	1
1998—Ohio State	11	58	2335	40.3	...	17	1
College totals (4 years)	47	237	9927	41.9	...	70	3

BARTON, ERIC — LB — RAIDERS

PERSONAL: Born September 29, 1977, in Alexandria, Va. ... 6-2/229.
HIGH SCHOOL: Edison (Alexandria, Va.).
COLLEGE: Maryland.
TRANSACTIONS/CAREER NOTES: Selected by Oakland Raiders in fifth round (146th pick overall) of 1999 NFL draft.
COLLEGE NOTES: Intercepted two passes for 15 yards (1998).

Year Team	G	SACKS
1995—Maryland	4	0.0
1996—Maryland	11	2.0
1997—Maryland	11	2.5
1998—Maryland	11	2.5
College totals (4 years)	37	7.0

BATES, D'WAYNE — WR — BEARS

PERSONAL: Born December 4, 1975, in Aiken, S.C. ... 6-2/215. ... Full name: D'Wayne Lavoris Bates.
HIGH SCHOOL: Silver Bluff (Aiken, S.C.).
COLLEGE: Northwestern.
TRANSACTIONS/CAREER NOTES: Selected by Chicago Bears in third round (71st pick overall) of 1999 NFL draft.
COLLEGE NOTES: Attempted one pass with a completion for 26 yards (1995); attempted one pass with a completion for 23 yards and a touchdown (1996); and attempted one pass without a completion (1998).

		RUSHING				RECEIVING				PUNT RETURNS				TOTALS	
Year Team	G	Att.	Yds.	Avg.	TD	No.	Yds.	Avg.	TD	No.	Yds.	Avg.	TD	TD	Pts.
1995—Northwestern	12	4	16	4.0	0	49	889	18.1	5	0	0	...	0	5	30
1996—Northwestern	12	2	14	7.0	0	75	1196	15.9	12	0	0	...	0	12	72
1997—Northwestern	1	0	0	...	0	3	40	13.3	0	0	0	...	0	0	0
1998—Northwestern	12	7	-18	-2.6	0	83	1245	15.0	9	15	109	7.3	0	9	54
College totals (4 years)	37	13	12	0.9	0	210	3370	16.0	26	15	109	7.3	0	26	156

BELL, TYRONE — CB — CHARGERS

PERSONAL: Born October 20, 1974, in West Point, Miss. ... 6-2/210. ... Full name: Tyrone Edward Bell.
HIGH SCHOOL: West Point (Miss.).
COLLEGE: North Alabama.
TRANSACTIONS/CAREER NOTES: Selected by San Diego Chargers in sixth round (178th pick overall) of 1999 NFL draft.
COLLEGE NOTES: Granted medical redshirt after one game (1996).

		INTERCEPTIONS			
Year Team	G	No.	Yds.	Avg.	TD
1994—North Alabama	8	0	0	...	0
1995—North Alabama	13	3	9	3.0	0
1996—North Alabama	1	0	0	...	0
1997—North Alabama	12	1	0	0.0	0
1998—North Alabama	10	6	29	4.8	0
College totals (5 years)	44	10	38	3.8	0

BENNETT, SEAN — RB — GIANTS

PERSONAL: Born November 9, 1975, in Evansville, Ind. ... 6-1/222. ... Full name: William Sean Bennett.
HIGH SCHOOL: Harrison (Ind.).
COLLEGE: Illinois (did not play football), then Evansville, then Northwestern.

– 447 –

TRANSACTIONS/CAREER NOTES: Selected by New York Giants in fourth round (112th pick overall) of 1999 NFL draft.
COLLEGE NOTES: Attempted five passes with two completions for 86 yards and one touchdown (1996).

Year Team	G	RUSHING Att. Yds. Avg. TD	RECEIVING No. Yds. Avg. TD	PUNT RETURNS No. Yds. Avg. TD	KICKOFF RETURNS No. Yds. Avg. TD	TOTALS TD Pts.
1994—Illinois			Did not play football.			
1995—Illinois			Did not play football.			
1996—Evansville	10	230 1189 5.2 9	44 740 16.8 10	0 0 ... 0	1 27 27.0 0	19 114
1997—Evansville	10	235 1667 7.1 16	24 260 10.8 4	6 81 13.5 0	1 34 34.0 0	20 120
1998—Northwestern	12	32 160 5.0 1	17 228 13.4 0	0 0 ... 0	0 0 ... 0	1 6
College totals (3 years)	32	497 3016 6.1 26	85 1228 14.4 14	6 81 13.5 0	2 61 30.5 0	40 240

BIDWELL, JOSH — P — PACKERS

PERSONAL: Born March 13, 1976, in Roseburg, Ore. ... 6-3/228. ... Full name: Joshua John Bidwell.
HIGH SCHOOL: Winston Churchill (Eugene, Ore.).
COLLEGE: Oregon (degree in English).
TRANSACTIONS/CAREER NOTES: Selected by Green Bay Packers in fourth round (133rd pick overall) of 1999 NFL draft.
HONORS: Named punter on THE SPORTING NEWS college All-America second team (1998).

Year Team	G	No.	Yds.	PUNTING Avg. Net avg. In. 20 Blk.
1994—Oregon			Redshirted.	
1995—Oregon	12	62	2249	36.3 34.8 10 0
1996—Oregon	11	56	2307	41.2 37.4 19 0
1997—Oregon	12	60	2248	37.5 38.9 15 0
1998—Oregon	12	51	2346	46.0 41.8 17 1
College totals (4 years)	47	229	9150	40.0 38.1 61 1

BISHOP, MICHAEL — QB — PATRIOTS

PERSONAL: Born May 15, 1976, in Willis, Texas. ... 6-0/195.
HIGH SCHOOL: Willis (Texas).
JUNIOR COLLEGE: Blinn College (Texas).
COLLEGE: Kansas State.
TRANSACTIONS/CAREER NOTES: Selected by New England Patriots in seventh round (227th pick overall) of 1999 NFL draft.
HONORS: Davey O'Brien Award winner (1998). ... Named quarterback on THE SPORTING NEWS college All-America first team (1998).

Year Team	G	PASSING Att. Cmp. Pct. Yds. TD Int. Avg. Rat.	RUSHING Att. Yds. Avg. TD	TOTALS TD Pts.
1995—Blinn College	...	191 102 53.4 1712 18 8 8.96 151.4	119 387 3.3 3	3 18
1996—Blinn College	...	152 67 44.1 972 9 11 6.39 102.9	69 265 3.8 3	3 20
1997—Kansas State	11	185 80 43.2 1557 13 8 8.42 128.5	147 556 3.8 9	9 54
1998—Kansas State	12	295 164 55.6 2844 23 4 9.64 159.6	177 748 4.2 14	14 84
Junior college totals (2 years)	...	343 169 49.3 2684 27 19 7.83 129.9	188 652 3.5 6	6 38
College totals (2 years)	23	480 244 50.8 4401 36 12 9.17 147.6	324 1304 4.0 23	23 138

BLY, DRE' — CB — RAMS

PERSONAL: Born May 22, 1977, in Chesapeake, Va. ... 5-9/197. ... Full name: Donald Andre Bly.
HIGH SCHOOL: Western Branch (Chesapeake, Va.).
COLLEGE: North Carolina.
TRANSACTIONS/CAREER NOTES: Selected after junior season by St. Louis Rams in second round (41st pick overall) of 1999 NFL draft.
HONORS: Named cornerback on THE SPORTING NEWS college All-America first team (1996). ... Named cornerback on THE SPORTING NEWS college All-America third team (1997).

Year Team	G	INTERCEPTIONS No. Yds. Avg. TD	PUNT RETURNS No. Yds. Avg. TD	KICKOFF RETURNS No. Yds. Avg. TD	TOTALS TD Pts.
1996—North Carolina	11	11 141 12.8 1	18 128 7.1 0	1 7 7.0 0	1 6
1997—North Carolina	11	5 55 11.0 1	19 127 6.7 0	2 35 17.5 0	1 6
1998—North Carolina	11	4 2 0.5 0	0 0 ... 0	2 32 16.0 0	0 0
College totals (3 years)	33	20 198 9.9 2	37 255 6.9 0	5 74 14.8 0	2 12

BOOKER, MARTY — WR — BEARS

PERSONAL: Born July 31, 1976, in Marrero, La. ... 5-11/218.
HIGH SCHOOL: Jonesboro-Hodge (Jonesboro, La.).
COLLEGE: Northeastern Louisiana.
TRANSACTIONS/CAREER NOTES: Selected by Chicago Bears in third round (78th pick overall) of 1999 NFL draft.

Year Team	G	RECEIVING No. Yds. Avg. TD
1994—Northeast Louisiana		Redshirted.
1995—Northeast Louisiana	11	8 138 17.3 1
1996—Northeast Louisiana	10	51 857 16.8 6
1997—Northeast Louisiana	9	44 621 14.1 5
1998—Northeast Louisiana	11	75 1168 15.6 11
College totals (4 years)	41	178 2784 15.6 23

1999 DRAFT PICKS

BOOTH, TONY — DB — PANTHERS

PERSONAL: Born August 3, 1975, in Richmond, Va. ... 6-1/195. ... Full name: Antoine Lamont Booth.
HIGH SCHOOL: Highland Springs (Richmond, Va.).
COLLEGE: James Madison.
TRANSACTIONS/CAREER NOTES: Selected by Carolina Panthers in seventh round (211th pick overall) of 1999 NFL draft.
COLLEGE NOTES: Returned one kickoff for 98 yards and a touchdown (1998).

		INTERCEPTIONS			
Year Team	G	No.	Yds.	Avg.	TD
1994—James Madison		Redshirted.			
1995—James Madison		Did not play.			
1996—James Madison	9	0	0	...	0
1997—James Madison	10	8	77	9.6	1
1998—James Madison	11	1	0	0.0	0
College totals (4 years)	30	9	77	8.6	1

BOSTON, DAVID — WR — CARDINALS

PERSONAL: Born August 19, 1978, in Humble, Texas. ... 6-1/215.
HIGH SCHOOL: Humble (Texas).
COLLEGE: Ohio State.
TRANSACTIONS/CAREER NOTES: Selected after junior season by Arizona Cardinals in first round (eighth pick overall) of 1999 NFL draft.
HONORS: Named wide receiver on THE SPORTING NEWS college All-America second team (1998).

		RUSHING				RECEIVING				PUNT RETURNS				TOTALS	
Year Team	G	Att.	Yds.	Avg.	TD	No.	Yds.	Avg.	TD	No.	Yds.	Avg.	TD	TD	Pts.
1996—Ohio State	12	0	0	...	0	33	450	13.6	7	32	297	9.3	1	8	48
1997—Ohio State	13	1	7	7.0	0	73	970	13.3	14	47	392	8.3	0	14	84
1998—Ohio State	12	2	1	0.5	0	85	1435	16.9	13	19	270	14.2	1	14	84
College totals (3 years)	37	3	8	2.7	0	191	2855	14.9	34	98	959	9.8	2	36	216

BOWENS, DAVID — LB — BRONCOS

PERSONAL: Born July 3, 1977, in Pontiac, Mich. ... 6-2/255.
HIGH SCHOOL: St. Mary's (Orchard Lake, Mich.).
COLLEGE: Michigan, then Western Illinois.
TRANSACTIONS/CAREER NOTES: Selected after junior season by Denver Broncos in fifth round (158th pick overall) of 1999 NFL draft.

Year Team	G	SACKS
1995—Michigan	13	4.0
1996—Michigan	12	12.0
1997—Michigan	Did not play.	
1998—Western Illinois	12	14.0
College totals (3 years)	37	30.0

BRADLEY, MELVIN — LB — CARDINALS

PERSONAL: Born August 15, 1976, in Barton, Ark. ... 6-1/269.
HIGH SCHOOL: Barton (Ark.).
COLLEGE: Arkansas.
TRANSACTIONS/CAREER NOTES: Selected by Arizona Cardinals in sixth round (202nd pick overall) of 1999 NFL draft.
COLLEGE NOTES: Intercepted one pass for 11 yards and recovered one fumble for 32 yards and a touchdown (1998).

Year Team	G	SACKS
1994—Arkansas	Redshirted.	
1995—Arkansas	3	0.0
1996—Arkansas	11	7.0
1997—Arkansas	11	4.0
1998—Arkansas	10	4.0
College totals (4 years)	35	15.0

BROOKS, AARON — QB — PACKERS

PERSONAL: Born March 24, 1976, in Newport News, Va. ... 6-4/203.
HIGH SCHOOL: Ferguson (Newport News, Va.).
COLLEGE: Virginia.
TRANSACTIONS/CAREER NOTES: Selected by Green Bay Packers in fourth round (131st pick overall) of 1999 NFL draft.

		PASSING								RUSHING				TOTALS	
Year Team	G	Att.	Cmp.	Pct.	Yds.	TD	Int.	Avg.	Rat.	Att.	Yds.	Avg.	TD	TD	Pts.
1994—Virginia		Redshirted.													
1995—Virginia	1	2	0	0.0	0	0	1	...	-100.0	0	0	...	0	0	0
1996—Virginia	11	89	37	41.6	517	1	7	5.81	78.3	30	65	2.2	3	3	18
1997—Virginia	11	270	164	60.7	2282	20	7	8.45	151.0	85	255	3.0	5	5	30
1998—Virginia	11	290	156	53.8	2319	12	9	8.00	128.4	84	227	2.7	5	5	30
College totals (4 years)	34	651	357	54.8	5118	33	24	7.86	130.2	199	547	2.7	13	13	78

BROOMFIELD, DONALD — DE — BENGALS

PERSONAL: Born June 10, 1976, in Lake City, Fla. ... 6-3/295. ... Full name: Donald Fred Broomfield.
HIGH SCHOOL: Baker County (Glen Saint Mary, Fla.).
COLLEGE: Clemson.
TRANSACTIONS/CAREER NOTES: Selected by Cincinnati Bengals in seventh round (249th pick overall) of 1999 NFL draft.

Year — Team	G	SACKS
1994—Clemson	Redshirted.	
1995—Clemson	4	0.0
1996—Clemson	8	1.0
1997—Clemson	12	1.0
1998—Clemson	11	1.0
College totals (4 years)	35	3.0

BROWN, DARWIN — CB — BRONCOS

PERSONAL: Born July 6, 1977, in Tyler, Texas. ... 5-10/170.
HIGH SCHOOL: John Tyler (Tyler, Texas).
COLLEGE: Texas Tech.
TRANSACTIONS/CAREER NOTES: Selected by Denver Broncos in fifth round (167th pick overall) of 1999 NFL draft.

		INTERCEPTIONS			
Year — Team	G	No.	Yds.	Avg.	TD
1995—Texas Tech	4	0	0	...	0
1996—Texas Tech	11	1	4	4.0	0
1997—Texas Tech	11	2	38	19.0	0
1998—Texas Tech	12	1	0	0.0	0
College totals (4 years)	38	4	42	10.5	0

BROWN, KRIS — K — STEELERS

PERSONAL: Born December 23, 1976, in Southlake, Texas. ... 5-10/204.
HIGH SCHOOL: Carroll (Southlake, Texas).
COLLEGE: Nebraska.
TRANSACTIONS/CAREER NOTES: Selected by Pittsburgh Steelers in seventh round (228th pick overall) of 1999 NFL draft.

		KICKING							
Year — Team	G	XPM	XPA	FGM	FGA	Lg.	50+	Pts.
1995—Nebraska	11	58	61	13	16	47	0-0	97
1996—Nebraska	11	50	51	12	19	51	0-0	86
1997—Nebraska	11	62	62	18	21	46	0-0	116
1998—Nebraska	12	47	48	14	21	48	0-0	89
College totals (4 years)	45	217	222	57	77	51	0-0	388

BROWN, NA — WR — EAGLES

PERSONAL: Born February 22, 1977, in Reidsville, N.C. ... 6-0/187. ... Full name: Na Orlando Brown.
HIGH SCHOOL: Reidsville (N.C.).
COLLEGE: North Carolina.
TRANSACTIONS/CAREER NOTES: Selected by Philadelphia Eagles in fourth round (130th pick overall) of 1999 NFL draft.

		RUSHING			RECEIVING				PUNT RETURNS				TOTALS	
Year — Team	G	Att.	Yds.	Avg.	TD	No.	Yds.	Avg.	TD	No.	Yds.	Avg.	TD	TD	Pts.
1995—North Carolina	8	0	0	...	0	3	45	15.0	0	0	0	...	0	0	0
1996—North Carolina	11	0	0	...	0	52	534	10.3	4	0	0	...	0	4	24
1997—North Carolina	11	0	0	...	0	55	610	11.1	4	8	83	10.4	0	4	24
1998—North Carolina	11	1	48	48.0	1	55	897	16.3	6	9	78	8.7	0	7	42
College totals (4 years)	41	1	48	48.0	1	165	2086	12.6	14	17	161	9.5	0	15	90

BRYANT, FERNANDO — CB — JAGUARS

PERSONAL: Born March 26, 1977, in Murfreesboro, Tenn. ... 5-10/180. ... Nephew of Don Griffin, cornerback with San Francisco 49ers (1986-93), Cleveland Browns (1994 and 1995) and Philadelphia Eagles (1996); and nephew of James Griffin, defensive back with Cincinnati Bengals (1983-85) and Detroit Lions (1986-89).
HIGH SCHOOL: Riverdale (Murfreesboro, Tenn.).
COLLEGE: Alabama.
TRANSACTIONS/CAREER NOTES: Selected by Jacksonville Jaguars in first round (26th pick overall) of 1999 NFL draft.
COLLEGE NOTES: Recovered one fumble for 15 yards (1997).

		INTERCEPTIONS				KICKOFF RETURNS				TOTALS	
Year — Team	G	No.	Yds.	Avg.	TD	No.	Yds.	Avg.	TD	TD	Pts.
1995—Alabama	11	0	0	...	0	0	0	...	0	0	0
1996—Alabama	12	3	13	4.3	0	0	0	...	0	0	0
1997—Alabama	11	3	106	35.3	1	15	416	27.7	0	1	6
1998—Alabama	11	2	0	0.0	0	2	50	25.0	0	0	0
College totals (4 years)	45	8	119	14.9	1	17	466	27.4	0	1	6

BRYANT, TONY — DE — RAIDERS

PERSONAL: Born September 3, 1976, in Marathon, Fla. ... 6-3/268.
HIGH SCHOOL: Marathon (Fla.).
JUNIOR COLLEGE: Copiah-Lincoln Junior College (Miss.).
COLLEGE: Florida State.
TRANSACTIONS/CAREER NOTES: Selected by Oakland Raiders in second round (40th pick overall) of 1999 NFL draft.
COLLEGE NOTES: Intercepted one pass (1997).

Year Team	G	SACKS
1995—Copiah-Lincoln	...	8.0
1996—Copiah-Lincoln	Statistics unavailable.	
1997—Florida State	12	7.0
1998—Florida State	12	7.0
College totals (2 years)	24	14.0

BRYSON, SHAWN — FB — BILLS

PERSONAL: Born November 30, 1976, in Franklin, N.C. ... 6-0/235. ... Full name: Adrian Shawn Bryson.
HIGH SCHOOL: Franklin (N.C.).
COLLEGE: Tennessee.
TRANSACTIONS/CAREER NOTES: Selected by Buffalo Bills in third round (86th pick overall) of 1999 NFL draft.

		RUSHING				RECEIVING				TOTALS	
Year Team	G	Att.	Yds.	Avg.	TD	No.	Yds.	Avg.	TD	TD	Pts.
1995—Tennessee	7	16	65	4.1	1	0	0	...	0	1	6
1996—Tennessee	8	18	94	5.2	1	2	10	5.0	0	1	6
1997—Tennessee	12	36	146	4.1	2	29	307	10.6	0	2	12
1998—Tennessee	12	21	200	9.5	4	19	167	8.8	1	5	30
College totals (4 years)	39	91	505	5.5	8	50	484	9.7	1	9	54

BRZEZINSKI, DOUG — G — EAGLES

PERSONAL: Born March 11, 1976, in Livonia, Mich. ... 6-4/305. ... Full name: Douglas Gregory Brzezinski.
HIGH SCHOOL: Detroit Catholic Central.
COLLEGE: Boston College.
TRANSACTIONS/CAREER NOTES: Selected by Philadelphia Eagles in third round (64th pick overall) of 1999 NFL draft.
HONORS: Named offensive guard on THE SPORTING NEWS college All-America first team (1998).
COLLEGE PLAYING EXPERIENCE: Boston College, 1994-1998. ... Games: 1994 (redshirted), 1995 (12), 1996 (12), 1997 (11), 1998 (11). Total: 46.

BURKE, THOMAS — DE — CARDINALS

PERSONAL: Born October 12, 1976, in Poplar, Wis. ... 6-2/264.
HIGH SCHOOL: Northwestern (Maple, Wis.).
COLLEGE: Wisconsin.
TRANSACTIONS/CAREER NOTES: Selected by Arizona Cardinals in third round (83rd pick overall) of 1999 NFL draft.
HONORS: Named defensive end on THE SPORTING NEWS college All-America first team (1998).

Year Team	G	SACKS
1995—Wisconsin	5	0.0
1996—Wisconsin	13	1.0
1997—Wisconsin	13	9.0
1998—Wisconsin	12	22.0
College totals (4 years)	43	32.0

IN MEMORIAM — BRANDON BURLSWORTH

PERSONAL: Born September 20, 1976, in Harrison, Ark. ... Died April 29, 1999. ... 6-3/308.
HIGH SCHOOL: Harrison (Ark.).
COLLEGE: Arkansas (degree in marketing management).
TRANSACTIONS/CAREER NOTES: Selected by Indianapolis Colts in third round (63rd pick overall) of 1999 NFL draft.
COLLEGE PLAYING EXPERIENCE: Arkansas, 1994-1998. ... Games: 1994 (redshirted), 1995 (13), 1996 (11), 1997 (11), 1998 (11). Total: 46.

CAMPBELL, DAN — TE — GIANTS

PERSONAL: Born April 13, 1976, in Glen Rose, Texas. ... 6-5/264. ... Full name: Daniel Allen Campbell.
HIGH SCHOOL: Glen Rose (Texas).
COLLEGE: Texas A&M.
TRANSACTIONS/CAREER NOTES: Selected by New York Giants in third round (79th pick overall) of 1999 NFL draft.

Year Team	G	RECEIVING No.	Yds.	Avg.	TD
1994—Texas A&M		Redshirted.			
1995—Texas A&M	4	0	0	...	0
1996—Texas A&M	12	8	103	12.9	0
1997—Texas A&M	12	12	143	11.9	2
1998—Texas A&M	13	7	68	9.7	1
College totals (4 years)	41	27	314	11.6	3

CARTY, JOHNDALE — S — FALCONS

PERSONAL: Born August 27, 1977, in Miami. ... 6-0/203.
HIGH SCHOOL: Hialeah (Fla.) Lakes.
COLLEGE: Utah State.
TRANSACTIONS/CAREER NOTES: Selected by Atlanta Falcons in fourth round (126th pick overall) of 1999 NFL draft.
COLLEGE NOTES: Credited with 1 1/2 sacks (1995); credited with one sack (1998).

		INTERCEPTIONS				PUNT RETURNS				KICKOFF RETURNS				TOTALS	
Year Team	G	No.	Yds.	Avg.	TD	No.	Yds.	Avg.	TD	No.	Yds.	Avg.	TD	TD	Pts.
1995—Utah State	10	0	0	...	0	0	0	...	0	1	43	43.0	0	0	0
1996—Utah State	11	1	0	0.0	0	0	0	...	0	0	0	...	0	0	0
1997—Utah State	11	6	39	6.5	0	1	18	18.0	0	0	0	...	0	0	0
1998—Utah State	7	1	5	5.0	0	1	5	5.0	0	0	0	...	0	0	0
College totals (4 years)	39	8	44	5.5	0	2	23	11.5	0	1	43	43.0	0	0	0

CESARIO, ANTHONY — G — JAGUARS

PERSONAL: Born July 19, 1976, in Pueblo, Colo. ... 6-6/312. ... Full name: Anthony Angelo Cesario Jr.
HIGH SCHOOL: South (Pueblo, Colo.).
COLLEGE: Colorado State.
TRANSACTIONS/CAREER NOTES: Selected by Jacksonville Jaguars in third round (88th pick overall) of 1999 NFL draft.
HONORS: Named offensive guard on THE SPORTING NEWS college All-America second team (1997 and 1998).
COLLEGE PLAYING EXPERIENCE: Colorado State, 1994-1998. ... Games: 1994 (redshirted), 1995 (12), 1996 (12), 1997 (13), 1998 (12). Total: 49.

CHIAVERINI, DARRIN — WR — BROWNS

PERSONAL: Born October 12, 1977, in Orange County, Calif. ... 6-1/205. ... Name pronounced shevv-er-RE-nee.
HIGH SCHOOL: Corona (Calif.).
COLLEGE: Colorado.
TRANSACTIONS/CAREER NOTES: Selected by Cleveland Browns in fifth round (148th pick overall) of 1999 NFL draft.
COLLEGE NOTES: Rushed once for 10 yards (1998).

Year Team	G	RECEIVING No.	Yds.	Avg.	TD
1995—Colorado	10	3	47	15.7	0
1996—Colorado	10	7	61	8.7	1
1997—Colorado	11	35	461	13.2	0
1998—Colorado	11	52	630	12.1	5
College totals (4 years)	42	97	1199	12.4	6

CHILDRESS, O.J. — LB — GIANTS

PERSONAL: Born December 6, 1976, in Hermitage, Tenn. ... 6-1/244. ... Full name: Orin J. Childress.
HIGH SCHOOL: McGavock (Nashville).
COLLEGE: Clemson.
TRANSACTIONS/CAREER NOTES: Selected by New York Giants in seventh round (231st pick overall) of 1999 NFL draft.
COLLEGE NOTES: Credited with two sacks (1998).
COLLEGE PLAYING EXPERIENCE: Clemson, 1995-1998. ... Games: 1995 (10), 1996 (12), 1997 (12), 1998 (9). Total: (43).

CLAIBORNE, CHRIS — LB — LIONS

PERSONAL: Born July 26, 1978, in Riverdale, Calif. ... 6-3/250.
HIGH SCHOOL: J.W. North (Riverside, Calif.).
COLLEGE: Southern California.
TRANSACTIONS/CAREER NOTES: Selected after junior season by Detroit Lions in first round (ninth pick overall) of 1999 NFL draft.
HONORS: Butkus Award winner (1998). ... Named inside linebacker on THE SPORTING NEWS college All-America first team (1998).
COLLEGE NOTES: Recovered one fumble for a touchdown (1996).

		INTERCEPTIONS				SACKS
Year Team	G	No.	Yds.	Avg.	TD	No.
1996—Southern California	12	2	34	17.0	0	0.0
1997—Southern California	11	0	0	...	0	7.0
1998—Southern California	13	6	159	26.5	2	5.0
College totals (3 years)	36	8	193	24.1	2	12.0

CLARK, DESMOND — TE/WR — BRONCOS

PERSONAL: Born April 20, 1977, in Lakeland, Fla. ... 6-3/255.
HIGH SCHOOL: Kathleen (Lakeland, Fla.).
COLLEGE: Wake Forest.
TRANSACTIONS/CAREER NOTES: Selected by Denver Broncos in sixth round (179th pick overall) of 1999 NFL draft.

		RECEIVING			
Year Team	G	No.	Yds.	Avg.	TD
1995—Wake Forest	9	24	236	9.8	1
1996—Wake Forest	11	61	782	12.8	6
1997—Wake Forest	11	72	950	13.2	5
1998—Wake Forest	10	59	866	14.7	8
College totals (4 years)	41	216	2834	13.1	20

CLOUD, MIKE — RB — CHIEFS

PERSONAL: Born July 1, 1975, in Charleston, S.C. ... 5-10/204. ... Full name: Michael Alexander Cloud.
HIGH SCHOOL: Portsmouth (R.I.).
COLLEGE: Boston College.
TRANSACTIONS/CAREER NOTES: Selected by Kansas City Chiefs in second round (54th pick overall) of 1999 NFL draft.

		RUSHING				RECEIVING				TOTALS	
Year Team	G	Att.	Yds.	Avg.	TD	No.	Yds.	Avg.	TD	TD	Pts.
1994—Boston College				Redshirted.							
1995—Boston College	12	102	626	6.1	2	8	44	5.5	0	2	12
1996—Boston College	12	68	359	5.3	1	6	57	9.5	1	2	12
1997—Boston College	10	136	886	6.5	8	20	225	11.3	0	8	48
1998—Boston College	11	308	1726	5.6	14	24	198	8.3	0	14	84
College totals (4 years)	45	614	3597	5.9	25	58	524	9.0	1	26	156

COADY, RICH — S — RAMS

PERSONAL: Born January 26, 1976, in Dallas. ... 6-0/203. ... Full name: Richard Joseph Coady IV. ... Son of Rich Coady, tight end/center with Chicago Bears (1970-74).
HIGH SCHOOL: J.J. Pearce (Dallas).
COLLEGE: Texas A&M.
TRANSACTIONS/CAREER NOTES: Selected by St. Louis Rams in third round (68th pick overall) of 1999 NFL draft.
COLLEGE NOTES: Credited with 1/2 sack (1996).

		INTERCEPTIONS			
Year Team	G	No.	Yds.	Avg.	TD
1994—Texas A&M			Redshirted.		
1995—Texas A&M	11	0	0	...	0
1996—Texas A&M	12	3	93	31.0	0
1997—Texas A&M	12	2	11	5.5	0
1998—Texas A&M	13	3	16	5.3	0
College totals (4 years)	48	8	120	15.0	0

COATS, TONY — G — BENGALS

PERSONAL: Born October 5, 1975, in Columbus, Ohio ... 6-6/305.
HIGH SCHOOL: South Kitsap (Port Orchard, Wash.).
COLLEGE: Washington.
TRANSACTIONS/CAREER NOTES: Selected by Cincinnati Bengals in seventh round (209th pick overall) of 1999 NFL draft. ... Signed by Bengals (May 6, 1999).
COLLEGE PLAYING EXPERIENCE: Washington, 1994-1998. ... Games: 1994 (redshirted), 1995 (12), 1996 (9), 1997 (11), 1998 (11). Total: 43.

COCHRAN, ANTONIO — DE — SEAHAWKS

PERSONAL: Born June 21, 1976, in Montezuma, Ga. ... 6-4/297. ... Full name: Antonio Desez Cochran.
HIGH SCHOOL: Macon County (Montezuma, Ga.).
JUNIOR COLLEGE: Middle Georgia College.
COLLEGE: Georgia.
TRANSACTIONS/CAREER NOTES: Selected by Seattle Seahawks in fourth round (115th pick overall) of 1999 NFL draft.
COLLEGE NOTES: Intercepted one pass (1996).

Year Team	G	SACKS
1995—Middle Georgia College	10	4.0
1996—Middle Georgia College	10	5.0
1997—Georgia	11	1.0
1998—Georgia	10	2.5
Junior college totals (2 years)	20	9.0
College totals (2 years)	21	3.5

COLEMAN, RODERICK — LB — RAIDERS

PERSONAL: Born August 16, 1976, in Philadelphia. ... 6-1/255.
HIGH SCHOOL: Simon Gratz (Philadelphia).
COLLEGE: East Carolina.
TRANSACTIONS/CAREER NOTES: Selected by Oakland Raiders in fifth round (153rd pick overall) of 1999 NFL draft.

Year — Team	G	SACKS
1995—East Carolina	12	3.0
1996—East Carolina	11	8.0
1997—East Carolina	11	15.0
1998—East Carolina	11	13.0
College totals (4 years)	45	39.0

COLLINS, BOBBY — TE — BILLS

PERSONAL: Born August 20, 1976, in York, Ala. ... 6-4/249. ... Full name: Bobby Eugene Collins.
HIGH SCHOOL: Sumter County (York, Ala.).
JUNIOR COLLEGE: East Mississippi Junior College.
COLLEGE: North Alabama.
TRANSACTIONS/CAREER NOTES: Selected by Buffalo Bills in fourth round (122nd pick overall) of 1999 NFL draft.
COLLEGE NOTES: Rushed once for six yards and caught one pass for a two point conversion (1997); rushed twice for six yards (1998).

		RECEIVING			
Year — Team	G	No.	Yds.	Avg.	TD
1995—East Mississippi College		Statistics unavailable.			
1996—East Mississippi College		Statistics unavailable.			
1997—North Alabama	11	11	202	18.4	3
1998—North Alabama	9	19	311	16.4	2
College totals (2 years)	20	30	513	17.1	5

COLLINS, CECIL — RB — DOLPHINS

PERSONAL: Born November 19, 1976, in Leesville, La. ... 5-10/209.
HIGH SCHOOL: Leesville (La.).
COLLEGE: Louisiana State, then McNeese State.
TRANSACTIONS/CAREER NOTES: Selected after junior season by Miami Dolphins in fifth round (134th pick overall) of 1999 NFL draft.

		RUSHING				RECEIVING				KICKOFF RETURNS				TOTALS	
Year — Team	G	Att.	Yds.	Avg.	TD	No.	Yds.	Avg.	TD	No.	Yds.	Avg.	TD	TD	Pts.
1996—Louisiana State								Ineligible.							
1997—Louisiana State	4	72	596	8.3	3	1	11	11.0	0	5	119	23.8	0	3	18
1998—McNeese State	2	28	117	4.2	1	0	0	...	0	0	0	...	0	1	6
College totals (2 years)	6	100	713	7.1	4	1	11	11.0	0	5	119	23.8	0	4	24

COLVIN, ROSEVELT — DE — BEARS

PERSONAL: Born September 5, 1977, in Indianapolis. ... 6-3/252.
HIGH SCHOOL: Broad Ripple (Indianapolis).
COLLEGE: Purdue.
TRANSACTIONS/CAREER NOTES: Selected by Chicago Bears in fourth round (111th pick overall) of 1999 NFL draft.
COLLEGE NOTES: Returned a blocked field goal attempt 62 yards for a touchdown (1997); recovered one fumble for 23 yards and a touchdown (1998).

Year — Team	G	SACKS
1995—Purdue	9	0.0
1996—Purdue	11	6.0
1997—Purdue	12	12.5
1998—Purdue	13	15.0
College totals (4 years)	45	33.5

COOK, RASHARD — S — BEARS

PERSONAL: Born April 18, 1977, in San Diego. ... 5-11/197.
HIGH SCHOOL: Samuel F.B. Morse (San Diego).
COLLEGE: Southern California.
TRANSACTIONS/CAREER NOTES: Selected by Chicago Bears in sixth round (184th pick overall) of 1999 NFL draft.
COLLEGE NOTES: Returned four kickoffs for 48 yards (1995); credited with four sacks (1997).

		INTERCEPTIONS			
Year — Team	G	No.	Yds.	Avg.	TD
1995—Southern California	12	0	0	...	0
1996—Southern California	11	0	0	...	0
1997—Southern California	11	3	22	7.3	0
1998—Southern California	13	2	1	0.5	0
College totals (4 years)	47	5	23	4.6	0

COUCH, TIM — QB — BROWNS

PERSONAL: Born July 31, 1977, in Hyden, Ky. ... 6-4/227. ... Full name: Timothy Scott Couch.
HIGH SCHOOL: Leslie Country (Hyden, Ky.).
COLLEGE: Kentucky.
TRANSACTIONS/CAREER NOTES: Selected after junior season by Cleveland Browns in first round (first pick overall) of 1999 NFL draft. ... Signed by Browns (April 17, 1999).
HONORS: Named quarterback on THE SPORTING NEWS college All-America third team (1998).

				PASSING						RUSHING				TOTALS	
Year Team	G	Att.	Cmp.	Pct.	Yds.	TD	Int.	Avg.	Rat.	Att.	Yds.	Avg.	TD	TD	Pts.
1996—Kentucky	7	84	32	38.1	276	1	1	3.29	67.2	24	-26	-1.1	0	0	0
1997—Kentucky	11	547	363	66.4	3884	37	19	7.10	141.4	66	-125	-1.9	3	3	18
1998—Kentucky	11	553	400	72.3	4275	36	15	7.73	153.3	64	-124	-1.9	1	1	6
College totals (3 years)	29	1184	795	67.1	8435	74	35	7.12	141.7	154	-275	-1.8	4	4	24

COVINGTON, SCOTT — QB — BENGALS

PERSONAL: Born January 17, 1976, in Laguna Niguel, Calif. ... 6-2/217.
HIGH SCHOOL: Dana Hills (Laguna Niguel, Calif.).
COLLEGE: Miami (Fla.).
TRANSACTIONS/CAREER NOTES: Selected by Cincinnati Bengals in seventh round (245th pick overall) of 1999 NFL draft.

				PASSING						RUSHING				TOTALS	
Year Team	G	Att.	Cmp.	Pct.	Yds.	TD	Int.	Avg.	Rat.	Att.	Yds.	Avg.	TD	TD	Pts.
1995—Miami (Fla.)	7	42	22	52.4	324	3	2	7.71	131.2	36	-20	-0.6	0	0	0
1996—Miami (Fla.)	8	125	73	58.4	919	4	4	7.35	124.3	13	-30	-2.3	1	1	6
1997—Miami (Fla.)	9	60	27	45.0	318	0	1	5.30	86.2	15	-12	-0.8	1	1	6
1998—Miami (Fla.)	11	270	159	58.9	2301	19	8	8.52	147.8	45	-192	-4.3	0	0	0
College totals (4 years)	35	497	281	56.5	3862	26	15	7.77	133.0	109	-254	-2.3	2	2	12

CRAFT, JASON — CB — JAGUARS

PERSONAL: Born February 13, 1976, in Denver. ... 5-9/175. ... Full name: Jason Donell Andre Craft.
HIGH SCHOOL: East (Denver).
JUNIOR COLLEGE: Denver Community College.
COLLEGE: Colorado State.
TRANSACTIONS/CAREER NOTES: Selected by Jacksonville Jaguars in fifth round (160th pick overall) of 1999 NFL draft. ... Signed by Jaguars (May 18, 1999).

		INTERCEPTIONS			
Year Team	G	No.	Yds.	Avg.	TD
1995—Colorado State		Did not play.			
1996—Colorado State		Did not play.			
1997—Colorado State	9	0	0	...	0
1998—Colorado State	12	4	56	14.0	0
College totals (2 years)	21	4	56	14.0	0

CULPEPPER, DAUNTE — QB — VIKINGS

PERSONAL: Born January 28, 1977, in Ocala, Fla. ... 6-4/255.
HIGH SCHOOL: Vanguard (Ocala, Fla.).
COLLEGE: Central Florida.
TRANSACTIONS/CAREER NOTES: Selected by Minnesota Vikings in first round (11th pick overall) of 1999 NFL draft.

				PASSING						RUSHING				TOTALS	
Year Team	G	Att.	Cmp.	Pct.	Yds.	TD	Int.	Avg.	Rat.	Att.	Yds.	Avg.	TD	TD	Pts.
1995—Central Florida	11	294	168	57.1	2071	12	10	7.04	123.0	85	17	0.2	5	5	30
1996—Central Florida	11	314	187	59.6	2565	19	15	8.17	138.6	94	102	1.1	2	2	12
1997—Central Florida	11	381	238	62.5	3086	25	10	8.10	146.9	136	438	3.2	5	5	30
1998—Central Florida	11	402	296	73.6	3690	28	7	9.18	170.2	141	463	3.3	12	12	72
College totals (4 years)	44	1391	889	63.9	11412	84	42	8.20	146.7	456	1020	2.2	24	24	144

CURRY, SCOTT — OT — PACKERS

PERSONAL: Born December 25, 1975, in Valier, Mont. ... 6-5/294.
HIGH SCHOOL: Valier (Mont.).
COLLEGE: Montana.
TRANSACTIONS/CAREER NOTES: Selected by Green Bay Packers in sixth round (203rd pick overall) of 1999 NFL draft.
COLLEGE PLAYING EXPERIENCE: Montana, 1994-1998. ... Games played unavailable.

DAFT, KEVIN — QB — TITANS

PERSONAL: Born November 19, 1975, in Long Beach, Calif. ... 6-1/184.
HIGH SCHOOL: Foothill (Calif.).

COLLEGE: California-Davis.
TRANSACTIONS/CAREER NOTES: Selected by Tennessee Titans in fifth round (151st pick overall) of 1999 NFL draft.

			PASSING							RUSHING				TOTALS	
Year Team	G	Att.	Cmp.	Pct.	Yds.	TD	Int.	Avg.	Rat.	Att.	Yds.	Avg.	TD	TD	Pts.
1994—California-Davis					Redshirted.										
1995—California-Davis	5	33	20	60.6	207	2	2	6.27	121.2	12	36	3.0	0	0	0
1996—California-Davis	7	46	27	58.7	381	3	2	8.28	141.7	13	38	2.9	0	0	0
1997—California-Davis	14	486	281	57.8	3696	33	18	7.60	136.7	80	6	0.1	1	1	6
1998—California-Davis	12	417	238	57.1	3317	30	8	7.95	143.8	57	15	0.3	0	0	0
College totals (4 years)	38	982	566	57.6	7601	68	30	7.74	139.4	162	95	0.6	1	1	6

DALTON, ANTICO — LB — VIKINGS

PERSONAL: Born in Eden, N.C. ... 6-1/242.
HIGH SCHOOL: Morehead (Eden, N.C.).
COLLEGE: Hampton University.
TRANSACTIONS/CAREER NOTES: Selected by Minnesota Vikings in sixth round (199th pick overall) of 1999 NFL draft.

Year Team	G	SACKS
1996—Hampton	6	0.0
1997—Hampton	8	7.5
1998—Hampton	11	13.5
College totals (3 years)	25	21.0

DANIEL, ROBERT — DE — PANTHERS

PERSONAL: Born October 19, 1975, in Dallas. ... 6-6/275.
HIGH SCHOOL: H. Grady Spruce (Dallas).
COLLEGE: Northwestern (La.) State.
TRANSACTIONS/CAREER NOTES: Selected by Carolina Panthers in sixth round (175th pick overall) of 1999 NFL draft.

Year Team	G	SACKS
1994—Northwestern State	8	0.0
1995—Northwestern State	10	0.0
1996—Northwestern State	11	2.5
1997—Northwestern State	Did not play—injured.	
1998—Northwestern State	11	4.0
College totals (4 years)	40	6.5

DAVIS, PERNELL — DT — EAGLES

PERSONAL: Born May 19, 1976, in Birmingham, Ala. ... 6-2/320.
HIGH SCHOOL: West End (Birmingham, Ala.).
COLLEGE: Alabama-Birmingham.
TRANSACTIONS/CAREER NOTES: Selected by Philadelphia Eagles in seventh round (251st pick overall) of 1999 NFL draft.

Year Team	G	SACKS
1995—Alabama-Birmingham	Redshirted.	
1996—Alabama-Birmingham	11	1.0
1997—Alabama-Birmingham	11	0.0
1998—Alabama-Birmingham	11	1.0
College totals (3 years)	33	2.0

DAVIS, RUSSELL — DL — BEARS

PERSONAL: Born March 28, 1975, in Fayetteville, N.C. ... 6-4/300. ... Full name: Russell Morgan Davis.
HIGH SCHOOL: E.E. Smith (Fayetteville, N.C.).
COLLEGE: North Carolina.
TRANSACTIONS/CAREER NOTES: Selected by Chicago Bears in second round (48th pick overall) of 1999 NFL draft.

Year Team	G	SACKS
1994—North Carolina	Redshirted.	
1995—North Carolina	8	3.0
1996—North Carolina	12	2.5
1997—North Carolina	10	3.0
1998—North Carolina	10	2.0
College totals (4 years)	40	10.5

DEARTH, JAMES — TE — BROWNS

PERSONAL: Born January 22, 1976, in Scurry, Texas. ... 6-3/269.
HIGH SCHOOL: Scurry-Rosser (Scurry, Texas).
COLLEGE: Tulsa, then Tarleton State (Texas).
TRANSACTIONS/CAREER NOTES: Selected by Cleveland Browns in sixth round (191st pick overall) of 1999 NFL draft.
COLLEGE NOTES: Played fullback (1995). ... Rushed once for minus five yards (1995). ... Played tight end (1996-98).

Year Team	G	RECEIVING No.	Yds.	Avg.	TD
1995—Tulsa	7	0	0	...	0
1996—Tarleton State	3	3	36	12.0	0
1997—Tarleton State	11	43	528	12.3	2
1998—Tarleton State	8	31	428	13.8	3
College totals (4 years)	29	77	992	12.9	5

DENSON, AUTRY — RB — BUCCANEERS

PERSONAL: Born December 8, 1976, in Davie, Fla. ... 5-10/202. ... Full name: Autry L. Denson.
HIGH SCHOOL: Nova (Davie, Fla.).
COLLEGE: Notre Dame.
TRANSACTIONS/CAREER NOTES: Selected by Tampa Bay Buccaneers in seventh round (233rd pick overall) of 1999 NFL draft.

Year Team	G	RUSHING Att. Yds. Avg. TD	RECEIVING No. Yds. Avg. TD	PUNT RETURNS No. Yds. Avg. TD	KICKOFF RETURNS No. Yds. Avg. TD	TOTALS TD Pts.
1995—Notre Dame	11	137 695 5.1 8	6 65 10.8 0	0 0 ... 0	4 39 9.8 0	8 48
1996—Notre Dame	11	202 1179 5.8 8	11 111 10.1 2	18 196 10.9 1	7 141 20.1 0	11 66
1997—Notre Dame	12	264 1268 4.8 12	30 175 5.8 1	7 68 9.7 0	5 93 18.6 0	13 78
1998—Notre Dame	11	251 1176 4.7 15	6 81 13.5 0	4 40 10.0 0	0 0 ... 0	15 90
College totals (4 years)	45	854 4318 5.1 43	53 432 8.2 3	29 304 10.5 1	16 273 17.1 0	47 282

DeVRIES, JARED — DE — LIONS

PERSONAL: Born June 11, 1976, in Aplington, Iowa. ... 6-4/280.
HIGH SCHOOL: Aplington-Parkersburg (Parkersburg, Iowa).
COLLEGE: Iowa.
TRANSACTIONS/CAREER NOTES: Selected by Detroit Lions in third round (70th pick overall) of 1999 NFL draft.
HONORS: Named defensive tackle on THE SPORTING NEWS college All-America third team (1997). ... Named defensive tackle on THE SPORTING NEWS college All-America first team (1998).

Year Team	G	SACKS
1994—Iowa	Redshirted.	
1995—Iowa	12	12.0
1996—Iowa	12	13.0
1997—Iowa	12	8.0
1998—Iowa	11	10.0
College totals (4 years)	47	43.0

DINGLE, ADRIAN — DE — CHARGERS

PERSONAL: Born June 25, 1977, in Holly Hill, S.C. ... 6-3/272. ... Full name: Adrian K. Dingle.
HIGH SCHOOL: Holly Hill-Roberts (Holly Hill, S.C.).
COLLEGE: Clemson.
TRANSACTIONS/CAREER NOTES: Selected by San Diego Chargers in fifth round (139th pick overall) of 1999 NFL draft.
COLLEGE NOTES: Intercepted one pass (1996).

Year Team	G	SACKS
1995—Clemson	12	2.0
1996—Clemson	12	6.0
1997—Clemson	11	4.5
1998—Clemson	11	10.5
College totals (4 years)	46	23.0

DINGLE, ANTONIO — NT — STEELERS

PERSONAL: Born October 7, 1976, in Fayetteville, N.C. ... 6-2/315. ... Full name: Antonio Demetric Dingle.
HIGH SCHOOL: South View (Hope Mills, N.C.).
COLLEGE: Virginia.
TRANSACTIONS/CAREER NOTES: Selected by Pittsburgh Steelers in seventh round (214th pick overall) of 1999 NFL draft.
COLLEGE NOTES: Intercepted one pass for 10 yards and a touchdown (1996).

Year Team	G	SACKS
1995—Virginia	12	3.0
1996—Virginia	11	2.0
1997—Virginia	11	2.0
1998—Virginia	11	2.0
College totals (4 years)	45	9.0

DOUGLAS, DAMEANE — WR — RAIDERS

PERSONAL: Born March 15, 1976, in Hanford, Calif. ... 6-0/187.
HIGH SCHOOL: Hanford (Calif.).
COLLEGE: California.
TRANSACTIONS/CAREER NOTES: Selected by Oakland Raiders in fourth round (102nd pick overall) of 1999 NFL draft.

Year Team	G	RUSHING Att. Yds. Avg. TD	RECEIVING No. Yds. Avg. TD	KICKOFF RETURNS No. Yds. Avg. TD	TOTALS TD Pts.
1994—California			Redshirted.		
1995—California	5	0 0 ... 0	5 38 7.6 1	3 7 2.3 0	1 6
1996—California	12	2 -5 -2.5 0	37 537 14.5 5	1 23 23.0 0	5 30
1997—California	11	1 1 1.0 0	53 610 11.5 3	5 56 11.2 0	3 18
1998—California	11	1 9 9.0 1	100 1150 11.5 4	4 81 20.3 0	5 30
College totals (4 years)	39	4 5 1.3 1	195 2335 12.0 13	13 167 12.8 0	14 84

DRIVER, DONALD — WR — PACKERS

PERSONAL: Born February 2, 1975, in Houston. ... 6-0/174. ... Full name: Donald Jerome Driver.
HIGH SCHOOL: Milby (Texas).
COLLEGE: Alcorn State.
TRANSACTIONS/CAREER NOTES: Selected by Green Bay Packers in seventh round (213th pick overall) of 1999 NFL draft.

Year Team	G	RECEIVING No. Yds. Avg. TD
1995—Alcorn State		Did not play.
1996—Alcorn State	11	12 429 35.8 1
1997—Alcorn State	11	21 556 26.5 6
1998—Alcorn State	11	55 1128 20.5 10
College totals (3 years)	33	88 2113 24.0 17

EDWARDS, ANTUAN — CB — PACKERS

PERSONAL: Born May 26, 1977, in Starkville, Miss. ... 6-1/208. ... Full name: Antuan Minye Edwards.
HIGH SCHOOL: Starkville (Miss.).
COLLEGE: Clemson.
TRANSACTIONS/CAREER NOTES: Selected by Green Bay Packers in first round (25th pick overall) of 1999 NFL draft.
COLLEGE NOTES: Recovered one fumble for 14 yards (1995); recovered two fumbles for 104 yards and one touchdown (1998).

Year Team	G	INTERCEPTIONS No. Yds. Avg. TD	PUNT RETURNS No. Yds. Avg. TD	KICKOFF RETURNS No. Yds. Avg. TD	TOTALS TD Pts.
1995—Clemson	12	0 0 ... 0	4 57 14.3 0	2 40 20.0 0	0 0
1996—Clemson	12	2 58 29.0 0	2 18 9.0 0	3 43 14.3 0	0 0
1997—Clemson	11	4 81 20.3 1	0 0 ... 0	12 280 23.3 0	1 6
1998—Clemson	10	2 56 28.0 0	6 82 13.7 0	13 350 26.9 0	1 6
College totals (4 years)	45	8 195 24.4 1	12 157 13.1 0	30 713 23.8 0	2 12

EDWARDS, TROY — WR — STEELERS

PERSONAL: Born April 7, 1977, in Shreveport, La. ... 5-9/192.
HIGH SCHOOL: Huntington (Shreveport, La.).
COLLEGE: Louisiana Tech.
TRANSACTIONS/CAREER NOTES: Selected by Pittsburgh Steelers in first round (13th pick overall) of 1999 NFL draft.
HONORS: Fred Biletnikoff Award winner (1998). ... Named wide receiver on THE SPORTING NEWS college All-America second team (1998).

Year Team	G	RUSHING Att. Yds. Avg. TD	RECEIVING No. Yds. Avg. TD	PUNT RETURNS No. Yds. Avg. TD	KICKOFF RETURNS No. Yds. Avg. TD	TOTALS TD Pts.
1995—LouisianaTech			Prop 48.			
1996—LouisianaTech	11	2 30 15.0 0	38 649 17.1 10	0 0 ... 0	21 424 20.2 0	10 60
1997—LouisianaTech	11	15 190 12.7 3	102 1707 16.7 13	2 6 3.0 0	12 241 20.1 0	16 96
1998—LouisianaTech	12	21 227 10.8 3	140 1996 14.3 27	13 235 18.1 1	16 326 20.4 0	31 186
College totals (3 years)	34	38 447 11.8 6	280 4352 15.5 50	15 241 16.1 1	49 991 20.2 0	57 342

EKUBAN, EBENEZER — DE — COWBOYS

PERSONAL: Born May 29, 1976, in Riverdale, Md. ... 6-3/281. ... Full name: Ebenezer Ekuban Jr.
HIGH SCHOOL: Bladensburg (Riverdale, Md.).
COLLEGE: North Carolina.
TRANSACTIONS/CAREER NOTES: Selected by Dallas Cowboys in first round (20th pick overall) of 1999 NFL draft.
COLLEGE NOTES: Played tight end (1995-96). ... Caught one pass for four yards and one touchdown (1995); caught five passes for 62 yards and one touchdown (1996).

Year Team	G	SACKS
1995—North Carolina	8	0.0
1996—North Carolina	10	0.0
1997—North Carolina	10	5.0
1998—North Carolina	11	7.0
College totals (4 years)	39	12.0

FARRIS, KRIS — OT — STEELERS

PERSONAL: Born March 26, 1977, in St. Paul, Minn. ... 6-8/322. ... Full name: Kristofer Martin Farris.
HIGH SCHOOL: Santa Margarita (Rancho Santa Margarita, Calif.).
COLLEGE: UCLA.

TRANSACTIONS/CAREER NOTES: Selected after junior season by Pittsburgh Steelers in third round (74th pick overall) of 1999 NFL draft.
HONORS: Outland Trophy winner (1998). ... Named offensive tackle on THE SPORTING NEWS college All-America first team (1998).
COLLEGE PLAYING EXPERIENCE: UCLA, 1995-1998. ... Games: 1995 (redshirted), 1996 (11), 1997 (12), 1998 (12). Total: 33.

FAULK, KEVIN — RB — PATRIOTS

PERSONAL: Born June 15, 1976, in Lafayette, La. ... 5-8/197.
HIGH SCHOOL: Carencro (Lafayette, La.).
COLLEGE: Louisiana State.
TRANSACTIONS/CAREER NOTES: Selected by New England Patriots in second round (46th pick overall) of 1999 NFL draft.
HONORS: Named kick returner on THE SPORTING NEWS college All-America second team (1998).
COLLEGE NOTES: Attempted one pass with a completion for seven yards and a touchdown (1996); attempted one pass without a completion (1997); and attempted one pass with a completion for 20 yards (1998).

			RUSHING				RECEIVING				PUNT RETURNS				KICKOFF RETURNS			TOTALS	
Year Team	G	Att.	Yds.	Avg.	TD	No.	Yds.	Avg.	TD	No.	Yds.	Avg.	TD	No.	Yds.	Avg.	TD	TD	Pts.
1995—Louisiana State	10	174	852	4.9	6	5	86	17.2	1	0	0	...	0	2	36	18.0	0	7	42
1996—Louisiana State	11	248	1281	5.2	13	10	134	13.4	0	24	375	15.6	1	14	313	22.4	0	14	84
1997—Louisiana State	9	205	1144	5.6	15	16	93	5.8	0	14	192	13.7	0	9	217	24.1	0	15	90
1998—Louisiana State	11	229	1279	5.6	12	22	287	13.0	3	9	278	30.9	1	23	265	11.5	1	17	102
College totals (4 years)	41	856	4556	5.3	46	53	600	11.3	4	47	845	18.0	2	48	831	17.3	1	53	318

FAZANDE, JERMAINE — FB — CHARGERS

PERSONAL: Born January 14, 1975, in Marrero, La. ... 6-2/262.
HIGH SCHOOL: Ehret (Marrero, La.).
COLLEGE: Oklahoma.
TRANSACTIONS/CAREER NOTES: Selected by San Diego Chargers in second round (60th pick overall) of 1999 NFL draft.
COLLEGE NOTES: Caught one pass for 12 yards (1998).

		RUSHING				TOTALS	
	G	Att.	Yds.	Avg.	TD	TD	Pts.
1994—Oklahoma				Redshirted.			
1995—Oklahoma	11	28	112	4.0	0	0	0
1996—Oklahoma	8	12	43	3.6	0	0	0
1997—Oklahoma	11	105	491	4.7	5	5	30
1998—Oklahoma	9	42	161	3.8	3	3	18
College totals (4 years)	39	187	807	4.3	8	8	48

FINN, JIM — RB — BEARS

PERSONAL: Born December 9, 1976, in Teaneck, N.J. ... 5-10/238.
HIGH SCHOOL: Bergen Catholic (Oradell, N.J.).
COLLEGE: Pennsylvania.
TRANSACTIONS/CAREER NOTES: Selected by Chicago Bears in seventh round (253rd pick overall) of 1999 NFL draft.
COLLEGE NOTES: Played defensive back (1995 and 1996). ... Intercepted three passes for 37 yards (1996). ... Attempted three passes with three completions for 70 yards and two touchdowns (1998).

			RUSHING				RECEIVING				KICKOFF RETURNS			TOTALS	
Year Team	G	Att.	Yds.	Avg.	TD	No.	Yds.	Avg.	TD	No.	Yds.	Avg.	TD	TD	Pts.
1995—Pennsylvania	8	0	0	...	0	0	0	...	0	0	0	...	0	0	0
1996—Pennsylvania	10	0	0	...	0	0	0	...	0	0	0	...	0	0	0
1997—Pennsylvania	10	155	801	5.2	11	10	98	9.8	1	10	191	19.1	0	12	72
1998—Pennsylvania	10	323	1450	4.5	17	20	134	6.7	0	0	0	...	0	17	102
College totals (4 years)	38	478	2251	4.7	28	30	232	7.7	1	10	191	19.1	0	29	174

FISHER, BRYCE — DT — BILLS

PERSONAL: Born May 12, 1977, in Renton, Wash. ... 6-2/251.
HIGH SCHOOL: Seattle Prep.
COLLEGE: Air Force.
TRANSACTIONS/CAREER NOTES: Selected by Buffalo Bills in seventh round (248th pick overall) of 1999 NFL draft.

Year Team	G	SACKS
1995—Air Force		Redshirted.
1996—Air Force	7	0.0
1997—Air Force	12	2.5
1998—Air Force	12	6.0
College totals (3 years)	31	8.5

FISHER, CHARLES — CB — BENGALS

PERSONAL: Born February 2, 1976, in Aliquippa, Pa. ... 6-0/186.
HIGH SCHOOL: Aliquippa (Pa.).
COLLEGE: West Virginia.
TRANSACTIONS/CAREER NOTES: Selected by Cincinnati Bengals in second round (33rd pick overall) of 1999 NFL draft.

Year Team	G	No.	Yds.	Avg.	TD
1994—West Virginia			Redshirted.		
1995—West Virginia	3	0	0	...	0
1996—West Virginia	12	1	0	0.0	0
1997—West Virginia	12	0	0	...	0
1998—West Virginia	12	3	30	10.0	0
College totals (4 years)	39	4	30	7.5	0

FLETCHER, DERRICK — OL — PATRIOTS

PERSONAL: Born September 9, 1975, in Aldine, Texas ... 6-6/348.
HIGH SCHOOL: Aldine (Texas).
COLLEGE: Baylor.
TRANSACTIONS/CAREER NOTES: Selected by New England Patriots in fifth round (154th pick overall) of 1999 NFL draft.
COLLEGE PLAYING EXPERIENCE: Baylor, 1994-1998. ... Games: 1994 (redshirted), 1995 (11), 1996 (10), 1997 (11), 1998 (11). Total: 43.

FOREMAN, JAY — LB — BILLS

PERSONAL: Born February 18, 1976, in Eden Prairie, Minn. ... 6-1/237. ... Full name: Jamal Foreman. ... Son of Chuck Foreman, running back with Minnesota Vikings (1973-79) and New England Patriots (1980).
HIGH SCHOOL: Eden Prairie (Minn.).
COLLEGE: Nebraska (degree in business administration).
TRANSACTIONS/CAREER NOTES: Selected by Buffalo Bills in fifth round (156th pick overall) of 1999 NFL draft.
COLLEGE NOTES: Intercepted two passes for 27 yards and a touchdown (1996).

Year Team	G	SACKS
1994—Nebraska		Redshirted.
1995—Nebraska	11	0.0
1996—Nebraska	12	0.5
1997—Nebraska	12	1.5
1998—Nebraska	12	3.0
College totals (4 years)	47	5.0

FRIEDMAN, LENNIE — G — BRONCOS

PERSONAL: Born October 13, 1976, in Livingston, N.J. ... 6-3/300.
HIGH SCHOOL: West Milford (N.J.).
COLLEGE: Duke.
TRANSACTIONS/CAREER NOTES: Selected by Denver Broncos in second round (61st pick overall) of 1999 NFL draft.
COLLEGE PLAYING EXPERIENCE: Duke, 1995-1998. ... Games: 1995 (7), 1996 (11), 1997 (11), 1998 (11). Total: 40.

GARDNER, BARRY — LB — EAGLES

PERSONAL: Born December 13, 1976, in Harvey, Ill. ... 6-0/248. ... Full name: Barry Allan Gardner.
HIGH SCHOOL: Thornton (Harvey, Ill.).
COLLEGE: Northwestern.
TRANSACTIONS/CAREER NOTES: Selected by Philadelphia Eagles in second round (35th pick overall) of 1999 NFL draft.

Year Team	G	No.	Yds.	Avg.	TD	SACKS No.
1994—Northwestern			Did not play.			
1995—Northwestern	11	1	-2	-2.0	0	0.0
1996—Northwestern	12	1	1	1.0	0	2.0
1997—Northwestern	12	2	17	8.5	0	1.0
1998—Northwestern	12	1	3	3.0	0	1.0
College totals (4 years)	47	5	19	3.8	0	4.0

GARMON, KELVIN — G — COWBOYS

PERSONAL: Born October 26, 1976, in Fort Worth, Texas. ... 6-2/329.
HIGH SCHOOL: Haltom (Fort Worth, Texas).
COLLEGE: Baylor.
TRANSACTIONS/CAREER NOTES: Selected by Dallas Cowboys in seventh round (243rd pick overall) of 1999 NFL draft.
COLLEGE PLAYING EXPERIENCE: Baylor, 1994-1998. ... Games: 1994 (redshirted), 1995 (9), 1996 (11), 1997 (11), 1998 (9). Total: (40).

GARY, OLANDIS — RB — BRONCOS

PERSONAL: Born May 18, 1975, in Washington, D.C. ... 5-11/218.
HIGH SCHOOL: Riverdale Baptist (Upper Marlboro, Md.).
COLLEGE: Marshall, then Georgia.
TRANSACTIONS/CAREER NOTES: Selected by Denver Broncos in fourth round (127th pick overall) of 1999 NFL draft.

GEORGE, TONY — S — PATRIOTS

PERSONAL: Born August 10, 1975, in Cincinnati. ... 5-11/200. ... Full name: Houston Antonio George.
HIGH SCHOOL: Winton Woods (Cincinnati).
COLLEGE: Florida.
TRANSACTIONS/CAREER NOTES: Selected by New England Patriots in third round (91st pick overall) of 1999 NFL draft.

			RUSHING				RECEIVING			KICKOFF RETURNS			TOTALS	
Year	Team	G	Att.	Yds.	Avg.	TD	No.	Yds.	Avg.	TD	No.	Yds.	Avg.	TD	TD	Pts.
1994—Marshall		7	34	262	7.7	3	4	14	3.5	...	1	16	16.0	0	3	18
1995—Marshall		11	69	514	7.4	9	5	18	3.6	0	1	35	35.0	0	9	54
1996—Georgia								Redshirted.								
1997—Georgia		11	66	381	5.8	7	7	75	10.7	1	0	0	...	0	8	48
1998—Georgia		11	143	698	4.9	10	10	117	11.7	0	0	0	...	0	10	60
College totals (4 years)		40	312	1855	5.9	29	26	224	8.6	1	2	51	25.5	0	30	180

			INTERCEPTIONS				SACKS
Year	Team	G	No.	Yds.	Avg.	TD	No.
1994—Florida			Redshirted.				
1995—Florida		12	1	0	0.0	0	0.0
1996—Florida		12	1	2	2.0	0	1.0
1997—Florida		11	2	89	44.5	1	3.0
1998—Florida		9	4	39	9.8	0	0.0
College totals (4 years)		44	8	130	16.3	1	4.0

GERMAINE, JOE — QB — RAMS

PERSONAL: Born August 11, 1975, in Mesa, Ariz. ... 6-0/203.
HIGH SCHOOL: Mountain View (Mesa, Ariz.).
JUNIOR COLLEGE: Scottsdale (Ariz.) Community College.
COLLEGE: Ohio State.
TRANSACTIONS/CAREER NOTES: Selected by St. Louis Rams in fourth round (101st pick overall) of 1999 NFL draft.

			PASSING								RUSHING			TOTALS	
Year	Team	G	Att.	Cmp.	Pct.	Yds.	TD	Int.	Avg.	Rat.	Att.	Yds.	Avg.	TD	TD	Pts.
1994—Scottsdale (Ariz.) CC		...	356	231	64.9	2729	18	5	7.67	143.2	0	0	...	0	0	0
1995—Ohio State						Redshirted.										
1996—Ohio State		12	147	80	54.4	1193	15	4	8.12	150.8	17	-61	-3.6	0	0	0
1997—Ohio State		13	210	129	61.4	1847	16	9	8.80	151.9	32	-132	-4.1	0	0	0
1998—Ohio State		12	384	230	59.9	3330	25	7	8.67	150.6	62	-83	-1.3	0	0	0
Junior college totals (1 year)		...	356	231	64.9	2729	18	5	7.67	143.2	0	0		0	0	0
College totals (3 years)		37	741	439	59.2	6370	56	20	8.60	151.0	111	-276	-2.5	0	0	0

GIBSON, AARON — OT — LIONS

PERSONAL: Born September 27, 1977, in Indianapolis. ... 6-4/375.
HIGH SCHOOL: Decatur Central (Indianapolis).
COLLEGE: Wisconsin.
TRANSACTIONS/CAREER NOTES: Selected by Detroit Lions in first round (27th pick overall) of 1999 NFL draft.
HONORS: Named offensive tackle on THE SPORTING NEWS college All-America second team (1998).
COLLEGE PLAYING EXPERIENCE: Wisconsin, 1995-1998. ... Games: 1995 (Prop 48), 1996 (9), 1997 (13), 1998 (12). Total: 34.

GLENN, LAMARR — FB — BUCCANEERS

PERSONAL: Born December 11, 1975, in Daytona Beach, Fla. ... 6-1/235.
HIGH SCHOOL: Seabreeze (Daytona Beach, Fla.).
COLLEGE: Florida State.
TRANSACTIONS/CAREER NOTES: Selected by Tampa Bay Buccaneers in sixth round (195th pick overall) of 1999 NFL draft.

			RUSHING				RECEIVING			TOTALS	
Year	Team	G	Att.	Yds.	Avg.	TD	No.	Yds.	Avg.	TD	TD	Pts.
1994—Florida State					Redshirted.							
1995—Florida State		...	8	21	2.6	0	0	0	...	0	0	0
1996—Florida State		12	8	49	6.1	0	3	18	6.0	0	0	0
1998—Florida State		12	15	41	2.7	1	1	6	6.0	0	1	6
College totals (3 years)		...	31	111	3.6	1	4	24	6.0	0	1	6

GLOVER, PHIL — LB — TITANS

PERSONAL: Born December 17, 1975, in Las Vegas, Nev. ... 5-11/239.
HIGH SCHOOL: Clark (Las Vegas, Nev.).
COLLEGE: Washington State, then Utah.
TRANSACTIONS/CAREER NOTES: Selected by Tennessee Titans in seventh round (222nd pick overall) of 1999 NFL draft.

Year Team	G	INTERCEPTIONS No.	Yds.	Avg.	TD	SACKS No.
1995—Washington State		Did not play.				
1996—Utah		Transfer student.				
1997—Utah	11	2	6	3.0	0	4.0
1998—Utah	6	1	0	0.0	0	0.0
College totals (2 years)	17	3	6	2.0	0	4.0

GRAMATICA, MARTIN — K — BUCCANEERS

PERSONAL: Born November 27, 1975, in Buenos Aires, Argentina. ... 5-8/180.
HIGH SCHOOL: La Belle (Fla.).
COLLEGE: Kansas State.
TRANSACTIONS/CAREER NOTES: Selected by Tampa Bay Buccaneers in third round (80th pick overall) of 1999 NFL draft.
HONORS: Named kicker on THE SPORTING NEWS college All-America first team (1997). ... Named kicker on THE SPORTING NEWS college All-America second team (1998).

				KICKING				
Year Team	G	XPM	XPA	FGM	FGA	Lg.	50+	Pts.
1994—Kansas State	12	38	39	6	9	40	0-0	56
1995—Kansas State	12	43	46	7	10	32	0-0	64
1996—Kansas State				Medical redshirt.				
1997—Kansas State	11	37	38	19	20	55	0-0	94
1998—Kansas State	12	69	69	22	31	65	0-0	135
College totals (4 years)	47	187	192	54	70	65	0-0	349

GREGG, KELLY — DT — BENGALS

PERSONAL: Born November 1, 1976, in Edmond, Okla. ... 6-0/285.
HIGH SCHOOL: Edmond (Okla.).
COLLEGE: Oklahoma.
TRANSACTIONS/CAREER NOTES: Selected by Cincinnati Bengals in sixth round (173rd pick overall) of 1999 NFL draft.

Year Team	G	SACKS
1995—Oklahoma	11	3.0
1996—Oklahoma	11	2.0
1997—Oklahoma	12	10.0
1998—Oklahoma	11	9.0
College totals (4 years)	45	24.0

GREISEN, CHRIS — QB — CARDINALS

PERSONAL: Born July 2, 1976, in Sturgeon Bay, Wis. ... 6-3/223.
HIGH SCHOOL: Sturgeon Bay (Wis.).
COLLEGE: Northwest Missouri State.
TRANSACTIONS/CAREER NOTES: Selected by Arizona Cardinals in seventh round (239th pick overall) of 1999 NFL draft.

		PASSING							RUSHING			TOTALS	
Year Team	G	Att.	Cmp.	Pct.	Yds.	TD	Int.	Avg.	Rat.	Att.	Yds.	Avg.	TD	TD	Pts.
1995—Northwest Missouri State	8	31	13	41.9	178	2	1	5.74	105.0	9	-27	-3.0	0	0	0
1996—Northwest Missouri State	7	18	11	61.1	170	1	0	9.44	158.8	13	34	2.6	0	0	0
1997—Northwest Missouri State	11	272	155	57.0	2456	23	7	9.03	155.6	53	49	0.9	1	1	6
1998—Northwest Missouri State	11	332	200	60.2	2937	25	14	8.85	151.0	44	20	0.5	5	5	30
College totals (4 years)	37	653	379	58.0	5741	51	22	8.79	150.9	119	76	0.6	6	6	36

HALE, RYAN — DT — GIANTS

PERSONAL: Born June 10, 1975, in Rogers, Ark ... 6-4/298.
HIGH SCHOOL: Rogers (Ark.).
COLLEGE: Arkansas.
TRANSACTIONS/CAREER NOTES: Selected by New York Giants in seventh round (225th pick overall) of 1999 NFL draft.

Year Team	G	SACKS
1994—Arkansas		Redshirted.
1995—Arkansas	6	0.0
1996—Arkansas	11	3.0
1997—Arkansas	11	5.0
1998—Arkansas	11	2.0
College totals (4 years)	39	10.0

HALEY, JERMAINE — DT — DOLPHINS

PERSONAL: Born February 3, 1973, in Fresno, Calif. ... 6-4/270.
HIGH SCHOOL: Hanford (Calif.).
JUNIOR COLLEGE: Butte Junior College (Calif.).
TRANSACTIONS/CAREER NOTES: Signed by Toronto Argonauts of CFL (May 1998). ... Selected by Miami Dolphins in seventh round (232nd pick overall) of 1999 NFL draft.

Year	Team	G	INTERCEPTIONS No.	Yds.	Avg.	TD	SACKS No.
1997—Butte College		11	2	45	22.5	0	23.0
1998—Toronto Argonauts CFL		16	0	0	...	0	7.0

HALL, CORY — S — BENGALS

PERSONAL: Born December 5, 1976, in Bakersfield, Calif. ... 6-0/205.
HIGH SCHOOL: South (Bakersfield, Calif.).
COLLEGE: Fresno State.
TRANSACTIONS/CAREER NOTES: Selected by Cincinnati Bengals in third round (65th pick overall) of 1999 NFL draft. ... Signed by Bengals (May 7, 1999).

Year	Team	G	INTERCEPTIONS No.	Yds.	Avg.	TD	SACKS No.
1995—Fresno State		5	0	0	...	0	0.0
1996—Fresno State		10	2	26	13.0	0	0.0
1997—Fresno State		8	1	0	0.0	0	3.5
1998—Fresno State		11	1	0	0.0	0	3.0
College totals (4 years)		34	4	26	6.5	0	6.5

HALL, DARRAN — WR/KR — TITANS

PERSONAL: Born September 8, 1975, in San Diego. ... 5-8/166. ... Full name: Darran Lamonta Hall.
HIGH SCHOOL: Lincoln (San Diego).
JUNIOR COLLEGE: Grossmont College (Calif.).
COLLEGE: Colorado State.
TRANSACTIONS/CAREER NOTES: Selected by Tennessee Titans in sixth round (186th pick overall) of 1999 NFL draft.

			RUSHING				RECEIVING				PUNT RETURNS				KICKOFF RETURNS				TOTALS	
Year	Team	G	Att.	Yds.	Avg.	TD	No.	Yds.	Avg.	TD	No.	Yds.	Avg.	TD	No.	Yds.	Avg.	TD	TD	Pts.
1996—Grossmont College		...	0	0	...	0	49	1239	25.3	13	0	0	...	0	0	0	...	0	13	78
1997—Colorado State		12	4	88	22.0	1	21	476	22.7	5	9	180	20.0	1	15	329	21.9	0	7	42
1998—Colorado State		11	7	65	9.3	2	44	629	14.3	2	26	302	11.6	0	6	95	15.8	0	5	30
Junior college totals (1 year)		...	0	0	...	0	49	1239	25.3	13	0	0	...	0	0	0	...	0	13	78
College totals (2 years)		23	11	153	13.9	3	65	1105	17.0	7	35	482	13.8	2	21	424	20.2	0	12	72

RECORD AS BASEBALL PLAYER

TRANSACTIONS/CAREER NOTES: Threw left, batted both. ... Selected by Cincinnati Reds organization in seventh-round of free agent draft (June 3, 1993).

							BATTING								FIELDING			
Year	Team (League)	Pos.	G	AB	R	H	2B	3B	HR	RBI	Avg.	BB	SO	SB	PO	A	E	Avg.
1993—Princeton (Appal.)	OF	49	142	17	28	3	0	0	5	.197	14	40	17	65	2	4	.944
1994—Princeton (Appal.)	OF	48	90	22	17	1	1	0	5	.189	33	29	19	49	2	3	.944
1995—Princeton (Appal.)	OF	9	25	3	3	0	0	0	1	.120	5	10	1	18	0	0	1.000
Totals (3 years)		106	257	42	48	4	1	0	11	.187	52	79	37	132	4	7	.951

HALL, JEFF — K — REDSKINS

PERSONAL: Born July 30, 1976, in Winchester, Tenn. ... 5-11/190. ... Full name: Paul Jeffery Hall.
HIGH SCHOOL: Franklin (Winchester, Tenn.).
COLLEGE: Tennessee.
TRANSACTIONS/CAREER NOTES: Selected by Washington Redskins in sixth round (181st pick overall) of 1999 NFL draft.

					KICKING			
Year	Team	G	XPM	XPA	FGM	FGA	Lg.	50+	Pts.
1994—Tennessee					Redshirted.				
1995—Tennessee	12	47	49	16	25	53	0-0	95
1996—Tennessee	12	47	49	10	18	46	0-0	77
1997—Tennessee	13	47	49	16	22	49	0-0	95
1998—Tennessee	12	47	47	19	24	47	0-0	104
College totals (4 years)	49	188	194	61	89	53	0-0	371

HATCHER, ARMON — S — BILLS

PERSONAL: Born July 15, 1976, in Diamond Bar, Calif. ... 6-0/212. ... Cousin of Billy Hatcher, outfielder with eight major league baseball teams (1981-95).
HIGH SCHOOL: Diamond Bar (Calif.).
COLLEGE: Oregon State.
TRANSACTIONS/CAREER NOTES: Selected by Buffalo Bills in sixth round (194th pick overall) of 1999 NFL draft.

			INTERCEPTIONS				KICKOFF RETURNS				TOTALS	
Year	Team	G	No.	Yds.	Avg.	TD	No.	Yds.	Avg.	TD	TD	Pts.
1994—Oregon State				Redshirted.								
1995—Oregon State		11	3	74	24.7	0	7	163	23.3	0	0	0
1996—Oregon State		11	2	-1	-0.5	0	22	444	20.2	0	0	0
1997—Oregon State		11	3	81	27.0	0	18	356	19.8	0	0	0
1998—Oregon State		11	5	60	12.0	0	0	0	...	0	0	0
College totals (4 years)		44	13	214	16.5	0	47	963	20.5	0	0	0

HEIDEN, STEVE — TE — CHARGERS

PERSONAL: Born September 21, 1976, in Rushford, Minn. ... 6-4/256.
HIGH SCHOOL: Rushford-Peterson (Rushford, Minn.).
COLLEGE: South Dakota State.
TRANSACTIONS/CAREER NOTES: Selected by San Diego Chargers in third round (69th pick overall) of 1999 NFL draft.

			RECEIVING			
Year Team		G	No.	Yds.	Avg.	TD
1995—South Dakota State		11	12	128	10.7	0
1996—South Dakota State		11	15	188	12.5	0
1997—South Dakota State		10	39	441	11.3	3
1998—South Dakota State		11	46	742	16.1	5
College totals (4 years)		43	112	1499	13.4	8

HEIMBURGER, CRAIG — G — PACKERS

PERSONAL: Born February 3, 1977, in Belleville, Ill. ... 6-2/314.
HIGH SCHOOL: East (Belleville, Ill.).
COLLEGE: Missouri.
TRANSACTIONS/CAREER NOTES: Selected by Green Bay Packers in fifth round (163rd pick overall) of 1999 NFL draft.
COLLEGE PLAYING EXPERIENCE: Missouri, 1995-1998. ... Games: 1995 (unavailable), 1996 (11), 1997 (12), 1998 (12).

HILL, MADRE — RB — BROWNS

PERSONAL: Born January 2, 1976, in Malvern, Ark. ... 5-11/199.
HIGH SCHOOL: Malvern (Ark.).
COLLEGE: Arkansas.
TRANSACTIONS/CAREER NOTES: Selected by Cleveland Browns in seventh round (207th pick overall) of 1999 NFL draft.

		RUSHING				RECEIVING				KICKOFF RETURNS				TOTALS	
Year Team	G	Att.	Yds.	Avg.	TD	No.	Yds.	Avg.	TD	No.	Yds.	Avg.	TD	TD	Pts.
1994—Arkansas	8	74	351	4.7	3	6	50	8.3	0	7	223	31.9	1	4	24
1995—Arkansas	12	307	1387	4.5	15	23	196	8.5	1	0	0	...	0	16	96
1996—Arkansas							Did not play.								
1997—Arkansas							Did not play.								
1998—Arkansas	11	160	669	4.2	7	3	26	8.7	0	1	12	12.0	0	7	42
College totals (3 years)	31	541	2407	4.4	25	32	272	8.5	1	8	235	29.4	1	27	162

HOLDMAN, WARRICK — LB — BEARS

PERSONAL: Born November 22, 1975, in Alief, Texas. ... 6-1/233. ... Full name: Warrick Donte Holdman.
HIGH SCHOOL: Elsik (Alief, Texas).
COLLEGE: Texas A&M.
TRANSACTIONS/CAREER NOTES: Selected by Chicago Bears in fourth round (106th pick overall) of 1999 NFL draft.
COLLEGE NOTES: Recovered one fumble for a touchdown (1998).

Year Team	G	SACKS
1994—Texas A&M		Redshirted.
1995—Texas A&M	9	2.0
1996—Texas A&M	12	2.5
1997—Texas A&M	12	5.0
1998—Texas A&M	13	7.0
College totals (4 years)	46	16.5

HOLT, TORRY — WR — RAMS

PERSONAL: Born June 5, 1976, in Gibsonville, N.C. ... 6-0/190.
HIGH SCHOOL: Eastern Guilford (Gibsonville, N.C.).
COLLEGE: North Carolina State.
TRANSACTIONS/CAREER NOTES: Selected by St. Louis Rams in first round (sixth pick overall) of 1999 NFL draft.
HONORS: Named wide receiver on THE SPORTING NEWS college All-America first team (1998).
COLLEGE NOTES: Attempted one pass with a completion for 45 yards and a touchdown (1998).

		RUSHING				RECEIVING				PUNT RETURNS				KICKOFF RETURNS				TOTALS	
Year Team	G	Att.	Yds.	Avg.	TD	No.	Yds.	Avg.	TD	No.	Yds.	Avg.	TD	No.	Yds.	Avg.	TD	TD	Pts.
1995—North Carolina State	11	2	2	1.0	0	17	261	15.4	1	5	20	4.0	0	13	274	21.1	0	1	6
1996—North Carolina State	7	2	9	4.5	0	24	415	17.3	1	1	-1	-1.0	0	7	143	20.4	0	3	18
1997—North Carolina State	11	3	6	2.0	0	62	1099	17.7	16	12	162	13.5	0	0	0	...	0	16	96
1998—North Carolina State	11	6	102	17.0	0	88	1604	18.2	11	20	273	13.7	2	0	0	...	0	13	78
College totals (4 years)	40	13	119	9.2	0	191	3379	17.7	31	38	454	11.9	2	20	417	20.9	0	33	198

HOPSON, TYRONE — OT — 49ERS

PERSONAL: Born May 28, 1976, in Owensboro, Ky. ... 6-2/305. ... Full name: Tyrone Hopson Jr.
HIGH SCHOOL: Daviess County (Owensboro, Ky.).

COLLEGE: Eastern Kentucky.
TRANSACTIONS/CAREER NOTES: Selected by San Francisco 49ers in fifth round (161st pick overall) of 1999 NFL draft.
COLLEGE PLAYING EXPERIENCE: Eastern Kentucky, 1995-1998. ... Games played unavailable.

HUARD, BROCK — QB — SEAHAWKS

PERSONAL: Born April 15, 1976, in Seattle. ... 6-5/228. ... Brother of Damon Huard, quarterback, Miami Dolphins.
HIGH SCHOOL: Puyallup (Wash.).
COLLEGE: Washington.
TRANSACTIONS/CAREER NOTES: Selected after junior season by Seattle Seahawks in third round (77th pick overall) of 1999 NFL draft.

			PASSING							RUSHING			TOTALS	
Year Team	G	Att.	Cmp.	Pct.	Yds.	TD	Int.	Avg.	Rat.	Att.	Yds.	Avg.	TD	TD Pts.
1996—Washington	11	217	108	49.8	1678	13	5	7.73	129.9	39	12	0.3	2	2 12
1997—Washington	10	244	146	59.8	2140	23	10	8.77	156.4	31	-82	-2.6	1	1 6
1998—Washington	9	315	168	53.3	1924	15	12	6.11	112.7	44	31	0.7	0	0 0
College totals (3 years)	30	776	422	54.4	5742	51	27	7.40	131.3	114	-39	-0.3	3	3 18

HUMPHREY, JAY — OT — VIKINGS

PERSONAL: Born June 20, 1976, in Dallas. ... 6-6/322. ... Full name: Jay Thomas Humphrey. ... Son of Tom Humphrey, center with Kansas City Chiefs (1974).
HIGH SCHOOL: Richardson (Texas).
COLLEGE: Texas.
TRANSACTIONS/CAREER NOTES: Selected by Minnesota Vikings in fourth round (125th pick overall) of 1999 NFL draft.
HONORS: Named offensive tackle on THE SPORTING NEWS college All-America first team (1998).
COLLEGE PLAYING EXPERIENCE: Texas, 1994-1998. ... Games: 1994 (redshirted), 1995 (6), 1996 (12), 1997 (11), 1998 (11). Total: 40.

HUNT, CLETIDUS — DT — PACKERS

PERSONAL: Born January 2, 1976, in Memphis, Tenn. ... 6-4/300. ... Name pronounced CLEE-tus.
HIGH SCHOOL: Whitehaven (Memphis, Tenn.).
JUNIOR COLLEGE: Northwest Mississippi Community College.
COLLEGE: Georgia, then Kentucky State.
TRANSACTIONS/CAREER NOTES: Selected by Green Bay Packers in third round (94th pick overall) of NFL draft.
COLLEGE NOTES: Intercepted one pass for no yards (1998).

Year Team	G	SACKS
1994—Northwest Mississippi CC	10	15.0
1995—Northwest Mississippi CC	10	6.0
1996—Georgia		Did not play.
1997—Kentucky State	11	2.0
1998—Kentucky State	11	10.0
Junior college totals (2 years)	20	21.0
College totals (2 years)	22	12.0

HUNT, ROBERT — G/OT — BUCCANEERS

PERSONAL: Born July 22, 1975, in Hampton, Va. ... 6-3/290. ... Full name: Robert Williams Hunt.
HIGH SCHOOL: Menchville (Va.).
COLLEGE: Virginia.
TRANSACTIONS/CAREER NOTES: Selected by Tampa Bay Buccaneers in seventh round (226th pick overall) of 1999 NFL draft.
COLLEGE PLAYING EXPERIENCE: Virginia, 1994-1998. ... Games: 1994 (redshirted), 1995 (3), 1996 (7), 1997 (11), 1998 (11). Total: 32.

IRVIN, SEDRICK — RB — LIONS

PERSONAL: Born March 30, 1978, in Miami. ... 5-11/217. ... Cousin of Michael Irvin, wide receiver, Dallas Cowboys.
HIGH SCHOOL: Southridge (Miami), then Miami High.
COLLEGE: Michigan State.
TRANSACTIONS/CAREER NOTES: Selected after junior season by Detroit Lions in fourth round (103rd pick overall) of 1999 NFL draft.
COLLEGE NOTES: Attempted three passes with two completions for 87 yards and one touchdown (1996); attempted two passes with one completion for 24 yards (1997); and attempted two passes with one completion for six yards (1998).

		RUSHING				RECEIVING				PUNT RETURNS				KICKOFF RETURNS				TOTALS	
Year Team	G	Att.	Yds.	Avg.	TD	No.	Yds.	Avg.	TD	No.	Yds.	Avg.	TD	No.	Yds.	Avg.	TD	TD Pts.
1996—Michigan State	12	237	1067	4.5	16	40	337	8.4	2	0	0	...	0	3	58	19.3	0	18 104
1997—Michigan State	12	246	1270	5.2	9	40	346	8.7	4	23	313	13.6	1	0	0	...	0	14 84
1998—Michigan State	12	272	1167	4.3	10	28	210	7.5	0	2	23	11.5	0	4	42	10.5	0	10 60
College totals (3 years)	36	755	3504	4.6	35	108	893	8.3	6	25	336	13.4	1	7	100	14.3	0	42 248

JACKSON, DEXTER — S — BUCCANEERS

PERSONAL: Born July 28, 1977, in Quincy, Fla. ... 6-0/189.
HIGH SCHOOL: James A. Shanks (Quincy, Fla.).

COLLEGE: Florida State.
TRANSACTIONS/CAREER NOTES: Selected by Tampa Bay Buccaneers in fourth round (113th pick overall) of 1999 NFL draft.
COLLEGE NOTES: Credited with two sacks (1996).

			INTERCEPTIONS			
Year Team		G	No.	Yds.	Avg.	TD
1995—Florida State		11	1	22	22.0	0
1996—Florida State		11	0	0	...	0
1997—Florida State		11	2	0	0.0	0
1998—Florida State		11	4	23	5.8	0
College totals (4 years)		44	7	45	6.4	0

JACKSON, SHELDON — TE — BILLS

PERSONAL: Born July 24, 1976, in Diamond Bar, Calif. ... 6-3/237.
HIGH SCHOOL: Damien (Diamond Bar, Calif.).
COLLEGE: Nebraska (degree in psychology).
TRANSACTIONS/CAREER NOTES: Selected by Buffalo Bills in seventh round (230th pick overall) of 1999 NFL draft.

		RECEIVING				KICKOFF RETURNS				TOTALS	
Year Team	G	No.	Yds.	Avg.	TD	No.	Yds.	Avg.	TD	TD	Pts.
1994—Nebraska				Redshirted.							
1995—Nebraska	10	6	52	8.7	2	0	0	...	0	2	12
1996—Nebraska	12	4	48	12.0	2	0	0	...	0	2	12
1997—Nebraska	12	11	189	17.2	2	1	13	13.0	0	2	12
1998—Nebraska	12	19	343	18.1	4	2	19	9.5	0	4	16
College totals (4 years)	46	40	632	15.8	10	3	32	10.7	0	10	52

JACKSON, TERRY — RB — 49ERS

PERSONAL: Born January 10, 1976, in Gainesville, Fla. ... 6-0/218. ... Full name: Terrance Bernard Jackson. ... Brother of Willie Jackson Jr., wide receiver, Cincinnati Bengals.
HIGH SCHOOL: P.K. Yonge (Gainesville, Fla.).
COLLEGE: Florida.
TRANSACTIONS/CAREER NOTES: Selected by San Francisco 49ers in fifth round (157th pick overall) of 1999 NFL draft.

		RUSHING				RECEIVING				TOTALS	
Year Team	G	Att.	Yds.	Avg.	TD	No.	Yds.	Avg.	TD	TD	Pts.
1995—Florida	12	122	780	6.4	6	20	188	9.4	0	6	36
1996—Florida	12	79	388	4.9	8	13	163	12.5	1	9	54
1997—Florida	4	15	39	2.6	0	8	135	16.9	3	3	18
1998—Florida	8	105	587	5.6	3	18	169	9.4	0	3	18
College totals (4 years)	36	321	1794	5.6	17	59	655	11.1	4	21	126

JAMES, EDGERRIN — RB — COLTS

PERSONAL: Born August 1, 1978, in Immokalee, Fla. ... 6-0/216. ... Full name: Edgerrin Teree James.
HIGH SCHOOL: Immokalee (Fla.).
COLLEGE: Miami (Fla.).
TRANSACTIONS/CAREER NOTES: Selected after junior season by Indianapolis Colts in first round (fourth pick overall) of 1999 NFL draft.
COLLEGE NOTES: Returned one kickoff for 35 yards (1997).

		RUSHING				RECEIVING				TOTALS	
Year Team	G	Att.	Yds.	Avg.	TD	No.	Yds.	Avg.	TD	TD	Pts.
1996—Miami (Fla.)	7	71	446	6.3	2	6	90	15.0	0	2	12
1997—Miami (Fla.)	10	184	1098	6.0	13	19	250	13.2	1	14	86
1998—Miami (Fla.)	11	242	1416	5.9	17	17	255	15.0	2	19	114
College totals (3 years)	28	497	2960	6.0	32	42	595	14.2	3	35	212

JANSEN, JON — OT — REDSKINS

PERSONAL: Born January 28, 1976, in Clawson, Mich. ... 6-6/302. ... Full name: Jonathan Ward Jansen.
HIGH SCHOOL: Clawson (Mich.).
COLLEGE: Michigan.
TRANSACTIONS/CAREER NOTES: Selected by Washington Redskins in second round (37th pick overall) of 1999 NFL draft.
COLLEGE PLAYING EXPERIENCE: Michigan, 1994-1998. ... Games: 1994 (redshirted), 1995 (13), 1996 (12), 1997 (12), 1998 (13). Total: 50.

JENKINS, MARTAY — WR — COWBOYS

PERSONAL: Born February 28, 1975, in Waterloo, Iowa ... 5-11/203.
HIGH SCHOOL: Waterloo (Iowa) North.
JUNIOR COLLEGE: North Iowa Area Community College.
COLLEGE: Nebraska-Omaha.
TRANSACTIONS/CAREER NOTES: Selected by Dallas Cowboys in sixth round (193rd pick overall) of 1999 NFL draft.

Year—Team	G	Rushing Att.	Yds.	Avg.	TD	Receiving No.	Yds.	Avg.	TD	Kickoff Returns No.	Yds.	Avg.	TD	Totals TD	Pts.
1995—Nebraska-Omaha						Did not play.									
1996—Nebraska-Omaha	11	4	42	10.5	1	36	848	23.6	8	15	346	23.1	0	9	54
1997—Nebraska-Omaha	1	0	0	...	0	2	51	25.5	2	2	39	19.5	0	1	6
1998—Nebraska-Omaha	11	10	171	17.1	3	29	540	18.6	3	7	212	30.3	1	7	42
College totals (3 years)	23	14	213	15.2	4	67	1439	21.5	13	24	597	24.9	1	17	102

JOHNSON, J.J. RB DOLPHINS

PERSONAL: Born April 20, 1974, in Mobile, Ala. ... 6-1/235. ... Full name: James E. Johnson.
HIGH SCHOOL: Davidson (Mobile, Ala.).
JUNIOR COLLEGE: East Mississippi Junior College.
COLLEGE: Mississippi State.
TRANSACTIONS/CAREER NOTES: Selected by Miami Dolphins in second round (39th pick overall) of 1999 NFL draft.
HONORS: Named running back on THE SPORTING NEWS college All-America second team (1998).

Year—Team	G	Rushing Att.	Yds.	Avg.	TD	Receiving No.	Yds.	Avg.	TD	Totals TD	Pts.
1995—East Mississippi College	8	117	592	5.1	11	0	0	...	0	11	66
1996—East Mississippi College	10	132	909	6.9	15	0	0	...	0	15	90
1997—Mississippi State	11	217	1069	4.9	12	5	56	11.2	0	12	72
1998—Mississippi State	12	236	1383	5.9	12	7	98	14.0	0	12	72
Junior college totals (2 years)	18	249	1501	6.0	26	0	0	...	0	26	156
College totals (2 years)	23	453	2452	5.4	24	12	154	12.8	0	24	144

JOHNSON, KEVIN WR BROWNS

PERSONAL: Born July 15, 1975, in Trenton, N.J. ... 5-10/188. ... Full name: Kevin L. Johnson.
HIGH SCHOOL: Hamilton West (Trenton, N.J.).
COLLEGE: Syracuse.
TRANSACTIONS/CAREER NOTES: Selected by Cleveland Browns in second round (32nd pick overall) of 1999 NFL draft.
COLLEGE NOTES: Attempted one pass with a completion for 50 yards and a touchdown (1997).

Year—Team	G	Rushing Att.	Yds.	Avg.	TD	Receiving No.	Yds.	Avg.	TD	Punt Returns No.	Yds.	Avg.	TD	Kickoff Returns No.	Yds.	Avg.	TD	Totals TD	Pts.
1995—Syracuse	3	2	14	7.0	0	0	0	...	0	0	0	...	0	2	31	15.5	0	0	0
1996—Syracuse	11	0	0	...	0	6	78	13.0	1	4	99	24.8	1	11	202	18.4	0	2	12
1997—Syracuse	12	6	26	4.3	0	32	612	19.1	3	2	12	6.0	0	14	514	36.7	2	5	30
1998—Syracuse	11	8	105	13.1	3	60	894	14.9	9	18	145	8.1	0	23	690	30.0	2	14	84
College totals (4 years)	37	16	145	9.1	3	98	1584	16.2	13	24	256	10.7	1	50	1437	28.7	4	21	126

JOHNSON, MALCOLM WR STEELERS

PERSONAL: Born August 27, 1977, in Washington, D.C. ... 6-5/215. ... Full name: Malcolm Alexander Johnson.
HIGH SCHOOL: Gonzaga (Washington, D.C.).
COLLEGE: Notre Dame (degree in marketing).
TRANSACTIONS/CAREER NOTES: Selected by Pittsburgh Steelers in fifth round (195th pick overall) of 1999 NFL draft.

Year—Team	G	Receiving No.	Yds.	Avg.	TD
1994—Notre Dame		Redshirted.			
1995—Notre Dame	11	0	0	...	0
1996—Notre Dame	11	25	449	18.0	2
1997—Notre Dame	12	42	596	14.2	2
1998—Notre Dame	12	43	692	16.1	6
College totals (4 years)	46	110	1737	15.8	10

JOHNSON, PARIS S CARDINALS

PERSONAL: Born January 18, 1976, in Chicago. ... 6-2/213.
HIGH SCHOOL: Oak Park-River Forest (Oak Park, Ill.).
JUNIOR COLLEGE: North Iowa Area Community College.
COLLEGE: Miami (Ohio).
TRANSACTIONS/CAREER NOTES: Selected by Arizona Cardinals in fifth round (155th pick overall) of 1999 NFL draft.
COLLEGE NOTES: Credited with one sack (1998).

Year—Team	G	Interceptions No.	Yds.	Avg.	TD
1996—Miami of Ohio		Redshirted.			
1997—Miami of Ohio	11	1	8	8.0	0
1998—Miami of Ohio	5	0	0	...	0
College totals (2 years)	16	1	8	8.0	0

1999 DRAFT PICKS

JOHNSON, STEVE — CB — SEAHAWKS

PERSONAL: Born March 24, 1976, in Powder Springs, Ga. ... 5-10/178. ... Full name: Steve Lamar Johnson.
HIGH SCHOOL: McEachern (Powder Springs, Ga.).
COLLEGE: Tennessee.
TRANSACTIONS/CAREER NOTES: Selected by Seattle Seahawks in sixth round (170th pick overall) of 1999 NFL draft.
COLLEGE NOTES: Granted medical redshirt after three games (1996).

		INTERCEPTIONS			
Year Team	G	No.	Yds.	Avg.	TD
1994—Tennessee	11	0	0	...	0
1995—Tennessee	12	0	0	...	0
1996—Tennessee	3	0	0	...	0
1997—Tennessee	13	1	0	0.0	0
1998—Tennessee	13	1	22	22.0	0
College totals (5 years)	52	2	22	11.0	0

JONES, BRYAN — LB — DOLPHINS

PERSONAL: Born December 21, 1975, in San Luis Obispo, Calif. ... 6-4/217. ... Full name: Bryan Jovan Jones.
HIGH SCHOOL: Arroyo Grande (Calif.).
COLLEGE: Oregon State.
TRANSACTIONS/CAREER NOTES: Selected by Miami Dolphins in fifth round (142nd pick overall) of 1999 NFL draft.
COLLEGE NOTES: Intercepted one pass (1997); intercepted one pass (1998).

Year Team	G	SACKS
1994—Oregon State		Redshirted.
1995—Oregon State	11	0.0
1996—Oregon State	11	5.5
1997—Oregon State	11	2.0
1998—Oregon State	11	5.5
College totals (4 years)	44	13.0

JONES, CHRIS — LB — VIKINGS

PERSONAL: Born September 30, 1976, in Monroe, Ga. ... 5-10/229. ... Full name: Christopher Jones.
HIGH SCHOOL: Monroe (Ga.).
COLLEGE: Clemson.
TRANSACTIONS/CAREER NOTES: Selected by Minnesota Vikings in fifth round (169th pick overall) of 1999 NFL draft.
COLLEGE NOTES: Credited with four sacks (1998).
COLLEGE PLAYING EXPERIENCE: Clemson, 1995-1998. ... Games: 1995 (12), 1996 (11), 1997 (12), 1998 (10). Total: 44.

JONES, JERMAINE — CB/KR — JETS

PERSONAL: Born July 25, 1976, in Morgan City, La. ... 5-8/173.
HIGH SCHOOL: Central Catholic (Morgan City, La.).
COLLEGE: Northwestern (La.) State.
TRANSACTIONS/CAREER NOTES: Selected by New York Jets in fifth round (162nd pick overall) of 1999 NFL draft.
COLLEGE NOTES: Played wide receiver (1995). ... Caught five passes for 114 yards and rushed one time for five yards (1995); credited with two sacks (1997); advanced one fumble for 74 yards and a touchdown and credited with one sack (1998).

		INTERCEPTIONS				PUNT RETURNS				KICKOFF RETURNS				TOTALS	
Year Team	G	No.	Yds.	Avg.	TD	No.	Yds.	Avg.	TD	No.	Yds.	Avg.	TD	TD	Pts.
1994—Northwestern State								Redshirted.							
1995—Northwestern State	11	0	0	...	0	0	0	...	0	0	0	...	0	0	0
1996—Northwestern State	11	2	32	16.0	0	4	29	7.3	0	1	16	16.0	0	0	0
1997—Northwestern State	11	5	30	6.0	0	0	0	...	0	0	0	...	0	0	0
1998—Northwestern State	11	6	232	38.7	2	4	132	33.0	2	18	406	22.6	0	3	18
College totals (4 years)	44	13	294	22.6	2	8	161	20.1	2	19	422	22.2	0	3	18

KATZENMOYER, ANDY — LB — PATRIOTS

PERSONAL: Born December 2, 1977, in Westerville, Ohio. ... 6-3/264. ... Full name: Andrew Warren Katzenmoyer.
HIGH SCHOOL: Westerville (Ohio) South.
COLLEGE: Ohio State.
TRANSACTIONS/CAREER NOTES: Selected after junior season by New England Patriots in first round (28th pick overall) of 1999 NFL draft.
HONORS: Butkus Award winner (1997). ... Named inside linebacker on The Sporting News college All-America third team (1997).

		INTERCEPTIONS				SACKS
Year Team	G	No.	Yds.	Avg.	TD	No.
1996—Ohio State	12	4	67	16.8	1	12.0
1997—Ohio State	13	2	25	12.5	1	2.0
1998—Ohio State	12	0	0	...	0	4.0
College totals (3 years)	37	6	92	15.3	2	18.0

KEARSE, JEVON — DE — TITANS

PERSONAL: Born September 3, 1976, in Fort Myers, Fla. ... 6-4/260.
HIGH SCHOOL: North Fort Myers (Fla.).
COLLEGE: Florida.
TRANSACTIONS/CAREER NOTES: Selected after junior season by Tennessee Titans in first round (16th pick overall) of 1999 NFL draft.
HONORS: Named outside linebacker on THE SPORTING NEWS college All-America second team (1998).
COLLEGE NOTES: Intercepted one pass for 13 yards (1998).

Year—Team	G	SACKS
1996—Florida	11	2.5
1997—Florida	11	6.5
1998—Florida	11	7.5
College totals (3 years)	33	16.5

KELLY, JEFF — LB — FALCONS

PERSONAL: Born December 13, 1975, in La Grange, Texas. ... 5-11/256.
HIGH SCHOOL: La Grange (Texas).
JUNIOR COLLEGE: Garden City (Kan.) Community College.
COLLEGE: Stephen F. Austin State, then Kansas State.
TRANSACTIONS/CAREER NOTES: Selected by Atlanta Falcons in sixth round (198th pick overall) of 1999 NFL draft.
HONORS: Named inside linebacker on THE SPORTING NEWS college All-America second team (1998).
COLLEGE NOTES: Recovered two fumbles for 25 yards and one touchdown (1998).

			INTERCEPTIONS			SACKS
Year—Team	G	No.	Yds.	Avg.	TD	No.
1994—Stephen F. Austin State	10	0	0	...	0	0.0
1995—Garden City CC	...	4	0	0.0	1	12.0
1996—Kansas State			Redshirted.			
1997—Kansas State	11	0	0	...	0	7.0
1998—Kansas State	11	3	18	6.0	0	6.0
Junior college totals (1 year)	...	4	0	0.0	1	12.0
College totals (2 years)	32	3	18	6.0	1	13.0

KELLY, REGGIE — TE — FALCONS

PERSONAL: Born February 22, 1977, in Aberdeen, Miss. ... 6-3/250. ... Full name: Reginald Kuta Kelly.
HIGH SCHOOL: Aberdeen (Miss.).
COLLEGE: Mississippi State.
TRANSACTIONS/CAREER NOTES: Selected by Atlanta Falcons in second round (42nd pick overall) of 1999 NFL draft.

			RECEIVING		
Year—Team	G	No.	Yds.	Avg.	TD
1995—Mississippi State	10	1	24	24.0	0
1996—Mississippi State	11	6	135	22.5	0
1997—Mississippi State	11	10	175	17.5	1
1998—Mississippi State	12	12	140	11.7	1
College totals (4 years)	44	29	474	16.3	2

KELSAY, CHAD — LB — STEELERS

PERSONAL: Born April 9, 1977, in Auburn, Neb. ... 6-2/252.
HIGH SCHOOL: Auburn (Neb.).
COLLEGE: Nebraska.
TRANSACTIONS/CAREER NOTES: Selected by Pittsburgh Steelers in seventh round (219th pick overall) of 1999 NFL draft.
COLLEGE NOTES: Intercepted one pass (1998).

Year—Team	G	SACKS
1995—Nebraska	11	2.0
1996—Nebraska	11	2.5
1997—Nebraska	12	3.0
1998—Nebraska	12	5.0
College totals (4 years)	46	12.5

KERNEY, PATRICK — DE — FALCONS

PERSONAL: Born December 30, 1976, in Trenton, N.J. ... 6-5/269. ... Full name: Patrick Manning Kerney.
HIGH SCHOOL: Taft (Watertown, Conn.).
COLLEGE: Virginia.
TRANSACTIONS/CAREER NOTES: Selected by Atlanta Falcons in first round (30th pick overall) of 1999 NFL draft.
HONORS: Named defensive end on THE SPORTING NEWS college All-America second team (1998).

Year—Team	G	SACKS
1995—Virginia	9	0.0
1996—Virginia	11	1.0
1997—Virginia	10	8.0
1998—Virginia	11	15.0
College totals (4 years)	41	24.0

KING, ERIC — G — CHIEFS

PERSONAL: Born July 27, 1975, in Pittsburgh. ... 6-4/290.
HIGH SCHOOL: North Allgheny (Wexford, Pa.).
COLLEGE: Richmond.
TRANSACTIONS/CAREER NOTES: Selected by Kansas City Chiefs in seventh round (220th pick overall) of 1999 NFL draft. ... Signed by Chiefs (May 6, 1999).
COLLEGE NOTES: Played tight end (1995). ... Caught three passes for 24 yards (1995).
COLLEGE PLAYING EXPERIENCE: Richmond, 1994-1998. ... Games: 1994 (redshirted), 1995 (6), 1996 (8), 1997 (11), 1998 (12). Total: 37.

KING, LAMAR — DE — SEAHAWKS

PERSONAL: Born August 10, 1975, in Boston. ... 6-3/294.
HIGH SCHOOL: Chesapeake (Md.).
JUNIOR COLLEGE: Montgomery College (Md.).
COLLEGE: Saginaw Valley State (Mich.).
TRANSACTIONS/CAREER NOTES: Selected by Seattle Seahawks in first round (22nd pick overall) of 1999 NFL draft.
COLLEGE NOTES: Intercepted two passes (1996); intercepted two passes for no yards (1997).

Year Team	G	SACKS
1995—Montgomery College	10	0.0
1996—Montgomery College	9	18.0
1997—Saginaw Valley State	11	15.5
1998—Saginaw Valley State	11	12.0
Junior college totals (2 years)	19	18.0
College totals (2 years)	22	27.5

KING, SHAUN — QB — BUCCANEERS

PERSONAL: Born May 29, 1977, in St. Petersburg, Fla. ... 6-0/221. ... Full name: Shaun Earl King.
HIGH SCHOOL: Gibbs (St. Petersburg, Fla.).
COLLEGE: Tulane.
TRANSACTIONS/CAREER NOTES: Selected by Tampa Bay Buccaneers in second round (50th pick overall) of 1999 NFL draft.

		PASSING								RUSHING			TOTALS	
Year Team	G	Att.	Cmp.	Pct.	Yds.	TD	Int.	Avg.	Rat.	Att.	Yds.	Avg.	TD	TD	Pts.
1995—Tulane	8	199	92	46.2	1046	2	7	5.26	86.7	46	-10	-0.2	3	3	18
1996—Tulane	11	273	132	48.4	1574	8	7	5.77	101.3	43	16	0.4	1	1	6
1997—Tulane	11	363	199	54.8	2567	24	14	7.07	128.3	124	511	4.1	5	5	30
1998—Tulane	11	328	223	68.0	3232	36	6	9.85	183.3	140	532	3.8	10	10	60
College totals (4 years)	41	1163	646	55.5	8419	70	34	7.24	130.4	353	1049	3.0	19	19	114

KLEINSASSER, JIMMY — TE — VIKINGS

PERSONAL: Born January 31, 1977, in Carrington, N.D. ... 6-3/272.
HIGH SCHOOL: Carrington (N.D.).
COLLEGE: North Dakota.
TRANSACTIONS/CAREER NOTES: Selected by Minnsota Vikings in second round (44th pick overall) of 1999 NFL draft.

		RUSHING				RECEIVING				TOTALS	
Year Team	G	Att.	Yds.	Avg.	TD	No.	Yds.	Avg.	TD	TD	Pts.
1995—North Dakota	10	0	0	...	0	11	146	13.3	0	0	0
1996—North Dakota	10	0	0	...	0	18	268	14.9	2	2	12
1997—North Dakota	9	0	0	...	0	13	190	14.6	3	3	18
1998—North Dakota	10	9	86	9.6	1	45	710	15.8	5	6	36
College totals (4 years)	39	9	86	9.6	1	87	1314	15.1	10	11	66

KONRAD, ROB — FB — DOLPHINS

PERSONAL: Born November 12, 1976, in Rochester, N.Y. ... 6-3/260. ... Full name: Robert L. Konrad.
HIGH SCHOOL: St. John's (Andover, Mass.).
COLLEGE: Syracuse.
TRANSACTIONS/CAREER NOTES: Selected by Miami Dolphins in second round (43rd pick overall) of 1999 NFL draft.

		RUSHING				RECEIVING				TOTALS	
Year Team	G	Att.	Yds.	Avg.	TD	No.	Yds.	Avg.	TD	TD	Pts.
1995—Syracuse	11	63	433	6.9	7	2	29	14.5	1	8	48
1996—Syracuse	10	93	361	3.9	3	12	149	12.4	0	3	18
1997—Syracuse	7	46	305	6.6	3	7	99	14.1	0	3	18
1998—Syracuse	11	93	417	4.5	7	20	196	9.8	2	9	54
College totals (4 years)	39	295	1516	5.1	20	41	473	11.5	3	23	138

KRIEWALDT, CLINT — LB — LIONS

PERSONAL: Born March 16, 1976, in Shiocton, Wis. ... 6-1/235.
HIGH SCHOOL: Shiocton (Wis.).

COLLEGE: Wisconsin-Stevens Point.
TRANSACTIONS/CAREER NOTES: Selected by Detroit Lions in sixth round (177th pick overall) of 1999 NFL draft.
COLLEGE NOTES: Intercepted one pass (1996); intercepted one pass (1997); intercepted one pass (1998).

Year Team	G	SACKS
1994—Wisconsin Stevens-Point	Redshirted.	
1995—Wisconsin Stevens-Point	10	2.5
1996—Wisconsin Stevens-Point	9	3.0
1997—Wisconsin Stevens-Point	10	2.0
1998—Wisconsin Stevens-Point	9	0.0
College totals (4 years)	**38**	**7.5**

LANDOLT, KEVIN   DT   JAGUARS

PERSONAL: Born October 25, 1975, in Burlington, N.J. ... 6-5/300.
HIGH SCHOOL: Holy Cross (Delran, N.J.).
COLLEGE: West Virginia.
TRANSACTIONS/CAREER NOTES: Selected by Jacksonville Jaguars in fourth round (121st pick overall) of 1999 NFL draft. ... Signed by Jaguars (May 18, 1999).

Year Team	G	SACKS
1994—West Virginia	Redshirted.	
1995—West Virginia	11	0.0
1996—West Virginia	12	4.0
1997—West Virginia	12	4.0
1998—West Virginia	12	8.0
College totals (4 years)	**47**	**16.0**

LEROY, EMARLOS   DT   JAGUARS

PERSONAL: Born July 31, 1975, in Albany, Ga. ... 6-2/298. ... Full name: Emarlos S. Leroy.
HIGH SCHOOL: Monroe (Ga.).
JUNIOR COLLEGE: Northwest Mississippi Community College.
COLLEGE: Georgia.
TRANSACTIONS/CAREER NOTES: Selected by Jacksonville Jaguars in sixth round (182nd pick overall) of 1999 NFL draft. ... Signed by Jaguars (May 27, 1999).
COLLEGE NOTES: Intercepted one pass (1998).

Year Team	G	SACKS
1995—Northwest Mississippi CC	Statistics unavailable.	
1996—Northwest Mississippi CC	7	9.0
1997—Georgia	11	1.0
1998—Georgia	11	2.5
Junior college totals (1 year)	**7**	**9.0**
College totals (2 years)	**22**	**3.5**

LOVERNE, DAVID   G   JETS

PERSONAL: Born May 22, 1976, in San Ramon, Calif. ... 6-3/299.
HIGH SCHOOL: De La Salle (Concord, Calif.).
COLLEGE: Idaho, then San Jose State.
TRANSACTIONS/CAREER NOTES: Selected by New York Jets in third round (90th pick overall) of 1999 NFL draft.
COLLEGE PLAYING EXPERIENCE: Idaho, 1994; San Jose State, 1995-1998. ... Games: 1994 (redshirted), 1995 (transfer student), 1996 (4), 1997 (11), 1998 (12). Total: 27.

LUCKY, MIKE   TE   COWBOYS

PERSONAL: Born November 23, 1975, in Antioch, Calif. ... 6-6/273. ... Full name: Michael Thomas Lucky.
HIGH SCHOOL: Antioch (Calif.).
COLLEGE: Arizona.
TRANSACTIONS/CAREER NOTES: Selected by Dallas Cowboys in seventh round (229th pick overall) of 1999 NFL draft.

			RECEIVING		
Year Team	G	No.	Yds.	Avg.	TD
1994—Arizona	Redshirted.				
1995—Arizona	11	5	99	19.8	0
1996—Arizona	11	14	168	12.0	2
1997—Arizona	12	15	191	12.7	2
1998—Arizona	12	11	142	12.9	0
College totals (4 years)	**46**	**45**	**600**	**13.3**	**4**

MACHADO, J.P.   G   JETS

PERSONAL: Born January 6, 1976, in Monmouth, Ill. ... 6-4/295.
HIGH SCHOOL: Monmouth (Ill.).
COLLEGE: Illinois.
TRANSACTIONS/CAREER NOTES: Selected by New York Jets in sixth round (197th pick overall) of 1999 NFL draft.
COLLEGE PLAYING EXPERIENCE: Illinois, 1994-1998. ... Games: 1994 (redshirted), 1995 (did not play), 1996 (11), 1997 (11), 1998 (11). Total: 33.

MAKOVICKA, JOEL — FB — CARDINALS

PERSONAL: Born October 6, 1975, in Brainard, Neb. ... 5-10/247.
HIGH SCHOOL: East Butler (Brainard, Neb.).
COLLEGE: Nebraska.
TRANSACTIONS/CAREER NOTES: Selected by Arizona Cardinals in fourth round (116th pick overall) of 1999 NFL draft.

Year — Team	G	RUSHING Att.	Yds.	Avg.	TD	RECEIVING No.	Yds.	Avg.	TD	TOTALS TD	Pts.
1994—Nebraska					Redshirted.						
1995—Nebraska	11	22	185	8.4	2	0	0	...	0	2	12
1996—Nebraska	10	23	119	5.2	0	3	28	9.3	0	0	0
1997—Nebraska	12	105	685	6.5	9	5	60	12.0	1	10	60
1998—Nebraska	12	97	458	4.7	2	4	67	16.8	0	2	12
College totals (4 years)	45	247	1447	5.9	13	12	155	12.9	1	14	84

MARTIN, CECIL — FB — EAGLES

PERSONAL: Born July 8, 1975, in Evanston, Ill. ... 6-0/235.
HIGH SCHOOL: Evanston (Ill.).
COLLEGE: Wisconsin.
TRANSACTIONS/CAREER NOTES: Selected by Philadelphia Eagles in sixth round (172nd pick overall) of 1999 NFL draft.

Year — Team	G	RUSHING Att.	Yds.	Avg.	TD	RECEIVING No.	Yds.	Avg.	TD	KICKOFF RETURNS No.	Yds.	Avg.	TD	TOTALS TD	Pts.
1994—Wisconsin								Redshirted.							
1995—Wisconsin	11	21	97	4.6	2	16	98	6.1	2	2	19	9.5	0	4	24
1996—Wisconsin	13	12	63	5.3	2	12	78	6.5	1	2	27	13.5	0	3	18
1997—Wisconsin	12	20	70	3.5	1	16	116	7.3	0	6	84	14.0	0	1	6
1998—Wisconsin	11	11	40	3.6	0	19	139	7.3	0	0	0	...	0	0	0
College totals (4 years)	47	64	270	4.2	5	63	431	6.8	3	10	130	13.0	0	8	48

McALISTER, CHRIS — CB — RAVENS

PERSONAL: Born June 14, 1977, in Pasedena, Calif. ... 6-1/206. ... Full name: Christopher James McAlister. ... Son of James McAlister, running back with Philadelphia Eagles (1975 and 1976) and New England Patriots (1978).
HIGH SCHOOL: Pasadena (Calif.).
JUNIOR COLLEGE: Mt. San Antonio College (Calif.).
COLLEGE: Arizona.
TRANSACTIONS/CAREER NOTES: Selected by Baltimore Ravens in first round (10th pick overall) of 1999 NFL draft.
HONORS: Named cornerback on THE SPORTING NEWS college All-America third team (1997). ... Named cornerback on THE SPORTING NEWS college All-America first team (1998).
COLLEGE NOTES: Credited with two sacks (1996); credited with 1/2 sack, rushed two times for 16 yards and caught one pass for minus three yards (1998).

Year — Team	G	INTERCEPTIONS No.	Yds.	Avg.	TD	PUNT RETURNS No.	Yds.	Avg.	TD	KICKOFF RETURNS No.	Yds.	Avg.	TD	TOTALS TD	Pts.
1995—Mt. San Antonio Junior College								Statistics unavailable.							
1996—Arizona	11	6	134	22.3	1	0	0	...	0	20	526	26.3	1	2	12
1997—Arizona	11	4	45	11.3	0	0	0	...	0	15	335	22.3	0	0	0
1998—Arizona	11	5	64	12.8	1	5	104	20.8	1	8	236	29.5	1	3	18
College totals (3 years)	33	15	243	16.2	2	5	104	20.8	1	43	1097	25.5	2	5	30

McCLURE, TODD — C — FALCONS

PERSONAL: Born February 16, 1977, in Baton Rouge, La. ... 6-1/292.
HIGH SCHOOL: Central (Baton Rouge, La.).
COLLEGE: Louisiana State.
TRANSACTIONS/CAREER NOTES: Selected by Atlanta Falcons in seventh round (237th pick overall) of 1999 NFL draft.
COLLEGE PLAYING EXPERIENCE: Louisiana State, 1995-1998. ... Games: 1995 (4), 1996 (11), 1997 (10), 1998 (11). Total: 36.

McCUTCHEON, DAYLON — CB — BROWNS

PERSONAL: Born December 9, 1976, in Walnut, Calif. ... 5-8/180. ... Son of Lawrence McCutcheon, running back with four NFL teams (1972-81).
HIGH SCHOOL: Bishop Amat (La Puente, Calif.).
COLLEGE: Southern California.
TRANSACTIONS/CAREER NOTES: Selected by Cleveland Browns in third round (62nd pick overall) of 1999 NFL draft.
HONORS: Named cornerback on THE SPORTING NEWS college All-America second team (1998).
COLLEGE NOTES: Caught five passes for 41 yards and rushed three times for 26 yards and one touchdown (1997).

Year — Team	G	INTERCEPTIONS No.	Yds.	Avg.	TD	PUNT RETURNS No.	Yds.	Avg.	TD	KICKOFF RETURNS No.	Yds.	Avg.	TD	TOTALS TD	Pts.
1995—Southern California	12	2	91	45.5	1	0	0	...	0	0	0	...	0	1	6
1996—Southern California	12	3	34	11.3	0	0	0	...	0	3	71	23.7	0	0	0
1997—Southern California	11	2	0	0.0	0	0	0	...	0	9	168	18.7	0	1	6
1998—Southern California	13	3	64	21.3	0	1	5	5.0	0	10	254	25.4	0	0	0
College totals (4 years)	48	10	189	18.9	1	1	5	5.0	0	22	493	22.4	0	2	12

McDONALD, DARNELL — WR — BUCCANEERS

PERSONAL: Born May 26, 1976, in College Park, Md. ... 6-3/190. ... Full name: Darnell Ali McDonald.
HIGH SCHOOL: Hayfield (Fairfax, Va.).
JUNIOR COLLEGE: Garden City (Kan.) Community College.
COLLEGE: Kansas State.
TRANSACTIONS/CAREER NOTES: Selected by Tampa Bay Buccaneers in seventh round (240th pick overall) of 1999 NFL draft.

		RECEIVING			
Year Team	G	No.	Yds.	Avg.	TD
1995—Garden City CC		Statistics unavailable.			
1996—Garden City CC	...	73	1165	16.0	10
1997—Kansas State	11	21	441	21.0	6
1998—Kansas State	12	75	1092	14.6	9
Junior college totals (1 year)	...	73	1165	16.0	10
College totals (2 years)	23	96	1533	16.0	15

McFARLAND, ANTHONY — DT — BUCCANEERS

PERSONAL: Born December 18, 1977, in Winnsboro, La. ... 6-0/292.
HIGH SCHOOL: Winnsboro (La.).
COLLEGE: Louisiana State.
TRANSACTIONS/CAREER NOTES: Selected by Tampa Bay Buccaneers in first round (15th pick overall) of 1999 NFL draft.
HONORS: Named defensive tackle on THE SPORTING NEWS college All-America second team (1998).
COLLEGE NOTES: Caught one pass for three yards and a touchdown (1995).

Year Team	G	SACKS
1995—Louisiana State	11	2.0
1996—Louisiana State	10	1.0
1997—Louisiana State	11	6.0
1998—Louisiana State	11	8.0
College totals (4 years)	43	17.0

McGARITY, WANE — WR — COWBOYS

PERSONAL: Born September 30, 1976, in San Antonio. ... 5-8/191. ... Full name: Wane Keith McGarity.
HIGH SCHOOL: Clark (San Antonio).
COLLEGE: Texas.
TRANSACTIONS/CAREER NOTES: Selected by Dallas Cowboys in fourth round (118th pick overall) of 1999 NFL draft.

		RUSHING				RECEIVING				KICKOFF RETURNS				TOTALS	
Year Team	G	Att.	Yds.	Avg.	TD	No.	Yds.	Avg.	TD	No.	Yds.	Avg.	TD	TD	Pts.
1995—Texas	12	26	112	4.3	3	9	113	12.6	0	4	40	10.0	0	3	18
1996—Texas	12	1	14	14.0	0	18	318	17.7	4	3	47	15.7	0	4	24
1997—Texas	3	1	-11	-11.0	0	10	169	16.9	1	4	107	26.8	0	1	6
1998—Texas	11	0	0	...	0	58	1087	18.7	9	0	0	...	0	9	54
College totals (4 years)	38	28	115	4.1	3	95	1687	17.8	14	11	194	17.6	0	17	102

McGREW, REGGIE — DT — 49ERS

PERSONAL: Born December 16, 1976, in Mayo, Fla. ... 6-1/301. ... Full name: Reginald Gerard McGrew.
HIGH SCHOOL: Lafayette (Mayo, Fla.).
COLLEGE: Florida.
TRANSACTIONS/CAREER NOTES: Selected after junior season by San Francisco 49ers in first round (24th pick overall) of 1999 NFL draft.

Year Team	G	SACKS
1995—Florida	Redshirted.	
1996—Florida	12	2.0
1997—Florida	7	1.5
1998—Florida	9	5.0
College totals (3 years)	28	8.5

McGRIFF, TRAVIS — WR — BRONCOS

PERSONAL: Born June 24, 1976, in Gainesville, Fla. ... 5-8/182. ... Full name: William Travis McGriff.
HIGH SCHOOL: P.K. Yonge (Gainesville, Fla.).
COLLEGE: Florida.
TRANSACTIONS/CAREER NOTES: Selected by Denver Broncos in third round (93rd pick overall) of 1999 NFL draft.
COLLEGE NOTES: Granted medical redshirt after three games (1994). ... Attempted one pass without a completion (1997); and attempted two passes with two completions for 59 yards and two touchdowns (1998).

		RUSHING				RECEIVING				PUNT RETURNS				TOTALS	
Year Team	G	Att.	Yds.	Avg.	TD	No.	Yds.	Avg.	TD	No.	Yds.	Avg.	TD	TD	Pts.
1994—Florida	3	0	0	...	0	3	31	10.3	0	0	0	...	0	0	0
1995—Florida	12	1	9	9.0	0	12	139	11.6	1	0	0	...	0	1	6
1996—Florida	8	0	0	...	0	14	167	11.9	0	0	0	...	0	0	0
1997—Florida	11	0	0	...	0	24	363	15.1	3	1	4	4.0	0	3	18
1998—Florida	11	2	-3	-1.5	1	70	1357	19.4	10	21	145	6.9	0	11	66
College totals (5 years)	45	3	6	2.0	1	123	2057	16.7	14	22	149	6.8	0	15	90

McKENZIE, MIKE — CB — PACKERS

PERSONAL: Born April 26, 1976, in Miami. ... 6-1/193.
HIGH SCHOOL: Norland (Miami).
COLLEGE: Memphis.
TRANSACTIONS/CAREER NOTES: Selected after junior season by Green Bay Packers in third round (87th pick overall) of 1999 NFL draft.

		INTERCEPTIONS			
Year Team	G	No.	Yds.	Avg.	TD
1995—Memphis		Redshirted.			
1996—Memphis	11	3	4	1.3	0
1997—Memphis	11	2	10	5.0	0
1998—Memphis	11	1	66	66.0	0
College totals (3 years)	33	6	80	13.3	0

McKINLEY, DENNIS — FB — CARDINALS

PERSONAL: Born November 3, 1976, in Kosciusko, Miss. ... 6-1/241. ... Full name: Dennis L. McKinley.
HIGH SCHOOL: Weir (Miss.) Attendance Center.
COLLEGE: Mississippi State.
TRANSACTIONS/CAREER NOTES: Selected by Arizona Cardinals in sixth round (206th pick overall) of 1999 NFL draft.

		RUSHING				RECEIVING				KICKOFF RETURNS				TOTALS	
Year Team	G	Att.	Yds.	Avg.	TD	No.	Yds.	Avg.	TD	No.	Yds.	Avg.	TD	TD	Pts.
1995—Mississippi State	7	0	0	...	0	0	0	...	0	0	0	...	0	0	0
1996—Mississippi State	11	8	44	5.5	0	2	17	8.5	0	0	0	...	0	0	0
1997—Mississippi State	11	17	98	5.8	2	2	22	11.0	0	2	10	5.0	0	2	12
1998—Mississippi State	12	24	130	5.4	2	4	40	10.0	0	2	32	16.0	0	2	12
College totals (4 years)	41	49	272	5.6	4	8	79	9.9	0	4	42	10.5	0	4	24

McLAUGHLIN, JOHN — DE — BUCCANEERS

PERSONAL: Born November 13, 1975, in Cleveland. ... 6-4/247.
HIGH SCHOOL: Hart (Newall, Calif.).
COLLEGE: Notre Dame, then California.
TRANSACTIONS/CAREER NOTES: Selected by Tampa Bay Buccaneers in fifth round (150th pick overall) of 1999 NFL draft.

Year Team	G	SACKS
1994—Notre Dame	9	0.0
1995—Notre Dame	8	2.0
1996—California		Transfer student.
1997—California	11	2.0
1998—California	11	3.0
College totals (4 years)	39	7.0

McNABB, DONOVAN — QB — EAGLES

PERSONAL: Born November 25, 1976, in Chicago. ... 6-2/226. ... Full name: Donovan Jamal McNabb.
HIGH SCHOOL: Mount Carmel (Chicago).
COLLEGE: Syracuse.
TRANSACTIONS/CAREER NOTES: Selected by Philadelphia Eagles in first round (second pick overall) of 1999 NFL draft.

		PASSING								RUSHING				TOTALS	
Year Team	G	Att.	Cmp.	Pct.	Yds.	TD	Int.	Avg.	Rat.	Att.	Yds.	Avg.	TD	TD	Pts.
1994—Syracuse		Redshirted.													
1995—Syracuse	11	207	128	61.8	1991	16	6	9.62	162.3	123	261	2.1	2	2	12
1996—Syracuse	11	215	118	54.9	1776	19	9	8.26	145.1	97	458	4.7	3	3	18
1997—Syracuse	12	265	145	54.7	2488	20	6	9.39	154.0	110	404	3.7	6	6	36
1998—Syracuse	11	251	157	62.5	2134	22	5	8.50	158.9	135	438	3.2	8	8	48
College totals (4 years)	45	938	548	58.4	8389	77	26	8.94	155.7	465	1561	3.4	19	19	114

McNOWN, CADE — QB — BEARS

PERSONAL: Born January 12, 1977, in Portland, Ore. ... 6-1/213. ... Full name: Cade B. McNown.
HIGH SCHOOL: San Benito (Hollister, Calif.), then West Linn (Ore.).
COLLEGE: UCLA.
TRANSACTIONS/CAREER NOTES: Selected by Chicago Bears in first round (12th pick overall) of 1999 NFL draft.
HONORS: Named quarterback on THE SPORTING NEWS college All-America third team (1997). ... Named quarterback on THE SPORTING NEWS college All-America second team (1998).

		PASSING								RUSHING				TOTALS	
Year Team	G	Att.	Cmp.	Pct.	Yds.	TD	Int.	Avg.	Rat.	Att.	Yds.	Avg.	TD	TD	Pts.
1995—UCLA	12	245	122	49.8	1698	7	8	6.93	110.9	71	311	4.4	5	5	30
1996—UCLA	11	336	176	52.4	2424	12	16	7.21	115.2	88	58	0.7	4	4	24
1997—UCLA	12	312	189	60.6	3116	24	6	9.99	166.0	79	26	0.3	4	4	24
1998—UCLA	12	357	207	58.0	3470	25	11	9.72	156.7	75	182	2.4	3	3	18
College totals (4 years)	47	1250	694	55.5	10708	68	41	8.57	138.7	313	577	1.8	16	16	96

MEGNA, MARC — LB — JETS

PERSONAL: Born July 30, 1976, in Fall River, Mass. ... 6-2/250.
HIGH SCHOOL: Durfee (Fall River, Mass.).
COLLEGE: Richmond.
TRANSACTIONS/CAREER NOTES: Selected by New York Jets in sixth round (183rd pick overall) of 1999 NFL draft.
COLLEGE NOTES: Intercepted one pass (1997); credited with one safety (1998).

Year—Team	G	SACKS
1994—Richmond	Redshirted.	
1995—Richmond	11	1.0
1996—Richmond	11	4.0
1997—Richmond	11	14.0
1998—Richmond	12	13.0
College totals (4 years)	**45**	**32.0**

MENENDEZ, RONDEL — WR — FALCONS

PERSONAL: Born May 18, 1975, in Louisville, Ky. ... 5-9/183.
HIGH SCHOOL: Eastern (Middletown, Ky.).
COLLEGE: Eastern Kentucky.
TRANSACTIONS/CAREER NOTES: Selected by Atlanta Falcons in seventh round (247th pick overall) of 1999 NFL draft.
COLLEGE NOTES: Granted medical redshirt after two games (1994). ... Returned one punt for six yards (1996); returned one punt for minus one yard (1997); returned three punts for 16 yards (1998).

		RUSHING				RECEIVING				KICKOFF RETURNS				TOTALS	
Year—Team	G	Att.	Yds.	Avg.	TD	No.	Yds.	Avg.	TD	No.	Yds.	Avg.	TD	TD	Pts.
1994—Eastern Kentucky	2	1	-5	-5.0	0	0	0	...	0	0	0	...	0	0	0
1995—Eastern Kentucky	12	2	-9	-4.5	0	6	105	17.5	0	4	75	18.8	0	0	0
1996—Eastern Kentucky	11	7	58	8.3	0	38	716	18.8	7	2	33	16.5	0	7	42
1997—Eastern Kentucky	12	3	28	9.3	0	54	1137	21.1	9	1	11	11.0	0	9	54
1998—Eastern Kentucky	9	5	100	20.0	1	52	1032	19.8	11	0	0	...	0	12	72
College totals (5 years)	**46**	**18**	**172**	**9.6**	**1**	**150**	**2990**	**19.9**	**27**	**7**	**119**	**17.0**	**0**	**28**	**168**

MILLER, BILLY — WR — BRONCOS

PERSONAL: Born April 24, 1977, in Los Angeles. ... 6-3/215.
HIGH SCHOOL: Westlake (Westlake Village, Calif.).
COLLEGE: Southern California.
TRANSACTIONS/CAREER NOTES: Selected by Denver Broncos in seventh round (218th pick overall) of 1999 NFL draft.

		RECEIVING			
Year—Team	G	No.	Yds.	Avg.	TD
1995—Southern California	2	3	27	9.0	0
1996—Southern California	7	17	273	16.1	2
1997—Southern California	11	56	649	11.6	2
1998—Southern California	13	49	623	12.7	3
College totals (4 years)	**33**	**125**	**1572**	**12.6**	**7**

MILLER, DEE — WR — PACKERS

PERSONAL: Born December 4, 1975, in Springfield, Ohio ... 6-0/194.
HIGH SCHOOL: South (Springfield, Ohio).
COLLEGE: Ohio State.
TRANSACTIONS/CAREER NOTES: Selected by Green Bay Packers in sixth round (196th pick overall) of 1999 NFL draft.

		RECEIVING			
Year—Team	G	No.	Yds.	Avg.	TD
1994—Ohio State		Redshirted.			
1995—Ohio State	13	5	47	9.4	0
1996—Ohio State	12	10	147	14.7	0
1997—Ohio State	13	58	981	16.9	5
1998—Ohio State	12	59	915	15.5	3
College totals (4 years)	**50**	**132**	**2090**	**15.8**	**8**

MINOR, KORY — LB — 49ERS

PERSONAL: Born December 14, 1976, in Inglewood, Calif. ... 6-0/247. ... Full name: Kory DeShaun Minor.
HIGH SCHOOL: Bishop Ahmat (La Puente, Calif.).
COLLEGE: Notre Dame.
TRANSACTIONS/CAREER NOTES: Selected by San Francisco 49ers in seventh round (234th pick overall) of 1999 NFL draft.

		INTERCEPTIONS				SACKS
Year—Team	G	No.	Yds.	Avg.	TD	No.
1995—Notre Dame	11	0	0	...	0	6.0
1996—Notre Dame	11	1	17	17.0	0	8.0
1997—Notre Dame	12	3	50	16.7	0	3.5
1998—Notre Dame	10	1	7	7.0	0	5.0
College totals (4 years)	**44**	**5**	**74**	**14.8**	**0**	**22.5**

1999 DRAFT PICKS

MIRANDA, PAUL — DB — COLTS

PERSONAL: Born May 2, 1976, in Thomasville, Ga. ... 5-10/184.
HIGH SCHOOL: Thomas County Central (Thomasville, Ga.).
JUNIOR COLLEGE: Holmes Junior College (Miss.), then Copiah-Lincoln Junior College (Miss.).
COLLEGE: Central Florida.
TRANSACTIONS/CAREER NOTES: Selected by Indianapolis Colts in fourth round (96th pick overall) of 1999 NFL draft.

			INTERCEPTIONS			SACKS	KICKOFF RETURNS				TOTALS	
Year Team	G	No.	Yds.	Avg.	TD	No.	No.	Yds.	Avg.	TD	TD	Pts.
1995—Holmes Junior College						Statistics unavailable.						
1996—Central Florida	9	0	0	...	0	0.0	0	0	...	0	0	0
1997—Central Florida	11	0	0	...	0	0.0	1	88	88.0	1	1	6
1998—Central Florida	11	2	72	36.0	1	1.0	25	644	25.8	0	1	6
College totals (3 years)	31	2	72	36.0	1	1.0	26	732	28.2	1	2	12

MITCHELL, DONALD — DB — TITANS

PERSONAL: Born December 14, 1976, in Beaumont, Texas. ... 5-9/185.
HIGH SCHOOL: Central (Beaumont, Texas).
COLLEGE: Southern Methodist.
TRANSACTIONS/CAREER NOTES: Selected by Tennessee Titans in fourth round (117th pick overall) of 1999 NFL draft.

		INTERCEPTIONS			
Year Team	G	No.	Yds.	Avg.	TD
1995—SMU	10	0	0	...	0
1996—SMU	9	0	0	...	0
1997—SMU	11	3	23	7.7	0
1998—SMU	11	3	40	13.3	0
College totals (4 years)	41	6	63	10.5	0

MONTGOMERY, JOE — RB — GIANTS

PERSONAL: Born June 8, 1976, in Robbins, Ill. ... 5-10/228.
HIGH SCHOOL: Richards (Oak Lawn, Ill.).
COLLEGE: Ohio State.
TRANSACTIONS/CAREER NOTES: Selected by New York Giants in second round (49th pick overall) of 1999 NFL draft.

		RUSHING				RECEIVING				TOTALS	
Year Team	G	Att.	Yds.	Avg.	TD	No.	Yds.	Avg.	TD	TD	Pts.
1994—Ohio State					Prop 48.						
1995—Ohio State					Redshirted.						
1996—Ohio State	8	68	460	6.8	0	0	...	0	2	12	
1997—Ohio State	6	30	105	3.5	0	2	7	3.5	0	0	0
1998—Ohio State	12	118	766	6.5	7	2	0	0.0	0	7	42
College totals (3 years)	26	216	1331	6.2	9	4	7	1.8	0	9	54

MOORE, DAMON — S — EAGLES

PERSONAL: Born September 15, 1976, in Fostoria, Ohio. ... 5-11/215.
HIGH SCHOOL: Fostoria (Ohio).
COLLEGE: Ohio State.
TRANSACTIONS/CAREER NOTES: Selected by Philadelphia Eagles in fourth round (128th pick overall) of 1999 NFL draft.
HONORS: Named strong safety on THE SPORTING NEWS college All-America first team (1998).

		INTERCEPTIONS				SACKS
Year Team	G	No.	Yds.	Avg.	TD	No.
1994—Ohio State			Redshirted.			
1995—Ohio State	12	2	22	11.0	0	0.0
1996—Ohio State	12	5	44	8.8	1	0.0
1997—Ohio State	13	3	38	12.7	0	1.0
1998—Ohio State	12	2	73	36.5	1	2.0
College totals (4 years)	49	12	177	14.8	2	3.0

MOREY, SEAN — WR — PATRIOTS

PERSONAL: Born February 26, 1976, in Marshfield, Mass. ... 5-11/190. ... Full name: Sean Joseph Morey.
HIGH SCHOOL: Marshfield (Mass.).
COLLEGE: Brown.
TRANSACTIONS/CAREER NOTES: Selected by New England Patriots in seventh round (241st pick overall) of 1999 NFL draft.

		RECEIVING			
Year Team	G	No.	Yds.	Avg.	TD
1995—Brown	10	34	454	13.4	7
1996—Brown	10	60	939	15.7	7
1997—Brown	10	74	1434	19.4	15
1998—Brown	10	83	1023	12.3	10
College totals (4 years)	40	251	3850	15.3	39

1999 DRAFT PICKS

MORONKOLA, DEE — CB — JAGUARS

PERSONAL: Born July 1, 1977, in Richmond, Calif. ... 5-9/203. ... Full name: Adesola A. Moronkola.
HIGH SCHOOL: DeAnza (Richmond, Calif.).
COLLEGE: Washington State.
TRANSACTIONS/CAREER NOTES: Selected by Jacksonville Jaguars in seventh round (242nd pick overall) of 1999 NFL draft. ... Signed by Jaguars (May 18, 1999).
COLLEGE NOTES: Recovered one fumble for a touchdown (1996).

		INTERCEPTIONS				PUNT RETURNS				KICKOFF RETURNS				TOTALS	
Year Team	G	No.	Yds.	Avg.	TD	No.	Yds.	Avg.	TD	No.	Yds.	Avg.	TD	TD	Pts.
1995—Washington State	5	1	0	0.0	0	0	0	...	0	10	234	23.4	0	0	0
1996—Washington State	11	2	42	21.0	0	0	0	...	0	10	247	24.7	0	1	6
1997—Washington State	11	2	0	0.0	0	0	0	...	0	8	128	16.0	0	0	0
1998—Washington State	11	2	0	0.0	0	6	33	5.5	0	16	504	31.5	2	2	12
College totals (4 years)	38	7	42	6.0	0	6	33	5.5	0	44	1113	25.3	2	3	18

MULITALO, EDWIN — OL — RAVENS

PERSONAL: Born September 1, 1974, in Daly City, Calif. ... 6-3/328. ... Full name: Edwin Moliki Mulitalo.
HIGH SCHOOL: Jefferson (Daly City, Calif.).
JUNIOR COLLEGE: Ricks College (Idaho).
COLLEGE: Arizona.
TRANSACTIONS/CAREER NOTES: Selected by Baltimore Ravens in fourth round (129th pick overall) of 1999 NFL draft.
COLLEGE PLAYING EXPERIENCE: Ricks College, 1992 and 1996; Arizona, 1997 and 1998. ... Games: 1992 (11), 1993 (Mormon mission), 1994 (Mormon mission), 1995 (Mormon mission), 1996 (10), 1997 (11), 1998 (13). Total NCAA: 24.

NAVIES, HANNIBAL — LB — PANTHERS

PERSONAL: Born July 19, 1977, in Berkeley, Calif. ... 6-2/240.
HIGH SCHOOL: Berkeley (Calif.).
COLLEGE: Colorado.
TRANSACTIONS/CAREER NOTES: Selected by Carolina Panthers in fourth round (100th pick overall) of 1999 NFL draft.

Year Team	G	SACKS
1995—Colorado	6	1.0
1996—Colorado	11	1.0
1997—Colorado	11	2.0
1998—Colorado	11	2.5
College totals (4 years)	39	6.5

NELSON, REGGIE — G — CHARGERS

PERSONAL: Born June 23, 1976, in Alexandria, La. ... 6-4/310.
HIGH SCHOOL: Alexandria (La.).
COLLEGE: McNeese State (degree in psychology).
TRANSACTIONS/CAREER NOTES: Selected by San Diego Chargers in fifth round (141st pick overall) of 1999 NFL draft.
COLLEGE PLAYING EXPERIENCE: McNeese State, 1995-1998. ... Games: 1995 (14), 1996 (11), 1997 (15), 1998 (12). Total: 52.

NEWMAN, KEITH — LB — BILLS

PERSONAL: Born January 19, 1977, in Tampa. ... 6-2/243. ... Full name: Keith Anthony Newman.
HIGH SCHOOL: Thomas Jefferson (Tampa).
COLLEGE: North Carolina.
TRANSACTIONS/CAREER NOTES: Selected by Buffalo Bills in fourth round (119th pick overall) of 1999 NFL draft.
COLLEGE NOTES: Intercepted one pass (1998).

Year Team	G	SACKS
1995—North Carolina	11	0.0
1996—North Carolina	11	1.0
1997—North Carolina	11	2.5
1998—North Carolina	11	4.0
College totals (4 years)	44	7.5

NGUYEN, DAT — LB — COWBOYS

PERSONAL: Born September 25, 1976, in Fulton, Texas. ... 5-11/231.
HIGH SCHOOL: Rockport-Fulton (Texas).
COLLEGE: Texas A&M (degree in agricultural development).
TRANSACTIONS/CAREER NOTES: Selected by Dallas Cowboys in third round (85th pick overall) of 1999 NFL draft.
HONORS: Lombardi Award winner (1998). ... Named inside linebacker on THE SPORTING NEWS college All-America first team (1998).
COLLEGE NOTES: Returned one kickoff for 46 yards and a touchdown (1995); recovered one fumble for 25 yards and a touchdown (1997).

				INTERCEPTIONS				SACKS
Year	Team	G	No.	Yds.	Avg.	TD		No.
1995—Texas A&M		11	0	0	...	0		0.0
1996—Texas A&M		12	3	38	12.7	1		1.5
1997—Texas A&M		12	1	32	32.0	1		0.0
1998—Texas A&M		13	2	28	14.0	0		4.0
College totals (4 years)		48	6	98	16.3	2		5.5

OGLE, KENDELL   LB   BROWNS

PERSONAL: Born November 25, 1975, in Hillside, N.J. ... 6-0/231.
HIGH SCHOOL: Hillside (N.J.).
COLLEGE: Maryland.
TRANSACTIONS/CAREER NOTES: Selected by Cleveland Browns in sixth round (187th pick overall) of 1999 NFL draft.
COLLEGE NOTES: Played running back (1994). ... Rushed twice for three yards and returns two kickoffs for 13 yards (1994); rushed five times for two yards (1996).

				INTERCEPTIONS				SACKS
Year	Team	G	No.	Yds.	Avg.	TD		No.
1994—Maryland		9	0	0	...	0		0.0
1995—Maryland				Redshirted.				
1996—Maryland		11	0	0	...	0		1.0
1997—Maryland		11	1	12	12.0	0		1.0
1998—Maryland		11	1	0	0.0	0		2.5
College totals (3 years)		42	2	12	6.0	0		4.5

OKEAFOR, CHIKE   DE   49ERS

PERSONAL: Born March 27, 1976, in West Lafayette, Ind. ... 6-4/248. ... Full name: Chikeze Russell Okeafor. ... Name pronounced CHEE-kay oh-KEY-fer.
HIGH SCHOOL: West Lafayette (Ind.).
COLLEGE: Purdue.
TRANSACTIONS/CAREER NOTES: Selected by San Francisco 49ers in third round (89th pick overall) of 1999 NFL draft.

Year	Team	G	SACKS
1994—Purdue		11	0.0
1995—Purdue		11	4.0
1996—Purdue		11	3.5
1997—Purdue		Redshirted.	
1998—Purdue		13	8.0
College totals (4 years)		46	15.5

PAGE, SOLOMON   OT   COWBOYS

PERSONAL: Born February 27, 1976, in Pittsburgh. ... 6-4/306.
HIGH SCHOOL: Brashear (Pittsburgh).
COLLEGE: West Virginia.
TRANSACTIONS/CAREER NOTES: Selected after junior season by Dallas Cowboys in second round (55th pick overall) of 1999 NFL draft.
COLLEGE PLAYING EXPERIENCE: West Virginia, 1995-1998. ... Games: 1995 (redshirted), 1996 (12), 1997 (12), 1998 (12). Total 36.

PARKER, ANTHONY   CB   49ERS

PERSONAL: Born December 4, 1975, in Denver. ... 6-1/200. ... Full name: Anthony E. Parker.
HIGH SCHOOL: Thornton (Colo.).
JUNIOR COLLEGE: Mesa (Ariz.) Community College.
COLLEGE: Weber State.
TRANSACTIONS/CAREER NOTES: Selected by San Francisco 49ers in fourth round (99th pick overall) of 1999 NFL draft.

				INTERCEPTIONS		
Year	Team	G	No.	Yds.	Avg.	TD
1994—Mesa (Ariz.) Community College			Statistics unavailable.			
1995—Mesa (Ariz.) Community College			Statistics unavailable.			
1996—Weber State			Redshirted.			
1997—Weber State		11	0	0	...	0
1998—Weber State		10	4	71	17.8	0
College totals (2 years)		21	4	71	17.8	0

PARKER, DEMONN   RB   PACKERS

PERSONAL: Born December 24, 1976, in Tulsa, Okla. ... 5-10/189.
HIGH SCHOOL: Washington (Tulsa, Okla.).
COLLEGE: Oklahoma.
TRANSACTIONS/CAREER NOTES: Selected after junior season by Green Bay Packers in fifth round (159th pick overall) of 1999 NFL draft.

			RUSHING				RECEIVING			KICKOFF RETURNS				TOTALS	
Year	Team	G	Att.	Yds.	Avg.	TD	No.	Yds.	Avg.	TD	No.	Yds.	Avg.	TD	TD	Pts.
1995—Oklahoma								Redshirted.								
1996—Oklahoma		11	180	1184	6.6	10	17	188	11.1	0	1	19	19.0	0	10	60
1997—Oklahoma		9	194	1143	5.9	6	11	140	12.7	0	0	0	...	0	6	36
1998—Oklahoma		11	205	1077	5.3	5	14	176	12.6	1	10	198	19.8	0	6	36
College totals (3 years)		31	579	3404	5.9	21	42	504	12.0	1	11	217	19.7	0	22	132

PARKER, LARRY — WR — CHIEFS

PERSONAL: Born July 14, 1976, in Bakersfield, Calif. ... 6-1/200.
HIGH SCHOOL: Bakersfield (Calif.).
COLLEGE: Southern California.
TRANSACTIONS/CAREER NOTES: Selected by Kansas City Chiefs in fourth round (108th pick overall) of 1999 NFL draft.

			RUSHING				RECEIVING				PUNT RETURNS				KICKOFF RETURNS				TOTALS	
Year	Team	G	Att.	Yds.	Avg.	TD	No.	Yds.	Avg.	TD	No.	Yds.	Avg.	TD	No.	Yds.	Avg.	TD	TD	Pts.
1994—Southern California		11	0	0	...	0	14	137	9.8	0	1	6	6.0	0	4	83	20.8	0	0	0
1995—Southern California		12	0	0	...	0	25	270	10.8	0	29	266	9.2	0	1	6	6.0	0	0	0
1996—Southern California		10	0	0	...	0	10	129	12.9	0	6	32	5.3	0	0	0	...	0	0	0
1997—Southern California								Redshirted.												
1998—Southern California		13	3	28	9.3	0	29	580	20.0	1	22	91	4.1	0	7	102	14.6	0	1	6
College totals (4 years)		46	3	28	9.3	0	78	1116	14.3	1	58	395	6.8	0	12	191	15.9	0	1	6

PAULK, JEFF — FB — FALCONS

PERSONAL: Born April 26, 1976, in Phoenix. ... 6-0/242. ... Full name: Jeffery Howard Paulk.
HIGH SCHOOL: Corona Del Sol (Tempe, Ariz.).
COLLEGE: Arizona State.
TRANSACTIONS/CAREER NOTES: Selected by Atlanta Falcons in third round (92nd pick overall) of 1999 NFL draft.

			RUSHING				RECEIVING			TOTALS	
Year	Team	G	Att.	Yds.	Avg.	TD	No.	Yds.	Avg.	TD	TD	Pts.
1994—Arizona State								Redshirted.				
1995—Arizona State		11	3	-1	-0.3	0	0	0	...	0	0	0
1996—Arizona State		11	42	267	6.4	1	0	0	...	0	1	6
1997—Arizona State		10	35	80	2.3	3	1	2	2.0	0	3	18
1998—Arizona State		11	41	208	5.1	2	1	18	18.0	0	2	12
College totals (4 years)		43	121	554	4.6	6	2	20	10.0	0	6	36

PERRY, JASON — S — CHARGERS

PERSONAL: Born August 1, 1976, in Passaic, N.J. ... 6-0/200.
HIGH SCHOOL: Paterson Catholic (N.J.).
COLLEGE: North Carolina State.
TRANSACTIONS/CAREER NOTES: Selected by San Diego Chargers in fourth round (104th pick overall) of 1999 NFL draft.
COLLEGE NOTES: Recovered one fumble for 36 yards and a touchdown (1998).

			INTERCEPTIONS				KICKOFF RETURNS				TOTALS	
Year	Team	G	No.	Yds.	Avg.	TD	No.	Yds.	Avg.	TD	TD	Pts.
1994—North Carolina State								Redshirted.				
1995—North Carolina State		10	2	33	16.5	0	2	59	29.5	0	0	0
1996—North Carolina State		11	0	0	...	0	0	0	...	0	0	0
1997—North Carolina State		8	0	0	...	0	0	0	...	0	0	0
1998—North Carolina State		11	4	27	6.8	0	2	38	19.0	0	1	6
College totals (4 years)		40	6	60	10.0	0	4	97	24.3	0	1	6

PETERSON, MIKE — LB — COLTS

PERSONAL: Born June 17, 1976, in Alachua, Fla. ... 6-2/229. ... Full name: Porter Michael Peterson.
HIGH SCHOOL: Santa Fe (Alachua, Fla.).
COLLEGE: Florida.
TRANSACTIONS/CAREER NOTES: Selected by Indianapolis Colts in second round (36th pick overall) of 1999 NFL draft.
HONORS: Named outside linebacker on THE SPORTING NEWS college All-America first team (1998).

Year	Team	G	SACKS
1994—Florida			Redshirted.
1995—Florida		11	1.0
1996—Florida		10	0.5
1997—Florida		10	2.0
1998—Florida		11	5.0
College totals (4 years)		42	8.5

PETITGOUT, LUKE — G — GIANTS

PERSONAL: Born June 16, 1976, in Milford, Del. ... 6-6/315. ... Full name: Lucas George Petitgout.
HIGH SCHOOL: Sussex Central (Georgetown, Del.).
COLLEGE: Notre Dame.
TRANSACTIONS/CAREER NOTES: Selected by New York Giants in first round (19th pick overall) of 1999 NFL draft.
COLLEGE PLAYING EXPERIENCE: Notre Dame, 1994-1998. ... Games: 1994 (redshirted), 1995 (3), 1996 (7), 1997 (11), 1998 (11). Total: 32.

PILLER, ZACH — OT — TITANS

PERSONAL: Born May 2, 1976, in Tallahassee, Fla. ... 6-5/332. ... Full name: Zachary Paul Piller.
HIGH SCHOOL: Lincoln (Tallahassee, Fla.).
COLLEGE: Georgia Tech, then Florida.
TRANSACTIONS/CAREER NOTES: Selected by Tennessee Titans in third round (81st pick overall) of 1999 NFL draft.
COLLEGE PLAYING EXPERIENCE: Georgia Tech, 1994; Florida, 1995-1998. ... Games: 1994 (11), 1995 (transfer student), 1996 (10), 1997 (8), 1998 (11). Total: 40.

PLUMMER, CHAD — WR — BRONCOS

PERSONAL: Born November 30, 1975, in Delray Beach, Fla. ... 6-3/223.
HIGH SCHOOL: Godby (Tallahassee, Fla.).
COLLEGE: Cincinnati.
TRANSACTIONS/CAREER NOTES: Selected by Denver Broncos in sixth round (204th pick overall) of 1999 NFL draft.
COLLEGE NOTES: Played quarterback (1995-1997). ... Attempted 47 passes with 25 completions for 459 yards, two touchdowns and two interceptions (1995); attempted 198 passes with 102 completions for 1,335 yards, seven touchdowns and eight interceptions (1996); attempted 190 passes with 87 completions for 1,178 yards, six touchdowns and 10 interceptions (1998).

		RUSHING				RECEIVING				TOTALS	
Year Team	G	Att.	Yds.	Avg.	TD	No.	Yds.	Avg.	TD	TD	Pts.
1995—Cincinnati	9	45	122	2.7	2	0	0	...	0	2	12
1996—Cincinnati	11	100	251	2.5	3	0	0	...	0	3	18
1997—Cincinnati	12	149	606	4.1	7	0	0	...	0	7	42
1998—Cincinnati	11	45	162	3.6	1	61	852	14.0	0	1	6
College totals (4 years)	43	339	1141	3.4	13	61	852	14.0	0	13	78

POINDEXTER, ANTHONY — S — RAVENS

PERSONAL: Born July 28, 1976, in Lynchburg, Va. ... 6-0/210. ... Full name: Anthony Scott Poindexter.
HIGH SCHOOL: Jefferson Forest (Forest, Va.).
COLLEGE: Virginia.
TRANSACTIONS/CAREER NOTES: Selected by Baltimore Ravens in seventh round (216th pick overall) of 1999 NFL draft.
HONORS: Named free safety on THE SPORTING NEWS college All-America first team (1997 and 1998).
COLLEGE NOTES: Recovered one fumble for 36 yards and a touchdown (1996); recovered one fumble for eight yards (1997).

		INTERCEPTIONS				SACKS	PUNT RETURNS				TOTALS	
Year Team	G	No.	Yds.	Avg.	TD	No.	No.	Yds.	Avg.	TD	TD	Pts.
1994—Virginia						Redshirted.						
1995—Virginia	12	1	12	12.0	0	1.0	0	0	...	0	0	0
1996—Virginia	11	4	58	14.5	0	0.0	2	14	7.0	0	1	6
1997—Virginia	10	4	55	13.8	0	0.0	1	11	11.0	0	0	0
1998—Virginia	7	3	16	5.3	0	2.0	0	0	...	0	0	0
College totals (4 years)	40	12	141	11.8	0	3.0	3	25	8.3	0	1	6

PORTER, JOEY — LB — STEELERS

PERSONAL: Born March 22, 1977, in Kansas City, Mo. ... 6-2/240. ... Full name: Joey Eugene Porter.
HIGH SCHOOL: Foothills (Calif.).
COLLEGE: Colorado State.
TRANSACTIONS/CAREER NOTES: Selected by Pittsburgh Steelers in third round (73rd pick overall) of 1999 NFL draft.
COLLEGE NOTES: Played running back (1995 and 1996). ... Rushed four times for 45 yards and caught one pass for nine yards (1995); rushed nine times for 165 yards and caught one pass for one yard (1996). ... Intercepted one pass (1998).

Year Team	G	SACKS
1995—Colorado State	12	0.0
1996—Colorado State	12	0.0
1997—Colorado State	12	6.0
1998—Colorado State	12	15.0
College totals (4 years)	48	21.0

PRICE, PEERLESS — WR — BILLS

PERSONAL: Born October 27, 1976, in Dayton, Ohio. ... 5-10/180. ... Full name: Peerless LeCross Price.
HIGH SCHOOL: Meadowdale (Dayton, Ohio).
COLLEGE: Tennessee.
TRANSACTIONS/CAREER NOTES: Selected by Buffalo Bills in second round (53rd pick overall) of 1999 NFL draft.

		RUSHING			RECEIVING				PUNT RETURNS				KICKOFF RETURNS				TOTALS	
Year Team	G	Att.	Yds.	Avg.	TD	No.	Yds.	Avg.	TD	No.	Yds.	Avg.	TD	No.	Yds.	Avg.	TD	TD	Pts.
1995—Tennessee	8	2	66	33.0	1	6	71	11.8	0	3	7	2.3	0	5	91	18.2	0	1	6
1996—Tennessee	11	0	0	...	0	32	609	19.0	3	0	0	...	0	0	0	...	0	3	18
1997—Tennessee	12	2	31	15.5	0	48	698	14.5	6	0	0	...	0	0	0	...	0	6	36
1998—Tennessee	12	3	25	8.3	0	61	920	15.1	10	1	-3	-3.0	0	14	389	27.8	1	11	66
College totals (4 years)	43	7	122	17.4	1	147	2298	15.6	19	4	4	1.0	0	19	480	25.3	1	21	126

PRINGLEY, MIKE — DE — LIONS

PERSONAL: Born May 22, 1976, in Linden, N.J. ... 6-4/270. ... Full name: Michael Charles Pringley.
HIGH SCHOOL: Linden (N.J.).
COLLEGE: North Carolina.
TRANSACTIONS/CAREER NOTES: Selected by Detroit Lions in seventh round (215th pick overall) of 1999 NFL draft.

Year — Team	G	SACKS
1994—North Carolina	Redshirted.	
1995—North Carolina	11	4.0
1996—North Carolina	10	3.0
1997—North Carolina	10	3.5
1998—North Carolina	11	4.0
College totals (4 years)	42	14.5

PRIOLEAU, PIERSON — CB — 49ERS

PERSONAL: Born August 6, 1977, in Charleston, S.C. ... 5-10/191. ... Full name: Pierson Olin Prioleau.
HIGH SCHOOL: Macedonia (S.C.).
COLLEGE: Virginia Tech.
TRANSACTIONS/CAREER NOTES: Selected by San Francisco 49ers in fourth round (110th pick overall) of 1999 NFL draft.
HONORS: Named strong safety on THE SPORTING NEWS college All-America third team (1997).

		INTERCEPTIONS			SACKS
Year — Team	G	No.	Yds.	Avg.	TD	No.
1995—Virginia Tech	11	0	0	...	0	0.0
1996—Virginia Tech	11	0	0	...	0	2.0
1997—Virginia Tech	11	1	73	73.0	0	1.0
1998—Virginia Tech	12	2	94	47.0	1	0.0
College totals (4 years)	45	3	167	55.7	1	3.0

RAINER, WALI — LB — BROWNS

PERSONAL: Born April 19, 1977, in Rockingham, N.C. ... 6-2/235. ... Full name: Wali Rashid Rainer.
HIGH SCHOOL: West Charlotte (N.C.).
COLLEGE: Virginia.
TRANSACTIONS/CAREER NOTES: Selected by Cleveland Browns in fourth round (124th pick overall) of 1999 NFL draft.

		INTERCEPTIONS			SACKS
Year — Team	G	No.	Yds.	Avg.	TD	No.
1995—Virginia	12	1	1	1.0	0	0.0
1996—Virginia	10	0	0	...	0	2.0
1997—Virginia	11	1	0	0.0	0	9.0
1998—Virginia	11	2	38	19.0	1	5.0
College totals (4 years)	44	4	39	9.8	1	16.0

REAGOR, MONTAE — DE — BRONCOS

PERSONAL: Born June 29, 1977, in Waxahachie, Texas. ... 6-2/256.
HIGH SCHOOL: Waxahachie (Texas).
COLLEGE: Texas Tech (degree in exercise and sports sciences).
TRANSACTIONS/CAREER NOTES: Selected by Denver Broncos in second round (58th pick overall) of 1999 NFL draft.
HONORS: Named defensive end on THE SPORTING NEWS college All-America second team (1997). ... Named defensive end on THE SPORTING NEWS college All-America first team (1998).
COLLEGE NOTES: Intercepted one pass for 10 yards (1997).

Year — Team	G	SACKS
1995—Texas Tech	11	3.0
1996—Texas Tech	11	4.0
1997—Texas Tech	11	10.5
1998—Texas Tech	11	7.0
College totals (4 years)	44	24.5

RHINEHART, COBY — CB — CARDINALS

PERSONAL: Born February 7, 1977, in Dallas. ... 5-10/187. ... Full name: Jacoby Rhinehart.
HIGH SCHOOL: Tyler Street Christian Academy (Dallas).
COLLEGE: Southern Methodist.
TRANSACTIONS/CAREER NOTES: Selected by Arizona Cardinals in sixth round (190th pick overall) of 1999 NFL draft.
COLLEGE NOTES: Advanced one fumble for 97 yards and a touchdown (1996); caught six passes for 80 yards and one touchdown and rushed four times for 79 yards and one touchdown (1998).

		INTERCEPTIONS			SACKS	PUNT RETURNS			TOTALS	
Year — Team	G	No.	Yds.	Avg.	TD	No.	No.	Yds.	Avg.	TD	TD	Pts.
1995—SMU	9	0	0	...	0	0.0	0	0	...	0	0	0
1996—SMU	11	2	7	3.5	0	0.0	15	105	7.0	0	1	6
1997—SMU	11	4	3	0.8	0	0.0	13	95	7.3	0	0	0
1998—SMU	12	2	1	0.5	0	1.0	6	32	5.3	0	2	12
College totals (4 years)	43	8	11	1.4	0	1.0	34	232	6.8	0	3	18

1999 DRAFT PICKS

– 481 –

ROGERS, CHARLIE — WR — SEAHAWKS

PERSONAL: Born June 19, 1976, in Cliffwood, N.J. ... 5-9/179. ... Full name: John Edward Rogers.
HIGH SCHOOL: Matawan Regional (Aberdeen, N.J.).
COLLEGE: Georgia Tech.
TRANSACTIONS/CAREER NOTES: Selected by Seattle Seahawks in fifth round (152nd pick overall) of 1999 NFL draft.

		RUSHING				RECEIVING				PUNT RETURNS				KICKOFF RETURNS				TOTALS	
Year Team	G	Att.	Yds.	Avg.	TD	No.	Yds.	Avg.	TD	No.	Yds.	Avg.	TD	No.	Yds.	Avg.	TD	TD	Pts.
1995—Georgia Tech	8	0	0	...	0	0	0	...	0	0	0	...	0	15	285	19.0	0	0	0
1996—Georgia Tech	11	115	551	4.8	2	17	240	14.1	1	2	60	30.0	0	26	626	24.1	0	3	18
1997—Georgia Tech	9	58	297	5.1	0	20	184	9.2	1	0	0	...	0	15	317	21.1	0	1	6
1998—Georgia Tech	10	47	439	9.3	3	21	233	11.1	1	30	425	14.2	2	2	36	18.0	0	6	36
College totals (4 years)	38	220	1287	5.9	5	58	657	11.3	3	32	485	15.2	2	58	1264	21.8	0	10	60

ROSENTHAL, MIKE — OT — GIANTS

PERSONAL: Born June 10, 1977, in Pittsburgh. ... 6-7/310. ... Full name: Michael Paul Rosenthal.
HIGH SCHOOL: Penn (Mishawaka, Ind.).
COLLEGE: Notre Dame.
TRANSACTIONS/CAREER NOTES: Selected by New York Giants in fifth round (149th pick overall) of 1999 NFL draft.
COLLEGE PLAYING EXPERIENCE: Notre Dame, 1995-1998. ... Games: 1995 (10), 1996 (7), 1997 (11), 1998 (11). Total: 39.

RUCKER, MICHAEL — DE — PANTHERS

PERSONAL: Born February 28, 1975, in St. Joseph, Mo. ... 6-5/258.
HIGH SCHOOL: Benton (St. Joseph, Mo.).
COLLEGE: Nebraska (degree in sociology).
TRANSACTIONS/CAREER NOTES: Selected by Carolina Panthers in second round (38th pick overall) of 1999 NFL draft.

Year Team	G	SACKS
1994—Nebraska		Redshirted.
1995—Nebraska	9	1.0
1996—Nebraska	12	7.0
1997—Nebraska	12	7.5
1998—Nebraska	12	1.5
College totals (4 years)	45	17.0

RUEGAMER, GREY — C/OT — DOLPHINS

PERSONAL: Born June 1, 1976, in Las Vegas, Nev. ... 6-5/304. ... Full name: Christopher Grey Ruegamer.
HIGH SCHOOL: Bishop Gorman (Las Vegas, Nev.).
COLLEGE: Arizona State.
TRANSACTIONS/CAREER NOTES: Selected by Miami Dolphins in third round (72nd pick overall) of 1999 NFL draft.
COLLEGE PLAYING EXPERIENCE: Arizona State, 1994-1998. ... Games: 1994 (redshirted), 1995 (5), 1996 (12), 1997 (12), 1998 (11). Total: 40.

RUTLEDGE, JOHNNY — LB — CARDINALS

PERSONAL: Born January 4, 1977, in Belle Glade, Fla. ... 6-2/245. ... Full name: Johnny Boykins Rutledge III.
HIGH SCHOOL: Glades Central (Belle Glades, Fla.).
COLLEGE: Florida.
TRANSACTIONS/CAREER NOTES: Selected by Arizona Cardinals in second round (51st pick overall) of 1999 NFL draft.
COLLEGE NOTES: Intercepted one pass for six yards (1998).

Year Team	G	SACKS
1995—Florida	11	0.0
1996—Florida	12	6.0
1997—Florida	11	4.0
1998—Florida	11	1.5
College totals (4 years)	45	11.5

SAMUEL, KHARI — LB — BEARS

PERSONAL: Born October 14, 1976, in New York. ... 6-2/242. ... Full name: Khari Iman Mitchell Samuel.
HIGH SCHOOL: Framingham (Mass.).
COLLEGE: Massachusetts.
TRANSACTIONS/CAREER NOTES: Selected by Chicago Bears in fifth round (144th pick overall) of 1999 NFL draft. ... Signed by Bears (May 27, 1999).

		INTERCEPTIONS				SACKS
Year Team	G	No.	Yds.	Avg.	TD	No.
1995—Massachusetts	11	1	0	0.0	0	7.0
1996—Massachusetts	11	0	0	...	0	6.0
1997—Massachusetts	11	0	0	...	0	3.0
1998—Massachusetts	14	3	61	20.3	1	2.0
College totals (4 years)	47	4	61	15.3	1	18.0

SANFORD, SULECIO   WR   BEARS

PERSONAL: Born March 23, 1976, in Milledgeville, Ga. ... 5-10/190.
HIGH SCHOOL: Milledgeville (Ga.).
JUNIOR COLLEGE: Georgia Military College.
COLLEGE: Middle Tennessee State.
TRANSACTIONS/CAREER NOTES: Selected by Chicago Bears in seventh round (221st pick overall) of 1999 NFL draft.
COLLEGE NOTES: Rushed twice for five yards (1997).

		RECEIVING				PUNT RETURNS				KICKOFF RETURNS				TOTALS	
Year Team	G	No.	Yds.	Avg.	TD	No.	Yds.	Avg.	TD	No.	Yds.	Avg.	TD	TD	Pts.
1995—Georgia Military College							Statistics unavailable.								
1996—Georgia Military College							Statistics unavailable.								
1997—Middle Tennessee State	9	27	407	15.1	5	5	84	16.8	1	6	96	16.0	0	6	36
1998—Middle Tennessee State	10	54	674	12.5	7	17	139	8.2	0	15	385	25.7	1	8	48
College totals (2 years)	19	81	1081	13.3	12	22	223	10.1	1	21	481	22.9	1	14	84

SAWYER, TALANCE   DE   VIKINGS

PERSONAL: Born June 14, 1976, in Bastrop, La. ... 6-2/252.
HIGH SCHOOL: Bastrop (La.).
COLLEGE: UNLV.
TRANSACTIONS/CAREER NOTES: Selected by Minnesota Vikings in sixth round (185th pick overall) of 1999 NFL draft.
COLLEGE NOTES: Played tight end (1995). ... Caught one pass for seven yards and a touchdown (1995).

Year Team	G	SACKS
1995—UNLV	8	0.0
1996—UNLV	12	4.5
1997—UNLV	11	7.0
1998—UNLV	...	4.0
College totals (3 years)	...	15.5

SCARLETT, NOEL   NT   VIKINGS

PERSONAL: Born January 21, 1974, in Atlanta. ... 6-3/320.
HIGH SCHOOL: Elbert County (Ga.).
COLLEGE: Langston University (Okla.).
TRANSACTIONS/CAREER NOTES: Selected by Minnesota Vikings in seventh round (236th pick overall) of 1999 NFL draft.

Year Team	G	SACKS
1996—Langston	10	2.0
1997—Langston	7	6.0
1998—Langston	10	9.5
College totals (3 years)	27	17.5

SCIOLI, BRAD   DE   COLTS

PERSONAL: Born September 6, 1976, in Bridgeport, Pa. ... 6-3/277. ... Full name: Brad Elliott Scioli.
HIGH SCHOOL: Upper Merion Area (King of Prussia, Pa.).
COLLEGE: Penn State.
TRANSACTIONS/CAREER NOTES: Selected by Indianapolis Colts in fifth round (138th pick overall) of 1999 NFL draft.
COLLEGE NOTES: Played tight end (1997). ... Intercepted one pass for 46 yards (1994); intercepted one pass for minus two yards (1995); caught nine passes for 171 yards (1997).

Year Team	G	SACKS
1994—Penn State	12	2.0
1995—Penn State	12	3.0
1996—Penn State		Redshirted.
1997—Penn State	11	0.0
1998—Penn State	11	10.0
College totals (4 years)	46	15.0

SCOTT, YUSUF   G   CARDINALS

PERSONAL: Born November 30, 1976 ... 6-2/324. ... Full name: Yusuf Jamall Scott.
HIGH SCHOOL: LaPorte (Texas).
COLLEGE: Arizona.
TRANSACTIONS/CAREER NOTES: Selected after junior season by Arizona Cardinals in fifth round (168th pick overall) of 1999 NFL draft.
COLLEGE PLAYING EXPERIENCE: Arizona, 1995-1998. ... Games: 1995 (redshirted), 1996 (11), 1997 (11), 1998 (12). Total: 34.

SHELTON, L.J.   OT   CARDINALS

PERSONAL: Born March 21, 1976, in Monrovia, Calif. ... 6-6/341. ... Full name: Lonnie Jewel Shelton. ... Son of Lonnie Shelton, forward with New York Knicks (1976-77 and 1977-78), Seattle SuperSonics (1978-79 through 1982-83) and Cleveland Cavaliers (1983-84 through 1985-86).

HIGH SCHOOL: Rochester (Rochester Hills, Mich.).
COLLEGE: Eastern Michigan.
TRANSACTIONS/CAREER NOTES: Selected by Arizona Cardinals in first round (21st pick overall) of 1999 NFL draft.
COLLEGE PLAYING EXPERIENCE: Eastern Michigan, 1994-1998. ... Games: 1994 (redshirted), 1995 (7), 1996 (11), 1997 (11), 1998 (11). Total: 40.

SHIELDS, SCOTT — S — STEELERS

PERSONAL: Born March 29, 1976, in San Diego. ... 6-4/228. ... Full name: Scott Paul Shields.
HIGH SCHOOL: Bonita Vista (Calif.).
COLLEGE: Weber State.
TRANSACTIONS/CAREER NOTES: Selected by Pittsburgh Steelers in second round (59th pick overall) of 1999 NFL draft.
COLLEGE NOTES: Played strong safety and kicker (1995-1998); played punter (1996-1998). ... Intercepted 10 passes for 101 yards (1996); intercepted seven passes for 100 yards and two touchdowns (1997); intercepted six passes for 77 yards (1998).

			PUNTING						KICKING				
Year Team	G	No.	Yds.	Avg.	Net avg.	In. 20	Blk.	XPM	XPA	FGM	FGA	Lg.	50+	Pts.
1994—Weber State							Redshirted.							
1995—Weber State	11	0	0	...	0.0	0	0	28	30	16	18	47	0-0	76
1996—Weber State	11	48	1940	40.4	0.0	7	1	35	38	18	24	52	0-0	89
1997—Weber State	11	48	2043	42.6	0.0	9	1	24	26	17	25	51	0-0	75
1998—Weber State	11	61	2597	42.6	0.0	21	0	24	24	16	23	55	0-0	72
College totals (4 years)	44	157	6580	41.9	0.0	37	2	111	118	67	90	55	0-0	312

SMITH, AARON — DE — STEELERS

PERSONAL: Born April 9, 1976, in Colorado Springs, Colo. ... 6-5/281.
HIGH SCHOOL: Sierra (Colorado Springs, Colo.).
COLLEGE: Northern Colorado.
TRANSACTIONS/CAREER NOTES: Selected by Pittsburgh Steelers in fourth round (109th pick overall) of 1999 NFL draft.

Year Team	G	SACKS
1994—Northern Colorado		Redshirted.
1995—Northern Colorado	11	8.0
1996—Northern Colorado	11	9.0
1997—Northern Colorado	11	15.5
1998—Northern Colorado	11	11.5
College totals (4 years)	44	44.0

SMITH, AKILI — QB — BENGALS

PERSONAL: Born August 21, 1975, in San Diego. ... 6-3/220. ... Full name: Kabisa Akili Maradu Smith.
HIGH SCHOOL: Lincoln (San Diego).
JUNIOR COLLEGE: Grossmont College (Calif.).
COLLEGE: Oregon.
TRANSACTIONS/CAREER NOTES: Selected by Cincinnati Bengals in first round (third pick overall) of 1999 NFL draft.
COLLEGE NOTES: Caught one touchdown pass for seven yards and a touchdown (1996).

		PASSING								RUSHING				TOTALS	
Year Team	G	Att.	Cmp.	Pct.	Yds.	TD	Int.	Avg.	Rat.	Att.	Yds.	Avg.	TD	TD	Pts.
1995—Grossmont College	...	...	...	...	2162	17	...	...	...	...	...	...	...	...	...
1996—Grossmont College	...	363	199	54.8	3212	32	...	8.85	158.2	78	343	4.4	5	5	30
1997—Oregon	11	200	108	54.0	1385	13	7	6.93	126.6	89	183	2.1	2	2	12
1998—Oregon	12	371	215	58.0	3763	32	8	10.14	167.3	82	184	2.2	4	4	24
Junior college totals (2 years)	...	...	...	...	5374	49	...	...	...	...	...	...	...	...	...
College totals (2 years)	23	571	323	56.6	5148	45	15	9.02	153.1	171	367	2.1	6	6	36

RECORD AS BASEBALL PLAYER

TRANSACTIONS/CAREER NOTES: Threw right, batted right. ... Selected by Pittsburgh Pirates organizaiton in seventh round of free-agent draft (June 3, 1993).

					BATTING								FIELDING		
Year Team (League)	Pos.	G	AB	R	H	2B	3B	HR	RBI	Avg.	BB	SO	SB	PO	A	E	Avg.
1993—GC Pirates (GCL)	OF	29	95	13	19	3	2	1	9	.200	10	18	1	31	2	4	.892
1994—GC Pirates (GCL)	OF	19	69	10	12	3	0	2	10	.173	2	18	0	18	1	0	1.000
Totals (2 years)		48	164	23	31	6	2	3	19	.189	12	36	1	49	3	4	.929

SMITH, DEREK — OT — REDSKINS

PERSONAL: Born April 13, 1976, in Portsmouth, Va. ... 6-6/309. ... Full name: Derek Gene Smith.
HIGH SCHOOL: Jefferson (Va.).
COLLEGE: Virginia Tech.
TRANSACTIONS/CAREER NOTES: Selected by Washington Redskins in fifth round (165th pick overall) of 1999 NFL draft.
COLLEGE PLAYING EXPERIENCE: Virginia Tech, 1994-1998. ... Games: 1994 (redshirted), 1995 (did not play), 1996 (11), 1997 (11), 1998 (12). Total: 34.

SMITH, HUNTER — P — COLTS

PERSONAL: Born August 9, 1977, in Sherman, Texas. ... 6-2/212. ... Full name: Hunter Dwight Smith.
HIGH SCHOOL: Sherman (Texas).
COLLEGE: Notre Dame.
TRANSACTIONS/CAREER NOTES: Selected by Indianapolis Colts in seventh round (210th pick overall) of 1999 NFL draft.

		PUNTING				
Year Team	G	No.	Yds.	Avg.	Net avg.	In. 20	Blk.
1995—Notre Dame	11	38	1382	36.4	.0	9	0
1996—Notre Dame	11	44	1906	43.3	.0	14	0
1997—Notre Dame	12	50	2132	42.6	.0	17	0
1998—Notre Dame	11	42	1750	41.7	.0	16	0
College totals (4 years)	45	174	7170	41.2	0.0	56	0

SMITH, LARRY — DT — JAGUARS

PERSONAL: Born December 4, 1974, in Folkston, Ga. ... 6-4/290.
HIGH SCHOOL: Valley Forge (Pa.).
COLLEGE: Florida State.
TRANSACTIONS/CAREER NOTES: Selected after junior season by Jacksonville Jaguars in second round (56th pick overall) of 1999 NFL draft. ... Signed by Jaguars (April 26, 1999).

Year Team	G	SACKS
1995—Florida State	Redshirted.	
1996—Florida State	10	0.0
1997—Florida State	11	3.0
1998—Florida State	10	3.0
College totals (3 years)	31	6.0

SMITH, MARQUIS — S — BROWNS

PERSONAL: Born January 13, 1975, in San Diego. ... 6-2/213.
HIGH SCHOOL: Patrick Henry (San Diego).
COLLEGE: California.
TRANSACTIONS/CAREER NOTES: Selected by Cleveland Browns in third round (76th pick overall) of 1999 NFL draft.

		INTERCEPTIONS			
Year Team	G	No.	Yds.	Avg.	TD
1994—California		Redshirted.			
1995—California	8	0	0	...	0
1996—California	12	3	25	8.3	0
1997—California	11	1	1	1.0	0
1998—California	11	1	0	0.0	0
College totals (4 years)	42	5	26	5.2	0

SMITH, TROY — WR — EAGLES

PERSONAL: Born July 30, 1977, in Greenville, N.C. ... 6-2/193.
HIGH SCHOOL: Rose (Greenville, N.C.).
COLLEGE: East Carolina.
TRANSACTIONS/CAREER NOTES: Selected by Philadelphia Eagles in sixth round (201st pick overall) of 1999 NFL draft.

		RECEIVING			
Year Team	G	No.	Yds.	Avg.	TD
1995—East Carolina	12	15	242	16.1	1
1996—East Carolina	11	16	226	14.1	2
1997—East Carolina	11	54	795	14.7	4
1998—East Carolina	10	44	719	16.3	3
College totals (4 years)	44	129	1982	15.4	10

SPIKES, CAMERON — G — RAMS

PERSONAL: Born November 6, 1976, in Bryan, Texas. ... 6-2/310. ... Full name: Cameron Wade Spikes.
HIGH SCHOOL: Bryan (Texas).
COLLEGE: Texas A&M.
TRANSACTIONS/CAREER NOTES: Selected by St. Louis Rams in fifth round (145th pick overall) of 1999 NFL draft.
COLLEGE PLAYING EXPERIENCE: Texas A&M, 1995-1998. ... Games: 1995 (12), 1996 (12), 1997 (10), 1998 (13). Total: 47.

SPRIGGS, MARCUS — DT — BROWNS

PERSONAL: Born July 26, 1976, in Washington, D.C. ... 6-4/314.
HIGH SCHOOL: Woodson (Washington, D.C.).
COLLEGE: Ohio State, then Troy (Ala.) State.
TRANSACTIONS/CAREER NOTES: Selected by Cleveland Browns in sixth round (174th pick overall) of 1999 NFL draft.

Year—Team	G	SACKS
1994—Ohio State	Redshirted.	
1995—Ohio State	8	0.0
1996—Troy State	Transfer student.	
1997—Troy State	10	3.0
1998—Troy State	10	6.5
College totals (3 years)	28	9.5

STILLS, GARY　　　　LB　　　　CHIEFS

PERSONAL: Born July 11, 1974, in Trenton, N.J. ... 6-2/238.
HIGH SCHOOL: Valley Forge (Pa.) Military Academy.
COLLEGE: West Virginia.
TRANSACTIONS/CAREER NOTES: Selected by Kansas City Chiefs in third round (75th pick overall) of 1999 NFL draft.

Year—Team	G	SACKS
1995—West Virginia	Prop 48.	
1996—West Virginia	11	4.0
1997—West Virginia	11	12.0
1998—West Virginia	8	10.0
College totals (3 years)	30	26.0

STIMSON, NATE　　　　LB　　　　REDSKINS

PERSONAL: Born March 4, 1976, in West Palm Beach, Fla. ... 6-2/253. ... Full name: Nathan Karl Stimson.
HIGH SCHOOL: Wellington (Fla.).
COLLEGE: Miami (Fla.), then Georgia Tech.
TRANSACTIONS/CAREER NOTES: Selected by Washington Redskins in fourth round (107th pick overall) of 1999 NFL draft.

Year—Team	G	SACKS
1994—Miami (Fla.)	Redshirted.	
1995—Georgia Tech	Transfer student.	
1996—Georgia Tech	9	1.0
1997—Georgia Tech	Did not play.	
1998—Georgia Tech	11	6.5
College totals (2 years)	20	7.5

STINCHCOMB, MATT　　　　OT　　　　RAIDERS

PERSONAL: Born June 3, 1977, in Lilburn, Ga. ... 6-5/297. ... Full name: Matthew Douglass Stinchcomb.
HIGH SCHOOL: Parkview (Lilburn, Ga.).
COLLEGE: Georgia.
TRANSACTIONS/CAREER NOTES: Selected by Oakland Raiders in first round (18th pick overall) of 1999 NFL draft.
HONORS: Named offensive tackle on THE SPORTING NEWS college All-America second team (1997 and 1998).
COLLEGE PLAYING EXPERIENCE: Georgia, 1995-1998. ... Games: 1995 (12), 1996 (11), 1997 (11), 1998 (10). Total: 44.

STOKLEY, BRANDON　　　　WR　　　　RAVENS

PERSONAL: Born June 23, 1976, in Blacksburg, Va. ... 5-11/197.
HIGH SCHOOL: Comeaux (La.).
COLLEGE: Southwestern Louisiana.
TRANSACTIONS/CAREER NOTES: Selected by Baltimore Ravens in fourth round (105th pick overall) of 1999 NFL draft.

			RECEIVING		
Year—Team	G	No.	Yds.	Avg.	TD
1994—Southwestern Louisiana	Redshirted.				
1995—Southwestern Louisiana	11	75	1121	14.9	9
1996—Southwestern Louisiana	11	81	1160	14.3	7
1997—Southwestern Louisiana	4	20	248	12.4	1
1998—Southwestern Louisiana	11	65	1173	18.0	8
College totals (4 years)	37	241	3702	15.4	25

STREETS, TAI　　　　WR　　　　49ERS

PERSONAL: Born April 20, 1977, in Matteson, Ill. ... 6-1/193.
HIGH SCHOOL: Thornton Township (Harvey, Ill.).
COLLEGE: Michigan.
TRANSACTIONS/CAREER NOTES: Selected by San Francisco 49ers in sixth round (171st pick overall) of 1999 NFL draft.

			RECEIVING		
Year—Team	G	No.	Yds.	Avg.	TD
1995—Michigan	8	5	43	8.6	0
1996—Michigan	12	44	730	16.6	2
1997—Michigan	12	28	476	17.0	6
1998—Michigan	13	67	1035	15.4	11
College totals (4 years)	45	144	2284	15.9	19

SWIFT, JUSTIN — TE — BRONCOS

PERSONAL: Born August 14, 1975, in Overland Park, Kan. ... 6-4/264.
HIGH SCHOOL: Blue Valley (Overland Park, Kan.).
COLLEGE: Kansas State.
TRANSACTIONS/CAREER NOTES: Selected by Denver Broncos in seventh round (238th pick overall) of 1999 NFL draft.

		RECEIVING			
Year Team	G	No.	Yds.	Avg.	TD
1994—Kansas State		Redshirted.			
1995—Kansas State	2	1	25	25.0	0
1996—Kansas State	8	5	63	12.6	0
1997—Kansas State	11	13	267	20.5	3
1998—Kansas State	12	23	342	14.9	4
College totals (4 years)	33	42	697	16.6	7

SYVRUD, J.J. — LB — JETS

PERSONAL: Born May 10, 1977, in Rock Springs, Wyoming. ... 6-3/265.
COLLEGE: Jamestown College.
TRANSACTIONS/CAREER NOTES: Selected by New York Jets in seventh round (235th pick overall) of 1999 NFL draft.
COLLEGE NOTES: Caught four touchdowns passes (1998).

Year Team	G	SACKS
1998—Jamestown College	...	17.0

TAIT, JOHN — OT — CHIEFS

PERSONAL: Born January 26, 1975, in Phoenix. ... 6-6/311.
HIGH SCHOOL: McClintock (Tempe, Ariz.).
COLLEGE: Brigham Young.
TRANSACTIONS/CAREER NOTES: Selected after junior season by Kansas City Chiefs in first round (14th pick overall) of 1999 NFL draft.
COLLEGE PLAYING EXPERIENCE: Brigham Young, 1993-1998. ... Games: 1993 (redshirted), 1994 (Mormon mission), 1995 (Mormon mission), 1996 (15), 1997 (9), 1998 (13). Total: 37.

TALTON, TY — S — LIONS

PERSONAL: Born May 10, 1976, in Beloit, Wis. ... 5-11/200. ... Full name: Tyree Talton.
HIGH SCHOOL: Turner (Beloit, Wis.).
COLLEGE: Northern Iowa.
TRANSACTIONS/CAREER NOTES: Selected by Detroit Lions in fifth round (137th pick overall) of 1999 NFL draft.
COLLEGE NOTES: Rushed nine times for 67 yards and one touchdown (1998).

		INTERCEPTIONS				PUNT RETURNS				KICKOFF RETURNS				TOTALS	
Year Team	G	No.	Yds.	Avg.	TD	No.	Yds.	Avg.	TD	No.	Yds.	Avg.	TD	TD	Pts.
1994—Northern Iowa								Redshirted.							
1995—Northern Iowa	13	8	57	7.1	0	0	0	...	0	3	87	29.0	0	0	0
1996—Northern Iowa	14	9	182	20.2	1	0	0	...	0	27	927	34.3	3	4	24
1997—Northern Iowa	11	3	21	7.0	0	1	5	5.0	0	25	604	24.2	0	0	0
1998—Northern Iowa	11	2	21	10.5	0	4	25	6.3	0	22	605	27.5	0	1	6
College totals (4 years)	49	22	281	12.8	1	5	30	6.0	0	77	2223	28.9	3	5	30

TERRY, CHRIS — OT — PANTHERS

PERSONAL: Born August 8, 1975, in Jacksonville. ... 6-5/295. ... Full name: Christopher A. Terry.
HIGH SCHOOL: Jean Ribault (Jacksonville).
COLLEGE: Georgia.
TRANSACTIONS/CAREER NOTES: Selected by Carolina Panthers in second round (34th pick overall) of 1999 NFL draft. ... Signed by Panthers (May 24, 1999).
COLLEGE NOTES: Played defensive end (1995 and 1996). ... Credited with one sack (1996).
COLLEGE PLAYING EXPERIENCE: Georgia, 1994-1998. ... Games: 1994 (redshirted), 1995 (6), 1996 (11), 1997 (11), 1998 (11). Total: 39.

TERRY, COREY — LB — COLTS

PERSONAL: Born March 6, 1976, in Warrenton, N.C. ... 6-3/258. ... Full name: Corey TeWana Terry.
HIGH SCHOOL: Warren County (N.C.).
JUNIOR COLLEGE: Garden City (Kan.) Community College.
COLLEGE: Tennessee.
TRANSACTIONS/CAREER NOTES: Selected by Indianapolis Colts in seventh round (250th pick overall) of 1999 NFL draft.

Year Team	G	SACKS
1992—Garden City CC		Redshirted.
1993—Garden City CC	...	21.0
1994—		Did not play.
1995—		Did not play.
1996—Tennessee	12	1.5
1997—Tennessee	12	4.0
1998—Tennessee	12	4.0
Junior college totals (1 year)	...	21.0
College totals (3 years)	36	9.5

THIGPEN, ERIC — S — FALCONS

PERSONAL: Born June 19, 1976, in Dolton, Ill. ... 6-0/199.
HIGH SCHOOL: Thornridge (Dolton, Ill.).
COLLEGE: Iowa.
TRANSACTIONS/CAREER NOTES: Selected by Atlanta Falcons in sixth round (200th pick overall) of 1999 NFL draft.
COLLEGE NOTES: Recovered one fumble for 29 yards and a touchdown (1998).

		INTERCEPTIONS			
Year Team	G	No.	Yds.	Avg.	TD
1994—Iowa			Redshirted.		
1995—Iowa	12	0	0	...	0
1996—Iowa	8	1	2	2.0	0
1997—Iowa	12	3	30	10.0	0
1998—Iowa	10	3	17	5.7	0
College totals (4 years)	42	7	49	7.0	0

THOMAS, RANDY — G — JETS

PERSONAL: Born January 19, 1976, in East Point, Ga. ... 6-4/301.
HIGH SCHOOL: Tri-Cities (East Point, Ga.).
JUNIOR COLLEGE: Copiah-Lincoln Junior College (Miss.).
COLLEGE: Mississippi State.
TRANSACTIONS/CAREER NOTES: Selected by New York Jets in second round (57th pick overall) of 1999 NFL draft.
HONORS: Named offensive guard on THE SPORTING NEWS college All-America second team (1998).
COLLEGE PLAYING EXPERIENCE: Copiah-Lincoln Junior College, 1995 and 1996; Mississippi State, 1997 and 1998. ... Games: 1995 (10), 1996 (10), 1997 (11), 1998 (12). Total Junior College: 20. Total NCAA: 23.

THORNTON, JOHN — DT — TITANS

PERSONAL: Born October 2, 1976, in Philadelphia. ... 6-2/304.
HIGH SCHOOL: Scotland School for Veterans' Children (Scotland, Pa.).
COLLEGE: West Virginia.
TRANSACTIONS/CAREER NOTES: Selected by Tennessee Titans in second round (52nd pick overall) of 1999 NFL draft.
COLLEGE NOTES: Intercepted one pass for three yards (1997).

Year Team	G	SACKS
1994—West Virginia		Redshirted.
1995—West Virginia	11	3.0
1996—West Virginia	12	5.0
1997—West Virginia	12	3.0
1998—West Virginia	12	4.0
College totals (4 years)	47	15.0

TUCKER, REX — OL — BEARS

PERSONAL: Born December 20, 1976, in Midland, Texas ... 6-5/285. ... Full name: Rex Truman Tucker. ... Brother of Ryan Tucker, center, St. Louis Rams.
HIGH SCHOOL: Lee (Midland, Texas).
COLLEGE: Texas A&M.
TRANSACTIONS/CAREER NOTES: Selected in third round by Chicago Bears (66th pick overall) of 1999 NFL draft.
COLLEGE PLAYING EXPERIENCE: Texas A&M, 1995-1998. ... Games: 1995 (12), 1996 (12), 1997 (13), 1998 (13). Total: 50.

TUMAN, JERAME — TE — STEELERS

PERSONAL: Born March 24, 1976, in Liberal, Kan. ... 6-3/250. ... Full name: Jerame Dean Tuman.
HIGH SCHOOL: Liberal (Kan.).
COLLEGE: Michigan.
TRANSACTIONS/CAREER NOTES: Selected by Pittsburgh Steelers in fifth round (136th pick overall) of 1999 NFL draft.
HONORS: Named tight end on THE SPORTING NEWS college All-America third team (1997).

Year—Team	G	RECEIVING No.	Yds.	Avg.	TD
1994—Michigan		Redshirted.			
1995—Michigan	10	9	71	7.9	1
1996—Michigan	12	33	524	15.9	5
1997—Michigan	11	29	437	15.1	5
1998—Michigan	12	27	247	9.1	2
College totals (4 years)	45	98	1279	13.1	13

UNDERWOOD, DIMITRIUS — DE — VIKINGS

PERSONAL: Born March 29, 1977, in Philadelphia. ... 6-6/276.
HIGH SCHOOL: E.E. Smith (Fayetteville, N.C.).
COLLEGE: Michigan State.
TRANSACTIONS/CAREER NOTES: Selected after junior season by Minnesota Vikings in first round (29th pick overall) of 1999 NFL draft.

Year—Team	G	SACKS
1995—Michigan State	11	0.0
1996—Michigan State	12	5.0
1997—Michigan State	12	8.0
1998—Michigan State		Did not play.
College totals (3 years)	35	13.0

VINSON, FRED — CB — PACKERS

PERSONAL: Born April 2, 1977, in North Augusta, S.C. ... 5-11/177. ... Cousin of Corey Chavous, defensive back, Arizona Cardinals.
HIGH SCHOOL: North Augusta (S.C.).
COLLEGE: Vanderbilt.
TRANSACTIONS/CAREER NOTES: Selected by Green Bay Packers in second round (47th pick overall) of 1999 NFL draft.

Year—Team	G	INTERCEPTIONS No.	Yds.	Avg.	TD
1995—Vanderbilt	11	0	0	...	0
1996—Vanderbilt	11	1	3	3.0	0
1997—Vanderbilt	11	0	0	...	0
1998—Vanderbilt	6	3	36	12.0	0
College totals (4 years)	39	4	39	9.8	0

WARE, BRAD — S — TITANS

PERSONAL: Born March 26, 1978, in Austell, Ga. ... 6-1/207. ... Full name: Bradley Genard Ware.
HIGH SCHOOL: McEachern (Powder Springs, Ga.).
COLLEGE: Auburn.
TRANSACTIONS/CAREER NOTES: Selected after junior season by Tennessee Titans in fourth round (114th pick overall) of 1999 NFL draft.
COLLEGE NOTES: Advanced one fumble 24 yards for a touchdown (1997).

Year—Team	G	INTERCEPTIONS No.	Yds.	Avg.	TD	SACKS No.
1996—Auburn	12	4	83	20.8	1	0.0
1997—Auburn	13	4	74	18.5	0	1.0
1998—Auburn	11	3	0	0.0	0	0.0
College totals (3 years)	36	11	157	14.3	1	1.0

WASHINGTON, MARCUS — DB — PATRIOTS

PERSONAL: Born February 26, 1975, in Mobile, Ala. ... 6-1/217.
HIGH SCHOOL: Harrison (Colorado Springs, Colo.).
COLLEGE: Colorado.
TRANSACTIONS/CAREER NOTES: Selected by New England Patriots in sixth round (180th pick overall) of 1999 NFL draft.
COLLEGE NOTES: Returned one punt for 16 yards and recovered one fumble for 24 yards (1995); recovered one fumble for 54 yards and a touchdown (1996).

Year—Team	G	INTERCEPTIONS No.	Yds.	Avg.	TD
1994—Colorado		Redshirted.			
1995—Colorado	11	0	0	...	0
1996—Colorado	11	0	0	...	0
1997—Colorado	11	3	43	14.3	1
1998—Colorado	10	2	60	30.0	1
College totals (4 years)	43	5	103	20.6	2

WATSON, CHRIS — CB — BRONCOS

PERSONAL: Born June 30, 1977, in Chicago. ... 6-1/192.
HIGH SCHOOL: Leo (Chicago).
COLLEGE: Eastern Illinois.

TRANSACTIONS/CAREER NOTES: Selected by Denver Broncos in third round (67th pick overall) of 1999 NFL draft.
COLLEGE NOTES: Credited with two sacks (1996); credited with one sack (1997); and rushed once for 18 yards (1998).

			INTERCEPTIONS				PUNT RETURNS				KICKOFF RETURNS				TOTALS	
Year Team	G	No.	Yds.	Avg.	TD	No.	Yds.	Avg.	TD	No.	Yds.	Avg.	TD	TD	Pts.
1995—Eastern Illinois	10	2	18	9.0	0	1	0	0.0	0	11	253	23.0	1	1	6
1996—Eastern Illinois	9	0	0	...	0	18	185	10.3	1	26	660	25.4	0	1	6
1997—Eastern Illinois	11	3	14	4.7	0	1	5	5.0	0	7	239	34.1	0	0	0
1998—Eastern Illinois	6	0	0	...	0	1	0	0.0	0	14	325	23.2	0	0	0
College totals (4 years)	36	5	32	6.4	0	21	190	9.0	1	58	1477	25.5	1	2	12

WEATHERS, ANDRE   CB   GIANTS

PERSONAL: Born August 6, 1976, in Flint, Mich. ... 6-0/189. ... Full name: Andre Lemelle Weathers.
HIGH SCHOOL: Flint (Mich.) Central.
COLLEGE: Michigan.
TRANSACTIONS/CAREER NOTES: Selected by New York Giants in sixth round (205th pick overall) of 1999 NFL draft.

		INTERCEPTIONS			
Year Team	G	No.	Yds.	Avg.	TD
1994—Michigan		Redshirted.			
1995—Michigan	8	0	0	...	0
1996—Michigan	11	0	0	...	0
1997—Michigan	11	2	53	26.5	0
1998—Michigan	13	3	26	8.7	0
College totals (4 years)	43	5	79	15.8	0

WEAVER, JED   TE   EAGLES

PERSONAL: Born August 11, 1976, in Bend, Ore. ... 6-4/246. ... Full name: Timothy Jed Weaver.
HIGH SCHOOL: Redmond (Ore.).
COLLEGE: Oregon.
TRANSACTIONS/CAREER NOTES: Selected by Philadelphia Eagles in seventh round (208th pick overall) of 1999 NFL draft.

		RECEIVING			
Year Team	G	No.	Yds.	Avg.	TD
1994—Oregon		Redshirted.			
1995—Oregon	1	0	0	...	0
1996—Oregon	11	2	6	3.0	1
1997—Oregon	12	2	48	24.0	0
1998—Oregon	12	39	623	16.0	5
College totals (4 years)	36	43	677	15.7	6

WEDDERBURN, FLOYD   OT   SEAHAWKS

PERSONAL: Born May 5, 1976, in Upper Darby, Pa. ... 6-5/333. ... Full name: Floyd E. Wedderburn.
HIGH SCHOOL: Upper Darby (Pa.).
COLLEGE: Penn State.
TRANSACTIONS/CAREER NOTES: Selected by Seattle Seahawks in fifth round (140th pick overall) of 1999 NFL draft.
COLLEGE PLAYING EXPERIENCE: Penn State, 1994-1998. ... Games: 1994 (redshirted), 1995 (did not play), 1996 (5), 1997 (10), 1998 (11). Total: 26.

WELBOURN, JOHN   G/OT   EAGLES

PERSONAL: Born March 30, 1976, in Torrance, Calif. ... 6-5/318.
HIGH SCHOOL: Peninsula (Palos Verdes, Calif.).
COLLEGE: California (degree in rhetoric).
TRANSACTIONS/CAREER NOTES: Selected by Philadelphia Eagles in fourth round (97th pick overall) of 1999 NFL draft.
COLLEGE PLAYING EXPERIENCE: California, 1994-1998. ... Games: 1994 (redshirted), 1995 (4), 1996 (8), 1997 (11), 1998 (11). Total: 34.

WEST, LYLE   S   GIANTS

PERSONAL: Born December 20, 1976, in Columbus, Ga. ... 6-0/210.
HIGH SCHOOL: Washington (Freemont, Calif.).
JUNIOR COLLEGE: Chabot College (Calif.).
COLLEGE: San Jose State.
TRANSACTIONS/CAREER NOTES: Selected by New York Giants in sixth round (189th pick overall) of 1999 NFL draft.

		INTERCEPTIONS			
Year Team	G	No.	Yds.	Avg.	TD
1995—Chabot College		Statistics unavailable.			
1996—Chabot College		Statistics unavailable.			
1997—San Jose State	11	5	27	5.4	0
1998—San Jose State	12	2	16	8.0	0
College totals (2 years)	23	7	43	6.1	0

WHITE, CHRIS — DE — JAGUARS

PERSONAL: Born September 28, 1976, in Shreveport, La. ... 6-3/280.
HIGH SCHOOL: Captain Shreve (Shreveport, La.).
COLLEGE: Southern.
TRANSACTIONS/CAREER NOTES: Selected by Jacksonville Jaguars in seventh round (246th pick overall) of 1999 NFL draft. ... Signed by Jaguars (May 27, 1999).

Year Team	G	SACKS
1996—Southern	10	3.0
1997—Southern	11	3.0
1998—Southern	11	4.0
College totals (3 years)	32	10.0

WILLIAMS, NICK — RB — BENGALS

PERSONAL: Born March 30, 1977, in Farmington Hills, Mich. ... 6-1/267. ... Full name: James Nicolas Williams.
HIGH SCHOOL: Harrison (Mich.).
COLLEGE: Miami (Fla.).
TRANSACTIONS/CAREER NOTES: Selected by Cincinnati Bengals in fifth round (135th pick overall) of 1999 NFL draft. ... Signed by Bengals (May 19, 1999).

		RUSHING				RECEIVING			TOTALS	
Year Team	G	Att.	Yds.	Avg.	TD	No.	Yds.	Avg.	TD	TD	Pts.
1995—Miami (Fla.)	8	1	3	3.0	0	0	0	...	0	0	0
1996—Miami (Fla.)	12	17	67	3.9	1	12	149	12.4	1	2	12
1997—Miami (Fla.)	10	13	40	3.1	0	6	55	9.2	0	0	0
1998—Miami (Fla.)	12	7	42	6.0	0	7	85	12.1	0	0	0
College totals (4 years)	42	38	152	4.0	1	25	289	11.6	1	2	12

WILLIAMS, RICKY — RB — SAINTS

PERSONAL: Born May 21, 1977, in San Diego. ... 5-10/236. ... Full name: Errick Lynne Williams.
HIGH SCHOOL: Patrick Henry (San Diego).
COLLEGE: Texas.
TRANSACTIONS/CAREER NOTES: Selected by New Orleans Saints in first round (fifth pick overall) of 1999 NFL draft. ... Signed by Saints (May 14, 1999).
HONORS: Named running back on THE SPORTING NEWS college All-America first team (1997 and 1998). ... Doak Walker Award winner (1997 and 1998). ... Heisman Trophy winner (1998). ... Walter Camp Award winner (1998). ... Maxwell Award winner (1998). ... Named College Football Player of the Year by THE SPORTING NEWS (1998).

		RUSHING				RECEIVING			TOTALS	
Year Team	G	Att.	Yds.	Avg.	TD	No.	Yds.	Avg.	TD	TD	Pts.
1995—Texas	12	166	990	6.0	8	16	224	14.0	0	8	48
1996—Texas	12	205	1272	6.2	12	25	291	11.6	2	14	84
1997—Texas	11	279	1893	6.8	25	20	150	7.5	0	25	150
1998—Texas	11	361	2124	5.9	27	24	262	10.9	1	28	168
College totals (4 years)	46	1011	6279	6.2	72	85	927	10.9	3	75	450

RECORD AS BASEBALL PLAYER

TRANSACTIONS/CAREER NOTES: Batted right, threw right. ... Selected by Philadelphia Phillies organization in eighth round of free-agent draft (June 1, 1995). ... Selected by Montreal Expos from Phillies organization in Rule 5 major league draft (December 14, 1998). ... Traded by Expos to Texas Rangers for cash considerations (December 15, 1998).

					BATTING								FIELDING		
Year Team (League)	Pos.	G	AB	R	H	2B	3B	HR	RBI	Avg.	BB	SO	SB	PO	A	E	Avg.
1995—Martinsville (Appal.)	OF	36	113	19	27	1	0	0	11	.239	6	32	13	51	5	3	.949
1996—Piedmont (S. Atl.)	OF	84	266	30	50	4	3	3	20	.188	18	87	17	117	9	9	.933
1997—Piedmont (S. Atl.)	OF	37	136	12	28	5	0	1	6	.206	9	44	10	58	0	3	.955
1998—Batavia (NY-Penn)	OF	13	53	7	15	0	0	3	.283	2	16	6	17	1	0	1.000
Totals (4 years)		170	568	68	120	10	3	4	40	.211	35	179	46	243	20	15	.946

WILLIAMS, RODNEY — P — RAMS

PERSONAL: Born April 25, 1977, in Decatur, Ga. ... 6-0/189. ... Full name: Rodney Colin Williams.
HIGH SCHOOL: DeKalb (Decatur, Ga.).
COLLEGE: Georgia Tech.
TRANSACTIONS/CAREER NOTES: Selected by St. Louis Rams in seventh round (252nd pick overall) of 1999 NFL draft.

		PUNTING				
Year Team	G	No.	Yds.	Avg.	Net avg.	In. 20	Blk.
1995—Georgia Tech	11	28	1068	38.1	32.3	11	0
1996—Georgia Tech	11	53	2034	38.4	36.9	16	2
1997—Georgia Tech	12	47	2145	45.6	40.9	19	0
1998—Georgia Tech	12	50	2126	42.5	40.0	19	0
College totals (4 years)	46	178	7373	41.4	38.1	65	2

WILSON, AL — LB — BRONCOS

PERSONAL: Born June 21, 1977, in Jackson, Tenn. ... 6-0/240. ... Full name: Aldra Kauwa Wilson.
HIGH SCHOOL: Central Merry (Jackson, Tenn.).
COLLEGE: Tennessee.
TRANSACTIONS/CAREER NOTES: Selected by Denver Broncos in first round (31st pick overall) of NFL draft.
HONORS: Named inside linebacker on THE SPORTING NEWS college All-America second team (1998).
COLLEGE NOTES: Intercepted one pass (1995).

Year Team	G	SACKS
1995—Tennessee	12	1.0
1996—Tennessee	11	1.0
1997—Tennessee	11	5.0
1998—Tennessee	9	4.0
College totals (4 years)	43	11.0

WILTZ, JASON — DT — JETS

PERSONAL: Born November 23, 1976, in New Orleans. ... 6-4/308.
HIGH SCHOOL: St. Augustine (New Orleans).
COLLEGE: Nebraska.
TRANSACTIONS/CAREER NOTES: Selected by New York Jets in fourth round (123rd pick overall) of 1999 NFL draft.
COLLEGE NOTES: Intercepted two passes for 32 yards (1998).

Year Team	G	SACKS
1994—Nebraska		Redshirted.
1995—Nebraska	3	0.0
1996—Nebraska	12	1.0
1997—Nebraska	11	2.0
1998—Nebraska	10	1.0
College totals (4 years)	36	4.0

WINFIELD, ANTOINE — CB — BILLS

PERSONAL: Born June 24, 1977, in Akron, Ohio. ... 5-8/180.
HIGH SCHOOL: Garfield (Ohio).
COLLEGE: Ohio State.
TRANSACTIONS/CAREER NOTES: Selected by Buffalo Bills in first round (23rd pick overall) of 1999 NFL draft.
HONORS: Named cornerback on THE SPORTING NEWS college All-America second team (1997). ... Jim Thorpe Award winner (1998). ... Named cornerback on THE SPORTING NEWS college All-America first team (1998).

		INTERCEPTIONS				SACKS
Year Team	G	No.	Yds.	Avg.	TD	No.
1995—Ohio State	13	0	0	...	0	0.0
1996—Ohio State	12	1	27	27.0	0	0.0
1997—Ohio State	13	2	25	12.5	0	3.0
1998—Ohio State	12	0	0	...	0	2.0
College totals (4 years)	50	3	52	17.3	0	5.0

WISNE, JERRY — G — BEARS

PERSONAL: Born July 28, 1976, in Rochester, Minn. ... 6-6/306. ... Full name: Gerald Edward Wisne.
HIGH SCHOOL: Jenks (Tulsa, Okla.).
COLLEGE: Notre Dame.
TRANSACTIONS/CAREER NOTES: Selected by Chicago Bears in fifth round (143rd pick overall) of 1999 NFL draft. ... Signed by Bears (May 27, 1999).
COLLEGE PLAYING EXPERIENCE: Notre Dame, 1995-1998. ... Games: 1995 (1), 1996 (9), 1997 (11), 1998 (9). Total: 30.

WONG, JOE — OT — DOLPHINS

PERSONAL: Born February 24, 1976, in Honolulu. ... 6-6/313. ... Full name: Hauoli Joseph Wong.
HIGH SCHOOL: Kailua (Honolulu).
COLLEGE: Hawaii, then Brigham Young.
TRANSACTIONS/CAREER NOTES: Selected by Miami Dolphins in seventh round (244th pick overall) of 1999 NFL draft.
COLLEGE PLAYING EXPERIENCE: Hawaii 1994-1995; Brigham Young 1996-1998. ... Games: 1994 (redshirted), 1995 (11), 1996 (transfer student), 1997 (11), 1998 (13). Total: 35.

WOODY, DAMIEN — C — PATRIOTS

PERSONAL: Born November 3, 1977, in Beaverdam, Va. ... 6-3/319. ... Full name: Damien Michael Woody.
HIGH SCHOOL: Patrick Henry (Beaverdam, Va.).
COLLEGE: Boston College.
TRANSACTIONS/CAREER NOTES: Selected after junior season by New England Patriots in first round (17th pick overall) of 1999 NFL draft.
COLLEGE PLAYING EXPERIENCE: Boston College, 1995-1998. ... Games: 1995 (redshirted), 1996 (10), 1997 (11), 1998 (11). Total: 32.

WRIGHT, KENNY — CB — VIKINGS

PERSONAL: Born September 14, 1977, in Ruston, La. ... 6-1/200.
HIGH SCHOOL: Ruston (La.).
COLLEGE: Arkansas, then Northwestern (La.) State.
TRANSACTIONS/CAREER NOTES: Selected after junior season by Minnesota Vikings in fourth round (120th pick overall) of 1999 NFL draft.

		INTERCEPTIONS			
Year Team	G	No.	Yds.	Avg.	TD
1995—Arkansas		Redshirted.			
1996—Northwestern State	6	1	15	15.0	0
1997—Northwestern State	11	2	19	9.5	0
1998—Northwestern State	11	2	84	42.0	0
College totals (3 years)	28	5	118	23.6	0

YANCEY, DAREN — DT — RAIDERS

PERSONAL: Born December 21, 1973, in Blackfoot, Idaho ... 6-5/305.
HIGH SCHOOL: Blackfoot (Idaho).
COLLEGE: Brigham Young.
TRANSACTIONS/CAREER NOTES: Selected by Oakland Raiders in sixth round (188th pick overall) of 1999 NFL draft.

Year Team	G	SACKS
1995—Brigham Young	11	0.0
1996—Brigham Young	13	4.0
1997—Brigham Young	11	1.0
1998—Brigham Young	13	6.0
College totals (4 years)	48	11.0

YEAST, CRAIG — WR — BENGALS

PERSONAL: Born November 20, 1976, in Danville, Ky. ... 5-7/160. ... Full name: Craig Nelson Yeast.
HIGH SCHOOL: Harrodsburg (Ky.).
COLLEGE: Kentucky.
TRANSACTIONS/CAREER NOTES: Selected by Cincinnati Bengals in fourth round (98th pick overall) of 1999 NFL draft.

		RUSHING				RECEIVING				PUNT RETURNS				KICKOFF RETURNS				TOTALS	
Year Team	G	Att.	Yds.	Avg.	TD	No.	Yds.	Avg.	TD	No.	Yds.	Avg.	TD	No.	Yds.	Avg.	TD	TD	Pts.
1995—Kentucky	10	5	6	1.2	0	24	337	14.0	2	0	0	...	0	8	117	14.6	0	2	12
1996—Kentucky	11	1	18	18.0	0	26	378	14.5	2	16	126	7.9	0	5	173	34.6	1	3	18
1997—Kentucky	11	1	14	14.0	0	73	873	12.0	10	7	109	15.6	1	15	345	23.0	1	12	72
1998—Kentucky	11	6	87	14.5	0	85	1311	15.4	14	11	33	3.0	0	14	410	29.3	1	15	90
College totals (4 years)	43	13	125	9.6	0	208	2899	13.9	28	34	268	7.9	1	42	1045	24.9	3	32	192

YOUNG, RYAN — OT — JETS

PERSONAL: Born June 28, 1976, in St. Louis. ... 6-5/337.
HIGH SCHOOL: Parkway Central (St. Louis).
COLLEGE: Kansas State.
TRANSACTIONS/CAREER NOTES: Selected by New York Jets in seventh round (223rd pick overall) of 1999 NFL draft.
COLLEGE PLAYING EXPERIENCE: Kansas State, 1994-1998. ... Games: 1994 (redshirted), 1995 (11), 1996 (11), 1997 (10), 1998 (12). Total: 44.

ZELLNER, PEPPI — DE — COWBOYS

PERSONAL: Born March 14, 1975, in Forsythe, Ga. ... 6-5/251. ... Full name: Hundens Zellner.
HIGH SCHOOL: Mary Persons (Forsythe, Ga.).
JUNIOR COLLEGE: Georgia Military College.
COLLEGE: Fort Valley (Ga.) State.
TRANSACTIONS/CAREER NOTES: Selected by Dallas Cowboys in fourth round (132nd pick overall) of 1999 NFL draft.

Year Team	G	SACKS
1994—Georgia Military College	Statistics unavailable.	
1995—Georgia Military College	Statistics unavailable.	
1996—Fort Valley State	3	0.0
1997—Fort Valley State	Played basketball.	
1998—Fort Valley State	12	3.0
College totals (2 years)	15	3.0

ZEREOUE, AMOS — RB — STEELERS

PERSONAL: Born October 8, 1976, in Hempstead, N.Y. ... 5-8/202.
HIGH SCHOOL: W.C. Mepham (Hempstead, N.Y.).

– 493 –

COLLEGE: West Virginia.
TRANSACTIONS/CAREER NOTES: Selected after junior season by Pittsburgh Steelers in third round (95th pick overall) of 1999 NFL draft.
HONORS: Named running back on THE SPORTING NEWS college All-America third team (1997).

			RUSHING				RECEIVING				KICKOFF RETURNS			TOTALS	
Year	Team	G	Att.	Yds.	Avg.	TD	No.	Yds.	Avg.	TD	No.	Yds.	Avg.	TD	TD	Pts.
1995—West Virginia								Redshirted.								
1996—West Virginia		11	222	1035	4.7	9	16	59	3.7	1	0	0	...	0	10	60
1997—West Virginia		11	281	1589	5.7	18	16	131	8.2	0	0	0	...	0	18	108
1998—West Virginia		11	283	1462	5.2	13	23	184	8.0	1	8	168	21.0	0	14	84
College totals (3 years)		33	786	4086	5.2	40	55	374	6.8	2	8	168	21.0	0	42	252

1999 DRAFT PICKS

HEAD COACHES

BILLICK, BRIAN — RAVENS

PERSONAL: Born February 28, 1954, in Fairborn, Ohio. ... Full name: Brian Harold Billick. ... Played tight end.
HIGH SCHOOL: Redlands (Calif.).
COLLEGE: Air Force, then Brigham Young.
TRANSACTIONS/CAREER NOTES: Selected by San Francisco 49ers in 11th round of 1977 NFL draft. ... Signed by 49ers for 1977 season. ... Released by 49ers (August 30, 1977). ... Signed by Dallas Cowboys (May 1978). ... Released by Cowboys before 1978 season.

HEAD COACHING RECORD

BACKGROUND: Assistant coach, University of Redlands (1977). ... Graduate assistant, Brigham Young (1978). ... Assistant public relations director, San Francisco 49ers NFL (1979 and 1980). ... Assistant coach and recruiting coordinator, San Diego State (1981-1985). ... Offensive coordinator, Utah State (1986-1988). ... Assistant coach, Stanford (1989-9191). ... Tight ends coach, Minnesota Vikings NFL (1992). ... Offensive coordinator, Vikings (1993-1998).

CARROLL, PETE — PATRIOTS

PERSONAL: Born September 15, 1951, in San Francisco. ... Full name: Peter C. Carroll.
HIGH SCHOOL: Larkspur (Calif.)-Redwood.
COLLEGE: Pacific (bachelor's degree in business administration, 1974; master's degree in physical education, 1978).

HEAD COACHING RECORD

BACKGROUND: Wide receivers coach, Pacific (1974). ... Defensive backs coach, Pacific (1975 and 1976). ... Assistant secondary coach, Arkansas (1977). ... Secondary coach, Iowa State (1978). ... Secondary coach, Ohio State (1979). ... Defensive coordinator, North Carolina State (1980-82). ... Offensive coordinator, Pacific (1983). ... Defensive backs coach, Buffalo Bills NFL (1984). ... Defensive backs coach, Minnesota Vikings NFL (1985-1989). ... Defensive coordinator, New York Jets NFL (1990-1993). ... Defensive coordinator, San Francisco 49ers NFL (1995 and 1996).

	REGULAR SEASON					POST-SEASON	
	W	L	T	Pct.	Finish	W	L
1994—New York Jets NFL	6	10	0	.375	5th/AFC Eastern Division	—	—
1997—New England NFL	10	6	0	.625	1st/AFC Eastern Division	1	1
1998—New England NFL	9	7	0	.563	4th/AFC Eastern Division	0	1
Pro totals (3 years)	25	23	0	.521	**Pro totals (2 years)**	1	2

NOTES:
1997—Defeated Miami, 17-3, in first-round playoff game; lost to Pittsburgh, 7-6, in conference playoff game.
1998—Lost to Jacksonville, 25-10, in first-round playoff game.

COSLET, BRUCE — BENGALS

PERSONAL: Born August 5, 1946, in Oakdale, Calif. ... Full name: Bruce Noel Coslet. ... Played tight end.
HIGH SCHOOL: Joint Union (Oakdale, Calif.).
COLLEGE: Pacific (degrees in history and psychology).
TRANSACTIONS/CAREER NOTES: Signed as non-drafted free agent by Cincinnati Bengals (1969). ... Released by Bengals before 1977 season.
PRO STATISTICS: 1973—Returned one kickoff for no yards and recovered one fumble. 1975—Rushed once for one yard and recovered two fumbles for two yards. 1976—Recovered two fumbles.

		RECEIVING				TOTALS		
Year Team	G	No.	Yds.	Avg.	TD	TD	Pts.	Fum.
1969—Cincinnati AFL	8	1	39	39.0	1	1	6	0
1970—Cincinnati NFL	14	8	97	12.1	1	1	6	0
1971—Cincinnati NFL	14	21	356	17.0	4	4	24	3
1972—Cincinnati NFL	10	5	48	9.6	1	1	6	0
1973—Cincinnati NFL	13	9	123	13.7	0	0	0	0
1974—Cincinnati NFL	14	2	24	12.0	0	0	0	0
1975—Cincinnati NFL	14	10	117	11.7	0	0	0	...
1976—Cincinnati NFL	14	5	73	14.6	2	2	12	0
AFL totals (1 year)	8	1	39	39.0	1	1	6	0
NFL totals (7 years)	93	60	838	14.0	8	8	48	3
Pro totals (8 years)	101	61	877	14.4	9	9	54	3

HEAD COACHING RECORD

BACKGROUND: Special teams/tight ends coach, San Francisco 49ers NFL (1980). ... Special teams/tight ends coach, Cincinnati Bengals NFL (1981-1983). ... Wide receivers coach, Bengals (1984 and 1985). ... Offensive coordinator, Bengals (1986-1989). ... Offensive coordinator, Bengals (1994-October 21, 1996).

	REGULAR SEASON					POST-SEASON	
	W	L	T	Pct.	Finish	W	L
1990—New York Jets NFL	6	10	0	.375	4th/AFC Eastern Division	—	—
1991—New York Jets NFL	8	8	0	.500	T2nd/AFC Eastern Division	0	1
1992—New York Jets NFL	4	12	0	.250	4th/AFC Eastern Division	—	—
1993—New York Jets NFL	8	8	0	.500	3rd/AFC Eastern Division	—	—
1996—Cincinnati NFL	7	2	0	.778	T3rd/AFC Central Division	—	—

	REGULAR SEASON					SEASON	
	W	L	T	Pct.	Finish	W	L
1997—Cincinnati NFL	7	9	0	.438	4th/AFC Central Division	—	—
1998—Cincinnati NFL	3	13	0	.188	5th/AFC Central Division	—	—
Pro totals (7 years)	43	62	0	.410	Pro totals (1 year)	0	1

NOTES:
1991—Lost to Houston, 17-10, in first-round playoff game.
1996—Replaced Dave Shula as head coach (October 21), with 1-6 record and club in fifth place.

COUGHLIN, TOM — JAGUARS

PERSONAL: Born August 31, 1946, in Waterloo, N.Y. ... Full name: Thomas Richard Coughlin.
HIGH SCHOOL: Waterloo (N.Y.) Central.
COLLEGE: Syracuse (bachelor's degree in education, 1968; master's degree in education, 1969).
COLLEGE NOTES: Played wingback (1965-67).

HEAD COACHING RECORD
BACKGROUND: Graduate assistant, Syracuse (1969). ... Quarterbacks/offensive backfield coach, Syracuse (1974-1976). ... Offensive coordinator, Syracuse (1977-1980). ... Offensive coordinator, Boston College (1980-1983). ... Receivers coach, Philadelphia Eagles NFL (1984 and 1985). ... Receivers coach, Green Bay Packers NFL (1986 and 1987). ... Receivers coach, New York Giants NFL (1988-1990).

	REGULAR SEASON					POST-SEASON	
	W	L	T	Pct.	Finish	W	L
1970—Rochester Tech	4	3	0	.571	Eastern College Athletic Conference	—	—
1971—Rochester Tech	5	2	1	.688	Eastern College Athletic Conference	—	—
1972—Rochester Tech	4	5	0	.444	Eastern College Athletic Conference	—	—
1973—Rochester Tech	3	5	1	.389	Eastern College Athletic Conference	—	—
1991—Boston College	4	7	0	.364	7th/Big East Conference	—	—
1992—Boston College	8	2	1	.773	3rd/Big East Conference	0	1
1993—Boston College	8	3	0	.727	3rd/Big East Conference	1	0
1995—Jacksonville NFL	4	12	0	.250	5th/AFC Central Division	—	—
1996—Jacksonville NFL	9	7	0	.563	2nd/AFC Central Division	2	1
1997—Jacksonville NFL	11	5	0	.688	T1st/AFC Central Division	0	1
1998—Jacksonville NFL	11	5	0	.688	1st/AFC Central Division	1	1
College totals (7 years)	36	27	3	.568	College totals (2 years)	1	1
Pro totals (4 years)	35	29	0	.547	Pro totals (3 years)	3	3

NOTES:
1992—Lost to Tennessee, 38-23, in Hall of Fame Bowl.
1993—Defeated Virginia, 31-13, in CarQuest Bowl.
1996—Defeated Buffalo, 30-27, in first-round playoff game; defeated Denver, 30-27, in conference playoff game; lost to New England, 20-6, in AFC championship game.
1997—Lost to Denver, 42-17, in first-round playoff game.
1998—Defeated New England, 25-10, in first-round playoff game; lost to New York Jets, 34-24, in coference playoff game.

COWHER, BILL — STEELERS

PERSONAL: Born May 8, 1957, in Pittsburgh. ... Full name: William Laird Cowher. ... Played linebacker.
HIGH SCHOOL: Carlynton (Crafton, Pa.).
COLLEGE: North Carolina State (bachelor of science degree in education, 1979).
TRANSACTIONS/CAREER NOTES: Signed as non-drafted free agent by Philadelphia Eagles (May 8, 1979). ... Released by Eagles (August 14, 1979). ... Signed by Cleveland Browns (February 27, 1980). ... On injured reserve with knee injury (August 20, 1981-entire season). ... Traded by Browns to Eagles for ninth-round pick (WR Don Jones) in 1984 draft (August 21, 1983). ... On injured reserve with knee injury (September 25, 1984-remainder of season).
PLAYING EXPERIENCE: Cleveland NFL, 1980 and 1982; Philadelphia NFL, 1983 and 1984. ... Games: 1980 (16), 1982 (9), 1983 (16), 1984 (4). Total: 45.
PRO STATISTICS: 1983—Recovered one fumble.

HEAD COACHING RECORD
BACKGROUND: Special teams coach, Cleveland Browns NFL (1985 and 1986). ... Defensive backs coach, Browns (1987 and 1988). ... Defensive coordinator, Kansas City Chiefs NFL (1989-1991).
HONORS: Named NFL Coach of the Year by THE SPORTING NEWS (1992).

	REGULAR SEASON					POST-SEASON	
	W	L	T	Pct.	Finish	W	L
1992—Pittsburgh NFL	11	5	0	.688	1st/AFC Central Division	0	1
1993—Pittsburgh NFL	9	7	0	.563	2nd/AFC Central Division	0	1
1994—Pittsburgh NFL	12	4	0	.750	1st/AFC Central Division	1	1
1995—Pittsburgh NFL	11	5	0	.688	1st/AFC Central Division	2	1
1996—Pittsburgh NFL	10	6	0	.625	1st/AFC Central Division	1	1
1997—Pittsburgh NFL	11	5	0	.688	T1st/AFC Central Division	1	1
1998—Pittsburgh NFL	7	9	0	.438	3rd/AFC Central Division	—	—
Pro totals (7 years)	71	41	0	.634	Pro totals (6 years)	5	6

NOTES:
1992—Lost to Buffalo, 24-3, in conference playoff game.
1993—Lost to Kansas City, 27-24 (OT), in first-round playoff game.
1994—Defeated Cleveland, 29-9, in conference playoff game; lost to San Diego, 17-13, in AFC championship game.
1995—Defeated Buffalo, 40-21, in conference playoff game; defeated Indianapolis, 20-16, in AFC championship game; lost to Dallas, 27-17, in Super Bowl XXX.
1996—Defeated Indianapolis, 42-14, in first-round playoff game; lost to New England, 28-3, in conference playoff game.
1997—Defeated New England, 7-6, in conference playoff game; lost to Denver, 24-21, in AFC championship game.

CUNNINGHAM, GUNTHER — CHIEFS

PERSONAL: Born June 19, 1949, in Munich, Germany. ... Full name: Gunther Manfred Cunningham.
COLLEGE: Oregon.
COLLEGE NOTES: Played linebacker and placekicker (1966-68).

HEAD COACHING RECORD

BACKGROUND: Defensive line coach, Oregon (1969-1971). ... Assistant coach, Arkansas (1972). ... Assistant coach, Stanford (1973-1976). ... Secondary coach, University of California (1977). ... Linebackers coach, University of California (1978). ... Defensive coordinator/defensive line coach, University of California (1979 and 1980). ... Defensive line/linebackers coach, Hamilton Tiger-Cats of CFL (1981). ... Defensive line coach, Baltimore Colts NFL (1982-1984). ... Defensive line coach, San Diego Chargers NFL (1985-1990). ... Linebackers coach, Oakland Raiders NFL (1991). ... Defensive coordinator, Raiders (1992 and 1993). ... Defensive line coach, Raiders (1994). ... Defensive coordinator, Kansas City Chiefs NFL (1995-1998).

DITKA, MIKE — SAINTS

PERSONAL: Born October 18, 1939, in Carnegie, Pa. ... Full name: Michael Keller Ditka. ... Played tight end.
HIGH SCHOOL: Aliquippa (Pa.).
COLLEGE: Pittsburgh.
TRANSACTIONS/CAREER NOTES: Selected by Chicago Bears in first round of 1961 NFL draft. ... Traded by Bears to Philadelphia Eagles for QB Jack Concannon and a pick in 1968 draft (April 26, 1967). ... Traded by Eagles to Dallas Cowboys for WR Dave McDaniels (January 18, 1969).
CHAMPIONSHIP GAME EXPERIENCE: Played in NFL championship game (1963 season). ... Played in NFC championship game (1970-1972 seasons). ... Played in Super Bowl V (1970 season). ... Member of Super Bowl championship team (1971 season).
HONORS: Named end on THE SPORTING NEWS college All-America first team (1960). ... Named NFL Rookie of the Year by THE SPORTING NEWS (1961). ... Named tight end on THE SPORTING NEWS NFL Western Conference All-Star team (1961-1965). ... Played in Pro Bowl (1961-1965 seasons). ... Inducted into Pro Football Hall of Fame (1988).
RECORDS: Shares NFL career record for most touchdowns by recovery of own fumbles—2.
PRO STATISTICS: 1962—Recovered one fumble for a touchdown. 1964—Recovered one fumble for a touchdown. 1971—Rushed twice for two yards, returned three kickoffs for 30 yards and recovered one fumble.

			RECEIVING				TOTALS		
Year Team	G	No.	Yds.	Avg.	TD	TD	Pts.	Fum.
1961—Chicago NFL	14	56	1076	19.2	12	12	72	0
1962—Chicago NFL	14	58	904	15.6	5	6	36	0
1963—Chicago NFL	14	59	794	13.5	8	8	48	0
1964—Chicago NFL	14	75	897	12.0	5	6	36	0
1965—Chicago NFL	14	36	454	12.6	2	2	12	0
1966—Chicago NFL	14	32	378	11.8	2	2	12	0
1967—Philadelphia NFL	9	26	274	10.5	2	2	12	0
1968—Philadelphia NFL	11	13	111	8.5	2	2	12	0
1969—Dallas NFL	12	17	268	15.8	3	3	18	1
1970—Dallas NFL	14	8	98	12.3	0	0	0	0
1971—Dallas NFL	14	30	360	12.0	1	1	6	0
1972—Dallas NFL	14	17	198	11.6	1	1	6	0
Pro totals (12 years)	158	427	5812	13.6	43	45	270	1

HEAD COACHING RECORD

BACKGROUND: Receivers coach, Dallas Cowboys NFL (1973 and 1974). ... Special teams/tight ends coach, Cowboys (1975, 1976 and 1980). ... Special teams/receivers coach, Cowboys (1977-1979 and 1981).
HONORS: Named NFL Coach of the Year by THE SPORTING NEWS (1985).

	REGULAR SEASON					POST-SEASON	
	W	L	T	Pct.	Finish	W	L
1982—Chicago NFL	3	6	0	.333	T11th/NFC	—	—
1983—Chicago NFL	8	8	0	.500	T2nd/NFC Central Division	—	—
1984—Chicago NFL	10	6	0	.625	1st/NFC Central Division	1	1
1985—Chicago NFL	15	1	0	.938	1st/NFC Central Division	3	0
1986—Chicago NFL	14	2	0	.875	1st/NFC Central Division	0	1
1987—Chicago NFL	11	4	0	.733	1st/NFC Central Division	0	1
1988—Chicago NFL	12	4	0	.750	1st/NFC Central Division	1	1
1989—Chicago NFL	6	10	0	.375	4th/NFC Central Division	—	—
1990—Chicago NFL	11	5	0	.688	1st/NFC Central Division	1	1
1991—Chicago NFL	11	5	0	.688	2nd/NFC Central Division	0	1
1992—Chicago NFL	5	11	0	.313	T3rd/NFC Central Division	—	—
1997—New Orleans NFL	6	10	0	.375	4th/NFC Western Division	—	—
1998—New Orleans NFL	6	10	0	.375	3rd/NFC Western Division	—	—
Pro totals (13 years)	118	82	0	.590	Pro totals (7 years)	6	6

NOTES:
- 1984—Defeated Washington, 23-19, in conference playoff game; lost to San Francisco, 23-0, in NFC championship game.
- 1985—Defeated New York Giants, 21-0, in conference playoff game; defeated Los Angeles Rams, 24-0, in NFC championship game; defeated New England, 46-10, in Super Bowl XX.
- 1986—Lost to Washington, 27-13, in conference playoff game.
- 1987—Lost to Washington, 21-17, in conference playoff game.
- 1988—Record includes two games missed due to heart attack suffered on November 1; assistant coach Vince Tobin was 2-0 during that time. Defeated Philadelphia, 20-12, in conference playoff game; lost to San Francisco, 28-3, in NFC championship game.
- 1990—Defeated New Orleans, 16-6, in first-round playoff game; lost to New York Giants, 31-3, in conference playoff game.
- 1991—Lost to Dallas, 17-13, in first-round playoff game.

DUNGY, TONY — BUCCANEERS

PERSONAL: Born October 6, 1955, in Jackson, Mich. ... Full name: Anthony Kevin Dungy. ... Played defensive back and quarterback. ... Name pronounced DUN-gee.
HIGH SCHOOL: Parkside (Jackson, Mich.).
COLLEGE: Minnesota (degree in business administration, 1978).
TRANSACTIONS/CAREER NOTES: Signed as non-drafted free agent by Pittsburgh Steelers (May 1977). ... Traded by Steelers to San Francisco 49ers for 10th-round pick in 1980 draft (August 21, 1979). ... Traded by 49ers with RB Mike Hogan to New York Giants for WR Jimmy Robinson and CB Ray Rhodes (March 27, 1980).
CHAMPIONSHIP GAME EXPERIENCE: Played in AFC championship game (1978 season). ... Played in Super Bowl XIII (1978 season).
PRO STATISTICS: 1977—Attempted eight passes with three completions for 43 yards and two interceptions, rushed three times for eight yards and fumbled once. 1978—Recovered two fumbles for eight yards. 1979—Recovered two fumbles.

		INTERCEPTIONS			
Year Team	G	No.	Yds.	Avg.	TD
1977—Pittsburgh NFL	14	3	37	12.3	0
1978—Pittsburgh NFL	16	6	95	15.8	0
1979—San Francisco NFL	15	0	0	...	0
Pro totals (3 years)	45	9	132	14.7	0

HEAD COACHING RECORD
BACKGROUND: Defensive backs coach, University of Minnesota (1980). ... Defensive assistant, Pittsburgh Steelers NFL (1981). ... Defensive backs coach, Steelers (1982 and 1983). ... Defensive coordinator, Steelers (1984-1988). ... Defensive backs coach, Kansas City Chiefs NFL (1989-1991). ... Defensive coordinator, Minnesota Vikings NFL (1992-1995).

	REGULAR SEASON					POST-SEASON	
	W	L	T	Pct.	Finish	W	L
1996—Tampa Bay NFL	6	10	0	.375	4th/NFC Central Division		
1997—Tampa Bay NFL	10	6	0	.625	2nd/NFC Central Division	1	1
1998—Tampa Bay NFL	8	8	0	.500	3rd/NFC Central Division		
Pro totals (3 years)	24	24	0	.500	Pro totals (1 year)	1	1

NOTES:
1997—Defeated Detroit, 20-10, in first-round playoff game; lost to Green Bay, 21-7, in conference playoff game.

FASSEL, JIM — GIANTS

PERSONAL: Born August 31, 1949, in Anaheim. ... Full name: James Fassel. ... Played quarterback.
HIGH SCHOOL: Anaheim (Calif.) High.
JUNIOR COLLEGE: Fullerton College (Calif.).
COLLEGE: Southern California, then Long Beach State (degree in physical education, 1972).
TRANSACTIONS/CAREER NOTES: Selected by Chicago Bears in seventh round of 1972 NFL draft. ... Released by Bears before 1972 season.

HEAD COACHING RECORD
BACKGROUND: Coach, Fullerton College (1973). ... Player/coach, Hawaii Hawaiians WFL (1974). ... Quarterbacks/receivers coach, Utah (1976). ... Offensive coordinator, Weber State (1977 and 1978). ... Offensive coordinator, Stanford (1979-1983). ... Offensive coordinator, New Orleans Breakers USFL (1984) ... Quarterbacks coach, New York Giants NFL (1991). ... Offensive coordinator, Giants (1992) ... Assistant head coach/offensive coordinator, Denver Broncos NFL (1993 and 1994). ... Quarterbacks coach, Oakland Raiders NFL (1995). ... Offensive coordinator/quarterbacks coach, Arizona Cardinals NFL (1996).
HONORS: Named NFL Coach of the Year by The Sporting News (1997).

	REGULAR SEASON					POST-SEASON	
	W	L	T	Pct.	Finish	W	L
1985—Utah	8	4	0	.667	2nd/Western Athletic Conference		
1986—Utah	2	9	0	.182	9th/Western Athletic Conference		
1987—Utah	5	7	0	.417	7th/Western Athletic Conference		
1988—Utah	6	5	0	.545	4th/Western Athletic Conference		
1989—Utah	4	8	0	.333	7th/Western Athletic Conference		
1997—New York Giants NFL	10	5	1	.656	1st/NFC Eastern Division	0	1
1998—New York Giants NFL	8	8	0	.500	3rd/NFC Eastern Division		
College totals (5 years)	25	33	0	.431			
Pro totals (2 years)	18	13	1	.578	Pro totals (1 year)	0	1

NOTES:
1997—Lost to Minnesota, 23-22, in first-round playoff game.

FISHER, JEFF — TITANS

PERSONAL: Born February 25, 1958, in Culver City, Calif. ... Full name: Jeffrey Michael Fisher. ... Played safety.
HIGH SCHOOL: Taft (Woodland Hills, Calif.).
COLLEGE: Southern California (degree in public administration, 1981).
TRANSACTIONS/CAREER NOTES: Selected by Chicago Bears in seventh round (177th pick overall) of 1981 NFL draft. ... On injured reserve with broken leg (October 24, 1983-remainder of season). ... On injured reserve with ankle injury entire 1985 season.
CHAMPIONSHIP GAME EXPERIENCE: Played in NFC championship game (1984 season).
PRO STATISTICS: 1981—Recovered one fumble. 1984—Recovered one fumble.

		INTERCEPTIONS				PUNT RETURNS				KICKOFF RETURNS				TOTALS		
Year Team	G	No.	Yds.	Avg.	TD	No.	Yds.	Avg.	TD	No.	Yds.	Avg.	TD	TD	Pts.	Fum.
1981—Chicago NFL	16	2	3	1.5	0	43	509	11.8	1	7	102	14.6	0	1	6	3
1982—Chicago NFL	9	3	19	6.3	0	7	53	7.6	0	7	102	14.6	0	0	0	2
1983—Chicago NFL	8	0	0	...	0	13	71	5.5	0	0	0	...	0	0	0	0
1984—Chicago NFL	16	0	0	...	0	57	492	8.6	0	0	0	...	0	0	0	4
1985—Chicago NFL								Did not play.								
Pro totals (4 years)	49	5	22	4.4	0	120	1125	9.4	1	14	204	14.6	0	1	6	9

HEAD COACHING RECORD

BACKGROUND: Defensive backs coach, Philadelphia Eagles NFL (1986-1988). ... Defensive coordinator, Eagles (1989 and 1990). ... Defensive coordinator, Los Angeles Rams NFL (1991). ... Defensive backs coach, San Francisco 49ers NFL (1992 and 1993). ... Defensive coordinator, Houston Oilers NFL (February 9-November 14, 1994). ... Oilers franchise moved to Tennessee for 1997 season.

	REGULAR SEASON					POST-SEASON	
	W	L	T	Pct.	Finish	W	L
1994—Houston NFL	1	5	0	.167	4th/AFC Central Division	—	—
1995—Houston NFL	7	9	0	.438	T2nd/AFC Central Division	—	—
1996—Houston NFL	8	8	0	.500	T3rd/AFC Central Division	—	—
1997—Tennessee NFL	8	8	0	.500	3rd/AFC Central Division	—	—
1998—Tennessee NFL	8	8	0	.500	2nd/AFC Central Division	—	—
Pro totals (5 years)	32	38	0	.457			

NOTES:
1994—Replaced Jack Pardee as head coach (November 14), with 1-9 record and club in fourth place.

GAILEY, CHAN — COWBOYS

PERSONAL: Born January 5, 1952, in Gainesville, Ga. ... Full name: Thomas Chandler Gailey.
HIGH SCHOOL: Americus (Ga.).
COLLEGE: Florida (degree in physical education, 1974).
COLLEGE NOTES: Played quarterback (1971-73).

HEAD COACHING RECORD

BACKGROUND: Graduate assistant, Florida (1974 and 1975). ... Defensive backfield coach, Troy State (1976-1979). ... Defensive backfield coach, Air Force (1979-1982). ... Assistant coach, Denver Broncos NFL (1985-1988). ... Offensive coordinator/wide receivers coach, Broncos (1989 and 1990). ... Wide receivers coach, Pittsburgh Steelers NFL (1994 and 1995). ... Offensive coordinator, Steelers NFL (1996 and 1997).

	REGULAR SEASON					POST-SEASON	
	W	L	T	Pct.	Finish	W	L
1983—Troy State	7	4	0	.636	T2nd/Gulf Coast Conference	—	—
1984—Troy State	9	1	0	.900	1st/Gulf Coast Conference	3	0
1991—Birmingham W.L.	5	5	0	.500	1st/North American West Division	0	1
1992—Birmingham W.L.	7	2	1	.750	2nd/North American West Division	0	1
1993—Samford	5	6	0	.455	Independent	—	—
1998—Dallas NFL	10	6	0	.625	1st/NFC Central Division	0	1
College totals (3 years)	21	11	0	.656	College totals (1 year)	3	0
W.L. totals (2 years)	12	7	1	.625	W.L. totals (2 years)	0	2
NFL totals (1 years)	10	6	0	.625	NFL totals (1 year)	0	1
Pro totals (3 years)	22	13	1	.625	Pro totals (3 years)	0	3

NOTES:
1984—Defeated Central State, 31-21, in first-round playoff game; defeated Towson State, 45-3, in semifinal playoff game; defeated North Dakota, 18-17, in championship game.
1991—Lost to Barcelona, 10-3, in first-round playoff game.
1992—Lost to Orlando, 45-7, in first-round playoff game.
1998—Lost to Arizona, 20-7, in first-round playoff game.

GREEN, DENNIS — VIKINGS

PERSONAL: Born February 17, 1949, in Harrisburg, Pa.
HIGH SCHOOL: John Harris (Harrisburg, Pa.).
COLLEGE: Iowa (degree in recreation education, 1971).
COLLEGE NOTES: Played flanker and running back (1968-70).

HEAD COACHING RECORD

BACKGROUND: Graduate assistant, Iowa (1972). ... Running backs/receivers coach, Dayton (1973). ... Running backs/receivers coach, Iowa (1974-1976). ... Running backs coach, Stanford (1977 and 1978). ... Special teams coach, San Francisco 49ers NFL (1979). ... Offensive coordinator, Stanford (1980). ... Receivers coach, 49ers (1986-1988).

	REGULAR SEASON					POST-SEASON	
	W	L	T	Pct.	Finish	W	L
1981—Northwestern	0	11	0	.000	10th/Big Ten Conference	—	—
1982—Northwestern	3	8	0	.273	T8th/Big Ten Conference	—	—
1983—Northwestern	2	9	0	.182	T8th/Big Ten Conference	—	—
1984—Northwestern	2	9	0	.182	9th/Big Ten Conference	—	—
1985—Northwestern	3	8	0	.273	T9th/Big Ten Conference	—	—
1989—Stanford	3	8	0	.273	T7th/Pacific-10 Conference	—	—
1990—Stanford	5	6	0	.455	T6th/Pacific-10 Conference	—	—
1991—Stanford	8	3	0	.727	T2nd/Pacific-10 Conference	0	1
1992—Minnesota NFL	11	5	0	.688	1st/NFC Central Division	0	1
1993—Minnesota NFL	9	7	0	.563	2nd/NFC Central Division	0	1
1994—Minnesota NFL	10	6	0	.625	1st/NFC Central Division	0	1
1995—Minnesota NFL	8	8	0	.500	4th/NFC Central Division	—	—
1996—Minnesota NFL	9	7	0	.563	2nd/NFC Central Division	0	1
1997—Minnesota NFL	9	7	0	.563	T3rd/NFC Central Division	1	1
1998—Minnesota NFL	15	1	0	.938	1st/NFC Central Division	1	1
College totals (8 years)	26	62	0	.295	College totals (1 year)	0	1
Pro totals (7 years)	71	41	0	.634	Pro totals (6 years)	2	6

NOTES:
1991—Lost to Georgia Tech, 18-17, in Aloha Bowl.
1992—Lost to Washington, 24-7, in first-round playoff game.
1993—Lost to New York Giants, 17-10, in first-round playoff game.
1994—Lost to Chicago, 35-18, in first-round playoff game.
1996—Lost to Dallas, 40-15, in first-round playoff game.
1997—Defeated New York Giants, 23-22, in first-round playoff game; lost to San Francisco, 38-22, in conference playoff game.
1998—Defeated Arizona, 41-21, in conference playoff game; lost to Atlanta, 30-27, in NFC championship game.

GRUDEN, JON — RAIDERS

PERSONAL: Born August 17, 1963, in Sandusky, Ohio. ... Son of Jim Gruden, scout, San Francisco 49ers; and brother of Jay Gruden, quarterback with Tampa Bay Storm of Arena League (1991-96).
HIGH SCHOOL: Clay (South Bend, Ind.).
COLLEGE: Dayton, then Tennessee (degree in communications, 1985).
COLLEGE NOTES: Played quarterback (1983-85).

HEAD COACHING RECORD

BACKGROUND: Graduate assistant, Tennessee (1986 and 1987). ... Passing game coordinator, Southeast Missouri State (1988). ... Wide receivers coach, Pacific (1989). ... Assistant coach, San Francisco 49ers NFL (1990) ... Wide receivers coach, University of Pittsburgh (1991). ... Offensive/quality control coach, Green Bay Packers NFL (1992). ... Wide receivers coach, Packers (1993 and 1994). ... Offensive coordinator, Philadelphia Eagles NFL (1995-1997).

	REGULAR SEASON					POST-SEASON	
	W	L	T	Pct.	Finish	W	L
1998—Oakland NFL	8	8	0	.500	T2nd/AFC Western Division	—	—

HOLMGREN, MIKE — SEAHAWKS

PERSONAL: Born June 15, 1948, in San Francisco. ... Full name: Michael George Holmgren. ... Played quarterback.
HIGH SCHOOL: Lincoln (San Francisco).
COLLEGE: Southern California (degree in business finance, 1970).
TRANSACTIONS/CAREER NOTES: Selected by St. Louis Cardinals in eighth round of 1970 NFL draft. ... Released by Cardinals (1970).

HEAD COACHING RECORD

BACKGROUND: Assistant coach, Sacred Heart Cathedral Prep School, San Francisco (1972 and 1973). ... Assistant coach, Oak Grove High School, San Jose, Calif. (1975-1980). ... Offensive coordinator/quarterbacks coach, San Francisco State (1981). ... Quarterbacks coach, Brigham Young (1982-1985). ... Quarterbacks coach, San Francisco 49ers NFL (1986-1988). ... Offensive coordinator, 49ers (1989-1991).

	REGULAR SEASON					POST-SEASON	
	W	L	T	Pct.	Finish	W	L
1992—Green Bay NFL	9	7	0	.563	2nd/NFC Central Division	—	—
1993—Green Bay NFL	9	7	0	.563	T2nd/NFC Central Division	1	1
1994—Green Bay NFL	9	7	0	.563	T2nd/NFC Central Division	1	1
1995—Green Bay NFL	11	5	0	.688	1st/NFC Central Division	2	1
1996—Green Bay NFL	13	3	0	.813	1st/NFC Central Division	3	0
1997—Green Bay NFL	13	3	0	.813	1st/NFC Central Division	2	1
1998—Green Bay NFL	11	5	0	.688	2nd/NFC/Central Division	0	1
Pro totals (7 years)	75	37	0	.670	Pro totals (6 years)	9	5

NOTES:
1993—Defeated Detroit, 28-24, in first-round playoff game; lost to Dallas 27-17, in conference playoff game.
1994—Defeated Detroit, 16-12, in first-round playoff game; lost to Dallas, 35-9, in conference playoff game.
1995—Defeated Atlanta, 37-20, in first-round playoff game; defeated San Francisco, 27-17, in conference playoff game; lost to Dallas, 38-27, in NFC championship game.
1996—Defeated San Francisco, 35-14, in conference playoff game; defeated Carolina, 30-13, in NFC championship game; defeated New England, 35-21, in Super Bowl XXXI.
1997—Defeated Tampa Bay, 21-7, in conference playoff game; defeated San Francisco, 23-10, in NFC championship game; lost to Denver, 31-24, in Super Bowl XXXII.
1998—Lost to San Francisco, 30-27, in first-round playoff game.

JAURON, DICK — BEARS

PERSONAL: Born October 7, 1950, in Swampscott, Mass. ... Full name: Richard Manuel Jauron. ... Played defensive back.
COLLEGE: Yale (degree in history).
TRANSACTIONS/CAREER NOTES: Selected by Detroit Lions in fourth round of 1973 NFL draft. ... Released by Lions (August 23, 1978). ... Signed by Cincinnati Bengals (August 29, 1978). ... On injured reserve with knee injury (November 12, 1980-remainder of season).
HONORS: Played in Pro Bowl (1974).

			INTERCEPTIONS			PUNT RETURNS				KICKOFF RETURNS				TOTALS		
Year Team	G	No.	Yds.	Avg.	TD	No.	Yds.	Avg.	TD	No.	Yds.	Avg.	TD	TD	Pts.	Fum.
1973—Detroit NFL	14	4	208	52.0	1	6	49	8.2	0	17	405	23.8	0	1	6	0
1974—Detroit NFL	14	1	26	26.0	0	17	286	16.8	0	2	21	10.5	0	0	0	0
1975—Detroit NFL	10	4	39	9.8	0	6	29	4.8	0	0	0	...	0	0	0	0
1976—Detroit NFL	6	2	0	0.0	0	0	0	...	0	0	0	...	0	0	0	0
1977—Detroit NFL	14	3	55	18.3	0	11	41	3.7	0	0	0	...	0	0	0	0
1978—Cincinnati NFL	16	4	52	13.0	1	3	32	10.7	0	0	0	...	0	1	6	0
1979—Cincinnati NFL	16	6	41	6.8	0	1	10	10.0	0	0	0	...	0	0	0	0
1980—Cincinnati NFL	10	1	11	11.0	0	0	0	...	0	0	0	...	0	0	0	0
Pro totals (8 years)	100	25	432	17.3	2	44	447	10.2	0	19	426	22.4	0	2	12	0

HEAD COACHING RECORD
BACKGROUND: Secondary coach, Buffalo Bills (1985). ... Defensive backs coach, Green Bay Packers (1986-94). ... Defensive coordinator, Jacksonville Jaguars (1995-1998).

JOHNSON, JIMMY — DOLPHINS

PERSONAL: Born July 16, 1943, in Port Arthur, Texas. ... Full name: James William Johnson.
HIGH SCHOOL: Thomas Jefferson (Port Arthur, Texas).
COLLEGE: Arkansas (degree in psychology, 1965).
COLLEGE NOTES: Played defensive line (1962-64).

HEAD COACHING RECORD
BACKGROUND: Defensive line coach, Louisiana Tech (1965). ... Assistant coach, Wichita State (1967). ... Defensive coordinator, Iowa State (1968 and 1969). ... Defensive line coach, Oklahoma (1970-1972). ... Defensive coordinator, Arkansas (1973-1976). ... Defensive coordinator, University of Pittsburgh (1977 and 1978).

	REGULAR SEASON					POST-SEASON	
	W	L	T	Pct.	Finish	W	L
1979—Oklahoma State	7	4	0	.636	3rd/Big Eight Conference	—	—
1980—Oklahoma State	3	7	1	.318	5th/Big Eight Conference	—	—
1981—Oklahoma State	7	4	0	.636	T3rd/Big Eight Conference	—	—
1982—Oklahoma State	4	5	2	.455	3rd/Big Eight Conference	—	—
1983—Oklahoma State	7	4	0	.636	T4th/Big Eight Conference	—	—
1984—Miami (Fla.)	8	4	0	.667	Independent	0	1
1985—Miami (Fla.)	10	1	0	.909	Independent	0	1
1986—Miami (Fla.)	11	0	0	1.000	Independent	0	1
1987—Miami (Fla.)	11	0	0	1.000	Independent	1	0
1988—Miami (Fla.)	10	1	0	.909	Independent	1	0
1989—Dallas NFL	1	15	0	.063	5th/NFC Eastern Division	—	—
1990—Dallas NFL	7	9	0	.438	4th/NFC Eastern Division	—	—
1991—Dallas NFL	11	5	0	.688	2nd/NFC Eastern Division	1	1
1992—Dallas NFL	13	3	0	.813	1st/NFC Eastern Division	3	0
1993—Dallas NFL	12	4	0	.750	1st/NFC Eastern Division	3	0
1996—Miami NFL	8	8	0	.500	4th/AFC Eastern Division	—	—
1997—Miami NFL	9	7	0	.563	T2nd/AFC Eastern Division	0	1
1998—Miami NFL	10	6	0	.625	T2nd/AFC Eastern Division	1	1
College totals (10 years)	78	30	3	.716	College totals (5 years)	2	3
Pro totals (8 years)	71	57	0	.555	Pro totals (5 years)	8	3

NOTES:
1980—Oklahoma State played to a 14-14 forfeit tie against Kansas (October 25).
1981—Lost to Texas A&M, 33-16, in Independence Bowl.
1983—Defeated Baylor, 24-14, in Bluebonnet Bowl.
1984—Lost to UCLA, 39-37, in Fiesta Bowl.
1985—Lost to Tennessee, 35-7, in Sugar Bowl.

1986—Lost to Penn State, 14-10, in Fiesta Bowl.
1987—Defeated Oklahoma, 20-14, in Orange Bowl.
1988—Defeated Nebraska, 23-3, in Orange Bowl.
1991—Defeated Chicago, 17-13, in first-round playoff game; lost to Detroit, 38-6, in conference playoff game.
1992—Defeated Philadelphia, 34-10, in conference playoff game; defeated San Francisco, 30-20, in NFC championship game; defeated Buffalo, 52-17, in Super Bowl XXVII.
1993—Defeated Green Bay, 27-17, in conference playoff game; defeated San Francisco, 38-21, in NFC championship game; defeated Buffalo, 30-13, in Super Bowl XXVIII.
1997—Lost to New England, 17-3, in first-round playoff game.
1998—Defeated Buffalo, 24-17, in first round playoff game; lost to Denver, 38-3, in conference playoff game.

MARIUCCI, STEVE — 49ERS

PERSONAL: Born November 4, 1955, in Iron Mountain, Mich. ... Full name: Steven Mariucci. ... Played quarterback.
HIGH SCHOOL: Iron Mountain (Mich.).
COLLEGE: Northern Michigan.
TRANSACTIONS/CAREER NOTES: Signed with Hamilton of the CFL for 1978 season.

HEAD COACHING RECORD

BACKGROUND: Quarterbacks/running backs coach, Northern Michigan (1978 and 1979). ... Quarterbacks/special teams coordinator, Cal State Fullerton (1980-1982). ... Assistant head coach, Louisville (1983 and 1984). ... Receivers coach, Orlando Renegades USFL (1985). ... Quality control coach, Los Angeles Rams NFL (fall 1985). ... Wide receivers/special teams coach, University of California (1987-1989). ... Offensive coordinator/quarterbacks coach, University of California (1990 and 1991). ... Quarterbacks coach, Green Bay Packers NFL (1992-1995).

	W	L	T	Pct.	Finish	POST-SEASON W	L
1996—California	6	6	0	.500	T5th/Pacific-10 Conference	0	1
1997—San Francisco NFL	13	3	0	.813	1st/NFC Western Division	1	1
1998—San Francisco NFL	12	4	0	.750	2nd/NFC Western Division	1	1
College totals (1 year)	6	6	0	.500	**College totals (1 year)**	0	1
Pro totals (2 years)	25	7	0	.781	**Pro totals (2 years)**	2	2

NOTES:
1996—Lost to Navy, 42-38, in Aloha Bowl.
1997—Defeated Minnesota, 38-22, in conference playoff game; lost to Green Bay, 23-10, in NFC championship game.
1998—Defeated Green Bay, 30-27, in first-round playoff game; lost to Atlanta, 20-18, in conference playoff game.

MORA, JIM — COLTS

PERSONAL: Born May 24, 1935, in Los Angeles. ... Full name: James Ernest Mora.
HIGH SCHOOL: University (Los Angeles).
COLLEGE: Occidental College (bachelor's degree in physical education, 1957), then Southern California (master's degree in education, 1967).
MISCELLANEOUS: Played for U.S. Marines at Quantico (1957) and Camp Lejeune (1958 and 1959).

HEAD COACHING RECORD

BACKGROUND: Assistant coach, Occidental College (1960-1963). ... Linebackers coach, Stanford (1967). ... Defensive assistant, University of Colorado (1967-1973). ... Linebackers coach, UCLA (1974). ... Defensive coordinator, University of Washington (1975-1977). ... Defensive line coach, Seattle Seahawks NFL (1978-1981). ... Defensive coordinator, New England Patriots NFL (1982).
HONORS: Named USFL Coach of the Year by THE SPORTING NEWS (1984). ... Name NFL Coach of the Year by THE SPORTING NEWS (1987).

	W	L	T	Pct.	Finish	POST-SEASON W	L
1964—Occidental	5	4	0	.556	3rd/Southern Calif. Intercollegiate Conference	—	—
1965—Occidental	8	1	0	.889	1st/Southern Calif. Intercollegiate Conference	—	—
1966—Occidental	5	4	0	.556	4th/Southern Calif. Intercollegiate Conference	—	—
1983—Philadelphia USFL	15	3	0	.833	1st/Atlantic Division	1	1
1984—Philadelphia USFL	16	2	0	.889	1st/Eastern Conference Atlantic Division	3	0
1985—Baltimore USFL	10	7	1	.583	4th/Eastern Conference	3	0
1986—New Orleans NFL	7	9	0	.438	4th/Western Division	—	—
1987—New Orleans NFL	12	3	0	.800	2nd/Western Division	0	1
1988—New Orleans NFL	10	6	0	.625	T1st/Western Division	—	—
1989—New Orleans NFL	9	7	0	.563	3rd/Western Division	—	—
1990—New Orleans NFL	8	8	0	.500	2nd/Western Division	0	1
1991—New Orleans NFL	11	5	0	.688	1st/Western Division	0	1
1992—New Orleans NFL	12	4	0	.750	2nd/Western Division	0	1
1993—New Orleans NFL	8	8	0	.500	2nd/Western Division	—	—
1994—New Orleans NFL	7	9	0	.438	T2nd/Western Division	—	—
1995—New Orleans NFL	7	9	0	.438	T3rd/Western Division	—	—
1998—Indianapolis NFL	3	13	0	.188	5th/AFCWestern Division	—	—
College totals (3 years)	18	9	0	.667			
USFL totals (3 years)	41	12	1	.769	**USFL totals (3 years)**	7	1
NFL totals (11 years)	94	81	0	.537	**NFL totals (4 years)**	0	4
Pro totals (14 years)	135	93	1	.592	**Pro totals (7 years)**	7	5

NOTES:
- 1983—Defeated Chicago, 44-38 (OT), in divisional playoff game; lost to Michigan, 24-22, in USFL championship game.
- 1984—Defeated New Jersey, 28-7, in conference playoff game; defeated Birmingham, 20-10, in conference championship game; defeated Arizona, 23-3, in USFL championship game.
- 1985—Defeated New Jersey, 20-17, in conference playoff game; defeated Birmingham, 28-14, in conference championship game; defeated Oakland, 28-24, in USFL championship game.
- 1987—Lost to Minnesota, 44-10, in wild-card playoff game.
- 1990—Lost to Chicago, 16-6, in conference playoff game.
- 1991—Lost to Atlanta, 27-20, in first-round playoff game.
- 1992—Lost to Philadelphia, 36-20, in first-round playoff game.

PALMER, CHRIS — BROWNS

PERSONAL: Born September 23, 1949, in Brewster, N.Y. ... Full name: Christopher J. Palmer.
COLLEGE: Southern Connecticut State.
COLLEGE NOTES: Played quarterback (1968-71).

HEAD COACHING RECORD

BACKGROUND: Wide receivers/defensive line coach, University of Connecticut (1972-1975). ... Wide receivers coach, Lehigh University (1975). ... Offensive coordinator, Colgate University (1976-1982). ... Offensive line coach, Montreal Concordes of CFL (1983). ... Wide receivers coach, New Jersey Generals of USFL (1984). ... Quaterbacks coach/offensive coordinator, New Jersey Generals of USFL (1985). ... Wide receivers coach, Houston Oilers NFL (1990-1992). ... Wide receivers coach, New England Patriots NFL (1993-1995). ... Quarterbacks coach, Patriots (1996). ... Offensive coordinator, Jacksonville Jaguars NFL (1997 and 1998).

	REGULAR SEASON					POST-SEASON	
	W	L	T	Pct.	Finish	W	L
1986—New Haven	8	2	0	.800	Independent	—	—
1987—New Haven	8	2	0	.800	Independent	—	—
1988—Boston University	4	7	0	.364	T7th/Yankee Conference	—	—
1989—Boston University	4	7	0	.364	6th/Yankee Conference	—	—
College totals (4 years)	24	18	0	.571			

PARCELLS, BILL — JETS

PERSONAL: Born August 22, 1941, in Englewood, N.J. ... Full name: Duane Charles Parcells.
HIGH SCHOOL: River Dell (Oradell, N.J.).
COLLEGE: Colgate, then Wichita State (degree in education, 1964).

HEAD COACHING RECORD

BACKGROUND: Defensive assistant coach, Hastings (Neb.) College (1964). ... Defensive line coach, Wichita State (1965). ... Linebackers coach, Army (1966-1969). ... Linebackers coach, Florida State (1970-1972). ... Defensive coordinator, Vanderbilt (1973 and 1974). ... Defensive coordinator, Texas Tech (1975-1977). ... Assistant coach, New York Giants NFL (1979). ... Lineackers coach, New England NFL (1980). ... Defensive coordinator/linebackers coach, New York Giants NFL (1981 and 1982). ... NFL analyst, NBC Sports (1991 and 1992).
HONORS: Named NFL Coach of the Year (1986).

	REGULAR SEASON					POST-SEASON	
	W	L	T	Pct.	Finish	W	L
1978—Air Force	3	8	0	.273	Independent	—	—
1983—New York Giants NFL	3	12	1	.219	5th/NFC Eastern Division	—	—
1984—New York Giants NFL	9	7	0	.563	T2nd/NFC Eastern Division	1	1
1985—New York Giants NFL	10	6	0	.625	T1st/NFC Eastern Division	1	1
1986—New York Giants NFL	14	2	0	.875	1st/NFC Eastern Division	3	0
1987—New York Giants NFL	6	9	0	.400	5th/NFC Eastern Division	—	—
1988—New York Giants NFL	10	6	0	.625	T1st/NFC Eastern Division	—	—
1989—New York Giants NFL	12	4	0	.750	1st/NFC Eastern Division	0	1
1990—New York Giants NFL	13	3	0	.813	1st/NFC Eastern Division	3	0
1993—New England NFL	5	11	0	.313	4th/AFC Eastern Division	—	—
1994—New England NFL	10	6	0	.625	T1st/AFC Eastern Division	0	1
1995—New England NFL	6	10	0	.375	4th/AFC Eastern Division	—	—
1996—New England NFL	11	5	0	.688	1st/AFC Eastern Division	2	1
1997—New York Jets NFL	9	7	0	.563	T2nd/AFC Eastern Division	—	—
1998—New York Jets NFL	12	4	0	.750	1st/AFC Eastern Division	1	1
College totals (1 year)	3	8	0	.273			
Pro totals (14 years)	130	92	1	.585	**Pro totals (8 years)**	11	6

NOTES:
- 1984—Defeated Los Angeles Rams, 16-10, in wild-card playoff game; lost to San Francisco, 21-10, in conference playoff game.
- 1985—Defeated San Francisco, 17-3, in wild-card playoff game; lost to Chicago, 21-0, in conference playoff game.
- 1986—Defeated San Francisco, 49-3, in conference playoff game; defeated Washington, 17-0, in NFC championship game; defeated Denver, 39-20, in Super Bowl XXI.
- 1989—Lost to Los Angeles Rams, 19-13 (OT), in conference playoff game.
- 1990—Defeated Chicago, 31-3, in conference playoff game; defeated San Francisco, 15-13, in NFC championship game; defeated Buffalo, 20-19, in Super Bowl XXV.
- 1994—Lost to Cleveland, 20-13, in first-round playoff game.
- 1996—Defeated Pittsburgh, 28-3, in conference playoff game; defeated Jacksonville, 20-6, in AFC championship game; lost to Green Bay, 35-21, in Super Bowl XXXI.
- 1998—Defeated Jacksonville, 34-24, in conference playoff game; lost to Denver, 23-10, in AFC championship game.

PHILLIPS, WADE — BILLS

PERSONAL: Born June 21, 1947, in Orange, Texas. ... Son of O.A. (Bum) Phillips, head coach with Houston Oilers (1975-80) and New Orleans Saints (1981-85).
HIGH SCHOOL: Port Neches-Groves (Neches, Texas).
COLLEGE: Houston (degrees in physical education and speech).
COLLEGE NOTES: Played linebacker (1966-68).

HEAD COACHING RECORD

BACKGROUND: Assistant coach, University of Houston (1969). ... Head coach, Orange (Texas) High School (1970-1972). ... Assistant coach, Oklahoma State (1973 and 1974). ... Assistant coach, Kansas (1975). ... Assistant coach, Houston Oilers NFL (1976-1980). ... Assistant coach, New Orleans Saints NFL (1981-November 25, 1985). ... Assistant coach, Philadelphia Eagles NFL (1986-1988). ... Defensive coordinator, Denver Broncos NFL (1989-January 25, 1993). ... Defensive coordinator, Buffalo Bills (1995-1997).

	REGULAR SEASON					POST-SEASON	
	W	L	T	Pct.	Finish	W	L
1985—New Orleans NFL	1	3	0	.250	3rd/NFC Western Division	—	—
1993—Denver NFL	9	7	0	.563	3rd/AFC Western Division	0	1
1994—Denver NFL	7	9	0	.438	4th/AFC Western Division	—	—
1998—Buffalo NFL	10	6	0	.625	T2nd/AFC Eastern Division	0	1
Pro totals (4 years)	27	25	0	.519	Pro totals (2 years)	0	2

NOTES:
1993—Lost to Los Angeles Raiders, 42-24, in first-round playoff game.
1998—Lost to Miami, 24-17, in first-round playoff game.

REEVES, DAN — FALCONS

PERSONAL: Born January 19, 1944, in Rome, Ga. ... Full name: Daniel Edward Reeves. ... Played running back.
HIGH SCHOOL: Americus (Ga.).
COLLEGE: South Carolina.
TRANSACTIONS/CAREER NOTES: Signed as non-drafted free agent by Dallas Cowboys for 1965 season.
CHAMPIONSHIP GAME EXPERIENCE: Played in NFL championship game (1966 and 1967 seasons). ... Played in NFC championship game (1970 and 1971 seasons). ... Played in Super Bowl V (1970 season). ... Member of Super Bowl championship team (1971 season).
HONORS: Named halfback on THE SPORTING NEWS NFL Eastern Conference All-Star team (1966).
PRO STATISTICS: 1965—Returned two kickoffs for 45 yards. 1966—Returned two punts for minus one yard, returned three kickoffs for 56 yards and fumbled six times. 1967—Fumbled seven times. 1969—Fumbled twice. 1970—Fumbled four times. 1971—Fumbled once.

		PASSING						RUSHING				RECEIVING			TOTALS	
Year Team	G	Att.	Cmp.	Pct.	Yds.	TD	Int.	Avg.	Att.	Yds.	Avg.	TD	No.	Yds.	Avg.	TD	TD	Pts.
1965—Dallas NFL	13	2	1	50.0	11	0	0	5.50	33	102	3.1	2	9	210	23.3	1	3	18
1966—Dallas NFL	14	6	3	50.0	48	0	0	8.00	175	757	4.3	8	41	557	13.6	8	16	96
1967—Dallas NFL	14	7	4	57.1	195	2	1	27.86	173	603	3.5	5	39	490	12.6	6	11	66
1968—Dallas NFL	4	4	2	50.0	43	0	0	10.75	40	178	4.5	4	7	84	12.0	1	5	30
1969—Dallas NFL	13	3	1	33.3	35	0	1	11.67	59	173	2.9	4	18	187	10.4	1	5	30
1970—Dallas NFL	14	3	1	33.3	14	0	1	4.67	35	84	2.4	2	12	140	11.7	0	2	12
1971—Dallas NFL	14	5	2	40.0	24	0	1	4.80	17	79	4.6	0	3	25	8.3	0	0	0
1972—Dallas NFL	14	2	0	0.0	0	0	0	...	3	14	4.7	0	0	0	...	0	0	0
Pro totals (8 years)	100	32	14	43.8	370	2	4	11.56	535	1990	3.7	25	129	1693	13.1	17	42	252

HEAD COACHING RECORD

BACKGROUND: Player/coach, Dallas Cowboys NFL (1970 and 1971). ... Offensive backs coach, Cowboys (1972 and 1974-1976). ... Offensive coordinator, Cowboys (1977-1980).
HONORS: Named NFL Coach of the Year by THE SPORTING NEWS (1993 and 1998).

	REGULAR SEASON					POST-SEASON	
	W	L	T	Pct.	Finish	W	L
1981—Denver NFL	10	6	0	.625	T1st/AFC Western Division	—	—
1982—Denver NFL	2	7	0	.222	12th/AFC	—	—
1983—Denver NFL	9	7	0	.563	T2nd/AFC Western Division	0	1
1984—Denver NFL	13	3	0	.813	1st/AFC Western Division	0	1
1985—Denver NFL	11	5	0	.688	2nd/AFC Western Division	—	—
1986—Denver NFL	11	5	0	.688	1st/AFC Western Division	2	1
1987—Denver NFL	10	4	1	.700	1st/AFC Western Division	2	1
1988—Denver NFL	8	8	0	.500	2nd/AFC Western Division	—	—
1989—Denver NFL	11	5	0	.688	1st/AFC Western Division	2	1
1990—Denver NFL	5	11	0	.313	5th/AFC Western Division	—	—
1991—Denver NFL	12	4	0	.750	1st/AFC Western Division	1	1
1992—Denver NFL	8	8	0	.500	3rd/AFC Western Division	—	—
1993—New York Giants NFL	11	5	0	.688	2nd/NFC Eastern Division	1	1
1994—New York Giants NFL	9	7	0	.563	2nd/NFC Eastern Division	—	—
1995—New York Giants NFL	5	11	0	.313	4th/NFC Eastern Division	—	—
1996—New York Giants NFL	6	10	0	.375	5th/NFC Eastern Division	—	—
1997—Atlanta NFL	7	9	0	.438	T2nd/NFC Western Division	—	—
1998—Atlanta NFL	14	2	0	.875	1st/NFC Western Division	2	1
Pro totals (18 years)	162	117	1	.580	Pro totals (8 years)	10	8

NOTES:
1983—Lost to Seattle, 31-7, in wild-card playoff game.
1984—Lost to Pittsburgh, 24-17, in conference playoff game.
1986—Defeated New England, 22-17, in conference playoff game; defeated Cleveland, 23-20 (OT), in AFC championship game; lost to New York Giants, 39-20, in Super Bowl XXI.
1987—Defeated Houston, 34-10, in conference playoff game; defeated Cleveland, 38-33, in AFC championship game; lost to Washington, 42-10, in Super Bowl XXII.
1989—Defeated Pittsburgh, 24-23, in conference playoff game; defeated Cleveland, 37-21, in AFC championship game; lost to San Francisco, 55-10, in Super Bowl XXIV.
1991—Defeated Houston, 26-24, in conference playoff game; lost to Buffalo, 10-7, in AFC championship game.
1993—Defeated Minnesota, 17-10, in first-round playoff game; lost to San Francisco, 44-3, in conference playoff game.
1998—Defeated San Francisco, 20-18, in conference playoff game; defeated Minnesota, 30-27, in NFC championship game; lost to Denver, 34-19, in Super Bowl XXXIII.

REID, ANDY — EAGLES

PERSONAL: Born March 19, 1958, in Los Angeles. ... Full name: Andrew Walter Reid.
COLLEGE: Brigham Young (bachelor's degree in physical education; master's degree in professional leadership, physical education and athletics).

HEAD COACHING RECORD

BACKGROUND: Graduate assistant, Brigham Young University (1982). ... Offensive coordinator, San Francisco State (1983-1985). ... Offensive line coach, Northern Arizona University (1986). ... Offensive line coach, University of Texas-El Paso (1987 and 1988). ... Offensive line coach, University of Missouri (1989-1992). ... Tight ends coach, Green Bay Packers NFL (1993-1996). ... Quarterbacks coach, Packers (1997 and 1998).

RHODES, RAY — PACKERS

PERSONAL: Born October 20, 1950, in Mexia, Texas. ... Full name: Raymond Earl Rhodes. ... Played wide receiver and defensive back.
HIGH SCHOOL: Mexia (Texas).
COLLEGE: Texas Christian, then Tulsa.
TRANSACTIONS/CAREER NOTES: Selected by New York Giants in 10th round of 1974 NFL draft. ... Traded by Giants with WR Jimmy Robinson to San Francisco 49ers for RB Mike Hogan and S Tony Dungy (March 27, 1980).
PRO STATISTICS: 1974—Rushed once for minus six yards, returned 10 punts for 124 yards and returned one kickoff for 27 yards. 1975—Rushed three times for minus four yards and recovered two fumbles. 1976—Rushed twice for 10 yards. 1977—Recovered two fumbles for 77 yards. 1979—Recovered two fumbles for seven yards. 1980—Recovered one fumble.

		INTERCEPTIONS				RECEIVING				TOTALS		
Year Team	G	No.	Yds.	Avg.	TD	No.	Yds.	Avg.	TD	TD	Pts.	Fum.
1974—New York Giants NFL	14	0	0	...	0	9	138	15.3	0	0	0	1
1975—New York Giants NFL	14	0	0	...	0	26	537	20.7	6	6	36	3
1976—New York Giants NFL	13	0	0	...	0	16	305	19.1	1	1	6	1
1977—New York Giants NFL	14	2	59	29.5	0	0	0	...	0	0	0	0
1978—New York Giants NFL	13	3	74	24.7	0	0	0	...	0	0	0	0
1979—New York Giants NFL	14	2	0	0.0	0	0	0	...	0	0	0	0
1980—San Francisco NFL	14	1	25	25.0	0	0	0	...	0	0	0	0
Pro totals (7 years)	96	8	158	19.8	0	51	980	19.2	7	7	42	5

HEAD COACHING RECORD

BACKGROUND: Assistant defensive backs coach, San Francisco 49ers NFL (1981). ... Defensive backs coach, 49ers (1982-1991). ... Defensive coordinator, Green Bay Packers NFL (1992 and 1993). ... Defensive coordinator, 49ers (1994).
HONORS: Named NFL Coach of the Year by THE SPORTING NEWS (1995).

	REGULAR SEASON					POST-SEASON	
	W	L	T	Pct.	Finish	W	L
1995—Philadelphia NFL	10	6	0	.625	2nd/NFC Eastern Division	1	1
1996—Philadelphia NFL	10	6	0	.625	T1st/NFC Eastern Division	0	1
1997—Philadelphia NFL	6	9	1	.406	3rd/NFC Western Division	—	—
1998—Philadelphia NFL	3	13	0	.188	5th/NFC Eastern Division	—	—
Pro totals (4 years)	29	34	1	.461	**Pro totals (2 years)**	1	2

NOTES:
1995—Defeated Detroit, 58-37, in first-round playoff game; lost to Dallas, 30-11, in conference playoff game.
1996—Lost to San Francisco, 14-0, in first-round playoff game.

RILEY, MIKE — CHARGERS

PERSONAL: Born July 6, 1953, in Wallace, Idaho ... Full name: Michael Joseph Riley.
HIGH SCHOOL: Corvallis (Ore.).
COLLEGE: Alabama (degree in social science); then Whitworth College, Wash. (master's degree).
HONORS: Named CFL Coach of the Year (1988 and 1990).

HEAD COACHING RECORD

BACKGROUND: Graduate assistant, University of California (1975). ... Graduate assistant, Whitworth College (1976). ... Defensive coordinator/secondary, Linfield College (1977-1982). ... Secondary coach, Winnipeg Blue Bombers of CFL (1983-1985). ... Defensive coordinator, Northern Colorado University (1986). ... Offensive coordinator/quarterbacks coach, University of Southern California (1993-1996).

					REGULAR SEASON	POST-SEASON	
	W	L	T	Pct.	Finish	W	L
1987—Winnipeg CFL	12	6	0	.667	1st/Eastern Division	0	1
1988—Winnipeg CFL	9	9	0	.500	2nd/Eastern Division	3	0
1989—Winnipeg CFL	7	11	0	.389	3rd/Eastern Division	1	1
1990—Winnipeg CFL	12	6	0	.667	1st/Eastern Division	2	0
1991—San Antonio W.L.	4	6	0	.400	—	—	—
1992—San Antonio W.L.	7	3	0	.700	—	—	—
1997—Oregon State	3	8	0	.273	10th/Pacific 10 Conference	—	—
1998—Oregon State	5	6	0	.455	T8th/Pacific 10 Conference	—	—
College totals (2 years)	8	14	0	.364			
W.L. totals (2 years)	11	9	0	.550			
CFL totals (4 years)	40	32	0	.556	CFL totals (4 years)	6	2
Pro totals (6 years)	51	41	0	.554			

NOTES:
1987—Lost to Toronto Argonauts, 19-3, in Divisional Finals of Grey Cup.
1988—Defeated Hamilton, 35-28, in Divisional Semi-finals of Grey Cup; defeated Toronto, 27-11, in Divisional Finals of Grey Cup; defeated B.C., 22-21, in Grey Cup Finals.
1989—Defeated Toronto, 30-7, in Divisional Semi-finals of Grey Cup; lost to Hamilton, 14-10, in Divisional Finals of Grey Cup.
1990—Defeated Toronto, 20-17, in Divisional Finals of Grey Cup; defeated Edmonton, 50-11, in Grey Cup finals.

ROSS, BOBBY — LIONS

PERSONAL: Born December 23, 1936, in Richmond, Va. ... Full name: Robert Joseph Ross.
HIGH SCHOOL: Benedictine (Richmond, Va.).
COLLEGE: Virginia Military Institute (degrees in English and history, 1959).
COLLEGE NOTES: Played quarterback and defensive back (1957-59).

HEAD COACHING RECORD
BACKGROUND: Head coach, Benedictine High School, Richmond, Va. (1959; record: 1-8-1). ... Served in military (1960-1962). ... Assistant coach, Colonial Heights (Va.) High School (1962). ... Head coach, Colonial Heights (Va.) High School (1963 and 1964). ... Freshman coach, Virginia Military Institute (1965). ... Defensive backs coach, VMI (1966). ... Offensive backs coach, William & Mary (1967 and 1968). ... Defensive backs coach, William & Mary (1969). ... Defensive coordinator, William & Mary (1970). ... Linebackers coach, Rice (1971). ... Linebackers coach, Maryland (1972). ... Special teams coach, Kansas City Chiefs NFL (1978 and 1979). ... Offensive backs coach, Chiefs (1980 and 1981).
HONORS: Named College Football Coach of the Year by THE SPORTING NEWS (1990).

					REGULAR SEASON	POST-SEASON	
	W	L	T	Pct.	Finish	W	L
1973—The Citadel	3	8	0	.273	T7th/Southern Conference	—	—
1974—The Citadel	4	7	0	.364	5th/Southern Conference	—	—
1975—The Citadel	6	5	0	.545	4th/Southern Conference	—	—
1976—The Citadel	6	5	0	.545	6th/Southern Conference	—	—
1977—The Citadel	5	6	0	.455	T3rd/Southern Conference	—	—
1982—Maryland	8	3	0	.727	2nd/Atlantic Coast Conference	0	1
1983—Maryland	8	3	0	.727	1st/Atlantic Coast Conference	0	1
1984—Maryland	8	3	0	.727	1st/Atlantic Coast Conference	1	0
1985—Maryland	8	3	0	.727	1st/Atlantic Coast Conference	1	0
1986—Maryland	5	5	1	.500	5th/Atlantic Coast Conference	—	—
1987—Georgia Tech	2	9	0	.182	8th/Atlantic Coast Conference	—	—
1988—Georgia Tech	3	8	0	.273	8th/Atlantic Coast Conference	—	—
1989—Georgia Tech	7	4	0	.636	T4th/Atlantic Coast Conference	—	—
1990—Georgia Tech	10	0	1	.955	1st/Atlantic Coast Conference	1	0
1991—Georgia Tech	7	5	0	.583	T2nd/Atlantic Coast Conference	1	0
1992—San Diego NFL	11	5	0	.688	1st/AFC Western Division	1	1
1993—San Diego NFL	8	8	0	.500	4th/AFC Western Division	—	—
1994—San Diego NFL	11	5	0	.688	1st/AFC Western Division	2	1
1995—San Diego NFL	9	7	0	.563	2nd/AFC Western Division	0	1
1996—San Diego NFL	8	8	0	.500	3rd/AFC Western Division	—	—
1997—Detroit NFL	9	7	0	.563	T3rd/NFC Central Division	0	1
1998—Detroit NFL	5	11	0	.313	4th/NFC Central Division	—	—
College totals (15 years)	90	74	2	.548	College totals (6 years)	4	2
Pro totals (7 years)	61	51	0	.545	Pro totals (4 years)	3	4

NOTES:
1982—Lost to Washington, 21-10, in Aloha Bowl.
1983—Lost to Tennessee, 30-23, in Florida Citrus Bowl.
1984—Defeated Tennessee, 28-27, in Sun Bowl.
1985—Defeated Syracuse, 35-18, in Cherry Bowl.
1990—Defeated Nebraska, 45-21, in Florida Citrus Bowl.
1991—Defeated Stanford, 18-17, in Aloha Bowl.

1992—Defeated Kansas City, 17-0, in first-round playoff game; lost to Miami, 31-0, in conference playoff game.
1994—Defeated Miami, 22-21, in conference playoff game; defeated Pittsburgh, 17-13, in AFC championship game; lost to San Francisco, 49-26, in Super Bowl XXIX.
1995—Lost to Indianapolis, 35-20, in first-round playoff game.
1997—Lost to Tampa Bay, 20-10, in first-round playoff game.

SEIFERT, GEORGE — PANTHERS

PERSONAL: Born January 22, 1940, in San Francisco ... Full name: George Gerald Seifert. ... Name pronounced SEE-fert.
HIGH SCHOOL: Polytechnic (San Francisco).
COLLEGE: Utah (bachelor's degree in zoology, 1963; master's degree in physical education, 1966).
MISCELLANEOUS: Served six months in U.S. Army after college.

HEAD COACHING RECORD
BACKGROUND: Graduate assistant, Utah (1964). ... Assistant coach, Iowa (1966). ... Defensive backs coach, Oregon (1967-1971). ... Defensive backs coach, Stanford (1972-1974 and 1977-1979). ... Defensive backs coach, San Francisco 49ers NFL (1980-1982). ... Defensive coordinator, 49ers (1983-1988).
HONORS: Named NFL Coach of the Year by THE SPORTING NEWS (1990 and 1994).

	REGULAR SEASON					POST-SEASON	
	W	L	T	Pct.	Finish	W	L
1965—Westminster (Utah)	3	3	0	.500	Independent	—	—
1975—Cornell	1	8	0	.111	8th/Ivy League	—	—
1976—Cornell	2	7	0	.222	T7th/Ivy League	—	—
1989—San Francisco NFL	14	2	0	.875	1st/NFC Western Division	3	0
1990—San Francisco NFL	14	2	0	.875	1st/NFC Western Division	1	1
1991—San Francisco NFL	10	6	0	.625	T2nd/NFC Western Division	—	—
1992—San Francisco NFL	14	2	0	.875	1st/NFC Western Division	1	1
1993—San Francisco NFL	10	6	0	.625	1st/NFC Western Division	1	1
1994—San Francisco NFL	13	3	0	.813	1st/NFC Western Division	3	0
1995—San Francisco NFL	11	5	0	.688	1st/NFC Western Division	0	1
1996—San Francisco NFL	12	4	0	.750	T1st/NFC Western Division	1	1
College totals (3 years)	6	18	0	.250			
Pro totals (8 years)	98	30	0	.766	**Pro totals (7 years)**	10	5

NOTES:
1989—Defeated Minnesota, 41-13, in conference playoff game; defeated Los Angeles Rams, 30-3, in NFC championship game; defeated Denver, 55-10, in Super Bowl XXIV.
1990—Defeated Washington, 28-10, in conference playoff game; lost to New York Giants, 15-13, in NFC championship game.
1992—Defeated Washington, 20-13, in conference playoff game; lost to Dallas 30-20 in NFC championship game.
1993—Defeated New York Giants, 44-3, in conference playoff game; lost to Dallas 38-21, in NFC championship game.
1994—Defeated Chicago, 44-15, in conference playoff game; defeated Dallas, 38-28, in NFC championship game; defeated San Diego, 49-26, in Super Bowl XXIX.
1995—Lost to Green Bay, 27-17, in conference playoff game.
1996—Defeated Philadelphia; 14-0, in first-round playoff game; lost to Green Bay, 35-14, in conference playoff game.

SHANAHAN, MIKE — BRONCOS

PERSONAL: Born August 24, 1952, in Oak Park, Ill. ... Full name: Michael Edward Shanahan.
HIGH SCHOOL: Franklin Park (East Leyden, Ill.).
COLLEGE: Eastern Illinois (bachelor's degree in physical education, 1974; master's degree in education, 1975).

HEAD COACHING RECORD
BACKGROUND: Graduate assistant, Eastern Illinois (1973 and 1974). ... Running backs/wide receivers coach, Oklahoma (1975 and 1976). ... Backfield coach, Northern Arizona (1977). ... Offensive coordinator, Eastern Illinois (1978). ... Offensive coordinator, University of Minnesota (1979). ... Offensive coordinator, University of Florida (1980-1983). ... Quarterbacks coach, Denver Broncos NFL (1984, 1989 and 1990). ... Offensive coordinator, Broncos (1985-1987 and 1991). ... Offensive coordinator, San Francisco 49ers NFL (1992-1994).

	REGULAR SEASON					POST-SEASON	
	W	L	T	Pct.	Finish	W	L
1988—L.A. Raiders NFL	7	9	0	.438	3rd/AFC Western Division	—	—
1989—L.A. Raiders NFL	1	3	0	.250	—	—	—
1995—Denver NFL	8	8	0	.500	T3rd/AFC Western Division	—	—
1996—Denver NFL	13	3	0	.813	1st/AFC Western Division	0	1
1997—Denver NFL	12	4	0	.750	2nd/AFC Western Conference	4	0
1998—Denver NFL	14	2	0	.875	1st/AFC Western Division	3	0
Pro totals (6 years)	55	29	0	.655	**Pro totals (3 years)**	7	1

NOTES:
1989—Replaced as Raiders coach by Art Shell (October 3) with club tied for fourth place.
1996—Lost to Jacksonville, 30-27, in conference playoff game.
1997—Defeated Jacksonville, 42-17, in first-round playoff game; defeated Kansas City, 14-10, in conference playoff game; defeated Pittsburgh, 24-21, in AFC championship game; defeated Green Bay, 31-24, in Super Bowl XXXII.
1998—Defeated Miami, 38-3, in conference playoff game; defeated New York Jets, 23-10, in AFC championship game; defeated Atlanta, 34-19, in Super Bowl XXXIII.

TOBIN, VINCE — CARDINALS

PERSONAL: Born September 29, 1943, in Burlington Junction, Mo.
HIGH SCHOOL: Maryville (Mo.).
COLLEGE: Missouri (bachelor's degree in physical education, 1965; master's degree in guidance and counseling, 1966).
COLLEGE NOTES: Played defensive back (1961-64).

HEAD COACHING RECORD
BACKGROUND: Graduate assistant, University of Missouri (1965 and 1966). ... Defensive ends coach, Missouri (1967-1970). ... Defensive coordinator, Missouri (1971-1976). ... Defensive coordinator, British Columbia Lions of CFL (1977-1982). ... Defensive coordinator, Philadelphia/Baltimore Stars USFL (1983-1985). ... Defensive coordinator, Chicago Bears NFL (1986-1992). ... Defensive coordinator, Indianapolis Colts NFL (1994 and 1995).

	\multicolumn{5}{c}{REGULAR SEASON}	\multicolumn{2}{c}{POST-SEASON}
	W	L	T	Pct.	Finish	W	L
1996—Arizona NFL	7	9	0	.438	4th/NFC Eastern Division	—	—
1997—Arizona NFL	4	12	0	.250	5th/NFC Eastern Division	—	—
1998—Arizona NFL	9	7	0	.563	2nd/NFC Eastern Division	1	1
Pro totals (3 years)	20	28	0	.417	Pro totals (1 year)	1	1

NOTES:
1998—Defeated Dallas, 20-7, in first-round playoff game; lost to Minnesota, 41-21, in conference playoff game.

TURNER, NORV — REDSKINS

PERSONAL: Born May 17, 1952, in LeJeune, N.C. ... Full name: Norval Eugene Turner. ... Brother of Ron Turner, head coach, University of Illinois.
HIGH SCHOOL: Alhambra (Calif.).
COLLEGE: Oregon (degree in history, 1975).

HEAD COACHING RECORD
BACKGROUND: Graduate assistant, Oregon (1975). ... Receivers coach, Southern California (1976-1979). ... Defensive backs coach, USC (1980). ... Quarterbacks coach, USC (1981-1983). ... Offensive coordinator, USC (1984). ... Receivers coach, Los Angeles Rams NFL (1985-1990). ... Offensive coordinator, Dallas Cowboys NFL (1991-1993).

	\multicolumn{5}{c}{REGULAR SEASON}	\multicolumn{2}{c}{POST-SEASON}
	W	L	T	Pct.	Finish	W	L
1994—Washington NFL	3	13	0	.188	5th/NFC Eastern Division	—	—
1995—Washington NFL	6	10	0	.375	3rd/NFC Eastern Division	—	—
1996—Washington NFL	9	7	0	.563	3rd/NFC Eastern Division	—	—
1997—Washington NFL	8	7	1	.531	2nd/NFC Eastern Division	—	—
1998—Washington NFL	6	10	0	.375	4th/NFC Eastern Division	—	—
Pro totals (5 years)	32	47	1	.406			

VERMEIL, DICK — RAMS

PERSONAL: Born October 30, 1936, in Calistoga, Calif. ... Full name: Richard Albert Vermeil. ... Brother of Al Vermeil, conditioning coach with San Francisco 49ers (1979-1982) and brother-in-law of Louie Giammona, running back with Philadelphia Eagles (1978-1982).
HIGH SCHOOL: Calistoga (Calif.).
JUNIOR COLLEGE: Napa College (degree in physical education, 1958).
COLLEGE: San Jose State (master's degree in physical edudation, 1959).
COLLEGE NOTES: Played quarterback (1956-59).

HEAD COACHING RECORD
BACKGROUND: Assistant coach, Del Mar High School, San Jose, Calif. (1959). ... Head coach, Hillsdale High School, San Mateo, Calif. (1960-1962; record: 17-9-1). ... Assistant coach, College of San Mateo (1963). ... Assistant coach, Stanford (1965-1968). ... Assistant coach, Los Angeles Rams NFL (1969 and 1971-1973). ... Assistant coach, UCLA (1970).
HONORS: Named NFL Coach of the Year by THE SPORTING NEWS (1979).

	\multicolumn{5}{c}{REGULAR SEASON}	\multicolumn{2}{c}{POST-SEASON}
	W	L	T	Pct.	Finish	W	L
1964—Napa College	8	1	0	.889	2nd/Golden Valley Conference	—	—
1974—UCLA	6	3	2	.636	T3rd/Pacific-8 Conference	—	—
1975—UCLA	8	2	1	.773	T1st/Pacific-8 Conference	1	0
1976—Philadelphia NFL	4	10	0	.286	4th/NFC Eastern Division	—	—
1977—Philadelphia NFL	5	9	0	.357	T4th/NFC Eastern Division	—	—
1978—Philadelphia NFL	9	7	0	.563	2nd/NFC Eastern Division	0	1
1979—Philadelphia NFL	11	5	0	.688	T1st/NFC Eastern Division	1	1

	REGULAR SEASON					SEASON	
	W	L	T	Pct.	Finish	W	L
1980—Philadelphia NFL............	12	4	0	.750	T1st/NFC Eastern Division	2	1
1981—Philadelphia NFL............	10	6	0	.625	2nd/NFC Eastern Division	0	1
1982—Philadelphia NFL............	3	6	0	.333	5th/NFC Eastern Division	—	—
1997—St. Louis NFL.................	5	11	0	.313	5th/NFC Western Division	—	—
1998—St. Louis NFL.................	4	12	0	.250	T4th/NFC Western Division	—	—
College totals (3 years)........	22	6	3	.758	**College totals (1 year)**	1	0
Pro totals (9 years)...............	63	70	0	.474	**Pro totals (4 years)**	3	4

NOTES:
1975—Defeated Ohio State, 23-10, in Rose Bowl.
1978—Lost to Atlanta, 14-13, in conference playoff game.
1979—Defeated Chicago, 27-17, in first-round playoff game; lost to Tampa Bay, 24-17, in conference playoff game.
1980—Defeated Minnesota, 31-16, in conference playoff game; defeated Dallas, 20-7, in NFC championship game; lost to Oakland, 27-10, in Super Bowl XV.
1981—Lost to New York Giants, 27-21, in conference playoff game.
1982—Only nine of 16 games were played due to the cancellation of games because of a players strike.

HEAD COACHES

1998 STATISTICAL LEADERS

AFC

RUSHING YARDS
Terrell Davis, Den. 2008
Marshall Faulk, Ind. 1319
Eddie George, Ten. 1294
Curtis Martin, NYJ..................1287
Ricky Watters, Sea. 1239

RUSHING ATTEMPTS
Terrell Davis, Den. 392
Curtis Martin, NYJ...................369
Eddie George, Ten. 348
Marshall Faulk, Ind. 324
Ricky Watters, Sea. 319

RUSHING TOUCHDOWNS
Terrell Davis, Den. 21
Fred Taylor, Jac. 14
Robert Edwards, N.E. 9
Ricky Watters, Sea. 9
Curtis Martin, NYJ........................8
Bam Morris, K.C. 8
Antowain Smith, Buf. 8

PASSER RATING
Vinny Testaverde, NYJ 101.6
John Elway, Den. 93.0
Neil O'Donnell, Cin. 90.2
Mark Brunell, Jac. 89.9
Doug Flutie, Buf.......................87.4

PASSING YARDS
Peyton Manning, Ind. 3739
Drew Bledsoe, N.E. 3633
Dan Marino, Mia......................3497
Vinny Testaverde, NYJ............3256
Steve McNair, Ten...................3228

PASS ATTEMPTS
Peyton Manning, Ind. 575
Dan Marino, Mia........................537
Steve McNair, Ten.....................492
Drew Bledsoe, N.E. 481
Kordell Stewart, Pit. 458

PASS COMPLETIONS
Peyton Manning, Ind. 326
Dan Marino, Mia........................310

Steve McNair, Ten.....................289
Drew Bledsoe, N.E. 263
Vinny Testaverde, NYJ..............259

PASSING TOUCHDOWNS
Vinny Testaverde, NYJ................29
Peyton Manning, Ind. 26
Dan Marino, Mia..........................23
John Elway, Den. 22
Drew Bledsoe, N.E. 20
Mark Brunell, Jac. 20
Doug Flutie, Buf. 20

PASS RECEPTIONS
O.J. McDuffie, Mia. 90
Marshall Faulk, Ind. 86
Rod Smith, Den. 86
Kayshawn Johnson, NYJ............83
Carl Pickens, Cin. 82

RECEIVING YARDS
Eric Moulds, Buf......................1368
Rod Smith, Den. 1222
Jimmy Smith, Jac. 1182
Keyshawn Johnson, NYJ........1131
Wayne Chrebet, NYJ 1083

RECEIVING TOUCHDOWNS
Joey Galloway, Sea....................10
Keyshawn Johnson, NYJ............10
Ed McCaffrey, Den. 10
Shannon Sharpe, Den. 10
Tim Brown, Oak. 9
Eric Moulds, Buf..........................9

INTERCEPTIONS
Ty Law, N.E.................................9
Terrell Buckley, Mia. 8
Sam Madison, Mia. 8
Shawn Springs, Sea. 7
Aaron Glenn, NYJ 6
Greg Jackson, S.D. 6
Lawyer Milloy, N.E. 6
Kurt Schulz, Buf. 6
Rod Woodson, Bal. 6

AVERAGE PUNT RETURN YARDS
(20 returns)
Reggie Barlow, Jac. 12.9
Jermaine Lewis, Bal. 12.7
Terrell Buckley, Mia. 12.2
Latario Rachal, S.D. 12.1
Desmond Howard, Oak. 12.0

PUNT RETURNS
Desmond Howard, Oak. 45
Reggie Barlow, Jac. 43
Kevin Williams, Buf. 37
Darrien Gordon, Den. 34
Jermaine Lewis, Bal. 32
Latario Rachal, S.D....................32

AVERAGE KICKOFF RETURN YARDS
(20 returns)
Corey Harris, Bal. 27.6
Steve Broussard, Sea. 26.9
Vaughn Hebron, Den. 26.4
Tremain Mack, Cin....................25.9
John Avery, Mia.......................25.2

KICKOFF RETURNS
Desmond Howard, Oak. 49
Kevin Williams, Buf. 47
Vaughn Hebron, Den. 46
Derrick Cullors, N.E. 45
Tremain Mack, Cin. 45

AVERAGE PUNTING YARDS
(40 punts)
Craig Hentrich, Ten. 47.2
Tom Rouen, Den. 46.9
Chris Gardocki, Ind. 45.4
Bryan Barker, Jac. 45.0
Lee Johnson, Cin.....................44.7

PUNTS
Leo Araguz, Oak. 98
Darren Bennett, S.D. 95
Klaus Wilmsmeyer, Mia. 93
Kyle Richardson, Bal. 90
Bryan Barker, Jac. 85

1998 STATISTICAL LEADERS

FIELD GOAL PERCENTAGE
(16 field goal attempts)
Al Del Greco, Ten. 923
Mike Vanderjagt, Ind. 871
John Carney, S.D. 867
Jason Elam, Den. 852
Pete Stoyanovich, K.C. 844

FIELD GOALS
Al Del Greco, Ten. 36
Steve Christie, Buf. 33
Adam Vinatieri, N.E. 31
Pete Stoyanovich, K.C. 27
Mike Vanderjagt, Ind. 27

POINTS SCORED BY KICKERS
Steve Christie, Buf. 140
Al Del Greco, Ten. 136
Jason Elam, Den. 127
Adam Vinatieri, N.E. 127
John Hall, NYJ........................120

POINTS SCORED BY NON-KICKERS
Terrell Davis, Den. 138
Fred Taylor, Jac. 102
Robert Edwards, N.E. 72
Joey Galloway, Sea. 72
Keyshawn Johnson, NYJ 66

SACKS
Michael Sinclair, Sea. 16.5
Michael McCrary, Bal..............14.5
Derrick Thomas, K.C. 12.0
Jason Gildon, Pit. 11.0
Lance Johnstone, Oak. 11.0

FUMBLES
Donald Hollas, Oak. 10
Drew Bledsoe, N.E. 9
Rich Gannon, K.C. 9
Dan Marino, Mia........................9
Craig Whelihan, S.D. 9
Ryan Leaf, S.D. 8
Warren Moon, Sea. 8

NFC

RUSHING YARDS
Jamal Anderson, Atl. 1846
Garrison Hearst, S.F. 1570
Barry Sanders, Det. 1491
Emmitt Smith, Dal. 1332
Robert Smith, Min. 1187

RUSHING ATTEMPTS
Jamal Anderson, Atl. 410
Barry Sanders, Det. 343
Emmitt Smith, Dal. 319
Garrison Hearst, S.F. 310
Adrian Murrell, Ari. 274

RUSHING TOUCHDOWNS
Jamal Anderson, Atl. 14
Emmitt Smith, Dal. 13
Leroy Hoard, Min. 9
Mike Alstott, T.B. 8
Skip Hicks, Was. 8
Adrian Murrell, Ari. 8

PASSER RATING
Randall Cunningham, Min. 106.0
Steve Young, S.F. 101.1
Chris Chandler, Atl.................100.9
Troy Aikman, Dal. 88.5
Steve Beuerlein, Car. 88.2

PASSING YARDS
Brett Favre, G.B. 4212
Steve Young, S.F....................4170
Jake Plummer, Ari. 3737

Randall Cunningham, Min. 3704
Trent Green, Was. 3441

PASS ATTEMPTS
Brett Favre, G.B. 551
Jake Plummer, Ari. 547
Steve Young, S.F......................517
Trent Green, Was. 509
Trent Dilfer, T.B........................429

PASS COMPLETIONS
Brett Favre, G.B. 347
Jake Plummer, Ari. 324
Steve Young, S.F......................322
Trent Green, Was. 278
Randall Cunningham, Min. 259

PASSING TOUCHDOWNS
Steve Young, S.F. 36
Randall Cunningham, Min. 34
Brett Favre, G.B. 31
Chris Chandler, Atl. 25
Trent Green, Was. 23

PASS RECEPTIONS
Frank Sanders, Ari. 89
Antonio Freeman, G.B. 84
Jerry Rice, S.F. 82
Herman Moore, Det. 82
Cris Carter, Min. 78

RECEIVING YARDS
Antonio Freeman, G.B. 1424

Randy Moss, Min. 1313
Tony Martin, Atl. 1181
Jerry Rice, S.F. 1157
Frank Sanders, Ari. 1145

RECEIVING TOUCHDOWNS
Randy Moss, Min. 17
Antonio Freeman, G.B. 14
Terrell Owens, S.F. 14
Cris Carter, Min. 12
Terance Mathis, Atl....................11

INTERCEPTIONS
Kwamie Lassiter, Ari..................8
Ray Buchanan, Atl. 7
Jimmy Hitchcock, Min. 7
Sammy Knight, N.O. 6
Eric Davis, Car. 5
Percy Ellsworth, NYG 5
Robert Griffith, Min. 5
Ronald McKinnon, Ari. 5
Deion Sanders, Dal.....................5
Tyrone Williams, G.B. 5

AVERAGE PUNT RETURN YARDS
(20 returns)
Deion Sanders, Dal. 15.6
Jacquez Green, T.B. 15.1
Andre Hastings, N.O. 14.0
Glyn Milburn, Chi. 11.6
Brian Mitchell, Was. 11.5

– 511 –

1998 STATISTICAL LEADERS

PUNT RETURNS
R.W. McQuarters, S.F. 47
Brian Mitchell, Was. 44
Winslow Oliver, Car. 44
Roell Preston, G.B. 44
Eric Metcalf, Ari. 43

AVERAGE KICKOFF RETURN YARDS
(20 returns)
Terry Fair, Det. 28.0
Tim Dwight, Atl. 27.0
Roell Preston, G.B. 26.3
Michael Bates, Car. 25.1
Glyn Milburn, Chi. 25.0

KICKOFF RETURNS
Glyn Milburn, Chi. 62
Michael Bates, Car. 59
Brian Mitchell, Was. 59
Roell Preston, G.B. 57
Eric Metcalf, Ari. 57

AVERAGE PUNTING YARDS
(40 punts)
Mark Royals, N.O. 45.6
Brad Maynard, NYG 45.2
Mitch Berger, Min. 44.7
Rick Tuten, St.L. 44.2
Matt Turk, Was. 44.1

PUNTS
Tom Hutton, Phi. 104
Brad Maynard, NYG................101
Rick Tuten, St.L. 95
Matt Turk, Was. 93
Mark Royals, N.O. 88

FIELD GOAL PERCENTAGE
(16 field goal attempts)
Gary Anderson, Min. 1.000
Doug Brien, N.O. 909
Jason Hanson, Det. 879
Ryan Longwell, G.B. 879
Richie Cunningham, Dal. 829

FIELD GOALS
Gary Anderson, Min. 35
Richie Cunningham, Dal. 29
Jason Hanson, Det. 29
Ryan Longwell, G.B. 29
Morten Andersen, Atl. 23

POINTS SCORED BY KICKERS
Gary Anderson, Min. 164
Ryan Longwell, G.B. 128
Richie Cunningham, Dal. 127
Morten Andersen, Atl. 120
Jason Hanson, Det. 114

POINTS SCORED BY NON-KICKERS
Randy Moss, Min. 106
Jamal Anderson, Atl. 98
Terrell Owens, S.F. 92
Emmitt Smith, Dal. 90
Antonio Freeman, G.B. 86

SACKS
Reggie White, G.B. 16.0
Chris Doleman, S.F. 15.0
Kevin Greene, Car. 15.0
Michael Strahan, NYG 15.0
Hugh Douglas, Phi. 12.5

FUMBLES
Trent Green, Was. 14
Steve Beuerlein, Car. 13
Kerry Collins, Car.-N.O. 13
Jake Plummer, Ari. 12
Tony Banks, St.L. 10